THE COMPLETE
ENCYCLOPEDIA
OF
SOCCER

PUBLISHER'S NOTE

In England, the home of soccer, the word most commonly used for the sport is 'football', and in homage to its origins, this is what the game is called in this book.

THIS IS A CARLTON BOOK

Copyright © Carlton Books Ltd, 1998

First published in 1998 by Carlton Books, 20 St Anne's Court, Wardour Street, London W1V 3AW

10 9 8 7 6 5 4 3 2 1

First published in the United States in 1999

A CIP catalogue record for this book is available from the British Library

ISBN 1 85868 487 0

Project Editor: Roland Hall
Project art direction: Paul Messam
Picture research: Justin Downing
Production: Sarah Schuman

Printed and bound in Italy

ACKNOWLEDGMENTS

Every soccer historian owes a major debt to his fellow writers, researchers and statisticians for their work down the years. Personal records provide a solid foundation but this work would not have been possible without having been able to draw on the enormous volume of published work worldwide on the subject of national and international soccer. Such resource falls into two categories – books and then newspapers and periodicals. Above all, it must be recorded that this book would not have been possible without the remarkable record provided by the London magazine *World Soccer* since its launch in October 1960. I would also like to thank Ron Hockings for his contribution. Further appreciated resources include:

Newspapers and periodicals:
A Bola (Portugal), *Corriere dello Sport* (Italy), *Don Balon* (Spain and Chile), *El Grafico* (Argentina), *FIFA News and Magazine* (Switzerland), *Foot* (Belgium), *France Football* (France), *Gazzetta dello Sport* (Italy), *Kicker* (Germany), *L'Equipe* (France), *Marca* (Spain), *Neue Fussball Woche* (former German Democratic Republic), *Nepsport* (Hungary), *Onze* (France), *Placar* (Brazil), *Planete Foot* (France), *Przeglad Sportowy* (Poland), *Soccer America* (United States), *Sovietski Sport* (former Soviet Union), *Sport* (Switzerland), *Sportul* (Romania), *Tuttosport* (Italy), *Voetbal International* (Holland), *World Soccer* (England).

Books and reference works:
Barrett, Norman: *World Soccer from A to Z* (Pan).
Bayona, Roman and Matteo, Carlos Lopez: *Enciclopedia Mundial del Futbol* (Oceano).
Beccantini, Roberto: *Dizionario Del Calcio* (Rizzoli).
Becker, Friedebert: *Europapokal* series (Copress).
Glanville, Brian and Weinstein, Jerry: *World Cup* series (Robert Hale and others).
Glanville, Brian: *The Footballer's Companion* (Eyre and Spottiswoode).
Gowarzewski, Andrzej: *Encyklopedia pitkarskich mistrzostw swiata* (Wydawnictwo SiT).
Hammond, Mike: *European Football Yearbook* series (Sports Projects).
Heimann, Karl-Heinz and Jens, Karl-Heinz: *Kicker-Almanach* series (Copress).
Henshaw, Richard: *Encyclopedia of World Soccer* (New Republic).
Hockings, Ron: *European Cups* (Kenneth Mason).
Huba, Karl-Heinz: *Fussball Europameisterschaft* (Copress).
Huba, Karl-Heinz: *Fussball Welt-geschichte* (Copress).
Jeffrey, Gordon: *European International Football* (The Sportsmans Book Club).
Jiminez Casado, Amparo: *Historia Del Futbol Espanol* (Aresa).
Jose, Colin: *NASL, A Complete Record of the North American Soccer League* (Breedon).
Lo Presti, Salvatore: *Annuario del Calcio Mondiale* series (Societa Editrice Torinese).
MacDonald, Roger: *Britain Versus Europe* (Pelham).
Meisl, Willy: *Soccer Revolution* (Phoenix).
Oliver, Guy: *The Guinness Book of World Soccer* (Guinness Publishing).
Puskas, Ferenc: *Captain of Hungary* (Cassell).
Raynor, George: *Football Ambasssador at Large* (Soccer Book Club).
Rethacker, Jean-Philippe, Thibert, Jacques: *La Fabuleuse Histoire Du Football* (Editions ODIL).
Rollin, Jack: *Rothmans Football Yearbook* series (Queen Anne Press then Headline).
Taylor, Frank: *The Day a Team Died* (Souvenir).
Walter Fritz: *3:2 Die Spiele Zur Weltmeisterschaft* (Copress).
Wilson, Neil: *The Sports Business* (Piatkus).

THE COMPLETE
ENCYCLOPEDIA
OF
SOCCER

The BIBLE of WORLD SOCCER

KEIR RADNEDGE
Executive editor, *World Soccer* magazine

CARLTON

CONTENTS

FOREWORD BY
GARY LINEKER

Welcome to the ultimate encyclopedia of the world's greatest sport. If proof were needed that football is an all-consuming passion from Newcastle to Nagoya, from Cape Town to Kuala Lumpur, look no further than the last World Cup. France played host to 32 teams from five continents. It was the biggest World Cup tournament ever, and FIFA, the sport's governing body, estimated that a cumulative audience of 35 billion people watched the 64 matches on television.

I was privileged to attend football's biggest party as both a TV presenter and a fan, and I'm already taking a keen interest in the next finals, which will be hosted jointly by Japan and South Korea in 2002. I travelled the world as an England international, and after happy days with Leicester City, Everton, Barcelona and Tottenham Hotspur, I ended my playing career in Japan with Grampus 8 in the early 1990s. Even then, football was booming in the Far East, and I can honestly say that Japanese supporters are as fanatical as any in the world.

Today, football is truly a dominant game. FIFA now has 198 member countries, and the traditional giants of the sport are no longer as dominant as they once were, as the likes of Croatia proved in France. Even the so-called "minnows" such as Morocco, Paraguay and Iran proved they are no longer pushovers, all of which can only bode well for the future. Football is constantly evolving; rules change, players are seemingly always on the move, and great teams come and go. But one thing remains certain: whenever there is a football match, there is drama, passion and excitement.

This informative and fascinating encyclopedia, compiled by *World Soccer* magazine's executive editor Keir Radnedge, celebrates all those qualities and more. Learn about the rise of legendary clubs such as Real Madrid, Juventus, Manchester United and Santos, as well as the incredible exploits of stars from past and present like Pele, Diego Maradona, Bobby Charlton, Johan Cruyff, Ronaldo, Zinedine Zidane and Alan Shearer. And above all, enjoy!

PREFACE

BY KEIR RADNEDGE

Call it association football, soccer, calcio, futbol, futebol or any of dozens of other linguistic variants; this is the greatest game in the world and much more.

This is the people's passion.

It is the common denominator between nations of political and armed antagonism. It is an alternative or an accompaniment to the smile which breaks down barriers. People with no other social or cultural connection may suddenly discover that the invocation of magic names such as "Pele… Real Madrid… Manchester United" can work a charm or spell.

And, for as many billions of people around the world as follow football, so they possess that many individual and powerful opinions about teams, clubs and players (and, of course, referees). But opinions can be fed only by knowledge about the game and that is what this book, in all modesty, is all about.

There remains an enormous hunger for information about the game. The 1998 World Cup Finals in France proved the point. A cumulative total of nearly 40 billion people worldwide watched the finals via television; some 2.5 million fans turned up at the stadia around France; and millions more around the world – and in Europe, in particular – raged in frustration that they were not among the lucky, comparitive few who got their hands on the gold dust which represented a match ticket.

Suddenly the World Cup had become not merely a specific sports tournament but the people's party – a fiesta, an international celebration for the common man, woman and child.

It may also be said that new perceptions about the interdependence of nations and peoples – perceptions championed particularly by the youth of the world – contributed in no small way to the success of France 98 as a spectacle in its own right.

It is to serve that vast constituency that it was decided to return to the original concept of a book about international football and start again – building the story of the modern game, its origins, its competition and its heroes on a deep statistical foundation. This book is the result. It is for every football fan… for those with a ticket and those without. The same passion devours all.

Writing and compiling this book has been a most daunting task in a sportswriting career which began in what now seem to have been the dark ages of the game in the faraway early 1960s.

Maybe the great mountaineers felt the same way in the Himalayan foothills with the peak of Everest lost up in the clouds. That we reached the summit was due to teamwork as in all the best traditions of the game. Lynn, my wife, and Aidan, my eldest son, put in long hours helping build the textual and statistical foundations.

Clubs provide an indispensible link to every aspect of football. They provide the opportunity for men and women, boys and girls to play within a structured competitive environment; they provide the talent which may ultimately graduate to the national teams for representative honours and the great tournaments such as the World Cup; they also serve as the focus through which fans channel their own vicarious enthusiasm for the game.

The initial competitions in which they met were simple knock-out events. This remains the oldest form of football tournament; in England the FA Cup is older than the Football League; in many other countries, too, such as Spain, the cup came first. It was easier to organize, for one thing.

But the game could not have turned professional without league competition though the switch from amateur to professional status caused all sorts of ructions which are hard to comprehend today when every player is equal, whether paid or unpaid. In Argentina the old amateur championship and the new professional set-up ran side by side for three years. In Colombia it was the impetus to go professional which created the famous pirate league of the late 1940s and early 1950s.

For many decades the national team was the pinnacle of achievement. But the advent of the European club competitions led to a change in the balance of power. Clubs such as Real Madrid, Milan, Juventus, Barcelona and Manchester United gained international status and fame in their own right.

Sponsorship and television subsequently brought financial power to such a degree that Silvio Berlusconi, media magnate and millionaire owner of Milan, could foresee a day when national team competitions would be overtaken in importance by international club leagues.

UEFA, the European federation, has tried to stay ahead of burgeoning club ambition in developing, then expanding, then redeveloping the UEFA Champions League. But an international superleague has been on the game's agenda for 40 years and no-one has yet seriously considered the implications of a Madrid, Milan or Manchester United stepping out of domestic competition. For this is where the bedrock of public support lies – in that sympathy and rivalry which the fan takes to the workplace, to the pub, to the bar – even to the family dinner table.

It's the same all around the world. A club's aura is not defined merely in terms of trophys won. It rests on the passion the club has aroused down the years by its style, by its failures as much as its successes, by the achievements and personalities of its finest players. It's woven into the walls of the stadium.

The clubs have an enduring, everyday permanence. Players and managers come and go, but the club remains – greater than the sum of all the individuals who pass through.

KEIR RADNEDGE, LONDON JULY 1998

The Origins of Football

Nothing unites people, nations, societies, individuals quite like association football. It is the modern opium of the masses; a *lingua franca* common to men and women, old and young, whose lives are otherwise so different they might be living on different planets. First world, Third world... at all extremes of the human spectrum, someone can be found kicking a football and imagining he – yes, or she – is scoring the winner in the World Cup Final.

The dreams it evokes govern people's lives around the world. It has developed its own culture and financial power. Billions of pounds, francs, marks and dollars are expended annually in its service. The football rolls not merely to serve the interests of 22 players on a rectangular patch of earth, but of a huge industry.

Association football, as the game came to be called, exists on two levels. It is, for the amateur, the provider of enormous pleasure (as well as addictive frustration) but it is also the most effective medium of showbusiness. Acting and singing are restricted by language and culture. Not football. A pensioner in Brighton and a child in Beijing share exactly the same emotions in participating in the ritual, as player or spectator, half a world apart.

The universal foundations have been traced by the world's scholars, all eager to claim for their own culture the origins of the greatest game of all. There is evidence of a form of football being played in China long before Julius Caesar brought the Roman game of *harpastum* to Britain.

China provides history's first football report, among the writings of the Han Dynasty 2000 years ago. Then Japan supported its bid to host the 2002 World Cup by noting 14-century-old records of a local game called *kenatt*. The rules may have changed down the centuries but the pursuit of what we term a football has remained one of man's most consistent entertainments. It was just so for the Greeks and the Romans. Pollux describes the pastime of *harpastum* in the following terms: "The players divided themselves into two bands. The ball was thrown upon the line in the middle. At the two ends behind the places where the players were stationed there were two other lines [which would seem to be equivalent to modern goal-lines], beyond which they tried to carry it, a feat that could not be done without pushing one another backward and forward." This suggests that harpastum was the origin of both rugby football and association football.

Ball games in Britain seem to have started as annual events staged over Shrovetide. As a rule these contests began in the market-place and involved two teams of unlimited numbers trying to propel a ball into the opposite side's goal, usually some convenient spot not too remote from the centre of town. It was very hostile, violent and extremely dangerous. Householders had to barricade their lower windows as the mobs did battle along the streets. The hero was the lucky player who eventually grounded the ball in goal. Not that it was always a ball. The followers of the rebel leader Jack Cade kicked a pig's bladder in the streets of London. In Chester it was even more distasteful. There the game originated as a celebration of victory over the marauding Danes, and the head of one of the vanquished army was used as a football. Later generations were content to boot a leather ball at their Shrove Tuesday festivals.

Banned by Royal Decree

There is a record of London schoolboys playing organized football before Lent in 1175, and so popular had the game become in the city's streets in the reign of Edward II that the merchants, fearing this most robust and violent activity was affecting their trade, petitioned the King to prohibit the game. On April 13, 1314, Edward II issued the following proclamation forbidding the practice as leading to a breach of the peace: "Forasmuch as there is great noise in the city caused by hustling over large balls, from which many evils may arise, which God forbid; we command and forbid on behalf of the King, on pain of imprisonment, such game to be used in the city in future." This was just one of many attempts to stamp out this popular activity. In 1349 Edward III tried to put an end to football because he felt the young men of the day were spending more time playing football than practising archery or javelin-throwing. He commanded his sheriffs to suppress "such idle practices."

Similar orders were issued by Richard II, Henry IV and James III, without any lasting effect. One such Royal proclamation in 1491 forbade the people to participate in football or golf: it was to be an offence if "in a place of the realme ther be used futeball, golfe, or other sik unprofitable sports." Despite these spoilsport measures the game flourished in the Tudor and Stuart epochs. It took Cromwell to suppress the activity effectively, after which football did not come back into vogue until the Restoration. Samuel Pepys, writing a hundred years after the event, describes how, in the great freeze of January 1565, "the streets were full of footballs." There were still no rules, the game basically being an excuse for an uninhibited ruck. Sir Thomas Elyot, in a well-known book entitled *The Governour,* published in 1564, waxes wroth against football, which he dismisses as "beastlike furie and extreme violence deserving only to be put in perpetual silence." But the lusty men of England were not to be denied their vigorous activity. During the reign of Elizabeth I football was played widely, and, in the absence of rules and referees, there were frequent and sometimes fatal accidents.

In the 17th century, football appears to have had various titles. In Cornwall it was termed "hurling," a name subsequently applied to hockey, while in Norfolk and parts of Suffolk it was known as "campynge" or "camping." Carew, in his *Survey of Cornwall*, suggests that the Cornish were the first to adopt regular rules. He records that no one was permitted to "but or handfast under the girdle," which presumably meant that tripping, charging or grabbing below the waist were prohibited. He states that it was also not allowed "to deal a foreball," which suggests it was forbidden to pass forward – another similarity with rugby football. Such rules were obviously not in general use. Strutt, in his *Sports and Pastimes*, describes football thus:

"When a match at Football is made, two parties, each containing an equal number of competitors, take the field and stand between two goals, placed at the distance of eighty or one hundred yards the one from the other. The goal is usually made with two sticks driven into the ground about two or three feet apart. The ball, which is commonly made of blown bladder and cased with leather, is delivered in the midst of the ground, and the object of each party is to drive it through the goal of their antagonists, which being achieved, the game is won. The abilities of the performers are best displayed in attacking and defending the goals, and hence the pastime was more frequently called a goal at Football than a game at Football. When the exercise becomes exceeding violent, the players kick each other's shins without the least ceremony, and some of them are over-thrown at the hazard of their limbs." It seems that "hacking" was as keenly relished in those days as it was when the game's modern renaissance began in the mid-19th century. By the end of the 20th century, of course, the very idea of "hacking" for its own sake would be viewed with horror.

A Unified Code

Football's sometime image as the working man's game overlooks one salient piece of history: it was the public schools, and Oxford and Cambridge Universities, which brought shape and order out of almost aimless violence. Nearly all the schools and numerous clubs which had mushroomed in the wake of the Industrial Revolution had their own sets of rules. Some allowed the ball to be handled, some did not; some limited the number of participants on each side, some did not. Some favoured hacking and tripping and grounding opponents by hand, while others

barred them. The overall situation was chaotic, to say the least; so, in 1846, the first serious attempt to unify a code of rules was instigated at Cambridge University by Messrs. H de Winton and J C Thring, who met representatives from the major public schools with a view to formulating a standardized set of rules. Their deliberations took seven hours, 55 minutes, and were published as the Cambridge Rules. These were well accepted and years afterwards, with very few alterations, became the Association Rules. There is no copy of the original regulations, and the earliest set of rules to which those of the Football Association may be traced are those issued by Mr Thring in 1862 when he was Assistant Master at Uppingham, a public school.

These were the rules for what he termed "The Simplest Game," and as they are so important to the development of Association football as we know it today they are worthy of reproduction. The Football Association came into being in October 1863 following a meeting at the Freemasons' Tavern, Great Queen Street, London, "for the purpose of forming an Association with the object of establishing a definite code of rules for the regulation of the game." Representatives of all the major clubs were present and they appointed Mr A Pember as president and Mr E C Morley as honorary secretary. Mr Morley was asked to write to the captains of the leading schools inviting them to co-operate in the movement, but at a second meeting, held a few days later, it was revealed replies from Harrow, Charterhouse and Westminster indicated they preferred to cling to their own rules. At a third meeting a letter of acceptance was read from Mr Thring of Uppingham School and considerable progress was made with the laws, which were published on December 1, 1863. At the sixth meeting, also held that month, the first committee of the Association was appointed. It consisted of: Mr J F Alcock (Forest Club), an elder brother of C W Alcock who was to come upon the scene later; Mr Warren (War Office); Mr Turner (Crystal Palace); Mr Steward (Crusaders); and the treasurer Mr Campbell (Blackheath); together with Messrs. Pember and Morley. It was at this meeting, however, that the split between the Rugby Unionists (as they were now termed) and the Associationists occurred. Blackheath withdrew their membership, though Campbell agreed to stay in office as treasurer. Another leading light was Lord Kinnaird who played in a record nine FA Cup Finals with Wanderers and the Old Etonians before being appointed to the FA Committee in 1868 and going on to become treasurer and then president.

Although there were no further major upsets, it seems there was still some uneasiness about the way the game should be played. At the FA's annual meeting in February 1866 a representative of the No Names (from Kilburn, north London) complained that only Barnes and Crystal Palace were playing strictly by association rules. All present, apart from the Lincoln club who withdrew, agreed that no member clubs should ever play under any other rules.

The association and the game grew steadily in public favour following the introduction of the FA Cup and international fixtures, but the comparatively peaceful progress enjoyed until 1880 was followed by a decade of drastic reforms. The number of rules of the association had by now increased from ten to 15. Scotland still refused to adopt the English throw-in, or the English understanding of the offside rule; apart from that, the two associations were on friendly terms with each other. But there loomed another crisis which was to become as significant as that which separated the associationists from the rugby followers. It was the advent of the paid player – the first professionals. By now the membership of the FA, including clubs and affiliated associations, amounted to 128, of which 80 belonged to the South of England, 41 to the North, six to Scotland and one to Australia. Amid persistent rumours that many of the Northern contingent were paying men to play for them, the following new rule (No. 16) was added in 1882:

"That any member of a club receiving remuneration or consideration of any sort, above his actual expenses and any wages actually lost by any such player taking part in any match, shall be debarred from taking part in either Cup, inter-Association or International contests, and any club employing such player shall be excluded from this Association." The liberty to pay "wages lost" was abused, and this falling away from amateurism was seen by those in the South as a reflection of an unsportsmanlike spirit.

Football had flourished with far greater rapidity in Scotland than in the rest of the UK, and English clubs looked north of the Border to strengthen their teams. The FA at first turned a blind eye, but its hand was forced by the Sheffield, Lancashire and Birmingham Associations, each of which held inquiries into charges of professionalism. In January 1883 an FA commission was appointed to look into the allegations. It consisted of C W Alcock, N L Jackson, J H Cofield, T Hindle and J R Harvey. They proved nothing. Yet the disquiet among the best amateur clubs continued and there was a veiled threat by some to boycott the FA Cup at the commencement of the 1883–84 season.

The row came to a head in 1884 when the Upton Park Club lodged a complaint against Preston North End on the grounds of professionalism. The case attracted wide publicity; and when William Sudell, the president of the Preston club and in effect the manager, admitted they did pay their players – and that he could prove that nearly every other important club in Lancashire and the Midlands did likewise – the cat was out of the bag. Preston were disqualified from that season's FA Cup but the frankness of Sudell's confession brought home to the FA councillors the need to face reality. At their next committee meeting C W Alcock proposed "that the time has come for the legalization of professionalism." This was seconded by Dr Morley but was by not a unanimous decision, and a concerted battle to repress the move raged until 1885 when the football professional was legalized.

Real rules

The rules which Kinnaird helped draft were taken around the world by the mixed bag of soldiers, sailors, civil servants, doctors, engineers and adventurers who built the British Empire. How ironic that arguably the most enduring legacy of their world-encompassing efforts should have been the absorption of Association football.

Naturally, the football spell worked first upon those European countries with a sea-coast. In Portugal, British university students played football in Lisbon in 1866. The Lisbon Football Club was founded in 1875 and the locals were forming their own clubs a decade later. In Spain, the first footballs were imported by British mining engineers to the northern Basque provinces in the 1890s. Today, pride in the historical link with football's "mother country" is evidenced still by the mere name of the Athletic Club of Bilbao (forced by Franco to become "Atletico" the club reverted to its historic title as soon as political shifts permitted. Not that the fans had ever taken any notice). British military personnel took the game to the great cities of Madrid and Barcelona. It was a Swiss, Hans Gamper, who founded FC Barcelona – but Real Madrid proudly recall an Englishman, Arthur Johnson, as their first trainer-manager at the turn of the century. Football was so important to Johnson that he arranged his wedding in the morning so as not to miss the afternoon's match. Football widows the world over may testify that nothing has changed in almost a century.

Athletics education in Italy in the 19th century had developed through the gymnastics schools, strongly influenced by the German academies. In 1896 the Italian gymnastics federation organized the first local football tournament between regional representative teams as a side-show to a weekend conference in Treviso. One of the pioneer societies was the Andrea Doria of Genoa, venerable ancestor of the present-day Sampdoria football club.

Contact between these societies and English sailors and merchants soon had the Italians won over to the merits of association football. A leading light was Edoardo Bosio, whose business took him between Turin and London. In March 1887 he brought a "proper football" home with him and fascinated his friends with his tales of the "matches" he had seen. In 1891 Bosio founded the Internazionale Football Club of Turin. More clubs sprang up, created both by Italians and by English residents, including the quaintly-named Genoa Cricket and Athletic Club in 1892 and the Milan Cricket and Football Club in 1899.

Of course, cricket soon fell by the wayside. But with Genoa and Milan, as with Bilbao in Spain, the historic link of the English names survives proudly to this day.

The first heroic player was Genoa's Dr Spensley who organized the first formal match against Bosio's FC Torinese on January 6, 1898. Genoa won with a goal by Mr Savage. Italy had awoken to modern football; though, with an eye to history, it borrowed

FIFA Presidents

1904–1906	**Robert Guerin** *(France)*
1906–1918	**Daniel Burley Woolfall** *(England)*
1921–1954	**Jules Rimet** *(France)*
1954–1955	**Rodolphe Seeldrayers** *(Belgium)*
1956–1961	**Arthur Drewry** *(England)*
1961–1974	**Sir Stanley Rous** *(England)*
1974–1998	**Joao Havelange** *(Brazil)*
1998–	**Joseph Blatter** *(Austria)*

the ancient Florentine title of Calcio.

To the north, France had its own history built around a football game called *la soule* whose roots are buried in Roman and Celtic folklore. But the game had been banned, on grounds of public order, by the end of the 18th century. It took British sailors, starting formally with Le Havre Athletic Club in 1872, to reintroduce the game's modern equivalent.

The game spreads

For many years, well into the 20th century, rugby proved a more popular import than soccer. Many rugby clubs were already thriving when, in 1891, British residents in Paris founded the country's first two clubs devoted exclusively to soccer. These were the all-Scottish White Rovers FC and Gordon FC (later renamed Standard). White Rovers beat their rivals 10–1 in 1892 in the first formal match recorded between French clubs. That same year Stade Français, the first club founded by Frenchmen, was created.

In Germany, too, association football faced early resistance, in this case from the established gymnastics and athletics societies. In many cases football crept in through the back door, being adopted as just one extra section of existing sports clubs. One of the most famous examples was TSV 1860 München, founded, obviously, in 1860 and proud of the fact. Originally the football section was just one of many teams. Now TSV 1860 München is renowned only for football and it is the basketball, orienteering, water-sport, handball, weightlifting, sailing, athletics, skiing, tennis and volleyball sections which have faded into the background, in the general public's perception at least. Football crossed the border into Germany through the North Sea ports of Hamburg and Bremen in 1870. An Oxford University XI toured Germany in 1875 in what is considered one of the first formal foreign tours by an English football club. The first German translation of the rules of the game was undertaken in Hamburg in 1876 and the game rapidly spread south via Berlin and on down to Dresden, Leipzig and Munich. Leipzig may be considered the birthplace of Germany's football organization since it saw the founding of the Deutscher Füßball-Bund in 1900. The DFB, still the governing body of German football, has proved a remarkably resilient organization down all the years of political turmoil.

Football's birth in Holland was a kick-about among British workmen at a textiles factory in Enschede in the 1860s. In the 1870s, students at a Jesuit college near Utrecht organized a team. So did British embassy staff in The Hague. But these were isolated developments. It took a Dutchman to popularize association football with his fellow-countrymen. Pim Mulier came upon a cross between football and rugby while attending boarding school in Noordwijk near Leiden in 1870. Few of his fellow-students were impressed. But nine years later, in a shop in Amsterdam, he saw a football for sale and all the old enthusiasm was rekindled. Mulier bought the ball, told friends about this strange British pastime and they played throughout the summer on a park in Haarlem. That September they formally set up what is now the oldest club in Holland: the Haarlemse Football Club. Parents and teachers were not so keen. The game was too rough. So Mulier ordered a copy of the "proper" rules from England, cut out the kicking and hacking, and won over many more converts. In 1885 he translated the rules into Dutch and, four years later, Haarlemse FC and nine other clubs formed a Dutch federation, later to become, with royal patronage, the present KNVB. Early royal enthusiasm was not confined to Holland. In neighbouring Belgium King Leopold II donated a league championship trophy as early as 1897; and the proliferation in Spain of clubs with the Real (or "Royal") prefix records the enthusiastic support of the pre-Franco monarchy.

To the north and east of Britain, sea and trade spread the soccer gospel. That is why Gothenburg is the traditional heart of Swedish soccer rather than the capital, Stockholm, and why old histories of the Russian game refer to the Charnock family's textile mills at Orekhovo as having given birth to the club which would one day be the foundation for the legendary Moscow Dynamo.

The varying regions of Europe also developed football along their own cultural lines. In Britain and northern Europe football was a robust outdoor enterprise for the hardy, around the Mediterranean it was an exercise in passion, while in central Europe it reflected a more languidly artistic temperament.

The late Willy Meisl, in the matchless book *Football Revolution*, left a vivid first-hand account of how football sparkled to life simultaneously in Prague, Vienna and Graz in the old Austrian monarchy.

Vienna depended on a large and influential British colony which ran many of the most fashionable shops as well as local gasworks which lit the streets. As in Italy and Spain, so in Austria, the English origins survive in club names such as First Vienna, which not only included Baron Rothschild's gardeners William Beale and James Black among its founding players but also adopted his blue and yellow racing colours.

Such was the enthusiasm generated by the first matches that when Vienna played the Vienna Cricket and Football Club in 1897 an entrance fee of sixpence was imposed "to reduce the number of spectators." M D Nicholson, who worked for Thomas Cook in Vienna, was the first president of the Austrian federation which was built up by the subsequent work of Hugo Meisl, son of a local banker who turned his back on the family business for the sake of football. It was Meisl who arranged touring visits by a string of British clubs and national teams, and imported the legendary coach Jimmy Hogan.

Budapest linked Vienna and Prague in a founding chain of central European football clubs and the Hungarian Alfred Schaffer earned the honorary title of "The Football King", long before the days of Puskas, Kocsis and Co.

Before the First World War brought organized football to a halt through Europe (barring Scandinavia) almost every country had its own thriving football association and active national team. Professionalism, in one form or another, was also developing apace. Association football was not merely an aesthetic exercise for the participant; it was rapidly becoming the major spectator entertainment in all four corners of the world.

South America joins in

In Brazil, British sailors were the first to play on its shores in 1874, and in 1878 men from the ship *Crimea* allegedly put on an exhibition match for the Princess Isabel. But Charles Miller, born in Sao Paolo, the son of English immigrants, who came to England to study and returned ten years later with kit and two new footballs after playing for Southampton, is acknowledged as the true inspiration of the game in Brazil. Miller encouraged the British workers in establishments such as the Gas Company, the London Bank and the Sao Paolo Railway, and the founders of the Sao Paolo Athletic Club – which was then exclusively concerned with cricket – to form football teams. The first real match was staged in April 1894 with the Rail team beating the Gas team 4–2. The first club comprising mainly Brazilians was established in 1898: the Associaçao Athletica Mackenzie College in Sao Paolo. Thus the game in South America is as old as it is on the European continent. The British influence is seen clearly in the names of some of the club sides: Corinthians in Brazil; Liverpool and Wanderers in Uruguay; and Everton and Rangers in Chile, while Argentina boasts Newells Old Boys and River Plate.

In Argentina, although football was begun in the last century by British residents of Buenos Aires, it was slow to catch on with the locals. The national side of 1911 was full of Englishmen, though one, Arnold Hutton, a star forward, declined to play in one match because he had agreed to play rugby for his club. But it was Italian immigrants who really triggered the game's popularity there, as indeed they did throughout much of Latin America.

Rules of The Simplest Game

1. A goal is scored whenever the ball is forced through the goal and under the bar, except it be thrown by hand.

2. Hands may be used only to stop a ball and place it on the ground before the feet.

3. Kicks must be aimed only at the ball.

4. A player may not kick the ball whilst in the air.

5. No tripping up or heel kicking allowed.

6. Whenever a ball is kicked beyond the side flags, it must be returned by the player who kicked it, from the spot it passed the flag line, in a straight line towards the middle of the ground.

7. When a ball is kicked behind the line of goal, it shall be kicked off from that line by one of the side whose goal it is.

8. No player may stand within six paces of the kicker when he is kicking off.

9. A player is out of play immediately he is in front of the ball, and must return behind the ball as soon as possible. If the ball is kicked by his own side past a player, he may not touch or kick it, or advance, until one of the other side has first kicked it, or one of his own side has been able to kick it on a level with, or in front of him.

10. No charging allowed when a player is out of play; that is, immediately the ball is behind him.

In Africa, not only English but French and, to a lesser extent, German and Portuguese colonial movements played predominant roles in introducing football. For Portugal, the investment paid off spectacularly: their outstanding team at the 1966 World Cup drew its finest players, Eusebio and Mario Coluna, from the colony of Mozambique. To develop into a coherent world-wide force, football needed a governing body with the power and authority to encourage international development through mutual co-operation and competition, as well as through control and refinement of the laws of the game.

Naturally, the English had no interest in such internationalization. A Dutch banker, C A W Hirschman, wrote to the Football Association with his idea in 1902. A similar suggestion was sent by the Union des Sociétés Françaises de Sports Athletiques in 1903. Sir Frederick Wall, secretary of the FA, replied: "The Council of the [British] Football Associations cannot see the advantages of such a federation but, on all matters upon which joint action was desirable, they would be prepared to confer."

So the English were absent when, on May 21, 1904, delegates from Belgium, Denmark, France, Holland, Spain, Sweden and Switzerland met in Paris to found the Federation Internationale de Football Association. In due course England relented a little and D B Woolfall became second president of FIFA. But it was his successor, a Frenchman, Jules Rimet, president from 1921 to 1954, who brought FIFA and world football through their adolescent years and moved FIFA to the neutral haven of Zürich, Switzerland, in 1932.

World powerbase

Football's presence at the Olympic Games grew increasingly important up until 1928. Then, as amateurism was pushed aside amid virtual sporting civil war in some countries, so Rimet inspired the creation of the all-embracing World Cup, launched in Uruguay in 1930. The South Americans were unimpressed when timorous Europe sent only four nations to compete. Mutual suspicion between the Old World and the New has never been far from the surface. It emerged in full political colours in 1974 when the incumbent English autocrat, Sir Stanley Rous, was defeated in elections for the FIFA presidency by Brazil's João Havelange. Havelange ushered in football's brave new world. He invoked the bankrolling potential of the twin powers of television and sponsorship to turn FIFA not only into the richest sports authority in the world but one of the globe's most powerful business corporations. His long-time aide and general secretary – and successor – Sepp Blatter would joke that "new nations find it hard to decide which to join first: the United Nations or FIFA." But it was no joke. Havelange invested World Cup profits in worldwide development programmes and a wide-ranging competitive structure. In 1974 there was just the World Cup. By

the end of 1996, when Havelange announced his intention to retire as FIFA president, FIFA controlled world championships in youth, junior, women's and indoor categories of football. Also by this time, with the promotion to independent regional status of Oceania, football's pyramid of power comprised FIFA at the apex, then the six regional confederations (Africa, Asia, Europe, North and Central America, Oceania, South America) which boasted a membership of 200 national associations.

The power of football's English founders had dwindled. England, Scotland, Wales and Northern Ireland were permitted to retain their independent status as a gesture to history. But that was worth only one vote apiece in the bi-annual FIFA Congress, precisely equal to the voting power of, say, the Faroe Islands. Even on the law-making International Board, the four British associations now had to share their power with four representatives from FIFA.

Back in 1904 FIFA and European football represented one and the same force. But by the mid-1950s the game was spreading apace as Europe's imperial shackles were slowly released in Africa, Asia and the Far East. Now Europe wanted to rebuild its power base. Thus, on June 15, 1954, in Basle, on the eve of the World Cup finals, the Union of European Football Associations (UEFA) was founded in Switzerland. Initially UEFA comprised 25 national federations; by 1996, after the fragmentation of the former Soviet Union and Yugoslavia, its membership had doubled. UEFA was founded to help focus its own members' increasing demand for international competition and co-operation. Within five years it had launched a European Championship for national teams as well as taking control of the prestigious European Cup for Champion Clubs (now the UEFA Champions League).

The two central individuals within UEFA are the president and the general secretary. Current president is Lennart Johansson of Sweden, who took up his mandate in 1990 after the retirement through ill-health of Jacques Georges of France. He is a former president of the Swedish federation and a vice-president of FIFA. German Gerhard Aigner has been general secretary since 1988. In addition to the club competitions, UEFA also supervises a wide range of other events, from the senior European Championship for national teams to youth events in various categories from Under-21 down, to a women's championship and a full range of coaching and development programmes. UEFA's ambition and financial power led, in 1996, to diplomatic warfare with FIFA over a perceived under-selling of World Cup television rights and the autocratic manner in which Havelange wielded control.

Across the world, similar confederations exist to govern the game in Africa, in Asia, in Oceania, in South America and in Central and North America. Their leaders fly the world, stay in the best hotels, enjoy the confidences of presidents and prime ministers. They represent a new aristocracy. Lord Kinnaird and his cronies might well have approved.

The Laws of Football

The Laws (not the rules) of football have been honed down to 17 in number, with numerous sub-clauses. This evolutionary process began in the mid-nineteenth century and continued through to the 1930s, when Stanley Rous recodified the Laws.

Recently the Laws were redrafted by FIFA. Law changes are made by the International Board, made up of eight members, four of them from the Home Countries of England, Scotland, Wales and Northern Ireland, and four from FIFA. It takes a threequarter majority to alter a Law. What follows is a summary of the Laws, as published by FIFA, simplified for general use.

The object of the game

The game is played by two teams, each consisting of 11 players, one of whom must be a goalkeeper. The goalkeeper must wear clothing that distinguishes him from his team-mates and does not clash with the colours worn by his opponents or the referee. Substitutes are allowed to each team, but once a player has been replaced that player may not re-enter the game. Each competition has its own rules which dictate how many substitutes per side are permitted. In international soccer it is now usually three, selected from seven named before the match, but this does vary. Most domestic competitions allow either two or three, the third being a goalkeeper, all of whom have to be named beforehand.

On the pitch the game is regulated in senior football by a referee and two linesmen, whereas in junior football it is permitted simply to have a referee.

The object of the game is to propel a ball by foot or any part of

England's David Beckham is shown a red card at the 1998 World Cup finals

The Officials

Originally soccer was played with an umpire and a referee rather like the game of tennis. Gradually it was necessary to introduce touch judges with the umpire's role transformed into that of the modern day referee who has two assistants, better known as linesmen, The assistant referees are qualified officials who specifically indicate ball in and out of play at throw-ins, corner kicks and goal kicks; who mainly are given the responsibility of deciding offside; who are required to attract the attention of the referee at substitutions and are generally there to aid and assist the referee.

The referee is the sole time-keeper and enforcer of the Laws. He therefore in order to carry these obligations into effect takes on to the field with him a stop watch, a whistle to start and stop the game, a pencil so as to write in all weather conditions, a note book or paper and a red and yellow card to administer punishment. In senior football he is usually entrusted with one match ball to take on to the pitch although he is required to inspect all match balls before the match starts to ensure they comply with the Laws.

The referee must report all misconduct to the appropriate body governing the game; he may refrain from punishing to play the advantage in favour of the attacking team and he can reverse his decision so long as the game has not been re-started. He should only accept the intervention of a linesman if the linesman is better placed to see the incident.

Referees are encouraged to absorb and administer the unwritten eighteenth Law shortly known as "common sense" and therefore he should indicate by means of approved signals various decisions. The referee will decide how to administer the game with his referee's assistants (formerly known as linesmen) and advise them where to stand. The usual system is known as the "diagonal system" and involves the referee being in the middle with each of the assistants being on either the right or left diagonal so that they are always in vision of each other. He will also discuss with them what positions to take up at penalties and corners. In addition,the three officials all compare watches before the start of the game.

Over a period of years the referees' outfit evolved from a jacket top and plus-fours trousers into a blazer and shorts, followed by a tunic top, which ultimately became an all-black outfit with white trimmings and socks to match. In recent years experiments have taken place with different colour outfits though FIFA generally requires referees to wear predominantly black.

---

the body other than the hands or arms into your opponents' goal. At each end of the field there is a goal consisting of two uprights placed eight yards (7.32m) apart (the inside measurement between the two posts), and joined at the top by a cross-bar eight feet in height (2.44m to the lower part of the bar) above the ground. The uprights and cross-bars should not exceed five inches (0.12m) in width and must be the same width. Normally these are made of wood or tubular steel. In senior football a net is is attached to the uprights and cross-bar or free-standing supports, to indicate clearly when a goal has been scored.

The field of play

The game is played on a pitch the surface of which is usually grass, although some competitions allow artificial surfaces of different types. The field of play is rectangular and measures between 100 to 130 yards (90–120m) in length and 50 to 100 yards (45–90m) in width. Under no circumstances can the pitch be square. The field of play is bounded by painted lines. Those down the longer side are known as the touch-lines, and those across the shorter side, on which the goals are positioned, as the goal-lines. All such boundary lines and other pitch markings, which should be no more than five inches (0.12m) wide, form part of the field of play.

Other pitch markings consist of a centre-line drawn across the pitch at a point midway between the two goal-lines. In the middle of this is placed a centre spot, from which play commences at the start of each half and after a goal is scored. A circle is drawn, with a ten-yard (9.15m) radius from the centre spot, within which no opponent is allowed to encroach until the ball is kicked into play. In each corner of the field, where the goal-line and touch-line meet, is a corner flag with a minimum height of five feet (1.5m). A quadrant with a one-yard (1m) radius is drawn at each corner of the field. As an optional extra, flags may be placed opposite the centre-line but must be at least one yard (1m) behind the touch-lines.

The goals are placed at the centre of each goal-line, and two lines are drawn at right angles to the goal-line six yards (5.5m) from the goal-posts. They extend into the field of play for a distance of six yards (5.5m) and are joined by a line of 20 yards (18.3m) parallel to the goal-line. This section defines the goal area. The goal area is enclosed within the larger penalty area, which is created by drawing two lines at right angles to the goal-line, 18 yards (16.5m) from each goal-post, which extend into the field of play a distance of 18 yards (16.5m) and are joined by a line of 44 yards (40.3m) parallel to the goal-line.

The penalty mark from where penalty kicks must be taken is marked twelve yards (11m) from the goal-line and facing the mid point of the goal. The Laws decree that there must be no encroachment when a penalty kick is taken. In order to ensure that all players apart from the kicker stand 10 yards (9.15m) from the ball until such a kick is taken, an arc with a radius of ten yards (9.15m), using the penalty spot as its centre, is drawn outside the area, and the players must stand outisde the area and outside this arc.

The game is played with a ball which must be round and made of leather or any other approved material, its circumference being between 27 and 28 inches (0.68–0.71m) and its weight between 14 and 16 ounces (396–453gm).

The object of the game is to score more goals than the opposition. In order to score a goal the whole of the ball must pass between the goal posts, under the cross-bar and across the goal-line. The whole of the ball must cross the whole of the line. If no goals are scored, or the teams have an equal number of goals, the match is termed a draw.

The duration of play

The match starts with a kick-off, with the ball placed on the centre spot and kicked forward by one of the attackers. Prior to that, the captains of the two teams meet the referee to spin a coin for choice of ends or kick-off. The winning captain generally makes the election for the first half, since the teams change ends to start the second half. The ball is in play once it has travelled its own circumference in the opponents' half of the pitch. The player taking the kick-off may not play the ball again until it has been touched by another player.

Play is divided into two equal halves, and in senior football a half lasts 45 minutes (although this can be reduced either by the rules of the competition or by agreement between the teams),

The Penalty Kick

This is for the serious offences mentioned. Taken from the penalty mark, it can be awarded irrespective of where the ball is at the time the offence is committed, provided that the ball is in play and the offence takes place in the penalty area. A goal may be scored directly from a penalty and the only players allowed in the penalty area until the ball has been kicked are the one taking the kick and the goalkeeper. If either team infringes these regulations, the kick will be retaken, except in the case of an infringement by the defending team where a goal has been scored. In that event the goal will normally be awarded, because to do otherwise would be to allow the offending team to gain an advantage from the infringement. Examples of when a retake is ordered are: where the goalkeeper saves the ball or the kick is missed, but the goalkeeper moved forward from goal-line before the kick was taken or there is encroachment by the defending side; where a goal is scored and there is encroachment by the attacking side; and, finally, where the kick is taken, whether or not a goal is scored, and there is encroachment by both sides. A match shall be extended at half-time or full-time to allow the penalty kick to be taken or retaken, but the extension shall last only until the moment that the penalty kick has been completed, whether it results in a goal, a miss or a save. Different rules apply in cup competitions when the teams are level at full-time and the game is to be decided by the taking of an initial five penalties by each side.

The Goalkeeper

The goalkeeper is the only player entitled to handle the ball, but he is only allowed to do this within his own penalty area. When he leaves his penalty area he becomes an ordinary player. He wears clothing which distinguishes him from all other members of his team, his opponents and the referee, and if he fails to do so he can be sent from the pitch until he complies with this ruling. The goalkeeper is the only other player apart from the penalty-taker to be in the penalty area at the time a kick is taken. He has to stand on the goal-line though a recent Law change allows him to move his feet before the ball is struck.

The goalkeeper is king in his own goal area and may not be charged except when he is holding the ball or obstructing an opponent in that particular area.

However, he is capable of being penalized more than any other player on the pitch. He may be penalized for taking more than four steps in any direction while in possession of the ball, whether holding or bouncing the ball or throwing it in the air and catching it again without releasing it into play; or if, having released the ball into play before, during or after the four steps, he touches it again with his hands before it has been touched or played by another player of the same team outside the penalty area, or by a player of the opposing team inside or outside the penalty area. Similarly, where a defending player deliberately kicks the ball to him, he is not permitted to touch it with his hands, and if he does he is penalized by the award of an indirect free-kick against him.

Finally, the goalkeeper is the only player to suffer the wrath of the Laws if he indulges in tactics which in the opinion of the referee are designed merely to hold up the game and thus waste time, giving an unfair advantage to his own team. These disadvantages are intended to balance out the advantage of being the only one who can legitimately handle the ball.

He is able to score a goal with a kick from his hands from his own penalty area, provided the ball is in play; and if he chooses to be just another player he can come out of his penalty area to score at the other end.

and there is a half-time interval lasting a minimum of five minutes.

To decide cup matches which are drawn after 90 minutes, extra time, usually of 15 minutes each way, is played. Some competitions allow for a penalty kick decider to occur to ascertain the winner. A 'golden goal' or 'sudden death' system in extra-time, with the first goal deciding the outcome, has already been employed in the finals of the 1996 European Championship and 1998 World Cup.

Equipment

A player's equipment consists of a jersey or shirt, shorts, socks, shinguards and footwear. The teams must wear colours that do not clash with each other or the referee. A player shall not wear anything that is dangerous to another player.

In play and out of play

The ball is in play at all times from the start of the match to the finish, including where an infringement of the Laws occurs (until a decision is given and the game is stopped by the referee). It is still in play when it rebounds inside the boundaries of the field from a goal-post, cross-bar or corner flag. The ball only goes out of play when it wholly crosses the boundaries of the field, whether on the ground or in the air.

When the ball leaves the field of play over the touch-line it re-enters the field by means of a throw-in. The throw is taken by a member of the team opposing that of the player who put it out of play. The throw must be taken from as close as possible to the point at which the ball left the field. If not taken from there it is described as a foul throw and the throw-in given to the other team. The thrower takes the ball in both hands and throws it from behind and over his head. He must face the pitch with both feet on the ground on or behind the touchline at the moment he delivers the throw.

When the ball leaves the field of play over the goal-line it is returned into play either by means of a goal-kick, if last touched by an attacker, or a corner kick, if last touched by a defender. At a goal-kick the defending side (usually the goalkeeper)

Brazil's Roberto Carlos, one of the modern experts of long-distance shooting, takes a corner against Italy at Le Tournoi 1997

restarts the game by kicking the ball from either half of his goal area, and the ball is not deemed to be in play until it has passed out of the penalty area. Any infringement of this procedure results in the kick being retaken.

At a corner-kick the ball is played from the quadrant, which is a quarter circle with a radius of one yard (1m) situated in the corner of the field. The ball must be within the quadrant, and the kick must be taken at the end of the defending side's goal-line nearest to where the ball went out of play. Again the player taking the corner-kick may not play the ball a second time until it has been touched by another player, and defenders must remain at a distance of ten yards (9.15m) until the ball has been kicked.

Where there is no other method of restarting the game,

following an injury, interference by spectators or for any other accidental reason, the restart is achieved by dropping the ball at the point where it was when play was suspended. The ball is deemed to be in play the moment it touches the ground, and no player may kick or attempt to kick the ball until that moment. In the event of a breach of this procedure the drop is retaken.

Offside

Arguably the most complex of the 17 Laws is Law 11, relating to "offside". Even the wording is difficult, which pronounces that "a player is offside if he is nearer his opponents' goal-line than the ball and interfering with play or an opponent at the moment the ball is last played unless . . ." Then follow four exceptions: (1) from restarts, namely goal-kicks, corner-kicks and throw-ins, but not free-kicks; (2) if a player is in his own half of the field; (3) if the ball was last played to him by an opponent; (4) if he is not nearer to the goal-line than at least two defenders, even if one is the goalkeeper.

In these cases he is not offside. The main problems come in deciding when the ball was last "played", and whether or not an attacker is "interfering". If the referee considers that an attacking player, albeit in an "offside position", is not interfering with play or with an opponent or seeking to gain an advantage by being in that offside position, he shall refrain from penalizing him and stopping play. A player who is level with the penultimate defender is not in an offside position. In such cases, the attacking player must be given the benefit of any doubt. A player cannot be offside if he is behind the ball when it is played, even if there are no defenders between him and the goal.

Infringements of the Laws

As football is a physical contact sport, infringements of the Laws will inevitably occur, giving rise to punishment by the referee in the form of "free-kicks". These free-kicks may be either "direct" or "indirect". The difference is that a goal may be scored directly from a direct free-kick but not from an indirect free-kick. At an indirect free-kick a second player must play the ball after the kicker before a goal can be scored.

A direct free-kick is awarded for more serious offences, and if these occur in the penalty area a penalty is awarded. All free-kicks (except penalties) are taken from the place where the infringement occurred unless they take place in the goal area. Then the attacking side take this indirect free-kick from that place on the goal-area line which is parallel to the goal-line and is nearest the infringement. For the defending side, the free-kick can be taken from anywhere inside the goal area.

Although opponents must be at least 10 yards (9.15m) from the ball at the moment the free-kick is taken, the attacking side has the option of waiving this rule should they consider that they would obtain greater advantage from taking the kick quickly. The referee may play what is known as the "advantage clause" and not award a free-kick if he considers that to play on is advantageous to the attacking team.

The more serious offences, for which a direct free-kick can be awarded, are intentional fouls or misconduct and are divided into nine categories, of which six are fouls against an opponent, two are against either an opponent or a team-mate, and one is technical. The six are: (a) tripping or throwing an opponent; (b)

jumping at an opponent; (c) charging an opponent from behind (unless he is obstructing); (d) holding an opponent; (e) pushing an opponent; (f) charging an opponent in a violent or dangerous manner. The two more serious offences are kicking or attempting to kick another player and striking or attempting to strike or spit at another player – or indeed the referee. The final offence is deliberately handling the ball which is defined as "carrying, propelling or striking the ball with the hand or arm". If any of these nine offences is committed by the defending side in their own penalty area, the referee will award a penalty, which is taken from the penalty mark.

Indirect free-kicks are awarded for eight main offences, which are: (a) dangerous (rather than violent) play; (b) charging fairly but at a time when the opponent does not have the ball within playing distance; (c) obstruction; (d) charging the goalkeeper except when he is holding the ball or is obstructing an opponent or has passed outside his goal area; (e) time-wasting by the goalkeeper; (f) the goalkeeper not releasing the ball in accordance with the laws; (g) any occasion when a player deliberately kicks the ball to his goalkeeper and the goalkeeper then touches it with his hand or hands, or when the goalkeeper deliberately handles the ball twice without an opponent touching it if he is not attempting to save the ball; (h) indulging in anything which the referee considers to be ungentlemanly conduct, including trying to circumvent the Laws – particularly the deliberate kick to the goalkeeper rule. In addition, an indirect free-kick is also awarded for the technical offence of offside.

The referee has power to punish these offences further if they are considered serious enough. A player shall be cautioned and shown the yellow card by the referee if he (a) enters or leaves the field of play without receiving a signal from the referee to do so; (b) persistently infringes the Laws of the Game; (c) shows, by word or actions, dissent from any decision given by the referee, or (d) is guilty of any act of ungentlemanly conduct, with particular reference to kicking the ball away after the award of a free-kick, encroaching from a "defensive wall" or standing in front of the ball to stop a free-kick being taken. For even more serious offences a player shall be shown the red card and sent off the field if (a) in the opinion of the referee a defending player impedes an opponent through unlawful means when that opponent has an obvious goalscoring opportunity; (b) any player is guilty of violent conduct or serious foul play, such as a violent tackle from behind with little or no attempt to play the ball, but also including spitting; (c) a defending player other than the goalkeeper in his own penalty area intentionally handles the ball to deny a goal or goalscoring opportunity; (d) any player uses foul or abusive language to anyone on the field of play; (e) a player after already having received a caution persists in misconduct.

Chapter 2

INTERNATIONAL
FOOTBALL
AND

COUPE
DU
MONDE
1938

TOURNAMENTS
COMPETITIONS

International Football Tournaments and Competitions

No sports competition on earth commands attention quite like the World Cup. This is the ultimate expression of the greatest game of all and the one game which unites the peoples of all nations – albeit not all of them countries in which association football is the No. 1 sport.

Competition has been the essence of the game since the very first international, played between Scotland and England in November 1872. Some competitions faded and disappeared. But the strongest, like the World Cup for nations, the European club tournaments and their South American and subsequent African and Asian counterparts, flourished as a worldwide competitive structure developed.

Scotland vs. England developed into the British Home Championship. South American students took the idea south of the equator and launched the South American Championship. Back in Europe, between the wars, the Mitropa Cup provided an international testing ground for the leading clubs of central and southern Europe.

Then came the World Cup itself. And so, by the start of the 1930s, the template for the competitive international structure that we know today, had been laid.

The 1950s brought a further expansion, with the success of the European cups for club sides and the launch of the European Championship for international sides. Each developing footballing region copied the competitive structures of Europe.

Now, the sheer weight of the international fixture list has forced football's world governing body, FIFA, into striving to impose a worldwide fixture schedule around which the game can organize itself harmoniously into the next century. Harmony is a key theme, since the increasing commercial and professional pressures have increased the antagonism between clubs and national associations on how and when players may be made available for the multiplicity of tournaments demanding their presence at both club and national level.

To qualify for the World Cup, many nations play around a dozen matches. When the various club competitions are added, top players can face around 70 games per year with very little let-up. The era of jet travel means players can fly between continents within hours and their countries expect them to do just that – to the annoyance of the clubs who pay their wages.

None of this was dreamed of by FIFA's founders when they put a cloak of reality over the vision of a world championship.

The first mention of the idea was at the congress of 1905. The proposal came from the Dutch representative, C A W Hirschmann. His idea was that a championship between national teams should be played at the end of each season; that congress would annually select the host association for the following year; that the competition format would be a knock-out system; that each association would pay its own costs; that any profits that were made should be split among the competing nations; that no country could select foreigners.

The first "world championship" – the term had already entered the minutes – was set for Switzerland in 1906. The British home nations would comprise one group; Spain, France, Belgium and Holland a second; Switzerland, Italy, Austria and Hungary a third; Germany, Denmark and Sweden a fourth.

All well and good – except that not one of those nations lodged a formal entry application. Grumpy words were exchanged at the 1906 congress. The idea was then pushed into the background until after the arrival on the scene of the now famous Frenchman Jules Rimet, who made his FIFA "debut" at the 1914 congress in Oslo.

In the meantime FIFA agreed, on Hirschmann's suggestion, to recognise the Olympic Games football tournament as a world amateur championship. There the matter rested until after the First World War when Rimet took over the FIFA presidency.

The success of the 1924 Olympic football tournament in Paris inspired him to re-examine the proposals for a World Cup. That work was given added impetus when, walking in Paris, he literally bumped into the Uruguayan diplomat Enrique Buero, who was then ambassador in Brussels. The two men had met at the Paris Olympics when Buero had accompanied Uruguay's winning team.

They exchanged greetings, reminisced over the Olympic football tournament and Buero said that, if Rimet was interested in pursuing the idea, the Uruguayan government might well consider not merely hosting a first World Cup but meeting all the costs of the competing nations. After all, in 1930, Uruguay would be celebrating its centenary and what more fitting way to do so than to welcome the world.

Rimet wrote later: "The World Cup was born in that happy meeting; surely providence at work."

Of course, Rimet needed no persuading about the launch of a World Cup. The rest of FIFA's expanding membership was another matter. He resurrected the idea at the 1927 congress and, a year later in Zurich, drove through formal acceptance of the concept that FIFA should organise a world championship every four years with the inaugural event in 1930.

In May 1929, at the congress of Barcelona, Spain, Holland, Hungary, Italy, Sweden and Uruguay applied to be the first hosts. Before the debate, Holland and Sweden withdrew in favour of Italy's candidature. Argentine delegate Adrian Beccar Varela then spoke up so forcefully on behalf of Uruguay that Spain, Hungary and Italy all withdrew.

Where were the British in all this? Gone. They had long since withdrawn fom FIFA in a row over the issue of broken time payments for amateurs. It's almost impossible now to understand the passion the issue invoked and the bitterness.

Thus the British home nations were absent from the first World Cup. Indeed, the rest of Europe very nearly missed the kick-off as well. When the logistics of travelling to Uruguay – a three-week boat trip – had sunk in, several of the European federations got cold feet. Two months before the competition, not one European entry had been received. Indeed, several European federations proposed switching the finals to convenient Italy. Rimet was furious. Argentina, Brazil, Paraguay, Peru, Chile, Mexico and Bolivia had accepted, as well as the United States. The Latin American federations were embittered by what they considered a European betrayal and threatened to withdraw from FIFA.

Rimet stood firm and put all his diplomatic skills to work. Eventually France, Belgium, Yugoslavia and, under the influence of King Carol, Romania all relented.

Their reward was an indelible place in football history.

Current world champions, France celebrate their 3–0 win over Brazil in July 1998

HISTORY OF THE WORLD CUP

Uruguay 1930

Lucien Laurent made history on Sunday, July 13, 1930, by scoring the first goal in World Cup history after 19 minutes of the Opening Match between France and Mexico. At the time the significance of the goal – beyond its simple value in this match – escaped him.

But then, the setting and the weather were modest indeed. Years later Laurent recalled: "The stadium we played in was only tiny. About 5,000 people would have filled it. And it was snowing! Remember, this was winter time in the southern hemisphere. It was a shock for us. We had come from mid-summer in Europe. Not that any of us cared. We were just thrilled to be there … ."

Altogether the Uruguayans had hoped for 16 nations at the finals. They had to make do with 13, including themselves.

The wonderful new Centenario stadium was not finished – shades of many future World Cups! – by the day of the Opening Match. France thus played Mexico in the little Pocitos stadium used by a local club side named Penarol. They did not make an auspicious start. After little more than 20 minutes goalkeeper Alex Thepot took a kick on the jaw in a collision with Mexico's Nicho Mejia and had to be helped from the pitch. No substitutes in those days – indeed no substitutes for another 40 years. Thus left-half Augustin Chantrel took over between the posts.

Even with 10 men, however, the French proved too good, running out 4–1 winners.

Two days later and the French bubble had burst. They lost 1–0 to Argentina. Burly centre-half Luisito Monti – later a hero with Juventus and Italy – scored the only goal nine minutes from time. The game had ended in chaos when Brazilian referee Almeida Rego blew for what he thought was time six minutes early as Langiller raced through for a possible equalizer. He was persuaded to bring the players back and restart the match but, by then, the French had lost their impetus.

As for Argentina, they would only get better. In their next match, against Mexico, Argentina brought in young Guillermo

FIFA president Jules Rimet presents the World Cup to Uruguayan officials

Stabile, known as "El Infiltrador". He scored three goals in Argentina's 6–3 victory – in a game of five penalties – and finished as the top scorer of the tournament.

Argentina topped Group 1, while from Group 2 Yugoslavia qualified with victories over Brazil and Bolivia. The United States were most impressive in Group 4, reaching the semi-finals without conceding a goal. Later the legend grew up that the American team was full of Scottish ex-professionals. That was not, in fact, the case but then, American soccer teams have always struggled to make the rest of the world take them seriously. Their hit-on-the-break tactics proved highly effective in the group matches. They defeated Belgium 3–0 in their first game and then Paraguay 3–0 next time out. Bert Patenaude scored once against Belgium and twice against Paraguay.

The World Cup's first ever hat-trick came from Uruguay's Pedro Cea in the semi-final 6–1 crushing of Yugoslavia. In the other semi-final Argentina dispatched the United States by the same margin to set up a repeat of the Olympic Final two years previously, which had been won by Uruguay.

A cordon of police and soldiers surrounded the Centenario stadium on the morning of the match, as they searched all fans for firearms. Not that all the fans made it to the match. Three thousand Argentine supporters boarded the Italian cruise ship Duilio in Buenos Aires… and never made it to Montevideo on the northern shores of the river Plate. Fog in the harbour prevented the ship from docking.

Inside the stadium more trouble was brewing. The Uruguayan and Argentine delegations could not agree which matchball to use. In the end they compromised, using an Argentine ball in the first half, a Uruguayan in the second.

Uruguay were happy with their team but not the Argentines. Controversy raged around the inclusion of Monti, whose aggressive style had infuriated the Uruguayan fans in many of his previous matches.

Another problem player was the Argentine inside-right, Pancho Varallo. He had broken a bone in his foot and spent the four days before the Final in bed. On the morning of the game he said he was not fit but one of the directors from Boca Juniors was a member of the selection committee. Boca had hired a boat to bring fans across the river Plate to see Varallo play … and, for that reason, he was told to shut up and get his boots on.

Ten minutes into the match Varallo twisted his foot and collapsed in pain. He was a passenger for the rest of the match.

Uruguay started in style, Pablo Dorado opening the scoring after 12 minutes. Argentina, weakened or not, hit back quickly to equalize through Carlos Peucelle, then forged ahead in the 35th minute with a disputed goal by Stabile, as the Uruguayans appealed for offside.

Twelve minutes into the second half – and now using the Uruguayan football, remember – the hosts hit back. Cea equalized then outside-left Santos Iriarte made it 3–2. Argentina

Uruguay vs. Argentina before the first ever World Cup Final

rallied. Five minutes remained when Varallo, ignoring the pain, shot for goal. Uruguay's Jose Andrade somehow scrambled the ball off the line with the Argentines angrily claiming the equaliser. As they plunged forward in desperation so Uruguay ran away for Castro to underline their victory with a fourth goal in the closing seconds.

Uruguay, first World Cup hosts, had become the first World Cup winners.

Italy 1934

Uruguay remain the only World Cup winners in history who did not defend their title. Upset by the Europeans' reluctance to participate in 1930, and plagued by players' strikes, they stayed at home. But now dozens of countries expressed an interest in either hosting or contesting the next World Cup.

FIFA's Berlin Congress of 1931 had before it two rival bids to host the 1934 finals from Spain and Hungary. Before addressing that matter, FIFA regulated that the maximum number of finalists should be 16 and that all qualifying matches should be played in the 12 months before the finals.

By 1932 both Spain and Hungary had had second thoughts and Italy and Sweden claimed host rights. Sweden ultimately

Hosts Italy open the 1934 World Cup with the fascist salute

withdrew, leaving Italy host to host the finals by default.

No fewer than 32 countries – 22 from Europe, eight from the Americas and one each from Asia and Africa – contested a qualifying series in which even hosts Italy had to take part, easily defeating Greece.

Uruguay, despite a late plea from Jules Rimet, remained resolutely aloof. Not only that, but they tried in vain to persuade Brazil and Argentina to join their boycott of the finals. In fact Argentina, riven by internal problems over the introduction of professionalism and angry at the way Italian clubs had poached their best players in 1930, sent a weakened team.

The 1934 World Cup may be considered the first soccer tournament to have been infiltrated by political concerns. The Italian dictator, Benito Mussolini, demanded not merely that the event run smoothly but that the Italian national team should prove ultimately superior.

Il Duce is supposed to have summoned Admiral Vaccaro, head of the Italian federation, to his palace in Rome.

"Admiral," said Mussolini, "Italy must win the World Cup."

Vaccaro replied: "Of course, Duce, that would be a wonderful achievement."

Mussolini interrupted coldly: "Admiral, I don't think you understood me … I said: Italy MUST win the World Cup."

Apocryphal or not, the development of the tournament certainly suggested that home advantage played a significant role in the Italians' ultimate victory. Not that Italy needed much outside help. Manager Vittorio Pozzo had fine players at his disposal. Goalkeeper Gianpiero Combi remains one of the greatest of all time; Argentine émigré Monti at centre-half was fearsome; Giuseppe Meazza and Giovanni Ferrari were two of the greatest European inside-forwards of the inter-war years.

They had no problems seeing off the United States 7–1 in their first match, Mussolini watching from the VIP box in the National Fascist Party stadium in Rome.

The competition was organized on a knock-out basis, which meant that Brazil, who were beaten 3–1 by Spain, and Argentina, who had been defeated 3–2 by Sweden, had travelled 8,000 miles to play just one solitary game.

The toughest tie of the quarter-finals saw Italy take on Spain in a match which rapidly escaped the control of Belgian referee Louis Baert, and in which Spain's legendary goalkeeper Ricardo Zamora played the game of his life.

After Luis Regueiro had opened the scoring for Spain on 31 minutes, the game grew more violent as the Italians grew more desperate. Eventually, when Mario Pizziolo shot, Italian forwards Meazza and Angelo Schiavio "sandwiched" Zamora, the ball ran loose and Ferrari equalized.

No fewer than seven Spanish players, including most crucially Zamora, were too battered and bruised to line up for the replay the following day when Meazza's 12th-minute header put Italy into the semi-finals. There they met Austria, who had been brought down to a rugged level themselves by Hungary in a quarter-final later described by their coach as "a brawl, not an exhibition of football".

A muddy pitch for the semi-final was not conducive to good football and Italy won when right-winger Enrico Guaita capitalized on a brilliant set-play routine, following a corner, to score in the 18th minute. Czechoslovakia, the conquerers of Romania and Switzerland, joined Italy in the Final after a 3–1 victory over Germany, with two goals by their star inside-forward Oldrich Nejedly.

Nejedly and left-wing partner Antonin Puc formed one of the most lethal attacking partnerships in European football. Their almost telepathic understanding enabled them to play in a manner described as being "as pure as Bohemian crystal".

Mussolini was in Rome for the Final expecting to see it

shattered. FIFA president Rimet was amazed and delighted that no fewer than 270 journalists attended to report the occasion and the Italians set up broadcast facilities to reach as far around the world as was then possible.

The football did not live up to the occasion. The first half produced few chances and no goals. Finally, in the 70th minute, the Czechoslovaks shocked their hosts by seizing the lead. Puc outplayed full-back Eraldo Monzeglio and shot past Combi.

Again Italy had come up against a brilliant goalkeeper in the Czechoslovak hero Frantisek Planicka. But, with eight minutes left, Italian left-winger Raimondo Orsi, through on goal, shaped to shoot with his left but hit the ball with his right boot. The ball spun crazily goalward, and though Planicka got his fingers to it, he could not prevent a goal.

The shot was a freak. Next day Orsi returned to the stadium to show the reporters how he had done it ... and gave up after 50 failed attempts.

For the first time, the World Cup Final went into an extra 30 minutes. Pozzo switched Orsi to centre-forward, the leg-weary centre-forward Schiavio he moved out to the right wing. Yet Schiavio it was who hit the Italian winner seven minutes into extra time.

"I didn't think I had the strength in me," said Schiavio later. "The ball sat up in front of me and I just swung my leg at it."

The result: Italy were world champions.

France 1938

Football came home for Jules Rimet in 1938 when his own France played host to the World Cup. Ironically, considering events much further down the line, FIFA had originally considered awarding the finals jointly to France, Holland and Belgium because it was feared the French did not have enough adequate stadiums.

In the end the French won the day – much to the anger of Argentina. They had thought the World Cup should return to South America. In protest they boycotted the 1938 finals and persuaded Colombia, Costa Rica, the United States, Mexico, El Salvador and Surinam to withdraw from the qualifying rounds in sympathy.

Already the shadow of war was cast across the tournament. Japan withdrew from the qualifying round because of the war with China. Austria, having qualified for the finals, were unable to take up their place because, by the summer of 1938, the country had been swallowed up after the Anschluss into Greater Germany.

FIFA invited England – despite the fact that they were not eligible as a non-member – to take the Austrians' place but the Football Association refused.

Further developments of the regulations saw FIFA decide that the holders should be seeded direct to the next finals as of right and that each nation should register a list of 22 players for the

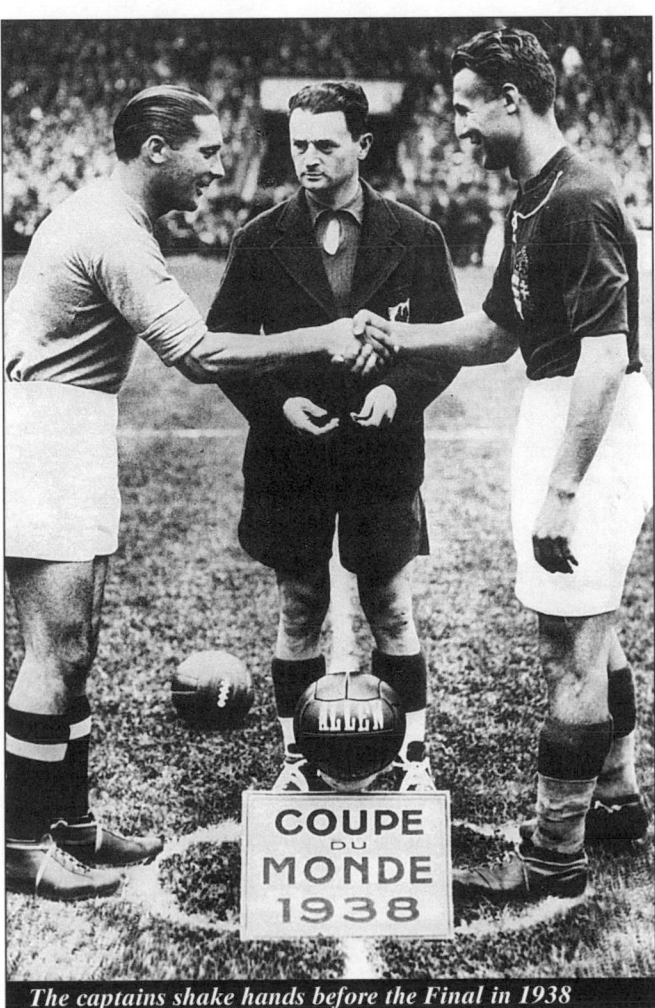

The captains shake hands before the Final in 1938

tournament. FIFA also agreed to pay the second-class travel costs for a delegation of 17 members with a daily allowance of three dollars per person per day. The fact that the 1934 Final had gone to extra time also concerned FIFA. It was decided that if the scores were level in the Final after extra time then a replay, also with extra time, would take place. If the scores were still level, then the countries would be declared joint winners.

Looking ahead, Brazil applied to host the 1942 finals, only to be told that FIFA had already accepted a bid by Germany …

Again the competitive format was a knock-out system with Sweden gaining a first-round bye because of Austria's absence. Remarkably, only Hungary, who eclipsed the Dutch East Indies 6–0, and France – 3–1 winners over Belgium – came through in 90 minutes. All the other ties went to extra time or replays.

Defending champions Italy were saved by their goalkeeper Aldo Olivieri, who made a blinding save from Norwegian centre-forward Knut Brynildsen in the last minute of the game to earn extra time. New star centre-forward Silvio Piola then struck the goal which saw them through.

Brazil emerged from the mud of Strasbourg after an 11-goal thriller. A hat-trick by their wonderfully agile centre-forward Lenidas da Silva gave the South Americans a 3–1 half-time lead, but the Poles ran riot after the break to force extra time. Ernst Wilimowski netted three times before Leonidas grabbed his own fourth to help Brazil to a 6–5 win!

The second round provided no shocks, though Brazil needed two games to eliminate 1934 runners-up Czechoslovakia and earn a semi final joust with Italy. Brazil were so confident that they rested Leonidas and inside-forward Tim from the semi-final in Marseille so they would be fresh for the Final … which they never reached. Italian captain Meazza converted the winning penalty. In the other semi-final, Hungary beat Sweden 5–1.

Italy's victory in 1934 had been tarnished by an uneasy sense that they had gained particular benefit from host status.

There was no such doubt in 1938. The political aura still hung strongly around the team. They were now kitted out not in Italy's traditional blue but in fascist all-black and the players gave a full-arm fascist salute when they lined up before kick-off. But they won the event fair and square in a foreign venue and deserved to do so.

Coach Vittorio Pozzo and his Italian winners in 1938

Brazil score against Spain in the host nation's 6–1 victory

Italy's opponents in the Final in the Stade Colombes in Paris were Hungary. The outcome was rarely in doubt once Gino Colaussi had drilled Italy ahead in the sixth minute after a scintillating run almost the length of the field from Amedeo Biavati. Pal Titkos equalized from close range within a minute but the goal only stung Italy to find their best form. Inside-forwards Meazza and Ferrari – the only survivors from the 1934 winning team – were in dazzling form.

Piola restored Italy's lead in the 15th minute, and Colaussi made it 3–1 in the 35th. In the 65th minute Sarosi forced the ball over the Italian line, but a magnificent back-heeled pass from Biavati set up Piola to smash in what proved to be the decisive goal in the 82nd minute.

Italy were world champions again ... and, with mankind set to descend into the horror and dislocation of a protracted global war, would remain so for 12 long years.

Brazil 1950

The first tournament after the war – for what was now known as the Jules Rimet trophy – was to prove a thriller, particularly enjoyable since the build-up to the tournament had verged on the chaotic. Jules Rimet himself is said to have kept the trophy under his bed for protection throughout the war.

Brazil, Argentina and Germany had originally applied to host the 1942 event that never was, but the Brazilians were the only ones in the ring for the championships scheduled for 1949, then put back to 1950. Before the qualifiers had even kicked off, Argentina, Ecuador, Peru, Belgium and Austria withdrew while Turkey and Scotland both pulled out having clinched their places in Brazil. The absence of Germany, and Communist countries like Hungary and Czechoslovakia, saw unsuccessful qualifiers France and Portugal invited to travel to Brazil, while

England had qualified by right to take their place in the finals for the first time.

Even with the participants safely gathered on South American soil, the finals themselves ran no more smoothly, with the enormous Maracana stadium not finished when Brazil opened against Mexico. Only Italy were granted the comfort of staying in one city for their group matches, one group consisted of just two teams – Uruguay and Bolivia – while the others boasted four apiece. France, having been granted a lifeline, chose to cut themselves adrift when faced with the nightmare logistics of participation. The tournament was reduced to 13 teams, as it had been in 1930: optimistic Uruguayan fans may have spotted the first favourable omen here.

The competition was arranged, as in 1930, on a pool basis. Brazil won Pool 1 despite a 2–2 draw with Switzerland, and Uruguay's 8–0 rout of Bolivia saw them effortlessly through Pool 4. The shocks came in Pools 2 and 3. A year earlier, eight Italian internationals had been among the fatalities when the entire Torino team was killed in an air crash, including captain Valentino Mazzola. A revamped Italian side started well enough, Riccardo Carapellese shooting them into a seventh-minute lead against Sweden. But by the break they were 2–1 down to goals from Jeppson and Sune Andersson. Jeppson grabbed another midway through the second half and, though Muccinelli replied and Carapellese hit the bar, this was Sweden's day. It was a setback the Italians were unable to overcome.

The greatest shock of all, however, was to beset England, rated by many as the finest team in the world. After a 2–0 victory over Chile, the game against the USA in Belo Horizonte seemed a formality. Instead it became a fiasco. England, having left out Stanley Matthews, hit the bar and found goalkeeper Borghi unbeatable. Then in the 37th minute the impossible happened. Bahr shot from the left and the Haiti-born Larry Gaetjens got a touch with his head – deliberate or accidental? – to divert the ball into the net. 1–0 to the USA, managed by Bill Jeffrey, a Scot! A single goal from Zarra in their final match against Spain formally ended England's hopes of progress, but the sucker-punch had already been thrown, by an American side which had long since lost the standing their 1930 counterparts had achieved.

There was no Final in this competition, Brazil, Uruguay, Sweden and Spain qualifying for the Final Pool. The hosts were favourites as they faced Uruguay in the last game (fortunately for the besieged organizers, a virtual Final) a point ahead, the talents of Ademir, Jair, Chico, Friaca and Zizinho having already humiliated Sweden and Spain, 7–1 and 6–1 respectively. A draw would make Brazil champions.

The pulsating action perfectly suited the occasion, watched by a 199,000-strong Maracana crowd – nearly all of whom had arrived to celebrate the hosts' first world title. But Brazil's inside-forward trio of Zizinho, Ademir and Jair, weaving gloriously through the Uruguayan defence, found goalkeeper Roque

Maspoli playing the game of his life. The giant Obdulio Varela proved another stumbling block, as did Rodriguez Andrade. They cracked in the 47th minute, Alcides Friaca shooting past Maspoli, but Uruguay's response was positive, and in the 65th minute Ghiggia's cross found Juan Schiaffino unmarked – his thunderous shot gave Barbosa no hope. Brazil were shaken, the fizz went out of their game, and when Ghiggia ran in to shoot home in the 79th minute they were beaten, victims of their own complacence. Indeed, Brazil manager Flavio Costa had warned before the game, "I'm afraid that my players will take the field on Sunday as though they had already had the championship shield sewn on their jerseys. It isn't an exhibition game. It is a match like any other, only harder than the others." Prophetic words, indeed.

After 20 years the World Cup had returned to Uruguay, their second triumph in their second finals appearance. For Brazil, shell-shocked in their own homes, streets and stadiums, the waiting game played on.

Switzerland 1954

Hungary arrived in Zurich as the hottest ever World Cup favourites. The magic of Puskas, Hidegkuti and Kocsis had added a new dimension to the beautiful game and, what is more, had proved an unbeatable combination in the 1952 Olympic tournament in Helsinki.

No one was really surprised when the Magyars rattled in 17 goals in their opening pool matches against South Korea and West Germany. Sandor Kocsis scored four against the Germans in an 8–3 win but Hungary were left a significant legacy by their opponents, centre-half Werner Liebrich delivering a fateful kick on Ferenc Puskas that caused the "Galloping Major" to limp from the action in the 30th minute. It was an injury from which he never fully recovered during the remainder of the tournament.

Hungary, of course, cruised into the quarter-finals, where they dispatched Brazil 4–2, but Germany had to win a play-off with Turkey to earn the right to face Yugoslavia.

England began with a 4–4 draw with Belgium, yet secured a quarter-final place with a 2–0 win over Switzerland. The Scots were not so successful. They failed to score and were beaten by Austria and Uruguay, neither of whom conceded a goal in their pool. Indeed, the Scots' 7–0 trouncing at the hands of Uruguay was an ignominious climax to the country's first appearance in the World Cup finals.

Stanley Matthews and Schiaffino took the individual honours as Uruguay beat England 4–2, the holders benefiting from some poor goalkeeping from England's Gil Merrick, but the competition was sullied by a notorious clash between Brazil and Hungary, which was dubbed "The Battle of Berne". Three players – Hungary's Jozsef Bozsik, and Nilton Santos and Humberto Tozzi of Brazil – were sent off by beleaguered English referee Arthur

Max Morlock scores West Germany's first goal in the 1954 final

Ellis, and a shameful fight ensued in the dressing-rooms afterwards, as the Brazilians – minus the stars of 1950, Zizinho, Ademir and Jair – added disgrace to their defeated disappointment. Puskas himself, watching the match from the stands, was later accused of striking the Brazilian centre-half Pinheiro with a bottle in the dressing-rooms.

If that was infamous, then the Austria-Switzerland tie was incredible. The Swiss, impressive throughout their hosting of the tournament, scored three in 20 minutes, and Austria replied with three in three minutes. In one seven-minute period, there were five goals! Eventually Austria came out 7–5 winners, even allowing themselves the luxury of a missed penalty, and admirably making up for their absence from the 1950 tournament, when they had judged themselves too young to compete. Wagner of Austria and Switzerland's Hügi notched up a hat-trick apiece, although Kocsis of Hungary would finish as the tournament's leading scorer, his 11 goals nearly double the tally of his closest contenders.

The Swiss captain Roger Bocquet had blatantly ignored his doctor's advice not to play, as he had been suffering with a tumour, but his determination not only to take the field once more before his operation, but to remain steadfast at centre-half, overrode their counsel.

Germany – having successfully gambled the odds in their group matches, fielding a weakened side against Hungary before defeating Turkey – just managed to scrape a victory over Yugoslavia, scoring a goal at the start, and another – which many claimed offside – at the end, of their quarter-final contest.

They were far more convincing in an amazing semi-final against Austria, running out 6–1 winners as the Austrian defence, led by Ernst Ocwirk, collapsed after being just a goal down at half-time. Goalkeeper Walter Zeman, surprisingly recalled to the line-up in place of Schmied, took the brunt of the criticism, for an unnerved display, although the Austrian defenders' lack of authority in the air assisted Germany's attackers. The other semi-final, pitting champions Uruguay against favourites Hungary, is considered by many the greatest game ever played, Czibor, Hidegkuti and Kocsis (twice) all getting on the scoresheet as the Magyars won 4–2 in extra time – for the first time, despite boasting the incandescent inside-forward Schiaffino, Uruguay tasted defeat in the World Cup.

Puskas returned for the Final, but it was a mistake. Although he scored the opening goal in a devastating start which saw Hungary score twice in eight minutes, his ankle was not fully recovered. Max Morlock replied for Germany in the 11th minute and Helmut Rahn blasted in two fine goals – the last only seven minutes from time – to win it for Germany. For the second successive World Cup, all expectations had been confounded, although the shock was perhaps greater this time around – indeed, this was the only match Hungary lost between 1950 and 1956. Puskas thought he had scored an equalizer, but it was ruled out for offside – for him, and the country his brilliance inspired, the greatest glory in the game was a crocked ankle too far.

Sweden 1958

After the disappointments, the deluge. Brazil enthralled the world in this competition, which was notable for the emergence of 4–2–4 and the outstanding individual talents of stars such as Didi, Garrincha, Vava and the teenager Pele. France too were to perform with style, Just Fontaine and Raymond Kopa providing the magic, while hosts Sweden provided their share of surprises.

Brazil's triumph crowned a World Cup which had seen the biggest entry yet, 48 countries taking part in the qualifying rounds. For the first, and only, time, all four British sides reached the finals, while Italy and Uruguay, winners of four of the five previous tournaments, were both absent.

For the first time since 1934, Argentina graced the competition, but their resources were severely limited by the flight of their biggest names to Europe – the irony was that Italy – who had repatriated Sivori, Angelillo, Maschio and Grillo – and Spain, who had welcomed Alfredo Di Stefano, both failed to qualify. Argentina did not last much longer, finishing bottom of their group, as did Scotland.

West Germany headed Pool 1, where Northern Ireland, who had eliminated Italy in the qualifying rounds, caused an upset by beating Czechoslovakia in a play-off to earn a quarter-final tie with France, who headed Pool 2 with Yugoslavia. Likewise Wales also made the quarter-finals, following a play-off with Hungary, and did themselves proud by limiting Brazil to one goal, inevitably scored by the 17-year-old prodigy, Pele. Brazil had comfortably emerged from a tough Pool 4 without conceding a goal, but England were knocked out when they lost 1–0 to the Soviet Union in another play-off, only four months after the Munich tragedy had robbed them of such key players as Duncan Edwards and Tommy Taylor.

Brazil had opened their campaign with a 3–0 defeat of Austria, followed by a goalless draw with England (the first ever in the World Cup Finals), before they introduced Pele, Garrincha and Zito to the world, watching the event on television for the first time, in a 2–0 defeat of the Soviet Union.

The new 4–2–4 formation deployed by Brazil took the entire footballing world by storm, radically unsettling their European opposition adhering rigidly to a 3–2–5 strategy, although France and Yugoslavia were delighting spectators with their flowing, attractive football.

As they had done four years earlier, though, West Germany ended Yugoslavia's challenge at the quarter-final stage, despite once more being the inferior side, an early goal from Rahn proving sufficient for the Germans. Northern Ireland followed Wales on the way back home, France's Fontaine taking his

Brazil's team in 1958. Back: D Santos, Zito, Bellini, N Santos, Orlando, Gilmar. Front: Garrincha, Didi, Pele, Vava, Zagallo

Pele scores against host nation Sweden in the 1958 World Cup Final which Brazil won 5–2

impressive tally to eight goals with a brace in the 4–0 win.

The semi-finals then pitted Sweden against West Germany and Brazil against France. Hans Schäfer blasted West Germany into the lead with a spectacular volley from 25 yards, but Sweden found some encouragement from the enthusiastic Gothenburg crowd, an oasis of fanaticism in a host country curiously indifferent to the spoils on display. The equalizer from Lennart Skoglund should not have been given – Nils Liedholm blatantly controlling the ball with a hand before setting up the chance – but when Ernst Juskowiak was sent off in the 57th minute, Sweden took full advantage to clinch their Final place with goals from Gunnar Gren and Kurt Hamrin.

In the other semi-final, Brazil took a second-minute lead against France thanks to a spectacular finish from Vava. Fontaine equalized within nine minutes, but Didi restored the lead for the South Americans, and in the second half young Pele ran riot with three more goals.

Sweden's English coach George Rayner had recalled such stars as Liedholm, Gren and Hamrin to his squad, and in a sensational start to the Final, it was Liedholm who kept his poise and balance to shoot Sweden into a fourth-minute lead. It was the first time in the tournament that Brazil had been behind. Six minutes later, however, it was 1–1, when Garrincha exploded down the right, and cut the ball back for Vava to run on to and fire firmly past Svensson. Already, this was proving a fascinating spectacle. Pele slammed a shot against a post, Zagallo headed out from beneath the Brazilian bar. In the 32nd minute the Garrincha-Vava combination struck again, and when Pele made it 3–1 in the 55th

minute with a touch of sheer magic, the game was won. Bringing a dropping ball down on a thigh in a crowded penalty area, the youngster hooked it over his head, spun and volleyed thunderously into the net. The first World Cup to be shown on television had produced a moment of magic to be re-run over and over.

Zagallo and Pele added further goals, either side of a dubious second Swedish goal from Agne Simonsson, who looked offside. At the final whistle the jubilant Brazilians paraded first their own flag, and then the Swedes'. In front of 199,000 of their own fans, in their own homeland, their 1950 predecessors had fallen short. Eight years later, Brazil, watched by a crowd of just 27,100, had come good, becoming the first side to win the trophy in a continent other than their own.

France's Fontaine had his own record, his phenomenal 13 goals setting a formidable standard. But there was no doubt that Brazil were the best in the world, and they had the prize, the pictures and the Pele to prove it.

Chile 1962

Brazil retained their world crown as Garrincha took centre stage and 4–3–3 became the subtle change. But this was a World Cup that was sadly marred by violence, with the hosts Chile at the centre of the storm.

Chile had been an unexpected choice to stage the event, FIFA's preference for their bid over that of Argentina being the latest setback in the Argentinians' unhappy relationship with the

Brazil's 1962 World Cup-winning squad

championships – even after the earthquake which hit Chile in May 1960 had caused serious damage and loss of life. Chile had a population of fewer than eight million, and only one sizeable stadium, but Carlos Dittburn, president of the Chilean Football Federation, refused to allow his country's grip on the tournament to be unloosed, declaring: "We have nothing, that is why we must have the World Cup", although he died a month before "his" tournament kicked off. The stadium in Arica was named in his memory, while some stirring performances from his nation's unfancied footballers provided an appropriate tribute.

In the qualification rounds Sweden and France, second and third respectively in 1958, both failed to make the trip to South America, as did Wales and Northern Ireland, quarter-finalists in Sweden, leaving England as Britain's sole representatives after Scotland had lost a play-off to Czechoslovakia. The Czechs, on the other hand, were getting ready to make more of an impact.

Once more, both Africa and Asia were left unrepresented on world football's greatest stage, with Morocco beaten by Spain, Israel by Italy and South Korea at the hands of Yugoslavia.

At the finals themselves, reigning European champions the

Soviet Union, and the team they beat in the 1960 European Championship Final, Yugoslavia, comfortably overcame the Uruguayan and Colombian challenge in Group 1, although the Soviets squandered 3–0 and 4–1 leads over the Colombians, being pegged back to a 4–4 draw. In Group 3 Brazil's only hiccup was a goalless draw with Czechoslovakia, who were to prove the surprise package of this tournament. That fixture also saw the premature departure of Pele from the 1962 event, a torn muscle forcing him out of action. The loss of the star of 1958 only emphasized, however, the exciting strength in depth the Brazilians now possessed, shifting the spotlight on to Garrincha instead. Vicente Feola had been compelled to stand down as manager due to illness, but his replacement by Aymore Moreira had made no apparent difference to the country's inimitable flair and finesse, even with six members of the side aged the wrong side of 30.

In Group 4, England got off to a bad start. Although the 21-year-old Bobby Moore emerged as an excellent talent, other big names like Johnny Haynes and Jimmy Greaves struggled to make an impact throughout the tournament. In their first match, Walter Winterbottom's side were unable early on to break down the massed Hungarian defence after Ron Springett was beaten by a thunderous long-range effort from Tichy. A Ron Flowers penalty equalized the scores, but the impressive Florian Albert clinched it for Hungary 18 minutes from time with a glorious individual goal. England did find some form to beat Argentina 3–1, with another Flowers penalty, a Charlton special and Greaves clinching their first World Cup finals victory since 1954, before a goalless draw with Bulgaria saw them through to the quarter-finals.

It was Group 2, however, which compelled the attention, certainly for the Chilean public, reluctant audiences for other groups, but assembled in their masses to support their own side. The most explosive passions, though, were on display on the pitch, most infamously in the so-called "Battle of Santiago", a day of shame for football.

The Chile-Italy tie possessed the potential to ignite: anti-Italian feeling stemmed from the European propensity to poach South American players, while two Italian journalists had inflamed tensions by dispatching disparaging articles about conditions in Chile. Wounded South American pride was exacerbated by three of the players named in Italy's starting line-up: Jose Altafini, who had played for Brazil in 1958, and the two Argentines, Omar Sivori and Kumberto Maschio, who had helped win the South American Championship in 1957.

The football contest, under the scowling eyes of 66,000 Chilean spectators, erupted into a violent confrontation, with spitting, fighting and two-footed tackles intended to maim. That referee Ken Aston sent only two players off was amazing in a game that sullied the name of football, with Italy's players rising to the bait offered by the home side. Italy's Giorgio Ferrini was dismissed after only eight minutes, though Chilean striker Leonel Sanchez – son of a professional boxer – was lucky to stay on the pitch after breaking Maschio's nose with a smart punch of his own, retaliation for a scything challenge. Even though Italy full-back Mario David followed Ferrini down the tunnel in the second half, Chile left it late to exploit their advantage, before goals from Ramirez and Toro clinched a place in the next round. Italy, in contrast, left the tournament in dishonour.

Spain were another side who had packed their line-up with foreigners, and like Italy, they fell by the wayside, finishing bottom of Group 3, despite Paraguay's Eulogio Martinez, Uruguay's Jose Santamaria and even the 36-year-old Hungarian Puskas, fresh from a hat-trick for Real Madrid in a European Cup Final, having taken the Spanish shilling.

Brazil, however, continued to thrill, even without Pele. After the opening round had been completed, with goal difference separating sides level on points for the first time, Garrincha mesmerized England to defeat, scoring two and creating one in the holders' 3–1 win, before taking Chile apart in the semi-final, only to be sent off for retaliation. In both matches, the 5'7"

Garrincha outjumped loftier centre-halves to power stunning headers into the net.

Chile had accounted for the Soviet Union in the quarter-finals, the Soviet goalkeeper Lev Yashin, arguably the finest goalkeeper ever, showing uncharacteristic fallibility. Both Chile goals, long-range efforts from Sanchez and Eladio Rojas, were blamed on the goalkeeper.

For the third consecutive tournament, Yugoslavia faced West Germany in the quarter-finals, but the eastern Europeans made it third-time lucky, with Detar Radakovic, playing at right-half with a bandaged head after colliding with Uwe Seeler, tormenting the German defence, and scoring the only goal with just four minutes left on the clock. Another eastern European side upset the odds in the other tie, Czechoslovakia having their goalkeeper Villem Schroiff to thank for an incredible display which denied Hungary the victory their overwhelming dominance deserved. Instead, a 13th-minute strike by Scherer, in a rare Czech counter-attack, surprised the Hungarians and proved enough to deny them a place in the semi-finals. Lajos Tichy thought he had scored an equalizer, only to see it contentiously ruled out for offside by the Russian referee, Latychev.

The Chilean challenge came to an inevitable conclusion against the might of the holders, with Brazil taking a two-goal lead within half an hour, both goals coming from the magic feet of Garrincha, and although goals from Toro and Sanchez gave Chile some reward for their efforts, a brace from Vava gave the Brazilians their rightful place in the Final. The match ended unhappily for Garrincha, his lonely walk off the field for an early bath accompanied by a barrage of boos and a flying bottle which cut open his head, but there was relief when he learned that FIFA had cleared him to play in the Final – far more important than jeers and scars.

Over 76,000 had watched the hosts take on the holders. In Vina del Mar, by stark contrast, a mere 5,000 watched the eastern Europeans lock horns, with Czechoslovakia earning their Final place at the expense of the unfortunate Yugoslavia, thanks to a couple of late goals from Scherer in a 3–1 win, and another inspired display between the posts from Schroiff.

After Chile had clinched third place thanks to a last-minute Rojas goal against Yugoslavia, the Czechs found themselves in front of an infinitely larger crowd than they had become accustomed to – and manager Rudolf Vytlacil's side, featuring Josef Masopust as chief architect, duly threatened to upset all the odds when Masopust cleverly gave them the lead over Brazil in the 16th minute. The equalizer, from Amarildo – Pele's replacement – was quickly registered but it was not until the 69th minute that Zito headed the favourites into the lead. Vava made it 3–1 when goalkeeper Schroiff fumbled a lob, a rare mistake by the goalkeeper who had played such an integral part in Czechoslovakia's surprise progress to the Final.

But Brazil succeeded where Hungary and Yugoslavia had

failed in the previous rounds, and demonstrated again to the world their stylish superiority. This time, it was Amarildo who took the plaudits, the dextrous speed of turn he showed to create Brazil's second goal being the highlight of an assured performance. Mario Zagallo, who would manage his country to glory in 1970 and then manage the national team, was another linchpin, working tirelessly in midfield, bursting into attack and down the wings. Brazil – 1962 vintage at least – had proved they could win over the world even without Pele.

England 1966

For the first time in 32 years the host nation was to win the title – and inspire an enduring national mythology in the process.

1966 is the date which resonates throughout English football, 4–2 the magic scoreline, and Kenneth Wolstenholme's famous commentary the soundtrack to England's wistful nostalgia for an elusive, imagined past perfect.

This was a series that had everything – passion, controversy, some fine football, and one of the greatest upsets of all time when North Korea knocked Italy out at Ayresome Park.

In a prescient battle to stage the finals, England were chosen above the West German bid at the 1960 FIFA Congress in Rome, after Spain had pulled out of the running, the first instance of "Football Coming Home" and the perfect companion-piece to the Football Association's centenary in 1963.

After a qualifying competition which had whittled seventy entries down to 16 qualifiers – and the theft of the trophy four months before kick-off, retrieved from a garden by a dog called Pickles – the tournament itself got off to a slow start, with England held 0–0 by Uruguay at Wembley. But in Group 2 West Germany quickly displayed their potential with a 5–0 win over Switzerland, Helmut Haller and Franz Beckenbauer each scoring twice. The hosts moved into gear with comfortable victories over France and Mexico. While Roger Hunt scored three times in the two games, the prolific Jimmy Greaves failed to find the net, and a gashed leg suffered against the French ruled him out of the quarter-final. Enter one Geoff Hurst … .

In a highly competitive Group 2, West Germany and Argentina proved too strong for Spain and Switzerland.

Brazil, alas, disappointed, failing to settle in the North-West, or to survive the close, decidedly unfriendly attentions of their opponents. Former stars like Garrincha, having been injured in a motor accident, Djalma Santos and Zito found it hard to keep up with the pace, and having beaten Bulgaria 2–0, they lost their first World Cup match since 1954 in a classic encounter with Hungary, for whom Albert was the dominating factor. They then succumbed to Portugal, whose striker Eusebio was to be one of the stars of the competition. Pele had been injured in the Bulgaria clash, complaining that "My legs ached as a result of Zhechev's constant tripping and kicking", and after missing the match with Hungary, he was desperately pitched into the line-up for the last group game despite being patently unfit. After being cynically hacked by Morais, Pele pledged he would never play in the World Cup again. Happily for Brazil, and football in general, he would be back. But this time, Brazilian hopes crumpled with him.

The Soviet Union, efficient and technically sound, cruised through to the quarter-finals without alarm. For Italy, however, there was a rude awakening. Having drawn 0–0 with France and lost 1–0 to the Soviets, and seen winger Bruno Mora break his leg, they had to beat North Korea to stay in the competition, but what seemed a formality turned into a nightmare. Before the tournament, manager Edmondo Fabbri had caused anger by omitting the Inter duo of Corso and Picchi, the Cagliari striker Riva, and experienced goalkeeper Sarti, but even his fiercest critics had not imagined the calamity that was to befall them. In the 42nd minute Pak Doo Ik dispossessed Gianni Rivera, advanced and crashed a searing shot past Enrico Albertosi. It was the only goal, and sent the derisive chants of "Ko-re-a!" echoing across Italian stadiums whenever the hapless Fabbri or his colleagues showed their faces. Since winning the 1934 and 1938 World Cups, Italy had lurched from one World Cup disaster to the next, but this was their lowest point, losing to the only country from outside Europe and South America to have qualified. A disgusted Italian public, welcoming the team home, expressed their frustration in a pelter of rotten fruit.

The Liverpool lunacies continued at Goodison Park with a sensational opening to Korea's quarter-final with Portugal. There was a goal in the opening minute, followed by a second and a third – and all for Korea. It was then that Eusebio proved his genius and, thanks to him and the towering Jose Torres, the Portuguese clawed back the deficit to win a sensational game 5–3. Just as memorable, though for less glorified reasons, was the clash at Wembley between England and Argentina, where the visiting captain, Antonio Rattin, not only talked himself into being sent off, but steadfastly refused to leave the pitch. Even when he had been removed from the pitch, England made heavy weather of exploiting their extra man, until Hurst, who had not played for England at the beginning of the year, made his first impression on the tournament, scoring the winner which took England into the World Cup semi-finals for the first time.

A World Cup veteran, Soviet goalkeeper Lev Yashin, redeemed himself for his aberrations of 1962 by heroically frustrating Hungary at Roker Park. Chislenko and Porkujan capitalized on defensive frailties at the other end to lead the Soviets to a 2–1 win, while West Germany romped to another resounding success, thumping nine-man Uruguay 4–0. The fact that a German referee had sent off an Argentine against England, and an English referee had dismissed two Uruguayans against Germany, did not escape many South Americans, fuelling blurry rumours of conspiracies. Uruguay and Argentina, defeated and disgruntled, boarded their planes back home.

England skipper Bobby Moore on top of the world in 1966

The England–Portugal semi-final produced an emotional classic, Bobby Charlton upstaging the mercurial Eusebio with what many felt was his greatest game for England, garnering congratulatory handshakes from the Portugese players after his scintillating second goal. This, unlike the England-Argentina quarter-final, was a wonderful advertisement for the game, providing the poignant final image of Eusebio's tears as he left the pitch – a late penalty, the eighth of his nine tournament goals, was not enough to take the game into extra time.

West Germany had edged out the Soviet Union, in a disappointing tie, to secure their place in the Final, and there they struck the first blow through Haller, after full-back Ray Wilson had shown an uncharacteristic lapse of concentration just 13 minutes into the match. England manager Alf Ramsey had caused a sensation before kick-off by omitting star striker Greaves, despite his return from injury, instead keeping together the forward partnership of Hurst and Liverpool's Roger Hunt. Greaves was distraught, but Ramsey's selection was spectacularly vindicated. It was Hurst who equalized, Germany having held the lead for just six minutes, and his West Ham colleague Martin Peters put England in front with just 12 minutes left. England, in unfamiliar red jerseys to Germany's white, felt that the Jules Rimet trophy was surely in their grasp. But a scrambled goal from Wolfgang Weber just before the final whistle forced the game into extra time, the first time the Final had gone to an extra period since 1934.

Ramsey refused to let the England players give in to weariness and disappointment, or to rue a shot sliced wide by Bobby Charlton just before the German equalizer. Instead, he pointed to the German players, barking, "Look at them! They're finished!" In the 100th minute controversy raged. The indefatigable Alan Ball crossed, and Hurst, coming in on the near post, hammered his shot goalward. It thumped against the underside of the bar and dropped – but which side of the line? Hunt obviously believed it was a goal, turning to celebrate rather than thump the ball reassuringly over the line. Swiss referee Gottfried Dienst was not sure, but the Soviet linesman Tofik Bakhramov was. 3–2 England! Any feeling of injustice felt by the Germans was quickly deemed irrelevant. With only seconds left, Moore swept a long ball upfield for Hurst to chase, and the big striker slammed his shot into the roof of Hans Tilkowski's net to become the first player ever to score a hat-trick in a World Cup Final. Thirty-two years later, Beckenbauer conceded that, despite the controversy over the third goal, England were the better side and deserved their victory.

Soon after the Final, Bobby Charlton was named European Footballer of the Year, while Moore had been voted best player of the tournament. It is therefore surprising to consider that before the tournament, Moore's place in the side was uncertain, the Leeds United winghalf Norman Hunter being thought of as a plausible alternative, especially since Moore had fallen foul of Ramsey's strict curfews on a 1964 tour in America.

Since that famous afternoon in July 1966, those vivid scenes, those red shirts, the heroes – Hurst, Moore, the Charltons – have entered the national psyche, the question "Where were you when Hurst scored his third?" reverberating through 30-plus years of pub conversations. The man who once asked Hurst himself the same question showed a rare ignorance. It had not been the highest-quality World Cup in history, big names like Brazil and Italy had disappointed, but it was certainly one of the most memorable, and, for English fans, the most perfectly complete.

Mexico 1970

Football triumphed again in Mexico, where the colourful free-flowing Brazilians delighted again, overcoming the heat, the altitude and, in a dramatic Final, Italy – the masters of defensive caution.

Appropriately, this was the first tournament to be seen by a television audience in full colour – and there was no spectacle more vivid than Pele, Rivelino, Tostao, Jairzinho and Gerson at their brilliant best. Not that television coverage was especially favourable to the players at the time, schedules demanding many matches took place at midday, the hottest time of the day at the hottest time of the Mexican year.

The gruelling conditions – the heat and the altitude – had been the main argument against Mexico being hosts, but Argentina once more found their bid rejected, before failing to even qualify for the tournament.

Other surprise fallguys in the qualifying rounds included Portugal, Hungary, Spain and Yugoslavia, while North Korea, the surprise package of 1966, forfeited their place after refusing to play Israel, who qualified from Asia.

Carlos Alberto, Brazilian captain in 1970, weighed down by achievement

Pele scores against Italy in the 1970 final

The most serious casualties, however, were the 2,000-plus lives lost in the so-called Fútbol War between El Salvador and Honduras, after tense relations between the two countries had been sparked into military confrontation by riots surrounding their three meetings in CONCACAF qualifiers.

Africa had cause for celebration, with Morocco becoming the first nation from that continent to attend the finals, where they acquitted themselves honourably, despite only taking one point in Group 4.

There were no surprises in Groups 1 and 2 where the Soviet Union and Mexico, and Italy and Uruguay qualified comfortably. Mexico, hosts and proud possessors of the majestic Azteca stadium, revelled in their newly exalted status, while Italy, determined to avoid the humiliation of recent World Cups, beat Sweden 1–0 before playing out two goalless draws, catenaccio at its most numbingly disciplined.

The fixture between Brazil and England in Group 3 provided the outstanding tie of the series, in what many anticipated as a rehearsal for the Final. England, though perceived by critics as too drearily workmanlike, still boasted the core of their 1966 winners in the shape of Banks, Moore, Ball, Hurst, Peters and the Charltons, while newcomers like Alan Mullery and Francis Lee had played encouragingly in the build-up to the tournament; since that famous day in July 1966, the holders had lost just four times in 35 matches, and had prepared well for

the inevitably torrid Mexican conditions.

Brazil, though, had succeeded the champions as favourites for 1970, after cruising through their qualification duties, inspired by the volatile coach, Joao Saldanha, whose previous job was … journalist. Despite the unexpected appointment – Saldanha had been an implacable critic of the side – the Brazilians, built around the Santos line-up, won all six qualifying matches, scoring 23 goals, before Saldanha went an impetuous step too far. His decisions, in November 1969, to drop four defenders and call up five new men, and in February 1970 to send home Toninho and Scala, had invited rumblings of discontent, made more audible after a defeat to Argentina. But it was his plans to drop Pele which finally cast him beyond the pale. After he had been found at the house of one of his critics brandishing a revolver, Saldanha's fanciful time in charge was brought to a suitably bizarre end.

His replacement was Mario Zagallo, World Cup-winning left-winger of 1958 and 1962, who called in Rivelino to play in his old position on the left flank, alongside Gerson in midfield. With the ingenious Tostao recovered from an eye injury, Brazil entered the 1970 tournament refreshed after recent turbulence, and determined to reclaim the title they had so disappointingly relinquished four years earlier. On arrival, they proved themselves more adept at public relations than the English, quickly winning over popular Mexican support, in sharp contrast to the querulous Ramsey and what a local newspaper called his "team of thieves and drunks".

The meeting with England fully lived up to its billing. In the 10th minute Jairzinho, a wonderful player of power and pace, delivered the perfect cross from the line. Pele timed his run and jump to perfection, and his header was hard and true, angled to bounce before passing just inside the left post. The shout of "Goal!" was already in the air when Gordon Banks, who had anticipated the ball going the other way, twisted athletically to pounce and incredibly push the wickedly bouncing ball over the bar. It was one of the greatest saves ever seen.

The only goal was scored in the second half by Jairzinho, who was to find the net in all of Brazil's six matches, becoming the only Cup-winning player to score in every round of a modern World Cup finals. At the final whistle, Pele made a point of seeking out Bobby Moore to exchange shirts, Moore's performances in 1970 even more majestic than in 1966, and all the more admirable since he had the blatantly false charges of stealing a bracelet in Bogota tailing him throughout and for some months after the finals.

Both sides qualified comfortably for the next round, but England faltered in the quarter-final. Without Banks, a victim of food poisoning, they squandered a two-goal lead to lose to West Germany in extra time. Peter Bonetti, Banks's replacement, had been on a winning side in all six of his previous England appearances, but he took the blame for Germany's comeback, as did Ramsey who replaced Bobby Charlton with the score at 2–1 to England. Two minutes earlier, Bonetti had allowed a Beckenbauer shot under his body into the net, and with only eight minutes left, England's confidence dented, Seeler back headed into the net to take the tie into a very unwelcome period of extra time.

Inevitably, the German matchwinner was Bayern Munich sharpshooter Gerd Müller – Das Bomber – who had scored seven goals in the three group matches, including consecutive hat-tricks against Bulgaria and Peru. He would add two more in the semi-final to claim the Golden Boot with 10 goals for the tournament, and his four goals in 1974 would make him the World Cup's leading goalscorer.

Defeat was particularly hard for the England players to take after their hero of 1966, Hurst, had seen a goal inexplicably ruled out by the referee Coerezza, and it was to be the last time Charlton, Bonetti, Labone and the hard-working Newton played for their country.

The clash between Peru and Brazil was delectable, the Peruvians – managed by another Brazilian World Cup winner, Didi – having produced performances which fully justified their presence in Mexico, after an earthquake just before the event had put their place in jeopardy. But Brazil were the one side destined to excel them, goals from Rivelino, Tostao (two) and Jairzinho securing a 4–2 triumph.

Italy's 4–1 win over hosts Mexico, staged – suicidally for the Mexicans – not in the inspiring Azteca but the 24,000-capacity stadium in Toluca, and Uruguay's single-goal triumph over the Soviet Union, guaranteed a Europe vs. South America Final.

The all-European semi-final between Italy and West Germany, however, defied all expectations. Italy, by now recognized masters of the defensive stalemate, sat back on an early Roberto Boninsegna goal, but were shaken out of their gameplan by a last minute Schnellinger equalizer. The extra time period was a thrilling 30 minutes, Müller giving Germany the lead only for Burgnich to level. It was then Italy's turn to regain the advantage, thanks to Riva, but Müller was there again to restore parity. Just a minute later, though, Rivera scored Italy's fourth, and this time there was no comeback from the Germans.

In the other semi-final, Uruguay took a 17th-minute lead through Luis Cubilla, but once Clodoaldo had put Brazil back on terms on the stroke of half-time, there was little doubt that

West German 'keeper Sepp Maier on his 1974 lap of honour

the favourites would confirm their place in the Final, which they did with second-half strikes from Jairzinho and Rivelino.

The Final proved a marvellous affirmation of attacking football, with both sides looking to clinch their third World Cup triumph and with it, permanent possession of the Jules Rimet trophy. Pele opened the scoring – the second player, after compatriot Vava, to score in two World Cup Finals – and made two more after Boninsegna had made it 1–1, capitalizing on a dreadful error by Clodoaldo. Gerson drove in a powerful cross-shot in the 66th minute, and the match was sewn up with goals from Jairzinho and Carlos Alberto, the final strike one of the finest goals ever scored. Clodoaldo began the move in Brazil's own half, sweeping the ball through to Jairzinho. Pele laid off his famous square pass into the marauding path of the Brazilian captain, whose brusque first-time shot crashed past the helpless Albertosi, to complete what was another wonderful World Cup for the Brazilians.

The Brazilian President, General Medici, had predicted before the match that his country would score four goals – and this was not a side in the habit of disappointing people.

Certainly they were too imaginative for even the stubborn Italian defence to subdue, and with Rivera only making an appearance for the Europeans with six futile minutes left to play, the sparkle of the Brazilian front five remained undimmed, for these 90 minutes and Brazilian football fantasies ever since.

West Germany 1974

European teams dominated this series in which West Germany regained the World Cup after 20 years. It was another triumph for positive tactics, as Holland and Poland – who had surprisingly eliminated England – demonstrated to the full the attributes of skill and technique. The term "Total Football" jinked into the football vocabulary, with Cruyff, Neeskens and Rep leading the Dutch masters who abandoned the rigidity of 4–2–4 and 4–3–3 to introduce the concept of "rotation" play. Rinus Michels was perhaps the only manager to have players versatile and skilful enough to make it work.

The main threat to Dutch success was, perversely, their own achievements. Ajax had won three European Cups in succession from 1971 to 1973, but players from the Amsterdam club did not get on with those from traditional rivals Feyenoord. The camp was further disrupted by mercenary financial concerns, even threatening a strike before the finals themselves. This has been a feature of many Dutch teams since.

In fact, for all their elegance, the Dutch had made heavy weather of qualifying, being held to a draw both home and away by neighbours Belgium, and had failed to reach the previous Nations European finals.

At least the Dutch had reached the World Cup finals, for the first time since 1938. The huge shock of the qualifying rounds was the elimination of England, who could only draw 1–1 with Poland in 1973, in a game they needed to win. One newspaper responded to the failure with the headline, "The end of the world", but it would be another eight years before England regained their place on the highest stage.

The Soviet Union were also absent, although their elimination provided one of the more peculiar episodes in World Cup history. Having drawn 0–0 with Chile in the first leg of a play-off, the Russians refused to play the return in the national stadium in Santiago, the scene earlier that year of a massacre of left-wing prisoners by the new right-wing regime of General Augusto Pinochet.

The Chileans refused to play the game elsewhere, and defiantly took the field on the scheduled matchday. The Soviet players, however, were nowhere to be seen, leaving the Chileans to score in an empty net into the bemusement of all concerned. Such scenes were not seen again until 1997, when Scotland took the field for a World Cup qualifier in Tallinn without their Estonian hosts. Whereas Scotland were compelled to replay the match at a different location, however, the Soviets were granted no reprieve, the game being awarded to Chile, and USSR hopes extinguished.

Hungary, Czechoslovakia, Austria, France and Portugal were the other World Cup veterans staying home as West Germany hosted its second major tournament in two years. They had staged the Olympic Games in 1972, just as Mexico had welcomed the two tournaments in quick succession in 1968 and 1970.

The murder of 11 Israeli athletes by Palestinian terrorists at the 1972 Games had provided a chilling backdrop, prompting tight security measures at the World Cup. Happily, a repeat of that tragedy was averted, with West Germany managing to ally on-the-field success with off-the-field safety.

Holland then, irresistible as their talents were, returned across the border with just the tag of "greatest team not to have won the World Cup", instead of the new FIFA trophy jubilantly lifted into the air by West German captain Franz Beckenbauer.

The original Jules Rimet trophy had been presented to Brazil in 1970 to keep, although in 1984 it would be stolen from the offices of the Brazilian football federation and melted down before it could be retrieved, Pickles-style. Brazil's hopes of getting their hands on the 1974 version were just as unavailing. Their final position of fourth was a misleading reward for a team sorely missing the retired Pele, Gerson and Tostao, relying instead on reductive defensiveness to cling on to their title.

The South American skills on display this time around came not from Brazil or Uruguay, both sterile rather than stylish, but Argentina, finally showing real promise after a troubled relationship with the World Cup. On a European tour, they had defeated West Germany, although their preparation had been jolted by the replacement of manager Sivori with Vladislao Cap, a less inspiring figure.

West Germany's 1974 winners cluster around coach Helmut Schon and skipper Franz Beckenbauer

Half of the 16 competing nations had been eliminated after the first series of group matches, under a new system which left the Final as the sole knock-out match of the tournament. The two Germanys qualified for the second phase comfortably, even though East Germany won the only match ever played between the two countries by a single goal. They were followed through by Holland and Sweden, and Poland from Group 4, where Argentina just pipped Italy on goal difference thanks to a 4–1 victory over Haiti, whom Italy had only managed to beat 3–1.

Group 2 proved to be the most competitive. Brazil, now sadly without the retired Pele, could only draw 0–0 with Yugoslavia and Scotland, the latter appearing in the finals for the first time since 1958. Zaire were to be the key factor. Scotland defeated them 2–0, but Yugoslavia overwhelmed them 9–0 to clinch pole position on goal difference. As they went into the final round Scotland needed victory over Yugoslavia to win the group. They could only draw 1–1, and Brazil squeezed through, by virtue of one goal, thanks to a 3–0 win over Zaire.

Holland, inevitably, looked impressive. They topped Group A to qualify for the Final without conceding a goal. Brazil, a shadow of their former selves, bowed out leaving us with one magic memory, their winning goal against East Germany. Jairzinho, standing on the end of the German wall facing a free-kick, ducked as Rivelino crashed his shot towards him, the ball

swerving past the bewildered goalkeeper Jurgen Croy. Argentina, still four years from their peak, lost to both Holland and Brazil before sharing two goals with East Germany. It was Holland's clash with Brazil, though, which commanded the attention, pitting the champions against the team many assumed were destined to claim their crown. After a goalless first half, Johan Neeskens and Johan Cruyff scored the goals which took the Dutch into the Final, in a match scarred by an ill-disciplined Brazilian side meting out the treatment former heroes like Pele had undergone in previous tournaments. Luis Pereira was sent off for scything Neeskens, who had been knocked cold in the first half by Mario Marinho. The Dutch responded with some brute force of their own, but Neeskens deposited his best revenge in the back of the Brazilian net, exquisitely lobbing Leao after exchanging passes with Cruyff, before Cruyff provided a dashing volley of his own after a pinpoint cross from Krol.

West Germany's passage was a little more uncertain. It hinged on their clash with the impressive Poles in the final game of Group B. On a waterlogged pitch, after delaying the kick-off while they sloughed off as much moisture as possible, they made their physical strength pay. Jan Tomaszewski saved an Uli Hoeness penalty, but the German atoned for his miss when his shot was deflected to "The Bomber", Gerd Müller, who booked the date with Holland. Yet had Sepp Maier in goal not made a breathtaking double save in the first half, from Grzegorz Lato and Robert Gadocha, it might have been different. It would not be the German goalkeeper's last significant contribution.

The Dutch produced the most dramatic opening to a Final in the history of the competition. Right from the kick-off the ball was fluently played into the German area, where Cruyff was brought down by Hoeness, leaving English referee Jack Taylor with little option but to point to the spot. Neeskens calmly calmly converted the first penalty awarded in a World Cup Final to record the fastest Final goal ever. And the Germans had yet to play the ball.

After being outplayed for the first quarter of the game, West Germany managed to get themselves off the hook. On a rare break from Dutch indulgence, Bernd Hölzenbein was homing in on goal when he was tripped by Wim Jansen, and Paul Breitner duly rammed in the resultant penalty himself to make it 1–1. A 43rd-minute goal from Gerd Müller was his 68th for his country, and proved to be his most important, clinching the World Cup.

But it was hard for Holland to blame anyone but themselves. Having taken an immediate advantage, they had failed to make their domination count with a second goal, and for all their luxurious touches, the final instinct was beyond them. Although the much-hyped duel between Beckenbauer and Cruyff – battling it out to replace Pele as the world's finest player – had gone the German's way, the hosts owed much of the glory to goalkeeper Sepp Maier. The highlight of his performance came when he blocked a formidable Neeskens volley. West Germany, indeed, could have had more goals, Müller erroneously called offside when clean through, and Jansen fortunate not to be penalised a second time for felling Hölzenbein in the area.

A higher winning margin for the hosts would have been even more unjustified, however. As it was, the Dutch side of 1974 entered the legends for their failure which looked, to the neutral observer, like a triumph. Holland were the best team, but West Germany were the champions. The Dutch would be back in a World Cup Final four years later, but without Cruyff. Like Puskas 20 years earlier, a prodigious talent had been denied the greatest glory – and again, it was the efficient Germans who had been too good on the day.

Argentina 1978

Ecstasy and euphoria greeted Argentina's eventual triumph on home soil, yet for the majority of neutrals the failure of Holland, as in 1974, to claim their rightful crown as the best team in the world left a void.

The home nation, backed by fanatical support and animated tickertape adoration in the River Plate stadium, staged a colourful and dramatic tournament. Yet their passage to the Final was not without controversy, both on and off the pitch.

After repeated frustrations in their attempts to stage the finals, Argentina were finally granted their wish in 1966, but by the time 1978 came around many people were concerned about the internal political situation of the country. Argentina's military government gave unnerving signals to the rest of the world, while organizations like Amnesty International stepped up campaigns highlighting the flagrant human rights abuses, so that at one stage a relocation of the event to Holland and Belgium emerged as a possible option.

One of the main rebel groups, the Monteneros, declared a ceasefire but the first president of the organizing committee, General Actis, was blown up, and a policeman was killed trying to remove another bomb from a press centre. Yet, despite the fears, the tournament itself passed without similar incident, while concerns about stadiums being ready were alleviated by the vast sums spent by the government on three new arenas.

The Argentine players, though, faced the responsibility of exploiting their home advantage and emulating neighbours Uruguay and Brazil by winning the greatest prize. Their opening game proved a torrid affair, despite the impassioned River Plate crowd roaring them on. Hungary, who had qualified at the expense of the Soviet Union, took the lead in 12 minutes through Zombori only for Leopoldo Luque to equalize three minutes later. The Hungarians were to have two players sent off before Ricardo Bertoni fired the winning goals. It was a deeply unsatisfactory way to begin a campaign, and the Hungarians seemed justified in their complaints. Their crimes had been in response to a treatment of constant bodychecks and fouls by the Argentines, left unpunished by referee Garrido. Instead, Hungary's most skilful players were the ones dismissed, Töröcsik for protesting his treatment, and then tripping Galván, and Nyilasi for barging Tarantini.

Michel Platini made his World Cup debut for France in the same group, but Italy and Argentina had already qualified for the second stage when they met to decide the final Group 1 places. The Italians played it tight and snatched the win through Bettega in the 67th minute – a mixed blessing for Argentina, who progressed into an easier group for the second round, but left the inspiring surroundings of Buenos Aires.

In Group 2 Poland carried on where they had left off in Germany, with slick precise play, although neither the Poles nor the West Germans were as strong as they had been four years previously, when they finished third and first respectively. The shock result featured Tunisia, who held holders West Germany to a goalless draw and could have won. The impressive performances of Tunisia – the first African side to win a match in the World Cup finals, when they comfortably disposed of Mexico – and Iran presented a case for increased African and Asian representation.

Brazil once again failed to inspire, preferring the physical approach to the artistry of their glory years, and only a very fortunate 1–0 victory over Austria, who topped their group, squeezed them into the second phase. Scotland, the only British representatives, suffered humiliation. Before the tournament, they had been spoken of as possible challengers for the title, by Rinus Michels and Miljan Miljanic – not to mention their own manager, Ally McLeod. He had pledged with rock-solid certainty that he would return home with the trophy, despite his omission of the young scoring sensation Andy Gray from his finals squad. Instead, the Tartan Army descending on Argentina – popular mythology, apocryphal, suggests some fans travelled by submarine – saw the Scots not only falter but flop at the first stage, the talents of Dalglish, Masson and Macari notwithstanding. Rocked by a 3–1 defeat by Peru, they received a further blow to morale when Willie Johnston failed a drugs test and was ordered home. A 1–1 draw with Iran added to the troubles but they went out in style against Holland, a fine solo goal from Archie Gemmill in a 3–2 win not quite enough to redeem the horrors of the previous 10 days.

The second group stage saw one group dominated by European countries, the other by South American sides, Poland the odd one out faced with Argentina, Brazil and Peru.

The Poles avoided finishing bottom of the group by putting a single goal past Peru with no reply, but the controversy destined to dog Argentina surrounded the hosts' final group game with Peru. Inept scheduling meant that Brazil's match with Poland was played earlier in the day, and a 3–1 win for Brazil ensured Argentina knew how many goals they needed to score to qualify ahead of their rivals. A 4–1 win would have sufficed – instead the Argentines put six past the hapless Peruvians, outraging Brazil who suspected foul play off the pitch. The Brazilians had already fallen foul of controversy earlier in the tournament when Welsh referee Clive Thomas had disallowed a last-minute Zico "winner" against Sweden, having blown the final whistle just before the ball crossed the line.

In the other group, while Italy and West Germany played not to lose, Holland thrilled with their adventurous attitude. The European entry to the 1978 tournament was generally disappointing, European champions Czechoslovakia and former World Cup winners England were among those who had failed to qualify, along with Sweden, Switzerland and Norway. Although the Dutch were without Cruyff and Van Hanegem, who had withdrawn from international football, manager Ernst Happel had maintained the slick stylishness and fluid movement of the 1974 line-up. The players were confident they could atone for their failure to win that tournament.

The "reprise" of the 1974 Final between them and Germany provided one of the best games of this series, the reigning champions finally finding their form, and twice taking the lead.

Argentina captain Daniel Passarella carried shoulder-high in triumph in 1978

A goal by René Van de Kerkhof eight minutes from time gave Holland the draw. This kept them on top of the group, despite Nanninga becoming the first substitute sent off in a World Cup, for laughing at a refereeing decision in the final minute of the match. The final score was 2–2 and, having summarily trounced Austria and defeated Italy, Holland were back in the Final, once more to face the tournament's hosts.

Argentina's manager, Cesar Menotti, had faced the traditional Argentine problem of players leaving the country for fame and fortune in Europe. His response was to ignore them, depending instead on home-based players – with one exception, the Valencia striker Mario Kempes.

It would be Kempes who made the Final, more dramatic than distinguished, his own. Characteristic of the tournament, however, the match had not kicked off before it was already enveloped in contention. Having kept the Dutch players waiting on the pitch for almost five minutes, the Argentines protested at the bandage René Van de Kerkhof had been wearing on his right arm for the previous five matches. Holland's reaction showed that they had been unsettled, a sequence of niggling fouls preventing the game from settling into an even pattern. Even so, the Argentines once more seemed to benefit from more lenient refereeing than their opposition. But it was the home side who broke the deadlock of a frustrating first half. Kempes clinically dispatched a cross from Luque to give them a half-time lead, although it took a crucial stop by Fillol to deny Rensenbrink just before the interval.

As the second half began with Holland still unable to convert their chances, and the Argentine defence hanging on resiliently, the Dutch replaced Rep with Nanninga to provide more of an aerial threat. Larrosa came on for Argentina in place of Osvaldo Ardiles, whose fitness had been in doubt during the build-up to the Final.

Finally, the Dutch pressure brought its reward when Nanninga soared to head an equalizer. With a minute of normal time left, Rensenbrink found himself in the perfect position to score a winner for the Dutch when put through by Krol. His shot rebounded from the post and Holland's chance had once more passed them by.

A combination of Menotti and the fanatical crowd somehow roused an Argentine side which had seemed spent, and extra time saw Holland suddenly struggling to stay in the game. Once more it was Kempes who provided Argentina's impetus, manouevring himself through the defence to force the ball home, much to the delight of the home crowd.

As the Dutch pushed more men forward with no tangible result, Kempes broke free one more time, this time laying the ball off for Bertoni to clinch the victory. There was a sense that Holland's artists were destined not to taste triumph; Argentina's first World Cup glory, on the other hand, had seemed compellingly natural as the tournament progressed.

Spain 1982

All the best things come to those who wait. Italy, who had not won the World Cup since their triumphs in 1934 and 1938, recovered from a lamentable start to deservedly win the 1982 World Cup. A slow start in which they drew all three games in Group 1 and qualified on the slenderest goal difference hardly augured well. Then the surprise emergence on to the world stage of Paolo Rossi transformed the Italians' prospects.

Rossi had been involved in an Italian match-fixing scandal, receiving a three-year suspension, later reduced to two years, for his pains. Returning to the fold just in time for the World Cup, he looked decidedly out of sorts in Italy's build-up and opening games. Like his return from suspension, though, he would show an exquisite sense of timing when it really counted.

The tournament organizers themselves also experienced problems early on in coming to terms with the competition. The finals draw was chaotic, as were the hotel and tickcting arrangements, which, combined with the fitful form of the Spanish national side, failed to inspire much confidence in the host nation for the month ahead.

Once again FIFA had adjusted the competition format, in part to accommodate an extra eight competitors, as Asia and Africa boasted two representatives apiece. The African nations were the more revelatory, Cameroon being unfortunate to miss out in Group 1. Italy qualified ahead of them on goal difference after both teams had drawn all three matches.

The other African side, Algeria, produced an even greater shock in Group 2. West Germany, who were to finish runners-up, suffered a shock 2–1 defeat in their opening tie against the Algerians. Like Italy, they got better as the tournament progressed. But their route to the Final left a sour taste in the mouth, particularly for Algeria. In an echo of the 1978 Argentina–Peru fiasco, West Germany and Austria met, knowing that a 1–0 German win would see both sides through to the next round at Algeria's expense. It would not be the last time this West German side would weather a storm of protest.

England, in contrast to the two eventual finalists, started with a bang then gradually fell away. Having qualified for the tournament despite defeats by Romania, Switzerland and Norway, Bryan Robson got them off to a dream start against France with a goal in 27 seconds. But although Ron Greenwood's team proved hard to beat, without the injured Kevin Keegan and Trevor Brooking they had little guile. France recovered from their opening defeat with a comfortable victory over Kuwait, as the young midfield of Platini, Giresse and Tigana began to stretch itself dextrously on the world stage. Two years later, they would win the European Championship on their own home soil.

But the fixture with Kuwait produced another element of farce into the proceedings, when Prince Fahad, the president of the Kuwaiti FA, invaded the pitch in protest at a French goal

Italy's Marco Tardelli celebrates his crucial goal in the 1982 final

– which the referee then obligingly disallowed.

Spain could have done with such assistance, struggling to negotiate Group 5, and fortunate to qualify for the next phase after a Gerry Armstrong goal had given Northern Ireland a famous victory over the hosts. Irish 17-year-old Norman Whiteside went down in history as the youngest player in a World Cup finals.

If Spain were disjointed and overwhelmed, then Brazil, in Group 6, looked back to their thrilling, flowing finest. Manager Tele Santana had been accused of including too many midfielders, but players of the quality of Socrates, Zico, Junior, Falcao and Eder put them on a different plateau to many of their opponents. They marked themselves out as clear, and popular, favourites to lift their fourth trophy. For one brief moment, when Scotland led the South Americans thanks to a David Narey goal, the Tartan Army glimpsed the second round and a stunning victory. Four breathtaking Brazilian strikes, however, restored normal service, and for the third consecutive World Cup, the Scots missed out on goal difference.

For the last time, the second round of the tournament split the teams into more groups, the strongest being Group C, featuring Brazil, Italy and the holders Argentina. Players like Kempes and Ardiles, winners in 1978, remained part of the Argentine set-up. But there was no doubting who the new star was this time: the 21-year-old Diego Maradona, boasting an exhilarating turn of pace, dazzling ball skills and audacity. Unfortunately for Maradona, who had made his debut at 16 in 1977 but had missed out on the 1978 triumph, this attention came not only from admirers across the world, but avengers on the pitch. The reigning champions lost to both Italy and Brazil, Maradona being treated appallingly by Italy's Claudio Gentile but receiving no sympathy from the referee. Five minutes from the end of the clash with Brazil, the boy wonder's patience snapped, and he was sent off for hacking at Batista. For all the hype, it would be another four years before Maradona truly made the World Cup his own.

With the holders eliminated, the final group match between Brazil and Italy assumed crucial importance, the action surpassing all expectations. Brazil, irresistible but too extravagant, conceded an early goal to Rossi, and though Zico soon equalized, Rossi once more penetrated the defence to restore Italy's advantage.

With just a quarter of the game left, though, the pendulum swung back in Brazil's favour, with a spectacular left-foot flourish from Falcao making it 2–2. Since Brazil only needed a draw to qualify for the semi-finals, the sensible course would have been to hold on for the remaining period of the match. Sensible, but anathema to the Brazilian spirit, and their relentless pursuit of more goals was punished when Rossi pounced again after Brazil's defence had failed to clear a corner. Dino Zoff made a crucial save to deny Cerezo at the death, but the undoubted hero was Rossi, who had gone from scandal to saviour. Suddenly Italy were leading contenders for a trophy for which even the most ardent *Azzurri* had almost given up hope.

The hosts, meanwhile, joined England in departing Group B, the West Germans going through after England had laboured to two goalless draws. A missed open goal by Keegan in the match with Spain was symbolic of England's campaign – they returned home unbeaten but had never been truly convincing.

In the semi-finals Rossi scored twice more to beat the impressive Poles, who would finish third for the second time in three tournaments, while West Germany and France, having grown in stature and confidence following that initial setback against England, were involved in a pulsating thriller. With Platini, Tigana and Giresse at their teasing best, many fancied France as winners. In a tense 90 minutes they carved out the better chances but failed to make them count, after a Platini penalty had equalized Littbarski's early opener. Penalties would play a crucial part later. For all the thrills and skills of the match, though, it was a vicious spill for which the game will be remembered, the German goalkeeper Toni Schumacher's brutal flying challenge pole-axing French substitute Patrick Battiston on the edge of the German penalty area. Battiston was carried unconscious from the pitch after the sickening foul, but Dutch referee Coerver inexplicably awarded a German goal-kick. Forced to reorganize their defence again, and, as Platini would later reveal, desperately anxious about whether Battiston was even alive, the French took a 3–1 lead in extra-time. The Germans hit back to 3–3, a controversial goal by substitute Rummenigge and a desperate equalizer by Fischer taking the game to a penalty shoot-out, the first in the history of the World Cup.

German sweeper Uli Stielike was the first player to miss, but as he knelt distraught, Schumacher saved from Didier Six, as he did from full-back Maxime Bossis, leaving Horst Hrubesch to strike the ball past Jean-Luc Ettori and take West Germany into the Final.

The Final did not live up to its billing. There was not a shot on target in the ragged opening 45 minutes including Antonio Cabrini's effort from a penalty, the left-back's miskick wide making him the first player to miss a spot-kick in the Final. But in the second half the Germans paid, in fatigue, the price of their extra-time victory over France, captain Rummenigge obviously not fully fit and the elusive Littbarski flawlessly subdued by Gentile. The German dressing-room at half-time was a simmering cauldron of dissent, with Stielike bemoaning the selection of Rummenigge. Italy, on the other hand, took control of the second half inspired by the effort of Marco Tardelli and counter-attacking pace of Bruno Conti after centre-forward Graziani had departed injured after only seven minutes. They were deserving winners. Inevitably it was Rossi who broke the

deadlock with a smart header after Gentile had turned up in attack to provide a sweet centre, before the effervescent Tardelli and Altobelli clinched the Italians' victory. Breitner's late consolation made him the third player to score in two Finals, but the West Germans' first defeat to a European neighbour since 1978 had been a formality. Italy had matched Brazil – as three-time winners of the World Cup.

Mexico 1986

The official film of the 1986 tournament was entitled "Hero", and there was no doubting who most deserved that accolade. After the frustration of Spain 1982, where he arrived heralded in hype and departed kicked and red-carded, Diego Maradona finished Mexico 1986 unquestionably accoladed as the world's finest footballer. But once again, the hero showed he could play the villain too – Maradona was arguably the most naturally

Maradona celebrates Argentina's second World Cup win

talented individual the World Cup had seen, but the infamous "Hand of God" incident revealed that he was also a simple cheat. But even those English fans cursing his audacity at having punched the ball past Peter Shilton in the quarter-final had to admire the same quality which took him on an unerring dance from his own half, through the English defence, before planting the ball into the net with clinical aplomb for his second goal. In 10 minutes, Maradona had provided the tournament's two abiding memories – the first, the most blatant disregard for the rules, the second, simply the finest goal scored in a World Cup.

But these were just the two most vivid moments in a tournament bestrode like a colossus by Maradona's diminutive but breathtakingly nimble figure.

Mexico staged its second World Cup finals in the wake of a tragic earthquake, and set records – for the time – with 52 matches played before 2,406,511 spectators. The intended hosts had been Colombia, but they would have struggled to accommodate even the originally planned 16-team event. Given the country's economic difficulties, and the dangers of the volatile drug trade, once FIFA had enlarged the tournament to 24 teams, a change of location was imperative. Mexico, though a surprise choice, above Brazil and the United States, became the first country to stage the finals for a second time. It was only 16 years since the last finals in Mexico. The heat and altitude promised similar difficulties to those faced in 1970, not helped again by a misguided scheduling of matches in the heat of the day (thanks, once more, to less-than-obliging television demands).

The qualifying tournament encouraged confidence in an excellent finals, all the big guns from Europe and South America clinching their places, save for Holland who lost to ancient rivals and neighbours Belgium in a play-off.

The tournament did not disappoint, being generally regarded as the most open and exciting since the last time in Mexico, with Maradona filling Pele's role as integral inspiration.

Of the early group games, the Soviet Union's 6–0 demolition of Hungary and Denmark's majestic 6–1 destruction of Uruguay were the highlights, while Italy, Argentina, West Germany, Brazil and European champions France all made it through to the knock-out stages. Platini, however, was sluggish as the French struggled to convince, and the Brazilians, the thrilling discovery of right-back Josimar notwithstanding, were worried by the fitness of stars Zico, Falcao and Socrates.

The only real disappointment, though, was Monterrey-based Group F, dubbed the 'group of sleep', with the first four games producing just two goals. England, having qualified for Mexico without losing a game, had been disrupted by a recurrence of skipper Bryan Robson's shoulder injury and uncertainty about manager Bobby Robson's confidence in midfielder Glenn Hoddle. Newly emerged star striker Gary Lineker, fresh from topping the First Division scoring charts in his only Everton season, was able to play with a plaster cast after injuring his arm.

But his side slumped to a shock 1–0 defeat to Portugal in their opening game, Carlos Manuel punishing a flat-footed English defence with just 15 minutes left. It grew worse for Bobby Robson's men in their second game, held to a goalless draw by unfancied Morocco. Bryan Robson departed the tournament injured and Ray Wilkins became the first England player sent off in a finals tournament for two bookings in as many minutes. Only in the final group game did England show the form expected of them, Hodge, Reid, Steven and Beardsley coming in for Robson, Wilkins, Waddle and Hateley, and producing a stunning first-half display, a Gary Lineker hat-trick securing a 3–0 win and passage into the second round.

Scotland were not so fortunate, losing to Denmark and West Germany under the managership of Aberdeen manager Alex Ferguson after Jock Stein had tragically died of a heart attack during the qualifying stages. Ferguson had caused a stir by omitting Liverpool centre-back Alan Hansen from his squad, a decision which upset club colleague Kenny Dalglish. He later withdrew with an injury to miss out on taking part in his fourth World Cup finals. Needing to win their final group match with Uruguay, Scotland could only manage a 0–0 draw – even after Batista had become the quickest dismissal in World Cup history, sent off after just 55 seconds by a referee many believe pulled out a red card by mistake.

With the second round restored to knock-out status after the group-based format of 1974, 1978 and 1982, Belgium's thrilling 4–3 victory over the Soviets was the most memorable encounter. With a quarter of an hour left of normal time, the Soviets, 2–1 ahead, were jolted by an equalizer from Jan Ceulemans. The goal looked offside, and with the initiative shifting to the Belgians in extra time, hat-trick-scoring Igor Belanov ended on the losing side as Belgium progressed. Having only scraped through their group as one of the best third-placed teams, Belgium, managed by Guy Thys, were to emerge as one of the genuine surprises of the knock-out stages.

Another surprise, another goal-feast, saw Denmark – many people's favourites, having routed Uruguay 6–1 – collapse 5–1 to an Emilio Butragueno-inspired Spain, despite taking an early lead through Manchester United winger Jesper Olsen. A defensive blunder, though, within minutes, gifted the ball to the Real Madrid striker, nickname "the Vulture", who calmly equalized. Butragueno helped himself to three more – the first player since Eusebio in 1966 to score four in one finals match – while a Goikoetxea penalty rammed home Spain's advantage. Denmark, without the suspended Klaus Berggren who had been sent off against West Germany, had contributed to another thrilling spectacle, but it would be their last appearance in the World Cup finals until 1998.

While Mexico eased past the insipid Bulgarians in the Azteca stadium, Brazil stepped up a gear to eliminate the team who had finished third four years earlier. Poland goalkeeper Jozsef

Gary Lineker and Peter Beardsley celebrate England's progress in the 1986 finals

Mlynarczyk, having just conceded three goals to England, picked the ball out of the net four times as Brazil gradually assumed superiority after an arrogantly casual Socrates penalty had given them a half-time lead. Josimar scored again in only his second international, while Edinho and a Careca penalty completed the scoring, the samba-kings becoming the first side to emerge as clear-cut favourites.

In an all-South American clash at Puebla, Argentina nudged past Uruguay with a goal from Pedro Pasculli, Maradona skipped through the cynical Uruguayans, showing no signs of the knee cartilage problems rumoured to have put his participation in the tournament in doubt.

The side who had stolen Argentina's crown in 1982, however, relinquished their hold on the trophy in a show of disappointing torpor. Italy, minus 1982 hero Rossi, slipped to a 2–0 defeat at the hands of France, for whom Platini scored the first goal – Italy manager Enzo Bearzot's use of Giuseppe Bergomi to try and control the French captain was abandoned as a failure at half-time. Bearzot himself would return home to be replaced by his assistant, Azeglio Vicini, the *Azzurri* having to wait another four years to attempt to regain the trophy on their own home soil.

Another 3–0 triumph sent England comfortably into a quarter-final clash with Argentina, their first meeting since the Falklands War. Paraguay's defenders had been unable to handle Lineker and Peter Beardsley legally, but the two strikers had the perfect response to their ill treatment, Lineker scoring twice and Beardsley once as England's newly restored confidence swept them through. The surprise winners of England's group, Morocco, saw their adventure end in the last minute of their clash with West Germany, a free-kick from Lothar Matthäus the only score of the game, though Moroccan manager José Faria had opted for a disappointingly negative strategy.

The first quarter-final fixture set an impossibly high standard for the others to follow, Brazil and France staging a compelling match in Guadalajara, an occasion which deserved a better resolution than the penalty shoot-out which eliminated the South American favourites. Careca gave Brazil the lead, only for Platini – inevitably – to equalize, but it was Zico who squandered Brazil's best chance, missing a penalty 17 minutes from the end of normal time, having just come on as a substitute.

Though France fashioned the better chances in extra time, neither side could break the deadlock without the return of the deadly shoot-out. Having lost to West Germany on penalties in 1982, the luck was with the French on this occasion at least. Following Zico's failure earlier in the match, both Socrates and Platini amazingly missed their spot-kicks while Zico this time scored, but French goalkeeper Joel Bats produced the decisive save from Julio Cesar. Luis Fernandez dispatched his shot and Brazil were out of the World Cup.

Maradona's exploits against England first outraged then

astonished those watching, and it was only with the appearance of substitute John Barnes that England scented a comeback, a Barnes cross being headed in by Lineker, his sixth goal of the tournament handing him the prestigious Golden Boot and a lucrative transfer to Spanish giants Barcelona. In a near replica of that move, Lineker once again got his head to a Barnes inswinger, but the ball somehow dropped beyond its target, and England were on their way back home, victims of a theft but victims of a genius too. Had Lineker forced an equalizer, all four quarter-finals could have been decided by penalties. Belgian goalkeeper Pfaff was the spot-kick-saving hero after Belgium and Spain had drawn 1–1, saving from Eloy.

West Germany, meanwhile, continued an underwhelming progress, knocking out the hosts on penalties after an energy-sapping goalless draw in Monterrey, despite the dismissal of Thomas Berthold after 65 minutes.

Schumacher, in the German goal, then came face to face once more with Patrick Battiston, the Frenchman he had nearly decapitated in 1982. There was to be no revenge for the French, however, although there was no need for extra time or penalties. An early goal from Andreas Brehme was the worst possible start for France, already handicapped by the absence of Rocheteau and the palpable unfitness of Platini. Schumacher, bête noir of the French, denied them consistently, before Rudi Völler added a second for Germany in the final minute.

In the other semi-final, Argentina also ran out 2–0 winners, both scored by Maradona, his second a stunner to compare with his second against England. Splintering the Belgian defence as he ran at them, Maradona feinted to his left before hooking an impeccable shot into the back of the net – the Argentine captain was head and shoulders above anyone else on the pitch.

How would German manager Franz Beckenbauer respond to Maradona? Matthäus was seconded to look after Maradona in the Final, but the surprise first scorer was Argentine centre-back Jose Luis Brown – without a club when he set off for Mexico – who nodded past the flailing Schumacher to open the scoring.

The goalkeeper was also blamed for Argentina's second, scored by Jorge Valdano, though the Germans constructed a characteristically gritty comeback after the arrival of substitute Karl-Heinz Rummenigge. Both goals came as a result of Brehme corners, the first one forced in by Rummenigge, the second by Völler with just eight minutes left.

But with players and spectators gearing up for another period of extra time, Maradona produced one more piece of magic within three minutes of the equalizer.

Expertly controlling the ball just inside his own half, Maradona slipped it subtly through to the onrushing Jorge Burruchaga, who charged on to slam the winner into the German net.

Rummenigge became the first player to captain the losing team in two Finals, but his opposing number, despite having a quiet Final, had achieved his rightful place as the world's number one

player and World Cup-winning captain. It would all be so different when the two countries met once more in the 1990 Final, but for now, Maradona – divine dancing feet and a "hand of God" – was the conquering hero.

Italy 1990

The 14th World Cup finals did not live up to the setting. There was a miserly shortage of goals, but perhaps the saddest failure of all was on the part of the established stars who failed to enhance their reputations. The occasion was saved by the Italians themselves, for this was the People's World Cup.

Like the event itself, there were high hopes of Italy's players, only for the final reckoning to bring frustration and disappointment. Before the tournament, they were clear favourites, boasting home advantage – the first European country to host the event twice – and a selection of the players who had won the European Under-21 title in 1986, including the stylish defender, Paolo Maldini. Azeglio Vicini, who had managed that side, was now the national team coach, though there were question marks over his reluctance to use Roberto Baggio in a position deep behind the main strikers. Indeed, it was up front where Italy's main concerns lay, with the fitness and form of Sampdoria striker Gianluca Vialli far from convincing. Toto Schillaci, who had just enjoyed a marvellous season with Juventus, had yet to prove himself on the international scene … though it would not be long before he did.

The main shock of the qualifying rounds was the failure of France, now managed by Michel Platini but in a state of transition. England, following their cataclysmic performance in the 1988 European Championship, when they had lost all three games, had qualified in second place to Sweden in their group. Manager Bobby Robson had announced he would be taking over at PSV Eindhoven after the tournament, after eight years in charge.

It was in the South American preliminary rounds, however, that the most unexpected event occurred. Mexico had been banned from the 1990 World Cup for fielding over-age players in the World Youth Cup, and they were followed on to the sidelines by Chile after some bizarre behaviour in a battle with Brazil. Trailing 1–0 in their final group match, a flare thrown from the crowd at Chilean goalkeeper Roberto Rojas prompted the whole team to leave the field, Rojas carried off by his colleagues – only for later investigations to discover that the flare had not hit him, his bleeding was self-inflicted, and the dubious plan had been hatched by the Chileans beforehand. Whatever the intentions had been behind this charade – how exactly did the Chileans expect it to succeed? – they faced a heavy punishment, a ban from the 1994 tournament.

With Mexico absent, just Costa Rica and the United States qualified from the CONCACAF region, with the Americans

Matthäus, Voller and Brehme lead West Germany's celebrations in Rome

having just been awarded the staging of the 1994 event.

Cameroon, qualifying along with Egypt from Africa, made the most interesting impression. The opening match saw one of the great shocks of World Cup history, when Cameroon, reduced to nine men, beat reigning champions Argentina by a single goal. The Argentines, Maradona notwithstanding, had endured a wretched build-up to the tournament, winning only once in their last 10 games, and that a 2–1 defeat of Israel.

Carlos Bilardo's use of Maradona in a more forward role, and his refusal to use the explosive River Plate striker Claudio Caniggia until the second half, played into the hands of Cameroon. Their willing pressing game may have tended toward abuse of themselves as well as their opponents – Kana Biyick was sent off on the hour for fouling Caniggia, who was again the victim of Massing, dismissed with two minutes left. But the pressure told on the Argentinians when both Sensini and goalkeeper Pumpido froze to allow François Omam Biyick to steal the only goal. It was a sensational, if a little sterile, opening to the tournament.

The North African side went on to prove that the victory was

by no means a freak result, beating Romania on the way to topping Group B. The hero of that match was Roger Milla, who had played in the 1982 World Cup, and whose two goals made him, at 38, the oldest player to score in a World Cup finals. Argentina scraped through in third place, after beating the Soviet Union in familiar surroundings to Maradona, the San Paolo stadium in Naples. Improbably, the Argentine captain got away with another crucial handball, flicking away from Kuznetsov to deny the Soviets the first goal of the match, before Troglio and Burruchaga wrapped up the points for the holders. A 4–0 triumph over Cameroon in their final match was small consolation for the Soviets, who had entered the tournament as many people's dark horses.

If the holders were rocking, the hosts were rolling. Italy cruised through Group A almost on autopilot, winning all three matches without conceding a goal, even if they only found the net four times themselves. In their opening match against Austria, the Italians struggled to find the killer instinct, until substitute Schillaci arrived in the right place at the right time to convert Vialli's cross, and cause heavy sighs of relief across the country.

The same starting line-up was used against the US, another single-goal triumph coming courtesy of Giannini, but it was in the final group game with Czechoslovakia that the hosts started to find their groove. Carnevale and Vialli dropped out, with their replacements Schillaci and Baggio hitting the goals in a 2–0 win, Baggio's swaggering solo effort one of the goals of the tournament. The sparse pockets of enthusiasm for the sport in the United States were hardly inflamed by their country's performances, though Caligiuri's individualistic strike in their 5–1 defeat by Czechoslovakia was a moment to remember.

It was an all-too-familiar story for Scotland in Group C, at their fifth consecutive World Cup, but once more destined to falter just short of the second round, having once again been drawn with Brazil. Only a lapse by goalkeeper Jim Leighton resulting in a Muller goal, and a glaring last-minute miss by Maurice Johnston, denied them a share of the spoils with the South Americans in their final match, after an encouraging defeat of Sweden. The damage had already been done in their opening-match defeat by Costa Rica. In fact, although that loss was judged a disgrace to rank with past disasters, the Costa Ricans were, along with Cameroon, one of the tournament's revelations, also defeating the hapless Swedes to book their place in the next round. There, only their hurried chasing of the game gave Czechoslovakia a misleading victorious scoreline, 4–1.

Where Scotland and Sweden fell by the wayside, the Europeans controlled Group D, West Germany hitting four past Yugoslavia, and five past the United Arab Emirates, in an untypically convincing start to a major tournament. The Yugoslavs, orchestrated by the intelligent Dragan Stojkovic, recovered well to coast past Colombia and the UAE, although a last-minute equalizer from Fredy Rincon against the Germans took Colombia into the second phase as well.

Uruguay also left it late in Group E, a last-gasp winner from Daniel Fonseca against South Korea shoehorning them through in third place, behind Spain and Belgium, while for the second successive World Cup, it was England's group which subjected those looking for attractive football to the most torrid test.

The clash between England and first-time qualifiers the Republic of Ireland – managed by English World Cup winner Jack Charlton – had been overshadowed by pre-match violence involving English "fans", but the on-field action itself was eminently forgettable. After Gary Lineker had quickly taken up where he'd left off in 1986, prodding home a ninth-minute goal, the two sides committed themselves to cancelling out each other's tedious long-ball tactics. An error by Steve McMahon gifted former Everton team-mate Kevin Sheedy an equalizer late on, and English newspapers pitched their tirades against Bobby Robson and his players even higher.

England would be the only team in the group to register a victory, Mark Wright's first and only international goal enough to defeat Egypt in their final group match, after a group full of draws. European champions Holland had performed disappointingly in their 1–1 tie with Egypt, stars like Ruud Gullit and Marco Van Basten despairingly out of sorts, before sharing a goalless draw with England. After the Republic had also held the Dutch, lots were drawn to place the two countries, and the luck was with the Irish, pairing them with Romania in the next round instead of West Germany.

The clash of the Dutch and the Germans was predictably full of incident, but also full of excitement, making it one of the most compelling games of the tournament. The Giuseppe Meazza stadium in Milan was a familiar setting for the stars of the occasion – the Germans Klinsmann, Brehme and Matthäus played for Inter, Holland's Van Basten, Gullit and Frank Rijkaard for Milan. Rijkaard made an early exit, sent off for spitting after an unseemly confrontation with the German striker Völler, also dismissed, which only added spice to the game. Left up front on his own, Jürgen Klinsmann produced perhaps his finest game for his country, giving the Germans the lead at the start of the second half, before Brehme scored the second with just six minutes left. A penalty from Ronald Koeman came too late to save the Dutch, who departed for home having seriously underperformed once more.

Another disappointment came with the premature exit of the Brazilians, punished for missing too many chances by Maradona's finest moment of the tournament, a perfect pass for Caniggia to stab home with just nine minutes left to take Argentina past their South American rivals.

In the only other second round game not to go to extra time, Italy eased past Uruguay with second-half goals from Schillaci and Serena, while the South American suffering continued with Colombia's defeat by the vibrant Cameroonians.

The Colombians had goalkeeper Rene Higuita to blame, his impulsive burst out of his area punished by the indefatigable Roger Milla, adding to the goal he had scored minutes earlier in the second half of extra time.

Spain, looking to win in Italy as the Italians had done in Spain eight years earlier, were unlucky to come up against Yugoslavia's Stojkovic on one of his most inspired days. His first goal was a piece of trickery which sold the whole stadium a monumental dummy, his second, three minutes into extra time, a vicious free-kick after Salinas had equalized for the Spanish.

The most dramatic extra-time climax came in Bologna, where substitute David Platt latched on to a perfectly flighted free-kick from England's young hero Paul Gascoigne to deny Belgium in the 119th minute, a matter of seconds from a penalty shoot-out. This was the moment that saw the full-scale arrival of both English players on the international scene, and it was no coincidence that they would both be playing their football in Italy's Serie A as the decade progressed.

England were joined in the last eight by the Republic of Ireland, who triumphed in a shoot-out with Romania to earn a

Toto Schillaci, top scorer at Italia '90

tilt at the hosts. Despite putting up their best performance of the tournament, the Republic succumbed to a goal by Schillaci, but returned home thrilled to have gone so far on their first World Cup finals adventure – even if they had failed to win a match in open play.

Nor did concerns about the manner of victory worry Argentina, who outbraved 10-man Yugoslavia in a shoot-out, the plaudits going to stand-in goalkeeper Sergio Goycochea, who had stepped up after Nery Pumpido had broken his leg in the group phase. Eastern European interest was finally extinguished with Czechoslovakia's defeat at the hands of West Germany, a first-half Matthäus penalty making the difference, with neither team making much of an impression in attack.

Once again it was Cameroon who provided the absorbing drama in the quarter-finals, recovering from going a goal down to England (David Platt again) to take a 2–1 lead, and being 10 minutes away from sensationally reaching the World Cup semi-finals, after a penalty from Kunde and a shrewd chip from Ekeke. For both goals, the inspiration was Milla, whose appearance as substitute had palpably unnerved the English defence.

The Cameroon players could not sustain their obvious superiority, however, the Tottenham combination of Gascoigne and Lineker winning England two penalties, one seven minutes from the end of normal time, the second halfway through extra time. On both occasions, Lineker kept his nerve, blasting a

relieved England into a semi-final with West Germany.

Having gone into the Cameroon match overwhelmingly expected to win, England became the underdogs for their clash with the Germans, but after a fitful World Cup campaign, finally produced an exhilarating, convincing team performance, outplaying their opponents for much of the game.

It was West Germany who took the lead, though, after a first half of few chances, when Paul Parker deflected a Brehme free-kick which dipped agonizingly beyond Shilton's reach into the England net. The Manchester United full-back made amends, though, with 10 minutes remaining, sweeping in a long ball which perplexed three Germany defenders, allowing Lineker to slip through with easeful control and a clinical finish.

England were performing heroics, becoming the first side in a World Cup to play extra time in three successive matches. Waddle and Buchwald hit the wordwork for each side, Platt had a goal ruled out for offside, but the emotional highpoint came when the masterful Gascoigne received his second booking of the tournament for a mistimed challenge on Berthold. The tears welled in his eyes as he realized he would miss the Final should England make it.

That they didn't is a testament to the West Germans' unfailing accuracy when it comes to penalty shoot-outs, successfully dispatching all five of theirs. England's fourth taker, Stuart Pearce, who was regular penalty-taker for what was then his club, Nottingham Forest, blasted his at Illgner's legs, and the outstanding Chris Waddle, needing to score, sent the ball so high and wide it may still be in orbit.

After a night of such tension and drama, once again the penalty shoot-out became the focus of anger and disappointment, particularly since the previous evening, Argentina had ousted the hosts by a similar means. Having opened the scoring early on through – who else? – Schillaci, Italy made the fatal error of sitting back to defend their lead, which was wiped out after 67 minutes by Caniggia's second goal of the tournament, and the first Italy had conceded. Schillaci's burst to prominence, and his Golden Boot-winning exploits, had invited the inevitable comparisons with Paolo Rossi, but the ultimate triumph of 1982 would elude the 1990 *Azzurri*. The unsatisfactory nature of Argentina's triumph – clinched by Goycochea's saves from Donadoni and Serena – was encapsulated by the absurdity of Caniggia's booking for deliberate handball, which ruled him out of the Final.

The third-place match between Italy and England would undoubtedly have made a much better final, Italy clinching a win thanks to some Higuita-style goalkeeping from Peter Shilton, in his 126th, and final, game for England.

The highlights of the tournament had included the drama in Milan, when Littbarski's goal seemed to have ended Colombia's dream before one of the great characters of the tournament, Carlos Valderrama, who had been carried off, returned to lay on an equalizer for Rincon. There had been the reckless stupidity of Higuita, the grace of Tomas Skuhravy, the Czech striker, and the magic of Yugoslavia's Stojkovic. There was also the sheer theatre of that semi-final shoot-out between West Germany and England.

But the lasting impression of Italia '90 was of the villain of the piece, Argentina, who had spoiled the script twice by ousting Brazil and Italy, to reach a Final they were to sully with their dour tactics and flagrant abuse of the rules. After the thrilling five-goal encounter between the two sides in the 1986 Final, this was not just a disappointment, but a disgrace. Maradona, the ringmaster four years earlier, was mercilessly jeered by the crowd and man-marked out of the game by Buchwald, his tears finding little sympathy as the Argentines became the first side to fail to score in a World Cup Final. Instead they collected the first red cards to be shown on such an occasion – to Monzon and Dezotti.

If Argentine displeasure had been provoked by that decision, they were incensed not only to be denied a penalty when Calderon went down in the German area, but to have one awarded against them 10 minutes later, and with only five minutes left to play, when Völler made a meal of an Argentine challenge. The unerring Brehme slotted home the penalty – an appropriate, if unhappy, way for this tournament to be finally settled

Germany had the glory of the golden World Cup trophy, after having lost two successive Finals, and could now boast to have won the title as many times as any other country.

For all the glee of stars like Klinsmann, Matthäus and the dependable Brehme, the abiding memories of Italia '90 will be the tears of two prodigal talents, Gascoigne and Maradona. .

USA 1994

History was made twice over at the 1994 World Cup finals. Brazil secured a fourth title to add to their triumphs in 1958, 1962 and 1970. But to do so they needed to win the first-ever penalty shoot-out at the end of extra time after the very first goalless Final, against Italy in the Rose Bowl in Pasadena.

FIFA introduced four radical measures in an attempt to improve the quality of the action: three points for a win instead of two in the first round group matches; a relaxation over the offside law by which play was to be stopped only if an attacking player was interfering with play; a crackdown on the tackle from behind in particular – for which a red card would be automatic – and violent conduct in general; and finally, injured players would be taken off the field immediately for treatment.

In simple statistical terms these changes added up to 15 sendings off and a record 235 bookings. But, on the positive side, they also computed to 141 goals in 52 matches, a match average of 2.71 and an improvement on Italia 90.

Doubts had been raised about the choice of the United States as host, Morocco's alternative bid having been rejected in 1988. The enthusiasm of American fans for "soccer" seemed lukewarm at best, and the North American Soccer League had folded abjectly in the early 1980s. But no new stadia were required for the event, and the tournament went on to boast the highest aggregate and average attendances in the history of the World Cup.

Most important of all, the football was of a consistently high standard, the participants emulating their counterparts in Mexico in 1970 and 1986, by shrugging off the arduous conditions with attacking, competitive displays.

One of the reasons the finals passed enjoyably and peacefully was perhaps the absence of England and their notorious followers. Graham Taylor's disastrous period in charge had seen a calamitous European Championship followed by chaotic defeats to Norway and Holland to deny England a place in the Finals for the first time since 1978 – even their final match against San Marino was touched by farce, the minnows scoring the fastest ever international goal after just nine seconds.

Yet again France failed to qualify, conceding last-gasp defeats to first Israel and then Bulgaria, having needed just one point from these two fixtures. The Bulgarians were inspired by late goals from striker Emil Kostadinov, but they also had French winger David Ginola to thank, his careless pass gifting them the winner in injury-time. European champions Denmark also spent the summer at home, falling behind Spain and the Republic of Ireland in their qualifying group.

The South American qualifiers threatened to deliver an even more sensational shock, after Brazil's 2–0 defeat to Bolivia left them needing to beat Uruguay in their final match. The recall of controversial striker Romario saved their blushes with a 2–0 win, maintaining the Brazilians' record of participating in every World Cup.

Argentina needed a lucky goal in a play-off with Australia, having lost 5–0 to Colombia in their worst ever defeat, a humiliation which saw Maradona recalled for one last throw of the dice. It would be a gamble with predictably unpredictable consequences.

The greatest tragedy of the qualifiers, however, was the death in an air crash of 18 of Zambia's national squad, on their way to a match in Senegal. The inexperienced players who carried on playing were desperately unlucky to miss out on the finals, needing only a draw against Morocco, but losing by a single goal.

A big shadow over the finals was cast by the death of Andres Escobar, the Colombian defender, shot a few days after returning home to Medellin. The exact reason for his murder is not known – gambling losses, probably involving drug barons, is thought to be the cause – but the centre-back had, inadvertently, scored an own goal against the United States in Colombia's 2–1 defeat.

That victory for the US was probably the most significant single result in the finals virtually ensuring the hosts a place in the second round. This success struck a chord with the domestic

Brazil's captain Dunga in triumph at Pasadena

audience which helped carry the World Cup along on a wave of excitement and enthusiasm surprising even the most optimistic of American soccer people.

However, the team of Group A were undoubtedly Romania, inspired by their attacking general Gheorghe Hagi. The well-organized Swiss team qualified in second place, but Colombia – among the pre-tournament favourites, many observers including Pele seduced by the talents of Valderrama controlling midfield and the trickery of Faustino Asprilla up front – played without conviction or pattern and were eliminated.

Group B offered clear favourites in Brazil and they did not disappoint their colourful, noisy and musical supporters. Brazil's strength was the striking partnership of Romario and Bebeto, adding lustre to a side more defensively sound than brilliantly creative. Romario either scored or had a creative hand in 10 of Brazil's 11 goals. Brazil topped the group with Sweden second, and the heroes of 1990, Cameroon, brought back down to earth with a bump. The Cameroon federation had been involved in a dispute over pay with the players, at one point putting the country's participation in dispute, and these concerns overshadowed their performances on the pitch. Against Brazil, 17-year-old Rigobert Song became the youngest player sent off in a World Cup finals, and the side bowed out with a 6–1 defeat at the hands of the similarly dissension-ridden Russia. The match will be remembered for Oleg Salenko's five goals, a record for

one World Cup match, and Roger Milla breaking his own record of being the oldest player to score in a World Cup, coming on as substitute to find the net at the age of 42.

Group C included the formal Opening Match in which holders Germany beat Bolivia 1–0, the sending-off of Bolivian substitute Marco Etcheverry posting a warning of the disciplinary strictures to come. The Germans appeared laboured, stealing a fortunate goal through Jürgen Klinsmann, and Stefan Effenberg was expelled from the squad at the end of the first round for making a rude gesture toward jeering German fans in the narrow 3–2 win over South Korea. This was the other group which provided only two, rather than three, second round qualifiers. Germany finished top followed by Spain, the unlucky South Koreans cursing their failure to achieve more than a goalless draw against Bolivia.

In Group D Argentina's Diego Maradona was his team's attacking inspiration in the opening 4–0 win over Greece – scoring one and helping Gabriel Batistuta to a hat-trick – and in the 2–1 follow-up defeat of Nigeria, but it was after this game that he failed a dope test which showed traces of the banned stimulant ephedrine. The tournament was over for Maradona and Argentina lost their next game, without him, 2–0 to Bulgaria. The Bulgarians thus qualified for the second round despite having crashed 3–0 to the entertaining World Cup newcomers Nigeria in the group's opening match. At their 18th and 19th attempts they had finally won not one but two World Cup matches, and were in the process of confounding the pessimistic predictions that had accompanied their elimination of France in the qualifiers.

Argentina had to settle for third place in the group, just enough to take them through, after a spectacular last-minute winner from Nigeria's Daniel Amokachi against the outclassed Greeks had seen the African side top the group on their World Cup debut.

Nigeria received an unfortunate reward, however, in the next round thanks to Italy's inability to finish higher than third in Group E. This was undoubtedly the tightest division, the six matches between the Italians, Norway, the Republic of Ireland and Mexico producing only eight goals.

The first of these came from a sweetly struck Ray Houghton volley, giving Ireland a shock 1–0 victory over Italy in their opening match, and Norway appeared on the verge of inflicting a second defeat on the group favourites when goalkeeper Gianluca Pagliuca was sent off. Remarkably, however, after Roberto Baggio had surprisingly made way for substitute goalkeeper Luca Marchegiani, Italy fought back to win with a goal from Dino Baggio when defeat would have resulted in almost certain elimination. Wasting that numerical superiority cost Norway dear. All four teams ended up on four points and zero goal difference, but Norway finished bottom of the group on goals scored and were thus eliminated. For the first time in a World Cup that all four teams in a group had finished with the same number of points.

Another favoured team who struggled in the first round were Holland. They beat Saudi Arabia only 2–1 in their first match then lost an exciting duel 1–0 to neighbours Belgium next time out. They escaped early elimination by defeating Morocco 2–1 in their final match, to qualify along with Belgium and World Cup newcomers Saudi Arabia – who beat Belgium 1–0 along the way. The Dutch had looked anything but convincing in the run-up to the finals. Marco Van Basten missing through injury and Ruud Gullit due to disagreements with coach Dick Advocaat, who was leading the team at the finals despite persistent rumours linking Johan Cruyff with the job.

The surprise package of the group were Saudi Arabia, who beat Belgium in their final group game with one of the most stunning goals seen in World Cup history. After just five minutes, midfielder Saeed Al Owairan coasted from his own half, through the Belgian defence to hammer the ball past the most impressive goalkeeper of the tournament, Preud'homme. In the same match, Majed Abdullah won his final cap for Saudi Arabia, the "Pele of the Desert" ending his international career with a FIFA-recognized world record of 147 caps.

The opening match of the second round saw Germany, as on the opening day, playing in Chicago. This time they defeated Belgium 3–2 in an exciting game which marked the successful return of veteran World Cup winner Rudi Völler, who scored twice. After taking a 3–1 lead into half-time, however, the Germans were disappointing in the second half. The Belgians only had a last-minute consolation from Philippe Albert to show for their superiority, but they had grounds for complaint for a penalty they were denied after Thomas Helmer fouled Josip Weber. They would not be the only ones to regret that decision: the man who made it, Swiss referee Kurt Röthlisberger, was sent home by FIFA.

The Republic of Ireland committed defensive suicide against Holland, losing 2–0 due to mistakes by full-back Terry Phelan and goalkeeper Packie Bonner, while Spain had an easy time in beating Switzerland 3–0 and Sweden saw off Saudi Arabia 3–1. Brazil also spoiled the Americans' Independence Day holiday by defeating the hosts more easily than the 1–0 scoreline suggests, despite the expulsion of Leonardo from the match – and the tournament – for a petulant elbow which fractured the jaw of Tab Ramos. Late in the game, the 37-year-old American defender Clavijo became the oldest player sent off in a World Cup.

The other three second round games were even more dramatic. Bulgaria defeated Mexico 3–1 on penalties – the first shoot-out of the finals – after an entertaining 1–1 draw, marred by two contentious sendings-off which took the impetus out of the game, Mexico's Luis Garcia following Bulgarian Kremenliev

Roberto Baggio: the penalty of failure

down the tunnel. As in their last World Cup appearance in 1986, Mexico failed in a shoot-out, despite the presence in goal of their multicoloured, sometime-striker Jorge Campos.

In Pasadena, Romania's Ilie Dumitrescu – pushed up front in place of the suspended Florin Raducioiu – played the game of his life in the match of the tournament, scoring twice and creating a third for Hagi in a 3–2 defeat of Argentina, crushed by Maradona's expulsion and an injury to Caniggia. Italy dramatically defeated Nigeria; with two minutes remaining the Italians were 1–0 down and had again been reduced to 10 men, this time by the dismissal of midfield substitute Gianfranco Zola for what the referee harshly judged to be retaliation. But having received a stroke of good fortune when the referee failed to send off Paolo Maldini for a professional foul on Yekini, Roberto Baggio snatched a last-minute equaliser and as the Nigerians sagged in extra time, he scored again, from the penalty spot.

In the quarter-finals, Sweden, themselves down to 10 men after Arsenal-bound Stefan Schwarz was sent off, defeated Romania on penalties after Kenneth Andersson had salvaged a 2–2 draw, the veteran goalkeeper Thomas Ravelli saving from Miodrag Belodedici to deny the Romanians the semi-final place they – and the mercurial Hagi especially – and many new admirers felt they deserved.

Roberto Baggio again confirmed his star rating with Italy's late second goal in their 2–1 victory over Spain, delicately placing the ball past Andoni Zubizarreta from an unpromising angle. Yet again fortune was on the side of the Italians, Mauro Tassotti going unpunished for an elbow which clattered Spanish striker Luis Enrique moments before Baggio's winner – at least, until FIFA imposed an eight-match ban, after which Tassotti never played for his country again.

Another tight game saw Brazil defeat Holland 3–2, the first time an opposing team had put Brazil's defence under serious sustained pressure. Indeed, Holland produced their best form of the tournament to recover a two-goal deficit – goals from a clearly offside Romario and Bebeto – thanks to timely strikes from Dennis Bergkamp and Aron Winter. With just nine minutes of normal time remaining, however, left-back Branco, in for Leonardo, somehow squeezed a dynamic free-kick through the wall and past Ed De Goey from 30 yards.

Completing the semi-final line-up were rank outsiders Bulgaria. Germany, with nine players from the winning 1990 side, went ahead through a Lothar Matthäus penalty. But the holders conceded two last-gasp goals, a free-kick from Hristo Stoichkov – on his way to sharing the Golden Boot with Salenko – and a glancing header from the tall, balding Iordan Lechkov, who played his club football in the Bundesliga. It was Germany's earliest elimination since their quarter-final failure in 1962 and Bulgaria, who had played 16 matches at the finals without winning one before this tournament, were into the semi-finals after what manager Dimitar Penev hailed as "the finest day in

the history of Bulgarian football". That was to prove the end of the road. The two-goal brilliance of Roberto Baggio lifted Italy into their fifth Final despite a rallying penalty from Stoichkov, although two shadows were cast over the Italians' success with Alessandro Costacurta's second yellow card of the tournament ruling him out of the Final, and a strained hamstring picked up by Baggio severely limiting his effectiveness.

In the other semi-final, Brazil encountered few difficulties in defeating a lacklustre and leg-weary Sweden 1–0 – again, Romario was the difference, heading the winner with 10 minutes left after Swedish captain Jonas Thern had been sent off for kicking Dunga.

The Swedes managed a measure of consolation in the third-place play-off, cruising against a deflated Bulgarian side who had already surpassed their own wildest hopes. Tomas Brolin was masterful in midfield, scoring the first, before laying on chances for Mild and Larsson to convert. Kenneth Andersson nodded in a Schwarz cross to complete a 4–0 triumph.

Italy gambled twice over, in playing superstar striker Roberto Baggio despite his lack of fitness, and in recalling veteran sweeper Franco Baresi for his first appearance after a cartilage operation following his injury against Norway in the first round. There was not even a place on the bench for the unlucky Zola.

In fact, Baresi was Italy's man of the match. The game saw Brazil employing their technical brilliance to try to outflank Italy's defensive discipline while the Italians sat back and waited for the right moment to unleash their rapid counter-attacks.

In direct contrast to the thrilling battle between the two sides in the 1970 Final, however, it was a game of few chances, most of which fell to Brazil. Romario misplaced a first-half header and Mazinho could not quite capitalize on a half-chance when Pagliuca spilled a Branco free-kick. In the 75th minute Pagliuca also allowed a long-range Mauro Silva effort to slip through his hands, but the ball bounced off the post and back into his arms. Pagliuca kissed the post in gratitude. Italy's best chance ended with Taffarel saving from Daniele Massaro, who had been first capped in 1982 but had only scored his first international goal less than three weeks previously against Mexico.

Roberto Baggio went close with one effort in each half of extra time while Brazil should again have taken the lead in the 109th minute when the industrious Cafu crossed to the far post and Romario put the ball fractionally the wrong side of the post from four yards out just beyond the far post. The extra-time introduction of Brazilian substitute Viola threatened to punish Italy, the teenager showing some delightful ball control and sparky enthusiasm, but both sides seemed exhausted in their seventh match of a gruelling tournament.

In the penalty shoot-out, Taffarel benefited immediately when Baresi shot over. Baresi sank to his knees in despair. Pagliuca then saved from Marcio Santos and Italy went briefly ahead as Demetrio Albertini scored from kick No. 2. Romario squared for Brazil, Evani netted for Italy and Branco for Brazil. This was the point at which it fell apart for Italy as Taffarel saved from Massaro and Brazil's captain, Dunga, after one of his most creative matches for his country, shot what proved the vital Brazilian kick. Baggio needed to score with Italy's last kick of the five to keep his country alive. Instead, he scooped the ball over the bar. Brazil were back on top of the world, Romario – voted Player of the Tournament – joyfully posing with the trophy alongside first Bebeto, and then a 17-year-old squad member called Ronaldo. He had not got a game in the tournament, but after 24 years of World Cup disappointment, the Brazilians now had plenty of reason to smile again.

France 1998

France won their "own" World Cup... and deservedly so. Previous host winners had usually triumphed in the shadow of controversy – as with Italy in 1934 and Argentina in 1978 who profited from the local political mood, England who benefited from benevolent refereeing in 1966 and West Germany who made the most of home comforts in 1974. Aime Jacquet's France, however, were demonstrably the best team in the finals. They secured the ultimate prize by beating Brazil 3–0 in the magnificent Stade de France .

Brazil are always carried along, wherever they go, on a cloud of hot air and hyperbole and Group A was no exception. Starting point was the fanciful suggestion that Ronaldo might challenge Just Fontaine's World Cup record of 13 goals. In fact, The Phenomenon found a goal of any sort beyond him in the 2–1 victory over Scotland with which Brazil began their campaign.

Group A was, in practical terms, two groups within one. Brazil were alone, out in front. Behind them came the other three, in a World Cup sub-group of their own.

All disappointed at one stage or another. Scotland began with great spirit in defeat by Brazil, should have done better than draw against Norway and subsided dismally after a bright start against Morocco, losing 3–0. Morocco were victims of their own erratic nature. With El Hadji and Tahar outstanding, they opened promisingly in a 2–2 draw against Norway, then collapsed 3–0 with a lack of conviction against Brazil. When they finally put it all together against Scotland it was, cruelly, not enough. Norway finally emerged from their shell in the last ten minutes of their last group game to snatch an amazing 2–1 win over Brazil and join them in the second round.

Italy always make even harder work of a World Cup than is necessary. Although they qualified impressively enough in the end they drew their first game 2–2 against Chile, while the other opening group game also finished all-square – Cameroon drawing 1–1 with Austria. Italy dispatched Austria and Cameroon without too much trouble, and they were joined in the second stage by Chile who drew all their three first-round matches.

In Group C France found out all about the odd unique

pressures of playing hosts as a World Cup the moment they walked out to the FIFA anthem to play their first game against South Africa in Marseille's magnificently refurbished Velodrome. To this extent France boss Jacquet was helped by the accident of the draw which served up perceived minnows South Africa and Saudi Arabia in the first two matches. Win those, Jacquet knew, and France would be in the second round. France did – with ease – and their 2–1 defeat of Denmark in the final pool match wasn't too disheartening for the Danes who also qualified after beating Saudi Arabia and taking a point from South Africa.

Group D had been proclaimed the "group of death" because it threw together the most evenly-balanced four nations – Bulgaria (fourth last time), Spain (quarter-finalists), Nigeria (second round) and Paraguay. In hindsight, the section should have been entitled the "group of suicide" as all except rank outsiders Paraguay managed to shoot themselves in the foot at one stage or another.

Spain set the trend on the group's opening day against Nigeria when a spectacular blunder by veteran goalkeeper Andoni Zubizarreta saw a 2–1 lead turned into a 3–2 defeat. The group remained wide open, however, because Bulgaria and Paraguay had played each other to a goalless stalemate. But Nigeria took decisive command of the race to the second round next time out when they defeated Bulgaria 1–0 while Paraguay held a hopelessly impotent Spanish side 0–0 in Saint-Etienne. Nigeria were now secure at the top of the group and again became a subject of controversy when Milutinovic rested half the team for their "meaningless" last match against Paraguay. The match may have meant nothing in terms of points or progress for Nigeria, but it meant everything to everyone else. Paraguay could qualify by defeating Nigeria; Spain or Bulgaria could qualify by defeating each other assuming Paraguay failed – as everyone expected – to beat Nigeria.

The surprise was that Nigeria appeared to have made no special plans for Paraguay and that complacency proved costly. Paraguay, driven on from the back by keeper-captain Jose Luis Chilavert, displayed a mettle which no-one had suspected to win 3–1. It mattered nothing that Spain thrashed the ragged defeatists of Bulgaria by 6–1... Paraguay were through and Spain were out.

If Group D was the "Group of Death" then Group E was the Group of Deja Vu. Holland and Belgium had played each other 130 times down the years and both they and Mexico had been in the same first-round group in the United States four years ago. The only outsiders in this family party were South Korea.

Mexico were by far the most entertaining side in the group. In their first match they had to come from 1–0 down against South Korea to win 3–1. In their second match they fought back in thrilling style to draw 2–2 with Belgium after being 2–0 down. Then they managed to repeat the trick against Holland – who led 2–0 after 18 minutes – in the last game after a mistake by Manchester United-bound Jaap Stam.

They qualified behind the Dutch who, after a dreary 0–0 draw

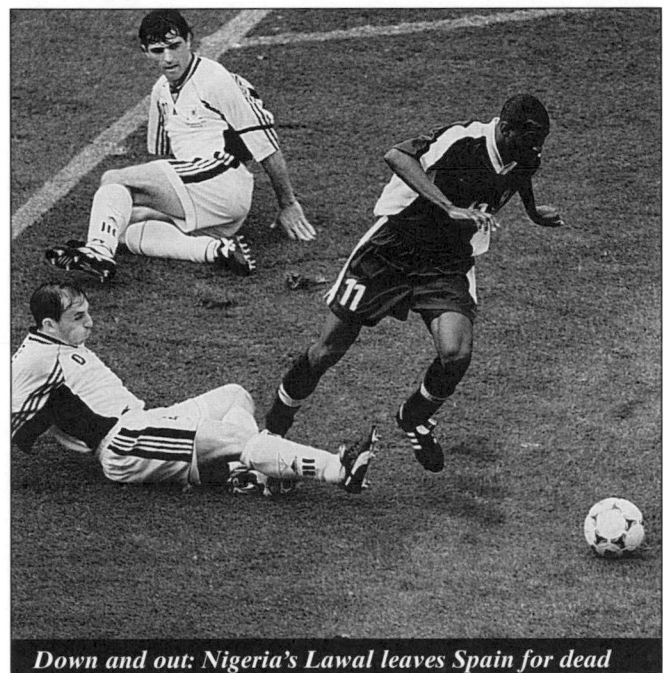
Down and out: Nigeria's Lawal leaves Spain for dead

against Belgium, found their touch against the Koreans with a 5–0 victory. Their draw with Mexico and Belgium's inability to defeat South Korea decided the outcome of the group.

Group F saw a rerun of another of the World Cup's classic confrontations between Germany and Yugoslavia. Yet the section will go down in football history not for this meeting of old football enemies but for the meeting of the United States and Iran.

Germany and Yugoslavia may have qualified for the second round, but it was the Iranians 2–1 defeat of the USA that captured the world's attention.

Romania and England went through from Group G as expected, although most forecasts suggested a reversal of the order. Much of the concern in Group G centred not, however, on the football but on the hooligans, the perpetual scar on the faces of England's football team abroad. All the PR about how wonderfully Europe's security forces had worked to ensure a peaceful World Cup was blown apart as English hooligans, along with the equally culpable Tunisians, smashed up various bars, shops and cars.

England defeated Tunisia and Colombia without any trouble, but sandwiched in between was a 2–1 defeat against Romania, the winning goal coming in the dying moments after a defensive blunder by defender Graeme Le Saux.

Group H managed to be simultaneously intriguing and predictable matching, as it did, Argentina and Croatia with newcomers Japan and Jamaica.

The two favourites found their two victories apiece over Japan and Jamaica a useful warm-up for heavier duties ahead – particularly Argentine striker Gabriel Batistuta who ended the first round as four-goal joint top scorer. That tally included the first hat-trick of the finals which he collected in the closing stages of the 5–0 thrashing of Japan.

Croatia struggled to impose themselves against Japan and Jamaica and finished runners-up after losing the last, decisive, tie against Argentina. Hector Pineda's first goal for his country handed Argentina top spot.

For Jamaica, the "Reggae Boyz" proved to be the entertainers of the tournament, along with their joyous fans. After the hammering they received at the hands of the Argentines, they showed wonderful resilience to bounce back with a 2–1 defeat of Japan. For the Japanese, co-hosts in 2002, the finals were not a pleasant experience. Along with the USA, Japan was the only country to lose all of its three pool matches.

One of the faults of the scheduling of France 98 was the absence of any break before first round and second. Thus the league campaigns ended the one day and the knock-out section began the next. There was no time to draw breath, no time to take stock, no time to praise the qualifiers or analyse the failures.

Not that Italy worried as Vieri struck his fifth goal in four games to defeat Norway in the first of the second round games, after he ran on to a through ball from Luigi Di Biagio, held off a challenge and then struck a perfect low shot just inside the far post in Marseille.

As for Brazil, coach Mario Zagallo damned Ronaldo with the faint praise of "having played a little better" as the Cup-holders stepped up their game in the Parc des Princes in Paris to crush Chile 4–1 and reach the quarter-finals. They scored four – two each to Ronaldo and Cesar Sampaio – came within a post's width of two more and might easily have had eight.

History was made in industrial town of Lens when France defeated Paraguay thanks to the first-ever golden goal in the World Cup – scored six minutes before the end of extra-time by central defender Laurent Blanc. France had not played played at their best, missing the inspiration of the suspended Zindane, but they had never ceased trying to create, pushing forward, searching for the goal which would represent their passport to the quarter-finals.

Denmark pulled off one of the shocks of the finals in thrashing Nigeria 4–1 to reach the quarter-finals. The third goal was the fastest ever by a substitute. Ebbe Sand stepped onto the pitch in the 59th minute and scored within 22 seconds.

Germany came from behind when a goal from Oliver Bierhoff four minutes from time in Montpellier earned them a place in the quarter-finals at the expense of Mexico. Germany were a goal down and struggling after the lively Mexicans took the lead thanks to a brilliant strike by Luis Hernandez, but when Klinsmann equalized there could only be one outcome.

Yugoslavia lost 2–1 to Holland who at looked to be running into form at just the right time to launch a serious challenge.

A penalty converted by Davor Suker two minutes into the second half against Romania in Bordeaux was enough to decide the flattest of the second-round ties and send Croatia into the quarter-finals at the first time of asking.

But the day's other tie, between England and Argentina in Saint-

Etienne was anything but flat. Indeed, it was probably the finest match of the finals.

England have had to pay a heavy price for the fortune of that famous third goal in the 1966 World Cup Final. For the third time in a major competition they went out on a penalty shoot-out.

But the failure to proceed to the quarter-finals may be blamed first on the failure against Romania in the first round which condemned England to finish second in the group, and secondly on the foolish behaviour of David Beckham in lifting a foot against Diego Simeone (who made the most of the opportunity) under the nose of the referee.

Beckham was sent off just after half-time with the score 2–2 and the game wide open. His absence meant withdrawing Michael Owen – who had earlier run from halfway to score the finest solo goal of the finals – into midfield and killed off England as an attacking force. It says everything about the way the remaining ten men performed that they held a talented and skilful Argentine attack at bay until the end of extra-time.

Now the world knew the eight teams who would comprise the quarter-finals, and for the players the end of the second round matches meant only one thing – a well-earned rest.

When the quarter-finals got under way, history painfully repeated itself for Italy, just as it had for England. France squeaked another round further thanks to a penalty shoot-out victory after a dull and dreary goalless draw in the Stade de France. Few chances were created, but Italy probably deserved to go out if only for their unadventurous and negative tactics.

As for Brazil, the suspicion had existed, ever since the Opening Match, that they were vulnerable in the centre of defence. No-one had tested the theory, Scotland and Morocco did not have the hardware; Norway tried for only the last 15 minutes of their group match; Chile could not provide Marcelo Salas and Ivan Zamorano with the necessary service. But it took Denmark only 95 seconds to find the key in Nantes.

A quick free kick by Peter Moller, Brian Laudrup nipped to the byline and pulled the ball back for Martin Jorgensen to shoot past Claudio Taffarel. Unfortunately for the Danes, subsequent opportunities to repeat the trick proved few and far between. Brazil had previously played their football in stops and starts, bits and pieces. But now the fun stopped and the real event started. The flips and tricks were still there, but applied to the serious cause of moving the ball forward in search of the inevitable equalizer. Goals from Bebeto and two from Rivaldo killed off the Danes who had drawn level at 2–2 shortly after half-time.

Down in Marseille, Argentina blamed the fatigue induced by their efforts against England for the 2–1 quarter-final defeat which provided Holland with belated revenge for the 1978 Final. Patrick Kluivert, restored in attack, opened the scoring and Claudio Lopez

Michael Owen: The boy who would be football king

levelled. Holland appeared at a disadvantage when leftback Arthur Numan was sent off for a second yellow card offence but the numbers were square in the 87th minute when Ortega head-butted Holland keeper Edwin Van de Sar. Two minutes later Argentina went out to a superb strike from Dennis Bergkamp.

Croatia sensationally reached their first World Cup semi-final trouncing Germany 3–0 in Lyon. It was a long time since Germany had been so decisively beaten, though the tie might have taken a different turn if Christian Wörns had received a yellow not a red card for a first-half clash with Davor Suker when the scoresheet was still blank. But the reality for the Germans was simple: age had caught up with the squad of veteran players.

By now most of the football world was holding its breath in hope of the event's dream final, hosts France against holders Brazil. First, however, there was the small matter of the semi-final stage when Brazil very nearly did not make it – squeezing through against Holland only by a virtue of a 4–2 victory in a penalty shoot-out after a 1–1 draw in Marseille.

Brazil just about deserved it on the balance of play after taking the lead within twenty seconds of the start of the second half when Roberto Carlos angled a crosses behind the Dutch defence and Ronaldo burst past Philip Cocu to score. Holland hit back. Frank De Boer saw a close-range jab fortuitously parried by Taffarel and Patrick Kluivert missed badly twice. Finally, with four minutes remaining, Frank De Boer crossed from the right and Kluivert, at last keeping the ball down, headed powerfully past Taffarel's left hand to send the tie into extra-time.

The way both sides began the penalty shoot-out promised a lengthy duel. But Cocu and Ronald De Boer, like so many before them, cracked under the pressure. Taffarel saved from both and Brazilian skipper Dunga had the personal satisfaction of knowing that it was his kick which took his country into their fifth Final.

The following day all France went wild – car cavalcades, hooters blaring and whistles shrilling, with nearly 400,000 thronging the Champs Elysees – after Les Bleus reached the Final for the first time in their history. The marvel of their 2–1 victory over Croatia in the Parc des Princes was not so much that France were the better team – which was never really in dispute – but that to prove it they had been forced to plumb depths of energy and determination never previously seen from any French national side. Not even the Kopa-Fontaine side of 1958 or even Michel Platini's European Championship-winners of 1984.

That greatest match of two-goal Lilian Thuram's career was marred only by the expulsion of Laurent Blanc for raising his hands in uncharacteristic fashion to Slaven Bilic. Television replays, however, showed that while Blanc flapped at Bilic who had been holding him in the penalty area, contact was minimal. Yet Bilic reacted as though he had been hit by a rifle bullet. Many people accused him of being a cheat after the incident. Certainly FIFA need to clamp down on those players who play-act in a deliberate attempt to get a fellow professional sent off.

For the first time, Marcel Desailly found himself up against a dangerous and testing centre-forward in Davor Suker. Just how dangerous was evidenced within 30 seconds of the start of the second half when Aljosa Asanovic found a hole in the heart of the French defence and Suker strode imperiously in from the right to shoot past Fabien Barthez.

Croatia were ahead, but within a minute of Suker's goal, France were level. Thuram, by far the outstanding right-back of the tournament, took the ball off Zvonimir Boban, fed Youri Djourkaeff then accelerated smoothly into position to convert the return pass into the equalizer. In the 70th minute Thuram, remarkably, did it again.

Croatia would ultimately achieve a double consolation. They ended their first-ever World Cup in third place after beating Holland 2–1 in the so-called "Losers' Final" while Suker was crowned the tournament's six-goal top scorer.

But these achievements were very much footnotes to history by comparison with events in the Stade de France on Sunday, July 12, when France took on Brazil.

The drama began long before kick-off when Ronaldo was taken ill at Brazil's hotel, falling victim to a stress attack provoked by a mixture of pressure, a stomach upset and allergic reaction to a cortizone injection for an ankle injury. Coach Zagallo initially omitted him from the team list submitted to FIFA. Then, when Ronaldo arrived late in the dressing rooms insisting he wanted to play, Zagallo was persuaded to change his mind.

Such chaos was the last thing Brazil's players needed in the hours before the most important match of their lives. No wonder they succumbed to the first-half French onslaught. Zidane headed goals in the 27th and 45th minutes to become the first man to score twice in normal time in a final since Brazil's own Pele and Vava 40 years earlier. French President Jacques Chirac and Prime Minister Lionel Jospin, tricolour scarves draped around their necks, shared the adolescent delight of Platini, who had unashamedly worn a France shirt beneath his suit jacket.

France moved the ball quickly and fluidly. Junior Baiano was all at sea in the heart of the Brazilian defence. Stephane Guivarc'h twice missed clear chances, Youri Djorkaeff failed with two more awkward openings. Brazil, in response, barely troubled keeper Barthez with one firm header from Rivaldo and a weak one from Bebeto the best they could offer.

Shocked Brazil, facing disaster and knowing it, attacked from the start of the second half with the individualistic Denilson now substituting for midfielder Leonardo. One chance fell to the off-colour Ronaldo but he shot at Barthez from close range. That was all Brazil managed even though Desailly was sent off for two yellow cards with 20 minutes to go. France, on the break, remained the more dangerous. Petit's breakaway goal in the second minute of overtime was no more than the French deserved.

Seconds later, it was all over. France, the country whose pioneers first launched the World Cup, were the new world champions.

WORLD CUP RESULTS

1930 URUGUAY

POOL 1

France 4	Mexico 1
Argentina 1	France 0
Chile 3	Mexico 0
Chile 1	France 0
Argentina 6	Mexico 3
Argentina 3	Chile 1

	P	W	D	L	F	A	Pts
Argentina	3	3	0	0	10	4	6
Chile	3	2	0	1	5	3	4
France	3	1	0	2	4	3	2
Mexico	3	0	0	3	4	13	0

POOL 2

Yugoslavia 2	Brazil 1
Yugoslavia 4	Bolivia 0
Brazil 4	Bolivia 0

	P	W	D	L	F	A	Pts
Yugoslavia	2	2	0	0	6	1	4
Brazil	2	1	0	1	5	2	2
Bolivia	2	0	0	2	0	8	0

POOL 3

Romania 3	Peru 1
Uruguay 1	Peru 0
Uruguay 4	Romania 0

	P	W	D	L	F	A	Pts
Uruguay	2	2	0	0	5	0	4
Romania	2	1	0	1	3	5	2
Peru	2	0	0	2	1	4	0

POOL 4

USA 3	Belgium 0
USA 3	Paraguay 0
Paraguay 1	Belgium 0

	P	W	D	L	F	A	Pts
USA	2	2	0	0	6	0	4
Paraguay	2	1	0	1	1	3	2
Belgium	2	0	0	2	0	4	0

SEMI-FINALS

Argentina 6 (Monti 20, Scopello 56, Stabile 69 87, Peucelle 80 85)
United States 1 (Brown 88)

Uruguay 6 (Cea 18 67 72, Anselmo 20 31, Iriarte 60)
Yugoslavia 1 (Sekulic 4)

THIRD-PLACE PLAY-OFF
Not held

FINAL
July 30 – Centenario, Montevideo
Uruguay 4 (Dorado 12, Cea 58, Iriarte 68, Castro 89)
Argentina 2 (Peucelle 20, Stabile 37)
HT: 1–2. Att: 93,000. Ref: Langenus (Bel)
URUGUAY: Ballestreros, Nasazzi, Mascheroni, Andrade, Fernandez, Gestido, Dorado, Scarone, Castro, Cea, Iriarte.
ARGENTINA: Botazzo, Della Torre, Paternoster, J Evaristo, Monti, Suarez, Peucelle, Varallo, Stabile, Ferreyra, M Evaristo.

TOP SCORER
Stabile (Arg) 8 goals.

1934 ITALY

FIRST ROUND

Italy 7	USA 1
Czech. 2	Romania 1
Germany 5	Belgium 2
Austria 3	France 2
(after extra time)	
Spain 3	Brazil 1
Switzerland 3	Holland 2
Sweden 3	Argentina 2
Hungary 4	Egypt 2

SECOND ROUND

Germany 2	Sweden 1
Austria 2	Hungary 1
Italy 1	Spain 1
(after extra time)	
Italy 1	Spain 0
(replay)	
Czech. 3	Switzerland 2

SEMI-FINALS
Czechoslovakia 3 (Nejedly 19 81, Krcil 71)
Germany 1 (Noack 62)

Italy 1 (Guaita 19)
Austria 0

THIRD-PLACE PLAY-OFF
Germany 3 (Lehner 1 42, Conen 27)
Austria 2 (Horvath 28, Sesta 54)

FINAL
June 10 – Flaminio, Rome
Italy 2 (Orsi 81, Schiavio 95)
Czechoslovakia 1 (Puc 71)
After extra time. HT: 0–0. 90 min: 1–1. Att: 55,000. Ref: Eklind (Swe)

ITALY: Combi, Monzeglio, Allemandi, Ferraris, Monti, Bertolini, Guaita, Meazza, Schiavio, Ferrari, Orsi.
CZECHOSLOVAKIA: Planicka, Zenisek, Ctyrocky, Kostalek, Cambal, Krcil, Junek, Svoboda, Sobotka, Nejedly, Puc.

TOP SCORER
Nejedly (Czech.) 5 goals.

1938 FRANCE

FIRST ROUND

Switzerland 1	Germany 1
(after extra time)	
Switzerland 4	Germany 2
(replay)	
Cuba 3	Romania 3
(after extra time)	
Cuba 2	Romania 1
(replay)	
Hungary 6	Dutch E. Ind. 0
France 3	Belgium 1
Czech. 3	Holland 0
(after extra time)	
Brazil 6	Poland 5
(after extra time)	
Italy 2	Norway 1
(after extra time)	

QUARTER-FINALS

Sweden 8	Cuba 0
Hungary 2	Switzerland 0
Italy 3	France 1
Brazil 1	Czech. 1
(after extra time)	
Brazil 2	Czech. 1
(replay)	

SEMI-FINALS
Italy 2 (Colaussi 55, Meazza 60)
Brazil 1 (Romeo 87)

Hungary 5 (Zsengeller 18 38 86, Titkos 26, Sarosi 61)
Sweden 1 (Nyberg 1)

THIRD-PLACE PLAY-OFF
Brazil 4 (Romeo 43, Leonidas 63 73, Peracio 80)
Sweden 2 (Jonasson 18, Nyberg 38)

FINAL
June 19 – Stade Colombes, Paris
Italy 4 (Colaussi 5 35, Piola 16 82)
Hungary 2 (Titkos 7, Sarosi 70)
HT: 2–1. Att: 55,000. Ref: Capdeville (Fra)
ITALY: Oliveiri, Foni, Rava, Serantoni, Andreolo, Locatelli, Biavati, Meazza, Piola, Ferrari, Colaussi.
HUNGARY: Szabo, Polgar, Biro, Szalay, Szucs, Lazar, Sas, Vincze, Sarosi, Zsengeller, Titkos.

TOP SCORER
Leonidas (Brazil) 8 goals.

1950 BRAZIL

POOL 1

Brazil 4	Mexico 0
Yugoslavia 3	Switzerland 0
Yugoslavia 4	Mexico 1
Brazil 2	Switzerland 2
Brazil 2	Yugoslavia 0
Switzerland 2	Mexico 1

	P	W	D	L	F	A	Pts
Brazil	3	2	1	0	8	2	5
Yugoslavia	3	2	0	1	7	3	4
Switzerland	3	1	1	1	4	6	3
Mexico	3	0	0	3	2	10	0

POOL 2

Spain 3	USA 1
England 2	Chile 0
USA 1	England 0
Spain 2	Chile 0
Spain 1	England 0
Chile 5	USA 2

	P	W	D	L	F	A	Pts
Spain	3	3	0	0	6	1	6
England	3	1	0	2	2	2	2
Chile	3	1	0	2	5	6	2
USA	3	1	0	2	4	8	2

POOL 3

Sweden 3	Italy 2
Sweden 2	Paraguay 2
Italy 2	Paraguay 0

	P	W	D	L	F	A	Pts
Sweden	2	1	1	0	5	4	3
Italy	2	1	0	1	4	3	2
Paraguay	2	0	1	1	2	4	1

POOL 4

Uruguay 8	Bolivia 0

	P	W	D	L	F	A	Pts
Uruguay	1	1	0	0	8	0	2
Bolivia	1	0	0	1	0	8	0

FINAL POOL

Uruguay 2	Spain 2
Brazil 7	Sweden 1
Uruguay 3	Sweden 2
Brazil 6	Spain 1
Sweden 3	Spain 1
Uruguay 2	Brazil 1

	P	W	D	L	F	A	Pts
Uruguay	3	2	1	0	7	5	5
Brazil	3	2	0	1	14	4	4
Sweden	3	1	0	2	6	11	2
Spain	3	0	1	2	4	11	1

THIRD PLACE
Sweden

FINAL (deciding match)
July 16 – Maracana, Rio de Janeiro
Uruguay 2 (Schiaffino 66, Ghiggia 79)
Brazil 1(Friaca 48)
HT: 0–0. Att: 199,854. Ref: Reader (Eng)
URUGUAY: Maspoli, M Gonzalez, Tejera, Gambetta, Varela, Andrade, Ghiggia, Perez, Miguez, Schiaffino, Moran.
BRAZIL: Barbosa, Augusto, Juvenal, Bauer, Danilo, Bigode, Friaca, Zizinho, Ademir, Jair, Chico.

TOP SCORER
Ademir (Bra) 9 goals.

1954 SWITZERLAND

POOL 1

Yugoslavia 1	France 0
Brazil 5	Mexico 0
France 3	Mexico 2
Brazil 1	Yugoslavia 1

	P	W	D	L	F	A	Pts
Brazil	2	1	1	0	6	1	3
Yugoslavia	2	1	1	0	2	1	3
France	2	1	0	1	3	3	2
Mexico	2	0	0	2	2	8	0

POOL 2

Hungary 9	Korea 0
W. Germany 4	Turkey 1
Hungary 8	W. Germany 3
Turkey 7	Korea 0

	P	W	D	L	F	A	Pts
Hungary	2	2	0	0	17	3	4
W. Germany	2	1	0	1	7	9	2
Turkey	2	1	0	1	8	4	2
Korea	2	0	0	2	0	16	0

PLAY-OFF
W. Germany 7   Turkey 2

POOL 3

Austria 1	Scotland 0
Uruguay 2	Czech. 0
Austria 5	Czech. 0
Uruguay 7	Scotland 0

	P	W	D	L	F	A	Pts
Uruguay	2	2	0	0	9	0	4
Austria	2	2	0	0	6	0	4
Czech.	2	0	0	2	0	7	0
Scotland	2	0	0	2	0	8	0

POOL 4

England 4	Belgium 4
England 2	Switzerland 0
Switzerland 2	Italy 1
Italy 4	Belgium 1

	P	W	D	L	F	A	Pts
England	2	1	1	0	6	4	3
Italy	2	1	0	1	5	3	2
Switzerland	2	1	0	1	2	3	2
Belgium	2	0	1	1	5	8	1

PLAY-OFF
Switzerland 4   Italy 1

QUARTER-FINALS

W. Germany 2	Yugoslavia 0
Hungary 4	Brazil 2
Austria 7	Switzerland 5
Uruguay 4	England 2

SEMI-FINALS
W. Germany 6 (Schafer 30, Morlock 49, F Walter 54 65, O Walter 60 89)
Austria 1 (Probst 51)

Hungary 4 (Czibor 13, Hidegkuti 47, Kocsis 111 116)
Uruguay 2 (Hohberg 75 86) (after extra time)

THIRD-PLACE PLAY-OFF
Austria 3 (Stojaspal 16, Cruz og 59, Ocwirk 79)
Uruguay 1 (Hohberg 21)

FINAL
July 4 – Wankdorf, Berne
W. Germany 3 (Morlock 11, Rahn 16 83)
Hungary 2 (Puskas 6, Czibor 8)
HT: 2–2. Att: 60,000. Ref: Ling (Eng)
GERMANY: Turek, Posipal, Kohlmeyer, Eckel, Liebrich, Mai, Rahn, Morlock, O Walter, F Walter, Schafer.
HUNGARY: Grosics, Buzansky, Lantos, Bozsik, Lorant, Zakarias, Czibor, Kocsis, Hidegkuti, Puskas, M Toth.

TOP SCORER
Kocsis (Hun) 11 goals.

1958 SWEDEN

POOL 1

W. Germany 3	Argentina 1
N. Ireland 1	Czech. 0
W.Germany 2	Czech. 2
Argentina 3	N. Ireland 1
W. Germany 2	N. Ireland 2
Czech. 6	Argentina 1

	P	W	D	L	F	A	Pts
W. Germany	3	1	2	0	7	5	4
Czech.	3	1	1	1	8	4	3
N. Ireland	3	1	1	1	4	5	3
Argentina	3	1	0	2	5	10	2

PLAY-OFF
N. Ireland 2   Czech. 1

POOL 2

France 7	Paraguay 3
Yugoslavia 1	Scotland 1
Yugoslavia 3	France 2
Paraguay 3	Scotland 2
France 2	Scotland 1
Yugoslavia 3	Paraguay 3

	P	W	D	L	F	A	Pts
France	3	2	0	1	11	7	4
Yugoslavia	3	1	2	0	7	6	4
Paraguay	3	1	1	1	9	12	3
Scotland	3	0	1	2	4	6	1

POOL 3

Sweden 3	Mexico 0
Hungary 1	Wales 1
Wales 1	Mexico 1
Sweden 2	Hungary 1
Sweden 0	Wales 0
Hungary 4	Mexico 0

	P	W	D	L	F	A	Pts
Sweden	3	2	1	0	5	1	5
Hungary	3	1	1	1	6	3	3
Wales	3	0	3	0	2	2	3
Mexico	3	0	1	2	1	8	1

PLAY-OFF

Wales 2	Hungary 1

POOL 4

England 2	Sov Union 2
Brazil 3	Austria 0
England 0	Brazil 0
Sov Union 2	Austria 0
Brazil 2	Sov Union 0
England 2	Austria 2

	P	W	D	L	F	A	Pts
Brazil	3	2	1	0	5	0	5
England	3	0	3	0	4	4	3
Sov Union	3	1	1	1	4	4	3
Austria	3	0	1	2	2	7	1

PLAY-OFF

Sov Union 1	England 0

QUARTER-FINALS

France 4	N. Ireland 0
W. Germany 1	Yugoslavia 0
Sweden 2	Sov Union 0
Brazil 1	Wales 0

SEMI-FINALS

Brazil 5 (Vava 2, Didi 38, Pele 53 64 76)
France 2 (Fontaine 8, Piantoni 83)

Sweden 3 (Skogland 30, Gren 81, Hamrin 88)
W. Germany 1 (Schafer 21)

THIRD-PLACE PLAY-OFF

France 6 (Fontaine 16 36 78 89, Kopa 27, Douis 50)
W. Germany 3 (Cieslarczyk 18, Rahn 52, Schafer 83)

FINAL

June 29 – Rasunda, Stockholm
Brazil 5 (Vava 9 32, Pele 55 89, Zagallo 68)
Sweden 2 (Liedholm 4, Simonsson 80)
HT: 2–1. Att: 49,737. Ref: Guigue (Fra)
BRAZIL: Gilmar, D Santos, N Santos, Zito, Bellini, Orlando, Garrincha, Didi, Vava, Pele, Zagallo.
SWEDEN: Svensson, Bergmark, Axbom, Borjesson, Gustavsson, Parling, Hamrin, Gren, Simonsson, Liedholm, Skoglund.

TOP SCORER

Fontaine (Fra) 13 goals.

1962 CHILE

GROUP 1

Uruguay 2	Colombia 1
Sov Union 2	Yugoslavia 0
Yugoslavia 3	Uruguay 1
Sov Union 4	Colombia 4
Sov Union 2	Uruguay 1
Yugoslavia 5	Colombia 0

	P	W	D	L	F	A	Pts
Sov Union	3	2	1	0	8	5	5
Yugoslavia	3	2	0	1	8	3	4
Uruguay	3	1	0	2	4	6	2
Colombia	3	0	1	2	5	11	1

GROUP 2

Chile 3	Switzerland 1
W. Germany 0	Italy 0
Chile 2	Italy 0
W. Germany 2	Switzerland 1
W. Germany 2	Chile 0
Italy 3	Switzerland 0

	P	W	D	L	F	A	Pts
W. Germany	3	2	1	0	4	1	5
Chile	3	2	0	1	5	3	4
Italy	3	1	1	1	3	2	3
Switzerland	3	0	0	3	2	8	0

GROUP 3

Brazil 2	Mexico 0
Czech. 1	Spain 0
Brazil 0	Czech. 0
Spain 1	Mexico 0
Brazil 2	Spain 1
Mexico 3	Czech. 1

	P	W	D	L	F	A	Pts
Brazil	3	2	1	0	4	1	5
Czech.	3	1	1	1	2	3	3
Mexico	3	1	0	2	3	4	2
Spain	3	1	0	2	2	3	2

GROUP 4

Argentina 1	Bulgaria 0
Hungary 2	England 1
England 3	Argentina 1
Hungary 6	Bulgaria 1
Argentina 0	Hungary 0
England 0	Bulgaria 0

	P	W	D	L	F	A	Pts
Hungary	3	2	1	0	8	2	5
England	3	1	1	1	4	3	3
Argentina	3	1	1	1	2	3	3
Bulgaria	3	0	1	2	1	7	1

QUARTER-FINALS

Yugoslavia 1	W. Germany 0
Brazil 3	England 1
Chile 2	Sov Union 1
Czech. 1	Hungary 0

SEMI-FINALS

Brazil 4 (Garrincha 9 31, Vava 49 77)
Chile 2 (Toro 41, L Sanchez 61)

Czech. 3 (Kadraba 49, Scherer 80 86)
Yugoslavia 1 (Jerkovic 69)

THIRD-PLACE PLAY-OFF

Chile 1 (Rojas 89)
Yugoslavia 0

FINAL

June 17 – Nacional, Santiago
Brazil 3 (Amarildo 18, Zito 69, Vava 77)
Czech. 1 (Masopust 16)
HT: 1–1. Att: 68,679. Ref: Latishev (SU)
BRAZIL: Gilmar, D Santos, N Santos, Zito, Mauro, Zozimo, Garrincha, Didi, Vava, Amarildo, Zagallo.
CZECH.: Scroiff, Tichy, Novak, Pluskal, Popluhar, Masopust, Pospichal, Scherer, Kvasnak, Kadraba, Jelinek.

TOP SCORERS

V Ivanov (SU), L Sanchez (Chl), Garrincha, Vava (Bra), Albert (Hun), Jerkovic (Yug) 4 goals each.

1966 ENGLAND

GROUP 1

England 0	Uruguay 0
France 1	Mexico 1
Uruguay 2	France 1
England 2	Mexico 0
Uruguay 0	Mexico 0
England 2	France 0

	P	W	D	L	F	A	Pts
England	3	2	1	0	4	0	5
Uruguay	3	1	2	0	2	1	4
Mexico	3	0	2	1	1	3	2
France	3	0	1	2	2	5	1

GROUP 2

W. Germany 5	Switzerland 0
Argentina 2	Spain 1
Spain 2	Switzerland 1
Argentina 0	W. Germany 0
Argentina 2	Switzerland 0
W. Germany 2	Spain 1

	P	W	D	L	F	A	Pts
W. Germany	3	2	1	0	8	2	5
Argentina	3	1	1	1	4	3	3
Spain	3	1	1	1	2	3	3
Switzerland	3	0	1	2	1	7	1

GROUP 3

Brazil 2	Bulgaria 0
Portugal 3	Hungary 1
Hungary 3	Brazil 1
Portugal 3	Bulgaria 0
Portugal 3	Brazil 1
Hungary 3	Bulgaria 1

	P	W	D	L	F	A	Pts
Portugal	3	3	0	0	9	2	6
Hungary	3	2	0	1	7	5	4
Brazil	3	1	0	2	4	6	2
Bulgaria	3	0	0	3	1	8	0

GROUP 4

Sov Union 3	N. Korea 0
Italy 2	Chile 0
Chile 1	N. Korea 1
Sov Union 1	Italy 0
N. Korea 1	Italy 0
Sov Union 2	Chile 1

	P	W	D	L	F	A	Pts
Sov Union	3	3	0	0	6	1	6
N. Korea	3	1	1	1	2	4	3
Italy	3	1	0	2	2	2	2
Chile	3	0	1	2	2	5	1

QUARTER-FINALS

England 1	Argentina 0
W. Germany 4	Uruguay 0
Portugal 5	N. Korea 3
Sov Union 2	Hungary 1

SEMI-FINALS

W. Germany 2 (Haller 44, Beckenbauer 68)
Sov Union 1 (Porkujan 88)

England 2 (R Charlton 30 79)
Portugal 1 (Eusebio 82)

THIRD PLACE PLAY-OFF

Portugal 2 (Eusebio 12, Torres 88)
Sov Union 1 (Metreveli 43)

FINAL

July 30 – Wembley Stadium
England 4 (Hurst 19 100, 119 Peters 77)
W. Germany 2 (Haller 13, Weber 89)

After extra time. HT: 1–1. 90 min: 2–2. Att: 96,924. Ref: Dienst (Swi)
ENGLAND: Banks, Cohen, Wilson, Stiles, J Charlton, Moore, Ball, Hunt, R Charlton, Hurst, Peters.
W. GERMANY: Tilkowski, Höttges, Schnellinger, Beckenbauer, Schülz, Weber, Haller, Overath, Seeler, Held, Emmerich.

TOP SCORER

Eusebio (Por) 9 goals.

1970 MEXICO

GROUP 1

Mexico 0	Sov Union 0
Belgium 3	El Salvador 0
Sov Union 4	Belgium 1
Mexico 4	El Salvador 0
Sov Union 2	El Salvador 0
Mexico 1	Belgium 0

	P	W	D	L	F	A	Pts
Sov Union	3	2	1	0	6	1	5
Mexico	3	2	1	0	5	0	5
Belgium	3	1	0	2	4	5	2
El Salvador	3	0	0	3	0	9	0

GROUP 2

Uruguay 2	Israel 0
Italy 1	Sweden 0
Uruguay 0	Italy 0
Sweden 1	Israel 1
Sweden 1	Uruguay 0
Italy 0	Israel 0

	P	W	D	L	F	A	Pts
Italy	3	1	2	0	1	0	4
Uruguay	3	1	1	1	2	1	3
Sweden	3	1	1	1	2	2	3
Israel	3	0	2	1	1	3	2

GROUP 3

England 1	Romania 0
Brazil 4	Czech. 1
Romania 2	Czech. 1
Brazil 1	England 0
Brazil 3	Romania 2
England 1	Czech. 0

	P	W	D	L	F	A	Pts
Brazil	3	3	0	0	8	3	6
England	3	2	0	1	2	1	4
Romania	3	1	0	2	4	5	2
Czech.	3	0	0	3	2	7	0

GROUP 4

Peru 3	Bulgaria 2
W. Germany 2	Morocco 1
Peru 3	Morocco 0
W. Germany 5	Bulgaria 2
W. Germany 3	Peru 1
Morocco 1	Bulgaria 1

	P	W	D	L	F	A	Pts
W. Germany	3	3	0	0	10	4	6
Peru	3	2	0	1	7	5	4
Bulgaria	3	0	1	2	5	9	1
Morocco	3	0	1	2	2	6	1

QUARTER-FINALS

W. Germany 3	England 2
(after extra time)	
Brazil 4	Peru 2
Italy 4	Mexico 1
Uruguay 1	Sov Union 0

SEMI-FINALS

Italy 4 (Boninsegna 7, Burgnich 99, Riva 104, Rivera 111)
W. Germany 3 (Schellinger 90, G Müller 95 110)
(after extra time)

Brazil 3 (Clodoaldo 45, Jairzinho 76, Rivelino 88)
Uruguay 1 (Cubilla 19)

THIRD-PLACE PLAY-OFF

W. Germany 1 (Overath 26)
Uruguay 0

FINAL

June 21 – Azteca, Mexico City
Brazil 4 (Pele 18, Gerson 66, Jairzinho 71, Carlos Alberto 86)
Italy 1 (Boninsegna 37)
HT: 1–1. Att: 107,000. Ref: Glockner (EG)
BRAZIL: Felix, Carlos Alberto, Brito, Wilson Piazza, Everaldo, Clodoaldo, Gerson, Rivelino, Jairzinho, Tostao, Pele.
ITALY: Albertosi, Burgnich, Cera, Rosato, Facchetti, Bertini (Juliano 75), Domenghini, De Sisti, Mazzola, Boninsegna (Rivera 84), Riva.

TOP SCORER

G Müller (WG) 10 goals.

1974 WEST GERMANY

GROUP 1

W. Germany 1	Chile 0
E. Germany 2	Australia 0
W. Germany 3	Australia 0
E. Germany 1	Chile 1
Australia 0	Chile 0
E.Germany 1	W. Germany 0

	P	W	D	L	F	A	Pts
E. Germany	3	2	1	0	4	1	5
W. Germany	3	2	0	1	4	1	4
Chile	3	0	2	1	1	2	2
Australia	3	0	1	2	0	5	1

GROUP 2

Brazil 0	Yugoslavia 0
Scotland 2	Zaire 0
Brazil 0	Scotland 0
Yugoslavia 9	Zaire 0
Yugoslavia 1	Scotland 1
Brazil 3	Zaire 0

	P	W	D	L	F	A	Pts
Yugoslavia	3	1	2	0	10	1	4
Brazil	3	1	2	0	3	0	4
Scotland	3	1	2	0	3	1	4
Zaire	3	0	0	3	0	14	0

GROUP 3

Holland 2	Uruguay 0
Bulgaria 0	Sweden 0
Holland 0	Sweden 0
Bulgaria 1	Uruguay 1
Holland 4	Bulgaria 1
Sweden 3	Uruguay 0

	P	W	D	L	F	A	Pts
Holland	3	2	1	0	6	1	5
Sweden	3	1	2	0	3	0	4
Bulgaria	3	0	2	1	2	5	2
Uruguay	3	0	1	2	1	6	1

GROUP 4

Italy 3	Haiti 1
Poland 3	Argentina 2
Argentina 1	Italy 1
Poland 7	Haiti 0
Argentina 4	Haiti 1
Poland 2	Italy 1

	P	W	D	L	F	A	Pts
Poland	3	3	0	0	12	3	6
Argentina	3	1	1	1	7	5	3
Italy	3	1	1	1	5	4	3
Haiti	3	0	0	3	2	14	0

SECOND ROUND – GROUP A

Brazil 1	E. Germany 0
Holland 4	Argentina 0
Holland 2	E. Germany 0
Brazil 2	Argentina 1
E.Germany 1	Argentina 1
Holland 2	Brazil 0

	P	W	D	L	F	A	Pts
Holland	3	3	0	0	8	0	6
Brazil	3	2	0	1	3	3	4
E. Germany	3	0	1	2	1	4	1
Argentina	3	0	1	2	2	7	1

GROUP B

Poland 1	Sweden 0
W. Germany 2	Yugoslavia 0
Poland 2	Yugoslavia 1
W. Germany 4	Sweden 2
Sweden 2	Yugoslavia 1
W. Germany 1	Poland 0

	P	W	D	L	F	A	Pts
W. Germany	3	3	0	0	7	2	6
Poland	3	2	0	1	3	2	4
Sweden	3	1	0	2	4	6	2
Yugoslavia	3	0	0	3	2	6	0

THIRD PLACE PLAY-OFF

Poland 1 (Lato 76)
Brazil 0

FINAL

July 7 – Olympiastadion, Munich
W. Germany 2 (Breitner 25 pen, G Muller 43)
Holland 1 (Neeskens 2 pen)
HT: 2–1. Att: 77,833. Ref: Taylor (Eng)
W. GERMANY: Maier, Vogts, Schwarzenbeck, Beckenbauer, Breitner, Bonhof, U Hoeness, Overath, Grabowski, G Müller, Hölzenbein.
HOLLAND: Jongbloed, Suurbier, Rijsbergen (De Jong 69), Haan, Krol, Jansen, Van Hanegem, Neeskens, Rep, Cruyff, Rensenbrink (R Van de Kerkhof 46).

TOP SCORER

Lato (Pol) 7 goals.

1978 ARGENTINA

GROUP 1

Argentina 2	Hungary 1
Italy 2	France 1
Argentina 2	France 1
Italy 3	Hungary 1
Italy 1	Argentina 0
France 3	Hungary 1

	P	W	D	L	F	A	Pts
Italy	3	3	0	0	6	2	6
Argentina	3	2	0	1	4	3	4
France	3	1	0	2	5	5	2
Hungary	3	0	0	3	3	8	0

GROUP 2

W. Germany 0	Poland 0
Tunisia 3	Mexico 1
Poland 1	Tunisia 0
W. Germany 6	Mexico 0
Poland 3	Mexico 1
W. Germany 0	Tunisia 0

	P	W	D	L	F	A	Pts
Poland	3	2	1	0	4	1	5
W. Germany	3	1	2	0	6	0	4
Tunisia	3	1	1	1	3	2	3
Mexico	3	0	0	3	2	12	0

GROUP 3

Austria 2	Spain 1
Sweden 1	Brazil 1
Austria 1	Sweden 0
Brazil 0	Spain 0
Spain 1	Sweden 0
Brazil 1	Austria 0

	P	W	D	L	F	A	Pts
Austria	3	2	0	1	3	2	4
Brazil	3	1	2	0	2	1	4
Spain	3	1	1	1	2	2	3
Sweden	3	0	1	2	1	3	1

GROUP 4

Peru 3	Scotland 1
Holland 3	Iran 1
Scotland 1	Iran 1
Holland 0	Peru 0
Peru 4	Iran 1
Scotland 3	Holland 2

	P	W	D	L	F	A	Pts
Peru	3	2	1	0	7	2	5
Holland	3	1	1	1	5	3	3
Scotland	3	1	1	1	5	6	3
Iran	3	0	1	2	2	8	1

SECOND ROUND – GROUP A

Italy 0	W. Germany 0
Holland 5	Austria 1
Italy 1	Austria 0
Austria 3	W. Germany 2
Holland 2	Italy 1
Holland 2	W. Germany 2

	P	W	D	L	F	A	Pts
Holland	3	2	1	0	9	4	5
Italy	3	1	1	1	2	2	3
W. Germany	3	0	2	1	4	5	2
Austria	3	1	0	2	4	8	2

GROUP B

Argentina 2	Poland 0
Brazil 3	Peru 0
Argentina 0	Brazil 0
Poland 1	Peru 0
Brazil 3	Poland 1
Argentina 6	Peru 0

	P	W	D	L	F	A	Pts
Argentina	3	2	1	0	8	0	5
Brazil	3	2	1	0	6	1	5
Poland	3	1	0	2	2	5	2
Peru	3	0	0	3	0	10	0

THIRD-PLACE PLAY-OFF

Brazil 2 (Nelinho 64, Dirceu 71)
Italy 1 (Causio 38)

FINAL

June 25 – Monumental, Buenos Aires
Argentina 3 (Kempes 37 104, Bertoni 114)
Holland 1 (Nanninga 81)
After extra time. HT: 1–0. 90 min: 1–1. Att: 77,260. Ref: Gonella (Ita)
ARGENTINA: Fillol, Olguin, Galvan, Passarella, Tarantini, Ardiles (Larrosa 66), Gallego, Kempes, Bertoni, Luque, Ortiz (Houseman 75).
HOLLAND: Jongbloed, Jansen (Suurbier 73), Brandts, Krol, Poortvliet, W Van de Kerkhof, Neeskens, Haan, R Van de Kerkhof, Rep (Nanninga 59), Rensenbrink.

TOP SCORER

Kempes (Arg) 6 goals.

1982 SPAIN

GROUP 1

Italy 0	Poland 0
Peru 0	Cameroon 0
Italy 1	Peru 1
Poland 0	Cameroon 0
Poland 5	Peru 1
Italy 1	Cameroon 1

	P	W	D	L	F	A	Pts
Poland	3	1	2	0	5	1	4
Italy	3	0	3	0	2	2	3
Cameroon	3	0	3	0	1	1	3
Peru	3	0	2	1	2	6	2

GROUP 2

Algeria 2	W. Germany 1
Austria 1	Chile 0
W. Germany 4	Chile 1
Austria 2	Algeria 1
Algeria 3	Chile 2
W. Germany 1	Austria 0

	P	W	D	L	F	A	Pts
W. Germany	3	2	0	1	6	3	4
Austria	3	2	0	1	3	1	4
Algeria	3	2	0	1	5	5	4
Chile	3	0	0	3	3	8	0

GROUP 3

Belgium 1	Argentina 0
Hungary 10	El Salvador 1
Argentina 4	Hungary 1
Belgium 1	El Salvador 0
Belgium 1	Hungary 1
Argentina 2	El Salvador 0

	P	W	D	L	F	A	Pts
Belgium	3	2	1	0	3	1	5
Argentina	3	2	0	1	6	2	4
Hungary	3	1	1	1	12	6	3
El Salvador	3	0	0	3	1	13	0

GROUP 4

England 3	France 1
Czech. 1	Kuwait 1
England 2	Czech. 0
France 4	Kuwait 1
France 1	Czech. 1
England 1	Kuwait 0

	P	W	D	L	F	A	Pts
England	3	3	0	0	6	1	6
France	3	1	1	1	6	5	3
Czech.	3	0	2	1	2	4	2
Kuwait	3	0	1	2	2	6	1

GROUP 5

Spain 1	Honduras 1
N. Ireland 0	Yugoslavia 0
Spain 2	Yugoslavia 1
N. Ireland 1	Honduras 1
Yugoslavia 1	Honduras 0
N. Ireland 1	Spain 0

	P	W	D	L	F	A	Pts
N. Ireland	3	1	2	0	2	1	4
Spain	3	1	1	1	3	3	3
Yugoslavia	3	1	1	1	2	2	3
Honduras	3	0	2	1	2	3	2

GROUP 6

Brazil 2	Sov Union 1
Scotland 5	N. Zealand 2
Brazil 4	Scotland 1
Sov Union 3	N. Zealand 0
Scotland 2	Sov Union 2
Brazil 4	N. Zealand 0

	P	W	D	L	F	A	Pts
Brazil	3	3	0	0	10	2	6
Sov Union	3	1	1	1	6	4	3
Scotland	3	1	1	1	8	8	3
N. Zealand	3	0	0	3	2	12	0

SECOND ROUND - GROUP A

Poland 3	Belgium 0
Sov Union 1	Belgium 0
Sov Union 0	Poland 0

	P	W	D	L	F	A	Pts
Poland	2	1	1	0	3	0	3
Sov Union	2	1	1	0	1	0	3
Belgium	2	0	0	2	0	4	0

GROUP B

W. Germany 0	England 0
W. Germany 2	Spain 1
England 0	Spain 0

	P	W	D	L	F	A	Pts
W. Germany	2	1	1	0	2	1	3
England	2	0	2	0	0	0	2
Spain	2	0	1	1	1	2	1

GROUP C

Italy 2	Argentina 1
Brazil 3	Argentina 1
Italy 3	Brazil 2

	P	W	D	L	F	A	Pts
Italy	2	2	0	0	5	3	4
Brazil	2	1	0	1	5	4	2
Argentina	2	0	0	2	2	5	0

GROUP D

France 1	Austria 0
N. Ireland 2	Austria 2
France 4	N. Ireland 1

	P	W	D	L	F	A	Pts
France	2	2	0	0	5	1	4
Austria	2	0	1	1	2	3	1
N.Ireland	2	0	1	1	3	6	1

SEMI-FINALS

Italy 2 (Rossi 22 73)
Poland 0

W.Germany 3 (Littbarski 18, Rummenigge 102, Fischer 107)
France 3 (Platini 27, Tresor 93, Giresse 97)
W. Germany 5–4 on pens, after extra time

THIRD PLACE PLAY-OFF

Poland 3 (Szarmach 41, Majewski 44, Kupcewicz 47)
France 2 (Girard 14, Couriol 75)

FINAL

July 11 – Estadio Santiago Bernabeu, Madrid
Italy 3 (Rossi 56, Tardelli 69, Altobelli 80)
W. Germany 1 (Breitner 82)
HT: 0–0. Att: 90,000. Ref: Coelho (Bra)
ITALY: Zoff, Bergomi, Collovati, Scirea, Gentile, Cabrini, Tardelli, Oriali, Conti, Rossi, Graziani (Altobelli 8 [Causio 88]).
W. GERMANY: Schumacher, Kaltz, K Förster, B Förster, Stielike, Briegel, Dremmler (Hrubesch 63), Breitner, Rummenigge (H Müller 70), Fischer, Littbarski.

TOP SCORER

Rossi (Ita) 6 goals.

1986 MEXICO

GROUP A

Bulgaria 1	Italy 1
Argentina 3	S. Korea 1
Italy 1	Argentina 1
Bulgaria 1	S. Korea 1
Argentina 2	Bulgaria 0
Italy 3	S. Korea 2

	P	W	D	L	F	A	Pts
Argentina	3	2	1	0	6	2	5
Italy	3	1	2	0	5	4	4
Bulgaria	3	0	2	1	2	4	2
S. Korea	3	0	1	2	4	7	1

GROUP B

Mexico 2	Belgium 1
Paraguay 1	Iraq 0
Mexico 1	Paraguay 1
Belgium 2	Iraq 1
Paraguay 2	Belgium 2
Mexico 1	Iraq 0

	P	W	D	L	F	A	Pts
Mexico	3	2	1	0	4	2	5
Paraguay	3	1	2	0	4	3	4
Belgium	3	1	1	1	5	5	4
Iraq	3	0	0	3	1	4	0

GROUP C

Sov Union 6	Hungary 0	
France 1	Canada 0	
Sov Union 1	France 1	
Hungary 2	Canada 0	
France 3	Hungary 0	
Sov Union 2	Canada 0	

	P	W	D	L	F	A	Pts
Sov Union	3	2	1	0	9	1	5
France	3	2	1	0	5	1	5
Hungary	3	1	0	2	2	9	2
Canada	3	0	0	3	0	5	0

GROUP D

Brazil 1	Spain 0
N. Ireland 1	Algeria 1
Spain 2	N. Ireland 1
Brazil 1	Algeria 0
Spain 3	Algeria 0
Brazil 3	N. Ireland 0

	P	W	D	L	F	A	Pts
Brazil	3	3	0	0	5	0	6
Spain	3	2	0	1	5	2	4
N. Ireland	3	0	1	2	2	6	1
Algeria	3	0	1	2	1	5	1

GROUP E

W. Germany 1	Uruguay 1
Denmark 1	Scotland 0
Denmark 6	Uruguay 1
W. Germany 2	Scotland 1
Scotland 0	Uruguay 0
Denmark 2	W. Germany 0

	P	W	D	L	F	A	Pts
Denmark	3	3	0	0	9	1	6
W. Germany	3	1	1	1	3	4	3
Uruguay	3	0	2	1	2	7	2
Scotland	3	0	1	2	1	3	1

GROUP F

Morocco 0	Poland 0
Portugal 1	England 0
England 0	Morocco 0
Poland 1	Portugal 0
England 3	Poland 0
Morocco 3	Portugal 1

	P	W	D	L	F	A	Pts
Morocco	3	1	2	0	3	1	4
England	3	1	1	1	3	1	3
Poland	3	1	1	1	1	3	3
Portugal	3	1	0	2	2	4	2

SECOND ROUND

Knock-out phase comprising the top two teams from each group plus the four best third-placed teams.

Mexico 2	Bulgaria 0
Belgium 4	Sov Union 3
(after extra time)	
Brazil 4	Poland 0
Argentina 1	Uruguay 0
France 2	Italy 0
W. Germany 1	Morocco 0
England 3	Paraguay 0
Spain 5	Denmark 1

QUARTER-FINALS

France 1	Brazil 1

(France 4–3 on pens after extra time)

W.Germany 0	Mexico 0

(W. Germany 4–1 on pens after extra time)

Argentina 2	England 1
Spain 1	Belgium 1

(Belgium 5–4 on pens after extra time)

SEMI-FINALS

Argentina 2 (Maradona 51 62)
Belgium 0

W. Germany 2 (Brehme 9, Völler 90)
France 0

THIRD PLACE PLAY-OFF

France 4 (Ferreri 27, Papin 42, Genghini 103, Amoros 108)
Belgium 2 (Ceulemans 10, Claesen 73)

FINAL

June 29 – Azteca, Mexico City
Argentina 3 (Brown 22, Valdano 56, Burruchaga 84)
W. Germany 2 (Rummenigge 73, Völler 82)
HT: 1–0. Att: 114,590. Ref: Arppi Filho (Brz)
ARGENTINA: Pumpido, Cuciuffo, Brown, Ruggeri, Giusti, Burruchaga (Trobbiani 89), Batista, Enrique, Olarticoechea, Maradona, Valdano.
W. GERMANY: Schumacher, Berthold, Jakobs, K Förster, Briegel, Brehme, Matthäus, Magath (D Hoeness 63), Eder, Rummenigge, K Allofs (Völler 46).

TOP SCORER

Lineker (Eng) 6 goals.

1990 ITALY

GROUP A

Italy 1	Austria 0
Czech. 5	USA 1
Italy 1	USA 0
Czech. 1	Austria 0
Italy 2	Czech. 0
Austria 2	USA 1

	P	W	D	L	F	A	Pts
Italy	3	3	0	0	4	0	6
Czech.	3	2	0	1	6	3	4
Austria	3	1	0	2	2	3	2
USA	3	0	0	3	2	8	0

GROUP B

Cameroon 1	Argentina 0
Romania 2	Sov Union 0
Argentina 2	Sov Union 0
Cameroon 2	Romania 1
Argentina 1	Romania 1
Sov Union 4	Cameroon 0

	P	W	D	L	F	A	Pts
Cameroon	3	2	0	1	3	5	4
Romania	3	1	1	1	4	3	3
Argentina	3	1	1	1	3	2	3
Sov Union	3	1	0	2	4	4	2

GROUP C

Brazil 2	Sweden 1
Costa Rica 1	Scotland 0
Brazil 1	Costa Rica 0
Scotland 2	Sweden 1
Brazil 1	Scotland 0
Costa Rica 2	Sweden 1

	P	W	D	L	F	A	Pts
Brazil	3	3	0	0	4	1	6
Costa Rica	3	2	0	1	3	2	4
Scotland	3	1	0	2	2	3	2
Sweden	3	0	0	3	3	6	0

GROUP D

Colombia 2	UAE 0
W. Germany 4	Yugoslavia 1
Yugoslavia 1	Colombia 0
W. Germany 5	UAE 1
W. Germany 1	Colombia 1
Yugoslavia 4	UAE 1

	P	W	D	L	F	A	Pts
W. Germany	3	2	1	0	10	3	5
Yugoslavia	3	2	0	1	6	5	4
Colombia	3	1	1	1	3	2	3
UAE	3	0	0	3	2	11	0

GROUP E

Belgium 2	S. Korea 0
Uruguay 0	Spain 0
Belgium 3	Uruguay 1
Spain 3	S. Korea 1
Spain 2	Belgium 1
Uruguay 1	S. Korea 0

	P	W	D	L	F	A	Pts
Spain	3	2	1	0	5	2	5
Belgium	3	2	0	1	6	3	4
Uruguay	3	1	1	1	2	3	3
S. Korea	3	0	1	2	1	7	1

GROUP F

England 1	Rep of Ireland 1
Holland 1	Egypt 1
England 0	Holland 0
Egypt 0	Rep of Ireland 0
England 1	Egypt 0
Holland 1	Rep of Ireland 1

	P	W	D	L	F	A	Pts
England	3	1	2	0	2	1	4
Rep of Ire	3	0	3	0	2	2	3
Holland	3	0	3	0	2	2	3
Egypt	3	0	2	1	1	2	2

SECOND ROUND

Knock-out phase comprising the top two teams from each group plus the four best third-placed teams.

Cameroon 2	Colombia 1
(after extra time)	
Czech. 4	Costa Rica 1
Argentina 1	Brazil 0
W. Germany 2	Holland 1
Rep of Ireland 0	Romania 0
(Rep of Ireland 5–4 on pens after extra time)	
Italy 2	Uruguay 0
Yugoslavia 2	Spain 1
England 1	Belgium 0
(after extra time)	

QUARTER-FINALS

Argentina 0	Yugoslavia 0
(Argentina 3–2 on pens after extra time)	
Italy 1	Rep of Ireland 0
W. Germany 1	Czech. 0
England 3	Cameroon 2
(after extra time)	

SEMI-FINALS

Argentina 1 (Caniggia 67)
Italy 1 (Schillaci 17)
(Argentina 4–3 on pens after extra time)

W. Germany 1 (Brehme 59)
England 1 (Lineker 80)
(West Germany 4–3 on pens after extra time)

THIRD-PLACE PLAY-OFF

Italy 2 (R Baggio 71, Schillaci 84)
England 1 (Platt 80)

FINAL

July 8 – Olimpico, Rome
W. Germany 1 (Brehme 84 pen)
Argentina 0
HT: 0–0. Att: 73,603. Ref: Codesal (Mex)
W. GERMANY: Illgner, Berthold (Reuter 74), Kohler, Augenthaler, Buchwald, Brehme, Hässler, Matthäus, Littbarski, Völler, Klinsmann.
ARGENTINA: Goycochea, Lorenzo, Sensini, Serrizuela, Ruggeri (*Monzon 46), Simon, Basualdo, Burruchaga (Calderon 53), Maradona, Troglio, **Dezotti.
*Monzon sent off, 65 min.
**Dezotti sent off, 86 min.

TOP SCORER:

Schillaci (Ita) 6 goals.

1994 UNITED STATES

GROUP A

USA 1	Switzerland 1
Colombia 1	Romania 3
USA 2	Colombia 1
Romania 1	Switzerland 4
USA 0	Romania 1
Switzerland 0	Colombia 2

	P	W	D	L	F	A	Pts
Romania	3	2	0	1	5	5	6
Switzerland	3	1	1	1	5	4	4
USA	3	1	1	1	3	3	4
Colombia	3	1	0	2	4	5	3

GROUP B

Cameroon 2	Sweden 2
Brazil 2	Russia 0
Brazil 3	Cameroon 0
Sweden 3	Russia 1
Russia 6	Cameroon 1
Brazil 1	Sweden 1

	P	W	D	L	F	A	Pts
Brazil	3	2	1	0	6	1	7
Sweden	3	1	2	0	6	4	5
Russia	3	1	0	2	7	6	3
Cameroon	3	0	1	2	3	11	1

GROUP C

Germany 1	Bolivia 0
Spain 2	S. Korea 2
Germany 1	Spain 1
S Korea 0	Bolivia 0
Bolivia 1	Spain 3
Germany 3	S. Korea 2

	P	W	D	L	F	A	Pts
Germany	3	2	1	0	5	3	7
Spain	3	1	2	0	6	4	5
S. Korea	3	0	2	1	4	5	2
Bolivia	3	0	1	2	1	4	1

GROUP D

Argentina 4	Greece 0
Nigeria 3	Bulgaria 0
Argentina 2	Nigeria 1
Bulgaria 4	Greece 0
Greece 0	Nigeria 2
Argentina 0	Bulgaria 2

	P	W	D	L	F	A	Pts
Nigeria	3	2	0	1	6	2	6
Bulgaria	3	2	0	1	6	3	6
Argentina	3	2	0	1	6	3	6
Greece	3	0	0	3	0	10	0

GROUP E

Italy 0	Rep of Ireland 1
Norway 1	Mexico 0
Italy 1	Norway 0
Mexico 2	Rep of Ireland 1
Rep of Ireland 0	Norway 0
Italy 1	Mexico 1

	P	W	D	L	F	A	Pts
Mexico	3	1	1	1	3	3	4
Rep of Ire	3	1	1	1	2	2	4
Italy	3	1	1	1	2	2	4
Norway	3	1	1	1	1	1	4

GROUP F

Belgium 1	Morocco 0
Holland 2	Saudi Arabia 1
Belgium 1	Holland 0
Saudi Arabia 2	Morocco 1
Morocco 1	Holland 2
Belgium 0	Saudi Arabia 1

	P	W	D	L	F	A	Pts
Holland	3	2	0	1	4	3	6
Saudi Arabia	3	2	0	1	4	3	6
Belgium	3	2	0	1	2	1	6
Morocco	3	0	0	3	2	5	0

SECOND ROUND

Germany 3	Belgium 2
Spain 3	Switzerland 0
Saudi Arabia 1	Sweden 3
Romania 3	Argentina 2
Holland 2	Rep of Ireland 0
Brazil 1	USA 0
Nigeria 1	Italy 2
(after extra time)	
Mexico 1	Bulgaria 1
(Bulgaria 3–1 on pens after extra time)	

QUARTER-FINALS

Italy 2	Spain 1
Holland 2	Brazil 3
Germany 1	Bulgaria 2
Sweden 2	Romania 2
(Sweden 5–4 on pens after extra time)	

Deschamps, Desailly and Barthez lead the French team to the trophy in 1998

SEMI-FINALS

Brazil 1 (Romario 80)
Sweden 0
Italy 2 (R Baggio 21 26)
Bulgaria 1 (Stoichkov 44 pen)

THIRD-PLACE PLAY-OFF

Sweden 4 (Brolin 8, Mild 30, H Larsson 37, K Andersson 39)
Bulgaria 0

FINAL

July 17 – Rose Bowl, Pasadena
Brazil 0
Italy 0
(Brazil 3–2 on pens after extra time)
HT: 0–0. 90 min: 0–0. Att: 94,000. Ref: Puhl (Hun)
BRAZIL: Taffarel, Jorginho (Cafu 21), Marcio Santos, Aldair, Branco, Mazinho, Mauro Silvo, Dunga, Zinho (Viola 106), Bebeto, Romario.
ITALY: Pagliuca, Mussi (Apolloni 34), Maldini, Baresi, Benarrivo, Donadoni, Albertini, D Baggio (Evani 95), Berti, Massaro, R Baggio.

TOP SCORERS

Salenko (Rus), Stoichkov (Bul) each 6 goals.

1998 FRANCE

GROUP A

Brazil 2	Scotland 1
Morocco 2	Norway 2
Brazil 3	Morocco 0
Scotland 1	Norway 1
Brazil 1	Norway 2
Scotland 0	Morocco 3

	P	W	D	L	F	A	Pts
Brazil	3	2	0	1	6	3	6
Norway	3	1	2	0	5	4	5
Morocco	3	1	1	1	5	5	4
Scotland	3	0	1	2	2	6	1

GROUP B

Italy 2	Chile 2
Austria 1	Cameroon 1
Chile 1	Austria 1
Italy 3	Cameroon 0
Chile 1	Cameroon 1
Italy 2	Austria 1

	P	W	D	L	F	A	Pts
Italy	3	2	1	0	7	2	7
Chile	3	0	3	0	4	4	3
Austria	3	0	2	1	3	4	2
Cameroon	3	0	2	1	2	5	2

GROUP C

S. Arabia 0	Denmark 1
France 3	S. Africa 0
France 4	S. Arabia 0
S. Africa 1	Denmark 1
France 2	Denmark 1
S. Africa 2	S. Arabia 2

	P	W	D	L	F	A	Pts
France	3	3	0	0	9	1	9
Denmark	3	1	1	1	3	3	4
S. Africa	3	0	2	1	3	6	2
S. Arabia	3	0	1	2	2	7	1

GROUP D

Paraguay 0	Bulgaria 0
Spain 2	Nigeria 3
Nigeria 1	Bulgaria 0
Spain 0	Paraguay 0
Nigeria 1	Paraguay 3
Spain 6	Bulgaria 1

	P	W	D	L	F	A	Pts
Nigeria	3	2	0	1	5	5	6
Paraguay	3	1	2	0	3	1	5
Spain	3	1	1	1	8	4	4
Bulgaria	3	0	1	2	1	7	1

GROUP E

S. Korea 1	Mexico 3
Holland 0	Belgium 0
Belgium 2	Mexico 2
Holland 5	S. Korea 0
Belgium 1	S. Korea 1
Holland 2	Mexico 2

	P	W	D	L	F	A	Pts
Holland	3	1	2	0	7	2	5
Mexico	3	1	2	0	7	5	5
Belgium	3	0	3	0	3	3	3
S. Korea	3	0	1	2	2	9	1

GROUP F

Germany 2	USA 0
Yugoslavia 1	Iran 0
Germany 2	Yugoslavia 2
USA 1	Iran 2
Germany 2	Iran 0
USA 0	Yugoslavia 1

	P	W	D	L	F	A	Pts
Germany	3	2	1	0	6	2	7
Yugoslavia	3	2	1	0	4	2	7
Iran	3	1	0	2	2	4	3
USA	3	0	0	3	1	5	0

GROUP G

England 2	Tunisia 0
Romania 1	Colombia 0
Colombia 1	Tunisia 0
Romania 2	England 1
Romania 1	Tunisia 1
Colombia 0	England 2

	P	W	D	L	F	A	Pts
Romania	3	2	1	0	4	2	7
England	3	2	0	1	5	2	6
Colombia	3	1	0	2	5	3	3
Tunisia	3	0	1	2	5	4	1

GROUP H

Argentina 1	Japan 0
Jamaica 1	Croatia 3
Japan 0	Croatia 1
Argentina 5	Jamaica 0
Argentina 1	Croatia 0
Japan 1	Jamaica 2

	P	W	D	L	F	A	Pts
Argentina	3	3	0	0	7	0	9
Croatia	3	2	0	1	4	2	6
Jamaica	3	1	0	2	3	9	3
Japan	3	0	0	3	1	5	0

SECOND ROUND

Italy 1	Norway 0
Brazil 4	Chile 1
France 1	Paraguay 0

(golden goal; after extra time)

Nigeria 1	Denmark 4
Germany 2	Mexico 1
Holland 2	Yugoslavia 1
Romania 0	Croatia 1
Argentina 2	England 2

(Argentina 4–3 on pens after extra time)

QUARTER-FINALS

Italy 0	France 0

(France 4–3 on pens after extra time)

Brazil 3	Denmark 2
Holland 2	Argentina 1
Germany 0	Croatia 3

SEMI-FINALS

Brazil 1 (Ronaldo 46)
Holland 1 (Kluivert 87)
(Brazil 4–2 on pens after extra time)

France 2 (Thuram 47 70)
Croatia 1 (Suker 46)

THIRD-PLACE PLAY-OFF

Holland 1 (Zenden 21)
Croatia 2 (Prosinecki 13, Suker 36)

FINAL

July 12 – Stade St Denis, Paris
Brazil 0
France 3 (Zidane 27 45, Petit 90)
HT: 0–2. 90 Att: 75,000. Ref: S Belqola (Mor)
BRAZIL: Taffarel, Cafu, Aldair, Junior Baiano, Roberto Carlos, Dunga, Cesar Sampaio (Edmundo 75), Leonardo (Denilson 46), Rivaldo, Bebeto, Ronaldo.
FRANCE: Barthez, Lizarazu, *Desailly, Leboeuf, Thuram, Petit, Deschamps, Karembeu (Boghossian 58), Zidane, Guivarc'h (Dugarry 66), Djorkaeff (Vieira 76).

*Desailly sent off, 68 min.

TOP SCORER

Suker (Cro) 6 goals.

HISTORY OF THE EUROPEAN CHAMPIONSHIP

FIFA, football's world governing body, was founded in Europe by Europeans. It is hard to escape the conclusion that in the early days of the twentieth century, Europe and the world were considered synonymous. The first discussions about a world championship envisaged what would have been, in effect, a European championship. But more than 50 years had to pass before that specific concept was brought to fruition.

Barely had Jules Rimet begun pressing his plans for a World Cup through FIFA in the mid-1920s, than his French federation colleague, Henri Delaunay, brought forward proposals for a European championship. February 5, 1927, was the specific date on which Delaunay first spoke up for such a competition. Not that he was opposed to a World Cup. But he foresaw huge logistical problems in going down that path and a European championship was, in his view, a more practical alternative – or even first step.

In fact, Delaunay was overruled. The idea of a world championship had caught light among FIFA's various national associations. Also, with Uruguay now the reigning Olympic champions, why restrict competition to Europe? Thus the idea was filed away in the pending tray while FIFA concentrated on launching and developing the World Cup. In truth, the European Championship had to wait until there was an administrative body in place which could run the event – and that had to wait until the creation of UEFA, the European football federation, in 1954.

Delaunay was an enthusiastic supporter of UEFA's foundation because he recognized its potential. Not only was the idea of a championship for European national teams in the air, many delegates were looking for closer cooperation and competition among clubs.

Sadly, Delaunay died the following year, 1955. But his son Pierre, who was also his successor as general secretary of the French federation, took up the baton. A meeting of UEFA's executive committee in the German city of Cologne, in the spring of 1957, took the historic decision to bring this 30-year-old concept to life.

By this time, any doubters within UEFA had seen two European club competitions kick off with unimagined success. The Champions Cup had been in existence less than two years, but it had gripped the imagination of European fans. Capacity crowds of between 70,000 and 100,000 were turning out in Lisbon, Madrid, Belgrade and Milan.

UEFA's Danish president, Ebbe Schwartz, proposed immediate steps to catch the mood with a championship for national teams. The Spanish, Hungarian and Greek federations were enthusiastic supporters. They envisaged a knock-out competition being launched in the autumn of 1958.

But they did not have the argument all their own way. The British countries viewed the idea with scepticism, fearing it would cut across their historic Home Championship. The West German federation, unhappy at the way in which Italian clubs were poaching their best players, were also opposed. That appears all the more surprising, looking back, because West Germany were then World Cup holders. But Cold War politics and travel restrictions were weighty considerations in the matter.

The UEFA executive decided to put the matter before congress on June 28, 1957, in Copenhagen. By this time, UEFA had 29 national association members. Some 26 were represented in Copenhagen; only Albania, Iceland and Wales were absent. A European Championship sub-committee, comprising Pierre Delaunay, Hungary's Guzstav Sebes and Spain's Agustin Pujol, issued a proposal document. They suggested a competition based on a direct knock-out basis. To meet fears of fixture congestion (!) they also suggested that each tie comprise just one match, not the two-leg, home-and-away variety in use in the Champions Cup.

Eventually, a vote was taken on whether to proceed. Some 14 federations voted in favour – Czechoslovakia, Denmark, East Germany, France, Greece, Hungary, Luxembourg, Poland, Portugal, Romania, Soviet Union, Spain, Turkey and Yugoslavia. Seven voted against – Belgium, Finland, Holland, Italy, Norway, Switzerland and West Germany. Five abstained – England, Northern Ireland, Scotland, the Republic of Ireland and Sweden.

Approval having been granted, UEFA moved on to consider a timetable for the competition's introduction. It decided the event should take place every four years, so as not to cut across the World Cup, and that the inaugural tournament should be played between autumn 1958 and the summer of 1960.

On August 6, 1958, UEFA formally launched the first European Championship with a draw for the first rounds and the decision to honour the vision of Henri Delaunay by naming the trophy in his memory.

On a financial note, UEFA decided to levy an entry fee of around £50. A levy of one per cent of gate receipts would go to FIFA and two per cent to UEFA. It was further decided to adopt the two-leg, home-and-away knock-out system which was continuing to prove such a success in the club competitions – not only the Champions Cup but also its cousin, the Inter-Cities Fairs Cup.

A decision was then taken on the final matches. A week would be set aside for the two semi-finals, third-place play-off and Final to be staged in one host country. The French federation having presented the new trophy – inspired by an idea from Ancient Greece – it was considered only fitting they should also host the first finals tournament.

Some 17 federations entered the first European Championship. That meant one preliminary tie was necessary. Czechoslovakia and the Irish Republic were drawn to contest it. In the meantime the Soviet Union literally set the ball rolling in Moscow on September 28, 1958, against Hungary.

The European Championship, destined to become the second most important tournament after the World Cup, was finally under way. Henri Delaunay had not lived to see the day, but his dream had come true.

Czech players are jubilant after their 6–5 penalty shoot-out win over France at Euro 96

France 1960

Europe's inaugural championship for national teams, in 1958–60, drew a cautious response from the various member associations of UEFA. Only 17 entered and Italy, West Germany – both future champions – and England were among the absentees. The first goal was scored by Anatoly Ilyin, an outside-left with Spartak Moscow, after four minutes. The Soviets and Hungarians had been drawn against each other in the first round proper. But the presence in the draw of 17 teams had meant a qualifying round was necessary to reduce the field to a practical number for the simple direct elimination system.

The qualifying tie was played after that initial first round meeting between the Soviet Union and Hungary. The Republic of Ireland met Czechoslovakia, winning 2–0 at home, but losing 4–0 away to go out 4–2 on aggregate. The Czechoslovaks went forward to beat Denmark 2–2, 5–1. No problems, either, for a French side still glowing from their third-place finish at the 1958 World Cup finals. France had been drawn against Greece and soon had the tie sewn up after winning 7–1 at home. World Cup marksman Just Fontaine scored twice, as did Reims team-mate Jean Vincent. The French could thus afford to send virtually a B side to Athens for the second leg which ended in a 1–1 draw.

Romania defeated Turkey 3–0, 0–2 while Austria steamrollered Norway by 1–0, 5–2 with future national coach Erich Hof scoring the away winner and two more goals back at home in Vienna. Yugoslavia beat Bulgaria 2–0, 1–1 and Portugal defeated East Germany – competing for the first time at senior international level – by 2–0, 3–2. Early tournament favourites Spain crushed Poland 7–2 on aggregate. Two goals apiece from Luis Suarez and Alfredo Di Stefano brought Spain a 4–2 win in Chorzow. Di Stefano scored again in the 3–0 return success.

The quarter-finals matched France against Austria, Portugal against Yugoslavia, Romania against Czechoslovakia and the Soviet Union against Spain.

The Austrians had no answer to Fontaine in the first leg as he scored a hat-trick which included a sensational goal when Fontaine met a cross from Francois Heutte full on the volley from 20 yards out. France won 5–2. Heutte scored himself when France won the return 4–2 in Vienna for a 9–4 aggregate. Thunderbolt specialist Bora Kostic was the hero of Yugoslavia's win over Portugal. Kostic scored the Slavs' late consolation in a 2–1 first leg defeat in Lisbon. He then scored twice to lead the Slavs to a 6–3 aggregate success. Czechoslovakia joined them in the finals after a comfortable 2–0, 3–0 win over Romania.

The remaining quarter-final was never played. Some 20 years after the Spanish civil war, the Spanish dictator, Francisco Franco, had no love for anything Soviet, not even a football team. The Soviets were thus barred from entering Spain to play football ... and the tie was awarded to them by default.

The finals were awarded to France – appropriately in Delaunay's honour – to host. They comprised two knock-out semi-finals, one third-place play-off plus the Final itself.

France should have been in that Final themselves. They led Yugoslavia 4–2 in their semi-final opener with 15 minutes to play. The Slavs, however, were spurred by a sense of injustice over the second of Heutte's two goals which should have been disallowed for offside. They thus battled back with astonishing results – putting three goals past Georges Lamia in the France goal within three minutes.

French fans excused the result on the grounds that playmaker Raymond Kopa and star striker Fontaine were out injured. Lamia, his confidence shattered by the Slavs' great revival, never played for France again.

The Soviet Union, including legendary goalkeeper Lev Yashin, thrashed Czechoslovakia 3–0 in Marseille in the other semi-final. Valentin Ivanov scored twice.

The Final was played in the old Parc des Princes – just like the first Champion Clubs Cup Final four years earlier. Also just like the club showdown, the referee was England's Arthur Ellis. The first goal was almost an own goal, Soviet skipper Igor Netto deflecting a strike from Milan Galic, though the latter was credited with the goal which came just two minutes before the interval. Soviet right-wing Slava Metreveli equalized four minutes after half-time to send the Final into extra time. Yugoslavia had been the better team. Only the brilliance of Lev Yashin in the Soviet goal had denied them victory. But in extra time they lost heart and defensive discipline. Soviet centre-forward Viktor Ponedelnik snatched his one chance of the game ... and the Soviet Union were first European champions.

Spain 1964

The Soviet Union, as holders, were favourites to retain the trophy in its second edition in 1964. The finals this time were played in Spain and proved something of a political triumph for football since, in the 1960 quarter-finals, Spain had withdrawn rather than play the Soviet Union. Now, four years on, Spain not only provided a host's welcome for the Soviet Union but met them in the Final – and beat them.

The qualifying competition was still organized on a direct elimination basis but this time with 29 countries on board. West Germany remained aloof but England competed for the first time ... and were instantly eliminated. Alf Ramsey's first competitive experience at national team level ended in a 2–5, 1–1 defeat by a French team inspired by Raymond Kopa. The political hitch this time surrounded the tie between neighbours Albania and Greece, who refused to play. The tie was awarded to the Albanians. The Soviet Union as holders, Austria and Luxembourg all benefited from the luck of the draw with a first-round bye.

Spain, under former Real and Atletico Madrid coach Jose Villalonga, were rebuilding. Villalonga had turned away from the mixed-nationality stars of Real and Barcelona and put his faith in the youngsters emerging from Spain's unfashionable provincial clubs. In the first round they opened with a 6–1 win over Romania, Valencia's Vicente Guillot scoring a hat-trick. Something similar was happening with Italy. New manager Edmundo Fabbri – nicknamed Topolino after the Little Mouse character in a popular cartoon – had thrown out the well-worn stars who had proved such an embarrassment only months earlier in the World Cup finals in Chile. He built a new side around the bright, emerging talents of Milan's Gianni Rivera and Inter's Sandro Mazzola. Fabbri used only one "non-Italian" in Angelo Benedetto Sormani, the Mantova centre-forward whose original claim to fame had been his status as "Pele's official deputy" at Santos. "New Italy" opened with a 6–0 win over Turkey in Bologna with two goals for Rivera and four from the Roma right-winger Alberto Orlando. Italy won the return 1–0 in Istanbul; Sormani scoring. Surprise failures were Czechoslovakia, who had finished World Cup runners-up in Chile. They fell to an athletic East Germany side coached by the Hungarian Karoly Soos. The GDR won 2–1 at home and forced a 1–1 draw in Prague.

In the second round Spain nearly came unstuck against Northern Ireland. Held 1–1 in Bilbao, Spain won 1–0 in Belfast with a second-half goal from the Real Madrid flyer, Francisco Gento. But Yugoslavia, the 1960 runners-up, went down 0–0, 2–3 to Sweden, and Holland suffered the indignity of defeat by Luxembourg. The Dutch – their football still light years removed from the "total football" revolution – drew 1–1 in the Grand Duchy but then lost 2–1 in Rotterdam. France avenged their 1962 World Cup qualifying defeat by Bulgaria while the new-look Italy fell to the Soviet holders. Goals from Ponedelnik and Igor Chislenko handed the Soviet Union a 2–0 win in Moscow but Italy were confident of reversing the damage in Rome. They might have done, as well, but then the young Mazzola had a penalty saved by Yashin and, in the end, it was all Italy could do to scramble to a 1–1 draw.

In the quarter-finals Spain found Irish opposition awaiting them once more. But the Republic put up much less testing opposition than the North. Spain won 5–1 at home in Seville with two goals apiece from Real Madrid's new right-winger starlet Amancio and the big Zaragoza centre-forward Marcelino. They also won in Dublin, 2–0. This time there were two goals for Barcelona's Pedro Zaballa. France, having disposed of England and Bulgaria in style, were outwitted by a Hungarian side who had found their first, post-Revolution hero in Ferencvaros centre-forward Florian Albert. He opened the scoring as Hungary won 3–1 in Paris and then 2–1 back in Budapest. France ended that 1963–64 season in disarray. They had won only three of 21 matches in three seasons, had lost Fontaine to injury and Kopa to suspension over a controversial interview in which he had attacked the retain-and-transfer system.

The Soviet Union beat Sweden 1–1, 3–1 while Denmark needed a play-off to shake off Luxembourg. Centre-forward Ole Madsen was Denmark's man of the moment. He had scored four goals, including a first leg hat-trick, against Malta in the first round, then another goal against Albania in the second. Against Luxembourg it was a one-man show. Madsen scored a hat-trick in the 3–3 draw in Luxembourg, both goals in the 2–2 tie in Copenhagen and then the decisive only goal of the play-off in Amsterdam.

UEFA had designated Spain as the venue for the finals even before the Spanish national team had qualified. They had to guarantee no political problems whoever qualified and so the Soviet Union – after the diplomatic bust-up of four years earlier – duly took their place in the finals. So did Hungary and Denmark. Whether by design or sheer luck of the draw, the Soviet Union played their semi-final in the more politically sympathetic Barcelona than in Madrid. They beat Denmark easily, by 3–0. The other semi-final saw hosts Spain defeat Hungary 2–1 after extra time. Amancio scored the winner, five minutes from the end. The Hungarians' consolation was to defeat Denmark 3–1 – also after extra time – in the third-place play-off. As for the Danes, they could at least boast in Madsen the tournament's 11-goal top scorer.

Amancio provided the eye-catching panache in Spain's attack but their key player was midfield general Luis Suarez. He came home for the finals after a superb season in which he had inspired Internazionale to win the European Champions Cup for the first time – beating Amancio's Real Madrid in the final. Suarez, who had made his name originally with Barcelona, was probably Europe's finest player at the time and he brought to the Spanish game a command and perception notably lacking in a raw, unimaginative Soviet side. Spain took an early lead in the Final in the Estadio Bernabeu through Jesus Pereda. Khusainov struck back for the Soviet Union but a second-half strike from Marcelino was the signal for Spanish celebrations. General Franco, watching from the VIP box, was reported to have greatly appreciated another victory over the forces of Communism.

Italy 1968

In 1968, for the second successive tournament, the hosts – Italy, this time – ended up as champions. But the *Azzurri* needed a replay before defeating Yugoslavia – who thus finished runners-up, just as they had done eight years earlier in France.

The dramatic success of the 1964 event was reflected in an increased entry for 1968 and UEFA's decision to organize the first round not on a knock-out basis but in mini-leagues. Some 31 of UEFA's 33 member nations entered, the only absentees being Iceland and Malta. West Germany, runners-up in the 1966 World Cup, decided they could no longer afford to miss the party and were one of the eight first-round seeds along with Spain, Portugal, the Soviet Union, Italy, Hungary, France and England.

For convenience it was decided to use the British Home Championship as the qualifying section for England, Scotland, Wales and Northern Ireland. England, the World Cup holders, finished one point clear of Scotland, who at least had the immense satisfaction of becoming the first nation to beat the new world champions when they won 3–2 at Wembley in April 1967 with goals from Denis Law, Bobby Lennox and Jim McCalliog. The Scots let themselves down, however, in being held to a 1–1 draw in Wales, then losing 1–0 in Northern Ireland. A 1–1 draw between Scots and English at Hampden Park in February 1968 then saw England safely through to the quarter-finals as group winners.

Spain, as holders, came safely through Group 1 but Portugal were pipped in Group 2 by Bulgaria. The penultimate match proved decisive, Bulgaria beating Eusebio and Co 1–0 in Sofia. A 63rd-minute goal from Dinko Dermendiev earned Bulgaria a decisive four-point advantage at the top of the table.

The Soviet Union and Italy each dropped only one point in winning their groups. Hungary also came through without too many problems, starting with a 2–2 draw away to a Dutch side whose second goal was scored by a much-vaunted youngster named Johan Cruyff. France surprisingly won a Group 7 which had been expected to fall to a Belgian side inspired by Paul Van Himst and leaning heavily on his Anderlecht side with their emphasis on possession football and the offside trap.

West Germany's debut in the European Championship was mixed. They began happily enough with a 6–0 thrashing of Albania in which new striker Gerd Müller scored four goals but they then lost 1–0 away to Yugoslavia. That should not have proved decisive in a three-team group. The Germans came to their concluding fixture, away to the Albanians, needing a simple win to qualify for the quarter-finals; they would be level on points with the Yugoslavs and possess a better goal difference. Surprisingly, they could only draw 0–0 in Tirana and Yugoslavia went through as group winners.

The one incident which scarred the qualifying section – and provided an unheeded warning of what was to come – occurred in Vienna's Prater stadium on November 5, 1967, when a pitch invasion by furious fans forced the game between Austria and Greece to be abandoned four minutes from time with the score 1–1. The hooligans, infuriated by the refereeing of the Hungarian official Gyula Gere, caused more than £40,000 worth of damage in and around the stadium.

For the quarter-finals, UEFA reverted to the two-leg direct elimination (knock-out) system. The top tie was the meeting of world champions England and European champions Spain. An 84th-minute goal from Bobby Charlton handed England a narrow victory at Wembley. Back in Madrid, Spain pulled level on aggregate with a 54th-minute strike from Amancio but England snapped back seven minutes later through Martin Peters. The Leeds wing-half Norman Hunter, renowned more for his defensive qualities, was surprise scorer of England's winner with

nine minutes remaining. Yugoslavia thrashed France 1–1, 5–1 while Italy and the Soviet Union both hit back decisively after first-leg defeats away to Bulgaria and Hungary respectively.

Italy had rebuilt yet again, after the humiliating defeat by North Korea at the 1966 World Cup finals. Fabbri, utterly discredited, had been sacked in favour of veteran coach Ferruccio Valcareggi who was spoiled for choice he had so many superb players from which to pick in Serie A – beginning in goal where Dino Zoff narrowly won the vote over Enrico Albertosi. In front of him was a watertight defence starring Inter's attacking left-back Giacinto Facchetti, a midfield balanced between the skill of Rivera and the strength of Giorgio Ferrini and a dream strike force comprising Mazzola and goal-hungry Pietro Anastasi and Luigi Riva.

For all that, the Italians had the utmost difficulty converting their apparent superiority into fact despite the added advantage of playing the finals in front of their own fans. Indeed, Valcareggi suggested later that he would have preferred to play the finals in a foreign country because it would have suited his players' catenaccio-inspired "hold-and-hit" mentality.

Instead, it took the good fortune of the toss of a coin for the Italians to earn a place in the Final after their semi against the Soviet Union finished goalless following extra time. In the other semi-final Yugoslavia beat England 1–0 in Florence in a match which was doubly disappointing for the reigning World Cup holders, who were making their finals debut. Not only did they lose but right-half Alan Mullery became the first England player to be sent off while representing his country in a senior international.

Yugoslavia, inspired by the left-wing skills of Dragan Dzajic, were given a better-than-evens chance of beating the pressure-frozen Italians in the Final in Rome's Stadio Olimpico. Dzajic – who had scored the only goal of the semi-finals – provided the Slavs with an early lead but Angelo Domenghini equalized controversially from a free-kick with 10 minutes remaining. Controversy was nothing new to the referee: he was Switzerland's Gottfried Dienst who had officiated two years earlier at the World Cup Final in which England beat West Germany with one of the most debated goals of all time. Two years further on and the European Championship saw extra time fail to provide any more goals so the Final went to a replay, again in Rome. Yugoslavia were now tiring badly. They resisted spiritedly in the opening minute and protested furiously that Gigi Riva's opening goal, after 12 minutes, should have been disallowed for offside. The referee who waved away their protests was, intriguingly, the Spaniard Jose Maria Ortiz de Mendibil who had been at the centre of another Italian controversy three years earlier over two controversial goals he "allowed" Internazionale to score in a Champions Cup semi-final against Liverpool. Once ahead, the hosts took control. Anatasi, about to cost Juventus a then world record £500,000 from Varese, scored their second goal on the half-hour. Italy were European champions for the first and, so far, only time.

Belgium 1972

Italy's attempt to retain the trophy in the 1970–72 series was brought to an abrupt end in the quarter-finals by Belgium, who then won the vote to host the finals of the newly re-baptized competition. What had thus far been formally known as the European Nations Cup now became the more accurate European Championship.

The most outstanding side in the competition was West Germany whose manager, Helmut Schön, had created a new team for this championship. It was a team which proved to be even more spectacular than the one which had recently finished third in the 1970 World Cup. The nucleus of the team was provided by the top German clubs of the era, Bayern Munich and Borussia Mönchengladbach. The creative combination of Bayern's revolutionary attacking sweeper, Franz Beckenbauer, and Borussia playmaker Gunter Netzer, lit up the European game. The assistance of adventurous young left-back Paul Breitner and supreme marksman Gerd Müller left no doubt that the right team had earned the crown of European champions.

The first round was again played on a mini-league basis, this time featuring eight groups of four national teams each. Then it was back to the two-leg, direct elimination quarter-finals. Again the entry was a record, with 32 nations competing and only Iceland, of the UEFA membership, remaining out – literally – in the cold. Hungary, England, the Soviet Union, Belgium and Yugoslavia each finished two points clear in their group, Italy finished three points ahead of Austria in Group 6 and the West Germans ran away with Group 8 – albeit after being held 1–1 at home by Turkey in Cologne in their first match. They dropped only one other point, being held 0–0 at home in Hamburg by Poland when it no longer mattered. The Germans finished four points clear of a Polish side they would see plenty more of in the next few years in both Olympic Games and World Cup.

The quarter-final draw matched Hungary against Romania, holders Italy against Belgium, the Soviet Union against Yugoslavia in a repeat of the inaugural Final, and West Germany against England. Here the Germans made history with their first victory at Wembley, where they overran their English hosts 3–1. It was marvellous, if belated, revenge for the 1966 World Cup Final. Nor could England complain. Beckenbauer and Netzer provided the creative magic, Breitner, Uli Hoeness and Herbert Wimmer the attacking energy, and Gerd Müller the deadly finishing. Indeed, years later many experts considered the 1972 German side to have been superior to the one which, in 1974, defeated Holland to win the World Cup itself.

The remaining quarter-finals saw the Soviets maintain their dominance over Yugoslavia, Belgium prise loose Italy's grip on the Henri Delaunay trophy and Hungary squeeze past Romania after a play-off in Belgrade. The away goals rule had yet to come into general use at this level so the play-off was ordered after the teams drew 1–1 in Budapest and 2–2 in Bucharest. They were, indeed, so closely matched that it appeared as if the play-off was heading for extra time with the teams locked at 1–1 after tit-for-tat first half goals for Hungary's Kocsis and Romania's Neagu. Then, in the final minute of normal time and with the Romanians waiting for the referee's whistle, Ferencvaros right-winger Szoke snatched the winner.

Belgium hosted the finals which saw the semis split evenly between eastern and western Europe. Anderlecht's Parc Astrid saw the Soviet Union defeat Hungary 1–0 with East German Rudi Glockner as referee. Antwerp witnessed West Germany defeat hosts Belgium 2–1 with Scotland's McMullan in charge. The difference in the interest aroused by the ties remains evident from the attendance figures. Almost 60,000 fans jammed into Antwerp's Bosuil stadium; a meagre 3,000 were scattered around the Parc Astrid. Belgium's consolation was to finish third after they beat Hungary three days later by 2–1 in the losers' play-off in Liege. Raoul Lambert from Brugge and Anderlecht's Van Himst scored the winners' goals.

Beckenbauer and his team were clear favourites to win the final in the Heysel Stadium in Brussels. The Soviet Union had rebuilt around a nucleus from the Ukraine club, Kiev Dynamo. Players such as sweeper Murtaz Khurtsilava, playmakers Viktor Kolotov and Antoly Konkov, and forward Vladimir Onishenko had brought new technical skill and tactical intelligence to a team thought previously to have been highly disciplined but pedestrian. Even the new, improved Soviet Union, however, proved no match for this German side. Netzer dominated midfield and hit a post before two typically opportunist strikes from Müller and another from Herbert Wimmer decided the match. The 3–0 scoreline remains the largest winning margin of any European Championship Final. It also barely reflected the manner in which West Germany dominated from start to finish. Müller finished as the tournament's 11-goal top scorer. He scored more than twice as many goals as the joint runners-up. East Germany's Hans Kreische, England's Martin Chivers and Holland's Cruyff and Piet Keizer each scored five goals. Müller was already by now established as the leading marksman in the overall history of the European Championship with 16 goals, followed by Madsen and Hungary's Ferenc Bene on 11.

Yugoslavia 1976

But if the 1972 finals had produced an outstanding team in West Germany, the 1976 event went three better by producing no fewer than four superbly competitive sides. Hosts Yugoslavia finished fourth after losing the third-place play-off to Holland – but there could be no embarrassment in that. These stand as probably the most thrilling finals of the "first" generation of the tournament – with the Final between Czechoslovakia and holders West Germany a dramatic classic. Once again the formula provided for a first round of eight mini-league groups of four nations apiece. Iceland came in from the cold this time but Albania did not enter – much to the relief of the rest of the Europe who found dealing with the isolationist Communist regime a political, bureaucratic and logistical nightmare.

The Czechoslovaks got off to a most unprepossessing start when they were trounced 3–0 by England at Wembley. Three goals in the last 18 minutes from Mick Channon and Colin Bell (two) condemned them to a defeat which gave no hint of the remarkable revival in store. England, their confidence sky-high, were held goalless at home by Portugal but then thrashed Cyprus 5–0 with Malcolm MacDonald scoring all five goals. The decisive match was the return between Czechoslovakia and England in Bratislava in October 1975. The afternoon of October 29 was chilled and foggy and Italian referee Michelotti had no option but to abandon the game after 17 minutes. The following day Czechoslovakia hit back from 1–0 down to win the return 2–1. They went on to finish a point clear of England at the top and head into the quarter-finals.

Wales were surprising winners of Group 2, Yugoslavia, Spain, the Soviet Union, Belgium and West Germany all coming through as predicted. The only other upset was in Group 5 in which minnows Finland had been drawn with three of Europe's most powerful nations in Italy, Holland (1974 World Cup runners-up) and Poland (1974 World Cup third place). The first keynote clash saw Holland beat Italy 3–1 in Rotterdam thanks to two goals from Cruyff. Italy then slipped further back after being held goalless in Rome by Poland, who subsequently seized command of the group by beating Holland 4–1 in Chorzow.

Cruyff and Co took their revenge with a 3–0 win in the return. Yet the Poles could still have made it had they beaten Italy in Warsaw. Instead they were held 0–0 and Holland, despite losing their last game 1–0 in Italy, went through as group winners on goal difference.

In the direct elimination quarter-finals Czechoslovakia, under the expert guidance of Vaclav Jezek, defeated the favoured Soviet Union 2–0, 2–2 in the most "political" of the ties. Holland, World Cup runners-up two years earlier and inspired by Johan Cruyff and Johan Neeskens, defeated neighbours Belgium. West Germany, reigning world as well as European champions, overran Spain and Yugoslavia won a bad-tempered tie with Wales to earn both a semi-final place and host rights.

The pattern of excitement was set when Czechoslovakia defeated Holland 3–1 after extra time in the first semi-final – the Dutch succumbing after referee Clive Thomas sent off Neeskens and Wim Van Hanegem. Then it was West Germany's turn to need extra time as they hit back from 2–0 down to beat hosts Yugoslavia 4–2.

The Germans had found a new Müller – Dieter Müller from Köln. He scored a hat-trick against Yugoslavia and led the German fightback in the Final after they had gone 2–0 down in 25 minutes to Czechoslovakia. One minute remained in normal time when Bernd Hölzenbein's equalizer sent the game into extra time. No more goals came and extra time ended amid chaos. The federations had agreed the previous day that, in the event of a draw, the match – and the championship – would be decided by a new-fangled penalty shoot-out. The Germans had taken the initiative under some pressure from club officials to bring the long drawn-out season to a close and allow their star players some sort of brief summer holiday. The Czechoslovak players, however, had no knowledge of this. As defender Koloman Gogh explained later: "When extra time ended we were all heading for the dressing-rooms when we were waved back. We didn't know what was going on." That makes it all the more remarkable that the Czechoslovaks regained their composure to become the first nation to win a major event on such a shoot-out.

In fact, the Czechoslovaks were better prepared. Masny, Nehoda, Ondrus, Jurkemik and midfield general Antonin Panenka were all experienced penalty-takers. Coach Vaclav Jezek had even taken the trouble, before the finals, to assemble a crowd at training especially ordered to whistle and jeer as his players practised penalties! The Germans, for the first and only time, were at sixes and sevens over the shoot-out. Dietz and Schwarzenbeck refused to take one and goalkeeper Sepp Maier had to insist on Franz Beckenbauer volunteering to take the possibly decisive No. 5. Marian Masny opened up for Czechoslovakia, Rainer Bonhof equalized; Zdenek Nehoda scored, Heinz Flohe levelled; Jan Ondrus converted, Hannes Bongartz squared it; Ladislav Jurkemik made no mistake, Uli Hoeness shot… over the bar. Panenka strolled up for the next kick, dummied one way, sending Maier in the wrong direction, and pushed the ball so gently the other way.

Czechoslovakia were champions of Europe not with a galaxy of stars but thanks to disciplined teamwork honed and perfected to such a degree by Jezek and assistant Jozef Venglos that they had gone 21 matches without defeat ... since that beating by England with which they started the campaign.

Italy 1980

It proved the end of an era. By 1978 such was the popularity of the tournament and the pressure for places in the finals, that UEFA decided to increase the scope of the finals to take in eight countries – split into two groups of four with the group-winners meeting in the Final. The expansion of the finals meant that the hosts – in this case Italy – had to be designated well in advance and their "reward" was to be seeded direct to the finals, as in the World Cup. That meant a qualifying tournament featuring 32 teams (Albania remaining absent) so the group balance was changed to feature three groups of five teams and four groups of four. England dropped only point in their eight games to run away with Group 1; West Germany dropped two points in their six games and strolled through Group 7. In all the other groups, there was only one point in it Belgium pipped Austria in Group 2, Spain beat Yugoslavia in Group 3, Holland outlasted Poland in Group 4, Czechoslovakia edged France in Group 5 and Greece surprisingly headed Hungary in Group 6.

Italy became the first nation to host the finals twice and were matched in their group with England, Belgium and Spain. The other finals group featured old rivals West Germany and Holland, title-holders Czechoslovakia and newcomers Greece.

The format was a little disappointing because the 12 group games produced only 22 goals. That, however, certainly did not reduce the passion among the crowds – particularly in Turin – where riot police unleashed tear gas to quell unrest among supporters during England's opening draw against Belgium in the old Stadio Communale.

Belgium beat Spain 2–1 in their next game but England's dreams of a place in the Final in Rome disintegrated as they lost 1–0 to their hosts, Juventus midfielder Marco Tardelli scoring the winner 10 minutes from the end. Belgium's goalless draw with Italy was enough to send them into their first major Final.

West Germany quickly established themselves as favourites by topping the other group thanks to a 1–0 revenge victory over Czechoslovakia, a 3–2 win over Holland – when the international game "discovered" an inspirational young midfielder named Bernd Schuster – and a goalless draw with Greece.

A 48,000 crowd, well below capacity, turned out for the Final. It would have been different if Italy had been playing but they had to settle for playing in the third-place play-off the previous evening in Naples against Czechoslovakia. A lacklustre game reached its nadir in a penalty shoot-out which the Czechoslovaks eventually won 9–8. Once again, as in the 1976 Final, the Czechoslovaks proved merciless from the penalty spot. Italy lost when centre-back Fulvio Collovati's effort was parried by keeper Jaroslav Netolocka. The Italians claimed that Netolicka had dropped the ball over the goal-line and that the shoot-out should have continued. Austrian referee Erich Linemayr disagreed. Even with that contrived finish, however, the match had proved massively anti-climactic and has gone down in football history as the last such match. UEFA scrapped the "losers' final" for all the subsequent championships.

West Germany's revival owed much to a new hero from Bayern Munich in flying forward Karl-Heinz Rummenigge. He scored the winner in the Germans' opening group match against Czechoslovakia and then justified his reputation in the Final against Belgium in Rome by contributing the inch-perfect corner from which giant Horst Hrubesch headed a last-minute winning goal. Earlier the Germans had taken the lead through Hrubesch in the 10th minute only for Belgium to equalize with a Rene Vandereycken penalty in the 72nd. The penalty punished a trip by West German sweeper Uli Stielike on the onrushing Francois

Van der Elst. Television replays appeared to show that the foul had been committed just outside the box but it was what Belgian manager Guy Thys described as "a moral penalty" and was just reward for the way the Belgians had attacked the entire event.

As for the West German winners, Rummenigge's efforts subsequently earned him the European Footballer of the Year award. As for Hrubesch, the two-goal hero of the Final could hardly believe his luck. At 29 he had suddenly emerged as an international hero only because Klaus Fischer, the Germans' regular centre-forward, had broken a leg in a league match earlier that spring.

France 1984

In 1984 France drove a coach and horses through the myth that host nations only succeed because of inordinately unfair advantages. After going close to winning the 1982 World Cup, this magnificent French side was unarguably the cream of the continent in the early 1980s, and they swept all before them to win the ultimate prize in the new Parc des Princes in Paris. For the first time, the entire UEFA membership – then it stood at 33 in the years before the fragmentation of the Soviet Union, Czechoslovakia and the former Yugoslavia – entered. France were seeded direct to the finals as hosts and the other qualifiers were the winners of the mini-leagues, which comprised four groups of five teams and three groups of four.

Belgium, runners-up in 1980 and then World Cup semi-finalists in 1982, maintained a remarkably consistent run of qualification success which would last right through the 1990s, by winning Group 1 with a three-point advantage over runners-up Switzerland. The other groups were all as tight as possible and went right to the wire. A single-point advantage was just enough for Portugal (over the Soviets in Group 2), Yugoslavia (ahead of Wales in Group 3), Denmark (ahead of England in Group 4) and Romania (ahead of Sweden in Group 5). The remaining groups, even more dramatically, were settled on goal difference. West Germany and Northern Ireland finished level on 11 points apiece in Group 6. The Germans had a far superior goals account yet they only narrowly scraped a 2–1 win at home to Albania in their decisive last match to pull level on points with the Irish. Group 7 ended amid a goal-scoring frenzy which helped persuade UEFA of the importance of ensuring that all last-round matches take place simultaneously, to avoid handing out any undue advantage.

Spain and Holland dominated the group. Holland played their last match on December 17, 1983, and duly beat minnows Malta 5–0 in Rotterdam, two goals falling to midfielder Frank Rijkaard. That meant that Spain went into their own last game against Malta, four days later, knowing that victory would pull them level with Holland on 13 points ... but would still not be enough to overtake. To go top, the Spaniards would need to win by a massive 11 goals! A 30,000 crowd turned out in Seville to see if a miracle was on the cards. It did not look like it when Carlos Santillana's 16th-minute goal was cancelled out by a shock equalizer from Degiorgio. Spain's Juan Senor even managed to miss a penalty so the first half ended with the Spaniards "only" 3–1 ahead, all the goals coming from Santillana. Degiorgio's goal had meant that Spain needed to reach 12 to top the group. Remarkably, that is exactly what they achieved. A second-half goal rush brought four goals for Hipolito Rincon, two for Manuel Sarabia, two for defender Antonio Maceda, one for Senor and one more for Santillana. The Dutch were furious but powerless – and also, of course, eliminated.

The changing balance of the international game was reflected in the make-up of the finals. France's brilliance emanated from the midfield trio of hard-working Luis Fernandez and Jean Tigana plus effervescent little Alain Giresse ... all topped off by the all-round attacking genius of Michel Platini. The presence of Denmark's rising force in the finals was another gesture towards a new balance of power within Europe, as was the failure of West Germany to reach the reconstituted knock-out semi-finals.

Denmark had reached the finals by winning their qualifying group in magnificent fashion and courtesy of a 1–0 win over England at Wembley. Former European Footballer of the Year Allan Simonsen converted the crucial penalty. Unfortunately, injury hampered Denmark's prospects in the finals which they opened with a 1–0 defeat by France, during which Simonsen broke his leg. Platini was the match-winner with the first of his nine goals in five games. His haul included hat-tricks against Belgium and Yugoslavia, a last-minute of extra time winner in the semi-final against Portugal, and the first goal of the Final itself against Spain.

The Spaniards misfired in their opening 1–1 draw against Romania and then had to be satisfied with another draw against Portugal. Their third match was against West Germany, who were unusually listless and dispirited. Maceda strode forward to hit a last-minute winner. Spain thus topped the group ahead of Portugal, who beat Romania 1–0 in the group's other match. Loss of the European crown duly cost West German coach Jupp Derwall his job. Within a matter of weeks Franz Beckenbauer had been appointed in his place. As for Spain, the fates continued to conspire in their favour as they beat Denmark in a penalty shoot-out in their semi-final in Lyon.

Finally, against France in the Final, Spain's remarkable luck ran out. Injuries and suspensions played havoc with coach Miguel Munoz's tactical plan before an uncharacteristic slip by goalkeeper-captain Luis Arconada, after 56 minutes, proved the decisive blow. Arconada, latest in a long line of outstanding Basque goalkeepers, allowed Platini's low drive from a free-kick to spin through his grasp and over the goal-line. This time Spain were doomed. France even overcame the sending-off of Yvon Le Roux after 84 minutes to score a second goal, through Bruno Bellone, in the final minute, but their lead had never been seriously threatened.

West Germany 1988

France were not the only nation for whom European Championship success had proved elusive. The same could have been said of Holland, World Cup runners-up in 1974 and 1978. But in 1988, in West Germany, the Dutch finally secured the major prize for which their pre-eminence in the international game had long since earned.

Holland's victory over the Soviet Union in the 1988 Final in Munich's Olympiastadion was serious evidence in favour of the Dutch approach to youth coaching and to all aspects of general football intelligence.

For the first event in three, the format was not changed. A qualifying section of mini-leagues was climaxed by two four-team groups in the finals, two direct elimination semi-finals and then the Final itself. In the qualifying round Italy, the Soviet Union, England and Holland swept all before them in their respective groups. Spain, Denmark and the Republic of Ireland – qualifying for the finals of a major tournament for the first time – all won through after a tight scrap.

The only hitch in the qualifying process occurred in Holland's home match against Cyprus on October 28, 1987. The Dutch won 8–0 but the result was later declared invalid by UEFA because a firework thrown from the crowd struck Cyprus goalkeeper Andreas Charitou. A replay was ordered which Holland also won, this time 4–0. Years later arguments still continued among Dutch soccer statisticians as to whether details from the first match should be credited to players' international records. The man with most at stake in terms of the history books was Dutch striker John Bosman. He scored five of Holland's eight goals in the first match but "only" a hat-trick in the replay.

England arrived in West Germany for the finals with the best record of any of the qualifiers, having won five and drawn one match, scoring 19 goals and conceding just one. But it appeared they had peaked too early and lost all three of their group matches. It started with a 1–0 setback against the Irish Republic newcomers and continuing with a devastating match against Holland, for whom Marco Van Basten scored a hat-trick. The Soviet Union completed their misery, winning 3–1.

Van Basten had been uncertain of his place with the Dutch at the start of the finals. It took the words of his friend and mentor Johan Cruyff to persuade him to stay with the squad. When, however, Van Basten was substituted toward the end of the England game, he shook hands with veteran coach Rinus Michels as he left the pitch. That handshake came to symbolize the new-found unity of spirit which carried the Dutch to ultimate victory.

West Germany topped the other group without appearing convincing – Italy were runners-up – and led Holland in their semi-final in Hamburg, thanks to a Lothar Matthäus penalty after a foul on Jürgen Klinsmann. Holland hit back immediately with Ronald Koeman thumping a penalty of their own and Van Basten snatched a late winner. The Soviet Union continued their fine record in the championships with 2–0 victory over Italy in the other semi-final.

In the Final, Holland met a Soviet side missing the significant defensive presence of Oleg Kuznetsov through suspension. Even Kuznetsov, however, would not have been able to control the attacking flair of Van Basten and skipper Ruud Gullit in the Dutch attack. Gullit scored the first goal and Van Basten the second – volleying home from Arnold Muhren's cross one of the greatest individual goals ever seen in any major international event.

The Soviet Union had a great chance to come back into the match when goalkeeper Hans Van Breukelen carelessly conceded a penalty midway through the second half. But he redeemed himself by saving Igor Belanov's spot-kick, and Holland were rarely troubled thereafter.

Nobody could have foreseen that this would be the Soviet Union's swan-song in these championships.

Sweden 1992

Sweden in 1992 saw Denmark come from nowhere to win the tournament for the first time, beating first Holland in the semi-finals and then Germany in the Final.

Political upheavals across the continent caused major disruption from the start of the qualifying groups. The former East Germany was consigned to history just as the qualifying tournament began and the GDR federation, as one of its last acts, withdrew from the event. This allowed key players, such as midfielder Matthias Sammer and forwards Thomas Doll and Andreas Thom, to play for a unified Germany in the finals.

The Soviet Union, in the throes of secession into independent states, was transformed into the Commonwealth of Independent States by the time the team flew in. Then there was Yugoslavia. They had been one of the more outstanding qualifiers. But the spring of 1992 saw the onset of the country's violent collapse. UEFA barred them from the finals on security grounds and recalled Denmark – the Slavs' qualifying group runners-up – in their stead and at two weeks' notice. Denmark manager Richard Moller Nielsen heard the news while he was in the middle of decorating his kitchen – the domestic task he had set himself for the summer.

Sweden was a suitably peaceable venue for the climax of a championship. The hosts, in the finals for the first time, deservedly topped Group A. Tomas Brolin's wonderful goal brought them a 2–1 victory over a disappointing England on the last matchday. Denmark were runners-up in the group, thanks to a 2–1 victory over an under-achieving French side managed by their old hero Platini (he would quit after their first-round

failure and later take on the co-presidency of the French organizing committee for the 1998 World Cup finals).

In Group B, Holland and Germany possessed too much firepower and experience for newcomers Scotland and the CIS, although Germany did need a last-minute goal from Thomas Hässler to snatch a point from their opening game against the CIS.

The two semi-finals produced great entertainment. Holland – imperious in qualifying – threw theirs away against Denmark, being held 2–2 and losing 5–4 on penalties. Remarkably, the decisive penalty miss was by Marco Van Basten, the hero four years earlier. Brolin scored again for Sweden in the other semi-final, but this time in vain in a 3–2 defeat by Germany.

Berti Vogts's men were clear favourites in the Final. But Denmark – from manager Moller Nielsen through goalkeeper Peter Schmeichel, skipper Lars Olsen, midfielder Kim Vilfort and forward Brian Laudrup – had not read the script. Goals from John Jensen and Vilfort – allied to the rock-solid inspiration of Peter Schmeichel and Olsen – had duly produced one of the greatest shocks in the competition's history.

England 1996

By now the European Championship was well established as the top national team event after the World Cup itself. Pressure to reach the finals was growing more intense all the time. UEFA thus decided to ask potential hosts for 1996 to submit bids based on a tournament not only for the established eight nations, but also for an enlarged 16-team competition.

As far as England were concerned, it was a case of the bigger the better. Their main club stadia had been redeveloped and converted into all-seater venues to comply with the recommendations of the Taylor report following the Hillsborough disaster. Add in the infrastructure, technological know-how and the attraction of "bringing football home" and England were streets ahead of the potential opposition (in fact, background political machinations had led to a tacit agreement whereby England would not bid to host the 1998 World Cup in return for French support for Euro 96).

The Football Association entrusted their foreign affairs expert, Glen Kirton, to organize Euro 96. His vision was that of a peaceful, enjoyable celebration of football which would do much to transform the image of English football which had been tarnished by hooliganism for close on two decades.

From that standpoint, the tournament was a massive success, a major public relations triumph for the game in general and England in particular. The only regret England took from the tournament was that Terry Venables's team did not also win the event for the first time. Instead, England were victims of an old jinx – a semi-final penalty shoot-out loss – and it was their German conquerors who went on to beat the outsiders from the Czech Republic 2–1 in the Final.

Germany thus secured a record third European Championship success and did so by taking advantage of the new and somewhat controversial golden goal rule. Substitute striker Oliver Bierhoff scored the event-stopping winner five minutes into extra time at Wembley. It was the first time a major senior tournament had been settled by this method. Ironically, one of the few managers to have declared himself in favour of the golden goal rule before the tournament had been the Czech Republic's Dusan Uhrin.

England had appeared unlikely to even reach the last four when they struggled to a 1–1 draw against Switzerland in Group A in the Opening Match. Perhaps it was the pressure of the nation's first serious competitive international since the autumn of 1993; perhaps it was the heat; perhaps it was the media fury provoked by the manner in which the players had let their hair down before the finals; perhaps it was the pressure of an occasion prefaced by a uniquely home-grown opening ceremony.

One of the tableaux – among the sky divers and the Red Arrows – was a pageant in which St George slew the dragon. To the disappointment of the Wembley crowd, England could not emulate their patron saint. A promising first half was followed by a weary standoff in the second. To match the pattern of play England scored first, through Alan Shearer, and Switzerland crowned their comeback with a late penalty equalizer from Kubilay Turkyilmaz.

But Opening Matches are always awkward, nerve-edged affairs. More important was that the game and the occasion was out of the way and the tournament proper could take off.

In Group A that meant quarter-final qualification for England and Holland but not without several surprising twists and turns. Scotland opened their campaign with a rousing 0–0 draw against Holland but they were fortunate when Swedish referee Leif Sundell failed to spot a handled, goal-line clearance by John Collins in the opening exchanges. If Sundell had not been unsighted then Scotland would not only have conceded but been reduced to 10 men by Collins's virtually certain expulsion.

The Tartan Army had long been concerned by their favourites' failure up front. It was to be their achilles heel in the so-called Battle of Britain against England at Wembley. Scotland's luckless skipper, Gary McAllister, even missed a penalty when his full-power spot-kick ricocheted over the bar off goalkeeper David Seaman's left elbow.

England, by contrast, crowned a spirited second-half display by scoring twice. First Alan Shearer headed his second goal of the tournament then Paul Gascoigne, prime target of tabloid attack, flicked a pass from Darren Anderton skilfully past Colin Hendry before volleying the Goal of the Tournament So Far.

On the face of it, the last matchday appeared to be a diplomatic straitjacket. A draw between England and Holland and both would qualify for the quarter-finals with Scotland and Switzerland comfortably eliminated.

But that was to reckon without the rapidly increasing confidence filling the England team – and the fatal complacency which Holland brought into the Wembley clash. England's finest display since at least the 1990 World Cup earned a 4–1 victory. Remarkably, the humiliated Dutch still qualified thanks to a late consolation goal from substitute Patrick Kluivert which rendered null and void Scotland's 1–0 win over the Swiss at Villa Park, Birmingham.

Group B opened with a temperamental clash between Bulgaria and Spain at Elland Road, Leeds. Bulgarian defender Petar Hubchev and Spain striker Juan Pizzi were sent off in a game from which Spain snatched a point courtesy of a first-touch goal from newly arrived substitute Alfonso. Bulgaria looked powerful and well-organized and were upset with the linesman whose mistaken flag denied them a superb "goal" by Hristo Stoichkov. Yet they failed to make it to the quarter-finals. Spain qualified after a second 1–1 draw, against France, and a dramatic 2–1 win over Romania. The Balkans' third defeat in three matches was not the way in which midfield general Gheorghe Hagi had hoped to celebrate his 100th international appearance.

France finished top of the group. They opened with a 1–0 win presented to them on a plate by Romania's eccentric goalkeeper Bogdan Stelea. He knocked over his own central defender, Gheorghe Mihali, chasing a cross which bobbled into goal off the head of Milan-bound striker Christophe Dugarry.

The subsequent 1–1 draw against Spain set France up for a decisive grudge match against Bulgaria. Over the years, the Bulgarians had consistently upset the French. Not this time, though, as Stoichkov allowed himself to be distracted by a personal duel with French defender Marcel Desailly and France ran out 1–0 winners.

The confrontation of eastern European pride and western European fantasy was repeated in Group D where international newcomers Croatia cruised through with the electric-heeled Portuguese. The victims were Turkey, as unanimously predicted, and, more notably, defending champions Denmark.

Croatia barely justified the popular belief that they were dark horses. They struggled to beat Turkey 1–0 in their first game thanks to a fine breakaway goal from Goran Vlaovic and, mistakenly shuffling the player pack, crashed 3–0 to Portugal in their group finale. The reason this did not prove fatal was down to a superb and even stunning second-half display against Denmark second time out.

Even the great Peter Schmeichel was outgunned by the inspiration of Croat striker Davor Suker. He scored twice – once from a penalty – created the other Croat goal for Zvonimir Boban and produced one of the finals' most outstanding pieces of individual virtuosity when he very nearly lobbed Schmeichel from the halfway line.

Croatia, however, had to give way at the top of the group to Portugal. The so-called "Brazilians of Europe" entertained fans with a fascinating brand of delicate touch and bewildering positional interchange. Their only weakness, going forward, appeared to be the lack of a killer touch in front of goal. Italian-based midfielder Rui Costa got into hot water with manager Antonio Oliveira over a comment to the media that Portugal needed a finisher such as his Fiorentina team-mate, Argentine Gabriel Batistuta.

It was not only Portugal who needed such a marksman in their team. Italy themselves were the shock first-round failures precisely because they could not score the goals they needed. First time out the Italians might have beaten Russia more easily than 2–1 had Fabrizio Ravanelli converted two easy chances in the closing 10 minutes after he arrived as a substitute.

Second-time out Italy should have at least salvaged a draw from a thrilling match against the Czech Republic. Italy played more than half the game with 10 men after the expulsion of defender Luigi Apolloni and would have gained the draw they merited had striker Pierluigi Casiraghi not missed from point-blank range in the last minute.

Similarly, third time out. That shock defeat by the badly under-rated Czechs left Italy needing to beat group leaders Germany at Old Trafford while depending, simultaneously, on the outcome of the Czechs' Anfield clash with homeward-bound Russia.

Italy, boasting the greatest depth of natural talent in the finals, dominated the entire 90 minutes. But they fell victim to an incident reminiscent of France's gallant semi-final failure against these same Germans in 1982. Again the German goalkeeper was the centre of controversy because, having committed a blatant foul, he was not sent off.

In 1982 it was Toni Schumacher; in 1996 it was Andy Köpke. Belgian referee Guy Goethals's failure to expel him for upending Casiraghi in the eighth minute had seismic consequences because Köpke then saved Gianfranco Zola's penalty.

Italy, for all their possession, for all their corners and free-kicks around the German penalty box, failed to create any clearcut chances. The Germans clung on by their fingertips, even after the expulsion of defender Thomas Strunz. Given no time to think by the Italians, they played from memory – surviving through practised years of tactical discipline and expertly-drilled defensive organization.

Ten minutes from time, when Russia went 3–2 ahead against the Czechs, Italy were in the quarter-finals. Two minutes from time, when Russia were pegged back to 3–3, Italy were out. Paolo Maldini may have been by far the greatest player on view at the finals. It mattered nothing. He – and Italy – were on their way home.

Oddly, the quality of football on view nose-dived once the knock-out stages had been reached. Only one of the quarter-finals provided any serious entertainment and even that – England vs. Spain – had to be settled by one of the six penalty shoot-outs which were ultimately needed.

England started like a train and it took the sharpest of goalkeeper Andoni Zubizarreta's reflexes to deny Alan Shearer in the opening minutes. As the match wore on, however, Spain drew some pretty patterns in midfield and veteran striker Julio Salinas had a goal ruled out for offside by the linesman – wrongly as television replays proved. Spain grew even more upset with French referee Marc Batta when he twice refused penalty claims – once when Paul Gascoigne tripped Alfonso and once when Tony Adams cleared away Jose Luis Caminero's foot as well as the ball.

Ultimately the match became the first in the history of the European Championship to be subject to the golden goal regulation – without success. Neither team managed an extra-time winner and so the outcome went to penalties. Stuart Pearce fired in one kick for England to avenge his 1990 World Cup failure and then David Seaman saved, decisively, from Spain's Miguel Angel Nadal.

Penalties were also needed after France and Holland failed to provide the contest expected of two of Europe's most creative nations. This time Holland's Clarence Seedorf was the luckless shoot-out scapegoat as France scraped into the last four to meet a Czech Republic side who had surprisingly defeated Portugal 1–0 at Villa Park with perhaps the goal of the tournament. Karel Poborsky, his shoulder-length hair twisting in the breeze, ran through the heart of the Portuguese defence then contrived a most delicate chip over Vitor Baia for the only goal.

The remaining quarter-final was the nastiest match of the tournament. Croatia, forgetting all their ambassadorial responsibilities, kicked Germany all over Old Trafford. It mattered not whether the ball was close at hand or on the opposite side of the pitch; the Croats kept on kicking. Yet referee Leif Sundell shut his eyes to the mayhem, most amazingly when Slaven Bilic kicked Christian Ziege on the ground in full view of the Swedish official.

Suker did score one superb goal but Germany survived the loss of injury-battered Jürgen Klinsmann and Fredi Bobic to win 2–1. Attacking sweeper Matthias Sammer was their hero: he provoked the handling offence which earned Germany's opening penalty goal by Klinsmann, then scored the second himself.

Of the two semi-finals, only one mattered to the hosts: England vs. Germany, the latest episode in one of international football's longest-running dramatic presentations.

Whoever won would be favourites for the Final – especially when the Czech Republic won another shoot-out to beat France after a 0–0 draw at Old Trafford. The French were toothless in the absence of injured centre-forward Christophe Dugarry. They leaned far too heavily on the creative talents of Youri Djorkaeff who came closest to a goal with a thundering drive which ricocheted off the Czech crossbar.

That meant another penalty shoot-out in which Nantes' Reynald Pedros emulated the semi-final failures of Didier Six and Maxime Bossis in the 1982 World Cup.

England vs. Germany also went to a penalty shoot-out. But, unlike France v Czech Republic, it also provided a night of exciting intensity which a 76,000 crowd at Wembley and 26 million domestic television viewers will never forget.

England secured a magnificent start, Shearer heading home in the third minute. Germany, with only one fit striker, responded with courage and invention and that lone raider, Stefan Kuntz, equalized in the 15th minute. The game was an emotional roller-coaster and produced, ultimately, one of the most thrilling extra-time spectacles Wembley has ever witnessed. Darren Anderton was an inch from the golden goal when his shot struck a post. Then Germany thought they had it as Kuntz headed past Seaman, only for referee Sandor Puhl to penalize the German for pushing.

And so to penalties.

Both England and Germany converted their five regulation efforts. Then Gareth Southgate ran up for England ... and pushed his kick low into the grateful arms of German keeper Köpke. Andy Möller ran up for Germany – and shot them into the Final.

Domestic euphoria might have been punctured like a balloon. Yet it said everything for the manner in which Euro 96 had gripped the public imagination that 73,611 turned out for the Final. The vast majority – English fans converted into honorary Czechs for the night – were celebrating when Patrick Berger fired home a 59th-minute penalty.

Germany had lost to underdogs in the Final – against Denmark – four years earlier in Sweden and history appeared about to repeat itself. Then German coach Berti Vogts played his hidden ace, bringing on substitute centre-forward 1Bierhoff. Within four minutes Bierhoff had headed the Germans level then, in the fourth minute of extra time, he fired home the golden goal.

The Czechs protested that Kuntz had been standing in an offside position but Italian referee Pierluigi Pairetto waved away their protests. An Italian linesman had proved a winner for Germany in the stadium where a Georgian had proved a loser in the World Cup 30 years earlier.

Unlike that World Cup, the hosts had not lifted the trophy. But they won just about everything else. Outgoing coach Terry Venables's last duty was to accept the UEFA Fairplay trophy and Shearer was crowned the tournament's five-goal top scorer. But, more than any individual, it was English football as a whole which was the winner. No game was blighted by hooliganism in or around the stadium. English football had been rehabilitated in the eyes of the world. What better time, then, than the day after the Final for the FA to announce England's candidacy to host the World Cup itself in 2006?

Holland/Belgium 2000

As for the European Championship, the first finals of the new millennium, in 2000, will be hosted jointly by Holland and Belgium. The expansion of the finals to incorporate 16 national teams had made it inevitable that event-sharing would be necessary and, in this way, UEFA set a precedent which FIFA would grudgingly follow when it awarded the 2002 World Cup to be hosted jointly by Japan and South Korea. The picturesque and historic Belgian city of Ghent was chosen as venue for the draw since the year 2000 will mark the 500th anniversary of the birth of Charles V, the monarch responsible for developing the city as the centre of the political, economic and cultural transformation which laid the foundations for the rise in power and strength of the Low Countries.

The draw itself was made on January 18, 1998 by two modern heroes in Paul Van Himst, whom many Belgians consider to be not only their greatest-ever player, but also the man who coached the national side to the World Cup finals in 1994 and the legendary Dutchman Johan Cruyff, the first player to ever win the European Footballer of the Year three times. UEFA decided to stay with the super-group formula rather than bow to a proposal – favoured by Germany – to return to the old formula by which only one group winner proceded to the finals. With Belgium and Holland both being seeded direct to the finals, this would have meant seven groups of three teams and seven groups of four teams.

That would, of course, have made a dramatic difference to fixture pressure on players, national associations and clubs. On the other hand, it would have severely reduced the potential television, sponsor, marketing and gate revenue. Sporting considerations were given short shrift as UEFA decided to stick with a formula involving five groups of five teams and four groups of six. The nine group winners plus the best runners-up will qualify automatically for the finals. The remaining eight runners-up will play each other in two-leg knock-out ties to determine the four remaining finalists.

The finals will be staged in nine cities across Holland and Belgium. The Dutch host cities are Amsterdam (Arena, 51,200 capacity), Arnhem (Gelredome, 30,000), Eindhoven (Philips Stadion, 30,200) and Rotterdam (De Kuip, 51,086). The Belgian host cities are Antwerp (Bosuil Eurostadion, 30,000), Bruges (Jan Breydelstadion, 30,000), Brussels (King Baudouin, 50,000) and Liege (Sclessin, 30,000).

The Opening Match will take place in the King Baudouin stadium in Brussels – the rebuilt Heysel – with the Final in the new Arena in Amsterdam.

The draw for the 2000 Championship:

Group 1: Italy, Denmark, Switzerland, Wales, Belarus.

Group 2: Norway, Greece, Georgia, Latvia, Slovenia, Albania.

Group 3: Germany, Turkey, Finland, Northern Ireland, Moldova.

Group 4: Russia, France, Ukraine, Iceland, Armenia, Andorra.

Group 5: England, Bulgaria, Sweden, Poland, Luxembourg.

Group 6: Spain, Austria, Israel, Cyprus, San Marino.

Group 7: Romania, Portugal, Slovakia, Hungary, Liechtenstein, Azerbaijan.

Group 8: Yugoslavia, Croatia, Rep Ireland, FYR Macedonia, Malta.

Group 9: Scotland, Czech Republic, Lithuania, Bosnia-Herzegovina, Faroe Islands, Estonia.

Even before the finals of the 1998 World Cup had opened, the Euro 2000 qualifying rounds had been set under way with Estonia beating the Faroe Islands 5–0 in Tallinn. Kristin Viikmae had the honour of scoring the opening goal in the championship while Faroes' goalkeeper Jens Knudson suffered the embarrassment, after 41 minutes, of being the first player sent off.

Goals ... drama ... just what the founders of the European Championship had hoped, way back in the mid-1950s.

EUROPEAN CHAMPIONSHIP FINAL STADIUMS

1960 AND 1984: FRANCE, PARIS
Parc des Princes

Capacity: *49,700*

Opened: *1897 (rebuilt 1932, 1972)*

Clubs: *Paris Saint-Germain, Racing Club*

Hosted: *1998 World Cup (six matches);1960 European Championship Final (Soviet Union 2, Yugoslavia 0); 1984 European Championship Final (France 2, Spain 0); 1956 European Cup Final (Real Madrid 4, Reims 3), 1975 (Bayern Munich 2, Leeds 0), 1981 (Liverpool 1, Real Madrid 0); 1978 European Cup-winners Cup Final (Anderlecht 4, FK Austria 0); 1994 European Cup-winners Cup Final (Zaragoza 2, Arsenal 1); 1998 UEFA Cup Final (Internazionale 3, Lazio 0)*

The original Parc des Princes played a significant role in the early history of the burgeoning European international competitions. It played host to the first Champions Club Cup Final in 1956 and then to the inaugural European Championship (then Nations Cup) Final in 1960, when the Soviet Union defeated Yugoslavia.

The Parc des Princes lies to the south-west of the centre of Paris and, as the name suggests, the area was a pleasure ground for royalty before the Revolution. The first stadium built on the site was a velodrome, which was constructed at the end of the last century and served, until 1967, as the finish for the Tour de France.

When professional football was introduced in 1932 it became home to Racing Club de France, but they enjoyed only limited success and the Stade Colombes remained the favourite ground for internationals and the 1938 World Cup. Nevertheless it held a particular atmosphere which suited club football and hosted a 38,000 sell-out crowd for the first European Cup Final in 1956, when Real Madrid beat Stade de Reims 4–3. The match was a home fixture for Reims since their own small stadium could not satisfy the demand for all the fans who wanted to follow their adventures in the first years of the Champions Cup. So they played all their big home matches in the Parc, including, of course, that first Final.

The old Parc was the venue for the opening European Championship four years later. But all those great matches proved was that France did not have a stadium worthy of its sporting ambition. This was rectified at the start of the 1980s when the creation of the Périphérique, the Paris ring road, contributed towards the urban redevelopment which brought with it the construction of the new two-tiered state-of-the-art stadium which bears the same name as the original.

It was the first in Europe with integral floodlighting and closed-circuit television.

Problems with the pitch dogged its early years, but these ills were cured by the time the Parc was needed to host three group matches and the Final of the 1984 European Championship, won in style by France's finest-ever national team, led by Michel Platini. France beat Spain 2–0 in the Parc to seize the trophy for the first and – so far – only time.

Paris itself has been a great under-achiever in soccer terms among European capitals. Racing Club went out of the professional soccer business in 1964 and a revived club did not last long some 20 years later. Instead, the flag for Paris football at top level has been waved by Paris Saint-Germain, an amalgamation of Paris FC and Saint-Germain. They moved into the new stadium in 1973, drew 20,000-plus crowds, became only the second Paris club to win the domestic championship and dominated the domestic game in the mid-1990s.

The death knell for the Parc as a major venue appeared to be sounded by the award of the 1998 World Cup finals to France. The all-concrete, near-50,000 capacity stadium designed by Roger Taillibert for both soccer and rugby union failed to meet FIFA's demand of a stadium with a minimum capacity of 80,000 for a Final. Thus the French government decided, in October

France vs. Spain at the 1984 European Championship. France won the game, and went on to be crowned champions of Europe

1993, to spend £300 million on a new stadium in the northern suburb of Saint-Denis. This was opened, amid much fanfare, in January 1998 when France beat Spain 1–0 in a friendly international.

The new Stade de France hosted the 1998 World Cup Final and eight other ties while the Parc hosted four group matches, one second-round match and the third-place play-off.

In May 1998 the Parc staged the first modern single-leg UEFA Cup Final in which Internazionale beat Lazio 3–0. That will not be the last big club match there, either. At around the same time, Paris Saint-Germain rejected proposals that they should switch to use the Stade de France as their regular home venue and signed on with the Parc for a further 10 years.

1964: SPAIN, MADRID
Santiago Bernabeu

Capacity: *105,000*

Opened: *1947*

Club: *Real Madrid*

Hosted: *1982 World Cup Final (Italy 3, West Germany 2); 1964 European Championship Final (Spain 2, Soviet Union 1); 1957 European Cup Final (Real Madrid 2, Fiorentina 0), 1969 (Milan 4, Ajax 1), 1980 (Nottingham Forest 1, Hamburg 0)*

It is thanks to the visionary foresight of long-time president Santiago Bernabeu that Real Madrid boast an imposing edifice on Madrid's most prestigious street, the Castellana, housing one of the world's foremost clubs and a trophy room bulging with silverware and displaying more than 5,000 items. Not all the trophies raised to the view of delighted fans have ended up in Real's own possession. The majesty and capacity of the Bernabeu means it has staged the World Cup Final and, in 1964, the second European Championship Final, when hosts Spain defeated the Soviet Cup-holders 2–1.

The ground, which began life as the Nuevo Chamartin stadium in 1944 on five hectares of prime land, was Bernabeu's brainchild. He was a lawyer who had been, in turn, player, captain, club secretary, coach and then, from 1942, president. The old stadium had been ravaged during the Spanish Civil War and Bernabeu decided that a super new stadium was needed if the club were to raise the funds needed to build a super new team. Real, who now include the King and Queen of Spain and president of the International Olympic Committee, Juan Antonio Samaranch, among their members, raised an astonishing 41 million pesetas by public subscription to finance the land purchase and first stage of building.

The stadium was opened, with a 75,000 capacity, for a testimonial match for veteran player Jesus Alonso against Belenenses of Lisbon in December 1947.

In the 1950s the finance raised by Real's dominance of the fledgling European Champions Cup enabled capacity within the distinctive white towers to be extended to 125,000. The name Estadio Santiago Bernabeu was adopted in 1955 and the floodlights were switched on in 1957 for the European Cup Final.

Bernabeu, who died in 1978, had plans for a new stadium north of the city but for once did not get his way and, instead, Spain's hosting of the 1982 World Cup led to more improvements. A total of 345,000 people watched three group matches and an outstanding Final in a stadium offering 30,200 seats and standing room for 60,000. Ten years further on, the third tier was completed and further remodelling increased the seating to 65,000 within a total capacity of 105,000.

Further expensive work was necessary – plunging Madrid deep into debt – in the early 1990s as the club sought to bring the stadium up to UEFA's all-seater standards. In 1997 one of Bernabeu's presidential successors, Lorenzo Sanz, reopened discussion on "moving house". Sanz argued that the Bernabeu stadium occupies valuable prime city centre land but lacks expansion space and – notoriously – no car parking facilities. He believed that selling the Bernabeu site would raise more than enough for Madrid to buy an edge-of-city site and construct a new state-of-the-art stadium.

1968 AND 1980: ITALY, ROME
Olimpico

Capacity: *80,000*
Opened: *1953*
Clubs: *Roma, Lazio*
Hosted: *1960 Olympic Final (Yugoslavia 3, Denmark 1); 1990 World Cup Final (West Germany 1, Argentina 0); 1968 European Championship Final (Italy 1, Yugoslavia 1; replay, Italy 2, Yugoslavia 0), 1980 (West Germany 2, Belgium 1); 1977 European Cup Final (Liverpool 3, Borussia Mönchengladbach 1), 1984 (Liverpool 1, Roma 1: Liverpool 4–2 on pens), 1996 (Juventus 1, Ajax 1: Juventus 4–2 on pens)*

European football has Benito Mussolini to thank, indirectly, for the magnificent bowl of the Stadio Olimpico in Rome. Not only did Mussolini make the trains run on time, but his regime also left the beautiful Foro Italico sports complex at the foot of Monte Mario as a legacy.

His original plan was to stage the 1944 Olympics there, much as Hitler used Berlin for propaganda purposes in 1936. Then the Second World War intervened. The main stadium was originally called Stadio dei Cipressi but was inaugurated in 1953 as the Olimpico by the legendary Hungarian team who beat Italy 3–0 in front of an 80,000 crowd. It then became the focal point of

the 1960 Olympic Games, and a home to both Roma and Lazio. In fact, the Stadio Olimpico is also the only venue which has staged the European Championship Final three times – simply because the first Final, in 1968, ended in a 1–1 draw between Italy and Yugoslavia and had to be replayed – Italy winning 2–0. The Olimpico was the Final venue again in 1980 when West Germany defeated Belgium 2–1.

Perhaps surprisingly all roads did not lead to Rome for the major European club finals until 1977 when Liverpool fans turned the stadium into a sea of red celebrating the first of their four Champions Cup triumphs. They returned for the 1984 Final to beat Roma, playing on their own ground but unable to take advantage. Liverpool eventually won on penalties.

To allow the stadium to stage 1990 World Cup games, individual seating had to be increased to 80,000 and a roof added to give two-thirds cover. Only in Italy could the wrangling and talking have gone on until May 1988. A year later the roof design was ditched, costs had risen to £75 million and the odds shifted

Italian captain Giacinto Facchetti in 1968

against the stadium being ready. Fraud squad investigators later seized all the accounts in one of the interminable investigations which followed the Tangentopoli scandals of the early 1990s.

1972: BELGIUM, BRUSSELS
King Baudouin, formerly Heysel

Capacity: *50,000*

Opened: *1927*

Club: *Anderlecht for major matches*

Hosted: *1972 European Championship Final (West Germany 3, Soviet Union 0); 1958 European Champions Cup Final (Real Madrid 3, Milan 2), 1966 (Real Madrid 2, Partizan Belgrade 1), 1974 (Bayern Munich 1, Atletico Madrid 1) and replay (Bayern Munich 4, Atletico Madrid 0), 1985 (Juventus 1, Liverpool 0); 1964 European Cup-winners Cup Final (Sporting Portugal 3, MTK Budapest 3), 1976 (Anderlecht 4, West Ham United 2), 1980 (Valencia 0, Arsenal 0: Valencia 5–4 on pens), 1996 (Paris Saint-Germain 1, Rapid Vienna 0)*

The King Baudouin stadium, as it is now, will play host to the Opening Match in the finals of the 2000 European Championship. Thus football history turns and turns, since the stadium – then known as the Heysel – was the central venue in 1972. It played host then to the semi-final in which the Soviet Union beat Hungary 1–0 and then the Final in which West Germany swept aside the Soviets under the imperious direction of Franz Beckenbauer and Gunter Netzer.

The original stadium was built in the north-west suburb of Brussels as a feature of the nation's centenary celebrations. The Stade du Centenaire, as it was then called, was opened in August 1930 with the world cycling championships. The first football match was an international in which Belgium beat Holland 4–1 the following month. It was Belgium's first international back on home soil since their historic trek to the first World Cup finals in Uruguay.

The stadium was used for all manner of sports events, including athletics, hockey, boxing and speedway. Floodlighting was added in 1957–58, when Expo'58 was held in Brussels – providing the Atomium as a ghostly backdrop to the stadium. That year Heysel first staged a European final when Real Madrid defeated Milan 3–2 in extra time to win the Champions Cup for the third successive year. Indeed, Heysel had staged more European club finals than any other stadium when it was chosen for the fateful, tragic, 1985 Champions Cup Final.

Heysel as it was, with the Atomioum's sinister backdrop

Czechoslovak players celebrate in 1976

Some 39 fans of Juventus died in a crush after a wall collapsed as they retreated from a marauding mob of Liverpool followers. Security was poor, crowd segregation controls were poor and the stadium was beginning to crumble. But it was easy for critics to be wise after the event. Without the hooligan element, none of those factors would have been brought into play.

The stadium was shut down for football and eventually razed and rebuilt. Only the outer shell of the west stand, with its offices and administrative facilities, survived. In May 1986, some 11 years after the tragedy, European football returned to Heysel when Paris Saint-Germain beat Rapid Vienna 1–0 to win the Cup-winners Cup Final.

1976: YUGOSLAVIA, BELGRADE
Crvena Zvezda

Capacity: *97,000*

Opened: *1927*

Club: *Red Star (Crvena Zvezda)*

Hosted: *1976 European Championship Final (Czechoslovakia 2, West Germany 2: Czechoslovakia 5–3 on pens); 1973 European Champions Cup Final (Ajax Amsterdam 1, Juventus 0)*

Yugoslavia was suddenly a popular venue for European football finals in the mid-1970s. The West had realized, belatedly, that Tito's Yugoslavia was not beholden to the Soviet Union and could serve as a useful bridge. The problem with taking European finals behind the Iron Curtain previously had been more financial than logistical since it was impossible to effect a balanced monetary account for UEFA's purposes.

That was not the case with Yugoslavia and thus the Champions Cup Final was played there in 1973 and then, after that experiment had been completed successfully, the finals of the European Championship three years later. They culminated in one of the most dramatic of European Championship Finals to date, when Czechoslovakia beat West Germany in a penalty shoot-out in the Red Star stadium.

The stadium had been built in 1927 in a comparatively upmarket suburb of Belgrade. It was used in the inter-war years by the Jugoslavija club, which represented Yugoslavia in the Mitropa Cup. After the war it was subsumed into the new Red Star (Crvena Zvezda in Serbo-Croat), who duly took over the stadium.

The ground was substantially rebuilt between 1959 and 1963, its expansion lifting capacity to around 80,000. Floodlights followed in 1971 and, by the time Europe's big events were imported, the stadium had earned the nickname of the "Marakana" – after the giant bowl in Brazil.

1988: WEST GERMANY, MUNICH
Olympiastadion

Capacity: *74,000*
Opened: *1972*
Club: *Bayern Munich*
Hosted: *1972 Olympic Final (Poland 2, Hungary 1); 1974 World Cup Final (West Germany 2, Holland 1); 1988 European Championship Final (Holland 2, Soviet Union 0); 1979 European Cup Final (Nottingham Forest 1, Malmo 0), 1993 (Marseille 1, Milan 0), 1997 (Borussia Dortmund 3, Juventus 1)*

Holland, beaten in the 1974 World Cup, returned to Munich 14 years later to win the European Championship in front of their West Germany hosts. There could have been few more spectacular venues than the individualistic Olympiastadion. Descriptions of it varied from a futuristic Bedouin tent to a steel and glass spider's web – although the desert analogy can feel rather tenuous in the depths of a Bavarian winter. It was built on the site of the airfield to which Neville Chamberlain flew in 1938 for his infamous ("Peace in our time") meeting with Hitler.

The tragic shadow of history fell across the stadium again at the end of the 1972 Olympics for which it had been built, when Arab terrorists took hostage and murdered Israeli athletes competing at the Games.

The bill for Behnisch and Otto's staggering creation at the centre of the green and pleasant Olympiapark came to 137 million marks. It was money well spent. The Park has become Germany's leading tourist attraction and a stunning venue for major events.

Bayern Munich, about to establish themselves as European giants with players such as Franz Beckenbauer, Paul Breitner and Gerd Müller, moved into the new stadium in 1972, two seasons before they lifted the first of their three successive European Champions Cups. Müller had helped to celebrate the opening by scoring all four goals in West Germany's 4–1 win over the Soviet Union in 1972. Two years later the stocky striker's place

Holland's Gullit and Koeman overwhelm Rudi Voller in the 1988 semi-final against West Germany

Shock winners Denmark celebrate in Gothenburg in 1992

in soccer's hall of fame was assured by his winning goal against Holland in the 1974 World Cup Final in front of his home fans.

The Dutch took happier memories away from the 1988 European Championship Final when they overcame the Soviets 2–0. The second goal, by Marco Van Basten, must count as one of the most spectacular in international football history. Most recently Borussia Dortmund became the first German club to win the European Champions Cup in 14 years by defeating favourites Juventus there by 3–1.

1992: SWEDEN, GOTHENBURG
Nya Ullevi

Capacity: *43,000*

Opened: *1958*

Club: *IFK Gothenburg*

Hosted: *1958 World Cup (six matches); 1992 European Championship Final (Denmark 2, West Germany 0); 1983 European Cup-winners Cup Final (Aberdeen 2, Real Madrid 1)*

Gothenburg has never been considered one of the great football capitals of the world but certainly no visiting team will ever go through with excessive confidence on the evidence of the European finals which have taken place there. Favourites have a tough time of it – the 1992 European Championship being a prime example. Denmark came from nowhere after the exclusion of Yugoslavia and achieved the two greatest triumphs in their football history in the Nya Ullevi.

First they beat Holland on penalties in the semi-final then they defeated Germany 2–0 in the Final. The surprise trend had been set a decade earlier however. The first time was when host club IFK Gothenburg defeated Hamburg in the UEFA Cup Final, the second time was when Scotland's Aberdeen defeated Real Madrid in the Cup-winners Cup Final.

Building the Nya (New) Ullevi took a year and cost far more than the organizing officials from the Swedish federation and the Gothenburg local authority had expected. It was opened in May 1958 in time for the World Cup finals, during which it staged six matches. These included Brazil vs. the Soviet Union – one quarter-final, a semi-final and the third-place play-off, in which France thrashed West Germany and Just Fontaine sealed his record of 13 goals in the tournament.

1996: ENGLAND, LONDON
Wembley

Capacity: *80,000*

Opened: *1923*

Club: *None*

Hosted: *1948 Olympic Final (Sweden 3, Yugoslavia 1); 1966 World Cup Final (England 4, West Germany 2 aet); 1996 European Championship Final (Germany 2, Czech Republic 1); 1963 European Cup Final (Milan 2, Benfica 1), 1968 (Manchester United 4, Benfica 1 aet), 1971 (Ajax 2, Panathinaikos 0), 1978 (Liverpool 1, Brugge 0), 1992 (Barcelona 1, Sampdoria 0 aet); 1965 Cup-Winners' Cup Final (West Ham 2, Munich 1860 0); 1993 (Parma 3, Antwerp 1)*

Wembley may be the ageing *grande dame* of stadiums but, steeped in history and with its distinctive twin towers, it remains the Mecca of English football and is revered by players and fans throughout the world. Wembley is synonymous with England internationals, the FA Cup Final, the epic World Cup Final of 1966 and the highly dramatic concluding matches in the 1996 European Championship. First Wembley held its breath during the penalty shoot-out in which Germany beat England in the semi-final. Then it witnessed the first major European event to be decided by the golden goal rule when Germany defeated the Czech Republic in the Final.

Unusually for a major stadium, Wembley is privately owned and financed by its staging of major soccer games, greyhound racing, rugby league, showpiece American football games, and ancillary sporting activities at the nearby 9,000-seater Arena.

In the 1920s the green fields of Wembley Park were chosen as the site for the 1923 Empire Exhibition. The then Empire stadium was built between January 22 and April 23. It was hailed as the largest monumental building of reinforced concrete in the world, and a troop of soldiers marched up and down the terracing in a unique safety check.

Since a crowd of "only" 53,000 had turned up for the 1922 FA Cup Final at Stamford Bridge, the authorities were concerned that Bolton and West Ham might not fill the new 126,000 capacity ground the following year. But on April 28 more than 200,000 people besieged Wembley, and that Bolton were eventually able to defeat West Ham 2–0 was due in no small part to the good nature of the crowd (in the presence of King George V), and a celebrated policeman on his white horse. The Wembley legend was born.

The watersheds of English football followed: the Cup was taken out of England for the only time by Cardiff in 1927; a year later Scotland destroyed England 5–1 with their famous forward line, dubbed the Wembley Wizards; Stanley Matthews had the 1953 Final "named" after him, when he inspired Blackpool to

beat Bolton 4–3 from 3–1 down. Later that year, Hungary changed world football by crushing England 6–3 there.

England held their heads high again in 1966, and when Manchester United became the first club to win the European Cup on a memorable June night two years later they could not have triumphed on more appropriate turf.

Wembley has moved with the times. The on-site exhibition centre was redeveloped while the stadium was remodelled in the 1980s at a cost of £60 million. Adapting to all-seater demands meant a capacity reduction from the historic 100,000. The addition of an Olympic Gallery beneath the roof edge kept an 80,000 level at which Wembley could take a pivotal role in England's hosting of the 1996 European Championship. Already plans were afoot to knock the old stadium down and replace it – thanks to vast grants from the National Lottery – with a new stadium appropriate to the needs of the twenty-first century.

Germany's golden boy Oliver Bierhoff in the Euro 96 Final

EUROPEAN CHAMPIONSHIP RESULTS

W. GERMANY: Maier, Hottges, Beckenbauer, Schwarzenbeck, Breitner, Hoeness, Netzer, Wimmer, Heynckes, G Müller, E Kremers.
SOV UNION: Rudakov, Dzodzuashvili, Khurtsilava, Kaplichni, Istomin, Kolotov, Troshkin, Konkov (Dolmatov 46), Baidachni, Banishevski (Kozenkevich 65), Onishenko.

1960 FRANCE

SEMI-FINALS

Yugoslavia 5 (Galic 11, Zanetic 55, Knez 75, Jerkovic 77 79)
France 4 (Vincent 12, Heutte 43 62, Wisnieski 52)

Sov Union 3 (V Ivanov 35 58, Ponedelnik 64)
Czech. 0

THIRD PLACE PLAY-OFF

Czech. 2 (Bubernik 58, Pavlovic 88)
France 0

FINAL

July 10 – Parc des Princes, Paris
Sov Union 2 (Metrevelli 49, Ponedelnik 113)
Yugoslavia 1 (Galic 41)
After extra time. HT: 0–1. 90 min: 1–1. Att: 17,966. Ref: Ellis (Eng)
SOV UNION: Yashin, Chekheli, Maslenkin, Krutikov, Voinov, Netto, Metrevelli, V Ivanov, Ponedelnik, Bubukhin, Meshki.
YUGOSLAVIA: Vidinic, Durkovic, Miladinovic, Jusufi, Zanetic, Perusic, Matus, Jerkovic, Galic, Sekularac, Kostic.

1964 SPAIN

SEMI-FINALS

Spain 2 (Pereda 35, Amancio 115)
Hungary 1 (Bene 85)
(After extra time)

Sov Union 3 (Voronin 19, Ponedelnik 40, V Ivanov 88)
Denmark 0

THIRD-PLACE PLAY-OFF

Hungary 3 (Bene 11, Novak 107 pen 110)
Denmark 1 (Bertelsen 81)
(After extra time)

FINAL

June 21 – Santiago Bernabeu, Madrid
Spain 2 (Pereda 6, Marcelino 83)
Sov Union 1 (Khusainov 8)
HT: 1–1. Att: 125,000. Ref: Holland (Eng)
SPAIN: Iribar, Rivilla, Olivella, Calleja, Zoco, Fuste, Amancio, Pereda, Marcelino, Suarez, Lapetra.
SOV UNION: Yashin, Shustikov, Shesternev, Mudrik, Voronin, Anichkin, Chislenko, V Ivanov, Ponedelnik, Korneyev, Khusainov.

1968 ITALY

SEMI-FINALS

Yugoslavia 1 (Dzajic 85)
England 0

Italy 0
Sov Union 0
(Italy on toss of a coin after extra time)

THIRD-PLACE PLAY-OFF

England 2 (Charlton 39, Hurst 63)
Sov Union 0

FINAL

June 8 – Olimpico, Rome
Italy 1 (Domenghini 80)
Yugoslavia 1 (Dzajic 38)
After extra time. HT: 0–1. 90min: 1–1. Att: 85,000. Ref: Dienst (Swi)
ITALY: Zoff, Castano, Burgnich, Guarneri, Facchetti, Ferrini, Juliano, Lodetti, Domenghini, Anastasi, Prati.
YUGOSLAVIA: Pantelic, Fazlagic, Holcer, Paunovic, Damjanovic, Acimovic, Trivic, Pavlovic, Petkovic, Musemic, Dzajic.

REPLAY

June 10 – Olimpico, Rome
Italy 2 (Riva 12, Anastasi 31)
Yugoslavia 0
HT: 2–0. Att: 50,000. Ref: Ortiz de Mendibil (Spa)
ITALY: Zoff, Salvadore, Burgnich, Guarneri, Facchetti, Rosato, De Sisti, Domenghini, Mazzola, Anastasi, Riva.
YUGOSLAVIA: Pantelic, Fazlagic, Paunovic, Holcer, Damjanovic, Acimovic, Trivic, Pavlovic, Hosic, Musemic, Dzajic.

1972 BELGIUM

SEMI-FINALS

Sov Union 1 (Konkov 53)
Hungary 0

W. Germany 2 (G Müller 24 72)
Belgium 1 (Polleunis 83)

THIRD-PLACE PLAY-OFF

Belgium 2 (Lambert 24, Van Himst 28)
Hungary 1 (Ku 53 pen)

FINAL

June 18 – Heysel, Brussels
W. Germany 3 (G Müller 27 57, Wimmer 52)
Sov Union 0
HT: 1–0. Att: 50,000. Ref: Marschall (Aut)

1976 YUGOSLAVIA

SEMI-FINALS

Czech. 3 (Ondrus 20, Nehoda 115, F Vesely 118)
Holland 1 (Ondrus og 74)
(After extra time)

W. Germany 4 (Flohe 65, D Müller 80 114 119)
Yugoslavia 2 (Popivoda 20, Dzajic 30)
(After extra time)

THIRD-PLACE PLAY-OFF

Holland 3 (Geels 27 106, W van der Kerkhof 39)
Yugoslavia 2 (Katalinski 43, Dzajic 82)
(After extra time)

FINAL

June 20 – Red Star, Belgrade
Czech. 2 (Svehlik 8, Dobias 25)
W. Germany 2 (D Müller 28, Hölzenbein 89)
After extra time. HT: 2–1. 90 min: 2–2. Czech 5–3 on pens. Att: 33,000. Ref: Gonella (Ita)
CZECH.: Viktor, Pivarnik, Ondrus, Capkovic, Gogh, Dobias, Panenka, Moder, Masny, Svehlik (Jurkemik 79), Nehoda.
W. GERMANY: Maier, Vogts, Beckenbauer, Schwarzenbeck, Dietz, Wimmer (Flohe 46), Bonhof, Beer (Bongartz 79), Hoeness, D Müller, Hölzenbein.

1980 ITALY

GROUP 1

W. Germany 1 (Rummenigge 55)
Czech. 0

Holland 1 (Kist 56 pen)
Greece 0

W. Germany 3 (K Allofs 15 60 68)
Holland 2 (Rep 75 pen, W van der Kerkhof 86)

Czech. 3 (Panenka 5, Vizek 25, Nehoda 63)
Greece 1 (Anastopoulos 11)

Czech. 1 (Nehoda 13)
Holland 1 (Kist 58)

W. Germany 0
Greece 0

	P	W	D	L	F	A	Pts
W. Germany	3	2	1	0	4	2	5
Czech.	3	1	1	1	4	3	3
Holland	3	1	1	1	4	4	3
Greece	3	0	1	2	2	4	1

GROUP 2

England 1 (Wilkins 32)
Belgium 1 (Ceulemans 38)

Italy 0
Spain 0

Belgium 2 (Gerets 17, Cools 64)
Spain 1 (Quini 35)

Italy 1 (Tardelli 78)
England 0

England 2 (Brooking 18, Woodcock 62)
Spain 1 (Dani 48 pen)

Italy 0
Belgium 0

	P	W	D	L	F	A	Pts
Belgium	3	1	2	0	3	2	4
Italy	3	1	2	0	1	0	4
England	3	1	1	1	3	3	3
Spain	3	0	1	2	2	4	1

THIRD-PLACE PLAY-OFF

Czech. 1 (Jurkemik 48)
Italy 1 (Graziani 74)
(Czech 9–8 on pens after extra time)

FINAL

June 22 – Olimpico, Rome
W. Germany 2 (Hrubesch 10 88)
Belgium 1 (Vandereycken 71 pen)
HT: 1–0. Att: 48,000. Ref: Rainea (Romania)
W. GERMANY: Schumacher, Kaltz, Stielike,
  K Forster, Dietz, Briegel (Cullmann 55), Schuster,
  H Müller, Rummenigge, Hrubesch, K Allofs.
BELGIUM: Pfaff, Gerets, L Millecamps, Meeuws,
  Renquin, Cools, Vandereycken, Van Moer,
  Mommens, Francois Van der Elst, Ceulemans.

1984 FRANCE

GROUP 1

France 1 (Platini 77)
Denmark 0

Belgium 2 (Vandenbergh 27, Grun 44)
Yugoslavia 0

France 5 (Platini 3 74 88, Giresse 32, Fernandez 43)
Belgium 0

Denmark 5 (Ivkovic og 7, Berggren 16, Arnesen 68,
  Elkjaer 81, Lauridsen 83)
Yugoslavia 0

France 3 (Platini 59 61 76)
Yugoslavia 2 (Sestic 31, Stojkovic 80)

Denmark 3 (Arnesen 40, Brylle 60, Elkjaer 83)
Belgium 2 (Ceulemans 25, Vercauteren 38)

	P	W	D	L	F	A	Pts
France	3	3	0	0	9	2	6
Denmark	3	2	0	1	8	3	4
Belgium	3	1	0	2	4	8	2
Yugoslavia	3	0	0	3	2	10	0

GROUP 2

W. Germany 0
Portugal 0

Spain 1 (Carrasco 20)
Romania 1 (Boloni 34)

W. Germany 2 (Völler 24 65)
Romania 1 (Coras 46)

Portugal 1 (Sousa 51)
Spain 1 (Santillana 72)

Spain 1 (Maceda 89)
W. Germany 0

Portugal 1 (Nene 80)
Romania 0

	P	W	D	L	F	A	Pts
Spain	3	1	2	0	3	2	4
Portugal	3	1	2	0	2	1	4
W. Germany	3	1	1	1	2	2	3
Romania	3	0	1	2	2	4	1

SEMI-FINALS

France 3 (Domergue 24 114, Platini 119)
Portugal 2 (Jordao 73 97)
(After extra time)

Spain 1 (Maceda 66)
Denmark 1 (Lerby 6)
(Spain 5–4 on pens after extra time)

FINAL

June 27 – Parc des Princes, Paris
France 2 (Platini 56, Bellone 90)
Spain 0
HT: 0–0. Att: 47,368. Ref: Christov (Cze)
FRANCE: Bats, Battiston (Amoros 72), *Le Roux,
  Bossis, Domergue, Fernandez, Giresse, Tigana,
  Platini, Lacombe (Genghini 79), Bellone.
*Le Roux sent off, 84 min.
SPAIN: Arconada, Urquiaga, Salva (Roberto 84),
  Gallego, Senor, Francisco, Victor, Camacho, Julio
  Alberto (Sarabia 76), Santillana, Carrasco.

1988 WEST GERMANY

GROUP 1

W. Germany 1 (Brehme 55)
Italy 1 (Mancini 51)

Spain 3 (Michel 5, Butragueno 52, Gordillo 67)
Denmark 2 (M Laudrup 25, Povlsen 85)

W. Germany 2 (Klinsmann 9, Thon 85)
Denmark 0

Italy 1 (Vialli 73)
Spain 0

W. Germany 2 (Völler 30 51)
Spain 0

Italy 2 (Altobelli 65, De Agostini 87)
Denmark 0

	P	W	D	L	F	A	Pts
W. Germany	3	2	1	0	5	1	5
Italy	3	2	1	0	4	1	5
Spain	3	1	0	2	3	5	2
Denmark	3	0	0	3	2	7	0

GROUP 2

Rep of Ireland 1 (Houghton 5)
England 0

Sov Union 1 (Rats 53)
Holland 0

Holland 3 (Van Basten 23 71 75)
England 1 (Robson 53)

Sov Union 1 (Protasov 75)
Rep of Ireland 1 (Whelan 38)

Sov Union 3 (Aleinikov 3, Mikhailichenko 28,
  Pasulko 72)
England 1 (Adams 16)

Holland 1 (Kieft 82)
Rep of Ireland 0

	P	W	D	L	F	A	Pts
Sov Union	3	2	1	0	5	2	5
Holland	3	2	0	1	4	2	4
Rep of Ire	3	1	1	1	2	2	3
England	3	0	0	3	2	7	0

SEMI-FINALS

Holland 2 (R Koeman 73 pen, Van Basten 88)
W. Germany 1 (Matthäus 54 pen)

Sov Union 2 (Litovchenko 59, Protasov 62)
Italy 0

FINAL

June 25 – Olympiastadion, Munich
Holland 2 (Gullit 33, Van Basten 54)
Sov Union 0
HT: 1–0. Att: 72,300. Ref: Vautrot (Fra)
HOLLAND: Van Breukelen, Van Aerle, R Koeman,
  Rijkaard, Van Tiggelen, Vanenburg, Wouters, E
  Koeman, Muhren, Gullit, Van Basten.
SOV UNION: Dasayev, Khidiatulin, Demianenko,
  Litovchenko, Aleinikov, Zavarov, Belanov,
  Mikhailichenko, Gotsmanov (Baltacha 69), Rats,
  Protasov (Pasulko 71).

1992 SWEDEN

GROUP A

Sweden 1 (Eriksson 26)
France 1 (Papin 59)

Denmark 0
England 0

France 0
England 0

Sweden 1 (Brolin 58)
Denmark 0

Denmark 2 (Larsen 7, Elstrup 78)
France 1 (Papin 58)
Sweden 2 (Eriksson 51, Brolin 84)
England 1 (Platt 3)

	P	W	D	L	F	A	Pts
Sweden	3	2	1	0	4	2	5
Denmark	3	1	1	1	2	2	3
France	3	0	2	1	2	3	2
England	3	0	2	1	1	2	2

GROUP B

Holland 1 (Bergkamp 7)
Scotland 0

Germany 1 (Hässler 90)
CIS 1 (Dobrovolski 63)

Germany 2 (Riedle 29, Effenberg 47)
Scotland 0

Holland 0
CIS 0

Holland 3 (Rijkaard 3, Rob Witschge 15,
 Bergkamp 73)
Germany 1 (Klinsmann 53)

Scotland 3 (McStay 6, McClair 17, McAllister 83 pen)
CIS 0

	P	W	D	L	F	A	Pts
Holland	3	2	1	0	4	1	5
Germany	3	1	1	1	4	4	3
Scotland	3	1	0	2	3	3	2
CIS	3	0	2	1	1	4	2

SEMI-FINALS

Germany 3 (Hässler 11, Riedle 59 88)
Sweden 2 (Brolin 64, Andersson 89)

Denmark 2 (H Larsen 5 32)
Holland 2 (Bergkamp 23, Rijkaard 85)
 (Denmark 5–4 on pens after extra time)

FINAL

June 26 – Nya Ullevi, Gothenburg
Denmark 2 (Jensen 18, Vilfort 78)
Germany 0
HT: 1–0. Att: 37,000. Ref: Galler (Swi)
DENMARK: Schmeichel, Sivebaek (Christiansen 66),
 K Nielsen, L Olsen, Piechnik, Christofte, Vilfort,
 J Jensen, H Larsen, B Laudrup, Povlsen.
GERMANY: Illgner, Reuter, Kohler, Helmer,
 Brehme, Buchwald, Effenberg (Thom 80),
 Sammer (Doll 46), Hässler, Klinsmann, Riedle.

1996 ENGLAND

GROUP A

England 1 (Shearer 23)
Switzerland 1 (Turkyilmaz 82 pen)

Holland 0
Scotland 0

Holland 2 (Jordi 66, Bergkamp 79)
Switzerland 0

England 2 (Shearer 52, Gascoigne 79)
Scotland 0

Scotland 1 (McCoist 36)
Switzerland 0

England 4 (Shearer 23 pen 57, Sheringham 51 62)
Holland 1 (Kluivert 78)

	P	W	D	L	F	A	Pts
England	3	2	1	0	7	2	7
Holland	3	1	1	1	3	4	4
Scotland	3	1	1	1	1	2	4
Switzerland	3	0	1	2	1	4	1

GROUP B

Spain 1 (Alfonso 74)
Bulgaria 1 (Stoichkov 65 pen)

France 1 (Dugarry 25)
Romania 0

Bulgaria 1 (Stoichkov 3)
Romania 0

France 1 (Djorkaeff 48)
Spain 1 (Caminero 85)

France 3 (Blanc 20, Penev og 62, Loko 90)
Bulgaria 1 (Stoichkov 68)

Spain 2 (Manjarin 11, Amor 84)
Romania 1 (Raducioiu 29)

	P	W	D	L	F	A	Pts
France	3	2	1	0	5	2	7
Spain	3	1	2	0	4	3	5
Bulgaria	3	1	1	1	3	4	4
Romania	3	0	0	3	1	4	0

GROUP C

Germany 2 (Ziege 26, Moller 32)
Czech Rep 0

Italy 2 (Casiraghi 5 52)
Russia 1 (Tsimbalar 20)

Czech Rep 2 (Nedved 5, Bejbl 36)
Italy 1 (Chiesa 18)

Germany 3 (Sammer 56, Klinsmann 77 90)
Russia 0

Italy 0
Germany 0

Czech Rep 3 (Suchoparek 7, Kuka 19, Smicer 89)
Russia 3 (Mostovoi 49, Tetradze 54,
 Beschastnikh 85)

	P	W	D	L	F	A	Pts
Germany	3	2	1	0	5	0	7
Czech Rep	3	1	1	1	5	6	4
Italy	3	1	1	1	3	3	4
Russia	3	0	1	2	4	8	1

Denmark 1 (B Laudrup 22)
Portugal 1 (Sa Pinto 53)

Croatia 1 (Vlaovic 85)
Turkey 0

Portugal 1 (Fernando Couto 66)
Turkey 0

Croatia 3 (Suker 53 pen 89, Boban 80)
Denmark 0

Portugal 3 (Figo 4, Joao Pinto 33, Domingos 83)
Croatia 0

Denmark 3 (B Laudrup 50 84, A Nielsen 69)
Turkey 0

	P	W	D	L	F	A	Pts
Portugal	3	2	1	0	5	1	7
Croatia	3	2	0	1	4	3	6
Denmark	3	1	1	1	4	4	4
Turkey	3	0	0	3	0	5	0

QUARTER-FINALS

England 0
Spain 0
 (England 4–2 on pens after extra time)

France 0
Holland 0
 (France 5–4 on pens after extra time)

Germany 2 (Klinsmann 21 pen, Sammer 59)
Croatia 1 (Suker 51)

Czech Rep 1 (Poborsky 53)
Portugal 0

SEMI-FINALS

Czech Rep 0
France 0
 (Czech Rep 6–5 on pens after extra time)

Germany 1 (Kuntz 16)
England 1 (Shearer 3)
 (Germany 6–5 on pens after extra time)

FINAL

June 30 – Wembley
Germany 2 (Bierhoff 73 94)
Czech Rep 1 (Berger 58 pen)
Germany on golden goal in extra time
HT: 0–0. 90 min: 1–1. Att: 76,000. Ref: Pairetto (Ita)
GERMANY: Köpke, Babbel, Sammer, Helmer,
 Strunz, Hässler, Eilts (Bode 46), Scholl (Bierhoff
 69), Ziege, Klinsmann, Kuntz.
CZECH REPUBLIC: Kouba, Hornak, Rada,
 Kadlec, Suchoparek, Poborsky (Smicer 88),
 Nedved, Bejbl, Berger, Nemec, Kuka.

OLYMPIC GAMES

Football has featured at the Olympics since 1896 but until the commercial revolution launched by International Olympic Committee (IOC) president Juan Antonio Samaranch, the amateur ethos of the Games sat uneasily at odds with mainstream professional football.

Trouble erupted as far back as the 1920s, when the four British Associations withdrew from FIFA in a row over broken time payments to players to compensate for loss of income from their regular jobs while they were away playing football.

Football was first seen at the Games in 1896, when a scratch tournament involving select teams from Denmark, Athens and Izmir was organized (The only recorded result was a 15–0 victory for the Danish XI against the Izmir XI). In Paris in 1900, football was again included as a demonstration sport, with Upton Park FC, representing England, beating France 4–0 in the only game played. In 1904 in St Louis, three North American teams entered a demonstration event which was won by Galt FC from Ontario representing Canada.

Football was finally accepted into the main programme for 1908 in London. The England amateur team (not a United Kingdom team), but still boasting many of the country's best players, beat Denmark 2–0 in the Final at White City.

Vivian Woodward, one of the outstanding players of the day and who scored the second goal, led England four years later in Stockholm. Denmark, the best amateur side on the continent, were again England's Final opponents, and again they ended up with the silver medal. Berry, Walden and Hoare (twice) scored for England in a 4–2 win. The Danish side included Nils Middelboe, later to play for Chelsea – one of Woodward's clubs.

The 1920 Games in Antwerp are remembered for the bad-tempered Final between Belgium and Czechoslovakia. Trailing by two goals, the Czechs accused the referee of being a "homer" and walked off midway through the second half. They were duly disqualified and an emergency tournament was staged to decide silver and bronze medals. Spain beat Holland 3–1 to claim silver.

In 1924 the Games returned to Paris and a South American nation, Uruguay, appeared for the first time. The Uruguayans brought with them dazzling ball skills which amazed the Europeans. They fielded some of the all-time greats of Uruguayan football: Nasazzi, Andrade, Vidal, Scarone, Petrone, Cea and Romano. No wonder Switzerland lost 3–0 in the final.

Four years later the Uruguayans returned, along with their great rivals Argentina, to take part in the 1928 Amsterdam Games. They met in the Final and Uruguay won 2–1 after a replay to retain the title. Uruguay's success confirmed the emergence of South America as a major footballing continent and provided enormous impetus towards the launch of the World Cup in 1930. Understanding, the Olympic title then assumed a less important role for the major players from Western Europe and South America.

The Americans did not want soccer at the Los Angeles Games of 1932 so Italy were the next Olympic champions, beating Austria 2–1 in the 1936 Final in Berlin. The Italians, under Vittorio Pozzo, thus emulated the Uruguayans in being both World Cup holders and Olympic champions simultaneously.

Sweden were surprise winners back in London in 1948. The Swedes, featuring Gunnar Gren, Gunnar Nordahl and Nils Liedholm (later nicknamed the Gre-No-Li trio when they all joined Milan), beat Yugoslavia 3–1 at Wembley.

Yugoslavia reached the Final again in Helsinki in 1952 – and lost again – this time to Hungary's "Magical Magyars." Ferenc Puskas and Zoltan Czibor scored in Hungary's 2–0 win which launched an era of Communist control.

Eastern European domination

Officially all players in eastern Europe were amateurs because Marxist-Leninist theory considered sport a leisure activity only. In practice, they were all professionals, holding jobs or armed service ranks on a nominal basis only. Western European football was now openly professional and could no longer compete.

A qualifying series was introduced for the 1956 Melbourne Games. Lev Yashin's Soviet Union won the gold medal, beating Yugoslavia 1–0 in the Final in front of an amazing 120,000 crowd at the Melbourne Cricket Ground.

Yugoslavia made it fourth time lucky in Rome, beating Denmark in the Final. Hungary clinched a hat-trick of titles when they beat Czechoslovakia in 1964 in Tokyo and Bulgaria in 1968 in Mexico City. Poland then ended the Hungarians' run by beating them 2–1 in in Munich in 1972. East Germany defeated Poland 3–1 in Montreal in 1976.

The increasing clamour over eastern European rule-bending provoked FIFA, in 1980, to bar any European or South American footballer who had played in a World Cup qualifier. The Eastern European satellites had one last hurrah in Moscow, where Czechoslovakia beat East Germany 1–0. But the new ruling which turned an official blind eye to professionalism, even if only an unsatisfactory compromise, did break the monopoly in 1984, when France won gold in Los Angeles.

The 1988 tournament in Seoul featured a host of top professional players and many emerging youngsters yet to play in the World Cup. Ironically, the Soviet Union again struck gold, beating Brazil 2–1 in the Final. The tournament also produced one of the biggest shocks in football history; Zambia beat Italy 4–0.

FIFA, bending further, turned the Olympic Games into an under-23 competition in time for Barcelona in 1992. Hosts Spain won a splendid final, beating Poland 3–2. They were unable to win gold again, however, four years later at the Atlanta Olympics.

None of the football matches were played in Atlanta itself – a discourtesy which grated with FIFA, particularly after the world body had bent the rules again to permit each nation to field three over-age players. The hope was that this would encourage mainstream nations to send a handful of star names whose presence would contribute promotional support to soccer in the United States.

In fact, it was not a mainstream nation who carried off gold but Nigeria, who thus made history as first African winners of the Olympic title. Relying on the experienced nucleus of their 1994 World Cup squad, the Nigerians beat favourites Brazil 4–3 in the semi-final and then Argentina 3–2 in the final in Athens, Georgia.

OLYMPIC GAMES FINALS RESULTS

1908 LONDON
England 2 (Chapman, Woodward)
Denmark 0
Att: 15,000

1912 STOCKHOLM
England 4 (Berry, Walden, Hoare 2)

Denmark 2 (Olsen 2)
Att: 4,000

1920 ANTWERP
Belgium 2 (Coppee, Larnoe)
Czechoslovakia 0
Att: 8,000

1924 PARIS
Uruguay 3 (Petrone, Cea, Romano)
Switzerland 0
Att: 41,000

1928 AMSTERDAM
Uruguay 1 (Ferreira)
Argentina 1 (Petrone)
Att: 40,000
Replay
Uruguay 2 (Figueroa, H Scarone)
Argentina 1 (Monti)
Att: 35,000

1932 LOS ANGELES
no tournament

1936 BERLIN
Italy 2 (Frossi 2)
Austria 1 (F Kainberger)
Att: 90,000

1948 LONDON
Sweden 3 (Gren 2, G Nordahl)
Yugoslavia 1 (Bobek)
Att: 60,000

1952 HELSINKI
Hungary 2 (Puskas, Czibor)
Yugoslavia 0
Att: 60,000

1956 MELBOURNE
Soviet Union 1 (Ilyin)
Yugoslavia 0
Att: 120,000

1960 ROME
Yugoslavia 3 (Galic, Matus, Kostic)
Denmark 1 (F Nielsen)
Att: 40,000

1964 TOKYO
Hungary 2 (Vojta og, Bene)
Czechoslovakia 1 (Brumousky)
Att: 65,000

1968 MEXICO CITY
Hungary 4 (Menczel 2, A Dunai 2)
Bulgaria 1 (Dimitrov)
Att: 100,000

1972 MUNICH
Poland 2 (Deyna 2)
Hungary 1 (Varadi)
Att: 50,000

1976 MONTREAL
East Germany 3 (Schade, Hoffmann, Hafner)
Poland 1 (Lato)
Att: 71,000

1980 MOSCOW
Czechoslovakia 1 (Svoboda)
East Germany 0 (Lato)
Att: 70,000

1984 LOS ANGELES
France 2 (Brisson, Xuereb)
Brazil 0
Att: 101,000

1988 SEOUL
Soviet Union 2 (Dobrovolski, Savichev)
Brazil 1 (Romario)
Att: 73,000

1992 BARCELONA
Spain 3 (Abelardo, Kiko 2)
Poland 2 (Kowalczyk, Staniek)
Att: 95,000

1996 ATHENS, GEORGIA
Nigeria 3 (Babayaro, Amokachi, Amunike)
Argentina 2 (C Lopez, Crespo)
Att: 45,000

COPA AMERICA

The South American Championship, known since 1975 as the Copa America, is the oldest surviving international football tournament outside the Olympic Games. It is contested every two years by the 10 members of CONMEBOL, the South American Confederation, and is 50 years older than its European equivalent.

The first tournament, in 1910, was not an official championship but one of the many "extraordinario" which have taken place down the years and served to confuse soccer historians and statisticians. The impetus came from the Argentine federation which wanted to organize a tournament involving themselves, Uruguay, Brazil and Chile. Brazil withdrew before the tournament began, but on May 29, 1910, Uruguay and Chile contested the very first South American Championship match in Buenos Aires.

Penarol's Jos Piendibene scored the first goal in the Copa America as Uruguay ran out 3–0 winners. Seven days later Argentina had an even easier 5–1 victory over Chile. Almost 40,000 crowded into the Gimnasia ground to see the great rivals Argentina and Uruguay battle it out for the inaugural title, but they were to be disappointed.

The fans burned one stand and the match was abandoned before it started. A day later a rearranged match was staged at Racing Club's ground, where only 8,000 saw Argentina win 4–1.

The second tournament, in 1916, is generally considered the first official such event and between then and 1959 the tournament was held, on average, every two years and in one host country. There was then a major hiatus in the 1960s when the international focus in South America was dominated by the newly-created Copa Libertadores for the champion clubs of the continent.

Uruguay won six of the first 11 South American championships. Argentina then gained the upper hand winning 11 of the 18 tournaments from the 1920s to the 1950s. Brazil, remarkably, won only three times in the first 60 years. They were unfortunate, however, in that when they were at their peak in the 1960s, only two tournaments were staged.

Successes for the rest of the South American nations have been few and far between. Peru won their titles in 1939 and 1975, Paraguay triumphed in 1953 and 1979. Most remarkably of all, Bolivia won in 1963 when they were hosts and took full advantage of the high-altitude conditions.

The tournament was traditionally played on a group basis with no final match (there were five championship play-offs). Television's demand for the drama of a final then imposed a change in format over the past decade. Now the Copa America features three first-round mini-leagues followed by direct elimination quarter- finals, semi-finals and final.

To make up the numbers – and generate greater television and sponsorship income – the Copa America was thrown open to two invited outsider nations from 1993 onwards. The first such expanded tournament took place in Ecuador with Mexico and the United States joining in. To the embarrassment of the South Americans, the Mexicans have once finished runners-up and reached the semi-finals on one other occasion.

Teething problems

At least most of the South American nations now take the Copa America seriously. This was not always the case. The stronger nations such as Brazil, Argentina and Uruguay often entered weak or B teams or even youth sides – generally because both European and also even domestic clubs refused to release star players. Indeed, 1975 was the first occasion on which all 10 CONMEBOL countries played. Argentina has played host to the official championship eight times, Uruguay six, Brazil, Chile and Peru four each.

The formal first tournament of 1916 was organized to celebrate Argentina's centenary of independence. Argentina and Uruguay again clashed in the decider – as they had done six years earlier – with Uruguay avenging their defeat of 1910.

The 1919 championship is considered to have been one of the most important in the history of the event. The Brazilian club Fluminense had built a 20,000-capacity stadium for the finals – a controversial decision with the club's membership, many of whom preferred yachting or cricket to football. Yet the final against Uruguay was considered such a success that the club raised funds to build other sports facilities nearby which attracted enormous interest both within Rio de Janeiro and far beyond. The game demonstrated football's ability to command attention. The final is also considered to have been a watershed in the history of football in Brazil which had been considered, until then, to be a sport favoured by the upper classes in their private clubs. Suddenly, football became the people's game.

Brazil reached the final by defeating Chile 6–0 and Argentina 3–1. Uruguay beat Chile 2–0 and Argentina 3–2. The final ended in a 2–2 draw so a replay was ordered. Thousands of fans who could not obtain tickets gathered in the streets around the offices of the *Jornal do Brasil* newspaper, to pick up what news they could about the progress of the match.

Brazil's hero was centre-forward Arthur Friedenreich, son of a German immigrant and a mulatto girl. But the stars of the game were the goalkeepers – 16-year-old Saporiti from Wanderers of Montevideo for Uruguay and Marcos Carneiro de Mendonça from host club Fluminense for Brazil. The 90 minutes failed to produce a goal. Neither did the standard 30 minutes' extra time. So the teams decided to play on until one of them scored – the first "golden goal" in international soccer history.

The teams had played a further 13 minutes – taking the match duration to two hours 13 minutes – when Saporiti could only parry a header from Neco and Friedenreich volleyed into the net. Brazil had won their first international prize.

Uruguay took their revenge against the champions by regaining the championship the following year (1920) in Chile. The competition was organized on a league basis during which the Uruguayans thrashed Brazil 6–0.

The championship was such a popular success that the big federations agreed it should be played every year, usually in September or October. Argentina won as hosts in 1921, defeating Uruguay in the decisive last match thanks to a single goal from the legendary Julio Libonatti.

Thus far, everything had taken place comparatively peacefully. The first cracks in temper and temperament occurred when the championship returned to Brazil in 1922. Brazil, Paraguay and Uruguay all finished the event with five points. But the Uruguayans were so incensed by the refereeing of their 1–0 defeat by Paraguay that they refused to stay on for a play-off series to decide the overall champion. Brazil thus won their second title by defeating Paraguay 3–1. Formiga scored twice with their third goal coming from Neco, one of Brazil's 1919 heroes.

Sulks forgotten, Uruguay played host in 1923 and won almost without raising a sweat. They won all three of their matches – 2–0 against Paraguay, 2–1 against Brazil and then 2–0 against old rivals Argentina.

This was one of the greatest Uruguayan national teams of all time. Seven members of the winning line-up – rightback and captain Jose Nasazzi, the halfback line of Andrade, Vidal and Ghierra plus the inside-forward trio of Petrone, Scarone and Cea were Olympic gold-medal winners a year later in Paris in 1924. In 1928 Nasazzi, Andrade, Scarone and Cea all won Olympic gold yet again, in Amsterdam.

Uruguay were South American Championship hosts and winners again in 1924 but did not defend their crown in 1925 when Argentina were hosts and winners. Argentina needed to hold Brazil to a draw in the concluding match in Boca Juniors' historic Bombonera ("Chocolate Box") stadium in Buenos Aires. They managed it despite a goal for Brazil by Friedenreich.

The Uruguayans returned to win in Chile in 1926, while Argentina were winners the first time Peru hosted the South American Championship in 1927 and then again, back in Buenos Aires, in 1929.

Confusion reigns

The next championship was delayed until 1935. The reasons were complex. First the 1930 World Cup finals got in the way then the federations became bogged down with problems over the introduction of professionalism. In Argentina, for example, two league championships ran simultaneously for four successive years between 1931 and 1934 before a peace deal was finally signed.

Impatience led the Peruvians to organize, in 1935, the first of several "unofficial" South American Championships. Uruguay sent a full-strength side, still captained by Nasazzi, and won again – defeating a weakened Argentina 3–0 in the concluding match in the Estadio Nacional in Lima.

The competition was notable as the first formal international tournament in which substitutes (two per team) were permitted.

Argentina's capital of Buenos Aires played host, in 1937, to the first official South American Championship in eight years. It was decided, after a great deal of bad-tempered wrangling at previous tournaments, that a play-off for the title would be held if two countries finished level on points.

Argentina and Brazil did precisely that though only after Argentina beat the Brazilians 1–0 in a tension-packed last league match. The Argentines were deserved winners with a fine team including all-time greats such as forwards De la Mata, Bernabe Ferreyra and Enrico Guaita – who had been a World Cup-winner with Italy in 1934 and picked up his Argentine nationality again after returning home to South America! Brazil's team included centre-half Oswaldo Brandao and inside forward Tim, both of whom would become outstanding and successful coaches.

Thus far the Big Three of Uruguay, Argentina and Brazil had dominated the competition. But 1939 saw the first outsiders break through when Peru won as hosts. Their hero was Teodoro Fernandez, one of the most popular Peruvian footballers of the era but almost forgotten nowadays. He scored a hat-trick in their opening 5–2 thrashing of Ecuador, two more in a 3–1 defeat of Chile then a further two in a 3–0 win over Paraguay.

Peru and Uruguay reached the concluding match level on six points apiece. Uruguay then concentrated so hard on ensuring that Fernandez did not add any more goals to his top-scoring seven that they left fatal gaps for his team-mates and Peru ran out 2–1 winners to top the table.

Uruguay finished runners-up again, this time to Argentina, in the unofficial tournament of 1941, then won the next official celebration a year later. But their star was on the wane. Power in the South American Championship was shifting to Argentina.

The late 1940s are legendary years in Argentine football history. They produced a stunning array of football talent. Top club were River Plate, whose brilliant forward line of Munoz, Moreno, Pedernera, Labruna and Loustau was nicknamed *La Maquina* – The Machine. They also had a young centre-forward in reserve named Alfredo Di Stefano.

The unofficial championship in Chile in 1945 produced a sensational exhibition of attacking football. Apart from Argentina, Brazil sent a forward line featuring a string of their own all-time greats such as Zizinho, Jair da Rosa Pinto, and an enormously controversial character, Heleno de Freitas. His brilliance forced Brazil's management to switch even the great Ademir de Menezes to outside-left.

The decisive match was played midway through the tournament. Argentina beat Brazil 3–1 with a hat-trick from Norberto Mendez and went on to finish a point ahead of them.

The Argentines also pipped Brazil in the official tournament of 1946 in Buenos Aires. Going into the last match – against Brazil – Argentina were one point ahead. Two more goals by Mendez provided Argentina with a 2–0 win and a further overall triumph, albeit "unofficial." The match lived in the memory, however, not for the football played but for a pitched battle between both sides after just 28 minutes of play. Bad feeling existed between the teams from a match three months before the tournament in which Brazil thrashed Argentina 6–2. Before the "revenge" in the championship, veterans captains Domingos of Brazil and Jose Saloman of Argentina exchanged bouquets of flowers as a goodwill gesture. Unfortunately, as one newspaper noted the next day, "the flowers must have been artificial."

Less than half an hour into the game Salomon suffered a double fracture of a leg in a collision with Jair. Argentina's Fonda flew at Jair and was himself attacked by Brazil's Chico – which was the signal for players and coaches from both sides to join in the fray. It took police intervention to break up the battle after which both sides were left with only nine men apiece to play on.

Argentina returned to win the title officially in Ecuador in December 1947. Three matches still remained to play after Argentina defeated Uruguay 3–1 – two more goals for Mendez plus another from Felix Loustau – but they could not be caught.

The power shifts again

By the time the next championship began in April 1949, however, Argentine football was in chaos. The mood of workers' unrest had infected football and the players had launched a famous strike for better pay and contract conditions. By the time the South American Championship began, stars such as Pedernera, Di Stefano, centre-half Nestor Rossi and goalkeeper Julio Cozzi had been lured away by the sky-high contracts to play in the pirate league of Colombia.

Argentina thus failed to enter the 1949 championship. Colombia, ironically, did send a team… and finished bottom. Winners were hosts Brazil, taking advantage of their opponents' confusion. They thrashed Paraguay 7–0 in the final in the Sao Januario stadium in Rio de Janeiro. Ademir scored a hat-trick in the final and was tournament top scorer with nine goals.

Playing hosts and emerging as winners was consolation for the Brazilians who had been expecting to host the World Cup itself then. However FIFA, after originally setting the first post-war finals for 1949, had set them back a year because of most countries' financial and administrative problems.

The delay also suited Brazil, who thus had an extra year in which to complete construction of their 200,000-capacity Maracana stadium. Not that they had any doubts over their ability to win the World Cup a year later. After all, on their way to winning the South American title they had beaten their most dangerous rivals, Uruguay, 5–1…

Brazil had taken the title in 1949 by thrashing Paraguay 7–0 in the concluding match. The same opponents lined up for the title play-off in 1953, in Lima. This time, however, Paraguay ran out winners by 3–2 and won the South American crown for the first time. Brazil's morale was clearly still somewhat fragile even three years after the shock of World Cup defeat.

Argentina returned for 1955 – when Brazil, still smarting from refereeing controversies in 1953, stayed away. Hosts Chile believed they could win for the first time but they lost the concluding match 1–0 to the Argentines. Rodolfo Micheli scored the only goal, making him the event's top marksman with eight.

The Argentines should have won again in 1956, with an inside-forward pairing matching the experience of the great Angel Labruna with the youthful cheek and flair of Enrique Omar Sivori. But complacency set in and they lost the decider – and thus their crown – to hosts Uruguay. Ambrois scored the only goal of the game.

The following year's championship, in Lima, Peru, in 1957, remains one of the fondest memories of Argentine football. They sent a team featuring one of the great inside forward trios in South American history – Humberto Maschio, Antonio Valentin Angelillo and Sivori.

No-one could withstand them. Argentina opened with an 8–2 destruction of Colombia; Maschio scored four goals, Angelillo two. They beat Ecuador 3–0 (Angelillo two and Sivori); beat Uruguay 4–0 (Maschio two, Angelillo and Sanfilippo); beat Chile 6–2 (Angelillo two, Maschio two, Sivori and Corbatta); and beat Brazil 3–0 (Angelillo, Maschio and Cruz). The Argentines lost their last match by 2–1 to hosts Peru, but they didn't care. The crown was already theirs. Not only that, but Argentina were the hot South American tip to win the World Cup the following year in Sweden.

A South American team did indeed win in Stockholm. But not Argentina. They flopped. The reason was simple: within weeks of the Triumph of Lima, Maschio, Angelillo and Sivori had all been lured away to Italy. Ever afterwards they were known bitterly, after the popular film of the day, as the "Angels With Dirty Faces".

Ironically Argentina pipped Brazil – Pele, Didi, Garrincha and Co. – to win the next South American title in 1959. But the tournament was marred by another pitched battle, this time after

50 minutes of Brazil's 3–1 win over Uruguay. No fewer than 10 players – seven Brazilians plus Uruguay's William Martinez, Nestor Gonçalves and Pepe Sasia – needed treatment in the hospital in the Monumental stadium in Buenos Aires before the match could continue.

Brazil won 3–1 with a hat-trick from Paulo Valentim. But they failed to win the title after drawing 1–1 with hosts Argentina in the last match. Argentina took the title instead. As one of the Brazilian player said afterwards: "After what happened against Uruguay, we didn't dare win."

Anyway, for now the South American Championship was small beer… and that very nearly spelled the end of it.

Championship on hold

Only two tournaments were staged in the 1960s and two in the 1970s. Many of the federations protested they could no longer obtain their best players for a month-long finals tournament and so the South American confederation experimented with different formats. In 1975, 1979 and 1983 the countries were split into preliminary round groups, playing each other home and away, followed by knock-out semi-finals and a two-leg final. It says everything about the attitude of the Big Three that Peru won in 1975 and Paraguay in 1979.

Player release had proved an even greater hurdle under this new format so, from 1987, CONMEBOL decided on a return to the old system of playing the entire tournament in one country. To reduce pressure on time the teams were split into three first-round groups followed by a knockout system and final. Television liked it, the sponsors liked it… and, with minor variations, that is how the Copa America, now staged every two years in what is, conveniently, the European close-season, has been successfully "reinvented." The 1987 tournament was played in Argentina and won by Uruguay, repeating their 1983 triumph. Brazil hosted the 1989 event and won their first title in 40 years, while Argentina won in 1991.

In 1993, in Ecuador, the tournament underwent another face-lift. Mexico and the United States were invited to take part as guests, and three first round groups produced eight quarter-finalists. Mexico almost spoiled the party by reaching the Final, where they lost 2–1 to Argentina.

Mexico and the US were invited again in 1995 in Uruguay and this time the North Americans reached the semi-finals before losing to Brazil. But Brazil lost in the Final to hosts Uruguay, 5–3 in a penalty shoot-out after a 1–1 draw.

The guests from Mexico reached the last four yet again in 1997 before going down 3–1 to hosts Bolivia. Fans in La Paz believed that their favourites were unbeatable in the rarefield atmosphere. But Brazil proved them wrong. Goals from Edmundo, Ronaldo and Ze Roberto earned the World Cup-holders a second crown – their fifth continental title.

Fans cheer on the United States at the Copa America

COPA AMERICA RESULTS

1910 ARGENTINA (unofficial)
1 Argentina
2 Uruguay
3 Chile

1916 ARGENTINA (unofficial)
1 Uruguay
2 Argentina
3 Brazil
4 Chile

1917 URUGUAY
1 Uruguay
2 Argentina
3 Brazil
4 Chile

1919 BRAZIL
1 Brazil (after play-off)
2 Uruguay
3 Argentina
4 Chile

Play-off: May 29 (Rio de Janeiro)
Brazil 1 (Friedenreich)
Uruguay 0
Att: 28,000. Ref: Barbera (Arg)
BRAZIL: Marcos, Pindaro, Bianco, Sergio, Amilcar, Fortes, Millon, Neco, Friedenreich, Heitor Dominguez, Arnaldo.
URUGUAY: Saporiti, M Varela, Foglino, Naguil, Zibechi, Vanzino, J Perez, H Scarone, Romano, Gradin, Marin.

1920 CHILE
1 Uruguay
2 Argentina
3 Brazil
4 Chile

1921 ARGENTINA
1 Argentina
2 Brazil
3 Uruguay
4 Paraguay

1922 BRAZIL
1 Brazil (after play-off)
2 Paraguay
3 Uruguay
4 Argentina
5 Chile

Play-off: Oct 22 (Rio de Janeiro)
Brazil 3 (Formiga 2, Neco)
Paraguay 1 (G Rivas)
Att: 20,000. Ref: Guevara (Chl)
BRAZIL: Kuntz, Palamone, Barto, Lais, Amilcar, Fortes, Formiga, Neco, Heitor Dominguez, Tatu, Rodriguez.
PARAGUAY: Denis, Mena, Porta, Miranda, Fleitas Solich, J Benitez, Capdevilla, Schaerer, I Lopez, G Rivas, Fretes.

1923 URUGUAY
1 Uruguay
2 Argentina
3 Paraguay
4 Brazil

1924 URUGUAY
1 Uruguay
2 Argentina
3 Paraguay
4 Chile

1925 ARGENTINA
1 Argentina
2 Brazil
3 Paraguay

1926 CHILE
1 Uruguay
2 Argentina
3 Chile
4 Paraguay
5 Bolivia

1927 PERU
1 Argentina
2 Uruguay
3 Peru
4 Bolivia

1929 ARGENTINA
1 Argentina
2 Paraguay
3 Uruguay
4 Peru

1935 PERU (unofficial)
1 Uruguay
2 Argentina
3 Peru
4 Chile

1937 ARGENTINA
1 Argentina (after play-off)
2 Brazil
3 Uruguay
4 Paraguay
5 Chile
6 Peru

Play-off: Feb 1 (Buenos Aires)
Argentina 2 (De la Mata 2)
Brazil 0
Att: 80,000. Ref: Macias (Arg)
ARGENTINA: Bello, Tarrio, Fazio, Sastre, Lazzatti, Martinez, Guaita, Varallo (De la Mata), Zozaya (Ferreyra), Cherro (Peucelle), E Garcia.
BRAZIL: Jurandir, Carnera, Jau, Britto, Brandao, Afonsinho, Roberto I (Carreiro), Luiz M Oliveira (Bahia), Cardeal (Carvalho Leite), Tim, Patesko.

1939 PERU
1 Peru
2 Uruguay
3 Paraguay
4 Chile
5 Ecuador

1941 CHILE (unofficial)
1 Argentina
2 Uruguay
3 Chile
4 Peru
5 Ecuador

1942 URUGUAY
1 Uruguay
2 Argentina
3 Brazil
4 Paraguay
5 Peru
6 Chile
7 Ecuador

1945 CHILE (unofficial)
1 Argentina
2 Brazil
3 Chile
4 Uruguay
5 Colombia
6 Bolivia
7 Ecuador

1946 ARGENTINA (unofficial)
1 Argentina
2 Brazil
3 Paraguay
4 Uruguay
5 Chile
6 Bolivia

1947 ECUADOR
1 Argentina
2 Paraguay
3 Uruguay
4 Chile
5 Peru
6 Ecuador
7 Bolivia
8 Colombia

1949 BRAZIL
1 Brazil (after play-off)
2 Paraguay
3 Peru
4 Bolivia
5 Chile
6 Uruguay
7 Ecuador
8 Colombia

Play-off: May 11 (Rio de Janeiro)
Brazil 7 (Ademir Menezes 3, Tesourinha 2, Jair Rosa Pinto 2)
Paraguay 0
Att: 55,000. Ref: Berrick (Eng)
BRAZIL: Barbosa, Augusto, Mauro, Ely, Danilo, Alvim, Noronha, Tesourinha, Zizinho, Ademir, Jair Rosa Pinto, Simao.
PARAGUAY: S Garcia, Gonzalez, Cespedes, Gavillan, Nardelli, Cantero, Fernandez (Barrios), Looez Fretes (Romero), Arce, D Benitez, Vazquez.

1953 PERU
1 Paraguay
2 Brazil
3 Uruguay
4 Chile
5 Peru
6 Bolivia
7 Ecuador

Play-off: Apr 1 (Lima)
Paraguay 3 (A Lopez, Gavilan, R Fernandez)
Brazil 2 (Baltazar 2)
Att: 35,000. Ref: Dean (Eng)
PARAGUAY: Riquelme, Herrera, Olmedo, Gavilan, Leguizamon, Hermosilla, Berni, A Lopez (Parodi), R Fernandez, Romero (Lacasia), Gomez (Gonzalez).
BRAZIL: Castilho, Djalma Santos, Haroldo II, Nilton Santos (Alfredo II), Bauer, Brandaozinho, Didi, Julinho, Baltazar, Pinga (Ipojucan), Claudio C Pinho.

1955 CHILE

1 Argentina
2 Chile
3 Peru
4 Uruguay
5 Paraguay
6 Ecuador

1956 URUGUAY (unofficial)

1 Uruguay
2 Chile
3 Argentina
4 Brazil
5 Paraguay
6 Peru

1957 PERU

1 Argentina
2 Brazil
3 Uruguay
4 Peru
5 Colombia
6 Chile
7 Ecuador

1959 ARGENTINA

1 Argentina
2 Brazil
3 Paraguay
4 Peru
5 Chile
6 Uruguay

1959 ECUADOR (unofficial)

1 Uruguay
2 Argentina
3 Brazil
4 Ecuador
5 Paraguay

1963 BOLIVIA

1 Bolivia
2 Paraguay
3 Argentina
4 Brazil
5 Peru
6 Ecuador
7 Colombia

1967 URUGUAY

1 Uruguay
2 Argentina
3 Chile
4 Paraguay
5 Venezuela
6 Bolivia

1975 (direct elimination tournament)

Final
1st leg: Oct 16 (Bogota)

Colombia 1 (P Castro)
Peru 0

2nd leg: Oct 22 (Lima)
Peru 2 (Oblitas, O Ramirez)
Colombia 0

Play-off: Oct 28 (Caracas, Venezuela)
Peru 1 (Sotil)
Colombia 0
Att: 30,000. Ref: Barreto (Uru)
PERU: Sartor, Soria, Melendez, Chumpitaz, Diaz, Cubillas, Ojeda, Quesada, P Rojas (Ramirez), Sotil, Oblitas.
COLOMBIA: Zape, Segovia, Zarate, Escobar, Bolanos, Ortiz, Calero, Umana (Retat), Arboleda, Diaz (P Castro), Campaz.

1979 (direct elimination tournament)

Final
1st leg: Nov 28 (Asuncion)
Paraguay 3 (C Romero 2, M Morel)
Chile 0

2nd leg: Dec 5 (Santiago)
Chile 1 (Rivas)
Paraguay 0

Play-off: Dec 11 (Buenos Aires, Argentina)
Paraguay 0
Chile 0
Att: 6,000
Paraguay on goal difference
PARAGUAY: R Fernandez, Espinola, Paredes, F Sosa, Torales, Florentin, Kiese, C Romero, Perez (Cibilis), M Morel, Aquino (Torres).
CHILE: Osben, Galindo, Valenzuela, Figueroa, E Escobar, M Rojas, Dubo (Estay), Rivas, Caszely, Fabbiani (Yanez), Veliz.

1983 (direct elimination tournament)

Final
1st leg: Oct 27 (Montevideo)
Uruguay 2 (Francescoli, Diogo)
Brazil 0
Att: 65,000. Ref: Ortiz (Par)
URUGUAY: R Rodriguez, Diogo, N Gutierrez, Acevedo, Agresta, W Gonzalez, Barrios, Cabrera, Aguilera (Bossio), Francescoli, Acosta (Ramos).
BRAZIL: Leao, Leandro, Marcio, Mozer, Junior, Jorginho, China (Tita), Renato Frederico, Renato Gaucho, Roberto Dinamite, Eder.

2nd leg: Nov 4 (Salvador)
Brazil 1 (Jorginho)
Uruguay 1 (Aguilera)
Att: 95,000. Ref: Perez (Per)
Uruguay 3–1 agg
BRAZIL: Leao, Paulo Roberto, Marcio, Mozer, Junior, Jorginho, China, Socrates, Tita (Renato Gaucho), Roberto Dinamite (Careca), Eder.
URUGUAY: R Rodriguez, Diogo, N Gutierrez, Acevedo, W Gonzalez, Barrios, Agresta, Cabrera, Aguilera (Bossio), Francescoli, Acosta (Ramos).

1987 ARGENTINA

Third place play-off
Colombia 2 (G Gomez, Galeano)
Argentina 1 (Caniggia)

Final: Jul 12 (Monumental, Buenos Aires)
Uruguay 1 (Bengochea 56)
Chile 0
HT: 0–0. Att: 35,000. Ref: Romualdo Arppi (Bra)
URUGUAY: Pereira, Dominguez, N Gutierrez, Trasante, Saldana, Matosas, Perdomo, P Bengoechea, Alzamendi (Pena), Francescoli, R Sosa.
CHILE: R Rojas, Reyes, E Gomez, Astengo, Hormazabal, Mardonez, Contreras, Puebla (Torro), Rubio, Letelier, Basay.

1989 BRAZIL

Final group
1 Brazil
2 Uruguay
3 Argentina
4 Paraguay

1991 CHILE

Final group
1 Argentina
2 Brazil
3 Chile
4 Colombia

1993 ECUADOR

Third place play-off
Colombia 1 (Valencia 84)
Ecuador 0

Final: Jul 4 (Guayaquil)
Argentina 2 (Batistuta 65 84)
Mexico 1 (Galindo 76 pen)
HT: 0–0. Att: 40,000. Ref: Marcio Rezende (Bra)
ARGENTINA: Goycochea, Basualdo, Borelli, Ruggeri (Caceres), Altamirano, Zapata, Redondo, Gorosito (L Rodriguez), Simeone, Acosta, Batistuta.
MEXICO: Campos, Gutierrez (Flores), Suarez, J Ramirez, F Ramirez, Patino (L Garcia), Ambriz, Galindo, Garcia Aspe, Hugo Sanchez, Zague Alves.

1995 URUGUAY

Third place play-off:
Colombia 4 (Quinonez 31, Valderrama 38, Asprilla 50, Rincon 76)
United States 1 (Moore 53 pen)

Final: Jul 23 (Montevideo)
Uruguay 1 (Bengoechea 48)
Brazil 1 (Tulio 30)
HT: 0–1. Att: 58,000. Ref: Brizio Carter (Mex)
Uruguay 5–3 on pens
URUGUAY: Alvez, Mendez, Herrera, Moas, Silva (Adinolfi), A Gutierrez, Dorta (P Bengoechea), Poyet, Francescoli, Fonseca (S Martinez), Otero.
BRAZIL: Taffarel, Jorginho (Beto), Andre Cruz, Aldair, Roberto Carlos, Cesar Sampaio, Zinho, Dunga, Juninho, Tulio, Edmundo.

1997 BOLIVIA

Third place play-off:
Mexico 1 (Hernandez 82)
Peru 0

Final: Jun 29 – La Paz
Brazil 3 (Edmundo 40, Ronaldo 79, Ze Roberto 90)
Bolivia 1 (E Sanchez 44)
HT: 1–1. Att: 50,000. Ref: Nieves (Uru)
BRAZIL: Taffarel, Cafu, Goncalves, Aldair, Roberto Carlos, Flavio Conceicao (Ze Roberto 62), Dunga, Leonardo (Mauro Silva 34), Denilson, Ronaldo, Edmundo (Paulo Nunes 67).
BOLIVIA: Trucco, S Castillo, Pena, Sandy, O Sanchez, Cristaldo, Baldivieso, Soria, Erwin Sanchez, Etcheverry, Moreno (Coimbra 74).

AFRICAN NATIONS CUP

The African Nations Cup is the blue ribbon event of African football, and the tournament is as old as the Confederation of African Football itself. Held every two years in a nominated country, the tournament has grown from humble beginnings to embrace the whole continent.

The first finals took place in Khartoum in 1957 to mark the founding of the continental confederation.

CAF, the Confederation Africain de Football to give it the formal title, was set up on June 7 and 8, 1957, at a meeting in the Hotel Avenida in Lisbon among delegates from Egypt, Sudan and South Africa. During that meeting Dr Abdel Hamil Mohaned from Sudan proposed that his country, which had gained independence in January 1956 and was building a national stadium in Khartoum, should organize the first African Cup of Nations.

The proposal was accepted. The new stadium in Khartoum was formally opened on September 30, 1956. Four months later CAF held its first general assembly in the Sudanese capital and set the Nations Cup under way.

The tournament, such as it was, involved only Sudan, Egypt and Ethiopia. South Africa, then members of FIFA, were initially due to take part, and had been scheduled to play Ethiopia in the semi- finals. The confederation told the South Africans it would accept only a multi-racial side but the South Africans replied that they would send only an all-black team or an all-white team. The CAF insisted again on a multi-racial team, South Africa refused and withdrew. Seven years later, in 1964, the South African FA would be suspended from FIFA pending the end of apartheid. They remained out in the cold until 1992, taking no further part in African or international football.

South Africa's withdrawal from the first tournament meant that Ethiopia were due a bye into the final. It was proposed that the event be reorganized on a mini-league basis but this was opposed by powerful Ethiopian delegate Ydnekatchew Tessema – later long-serving president of CAF – on the grounds that his country had already been declared "qualified" for the final.

Thus the other semi-final went ahead as had been originally drawn and saw hosts Sudan lose 2–1 to Egypt in front of 30,000 disappointed home fans. El Diba, who had scored Egypt's winner against Sudan, then proved too much for Ethiopia in the final – scoring all the Pharaohs' goals in their 4–0 win.

The same three nations took part in the second Nations Cup tournament, which Egypt hosted in 1959. The tournament was played on a league basis to make the trip worthwhile for Ethiopia and Sudan. The outcome was the same, with Egypt retaining the trophy. Once again they beat Ethiopia 4–0, with Mahmoud Al-Gohari scoring a hat-trick. Sudan then defeated Ethiopia 1–0 to set up a concluding match against Egypt which was also the tournament decider. Issam put Egypt ahead after 12 minutes only for Manzul to equalize for Sudan midway through the second half. Issam then snatched a winner for Egypt in injury time.

The rest of Africa remained largely unimpressed. Many of today's proud and ambitious nations had yet to free themselves from colonial status and those who were independent lacked both the financial and logistical resources to compete.

Tunisia and Uganda were the only newcomers when Ethiopia hosted the third tournament at the Haile Selassie stadium in Addis Ababa in 1962. Egypt were pre-tournament favourites and justified their status by defeating Uganda 2–1 in the semi-finals. Hosts Ethiopia defeated Tunisia 4–2 in the other tie – and then prevented the Egyptians completing a hat-trick of consecutive titles by beating them 4–2 in a dramatic final which went to extra time. Emperor Haile Selassie handed over the trophy to Ethiopian captain Luciano Vassallo who was also one of their heroes after scoring twice in the semi-final.

The tournament opens up

Ghana and Nigeria joined the fray for the 1963 tournament, which was held in Ghana. Their arrival on the scene enabled the confederation to expand the tournament format. This was expanded to feature two mini-league groups of three nations each. The winners of each group then proceeded to the final. In this case that meant Ghana and Sudan. The hosts were accepted abroad as a dynamic rising force in the African game: the previous year the national team had beaten the great Spanish club, Real Madrid 4–3, albeit only in a pre-season friendly match. It was no more than observers expected when they strolled to Nations Cup victory – beating Sudan 3–0 in the final in Accra – and went on to become the true dominant force in African football during the decade. Twice they would win the Nations Cup, twice they would finish as runners-up.

The fifth edition of the Nations Cup was staged two years later, in Tunisia. The tournament assumed a far greater importance than before because it took place in the wake of a political dispute with FIFA. The African confederation had been furious when FIFA refused to grant Africa one guaranteed place for one of its countries at the 1966 World Cup finals in England. As a result, the CAF instructed its members not to enter the World Cup – which they did not.

Thus the 1965 Nations Cup was important in demonstrating the technical and adminstrative progress being made in Africa. Six nations took part again. Tunisia topped their first-round group ahead of Senegal and Ethiopia while favourites Ghana headed their group over Ivory Coast and Congo Kinshasa (later

Zaire and now Democratic Republic of Congo). Osei Kofi and Ben Acheampong did the attacking damage for Ghana. They both scored in the group wins over Congo (by 5–2) and Ivory Coast (4–1) and were reason enough for Ghana to consider themselves favourites in the final.

Tunisia, however, had other ideas – and some fine players, including most notably the goalkeeper Attouga, considered the best in Africa in the 1960s as well as midfielder Majid Chetali who later took Tunisia to the World Cup finals as manager in 1978.

Chetali also scored the Tunisians' opening goal and they led 2–1 with just over 10 minutes to go. Then Kofi equalized for a relieved Ghana to send the final into extra time for the first time. Ghana eventually emerged as 3–2 winners and still champions.

Various rule changes were instituted ahead of the 1968 tournament. For one thing, an explosion in interest meant no fewer than 15 other nations had entered, along with finals hosts Ethiopia and holders Ghana. CAF thus decided to introduce a qualifying competition and decreed that the finals would take place once every two years.

The qualifying tournament did not run smoothly. Africa's complex political problems meant that Tanzania refused to face Congo Kinshasa in one qualifying play-off – allowing them a walkover to the finals – while Egypt pulled out in another squabble despite having won 1–0 away to Uganda in the first leg of their qualifying play-off.

A rule which had been introduced in 1965 and restricted each country to only two overseas-based players per team had also caused controversy. The idea had been to encourage development of the game within Africa and press players to stay home rather than move to Europe. Most players, however, considered steady club wages in Europe as far more of an attraction than playing in the African Nations Cup so, in 1982, the rule was rescinded.

The 1968 finals tournament was staged in Ethiopia and the hosts duly delighted their fans by topping their first-round group to qualify for the semi-finals. Here they lost 3–2 to Congo Kinshasa who thus went onto face reigning champions Ghana in the Final in Addis Ababa. Ghana had not looked particularly impressive but it was still something of a shock when Congo Kinshasa beat them 1–0 in the final with a goal by Kalala. Ghana returned for the 1970 Final in Khartoum, but lost 1–0 to the hosts Sudan.

Onto the world stage

In 1972, in Yaounde, Zaire's neighbours Congo won the title, beating Mali 3–2 in the Final. But Zaire returned in 1974 to face Zambia in the Final. A 2–2 draw in the first game was followed by a 2–0 win for Zaire, who travelled to the World Cup finals a few months later as reigning African champions and the first African side to reach the finals of the world's premier event. Here

Zaire striker Ndaye scored twice in the first match and repeated the trick in the second. It was the first time that the African Nations Cup had required a replay.

Guinea won numerous club honours during the 1970s, but these triumphs were never reflected at national level. They went closest to winning the African title in 1976 in Ethiopia. A final round group replaced the semi-finals and Final, and Guinea needed a win in their final match against Morocco to take the title. Cherif gave them the lead after 33 minutes, but an equalizer by Baba four minutes from time gave Morocco a 1–1 draw and the title by a point.

Morocco, like their North African neighbours, have not done particularly well in the African Nations Cup. Despite qualifying for the World Cup finals on three occasions, 1976 remains Morocco's only African title. Given the success of North African clubs in continental competitions, it is curious that the national sides have not matched them.

Nigeria won their first African Nations Cup title on home soil in 1980. The semi-finals featured the hosts, Algeria, Egypt and Morocco, but again the North Africans revealed a dislike for travelling. Paired with Algeria in the Final, and spurred on by a crowd of 80,000 in Lagos, the Nigerians won 3–0 with goals by Odegbami (two) and Lawal.

The 1982 tournament in Libya saw the return of Ghana to the African throne. The two-overseas-players rule, which had become impractical with so many of them earning a living in Europe, was abolished, and nations could choose their best line-ups once again. In the opening game of the tournament Libya beat Ghana 2–0, but both countries progressed to the Final.

This time round the Ghanaians made their greater experience count as they fought out a 1–1 draw before taking the trophy for a record fourth time with a 7–6 penalty shoot-out victory.

Cameroon emerged for their only victory in the 1984 finals in the Ivory Coast. Having squeezed past Algeria in the semi-finals, on penalties, they beat Nigeria 3–1 in the Final. Their side contained many who had performed so well at the 1982 World Cup finals in Spain, including the incomparable Roger Milla.

In 1986 Egypt hosted the tournament, which was marked by incidents on and off the field. A week before the tournament began, security police conscripts in Egypt rioted. A curfew was imposed and there was the very real threat that the finals would have to be cancelled. Thankfully the curfew was lifted so that the tournament could take place, but tanks and armoured cars still surrounded the stadiums to prevent further trouble.

On the pitch many of the teams complained about the standard of refereeing, and there were several angry outbursts from players and managers. Morocco manager Jos Faria was even prompted to describe one match as being rougher than the England vs. France Rugby Union international which was staged at about the same time!

Defending champions Cameroon again reached the Final,

where they met the hosts Egypt. The tournament as a whole had been laden with defensive play, and the Final was no exception. After a very dull 0–0 draw the hosts won the Cup, 5–4 on penalties, to the delight of the 100,000 crowd at Cairo's International Stadium.

Cameroon recovered from this disappointment by winning the 1988 title in Morocco. In the semi-finals, they beat the hosts by a single goal while Nigeria needed penalties to get past Algeria. A crowd of 50,000 in Casablanca saw Cameroon win 1–0 with a goal by Emmanuel Kunde after 55 minutes.

Nigeria's final failings

Two years later, in Algiers, the Nigerians again reached the Final. Unfortunately for them, they met the hosts and were again beaten by a single goal, from Oudjani after 38 minutes, in front of 80,000 fans. For the poor Nigerians, it was their third final defeat in four tournaments.

In 1992 a new name was added to the list of winners: the Ivory Coast. The tournament, held in Senegal for the first time, was expanded to 12 teams in the final round because of the ever-increasing number of countries taking part – even tiny nations such as Burkina Faso, Swaziland and the Seychelles now consider the African Nations Cup a worthwhile exercise.

The Ivory Coast and their western neighbours Ghana reached the Final, although the Ivorians needed penalties to overcome Cameroon in the semi-finals. The Final finished goalless and, in one of the most amazing penalty shoot-outs ever seen, the Ivory Coast won 11–10.

Zambia suffered a catastrophe in April 1993, when the plane carrying their squad to a World Cup match in Senegal crashed into the sea off Gabon, en route from a Nations Cup quailifier in Mauritius. All 30 people on board, including 18 players, died. But several European-based players were not on the flight, and the Zambians rebuilt their team around them, completed their qualifying programme and duly qualified for the 1994 finals in Tunisia. Neutrals must have been hoping that Zambia would win, but they fell to Nigeria who, in their fourth final in 10 years, triumphed 2–1. Emmanuel Amunike scored both goals and this same Nigerian team went on to give an excellent account of themselves by reaching the second round of the World Cup finals in the United States a few months later.

To overcome the problem of getting European-based players released, the bi-annual tournament was now held in the early part of the year, when many European countries are taking their winter break. The tournament has come a long way since 1957 with the expanded 1998 finals featuring a record 16 teams.

Much of the expanding profile of the event was owed to the return to the African and international fold of South Africa. They had failed to qualify for the 1994 finals, the first available Nations Cup after their return to respectability. But the richest country on the African continent then stepped in late to become the emergency venue for the 1996 finals after Kenya withdrew as hosts through lack of funds.

With the home fans still celebrating their success in winning rugby union's World Cup in 1995, South Africa surprised the continent by proving too strong for everybody and with a number of players now based in northern Europe, they won the trophy. Their task was made easier by Nigeria's decision to pull out of the tournament a few days before the opening ceremony.

The Nigerian government, to the bitter disappointment of their own players, claimed they dare not send a delegation to South Africa because of security concerns. They were the losers. South Africa beat Cameroon 3–0 and Angola 1–0 and qualified for the quarter-finals despite losing their last group match 1–0 to Egypt. In the quarter-finals goals from Mark Fish and John Moshoeu brought a 2–1 win over Algeria. Moshoeu then scored twice more in a comfortable 3–0 win over Ghana in the semi-finals.

By now, South African morale was high. In front of President Nelson Mandela, two goals from Mark Williams secured a 2–0 victory over Tunisia.

More new hosts

Away from home two years later, in 1998, South Africa fell just short of retaining the cup in Burkina Faso – whose choice as host nation was a gamble which just about came off for CAF.

Egypt ended almost a decade in the doldrums by regaining the title but the tournament itself was full of shocks with few of the established nations living up to their reputations and traditions. Ghana failed to qualify from the first round and Morocco, Cameroon and Tunisia were all eliminated in the quarter-finals.

Egypt's victory owed much to the experience of their coach, Mahmoud Al-Gohari, who thus gained the unique distinction of the first man to win the Nations Cup as both player and coach – having been top scorer for the winning Egyptian side back in 1959. His key men were central defender Hany Ramzy – with vast experience from playing in France, Switzerland and Germany – forward Hazem Imam from Italian club Udinese and prolific-scoring striker Hossam Hassan.

The tournament's two top-scoring players – Hassan for Egypt and McCarthy for South Africa – both reached the final, but neither scored. Egypt made an ideal start. South Africa's defence retreated as Ahmed Hassan advanced, offering time and space to strike a shot which took a deflection off defender Mark Fish and flashed past goalkeeper Brian Baloyi. Eight minutes later Tarek Mostafa shot home after a quick free kick by Hany Ramzy. Egypt, original winners of the Nations Cup, thus ended a 12-year drought and equalled Ghana's record of four victories.

AFRICAN NATIONS CUP RESULTS

1957 SUDAN

Semi-finals
Ethiopia vs. South Africa
Ethiopia walkover
Egypt 2 Sudan 1

Final: Feb 16 (Khartoum)
Egypt 4 (El Diba 4)
Ethiopia 0
Att: 15,000. Ref: Youssef (Sud)
EGYPT: Brascos, Mossaad, Dali, Fanaguili, Hanafi, Sanir Kotb, Ibrahim Tewfik, El Diba, Raafat Attia, Alaa, Adelfatah Hamdi.
ETHIOPIA: Gila, Ayele, Adale, Adamu, Asefaw, Berhe, Kebede, Zewode, Abreha, Nertsere, Berhane.

1959 EGYPT

League:

Egypt 4	**Ethiopia 0**
Sudan 1	**Ethiopia 0**
Egypt 2	**Sudan 1**

1 Egypt
2 Sudan
3 Ethiopia

1962 ETHIOPIA

Semi-finals

Ethiopia 4	**Tunisia 2**
Egypt 2	**Uganda 1**

Third place play-off
Tunisia 3   **Uganda 0**

Final: Jan 21 (Addis Ababa)
Ethiopia 4 (Girma 74, Menguitsou 84 117, Italo 101)
Egypt 2 (Abdelfattah Badawi 35, 75)
HT: 0–1. After extra time. 90min: 2–2. Att: 20,000. Ref: Brooks (Uga)
ETHIOPIA: Gila, Kiflom, Asmelash, Berhe, Awade, Tesfaye, Luciano, Girma, Menguistou, Italo, Guetacheou.
EGYPT: Adel Heykal, Admed Mostafa, Raafat, Tarak, Fanaguili, M Badaw, Chehta, Abdelfattah Badawi, Salah Selim, Taha, Cherbini.

1963 GHANA

Third place play-off (group runners-up)
Egypt 3 Ethiopia 0

Final: Dec 1 (Accra)
Ghana 3 (Aggrey-Fynn 62 pen, Mfum 72 82)
Sud an 0
HT: 0–0. Att: 50,000. Ref: Abdelkader (Tun)
GHANA: Ankrah, Crentsil, Aggrey-Fynn, Odametey, Simmons, Obiley, Adarkwa, Ofei Dodo, Mfum, Acquah, Salisu.
SUDAN: Sabbit, Samir, Kabir, Amin, Omar, Zarzour, Magod, Ibrahima, Djaksa, Nagy, Jagdoul.

1965 TUNISIA

Third place play-off (group runners-up)

Ivory Coast 1   **Senegal 0**

Final: Nov 21 (Zouiten, Tunis)
Ghana 3 (Odoi 37, 96, O Kofi 79)
Tunisia 2 (Chetali 47, Chaibi 67)
HT: 1–0. Att: 30,000. Ref: Chekaimi (Alg)
GHANA: Naawu, Ben Kusi, Acquah, Odametey, Evans, Kwamenti, Mensah, Osei Kofi, Jones, Kofi Oare, F Odoi.
TUNISIA: Attouga, Benzerti, Douiri, Habacha, Lamine, Chetali, Chaibi, Sassi, Gribaa, Delhoum, Djedidi.

1968 ETHIOPIA

Semi-finals

Congo Kinshasa 3	**Ethiopia 2**
after extra time	
Ghana 4	**Ivory Coast 3**

Third place play-off
Ivory Coast 1 Ethiopia 0

Final: Jan 21 (Addis Ababa)
Congo Kinshasa 1 (Kalala 66)
Ghana 0
HT: 0–0. Att: 12,000. Ref: Al Diba (Egy)
CONGO KINSHASA: Kazadi, Mange, Katumba, Tshimanga, Mukombo, Kibongo, Kassongo, Kalala, Kidimu, Kembo, Mungamuni.
GHANA: Naawu, Crentsil, Eshun, Odametey, Kusi, Sunday, Acquah, Osei Kofi, Attuquayefio, Mfum, Malik.

1970 SUDAN

Semi-finals

Ghana 2	**Ivory Coast 1**
after extra time	
Sudan 2	**Egypt 1**
after extra time	

Third place play-off
Egypt 3   **Ivory Coast 1**

Final: Feb 16 (Khartoum)
Sudan 1 (El Issed 12)
Ghana 0
HT: 1–0. Att: 35,000. Ref: Tesfaye (Eth)
SUDAN: Aziz, Kaunda, Suliman, Amin, Samir, Bushra, Bushara, El Issed, Dahish, Djaksa, Hasabu.
GHANA: Mensah, Boye, Mingle, Eshun, Acquah, Ghartey, Attuquayefio, Sunday, Folley, Owusu, Malik.

1972 CAMEROON

Semi-finals

Congo 1	**Cameroon 0**
Mali 4	**Zaire 3**
after extra time	

Third place play-off
Cameroon 5   **Zaire 2**

Final: Mar 5 (Yaounde)
Congo 3 (Mbono 57 59, M'Pele 63)
Mali 2 (Diakhite 42, Moussa Traore 75)
HT: 0–1. Att: 5,000. Ref: Aoussi (Alg)
CONGO: Matsima, Dengaky, Ngassaki, Ndolou, Niangou, Minga, Balekita, M'Pepe, Bahamboula, Matongo (Ongania), Moukila (Mbono).
MALI: M Keita, Moctar, Sangare, Kidian, Cheikna, Bakary, O Traore, Toure (M Traore), Salif Keita (Adama Traore), Fantamady Keita, Moussa Diakite.

1974 EGYPT

Semi-finals

Zaire 3	**Egypt 2**
Zambia 4	**Congo 2**
after extra time	

Third place play-off
Egypt 4   **Congo 0**

Final: Mar 12 (Cairo)
Zaire 2 (*Ndaye 65 117*)
Zambia 2 (*Kaushi 40, Sinyangwe 120*)
HT: 0–1. After extra time. 90min: 1–1. Att: 5,000. Ref: Gamar (Lby)
ZAIRE: Kazadi, Mwepu, Bwanga, Lobilo, Ngoie, Mavuba, Mana, Mayanga, Ndaye, Kidumu, Kakoko.
ZAMBIA: Mwape, Musenge, Chama, Makwaza, Mbaso, Simulowe, Simulombo, Mapulanga, Chanda, Kaushi, Sinyangwe.

Replay: Mar 14 (Cairo)
Zaire 2 (*Ndaye 30 76*)
Zambia 0
HT: 1–0. Att: 1,000. Ref: Gamar (Lby)
ZAIRE: Kazadi, Mwepu, Mukombo, Bwanga, Lobilo, Mana, Mayanga, Mavuba, Ndaye, Kidumu, Kakoko.
ZAMBIA: Mwape, Musenge, Chama, Makwaza, Mbaso, Simutowe, Mapulanga, Simulambo, Chanda, Sinyangwe, Kaushi.

1976 ETHIOPIA

Group format

Concluding match: Mar 14 (Addis Ababa)
Morocco 1 (Baba 86)
Guinea 1 (Cherif 33)
HT: 0–1. Att: 4,000. Ref: Chayu (Zam)
MOROCCO: Mazzaz, Cherif, Baba, Glaoua, Mehdi (Guezzar), Larbi, Semmat, Zahraoui, Taza, Faras, Abouali (Dolmy).
GUINEA: Sylla, Bangoura, Morcire, Cherif, Diarra, I Sylla, Papa Camara, Jancky, Sory, N'Jo Lea, Bangaly (Mory Kone).

Final placings:
1 Morocco
2 Guinea
3 Nigeria
4 Egypt

1978 GHANA

Semi-finals

Ghana 1	**Tunisia 0**
Uganda 2	**Nigeria 1**

Third place play-off
Nigeria walkover after Tunisia withdrew at 30 min

Final: Mar 18 (Accra)
Ghana 2 (Afriye 38 64)
Uganda 0
HT: 1–0. Att: 40,000. Ref: El Ghoul (Lby)
GHANA: Carr, Paha, Quaye, Acquaye, Dadzie, Kyenkyehene, Yawson, Seidi, Afriye, Razak, Ahmed.
UGANDA: Ssali, Semwanga, Musenza, Lwanga, Kirundu, Kiganda, Nasur, Nsereko, Omondi, Kisitu, Isabirye (Lubega).

1980 NIGERIA

Semi-finals

Nigeria 1   **Morocco 0**
Egypt 2   **Algeria 2**
Algeria 4–2 on pens after extra time

Third place play-off

Morocco 2   **Egypt 0**

Final: Mar 22 (Lagos)

Nigeria 3 (Odegbami 2 42, Lawal 50)
Algeria 0
HT: 2–0. Att: 80,000. Ref: Tesfaye (Eth)
NIGERIA: Best, Adiele, Chukwu, Tunde, Isima, Atuegbu, Odiye, Owolabi, Odegbami, lawal, Amesiemaka.
ALGERIA: Cerbah, Mersekane, Horr, Kheddis, Kouici, Mahyouz, Fergani, Belloumi, Bensaoula (Madjer), Benmiloudi (Guemri), Assad.

1982 LIBYA

Semi-finals

Ghana 3   **Algeria 2**
after extra time
Libya 2   **Zambia 1**

Third place play-off

Zambia 2   **Algeria 0**

Final: Mar 19 (Tripoli)

Ghana 1 (Al Hassan 35)
Libya 1 (Beshari 70)
HT: 1–0. After extra time. 90min: 1–1. Ghana 7–6 on pens after extra time. Att: 50,000. Ref: Sohan Ramlochun (Mau)
GHANA: Owusu, Haruna Yusif, L Sampson, Paha, Kwame Sampson, Asase, Quarshie, Kofi Badu (Abedi Pele), Essien (Opoku Nti), Al Hassan, Abbrey Kofi.
LIBYA: Kouafi, El Ageli, Zeiw, Sola, Beshari, Majdoub (El Borosi), Garana, El Fergani (Abubaker), Ferjani, Issawi, Gonaim.

1984 IVORY COAST

Semi-finals

Nigeria 2   **Egypt 2**
Nigeria 8–7 on pens after extra time
Cameroon 0   **Algeria 0**
Cameroon 5–4 on pens after extra time

Third place play-off

Algeria 3   **Egypt 1**

Final: Mar 17 (Abidjan)

Cameroon 3 (Ndjeya 32, Abega 79, Ebongue 84)
Nigeria 0
HT: 1–0. Att: 50,000. Ref: Bennaceur (Tun)
CAMEROON: Bell, Toube, Ndjeya, Doumbe Lea, Sinkot, Abega, Mbida, Aoudou, Ebongue, Milla, Djonkep (Kunde).
NIGERIA: Okala, Kingsley, Keshi, Eboigbe, Shofoluwe, Lawal, Adesina (Okoku), Edobor, Ali Bala (Temile), Nwosu, Etokebe.

1986 EGYPT

Semi-finals

Egypt 1   **Morocco 0**
Cameroon 1   **Ivory Coast 0**

Third place play-off

Ivory Coast 3   **Morocco 2**

Final: Mar 21 (Cairo)

Egypt 0
Cameroon 0

HT: 0–0. 90mins: 0–0. After extra time. Egypt 5–4 on pens. Att: 100,000. Ref: Bennaceur (Tun)
EGYPT: Batal, Yassine, Ali Shehata, Omar (Moyhoub), Sedki, Kassem, Abdelghani, Abou Zeid (Yehia), Andelhamid, Abdou, El Khatib.
CAMEROON: N'Kono, Ndip, Aoudou, Kunde, Sinkot, Mbouh, Kana, Mbida, Ebongue (Oumarou), Milla, Mfede.

1988 MOROCCO

Semi-finals

Cameroon 1   **Morocco 0**
Nigeria 1   **Algeria 1**
Nigeria 9–8 on pens after extra time

Third place play-off

Algeria 1   **Morocco 1**
Algeria 4–3 on pens after extra time

Final: Mar 27 (Casablanca)

Cameroon 1 (Kunde 55)
Nigeria 0
HT: 1–0. Att: 50,000. Ref: Idrissa (Sen)
CAMEROON: Bell, Massing, Kunde, Ntamark, Tataw, Mbouh, Mfede, K Biyik, Makanaky, Milla, Olleolle (Abena).
NIGERIA: Rufai, Sofoluwe, keshi, Eboigbe, Omokaro, Nwosu, Okosieme, Eguavon, Folorunso (Edobor), Okwaraji, Yekini.

1990 ALGERIA

Semi-finals

Algeria 2   **Senegal 1**
Nigeria 2   **Zambia 0**

Third place play-off

Zambia 1   **Senegal 0**

Final: Mar 16 (Algiers)

Algeria 1 (Oudjani 38)
Nigeria 0
HT: 1–0. Att: 80,000
ALGERIA: Demani, Benhalima, Kegharia, Serrar, Ait-Abderrahmane, El Ouzani (Neftah), Amani, Saib, Madjer, Oudjani (Rahim), Menad.
NIGERIA: Agui, Okechukwu, Anijekwu, Semitoje, Uwe (Aminu), Adesina, Kpakor, Oliha, Oguniana (Amokachi), Yekini, Elahor.

1992 SENEGAL

Semi-finals

Ivory Coast 0   **Cameroon 0**
Ivory Coast 3–1 on pens after extra time
Ghana 2   **Nigeria 1**

Third place play-off

Nigeria 2   **Cameroon 1**

Final: Jan 26 (Dakar)

Ghana 0
Ivory Coast 0
HT: 0–0. 90 mins: 0–0. After extra time. Ghana 11–10 on pens. Att: 60,000. Ref: Sene (Sen)
GHANA: Ansah, Armah, Ampeah, Baffoe, Asare, Abroah, Gyamfi (Naawu), Lamptey, Mensah, Opoku, Yeboah.
IVORY COAST: Gouamene, Aka, Sam, Sekana, Hobou, Gadji Celi, Magui, Otokore (M Traore), Sie, A Traore (Kassy Kouadio), Tieni.

1994 TUNISIA

Semi-finals

Nigeria 2   **Ivory Coast 2**
Nigeria 4–2 on pens after extra time
Zambia 4   **Mali 0**

Third place play-off

Ivory Coast 2   **Mali 1**

Final: Apr 10 (Tunis)

Nigeria 2   (Amunike 5 46)
Zambia 1   (Litana 3)
HT: 1–1. Att: 25,000. Ref: Lim Kee Chong (Mau)
NIGERIA: Rufai, Eguavon, Okafor, Okechukwu, Iroha, Finidi George (Siasia), Oliseh, Okocha (Ugbade), Amuinike, Yekini, Amokachi.
ZAMBIA: Phiri, M Malitoli, Chongo, Litana, Chiyangi, Joel Bwalya (Johnson Bwalya), Sakala, Muklenga (Makwaza), K Malitoli, Saileti, Kalusha Bwalya.

1996 SOUTH AFRICA

Semi-finals

Tunisia 4   **Zambia 2**
South Africa 3 Ghana   0

Third place play-off

Zambia 1   **Ghana 0**

Final: Feb 3 (Johannesburg)

South Africa 2 (Williams 73 74)
Tunisia 0
HT: 0–0. Att: 80,000. Ref: Massembe (Uga)
SOUTH AFRICA: Arendse, Motaung, Tovey, Fish, Radebe, Moshoeu, Tinkler, Buthelezi (Mkalele 50), Khumalo, Bartlett, Masinga (Williams 64).
TUNISIA: El Ouaer, Jaballah, Chouchane, Boukadida, Ben Rekhissa, Bouazizi (Ben Hassen 30), Kodhbana (Hanini 46), Fekih, Beya, Sellimi, Slimane.

1998 BURKINA FASO

Semi-finals

South Africa 2
Democratic Republic of Congo 1
after extra time
Egypt 2   **Burkina Faso 0**

Third place play-off

DR Congo 4   **Burkina Faso 4**
DR Congo 4–1 on pens

Final: Feb 28 (Ougadougou)

Egypt 2 (Ahmed Hassan 5, Tarek Mostafa 13)
South Africa 0
HT: 2–0. Att: 40,000. Ref: Belgola (Mor)
EGYPT: Al Sayed, Al Sakka, Hadi Medhat, Kamouna, Omara, Radwan, A Hassan, Hani Ramzy, Mostafa Tarek (Osama Nabih 78), Hazam (Sabri 55), H Hassan.
SOUTH AFRICA: Baloyi, Rabutla, Fish, Jackson, Augustine (Fortune 49), Radebe, Moeti, Mkalele, McCarthy, Masinga (Ndlanya 80).

ASIAN GAMES AND ASIAN CUP

The Asian Games was launched in 1951 and the Asian Cup for national teams in 1956. For most of the early years they were dominated by South Korea and Iran but the balance of power then shifted towards the Gulf states before Japan, encouraged by their J League-inspired revolution, started to contest power both on and off the pitch.

The 1950s and early 1960s were expansive years for FIFA and the world of football. Not only were the European and African confederations founded in that decade but so was the Asian Football Confederation – created in 1954, to be exact, by Hong Kong, India, Indonesia, Japan, South Korea, Malaysia, Philippines, Singapore and South Vietnam. Nationalist China (commonly known as Taiwan and later, formally, as Chinese Tapei) were admitted in 1955 and Israel in 1956. The Middle East "Gulf" states followed on into membership themselves during the 1960s and 1970s. Now the AFC has its headquarters in Ipoh, capital of Malaysia, though the first offices were in Hong Kong before moving to their present location.

In all this time the AFC had not stopped expanding and developing its portfolio of competitions which, by now, includes the Asian Cup, the football tournament at the Asian Games, the Asian Club Championship, the Asian youth tournaments and even an Asian women's football championship (the world's first).

The original Asian international tournament was the football section of the Asian Games. Originally open only to amateur players, the games are staged every four years in a host country, midway between each Olympiad. Surprisingly the soccer tournament has retained much of its significance – which is more than the football tournament of the "real" Olympic Games can boast.

India, Indonesia, Afghanistan, Japan, Iran and Burma attended the first tournament in 1951 – the Arab states staying away until the early 1970s. India's successes in the early years proved ultimately illusory but South Korea have been consistently successful as befits the Asian region's most consistent World Cup finals qualifiers.

India hosted the first Asian Games. Some 11 nations took part and six contested the football tournament in which matches lasted 80 rather than the statutory 90 minutes. This was because the Asian Games were ostensibly about amateur rather than professional athletes. Hosts India defeated Indonesia in the first round, Afghanistan in the semi-finals and Iran – narrowly – in the final.

The next Games were hosted in Manila, capital of Philippines. South Korea and Hong Kong drew 3–3 in the opening match but the South Koreans were later surprisingly beaten by Taiwan, masquerading as China, in the final. Taiwan beat South Korea again in the 1958 final before the Koreans completed a hat-trick of silver medals by losing the 1962 final by 2–1 to India in Jakarta, Indonesia.

For its first 20 years in existence, the AFC was dominated by a powerful alliance of East and Southeast Asians. In the early 1960s and 1970s, however, other countries decided they wanted to muscle in on the policy-making and power-broking, notably Iran and Hong Kong. This, plus the steady expansion in membership, provoked political problems far more complex than anything seen in any of the other regional, geographical confederations.

Iran made their presence felt from a playing point of view by reaching the final of the 1966 Asian Games football final in Bangkok, Thailand. Here they lost 1–0 to Burma – for whom victory, with a second-half goal from Aung Khin remains one of the greatest football achievements. The 1970 Asian Games were also staged in Bangkok and once again Burma were winners, albeit this time they had to share the prize and title with South Korea after a 0–0 draw in the final.

Politics interfere

Tehran was host city to the Asian Games in 1974 but already political trouble was boiling up. The Gulf states stayed away because of Israel's presence at the Games. Hosts Iran beat Israel 1–0 in the final but that was the last time an Israeli team was seen at the event. A year later in 1975, despite warnings from FIFA, AFC Congress voted to expel both Israel and Nationalist China. FIFA told the AFC this was, in effect, illegal and ordered the reinstatement of the two countries. The AFC refused and FIFA president Joao Havelange was engaged in a string of peace-seeking manoeuvres – none of which succeded in persuading the AFC to think again.

Only when Havelange, employing both great patience and a little negotiating bluff, achieved the political coup of bringing Communist China into FIFA did the tension subside. Havelange managed skilfully to maintain Chinese Taipei within membership of the AFC while, simultaneously, bringing mainland China on board. On the Israel issue, however, even he had to admit defeat. Ultimately, of course, Israel became "European."

Mainland China thus made their Asian Games debut at the 1978 event back in Bangkok. They even took the bronze medals.

Asian football power on the pitch now began to match the trends becoming obvious in the World Cup. Kuwait, World Cup finalists in 1982, were Asian Games runners-up that same year to Iraq. Four years later South Korea, themselves World Cup finalists that year, secured the Asian Games title with a 2–0 victory over Saudi Arabia in the final. The fact that the South Koreans were also event hosts, was of course an asset.

Politics intervened again in the 1990s. Iran won the 1990 Asian Games football title before disappearing, of their own volition for several years, off the face of the international football map. A significant change in the balance of power within the Asian confederation was then threatened after the collapse of the Soviet Union, with seven of the newly-independent states falling into the Asian arena. One of those, Uzbekistan, promptly surprised the long-established members by beating China 4–2 to win the 1994 Asian Games title.

Each geographical region of world football has its own competitive rhythm. For Europeans, that means a two-year campaign ending in European Championship or World Cup finals. Africa, South America and Central and North America now stage their national team championship tournament every two years. As for Asia, the competitive pattern swings between Asian Games and Asian Cup – which both take place every four years but with two years between each.

The Asian Cup

The Asian Cup, the regional contest for national teams, has been held every Olympic year. Qualifying rounds are staged across Asia followed by a 16-nation finals. The first four finals tournaments in 1956, 1960, 1961 and 1968 were played on strict league system. In 1972 the curren5 system was adopted with mini-leagues in the first round followed by a knock-out system and one-off final.

Political snags marked the first tournament. Ten nations entered, split into three qualifying groups with Hong Kong seeded direct to the finals as hosts. South Korea topped one group, South Vietnam another and Israel another… because both Afghanistan and Pakistan refused to play them. The finals were played on a mini-league basis with South Korea emerging as winners thanks to a 2–1 victory over Israel, who finished one point behind.

The outcome was the same in Seoul in 1960. Again South Korea topped the four-team finals mini-league with Israel their runners-up. Israel then won – at last – as hosts in 1964. Mordechai Spiegler, their greatest player, scored the opening goal in their all-important 2–0 win over ultimate runners-up India.

Host advantage proved precisely that also for Iran in 1968. That was the first of their hat-trick of victories, with follow-up successes in 1972 and 1976. Further evidence of their progress followed under the management of Frank O'Farrell who guided them to the 1978 World Cup finals where they achieved a notable 1–1 draw against Scotland.

The Asian Cup in the 1980s and 1990s saw the massive investment made in football by the Gulf states begin to pay off. Kuwait beat South Korea 3–0 in the 1980 final while Saudi Arabia won three of the next four (1984, 1988 and 1996) and were runners-up to Japan in 1992.

In 1996 the Saudis achieved their history-equalling third title, in between consecutive World Cup finals appearances, by defeating their United Arab Emirates hosts 4–2 in a penalty shoot-out after the final ended in a goalless draw. The Saudis thus equalled Iran's record of three Asian Cup titles. Ironically, they beat Iran on penalties in the semi-finals. Midfield general Khalid Al Muwalid converted the crucial penalty in the Final after UAE's Hassan Ahmed saw his kick rebound off a post. Saudi Arabia celebrated despite having had 19-year-old defender Hussein Sulimani sent off for his second bookable offence in the 86th minute. Saudi Arabia's success was all the more notable in that star forward Saeed Al-Owairan and two other national team-mates were suspended.

Hosts' disappointment

The home fans took defeat badly, racing from the stadium to leave only the 5,000 flag-waving Saudis celebrating victory and watching their heroes collecting the cup. It was the first time in seven that a host nation had lost the Final. Even some of the police and security guards were so overcome – some sobbing openly – that they left their posts to join the mourning fans.

In the third place play-off Iran beat Kuwait 3–2 in another penalty-shootout after a 1–1 draw. Iran gained further consolation in having strikers Ali Daei and Khodadad Azizi collect the top scorer and best player awards respectively. The Iranians also won the fair play award.

Kuwait reached the last four thanks not only to their own abilities but a little political fortune when Iraq were knocked out in the quarter-finals by the UAE. A major political storm would have erupted had Iraq won since they were due to face Kuwait in the semi-finals – and the Kuwaitis had insisted all along that they would walk out on the finals rather than play football against their military enemies.

Japan and South Korea, due to be World Cup co-hosts in 2002, were disappointing quarter-final failures. The Koreans won only one game out of four and were thrashed 6–2 by Iran in the quarter-finals. Reigning Cup-holders Japan won all three group matches then fell 2–0 to Kuwait. Both Korea and Japan blamed poor preparation and long domestic seasons but it would not be wide of the mark to suggest that both considered the Asian Cup far less important than the upcoming World Cup qualifying competition… from which they duly progressed to the finals in France, although neither managed to progress past their respective group stages.

ASIAN GAMES RESULTS

1951 NEW DELHI
Semi-finals
India 3	**Afghanistan 0**
Iran 3	**Japan 2**

Final
India 1	**Iran 0**

1954 MANILA
Semi-finals
Taiwan 4	**Indonesia 2**
South Korea 2	**Burma 2**

South Korea after drawing lots

Third place play-off
Burma 5	**Indonesia 4**

Final
Taiwan 5	**South Korea 2**

1958 TOKYO
Semi-finals
Taiwan 1	**Indonesia 0**
South Korea 3	**India 1**

Third place play-off
Indonesia 4	**India 1**

Final
Taiwan 3	**South Korea 2**

1962 JAKARTA
Semi-finals
India 3	**South Vietnam 2**
South Korea 3	**Malaysia 1**

Third place play-off
Malaysia 4	**South Vietnam 1**

Final
India 2	**South Korea 1**

1966 BANGKOK
Semi-finals
Iran 1	**Japan 0**
Burma 2	**Singapore 0**

Third place play-off
Japan 2	**Singapore 2**

Final
Burma 1	**Iran 0**

1970 BANGKOK
Semi-finals
Burma 2	**India 0**
South Korea 2	**Japan 1**

Third place play-off
India 1	**Japan 0**

Final
Burma 0	**South Korea 0**

title shared

1974 TEHRAN
Semi-finals
Group A:
Iran 6pts, Malaysia 3, Iraq 2, South Korea 1.

Group B:
Israel 6, North Korea 3, Kuwait 2, Burma 1.

Third place play-off
Malaysia 2	**North Korea 1**

Final
Iran 1	**Israel 1**

1978 BANGKOK
Semi-finals
Group A:
South Korea 6pts, China 4, Thailand 2, Malaysia 0.

Group B:
North Korea 5, Iraq 4, Kuwait 3, India 0.

Third place play-off
China 1	**Iraq 0**

Final
South Korea 0	**North Korea 0**

title shared

1982 NEW DELHI
Semi-finals
Iraq 1	**Saudi Arabia 0**
Kuwait 3	**North Korea 2**

Third place play-off
Not contested

Final
Iraq 1	**Kuwait 0**

1986 SEOUL
Semi-finals
South Korea 4	**Indonesia 0**
Saudi Arabia 2	**Kuwait 2**

Saudi Arabia 5–4 on pens

Third place play-off
Kuwait 5	**Indonesia 0**

Final
South Korea 2	**Saudi Arabia 0**

1990 BEIJING
Semi-finals
Iran 1	**South Korea 0**
North Korea 1	**Thailand 0**

Third place play-off
South Korea 1	**Thailand 0**

Final
Iran 0	**North Korea 0**

Iran 4–1 on pens

1994 HIROSHIMA
Semi-finals
Uzbekistan 1	**South Korea 0**
China 2	**Kuwait 0**

Third place play-off
Kuwait 2	**South Korea 1**

Final
Uzbekistan 4	**China 2**

ASIAN CUP RESULTS

1956 HONG KONG (league format)
1 South Korea
2 Israel
3 Hong Kong
4 South Vietnam

1960 SOUTH KOREA (league format)
1 South Korea
2 Israel
3 Taiwan
4 South Vietnam

1964 ISRAEL (league format)
1 Israel
2 India
3 South Korea
4 Hong Kong

1968 IRAN (league format)
1 Iran
2 Burma
3 Israel
4 Taiwan
5 Hong Kong

1972 THAILAND (fianls tournament)
Semi-finals

Iran 2   **Cambodia 1**
South Korea 1   **Thailand 1**
South Korea 2–1 on pens

Third place play-off
Thailand 2   **Cambodia 2**
Thailand 5–3 on pens

Final: May 19 (Bangkok)
Iran 2 (Jabary 48, Khalani 107)
South Korea 1 (Lee Whae-taek 65)
HT: 0–0. 90min: 1–1. After extra time. Att: 8,000

1976 IRAN
Semi-finals

Iran 2   **China 0**
Kuwait 3   **Iraq 2**

Third place play-off
China 1   **Iraq 0**

Final: Jun 13 (Tehran)
Iran 1
Kuwait 0
Att: 40,000

1980 KUWAIT
Semi-finals

Kuwait 2   **Iran 1**
South Korea 2   **North Korea 1**

Third place play-off
Iran 3   **North Korea 0**

Final: Sep 28 (Kuwait City)
Kuwait 3
South Korea 0
Att: 35,000
Semi-finals
Saudi Arabia 1   **Iran 1**
Saudi Arabia 5–4 on pens
China 1   **Kuwait 0**

Third place play-off
Kuwait 1   **Iran 1**
Kuwait 5–3 on pens

Final: Dec 16 (Singapore)
Saudi Arabia 2 (Shaye Nafisah 10,
  Majid Abdullah 47)
China 0
HT: 1–0. Att: 40,000

1988 QATAR
Semi-finals

Saudi Arabia 1   **Iran 0**
South Korea 2   **China 1**

Third place play-off
Iran 0   **China 0**
Iran 3–0 on pens

Final: Dec 19 (Doha)
Saudi Arabia 0
South Korea 0
HT: 0–0. 90 min: 0–0. After extra time. Att: 25,000
Saudi Arabia 4–3 on pens

1992 JAPAN
Semi-finals

Japan 3   **China 2**
Saudi Arabia 2   **UAE 0**

Third place play-off
China 1   **UAE 1**
China 4–3 on pens

Final: Nov 8 (Hiroshima)
Japan 1 (Takagi 36)
Saudi Arabia 0
HT: 1–0. Att: 40,000. Ref: Al Sharif (Syr)
JAPAN: Maekawa, Horlike, Hasiratani, Ihara, Tsunami, Ramos, Kitazawa, Yoshida (Katsuya), Fukuda, Miura, Takagi.
SAUDI ARABIA: Al Shujaa, Al Dosari, Al Khlawi, Al Roomi, Al Alwi, Amin, Al Bishi, Al Muwallid, Al Thunayan, Falatah (Al Mehalel), Al Owairan.

1996 UNITED ARAB EMIRATES
Semi-finals

Iran 0   **Saudi Arabia 0**
Saudi Arabia 4–3 on pens
UAE 1   **Kuwait 0**

Third place play-off
Iran 1 Kuwait 1
Iran 3–2 on pens

Final: Dec 21 (Abu Dhabi)
UAE 0
Saudi Arabia 0
HT: 0–0. 90min: 0–0. After extra time. Saudi Arabia 4–2 on pens. Att: 60,000 Ref: Mohammed Nazri Abdullah (Mal)
UAE: Muhsin Fairouz, Munther Abdulla, Yousef Saleh, Ismail Ismail, Bakhit Saad (Abdulaziz Mohamed 46), Adnan Al Talyani (Khamis Saad 91), Hassan Mubarak, Mohamed Mohamed, Hassan Ahmed, Ahmed Ahmed, Adel Ahmed (Zuhair Bkhait 46).
SAUDI ARABIA: Mohammed Al Daeyea, Mohammed Al Jahani, Mohammed Al Khilaiwi (Ibrahim Al Harbi 77), Abdullah Zubrom, Khalid Al Temawi, Sami Al Jaber (Abdullah Al Dossary 62), Fahad Mahalel (Hamzah Falatah 80), Sulimani*, Khalid Al Muwalid, Yousif Al Thunai, Khamis Al Dossary. *Sent off, 83 min.

CONCACAF CHAMPIONSHIP

What is now the CONCACAF Gold Cup for national teams in North and Central America has been contested, under various formats and with varying numbers of participants, since 1941. Costa Rica has the most outstanding record, with 10 victories, including three in a row between 1960 and 1963.

In 1991 the United States came on board as part of their pre-World Cup enthusiasm for all things soccer. Sponsors came running and the tournament was upgraded to its present title and vastly improved status. The Americans beat Honduras on penalties in that 1991 final but Mexico then justified their traditional role as top regional power by winning in 1993, 1996 and 1998.

In 1996 the Mexicans beat invited guests Brazil, who sent an under-23 Olympic team, by 2–0 in the final in front of 88,000 in Los Angeles. In 1998 Mexico beat their United States hosts 1–0 with a goal by Luis Hernandez. Ironically Brazil, again the crowd-pulling invited guests, finished in third place despite using not far short of their full-strength national team.

The history of CONCACAF goes back to 1924 and the seventh Olympic Games in Paris. Olympic officials from the region set up the Congreso Deportivo Centroamericano, later renamed the Organizacion Deportiva Centroamericano y del Caribe (ODCC) and launched their own regional mini-Olympics in 1930 in Havana, Cuba. Soccer was one of a dozen events. A second Games was held in 1935 but it was not until a third took place in Panama City in 1938 that the concept of a separate governing body for soccer was taken on board. Thus the Confederacion Centroamericano y del Caribe de Futbol (CCCF) was founded.

This was set up initially only to run football at the Central American and Caribbean Games. But officials meeting at the Games decided to extend the life of what had been, initially, only a one-off committee by empowering it to run a regular competition for national teams in the region. One of the most important decisions was to throw that competition open to all countries and players, thus permitting both amateurs and professionals.

The creation of the event was greeted with enthusiasm – but enthusiasm which melted away when national associations had to find funds to permit their teams to take part. Thus no more than six countries competed in the first four tournaments – even though the membership of the CCCF included Colombia, Costa Rica, El Salvador, Curacao (later part of Netherlands Antilles), Dominican Republic, Guetemala, Haiti, Honduras, Jamaica, Nicaragua, Panama, Puerto Rico and Venezuela (of course, Colombia and Venezuela later left the CCCF to join CONMEBOL, the South American Confederation).

As far as the regional championship went, the most loyal adherents were Costa Rica and El Salvador, followed by Guatemala, Panama and Nicaragua. Occasional appearances were put in by the likes of Honduras, Curacao and Nicaragua.

The tournament struggled along from 1941 to 1961, coming to life every two or three years. Ten editions of the championship took place in those 20 years with Costa Rica dominating. They were proclaimed champions on seven occasions. El Salvador, Panama and Haiti claimed one triumph each. Without the presence of Mexico, however, the regional soccer giant, the tournament lacked credibility as a true championship.

Tournaments merge

Running on parallel tracks was a North American Football Confederation Championship which took place twice during the 1940s and was won each time by Mexico. The confederation itself had been founded in 1939 by Cuba, Mexico and the United States – Canada staying aloof. War-time concerns meant that the first championship could not be undertaken until 1947. It was staged in Havana, Cuba, all three nations played each other in a round robin format and it was all over and done with in a week.

The United States did not have a national team and thus sent, instead, the Ponta Delgada Football Club from Fall River, Masachusetts – one of the cradles of American soccer. Teamwork counted for nothing: the Americans were well beaten by both Mexico and Cuba.

The convention was that the winners of one edition should be rewarded with the right to host the next finals. Thus the 1949 event was staged in Mexico City. This time the tournament lasted three weeks with everyone playing the other nations twice. Mexico won again and were, again, unbeaten. Cuba and the United States made it easy for the Mexicans by each winning one of their mutual games.

Further complicating matters was the creation, in 1946, of a Pan American Football Confederation. This was set up by officials meeting in Barranquilla, Colombia, and encompassed nations from South America, Central America and Caribbean and North American regions. However, it did not even survive a decade and organised only one Pan American Championship. Brazil triumphed by winning four matches and drawing one.

Clearly, the existence of three inefficient organizing bodies and three stuttering championships was not in the long-term interests of the game in the region. All that changed – though it took time

– after CONCACAF was set up to govern football in Central and North America in the early 1960s.

One of the major projects of the new authority was to put the regional championship on the sort of sound footing long evident in the South American Championship and just emulated in Europe by the creation of the European Championship (or Nations Cup, as it was originally entitled). The founding members were Cuba, Guatemala, Honduras, Mexico and Netherlands Antilles. Now membership stands at 33 plus two associate members and CONCACAF boasts offices in Guatemala City (the original HQ), Manhattan (New York) and Port of Spain (home of CONCACAF president Jack Warner).

Initially, the same sort of problems were apparent – a lack of both financial resources and administrative commitment. What had been the CCCF championship was extended to become the biennial CONCACAF championship in 1963, though the United States and Canada – the countries seen as most in need of "missionary work" – stayed away in both 1963 and 1965.

Costa Rica won the first "new" championship in 1963, under the guidance of Eduardo Toba, who was later, briefly, national manager of Spain. Toba's team surprisingly beat a Mexican side who had done comparatively well the previous year at the 1962 World Cup where they scored a 3–1 win over ultimate runners-up Czechoslovakia. The Mexicans took their revenge in 1965 with goalkeeper Ignacio Calderon and playmaker Javier Barba the stars.

Added value

In 1972–73 and 1976–77, an attempt to improve the value and image of the CONCACAF Championship was made by using it as the regional qualifying competition for the World Cups of 1974 and 1978 respectively – just as the British Home Championship had been used as a qualifying tournament in the early 1950s. Even then, it was hard to raise interest though more West Indian associations such as Antigua, Barbados and Jamaica came on board.

The 1972–73 series featured just 11 nations and the 1976–77 series featured 16. Each time the ultimate winners took up CONCACAF's one allotted place at the World Cup. Haiti caused a minor stir in West Germany in 1974 when star striker Emmanuel Sanon opened the scoring in their first match against Italy but Mexico succumbed without a fight in Argentina in 1978.

Taking the CONCACAF championship back out of the World Cup equation reduced its status, particularly since no-one showed any interest in changing the four-year cycle into which it had fallen. Mexico remained the major soccer power in the region but even they hardly took the event seriously – as evidenced by the fact that the three tournaments in the 1980s were all won by outsiders: Honduras in 1981, Canada in 1985 and Costa Rica in 1989.

One year later came a major development when Trinidadian law lecturer Jack Warner effectively ousted Mexico's Joaquin Soria as president of CONCACAF. One of Warner's priorities was to raise the status of the CONCACAF championship and, by using his excellent contacts within the burgeoning US soccer fraternity, he brought a raft of sponsors on board. A new trophy was created – the Gold Cup – and a 250,000-dollar prize fund was raised, immediately exciting attention from all the region's member associations.

The CONCACAF Gold Cup

The first revamped CONCACAF Gold Cup featured Carribean, Central American and North American qualifying sections and then a two-week finals tournament in Los Angeles featuring eight nations split into two groups of four followed by a knock-out section. The American hosts beat Honduras 4–3 on penalties after a 0–0 draw in the Final. Two years later – the Gold Cup having reverted to the biennial schedule – the finals tournament was staged jointly in Dallas and Mexico City and this time the Mexicans came out on top, beating the US 4–0 in the final in the Estadio Azteca. Mexico then retained the trophy in both 1996 and 1998.

The 1998 event was notable for two reasons. One was the presence of debutant World Cup finalists Jamaica, albeit thanks to Canadian generosity in withdrawing after the Jamaicans had failed to qualify from the Carribean qualifying section. The second point of note was the difficulty incurred by guests Brazil – including superstars Romario, Denilson, Roberto Carlos and co. – who were held 0–0 by Jaimaica and 1–1 by Guatemala in the first round and then beaten 1–0 by the US in the semi-finals. That all added up to signs of significant progress in playing standards within CONCACAF. Precisely what the CONCACAF Gold Cup and its variously-entitled predecessor tournaments had been created to encourage.

CONCACAF CHAMPIONSHIP (GOLD CUP) RESULTS

1941 COSTA RICA

1 Costa Rica
2 El Salvador
3 Curacao
4 Panama
5 Nicaragua

1943 EL SALVADOR

1 El Salvador
2 Costa Rica
3 Guatemala
4 Nicagarua

1946 COSTA RICA

1 Costa Rica
2 Guatemala
3 El Salvador
4 Honduras
5 Panama
6 Nicaragua

1948 GUATEMALA

1 Costa Rica
2 Guatemala
3 Curacao
4 El Salvador
5 Panama

1951

Winners: Panama

1953

Winners: Costa Rica

1955

Winners: Costa Rica

1957 CURACAO

1 Haiti
2 Curacao
3 Honduras
4 Panama
5 Cuba

1960 CUBA

1 Costa Rica
2 Netherlands Antilles
3 Honduras
4 Surinam
5 Cuba

1961 COSTA RICA

1 Costa Rica
2 El Salvador
3 Honduras
4 Haiti

1963 EL SALVADOR

1 Costa Rica
2 El Salvador
3 Netherlands Antilles
4 Honduras

1965 GUATEMALA

1 Mexico
2 Guatemala
3 Costa Rica
4 El Salvador
5 Netherlands Antilles
6 Haiti

1967 HONDURAS

1 Guatemala
2 Mexico
3 Honduras
4 Trinidad and Tobago
5 Haiti
6 Nicaragua

1969 COSTA RICA

1 Costa Rica
2 Guatemala
3 Netherlands Antilles
4 Mexico
5 Trinidad and Tobago
6 Jamaica

1971 TRINIDAD AND TOBAGO

1 Mexico
2 Haiti
3 Costa Rica
4 Cuba
5 Trinidad and Tobago
6 Honduras

1973

Winners: Haiti

1977

Winners: Mexico

1981

Winners: Honduras

1985

Winners: Canada

1989

Winners: Costa Rica

1991 UNITED STATES

Semi-finals
United States 2   **Mexico**   0
Honduras 2   **Costa Rica**   0

Third place play-off
Mexico 2   **Costa Rica**   0

Final: Jul 7 (Los Angeles Coliseum)
United States 0
Honduras 0
Att: 39,000 United States 4–3 on pens
UNITED STATES: Meola, Caligiuri, Balboa, Doyle, Clavijo, Quinn, Henderson, Murray (Kinnear), Perez, Vermes, Wynalda (Eck).
HONDURAS: Rivera (Cruz), Castro, Martinez, Flores, Zapata, Anariba, Yearwood, Funez, Espinoza, Calix, Bennett (Vallejo).

1993 MEXICO CITY (unless stated)

Semi-finals
Mexico 6   **Jamaica**   1
United States 1   **Costa Rica 0**
(in Dallas)

Third place play-off
Costa Rica 1   **Jamaica**   1

Final: Jul 25
Mexico 4 (Ambriz 12, Doyle og 31, Zague Alves 71, Cantu 80)
United States 0
HT: 2–0. Att: 105,000. Ref: Sawtell (Can)
MEXICO: Campos, Suarez, Ambriz, J Ramirez, Perales, R Ramirez, Hernandez, Salvador (Noriega 76), Mora (Cantu 76), Del Olmo, Rodriuguez, Alves Zague.
UNITED STATES: Meola, Doyle, Lalas, Kooiman, Dooley, Henderson, Harkes, Wynalda, Jones (Kinnear 53), Armstrong, Wegerle (Moore 80).

1996 (finals in US)

Semi-finals
United States 0   **Brazil**   1
Mexico 1   **Guatemala 0**

Third place play-off
United States 3   **Guatemala 0**

Final: Jan 21 (Los Angeles)
Mexico 2 (Luis Garcia 54, Blanco 75)
Brazil 0
HT: 0–0. Att: 88,155. Ref: Ramesh Ramdhan (Tri)
MEXICO: Campos, Villa, Davino, Suarez, Gutierrez, Lara, Ramon Ramirez, Garcia Aspe, Del Olmo (Pelaez 90), Luis Garcia, Blanco (Hernandez 81).
BRAZIL: Dida, Andre Luis, Narciso, Carlinhos, Ze Maria, Arilson (Ze Elias 68), Amaral (Beto 64), Flavio Conceicao, Jamelli (Leandro 64), Savio, Caio.

1998 (finals in US)

Semi-finals
United States 1   **Brazil**   0
Mexico 1   **Jamaica**   0

Third place play-off
Brazil 1   **Jamaica**   0

Final: Feb 15 (Los Angeles)
Mexico 1 (Luis Hernandez 43)
United States 0
HT: 1–0. Att: 91,255. Ref: Ramesh Ramdhan (Tri)
MEXICO: Perez, Villa, Davino, Pardo, Carmona, Suarez, Ramon Ramirez (Alfaro 86), Medina (Lara 67), Blanco, Lozano (Luna 56), Hernandez.
US: Keller, Burns, Lalas (McBride 82), Pope, Agoos, Hejduk (Reyna 76), Harkes, Moore, Jones, Wynalda, Wegerle (Preki 46).

FIFA UNDER-17 AND YOUTH CHAMPIONSHIPS

FIFA has made no secret of its desire to encourage football at grass roots level and in the Third World, and the Under-17 (Junior) and Under-20 (Youth) World Championships are crucial elements of that process.

It was inevitable that opportunities for the developing nations would be restricted within the senior World Cup, however steadily they expanded. But the launch of a World Youth Cup in 1985 was the vehicle with which then FIFA president Joao Havelange planned to offer greater participatory and organizational openings to the nations of Africa and Asia.

The first World Youth Cup was staged in Tunisia in 1977, where the Soviet Union triumphed, to be followed by Argentina's success in Japan in 1979. This was the tournament which 'made' the World Youth Cup because the Argentines were managed by their World Cup-winning coach Cesar Luis Menotti and were inspired in attack by Diego Maradona.

The status of the event was confirmed as a world championship – a meaningless gesture outside the formalities of FIFA – for the 1981 finals in Australia. West Germany beat surprise opposition Qatar in the final. Mexico, in 1983, saw Brazil beat Argentina 1–0 at the conclusion of a sensationally successful event in which the 32 matches drew 1.3 million spectators, an average of 40,625 per game.Notable was the presence of a Chinese team, the first to appear in the finals of an official FIFA event.

The year 1985 saw not only the fifth World Youth Cup but the first World Under-17 Championship, won by Nigeria – the first world title success for an African nation. The Nigerians not only repeated their victory in 1993 but served as pathfinders for Ghana, under-17 champions in 1991 and 1995.

Intriguingly, the 'elder' event, the World Youth Cup for the under-20s, remained the property of Europe and South America. Title hat-tricks were achieved by Brazil (1983, 1985 and 1993) and Argentina (1979, 1995 and 1997).

Future superstars lit up the under-17 and under-20 events. Future Bayern Munich striker Marcel Witeczek was top scorer (eight goals) at the first under-17 event in 1985 and at the under-20 event (with seven goals) two years later. European Champions Cup-winning glory with Ajax would beckon Nwanko Kanu, an inspiration for Nigeria's 1993 winners at under-17 level. In the World Youth Cup – apart from Maradona and eight-goal top-scoring team-mate Ramon Diaz in 1979 – the spotlight fell on the likes of Holland's Marco Van Basten in 1983 and later on Portugal's triumphant Joao Vieira Pinto, Rui Costa and Luis Figo.

Joseba Exteberria, Spain's tournament top scorer with five goals in Qatar, in 1995, went on to play for the senior squad at France 98.

One of the most memorable World Youth Cups was staged in Chile, in 1987, when Yugoslavia defeated West Germany in a penalty shoot-out after a 1–1 draw in the final. The German team included not only youth specialist Witeczek but Andy Möller, who would go on to greater things in midfield at the 1990 World Cup and win the European Champions Cup (in 1997 with Borussia Dortmund) and UEFA Cup (in 1993 with Juventus). Even more intriguingly, the Yugoslavs fielded four future stars of Croatia in defender Robert Jarni, midfielders Zvonimir Boban and Robert Prosinecki – voted best player – and striker Davor Suker. All of these players made names for themselves in the World Cup eleven years later as the little-fancied Croatia made it to the semi-finals before running out of steam against eventual winners France. Suker won the Golden Boot, claiming the last of his six goals against Holland in the third place play-off, which Croatia won 2–1.

FIFA's ambition of taking the hosting of the event to the developing world sometimes, predictably, misfired. Ecuador lost out on staging the under-17 finals in 1991 at short notice because of a cholera outbreak. Then Nigeria, again with health the main concern, missed out on the 1995 under-20 finals at comparatively short notice. FIFA president, Joao Havelange, had to fly out in person to offer formal apologies, so upset was African football in general by the controversy.

If nothing else, that just proved how important the world youth tournaments had become.

WORLD UNDER-17 CHAMPIONSHIP RESULTS

1985 CHINA

Semi-finals
Nigeria 1   **Guinea 1**
Nigeria 4–2 on pens
West Germany 4   **Brazil 3**

Third place play-off
Brazil 4   **Guinea 1**

Final: Aug 11 (Beijing)
Nigeria 2 (Akpoborie 4, Adamu 79)
W Germany 0
HT: 1–0. Att: 80,000. Ref: Bambridge (Aus)
NIGERIA: Agbonsevbage, Duere, Ugbade, Atere, Numa, Aikhionbore, Babatunde, Adamu, Akpoborie (Nakade), Igbinoba, Momoh.
WEST GERMANY: Ogrinc, Lewe, Schneider, Konerding, Gabriel, Gartmann, Jester, Dammeier, Schlichting (Mirwald), Witeczek, Radojewski (Simon).

1987 CANADA

Semi-finals
Soviet Union 5   **Ivory Coast 1**
Nigeria 1   **Italy 0**

Third place play-off
Ivory Coast 2   **Italy 1**

Final: Jul 25 (Toronto)
Sov Union 1 (Nikiforov 6)
Nigeria 1 (Osundo 11)
HT: 1–1. Soviet Union 3–1 on pens. Att: 14,997. Ref: Wright (Bra)
SOVIET UNION: Okrozhidze, Asadov, Mokritski, Bezhenar, Moroz, Matveyev, Vysokos (Kadyrov 40), Mushinka, Nikiforov, Kasimov, Arutyunyan (Rusin 51).
NIGERIA: Isa, Oyekale, Abdulahi, Duere (Jibrin 57), Fetuga, Peter, Energwea, Nwosu, Mohammed, Osundo, Emoedofu.

1989 SCOTLAND

Semi-finals
Saudi Arabia 1   **Bahrain 0**
Scotland 1   **Portugal 0**

Third place play-off
Portugal 3   **Bahrain 0**

Final: June 24 (Glasgow)
Saudi Arabia 2 (Al-Reshoudi 49, Al-Terair 65)
Scotland 2 (Downie 7, Dickov 25)
HT: 0–2. 90min: 2–2. After extra time. Saudi Arabia 5–4 on pens. Att: 51,674. Ref: Escobar (Gua)
SAUDI ARABIA: Al Deayea, Abdulshkor, Burshaid, Al Theyneyan, Al Alivi, Al Hammali, Al Hamdi, Al Reshoudi, Al Terair, Al Roalhi (Al Mosa 99), Al Shamrani.
SCOTLAND: Will, Bain, McMillan, Marshall, Beattie, Downie (Murray 98), Lindsay, O'Neill, Bollan, McGoldrick (McLaren 82), Dickov.

1991 ITALY

Semi-finals
Ghana 0   **Qatar 0**
Ghana 4–2 on pens
Spain 1   **Argentina 0**

Third place play-off
Argentina 1   **Qatar 1**
Argentina 4–1 on pens

Final: Aug 31 (Florence)
Ghana 1 (Duah 77)
Spain 0
HT: 0–0. Att: 5,000. Ref: Sundell (Swe).
GHANA: Owu, Nimo, Barnes, Asare, Mbeah, Lamptey, Opuko, Gargo, Duah, Preko (Bronw), Addo.
SPAIN: Javier, Chocarro, Castro, Exposito, Juan Carlos, Gerardo, Vaqueriza (Gerardo), Sandro (Velasco), Emilio, Murgi, Toni.

1993 JAPAN

Semi-finals
Nigeria 2   **Poland 1**
Ghana 3   **Chile 0**

Third place play-off
Chile 1   **Poland 1**
Chile 4–2 on pens

Final: Sep 4 (Tokyo)
Nigeria 2 (Oruma 3, Anosike 74)
Ghana 1 (Fameye 83)
HT: 1–0. Att: 30,000. Ref: Castrill (Arg).
NIGERIA: Okhennoboh, Oparaku, Babayaro, Okenedo, Anyanwu, Ojigwe, Oruma, Kanu, Odini (Ogbebor 63), Choji (Okougha 24), Anosike.
GHANA: Jarra, Barnes, Kuffour, Opoku, Edusei, Antwi (Muftawu 71), Fameye, Addo, Duah, Dadzie, Armah (Sarpong 14).

1995 ECUADOR

Semi-finals
Brazil 3   **Argentina 0**
Ghana 3   **Oman 1**

Third place play-off
Argentina 2   **Oman 0**

Final: Aug 21 (Guayaquil)
Ghana 3 (Bentile 38 50, Idrisu 43)
Brazil 2 (Juan Santos 48, Marco Antonio 89)
HT: 2–0. Att: 22,000. Ref: Irvine (NI)
GHANA: Abu, Allotey, Amanianpong, Camara, Ansah, Idrisu, Bentile, Amoako, Issaka, Gyan, Sule.
BRAZIL: Julio Cesar, Djimi (Eduardo 46), Bel, Juan Santos, Rodriguez, Helder (Nascimento 46), Carlos Alberto (Marica 63), Marcelo Rocha, Kleber, Marco Antonio, Rodrigo.

1997 EGYPT

Semi-finals
Brazil 4   **Germany 0**
Ghana 2   **Spain 1**

Third place play-off
Spain 2   **Germany 1**

Final: Sep 21 (Cairo)
Brazil 2 (Matuzalem 63, Andrey 87)
Ghana 1 (Afriyie 39)
HT: 0–1. Att: 45,000. Ref: Hauge (Nor)
BRAZIL: Fabio, Andrey (Henrique 88), Fernando, Jorginho, Diogo (Giovani 54), Ferrugem, Carlos Gaviao, Matuzalem, Abel, Fabio Pinto, Ronaldo.
GHANA: Boateng, Razak, Awuley Quaye (Owusu 55), Rahamani, Mohamed, Abbey (Coffie 73), Adjogu, Attram, Ansah, Dan Quaye, Afriyie.

WORLD YOUTH CUP RESULTS

1977 TUNISIA

Semi-finals
Soviet Union 0   **Uruguay 0**
Soviet Union 4–3 on pens
Mexico 1   **Brazil 1**
Mexico 5–3 on pens

Third place play-off
Brazil 4   **Uruguay 4**

Final: Jul 10 (Tunis)
Soviet Union 2 (Bessonov 43 52)
Mexico 2 (Garduno 50, Manzo 59)
HT: 1–0. Att: 5,000. Ref: Vautrot (Fra)
Soviet Union 9–8 on pens.
SOVIET UNION: Novikov (Sivukha), Krayachko, Baltacha, Kaplun, Iliyn, Bal, Bessonov, Khidiatulin, Bichckov, Bodrov, Sopko.
MEXICO: Paredes, Mora, Rubio, Alvarez, Lopes, Rergis, Cosio, Rodriguez, Manzo, Garduno, Placencia.

1979 JAPAN

Semi-finals
Argentina 2   **Uruguay 0**
Soviet Union 1   **Poland 1**

Third place play-off
Uruguay 1   **Poland 1**
Uruguay 5–3 on pens

Final: Sep 7 (Tokyo)
Argentina 3 (Alves 68, Diaz 71, Maradona 76)
Sov Union 1 (Ponomarev 52)
HT: 0–0. Att: 52,000. Ref: Wright (Bra)
ARGENTINA: Garcia, Carabelli, Simon, Rossi, Alves, Barbas, Rinaldi (Mezza 49), Maradona, Escudero (Torres 80), Diaz, Calderon.
SOVIET UNION: Chanov, Yanushevski (Olefirenko 56), Khachatrian, Ovchinnikov, Polukarov, Dumansski (Mikhalevski 60), Ponomarev, Radenko, Gurinovich, Taran, Stukashev.

1981 AUSTRALIA

Semi-finals
W Germany 1   **Romania 0**
Qatar 2   **England 1**

Third place play-off
Romania 1   **England 0**

Final: Oct 18 (Sydney)
West Germany 4 (Loose 26 66, Wohlfarth 42, Anthes 86)
Qatar 0
HT: 2–0. Att: 18,531. Ref: Coelho (Bra)
WEST GERMANY: Volborn, Winklhofer, Zorc, Schmidkunz, Trieb, Sievers (Brunner 66), Schön,

Loose, Anthes, Wohlfarth, Brummer (Herbst 85).
QATAR: Ahmed Younes, M Alsowaidi, Mohd
Duham, Ahmed Adil, Almas, Afifa, Beleal, Salem,
Alsada, Maayouf, Mohamadi, E Almuhannadi
(Khamis Alsowaidi 57).

1983 MEXICO

Semi-finals
Brazil 2   **South Korea 1**
Argentina 1   **Poland 0**

Third place play-off
Poland 2   **South Korea 1**

Final: Jun 19 (Mexico City)
Brazil 1 (Geovani 39)
Argentina 0
HT: 1–0. Att: 110,000. Ref: Biguet (Fra)
BRAZIL: Hugo, Heitor, Boni, Guto, Jorginho,
Dunga, Geovani, Gilmar (Demetrio 70),
Mauricinho, Marinho (Bebeto 82), Paulinho.
ARGENTINA: Islas, Basualdo, Borelli, Theiler,
Oliveira, Gaona (Graciani 75), Vanemarak,
Zarate, Garcia, Gabrich, Dezotti.

1985 SOVIET UNION

Semi-finals
Brazil 2   **Nigeria 0**
Argentina 1   **Poland 0**

Third place play-off
Poland 2   **South Korea 1**

Final: Sep 7 (Moscow)
Brazil 1 (Henrique 92)
Spain 0
HT: 0–0. 90mins: 0–0. After extra time. Att: 45,000. Ref:
Syme (Sco)
BRAZIL: Taffarel, Luciano, Luis Carlos, Henrique,
Dida, Joao Antonio, Tostin, Silas (Janivaldo 116),
Muller, Gerson (Antonio 110), Balaio.
SPAIN: Unzue, Tirado, Lizarralde, Arozarena,
Mendiondo, Marcelino (Nayim 76), Paz, Gay,
Fernando, Losado, Goicoechea (Francis 65).

1987 CHILE

Semi-finals
Yugoslavia 2   **East Germany 1**
West Germany 4   **Chile 0**

Third place play-off
East Germany 1   **Chile 1**
East Germany 3–1 on pens

Final: Oct 25 (Santiago)
Yugoslavia 1 (Boban 85)
West Germany 1 (Witeczek 87)
HT: 0–0. 90min: 1–1. After extra time. Yugoslavia 5–4
on pens. Att: 68,000. Ref: Loustau (Arg)
YUGOSLAVIA: Lekovic, Brnovic, Jarni, Pavlicic,
Jankovic, Mijucic, Boban, Pavlovic (Zirojevic 88),
Suker, Petric, Skoric.
West GERMANY: Brunn, Luginger, Metz, Strehmel,
Spyrka, Schneider, Reinhardt, Möller, Dammeier
(Heidenreich 106), Eichenauer (Epp 74),
Witeczek.

1989 SAUDI ARABIA

Semi-finals
Portugal 1   **Brazil 0**
Nigeria 2   **United States 1**

Third place play-off
Brazil 2   **United States 0**

Final: Mar 3 (Riyadh)
Portugal 2 (Abel 44, Jorge Couto 76)
Nigeria 0
HT: 1–0. Att: 65,000. Ref: Schmidhuber (WG)
PORTUGAL: Bizarro, Abel, Valido, Paulo Madeira,
Morgado, Filipe, Helio, Toze, Amaral (Paulo Alves
88), Joao Vieira Pinto (Folha 90), Jorge Couto.
NIGERIA: Amadi (Ikeji 81), Elijah, Onyemachara,
Chinedu, Charity, Oladimeji, Adepoju, Ogaba,
Nwosu, Balogan (Osundo 49), Ohenhen.

1991 PORTUGAL

Semi-finals
Portugal 1   **Australia 0**
Brazil 3   **Soviet Union 0**

Third place play-off
Soviet Union 1   **Australia 1**
Soviet Union 5–4 on pens

Final: Jun 30 (Lisbon)
Portugal 0
Brazil 0
HT: 0–0. 90min: 0–0. After extra time. Portugal 4–2 on
pens. Att: 130,000. Ref: Lamolina (Arg)
PORTUGAL: Brassard, Nelson (Tulipa 10; Nuno
Capucho 70), Rui Bento, Jorge Costa, Paulo Torres,
Peixe, Rui Costa, Gil, Luis Figo, Toni, Joao Vieira
Pinto.
BRAZIL: Roger, Zelao, Andrei, Castro, Roberto
Carlos, Rodrigao, Marquinhos, Djair, Luis
Fernando (Serginho 98), Paulo Nunes (Ramon 60),
Elber.

1993 AUSTRALIA

Semi-finals
Brazil 2   **Australia 0**
Ghana 2   **England 1**

Third place play-off
England 2   **Australia 1**

Final: Mar 20 (Sydney)
Brazil 2 (Yan 50, Gian 88)
Ghana 1 (Duah 15)
HT: 0–1. Att: 40,000. Ref: Cakar (Tur)
BRAZIL: Dida, Juarez, Bruno, Gelson, Hermes,
Pereira (Caico 62), Marcelinho, Yan, Cate, Adriano
(Argel 89), Gian.
GHANA: Owu, Kuffour, Nimo, Banini, Asare, Addo,
Gargo, Lamptey, Akonnor (Boateng 86), Ahinful,
Duah.

1995 QATAR

Semi-finals
Argentina 3   **Spain 0**
Brazil 1   **Portugal 0**

Third place play-off
Portugal 3   **Spain 2**

Final: Apr 28 (Doha)
Argentina 2 (Biagini 26, Guerreiro 86)
Brazil 0
HT: 1–0. Att: 50,000. Ref: Gallagher (Eng)
ARGENTINA: Irigoytia (pezutti 88), Lombardi,
Pena, Sorin, Dominguez, Larrosa, Juan, Ibagaza,
Coyette, Chaparro (Arangio 62), Biagini
(Guerreiro 83).
BRAZIL: Fabio, Dedimar, Fabiano, *Cesar,
Leonardo, Elder (Luizao 57), Ze Elias, Murilo
(Claudinho 72), Reinaldo (Denilson 81), Caio,
Glacio.
*Sent off, 78 min.

1997 MALAYSIA

Semi-finals
Argentina 1   **Republic of Ireland 0**
Uruguay 3   **Ghana 2**
after extra time

Third place play-off
Republic of Ireland 2   **Ghana 1**

Final: Jul 5 (Shah Alam)
Argentina 2 (Cambiasso 25, Quintana 41)
Uruguay 1 (Garcia 15)
HT: 2–1. Att: 50,000. Ref: Manei (Kuw)
ARGENTINA: Franco, Cufre, Serrizuela, Cubero,
Placente, Samuel, Scaloni (Rodriguez 83),
Cambiasso, Riquelme, Quintana (Aimar 54),
Romeo (Perezlindo 76).
URUGUAY: Munua, Diaz, Rivas, Melono
(Cartagena 63), Pellegrin (Lopez 46), Perea,
Garcia, Callejas (Regueiro 79), Coelho, Zalayeta,
Olivera.

WOMEN'S WORLD CHAMPIONSHIP

The Women's World Cup – though that is not quite its official title – was launched in 1991 as a further plank in FIFA's bid to make soccer more user-friendly to a United States audience ahead of the men's World Cup finals three years later.

The reasoning was perfectly obvious: the United States has shown a far greater commitment and enthusiasm for organized women's soccer than any other country. Appropriately, the Americans were winners of the inaugural women's event that year in China. The US, led by the outstanding Michelle Akers-Stahl, beat Norway 2–1 in the final.

Norway took their revenge four years later, in Sweden. This time they boasted the outstanding player in the tournament in Helge Riise. The impact she made in her native land can be assessed from the fact Egil Olsen, coach to the men's national team, included her among his three nominations in the annual FIFA Footballer of the Year award. In the 1995 final, the Norwegians defeated Germany 2–0 in Stockholm. Riise scored the first goal in front of more than 17,000 fans.

A year later, women's soccer was included in the Olympic Games for the first time, largely thanks to pressure exerted by the American soccer community because the Games were being staged in Atlanta. A world record crowd for a women's soccer match saw the US beat China 2–1 in the final in Athens, Georgia.

American captain Julie Foudy subsequently put the vast majority of male players to shame with her concerns over wider issues within the game. When a major sports outfitter began sponsorship negotiations with the US women's team, Fowdy made a point of accompanying company executives to Pakistan to assure herself child labour was not being exploited in the manufacture of footballs. Foudy duly received a FIFA fair play award for her effort.

Further evidence of the respect being won by the women's game came in 1997, with an invitation to top Canadian referee Sonia Denoncourt to take charge of top-level men's league matches in Brazil, one of the most testing soccer arenas in the world.

WOMEN'S WORLD CHAMPIONSHIP RESULTS

1991 CHINA

Semi-finals
| United States 5 | Germany 2 |
| Norway 4 | Sweden 1 |

Third place play-off
| Sweden 4 | Germany 0 |

Final: Nov 30 (Guangzhou)
United States 2 (Akers-Stahl 20 77)
Norway 1 (Medalen 28)
HT: 1–1. Att: 65,000. Ref: Zhuk (SU)
US: Harvey, Heinrichs, Higgins, Werden, Hamilton, Hamm, Akers-Stahl, Foudy, Jennings, Lilly, Biefeld.
NORWAY: Seth, Zaborowski, Espeseth, Nyborg, Carleen, Haugen, Store, Riise, Medalen, Hegstad, Svensson

1995 SWEDEN

Semi-finals
| Norway 1 | United States 0 |
| Germany 1 | China 0 |

Third place play-off
| United States 2 | China 0 |

Final: Jun 18 (Stockholm)
Norway 2 (Riise 37, Pettersen 41)
Germany 0
HT: 2–0. Att: 17,000. Ref: Jonsson (Swe)
NORWAY: Nordby, Svensson, Nymark, N Andersen, Espeseth, Myklebust, Riise, Haugen, A Andersen, Aarones, Medalen.
GERMANY: Goller, Bernhard, Austermühl, Lohn, Mohr, Neid, Wiegmann, Viss, Pohlmann (Wünderlich), Meinert (Smisek), Prinz (Brocker).

OLYMPIC GAMES RESULTS

1996 ATLANTA

Semi-finals
China 3	Brazil 2
United States 2	Norway 1
(after extra time)	

Bronze medal play-off
| Norway 2 | Brazil 0 |

Final: Aug 1 (Athens, Georgia)
United States 2 (MacMillan 18, Milbrett 68)
China 1 (Sun Wen 31)
HT: 1–1. Att: 76,481. Ref: Skovgang (Nor)
US: Scurry, Overbeck, Chastain, Fawcett, MacMillan, Foudy, Lilly, Venturini, Hamm (Gabarra 90), Akers, Milbrett (Roberts 71).
CHINA: Gao Hong, Fan Yunjie, Wang Liping (Yu Honggi 87), Xie Huilin, Zhao Lihong, Shui Qingxia, Liu Ailing, Sun Qingmei, Liu Ying, Sun Wen, Shi Guihong (Wei Haiying 70).

EUROPEAN YOUTH AND UNDER–21 CHAMPIONSHIPS

The International football federations have always considered a key function to be the development of football at junior levels, and this has seen the creation of a wide variety of age level competitions in all confederations and regions. The tournaments do not, generally, receive much publicity compared with the senior events, but their value is inestimable.

The veteran tournament is what is now the UEFA Youth Championship for under-18s, but which began life in 1948 as the European Youth Cup. In 1981, it was promoted in status to become a formal championship and many of the game's professional heroes gained their first taste of international success at this level.

By the mid-1960s, the need had become clear for a tournament which bridged the international competitive gap between the youth event and the senior World Cup and European Championship. So, in June 1967, UEFA launched the European Under-23 Challenge Cup. It was a modest enough concept. So few countries were interested that it was played on a challenge round basis – the holders played at home against another nation, drawn at random. Bulgaria were the first winners, defended successfully three times and were then beaten by Yugoslavia – who defended on three more occasions.

Clearly that was only a start. Many more nations expressed an interest and, in 1970, the first European Under-23 Championship was launched. The first tournament attracted 23 entries and took two years to complete. The format featured eight preliminary groups whose winners entered direct elimination quarter and semi-finals. Then, in the first final, Czechoslovakia beat the Soviet Union 2–2, 3–1 over two legs.

Among the youthful Czechoslovaks was a centre-forward in Zdenek Nehoda, who would captain their team at the 1982 World Cup finals in Spain. The scorer of two of the Soviets' three goals was a speedy left winger named Oleg Blokhin, who would go on to win more than 100 senior caps and become European Footballer of the Year.

The under-23 championship lasted four more years. In the 1974 final, Hungary beat the former East Germany – then a major power in age group international football – before the Soviets stormed back in 1976. At that point, UEFA took a new look at the event and decided the under-23 age limit was no longer realistic. Players were developing into senior internationals at a lower age and thus, from 1975 onwards, the tournament was converted into an under-21 championship.

UEFA also decided then, that the first round groups should fall into line with the draw for the European Championship and World Cup so the matches of seniors and juniors could be scheduled simultaneously and squads could travel together. This eased administration and financial pressures and further increased the popularity of the event which continued to produce star names.

It was in inspiring France to victory in the under–21 event, in 1988, that the youthful Eric Cantona first came to the notice of an international audience. No fewer than nine of the Italian and Spanish squads who contested the 1996 final were pressing for places in their countries' World Cup finals squads just two years later. Such successful graduates included Italians Fabio Cannavaro, Christian Panucci, Alessandro Nesta and Alessio Tacchinardi as well as Spain's Santi Denia, Ivan De la Pena, Jordi Lardin, Fernando Morientes and Raul Gonzalez.

The 'package' of such age group tournaments more than adequately filled the gap left by the hardly surprising failure of UEFA's short-lived amateur championship.

EUROPEAN UNDER-23 CHALLENGE CUP RESULTS

1967
Challenge round format
Bulgaria 3	**East Germany 2**
Bulgaria 6	**Finland 0**
Bulgaria2	**Czechoslovakia 1**

Winners: Bulgaria

1968
Challenge round format
Bulgaria 3	**Holland 1**
Yugoslavia 2	**Bulgaria 1**

1969
Challenge round format
Yugoslavia 3	**Spain 0**
Yugoslavia 2	**Sweden 0**

1970
Challenge round format
Yugoslavia 5	**Greece 1**

EUROPEAN UNDER-23 CHAMPIONSHIP RESULTS

1970–72
Semi-finals
Czechoslovakia bt Greece 2–0, 2–1
4–2 agg
Soviet Union bt Bulgaria 4–0, 3–3
7–3 agg

Final
Czechoslovakia bt Soviet Union 2–2, 3–1
5–3 agg

1972–74
Semi-finals
Hungary bt Soviet Union 0–2, 2–0
4–3 on pens, agg 2–2
East Germany bt Poland 0–0, 2–2
away goals, agg 2–2

Final
Hungary bt East Germany 2–3, 4–0
6–3 agg

1974–76
Semi-finals
Hungary bt Yugoslavia 3–2, 1–1
4–3 agg
Soviet Union bt Holland 3–0, 0–1
3–1 agg

Final
Sov Union bt Hungary 1–1, 2–1
3–2 agg

EUROPEAN UNDER-21 CHAMPIONSHIP RESULTS

1976–78
Semi-finals
E Germany bt Bulgaria 1–2, 3–1
4–3 agg
Yugoslavia bt England 2–1, 1–1
3–2 agg

Final
Yugoslavia bt East Germany 1–0, 4–4
5–4 agg

1978–80
Semi-finals
Soviet Union bt Yugoslavia 3–0, 1–0
4–0 agg
East Germany bt England 2–1, 1–0
3–1 agg

Final
Soviet Union bt East Germany 0–0, 1–0
1–0 agg

1980–82
Semi-finals
West Germany bt Soviet Union 4–3, 5–0
9–3 agg
England bt Scotland 1–0, 1–1
2–1 agg

Final
England bt West Germany 3–1, 2–3
5–4 agg

1982–84
Semi-finals
England bt Italy 3–0, 0–1
3–1 agg
Spain bt Yugoslavia 1–0, 2–0
3–0 agg

Final
England bt Spain 1–0, 2–0
3–0 agg

1984–86
Semi-finals
Italy bt England 2–0, 1–1
3–1 agg
Spain bt Hungary 1–3, 4–1
5–4 agg

Final
Spain bt Italy 1–2, 2–1
3–0 on pens, 3–3 agg

1986–88
Semi-finals

France bt England 4–2, 2–2
6–4 agg
Greece bt Holland 5–0, 0–2
5–2 agg

Final
France bt Greece 0–0, 3–0
3–0 agg

1988–90
Semi-finals
Yugoslavia bt Italy 0–0, 2–2
away goals, 2–2 agg
Soviet Union bt Sweden 1–1, 2–0
3–1 agg

Final
Soviet Union bt Yugoslavia 4–2, 3–1
7–3 agg

1990–92
Semi-finals
Italy bt Denmark 1–0, 2–0
3–0 agg
Sweden bt Scotland 0–0, 1–0
1–0 agg

Final
Italy bt Sweden 2–0, 0–1
2–1 agg

1994 FRANCE
Semi-finals
Italy 0	**France 0**
Italy 5–3 on pens	
Portugal 2	**Spain 0**

Third place play-off
Spain 2	**France 1**

Final: Apr 20 (Montpellier)
Italy 1 (Orlandini 98)
Portugal 0
HT: 0–0. 90min: 0–0. After extra time. Ref: Muhmenthaler (Swi)
ITALY: Toldo, Colonnese, Panucci, Cannavaro, Cherubini, Berretta, Scarchilli, Marcolin, Muzzi, Inzaghi (Orlandini 84), Carbone.
PORTUGAL: Brassard, Nelson, Jorge Costa, Paulo Torres, Rui Bento, Abel Xavier, Luis Figo, Nuno Capucho, Rui Costa, Joao Vieira Pinto, Toni (Sa Pinto 79).

1996 SPAIN
Semi-finals
Italy 1	**France 0**
Spain 2	**Scotland 1**

Third place play-off
France 1	**Scotland 0**

Final: May 31 (Barcelona)
Italy 1 (Idiakez og 37)
Spain 1 (Raul 42)
HT: 1–1. 90mins: 1–1. After extra time. Italy 4–2 on pens. Att: 35,000. Ref: Benko (Aut)
ITALY: Pagotto, Panucci, Cannavaro, Fresi, Galante (Pistone 59), Nesta, Ametrano, Brambilla, Tommasi (Tacchinardi 74), Amoruso, Totti (Morfeo 74).
SPAIN: Mora, Mendieta, Santi, Corino, Aranzabal, Roberto, De la Pena, Jose Ignacio (Oscar 46), Lardin (Morientes 49), Raul, Idiakez (De Pedro 46).

YOUTH (UNDER-18) CHAMPIONSHIP RESULTS

1948 ENGLAND
Semi-finals

Holland 2	Italy 1
England 3	Belgium 1

Third place play–off

Belgium 3	Italy 1

Final

England 3	Holland 2

1949 HOLLAND
Semi-finals

Holland 2	Northern Ireland 0
France 4	Belgium 0

Third place play-off

Belgium 5	Northern Ireland 0

Final

France 4	Holland 1

1950 AUSTRIA
Semi-finals

Austria 5	Luxembourg 1
France 4	Holland 1

Third place play-off

Holland 6	Luxembourg 0

Final

Austria 3	France 2

1951 FRANCE
Semi-finals

Austria 3	Belgium 1
Yugoslavia 2	Northern Ireland 1

Third place play-off

Belgium 1	Northern Ireland 0

Final

Yugoslavia 3	Austria 2

1952 SPAIN
Semi-finals

Spain 4	England 1
Austria 2	Belgium 2
toss of coin	

Third place play-off
not contested

Final

Spain 0	Belgium 0
Spain, on tournament goal average	

1953 BELGIUM
Semi-finals

Hungary 2	Turkey 0
Yugoslavia 3	Spain 1

Third place play-off

Turkey 3	Spain 2

Final

Hungary 2	Yugoslavia 0

1954 WEST GERMANY
Semi-finals

Spain 1	Argentina 0
West Germany 2	Turkey 1

Third place play-off

Argentina 1	Turkey 0

Final

Spain 2	West Germany 2
Spain, on toss of coin	

1955 ITALY
No finals tournament

1956 HUNGARY
No finals tournament

1957 SPAIN
Semi-finals

Spain 3	Italy 0
Austria 3	France 3

Third place play-off

Italy 0	France 0
shared	

Final

Austria 3	Spain 2

1958 LUXEMBOURG
Semi-finals

Italy 3	France 0
England 1	Romania 0

Third place play-off

France 3	Romania 0

Final

Italy 1	England 0

1959 BULGARIA
Semi-finals

Bulgaria 3	East Germany 0
Italy 1	Hungary 0

Third place play-off

Hungary 6	East Germany 1

Final

Bulgaria 1	Italy 0

1960 AUSTRIA
Semi-finals

Hungary 2	Portugal 1
Romania 4	Austria 1

Third place play-off

Portugal 2	Austria 1

Final

Hungary 2	Romania 1

1961 Portugal

Semi-finals

Portugal 4	Spain 1
Poland 2	West Germany 1

Third place play-off

W Germany 2	Spain 1

Final

Portugal 4	Poland 0

1962 ROMANIA
Semi-finals

Yugoslavia 6	Czech 2
Romania 4	Turkey 0

Third place play-off

Czechoslovakia 1	Turkey 1
Czechoslovakia, on toss of coin	

Final

Romania 4	Yugoslavia 1

1962–63 ENGLAND
Semi-finals

England 1	Scotland 0
Northern Ireland 3	Bulgaria 3
Northern Ireland, on toss of coin	

Third place play-off

Scotland 4	Bulgaria 2

Final

England 1	Northern Ireland 1

1964 HOLLAND
Semi-finals

Spain 3	Scotland 2
England 4	Portugal 0

Third place play–off

Portugal 3	Scotland 2
after extra time	

Final

England 4	Spain 0

1965 WEST GERMANY
Semi-finals

England 3	Italy 1
East Germany 2	Czechoslovakia 1

Third place play-off

Czechoslovakia 4	Italy 1

Final

East Germany 3	England 2

1966 YUGOSLAVIA

Semi-finals
Italy 1	Spain 0
Soviet Union 1	Yugoslavia 0

Third place play-off
Yugoslavia 2	Spain 0

Final
Italy 0	Soviet Union 0

title shared

1966–67 TURKEY

Semi-finals
Soviet Union 2	Turkey 1
England 2	France 0

Third place play-off
Turkey 1	France 1

Turkey, on toss of coin

Final
Soviet Union 1	England 0

1967–68 FRANCE

Semi-finals
Czechoslovakia 3	Portugal 1
France 3	Bulgaria 1

Third place play-off
Portugal 4	Bulgaria 2

Final
Czechoslovakia 2	France 1

1968–69 EAST GERMANY

Semi-finals
Bulgaria 3	Soviet Union 0
East Germany 2	Scotland 2

Third place play-off
Soviet Union 1	Scotland 0

Final
Bulgaria 1	East Germany 1

Bulgaria, on toss of coin after extra time

1969–70 SCOTLAND

Semi-finals
Holland 1	Scotland 0
East Germany 1	France 1

East Germany, on toss of coin

Third place play-off
Scotland 2	France 0

Final
East Germany 1	Holland 1

East Germany, on toss of coin after extra time

1970–71 CZECHOSLOVAKIA

Semi-finals
Portugal 2	East Germany 1
England 1	Soviet Union 1

England 4–2 on pens

Third place play-off
East Germany 1	Soviet Union 1

East Germany 5–3 on pens

Final
England 3	Portugal 3

1972 SPAIN

Semi-finals
England 1	Poland 0
West Germany 2	Spain 2

West Germany on pens

Third place play-off
Poland 0	Spain 0

Poland, on pens

Final
England 2	West Germany 0

1973 ITALY

Semi-finals
England 1	Italy 0
East Germany 1	Bulgaria 0

Third place play-off
Italy 1	Bulgaria 0

Final
England 3	East Germany 2

after extra time

1974 SWEDEN

Semi-finals
Bulgaria 2	Scotland 0
Yugoslavia 1	Greece 0

Third place play-off
Scotland 1	Greece 0

Final
Bulgaria 1	Yugoslavia 0

1975 SWITZERLAND

Semi-finals
Finland 1	Turkey 0
England 3	Hungary 1

Third place play-off
Hungary 2	Turkey 2

Hungary, on pens

Final
England 1	Finland 0

1976 HUNGARY

Semi-finals
Hungary 1	France 1

Hungary, on pens
Soviet Union 3	Spain 0

Third place play-off
Spain 3	France 0

Final
Soviet Union 1	Hungary 0

1977 BELGIUM

Semi-finals
Belgium 1	Soviet Union 1

Belgium, 4–2 on pens
Bulgaria 2	West Germany 1

Third place play-off
Soviet Union 7	West Germany 2

Final
Belgium 2	Bulgaria 1

1978 POLAND

Semi-finals
Yugoslavia 2	Scotland 2

Yugoslavia, on pens
Soviet Union 2	Poland 0

Third place play-off
Poland 3	Scotland 1

Final
Soviet Union 3	Yugoslavia 0

1979 AUSTRIA

Semi-finals
Yugoslavia 3	France 0
Bulgaria 1	England 0

Third place play-off
England 0	France 0

England 4–2 on pens

Final
Yugoslavia 1	Bulgaria 0

1980 EAST GERMANY

Semi-finals
Poland 2	Italy 0
England 1	Holland 0

Third place play-off
Italy 3	Holland 0

Final
England 2	Poland 1

1981 WEST GERMANY

Semi-finals
West Germany 1	France 1

West Germany 4–3 on pens
Poland 4	Spain 4

Poland 6–5 on pens

Third place play-off
France 1	Spain 1

France 2–0 on pens

Final
West Germany 1	Poland 0

1982 FINLAND

Semi-finals
Czechoslovakia 1	Soviet Union 0
Scotland 2	Poland 0

Third place play-off
Soviet Union 3	Poland 1

Final
Scotland 3	Czechoslovakia 1

1983 ENGLAND

Semi-finals
Czechoslovakia 1	England 1

Czechoslovakia 4–2 on pens
France 1	Italy 0

Third place play-off
England 1	Italy 1

England, 4–2 on pens

Final
France 1	Czechoslovakia 0

1984 SOVIET UNION

Semi-finals

Hungary 2	Poland 0
Soviet Union 2	Republic of Ireland 1

Third place play-off

Poland 2	Republic of Ireland 1

Final

Hungary 0	Soviet Union 0

Hungary 3–2 on pens

1984–86 YUGOSLAVIA

Semi-finals

East Germany 1	West Germany 0
Italy 1	Scotland 0

Third place play-off

West Germany 1	Scotland 0

Final

East Germany 3	Italy 1

1986–88 CZECHOSLOVAKIA

Semi-finals

Portugal 2	Spain 0
Soviet Union 3	East Germany 3

Third place play-off

East Germany 2	Spain 0

Final

Soviet Union 3	Portugal 3

after extra time

1988–90 HUNGARY

Semi-finals

Soviet Union 3	England 1
Portugal 2	Spain 1

Third place play-off

Spain 1	England 0

Final

Soviet Union 0	Portugal 0

Soviet Union, 4–2 on pens

1990–92 GERMANY

Semi-finals

Portugal 1	England 1

Portugal, 12–11 on pens

Turkey 2	Norway 1

Third place play-off

Norway 1	England 1

Norway, 8–7 on pens

Final

Turkey 2	Portugal 1

Golden Goal

1992–93 ENGLAND

Third place play-off

Spain 2	Portugal 1

Final

England 1	Turkey 0

1993–94 SPAIN

Third place play-off

Spain 5	Holland 2

Final

Portugal 1	Germany 1

Portugal, 5–2 on pens

1994–95 GREECE

Third place play-off

Greece 5	Holland 0

Final

Spain 4	Italy 1

1996 FRANCE

Third place play-off

England 3	Belgium 2

Golden Goal

Final

France 1	Spain 0

1997 ICELAND

Third place play-off

Spain 2	Republic of Ireland 1

Final

France 1	Portugal 0

Golden Goal

EUROPEAN YOUTH (UNDER-16) CHAMPIONSHIP RESULTS

1980–82 ITALY

Semi-finals

Italy 1	Finland 1

Italy, 4–2 on pens

West Germany 2	Yugoslavia 1

Third place play-off

Yugoslavia 0	Finland 0

Yugoslavia, 4–2 on pens

Final

Italy 1	West Germany 0

1982–84 WEST GERMANY

Semi-finals

West Germany 5	Yugoslavia 1
Soviet Union 2	England 0

Third place play-off

England 1	Yugoslavia 0

Final

West Germany 2	Soviet Union 0

1985 HUNGARY

Semi-finals

Spain 0	Greece 0

Spain, 4–3 on pens

Soviet Union 5	East Germany 3

Third place play-off

Spain 1	East Germany 0

Final

Soviet Union 4	Greece 0

1986 GREECE

Semi-finals

Italy 2	East Germany 2

Italy, 4–2 on pens

Spain 2	Soviet Union 1

Third place play-off

Soviet Union 1	East Germany 1

Soviet Union, 8–7 on pens

Final

Spain 2	Italy 1

1987 FRANCE

Semi-finals

Italy* 1	Turkey 0
Soviet Union 0	France 0

Soviet Union, 3–0 on pens

Third place play-off

France 3	Turkey 3

Final

Italy* 1	Soviet Union 0

*Italy were stripped of the title after it was discovered they had fielded an over-age player in the semi-final and final. Title declared vacant.

1988 SPAIN

Semi-finals

Spain 3	West Germany 0
Portugal 4	East Germany 0

Third place play-off

East Germany 0	West Germany 0

East Germany, 5–4 on pens

Final

Spain 0	Portugal 0

Spain, 4–2 on pens

1989 DENMARK

Semi-finals

Portugal 2	Spain 1
East Germany 3	France 0

Third place play-off

France 3	Spain 2

Final

Portugal 4	East Germany 1

1990 EAST GERMANY

Semi-finals
Yugoslavia 4	**Poland 1**
Czechoslovakia 0	**Portugal 0**

Czechoslovakia, 5–3 on pens

Third place play-off
Poland 3	**Portugal 2**

Final
Czechoslovakia 3	**Yugoslavia 2**

after extra time

1991 SWITZERLAND

Semi-finals
Spain 1	**Greece 0**
Germany 1	**France 1**

Germany, 5–4 on pens

Third place play-off
Greece 1	**France 1**

Greece, 5–4 on pens

Final
Spain 2	**Germany 0**

1992 CYPRUS

Semi-finals
Germany 0	**Italy 0**

Germany, 6–5 on pens
Spain 3	**Portugal 1**

Third place play-off
Italy 1	**Portugal 0**

Final
Germany 2	**Spain 1**

1993 TURKEY

Semi-finals
Italy 0	**Czech Republic 0**

Italy, 5–4 on pens
Poland 2	**France 1**

Third place play-off
Czech Republic 2	**France 1**

Final
Poland 1	**Italy 0**

1994 REPUBLIC OF IRELAND

Semi-finals
Denmark 2	**Ukraine 2**

Denmark, 7–6 on pens
Turkey 1	**Austria 0**

Third place play-off
Ukraine 2 Austria 0	

Final
Turkey 1	**Denmark 0**

1995 BELGIUM

Semi-finals
Spain 2	**France 0**
Portugal 3	**Germany 1**

Third place play-off
Germany 2	**France 1**

Golden Goal

Final
Portugal 2	**Spain 0**

1996 AUSTRIA

Semi-finals
Portugal 3	**Greece 0**
France 1	**Israel 0**

Third place play-off
Israel 3	**Greece 2**

Final
Portugal 1	**France 0**

1997 GERMANY

Semi-finals
Spain 2	**Germany 1**
Austria 0	**Switzerland 0**

Austria, 6–5 on pens

Third place play-off
Germany 3	**Switzerland 1**

Final
Spain 0	**Austria 0**

Spain, 5–4 on pens

UEFA AMATEUR CHAMPIONSHIP

1966–77 SPAIN

Semi-finals
Austria 1	**Turkey 0**

after extra time
Scotland 3	**Spain 1**

after extra time

Final
Austria 2	**Scotland 1**

1969–70 ITALY

Semi-finals
Spain 6	**Italy 0**
Holland 4	**Yugoslavia 0**

Third place play-off
Yugoslavia 3	**Italy 0**

Final
Spain 2	**Holland 1**

in replay after 1–1 draw

1973–74 YUGOSLAVIA

Semi-finals
West Germany 1	**Holland 1**

West Germany, 4–2 on pens
Yugoslavia 2	**Spain 1**

after extra time

Third place play-off
Spain 2	**Holland 2**

Spain, 5–3 on pens

Final
West Germany vs. Yugoslavia
shared title (match cancelled, waterlogged pitch)

1977–78 GREECE

Semi-finals
Greece 2	**Republic of Ireland 0**
Yugoslavia 0	**West Germany 0**

Yugoslavia, 3–1 on pens

Third place play-off
West Germany 3	**Republic of Ireland 0**

Final
Yugoslavia 2	**Greece 1**

after extra time

Chapter 3

INTERNATIONAL CLUB

COMPETITIONS

WORLD CLUB CUP

The World Club Cup represents "world" football as it used to be considered by the patronising conversatives of Europe and South America. That is, it is a challenge match for the right to the global title but contested between "only" the champion clubs of Europe and South America.

FIFA is expected to bring forward proposals for a world club championship which will include Africa, Asian, Central and North America and Oceania but that may have to wait.

In the meantime the World Club Cup continues as the only regular contest of that category. It is also known as the Intercontinental Club Cup or the Europe/South America Cup.

Henri Delaunay, UEFA general secretary in the mid-1950s, first suggested the idea of a challenge match between the champions of Europe and South America in a letter to CONMEBOL, the South American Confederation. His idea provided the impetus for the South Americans to set up the Copa Libertadores (the South American Club Cup) in imitation of the hugely-successful European Champion Clubs Cup.

Between the first final in 1960 and 1980, ties in the World Club Cup were played on a home and away basis, and up until 1968 the result was decided by points, not the aggregate score. This meant that if the clubs won one match each or both were drawn, a decider had to be played. Until 1964 this decider had, for pragmatic reasons of logistics, to take place in the stadium of the team who played at home in the second leg, giving them a massive advantage. Then for another four years the decider at least had to be played on that club's continent.

Despite these tortuous rules, the competition got off to a flying start in 1960, when Real Madrid met Penarol of Uruguay. Madrid had just won their fifth European Cup in a row, with a 7–3 demolition of Eintracht Frankfurt, while Penarol had become the first winners of the Copa Libertadores.

The first leg took place on a quagmire of a pitch in Montevideo's Centenario stadium before a soaking wet 80,000 crowd. It was appropriate that the venue which had seen the first World Cup Final back in 1930 should see the launch of the club world's equivalent.

Penarol might have had two penalties early on, once when Carlo Borges was "taken out" by Madrid skipper Jose Maria Zarraga, then when Marquitos appeared to trip Juan Eduardo Hohberg. But referee Praudade of Argentina was unmoved by the roar of the crowd. Goalkeepers Luis Maidana of Penarol and Rogelio Dominguez of Madrid excelled themselves in keeping clean sheets. As tension increased towards the end so the referee had to sort out a touchline slanging match between coaches Miguel Munoz of Madrid and Hector Scarone of Penarol.

The return, before 125,000 in Madrid, witnessed a massacre. Madrid's great Hungarian, Ferenc Puskas, scored three goals in the first nine minutes and right winger Chus Herrera grabbed a fourth just before half-time. Francisco Gento made it five in the 52nd minute and a Penarol side sadly missing injured midfield anchor Nestor Goncalves gained only a 71st-minute consolation by Borges.

A year later it was Penarol's turn to chalk up five goals but not until after the emerging Portuguese eagles, Benfica, had given them a testing time of it. A solitary goal from Mario Coluna handed Benfica victory in the first leg in Lisbon but – missing key central defender Germano – they crashed 5–0 to Penarol back in Montevideo. Today's regulations would have seen Penarol declared winners on aggregate but in those days its was points which counted. Each team had won their home leg and thus a decider was necessary, again in Montevideo.

Benfica, in desperation, flew out their new sensation Eusebio for the play-off. But though he scored with a typucal 30-yard scorcher in the 11th minute, Pepe Sasia replied with a double – the first a penalty – to turn Penarol into Uruguay's first world club champions.

Pele's triumph

Benfica represented Europe again in 1962, but this time they ran headlong into Brazil's Santos... and Pele. Santos were everyone's unofficial world champions long before the occasion itself. The first leg was played in Rio's 200,000-capacity Maracana stadium and while the great man scored twice for Santos, Benfica hit back bravely through the Angolan Santana, to go down only 3–2.

That gave their players, officials and fans a false sense of optimism for the return. Pele rose to new heights, added a further three goals to the two he had grabbed in Rio and helped lay on two others for Coutinho and the cannonball-shot left winger Pepe. This time even Eusebio was powerless.

Santos, in 1963, became one of only four sides to retain the trophy when they beat Milan but the tie provided a nasty taste of things to come. The Brazilians flew to Italy for the first leg without centre-back and 1962 World Cup-winning skipper Mauro and suffered badly in attack where Pele was brilliantly policed by Giovanni Trapattoni. Even so, he managed to score both Santos' goals in a 4–2 defeat. Amarildo, Brazil's World Cup-winning deputy for injured Pele in the 1962 World Cup Final, scored twice for Milan.

Back in Rio, though Santos had Mauro back, both midfield dynamo Zito and Pele were out injured. It looked all over after 16 minutes when Milan led 2–0 with goals from another Brazilian,

Jose Altafini, and Bruno Mora. But Santos fought back in the second half. Pepe smashed home two free kicks and the Brazilians won 4–2 to set up a play-off back in the Maracana.

This was the time and place when the World Club Cup turned ugly. The 165,000 crowd jeered Milan from the outset. Both sides became frustrated at the lack of openings and tempers soon frayed. The Italians argued ceaselessly with referee Juan Brozzi of Argentina (later struck off the FIFA list).

In the 34th minute Milan sweeper and skipper Cesare Maldini flattened Almir, Pele's deputy, and was sent off. Dalmo converted the penalty for the only goal.

That was not all. Just before half-time Almir kicked goalkeeper Balzarini and the Italian was carried off to have three stitches in his head and three in his hand. Three minutes later Santos defender Ismael attacked Amarildo and was sent to join Maldini.

The next two competitions were contested by Internazionale of Italy and Independiente of Argentina, with Inter winning on both occasions. Both ties were "Anti-Matches" because both clubs were, in their respective continents, leading a ruthless, defensive revolution.

In 1964 the first leg was played in Avellaneda and Independiente, despite being reduced to ten men by injury to fullback Tomas Rolan, won with a lucky goal in the 57th minute. Mario Rodriguez was the scorer – his tame shot creeping over the goal-line after a rare slip by Giuliano Sarti. Back in Milan Inter turned the tie around with first-half goals from Sandro Mazzola and Mario Corso. A further goal by Corso, with 10 minutes remaining in extra-time in the play-off in Madrid, handed Inter the crown.

They found it easier the following year. This time the first leg was in Milan where Inter, through Spaniard Joaquin Peiro and Mazzola (two) found Independiente far less resistant than a year earlier. Back in Avellaneda the Argentines threw everything at Inter… including stones, bottles and sticks. Inter coach Helenio Herrera suffered a head injury from one such missile. Out on the pitch Independiente hit posts and bar several times but, with Sarti making amends for his blunder of the previous year, Inter retained the crown.

In 1966 Penarol returned to win for the third time, beating Real Madrid 2–0 in both legs, with Ecuadorian Pedro Spencer scoring three of the Uruguayans' goals.

But, after this generally encouraging start, the World Club Cup ran into severe problems in the late 1960s and early 1970s, mainly due to different styles of play and behaviour.

The 1967 series paired Argentina's Racing Club with Scotland's Celtic. Feelings in Argentina were still running high over their 1966 World Cup quarter-final elimination by England, and the matches degenerated into bad-tempered farce. After a 1–0 Celtic win in Glasgow, the return in Buenos Aires was chaotic.

Celtic goalkeeper Ronnie Simpson was struck by a missile from the crowd before the kick-off and had to be replaced by John Fallan. Tommy Gemmell dared to put Celtic ahead from a 22nd-minute penalty after goalkeeper Mario Cejas had brought down Jimmy Johnstone. But Rafo equalized and Cardenas snatched a second for Racing just after the interval, setting up a Montevideo play-off which was doomed before it began.

Cardenas scored the only goal after 56 minutes, but that was a rare moment of football during a sad 90 minutes in which the players appeared more concerned with settling the scores which had built up over the previous two games. Paraguayan referee Rodolfo Osorio ordered six players off including Celtic's Johnstone, Bobby Lennox, John Hughes and Bertie Auld – though Auld ignored the order and, since the game was almost over, the referee overlooked the fact that he stayed on the pitch.

Pitched battles

It was extremely unfortunate, therefore, that the next team to represent South America – for three years running – was the ruthless Estudiantes de La Plata of Argentina.

When they faced Manchester United in 1968 animosity from the previous year still hung in the Argentine air. The fine difference that Celtic were Scottish and United English was lost on the media and fans in general. Estudiantes, coached in all the tricks of the game by Osvaldo Zubeldia, were the most infamously unpleasant side to emerge from South America.

United held their tempers remarkably but lost the first leg to a goal headed in by Conigliaro.

Referee Sosa Miranda disallowed a 38th-minute "goal" by United's David Sadler then sent off Nobby Stiles ten minutes from time for a gesture to a linesman who had wrongly flagged him offside. Stiles had already played most of the game with a gash over his left eye after being butted by Carlos Bilardo, while Bobby Charlton needed three stitches in a leg wound after being "raked" by Carlos Pachame. The return at Old Trafford was a poor game. A goal inside five minutes from Juan Veron knocked the wind out of United's sails. They equalized eventually through Willie Morgan but there were more expulsions – for George Best and defender Medina after a scuffle.

Under the competition's revised rules, the Argentine clubs claimed a 2–1 aggregate win. The violence was so bad that FIFA president Sir Stanley Rous was prompted to write a letter of complaint to the Estudiantes hierarchy.

The following year, 1969, Milan came off even worse than United. After winning 3–0 at home with two goals from Brazilian Angelo Sormani and one from Franco-Argentine Nestor Combin, Milan were savaged in South America.

Combin had a terrible time. Aguirre Suarez, one of Estudiantes' noted hatchet men against United, broke Combin's nose with a blow of the elbow – and later Combin was threatened with imprisonment for not having undertaken his statutory

Argentine national service.

Among other vicious incidents on the pitch Poletti, the Argentine goalkeeper, committed an awful foul on Milan winger Pierino Prati, kicking him in the back as he lay injured awaiting treatment. Argentine state President Ongania was so embarrassed by the violence of his own men that he had Aguirre Suarez, Poletti and Manera all held in jail overnight after the match. Poletti was later banned for life but Aguirre Suarez enjoyed a successful extension of his career in Spain.

Again goal aggregate was decisive. So although goals from Suarez and Conigiliaro brought Estudiantes a second-leg victory, Milan were spared the ferocity of a play-off by virtue of a 4–2 overall success.

Sadly, Estudiantes did not learn their lesson, and things were as bad in 1970 when they played Feyenoord, who came out on top after drawing the drawing the first leg in Buenos Aires. In the return in Rotterdam, Feyenoord's bespectacled Van Daele had his glasses smashed early in the game but still scored the winner.

Feyenoord made it known that they would not have taken part in a decider if it had been needed, and the following year their countrymen, Ajax, went a step further by refusing to play against Nacional of Uruguay. Panathinaikos, beaten finalists in the European Cup, were appointed by UEFA to replace Ajax, and put up a brave performance before losing 3–2 on aggregate.

After such violent clashes, the value of the competition came into question, and it looked as if the World Club Cup would fade into history. Ajax did restore some credibility with a fine 4–1 aggregate win over Independiente in 1972, despite some rough treatment for Johan Cruyff, but the trend they started the year before continued throughout the 1970s.

European boycott

Rather than risk their valuable players being mangled by the South Americans, Ajax, Liverpool, Bayern Munich and Nottingham Forest refused to take part, reducing the competition to a sideshow. On all bar two occasions, 1975 and 1978 (when the competition was not held), the beaten European Cup finalists substituted for the real champions – Atletico Madrid even managing a victory in 1974 against Independiente, who were making the fourth of their six appearances in the event.

Clearly this situation could not continue and it was Japan who came to the rescue. In 1980 the format of the World Club Cup was changed. The two-legged tie was replaced by a single game at the National Stadium in Tokyo with the motor car manufacturer Toyota as sponsor.

In the succeeding years the tournament regained much of its credibility with the European club champions consistently taking part every time. The South Americans won the first five matches

played in Tokyo with Flamengo outstanding in a Zico-inspired 3–0 win over Liverpool in 1981. Europe enjoyed more success in the second half of the decade. Victories for Juventus, FC Porto and Milan (twice) were interspersed with wins for River Plate of Argentina and Nacional of Uruguay.

In 1991 Red Star Belgrade became the first Eastern European side to win when they beat Chile's Colo Colo 3–0. In the meantime, Barcelona and Milan (twice), however highly-rated in Europe, were successively dismissed by Sao Paulo (twice) and Argentina's Velez Sarsfield. While European commentators called Milan the world's best, their duel with Sao Paulo suggested otherwise. The Brazilians were coached by ex-World Cup boss Tele Santana and well-balanced through the experience of veterans Toninho Cerezo and Muller and new heroes Rai, Cafu and Juninho.

It was not until 1995 that Europe regained the trophy. First Ajax needed a penalty shoot-out to defeat Gremio from Brazil. Then Juventus took over with a win over River Plate.

In 1997, Borussia Dortmund maintained European hegemony by seeing off the challenge of Brazil's Cruzeiro by 2–0. One goal in each half from skipper Michael Zorc and Heiko Herrlich brought Germany their first world club crown since Bayern Munich defeated those same South American champions 21 years earlier in the old two-match, home-and-away format.

Bending the rules

Cruzeiro made no friends with the way they had set about pursuing the rewards in both cash and prestige which are available to the world club champions. Shamelessly, they borrowed three players – including 1994 World Cup-winning hero Bebeto – just for Tokyo. Another loan target, international striker Palhinha who played for Spain's Mallorca, refused to join Cruzeiro's dirty tricks brigade. "What – go back to Brazil to play a match in Tokyo?" he said. "I don't think Mallorca's fans would be too happy."

Bebeto, fellow Brazil striker Donizete and defender Goncalves did, however, join the South American champions for a three-week stint which ended immediately after the final. Bebeto and Donizete formed Cruzeiro's temporary new attack while Goncalves took command of the centre of defence. Cruzeiro thus capitalized ruthlessly on the advanced play-off stage of the Brazilian national championship. 18 of the 26 original clubs had been eliminated – including not only Cruzeiro but Bebeto's Vitoria, Donizete's Corinthians, Goncalves' Botafogo… which is why the players were available. They were allowed to get away with it because no authority has executive control over the World Club Cup. It is organized by the Japanese federation with the cooperation of the European and South American governing bodies, UEFA and CONMEBOL. As UEFA spokesman Frits

Ahlstrom said: "We have no jurisdiction over the South American team. They have to prepare as they think fit."

Ironically it was a Brazilian, Julio Cesar, who took perhaps the most significant role in seeing that justice was done as he effectively marked Bebeto out of the game. Dortmund's Michael Zorc opened the scoring after 34 minutes when he fired home

a cross from Stephane Chapuisat. Cruzeiro's efforts in search of an equalizer subsided early in the second half when right-back Victor was sent off. Dortmund duly took advantage by claiming a second goal through midfielder Heiko Herrlich.

But how much longer the Tokyo party will last is open to question.

Kenny Dalglish of Liverpool in the 1984 World Club Cup. Their opponents were Independiente from Argentina

WORLD CLUB CUP RESULTS

1960

1ST LEG

July 3 (Centenario, Montevideo)
Penarol 0
Real Madrid 0
Att: 75,000. Ref: Prauddade (Arg)
PENAROL: Maidana, Martinez, Aguirre, Pino, Salvador, Goncalves, Cubilla, Linazza, Hohberg, Spencer, Borges.
MADRID: Dominguez, Marquitos, Pachin, Vidal, Santamaria, Zarraga, Canario, Del Sol, Di Stefano, Puskas, Gento.

2ND LEG

(Santiago Bernabeu, Madrid)
Real Madrid 5 (Puskas 3 9, Di Stefano 4, Herrera 44, Gento 54)
Penarol 1(Borges 69)
HT: 4–0. Att: 125,000. Ref: Aston (Eng)
MADRID: Dominguez, Marquitos, Pachin, Vidal, Santamaria, Zarraga, Herrera, Del Sol, Di Stefano, Puskas, Gento.
PENAROL: Maidana, Martinez, Aguirre, Pino, Mayewski, Salvador, Cubilla, Linazza, Hohberg, Spencer, Borges.
Winners: Real Madrid

1961

1ST LEG

Sep 17 (Lisbon)
Benfica 1 (Coluna 60)
Penarol 0
HT: 0–0. Att: 50,000. Ref: Ebert (Swi)
BENFICA: Costa Pereira, Angelo, Saraiva, Mario Joao, Neto, Cruz, Jose Augusto, Santana, Aguas, Coluna, Cavem.
PENAROL: Maidana, Gonzalez, Martinez, Aguerre, Cano, Goncalves, Ledesma, Spencer, Cubilla, Cabrera, Sasia.

2ND LEG

Sep 17 (Centenario, Montevideo)
Penarol 5 (Sasia 10, Joya 18 28, Spencer 42 60)
Benfica 0
HT: 4–0. Att: 56,000. Ref: Nalfoino (Arg)
PENAROL: Maidana, Gonzalez, Martinez, Cano, Aguerre, Goncalves, Ledesma, Cubilla, Sasia, Spencer, Joya.
BENFICA: Costa Pereira, Angelo, Saraiva, Mario Joao, Neto, Cruz, Jose Augusto, Santana, Mendes, Coluna, Cavem.

PLAY-OFF

Sep 19 (Centenario, Montevideo)
Penarol 2 (Sasia 6 41)
Benfica 1 (Eusebio 35)
HT: 2–1. Att: 62,000. Ref: Praddaude (Arg)
PENAROL: Maidana, Gonzalez, Martinez, Aguerre, Cano, Goncalves, Cabrera, Cubilla, Ledesma, Sasia, Spencer.
BENFICA: Costa Pereira, Angelo, Humberto, Cruz, Neto, Coluna, Augusto, Eusebio, Aguas, Cavem, Simoes.
Winners: Penarol

1962

1ST LEG

Sep 19 (Maracana, Rio de Janeiro)
Santos 3 (Pele 31 86, Coutinho 64)
Benfica 2 (Santana 58 87)
HT: 1–0. Att: 90,000. Ref: Ramirez (Par)
SANTOS: Gilmar, Lima, Mauro, Calvet, Dalmo, Zito, Mengalvio, Dorval, Coutinho, Pele, Pepe.
BENFICA: Costa Pereira, Jacinto, Raul, Humberto, Cruz, Cavem, Coluna, Jose Augusto, Santana, Eusebio, Simoes.

2ND LEG

Oct 11 (Estadio da Luz, Lisbon)
Benfica 2 (Eusebio 87, Santana 89)
Santos 5 (Pele 17 28 64, Coutinho 49, Pepe 77)
HT: 0–2. Att: 75,000. Ref: Schwinte (Fra)
BENFICA: Costa Pereira, Jacinto, Raul, Humberto, Cruz, Cavem, Coluna. Jose Augusto, Santana, Eusebio, Simoes.
SANTOS: Gilmar, Olavo, Mauro, Calvet, Dalmo, Lima, Zito, Dorval, Coutinho, Pele, Pepe.
Winners: Santos

1963

1ST LEG

Oct 16 (San Siro, Milan)
Milan 4 (Trapattoni 4, Amarildo 15 65, Mora 80)
Santos 2 (Pele 59 87)
HT: 2–0. Att: 80,000. Ref: Haberfellner (Aut)
MILAN: Ghezzi, David, Maldini, Trapattoni, Trebbi, Pelagalli, Lodetti, Rivera, Mora, Altafini, Amarildo.
SANTOS: Gilmar, Lima, Haroldo, Calvet, Geraldino, Zito, Mengalvio, Dorval, Coutinho, Pele, Pepe.

2ND LEG

Nov 14 (Maracana, Rio de Janeiro)
Santos 4 (Pepe 50 67, Almir 60, Lima 63)
Milan 2 (Altafini 12, Mora 17)
HT: 0–2. Att: 150,000. Ref: Brozzi (Arg)
SANTOS: Gilmar, Ismael, Dalmo, Mauro, Haroldo, Lima, Mengalvio, Dorval, Coutinho, Pele, Pepe.
MILAN: Ghezzi, David, Maldini, Trapattoni, Trebbi, Pelagalli, Lodetti, Rivera, Mora, Altafini, Amarildo.

PLAY-OFF

Nov 16 (Maracana, Rio de Janeiro)
Santos 1 (Dalmo 26)
Milan 0
HT: 1–0. Att: 121,000. Ref: Brozzi (Arg)
SANTOS: Gilmar, Ismael, Dalmo, Mauro, Haroldo, Lima, Mengalvio, Dorval, Coutinho, Almir, Pepe.
MILAN: Balzarini (Barluzzi), Pelagalli, Maldini, Trebbi, Benitez, Lodetti, Trapattoni, Mora, Altafini, Amarildo, Fortunato.
Winners: Santos

1964

1ST LEG

Sep 9 (Cordero, Avellaneda)
Independiente 1 (Rodriguez 60)
Internazionale 0
HT: 0–0. Att: 70,000. Ref: Marques (Bra)
INDEPENDIENTE: Santoro, Ferreiro, Guzman, Maldonado, Rolan, Acevedo, Mura, Bernao, Prospitti, Rodriguez, Savoy.
INTERNAZIONALE: Sarti, Burgnich, Guarneri, Picchi, Facchetti, Tagnin, Suarez, Corso, Jair, Mazzola, Peiro.

2ND LEG

Sep 23 (San Siro, Milan)
Internazionale 2 (Mazzola 8, Corso 39)
Independiente 0
HT: 2–0. Att: 70,000. Ref: Gere (Hun)
INTER: Sarti, Burgnich, Guarneri, Picchi, Facchetti, Malatrasi, Suarez, Corso, Jair, Mazzola, Milani.
INDEPENDIENTE: Santoro, Ferreiro, Paflik, Maldonaldo, Decaria, Acevedo, Prospitti, Suarez, Mura, Rodriguez, Savoy.

PLAY-OFF

Sep 26 (Santiago Bernabeu, Madrid, Spain)
Internazionale 1 (Corso 120)
Independiente 0
HT: 0–0. 90min: 0–0. Aftra extra time. Att: 45,000. Ref: De Mendibil (Spa)
INTERNAZIONALE: Sarti, Malatrasi, Guarneri, Picchi, Facchetti, Tagnin, Suarez, Corso, Domenghini, Perio, Milani.
INDEPENDIENTE: Santoro, Guzman, Paflik, Decaria, Maldonaldo, Acevedo, Prospitti, Suarez, Bernao, Rodriguez, Savoy.
Winners: Internazionale

1965

1ST LEG

Sep 8 (San Siro, Milan)
Internazionale 3 (Peiro 3, Mazzola 23 61)
Independiente 0
HT: 2–0. Att: 70,000. Ref: Kreitlein (WG)
INTERNAZIONALE: Sarti, Burnich, Guarneri, Picchi, Facchetti, Bedin, Suarez, Corso, Jair, Mazzola, Peiro.
INDEPENDIENTE: Santoro, Pavoni, Guzman, Navarro, Ferreiro, Acevedo, De la Mata, Avallay, Bernao, Rodriguez, Savoy.

2ND LEG

Sep 15 (Cordero, Avellanada)
Independiente 0
Internazionale 0
HT: 0–0. Att: 70,000. Ref: Yamasaki (Per)
INDEPENDIENTE: Santoro, Navarro, Pavoni, Guzman, Ferreiro, Rolan, Mori, Bernao, Mura, Avallay, Savoy.
INTERNAZIONALE: Sarti, Burgnich, Guarneri, Picchi, Facchetti, Bedin, Suarez, Corso, Jair, Mazzola, Peiro.
Winners: Internazionale

1966

1ST LEG

Oct 12 (Centenario, Montevideo)
Penarol 2 (Spencer 39 82)
Real Madrid 0
HT: 1–0. Att: 70,000. Ref: Vicuna (Chl)
PENAROL: Mazurkiewicz, Forlan, Lezcano, Varela, Gonzalez, Goncalves, Cortes, Rocha, Abbadie, Spencer, Joya.
REAL MADRID: Betancort, Pachin, De Felipe, Zoco, Sanchis, Felix Ruiz, Pirri, Velasquez, Serena, Amancio, Bueno.

2ND LEG

Oct 26 (Santiago Bernabeu, Madrid)
Real Madrid 0
Penarol 2 (Rocha 28, Spencer 37)
HT: 0–2. Att: 70,000. Ref: Lo Bello (Ita)
REAL MADRID: Betancort, Calpe, De Felipe, Zoco, Sanchis, Pirri, Grosso, Velasquez, Serena, Amancio, Gento.
PENAROL: Mazurkiewicz, Gonzalez, Lezcano, Varela, Caetano, Rocha, Goncalves, Cortes, Abbadie, Spencer, Joya.
Winners: Penarol

1967

1ST LEG

Oct 18 (Hampden Park, Glasgow)
Celtic 1 (McNeill 67)
Racing Club 0
HT: 0–0. Att: 103,000. Ref: Gardeazabal (Spa)
CELTIC: Simpson, Craig, McNeill, Gemmell, Murdoch, Clark, Johnstone, Lennox, Wallace, Auld, Hughes.
RACING CLUB: Cejas, Martin, Perfumo, Basile, Diaz, Rulli, Mori, Maschio, Cardenas, Rodriguez, Raffo.

2ND LEG

Nov 1 (Mozart y Cuyo, Avellanada)
Racing Club 2 (Raffo 32, Cardenas 48)
Celtic 1 (Gemmell 20)
HT: 1–1. Att: 80,000. Ref: Esteban (Spa)
RACING CLUB: Cejas, Perfumo, Chabay, Basile, Martin, Rulli, Maschio, Raffo, Cardoso, Cardenas, Rodriguez.
CELTIC: Fallon, Craig, Clark, McNeill, Gemmell, Murdoch, ONeill, Johnstone, Wallace, Chalmers, Lennox.

PLAY-OFF

Nov 4 (Centenario, Montevideo)
Racing Club 1 (Cardenas 55)
Celtic 0
HT: 0–0. Att: 65,000. Ref: Osario (Par)
RACING CLUB: Cejas, Perfumo, Chabay, Martin, Basile, Rulli, Maschio, Raffo, Cardoso, Cardenas, Rodriguez.
CELTIC: Fallon, Craig, Clark, McNeill, Gemmell, Murdoch, Auld, Johnstone, Lennox, Wallace, Hughes.
Winners: Racing Club

1968

1ST LEG

Sep 25 (Bombonera, Buenos Aires)
Estudiantes de La Plata 1 (Conigliaro 28)
Manchester United 0
HT: 1–0. Att: 65,000. Ref: Miranda (Par)
ESTUDIANTES: Poletti, Suarez, Medina, Malbernat, Pachame, Madero, Ribaudo, Bilardo, Conigliaro, Togneri, Veron.
MANCHESTER UNITED: Stepney, Dunne, Foulkes, Sadler, Burns, Crerand, Stiles, Charlton, Morgan, Law.

2ND LEG

Oct 16 (Old Trafford, Manchester)
Manchester United 1 (Morgan 8)
Estudiantes de La Plata 1 (Veron 5)
HT: 1–1. Att: 60,000. Ref: Machin (Fra)
MANCHESTER UNITED: Stepney, Dunne, Foulkes, Brennan, Sadler, Crerand, Charlton, Morgan, Kidd, Law (Sartori), Best.
ESTUDIANTES: Poletti, Malbernat, Aguirre, Suarez, Medina, Bilardo, Pachame, Madero, Togneri, Ribaudo, Conigliaro, Veron (Echecopar).
Winners: Estudiantes de La Plata

1969

1ST LEG

Oct 8 (San Siro, Milan)
Milan 3 (Sormani 8 73, Combin 44)
Estudiantes de La Plata 0
HT: 2–0. Att: 80,000. Ref: Machin (Fra)
MILAN: Cudicini, Malatrasi, Anquilletti, Rosato, Schnellinger, Lodetti, Rivera, Fogli, Sormani, Combin (Rognoni), Prati.
ESTUDIANTES: Poletti, Suarez, Manera, Madero, Malbernat, Bilardo, Togneri, Echecopar (Ribaudo), Flores, Conigliaro, Veron.

2ND LEG

Oct 22 (Bombonera, Buenos Aires)
Estudiantes de La Plata 2 (Conigliaro 43, Aguirre Suarez 44)
Milan 1 (Rivera 30)
HT: 2–1. Att: 65,000. Ref: Massaro (Chl)
ESTUDIANTES: Poletti, Manera, Aguirre, Suarez, Madero, Malbernat, Bilardo, (Echecopar), Romero, Togneri, Conigliaro, Taverna, Veron.
MILAN: Cudici, Malatrasi (Maldera), Anquilletti, Rosato, Schnellinger, Foglio, Lodetti, Rivera, Sormani, Combin, Prati (Rognoni).
Winners: Milan, 4–2 agg

1970

1ST LEG

Aug 26 (Bombonera, Buenos Aires)
Estudiantes de La Plata 2 (Echecopar 6, Veron 10)
Feyenoord 2 (Kindvall 21, Van Hanegem 65)
HT: 2–1. Att: 65,000. Ref: Glockner (EG)
ESTUDIANTES: Errea, Pagnanini, Spadaro, Togneri, Malbernat, Bilardo (Solari), Pacheme, Echecopar (Rudski), Conigliaro, Flores, Veron.
FEYENOORD: Treytel, Romeyn, Israel, Laseroms, Van Duivenbode, Hasil, Jansen, Van Hanegem (Boskamp), Wery, Kindvall, Moulijn.

2ND LEG

Sep 9 (Feyenoord Stadion, Rotterdam)
Feyenoord 1 (Van Daele 65)
Estudiantes de La Plata 0
HT: 0–0. Att: 70,000. Ref: Tejada (Per)
FEYENOORD: Treytel, Romeyn, Israel, Laseroms, Van Duivenbode, Hasil (Boskamp), Van Hanegem, Jansen, Wery, Kindvall, Moulijn (Van Daele).
ESTUDIANTES: Pezzano, Malbernat, Spadaro, Togneri, Medina (Pagnanini), Bilardo, Pacheme, Romero, Conigliaro (Rudzki), Flores, Veron.
Winners: Feyenoord, 3–2 agg

1971

1ST LEG

Dec 15 (Athens)
Panathinaikos 1 (Filakouris 48)
Nacional Montevideo 1 (Artime 50)
HT: 0–0. Att: 60,000
PANATHINAIKOS: Ekonomopoulos, Tonaras (Vlachos), Kapsis, Sourpis, Athanasopoulos, Eleftherakis, Filikouris, Dimitriou, Kouvas, Antoniadis, Domazos.
NACIONAL: Manga, Masnik, Brunel, Ubinas, Montero Castillo, Blanco, Cubilla, Maneiro, Esoarrago (Duarte), Artime, Morales.

2ND LEG

Dec 29 (Centenario, Montevideo)
Nacional 2 (Artime 34 75)
Panathinaikos 1 (Filakouris 89).
HT: 1–0. Att: 70,000
NACIONAL: Manga, Ubinas, Masnik, Brunel, Blanco, Maneiro, Montero Castillo, Cubilla (Mujica), Esparrago, Artime, Mamelli (Bareno).
PANATHINAIKOS: Ekonomopoulos, Mitropoulos, Kapsis, Sourpis, Athanasopoulos, Kamaras (Filikouris), Domazos, Eleftherakis, Dimitriou, Antoniadis, Kouvas.
Winners: Nacional, 3–2 agg

1972

1ST LEG

Sep 6 (Mozart y Cuyo, Avellaneda)
Independiente 1 (Sa 82)
Ajax 1 (Cruyff 6)
HT: 0–1. Att: 65,000. Ref: Bakhramov (SU)
INDEPENDIENTE: Santoro, Commisso, Lopez, Sa, Pavoni, Pastoriza, Semenewicz, Raimondo (Bulla), Balbuena, Maglioni, Mircoli.
AJAX: Stuy, Suurbier, Hulshoff, Blankenburg, Krol, Haan, Neeskens, G Muhren, Swart, Cruyff (A Muhren), Keizer.

2ND LEG

Sep 28 (Olympish Stadion, Amsterdam)
Ajax 3 (Neeskens 12, Rep 16 78)
Independiente 0
HT: 2–0. Att: 60,000. Ref: Romey (Par)
AJAX: Stuy, Suurbier, Hulshoff, Blankenburg, Krol, Haan, Neeskens, G Muhren, Swart (Rep), Cruyff, Keizer.
INDEPENDIENTE: Santoro, Commisso, Sa, Lopez, Pavoni, Pastoriza, Garisto (Magan), Semenewicz, Balbuena, Maglioni, Mircoli (Bulla).
Winners: Ajax, 4–1 agg

1973

Nov 28 (Olimpico, Rome) single match
Independiente 1 (Bochini 40)
Juventus 0
HT: 1–0. Att: 35,000. Ref: Belcourt (Bel)
INDEPENDIENTE: Santoro, Commisso, Lopez, Sa, Pavoni, Raimondo, Galvan, Bochini, Balbuena, Maglioni, Bertoni (Semenewicz).
JUVENTUS: Zoff, Spinosi (Viola), Salvadore, Morini, Marchetti, Causio, Cuccureddu, Gentile, Altafini, Anastasi, Bettega (Longobucco).

1974

1ST LEG

Mar 12 (Mozart y Cuyo, Avellaneda)
Independiente 1 (Balbuena 33)
Atletico Madrid 0
HT: 1–0. Att: 60,000. Ref: Corver (Hol)
INDEPENDIENTE: Perez, Commisso, Lopez, Sa, Pavoni, Rodriguez, Galvan, Bocchini, Balbuena, Rojas, Bertoni.
ATLETICO: Reina, Melo, Heredia, Benegas, Capon, Eusebio, Alberto, Adelardo, Irureta, Garate, Ayala.

2ND LEG

Apr 10 (Vicente Calderon, Madrid)
Atletico Madrid 2 (Irureta 21, Ayala 86)
Independiente 0
HT: 1–0. Att: 45,000. Ref: Robles (Chl)
AT MADRID: Pacheco, Melo, Heredia, Eusebio, Capon, Adelardo, Irureta, Alberto (Salcedo 61), Aguilar, Garate, Ayala.
INDEPENDIENTE: Perez, Commisso, Lopez, Carrica, Pavoni, Saggioratto, Galvan, Bochini, Balbuena, Rojas (Rodriguez 68), Bertoni.
Winners: Atletico, 2–1 agg

1975

Bayern Munich vs. Independiente: not contested

1976

1ST LEG

Nov 23 (Olympiastadion, Munich)
Bayern Munich 2 (Müller 80, Kapellmann 83)
Cruzeiro 0
HT: 0–0. Att: 22,000. Ref: Pestarino (Arg)
BAYERN MUNICH: Maier, Andersson, Beckenbauer, Schwarzenbeck, Horsmann, Durnberger, Kapellmann, Torstensson, U Hoeness, G Müller, K Rummenigge.
CRUZEIRO: Raul, Nelinho, Moraes, Osiris, Vanderlay, Ze Carlos, Piazza, Eduardo, Jairzinho, Palinha, Joaozinho.

2ND LEG

Dec 21 (Mineirao, Belo Horizonte)
Cruzeiro 0
Bayern Munich 0
HT: 0–0. Att: 114,000. Ref: Partridge (Eng)
CRUZEIRO: Raul, Moraes, Osiris, Piazza (Eduardo), Nelinho, Vanderlay, Dirceu (Forlan), Ze Carlos, Jairzinho, Palinha, Joaozinho.

BAYERN MUNICH: Maier, Andersson, Beckenbauer, Schwarzenbeck, Horsmann, Weiss, U Hoeness, Kapellmann, Torstensson, G Müller, K Rummenigge.
Winners: Bayern, 2–0 agg

1977

1ST LEG

Mar 22 (Bombonera, Buenos Aires)
Boca Juniors 2 (Mastrangelo 16, Ribolzi 51)
Borussia Mönchengladbach 2 (Hannes 24, Bonhof 29)
HT: 1–2. Att: 50,000. Ref: Doudine (Bul)
BOCA: Santos, Pernia, Sa, Mouzo, Bordon, Benitez (Ribolzi), Sune, Zanabria, Mastrangelo, Pavon (Alvarez), Salinas.
BORUSSIA: Kleff, Vogts, Hannes, Wohlers, Bonhof, Schafer, Wimmer, (Danner), Kulik, Del'Haye, Nielsen, Lienen.

2ND LEG

Mar 26 (Wildpark Stadion, Karlsruhe)
Borussia Mönchengladbach 0
Boca Juniors 3 (Zanabria 2, Mastrangelo 33, Salinas 35)
HT: 0–3. Att: 21,000. Ref: Cerullo (Uru)
BORUSSIA: Kneib, Vogts, Hannes, Wohlers (Schafer), Ringels, Kulik, Simonsen, Nielsen, Larsen (Lienen), Bruns, Gores.
BOCA: Gatti, Pernia, Tesare, Bordon, Suarez, Zanabria, Sune, Salinas, Mastrangelo, Saldano (Veglio), Felman.
Winners: Boca Juniors, 5–2 agg

1978

Liverpool vs. Boca Juniors: not contested

1979

1ST LEG

Nov 18 (Malmo Stadion, Malmo)
Malmo 0
Olimpia 1 (Isasi 41)
HT: 0–1. Att: 4,000. Ref: Partridge (Eng)
MALMO: Moller, R Andersson, Johnsson, Erlandsson, Prytz, Hansson, Ljungberg, Malmberg, Arvidsson, Sjoberg, Kinvall.
OLIMPIA: Almeida, Paredes, Piazza, Souza, Solalinde, Kiese, Delgado, Torres, Ortiz, Cespedes, Isasi.

2ND LEG

Mar 3 (Manuel Ferreira, Asuncion)
Olimpia 2 (Solalinde 40 pen, Michelagnoli 71)
Malmo 1 (Earlandsson 48)
HT: 1–0. Att: 35,000. Ref: Cardellino (Uru)
OLIMPIA: Almeida, Solalinde, Paredes, Sosa, Do Bartolomeo, Torres, Kiese, Talavera (Michelagnoli), Isasi, Valik, Aquino.
MALMO: Moller, R Andersson, Parkins, Johnsson, Vidsson, M Andersson, Olsson (Hansson), Prytz, Erlandsson, Sjoberg (Malmberg), T Andersson.
Winners: Olimpia, 3–1 agg

1980

Feb 11 (National Stadium, Tokyo)
Nacional 1 (Victorino 10)
Nottingham Forest 0
HT: 1–0. Att: 62,000. Ref: Klein (Isr)
NACIONAL: Rodriguez, Moreira, Blanco, Enriquez, Gonzalez, Milar, Esparrago, Luzardo, Morales, Bica, Victorino.
NOTTINGHAM FOREST: Shilton, Anderson, Lloyd, Burns, F Gray, Ponte (Ward), O'Neill, S Gray, Robertson, Francis, Wallace.

1981

Dec 13 (Tokyo)
Flamengo 3 (Nunes 13 41, Adilio 34)
Liverpool 0
HT: 3–0. Att: 62,000. Ref: Vasquez (Mex)
FLAMENGO: Raul, Leandro, Junior, Mozer, Marinho, Adilio, Tita, Andrade, Zico, Lico, Nunes.
LIVERPOOL: Grobbelaar, Neal, Lawrenson, Hansen, Thompson, R Kennedy, Lee, McDermott (Johnson), Souness, Dalglish, Johnston.

1982

Dec 12 (Tokyo)
Penarol 2 (Jair 27, Charrua 68)
Aston Villa 0
HT: 1–0. Att: 62,000. Ref: Calderon (CR)
PENAROL: Fernandez, Diogo, Oliveira, Morales, Gutierrez, Saralegui, Bossio, Jair, Ramos (Charrua), Morena, Silva.
ASTON VILLA: Rimmer, Jones, Evans, McNaught, Williams, Bremner, Mortimer, Cowans, Shaw, Withe, Morley.

1983

Dec 11 (Tokyo)
Gremio 2 (Renato 37 93)
Hamburg 1 (Schroder 85)
HT: 1–0. 90min: 1–1. After extra time. Att: 62,000. Ref: Vautrot (Fra)
GREMIO: Mazaropi, Paulo Roberto, Baidek, De Leon, Magalhaes, Sergio, Paulo, Cesar (Caio), Osvaldo (Bonamigo), China, Renato, Tarciso.
HAMBURG: Stein, Wehmeyer, Jakobs, Hieronmus, Schroder, Hartwig, Groh, Rolff, Magath, Wuttke, Hansen.

1984

Dec 9 (Tokyo)
Independiente 1 (Percudiani 6)
Liverpool 0
HT: 1–0. Att: 62,000. Ref: Romouldo (Bra)
INDEPENDIENTE: Goyen, Villaverde (Monzon), Enrique, Clausen, Trossero, Marangoni, Burruchaga, Giusti, Bochini, Percudani, Barberon.
LIVERPOOL: Grobbelaar, Neal, A Kennedy, Gillespie, Hansen, Nicol, Dalglish, Molby, Wark (Whelan), Rush, Johnston.

1985

Dec 8 (Tokyo)
Juventus 2 (Platini 63, M Laudrup 82)
Argentinos Juniors 2 (Ereros 55, Castro 75)
HT: 0–0. 90min: 2–2. After extra time. Juventus 4–2 on pens. Att: 62,000. Ref: Roth (WG)
JUVENTUS: Tacconi, Favero, Brio, Scirea (Pioli), Cabrini, Bonini, Manfredonia, Platini, Mauro (Briaschi), Serena, M Laudrup.
ARGENTINOS JUNIORS: Vidalele, Villaba, Pavoni, Olguin, Domenech, Videla, Batista, Commisso (Coris), Casro, Borghi, Ereros (Lopez).

1986

Dec 14 (Tokyo)
River Plate 1 (Alzamendi 28)
Steaua Bucharest 0
HT: 1–0. Att: 62,000. Ref: Martinez Bazan (Uru)
RIVER PLATE: Pumpido, Gordillo, Gutierrez, Montenegro, Ruggeri, Alfaro (Sperando), Alonso, Enrique, Gallego, Alzamendi, Funes.
STEAUA: Stingaciu, Iovan, Bumbescu, Belodedici, Barbulescu (Majaru), Weisenbacher, Stoica, Balint, Balan, Lacatus, Piturca.

1987

Dec 13 (Tokyo)
FC Porto 2 (Gomes 41, Madjer 108)
Penarol 1 (Viera 80)
HT: 1–0. 90min: 1–1. After extra time. Att: 45,000. Ref: Wohrer (Aut)
FC PORTO: Mlynarczyk, Joao Pinto, Geraldao, Lima Pereira, Inacio, Rui Barros (Quim), Magalhaes, Andre, Sousa, Gomes, Madjer.
PENAROL: Pereira, Herrera (Goncalves), Rotti, Trasante, Dominguez Perdomo, Viera, Aguirre, Cabrera (Matosas), Vidal, Da Silva.

1988

Dec 11 (Tokyo)
Nacional 2 (Ostolaza 7, 119)
PSV Eindhoven 2 (Romario 75, R Koeman 109)
HT: 1–0. 90min: 1–1. After extra time. Nacional 7–6 on pens. Att: 62,000. Ref: Palacios (Col)
NACIONAL: Sere, Gomez, De Leon, Revelez, Saldana, Ostolazza, Vargas (Moran), Lemos, De Lima, Cardaccio (Carrelo), Castro.
PSV EINDHOVEN: Van Breukelen, Gerets, Koot, Koeman, Heintze (Valckx), Lerby, Van Aerle, Vanenburg (Gillhaus), Romario, Kieft, Ellerman.

1989

Dec 17 (Tokyo)
Milan 1 (Evani 118)
Atletico Nacional Medellin 0
HT: 0–0. 90min: 0–0. After extra time. Att: 62,000. Ref: Fredriksson (Swe)
MILAN: Galli, Baresi, Tassotti, Maldini, Fuser (Evani), Costacurta, Donadoni, Rijkaard, Ancelotti, Van Basten, Massaro (Simone).
NACIONAL: Higuita, Escobar, Gomez, Herrera, Cassiani, Perez, Arango (Restrepo), Alvarez, Arboleda (Uzurriaga), Garcia, Trellez.

1990

Dec 9 (Tokyo)
Milan 3 (Rijkaard 43 65, Stroppa 62)
Olimpia 0
HT: 1–0. Att: 60,000. Ref: Wright (Bra)
MILAN: Pazzagli, Baresi, Tassotti, Costacurta, Maldini (Galli), Carbone, Donadoni (Guerreiro), Rijkaard, Stroppa, Gullit, Van Basten.
OLIMPIA: Almeida, Fernandez, Caceras, Guasch, Ramirez, (Chamac), Suarez, Hoyn, (Cubilla), Balbuena, Monzon, Amarilla, Samaniego.

1991

Dec 8 (Tokyo)
Red Star Belgrade 3 (Jugovic 19 58, Pancev 72)
Colo Colo 0
HT: 1–0. Att: 60,000. Ref: Rothlisberger (Swi)
RED STAR: Milojevic, Radinovic, Vasilijevic, Belodedic, Najdoski, Jugovic, Stosic, Ratkovic, Savicevic, Mikhailovic, Pancev.
COLO COLO: Moron, Garrido, Margas, M Ramirez, Salvatierra, (Dabrowski), Mendoza, Vilches, Barticciotto, Pizarro, Yanez, Martinez (Rubio).

1992

Dec 13 (Tokyo)
Sao Paulo 2 (Rai 26, 79)
Barcelona 1 (Stoichkov 13)
HT: 1–1. Att: 80,000. Ref: Loustau (Arg)
SAO PAULO: Zetti, Victor, Adilson, Cafu, Pintado, Luiz, Rai, Toninho, Cerezo (Dinho), Palinha, Muller.
BARCELONA: Zubizarreta, Ferrer, R Koeman, Witschge, Guardiola, Eusebio, Amor, Bakero (Goikoetxea), Beguiristain (Nadal).

1993

Dec 12 (Tokyo)
Sao Paulo 3 (Palinha 20, Cerezo 59, Mller 86)
Milan 2 (Massaro 48, Papin 82)
HT: 1–0. Att: 52,000. Ref: Quiniou (Fra)
SAO PAULO: Zetti, Cafu, Valber, Doriva, Andre, Dinho, Leonardo, Toninho, Cerezo, Palinha (Juninho), Muller.
MILAN: Rossi, Panucci, Costacurta, Baresi, Maldini, Donadoni, Desailly, Albertini (Tassotti), Massaro, Raducioiu (Orlando), Papin.

1994

Dec 1 (Tokyo)
Velez Sarsfield 2 (Trotta 50 pen, Asad 57)
Milan 0
HT: 0–0. Att: 65,000. Ref: Torres (Col)
VELEZ Sarsfield: Chilavert, Almandoz, Trotta, Sotomayor, Cardoza, Gomez, Basualdo, Bassedas, Pompei, Asad, Flores.
MILAN: Rossi, Tassotti, Costacurta, Baresi, Maldini, Donadoni, Albertini, Desailly, Boban, Savicevic (Simone), Massaro (Panucci).

1995

Nov 28 (Tokyo)
Ajax 0
Gremio 0
HT: 0–0. 90min: 0–0. After extra time. Ajax 4–3 on pens. Att: 62,000. Ref: Elleray (Eng)
AJAX: Van der Sar, Reiziger, F de Boer, Bogarde, Blind, R de Boer, Davids, Litmanen (Reuser 94), Finidi George, Kluivert, Overmars (Kanu 68).
GREMIO: Danlrei, Arce, Rivarola, Adilson, Roger, Dinho, Goiano, Arulson (Luciano 61), Carlos Miguel (Gelson 97), Paulo Nunes, Jardel (Magno 79).

1996

Nov 26 (Tokyo)
Juventus 1 (Del Piero 82)
River Plate 0
HT: 0–0. Att: 55,000. Ref: Rezende de Freitas (Bra)
JUVENTUS: Peruzzi, Ferrara, Porrini, Torricelli, Montero, Di Livio, Deschamps, Jugovic, Zidane (Tacchinardi 86), Del Piero, Boksic.
RIVER PLATE: Bonano, Diaz, Berizzo, Ayala, Sorin, Astrada, Montserrat, Berti (Gancedo 75), Ortega, Francescoli, Cruz (Salas 84).

1997

Dec 2 (Tokyo)
Borussia Dortmund 2 (Zorc 34, Herrlich 85)
Cruzeiro 0
HT: 1–0. Att: 46,953. Ref: Garcia Aranda (Spa)
DORTMUND: Klos, Reuter, Feiersinger, Julio Cesar, Freund, Paulo Sousa, Möller, Zorc (Kirovski 80), Heinrich, Herrlich, Chapuisat (Decheiver 75).
CRUZEIRO: Dida, Vitor, Joao Carlos, Goncalves, Elivelton, Roberto Palacios (Marcelo 64), Ricardinho, Fabinho, Cleison, Bebeto, Donizete.

COPA LIBERTADORES (SOUTH AMERICAN CLUB CUP)

The Copa Libertadores is South America's premier club event, but has had an erratic history. A South American champion clubs cup had been organized by Chile's Colo Colo as early as 1948, but the competition, won by Brazil's Vasco da Gama, was a financial disaster and was not staged again. But UEFA's success with the European Cup prompted the South American confederation, CONMEBOL, to consider giving the competition another chance, and the lucrative lure of the World Club Cup swayed the balance in favour of trying again.

An executive committee meeting in 1958 included this item on the agenda after a suggestion from UEFA to co-organize a two-leg annual play-off between the European Champion Clubs Cup winners and a top South American team. It was not until 1959, however, that CONMEBOL decided to go ahead, and the regulations of a South American Champions Cup were not approved until after yet another meeting in Montevideo on February 18, 1960.

CONMEBOL's leading lights – who included future president Teofilo Salinas Fuller of Peru and future FIFA president Joao Havelange of Brazil – considered such an event would be a valuable means of bringing South American nations closer together through sport. It did not escape their attention, either, than such a competition could be highly profitable. Ironically, it was neither as can be seen from the angry incidents provoked down the years and by the number of clubs who have been reduced to the brink of bankruptcy by a mixture of player greed and high travel costs.

Yet for all that, the competition caught the imagination of the fans to such an extent that it soon overshadowed the South American Championship. Indeed, the Copa America came close to extinction because clubs refused to release their players for national team duty while they remained in club cup contention.

The new cup even began to overshadow domestic competition with clubs deliberately fielding weakened teams in the league to rest players for the cup. In the late 1970s Boca Juniors, under controversial coach Juan Carlos Lorenzo, fielded one team in the Argentine league championship and a different – far better – team in the international competition. Boca's victories in the cup in both 1977 and 1978 meant not a whisper of complaint was heard from fans or directors.

The first tournament was held in 1960. It was opened to the champion clubs of the ten South American nations, and seven took part in the competition which was organised on a direct elimination, two-leg basis. The final, then as now, was played over two legs. In the early years the result was resolved by games won, not goal difference. Later, goal difference came into the equation when any necessary play-off failed to produce a winner. In due course aggregate scores and penalties eventually replaced the play-off altogether.

At first there was little interest in the new event, largely because league championships have always been more popular than cup competitions in South America. The very first match was played in Buenos Aires on April 20, 1960, at the Huracan stadoum between hosts San Lorenzo de Almagro, the 1959 Argentine champions, and Esporte Clube de Bahia, who had won their state championship in Brazil and then beaten Santos for the honour of representing their country.

The first winners

San Lorenzo, their attack led by the erratically brilliant marksman Jose Sanfilippo, won 3–0 in front of a crowd which numbered a mere 6,650. San Lorenzo went through to the semi-finals and were drawn to play Penarol of Montevideo.

Uruguayan fans had proved much more enthusiastic than their Argentine counterparts about the tournament. When both legs ended in draws San Lorenzo gave up the option of home advantage for financial reasons to return to Montevideo for the play-off. Penarol won 2–1 to reach the final where they subsequently defeated Olimpia of Paraguay 1–0 in Montevideo and then drew 1–1 away.

Penarol, founded originally as a railway sports club, were the South American equivalent of Real Madrid in understanding, quicker than most, the potential of international club success – and in putting together a team good enough to dominate it. Luis Maidana was one of South America's top goalkeepers, William Martinez a rock-like centre back and Nestor Goncalves a midfield anchor in the great traditions of the old, attacking centre-half. Above all, Penarol benefited from the presence in attack of Pedro Spencer, Ecuador's greatest-ever footballer, and still record-holding marksman with more than 50 goals in the history of the Copa Libertadores.

Penarol retained the club crown in 1961. This time nine countries entered clubs with Ecuador and Peru joining in. The tournament was again organized under a two-leg direct elimination format. Penarol beat Universitario of Peru in the quarter-finals, repeated their 1960 victory over Olimpia in the semi-finals and disposed of Brazil's Palmeiras in the final.

Penarol won 1–0 at home, with Spencer scoring just as he had in the final opener the previous year, and drew 1–1 away.

Significantly, terrace interest was on the increase. More than 50,000 watched the first leg of the final in Montevideo and 40,000 Brazilians turned out for the return in Sao Paulo.

The following year, 1962, the format of the competition changed as more teams entered. The home-and-away knock-out method was replaced by groups, played for points, up until the final. Uruguay was permitted two entries – Nacional joining in thanks to the status of their old rivals, Penarol, as champions. Pele's Santos entered for the first time and won their first round group, as did Nacional and Chile's Universidad Catolica. Penarol were granted a bye to the semi-finals where, under the rules, they had to be drawn against Nacional to prevent the possibility of two clubs from the same country meeting in the final. A tight tie ended in Penarol winning on aggregate after a 1–1 draw in a play-off. In the other semi-final Santos squeezed past Universidad Catolica by 1–1 and 1–0.

The final between Penarol and Santos, brought all manner of problems. The first leg was played in the Centenario stadium in Montevideo and resulted in a surprise 2–1 win for Santos even though they missed the injured Pele. His "twin," Coutinho, scored both goals with Spencer replying for Penarol.

The second leg, back in Brazil, remains the longest game on record in the competition – lasting three and a half hours from first to final whistle. Penarol, thanks to goals from Spencer and Pepe Sasia (two) were leading 3–2 shortly after half-time when Chilean referee Carlos Robles was knocked unconscious by a stone thrown from the crowd. When he came round, he suspended the game.

After more than an hour's confusion, the game was restarted and Santos – who had scored earlier through Dorval and Mengalvio – equalised just as a linesman, raising his flag, was knocked out by another stone from the terraces. That prompted Robles to suspend the game, this time briefly, once more.

At the long-delayed end of the match the Brazilians believed they had done enough to win. However, at the inevitable inquiry, referee Robles said he had only restarted the game the first time under pressure from Brazilian officials and out of concern for his own personal safety. Thus the confederation reverted the result to 3–2 to Penarol and ordered a play-off.

This took place in the Monumental stadium in Buenos Aires – home of River Plate – and saw Pele make his final debut. His presence proved decisive as Santos won 3–0 to settle all the arguments.

Santos retained their trophy a year later, beating Boca Juniors home and away, but had been helped by the rule which gave the holders a bye into the semi-finals. Boca, managed by Adolfo Pedernera, had an excellent team but Santos deserved to win thanks to the telepathic attacking brilliance of Pele and Coutinho. Coutinho scored twice in the Brazilian club's 3–2 first leg win

in Maracana and he and Pele claimed the goals when Santos won 2–1 in Buenos Aires in the return.

Boca striker Sanfilippo – top marksman in the cup that year with seven goals – scored all Boca's goals in the final. Both games were weatched by 50,000-plus crowds and the Buenos Aires leg set a gate receipts record for any South American club match.

Increasing interest

Pele's inspiration of Santos' double success provided the new club cup with the image boost it needed. Interest in the competition increased dramatically, and by 1964 every CONMEBOL country entered. Boca's run to the Final was another important factor, as it encouraged the other Argentine clubs to take the competition more seriously (Uruguay had always regarded it as a serious event because it needed an outlet for Penarol and Nacional, who always finished first and second in the Uruguayan league).

Argentine clubs came to the fore as Independiente became champions in 1964 and retained the trophy in 1965.

By now Venezuela had come on board to complete the entry complement. But the competition's expansion proved a thorny subject. Penarol were prime movers. They had always relied more on international matches and tours for revenue rather than domestic competition. Thus they pressed CONMEBOL to admit two clubs per country – champions and runners-up – as this would not only increase the number of matches and gate and TV revenue but also virtually guarantee themselves a permanent presence in the event.

Washington Cataldi, long-serving Penarol president and CONMEBOL director, laid his proposal before the confederation in November 1965. It met strong opposition from Argentina, Brazil and Chile who considered it would make the competition too long and unwieldy. However a majority – Colombia, Ecuador, Paraguay, Peru Venezuela and of course Uruguay – voted in favour. The Brazilians were furious and reacted by boycotting the cup in both 1966 and 1967.

It was not only the format of the tournament which was changed – so was the name. Up until then it had been known as the South American Champions Cup. But permitting access to runners-up demanded a new title. CONMEBOL settled on the Copa Libertadores in honour of the national heroes who led the fight for independence from Europe's old colonial powers.

Thus the 1966 tournament involved no fewer than 95 games even without the Brazilians. Penarol, the winners, played a then record 17 games to regain the title. Again controversy occurred. A play-off with River Plate was needed in the Final, and, having led 2–0 with 20 minutes remaining, River Plate eventually lost 4–2 after extra time. Argument over who to blame for that defeat continued for years. Some blamed coach Renato Cesarini for switching central midfielder Jorge Solari to right-back because of injury to Sainz. Others blamed the poor performances of two former Penarol players in River's side, Roberto Matosas and Luis Cubilla. Matosas lucklessly deflected a shot into his own net for Penarol's late equaliser at 2–2.

Daniel Onega's 17 goals for River Plate that year is a record which will probably never be beaten. Years later Onega admitted that he remembered the "one which got away" more than the ones he scored. In the last minute of normal time, with the score 2–2, Onega fired a cross hastily over the bar from close range. If it had gone in River would have been champions. Instead, they had to wait another 20 years to lay their hands on the cup.

The 1967 Final, between Argentina's Racing Club and Uruguay's Nacional, witnessed the birth of the win-at-all-costs approach to the competition, especially from the Argentinians. The three-game final series was peppered with poor gamesmanship and rough play.

Racing's win marked the beginning of a period of Argentine dominance, especially by the small-town club Estudiantes de La Plata, who won the Copa Libertadores three years running (1968–70) on the back of a single Argentine championship in 1967. Estudiantes were the worst offenders when it came to gamesmanship. Every conceivable method was employed to distract opponents, from verbal harassment and time-wasting to spitting and even pricking opponents with pins when out of the referee's view. Estudiantes made few friends and very little money. Indeed, their hat-trick of titles earned them a net loss of $1,600,000. As a result their president committed suicide, the board resigned and their replacements were forced to sell their best players at knock-down prices.

One of them, star marksman Juan Ramon Veron, explained later: "We tried to find out everything possible about our rivals individually. Not just the way they played but their habits, their characters, their weaknesses and even about their private lives so we could goad them on the pitch, get them to react and risk being sent off."

Carlos Bilardo, later Argentina's World Cup-winning national team coach in 1986, said: "Nothing was left to chance. We worked hard in training on all our corner, free kick and throw-in routines. We had secret signs and phrases which we used to trap the opposition. For example, defenders used to shout: 'Let's go up'. So the opposition moved back to avoid being caught offside… and we just watched them go. This really disrupted other teams' attacking play."

Estudiantes' ruthless cynicism reached its peak when the second leg of their third Final against Penarol ended in a free-for-all between both sets of players in the middle of the pitch. The disciplinary committee was lenient – but did come down heavily on Boca Juniors a year later, after a battle between the players in a tie against Peru's Sporting Cristal in Buenos Aires, which resulted in all of them being locked up in prison!

Serious trouble

Top-level diplomatic negotiations earned the players' release the following day, and they were all promptly suspended by the clubs. CONMEBOL punished Boca by closing their stadium for cup games, a strange move given that the fans were generally well-behaved – it was the players who had been the problem!

Boca refused to accept this and duly turned up at their stadium for their next match. Their opponents, Universitario of Peru, did not – on the express orders of CONMEBOL's Peruvian president Salinas Fuller. Universitario were awarded the points and Boca were expelled from the competition.

With the ever-increasing disruption caused to domestic championships, Argentina joined Brazil in a boycott in 1969, prompting CONMEBOL to streamline the competition by reducing the number of group matches. Argentina's Independiente then embarked on an unprecedented sequence of victories, winning four times in succession from 1972 to 1975.

The Brazilians, who returned in 1970, also began to enjoy some success, with Cruzeiro, Flamengo and Gremio winning between 1976 and 1983. Overall, however, Brazil's record in the tournament was initially as disappointing as their record in the Copa America. Indeed, until the 1990s Brazilian clubs had won only five times. Yet in the same period, Argentine clubs won 15 times and the Uruguayans seven times. Between 1963 and 1979, Argentine clubs appeared in all 17 finals, winning 12 of them.

Boca Juniors won the trophy for Argentina in 1977 and 1978, but in 1979 Olimpia of Paraguay broke the Argentina-Uruguay-Brazil domination of the competition. Olimpia's breakthrough marked a new era for the competition, which became more even and open. Argentine clubs still enjoyed success – Independiente, Argentinos Juniors and River Plate all tasted victory – but the smaller nations were starting to make an impression.

Chilean champions Cobreloa reached two successive finals in 1981 and 1982, and were followed by Colombia's America Cali, who lost three successive finals from 1985.

Uruguay came back into contention with wins by Nacional (1980 and 1988) and by Penarol (1982 and 1987), but no Uruguayan club has won the Copa Libertadores since 1988 and a decade separated the two Argentine triumphs of River Plate in 1986 and 1996.

In 1989 Nacional of Medellin won the trophy for Colombia for the first time, beating Olimpia 5–4 on penalties after a 2–2 aggregate draw. Olimpia returned the following year to win for the second time, beating Barcelona of Ecuador in the Final, and made it a hat-trick of Final appearances in 1991 when they lost to Chile's Colo Colo.

The rest of the 1990s has been Brazilian-dominated. In 1992 Sao Paulo beat Newell's Old Boys of Argentina, to win Brazil's first Copa Libertadores for almost a decade. The Sao Paulo side, containing many Brazil internationals such as Rai, Cafu, Palinha and Muller, won again in 1993, beating Chile's Universidad Catolica 5–3 on aggregate, to become the first club to retain the trophy since 1978.

Sao Paulo almost made it a hat-trick in 1994 but lost out ,on penalties, to Velez Sarsfield. A year later, Gremio took Brazilian revenge, beating Nacional of Colombia in the Final. The 1996 Final saw a repeat of 1986, with River Plate once again beating America Cali. Then it was Brazil's turn again, with Cruzeiro regaining the crown they had previously worn back in 1976.

The Copa Libertadores developed, slowly, into a respectable competition which attracts all the continent's leading clubs. There are still moments of controversy and high drama, but that is all of South American football.

Such is the excitement generated that it is worth putting up with the constantly changing format which, at present, involves five first-round groups playing 60 matches to eliminate just five teams. It will grow still bigger as neighbouring countries from central and, perhaps one day, North America are invited to join in. The 1998 competition, for example, saw Mexican clubs taking part for the first time.

COPA LIBERTADORES RESULTS

1960 FINAL

1st leg: Jun 12 (Montevideo)
Penarol (Uru) 1 (Spencer 79)
Olimpia (Par) 0
HT: 0–0. Att: 50,000. Ref: Robles (Chl)

2nd leg: Jun 19 (Asuncion)
Olimpia 1 (Recalde 28)
Penarol 1 (Cubilla 83)
HT: 1–0. Att: 35,000. Ref: Prauddade (Arg)
Winners: Penarol

1961 FINAL

1st leg: Jun 9 (Montevideo)
Penarol (Uru) 1 (Spencer 89)
Palmeiras (Bra) 0
HT: 0–0. Att: 50,000. Ref: Prauddade (Arg)

2nd leg: Jun 11 (Sao Paulo)
Palmeiras 1 (Nardo 77)
Penarol 1 (Sasia 2)
HT: 0–1. Att: 40,000. Ref: Prauddade (Arg)
Winners: Penarol

1962 FINAL

1st leg: Jul 28 (Montevideo)
Penarol (Uru) 1 (Spencer 18)
Santos (Bra) 2 (Coutinho 29 70)
HT: 1–1. Att: 50,000. Ref: Robles (Chl)

2nd leg: Aug 2 (Santos)
Santos 2 (Dorval 27, Mengalvio 50)
Penarol 3 (Spencer 73, Sasia 18 48)
HT: 1–0. Att: 30,000. Ref: Robles (Ch)

Play-off: Aug 30 (Buenos Aires, Argentina)
Santos 3 (Coutinho 11, Pele 48 89)
Penarol 0
HT: 1–0. Att: 36,000. Ref: Horn (Hol)
Winners: Santos

1963 FINAL

1st leg: Sep 3 (Rio de Janeiro)
Santos (Bra) 3 (Coutino 2 21, Lima 28)

Boca Juniors (Arg) 2 (Sanfilippo 43 89)
HT: 3 1. Att: 55,000. Ref: Bois (Fra)

2nd leg: Sep 11 (Buenos Aires)
Boca Juniors 1 (Sanfilippo 46)
Santos 2 (Coutinho 50, Pele 82)
HT: 0–0. Att: 50,000. Ref: Bois (Fra)
Winners: Santos

1964 FINAL

1st leg: Aug 6 (Montevideo)
Nacional (Uru) 0
Independiente (Arg) 0
Att: 65,000. Ref: Horn (Hol)

2nd leg: Aug 12 (Avellaneda)
Independiente 1 (Rodriguez 35)
Nacional 0
HT: 1–0. Att: 45,000. Ref: Larrosa (Par)
Winners: Independiente

1965 FINAL

1st leg: Apr 9 (Avellaneda)
Independiente (Arg) 1 (Bernao 83)
Penarol (Uru) 0
HT: 0–0. Att: 45,000. Ref: Yamasaki (Per)

2nd leg: Apr 12 (Montevideo)
Penarol 3 (Goncalves 14, Reznik 43, Rocha 46)
Independiente 1 (De la Mata 88)
HT: 2–0. Att: 65,000. Ref: Yamasaki (Per)

Play-off: Apr 15 (Santiago, Chile)
Independiente 4 (Acevedo 10, Bernao 27, Avallay 33, Mura 82)
Penarol 1 (Joya 44)
HT: 3–1. Att: 35,000. Ref: Yamasaki (Per)
Winners: Independiente

1966 FINAL

1st leg: May 12 (Montevideo)
Penarol (Uru) 2 (Abaddie 75, Joya 85)
River Plate (Arg) 0
HT: 0–0. Att: 49,000. Ref: Goicoechea (Arg)

2nd leg: May 18 (Buenos Aires, Monumental)
River Plate 3 (D Onega 38, Sarnari 52, E Onega 73)
Penarol 2 (Rocha 32, Spencer 50)
HT: 1–1. Att: 60,000. Ref: Codesal (Uru)

Play-off: May 20 (Santiago, Chile))

Penarol 4 (Spencer 57 101, Abbadie 72, Rocha 109)
River Plate 2 (D Onega 37, Solari 42)
HT: 0–2. 90min: 2–2. After extra time. Att: 39,000. Ref: Vicuna (Chl)
Winners: Penarol

1967 FINAL

1st leg: Aug 15 (Avellaneda)
Racing Club (Arg) 0
Nacional (Uru) 0
Att: 54,000. Ref: Orozco (Per)

2nd leg: Aug 25 (Montevideo)
Nacional 0
Racing Club 0
Att: 54,000. Ref: Orozco (Per)

Play-off: Aug 29 (Santiago, Chile)
Racing Club 2 (Cardozo 14, Raffo 43)
Nacional 1 (Esparrago 79)
HT: 2–0. Att: 25,000. Ref: Orozco (Per)
Winners: Racing Club

1968 FINAL

1st leg: May 2 (La Plata)
Estudiantes de La Plata (Arg) 2 (Veron 83, Flores 87)
Palmeiras (Bra) 1 (Servillio 50)
HT: 0–0. Att: 35,000. Ref: Marino (Uru)

2nd leg: May 7 (Sao Paulo)
Palmeiras 3 (Tupazinho 10 68, Reinaldo 54)
Estudiantes 1 (Veron 72)
HT: 1–0. Att: 85,000. Ref: Massaro (Chl)

Play-off: May 15 (Montevideo, Uruguay)
Estudiantes 2 (Ribaudo 13, Veron 82)
Palmeiras 0
HT: 1–0. Att: 35,000. Ref: Orozco (Per)
Winners: Estudiantes de La Plata

1969 FINAL

1st leg: May 15 (Montevideo)
Nacional (Uru) 0
Estudiantes de La Plata (Arg) 1 (Flores 66)
HT: 0–0. Att:50,000. Ref: Massaro (Chl)

2nd leg: May 22 (La Plata)
Estudiantes 2 (Flores 31, Conigliaro 37)
Nacional 0
HT: 1–0. Att: 30,000. Ref: Delgado (Col)
Winners: Estudiantes de La Plata

1970 FINAL

1st leg: May 21 (La Plata)
Estudiantes de La Plata (Arg) 1 (Togneri 87)
Penarol (Uru) 0
HT: 0–0. Att: 36,000. Ref: Robles (Chl)

2nd leg: May 27 (Montevideo)
Penarol 0
Estudiantes 0
HT: 0–0. Att: 50,000. Ref: Larrosa (Par)
Winners: Estudiantes de La Plata

1971 FINAL

1st leg: May 26 (La Plata)
Estudiantes de La Plata (Arg) 1 (Romeo 60)
Nacional (Uru) 0
HT: 0–0. Att: 32,000. Ref: Canessa (Chl)

2nd leg: Jun 2 (Montevideo)
Nacional 1 (Masnik 17)
Estudiantes 0
HT: 1–0. Att: 62,000. Ref: Favilli Neto (Bra)

Play-off: Jun 9 (Lima, Peru)
Nacional 2 (Esparrago 22, Artime 65)
Estudiantes 0
HT: 1–0. Att: 42,000. Ref: Hormazabal (Chl)
Winners: Nacional

1972 FINAL

1st leg: May 17 (Lima)
Universitario (Per) 0
Independiente (Arg) 0
Att: 45,000. Ref: Marques (Bra)

2nd leg: May 24 (Avellaneda)
Independiente 2 (Maglioni 6 60)
Universitario 1 (Rojas 79)
HT: 1–0. Att: 65,000. Ref: Favilli Neto (Bra)
Winners: Independiente

1973 FINAL

1st leg: May 22 (Avellaneda)
Independiente (Arg) 1 (Mendoza 75)
Colo Colo (Chl) 1 (Caszely 71)
HT: 0–0. Att: 65,000. Ref: Lorenzo (Uru)

2nd leg: May 29 (Santiago)
Colo Colo 0
Independiente 0
Att: 77,000. Ref: Arppi Filho (Bra)
Play-off: Jun 6 (Montevideo, Uruguay)
Independiente 2 (Mendoza 25, Giachello 107)
Colo Colo 1 (Caszely 39)
HT: 1–1. 90min: 1–1. After extra time. Att: 45,000. Ref: Romei (Par)
Winners: Independiente

1974 FINAL

1st leg: Oct 12 (Sao Paulo)
Sao Paulo (Bra) 2 (Rocha 48, Mirandinha 50)
Independiente (Arg) 1 (Saggioratto 28)
HT: 0–1. Att: 51,000. Ref: Perez (Per)

2nd leg: Oct 16 (Avellaneda)
Independiente 2 (Bochini 34, Balbuena 48)
Sao Paulo 0
HT: 1–0. Att: 48,000. Ref: Barreto (Uru)

Play-off: Oct 19 (Santiago, Chile)
Independiente 1 (Pavoni 37)
Sao Paulo 0
HT: 1–0. Att: 27,000. Ref: Orozco (Per)
Winners: Independiente

1975 FINAL

1st leg: Jun 18 (Santiago)
Union Espanola (Chl) 1 (Ahumada 87)
Independiente (Arg) 0
HT: 0–0. Att:43,000. Ref: Bazan (Uru)

2nd leg: Jun 25 (Avellaneda)
Independiente 3 (Rojas 1, Pavoni 58, Bertoni 83)
Union Espanola 1 (Las Heras 56)
HT: 1–0. Att: 52,000. Ref: Barreto (Uru)

Play-off: Jun 29 (Asuncion)
Independiente 2 (Ruiz Moreno 29, Bertoni 65)
Union Espanola 0
HT: 1–0. Att: 45,000. Ref: Perez (Per)
Winners: Independiente

1976 FINAL

1st leg: Jul 21 (Belo Horizonte)
Cruzeiro (Bra) 4 (Nelinho 22, Palinha 29 40, Waldo 80)
River Plate (Arg) 1 (Mas 62)
HT: 3–0. Att: 58,000. Ref: Llobregat (Ven)

2nd leg: Jul 28 (Buenos Aires)
River Plate 2 (J J Lopez 10, Gonzalez 76)
Cruzeiro 1 (Palinha 48)
HT: 1–0. Att: 45,000. Ref: Bazan (Uru)

Play-off: Jul 30 (Santiago, Chile)
Cruzeiro 3 (Nelinho 24, Ronaldo 55, Joazinho 88)
River Plate 2 (Mas 59, Urquiza 64)
HT: 1–0. Att: 35,000. Ref: Martinez (Chl)
Winners: Cruzeiro

1977 FINAL

1st leg: Sep 6 (Buenos Aires)
Boca Juniors (Arg) 1 (Veglio 3)
Cruzeiro (Bra) 0
HT: 1–0. Att: 50,000. Ref: Cerullo (Uru)

2nd leg: Sep 11 (Belo Horizonte)
Cruzeiro 1 (Nelinho 76)
Boca Juniors 0
HT: 0–0. Att: 55,000. Ref: Orozco (Per)

Play-off: Sep 14 (Montevideo, Uruguay)
Boca Juniors 0
Cruzeiro 0
Att: 45,000. Ref: Llobregat (Ven)
Winners: Boca 5–4 on pens after extra time

1978 FINAL

1st leg: Nov 23 (Cali)
Deportivo Cali (Col) 0
Boca Juniors (Arg) 0
Att: 35,000. Ref: Ortiz (Par)

2nd leg: Nov 28 (Buenos Aires)
Boca Juniors 4 (Perotti 15 85, Mastrangelo 60, Salinas 71)
Deportivo Cali 0
HT: 1–0. Att: 45,000. Ref: Nunez (Per)
Winners: Boca Juniors

1979 FINAL

1st leg: Jul 22 (Asuncion)
Olimpia (Par) 2 (Aquino 3, Piazza 27)
Boca Juniors (Arg) 0
HT: 2–0. Att: 45,000. Ref: Castro (Chl)

2nd leg: Jul 27 (Buenos Aires)
Boca Juniors 0
Olimpia 0
Att: 50,000. Ref: Cardelino (Uru)
Winners: Olimpia (Par)

1980 FINAL

1st leg: Jul 30 (Porto Alegre)
Internacional Porto Alegre (Bra) 0
Nacional (Uru) 0
Att: 80,000. Ref: Romero (Arg)

2nd leg: Aug 6 (Montevideo)
Nacional 1 (Victorino 35)
Internacional 0
HT: 1–0. Att: 75,000. Ref: Perez (Per)
Winners: Nacional

1981 FINAL

1st leg: Nov 13 (Rio de Janeiro)
Flamengo (Bra) 2 (Zico 12 30)
Cobreloa (Chl) 1 (Merello 65)
HT: 2–0. Att: 114,000. Ref: Esposito (Arg)

2nd leg: Nov 20 (Santiago)
Cobreloa 1 (Merello 79)
Flamengo 0
HT: 0–0. Att: 61,000. Ref: Barreto (Uru)

Play-off: Nov 23 (Montevideo, Uruguay)
Flamengo 2 (Zico 18 79)
Cobreloa 0
HT: 1–0. Att: 35,000. Ref: Cerullo (Uru)
Winners: Flamengo

1982 FINAL

1st leg: Nov 26 (Montevideo)
Penarol (Uru) 0
Cobreloa (Chl) 0
HT; 0–0. Att: 70,000

2nd leg: Nov 30 (Santiago)
Cobreloa 0
Penarol 1 (Morena 89)
HT; 0–0. Att: 70,000
Winners: Penarol

1983 FINAL

1st leg: Jul 22 (Montevideo)
Penarol (Uru) 1 (Morena 35)
Gremio (Bra) 1 (Tita 12)
HT: 1–1. Att: 65,000. Ref: Nitti (Arg)

2nd leg: Jul 28 (Porto Alegre)
Gremio 2 (Caio 9, Cesar 87)
Penarol 1 (Morena 70)
HT: 1–0. Att: 75,000. Ref: Perez (Per)
Winners: Gremio

1984 FINAL

1st leg: Jul 24 (Porto Alegre)
Gremio (Bra) 0
Independiente (Arg) 1 (Burruchaga 24)
HT: 0–1. Att: 55,000

2nd leg: Jul 27 (Avellaneda)
Independiente 0
Gremio 0
HT: 0–0. Att: 75,000
Winners: Independiente

1985 FINAL

1st leg: Oct 17 (Buenos Aires)
Argentinos Juniors (Arg) 1 (Comisso 40)
America Cali (Col) 0
HT: 1–0. Att: 50,000. Ref: Escobar (Par)

2nd leg: Oct 22 (Cali)
America Cali 1 (Ortiz 3)
Argentinos Juniors 0
HT: 1–0 Att: 50,000. Ref: Felix (Bra)

Play-off: Oct 24 (Asuncion, Paraguay)
Argentinos Juniors 1 (Comisso 37)
America Cali 1 (Gareca 42)
HT: 1–1. Att: 35,000. Ref: Silva (Chl)
Winners: Argentinos Juniors 5–4 on pens after extra
time

1986 FINAL

1st leg: Oct 22 (Cali)
America Cali (Col) 1 (Cabanas 47)
River Plate (Arg) 2 (Funes 22, Alonso 25)
HT: 0–2. Att: 55,000. Ref: Cardellino (Uru)

2nd leg: Oct 29 (Buenos Aires)
River Plate 1 (Funes 70)
America Cali 0
HT: 0–0. Att: 85,000. Ref: Wright (Bra)
Winners: River Plate

1987 FINAL

1st leg: Oct 21 (Cali)
America Cali (Col) 2 (Battaglia 21, Cabanas 35)
Penarol (Uru) 0
Att: 45,000. Ref: Wright (Bra)

2nd leg: Oct 28 (Montevideo)
Penarol 2 (Aguirre 58, Villar 86)
America Cali 1 (Cabanas 19)
HT: 0–1. Att: 70,000. Ref: Calabria (Arg)

Play-off: Oct 31 (Santiago, Chile)
Penarol 1 (Aguirre 119)
America Cali 0
HT: 0–0. 90min: 0–0. After extra time. Att: 30,000. Ref:
Silva (Chl)
Winners: Penarol

1988 FINAL

1st leg: Oct 19 (Rosario)
Newell's Old Boys (Arg) 1
(Gabrich 60)Nacional (Uru) 0
HT: 0–0. Att: 45,000. Ref: Silva (Chl)

2nd leg: Oct 26 (Montevideo)
Nacional 3 (Vargas 10, Ostolaza 30, De Leon 81)
Newell's Old Boys 0
HT: 2–0. Att: 75,000. Ref: Coelho (Bra)
Nacional 3–1 agg

1989 FINAL

1st leg: May 24 (Asuncion)
Olimpia (Par) 2 (Bobadilla 36, Sanabria 60)
Atletico Nacional Medellin (Col) 0
HT: 1–0. Att: 50,000. Ref: Wright (Bra)

2nd leg: May 31 (Bogota)
Atletico Nacional 2 (Amarilla 46, Usurriaga 64)
Olimpia 0
HT: 0–0. 90min: 2–0. Att: 50,000. Ref: Loustau (Arg)
Winners: Atletico Nacional 5–4 on pens after extra
time

1990 FINAL

1st leg: Oct 3 (Asuncion)
Olimpia (Par) 2 (Amarilla 47, Samaniego 65)
Barcelona (Ecu) 0
HT: 0–0. Att: 35,000. Ref: Cardellino (Uru)

2nd leg: Oct 10 (Guayaquil)
Barcelona 1 (Trobbiani 61)
Olimpia 1 (Amarilla 80)
HT: 0–0. Att: 55,000. Ref: Montalban (Per)
Winners: Olimpia, 3–1 agg

1991 FINAL

1st leg: May 29 (Asuncion)
Olimpia (Par) 0
Colo Colo (Chl) 0
HT: 0–0. Att: 48,000. Ref: Filippi (Uru)

2nd leg: Jun 5 (Santiago)
Colo Colo 3 (Perez 13 18, Herrera 85)
Olimpia 0
HT: 2–0. Att: 64,000. Ref: Wright (Bra)
Winners: Colo Colo, 3–0 agg

1992 FINAL

1st leg: Jun 10 (Rosario)
Newell's Old Boys (Arg) 1 (Berizzo 38)
Sao Paulo (Bra) 0
HT; 1–0. Att: 45,000. Ref: Silva (Chl)

2nd leg: Jun 17 (Sao Paulo)
Sao Paulo 1 (Rai 65)
Newell's Old Boys 0
HT: 0–0. Att: 105,000. Ref: Cadena (Col)
Winners: Sao Paulo, 3–2 on pens after extra time

1993 FINAL

1st leg: May 19 (Sao Paulo)
Sao Paulo (Bra) 5 (Lopez og 31, Dinho 41, Gilmar
55, Rai 61, Muller 65)
Universidad Catolica (Chl) 1 (Almada 85pen)
HT: 2–0. Att: 99,000. Ref: Torres (Col)

2nd leg: May 26 (Santiago)
Universidad Catolica 2 (Lunari 9, Almada 16pen)
Sao Paulo 0
HT: 2–0. Att: 50,000. Ref: Escobar (Par)
Winners: Sao Paulo, 5–3 agg

1994 FINAL

1st leg: Aug 24 (Buenos Aires)
Velez Sarsfield (Arg) 1 (Asad 35)
Sao Paulo (Bra) 0
HT: 1–0. Att: 50,000. Ref: Torres (Col)

2nd leg: Aug 31 (Sao Paulo)
Sao Paulo 1 (Muller 32pen)
Velez Sarsfield 0
HT: 1–0. Att: 92,000. Ref: Filippi (Uru)
Winners: Velez 5–3 on pens after extra time

1995 FINAL

1st leg: Aug 24 (Porto Alegre)
Gremio (Bra) 3 (Marulanda og 36, Jardel 40, Paulo
Nunes 56)
Atletico Nacional (Col) 1 (Angel 71)
HT: 2–0. Att: 90,000. Ref: Rodas (Ecu)

2nd leg: Aug 30 (Medellin)
Atletico Nacional 1 (Aristizabal 13)
Gremio 1 (Dinho 85)
HT: 1–0. Att: 45,000. Ref: Imperatore (Chl)
Winners: Gremio, 4–2 agg

1996 FINAL

1st leg: Jun 19 (Cali)
America Cali (Col) 1 (De Avila 72)
River Plate (Arg) 0
HT: 0–0. Att: 50,000. Ref: Velasquez (Par)

2nd leg: Jun 26 (Buenos Aires)
River Plate 2 (Crespo 7, 14)
America Cali 0
HT: 2–0. Att: 80,000. Ref: Matto (Uru)
Winners: River Plate, 2–1 agg

1997 FINAL

1st leg: Aug 6 (Lima)
Sporting Cristal (Per) 0
Cruzeiro (Bra) 0
Att: 45,000. Ref: Moreno (Ecu)

2nd leg: Aug 13 (Belo Horizonte)
Cruzeiro 1 (Elivelton 75)
Sporting Cristal 0
HT: 0–0. Att: 75,000. Ref: Castrilli (Arg)
Winners: Cruzeiro, 1–0 agg

SOUTH AMERICAN SUPER COPA

The success of the Copa Libertadores and the example of Europe's three club competitions made it inevitable the big South American clubs would push for an expansion of international opportunities.

What is surprising, looking back, is that it took so long to bring these projects to life – particularly since the likes of River Plate, Penarol, Flamengo and the rest desperately needed not merely the excitement and prestige offered by regular international competition, but the revenue.

In Argentina, for example, only the "classic" derby against Boca Juniors guaranteed River Plate a full house. In an increasingly impoverished Uruguayan football environment, Penarol's only big match was the derby against old enemies Nacional.

Thus, in 1988, the South American confederation launched the South American Super Cup, or Trofeo Havelange as it became known in honour of the then FIFA president from Brazil, who had been a long-time executive committee member of CONMEBOL.

Creating new competitions after the European models was not simple. For one thing, the concept of the domestic knock-out competition had never caught on in South America. So the possibility of a Cup-winners Cup did not exist. Also, because the domestic championship runners-up were already admitted to the Copa Libertadores, the prospect of copying the UEFA Cup – open to high-placed non-champions – was compromised.

The solution – and one which suited the big clubs ideally - was to create a super cup which was open annually to all previous winners of the Copa Libertadores. Thus, at a stroke, the River Plates, Penarols and Flamengos were guaranteed regular annual international competition – a huge relief to their accountants and bank managers.

The media initially dismissed the Super Copa as an unnecessary tournament, but it rapidly gained in popularity because it perpetuated competition among the continent's top clubs. It was originally organized on a direct elimination, two-leg basis. That might ultimately be varied – after the manner of Europe's Champions League – as pressure grows for a South American super league.

In fact, the creation of a multi-club super cup demonstrated that South America was a lot further down the road towards an international club super league than Europe.

First winners were Racing Club of Avellaneda, for whom the competition an immense relief, rescuing the club from the competitive and financial backwaters of Argentina. Racing, who had won the Copa Libertadores only once, defeated Argentina rivals River Plate in the semi-finals, and then Cruzeiro of Brazil in the two-leg final. Hero of their victory was goalkeeper Ubaldo Fillol, veteran of Argentina's 1978 World Cup triumph… and, ironically, once a hero of River Plate.

Not that the Super Copa has been about veterans and past glories. In 1993, for example, Cruzeiro reached only the quarter-finals before losing on penalties to Nacional of Uruguay. But they shared the end-of-competition honours since they boasted the competition's eight-goal top scorer in a 16-year-old striker… named Ronaldo.

In 1998, World Cup year, the Super Copa was suspended because of fixture date pressure. Its resumption depends largely on the success of two new club tournaments for South and Central American clubs – the Mercosur and Merconorte cups.

SUPER COPA RESULTS

1988

Semi-finals
Racing Club (Arg) bt River Plate (Arg) 2–1, 1–1
(3–2 agg)
Cruzeiro (Bra) bt Nacional (Uru) 2–3, 1–0
(away goals, 3–3 agg)

Final
1st leg: Jun 13 (Avellaneda)
Racing 2 (Fernandez 44, Colombatti 90)
Cruzeiro 1 (Robson 37)
HT: 1–1. Att: 50,000

2nd leg: Jun 18 (Belo Horizonte)
Cruzeiro 1 (Robson 82)
Racing 1 (Catalan 43)
HT: 0–1. Att: 75,000
Winners: Racing, 3–2 agg

1989

Semi-finals
Boca Juniors (Arg) bt Gremio (Bra) 0–0, 2–0
(2–0 agg)
Independiente (Arg) bt Argentinos Juniors (Arg) 1–0, 2–1
(3–1 agg)

Final
1st leg: Nov 23 (Buenos Aires)
Boca Juniors 0
Independiente 0
HT: 0–0. Att: 45,000

2nd leg: Nov 29 (Avellaneda)
Independiente 0
Boca Juniors 0
HT: 0–0. Att: 60,000
Winners: Boca Juniors, 5–3 on pens, 0–0 agg

1990

Semi-finals
Nacional (Uru) bt Estudiantes de La Plata (Arg) 0–0, 0–0
(5–3 on pens, 0–0 agg)
Olimpia (Par) bt Penarol (Uru) 1–2 6–0
(7–2 agg)

Final
1st leg: Jan 5, 1991 (Montevideo)
Nacional 0
Olimpia 3 (Gonzalez 55, Amarilla 81, Samaniego 87)
HT: 0–0. Att: 45,000. Ref: Wright (Bra)

2nd leg: Jan 11, 1991 (Asuncion)
Olimpia 3 (Samaniego 27, Amarilla 50, Monzon 69)
Nacional 3
(Cardaccio 5, Moran 31, Wilson Nunes 34)
HT: 1–3. Att: 40,000. Ref: Loustau (Arg)
Winners: Olimpia, 6–3 agg

1991

Semi-finals
Cruzeiro (Bra) bt Olimpia (Par) 1–1, 0–0
(5–3 on pens, 1–1 agg)
River Plate (Arg) bt Penarol (Uru) 2–0, 3–1
(5–1 agg)

Final
1st leg: Nov 13 (Buenos Aires)
River Plate 2 (Rivarola 30, Higuain 89)
Cruzeiro 0
HT: 1–0. Att: 60,000. Ref: Orellana (Ecu)

2nd leg: Nov 20 (Belo Horizonte)
Cruzeiro 3 (Ademir 34, Tilico 52, Marquinhos 75)
River Plate 0
HT: 1–0. Att: 80,000. Ref: Silva (Chl)
Winners: Cruzeiro 3–2 agg

1992

Semi-finals
Cruzeiro (Bra) bt Olimpia (Par) 1–0, 2–2
(3–2 agg)
Racing Club (Arg) bt Flamengo (Bra) 3–3, 1–0
(4–3 agg)

Final
1st leg: Nov 18 (Belo Horizonte)
Cruzeiro 4 (Roberto Gaucho 31 57, Luis Fernando 69, Boiadeiro 84)
Racing Club 0
HT: 1–0. Att: 77,000. Ref: Torres (Col)

2nd leg: Nov 25 (Buenos Aires)
Racing Club 1 (Garcia 84pen)
Cruzeiro 0
HT: 0–0. Att: 20,000. Ref: Escobar (Par)
Winners: Cruzeiro 4–1 agg

1993

Semi-finals
Sao Paulo (Bra) bt Atletico Nacional Medellin (Col) 1–0, 1–2
(5–4 pens, 2–2 agg)
Flamengo (Bra) bt Nacional (Uru) 2–1, 3–0
(5–1 agg)

Final
1st leg: Nov 17 (Rio de Janeiro)
Flamengo 2 (Marquinhos 35 47)
Sao Paulo 2 (Leonardo 16, Juninho 87)
HT: 1–1. Att: 50,000. Ref: Rezende (Bra)

2nd leg: Nov 24 (Sao Paulo)
Sao Paulo 2 (Leonardo 61, Juninho 80)
Flamengo 2 (Renato Gaucho 9, Marquinhos 62)
HT: 0–1. Att: 70,000. Ref: Marsilia (Bra)
Winners: Sao Paulo 5–3 on pens, 4–4 agg

1994

Semi-finals
Independiente (Arg) bt Cruzeiro (Bra) 0–1, 4–0
(4–1 agg)
Boca Juniors (Arg) bt Sao Paulo (Bra) 2–0, 0–1
(2–1 agg)

Final
1st leg: Nov 3 (Buenos Aires)

Boca Juniors 1 (Martinez 25)
Independiente 1 (Rambert 72)
HT: 1–0. Att: 45,000. Ref: Ruscio (Arg)
2nd leg: Nov 9 (Avellaneda)
Independiente 1 (Rambert 55)
Boca Juniors 0
HT: 0–0. Att: 60,000. Ref: Lamolina (Arg)
Winners: Independiente, 2–1 agg

1995

Independiente (Arg) bt River Plate (Arg) 2–2, 0–0
(4–1 on pens, 2–2 agg)
Flamengo (Bra) bt Cruzeiro (Bra) 1–0, 3–1
(4–1 agg)

Final
1st leg: Nov 29 (Avellaneda)
Indepediente 2 (Mazzoni 1, Domizi 72)
Flamengo 0
HT: 1–0. Att: 55,000. Ref: Imperatore (Chl)

2nd leg: Dec 6 (Rio de Janeiro)
Flamengo 1 (Romario 62)
Independiente 0
HT: 0–0. Att: 70,000. Ref: Gonzalez (Par)
Winners: Independiente, 2–1 agg

1996

Semi-finals
Velez Sarsfield (Arg) bt Santos (Bra) 2–1, 1–1
(3–2 agg)
Cruzeiro (Bra) bt Colo Colo (Chl) 3–2, 4–0
(7–2 agg)

Final
1st leg: Nov 20 (Belo Horizonte)
Cruzeiro 0
Velez Sarsfield 1 (Chilavert 87pen)
HT: 0–0. Att: 80,000. Ref: Ruiz (Col)

2nd leg: Dec 4 (Buenos Aires)
Velez Sarsfield 2 (Camps 4, Gelson og 8)
Cruzeiro 0
HT: 2–0. Att: 50,000. Ref: Ruiz (Col)
Winners: Velez Sarsfield, 3–0 agg

1997

Semi-finals
River Plate (Arg) bt Nacional (Uru) 2–0, 1–2
(3–2 agg)
Sao Paulo (Bra) bt Colo Colo (Chl) 3–1 1–0
(4–1 agg)

Final
1st leg: Dec 5 (Sao Paulo)
Sao Paulo 0
River Plate 0
Att: 70,000. Ref: Sanchez (Chl)

2nd leg: Dec 17 (Buenos Aires)
River Plate 2 (Salas 47 58)
Sao Paulo 1 (Dodo 51)
HT: 0–0. Att: 70,000. Ref: Aquino (Par)
Winners: River Plate, 2–1 agg

1998

Not contested

SOUTH AMERICAN RECOPA

The value of the creation of the Super Copa was doubled by the simultaneous launch of the Recopa – a neat Spanish term originally used in Europe by the the Madrid media to describe the European Cup-winners Cup.

The South American formalized the term by adopting it for what was, confusingly, their own version of the European Supercup – for the Recopa matched annually the winners of the Copa Libertadores with the winners of the Super Copa.

This did cause occasional confusion since South American clubs were given free rein to enter as many competitions as they qualified for. Thus the big clubs could participate simultaneously in both of the international competitions – not an option in the European club events.

Thus, in 1990, no Recopa final could be held because Olimpia of Paraguay had, remarkably, won the Copa Libertadores and the Super Copa. They were granted the right to proclaim themselves Recopa winners – thus completing a unique treble

– thanks to a walkover victory over... themselves.

The increasingly strong links being developed between North and South American and Japanese football, led to the Recopa final ultimately being turned into a promotional weapon in the fight to establish the professional game in both the United States and Japan.

Thus, the Recopa was staged in Miami's Orange Bowl in 1990 and in Kobe, Japan, in 1991 – which ultimately became an apparently permanent venue for the match. The Japanese turned out enthusiastically to support the event – since it usually featured at least one club from their favourite football nation, Brazil – and South American television paid handsomely to beam the match back to its home continent.

RESULTS

1988

1st leg: Jan 31, 1989 (Montevideo)
Nacional (Uru) 1 (Fonseca)
Racing Club (Arg) 0
HT: 1–0. Att: 45,000

2nd leg: Feb 6, 1989 (Avellaneda)
Racing Club 0
Nacional 0
HT: 0–0. Att: 38,500
Winners: Nacional 1–0 agg

1989

Mar 17, 1990 (Miami, USA)
Boca Juniors (Arg) 1 (Latorre)
Atletico Nacional Medellin (Col) 0
HT: 0–0. Att: 25,000

1990

No play-off: Olimpia acclaimed as winners since they had won the Copa Libertadores and the Super Copa

1991

Apr 19, 1992 (Kobe, Japan)
Colo Colo (Chl) 0
Cruzeiro (Bra) 0
HT: 0–0. Att: 35,000
Winners: Colo Colo, 5–4 on pens

1992

1st leg: Sep 26, 1993 (Sao Paulo)
Sao Paulo (Bra) 0
Cruzeiro (Bra) 0
HT: 0–0. Att: 75,000

2nd leg: Sep 29, 1993 (Belo Horizonte)
Cruzeiro 0
Sao Paulo 0
HT: 0–0. Att: 50,000
Winners: Sao Paulo, 4–2 on pens

1993

Apr 3, 1994 (Kobe, Japan)
Sao Paulo (Bra) 3 (Leonardo 12, Guilherme 73, Muller 87)
Botafogo (Bra) 1 (Cavalo 68)
HT: 1–0. Att: 32,000

1994

Apr 9, 1995 (Tokyo, Japan)
Independiente (Arg) 1 (Serrizuela 70)
Velez Sarsfield (Arg) 0
HT: 0–0. Att: 40,000. Ref: Lamolina (Arg)

1995

Apr 7, 1996 (Kobe, Japan)
Gremio (Bra) 4 (Jardel 18, Carlos Miguel 44, Adilson 69pen, Paulo Nunes 79)
Independiente (Arg) 1 (Burruchaga 25 pen)
HT: 2–1. Att: 28,00. Ref: Gonzalez (Par)

1996

Apr 13, 1997 (Kobe, Japan)
Velez Sarsfield (Arg) 1 (Chilavert 29 pen)
River Plate (Arg) 1 (Francescoli 82 pen)
HT: 1–0. Att: 35,000. Ref: Jorge Nieves (Uru)
Winners: Velez Sarsfield, 4–2 on pens

COPA INTERAMERICANA

IN 1993, the South American international club scene was further complicated by the creation of the Copa CONMEBOL, which corresponded roughly to the European UEFA Cup in that it was named after the confederation and featured the two next-best clubs in the domestic championships who had not qualified for the top event – in South America's case, the Copa Libertadores.

L ike the Super Copa, this was also viewed at first as just another sop to the big clubs. Those previous Libertadores winners who missed out on the current season's event could thus still take part in two international events – the Super Copa and the Copa CONMEBOL.

Thus, in 1993, Penarol of Uruguay were eliminated in the first round of the Super Copa but reached the final of the Copa

CONMEBOL – where they lost to Brazil's Botafogo. The Uruguayans were not happy in defeat since, had the European rule of away goals counting double applied, they would have won the final. Held 1–1 at home in Montevideo, Penarol forced a 2–2 draw in Rio de Janeiro. Simple aggregate being decisive, the final then went – to the Uruguayans' consternation – to a penalty shoot-out, which they lost 3–1.

RESULTS

1993

Semi-finals
**Botafogo (Bra) bt Atletico Mineiro (Bra)
1–3, 3–0**
(4–3 agg)
Penarol (Uru) bt San Lorenzo (Arg) 1–0, 1–2
(4–2 on pens, 2–2 agg)

Final
1st leg: Sep 22 (Montevideo)
Penarol 1 (Otero 37)
Botafogo 1 (Perivaldo 4)
HT: 1–1. Att: 50,000. Ref: Escobar (Par)

2nd leg: Sep 29 (Rio de Janeiro)
Botafogo 2 (Eliel 50, Sinval 70)
Penarol 2 (Berngoechea 33, Otero 89)
HT: 0–1. Att: 80,000. Ref: Lamolina (Arg)
Winners: Botafogo 3–1 on pens, 3–3 agg

1994

Semi-finals
**Penarol (Uru) bt Universidad de Chile (Chl)
2–0, 1–1**
(3–1 agg)
**Sao Paulo (Bra) bt Corinthians (Bra) 4–3,
2–3**
(5–4 on pens, 6–6 agg)

Final
1st leg: Dec 9 (Sao Paulo)
Sao Paulo 6 (Caio 4, 75, Cate 58 59 90, Toninho 73)
Penarol 1 (Aguilera 4)
HT: 1–1. Att: 85,000. Ref: Guerrero (Chl)

2nd leg: Dec 21 (Montevideo)
Penarol 3 (Martin Rodriguez 57 73, Dario Silva 72)
Sao Paulo 0
HT: 0–0. Att: 20,000. Ref: Castrilli (Arg)
Winners: Sao Paulo, 6–4 agg

1995

Semi-finals
**Atletico Mineiro (Bra) bt America Cali (Col)
3–4, 1–0**
(4–3 on pens, 4–4 agg)
**Rosario Central (Arg) bt Colegiales (Par)
2–0, 3–1**
(5–1 agg)

Final
1st leg: Dec 12 (Belo Horizonte)
Atletico Mineiro 4 (Ezio 7, Cairo 55, Paulo Roberto 60, Carlos 89)
Rosario Central 0
HT: 1–0. Att: 80,000. Ref: Velazquez (Par)

2nd leg: Dec 19 (Rosario)
Rosario Central 4 (Da Silva 22, Carbonari 38 89, Cardetti 40)
Atletico Mineiro 0
HT: 3–0. Att: 45,000. Ref: Filippi (Uru)
Winners: Rosario Central, 4–3 on pens, 4–4 agg

1996

Semi-finals
Independiente Santa Fe (Col) bt Vasco da Gama (Bra) 1–2, 1–0
(6–5 on pens, 2–2 agg)
**Lanus (Arg) bt Rosario Central (Arg) 3–0,
3–1**
(6–1 agg)

Final
1st leg: Nov 20 (Lanus)
Lanus 2 (Mena 31pen, Ibagaza 79)
Independiente Santa Fe 0
HT: 1–0. Att: 35,000. Ref: Robles (Chl)

2nd leg: Dec 12 (Santa Fe)
Independiente SF 1 (Wittingham 4pen)
Lanus 0
HT: 1–0. Att: 50,000. Ref: Pereira (Bra)
Winners: Lanus, 2–1 agg

1997

Semi-finals
Lanus (Arg) bt Colon (Arg) 2–0, 0–0
(2–0 agg)
**Atletico Mineiro (Bra) bt Universitario Lima
(Per) 2–0, 4–0**
(6–0 agg)

Final
Nov 7 (Buenos Aires) 1st leg
Lanus 1 (Ibagaza 18)
Atletico Mineiro 4 (Bruno 41, Serrizuela og 55, Hernani 60, Valdir 79)
HT: 1–1. Att: 20,000. Ref: Gallesio (Uru)

Dec 17 (Belo Horizonte) 2nd leg
Atletico Mineiro 1 (Jorginho 9)
Lanus 1 (Trimarchi 58)
HT: 1–0. Att: 15,000. Ref: Gonzalez (Par)
Winners: Atletico Mineiro, 5–2 agg

SOUTH AMERICAN COPA CONMEBOL

THE increasing value of a link with Mexican and then United States soccer grew steadily more obvious throughout the 1960s. Mexico not only boasted some of the richest clubs in the Americas but also access to major television and sponsorship.

The opportunity to gain added prestige through laying claim to being the champion club of the entire American continent was also a valuable attraction in making a regular match between the club champions of South America and those of Central and North America.

The competition has stuttered along, largely because the South American clubs had problems either finding fixture space or because the concept never appealed to their fans. Estudiantes de La Plata from Argentina were the first winners in 1969, but it was two years before the competition was continued and there were further breaks throughout the 1970s and 1980s.

The lack of interest in South America is evidenced by the ready manner in which Argentina clubs in particular, in the competition's early years, sold their right to home advantage – playing both ties either in the CONCACAF host's home or on neutral territory in between, a ploy which also reduced match costs. In recent years, the Libertadores winners have also developed a tendency to leave the Interamericana to their runners-up, while they concentrated on the more important World Club Cup in Tokyo.

The incorporation, from 1998, of Mexican clubs in the Copa Libertadores may finally prove the last nail in the coffin of the Interamericana. After all, the competition had thus, in effect, been swallowed up by its southern neighbour.

Quite which year the competition should belong to remains a thorny problem for South American soccer statisticians. Sometimes, the Copa Libertadores and the CONCACAF Club Championship, though they began in the same year, ended in a different year, usually because the CONCACAF competition took much longer to complete.

The pragmatic conclusion is therefore to treat each tie as appropriate to the year in which it took place.

RESULTS

1968

1st leg: Feb 13 (Mexico City)
Toluca (Mex) 1 (Linares)
Estudiantes de La Plata (Arg) 2 (Conigliaro, Bilardo)
HT: 1–1. Att: 100,000

2nd leg: Feb 19 (La Plata)
Estudiantes de La Plata 1 (Veron)
Toluca 2 (Linares, Albino)
HT: 1–0. Att: 45,000

Play-off: Feb 21 (Montevideo)
Estudiantes de La Plata 3 (Conigliaro 2, E Flores)
Toluca 0
HT: 2–0. Att: 35,000

1969

Not contested

1970

Not contested

1971

1st leg: Jul 15 (Mexico City)
Cruz Azul (Mex) 1 (Pulido)
Nacional (Uru) 1 (Mamelli)
HT: 1–0. Att: 75,000

2nd leg: Nov 7 (Montevideo)
Nacional 2 (Mamelli, B Castro)

Cruz Azul 1 (Bustos)
HT: 1–1. Att: 40,000
Winners: Nacional, 3–2 agg

1972

1st leg: Jun 17 (San Pedro Sula, Honduras)
Olimpia (Hon) 1 (Brand)
Independiente (Arg) 2 (Semenewicz, Maglioni)
HT: 0–0. Att: 20,000

2nd leg: Jun 20 (Tegucigalpa, Honduras)
Olimpia 0
Independiente 2 (Maglioni, Balbuena)
HT: 0–2. Att: 15,000
Winners: Independiente, 4–1 agg

1973

Not contested

1974

Nov 24 (Guatemala City) 1st leg
Municipal 0
Independiente (Arg) 1 (Bochini)
HT: 0–0. Att: 30,000

Nov 26 (Guatemala City) 2nd leg
Municipal 1 (Mitrovich)
Independiente 0
HT: 0–0. Att: 25,000
Winners: Independiente 4–2 on pens, 1–1 agg

1975

Not contested

1976

1st leg: Aug 26 (Caracas, Venezuela)
Independiente (Arg) 2 (Bochini, Villaverde)
Atletico Espanol (Mex) 2 (Ramirez, Borbolla)
HT: 1–1. Att: 22,000
2nd leg: Aug 29 (Caracas, Venezuela)
Independiente 0
Atletico Espanol 0
HT: 0–0. Att: 15,000
Winners: Independiente 4–2 on pens, 2–2 agg

1977

1st leg: Mar 28 (Buenos Aires)
Boca Juniors (Arg) 3 (Salinas 2, Mastrangelo)
America (Mex) 0
HT: 1–0. Att: 45,000

2nd leg: Apr 17 (Mexico City)
America 1 (Kiese)
Boca Juniors 0
HT: 1–0. Att: 100,000

Play-off: Apr 19 (Mexico City)
America 2 (Acevedo, Reynoso)
Boca Juniors 1 (Pavon)
HT: 2–1. Att: 105,000

1978

Not contested

1979

Not contested

1980

1st leg: Feb 18, 1980 (San Salvador)
Deportivo FAS (ESv) 3 (Casadel 2, Abraham)
Olimpia (Par) 3 (Solalinde, Yaluk, Isasi)
HT: 1–1. Att: 35,000

Mar 17, 1980 (Asuncion)
Olimpia 5 (Aquino, Michelagnoli 2, Ortiz 2)
Deportivo FAS 0
HT: 3–0. Att: 35,000
Winners: Olimpia, 8–3 agg

1981

1st leg: Mar 25 (Mexico City)
UNAM (Mex) 3 (Hugo Sanchez 2, Ferreti)
Nacional (Uru) 1 (Esparrago)
HT: 1–0. Att: 100,000

Apr 8 (Montevideo) 2nd leg
Nacional 3 (J Cabrera 2, W Cabrera)
UNAM 1 (Vargas)
HT: 2–1. Att: 45,000

Play-off: May 15 (Los Angeles, USA)
UNAM 2 (Ferreti, Vargas)
Nacional 1 (J Cabrera)
HT: 2–1. Att: 35,000

1982

Not contested

1983

Not contested

1984

Not contested

1985

Not contested

1986

Dec 11 (Port of Spain, Trinidad)
Defence Force 0
Argentinos Juniors 1 (Valdez)
HT: 0–1. Att: 30,000

1987

1st leg: Jul 21 (San Jose)
Liga Deportiva Alajuelense 0
River Plate 0
HT: 0–0. Att: 16,000

2nd leg: Aug 16 (Buenos Aires)
River Plate 3 (Villazan, Funes, Enrique)
Liga Deportiva Alajuelense 0
HT: 2–0. Att: 50,000
Winners: River Plate, 3–0 agg

1988

Not contested

1989

1st leg: Mar 5 (Tegucigalpa, Honduras)
Olimpia (Hon) 1 (Rivera)
Nacional (Uru) 1 (Fonseca)
HT: 1–1. Att: 30,000

2nd leg: Mar 30 (Montevideo)
Nacional 4 (Fonseca, Ostolaza, Noe 2)
Olimpia 0
HT: 2–0. Att: 35,000
Winners: Nacional, 5–1 agg

1990

1st leg: Jul 25 (Medellin)
Atletico Nacional (Col) 2 (Fajardo, Galeano)
UNAM (Mex) 0
HT; 1–0. Att: 40,000

2nd leg: Aug 1 (Mexico City)
UNAM 1 (Negrete)
Atletico Nacional Medellin 4 (Restrepo 2, Galeano, Arango)
HT: 0–1. Att: 85,000
Winners: Atletico Nacional Medellin, 6–1 agg

1991

1st leg: Oct 1 (Asuncion)
Olimpia (Par) 1 (Gonzalez)
America MC (Mex) 1 (Edu)
HT: 1–0. Att: 40,000

2nd leg: Oct 12 (Mexico City)
America 2 (Toninho 2)
Olimpia 1 (Gonzalez)
HT: 1–1. Att: 60,000
Winners: America MC, 3–2 agg

1992

1st leg: Sep 9 (Puebla)
Puebla (Mex) 1 (Silmar)
Colo Colo (Chl) 4 (Barticciotto 3, Adomaitis)
HT: 1–2. Att: 8,000

2nd leg: Sep 22 (Santiago)
Colo Colo 3 (Rubio, Mendoza, Adomaitis)
Puebla 1 (Rotlan)
HT: 1–1. Att: 55,000
Winners: Colo Colo, 7–2 agg

1993

Not contested

1994

1st leg: Sep 15 (San Jose, Costa Rica)
Deportivo Saprissa (CR) 3 (Myers 20, Fonseca 64, Wanchope 84)
Universidad Catolica (Chl) 1 (S Vasquez 71)
HT: 1–0. Att: 30,000. Ref: Escobar (Par)

Oct 1 (Santiago) 2nd leg
Universidad Catolica 5 (Romero 28, Acosta 30, Olmos 89, Ardiman 102, Barrera 111)
Deportivo Saprissa 1 (Wanchope 35)
HT: 3–0. 90min: 3–1. Att: 50,000. Ref: Chapell (Per)
Winners: Universidad Catolica, 6–4 agg after extra time

1995

Not contested

1996

1st leg: Feb 17 (Cartago, Costa Rica)
Cartagines (CR) 0
Velez Sarsfield (Arg) 0
Att: 30,000. Ref: Archundia (Mex)

2nd leg: Feb 24 (Buenos Aires)
Velez Sarsfield 2 (Flores 3, 76)
Cartagines 0
HT: 1–0. Att: 45,000. Ref: Dluznievski (Uru)
Winners: Velez Sarsfield, 2–0 agg

1997

Apr 3 (San Jose, Costa Rica)
Deportivo Saprissa (CR) 2 (Mahia 38, Wanchope 89)
Atletico Nacional Medellin 3 (Col) (Comas 27, Gomez 35, Gaviria 70)
HT: 1–2. Att: 35,000. Ref: Alcala (Mex)

EUROPEAN CHAMPIONS CLUB CUP/ UEFA CHAMPIONS LEAGUE

Sport in general – association football especially, and the European Champions Cup in particular – may claim to have been the greatest unifying force in Europe in the 20th century.

Of course, the communications revolution and increasing ease of travel helped. But these were mere mechanics. It was the sporting ideal of peaceable, competitive interaction which channelled the historic antagonisms of Europe into more acceptable – and entertaining – confrontations.

In the late 1920s, the associations of federal Europe had created, under the visionary impulse of Austria's Hugo Meisl, the Mitropa Cup (a contraction of the German *Mittel Europa* – Central Europe). Italy, Austria, Hungary and Czechoslovakia were the dominant partners, though as the competition's success grew, so their neighbours wanted to join in.

The Mitropa Cup pioneered the format later to become so familiar. It was a knockout competition but each pair of teams played each other home and away with the aggregate score deciding who progressed into the next round. Rapid and FK Austria of Vienna, Slavia and Sparta of Prague, Bologna and Ambrosiana-Inter of Italy were the giants of the age.

The Mitropa staggered back into life after World War Two but the spirit had vanished just as the cold war barriers had gone up between old neighbours. Football's focus of club power shifted west as the top clubs of Italy, Spain, France and Portugal created the Latin Cup. This was an end-of-season tournament played – in a single venue and in a single-match knock-out formula – between the newly-crowned champions of each country. "National" points were allocated and, every four years, they were totalled up to provide an overall winning country.

Real Madrid, Barcelona and Benfica developed their initial taste for European competitive drama in the Latin Cup.

Elsewhere, the end was the same if the means were different. The fledgling fascination of continental football, sparked by the legendary Hungarians of Ferenc Puskas in 1953, provoked progressive Wolverhampton Wanderers into arranging a series of international friendlies under their recently installed floodlighting system.

They beat Honved, the Budapest side which provided Hungary's national team nucleus, and also Moscow Spartak. The English newspapers, in their comfortable xenophobia, instantly proclaimed Wolves the champions of Europe.

That was like a red rag to a bull for Gabriel Hanot, a former French international who had become editor of the Parisian sports newspaper *L'Equipe*. He had seen the developments at Real Madrid, as well as the thrilling power of a Milan team built around their Swedish Gre-No-Li trio (Gunnar Gren, Gunnar Nordahl, Nils Liedholm) and he was thrilled by the potential of a "local" Reims club with a twinkle-toed creative centre-forward named Raymond Kopa.

Hanot took out a page of his newspaper to propose a "real" European club cup. He invited representatives of leading clubs from all over Europe to a meeting in Paris, and they laid down the concept of a midweek knockout competition based on the two-leg aggregate system. Some clubs were more enthusiastic than others.

Real Madrid, whose ambition knew no bounds under the leadership of president Santiago Bernabeu and secretary Raimundo Saporta, were signing some of the world's finest players and wanted a stage on which to parade them. This was it.

On the other hand Chelsea, League champions in 1955, were ordered by the English football authorities not to go near this disruptive, unauthorized, extra-curricular activity.

English out again

So, like most international football competitions, the English missed the start. That was, precisely, on September 4, in front of 60,000 in Lisbon where Sporting Clube de Portugal drew 3–3 with Partizan of Belgrade. Four days later, Real Madrid set their own ball rolling when they defeated Servette of Geneva 2–0 in Switzerland. Appropriately it was Madrid's right half and captain – and later coach – Miguel Munoz, who scored their first goal.

This was football in a different era. Television was a new technological toy which caught fading images of the first final but nothing else. There were no sponsors, no commercial side-shows. Football was king – and the glamour of Real Madrid, winning for the first five years in a row, provided the magical lustre which launched the European Champions Cup on its journey into the sporting stratosphere.

Even now, with its format changed to incorporate a league system with million-pound bonuses on offer, it remains the most prestigious club event in the world.

The French having dreamed up the idea, the first final was staged, appropriately, in the old Parc des Princes in Paris. England did make one contribution – providing referee Arthur Ellis. Under his control Reims raced into a lead of 2–0 then 3–1. Madrid stormed back to win 4–3. Their Argentine-born centre-forward Alfredo Di Stefano, inside forward compatriot Hector Rial and flying left winger Francisco Gento were on their way towards football immortality.

Kings of Europe: Real Madrid's Marquitos, skipper Jose Maria Zarraga and Canario collect the 1960 Champions Cup

The next season the English joined up in the shape of Manchester United's Busby Babes. They had been ordered not to compete but manager Matt Busby shared the same vision as Madrid, and went his own way – to triumph and disaster.

United opened with a 10–0 thrashing of Belgian champions Anderlecht but were ultimately too inexperienced to cope with the semi-final sophistication of Madrid for whom Di Stefano covered huge tracts of the pitch – one moment clearing from his own penalty area, the next shooting for goal at the other end.

Real Madrid's defence was not up to the standard of their attack – in fact, they needed a replay to defeat Rapid Vienna along the way and would have been eliminated had today's away goals rule then applied – but they could always summon up the necessary goals. Raymond Kopa, leading light with Reims in the first European Cup, starred in the 3–1 home victory over United and the 2–2 draw in Manchester.

The final was to be hosted by the previous year's winners. Thus Madrid beat Italy's Fiorentina 2–0, with goals from Di Stefano (penalty) and Gento in their own Estadio Bernabeu in front of 110,000 delighted Spaniards. The next season, 1957–58, was overshadowed by tragedy though it also produced a classic final and the first which went to extra time. Benfica of Portugal and Dutch club Ajax competed for the first time – Ajax losing to Vasas of Hungary in the quarter-finals while Benfica were beaten in the second round by Seville (invited as a second Spanish entry since they had finished league runners-up to Madrid, who benefited from the holders' automatic right of participation).

Also in the quarter-finals, Manchester United scored a thrilling victory over Red Star Belgrade only for their plane to crash on take-off after a refuelling stop in Munich on the way home. Eight players were killed, including England stalwarts Roger Byrne, Duncan Edwards and Tommy Taylor – and a weakened United lost to Milan in the semi-finals.

Milan, beaten by Madrid in the 1956 semi-finals, came within a whisker of revenge in the final in the Heysel stadium in Brussels. In the shadow of the Atomium, Di Stefano kept Madrid in the game virtually single-handed and also contributed one of the goals with which they eventually triumphed 3–2 in extra time.

In 1959–60, Reims returned to the attack with a forward line spearheaded by Just Fontaine, who had scored a record-breaking 13 goals at the World Cup finals in 1958 in Sweden. He opened his European club account with a four-goal display at Ards in Northern Ireland.

Spain again

Two Madrid clubs competed this time, Real as holders and neighbours Atletico by special invitation after finishing runners-up to Real. They came face to face in the semi-finals. Under present rules, Atletico would have won on away goals. Instead, after winning at home and losing away, they went down 2–1 in a replay. Madrid, although having Kopa limping for much of the clash, defeated Reims 2–0 in the final, despite a missed penalty.

England's challenge was represented by Wolves who proved a shadow of the team in competition that they had been in those famous friendlies. After being granted a first-round bye, they fell to West German champions Schalke. The gap between the top English and European clubs was brutally exposed in 1959–60. Wolves were thrashed in the quarter-finals by Barcelona who were themselves beaten by Real Madrid in the semis.

Madrid then exemplified all the class, excitement and drama of the event in the most famous match in its history – their 7–3 demolition of Eintracht Frankfurt at Hampden Park, Glasgow, in May, 1960, before a record crowd for a final. Di Stefano scored three of Madrid's goals with the other four all contributed by the great Hungarian Ferenc Puskas.

It was not that Frankfurt were a poor team – anything but. They had, after all, just put 12 goals past Scottish champions Rangers in the semi-finals and opened the scoring against Madrid in the final.

Looked at today, the final makes strange viewing, considering the space in which the players had time to work. But the flow of goals remains breathtaking with Di Stefano and Puskas, who set a then record with 12 goals in the season's competition, supported brilliantly by Francisco Gento, Jose Santamaria and by the hard-working inside right from Real Betis, Luis Del Sol.

Time for change

That was also the beginning of the end. Madrid were eliminated in the second round the following season by rivals Barcelona – led by a veteran Hungarian of their own in Ladislav Kubala and by possibly the greatest Spanish footballer of all time in Luis Suarez. He scored both Barcelona's goals in the 2–2 draw in Madrid in the first leg and the Catalans won the return 2–1 against a Madrid side who had defender Pachin at half-pace for much of the game and no luck with several refereeing decisions.

Barcelona then needed a play-off in Brussels to defeat Germany's Hamburg in the semi-finals. The semi-finals also saw the Cup's first serious crowd trouble when Austrian fans ran amok in Vienna as Rapid headed for defeat against Benfica. Barcelona were favourites for the final in Berne but Benfica played magnificently to win 3–2 after Barcelona hit both posts and the bar. Sandor Kocsis and left-winger Zoltan Czibor thus took away another bitter memory from the stadium where, seven years earlier, they had ended up as surprise losers with Hungary in the World Cup Final.

For the following season, 1961–62, Benfica had reinforced their attack in formidable fashion with the addition of their new Mozambique-born striker, Eusebio. The quarter-finals provided some classic action. The Czech army team, Dukla, guided from midfield by Josef Masopust, fell to a Tottenham double-winning

side reinforced by Jimmy Greaves. Then Italy's Juventus (Omar Sivori, John Charles and all) went down to Real Madrid, though not until after a play-off in Paris. Juventus had earned the extra chance after becoming the first team in Champions Cup history to beat Madrid in their own Estadio Bernabeu.

The Tottenham bubble burst in the semi-finals. Manager Bill Nicholson used Tony Marchi, back from Torino, as an extra defender in away legs but the tactic failed in Lisbon where Spurs lost 3–1 to Benfica. The return was a soon-to-be-typical White Hart Lane European special, but Benfica survived to go on and defeat Real Madrid – after being 3–1 down – in yet another fantastic final, this time in Amsterdam.

Season 1962–63 saw the first Italian success. Milan had been original entrants in the Champions Cup, lost one final (in 1958) and had no intention of losing another. They boasted a superb, cosmopolitan team but, for all the midfield wisdom of Brazil's Dino Sani, the goals of Brazil's Jose Altafini and the tight marking of Peruvian Victor Benitez, it was Italy's own Gianni Rivera who was the No. 1.

The British challenge was provided by Ipswich for England and Dundee for Scotland but neither proved to be up to the Milan challenge. Ipswich were rolled over in the second round while Dundee, after fine victories over Cologne, Sporting Lisbon and Anderlecht, fell to Milan in the semi-finals.

Benfica did not have an easy time reaching Wembley, the first English staging of Europe's top club event. Eusebio scored a second-round hat-trick against Norrkoping but then Dukla Prague, followed by Feyenoord, tested Portuguese creativity and resilience to the limits. Perhaps they came to face Milan at Wembley believing that the hardest part was behind them – especially after Eusebio outpaced Giovanni Trapattoni to shoot them ahead. But Milan had planned for a full 90 minutes and Gianni Rivera twice sent Jose Altafini away for the two goals which earned him a one-season record of 14.

Teams tighten up

The nature of the game was changing. The free-flowing attacking football of the 1950s had given way to a much more pragmatic, physical style. The rewards for victory and the pressure for achievement were increasing all the time and, in the circumstances, it was hardly surprising that Italians dominated the competition in this era. Helenio Herrera's Internazionale were the most adept exponents of this new, negative football, marking tightly at the back and using a sweeper, in skipper Armando Picchi, who was never to be found anywhere except behind his own defenders. Inter had also bought Luis Suarez from Barcelona to run midfield and revealed the youthful Sandro Mazzola – the equal of Rivera – in attack. Inter had too much all-round strength for Everton, Monaco, Partizan Belgrade and Borussia Dortmund and then too much physical resistance against an ageing, fading Real Madrid in the final in Vienna. Mazzola scored two of Inter's goals in the victory to finish as the competition's joint-top scorer.

Liverpool announced their arrival on the Champions Cup scene by reaching the 1964–65 semi-finals. Bill Shankly's men beat Anderlecht home and away in the second round, but needed the toss of a coin to beat Cologne after a dramatic play-off in Rotterdam in the quarter-finals. They harboured brief ambitions of beating Inter in the semi-finals. But, after winning 3–1 at home, Liverpool were outmanoeuvred in Milan. Inter's Spanish forward, Joaquin Peiro, "stole" a bounced ball from keeper Tommy Lawrence for one goal and attacking full-back Giacinto Facchetti scored a brilliant winner.

In the final, also staged in the San Siro, Inter faced Benfica. The Portuguese, appearing in their fourth final in five years, had everything against them: the venue, the crowd, the monsoon rain which wrecked their delicate passing and the injury which cost them the services of veteran goalkeeper Costa Pereira. Inter won with a single goal from Brazilian right-winger Jair and appeared to possess the discipline and iron will to dominate Europe for years. However, the British challenge was growing ever stronger. Manchester United, in 1965–66, became favourites after a thrilling 5–1 victory over Benfica in Lisbon in the quarter-finals – only to blow up against Partizan Belgrade next time out. The Yugoslavs became the first eastern European team to reach the final where their opponents – surprising semi-final victors themselves over holders Inter – were a new Real Madrid.

Di Stefano and Puskas had gone, succeeded by a new generation nicknamed the "Ye-ye" team in regard of that era's youth culture. They certainly had too much rhythm for Partizan and hit back from 1–0 down to win 2–1 with two goals inside six second-half minutes from Amancio and Serena. That was Madrid's sixth – and, for 32 years, last – Champions Cup.

Neither Liverpool nor Manchester United, surprisingly, achieved the first British success which had been on the cards for several years. Instead it was Scotland's Celtic who brought the Cup back for the first time when they defeated Inter 2–1 in Lisbon's Stadium of Light in 1967. Jock Stein's men overcame the shock of an early penalty by Mazzola to win with second-half goals from Tommy Gemmell and Steve Chalmers.

Rule Britannia

British domination was extended the following season when Manchester United – amid high emotion – marked the 10th anniversary of the Munich air disaster by securing the trophy their predecessors had been pursuing. This time there was no late slip-up, as against Partizan Belgrade at the semi-final stage in 1966, to stand between Matt Busby, Bobby Charlton, Bill Foulkes and destiny.

Bobby Charlton achieves Manchester Utd's dream in 1968

United beat Hibernians of Malta in the first round, Sarajevo in the second, Poland's Gornik Zabrze in the quarter-finals and old rivals Real Madrid in the semi-finals. In Madrid, United appeared eliminated when they went 3–1 down in the second leg. But they stormed back against all the odds and a goal from defender Bill Foulkes turned the aggregate tables.

Benfica beat Juventus in the semi-finals and resisted bravely against United and the pressure of the Wembley crowd for the first 90 minutes of the final. A late save by goalkeeper Alex Stepney from Eusebio earned United extra time when their superior fitness and ambition lifted them to three further goals and a 4–1 win. Munich survivor Bobby Charlton scored twice before being presented with the Cup as United's captain.

Their reign, however, lasted less than a year. Milan beat them in the 1969 semi-finals and then thrashed a naive, youthful Ajax 4–1 in the final in the Estadio Bernabeu, in Madrid. With hindsight, Milan's success was less significant than Ajax's presence in the final. A year later, Feyenoord became the first Dutch champions of Europe when they defeated Celtic 2–1 in extra-time in Milan, then Ajax themselves embarked upon the three-year run in which their "total football" enthralled the world game.

In 1971 Ajax collected their first Cup by defeating Panathinaikos of Athens, first Greek finalists and coached by ex-Honved and Real Madrid star Ferenc Puskas, 2–1 at Wembley. Their towering centre-forward Anton Antoniadis had scored freely on the way to the final, including two goals when

Ajax win their first Champions Cup at Wembley in 1971

Panathinaikos overcame a 4–1 first leg defeat by Red Star Belgrade in the semi-finals. But Ajax contained him easily and goals by Van Dijk and Arie Haan did the rest.

A new regime

"Total football" was perhaps the ultimate expression of modern football – involving footballers of high technical and intellectual competence switching and inter-changing to suit the state of the game. All of it was threaded together by the central genius of Johan Cruyff who also scored most of the goals – including the single effort which was, over 180 minutes, enough to defeat Benfica in the 1972 semi-finals.

Inter, with fortune on their side, qualified to meet Ajax in the final. In the second round, the Italians had been thrashed 7–1 by Borussia Mönchengladbach in Germany but obtained a replay in Berlin after protesting that Roberto Boninsegna had been struck by a soft drink can. While UEFA was deliberating, Inter won the second leg 4–2 then held out for a 0–0 draw in the replayed first leg. They beat Celtic on a penalty shoot-out in the semi-finals but, in the final in Rotterdam, their luck ran out. Two more goals for Cruyff secured Ajax's second Cup.

Next season, 1972–73, was Ajax's swan-song but they became the first team since Real Madrid to win the Champions Cup three years running. This they achieved thanks to a 1–0 win over Juventus in the final which was a much clearer victory than the result might indicate. Ajax scored through Johnny Rep after only

four minutes and played such wonderful, sweeping football over the next quarter of an hour that they could have won by a hatful of goals. It was almost as if they became bored with their own domination.

But, while Ajax could not score any more goals, Juventus could not score any at all despite the presence in their ranks of the veteran Brazilian striker Altafini, of £500,000 centre-forward Pietro Anastasi and of German World Cup star Helmut Haller.

England's challenge had been carried by Brian Clough's Derby County, who beat Benfica before falling to Juventus in the semi-finals – where penalty expert Alan Hinton missed a decisive spot-kick in the second leg at the Baseball Ground. Further controversy surrounded events in the first leg when Juve's Helmut Haller paid a "courtesy call" on German referee Kurt Tschenscher at half-time in Turin. Derby's protests were ignored.

No German team had, up to then, won the Champions Cup. Indeed, Bayern Munich had been put very firmly in their place in the 1973 quarter-finals by Ajax. But now the Ajax bubble had been punctured. Cruyff had been sold to Barcelona for a world record £922,000, coach Stefan Kovacs had gone and Ajax were eliminated in the second round by CSKA Sofia.

Franz Beckenbauer's Bayern Munich immediately took over as new favourites – a status they ultimately merited though not without difficulty. Reaching the final in the Heysel stadium in Brussels was not so hard. But once there, Bayern were within seconds of defeat in extra time by Atletico Madrid. Atletico had three players sent off in a battle of a semi-final against Celtic, but they held Bayern goalless through 90 minutes in Brussels then seized the lead through a free-kick from Luis Aragones. Bayern hit back, with a speculative low drive from centre-back Georg Schwarzenbeck, in the last seconds of injury time.

That meant a replay – the first and last in the history of the event. This time fatigue caught up with Atletico and Bayern won with two goals apiece from Uli Hoeness and Gerd Müller who became that season's eight-goal top scorer.

Bayern retained the Cup in 1975, but the final was marred by the first major eruption of a decade of English hooligan violence in Europe. Angry Leeds United fans ripped out seats in the new Parc des Princes in the closing minutes of their defeat.

They were furious that a "goal" by Peter Lorimer had been ruled out though referee Kitabdjian was later justified by film showing Billy Bremner in the centre of goalmouth, offside and clearly interfering with play.

Bayern, however, wer certainly lucky. Swedish defender Bjorn Andersson was injured in the second minute by a "careless" tackle and a gamble on Uli Hoeness' fitness was quickly exposed as well. Bayern brought on Klaus Wunder up front and withdrew Gerd Müller into midfield where he played with a poise and vision which surprised all those observers who had thought him nothing but a penalty-box poacher.

The Germans duly completed their hat-trick the following season, though in unconvincing fashion. They beat Jeunesse d'Esch of Luxembourg 8–1 on aggregate in the first round to only squeeze past Malmo 2–1 in the second. They were then in turn magnificent and irresistible in disposing of Benfica 0–0, 5–1 in the quarter finals and Real Madrid 1–1, 2–0 in the semis. Gerd Müller's wonderful opportunism was the key. He scored two of the five goals against Benfica and all three against Madrid.

Bayern's Final opponents were the first French team to reach that exalted stage since Reims faced Real Madrid in Stuttgart, in 1959. St Etienne dominated the first half at Hampden Park, yet the only goal fell to Bayern, 12 minutes into the second half when Franz Roth drove home a low 25-yard drive from a free-kick which caught goalkeeper Yvan Curkovic unsighted.

England take over

Spain, Portugal, Italy, Holland and Germany had all enjoyed their eras of dominance. Now it was the turn of English football – starting with Liverpool in 1977. Under Bill Shankly then Bob Paisley, Liverpool had been irresistible for more than a decade in England. It had been only a question of time before they translated that into European success.

Liverpool had already won the UEFA Cup and reached the final of the Cup-winners Cup before taking the last step – beating Borussia Mönchengladbach 3–1 in Rome in what was Kevin Keegan's competitive farewell before his transfer to Hamburg.

Liverpool went marching on a year later, better than ever after filling the Keegan void with the very player best equipped for the challenge in Celtic's Kenny Dalglish. He had joined the Scottish club on the day they won the Champions Cup a decade earlier and completed the circle of achievement by scoring the goal which, for Liverpool, defeated Club Brugge in the 1978 final.

The Belgians had reached Wembley with victories over KuPa of Finland, Panathinaikos, Atletico Madrid and Juventus. But injuries upset all coach Ernst Happel's tactical planning and he opted, in the end, for a highly-defensive formation and a minimal attack in which Hungarian Lajos Ku was making his European debut for the club.

Liverpool's second defence was short-lived, upset in the autumn of 1978 by a Nottingham Forest now managed by former Derby boss Brian Clough, who had become a cult figure in England – a media superstar with strong motivational powers.

His reputation never travelled to the continent but at least Nottingham Forest's two Champions Cup victories at the turn of the decade ensured a place for his name in the history books.

Forest began with a gesture of intent by eliminating Liverpool. They won 2–0 at home then drew 0–0 at Anfield. AEK Athens fell next, then Grasshopper Zurich and Koln in the semi-finals. The Germans thought they had achieved most of their task when they drew 3–3 at the City Ground in the first leg, but a single goal from Ian Bowyer did the trick for Forest in Germany.

One goal was also enough in the final against Malmo, the first Swedish side to progress so far. The scorer was Trevor Francis, England's first million-pound player when Clough signed him in mid-season from Birmingham City. A diving header shortly before half-time was all it took in Munich's Olympiastadion. For the first time, both managers in the final were English – Clough for Forest and Bob Houghton of Malmo.

The opposition to Forest's title defence appeared daunting the following term. Real Madrid, Ajax, FC Porto, Milan, Hamburg and Liverpool were considered better all-round outfits. But the luck of the draw meant Porto knocked out Milan and were then eliminated by Real Madrid – who, in turn, fell to Hamburg in the semi-finals. Madrid won 2–0 at home with goals from centre-forward Carlos Santillana but crashed 5–1 in West Germany. Madrid were furious at their failure since the final had already been allocated to their own Estadio Bernabeu.

Instead Hamburg, led by Kevin Keegan, took on Nottingham Forest there. Once again, Forest needed just one goal – scored after 19 minutes of the first half by their Scottish international left-winger John Robertson.

The Cup stayed in England for a fifth successive year in 1981 when Liverpool recovered to secure their third European triumph in five seasons with a goal from left-back Alan Kennedy – bursting through a half-hearted tackle from Real Madrid's Rafael Garcia Cortes to thump home an angled drive.

Madrid's first appearance in the final for 15 years thus ended in anti-climax.

Holders Forest fell in the first round to the ever-threatening giant-killers of CSKA Sofia. CSKA won 1–0 home and away but Liverpool finally wreaked English football's revenge in the quarter-finals and then defeated Bayern Munich on the away goals rule in the semi-finals. Madrid defeated Limerick, Honved and Moscow Spartak before renewing, in the semi-finals, their great rivalry with Internazionale. Goals from Santillana and Juanito brought Madrid victory in the Bernabcu while one from sweeper Graziano Bini was not enough in the second leg for the Italian champions.

Aston Villa maintained the English grip in 1982. They had won their first League title in 71 years under the management of Ron Saunders but he parted company with the club within months and Villa's European campaign was plotted by Tony Barton, his former assistant.

British teamwork

Barton, unprepossessing but popular, put together a side which was a team in the very sense of the word – players dedicated to the club and to each other out on the pitch. Gordon Cowans pulled the strings in midfield, Tony Morley provided fireworks on the left wing and centre-forward Peter Withe contributed power through the middle. It was Withe who scored the only goal in the final against Bayern Munich, though he very nearly fell over his own feet before toe-poking the ball home from inside the six-yard box. Villa's success on the day in Rotterdam was even more remarkable considering they lost goalkeeper Jimmy Rimmer to injury only a few minutes into the game. Nigel Spink barely had time to say: "My Mum will be pleased," before sprinting off the bench and into action.

The Athens final of 1983 underlined the point that favouritism is a double-edged sword once more, as the galaxy of superstars from Juventus had been expected to run rings around the workmen of Hamburg. Juve were perhaps the most star-studded team of the era, with Frenchman Michel Platini, Poland's Zbigniew Boniek and Italian World Cup winners Dino Zoff, Claudio Gentile, Antonio Cabrini, Gaetano Scirea, Marco Tardelli and Paolo Rossi. They beat holders Aston Villa 2–1 away and 3–1 at home in the quarter-finals. But in the final, a goal from Hamburg midfielder Felix Magath proved too much for them.

Hamburg's success meant yet another appearance at the peak of the club game for Austrian master coach Ernst Happel, who had won with Feyenoord in 1970 and finished runner-up with Club Brugge in 1978. His defeated opposite number on the Juventus bench was Giovanni Trapattoni who had won the Champions Cup as a player with Milan in 1963 and 1969.

That Hamburg victory was not the precursor of a German revival – just a blip on the Anglo-Italian screen. Liverpool, in

1984, returned to win again in Rome, where they had secured their first Champions Cup against Borussia Mönchengladbach.

It was nothing like as clear cut as in 1977 and Liverpool, with Joe Fagan having succeeded Bob Paisley as manager, needed a penalty shoot-out to defeat the home side. Roma, under Nils Liedholm, had beaten CSKA Sofia, Dynamo Berlin and Dundee United on their way to the final. They boasted Brazil's Toninho Cerezo and Paulo Roberto Falcao in midfield plus Italy's Bruno Conti, Francesco Graziani and Roberto Pruzzo in attack.

Roma hit back through Pruzzo just before half-time to square Phil Neal's first goal. But the longer the match went on, the more fragile Roma's self-confidence appeared. When it came to the shoot-out, Falcao, hero of the local fans, would not take a penalty and Bruce Grobbelaar's wobbly knees did the rest. Conti and Graziani were Roma's unlikely failures in the spot-kick decider.

The 1985 Champions Cup Final is listed in the record books as having been won 1–0 by Juventus. It is an occasion frequently recalled – but never for the football.

The Heysel disaster

May 29, 1985, was the day of the Heysel stadium disaster when 39 Juventus fans were killed, crushed against or falling through a weak retaining wall after being charged across the terracing by a mob of Liverpool fans. It was the most horrific international display of the evils of hooliganism.

Criminal charges were laid and proved against Belgian and UEFA officials, despite highly-debatable protests. Video was used to track down some of the hooligans. Controversy reigned over whether UEFA had been correct in going ahead with the match. But it did keep the remainder of the crowd in the stadium, preventing more trouble on the streets of Brussels and not clogging up traffic lanes cleared for the emergency services.

The match was decided by a penalty by Michel Platini, but it was not a night to be remembered with pride and provoked the removal of English clubs from Europe for five years.

Yet, oddly, in the first post-Heysel season there was an English presence in the Champions Cup Final, in the presence of Barcelona's coach, Terry Venables.

Barcelona reached the 1986 final believing that they needed merely to turn up to win. The venue was the Sanchez Pizjuan stadium in Seville, and their opposition were the little known, little-appreciated Steaua of Bucharest. No eastern European club had ever won the Champions Cup and Steaua were not considered in the same class as, say, Red Star Belgrade or Kiev Dynamo. On the night, however, Barcelona's attack was swallowed up by a Romanian defence superbly marshalled by Miodrag Belodedici. Even when it went to a penalty shoot-out, Barca could not put the ball in the net. Steaua duly made history.

In 1987, FC Porto became the first Portuguese club since

Benfica 25 years earlier to win the Champions Cup when they hit back with style and panache against Bayern Munich in the Prater stadium in Vienna. This was not the Bayern of Beckenbauer and Müller, but a more prosaic team who, despite snatching an early lead through Ludwig Kogl, never controlled the match. Porto, weakened by injury before the kick-off, deserved victory, late as their two goals were.

The 1986 Cup-holders, Steaua, were given a bye through the first round then were eliminated by Belgium's Anderlecht in the second round. Anderlecht won 3–0 at home with two goals from Australian international Eddie Krncevic and went down only 1–0 in Bucharest. Anderlecht then collapsed next time out against Bayern, losing 5–0 in Munich in the first leg of the quarter-finals. Bayern kept the goals running when they beat Real Madrid in the first leg of their semi-final, with Lothar Matthäus scoring twice. Madrid had already disposed of the 1985 champions, Juventus. In the other semi-final, favoured Kiev fell 2–1 away and home against Porto, for whom Paulo Futre had emerged as a major new force in the European game.

Dutch resurgence

He was sold to Atletico Madrid, within weeks of success and Porto also lost the Cup. PSV Eindhoven became the third Dutch club to see their name engraved on the Cup when they defeated Benfica in a penalty shoot-out after a goalless draw in Stuttgart.

Milan crowned in Barcelona in 1989

PSV had been most observers' favourites for the trophy and the only surprise was that Benfica made them work so hard in the final. This was, after all, the year in which a second generation of Dutch football achieved a European monopoly with PSV winning the Champions Cup and the national team winning the European Championship. PSV provided goalkeeper Hans Van Breukelen, defenders Berry Van Aerle and Ronald Koeman as well as midfielder Gerald Vanenburg to the Dutch effort.

In the final, Koeman converted PSV's first kick in the penalty shoot-out while Van Breukelen saved the decisive, last, penalty.

In the mid-1980s, Milan, one of the original Champions Cup contestants back in 1955–56, had been taken over by the millionaire businessman and media magnate Silvio Berlusconi. He was a long-standing fan of the club but, more, he had a grand commercial vision which would help reshape football as a business in its own right and as a commercial contributor.

Berlusconi poured £20 million into Milan initially to pay off the debts of the old regime and buy Dutch superstars Ruud Gullit and Marco Van Basten (joined a year later by Frank Rijkaard). Results were spectacular. In 1988, Milan won the Italian title, in 1989 they won the Champions Cup and their domination of the European game lasted to the mid-1990s.

Milan were among the television stars of Berlusconi's electronic empire and he even flew in his own TV crews and equipment to Barcelona for the 1989 final when Spanish technicians went on strike. His investment was rewarded with Milan's sweeping 4–0 victory. Gullit and Van Basten scored twice.

Milan appeared bound to dominate the Champions Cup in the manner of Real Madrid in the early days. But they did not have it as easy as Berlusconi might have hoped. In 1989–90, they disposed of HJK Helsinki in the first round 5–0 overall, but squeezed past Real Madrid 2–1 in the second round and needed extra time against Mechelen in the quarter-finals and Bayern Munich in the semis. In the final, Milan met Benfica, with a goal from Frank Rijkaard after 67 minutes deciding the Portuguese club's fifth defeat at this stage.

Benfica's presence in the final infuriated French fans after their semi-final victory over Marseille. The French champions, owned by millionaire businessman Bernard Tapie – as major a personality in his own land as Berlusconi in his – believed they could become the first French club to win the Cup. They beat Benfica 2–1 at home in the semi-finals and, at 0–0 in the closing stages in Lisbon, appeared on the verge of reaching the final. Then Vata struck for Benfica, a goal which delighted the Portuguese fans and angered the French, since it had been preceded by a clear handball. The referee was unsighted. Benfica, and not Marseille, went through.

Tapie had to wait just one year before Marseille did pierce the semi-final barrier. But the 1991 final will go down as a Champions Cup paradox. First, the venue. The San Nicola stadium in Bari had been built for the 1990 World Cup but appeared something of a white elephant on the fringe of the south-eastern Italian port. Then the match. Milan had walked off the pitch in Marseille in a sulk after a floodlight failure held up their quarter-final and lost their title virtually by default. In their absence, Marseille and Red Star Belgrade were the best finalists available.

Both were capable of glorious attacking football, as Marseille displayed regularly in France and Red Star achieved in Europe, most notably in their semi-final victory over Bayern Munich. The final, however, was a negative, fear-ridden bore.

Marseille's veteran Belgian coach, Raymond Goethals, used his midfielders to protect defence rather than support attack; Red Star's Ljubko Petrovic left Darko Pancev isolated upfield. Hardly surprisingly, it was 0–0 at the end of extra time and went to penalties – the fourth Champions Cup Final decided in this manner. Manuel Amoros, experienced World Cup veteran, missed Marseille's first kick and Red Star converted all theirs to win 5–3. Sweeper Miodrag Belodedici became the first player to win the Cup with two different clubs, after having collected a winner's medal in 1986 with Steaua Bucharest.

Another echo of 1986 was heard in 1992 when Barcelona, beaten finalists six years earlier, achieved their long-awaited Champions Cup success. The Catalan giants had appeared jinxed in the one competition they wanted to win above all others. To succeed they had to safely negotiate a new mini-league structure which UEFA had dropped, experimentally, into the spring slot previously taken up by the quarter and semi-finals.

In Group B of the mini-league, Barcelona triumphed over Sparta Prague, Benfica and Kiev Dynamo while Group A saw Italy's Sampdoria outrun Red Star Belgrade (now homeless in European competition because of the Yugoslav conflict), Anderlecht and Panathinaikos.

The final was a repeat of the 1988 Cup-winners Cup showdown, but the 90 minutes ended without a goal despite some high-quality football. No need for penalties this time, though. Eight minutes before the end of extra time, Barcelona were awarded a free-kick almost 30 yards from goal. Ronald Koeman thundered his drive beyond keeper Gianluca Pagliuca.

Barcelona celebrated in style. They had brought their "real" kit to replace the change strip they had played in and it was in their traditional red and blue that they collected the Cup for which they had waited so long.

Into the big league

UEFA now formalized the mini-league system into the newly-baptized UEFA Champions League. The European governing body had called a special meeting to reshape its statutes and secure authority to market the entire competition as it saw fit – with exclusive sponsorship and television contracts.

Rules and regulations also played a role in the early rounds of the 1992–93 season when Stuttgart fielded one foreigner too many against Leeds. The English champions won the duly-ordered replay then fell to Rangers – who went on into the Champions League. The Scottish champions very nearly reached the final too, but were pipped by Marseille, who faced Milan in Munich.

A goal from Basile Boli brought France their first-ever Champions Cup but, even that night, whispers were circulating about Marseille's match-fixing past. The whispers were not developed for several weeks after what appears, with hindsight, to have been a media and official conspiracy to allow Marseille's players their triumph. Ultimately, it emerged Marseille had fixed the League match before the final, against Valenciennes, so they could concentrate on facing Milan knowing the French title was once again safely theirs.

The ripples of corruption continued. Marseille were stripped of their 1993 French title and subsequently relegated as further punishment. They were not stripped of their European crown, but they were immediately barred from defending the Cup.

It was not until the spring of 1997 that the disgraced Tapie was jailed for match-fixing. By then, it had become clear Marseille had fixed far more than just the infamous match with Valenciennes.

The credibility of the Champions Cup was on the line in 1993–94, but Milan rose to that challenge in style throughout the competition, ultimately defeating Barcelona in Athens, in the final, with one of the finest displays of football seen in the event for more than 20 years. By now, English clubs were back in Europe but both they and German sides struggled to keep pace with the tactical and technical developments of the international club game.

The glorious old Champions Cup was history. In 1992–93, the winners of the two mini-league groups (which had replaced the quarter and semi-finals) had moved directly to the final. But in 1993–94, partly to prevent a glut of "dead" matches in the groups, knockout semi-finals were introduced. The top team in each group played the runners-up from the other in single-leg ties for which the group leaders, as reward, played hosts.

In 1993–94, that meant Milan at home to Monaco and Barcelona at home to FC Porto. Milan won comfortably despite playing more than half the match against the French champions with only ten men after the first-half expulsion of central defender Alessandro Costacurta.

The Italian champions took the lead after 14 minutes when Monaco failed to mark up at a left-wing corner from Zvonimir Boban and French international Marcel Desailly rose to head past Jean-Luc Ettori in the Monaco goal. Milan were reduced to 10 men five minutes before half-time when Costacurta was sent off for tripping Monaco's German striker, Jürgen Klinsmann. He was not the only Milan player who would miss the final. Captain and sweeper Franco Baresi was shown a yellow card and because it was his third of the campaign he, too, was

Red Star Belgrade hold the trophy up high after their penalty shoot-out victory over Marseille in 1991

condemned to missing Milan's seventh final appearance.

Despite their handicap, Milan dominated the second half. Demetrio Albertini scored with a superb long-range shot after a free-kick and Daniele Massaro volleyed a magnificent third goal after a defence-splitting, crossfield pass from Christian Panucci. As Milan coach Fabio Capello, said: "It was an extraordinary performance to win such an important game so decisively with only ten men."

In the other semi-final, Barcelona had to wait only 10 minutes before the path to the final opened up before them. That was how long it took for Bulgarian World Cup striker Hristo Stoichkov to open the scoring against Porto from close range after an attack organised by Romario and Sergi. The same three players were involved in the second goal after 35 minutes. Again Romario found Sergi in space on the left and the lethal Stoichkov pounced in front of goal. Porto never seriously threatened Barcelona goalkeeper Andoni Zubizarreta and lost all hope of recovery when captain Joao Pinto was sent off in the 61st minute for a second yellow-card offence.

Dutchman Ronald Koeman scored Barcelona's third goal in the 72nd minute – unusually for him, the goal was neither a penalty nor a free-kick. Koeman accelerated through a gap which the depleted Porto had left in midfield and drove a typically powerful shot beyond the reach of Vitor Baia. After the match, Sergi said: "This was probably our best game of the season." But the final would be another matter entirely.

Barcelona were many neutrals' favourites because of the one-touch, perpetual motion style favoured by coach Cruyff. Also, Milan had selection problems. They suffered through the suspension of key central defenders Costacurta and Baresi and the further absence, through injury, of spearhead Van Basten. The exigencies of UEFA's foreigners rules meant, also, that coach Fabio Capello had to leave Romania centre-forward Florin Raducioiu and Denmark forward Brian Laudrup in the stands.

Barcelona boasted an attack spearheaded by a fearsome partnership in Brazil's Romario and Bulgaria's Stoichkov. But they saw very little of the ball. Instead, Milan took the game by the scruff of the neck with Frenchman Desailly providing the power and Yugoslav Dejan Savicevic all the skill and inspiration. Daniele Massaro (two), Savicevic and Desailly scored the goals. Desailly, signed the previous autumn from Marseille, thus became the first man to win the Champions Cup with two different clubs in successive seasons.

Towards a super league

The Champions League took a major step forward in the following, 1994–95, season under a redevelopment which clearly addressed the "European league" concept of which so many people had dreamed so long. Now the event expanded to accommodate four groups of four teams – but in a different competitive sequence. Thus, a preliminary knockout round was played in August and the four Champions League groups from September to December, then the competition stepped back into line with the Cup-winners Cup and the UEFA Cup with two-leg quarter and semi-finals in the spring. One byproduct, which upset the smaller nations, was that champion clubs outside the top 24 countries were removed from the Champions League set-up and dumped into the expanded UEFA Cup.

The value of the Champions League from the financial aspect was undeniable and the pace of its expansion owed much to television pressure. Competing clubs were guaranteed income from three home matches on top of appearance money and bonuses per point. UEFA, through lucrative exclusive TV and sponsorship deals, was assured an annual income with which all the junior competitions plus various development agencies could be funded, and still leave plenty over. TV channels in all the mainstream western European countries gained the virtual security of an ongoing national interest through the legitimate fixing of entry procedures – with the UEFA coefficient being used to seed top-nation clubs direct into the mini-leagues.

UEFA also claimed sporting advantages: that players appreciated the opportunity to play their football released from the pressures of sudden-death; that referees acknowledged the assistance this provided in controlling the temperature of games; and fans throughout Europe, in the stadia and through television, "have all become winners from the entertainment."

In fact, the competition paid in reduced drama and glamour for the necessary compromise with TV and sponsors. But football was becoming big business and UEFA acknowledged it needed to edge down the superleague path to keep the big clubs happy.

A further development of that process was UEFA's decision in 1994 – again, at the initial behest of TV and sponsors – to clear Wednesday nights for Champions League only. Thus Tuesday became the designated night for UEFA Cup ties and Thursday the official day for the Cup-winners Cup.

So the 1994–95 Champions League made football history, bringing UEFA ever closer to their long-dreamed of European superleague.

Results also showed that not all of the self-obsessed giants of the European club game were as good as they thought. In Group A, for example, IFK Gothenburg were the surprise winners ahead of the 1994 finalists Barcelona and the well-fancied Manchester United the most notable of failures. Although they finished level on points with Barcelona, they were eliminated for failing in the head-to-head contest against the Spanish champions. Barcelona reached the quarter-finals after struggling to a 1–1 draw at home against IFK in their last match. If Barcelona had not drawn then Manchester United – winning at home simultaneously against Galatasaray – would have finished one vital point ahead.

Barcelona opened with a 2–1 victory over Galatasaray then conceded two late goals to lose by the same margin in Gothenburg. This confirmed their duels with Manchester United as the key to the group. Johan Cruyff's Spanish champions secured a 2–2 draw at Old Trafford then thrashed United 4–0 at home with one superb goal from Romario and two equally adept from Stoichkov.

Manchester United's misery

United fretted over the foreign player restrictions which cost them Danish goalkeeper Peter Schmeichel and the four-game suspension which kept Eric Cantona out of action. The result was their biggest defeat in Europe since they had lost to Porto by the same score in a Cup-winners Cup-tie in October 1977 and their biggest defeat in any game since a 4–0 reverse at Liverpool in September 1990.

IFK followed up their retention of the Swedish title by winning 1–0 at Galatasaray of Turkey and taking over the group leadership. Their next victory – 3–1 at home to Manchester United – earned them a quarter-final place with a game to spare. Jesper Blomqvist, coveted by many leading clubs, Magnus Erlingmark and captain Pontus Kamark (penalty) scored IFK's goals.

United missed Schmeichel, Roy Keane, Ryan Giggs and Lee Sharpe through injury, but manager Alex Ferguson did not look for excuses, saying: "It was a terrible result for us. We cannot expect to come away with anything from matches like this when we concede goals like we did in Barcelona (a 4–0 defeat) and in Sweden. You can make excuses if you want to but at the end of the day we weren't good enough."

In Group B, Paris Saint-Germain were the only team to end the mini-league stage with a 100 per cent record, having won all their games. Bayern Munich, with Lothar Matthäus reverting from sweeper to midfield just in time, followed them thanks to a decisive 4–1 win over Kiev Dynamo on the last matchday. Jean-Pierre Papin, fully fit just briefly, scored twice.

PSG, who had emerged through the preliminary round, took a much more impressive route to the quarter-finals. First they scored an impressive 2–0 victory over Bayern Munich. George Weah and Daniel Bravo scored a goal in each half. They followed up with a 2–1 win over Moscow Spartak in Russia and the "double" over Kiev Dynamo. Paris won 2–1 in the Ukraine then 1–0 at home in the Parc des Princes, securing an early place in the last eight with a second-half header from Weah.

Group C was the flattest. Benfica and Hajduk Split drew 0–0 in Croatia on the opening matchday and there was little else to separate them for most of the campaign. Both clubs went on to qualify for the quarter-finals. Hajduk were one of three quarter-finalists to have progressed all the way through from the preliminary rounds.

Argentina's Claudio Caniggia proved crucial to the Portuguese champions' progress, scoring twice in their important 3–1 win over Anderlecht. Caniggia might have celebrated with a hat-trick but missed a penalty two minutes after half-time. He scored again in Benfica's next 2–1 home win over Steaua Bucharest but missed the return in Romania after aggravating an injury on the eve of the game. Benfica secured a 1–1 draw while Hajduk justified claims of the tightest defence in the early stages of the Champions League – with one goal conceded in four games – as they drew 0–0 at Anderlecht.

Now Benfica and Hajduk needed only a draw in Lisbon on November 23 in the fifth matchday to both secure quarter-finals places with one round of matches to go. Benfica defeated Hajduk 2–1 but both teams qualified as Steaua and Anderlecht eliminated each other by drawing 1–1 in Romania. Brazilian-born Isaias Soares and Portugal's Joao Vieira Pinto scored for Benfica. Midfielder Stjepan Andrijasavic provided a consolation for the Croats in their first group defeat.

Group D saw Ajax dominate the keynote confrontation with holders Milan. The Dutch champions won home and away, finishing their programme unbeaten, to establish themselves as new favourites to win the Cup.

Milan's defending champions squeezed through courtesy only of a 1–0 victory over Casino Salzburg in Vienna on the last matchday. The clubs had finished level on points but Milan, like Barcelona in Group A, qualified ahead of Salzburg thanks to the head-to-head results between the clubs.

Milan miss Meazza

Milan made a poor start when they lost their opening match 2–0 at Ajax. The Italian club were then engulfed in controversy after Salzburg goalkeeper Otto Konrad was struck on the head by a bottle during the match in the Stadio Meazza. Konrad played on after treatment but was later substituted after Marco Simone shot Milan 2–0 ahead. Konrad spent the night in hospital while Salzburg, without him, lost 3–0. They also appealed to UEFA for the match result to be reversed or for a replay to be ordered on neutral territory. UEFA's decision was to remove the two points Milan had gained from winning the match and order them to play their next two home matches away from the Meazza.

Significantly, UEFA allowed Milan to keep the 3–0 victory margin. This meant that not only did they collect the victory bonus but they also had a significant technical advantage going into the last matchday against Salzburg.

Ajax beat AEK Athens 2–1 in Greece with goals from Finland's Jari Litmanen and Patrick Kluivert. Not until the third matchday did Ajax drop their first point, held goalless by Salzburg in Vienna.

Milan hung on for a goalless draw at AEK Athens then beat the Greek champions in their temporary "home" of Trieste. Defender Christian Panucci scored two second-half goals in seven minutes to secure a 2–1 victory after midfielder Toni Savevski had given AEK an early advantage.

Ajax, at home to Salzburg, snatched a draw thanks only to a late goal from Litmanen. Then they beat Milan 2–0 for a second time, on this occasion in Trieste. One further strike from Litmanen in the second minute and an own goal by Milan's

captain and sweeper Franco Baresi in the 66th confirmed Ajax as group winners with one round of games remaining. Milan were thus forced to beat Salzburg in Vienna on the last matchday to qualify for the quarter-finals – a task they accomplished thanks to a lone goal from Daniele Massaro.

The fixture pressure developed by the Champions League has forced many European nations to reduce the length of the winter break they had traditionally enjoyed. Three of the eight quarter-finalists in 1995 were affected significantly: Hajduk Split, IFK and Bayern Munchen. The other five found the mid-winter gap in UEFA competition having varied effects on their ambitions.

Bayern had to play IFK. The Swedes, the one UEFA Champions League club actually in their close-season, wandered around Europe playing a series of friendly matches to regain fitness after the Christmas break and prepare tactics for a duel they felt confident they could win. That confidence was strengthened when skipper Lothar Mätthaus fell awkwardly during one of Bayern's own friendly matches and was subsequently ruled out for the rest of the season.

Hajduk also busied themselves in a friendly way for their meeting with Ajax and used the winter break to contract several new players. They arrived in time to beat UEFA's eligibility deadline as did a handful of new signings at Barcelona. But more significant in the Spanish champions' preparation for the impatiently-awaited duel with Paris Saint-Germain was a transfer AWAY from Nou Camp. World Cup hero Romario, homesick for his native Brazil, persuaded the Spanish champions to sell him to Flamengo of Rio de Janeiro. At once, the balance of the tie shifted towards France.

Milan had also made international headlines during the Italian "transfer window". They, too, "lost" a player and a famous one in veteran Dutchman Ruud Gullit. But his departure back to Sampdoria was considered only good sense from both technical and tactical standpoints.

Yet it was not one of Milan's foreign superstars who made all the difference against Benfica, but home-grown Italian Marco Simone. He scored twice in a 12-minute spell midway through the second half of the first leg which saw Milan welcomed home to the Stadio Meazza after their enforced exile to Trieste. Milan, who had won the European Supercup against Arsenal while waiting, might even have won the return against Benfica but Simone and Zvonimir Boban were foiled by the posts and a 0–0 draw was good enough.

As for Ajax, their youthful endeavours in the first round had turned them into favourites to win the Cup. Louis Van Gaal and his team – with an average age of 23, despite the presence of 32-year-old Rijkaard in midfield – had no problems with Hajduk. Ajax drew 0–0 away when they might have won but made no mistake back in Amsterdam. Defender Frank de Boer outscored attacking brother Ronald for once, scoring twice in a comprehensive 3–0 success.

However, the normal European pattern of draw-away-win-at-home was upset in Munich and Gothenburg. Bayern, having strengthened their attack with the mid-winter arrival of Bulgaria's Emil Kostadinov, had been further weakened by the losses of Papin and Swiss winger Alain Sutter. A gloomy 45,000 crowd saw Bayern held 0–0 in the Olympiastadion and must have held out little hope for the visit to Sweden.

What optimism existed was further reduced when, after only 22 minutes of the return, goalkeeper Sven Scheuer was sent off for bringing down IFK's Mikael Martinsson outside the penalty box. This was when coach Giovanni Trapattoni pulled out all the tactical stops (taking off Kostadinov to bring on substitute goalkeeper Gospodarek) and Bayern's remaining players produced spirit and inspiration which proved overwhelming. They seized a two-goal lead through Alex Zickler and Christian Nerlinger before settling for a 2–2 draw and qualification on the away goals rule.

Finally, in the long-designated "tie of the round," Barcelona conceded a crucial advantage to Paris Saint-Germain when the French champions snatched a 1–1 draw in Nou Camp thanks to yet another goal from the inevitable Weah – once again crowned African Footballer of the Year. Barcelona had opened through their new Russian, Igor Korneyev, but there was, of course, no Romario to extend the lead.

Lucky for some

Football success also depends on good fortune and, for half the match back in Paris, it seemed as if the fates were with Barcelona. PSG hit the post five times and Barcelona snatched the lead just after the break through Jose Bakero. Catalan hopes turned, however, to disillusion in the closing 18 minutes as PSG gained overdue reward for their near-misses, first through Rai then through Vincent Guerin. PSG were through to their third consecutive European semi-final; Barcelona, beaten in the final the previous year, had fallen this time two rounds short.

Footballers are generally agreed that, if there is anything worse than losing a final, it is losing a semi-final. At least finishing runners-up, the players have the satisfaction of knowing they reached the big occasion. They may then convince themselves that only a bad bounce or ill fortune prevented them walking off with a winners' medal.

Ajax and Bayern had old scores to settle in the first semi-final. In the early 1970s, when Ajax were dominating the European game, they outclassed even a Bayern team featuring of Franz Beckenbauer, Uli Hoeness and Gerd Müller. Now Bayern, who subsequently recorded their own Cup hat-trick, appeared once again in their path with Beckenbauer and Hoeness in key roles, albeit as club president and general manager this time.

Memories of the days of Johan Cruyff, Piet Keizer, Rudi Krol,

Johan Neeskens and the days of "total football" came flooding back. Not so much in the goalless first leg in the Olympiastadion, but rather in the return in Amsterdam, when Ajax secured their place in the final with a 5–2 victory. One goal for Litmanen, another for the Nigerian Finidi George and a third for Ronald de Boer, provided Ajax with a 3–1 interval lead. Only one brief incident in the second half worried the Dutch: when defender Danny Blind handled in the penalty box. Hungarian referee Sandor Puhl awarded a yellow card rather than a red and not only did Ajax qualify for the final – so did their skipper.

The other semi-final was the clash between French (and Brazilian) flair and cosmopolitan class. An intriguing element was Milan's admiration for Paris' attacking leader, Weah. In the event, Milan's experience and command of the big occasion meant neither Paris nor their Liberian hero had much of a look-in. David Ginola struck Sebastiano Rossi's bar with a thunderous free-kick six minutes from the end, but that was their last chance not only in the match but, effectively, in the tie. In the very last minute, Boban stole away to convert a cross from Savicevic.

The former Red Star forward was Milan's hero in the second leg, demonstrating once again the form which destroyed Barcelona in the previous season's final. This time, Savicevic was not so much creator as finisher, scoring both Milan's goals in a 2–0 victory which secured a 3–0 aggregate success – and earned Savicevic, from the French media, comparisons with their 1980s hero Michel Platini.

Thus Ajax and Milan progressed to the dizzy heights of the final, in Vienna, where a goal from 18-year-old substitute Patrick Kluivert, with five minutes remaining, earned the Dutch their fourth Champions Cup triumph.

Kluivert's conversion of a pass from ex-Milan hero Frank Rijkaard secured Ajax's first Champions' triumph since 1973. For Ajax, victory offered revenge for their defeat by Milan in the 1969 final and guaranteed them the honour of being top seeds, as holders, in the following season's Champions League. For Milan, defeat meant they had failed to equal Real Madrid's record of six wins in European club football's most prestigious competition. Having lost their domestic title to Juventus, coach Fabio Capello and his men were also not destined to return for several years.

Rijkaard's contribution was a perfect farewell to international football. The 32-year-old midfielder scored Milan's winner in the 1990 final against Portugese side Benfica in the same Viennese stadium. This time Rijkaard, who had already announced his end-of-season retirement, created the decisive goal. Rijkaard said later: "I feel sorry for my Italian friends but sometimes football is like that."

Back in Holland, the city of Amsterdam erupted into a jubilant mass of red and white as thousands of fans poured into the city centre to celebrate. Fans danced on tram stop shelters, waving red banners and scarfs. Some wore T-shirts demanding Louis for president, referring to Ajax coach Louis Van Gaal.

Kluivert was not the only 18-year-old substitute who tormented Milan in the climactic last few minutes of the 1994–95 UEFA Champions League campaign. He had entered soon after Nkankwo Kanu, had joined the action to disturb Milan's defensive control. The plan was for their young legs to wear down the Italian club's elder statesmen. "Milan were more experienced than us," said Ajax coach Van Gaal. "That's why in the second half I put two 18-year-old boys on the field and they won it for us."

Milan, who included only one player aged under 25, ran into problems before the kick-off when forward Savicevic failed a fitness test on a damaged thigh muscle. The closest they came to a goal was on the stroke of half-time when a volley from Marco Simone was fisted for a corner by Edwin Van der Sar.

Ajax dominate Milan

Ajax followed up their victory over Milan by completing the Dutch league season with yet another championship and an unbeaten record. They also, of course, now boasted a hat-trick of victories over Milan in Europe for the season. As Capello said: "Any team who can beat the holders three times in one season deserve to win the Cup."

Milan did take one prize home to Italy. Midfielder Desailly was selected by a panel of leading football writers as Man of the Match. As befitted this brave new commercial world, the award was, of course, sponsored by a credit card company.

The sponsors, and UEFA, could not have been happier. A survey by the Luzern agency TEAM Marketing, which undertook all the TV and commercial liaison work, revealed that a staggering 3.64 billion viewers in 33 European countries watched the UEFA Champions League matches in the 1994–95 season. This represented an increase of 1.4 billion viewers (61 per cent) over the previous season.

UEFA, for 1995–96, maintained the mixture of the autumn group section with the spring knock-out sequence. The first eight clubs, including holders Ajax, qualified automatically for the group stage. The clubs seeded from nine to 24 played in a qualifying, direct elimination round in August. The winners of those eight ties were then drawn in the groups. Those domestic champions seeded 25 and below were redirected into the UEFA Cup.

The hidden agenda for the new Champions League was to offer the big clubs semi-permanent membership of a football elite. Thus the groups included five clubs who had previously won the Champion Clubs Cup: FC Porto (once previous winners) in Group A; Juventus and Steaua Bucharest (each winners once previously) in Group C; and Ajax (holders and four-times winners) and Real Madrid (six) in Group D. Four other competing clubs had achieved success in other UEFA competitions: Dynamo Kiev (Cup-winners Cup) in Group A;

Rangers and Borussia Dortmund (both Cup-winners Cup) in Group C; and Ferencvaros (UEFA/Fairs Cup) in Group D.

Kiev Dynamo were one of the eight clubs who had emerged from the qualifying round. However, they were expelled from Group A following corruption allegations (which the club denied) concerning their initial 1–0 home win over Panathinaikos. Spanish referee Antonio Lopez Nieto alleged he and his assistants had been offered expensive fur coats by Kiev's directors on the eve of the match. The result was expunged from the records and the Danish club Aalborg, who had been beaten by Kiev in the qualifying round, were promoted into Group A in their place. Kiev were subsequently banned from European competition for three seasons but this punishment was later suspended as a goodwill gesture towards the financially-strapped Ukraine federation.

Group A saw Panathinaikos and Nantes reach the quarter-finals, surprisingly edging out Porto after a group which produced the fewest goals (26) but also the tightest series of matches. The Portuguese appeared to have made a sound start when they forced a goalless draw in Nantes. The French champions had been slow to find their form at home and abroad and suffered a further setback next time, losing 3–1 to Panathinaikos. The Greek champions owed victory to two goals from Polish striker Kryzstof Warzycha. But there were no more slip-ups by the French. They took six of their eight points from away and home wins over Aalborg and qualified in second place.

Spartak were in thrilling form throughout Group B, which they completed as the only club with a 100 per cent record. Their policy of using their Champions League cash to bring home internationals stars such as striker Sergei Yuran, midfielder Vasili Kulkov and goalkeeper Stanislav Cherchesov paid a rich dividend. But English champions Blackburn Rovers provided one of the major disappointments of the competition. A misjudgment by goalkeeper Tim Flowers, rushing from his goal and colliding with defender Graeme Le Saux, presented Yuran with the only goal of their first match. From that point, Spartak never looked back and Blackburn never looked like qualifying.

Spartak appeared to be in haste to secure all the points needed before the icy weather turned Moscow matches into a lottery. They defeated Legia Warsaw more easily than the 2–1 scoreline sugested then hit back from 2–0 down in Norway to beat Rosenborg Trondheim 4–2 in the most thrilling match of the group. Substitute Valeri Kechinov scored twice in the last 15 minutes after replacing Valeri Shmarov.

First quarter-finalists

The fourth matchday brought Spartak the accolade of being the first certain quarter-finalists after they overwhelmed Rosenborg once more, this time 4–1. Confused Blackburn fell 3–0 in Moscow

– England internationals David Batty and Le Saux exchanging blows after a defensive mix-up – before Spartak rounded off their campaign with a 1–0 win in Warsaw. Legia also celebrated in defeat, reaching the quarter-finals as group runners-up.

Juventus were the kings of Group C. Remarkably, they had sold Italy's 1994 World Cup hero Roberto Baggio to Milan before the start of the season but the emergence of Alex Del Piero inspired the early victories which lifted them into the last eight with two matchdays remaining. Borussia Dortmund, always expected to be their most resilient challengers, finished second.

Dortmund were not, however, in the same class. Juventus demonstrated the point when they won 3–1 in Germany on the first matchday. They did so despite falling behind to a goal from Andy Möller – a Juventus old boy – after only 38 seconds. Then Del Piero set to work. First, he created an equaliser for Michele Padovano, then scored himself to provide Juve with a 2–1 interval lead. Midway through the second half Del Piero struck again, helping provide a third goal for Antonio Conte.

The other group opening match saw Steaua Bucharest defeat Rangers of Glasgow 1–0 in Romania. But already the class divide was clear. Juventus were head and shoulders above the rest. They underlined the point with successive home wins against Steaua (3–1) and Rangers (4–1). Del Piero scored one and made one each time, then opened the scoring in a 4–0 win in Glasgow. The pressure off, a quarter-final place achieved, Juventus eased up. They lost at home to Dortmund then drew in Bucharest.

Steaua's failure to win meant they were also frozen out with Dortmund qualifying for the quarters as Juventus's runners-ups.

Ajax, in Group D, began their title defence in precisely the way they ended the 1994–95 event – with a 1–0 win. This time Real Madrid, another of European football's greatest names, were the victims. Winger Marc Overmars struck home a right-foot shot after 14 minutes. The Dutch champions went straight to the top of the table and never lost command of a group in which Real finished runners-up with Hungary's Ferencvaros and Grasshopper of Switzerland the also-rans.

Tough at the bottom

Grasshopper took only two points from their six matches, the poorest record of any of the 16 UEFA Champions League clubs. They never recovered from a bad start – losing 3–0 at home to Ferencvaros after the expulsion of Sweden's Mats Gren then going down 2–0 in Madrid, where Ivan Zamorano struck Real's first goals in the competition. Teenage striker Raul then became the youngest player to score a Champions League hat-trick in a 6–1 thrashing of Ferencvaros.

Raul also scored Madrid's goal in the 1–1 return draw in Budapest on the fourth matchday, but he was silenced when the Dutch went to Spain. Ajax extended their record unbeaten

European run to 16 matches with a stylish 2–0 victory which earned a standing ovation from the Real supporters. Overmars, Litmanen and Kluivert all struck the woodwork before the latter two claimed the decisive goals in a ten-minute spell midway through the second half. Litmanen's strike earned him the accolade of six-goal top scorer in the Champions League.

In the quarter-finals, the group winners did not have everything all their own way. Panathinaikos, Juventus and Ajax qualified for the semi-finals but Moscow Spartak – after finishing Group B with a 100 per cent record – were defeated over two legs by French champions Nantes.

The first leg was played in France where goals from Japhet N'Doram and Nicolas Ouedec provided a 2–0 victory over a Russian team which was ring-rusty after the winter close-season. Spartak also suffered from the mid-winter departures of key players such as goalkeeper Stanislav Cherchesov, skipper Viktor Onopko, midfielder Vasili Kulkov and striker Sergei Yuran to clubs in Austria, Spain and England. Yuri Nikiforov offered Spartak brief hope of a remarkable recovery in the second leg. He scored twice in the first half to bring Spartak level on aggregate. But Nantes responded with two goals from Ouedec in the second half and secured a 4–2 victory on aggregate.

No such problems for Ajax against Borussia Dortmund. The tie was virtually decided by the first leg in Germany. Ajax won 2–0 with a goal in each half from Edgar Davids and Kluivert. Dortmund's hopes of springing a second-leg surprise were wrecked when skipper and sweeper Matthias Sammer was sent off in the 65th minute. As predicted, Dortmund rarely threatened in the second leg which Ajax won 1–0 with a goal from 18-year-old Kiki Musampa.

Clash of outsiders

Legia Warsaw were matched with Panathinaikos. The first leg, in freezing conditions in Warsaw, was dominated by Polish goalkeeper Jozef Wandzik – who played against his compatriots for Panathinaikos. A string of fine saves secured a goalless draw and Panathinaikos wrapped up the tie by winning 3–0 in Athens. Two of their goals were scored by another Polish export, striker Krzysztof Warzycha.

The outstanding quarter-final was between Real Madrid and Juventus, both former champions and whose rivalry in this competition went back 34 years. Real approached the tie amid uncertainty after the replacement of coach Jorge Valdano by Arsenio Iglesias. Nevertheless, he had cause to celebrate when a first-half goal from Raul brought Madrid victory at home. In the second leg Juventus turned the tie around by winning 2–0 in Turin and 2–1 on aggregate.

The semi-finals, with a pre-ordained "draw," matched Ajax against Panathinaikos of Athens and Juventus against Nantes.

Ajax and Juventus were expected to have few problems and Juventus were, indeed, always in control at home and away.

Ajax could not say the same. They appeared to have suffered a major setback in their title defence when they ended their last European tie in the old Olympic stadium with a 1–0 defeat. Panathinaikos won with an 87th-minute goal from Krzysztof on an assist from Giorgios Donis. Ajax coach Louis Van Gaal said: "We played all the match in their half but did nothing with our chances. We will need to get our act together for the return. But we are not beaten yet."

Away goals count

His words proved prophetic as Ajax went on to defy the Greek champions and their noisy 75,000 supporters in Athens. Litmanen levelled the aggregate score after only four minutes and Ajax, despite the absence of injured Kluivert, dominated possession. Yet it was not until 13 minutes from the end that Litmanen scored their second. Panathinaikos now needed to score three times to overcome Ajax's away goals advantage. Their desperation left gaps in defence and Nordin Wooter took advantage to score Ajax's third for a win of 3–0 on the night and 3–1 on aggregate.

Juventus won their first leg in Turin against Nantes 2–0 with second-half goals from captain Gianluca Vialli and midfielder Vladimir Jugovic. Their task was assisted by the fact Nantes had to play more than half the match with only 10 men after the expulsion of midfielder Bruno Carotti just on half-time for having been shown a second yellow card. Three minutes into the second half, Juventus took the lead through Vialli. Surprisingly, it was his first goal in the competition that season – and he followed up with another after just 17 minutes of the return in France. Juventus led 1–0 and later 2–1. An eventual 3–2 defeat was academic since they had won 4–3 on aggregate.

Vialli said: "I was criticised after the first leg so I was pleased to put the record straight. Playing against Ajax will be an ideal final. We will be the underdogs but we don't mind that… "

Prophetic words, again. Juventus won the final in Rome's Olympic Stadium by defeating the Dutch title-holders 4–2 on penalties after a 1–1 draw, following extra time. It was the second time Juventus had won the Cup (after 1985) and the second time Ajax had lost the final. Juventus were ecstatic. Chief executive and former star forward Roberto Bettega, said: "This is for real. We have never really considered 1985 as a victory because of what happened in the Heysel stadium. We have waited a long time."

The Italian club thus crowned two remarkable seasons under coach Marcello Lippi and no-one disputed their success, even though it took a penalty shoot-out. Lippi praised his men for the manner in which they maintained the pace of their game throughout the 120 minutes; Ajax coach Louis Van Gaal conceded the Italian tactics exposed the frailties of his team.

The early openings fell to Juventus. First, Del Piero needed just a little too long to control a crossfield pass from Vialli, then Fabrizio Ravanelli fired hastily high and wide after a misjudgment by Ajax goalkeeper Van der Saar. Worse was to come for both Ajax and their keeper when he and Frank de Boer allowed Ravanelli to slip a bouncing ball from between them and shoot home the opening goal from the narrowest of angles.

Ajax worked hard to make amends and equalised four minutes before half-time. Frank de Boer surprised Angelo Peruzzi with a free-kick and Litmanen pounced for a goal which established him as the competition's overall nine-goal top scorer. The rest of the match was mainly Juventus. Vialli hit the bar and was foiled three times, brilliantly, by the reflexes of Van der Saar.

The first period of extra time was goalless and chance-less. The second period offered more – Van der Sar saving twice from Vialli and Del Piero hitting the goalkeeper in the very last minute. The only time Ajax had an advantage was in taking the first penalty of the shoot-out… and they missed it.

Lippi, whose two-year reign at Juventus had already brought success in Italian League and Cup and now Europe, said: "I think we deserved to win over the 90 minutes and then again over the 120 minutes, without going to penalties. We looked sharp, well-prepared, calm. We kept up the pace we had set ourselves – right to the end. We knew what we wanted and how to go about it and that was our great strength. With all due respect to Ajax, victory was more important to us and I think that was evident in the way we played. Winning the League last year was wonderful because it was the first major prize I had ever won as a coach. But this is different again. I'm sure it will go down in the history of Juventus's greatest moments."

Lifting the Cup high towards the fans proved to be Vialli's last duty as Juventus captain since he announced, two days later, his impending transfer to the English club Chelsea. He said: "This is the perfect climax to so many years of hard work because I was very close to this cup once before, four years ago, when I was with Sampdoria and Barcelona beat us."

Ajax lacked the injured Overmars and had the de Boer twins and substitute Kluivert struggling for fitness. But Van Gaal, said: "We didn't play well enough and Juventus put us under a great deal of pressure, especially at the back which is where we start to build our game. We just missed too many players at 100 per cent to be able to give a good performance. But I must give Juventus all credit for the way they played."

Van Gaal knew the outcome, even before the penalty shoot-out. "You can tell, when you get to the start of penalties, who is going to win," he added. "When you have only a few players volunteering then you know you have lost. It's about confidence and morale. By contrast, look at the way Ferrara took the first penalty for Juventus! That was the confidence of a man who knew his team were going to win."

The Bosman ruling

By the time the 1996–97 campaign was set under way, a significant new factor had entered the equation. In December 1995, a little-known Belgian midfielder named Jean-Marc Bosman had successfully challenged the football establishment in the European Court of Justice. One effect of the judgment was to formalize every player's right to a free transfer when changing clubs between countries within the European Union. The second effect, most relevant to the UEFA club competitions, was to outlaw the practice of restricting the number of players per club on grounds of nationality – at least as far as EU citizen players were concerned. The Bosman freedoms, enmeshed with the Champions League TV and sponsorship cash bonanza, helped tighten the grip of Europe's big clubs on Europe's biggest prize.

Oddly, in that loadsamoney climate, the 1996–97 group stages saw the end of the Milan era. Their dreams of winning the Cup for a record-equalling sixth time were blown away in the last matchday of Group A, when the unlikely Norwegians of Rosenborg went to the Stadio Meazza needing nothing less than victory… and beat the Italians 2–1. Porto won the group.

Milan, back briefly under the guidance of Arrigo Sacchi who had resigned as manager of Italy the previous Sunday, had needed only a point against Rosenborg. But they fell behind when Harald Brattbakk scored after 29 minutes and lost the match to a 69th-minute winner from Vegard Heggem after Milan's French international Christophe Dugarry had equalised on the stroke of half-time. It was an astonishing defeat for the Italians, who had beaten the Norwegians 4–1 away earlier in the competition and, despite a poor run in Serie A, had always been favourites to qualify from group D with Porto.

The result deprived the competition of what would have been a fascinating all-Italian quarter-final between Milan and the newly-crowned world club champions Juventus. Milan's owner Silvio Berlusconi, said the defeat was "the lowest point in our luck and in the League since I have been at Milan".

While Milan were sinking, European pedigree was floating to the surface elsewhere on the continent. In Group A, Ajax, bidding to reach their third consecutive Champions Cup Final but needing an away win from their last game to qualify, rose to the challenge and beat Grasshopper Zurich 1–0 in Switzerland. Kluivert scored Ajax's vital goal after 31 minutes to keep alive the Dutch champions' remarkable record of not having lost an away tie in Europe for three seasons. Ajax qualified in second place, level on points with Champions League debutants Auxerre, who clinched their quarter-final place with a 2–1 win over Rangers, in France.

In Group C, Manchester United, lying third before last night kick-off, defeated Rapid Vienna 2–0 on a chilly day in Austria and had Juventus to thank for snuffing out Fenerbahce's

quarter-final hopes by the same scoreline in Turin. Giggs and Cantona scored for the English champions, whose fans spent as much time listening out for the score from Turin as watching their own side's level-headed performance in sub-zero temperatures. If Fenerbahce had beaten Juventus, United's win would not have been enough to take them through. In the event, goals from Michele Padovano and Nicola Amoruso gave Juve victory and calmed English nerves. Atletico Madrid beat Widzew Lodz 1–0 in their final group fixture to win Group B ahead of Borussia Dortmund, who finished runners-up despite winning their final match against Steaua Bucharest 5–3.

In the quarter-finals, victories for Ajax, Juventus, Manchester United and Borussia Dortmund represented a triumph for the status quo. But Ajax very nearly did not make it. Nigerian star Tijani Babangida scored a minute from the end of extra time to secure the decisive 3–2 win over Atletico Madrid which set up a repeat of the previous season's final against Juventus. With the scores level at 2–2 and 3–3 overall after the first leg tie in Amsterdam, Babangida, one of Nigeria's 1996 Olympic gold medal-winning heroes, first hit the post then snatched the winner.

Juventus reached the last four by beating Rosenborg 2–0 and 3–1 overall. French midfielder Zinedine Zidane took advantage of a blunder by Rosenborg keeper Jorn Jamtfall to score in the 29th minute. The clearance hit the Juventus midfielder and rebounded into the net. Amoruso enhanced the victory margin with an 89th-minute penalty.

Manchester United became the first English semi-finalists for 12 years and took a step closer a poignant return to Munich – where the final would be staged – when they beat Porto 4–0 at home and forced a 0–0 draw away. United withstood a barrage of early pressure from Porto, unaware of problems outside the ground where 20 fans were injured after clashes with police amid security chaos. In the other quarter-final, Borussia Dortmund beat Auxerre 4–1 on aggregate.

Repeat fixtures

The semi-finals produced a repeat between Juventus and Ajax but none of the 1996 final's nail-biting tension. First-half goals from Amoruso and Christian Vieri earned a 2–1 win for Juve in Amsterdam and they ran away 4–1 with the second leg. A 70,000 crowd in the Delle Alpi stadium saw veteran Attilio Lombardo head in a corner for the first goal then set up Vieri for a second. Mario Melchiot replied for the Dutch with 15 minutes to go before Amoruso and Zidane scored Juve in quick succession.

In the other tie, Borussia Dortmund achieved the rare feat of winning home and away against Manchester United. An own goal from Gary Pallister provided victory in Dortmund, a strike from Lars Ricken victory at Old Trafford. With veteran Jurgen Kohler in brilliant form at the heart of the Dortmund defence and goalkeeper Stefan Klos making stunning stops from Andy Cole and substitute Giggs, the Germans survived tremendous pressure in front of a 55,000 crowd.

"I think we did most things quite well," said United manager Alex Ferguson. "Obviously losing the goal so early in the game was a bit of a handicap, but we could have overcome that if we had taken any of the chances. Next season we will be back."

Even though the final was in Munich, Juventus were almost everyone's clear favourites. Dortmund were there, so it appeared, to make up the numbers. In the event, however, Dortmund caused the biggest final upset for more than a decade when they beat the Italians 3–1 to secure their first European trophy since they won the Cup-winners Cup in 1965.

Dortmund took the lead with their first shot of the match after 29 minutes when Juve failed to clear a corner. Paul Lambert centred and Karlheinz Riedle chested the ball down before shooting home. Riedle made it 2–0 when he rose unmarked to head home another Andy Möller corner four minutes later. Substitute Lars Ricken scored the goal of the match only 16 seconds after coming on. He lobbed Angelo Peruzzi from 30 metres after spotting the goalkeeper off his line. Del Piero scored Juve's consolation with a close-range flick to end a move engineered by Croatia striker Alen Boksic.

All change again

For 1997–98, UEFA decided on a further, highly controversial, expansion. The big Spanish and Italian clubs had been pressing to be permitted more than one entry into the Champions League. So, in 1996, UEFA decided to admit the league runners-up from the top eight countries according to the coefficient. They created room by expanding the league from four to six groups with group winners plus the two runners-up with the best records proceeding to the quarter-finals. Naturally, this provoked renewed accusations that UEFA was putting business before sporting interests at the behest of a small but powerful inner cabal.

UEFA did, however, also act to reintegrate the smaller and less successful nations into the Champions League by virtue of an extra qualifying round. Instead of shuffling off the minnows into the UEFA Cup, the competitions committee decided all 48 eligible champions plus the holders of the Cup should be seeded according to their countries' coefficient rating. The top eight clubs – including the holders whatever their coefficient – were seeded direct to the mini-league section with one seed each in four groups and two in each of the other two groups.

The clubs seeded between 17 and 32 were drawn to play the clubs seeded 33 to 48 in a two-leg knock-out preliminary round to be staged at the end of July. The losers were eliminated from European competition while the 16 winners went on to the second qualifying round in August where they faced the clubs seeded nine to 16 plus the eight clubs who finished as runners-up in the top eight European nations. The winners went on into the six groups of the Champions League 'proper' while the losers were granted a consolation place in the UEFA Cup.

Allowing runners-up into the Champions Cup was not totally new. Several of the clubs who launched the event in that inaugural season of 1955–56 were not champions because the competition had been organized, initially, by invitation. Then Real Madrid's subsequent domination persuaded UEFA to allow the Spanish runners-up to enter in 1956–57 (Bilbao), 1957–58 (Seville) and 1958–59 (Atletico Madrid).

The runners-up who kicked off a new era in the second qualifying round for the 1997–98 Champions League were Barcelona (Spain), Newcastle (England), Feyenoord (Holland), Bayer Leverkusen (Germany), Paris Saint-Germain (France), Parma (Italy), Sporting (Portugal) and Besiktas (Turkey). The one anomaly was the presence in the August draw of Turkish champions Galatasaray and runners-up Besiktas. UEFA's eight top-seeded countries had all been promised two Champions League places but the award of a direct seeding to holders Dortmund meant pushing Turkey, in effect, into ninth place in the order of preference. Thus both their champions and runners-up entered the Champions League in the second qualifying round. Happily, both won through to the group stage. Only one of the runners-up progressed to the quarter-finals, Leverkusen.

In effect the groups were decided over two matchdays. Borussia Dortmund, Manchester United, Kiev Dynamo and Bayern Munich had a comparatively easy ride, all sewing up group leadership with a game to play and a fortnight remaining. That still left plenty of drama for the sixth and final matchday.

Juventus had a close call from Group B. They qualified as one of the two group runners-up with best records because, while they were beating group winners Manchester United 1–0, Rosenborg Trondheim could only draw 2–2 with Olympiakos Piraeus in Group D. Juventus owed their victory to a goal from Filippo Inzaghi with six minutes remaining. It would not have been enough if Olympiakos' Predrag Djodjevic had not scored two minutes from time to salvage a 2–2 draw for the Greeks and eliminate furious Rosenborg. The Serb scored with a free-kick from the edge of the penalty box.

Rosenborg would have gone through to the quarter-finals with 13 points as one of the two best second-place teams had they held on for a victory. Instead, they finished with 11 and went out. Juventus went through with 12 points and Leverkusen got in with 13 as the other "best runners-up" (Points scored, goal difference, goals scored were the deciding factors).

Juve hero Inzaghi, said: "I didn't realise we had qualified until I saw my team-mates jumping up and down on the touchlines. This must be the most important goal of my career."

Real Madrid left it to the last match to win Group D after thrashing Porto 4–0. Croatia's Davor Suker scored twice with

Real Madrid – the original champions – celebrate their 1998 victory over Juventus

the other two coming from Fernando Hierro and Brazilian left-back Roberto Carlos. In Group F, Leverkusen and Monaco played out a 2–2 draw which was good enough for both to get through. Monaco qualified as group winners with 13 points and Leverkusen, with an inferior goal difference, took second spot. Monaco hit back with late goals from Christophe Pignol and Thierry Henry after Stefan Beinlich and Erik Meijer had given the Germans a 2–– lead after 57 minutes. As it turned out, when the mathematical dust had settled, both clubs would have qualified even if one had lost the match.

German talent tells

Leverkusen's progress meant that, along with holders Borussia Dortmund who won Group A, and Group E winners Bayern Munich, Germany had three sides in the quarter-finals. They had only one left after that phase however, Leverkusen falling to Real Madrid and Dortmund knocking out domestic rivals Bayern.

Madrid beat Leverkusen 1–1, 3–0 and 4–1 on aggregate. The margin would have been greater but for the superb form of Leverkusen goalkeeper Dirk Heinen in the second leg in Spain. He pulled off two superb first-half saves from Raul but had no answer when French international Christian Karembeu scored four minutes into the second half. Karembeu had only just joined Madrid after a long battle to obtain his freedom from Sampdoria, but the wait had been worth it since he had also scored Madrid's

goal in the first leg. New striking hero Fernando Morientes and defender Hierro, from the penalty spot, extended Madrid's lead.

Dortmund needed an extra-time goal from Stephane Chapuisat to lift them into the semi-finals at the expense of Bayern. The goal after 109 minutes was the only one that either side managed in the two legs, the opening match in Munich having finished 0–0 and the first 90 minutes of the Dortmund return also scoreless. Switzerland spearhead Chapuisat gave Bayern goalkeeper Oliver Kahn no chance with a left-foot volley.

Juventus cruised through in the end against Kiev Dynamo but, again, they did not make life easy for themselves. Held 1–1 at home, Juve then had to win in the Ukraine capital, which they did 4–1. As coach Lippi, said: "When this team have to rise to the occasion they always manage it." Inzaghi scored a hat-trick and Del Piero completed the rout a minute from time.

Completing the semi-final line-up were Monaco, who beat a Manchester United fading at home and abroad. Perhaps United were complacent after forcing a 0–0 draw in the Principality. But at Old Trafford, Alex Ferguson's men fell behind to an early strike by David Trezeguet and went out on the away goals rule despite a second-half reply from striker Ole Gunnar Solskjaer. Ferguson said: "I don't think they were on top, they only had one shot and that was the goal. It was an away goal and it was a killer. But we'll be back."

Monaco coach Jean Tigana, said: "The highest point in my career as a player was when France beat Brazil in the 1986 World Cup in Mexico. This is the highest point as a coach."

It was also almost the end of road for Tigana and Monaco. They fell 6–4 on aggregate in the semi-finals to Juventus while Real Madrid, defeating holders Dortmund 2–0 overall, set up what Juve's Lippi described as "the dream final."

Juventus dominated the first leg to win 4–1 thanks to a hat-trick from Del Piero – two from penalties after trips on Inzaghi and Zidane – and a late goal from Zidane himself. In Monte Carlo, Juventus extended their 4–1 advantage after only 14 minutes of the return through reserve striker Amoruso. Monaco hit back with spirit to win the match 3–2 but Juve, 6–4 clear overall, were never in danger.

Real trouble

Chaos theory turned into reality in the other semi-final, between Real Madrid and Dortmund in the Estadio Bernabeu, after what was later described as the most embarrassing incident in Real's 96 years. A few minutes before kick-off, a group of Real's notorious Ultra Sur hooligan supporters climbed up on terrace fencing and brought down the ball catch netting. One post fell onto the goal in front, smashing the bar and uprooting the posts. Dutch referee Mario Van der Ende took both teams off the pitch and the kick-off was delayed 45 minutes. No spare goal could be found in the Bernabeu so groundstaff had to break into Madrid's training ground three miles away to find a replacement.

When the match did get under way, goals from Morientes and Karembeu earned Real a win but they also collected a massive from UEFA for the security failures. Dortmund appealed that they should be awarded the match, then withdrew, agreeing they had accepted Van der Ende's decision to postpone the kick-off.

The second leg, by comparison, was a tame goalless draw.

Thus the scene was set for Juventus vs. Real Madrid, the sort of final shakedown associated with the glamourous early years of the Champions Cup; the years when the competition was more about the glory than the money. Yet even the final was bedevilled by logistical confusion when, a week from the big night in the Amsterdam ArenA, Dutch air traffic controllers refused to accept charter flights bringing not only Spanish and Italian fans but the Juventus team. UEFA gave the Dutch federation 24 hours to sort it out and eventually the Government declared a temporary lifting of flight restrictions to avert a public relations disaster.

The expectation ahead of the final was almost too much. Madrid and Juventus shared the same tradition: they had won more domestic championships than any of their envious rivals and they had known the glory of winning the most prestigious trophy in European football – Juventus twice, Real Madrid six times. They had met three times before in Europe. In the Champions Cup in 1961–62, Real beat Juventus – John Charles and all – in a quarter final play-off. Some 25 years later, in the second round, the Spaniards won again, this time after a penalty shoot-out. But in the quarter-finals two years earlier, it was Juventus's turn to celebrate a 2–1 aggregate victory.

As in 1997, Juventus were favourites. As in 1997, they were defeated. A technically engrossing game played at remarkable pace saw Juventus seize early control only for Real – with Clarence Seedorf tireless in midfield and Hierro a tower of strength at the back – "think" their way back into the match.

Real had lost form so badly in the Spanish League that they had finished outside the top two places which would have guaranteed a Champions League return the following season. Juventus, Italian champions once again, did not have that problem.

In the second half, Real grew in confidence and, in the 66th minute, striker Predrag Mijatovic seized on a loose ball on the edge of the six-yard box, stepped wide of keeper Peruzzi and scored the only goal of the game. Real – original champions of Europe – were back where they knew they belonged.

Champions Cup or Champions League... whatever its title, this was still THE prize to win.

The UEFA Champions League is now established, beyond all doubt, as the most prestigious international club competition in Europe, if not the world. Its high profile has been enhanced by the proven success of the competition format allied to the strength of the partnerships developed with sponsors and broadcasters.

The intense interest in the UEFA Champions League has been reflected in media discussion over the manner in which the competition may expand. Such interest only serves to underline the allure of the event and the worldwide interest in sharing in it – if not as direct participants, then at the least as tele-spectators.

Enormous developments in travel and communications since the launch of the original European Champion Clubs' Cup in the mid-1950s have enabled UEFA to capitalise on the success of this flagship competition. It should never be overlooked that the participating clubs are not the competition's only beneficiaries: the smallest federations and their clubs and the less glamorous of UEFA's competitions all profit from the Champions League's success.

At present, the UEFA Champions League has been "held" to a format featuring a qualifying round, four groups of four clubs and then direct elimination, two leg ("knock-out") quarter-finals and semi-finals leading up to the single-match final. But this format is not fixed in stone. UEFA is currently considering the most appropriate method of expanding the event.

The European football family can only benefit - from UEFA, to the clubs and players, to the sponsors and broadcasters and, above all, to the fans."

— *UEFA president Lennart Johansson, reviewing the dramatic success of the Champions League in 1996*

EUROPEAN CHAMPIONS CUP RESULTS

* denotes captain

1955–56

SEMI-FINALS:

Real Madrid bt Milan 4–2, 1–2
(5–4 agg)
Reims bt Hibernian 2–0, 1–0
(3–0 agg)

FINAL

June 13 (Parc des Princes, Paris)
Real Madrid 4 (Di Stefano 15, Rial 30 79, Marquitos 71)
Reims 3 (Leblond 6, Templin 10, Hidalgo 62)
HT: 2–2. Att: 38,239. Ref: Ellis (Eng).
REAL: Alonso, Atienza, Lesmes, Munoz*, Marquitos, Zarraga, Joseito, Marsal, Di Stefano, Rial, Gento. Coach: Villalonga.
REIMS: Jacquet, Zimny, Giraudo, Leblond, Jonquet*, Siatka, Hidalgo, Glowacki, Kopa, Bliard, Templin. Coach: Batteux.

1956–67

SEMI-FINALS

Real Madrid bt Manchester Utd 3–1, 2–2
(5–3 agg)
Fiorentina bt Red Star Belgrade 1–0, 0–0
(1–0 agg)

FINAL

May 30 (Santiago Bernabeu, Madrid)
Real Madrid 2 (Di Stefano 70 pen, Gento 76)
Fiorentina 0
HT: 0–0. Att: 120,000. Ref: Horn (Hol).
REAL: Alonso, Torres, Lesmes, Munoz*, Marquitos, Zarraga, Kopa, Mateos, Di Stefano, Rial, Gento. Coach: Villalonga.
FIORENTINA: Sarti, Magnini, Cervato*, Scaramucci, Orzan, Segato, Julinho, Gratton, Virgili, Montuori, Prini. Coach: Bernardini.

1957–58

SEMI-FINALS

Real Madrid bt Seville 8–0, 2–2
(10–2 agg)
Milan bt Manchester United 1–2, 4–0
(5–2 agg)

FINAL

May 29 (Heysel, Brussels)
Real Madrid 3 (Di Stefano 74, Rial 79, Gento 107)

Milan 2 (Schiaffino 59, Grillo 78)
HT: 0–0. After extra time . 90 min: 2–2. Att: 70,000. Ref: Alsteen (Bel).
REAL: Alonso*, Atienza, Lesmes, Santisteban, Santamaria, Zarraga, Kopa, Joseito, Di Stefano, Rial, Gento. Coach: Carniglia.
MILAN: Soldan, Fontana, Beraldo, Bergamaschi, C Maldini, Radice, Danova, Liedholm*, Schiaffino, Grillo, Cucchiaroni. Coach: Puricelli.

1958–59

SEMI-FINALS

Real Madrid bt Atletico Madrid 2–1, 0–1, 2–1
(5–3 agg)
Reims bt Young Boys 1–0, 0–3
(3–1 agg)

FINAL

June 3 (Neckar, Stuttgart)
Real Madrid 2 (Mateos 2, Di Stefano 47)
Reims 0
HT: 1–0. Att: 72,000. Ref: Dusch (Fra).
REAL: Dominguez, Marquitos, Zarraga*, Santisteban, Santamaria, Ruiz, Kopa, Mateos, Di Stefano, Rial, Gento. Coach: Carniglia.
REIMS: Colonna, Rodzik, Giraudo, Penverne, Jonquet*, Leblond, Lamartine, Bliard, Fontaine, Piantoni, Vincent. Coach: Batteux.

1959–60

SEMI-FINALS

Real Madrid bt Barcelona 3–1, 3–1
(6–2 agg)
Eintracht Frankfurt bt Rangers 6–1, 6–3
(12–4 agg)

FINAL

May 18 (Hampden Park, Glasgow)
Real Madrid 7 (Di Stefano 26 29 74, Puskas 44 56 pen 60 71)
Eintracht Frankfurt 3 (Kress 18, Stein 72 76)
HT: 3–1. Att: 127,621. Ref: Mowat (Sco).
REAL: Dominguez, Marquitos, Pachin, Vidal, Santamaria, Zarraga*, Canario, Del Sol, Di Stefano, Puskas, Gento. Coach: Munoz.
EINTRACHT: Loy, Lutz, Hofer, Weilbacher, Eigenbrodt, Stinka, Kress, Lindner, Stein, Pfaff*, Meier. Coach: Osswald.

1960–61

SEMI-FINALS

Benfica bt Rapid Vienna 3–0, 1–1
(4–1 agg)
Barcelona bt Hamburg 1–0, 1–2, 1–0
(3–2 agg)

FINAL

May 31 (Wankdorf, Bern)
Benfica 3 (Aguas 30, Ramallets og 31, Coluna 54)
Barcelona 2 (Kocsis 20, Czibor 75)

HT: 2–1. Att: 33,000. Ref: Dienst (Swi).
BENFICA: Costa Pereira, Mario Joao, Angelo, Germano, Cruz, Jose Augusto, Santana, Aguas*, Coluna, Cavem. Coach: Guttmann.
BARCELONA: Ramallets*, Foncho, Gracia, Verges, Garay, Gensana, Kubala, Kocsis, Evaristo, Suarez, Czibor. Coach: Orizaola.

1961–62

SEMI-FINALS

Benfica bt Tottenham Hotspur 3–1, 1–2
(4–3 agg)
Real Madrid bt Standard Liege 4–0, 2–0
(6–0 agg)

FINAL

May 2 (Olympic, Amsterdam)
Benfica 5 (Aguas 25, Cavem 34, Coluna 61, Eusebio 68 pen, 78)
Real Madrid 3 (Puskas 17, 23, 38)
HT: 2–3. Att: 68,000. Ref: Horn (Hol).
BENFICA: Costa Pereira, Mario Joao, Angelo, Cavem, Germano, Cruz, Jose Augusto, Eusebio, Aguas*, Coluna, Simoes. Coach: Guttmann.
REAL: Araquistain, Casado, Miera, Felo, Santamaria, Pachin, Tejada, Del Sol, Di Stefano, Puskas, Gento*. Coach: Munoz.

1962–63

SEMI-FINALS

Milan bt Dundee 5–1, 0–1
(5-2 agg)
Benfica bt Feyenoord 0–0, 3–1
(4–1 agg)

FINAL

May 22 (Wembley)
Milan 2 (Altafini 58 66)
Benfica 1 (Eusebio 18)
HT: 0–1. Att: 45,000. Ref: Holland (Eng).
MILAN: Ghezzi, David, Trebbi, Benitez, C Maldini*, Trapattoni, Pivatelli, Dino Sani, Altafini, Rivera, Mora. Coach: Rocco.
BENFICA: Costa Pereira, Cavem, Cruz, Humberto, Raul, Coluna*, Jose Augusto, Santana, Torres, Eusebio, Simoes. Coach: Riera.

1963–64

SEMI-FINALS

Internazionale bt Borussia Dortmund 2–2, 2–0
(4–2 agg)
Real Madrid bt FC Zurich 2–1, 6-0
(8–1 agg)

FINAL

May 27 (Prater, Vienna)
Internazionale 3 (Mazzola 43 76, Milani 62)
Real Madrid 1 (Felo 69)
HT: 1–0. Att: 72,000. Ref: Stoll (Aut).
INTER: Sarti, Burgnich, Facchetti, Tagnin, Guarneri,

Picchi*, Jair, Mazzola, Milani, Suarez, Corso. Coach: Herrera.
REAL: Vicente, Isidro, Pachin, Muller, Santamaria, Zoco, Amancio, Felo, Di Stefano, Puskas, Gento*. Coach: Munoz.

1964–65

SEMI-FINALS

Internazionale bt Liverpool 1–3, 3–0
(4–3 agg)
Benfica bt Vasas Gyor 1–0, 4–0
(5–0 agg)

FINAL

May 27 (San Siro, Milan)
Internazionale 1 (Jair 42)
Benfica 0
HT: 1–0. Att: 80,000. Ref: Dienst (Swi).
INTER: Sarti, Burgnich, Facchetti, Bedin, Guarneri, Picchi*, Jair, Mazzola, Peiro, Suarez, Corso. Coach: Herrera.
BENFICA: Costa Pereira, Cavem, Cruz, Neto, Germano, Raul, Jose Augusto, Eusebio, Torres, Coluna*, Simoes. Coach: Schwartz.

1965–66

SEMI-FINALS

Real Madrid bt Internazionale 1–0, 1–1
(2–1 agg)
Partizan Belgrade bt Manchester United 2–0, 0–1
(2–1 agg)

FINAL

May 11 (Heysel, Brussels)
Real Madrid 2 (Amancio 70, Serena 76)
Partizan Belgrade 1 (Vasovic 55)
HT: 0–0. Att: 55,000. Ref: Kreitlein (WG).
REAL: Araquistain, Pachin, Sanchis, Pirri, De Felipe, Zoco, Serena, Amancio, Grosso, Velazquez, Gento*. Coach: Munoz.
PARTIZAN: Soskic, Jusufi, Mihajlovic, Becejac, Rasovic, Vasovic*, Bajic, Kovacevic, Hasanagic, Galic, Pirmajer. Coach: Gegic.

1966–67

SEMI-FINALS

Celtic bt Dukla Prague 3–1, 0–0
(3–1 agg)
Internazionale bt CSKA Sofia 1–1, 1–1, 1–0
(3–2 agg)

FINAL

May 25 (Lisbon)
Celtic 2 (Gemmell 62, Chalmers 83)
Internazionale 1 (Mazzola 6 pen)
HT: 0–1. Att: 55,000. Ref: Tschenscher (WG).
CELTIC: Simpson, Craig, Gemmell, Murdoch, McNeill*, Clark, Johnstone, Wallace, Chalmers, Auld, Lennox. Manager: Stein.
INTER: Sarti, Burgnich, Facchetti, Bedin, Guarneri, Picchi*, Domenghini, Bicicli, Mazzola, Cappellini, Corso. Coach: Herrera.

1967–68

SEMI-FINALS

Manchester United bt Real Madrid 1–0, 3–3
(4–3 agg)
Benfica bt Juventus 2–0, 1–0
(3–0 agg)

FINAL

May 29 (Wembley)
Manchester United 4 (Charlton 54 98, Best 92, Kidd 95)
Benfica 1 (Jaime Graca 78)
HT: 0–0. After extra time . 90 min: 1–1. Att: 100,000. Ref: Lo Bello (Ita).
UNITED: Stepney, Brennan, A Dunne, Crerand, Foulkes, Stiles, Best, Kidd, Charlton*, Sadler, Aston. Manager: Busby.
BENFICA: Henrique, Adolfo, Humberto, Jacinto, Cruz, Jaime Graca, Jose Augusto, Coluna*, Eusebio, Torres, Simoes. Coach: Gloria.

From this season, teams level on aggregate after 90 minutes of the second leg were split by the away goals counting double rule. If the aggregate was still level, extra time was played in the first two rounds, with a play-off maintained from the quarter-finals onwards.

1968–69

SEMI-FINALS

Milan bt Manchester United 2–0, 0–1
(2–1 agg)
Ajax bt Spartak Trnava 3–0, 0–2
(3–2 agg)

FINAL

May 28 (Santiago Bernabeu, Madrid)
Milan 4 (Prati 7 39 74, Sormani 66)
Ajax Amsterdam 1 (Vasovic 61 pen)
HT: 2–0. Att: 50,000. Ref: Ortiz de Mendibil (Spa).
MILAN: Cudicini, Anquilletti, Schnellinger, Malatrasi, Rosato, Trapattoni, Hamrin, Lodetti, Sormani, Rivera*, Prati. Coach: Rocco.
AJAX: Bals, Suurbier (Muller 46), Van Duivendobe, Vasovic*, Hulshoff, Pronk, Groot (Nuninga 46), Swart, Cruyff, Danielsson, Keizer. Coach: Michels.

1969–70

SEMI-FINALS

Feyenoord bt Legia Warsaw 0–0, 2–0
(2–0 agg)
Celtic bt Leeds United 1–0, 2–1
(3–1 agg)

FINAL

May 6 (San Siro, Milan)
Feyenoord 2 (Israel 29, Kindvall 116)
Celtic 1 (Gemmell 31)
HT: 1–1. After extra time. 90min: 1–1. Att: 53,187. Ref: Lo Bello (Ita).
FEYENOORD: Pieters Graafland, Romeijn (Haak 107), Van Duivendobe, Jansen, Israel*, Hasil, Wery, Laseroms, Kindvall, Van Hanegem, Moulijn. Coach: Happel.
CELTIC: Williams, Hay, Gemmell, Murdoch, McNeill*, Brogan, Johnstone, Wallace, J Hughes, Auld (Connelly 77), Lennox. Manager: Stein.

1970–71

SEMI-FINALS

Ajax bt Atletico Madrid 0–1, 3–0
(3–1 agg)
Panathinaikos bt Red Star Belgrade 1–4, 3–0
(agg 4–4, away goals)

FINAL

June 2 (Wembley)
Ajax Amsterdam 2 (Van Dijk 5, Haan 87)
Panathinaikos 0
HT: 1–0. Att: 90,000. Ref: Taylor (Eng).
AJAX: Stuy, Suurbier, Neeskens, Vasovic*, Rijnders (Blankenburg 46), Hulshoff, Swart (Haan 46), Van Dijk, Cruyff, G Muhren, Keizer. Coach: Michels.
PANATHINAIKOS: Ekonomopoulos, Tomaras, Vlahos, Elefterakis, Kamaras, Sourpis, Gramos, Filakouris, Antoniadis, Domazos*, Kapsis. Coach: Puskas.

From this season, if aggregate scores and away goals were level at the end of 90 minutes of the second leg, extra time was played and, if the scores were still level, a penalty shoot-out determined the winners. A drawn final would go to a replay until 1975.

1971–72

SEMI-FINALS

Ajax bt Benfica 1–0, 0–0
(1–0 agg)
Internazionale bt Celtic 0–0, 0–0
(0–0 agg, 5–4 on pens)

FINAL

May 31 (De Kuijp, Rotterdam)
Ajax Amsterdam 2 (Cruyff 48 77)
Internazionale 0
HT: 0–0. Att: 61,000. Ref: Helies (Fra).
AJAX: Stuy, Suurbier, Krol, Blankenburg, Hulshoff, Neeskens, Swart, G Muhren, Cruyff, Haan, Keizer*. Coach: Kovacs.
INTER: Bordon, Burgnich, Facchetti, Bellugi, Giubertoni (Bertini 12), Oriali, Jair (Pellizzaro 58), Bedin, Boninsegna, Mazzola*, Frustalupi. Coach: Invernizzi.

1972–73

SEMI-FINALS

Ajax bt Real Madrid 2–1, 1–0
(3–1 agg)
Juventus bt Derby County 3–1, 0–0
(3–1 agg)

FINAL

May 30 (Belgrade)
Ajax Amsterdam 1 (Rep 4)
Juventus 0
HT: 1–0. Att: 93,000. Ref: Gugulovic (Yug).
AJAX: Stuy, Suurbier, Krol, Blankenburg, Hulshoff, Neeskens, Haan, G Muhren, Cruyff, Rep, Keizer*. Coach: Kovacs.
JUVENTUS: Zoff, Longobucco, Marchetti, Furino, Morini, Salvadore*, Causio (Cuccureddu 78), Altafini, Anastasi, Capello, Bettega (Haller 63). Coach: Vycpalek.

1973–74

SEMI-FINALS
Bayern Munich bt Ujpest Dozsa 1–1, 3–0
(4–1 agg)
Atletico Madrid bt Celtic 0–0, 2–0
(2–0 agg)

FINAL
May 15 (Heysel, Brussels)
Bayern Munich 1 (Schwarzenbeck 120)
Atletico Madrid 1 (Luis Aragones 113)
HT: 0–0. After extra time. 90 min: 0–0. Att: 65,000. Ref: Loraux (Bel).
BAYERN: Maier, Hansen, Breitner, Schwarzenbeck, Beckenbauer*, Roth, Torstensson (Dürnberger 76), Zobel, G Müller, Hoeness, Kapellmann. Coach: Lattek.
ATLETICO: Reina, Melo, Capon, Adelardo*, Heredia, Eusebio, Ufarte (Becerra 69), Luis, Garate, Irureta, Salcedo (Alberto 91). Coach: Lorenzo.

Replay – May 17 (Heysel, Brussels)
Bayern Munich 4 (Hoeness 28 81, Müller 57 70)
Atletico Madrid 0
HT: 1–0. Att: 23,000. Ref: Delcourt (Bel).
BAYERN: Maier, Hansen, Breitner, Schwarzenbeck, Beckenbauer*, Roth, Torstensson, Zobel, G Müller, Hoeness, Kapellmann. Coach: Lattek.
ATLETICO: Reina, Melo, Capon, Adelardo* (Benegas 61), Heredia, Eusebio, Ufarte (Becerra 65), Luis, Garate, Irureta, Salcedo (Alberto). Coach: Lorenzo.

1974–75

SEMI-FINALS
Bayern Munich bt St Etienne 0–0, 2–0
(2–0 agg)
Leeds United bt Barcelona 2–1, 1–1
(2–2 agg)

FINAL
May 28 (Parc des Princes, Paris)
Bayern Munich 2 (Roth 71, Müller 81)
Leeds United 0
HT: 0–0. Att: 48,000. Ref: Kitabdjian (Fra).
BAYERN: Maier, B Andersson (Weiss 4), Dürnberger, Schwarzenbeck, Beckenbauer*, Zobel, Torstensson, Roth, G Müller, Hoeness (Wunder 42), Kapellmann. Coach: Cramer.
LEEDS: Stewart, Reaney, F Gray, Bremner*, Madeley, Hunter, Lorimer, A Clarke, Jordan, Giles, Yorath (E Gray 80). Manager: Armfield.

1975–76

SEMI-FINALS
Bayern Munich bt Real Madrid 1–1, 2–0
(3–1 agg)
St Etienne bt PSV Eindhoven 1–0, 0–0
(1–0 agg)

FINAL
May 12 (Hampden Park, Glasgow)
Bayern Munich 1 (Roth 57)
St Etienne 0
HT: 0–0. Att: 54,684. Ref: Palotai (Hun).

BAYERN: Maier, Hansen, Horsmann, Schwarzenbeck, Beckenbauer*, Roth, Kapellmann, Dürnberger, G Müller, Hoeness, Rummenigge. Coach: Cramer.
ST ETIENNE: Curkovic, Janvion, Repellini, Piazza, Lopez, Bathenay, Santini, Larque*, P Revelli, H Revelli, Sarramagna (Rocheteau 82). Coach: Herbin.

1976–77

SEMI-FINALS
Liverpool bt FC Zurich 3–1, 3–0
(6–1 agg)
Borussia Mönchengladbach bt Kiev Dynamo 0–1, 2–0
(2–1 agg)

FINAL
May 25 (Olimpico, Rome)
Liverpool 3 (McDermott 27, Smith 65, Neal 82 pen)
Borussia Mönchengladbach 1 (Simonsen 51)
HT: 1–0. Att: 57,000. Ref: Wurtz (Fra).
LIVERPOOL: Clemence, Neal, Jones, Smith, R Kennedy, E Hughes*, Keegan, Case, Heighway, McDermott, Callaghan. Manager: Paisley.
MÖNCHENGLADBACH: Kneib, Vogts*, Klinkhammer, Wittkamp, Bonhof, Wohlers (Hannes 79), Simonsen, Wimmer (Kulik 24), Stielike, Schafer, Heynckes. Coach: Lattek.

1977–78

SEMI-FINALS
Liverpool bt Borussia Mönchengladbach 1–2, 3–0
(4–2 agg)
Club Brugge bt Juventus 0–1, 2–0
(2–1 agg)

FINAL
May 10 (Wembley)
Liverpool 1 (Dalglish 64)
Club Brugge 0
HT: 0–0. Att: 92,000. Ref: Corver (Hol)
LIVERPOOL: Clemence, Neal, R Kennedy, E Hughes*, Thompson, Hansen, Dalglish, Case (Heighway 63), Fairclough, McDermott, Souness. Manager: Paisley.
BRUGGE: Jensen, Bastijns*, Maes (Volders 70), Krieger, Leekens, Cools, De Cubber, Vandereycken, Simeon, Ku (Sanders 60), Sorensen. Coach: Happel.

1978–79

SEMI-FINALS
Nottingham Forest bt FC Köln 3–3, 1–0,
(4–3 agg)
Malmo bt FK Austria 0–0, 1–0
(1–0 agg)

FINAL
May 30 (Olympia, Munich)
Nottingham Forest 1 (Francis 44)
Malmo 0

HT: 1–0. Att: 57,500. Ref: Linemayr (Aut).
FOREST: Shilton, V Anderson, Clark, McGovern*, Lloyd, Burns, Francis, Bowyer, Birtles, Woodcock, Robertson. Manager: Clough.
MALMO: Moller, R Andersson, Jonsson, M Andersson, Erlandsson, Tapper* (Malmberg 34) Ljungberg, Prytz, Kinnvall, Hansson (T Andersson 82), Cervin. Coach: Houghton.

1979–80

SEMI-FINALS
Nottingham Forest bt Ajax 2–0, 0–1
(2–1 agg)
Hamburg bt Real Madrid 0–2, 5–1
(5–3 agg)

FINAL
May 28 (Santiago Bernabeu, Madrid)
Nottingham Forest 1 (Robertson 19)
Hamburg 0
HT: 1–0. Att: 51,000. Ref: Garrido (Por).
FOREST: Shilton, V Anderson, F Gray (Gunn 84), McGovern*, Lloyd, Burns, O'Neill, Bowyer, Birtles, Mills (O'Hare 68), Robertson. Manager: Clough.
HAMBURG: Kargus, Kaltz, Nogly*, Jakobs, Buljan, Hieronymus (Hrubesch 46), Keegan, Memering, Milewski, Magath, Reimann. Coach: Zebec.

1980–81

SEMI-FINALS
Liverpool bt Bayern Munich 0–0, 1–1
(agg 1–1, away goals)
Real Madrid bt Internazionale 2–0, 0–1
(2–1 agg)

FINAL
May 27 (Parc des Princes, Paris)
Liverpool 1 (A Kennedy 82)
Real Madrid 0
HT: 0–0. Att: 48,360. Ref: Palotai (Hun).
LIVERPOOL: Clemence, Neal, A Kennedy, R Kennedy, Thompson*, Hansen, Dalglish (Case 87), Lee, Johnson, McDermott, Souness. Manager: Paisley.
REAL: Agustin, Garcia Cortes (Pineda 87), Camacho, Angel, Sabido, Garcia Navajas, Juanito, Del Bosque, Santillana, Stielike, Cunningham. Coach: Boskov.

1981–82

SEMI-FINALS
Aston Villa bt Anderlecht 1–0, 0–0
(1–0 agg)
Bayern Munich bt CSKA Sofia 3–4, 4–0
(7–4 agg)

FINAL
May 26 (De Kuyp, Rotterdam)
Aston Villa 1 (Withe 67)
Bayern Munich 0
HT: 0–0. Att: 45,000. Ref: Konrath (Fra).

VILLA: Rimmer (Spink 10), Swain, Williams, Mortimer*, Evans, McNaught, Bremner, Shaw, Withe, Cowans, Morley. Manager: Barton.
BAYERN: Möller, Dremmler, Horsmann, Dürnberger, Augenthaler, Weiner, Kraus (Niedermayer 79), Breitner, D Hoeness, Mathy (Göttler 52), Rummenigge. Coach: Csernai.

1982–83

SEMI-FINALS

Hamburg bt Real Sociedad 1–1, 2–1
(3–2 agg)
Juventus bt Widzew Lodz 2–0, 2–2
(4–2 agg)

FINAL

May 25 (Olympic, Athens)
Hamburg 1 (Magath 9)
Juventus 0
HT: 1–0. Att: 73,500. Ref: Rainea (Rom).
HAMBURG: Stein, Kaltz, Wehmeyer, Jakobs, Hieronymus, Rolff, Milewski, Groh, Hrubesch*, Magath, Bastrup (Von Heesen 56). Coach: Happel.
JUVENTUS: Zoff, Gentile, Cabrini, Bonini, Brio, Scirea*, Bettega, Tardelli, P Rossi (Marocchino 56), Platini, Boniek. Coach: Trapattoni.

1983–84

SEMI-FINALS

Liverpool bt Dinamo Bucharest 1–0, 2–1
(3–1 agg)
Roma bt Dundee United 0-2, 3–0
(3–2 agg)

FINAL

May 30 (Olimpico, Rome)
Liverpool 1 (Neal 15)
Roma 1 (Pruzzo 38)
HT: 1–1. After extra time. 90 mins: 1–1. Liverpool 4–2 on pens. Att: 69,693. Ref: Fredriksson (Swe).
LIVERPOOL: Grobbelaar, Neal, A Kennedy, Lawrenson, Whelan, Hansen, Dalglish (Robinson 94), Lee, Rush, Johnston (Nicol 72), Souness*. Manager: Fagan.
ROMA: Tancredi, Nappi, Bonetti, Righetti, Falcao, Nela, Conti, Toninho Cerezo (Strukely 115), Pruzzo (Chierico 64), Di Bartolomei*, Graziani. Coach: Liedholm.

1984–85

Juventus bt Bordeaux 3–0, 0–2
(3–2 agg)
Liverpool bt Panathinaikos 4–0, 1–0
(5–0 agg)

FINAL

May 29 (Heysel, Brussels)
Juventus 1 (Platini 57 pen)
Liverpool 0
HT: 0–0. Att: 60,000. Ref: Daina (Swi).
JUVENTUS: Tacconi, Favero, Cabrini, Bonini, Brio, Scirea, Briaschi (Prandelli 84), Tardelli, P Rossi

(Vignola 89), Platini, Boniek. Coach: Trapattoni.
LIVERPOOL: Grobbelaar, Neal, Beglin, Lawrenson (Gillespie 3), Nicol, Hansen, Dalglish, Whelan, Rush, Walsh (Johnston 46), Wark. Manager: Fagan.

1985–86

SEMI-FINALS

Steaua Bucharest bt Anderlecht 0–1, 3–0
(3–1 agg)
Barcelona bt IFK Gothenburg 0–3, 3–0
(agg 3–3, 5–4 on pens)

FINAL

May 7 (Sanchez Pizjuan, Seville)
Steaua Bucharest 0
Barcelona 0
HT: 0–0. After extra time. 90 min: 0–0. Steaua 2–0 on pens. Att: 75,000. Ref: Vautrot (Fra).
STEAUA: Ducadam, Belodedici, Iovan*, Bumbescu, Barbulescu, Balint, Balan (Iordanescu 72), Boloni, Majaru, Lacatus, Piturca (Radu 107). Coach: Jenei.
BARCELONA: Urruti, Gerardo, Migueli, Alexanco*, Julio Alberto, Victor, Marcos, Schuster (Moratalla 85), Pedraza, Archibald (Pichi Alonso 106), Carrasco. Coach: Venables.

1986–87

SEMI-FINALS

FC Porto bt Kiev Dynamo 2–1, 2–1
(4–2 agg)
Bayern Munich bt Real Madrid 4–1, 0–1
(4–2 agg)

FINAL

May 27 (Prater, Vienna)
FC Porto 2 (Madjer 77, Juary 81)
Bayern Munich 1 (Kogl 25)
HT: 0–1. Att: 62,000. Ref: Ponnet (Bel).
PORTO: Mlynarczyk, Joao Pinto*, Eduardo Luis, Celso, Ignacio (Frasco 66), Quim (Juary 46), Jaime Magalhaes, Sousa, Andre, Futre, Madjer. Coach: Jorge.
BAYERN: Pfaff, Winkelhofer, Nachtweih, Eder, Pflugler, Flick (Lunde 82), Brehme, Hoeness, Matthäus, Kogl, Rummenigge*. Coach: Lattek.

1987–88

SEMI-FINALS

PSV Eindhoven bt Real Madrid 1–1, 0–0
(agg 1–1, away goals)
Benfica bt Steaua Bucharest 0–0, 2–0
(2–0 agg)

FINAL

May 25 (Neckar, Stuttgart)
PSV Eindhoven 0
Benfica 0
HT: 0–0. After extra time. 90 mins: 0–0. PSV 6–5 on pens. Att: 68,000. Ref: Agnolin (Ita).
PSV: Van Breukelen, Gerets*, Nielsen, R Koeman, Heintze, Lerby, Linskens, Van Aerle, Kieft,

Vanenburg, Gillhaus (Janssen 107). Coach: Hiddink.
BENFICA: Silvino, Veloso, Dito, Mozer, Alvaro, Chiquinho, Sheu*, Elzo, Pacheco, M Magnusson (Hajri 112), Rui Aguas (Valdo 56). Coach: Toni.

1988–89

SEMI-FINALS

Milan bt Real Madrid 1–1, 5–0
(6–1 agg)
Steaua Bucharest bt Galatasaray 4–0, 1–1
(5–1 agg)

FINAL

May 24 (Nou Camp, Barcelona)
Milan 4 (Gullit 18 38, Van Basten 27 46)
Steaua Bucharest 0
HT: 3–0. Att: 100,000. Ref: Tritschler (WG).
MILAN: G Galli, Tassotti, P Maldini, Colombo, Costacurta (F Galli 74), F Baresi*, Donadoni, Rijkaard, Van Basten, Gullit (Virdis 60), Ancelotti. Coach: Sacchi.
STEAUA: Lung, Petrescu, Ungureanu, Bumbescu, Stoica*, Iovan, Lacatus, Minea, Piturca, Hagi, Rotariu (Balint 46). Coach: Iordanescu.

1989–90

SEMI-FINALS

Milan bt Bayern Munich 1–0, 1–2
(agg 2–2, away goals)
Benfica bt Marseille 1–2, 1–0
(agg 2–2, away goals)

FINAL

May 23 (Prater, Vienna)
Milan 1 (Rijkaard 67)
Benfica 0
HT: 0–0. Att: 58,000. Ref: Kohl (Aut).
MILAN: G Galli, Tassotti, P Maldini, Colombo (F Galli 89), Costacurta, F Baresi*, Ancelotti (Massaro 67), Rijkaard, Van Basten, Gullit, Evani. Coach: Sacchi.
BENFICA: Silvino, Jose Carlos, Ricardo, Samuel, Aldair, Thern, Vitor Paneira (Vata 78), Jaime Pacheco* (Cesar Brito 59), Hernani, Valdo, M Magnusson. Coach: Eriksson.

1990–91

SEMI-FINALS

Red Star Belgrade bt Bayern Munich 2–1, 2–2
(4–3 agg)
Marseille bt Moscow Spartak 3–1, 2–1
(5-2 agg)

FINAL

May 29 (San Nicola, Bari)
Red Star Belgrade 0
Marseille 0
HT: 0–0. After extra time. 90 min: 0–0. Red Star 5–3 on pens. Att: 58,000. Ref: Lanese (Ita).
RED STAR: Stojanovic*, Jugovic, Marovic, Sabanadzovic, Belodedici, Najdovski, Mihajlovic,

Savicevic (Dodic 84), Pancev, Prosinecki, Binic. Coach: Petrovic.
MARSEILLE: Olmeta, Amoros, Di Meco (Stojkovic 112), Boli, Mozer, Germain, Casoni, Waddle, Papin*, Pele, Fournier (Vercruysse 75). Coach: Goethals.

From this season, UEFA developed a mini-league format within the Champions Cup. The first season, 1991–92, was an experiment. From the following season the mini-league was formalised as the UEFA Champions League, geared to exclusive pan-European sponsorship and television arrangements. Initially, the Champions League compromised two groups replacing the quarter and semi-final stages. From 1994–95, the group stage expanded to four mini-leagues, replacing the first and second rounds. From 1996–97, the group stage was expanded to six mini-leagues and entry to the overall competition was expanded to include the national championship runners-up of Europe's top leagues.

1991–92

QUARTER-FINAL GROUPS

Group I

	P	W	D	L	F	A	Pts
Sampdoria	6	3	2	1	10	5	8
Red Star	6	3	0	3	9	10	6
Anderlecht	6	2	2	2	8	9	6
Panathinaikos	6	0	4	2	1	4	4

Group II

	P	W	D	L	F	A	Pts
Barcelona	6	4	1	1	10	4	9
Sparta Prague	6	2	2	2	7	7	6
Benfica	6	1	3	2	8	5	5
Kiev Dynamo	6	2	0	4	3	12	4

FINAL

May 20 (Wembley)
Barcelona 1 (Koeman 111)
Sampdoria 0
HT: 0–0. After extra time. 90 min: 0–0. Att: 70,827. Ref: Schmidhuber (Ger).
BARCELONA: Zubizarreta*, Nando, Ferrer, R Koeman, Juan Carlos, Bakero, Salinas (Goikoetxea 64), Stoichkov, M Laudrup, Guardiola (Alexanco 113), Eusebio. Coach: Cruyff.
SAMPDORIA: Pagliuca, Mannini, Katanec, Pari, Vierchowod, Lanna, Lombardo, Toninho Cerezo, Vialli (Buso 100), Mancini*, Bonetti (Invernizzi 72). Coach: Boskov.

1992–93

QUARTER-FINAL GROUPS

Group I

	P	W	D	L	F	A	Pts
Marseille	6	3	3	0	14	4	9
Rangers	6	2	4	0	7	5	8
Club Brugge	6	2	1	3	5	8	5
CSKA Moscow	6	0	2	4	2	11	2

Group II

	P	W	D	L	F	A	Pts
Milan	6	6	0	0	11	1	12
IFK Gothenburg	6	3	0	3	7	8	6
FC Porto	6	2	1	3	5	5	5
PSV Eindhoven	6	0	1	5	4	13	1

FINAL

May 26 (Olympiastadion, Munich)
Marseille 1 (Boli 43)
Milan 0
HT: 1–0. Att: 64,400. Ref: Rothlisberger (Swi).
MARSEILLE: Barthez, Angloma (Durand 64), Boli, Desailly, Pele, Eydelie, Sauzee, Deschamps*, Di Meco, Boksic, Voller (Thomas 78). Coach: Goethals.
MILAN: Rossi, Tassotti, Costacurta, F Baresi*, Maldini, Donadoni (Papin 56), Albertini, Rijkaard, Lentini, Van Basten (Eranio 85), Massaro. Coach: Capello.

1993–94

QUARTER-FINAL GROUPS

Group A

	P	W	D	L	F	A	Pts
Barcelona	6	4	2	0	13	3	10
Monaco	6	3	1	2	9	4	7
Moscow Spartak	6	1	3	2	6	12	5
Galatasaray	6	0	2	4	1	10	2

Group B

	P	W	D	L	F	A	Pts
Milan	6	2	4	0	6	2	8
FC Porto	6	3	1	2	10	6	7
Werder Bremen	6	2	1	3	11	15	5
Anderlecht	6	1	2	3	5	9	4

SEMI-FINALS

Milan bt Monaco 3–0
Barcelona bt FC Porto 3–0

FINAL

May 18 (Olympic, Athens)
Milan 4 (Massaro 22 45, Savicevic 47, Desailly 59)
Barcelona 0
HT: 2–0. Att: 70,000. Ref: Don (Eng).
MILAN: S Rossi, Tassotti*, Panucci, Desailly, F Galli, P Maldini (Nava 84), Donadoni, Albertini, Boban, Savicevic, Massaro. Coach: Capello.
BARCELONA: Zubizarreta*, Ferrer, Guardiola, R Koeman, Nadal, Bakero, Sergi (Quique 73), Stoichkov, Amor, Romario, Beguiristain, Coach: Cruyff.

1994–95

LEAGUE TABLES

Group A

	P	W	D	L	F	A	Pts
IFK Gothenburg	6	4	1	1	10	7	9
Barcelona	6	2	2	2	11	8	6
Manchester Utd.	6	2	2	2	11	11	6
Galatasaray	6	1	1	4	3	9	3

Group B

	P	W	D	L	F	A	Pts
Paris St-Germain	6	6	0	0	12	3	12
Bayern Munich	6	2	2	2	8	7	6
Moscow Spartak	6	1	2	3	8	12	4
Kiev Dynamo	6	1	0	5	5	11	2

Group C

	P	W	D	L	F	A	Pts
Benfica	6	3	3	0	9	5	9
Hajduk Split	6	2	2	2	5	7	6
Steaua Bucharest	6	1	3	2	7	6	5
Anderlecht	6	0	4	2	4	7	4

Group D

	P	W	D	L	F	A	Pts
Ajax Amsterdam	6	4	2	0	9	2	10
Milan	6	3	1	2	6	5	5
Austria Salzburg	6	1	3	2	4	6	5
AEK Athens	6	0	2	4	3	9	2

QUARTER-FINALS

Ajax bt Hajduk Split 0–0, 3–0
(3–0 agg)
Bayern Munich bt IFK Gothenburg 0–0, 2–2
(2–2 agg, away goals)
Paris St-Germain bt Barcelona 1–1, 2–1
(3–2 agg)
Milan bt Benfica 2–0, 0–0
(2–0 agg)
Ajax bt Bayern Munich 0–0, 5-2
(5-2 agg)
Milan bt Paris St-Germain 2–0, 1–0
(3–0 agg)

FINAL

May 24 (Ernst-Happel Stadion, Vienna)
Ajax 1 (Kluivert 83)
Milan 0
HT: 0–0. Att: 49,500. Ref: Craciunescu (Rom).
AJAX: Van der Sar, Reiziger, Blind*, F de Boer, Seedorf (Kanu 52), Rijkaard, Litmanen (Kluivert 65), Davids, George, R de Boer, Overmars. Coach: Van Gaal.
MILAN: S Rossi, Panucci, Costacurta, F Baresi*, P Maldini, Donadoni, Albertini, Desailly, Boban (Lentini 83), Massaro (Eranio 89), Simone. Coach: Capello.

1995–96

LEAGUE TABLES

Group A

	P	W	D	L	F	A	Pts
Panathinaikos	6	3	2	1	7	3	11
Nantes	6	2	3	1	8	6	9
FC Porto	6	1	4	1	6	5	7
Aalborg	6	1	1	4	5	12	4

Group B

	P	W	D	L	F	A	Pts
Moscow Spartak	6	6	0	0	15	4	18
Legia Warsaw	6	2	1	3	5	8	7
Rosenborg	6	2	0	4	11	16	6
Blackburn Rovers	6	1	1	4	5	8	4

Group C

	P	W	D	L	F	A	Pts
Juventus	6	4	1	1	15	4	13
Bor Dortmund	6	2	3	1	8	8	9
Steaua Bucharest	6	1	3	2	2	5	6
Rangers	6	0	3	3	6	14	3

Group D

	P	W	D	L	F	A	Pts
Ajax	6	5	1	0	15	1	16
Real Madrid	6	3	1	2	11	5	10
Ferencvaros	6	1	2	3	9	19	5
Grasshopper	6	0	2	4	3	13	2

QUARTER-FINALS

Ajax bt Bor Dortmund 2–0, 1–0
(3–0 agg)
Panathinaikos bt Legia Warsaw 0–0, 3–0
(3–0 agg)
Nantes bt Moscow Spartak 2–0, 2–2
(4–2 agg)
Juventus bt Real Madrid 0–1, 2–0
(2–1 agg)

SEMI-FINALS

Juventus bt Nantes 2–0, 2–3
(4–3 agg)
Ajax bt Panathinaikos 0–1, 3–0
(3–1 agg)

FINAL

May 22 (Olimpico, Rome)
Juventus 1 (Ravanelli 12)
Ajax 1 (Litmanen 40)
HT: 1–1. After extra time. 90 min: 1–1. Juventus 4–2 on pens. Att: 70,000. Ref: Diaz Vega (Spa).
JUVENTUS: Peruzzi, Torricelli, Ferrara, Vierchowod, Pessotto, Conte (Jugovic 43), Paulo Sousa (Di Livio 56), Deschamps, Vialli*, Del Piero, Ravanelli (Padovano 76). Coach: Lippi.
AJAX: Van der Sar, Silooy, Blind*, F de Boer (Scholten 67), Bogarde, George, R de Boer (Wooter 91), Litmanen, Davids, Kanu, Musampa (Kluivert 46). Coach: Van Gaal.

1996–97

LEAGUE TABLES

Group A

	P	W	D	L	F	A	Pts
Auxerre	6	4	0	2	8	4	12
Ajax Amsterdam	6	4	0	2	8	4	12
Grasshopper	6	3	0	3	8	5	9
Rangers	6	1	0	5	5	13	3

Group B

	P	W	D	L	F	A	Pts
Atletico Madrid	6	4	1	1	12	4	13
Bor Dortmund	6	4	1	1	14	8	13
Widzew Lodz	6	1	1	4	6	10	4
Steaua Bucharest	6	1	1	4	5	15	4

Group C

	P	W	D	L	F	A	Pts
Juventus	6	5	1	0	11	1	16
Manchester Utd	6	3	0	3	6	3	9
Fenerbahce	6	2	1	3	3	6	7
Rapid Vienna	6	0	2	4	2	12	2

Group D

	P	W	D	L	F	A	Pts
FC Porto	6	5	1	0	12	4	16
Rosenborg	6	3	0	3	7	11	9
Milan	6	2	1	3	13	11	7
IFK Gothenburg	6	1	0	5	7	13	3

QUARTER-FINALS

Ajax bt Atletico Madrid 1–1, 3–2
(4–3 agg)
Juventus bt Rosenborg 1–1, 2–0
(3–1 agg)
Bor Dortmund bt Auxerre 3–1, 1–0
(4–1 agg)
Manchester Utd bt FC Porto 4–0, 0–0
(4–0 agg)

SEMI-FINALS

Juventus bt Ajax 2–1, 4–1
(6–2 agg)
Bor Dortmund bt Manchester Utd 1–0, 1–0
(2–0 agg)

FINAL

May 28 (Olympiastadion, Munich)
Borussia Dortmund 3 (Riedle 29 34, Ricken 71)
Juventus 1 (Del Piero 64)
HT: 2–0. Att: 65,000. Ref: Puhl (Hun).
DORTMUND: Klos, Kohler, Sammer*, Kree, Reuter, Lambert, Paulo Sousa, Möller (Zorc 88), Heinrich, Riedle, Chapuisat (Ricken 70). Coach: Hitzfeld.
JUVENTUS: Peruzzi, Porrini (Del Piero 46), Ferrara, Montero, Iuliano, Di Livio, Deschamps, Zidane, Jugovic, Vieri (Amoruso 73), Boksic (Tacchinardi 87). Coach: Lippi.

1997–98

LEAGUE TABLES

Group A

	P	W	D	L	F	A	Pts
Bor Dortmund	6	5	0	1	14	3	15
Parma	6	2	3	1	6	5	9
Sparta Prague	6	1	2	3	6	11	5
Galatasary	6	1	1	4	4	11	4

Group B

	P	W	D	L	F	A	Pts
Manchester Utd	6	5	0	1	14	5	15
Juventus	6	4	0	2	12	8	12
Feyenoord	6	3	0	3	8	10	9
Kosice	6	0	0	6	2	13	0

Group C

	P	W	D	L	F	A	Pts
Kiev Dynamo	6	3	2	1	13	6	11
PSV Eindhoven	6	2	3	1	9	8	9
Newcastle Utd	6	2	1	3	7	8	7
Barcelona	6	1	2	3	7	14	5

Group D

	P	W	D	L	F	A	Pts
Real Madrid	6	4	1	1	15	4	13
Rosenborg	6	3	2	1	13	8	11
Olympiakos	6	1	2	3	6	14	5
Porto	6	1	1	4	3	11	4

Group E

	P	W	D	L	F	A	Pts
Bayern Munich	6	4	0	2	13	6	12
Paris Sr-Germain	6	4	0	2	11	10	12
Besiktas	6	2	0	4	6	9	6
IFK Gothenburg	6	2	0	4	4	9	6

Group F

	P	W	D	L	F	A	Pts
Monaco	6	4	1	1	15	8	13
B. Leverkusen	6	4	1	1	11	7	13
Sporting Lisbon	6	2	1	3	9	11	7
Lierse	6	0	1	5	3	12	1

QUARTER-FINALS

Bor Dortmund bt Bayern Munich 0–0, 1–0
(1–0 agg)
Juventus bt Kiev Dynamo 1–1, 4–1
(5–2 agg)
Monaco bt Manchester Utd 0–0, 1–1
(on away goals, 1–1 agg)
Real Madrid bt Bayer Leverkusen 1–1, 3–0
(4–1 agg)

SEMI-FINALS

Real Madrid bt Bor Dortmund 2–0, 0–0
(2–0 agg)
Juventus bt Monaco 4–1, 2–3
(6–4 agg)

FINAL

May 20 (Amsterdam)
Real Madrid 1 (Mijatovic 66)
Juventus 0
HT: 0–0. Att: 50,000. Ref: Krug (Ger)
REAL: Illgner, Panucci, Sanchis, Hierro*, Roberto Carlos, Karembeu, Redondo, Seedorf, Raul (Amavisca 90), Mijatovic (Suker 90), Morientes (Jaime 83). Coach: Heynckes.
JUVENTUS: Peruzzi*, Torricelli, Iuliano, Montero, Di Livio (Tacchinardi 46), Deschamps (Conte 78), Davids, Pessoto (Fonseca 71), Zidane, Inzaghi, Del Piero, Coach: Lippi.

EUROPEAN CUP-WINNERS CUP

The European Cup-winners Cup – or Recopa as the Spanish neatly describe it – was an inevitable development after the demonstrable instant success of the Champions Cup.

In the winter of 1959–60, representatives from a number of European federations began discussing, informally, the launching of a competition for national cup winners. On February 13, 1960, the European Cup-winners Cup was officially set up at a meeting in Vienna involving the federations of Austria, Belgium, West Germany, France, Italy, Yugoslavia, Switzerland, Spain, Czechoslovakia and Hungary.

At that time, only half the federations in Europe organized cup competitions following the traditional direct-elimination format which had been established in the 19th century within English football. But the launching of the Cup-winners Cup galvanized every country in Europe into launching or raising the status of its own domestic event.

Just ten clubs entered the first Cup-winners Cup and a draw was made for a preliminary round of two matches so as to cut the entry to an effective. The opening match was played in East Berlin on August 1, 1960. It saw the East German army team, Vorwarts, beat Red Star Brno of Czechoslovakia 2–1. The historic first goal was scored, after 42 minutes of the first half, by Vorwarts. Brno, however, won the return 2–0 and thus the tie 3–2 on aggregate. The other preliminary tie saw Rangers – still smarting from their 12–4 aggregate bludgeoning at the hands of Eintracht Frankfurt in the previous season's Champions Cup semi-finals – beat Ferencvaros of Hungary.

Effectively, the first full round of the initial Cup-winners Cup was the quarter-final stage. Red Star Brno fell to Dinamo Zagreb, Rangers put a total of 11 goals past West Germany's Borussia Mönchengladbach, Fiorentina of Italy hit nine against Switzerland's Lucerne over two legs and English FA Cup holders Wolves beat FK Austria 5–0 at Molineux after losing 2–0 in Vienna. After a 3–0 win away, the Scots put eight in at Ibrox. Rangers then won the all-British semi-final, beating Wolves 3–1 overall while Fiorentina defeated Zagreb 4–2 on aggregate.

The Florence club's star thus far was Brazilian forward Angelo Benedetto Sormani, nicknamed Antoninho. He had scored a hat-trick against Lucerne in the quarter-final and the first goal against Zagreb in the semi-final. Injury kept him out of the final against Rangers but Fiorentina had other weapons in their armoury. This was the one and only Cup-winners Final to be played over two legs. Fiorentina won them both, 2–0 and 2–1. Home-grown Luigi Milan scored twice at Ibrox then he and Swedish goal-poacher Kurt Hamrin finished the job in the Stadio Comunale. Alex Scott scored Rangers' consolation.

Fiorentina thus became the first Italian club to win a major European trophy, five months before Roma won the long-delayed Fairs Cup Final for that same season.

A clubs' committee had run the 1960–61 tournament but its success prompted a formal organizational takeover by UEFA. This, in turn, legitimized the event and thus 23 clubs entered the next, 1961–62, competition. The first round – from which Fiorentina were exempted as holders – saw one of the most remarkable ties in European club history between Swiss club La Chaux-de-Fonds and Leixoes of Portugal. Chaux-de-Fonds won 6–2 at home... then crashed 5–0 away.

Fiorentina, having been among nine clubs granted a bye, duly crushed Rapid Vienna 3–1, 6–2 in the second round. Aurelio Milani scored one goal in Vienna, a hat-trick in Florence then another goal to spearhead the quarter-final victory over ZVL Zilina of Czechoslovakia. They then beat Ujpest Dozsa in the semi-finals to reach the final against Atletico Madrid.

The Spanish club beat now-defunct Sedan of France then England's Leicester City, deputizing for Tottenham who had won the English League and Cup double the previous term. In the quarter-finals they disposed of Werder Bremen then Carl Zeiss Jena of the former East Germany in the semis.

On three occasions in the first ten years of the Cup-winners Cup, a replay was needed and 1962 was the first time. A poor final at Hampden Park, Glasgow, saw Fiorentina and Atletico draw 1–1 after extra time. When a replay was eventually organized – four months later in Stuttgart – Atletico won 3–0.

History is made

It was in the Cup-winners Cup that Tottenham Hotspur made football history in 1962–63 by becoming the first British club to win a European trophy. But their thunder was stolen in the early stages by the Welsh non-League club Bangor City, holders of the Welsh Cup. Amazingly, they beat mighty Napoli of Italy 2–0 in the first leg and lost only 3–1 in the Stadio San Paolo. If the away goals rule had been operative, Bangor would have progressed. But it was not... and Napoli won the play-off at Highbury 2–1.

Tottenham had reached the Champions Cup semi-finals the previous season, before falling to Benfica. The experience stood them in good stead now, particularly in their superb 5–2, 3–2 win over Rangers in the second round. Slovan Bratislava were defeated 5–2 on aggregate in the quarter-finals before OFK Belgrade were brushed aside by the same score in the semis.

Atletico Madrid, the holders, were waiting in the final, in Rotterdam. But they were no match for rampant Spurs, despite the absence of injured powerhouse left-half Dave Mackay. Little

West Ham on their way to victory in 1965 – beating Real Zaragoza 2–1 at Upton Park

left-winger Terry Dyson and, inevitably, Jimmy Greaves each scored twice. The decisive goal was Dyson's first after 67 minutes. Atletico, 2–0 down at the interval, had stormed back into the match after the break and pulled a goal back with an Enrique Collar penalty. Everything hung in the balance when Dyson, from way out on the left, lifted a high swirling cross towards the Atletico goal. Keeper Madinbeytia misjudged the flight and the ball dropped over his head into the net. Spurs were suddenly 3–1 up and they never looked back, winning 5–1.

The Cup-winners Cup offered Mackay more bad luck the following season. When Spurs entered the second round against English FA Cup winners Manchester United, Mackay broke his leg again and – with substitutions not possible at the time – the holders went out. Two goals each from David Herd and Bobby Charlton saw United to victory at Old Trafford following a 2–0 defeat at White Hart Lane. But the Reds were duly taken apart by Sporting from Lisbon in the quarter-finals. United won 4–1 at home, inspired by a Denis Law hat-trick, then crashed 5–0 in Lisbon where Sporting's Osvaldo Silva replied with a treble of

his own. United paid the penalty for complacency. They should have been warned by the way in which Sporting had won an earlier home tie 16–1 against Apoel Nicosia of Cyprus. Mascarenhas scored six, Figueiredo three.

There was a nasty shock awaiting another British entry, Celtic, in the semi-finals. They wanted to go one better than old rivals Rangers, who had been runners-up in 1961. Celtic thought they were on their way, too, after beating MTK Budapest 3–0 in their semi-final first leg at Parkhead. Unfortunately, the Hungarians won the return 4–0.

Replay it again

The final in the Heysel stadium was an entertaining scrap. MTK led 1–0, went 2–1 down then led 3–2 before earning a 3–3 draw. That meant another replay, which Sporting won 1–0 in Antwerp with a goal direct from a corner by Morais. At least the replay drew a bigger crowd (13,924) then the original final (3,208).

This was the decade in which English clubs came to dominate the Cup-winners Cup. But their British neighbours also joined in the fun. In 1964–65, for example, holders Sporting Lisbon were put out by Welsh club Cardiff City, then in the old Second Division and enjoying the first of many Cup-winners Cup adventures. Remarkably, they even won 2–1 win in Lisbon thanks to opportunist goals from Greg Farrell and Derek Tapscott. Cardiff then went close to upsetting the Fairs Cup holders Real Zaragoza in the quarter-finals. They forced a 2–2 draw in Spain but lost 1–0 at Ninian Park.

Zaragoza, favourites to win the Cup, then lost out to Ron Greenwood's West Ham in the semi-finals. West Ham had stuttered past Gent, Sparta Prague and Lausanne in previous rounds. Goals from Brian Dear and Johnny Byrne secured only a 2–1 win at Upton Park but a strike by John Sissons earned a 1–1 draw in La Romareda and West Ham's ticket to the final. In the other semi, TSV 1860 Munich beat Italy's Torino 0–2, 3–1 and 2–0 in a play-off. Defensive half-back Otto Luttrop made up for an own goal in Turin with two thunderous strikes in the second leg and Munich's second in the play-off.

At Wembley, however, he had little chance to show off his prowess. Instead, a match of outstanding football – and sportsmanship – was decided by two goals in three minutes from Alan Sealey, playing the game of his life. Victory also contributed to the legend of the late Bobby Moore. The previous year he had captained West Ham to FA Cup victory at Wembley; 1965 brought Cup-winners Cup success on the same pitch; and 1966 saw Moore hold aloft the World Cup on England's behalf, again at Wembley.

England roll on...

Liverpool were favoured to provide a third English victory in the Cup-winners Cup in 1966, but they lost in extra time to Borussia Dortmund at Hampden Park. As for West Ham, they reached the semi-finals, where they lost both legs to Dortmund – the only non-British club who had progressed that far.

The Germans beat Floriana of Malta 5–1, 8–0 but had nearly slipped up against CSKA Sofia. They took a 3–0 lead against the Bulgarian army club only to come close to letting it slip in a 4–2 defeat in Bulgaria. In the quarter-finals, they drew 1–1 at Atletico Madrid and won 1–0 at home. Powerful left-winger Lothar Emmerich was Dortmund's hero with 14 goals, which remains a Cup-winners Cup record. Emmerich, a World Cup runner-up against England in 1966, scored six goals in Borussia's 8–0 win over Floriana – another individual record which Enmmerich shares with Milanov of Levski Spartak who scored six against Lahden Reipas in the 1976–77 Cup-winners Cup.

The final, back at Hampden Park, matched Borussia with Liverpool who had endured a much more testing ride – defeating Juventus 2–1, Standard Liege 5–2, Honved 2–0 and Celtic 2–1. Displaying all the resilience for which they would become renowned, Liverpool hit back from 1–0 down against Juventus and Celtic. Each time, they owed ultimate success to goals from raiding right-back Chris Lawler and centre-forward Ian St John.

The final was a step too far, however. Dortmund sweeper Wolfgang Paul was a tower of strength as Liverpool forced the Germans back for long periods. As so often happens, Dortmund then broke away to score through Sigi Held who, along with Emmerich and keeper Hans Tilkowski, would face England in the World Cup Final two months later. Roger Hunt quickly equalized for Liverpool but it was still 1–1 at the end of the regulation 90 minutes. In extra time, a remarkable goal from right winger "Stan" Libuda – lofted beyond goalkeeper Tommy Lawrence and skipper Ron Yeats from way out on the right wing – provided Dortmund with a first-ever European club triumph for German football. Liverpool would have to wait until the 1970s before they could taste success in the Champions Cup and UEFA Cup – yet the Cup-winners Cup continued to elude them.

Germany needed extra time to beat Britain again the following year. This time, Bayern Munich were the winners and Rangers the losers, 1–0 in Nuremberg. This was also the season which saw the Cup-winners Cup experiment by scrapping play-offs and introducing the rule of away goals counting double in the event of clubs finishing all-square on aggregate.

Bayern were laying the foundations for their Champions Cup domination of the mid-1970s. Goalkeeper Sepp Maier, sweeper and skipper Franz Beckenbauer, goal-scoring midfielder Franz Roth and supreme goal-grabber Gerd Müller already made up the backbone of the team. Bayern progressed to the semi-final with three narrow victories – 4–3 against Tatran Presov of Czechoslovakia and Ireland's Shamrock Rovers and 2–1 against Rapid Vienna. They then won 2–0 at home and 3–1 away against Standard Liege in the semi-finals. Müller scored all five goals and ended up the tournament's eight-goal top scorer.

Coin flip decides

Rangers had succeeded where neighbours Celtic had failed the previous season, by reaching the final. Six days earlier, Celtic had won the Champions Cup in Lisbon and Rangers desperately wanted to complete a city double. To reach the final, they beat Glentoran of Northern Ireland 5–1 on aggregate then eliminated holders Borussia Dortmund 2–1 overall, before facing Spain's Real Zaragoza in the quarter-finals. Both teams won their home leg 2–0 so the new away goals rule was rendered useless. Instead, it took the toss of a coin to decide that Rangers should go through to play Slavia Sofia in the semi-finals. Left-winger Davie Wilson scored the only goal in Sofia; right-winger Willie Henderson scored the only goal at Ibrox.

Nuremberg, for the final, was home from home for Bayern but the advantage appeared lost on them. A match between two cautious teams produced few chances and, for the fourth time in the fledgling competition, the final went to extra time. It was settled, ultimately, not by Müller but by bullish midfielder Franz Roth, 11 minutes from the end of the additional half-hour. Roth, very much one of the journeymen in Bayern's team, would later lay further claim to fame by scoring their lone-goal winner in the 1976 Champions Cup Final against St Etienne.

Bayern's success meant a two-year German command of the Cup-winners Cup, but that was as long as it lasted. The following season their grip was broken by Milan who emphasised their takeover by beating holders Bayern in the semi-finals. Milan won 2–0 at home with goals from Sormani – a Fiorentina hero in the original tournament in 1960–61 – and Pierino Prati. An iron-clad defence built around the rock-like talents of Giovanni Trapattoni and West Germany's own Karl-Heinz Schnellinger held out for a goalless draw in Munich. Milan could thus not have had a happier debut in the Cup-winners Cup. In the first round, they defeated Bulgaria's Levski Sofia 6–2, then went through on the away goals rule against Gyor of Hungary. Play-offs had been brought back, temporarily, to split clubs level on aggregate in the quarter and semi-finals. Three of the four quarter-finals had to be settled this way with Milan beating Standard Liege 2–0 (Prati and Gianni Rivera on target) after 1–1 draws in Italy and Belgium.

The most fascinating of the marathon quarter-finals, however, was the tie between Cardiff City and Moscow Torpedo. Cardiff won 1–0 at Ninian Park but then, ridiculous as it seems now, had to travel some 3,000 miles to the heart of Soviet Asia for the return leg because Moscow grounds were still frozen and unplayable. A 32nd-minute goal from Gerskovich in Tashkent, Uzbekistan, sent the tie into extra time and earned, ultimately, a play-off in the more convenient location of Augsburg, West Germany. Here, despite being forced by injuries and suspension to field five reserves, Cardiff won 1–0 with a goal shortly before half-time from Norman Dean. It appeared an appropriate reward.

Regular finalists from Germany

No other Welsh club has ever reached a European semi-final, but this was where the Cardiff adventure hit the buffers. Another fine result in Germany followed when Dean's goal earned a 1–1 draw at Hamburg. But Uwe Seeler and co. hit back to win 3–2 in Wales and reach the final against Milan. Seeler, West Germany's 1966 World Cup captain, scored Hamburg's second goal. It was the fourth successive year a German side had reached the final. Hamburg had previously beaten Randers Freja of Denmark, the Poles of Wislaw Krakow and Lyon – after the inevitable quarter-final play-off.

Hamburg hopes of extending German possession of the Cup-winners Cup were destroyed in the Rotterdam final by two goals from Milan's Swedish veteran Kurt Hamrin. He knew all about the Cup-winners Cup, having been a key member of the Fiorentina side who won the 1961 final against Rangers. In fact, a 2–0 margin hardly did justice to Milan's command of the match. The following season, their talents were further rewarded when Rivera and co. thrashed emerging Ajax, in Madrid, to win the Champions Cup itself.

The 1968–69 European club competitions were enveloped in controversy following the Soviet invasion of Czechoslovakia. A number of leading western European clubs, under Government pressure, demanded UEFA scrap the original draw in the Champions Cup and Cup-winners Cup and make a new one which would keep Nato and Warsaw Pact clubs apart. In the Cup-winners Cup, the draw made in Berne, on July 10, had included the following ties: Altay (Turkey) vs. Gornik (Poland), Bordeaux vs. Spartak Sofia (Bulgaria), Gyor (Hungary) vs. Lyn Oslo, Dinamo Bucharest vs. Cologne, Moscow Dynamo vs. Olympiakos (Greece), Union Berlin (East Germany) vs. FK Bor (Yugoslavia) and Slovan Bratislava (Czechoslovakia) vs. KR (Iceland). On August 31, UEFA decided to redraw those specific ties, thus: Altay vs. Lyn, Bordeaux vs. Cologne, Olmpiakos vs. KR Reykjavik… and Spartak Sofia vs. Gornik, Moscow Dynamo vs. Union Berlin, Dinamo Bucharest vs. Gyor, Slovan Bratislava vs. FK Bor.

The Soviet federation protested immediately that politics should not impinge on a sporting competition and leaned on the federations from the rest of the Warsaw Pact to toe the line. When UEFA refused to reinstate the original draw, five of the eastern European clubs withdrew: Spartak Sofia, Gornik, Moscow Dynamo, Union Berlin and Gyor. The Romanian federation dissociated itself from the protest and thus Dinamo Bucharest were awarded a walkover against Gyor. Slovan Bratislava, from the offended Czechoslovakia, accepted the redraw and, with delicious irony, went on to win the Cup. They thus became the first eastern European club to win one of the two top club competitions, though Ferencvaros of Hungary and Dinamo Zagreb of the former Yugoslavia had already been successful in the "third" event, the Fairs Cup.

Slovan beat Bor 3–2 then did well to defeat Portugal's Porto 4–2. In the quarter-finals, they faced Italy's Torino who had, with Spain's Barcelona, benefited from the disruption in the draw by being granted a bye through the second round. The break proved of no value. A Karol Jokl goal brought Slovan a 1–0 win in Turin which the Czechoslovaks extended with a 2–1 success at home. In the semi-finals they drew 1–1 in Scotland against Dumfermline Athletic –conquerors of England's West Bromwich Albion – and won 1–0 at home.

Final rivals Barcelona, veteran campaigners in Europe, had cruised through, scoring 15 goals in their ties against Lugano (Switzerland), Lyn Oslo and Cologne. It was thought they had

AC Milan's Cup-winning captain, Luigi Rivera, receives the cup in 1973

merely to turn up at the Sankt-Jakob stadium in Basle to carry off the cup. Slovan, coached by former World Cup hero Michal Vican, had other ideas and snatched the lead after only a minute through fine left-winger Ludovit Cvetler. When Jose Zaldua equalised, direct from a corner after 15 minutes, it appeared Barcelona had got their act together. But they allowed themselves to be caught by further sucker punches before half-time from Vladimir Hrivnak and Jan Capkovic.

Substitutes had been permitted in European club competitions this season for the first time and Barcelona's French coach, Salvador Artigas, took advantage to throw in extra forwards Jesus Pereda and Jorge Mendonca. The sum total of

their huffing and puffing, however, was a single second-half goal from Carlos Rexach. Once again, as in the Champions Cup in Berne, in 1961, Barcelona had gone to Switzerland for a European club final and come away empty-handed. Slovan Bratislava had made their sporting point.

British clubs regained control at the start of the 1970s through Manchester City, Chelsea and Rangers before Leeds United failed against Milan in 1973.

In 1969–70, the Eastern Bloc returned after their previous year's boycott as if nothing had happened. The spell broken, holders Slovan were themselves quickly eliminated in the first round by Dinamo Zagreb of the former Yugoslavia. Slovan were three goals down inside an hour of the first leg in Zagreb, to strikes from Miljkovic, Novak and Gucmirtl. They could only draw 0–0 at home and were thus eliminated. Dinamo Zagreb subsequently beat Marseille before losing to Schalke in the quarter-finals.

The Italian challenge this season came from Roma, who beat PSV Eindhoven in the second round on the toss of a coin, then defeated the Turks of Goztepe Izmir, conquerors of Cardiff City, in the quarter-finals. Fabio Capello, later highly successful coach of Milan and Real Madrid, scored decisive goals against PSV and Goztepe. In the semi-finals, Roma met Gornik Zabrze from the heart of Poland's Silesia minefields. The first meeting in Rome ended 1–1 and the return finished 2–2 after extra time, Capello scoring again for Roma. The rules decreed a play-off, in Strasbourg. Capello scored the Roma goal but again the match went to extra time, after which Gornik won on the toss of a coin.

Already awaiting them in the final were England's Manchester City. Flamboyantly managed by Joe Mercer and Malcolm Allison, City had beaten Bilbao of Spain 6–3 and Belgium's Lierse 8–0, with future chairman Francis Lee scoring twice both home and away. City needed extra time to beat Academica, from the Portuguese university city of Coimbra, in the quarter-final, then crushed Schalke 04 5–2 on aggregate in the semi-final. Reinhard Libuda, destroyer of Liverpool in the 1966 final, scored home and away but his goals were mere consolations.

Gornik appeared awkward opponents in the final, their defence built around the young giant Jerzy Gorgon and their attack inspired by a rising star in Wlodek Lubanski. He scored three times in the second-round win over Rangers, once in the quarter-final dismissal of Levsky-Spartak Sofia and twice in the tension-packed semi-final against Roma. Not, however, against Manchester City in the final.

Triumph for Manchester's blues

A meagre crowd of 7,968 turned out in the rain, in Vienna, to see City collect their first, and so far last, European trophy. Neil Young opened the scoring from close range after 12 minutes and Lee scored a second from a penalty after Young had been fouled. Lubanski created a goal, midway through the second half, for Stanislaw Oslizlo but it was too little too late for Gornik, who remain the only Polish side to have reached a European final.

City appeared on the brink of even greater things. This was their fourth major prize in three seasons after the League title in 1968, the FA Cup in 1969 and the League Cup in 1970. Strangely, their success went almost unnoticed in England where almost all the attention that night was focused on Manchester United's Old Trafford home, where Chelsea were beating Leeds United in an FA Cup Final replay. That victory opened the European door once more for Chelsea – and they took full advantage in a 1970–71 campaign dominated by British clubs.

Cardiff City, for example, beat Pezoporikos of Cyprus 8–0 then French Cup winners Nantes 7–2. Centre-forward John Toshack scored two goals against the Cypriots and three against Nantes. However, he went goalless against Real Madrid in the quarter-finals where Cardiff, despite winning 1–0 at home were eliminated after falling 2–0 in the Estadio Bernabeu.

Scotland's Aberdeen enjoyed no luck, losing to the Hungarian army team Honved, in the first round. But they did, at least, make history as the first club beaten on the new-fangled penalty shoot-out. Honved, in their turn, were beaten 3–0 by Manchester City, the latter having squeezed past Linfield of Northern Ireland on the away goals rule in the first round, thanks to a strike in Belfast from Lee. They then had a close call against old rivals Gornik in the quarter-finals, being taken to a play-off which they ultimately won 3–1 in Copenhagen. Goals from Young, Tommy Booth and Lee won the day. Lubanski replied for Gornik and thus became the competition's top scorer for the second successive season – again with eight goals.

In the semi-finals, Real Madrid beat PSV Eindhoven 0–0, 2–1 while City fell to Chelsea. They had beaten Aris Salonika and CSKA Sofia before thrilling the Stamford Bridge faithful in the quarter-finals by hitting back from a 2–0 defeat to beat Club Brugge 4–2. City came to the semi-finals in the midst of an injury crisis. Lacking Mike Doyle and Colin Bell, they lost the first leg at Stamford Bridge to a goal just after half-time from Derek Smethurst. The margin was the same at Maine Road. City's will to win was punctured just before half-time after a bizarre own goal by goalkeeper Ron Healey.

The final, in Athens, was Real Madrid's ninth in Europe though their first outside of the Champions Cup. Chelsea took a 56th-minute lead through Peter Osgood and their fans were celebrating another Cup success when, in injury time, John Dempsey's mis-kicked clearance offered Ignacio Zoco the equaliser. Only the brilliance of goalkeeper Peter Bonetti held Real at bay in extra time and earned Chelsea's fans an extra two-days' holiday in Greece before the replay in the Karaiskaki stadium. This time, Chelsea determined not to relax their grip. Dempsey and Osgood's first-half goals were just enough to see the Londoners through after Fleitas pulled one back in the 75th minute for Real. Defeat was a poignant exit from the European stage of left-winger Francisco Gento, Real's last survivor from the great teams of the late 1950s and early 1960s.

Rangers maintained the British grip on the Cup-winners Cup in 1972, but their victory in the final over Moscow Dynamo – thus far the only Russian club to have reached a European final – has been remembered for all the wrong reasons. Rangers reached the decider with victories over Rennes, Sporting Lisbon – with Colin Stein scoring four of their six goals – Torino, and the Bayern Munich side on whose Maier-Beckenbauer-Müller foundation West Germany would win the European

Championship in great style, a few months later. Goals by Sandy Jardine and Derek Parlane at Ibrox secured belated semi-final revenge for Rangers' defeat in the 1967 final. Earlier, Bayern had knocked Liverpool, who had entered the Cup as deputies for England's 1971 League and Cup double-winners Arsenal.

Holders Chelsea enjoyed their newly-won status, opening up their Cup defence by swamping Luxembourg's Jeunesse Hautcharage 21–0, a record aggregate score for any European tie. Osgood scored eight goals, three in Chelsea's 8–0 away win and five in the 13–0 victory at Stamford Bridge being enough to secure him the honour of tournament top scorer – even though he did not score again. Chelsea were beaten in the second round by Sweden's Atvidaberg, who drew 0–0 at home then sneaked through on away goals after drawing 1–1 in London.

Away goals and shoot-outs decide

For the first time in a European competition, all rounds were decided on away goals or penalties. Play-offs were scrapped, except for the final. Moscow Dynamo took advantage of the rule change by defeating Union Berlin of East Germany 4–1 in a semi-final shoot-out.

The final was staged in Barcelona's Nou Camp. The locals were not interested and the meagre attendance of 24,701 was dominated by Rangers fans who enjoyed the sight of their favourites seizing a 3–0 lead within 49 minutes. Colin Stein scored after 24 minutes and Willie Johnston either side of the break. Moscow, apparently overawed by the occasion until then, suddenly woke up. Yestrekov pulled one goal back and Makhovikov got a second with three minutes remaining. Rangers hung on but their fans, who had caused trouble before and during the game, took the final whistle as the signal to run amok. One supporter died and hundreds were injured and arrested. Rangers took the brunt of the punishment for the hooliganism. UEFA banned them from European competition for two seasons. This was commuted, on appeal, to one season and Rangers' next appearance in Europe was back in the Cup-winners Cup in 1973–74, when they fell in the second round to Borussia Mönchengladbach.

The Cup-winners Cup has generally been a comparatively peaceful haven of the European club game, apart from the Rangers riot in 1972 and, a year later, a controversial final in which Milan ended British control by defeating Leeds United in Salonika, Greece.

Welsh heroics that season were provided by Wrexham of the old Third Division. They defeated Zurich in the first round before losing on away goals to Hajduk Split. Hajduk also ended Scottish hopes when they beat Hibernian in the quarter-finals. Hibs had previously eliminated Sporting Lisbon and Besa of Albania, with John O'Rourke scoring a hat-trick in each tie. He

did not score against Hajduk, however, and Hibs lost 5–4 on aggregate.

British hopes thus rested with Don Revie's awesome Leeds. They progressed relentlessly to the semi-finals with victories over Ankaragucu of Turkey, East Germany's Carl Zeiss Jena and Rapid Bucharest of Romania. There was only one goal in the semi-final against Hajduk Split and it was scored in the first leg at Elland Road, after 20 minutes, by Allan Clarke. In the other semi-final, Milan beat Sparta Prague 1–0 in both legs, having previously seen off Red Boys of Luxembourg, Legia Warsaw and Moscow Spartak. In the semi-finals Luciano Chiarugi scored the only goal in Milan and in Prague.

Chiarugi, 26-year-old graduate of the vaunted Fiorentina youth system, also scored the only goal of the final after a mere four minutes. But memories of his goal – his seventh of the campaign – have long since become submerged beneath controversy over the refereeing of Christos Michas, the Greek official.

Michas had refereed Milan's second round, first leg tie against Legia Warsaw and infuriated the Poles by failing to crack down on some rugged tackling and hustling by Italian defender Roberto Rosato. It was reported some members of the Greek federation had opposed the appointment because of his Italian business connections. Leeds might have been favourites in normal circumstances, but they were seriously weakened by the absence through injury of midfield general Johnny Giles and winger Eddie Gray, and through the suspension of skipper Billy Bremner and striker Clarke. Milan had their own injury problems, missing defender Schnellinger and forward Prati.

The only goal came after four minutes. Michas awarded Milan a contentious free-kick and Chiarugi fired it through a poorly-secured defensive wall. Goalkeeper David Harvey was unsighted and the ball ricocheted off a post into the net. Minutes later, a header from Sogliano flew just wide and, after that, Milan shut up shop. The vast majority of the 50,000 crowd got behind Leeds' attempts to battle back. Peter Lorimer went close a couple of times and Milan goalkeeper Walter Vecchi dealt comfortably with the rest of Leeds's crosses and goal attempts.

The Italians hardly ventured out of their own half, blatantly wasting time. Yet when Paul Reaney took his time over setting up a free-kick, Michas booked him. When Chiarugi and Terry Yorath squared up, Michas turned his back. When Anquilletti pulled down Jones in a rugby tackle in the penalty area, the referee waved away appeals.

The longer it went on, the worse it got. Milan flexed their attacking muscles briefly, early in the second half and Harvey saved well from Albertino Bigon. But it was Vecchi, at the other end, who saw most of the action. All manner of fouls went on behind the referee's back as Milan sought to interrupt Leeds's pattern of play. In the 89th minute, Norman Hunter charged upfield, shrugged off two attempted fouls then raged at Milan skipper Gianni Rivera after being finally brought to a halt.

Sogliano weighed in and Michas sent off Sogliano and Hunter.

The Cup presentation to Milan's players provoked whistles and jeers and a hail of cushions. Laughter broke out outside the dressing-room when Milan coach Nereo Rocco described it as "a good game." Leeds boss Revie, on the other hand, asked whether his team should have had three penalties, said: "That's the understatement of the year. The refereeing was scandalous."

Too late for Leeds, fate took a hand. Milan lost 5–3 to Verona the next weekend and Juventus pipped them to the Italian title by one point. As for Michas, he was later suspended by his own federation. Justice was done, but belatedly. Too late for Leeds and too late for Revie, who left the club after the Salonika trip to take over as manager of England. It was thus his successor, Jimmy Armfield, who would guide Leeds to another European final defeat the following season, in the Champions Cup, in Paris.

Milan's failure to win the Italian league meant that, in 1973–74, they returned to the Cup-winners Cup as holders – and with a nasty shock in store when they returned to the final to face East Germany's Magdeburg after victories over Rapid Vienna, PAOK Salonika and Borussia Mönchengladbach.

Only one British club reached the quarter-finals – Glentoran from Northern Ireland who scored 4–2 aggregate victories over Chimia Ramnicu Vilcea of Romania and Brann Bergen of Norway before losing home and away against Borussia Mönchengladbach. The home leg was a sad day for Glentoran: centre-half Walker broke a leg and, that same night, midfielder Roy Stewart died of a heart attack. Welsh contestants Cardiff City lost in the first round to Sporting Lisbon while Scotland's Rangers – back in Europe after their year's suspension – fell to Borussia in the second round. England hopes rested on Second Division Sunderland, who had shocked Leeds in the FA Cup Final the previous May. They beat Vasas of Hungary 3–0 on aggregate in the first round then fell 2–1, 0–2 to Sporting Lisbon.

East Germany's only victory

Magdeburg became the first East German side to reach a European club final thanks to the power and skill of international forwards such as Jürgen Sparwasser, Martin Hoffmann and Jurgen Pommerenke. To reach the last four, they defeated Holland's NAC Breda, Banik Ostrava of Czechoslovakia and Bulgaria's Beroe Stara Zagora. In the semi-finals, they beat Sporting 3–2 on aggregate with Sparwasser scoring in both legs.

Milan did not go to Rotterdam for the final in the happiest frame of mind. Chiarugi, their match-winner the previous year against Leeds, was suspended and assistant coach Giovanni Trapattoni had taken over as caretaker-boss following the resignations of Rocco and then Cesare Maldini. Nevertheless, the presence of the likes of Rivera and Schnellinger was enough to establish them as clear favourites – one reason, perhaps, why

only 4,641 fans turned out in the Feyenoord stadium.

Those who did bother to attend witnessed a major shock as unfancied, little-known Magdeburg won 2–0 to become the only East German club to win a European trophy. They deserved it, too. Milan reserve defender Enrico Lanzi put through his own goal five minutes before half-time as he tried to cut out a cross from Detlef Raugust. Milan went close on the hour when Wolfgang Abraham cleared a Rivera header off the line. Then, 15 minutes from time, Wolfgang Seguin made it 2–0, converting a cross from Axel Tyll.

Magdeburg had made history. A few weeks later, Sparwasser and Hoffmann starred in the East German national side who beat West Germany 1–0 in their only meeting, in the World Cup finals, in Hamburg. Sparwasser, who scored, would later take advantage of a trip to the West for a veterans' tournament, to defect.

A far finer representative of Warsaw Pact football emerged to carry off the Cup-winners Cup a year later, in 1974–75. Kiev Dynamo were a class above most of the rest of Europe. They despatched Ferencvaros of Hungary 3–0 in the 1975 final with a mixture of skill, pace and tactical intelligence which drew comparisons with the impact made by the Moscow Dynamo side of the late 1940s.

Kiev beat CSKA Sofia, Eintracht Frankfurt, Bursaspor of Turkey and PSV Eindhoven on their way to the final. Ferencvaros took a measure of revenge against Britain for their defeat by Leeds in the 1968 Fairs Cup Final by defeating Cardiff City and Liverpool. Bill Shankly's men had earlier set a club record in thrashing Stromgodset of Norway 11–0 at Anfield. Remarkably, nine different players got their name on the scoresheet –Phil Boersma (two), Peter Thompson (two), Alec Lindsay (penalty), Steve Heighway, Tommy Smith, Peter Cormack, Emlyn Hughes, Ian Callaghan and Ray Kennedy. The only "absentees" were goalkeeper Ray Clemence and Brian Hall.

In the final, in Basle, Oleg Blokhin was superb and rounded off Kiev's success by scoring their third goal in the 67th minute. He was aided and abetted by deep-lying centre-forward Leonid Buryak and right-winger Vladimir Onischenko, who took his total for the campaign to seven goals by scoring twice in the first half.

As for Kiev, having become the first Soviet club to land a European trophy, they went on to collect a second – barely raising a sweat in defeating Bayern Munich to lift the European Supercup. But their prospects of achieving greater things were undermined by the Soviet federation which demanded Kiev turn out, en bloc, as the national team in the World Cup qualifiers and the Olympic Games. Even outstanding players such as midfield general Viktor Kolotov and striker Blokhin could not withstand the physical and mental pressures and Kiev quickly ran out of steam.

Belgium's Anderlecht were next to try empire-building in the Cup-winners Cup and enjoyed more consistent success than most. The Belgian club reached the final three years in a row in the late 1970s, defeat by Hamburg in 1977 being sandwiched between entertaining victories over West Ham United and FK Austria. Anderlecht's dominance owed much to their Dutch neighbours from whom they had acquired goalkeepers Jan Ruiter and Nico De Bree, centre-half Johnny Dusbaba, midfield fulcrum Arie Haan and goal-scoring left-winger Rob Rensenbrink.

The 1975–76 competition was far from a classic. Anderlecht, on their way to the final, lost to Rapid in Bucharest and to Borac Banja Luka in Yugoslavia and only drew 1–1 in Wrexham. The Welsh Cup winners considered themselves unfortunate to be beaten by the odd goal in three in the quarter-finals. Rensenbrink scored the late equaliser which earned Anderlecht a 1–1 draw at the Racecourse Ground and 2–1 win on aggregate. The Dutchman was on target in both legs of the semi-final where Anderlecht had fewer problems beating Sachsenring Zwickau of East Germany.

Their opponents in the final were West Ham United, winners in 1965. The Hammers defeated Finland's Reipas Lahti in the first round then Ararat Yerevan, then of the Soviet Union now of Armenia, in the second. Den Haag surprised West Ham in the quarter-finals, winning 4–2 in Holland with a hat-trick from Mansveld but West Ham recovered 3–1 at Upton Park and went through on away goals. In the semi-final they beat Eintracht Frankfurt 1–2, 3–1. Trevor Brooking, whose goals were few and far between, scored twice in the second leg in London.

West Ham knew the odds were stacked against them in the final from the outset since it was to be played in the Heysel stadium which Anderlecht often used as their home stadium for big European games. The two previous Cup-winners finals had drawn barely 16,000 fans but 51,296 filled the Heysel to celebrate the first European club success for a Belgian club. West Ham tried hard to spoil the party, with Pat Holland opening the scoring after 28 minutues. But Anderlecht recovered with poise and pace to win 4–2. Rensenbrink and Francois van der Elst – later to play for West Ham – scored two goals each. Keith Robson brought West Ham back into the game briefly when he equalised for 2–2 midway though the second half. Four minutes later, West Ham conceded a penalty, Rensenbrink converted and the Belgians had regained a lead they never again relinquished.

Hamburg win for West Germany

No club had ever won the Cup-winners Cup twice in a row but Anderlecht appeared poised to beat the jinx when they reached the final again in 1976–77, only to be beaten by Hamburg, who thus became the first German winners of the Cup since Bayern Munich a decade earlier. Hamburg were tested seriously only by Atletico Madrid in the semi-finals. A 55th-minute goal from midfield general Felix Magath kept them alive in a 3–1 defeat in Spain in the first leg. Back in Germany, attacking full back Manni Kaltz scored after 19 mintes and Willi Reimann shot Hamburg level on aggregate three minutes later. Ferdinand Keller scored the 27th-minute winner.

The final was staged in the Olympic Stadium in Amsterdam. Anderlecht should have been able to win but, just when it mattered, their cohesion and passing accuracy deserted them. Hamburg won it with two goals in the last ten minutes. Left-winger Georg Volkert scored the first from a penalty, Magath claimed a second in the last minute.

Anderlecht were back for yet another tilt at the Cup-winners Cup in 1977–78. They had not only lost the Cup-winners Final in 1977 but also the Belgian Cup Final 4–3 to Club Brugge. However, Brugge had also won the Belgian title – pipping Anderlecht by one point –so Anderlecht entered the Cup-winners Cup by default.

English football had what was perceived as their most redoubtable Cup-winners Cup challenger for years in Manchester United, but they very nearly did not make it past the first leg in the first round. United had endured a turbulent summer after beating Liverpool in the FA Cup Final. Manager Tommy Docherty had been dismissed after leaving his wife to set up home with Mary Brown, the wife of United's club physiotherapist. Then crowd trouble in St Etienne led to United – who had drawn 1–1 there – being first banned from the Cup-winners Cup then reinstated and ordered to play the second leg of their tie 300 kilometres from Manchester. Their choice was Home Park, Plymouth, where United won 2–0 with goals from Stuart Pearson and Steve Coppell. In the second round, they crashed 4–0 at Porto and were unable to make up the leeway at Old Trafford, where they won an exciting match 5–2.

Porto defeated Anderlecht 1–0 in the first leg of the quarter-finals but that was the last goal the Belgians conceded in the competition that season. They won the return 3–0 against Porto then defeated Twente Enschede 1–0, 2–0 in the semi-finals. Anderlecht's most satisfying victory on the way to the final, however, was in the second round when they won 2–1 away to Hamburg, who had beaten them in the previous season's final. Kevin Keegan's goal in the return could only equal Van der Elst's earlier effort and Anderlecht progressed 3–2 on aggregate.

In the final, Anderlecht faced FK Austria, whose greatest international club era was back in the Mitropa Cup days of the 1930s. The 1978 team had none of the power of their predecessors. They had scraped past Cardiff City and Lokomotiv Kosice of Poland then beaten Hajduk Split and Moscow Dynamo only in penalty shoot-outs. Despite the midfield efforts of Herbert Prohaska, they were no match for Anderlecht in the Parc des Princes and collapsed 4–0. Rensenbrink scored another two goals, as did attacking full back Gilbert Van Binst.

The 1978–79 competition produced one of the most exciting finals, in which Barcelona defeated unfancied Fortuna

Willie Miller carries off the Cup for Aberdeen in 1983

Düsseldorf 4–3 in extra time. Barcelona thus made amends for their surprising defeat in 1969 by Slovan Bratislava of the former Czechoslovakia. They also eliminated holders Anderlecht in the second round. Anderlecht won 3–0 at home with two goals from Van der Elst but were unnerved by the wall of sound which greeted them at the Nou Camp. Barcelona's Austrian hitman Hans Krankl, scored after eight minutes with Juan Carlos Heredia making it 2–0 by half-time. Anderlecht resisted bravely in the second half but, with four minutes remaining, Rafael Zuviria scored again to send the tie into extra time. With no futher goals, Barcelona won 4–1 on penalties.

Barcelona then beat Ipswich luckily in the quarter-finals on away goals. Barca lost 2–1 at Portman Road to two goals from Eric Gates but picked up one goal on the break through Esteban after Krankl was allowed too much space. Centre-half Migueli scored the only goal of the return but that was just enough, and Barcelona won 1–0 home and away against Beveren in the semi-finals. A penalty in each leg did the damage – Carlos Rexach scoring in Belgium, Krankl in the last minute back in Catalonia.

Surprise finalists opposite Barcelona were West Germany's Fortuna Düsseldorf whose solid teamwork was topped off with the outstanding finishing qualities of West German international Klaus Allofs. Narrow victories were the order of the day. Düsseldorf beat Universitatea Craiova of Romania 4–3, 1–1 in the first round, Aberdeen 3–0, 0–2 in the second, Servette of Switzerland on away goals in the quarter-finals and Czechoslovakia's Banik Ostrava 4–3 in the semi-finals.

A stunning Final

The Final, in front of 58,500 in the Sankt-Jakob stadium, Basle, provided superb entertainment. The teams were level at 2–2 at the end of the first half and after 90 minutes. Winger Rexach and Krankl made it 4–2 then Wolfgang Seel pulled Düsseldorf close with a penalty to set up a frantic last six minutes. At last, ten years since Barcelona had lost in this same stadium, in this same final, to Slovan Bratisalava, they had won the Cup-winners Cup.

Season 1979–80 saw Arsenal make their debut on the Cup-winners Cup scene. Under the managerial guidance of Terry Neill, Arsenal had rebuilt their dreams around a nucleus of outstanding discoveries such as Irish midfielder Liam Brady. Fenerbahce of Turkey were the first round opposition. Arsenal coach Don Howe had worked in Turkey for their rivals, Galatasaray, and was under no illusions about the task in hand. Goals from Alan Sunderland and Willie Young brought a 2–0 win at Highbury while a goalless draw in Istanbul earned a second-round meeting with the East Germans of Magdeburg.

Five years earlier, Magdeburg had surprised Europe by winning the Cup. But by now, the edge had gone off the team.

Arsenal won only 2–1 at home but defied East German overconfidence to secure a 2–2 draw beyond the Iron Curtain.

The beauty of the Cup-winners Cup – compared with the UEFA Cup – is that two aggregate victories lift a club into the quarter-finals. Here, Arsenal gained a bonus by being drawn against the Swedes of IFK Gothenburg. The Angels of Gothenburg were not quite yet the outstanding side who would upset a lot of form favourites in the Champions League. They were also rusty after their winter break and crashed 5–0 at Highbury. Arsenal might have won more easily but strolled confidently to a 0–0 draw in Sweden.

So far so good. Arsenal had played six games, won three and drawn three. But Juventus in the semi-finals were a far tougher test. They even took the lead at Highbury and, though midfielder Marco Tardelli was sent off and Roberto Bettega put through his own goal, held out for a 1–1 draw.

Highbury hopes dashed

The return could not have come at a more challenging time for the Gunners who went to Turin in the middle of an FA Cup semi-final saga with Liverpool. Remarkably, they won 1–0, with a goal from youngster Paul Vaessen, who was then unknown to most English fans let alone the Italians. That was Arsenal's last celebration of the season. Liverpool left them trailing in the League, they lost 1–0 to West Ham in the FA Cup Final… and fell to Valencia of Spain in the final of the Cup-winners Cup.

The Heysel stadium, scene only five years later of the most horrific events at any European final, was the venue. Valencia boasted Mario Kempes, Argentina's World Cup-winning inspiration from 1978. Not that he ever threatened Arsenal. David O'Leary covered his every stride across the penalty box. After a stifling, defence-dominated, fear-ridden match, Kempes failed even in the penalty shoot-out. But so did Brady – being watched by Barcelona and Juventus – and so, conclusively, did Graham Rix. Valencia thus triumphed 5–4 on penalties.

Kempes had been top scorer in the 1979–80 Cup-winners Cup with nine goals yet, though Valencia strengthened their attack with the purchase of Uruguay centre-forward Fernando Morena, they crashed out of the 1980–81 competition in the second round, to Carl Zeiss Jena. The East Germans duly progressed – with victories over Newport County and Benfica – to the final. Their opponents in Düsseldorf were Tbilisi Dinamo, then representing the Soviet Union and the top club in Georgia. Tbilisi played football on a technical and intellectual level far above the run of the mill Soviet game. Alexander Chivadze was a commanding sweeper, David Kipiani one of the shrewdest of midfield generals and Ramaz Shengelia one of the quickest-breaking of goalscoring wingers. Jena surprised Tbilisi by taking the lead in the final but that merely stung the Georgians into raising their game and creating goals for Vladimir Gutsayev and Vitali Daraselia.

Tbilisi had the talent to go all the way again in 1981–82. But, having reached the semi-finals, they were surprisingly beaten by the down-to-earth commitment and discipline of Standard Liege. The Belgians won 1–0 at home and away with goals from Jos Daerden. Tbilisi officials did not dare say so at the time but privately they blamed the Soviet federation for having taken the national team to South America for a lucrative friendly against Argentina the previous weekend. Six Tbilisi players were called up and they arrived back, tired and dispirited, barely two days before the second leg in Liege.

Standard were far from happy at having to play Barcelona in the final since UEFA had also chosen Nou Camp as the venue. They hoped only that they might take advantage of unrest within the Catalan camp. Barcelona had just lost any hope of regaining the Spanish title after a 3–1 League defeat by Real Madrid, coach Udo Lattek was under pressure, a question mark hung over the contract renewal of Danish star Allan Simonsen, midfielders Bernd Schuster and Victor were injured and defender Estella was suspended.

The Belgians came to Barcelona with an unbeaten record in the competition and with the confidence engendered by just having sewn up their own domestic title. Coach Raymond Goethals, Anderlecht's winning boss in 1978, could not have wished for a better start when Guy Vandersmissen converted an indirect free-kick from Dutchman Arie Haan after only seven minutes. Barcelona, after being denied a penalty claim and wasting two easy chances, equalised in first-half injury time with a header from Simonsen after a free-kick by Esteban. Centre-forward Quini scored what proved the winner after 61 minutes and the match ended amid a flurry of cards and bad temper with Standard's Walter Meeuws sent off for a trip on Carrasco.

Barcelona celebrated long into the night, the directors at the nearby Princesa Sofia hotel, the players at a restaurant owned by Martinez, one of their reserves. Simonsen and Lattek had extra reason to celebrate. The former had earned a new contract with his goal while Lattek had become the first coach to win all three European prizes after collecting the Champions Cup with Bayern Munich and the UEFA Cup with Borussia Mönchengladbach.

Spain could have held onto the Cup-winners Cup in 1983 in the shape of Real Madrid, but a provincial Scottish club had other ideas. Aberdeen rose in the the 1980s to challenge and overthrow, briefly, the traditional giants of the Scottish game in Rangers and Celtic. Optimistic observers of the time described Aberdeen's arrival as a revolution. In fact, hindsight proved it to have been a brief insurrection – a talented generation of players under the command of an exceptional manager in Alex Ferguson. Also, while Aberdeen won the League three times in six seasons, they were more honestly what is known as a cup team. They won the Scottish Cup three times in a row and five times in nine seasons. And, of course, they won the Cup-winners Cup.

To reach the final, the Dons had to play an extra two matches after having been drawn in the preliminary round where they beat Sion of Switzerland 11–1 on aggregate. Albania's Dinamo Tirana, Lech Poznan of Poland, Bayern Munich and Belgium's Waterschei went the same way. On the other side of the draw, Real Madrid beat Baia Mare of Romania, Ujpest Dozsa, Internazionale and FK Austria. The Viennese had done Madrid and Aberdeen a favour by surprisingly eliminating holders Barcelona in the quarter-finals. Barcelona had a new superstar on board in Diego Maradona, who scored a hat-trick against Apollon Limassol on his European club debut and two more vital goals in the second-round defeat of Red Star Belgrade. But by the time the quarter-finals came around, Maradona had been cruelly removed from the game by Andoni Goikotxea, the so-called Butcher of Bilbao, in a League match. Barcelona, without him, fell to FK Austria on away goals.

The final between Aberdeen and Real Madrid took place in streaming rain, in Gothenburg. Ian Black put Aberdeen ahead after seven minutes and Juanito equalised from a penalty as many minutes later. A match in which physical strength and commitment mattered more than technique was decided Aberdeen's way by John Hewitt, with eight minutes of extra time remaining. Madrid's old hero, Alfredo Di Stefano, merely shrugged his shoulders at the final whistle. He had guided Valencia to victory in the Cup-winners Cup in 1980, but repeating the trick as coach to the club he inspired as a player had proved beyond him.

The big guns make good

The profile of the Cup-winners Cup had never been higher than in the early 1980s with the presence in successive finals of Barcelona, Real Madrid and then, in 1983–84, Juventus. The Fiat-owned club were embarking on a long period at the forefront of the Italian and the European game, inspired on the pitch initially by the magical talents of Frenchman Michel Platini, Poland's Zbigniew Boniek and Italian Paolo Rossi.

No wonder Lechia Gdansk of Poland, Paris Saint-Germain, Finland's Valkeakosken Haka and, in the semi-finals, Manchester United, found Juventus too good for them. Much the same was true for Porto in the final in Basle. Beniamino Vignola opened the scoring after 13 minutes, Sousa equalised and Boniek scored what proved the winner four minutes before half-time. Juve coach Giovanni Trapattoni had succeeded amid acclaim instead of the derision which he had experienced with Milan in Salonika, in 1973.

As for Platini, life just got better and better. A few weeks after winning the Cup-winners Cup he was scoring the goals and captaining France to victory in the European Championship.

It was now 14 seasons since an English club had won the tournament which once appeared tailor-made for teams brought up on the knock-out traditions of the FA Cup. Everton put that right in 1984–85 but, instead of beginning a new start, it was the end of an era. Everton were a team without stars, though goalkeeper Neville Southall, midfielder Peter Reid and Scottish striker Andy Gray would prove enduring personalities within English football – albeit Gray, indirectly, through the media of satellite television rather than directly within the game.

Everton rolled over University College Dublin, Inter Bratislava, Fortuna Sittard and Bayern Munich on their way to the final against Rapid Vienna, in Rotterdam. Rapid had been strengthened in attack by the return of Hans Krankl from Barcelona but, though he scored, had to wait until the 84th minute for his goal. By that time, Everton were two-up through Gray and Trevor Steven and there was another to come, in the dying minutes, from Kevin Sheedy.

"Everton looked to me like the best team in Europe," said Krankl later. Whether they were or not was never tested. Everton should have taken their teamwork – and the striking addition of summer signing Gary Lineker – into the Champions Cup. But two weeks after the triumph of Rotterdam came the disaster of Heysel when hooligan followers of Everton's city neighbours Liverpool, provoked the deaths of 39 Italian fans in Brussels. English clubs were subsequently withdrawn then formally banned from Europe. Everton's reign was before it had begun.

Kiev Dynamo returned to the Cup-winners Cup in triumph in 1986. A new team had been built around Oleg Blokhin just as stylish, skilled and impressive as Kiev's 1975 winners. In 1986, just as in 1975, they won the Cup-winners Cup Final 3–0. Their victims this time were Atletico Madrid, whose Argentine World Cup-winning goalkeeper Ubaldo Fillol was helpless against the efforts of Alexander Zavarov and, in the closing minutes, Blokhin and Vadim Yevtushenko.

Having won the Soviet championship, Kiev moved into the Champions Cup in 1986–87 and left the Cup-winners Cup open for a new name to be engraved on the trophy. Scotland's Aberdeen were the only previous winners in the first round draw and they went no further, losing 4–2 on aggregate to Sion, of Switzerland. The big names in the event were Ajax and Benfica so once the Portuguese had fallen to Bordeaux in the second round, it left the Dutch club, now coached by former player Johan Cruyff, out on their own. They had few problems. Bursaspor were beaten 2–0, 5–0 in the first round with John Bosman and Marco Van Basten scoring all the goals. Van Basten scored one in each leg, Bosman scored one in the first leg and four in the return.

Olympiakos Piraeus were beaten 4–0, 1–1 in the second round and Malmo 0–1, 3–1 in the quarter-finals. Cruyff was so keen to bring a teenager named Dennis Bergkamp into the action that he flew him out on the day of the game in Sweden because his protege had to sit an exam the previous afternoon. In the semi-finals, Ajax beat Real Zaragoza 3–2, 3–0 and should have beaten Lokomotive Leipzig by a wider margin than 1–0 in the final, in Athens. Van Basten scored the decisive goal after 21 minutes.

Ajax were back in the final the following season, 1987–88, but not Van Basten or Cruyff. The tall, angular centre-forward had been sold to Milan within a month of the 1987 Cup-winners success while Cruyff had been lured to Barcelona. Bosman remained to lead the Ajax attack but without success in the final against the unrated, unfancied Belgians of Mechelen (whom Bosman joined within weeks of the final). Young full-back Danny Blind was sent off by German referee Dieter Pauly after only 16 minutes and Mechelen upset all the forecasts with a 1–0 win courtesy of a 53rd-minute goal from Pieter Den Boer, a Dutchman.

The Cup-winners Cup could not, it seemed, be wrapped up safely now without a Dutch influence being brought to bear. Ajax had won in 1987, a Dutchman had won it for Mechelen in 1988 and a Dutchman was the winning coach in 1989 – Cruyff, with Barcelona. His reign at Nou Camp would last nine years and encompass a record four-year domination of the Spanish championship as well as bring the club their much-coveted Champions Cup in 1992. In the meantime, as a form of warm-up, they won the Cup-winners Cup, beating Sampdoria of Italy 2–0 in the final, in Berne. Julio Salinas and Lopez Rekarte scored the goals. Gary Lineker won his only European club medal in this game albeit playing in the unfamiliar, wide-right role in which Cruyff wanted him. Little wonder that Lineker, top scorer in the World Cup finals three years earlier, had scored only four of Barcelona's 16 goals on their way to the final.

Sampdoria's sudden success

Sampdoria's consolation in 1989 was to win their domestic cup for a second successive year and not only bounce straight back into the Cup-winners Cup but win it. Their opponents on a chilly May evening in the Ullevi stadium, Gothenburg were former kings of the event Anderlecht. The Belgians had collected the major scalp in defeating Barcelona in the second round. Anderlecht won 2–0 in Brussels and were 2–0 down at the end of normal time in Spain. An extra-time goal by Van der Linden took them through. As for Sampdoria, no-one got that close. They beat Brann Bergen 3–0 on aggregate, Borussia Dortmund 3–1, Grasshopper Zurich 4–1 and Monaco 4–2.

The final was expected to be a competition between Anderlecht spearhead Luc Nilis and Samp's Gianluca Vialli. Nilis had contributed four goals to Anderlecht's campaign, Vialli five for the Italians. That marginal could be seen, with hindsight, to have been reflected in the outcome of the final. Sampdoria won in extra time with two goals from Vialli. Nilis was virtually anonymous, a disappointing performance which not only deprived Anderlecht of a third Cup-winners Cup but cost Nilis a place in Belgium's squad at the World Cup finals in Italy.

England's national team reached the semi-finals of the World Cup but the summer of 1990 was also an important one for English clubs. Lennart Johansson was voted in as president of UEFA and moved swiftly, in line with one of his campaign promises, to bring English clubs back into Europe. The process was a gradual one, beginning with Manchester United in the 1990–91 Cup-winners Cup. If all went well, then the other competitions would open up to England.

All did, indeed, go well – so well, that United ended the season dancing in delight around the Feyenoord stadium in Rotterdam after winning the Cup. The first English club tie in Europe for five years saw Pecsi Munkas of Hungary beaten 2–0 at Old Trafford. Clayton Blackmore thundered home the all-

important opening goal from 25 yards after nine minutes and Neil Webb added a second goal seven minutes later. United won the return 1–0 then beat European neighbours Wrexham, holders of the Welsh Cup, in a gift of a second round tie.

The quarter-final, against Montpellier of France, was a more complex affair. Brian McClair opened the scoring within a minute of the kick-off at Old Trafford but a Lee Martin own goal handed Montpellier the draw. An unnecessary extra level of tension was built into the second leg because of an incident involving Welshman Mark Hughes which provoked the expulsion of Montpellier defender Pascal Baills at Old Trafford. United responded by stepping their game up a gear and winning the away leg 2–0 with goals either side of half-time from Blackmore and Steve Bruce (penalty). Legia Warsaw, who had eliminated holders Sampdoria, went down tamely in the semi-final and United found themselves facing Barcelona in the final.

This was a dream final for Hughes against his old club.

Fairytale success for Arsenal in Copenhagen in 1994

Barcelona had the tougher passage, beating Trabzonspor, Fram Reykjavik, Kiev Dynamo and Juventus. But in the final, suspension robbed them of feisty midfielder Guillermo Amor and goalkeeper, Andoni Zubizarreta. His deputy, Carlos Busquets, had never played a first-team competitive match before the final but he nervelessly held United at bay until the 67th minute when Hughes prodded a header from Bruce over the goal-line. Hughes struck again with an angled drive which brought up United's century for the season. Dutchman Ronald Koeman scored for Barcelona with a trademark free-kick but that was mere consolation. United were triumphant in Europe and hundreds of thousands duly lined the homecoming route from Ringway airport to Manchester city centre.

The 1991–92 competition brought United down to earth as they crashed out in the second round to Atletico Madrid. United manager Alex Ferguson blamed UEFA's newly-redrawn restrictions on foreign players which meant that, for English clubs in Europe, all Scots, Welsh and Irish players counted as foreigners. The selection juggling this demanded hindered English clubs' prospects for four years until the Bosman case drove a coach and horses through UEFA's restrictive practices.

First time for Bremen

In United's absence, the Cup-winners Cup field was wide open and Werder Bremen added a new name to the role of honour when they defeated Monaco 2–0 in the final, in Lisbon. A mere 15,000 spectators were virtually lost in the giant Stadio da Luz of Benfica. Klaus Allofs, a Cup-winners runner-up with Düsseldorf in 1979, collected a winner's medal after scoring the opening goal which set Bremen on their way to a 2–0 victory.

Yet another new name followed Bremen in 1993 when Italy's rising power of Parma, owned and financed by the Parmalat dairy products corporation, took the cream. Coach Nevio Scala brought his team to Wembley for the final with one doubt, unpredictable Colombian forward Faustino Asprilla. He had scored vital goals in early-round victories over Ujpest Dozsa, Sparta Prague and Atletico Madrid but had then flown home to Colombia for an international break and returned with a mysterious leg injury. Asprilla claimed he was fit for the final and had earned the right to play. Scala disagreed but, even without Asprilla, Parma had far too much firepower for their willing but limited opponents, Royal Antwerp. Italy defender Lorenzo Minotti scored after ten minutes, forwards Alessandro Melli and Stefano Cuoghi in the second half. Earlier, Francis Severeyns scored a brief equaliser but Parma never appeared seriously endangered.

An interested spectator was Arsenal manager George Graham, a keen student of the international game. The lessons Graham had imbibed were put into practice with the greatest success on Arsenal's behalf in the Cup-winners Cup in 1993–94. Arsenal ultimately carried off the Cup – belated success after their narrow failure in 1980 – and earned extra credit for doing so in a season when the secondary competition carried more glamour than the Champions Cup. Apart from Arsenal, the main challengers to holders Parma included Real Madrid, Ajax, Benfica and the rising French power, Paris Saint-Germain.

OB Copenhagen were no problem in the first round. Arsenal won 3–2 on aggregate before sensationally thrashing Belgium's Standard Liege 10–0 overall in the second round. Two goals from Ian Wright inspired a 3–0 success at home which provoked all sorts of internal problems at Liege. The Belgians were in no mood for the second leg and even their own fans ended up cheering Arsenal who scorched to a 7–0 success in the Sclessin stadium.

Arsenal had not progressed beyond the quarter-finals in a European competition since the 1980 Cup-winners Cup. Graham was determined that, this time, there would be no slip-ups. Accordingly, he plotted the tactical battle with Torino in the last eight down to the last detail. The first leg, in Turin, ended 0–0. The second leg, at Highbury, was decided by a 65th-minute goal from skipper Tony Adams, heading home a Paul Davis free-kick.

The semi-finals matched Arsenal against PSG. The French, having defeated Real Madrid with some panache in the quarter-finals, were the neutrals' favourites. They had gone 35 matches without defeat, were virtually certain of winning the French League and could indulge their own European fantasies.

Not for much longer. In the 35th minute, another penetrating Davis free-kick split the offside trap and Wright was in place to score. The French equalised through David Ginola early in the second half, then the tide turned again. Kevin Campbell headed home after only seven minutes of the second leg and Arsenal exerted a vice-like grip on the rest of the match to secure their tickets to Copenhagen for the final.

Parma gunned down

Still no club had managed to retained the trophy. Parma believed they could break that jinx and might well have done so had Sweden's Tomas Brolin taken advantage of two gilt-edged opportunities in the first 15 minutes in the Parkstadion. Four more minutes were all it took for Arsenal to take charge. Parma skipper Lorenzo Minotti miscued a clearance and Alan Smith, hardly believing his luck, strode forward for a left-foot shot which clipped the inside of the near post and ricocheted into the far corner.

This was, to all intents and purposes, the long-awaited springboard towards a place in the European superleague to which Arsenal aspired. Progress off the pitch, under the eagle eye of vice-chairman David Dein, saw the redevelopment of the club's home ground at Highbury underpinned by an aggressive commercial and promotional policy.

But football has an odd habit of upsetting the best-laid plans and Arsenal's defence of the Cup-winners Cup in 1994–95 proved the point. Just like Parma the previous season, they found their way back to the final. Then, just like Parma the previous season, they lost it.

Ironically, this Cup-winners Cup did not contain anything like the same quality of potential opposition. Ian Wright was the individual star. He scored three goals in the 6–1 defeat of Omonia of Cyprus in the first round and two more in the 4–3 elimination of Denmark's Brondby in the second round. Wright scored the

goals, home and away, with which Arsenal overcame Auxerre of France 2–1 on aggregate in the quarter-finals. He then scored in each leg of the semi-final against Sampdoria – before England goalkeeper David Seaman took on the hero's mantle.

Arsenal beat Sampdoria 3–2 at home and lost 3–2 away. That meant Arsenal's first penalty shoot-out since the painful failure against Valencia in 1980. Now it was Arsenal's turn to find fortune's smile. Seaman saved the kicks of Sinisa Mihajlovic, Vladimir Jugovic and Attilio Lombardo and the Gunners had survived by a 3–2 shoot-out margin.

But Seaman's unhappy "reward" for his semi-final heroics was to be the scapegoat in the final, against Spain's barely-rated Real Zaragoza in Paris.

Bobby Robson's Barcelona triumph in Rotterdam

Freak goal settles it

A tight match saw Zaragoza snatch the lead with a superb strike-on-the-turn by Argentine forward Juan Esnaider midway through the second half. Arsenal needed a touch of Ian Wright's magic but, for the first time in the competition, he found the way to goal blocked and it was left to the young Welshman, John Hartson, to score the equalizer which earned extra time.

As the match drew on, so loomed the prospect of a penalty shoot-out in which Arsenal, with Seaman to fill the goalmouth, would be favourites. But, with Italian referee Ceccarini looking at his watch, Zaragoza struck the fantastic, decisive blow. Midfielder Nayim, way out on the right, hit a towering lob high in the direction of goal. The lights in the Parc des Princes are hung from the roof of the stand and Seaman, looking up into the lights as he ran back, lost the trajectory of the ball... which fell behind him, just under the bar, and into the net.

It was a fearsomely dramatic way in which to lose a match – let alone a cup. As for Zaragoza, they also failed the title defence challenge in 1995–96. They lost to fellow Spanish outfit Deportivo La Coruna in the quarter-finals. One round later and Deportivo succumbed to Paris Saint-Germain who went on to beat Rapid Vienna 1–0 in a one-sided final in the redeveloped King Baudouin (formerly Heysel) stadium. Paris then went close to breaking the holders' hoodoo, reaching the 1997 final... only to lose 1–0 to Barcelona in the same De Kuip stadium in Rotterdam where the Catalans had lost to Manchester United in 1991.

Barcelona's coach Robson did possess one enormous advantage not available to Cruyff, his predecessor, and not available, either, to managerial successor Louis Van Gaal from Ajax. That advantage was, simply, Ronaldo.

Barcelona had paid PSV Eindhoven £12.9 million for the Brazilian striker in the summer of 1996. He was widely regarded as the finest footballer in the world and his record, while in Barcelona, justified the accolade. Of course, Barcelona were not a one-man team. Robson had brought in his old favourites from his Portuguese days such as goalkeeper Vitor Baia and forward Luis Figo. But it was Ronaldo who dominated the headlines.

Under the traditional rules, Barcelona should have defended the Cup-winners Cup in 1997–98. However, the fact that they did not held great significance for the status and image of the Cup-winners Cup.

This was the season in which UEFA allowed the runners-up of Europe's top eight nations into the Champions League. The decision meant an inevitable slip in quality in the Cup-winners Cup. Indeed, UEFA accepted the likely inevitable by ruling that, where both domestic cup finalists had qualified for the Champions League, a country would be expected to stage a play-off between the losing semi-finalists to sort out a representative for the Cup-winners Cup.

Competition devalued

All the pessimistic comments about the future of the Cup-winners Cup appeared justified by the entry for 1997–98. None of the "greats" were in evidence. England's Chelsea, managed at the time in idiosyncratic style by Ruud Gullit.

Chelsea and Stuttgart were well-balanced opponents in the final, in Stockholm. Both ended the season in fourth place in the league, with the comfort of knowing that win or lose in Stockholm, they were guaranteed a place in Europe the next season through the UEFA Cup.

Chelsea had reached Stockholm with victories over Slovan Bratislava, snowbound Tromso of Norway, Betis and Vicenza. Stuttgaft overcame IBV of Iceland, Germinal Ekeren of Belgium, Slavia Prague and Lokomotiv Moscow. The Londoners were at full strength after the return from serious injury of Uruguayan midfielder Gustavo Poyet, a Cup-winners Cup winner in 1995 with Zaragoza. Stuttgart missed defenders Frank Verlaat and Martin Spanring through suspension and gambled on top-scoring striker Fredi Bobic, even though he was only half-fit.

Chelsea had no need this time, as in 1971, of anything beyond the 90 minutes. A superb goal from Italy's Gianfranco Zola 23 seconds after coming on as a second-half substitute earned a 1–0 win. Zola, out of the Chelsea side for three weeks through injury, replaced Norwegian Tore Andre Flo in the 71st minute and with his second touch collected a perfect pass from Dennis Wise and blasted a shot past Stuttgart keeper Franz Wohlfahrt.

In a disappointing game, both sides finished with ten men after Chelsea's Dan Petrescu was sent off five minutes from time Gerhard Poschner followed him on the stroke of full time. Stuttgart's best chance fell to Nigerian striker Jonathan Akpoborie in the ninth minute but he hesitated with only goalkeeper Ed De Goey to beat and missed. Zola said: "This is one of the best moments of my career." Little did he know one of the worst was just around the corner... when Cesare Maldini left Zola out of his World Cup squad for France 98.

The Cup-winners Cup remains, officially, the second competition in status in Europe behind the Champions League and ahead of the UEFA Cup. But how long that may last is open to question. The absence of a third round (in November-December) makes the Cup-winners Cup financially unpopular compared with the UEFA Cup. Indeed, Stuttgart, before the 1998 final, had lobbied UEFA in vain pursuit of permission to enter the UEFA Cup in 1998–99 (for which they had qualified) rather than defend the Cup-winners Cup, should have won it.

"Football clubs have more to think about nowadays than the mere pleasure of the sport," said Stuttgart president Gerhardt Mayer-Vorfelder.

In such an increasingly business-orientated climate one can only question the long-term future of the competition.

EUROPEAN CUP-WINNERS CUP RESULTS

1960–61

SEMI-FINALS

Fiorentina bt Dinamo Zagreb 3–0, 1–2
(4–2 agg)

Rangers bt Wolverhampton Wanderers 2–0, 1–1
(3–1 agg)

FINAL

1st leg: May 17 (Ibrox, Glasgow)
Rangers 0
Fiorentina 2 (Milani 12 88)
HT: 0–1. Att: 80,000. Ref: Steiner (Aut).
RANGERS: Ritchie, Shearer, Caldow, Davis, Paterson, Baxter, Wilson, McMillan, Scott, Brand, Hume.
FIORENTINA: Albertosi, Robotti, Castelletti, Gonfiantini, Orzan, Rimbaldo, Hamrin, Micheli, Da Costa, Milani, Petris.

2nd leg: May 27 (Comunale, Florence)
Fiorentina 2 (Milani 12, Hamrin 88)
Rangers 1 (Scott 60)
HT: 1–0. Att: 50,000. Ref: Hernadi (Hun)
FIORENTINA: Albertosi, Robotti, Castelletti, Gonfiantini, Orzan, Rimbaldo, Hamrin, Micheli, Da Costa, Milani, Petris.
RANGERS: Ritchie, Shearer, Caldow, Davis, Paterson, Baxter, Scott, McMillan, Millar, Brand, Wilson.
Winners: Fiorentina 4–1 agg

1961–62

SEMI-FINALS

Atletico Madrid bt Motor Jena 1–0, 4–0
(5–0 agg)

Fiorentina bt Ujpest Dozsa 2–0, 1–0
(3–0 agg)

FINAL

May 10 (Hampden Park, Glasgow)
Atletico Madrid 1 (Peiro 11)
Fiorentina 1 (Hamrin 27)
HT: 1–1. Att: 27,000. Ref: Wharton (Sco).
ATLETICO: Madinabeytia, Rivilla, Calleja, Ramirez, Griffa, Glaria, Jones, Adelardo, Mendona, Peiro, Collar.
FIORENTINA: Albertosi, Robotti, Castelletti, Malatrasi, Orzan, Marchesi, Hamrin, Ferretti, Milan, Dell'Angelo, Petris.

Replay: September 5 (Neckarstadion, Stuttgart)
Atletico Madrid 3 (Jones 8, Mendonca 27, Peiro 59)
Fiorentina 0
HT: 2–0. Att: 38,000. Ref: Tschenscher (WG).
ATLETICO: Madinabeytia, Rivilla, Calleja, Ramirez, Griffa, Glaria, Jones, Adelardo, Mendona, Peiro, Collar.
FIORENTINA: Albertosi, Robotti, Castelletti, Malatrasi, Orzan, Marchesi, Hamrin, Ferretti, Milani, Dell'Angelo, Petris.

1962–63

SEMI-FINALS

Tottenham Hotspur bt OFK Belgrade 2–1, 3–1
(5–2 agg)

Atletico Madrid bt Nürnberg 1–2, 2–0
(3–2 agg)

FINAL

May 15 (Feyenoord, Rotterdam)
Tottenham Hotspur 5 (Greaves 16 80, White 35, Dyson 67 85)
Atletico Madrid 1 (Collar 47)
HT: 2–0. Att: 49,000. Ref: Van Leuwen (Hol)
TOTTENHAM: Brown, Baker, Henry, Blanchflower, Norman, Marchi, Jones, White, Smith, Greaves, Dyson.
ATLETICO: Madinabeytia, Rivilla, Griffa, Rodriguez, Ramiro, Glaria, Jones, Adelardo, Chuzo, Mendona, Collar.

1963–64

SEMI-FINALS

Sporting Lisbon bt Olympique Lyon 0–0, 1–1, 1–0
(play-off, 1–1 agg)

MTK Budapest bt Celtic 0–3, 4–0
(4–3 agg)

FINAL

May 13 (Heysel, Brussels)
Sporting Lisbon 3 (Mascarenhas 40, Figueiredo 45 80)
MTK Budapest 3 (Sandor 18 75, Kuti 73)
HT: 2–1. Att: 30,000. Ref: Van Nuffel (Bel)
SPORTING: Carvalho, Gomes, Peridis, Battista, Carlos, Geo, Mendes, Oswaldo, Mascarenhas, Figueiredo, Morais.
MTK: Kovalik, Keszei, Dansky, Jenei, Nagy, Kovacs, Sandor, Vasas, Kuti, Bodor, Halapi.

Replay: May 15 (Antwerp)
Sporting Lisbon 1 (Morais)
MTK Budapest 0
HT: 1–0. Att: 19,000. Ref: Versyp (Bel)
SPORTING: Carvalho, Gomes, Peridis, Battista, Carlos, Geo, Mendes, Oswaldo, Mascarenhas, Figueiredo, Morais.
MTK: Kovalik, Keszei, Dansky, Jenei, Nagy, Kovacs, Sandor, Vasas, Kuti, Bodor, Halapi.

1964–65

SEMI-FINALS

West Ham United bt Real Zaragoza 2–1, 1–1
(3–2 agg)

Munich 1860 bt Torino 0–2, 3–1, 2–0
(play-off, 3–3 agg)

FINAL

May 19 (Wembley)
West Ham United 2
Sealey 70 72)
1860 Munich 0
HT: 0–0. Att: 100,000. Ref: Zsolt (Hun)
WEST HAM: Standen, Kirkup, Burkett, Peters, Brown, Moore, Sealey, Boyce, Hurst, Dear, Sissons.
TSV 1860: Radenkovic, Wagner, Kohlars, Reich, Bena, Luttrop, Heiss, Küppers, Brunnemeier, Grosser, Rebele.

1965–66

SEMI-FINALS

Borussia Dortmund bt West Ham United 2–1, 3–1
(5–2 agg)

Liverpool bt Celtic 0–1, 2–0
(3–1 agg)

FINAL

May 5 (Hampden Park, Glasgow)
Borussia Dortmund 2 (Held 62, Libuda 109)
Liverpool 1 (Hunt 68)
HT: 0–0. 90min: 1–1. After extra time. Att: 41,000. Ref: Schwinte (Fra)
BORUSSIA: Tilkowski, Cyliax, Redder, Kurrat, Paul, Assauer, Libuda, Schmidt, Held, Sturm, Emmerich.
LIVERPOOL: Lawrence, Lawler, Byrne, Milne, Yeats, Stevenson, Callaghan, Hunt, St John, Smith, Thompson.

1966–67

SEMI-FINALS

Bayern Munich bt Standard Liege 2–0, 3–1
(5–1 agg)

Rangers bt Slavia Sofia 1–0, 1–0
(2–0 agg)

FINAL

May 31 (Frankenstadion, Nuremberg)
Bayern Munich 1 (Roth 108)
Rangers 0
HT: 0–0. 90min: 0–0. After extra time. Att: 69,000. Ref: Lo Bello (Ita)
BAYERN: Maier, Nowak, Kupferschmidt, Beckenbauer, Olk, Roth, Koulmann, Nafziger, Ohlhauser, G Müller, Brenniger.
RANGERS: Martin, Johansen, Provan, Greig, McKinnon, Jardine, D Smith, Henderson, Hynd, A Smith, Johnston.

1967–68

SEMI-FINALS

Hamburg bt Cardiff City 1–1, 3–2
(4–3 agg)

Milan bt Bayern Munich 2–0, 0–0
(2–0 agg)

FINAL

May 23 (Feyenoord, Rotterdam)
Milan 2 (Hamrin 3 19)
Hamburg 0
HT: 2–0. Att: 53,000. Ref: De Mendibil (Spa)
MILAN: Cudicini, Anquilletti, Schnellinger, Scala, Rosato, Trapattoni, Hamrin, Lodetti, Sormani, Rivera, Prati.
HAMBURG: Ozcan, Sandmann, Schulz, Horst, Kurbjuhn, Dieckmann, Kramer, B Dörfel, Seeler, Hönig, G Dörfel.

1968–69

SEMI-FINALS

Slovan Bratislava bt Dunfermline Athletic 1–1, 1–0
(2–1 agg)
Barcelona bt FC Köln 2–2, 4–1
(6–3 agg)

FINAL

May 21 (St Jakob, Basle)
Slovan Bratislava 3 (Cvetler 2, Hrivnak 30, Jan Capkovic 42)
Barcelona 2 (Zaldua 16, Rexach 52)
HT: 3–1. Att: 19,000. Ref: Van Raven (Hol)
SLOVAN: Vencel, Filo, Horvath, Hrivnak, Zlocha, Hrdlicka, Josef Capkovic, Cvetler, Moder (Hatar 67), Jokl, Jan Capkovic.
BARCELONA: Sadurni, Franch (Pereda 11), Eladio, Rife, Olivella, Zabalza, Pellicer, Castro (Mendona 46), Zaldua, Fuste, Rexach.

1969–70

SEMI-FINALS

Manchester City bt Schalke 0–1, 5–1
(5–2 agg)
Gornik Zabrze bt Roma 1–1, 2–2, 1–1
(Gornik on toss of coin after play-off, 3–3 agg)

FINAL

May 29 (Prater, Vienna)
Manchester City 2 (Young 11, Lee 43)
Gornik Zabrze 1 (Oslizlo 70)
HT: 2–0. Att: 8,000. Ref: Schiller (Aut)
MANCHESTER CITY: Corrigan, Book, Pardoe, Booth, Heslop, Doyle (Bowyer 23), Towers, Oakes, Bell, Lee, Young.
GORNIK: Kostka, Oslizlo, Florenski (Kuchta 85), Gorgon, Olek, Latocha, Szoltysik, Wilczek (Skowronek 75), Szarynski, Banas, Lubanski.

1970–71

SEMI-FINALS

Chelsea bt Manchester City 1–0, 1–0
(2–0 agg)
Real Madrid bt PSV Eindhoven 0–0, 2–1
(2–1 agg)

FINAL

May 19 (Karaiskaki, Piraeus)
Chelsea 1 (Osgood 55)
Real Madrid 1 (Zoco 30)
HT: 0–1. 90 min: 1–1. After extra time. Att: 42,000. Ref: Scheurer (Swi)
CHELSEA: Bonetti, Boyle, Dempsey, Webb, Harris, Hollins (Mulligan 91), Hudson, Cooke, Weller, Osgood (Baldwin 86), Houseman.
REAL: Borja, Jose Luis, Benito, Zoco, Zunzunegui, Pirri, Grosso, Velazquez, Miguel Perez (Fleitas 65), Amancio, Gento (Grande 70).

Replay: May 21 (Karaiskaki, Piraeus)
Chelsea 2 (Dempsey 31, Osgood 39)
Real Madrid 1 (Fleitas 75)
HT: 2–0. Att: 19,917. Ref: Bucheli (Swi)
CHELSEA: Bonetti, Boyle, Dempsey, Cooke, Harris, Weller, Baldwin, Webb, Hudson, Osgood (Smethurst 73), Houseman.
REAL: Borja, Jose Luis, Benito, Zoco, Zunzunegui, Pirri, Velazquez (Gento 75), Fleitas, Amancio, Grosso, Bueno (Grande 60).

1971–72

SEMI-FINALS

Rangers bt Bayern Munich 1–1, 2–0
(3–1 agg)
Moscow Dynamo bt Dynamo Berlin 1–1, 1–1
(4–1 on pens, 2–2 agg)

FINAL

May 24 (Nou Camp, Barcelona)
Rangers 3 (Stein 23, Johnston 40 49)
Moscow Dynamo 2 (Estrekov 60, Makovikov 87)
HT: 2–0. Att: 24,000. Ref: De Mendibil (Spa)
RANGERS: McCloy, Jardine, Johnstone, Smith, Mathieson, Greig, Conn, MacDonald, McLean, Stein, Johnston.
DYNAMO: Pilgui, Basalev, Dolmatov, Zikov, Dobonosov (Gershkovich 69), Zhukov, Yakubik (Estrekov 56), Sabo, Baidachni, Makovikov, Yevreshukin.

1972–73

SEMI-FINALS

Milan bt Sparta Pargue 1–0, 1–0
(2–0 agg)
Leeds United bt Hajduk Split 1–0, 0–0
(1–0 agg)

FINAL

May 16 (Kaftantzoglio, Salonica)
Milan 1 (Chiarugi 5)
Leeds United 0
HT: 1–0. Att: 45,000. Ref: Michas (Gre)
MILAN: Vecchi, Sabadini, Zignoli, Anquilletti, Turone, Rosato (Dolci 59), Rivera, Benetti, Sogliano, Bigon, Chiarugi.
LEEDS UTD: Harvey, Reaney, Cherry, Bates, Madeley, Hunter, F Gray (McQueen 54), Yorath, Lorimer, Jordan, Jones.

1973–74

SEMI-FINALS

FC Magdeburg bt Sporting Lisbon 1–1, 2–1
(3–2 agg)
Milan bt Borussia Mönchengladbach 2–0, 0–1
(3–1 agg)

FINAL

May 8 (Feyenoord, Rotterdam)
FC Magdeburg 2 (Lanzi og 40, Seguin 74)
Milan 0
HT: 1–0. Att: 4,000. Ref: Van Gemert (Hol)
MAGDEBURG: Schlze, Enge, Zapf, Tyll, Abraham, Seguin, Pommerenke, Gaube, Raugust, Sparwasser, Hoffmann.
MILAN: Pizzaballa, Sabadini, Anquilletti, Lanzi, Schnellinger, Benetti, Maldera, Rivera, Tresoldi, Bigon, Bergamaschi (Turini 60).

1974–75

SEMI-FINALS

Kiev Dynamo bt PSV Eindhoven 3–0, 2–1
(5–1 agg)
Ferencvaros bt Red Star Belgrade 2–1, 2–2
(4–3 agg)

FINAL

May 14 (St Jakob, Basle)
Kiev Dynamo 3 (Onischenko 18 39, Blokhin 67)
Ferencvaros 0
HT: 2–0. Att: 10,000. Ref: Davidson (Sco)
DYNAMO Kiev: Rudakov, Troshkin, Matvienko, Reshko, Fomenko, Muntian, Konkov, Buryak, Kolotov, Onishenko, Blokhin.
FERENCVAROS: Geczi, Martos, Megyesi, Pataki, Rab, Nyilasi (Ohnhaus 60), Juhasz, Mucha, Szabo, Magyar, Mate.

1975–76

SEMI-FINALS

Anderlecht bt Sachsenring Zwickau 3–0, 2–0
(5–0 agg)
West Ham United bt Eintracht Frankfurt 1–2, 3–1
(4–3 agg)

FINAL

May 5 (Heysel, Brussels)
Anderlecht 4 (Rensenbrink 42 73, Van der Elst 48 87)
West Ham United 2 (Holland 28, Robson 68)
HT: 1–1. Att: 58,000. Ref: Wurtz (Fra)
ANDERLECHT: Ruiter, Lomme, Van Binst, Thissen, Broos, Dockx, Coeck (Vercauteren 32), Haan, Van der Elst, Ressel, Rensenbrink.
WEST HAM: Day, Coleman, Lampard (A Taylor 47), T Taylor, McDowell, Bonds, Brooking, Paddon, Holland, Jennings, Robson.

1976–77

SEMI-FINALS

Hamburg bt Atletico Madrid 1–3, 3–0
(4–3 agg)
Anderlecht bt Napoli 0–1, 2–0
(2–1 agg)

FINAL

May 11 (Olympisch, Amsterdam)
Hamburg 2 (Volkert 78, Magath 88)
Anderlecht 0
HT: 0–0. Att: 66,000. Ref: Partridge (Eng)
HAMBURG: Kargus, Kaltz, Ripp, Nogly, Hidien, Memering, Magath, Keller, Steffenhagen, Reimann, Volkert.
ANDERLECHT: Ruiter, Van Binst, Van den Daele, Thissen, Broos, Dockx (Van Poucke 81), Coeck, Haan, Van der Elst, Ressel, Rensenbrink.

1977–78

SEMI-FINALS

Anderlecht bt Twente Enschende 1–0, 2–0
(3–0 agg)
Moscow Dynamo bt FK Austria 0–0, 1–0
(1–0 agg)

FINAL

May 3 (Parc des Princes, Paris)
Anderlecht 4 (Rensenbrink 13 41, Van Binst 45 80)
FK Austria 0
HT: 2–1. Att: 48,000. Ref: Alginder (WG)
ANDERLECHT: De Bree, Van Binst, Thissen, Dusbaba, Broos, Van der Elst, Haan, Nielsen, Coeck, Vercauteren (Dockx 87), Rensenbrink.
AUSTRIA: Baumgartner, R Sara, J Sara, Obermayer, Baumeister, Prohaska, Daxbacher (Martinez 60), Gasselich, Morales (Dragan 74), Pirkner, Parits.

1978–79

SEMI-FINALS

Barcelona bt Beveren 1–0, 1–0
(2–0 agg)
Fortuna Düsseldorf bt Banik Ostrava 3–1, 1–2
(4–3 agg)

FINAL

May 16 (St Jakob, Basle)
Barcelona 4 (Sanchez 5, Asensi 34, Rexach 104, Krankl 111)
Fortuna Düsseldorf 3 (K Allofs 8, Seel 41 114)
HT: 2–2. 90min: 2–2. After extra time. Att: 58,000. Ref: Palotai (Hun)
BARCELONA: Artola, Zuviria, Migueli, Costas (Martinez 66), Albaledejo (De la Cruz 57), Sanchez, Neeskens, Asensi, Rexach, Krankl, Carrasco.
FORTUNA: Daniel, Baltes, Zewe, Zimmermann (Lund 84), Brei (Weikl 24), Kohnen, Schmitz, T Allofs, Bommer, K Allofs, Seel.

1979–80

SEMI-FINALS

Valencia bt Nantes 1–2, 4–0
(5–2 agg)
Arsenal bt Juventus 1–1, 1–0
(2–1 agg)

FINAL

May 15 (Heysel, Brussels)
Valencia 0
Arsenal 0
HT: 0–0. 90min: 0–0. After extra time. Valencia 5–4 on pens Att: 36,000. Ref: Christov (Cze)
VALENCIA: Pereira, Carrete, Botubot, Arias, Tendillo, Solsona, Saura, Bonhof, Subirats (Castellanos 112), Kempes, Pablo.
ARSENAL: Jennings, Rice, Nelson, O'Leary, Young, Rix, Talbot, Price (Hollins 105), Brady, Sunderland, Stapleton.

1980–81

SEMI-FINALS

Tbilisi Dynamo bt Feyenoord 3–0, 0–2
(3–2 agg)
Carl Zeiss Jena bt Benfica 2–0, 0–1
(2–1 agg)

FINAL

May 13 (Rheinstadion, Düsseldorf)
Tbilisi Dynamo 2 (Gutsayev 67, Daraselia 86)
Carl Zeiss Jena 1 (Hoppe 63)
HT: 0–0. Att: 9,000. Ref: Lattanzi (Ita)
DYNAMO: Gabelia, Kostava, Chivadze, Khisanishvili, Tavadze, Svanadze (Kakilashvili 67), Sulakvelidze, Daraselia, Gutsayev, Kipiani, Shengalia.
CARL ZEISS: Grapenthin, Bruer, Kurbjuweit, Schnphase, Schilling, Hoppe (Overmann 88), Krause, Lindemann, Bielau (Topfer 76), Raab, Vogel.

1981–82

SEMI-FINALS

Barcelona bt Tottenham Hotspur 1–1, 1–0
(2–1 agg)
Standard Liege bt Tbilisi Dynamo 1–0, 1–0
(2–0 agg)

FINAL

May 12 (Nou Camp, Barcelona)
Barcelona 2 (Simonsen 44, Quini 63)
Standard Liege 1 (Vandersmissen 7)
HT: 1–1. Att: 100,000. Ref: Eschweller (WG)
BARCELONA: Urruti, Gerardo, Migueli, Alesanco, Manolo, Sanchez, Moratalla, Estaban, Simonsen, Quini, Carrasco.
STANDARD: Preud'homme, Gerets, Poel, Meeuws, Plessers, Vandersmissen, Daarden, Haan, Botteron, Tahamata, Wendt.

1982–83

SEMI-FINALS

Aberdeen bt Watershei 5–1, 0–1
(5–2 agg)
Real Madrid bt FK Austria 2–2, 3–1
(5–3 agg)

FINAL

May 11 (Nya Ullevi, Gothenburg)
Aberdeen 2 (Black 4, Hewitt 112)
Real Madrid 1 (Juanito 15)
HT: 1–1. 90min: 11. After extra time. Att: 17,000. Ref: Menegali (It)
ABERDEEN: Leighton, Rougvie, McLeish, Miller, McMaster, Cooper, Strachan, Simpson, McGhee, Black (Hewitt 87), Weir.
MADRID: Agustin, Juan Josc, Mctgod, Bonct, Camacho (San Jose 91), Angel, Gallego, Stielike, Isidro (Salguero 103), Juanito, Santillana.

1983–84

SEMI-FINALS

Juventus bt Manchester United 1–1, 2–1
(3–2 agg)
FC Porto bt Aberdeen 1–0, 1–0
(2–0 agg)

FINAL

May 16 (St Jakob, Basle)
Juventus 2 (Vignola 12, Boniek 41)
FC Porto 1 (Sousa 29)
HT: 2–1. Att: 60,000. Ref: Galler (Swi)
JUVENTUS: Tacconi, Gentile, Brio, Scirea, Cabrini, Tardelli, Bonini, Vignola (Caricola 89), Platini, Rossi, Boniek.
PORTO: Ze Beto, Joao Pinto, Lima Pereira, Enrico, Eduardo Luis (Costa 82), Jaime Magalhaes (Walsh 65), Frasco, Pacheco, Sousa, Gomes, Vermelinho.

1984–85

SEMI-FINALS

Everton bt Bayern Munich 0–0, 3–1
(3–1 agg)
Rapid Vienna bt Moscow Dynamo 3–1, 1–1
(4–2 agg)

FINAL

May 15 (Feyenoord, Rotterdam)
Everton 3 (Gray 57, Steven 72, Sheedy 85)
Rapid Vienna 1 (Krankl 85)
HT: 0–0 Att: 50,000. Ref: Casarin (Ita)
EVERTON: Southall, Stevens, Van Den Hauwe, Ratcliffe, Mountfield, Reid, Steven, Bracewell, Sheedy, Gray, Sharp.
RAPID: Konsel, Lainer, Weber, Garger, Brauneder, Hrstic, Kranjcar, Kienast, Weinhofer (Panenka 67), Pacult (Gross 60), Krankl.

1985–86

SEMI-FINALS

Kiev Dynamo bt Dukla Prague 3–0, 1–1
(4–1 agg)
Atletico Madrid bt Bayer Uerdingen 1–0, 3–2
(4–2 agg)

FINAL

May 2 (Gerland, Lyon)
Kiev Dynamo 3 (Zavarov 4, Blokhin 85, Yevtushenko 87)
Atletico Madrid 0
HT: 1–0. Att: 50,000. Ref: Wohrer (Aut)
DYNAMO: Chanov, Bessonov, Baltacha (Bal 38), Kuznetsov, Demianenko, Yaremchuk, Yakovenko, Zavarov (Yevtushenko 70), Rats, Belanov, Blokhin.
ATLETICO: Fillol, Tomas, Arteche, Ruiz, Clemente, Julio Prieto, Landaburu (Quique Setien 61), Marina, Quique, Da Silva, Cabrera.

1986–87

SEMI-FINALS

Ajax bt Real Zaragoza 3–2, 3–0
(6–2 agg)
Lokomotive Leipzig bt Bordeaux 1–0, 0–1
(6–5 on pens, 1–1 agg)

FINAL

May 13 (Olympic, Athens)
Ajax 1 (Van Basten 21)
Lokomotive Leipzig 0
HT: 1–0. Att: 35,000. Ref: Agnolin (Ita)
AJAX: Menzo, Silooy, Rijkaard, Verlaat, Boeve, Wouters, Winter, A Muhren (Scholten 83), Van't Schip, Van Basten, Rob Witschge (Bergkamp 66)
LOKOMOTIVE: Mller, Kreer, Baum, Lindner, Ztzsche, Scholz, Liebers (Khn 76), Bredow, Marschal, Richter, Edmond (Leitzke 55)

1987–88

SEMI-FINALS

Mechelen bt Atalanta 2–1, 2–1
(4–2 agg)
Ajax bt Marseille 3–0, 1–2
(4–2 agg)

FINAL

May 11 (Meinau, Strasbourg)
Mechelen 1 (Den Boer 53)
Ajax 0
HT: 0–0. Att: 40,000. Ref: Pauly (WG)
MECHELEN: Preud'homme, Clijsters, Sanders, Rutjes, Deferm, Hofkens, (Theunis 73), Emmers, Koeman, De Wilde (Demesmaeker 60), Den Boer, Ohana.
AJAX: Menzo, Blind, Wouters, Larsson, Verlaat (Meijer 73), Van't Schip (Bergkamp 57), Winter, A Muhren, Scholten, Bosman, Rob Witschge.

1988–89

SEMI-FINALS

Barcelona bt CSKA Sofia 4–2, 2–1
(6–3 agg)
Sampdoria bt Mechelen 1–2, 3–0
(4–2 agg)

FINAL

May 10 (Wankdorf, Berne)
Barcelona 2 (Salinas 4, Lopez Rekarte 79)
Sampdoria 0
HT: 1–0. Att: 45,000. Ref: Courtney (Eng)
BARCELONA: Zubizarreta, Aloisio, Alexanco, Urbano, Milla (Soler 61), Amor, Eusebio, Roberto, Lineker, Salinas, Beguiristain (Lopez Rekarte 74)
SAMPDORIA: Pagliuca, L Pellegrini (Bonomi 54), Mannini (S Pellegrini 27), Lanna, Salsano, Pari, Victor, Toninho Cerezo, Dossena, Vialli, Mancini.

1989–90

SEMI-FINALS

Sampdoria bt Monaco 2–2, 2–0
(4–2 agg)
Anderlecht bt Dinamo Bucharest 1–0, 1–0
(2–0 agg)

FINAL

May 9 (Nya Ullevi, Gothenburg)
Sampdoria 2 (Vialli 105 107)
Anderlecht 0
HT: 0–0. 90min: 0–0. After extra time. Att: 20,000. Ref: Galler (Swi)
SAMPDORIA: Pagliuca, L Pellegrini, Mannini, Vierchwood, Carboni, Pari, Katanec (Salsano 92), Invernizzi (Lombardo 55), Dossena, Vialli, Mancini.
ANDERLECHT: De Wilde, Grun, Marchoul, Keshi, Kooiman, Vervoot, Musonda, Gudjohnson, Jankovic (Oliveira 116), Degryse (Nilis 104), Van der Linden.

1990–91

SEMI-FINALS

Manchester United bt Legia Warsaw 3–1, 1–1
(4–2 agg)
Barcelona bt Juventus 3–1, 0–1
(3–2 agg)

FINAL

May 15 (Feyenoord, Rotterdam)
Manchester United 2 (Bruce 67, Hughes 74)
Barcelona 1 (Koeman 79)
HT: 0–0. Att: 48,000. Ref: Karlsson (Swe)
UNITED: Sealey, Irwin, Bruce, Pallister, Blackmore, Phelan, Robson, Ince, Sharpe, Hughes, McClair.
BARCELONA: Busquets, Alexanco (Pinilla 72), Nando, R Koeman, Ferrer, Goikotxea, Eusebio, Bakero, Beguiristain, Salinas, M Laudrup.

1991–92

SEMI-FINALS

Werder Bremen bt Club Brugge 0–1, 2–0
(2–1 agg)
Monaco bt Feyenoord 1–1, 2–2
(away goals, 3–3 agg)

FINAL

May 6 (Benfica, Lisbon)
Werder Bremen 2 (K Allofs 41, Rufer 54)
Monaco 0
HT: 1–0. Att: 15,000. Ref: D'Elia (Ita)
WERDER: Rollmann, Bockenfeld, Borowka, Bratseth, Wolter (Schaaf 34), Eilts, Votava, Bode, Neubarth (Kohn 75), Rufer, K Allofs.
MONACO: Ettori, Valery (Djorkaeff 62), Mendy, Sonor, Gnako, Rui Barros, Dib, Petit, Passi, Fofana (Clement 59), Weah.

1992–93

SEMI-FINALS

Parma bt Atletico Madrid 2–1, 0–1
(away goals, 2–2 agg)
Antwerp bt Moscow Spartak 0–1, 3–1
(3–2 agg)

FINAL

May 12 (Wembley)
Parma 3 (Minotti 9, Melli 30, Cuoghi 83)
Antwerp 1 (Severeyns 11)
HT: 2–1. Att: 37,000. Ref: Assenmacher (Ger)
PARMA: Ballotta, Benarrivo, Di Chiara, Minotti, Apolloni, Grun, Zoratto (Pin 25), Cuoghi, Osio (Pizzi 65), Melli, Brolin.
ANTWERP: Stojanovic, Brockaert, Taeymans, Smidts, Van Rethy, Segers (Moukrim 85), Kiekens, Jakovljevic (Van Veirdeghem 57), Lehnoff, Severeyns, Czerniatynski.

1993–94

SEMI-FINALS

Arsenal bt Paris Saint-Germain 1–1, 1–0
(2–1 agg)
Parma bt Benfica 1–2, 1–0
(away goals, 2–2 agg)

FINAL

May 4 (Parkstadion, Copenhagen)
Arsenal 1 (Smith 19)
Parma 0
HT: 1–0. Att: 33,765. Ref: Krondl (Cze)
ARSENAL: Seaman, Dixon, Winterburn, Davis, Bould, Adams, Campbell, Morrow, Smith, Merson (McGoldrick 86), Selley.
PARMA: Bucci, Benarrivo, Di Chiara, Minotti, Apolloni, Sensini, Brolin, Pin (Melli 70), Crippa, Zola, Asprilla.

1994–95

SEMI-FINALS

Real Zaragoza bt Chelsea 3–0, 1–3
(4–3 agg)
Arsenal bt Sampdoria 3–2, 2–3
(3–2 on pens, 5–5 agg)

FINAL

May 10 (Parc des Princes, Paris)
Real Zaragoza 2 (Esnaider 68, Nayim 119)
Arsenal 1 (Hartson 77)
HT: 0–0. 90min: 1–1. After extra time. Att: 42,424. Ref: Ceccarini (Ita)
ZARAGOZA: Cedrun, Belsue, Solana, Caceres, Aragon, Nayim, Aguado, Poyet, Esnaider, Higuera (Garcia Sanjuan 66; Geli 114), Pardeza.
ARSENAL: Seaman, Dixon, Schwarz, Winterburn (Morrow 47), Adams, Linighan, Keown (Hillier 46), Parlour, Merson, Wright, Hartson.

1995–96

SEMI-FINALS

Paris Saint-Germain bt Deportivo La Coruna 1–0, 1–0
(2–0 agg)
Rapid Vienna bt Feyenoord 1–1, 3–0
(4–1 agg)

FINAL

May 8 (King Baudouin, Brussels)
Paris Saint-Germain 1 (N'Gotty 28)
Rapid Vienna 0
HT: 1–0. Att: 37,500. Ref: Pairetto (Ita)
PSG: Lama, Roche, Le Guen, N'Gotty, Fournier (Llacer 76), Bravo, Guerin, Colleter, Djorkaeff, Loko, Rai (Dely Valdes 11).
RAPID: Konsel, Hatz, Ivanov, Schttel, Heraf, Guggi, Stger, Khbauer, Marasek, Jancker, Stumpf (Barisic 46).

1996–97

SEMI-FINALS

Barcelona bt Fiorentina 1–1, 2–0
(3–1 agg)
Paris Saint-Germain bt Liverpool 3–0, 0–2
(3–2 agg)

FINAL

May 14 (Feyenoord, Rotterdam)
Barcelona 1 (Ronaldo 37 pen)
Paris Saint-Germain 0
HT: 1–0. Att: 50,000. Ref: Merk (Ger)
BARCELONA: Vitor Baia, Ferrer, Fernando Couto, Abelardo, Sergi, Popescu (Amor 46), Guardiola, Figo, de la Pena (Stoichkov 85), Luis Enrique (Pizzi 89), Ronaldo.
PARIS S-G: Lama, Fournier (Algerino 58), N'Gotty, Le Guen. Domi, Leroy, Guerin (Dely Valdes 68), Rai, Cauet, Loko (Pouget 78), Leonardo.

1997–98

SEMI-FINALS

Chelsea bt Vicenza 0–1, 3–1
(3–2 agg)
Stuttgart bt Lokomotiv Moscow 2–1, 1–0
(3–1 agg)

FINAL

May 13 (Rasunda, Stockholm)
Chelsea 1 (Zola 71)
Stuttgart 0
HT: 0–0. Att: 30,216. Ref: Braschi (Ita)
CHELSEA: De Goey, Petrescu**, Clarke, Leboeuf, Duberry, Granville, Poyet (Newton 80), Wise*, Di Matteo, Flo (Zola 71), Vialli
STUTTGART: Wohlfahrt, Yakin, Berthold, Hagner* (Ristic 78), Haber (Djordjevic 74), Schneider (Endress 55), Soldo, Poschner**, Balakov, Akpoborie, Bobic.
**Sent off : Petrescu 84 min, Poschner 90 min.

Sampdoria beat Anderlecht 2–0 to win the 1990 Cup-winners Cup

INTER-CITIES FAIRS/UEFA CUP

The competition now known as the UEFA Cup is, in origins, the oldest of the present trio of European club tournaments. It was the brainchild of the Swiss vice-president of FIFA, Ernst Thommen.

He first proposed in 1950 the creation of an international competition between clubs – or city select teams – from those cities which hosted industrial fairs.

Thommen found allies in top officials such as prospective FIFA president Sir Stanley Rous (who drafted the initial regulations) and Italy's Ottorino Barassi and they eventually launched their project – totally independently from the European Champion Clubs Cup – in 1955.

In April of that year, 12 representatives from European trade fair cities from 10 countries met in Basle to lay down the rules. They decided each city should be represented by a club or a city select team, or both – as long as no more than two teams competed simultaneously from any one city. It was also agreed the matches should be timed to coincide with the cities' trade fairs.

That was one reason why the first edition of the Industrial Inter-City Fairs Cup took three years to complete! Yet, oddly enough, it foreshadowed by nearly 40 years, the UEFA Champions League in that the first round of the first competition was organized in four mini-leagues. The group winners would qualify for two-leg knock-out semi-finals, followed by a two-leg final.

The first match took place on June 4, 1955, when Basle lost 5–0 at home to London, who went on to reach the semi-finals along with Barcelona, Lausanne and Birmingham City.

London's line-up was a fascinating mixture of players from across the capital including Tottenham's Ron Reynolds in goal, Chelsea's Peter Sillett at right-back, West Ham's Harry Hooper and Charlton's Bill Kiernan on the wings, with an inside forward trio of Johnny Haynes (Fulham), Cliff Holton (Arsenal) and Eddie Firmani (Charlton).

Alois Penning, of West Germany, was the referee in front of a 10,000 crowd who witnessed what remains a largely unremarked piece of history – the first substitute in a "modern" European club tie. He was Brian Nicholas who was between clubs – just about to leave Queens Park Rangers of the Third Division to join Chelsea. Nicholas, a Welshman from Aberdare, appeared in the 65th minute as a substitute for an injured future team-mate, Chelsea's Derek Saunders.

London won 5–0. Firmani scored the historic first goal after 35 minutes with the rest coming from Hooper and a first European club competition hat-trick for Holton.

The first home match ever played by a London team in a European competition was, interestingly, at Wembley. That was where the London select lost 2–0 to Frankfurt on October 26, 1955. A 35,000 crowd turned out to see a London team who included only two of the men who had made history in

Switzerland in June – full-backs Sillett and Dan Willemse. To add to the sense of historical fascination, the Frankfurt line-up included two players, in centre-forward Richard Kress and inside left Alfred Pfaff, who would re-enter football history in 1960 as senior members of the Eintracht Frankfurt side beaten 7–3 by Real Madrid in the most famous of Champions Cup finals at Hampden Park, Glasgow.

London had to wait until May 4, 1956, to play their next match, winning 1–0 at home to Basle with an 87th-minute goal from Tottenham left-winger George Robb. They lost their last group match 1–0 at Frankfurt almost a year later – on March 27, 1957 – but defeat was not enough to prevent them topping the group and qualifying for the semi-finals. London's ever-changing line-up this time included a West Ham half-back Malcolm Allison.

The semi-final draw saw London matched against Lausanne-Sports of Switzerland and Barcelona against Birmingham City.

Barcelona's cosmopolitan line-up included superstars of the era such as Hungary's Ladislao Kubala, Spain's Luis Suarez, Brazil's Evaristo de Macedo and Paraguayan striker Eulogio Martinez. Birmingham's only claim to fame was having reached the FA Cup Final in 1956, when they lost 3–1 to Manchester City.

Birmingham City won 4–3 in their home leg at St Andrew's and were within one minute of reaching the final after holding out bravely and efficiently in Barcelona. Then, with the referee looking to his watch and his linesman, Kubala snatched the goal which decided the match. Nowadays it would have been decisive for the tie as well – since Barcelona had scored three away goals. But such sophistications had not been built into the competition rules in those pioneering days. The clubs were level on aggregate so the organizing committee had decreed a play-off.

Neutral ground

It had to take place on neutral territory and was thus arranged for the Sankt-Jakob stadium in Basle, Switzerland. So evenly balanced were the sides they were level at 1–1 with the end of the match rapidly approaching. Then, just as in Barcelona, Kubala took the game into his own hands and scored the tie-breaker. This time his goal did send Barcelona through to the final.

The other semi-final saw the London XI face Lausanne – the one and only time that this particular Swiss club have ever reached a European semi-final.

The first leg was played in Switzerland and saw Lausanne win 2–1 with two goals from their World Cup inside forward Roger

Vonlanthen. London replied through Arsenal's little Irish left-winger, Joe Haverty. His reward was to be omitted from the return, even though the second leg was staged at Highbury – on October 23, 1957. A crowd of only 16,723 saw Chelsea's teenage wonder Jimmy Greaves square the aggregate after 10 minutes and Holton win match and tie with a second London goal a quarter of an hour from the end.

The first leg of the final between London and Barcelona was staged at Chelsea's Stamford Bridge on March 5, 1958. The choice of venue was hugely ironic since Chelsea had been barred by the Football League from entering the inaugural European Champion Clubs Cup in 1955–56. Quite why a London XI was permitted, simultaneously, to enter the Fairs Cup remains a mystery ... until one realises Sir Stanley Rous, general secretary of the Football Association, was also a leading light behind the launch of the Fairs Cup. Also, the Fairs Cup was seen in those days as an event for international representative teams rather than specific clubs.

Barcelona borrowed several players from neighbours Espanyol for early matches while Basle relied almost entirely on FC Basle. The Frankfurt team which played London was more of a regional selection – including players not only from FSV Frankfurt, Eintracht Frankfurt and Kickers Offenbach.

Barcelona took a seventh-minute lead in the first leg of the final through Spanish international right-winger Justo Tejada who would later become one of only a handful of players to transfer from the Catalan giants to their hated domestic rivals Real Madrid. The lead stood for only three minutes before Greaves delighted the 45,466 home fans with a typically opportunist equaliser. Barcelona seized the lead again through Paraguayan Eulogio Martinez after 35 minutes and thought they had the match won until West German referee Albert Dusch – both his linesman, incidentally, were English – awarded London an 88th-minute penalty which Fulham's Jim Langley converted.

Dusch was also the referee for the return in Barcelona's wonderful new Nou Camp stadium on May 1, 1958. A capacity crowd of 70,000 turned out. London fielded a strong side including Arsenal goalkeeper Jack Kelsey, left-half Dave Bowen, inside forwards Vic Groves and Jimmy Bloomfield plus Tottenham's Danny Blanchflower, Terry Medwin and Bobby Smith.

But they were no match for the Catalans. Barcelona had made a significant change compared with the first leg, bringing in a home-grown inside left named Luis Suarez who would shine brighter than almost all the cosmpolitan stars hired by the club down the years. Suarez struck twice in the first eight minutes and, as they tried to chase the match and the tie, so London were sliced apart on the break.

Martinez made it 3–0 just before half-time. In the second half, Barcelona doubled the score through wing-half Martin Verges and two goals from Brazilian centre-forward Evaristo. They won 6–0 on the day, 8–2 on aggregate. Almost three years after it began, the first edition of the Industrial Inter-Cities Fairs Cup had been completed.

The organizing committee agreed the second edition of the tournament should be kept to a tighter schedule and thus decided to drop the mini-leagues first round in favour of a direct elimination format after the manner of the Champions Cup which was, by now, a roaring success. Invitations were issued again and entries received from an increased number of 16 cities. In most cases, these volunteered their senior club side to represent them in preference to a city select team. The Fairs Cup committee was reluctant to go down this path, fearing it meant a watering-down of the original concept. But fixture practicalities meant it was inevitable.

Multiple cup entries

This also meant that, for the first and only time, it was possible to find clubs competing simultaneously in two European club competitions – an option which UEFA would later deny clubs. By the 1990s, UEFA's strategy of dictating fixture dates for the various rounds of the competitions meant dual representation would be impossible.

Thus the 1958–60 Fairs Cup entry included Barcelona and Red Star Belgrade who would also be competing, in 1959–60, in the Champions Cup. Dinamo Zagreb competed in the Champions Cup in 1958–59. The 1958–60 Fairs Cup also saw the European club debut of Internazionale, of Milan, who marked their arrival with a 7–0 first round thrashing of French club Lyon. England again had two entries – Birmingham City thanks to their semi-final progress in 1955–58 and Chelsea. The Stamford Bridge club represented London and thus achieved some sort of amends for their failure to take up the preferred place in the original Champions Cup, in 1955–56.

Chelsea got off to a successful start, with a 3–1, 4–1 win over Frem Copenhagen, but fell to Belgrade in the quarter-finals.

Ultimately Barcelona, coached by the legendary Helenio Herrera, won the Fairs Cup again and without losing a match. Their team was even better now. Just as Real Madrid had strengthened their attack with Ferenc Puskas, so Barcelona had gained from the tragedy of the Hungarian revolution. The persuasive powers of Ladislav Kubala had led to Barcelona signing two of the stars of the magical Magyars team of the early 1950s, in inside right Sandor Kocsis and left-winger Zoltan Czibor.

In the first round, Barcelona beat Basle 2–1, 5–2, in the quarter-finals they thrashed Inter 4–2, 4–0 and in the semi-finals they won 3–1 in Belgrade, then drew the return 1–1.

For the second successive final, Barcelona were matched against Birmingham City – a comparatively forgotten English football success story. In later years, from the way the history of English clubs in Europe is recounted, one would almost think that

Manchester United and Liverpool set the trend. In fact, it was the Midlands clubs such as Wolverhampton Wanderers in the Champions Cup and Birmingham City in the Fairs Cup who consolidated the interest originally aroused by Manchester United.

To reach their second Fairs Cup Final, Birmingham won 2–2, 2–0 against Cologne, 1–0, 3–3 against Zagreb and 4–2, 4–2 against Belgian club Union St-Gilloise.

The first leg of the final was played on March 29, 1960, at St Andrew's. A heavy pitch assisted Barcelona's defensive efforts and that, along with the fine form of international goalkeeper Antonio Ramallets, meant the 90 minutes ended goalless. But there was no doubting Barcelona's command of the return which they won 4–1, with goals from Eugelio Martinez, Czibor (two) and Coll. Birmingham's consolation was provided by Harry Hooper – who had played for London in the first Fairs Cup.

The 1960–61 Fairs Cup again featured 16 teams but this time was tightened further to one season, so as to fall in line with the Champions Cup and the newly-created Cup-winners Cup. Barcelona returned to defend the trophy while simultaneously taking up their right, as Spanish champions, to enter the Champions Cup. In the Champions Cup, they eliminated five-times champions Real Madrid while, in the Fairs Cup, they progressed with a 1–1, 4–3 victory over Zagreb.

The pressures of competing in all directions proved ultimately too much when Barcelona came up against Hibernian of Edinburgh in the Fairs Cup quarter-finals. Barcelona had beaten Hibs 5–1 in a pre-season friendly but were complacent going into the first leg in Spain. It finished in a 4–4 draw while the return in Scotland ended in a 3–2 win for the hosts. It was a stormy old night, however, with Barcelona's players losing their tempers. West German referee Johannes Malka famously complained, later: "If I have to referee Barcelona again then I shall wear spikes and carry a gun."

The semi-finals saw Hibernian drawn against Roma and Internazionale matched with Birmingham City. Roma had beaten Fairs Cup regulars Union St-Gilloise in the first round and Cologne in a quarter-final play-off, in Rome. When the two teams finished level on aggregate after the second leg, they tossed for host rights for the play-off and the Italians came up winners.

As for Inter, they rattled 14 goals past West German club Hannover 96 in the first round, winning 8–2, 6–1, before beating Belgrade 5–0, 1–1. Intriguingly, looking back, they proved no match for Birmingham in the semi-finals – the English club winning 2–1 in the San Siro stadium in Milan, and back at St Andrew's, to reach their second successive final.

Their opponents were Roma who, after beating Cologne in a quarter-final play-off, had been taken to another extra tie in the semi-finals by Hibernian. The clubs drew 2–2 in Edinburgh and 3–3 in Rome. Roma won the right to stage a play-off and thrashed the Scots 6–0. Their new Argentine centre-forward, Pedro Manfredini, scored four goals.

The haphazard nature of these early European competitions, and the Fairs Cup in particular, was evidenced from the fact Birmingham did not play Roma in the final until the autumn. St Andrew's staged the first leg on September 27, when the teams played out a 2–2 draw – Mike Hellawell and Brian Orritt's goals being matched by strikes from Manfredini.

The return was played in the Olympic stadium in Rome on October 11 – well after the new season's competitions had begun. Brian Farmer put through his own goal for the first strike, Pestrin made it 2–0. Roma thus won 4–2 on aggregate and became the first Italian winners of a competition which that countries' teams would come to dominate in the 1990s.

Clean sweep for 'keeper

Roma goalkeeper Fabio Cudicini would, in due course, become the first player to win all three European club competitions. Cudicini later joined Milan and won, with them, the Cup-winners Cup in 1968 and the Champions Cup in 1969. Oddly enough, he was never considered good enough to merit selection for the Italian national team.

Already, the general pattern of the early years of the European club competitions had been set: Latin Europe – Italy, Portugal and Spain – had the dominant clubs in Europe. English clubs had a lot to learn while West Germany, only just about to launch itself into a unified league and full-time professionalism, had much ground to make up.

The excellent record of Barcelona in the three editions of the Fairs Cup played thus far persuaded the Spanish federation to press for UEFA to permit an expanded entry into the Fairs Cup. Thus, in 1961–62, Spain sent Valencia, Barcelona and Espanyol into the Fairs Cup. An increasing interest in European competition in general, and the Fairs Cup in particular, meant an expansion of the event to 28 teams, thus providing an extra round of competition.

The 1961 runners-up, Birmingham City, were eliminated in the second round this time by Espanyol who themselves lost to Red Star Belgrade in the quarter-finals. Thus, the semi-finals matched Spain against Eastern Europe with Red Star drawn against Barcelona and MTK Budapest paired with Valencia. Spanish domination was never in doubt. Valencia – who scored a Fairs Cup record of 26 goals – thrashed MTK 3–0, 7–3 while Barcelona brushed aside Red Star 6–1 on aggregate.

Barcelona went into the final as favourites, thanks to their competitive experience and despite the sale the previous year of Luis Suarez to Internazionale and the retirement of Kubala. But Valencia, at home in the first leg, had other ideas. They had already eliminated Nottingham Forest, Lausanne and Internazionale – then coached by Helenio Herrera – as well as MTK in the semi-finals and had no intention of letting "mere" Spanish opposition upset them. Thus they ran out 6–2 winners. Vicente Guillot scored a hat-trick for Valencia while Kocsis claimed the two consolation goals for a thoroughly shell-shocked Barcelona.

Kocsis and Guillot again shared the honours for their respective clubs as the return ended in a 1–1 draw before 60,000 in Nou Camp. Valencia had won their first European trophy, 7–3 on aggregate.

In the 1962–63 Fairs Cup, the full quota of 32 teams was taken up for the first round though, to Valencia's irritation, there was no automatic pass through the first round for the holders. Thus, they set out on what became a Scottish campaign. In the first round, Valencia beat Celtic 4–2, 2–2, in the second round they saw off Dunfermline 1–0 in a play-off in Lisbon, and in the quarter-finals they disposed of Hibernian. The Dunfermline tie was remarkable. The Scots, managed by future Scotland boss Jock Stein, lost 4–0 in Spain but recovered remarkably to win 6–2 at East End Park – before losing the play-off.

In the semi-finals, Valencia beat former champions Roma and thus qualified to face Dinamo Zagreb – then from Yugoslavia – who had become the first eastern European side to reach one of the club finals. Dinamo, later to become FC Croatia after the Balkan troubles of the early 1990s, had beaten Porto, Union St-Gilloise, Bayern Munich and Ferencvaros on their way to the final. But, once there, they proved no match for Valencia.

Goals from Brazilians Waldo and Urtiaga brought Valencia a 2–1 victory in Zagreb which was extended by a 2–0 home success in the return. Mano and Nunez scored the goals in the Mestalla stadium.

Valencia very nearly made it a hat-trick in 1963–64, when the Fairs Cup once again produced an all-Spanish final. Valencia squeezed through to their third successive final with a series of narrow victories over Shamrock Rovers, Rapid Vienna, Ujpest Dozsa and Cologne.

Spanish superiority

British clubs had a sorry time of it. Hearts lost to Lausanne in the first round after a play-off while Arsenal, Sheffield Wednesday and Partick Thistle all went out in the second round.

Zaragoza, the challengers to Valencia in the final, thrashed Iraklis of Salonika and Lausanne, then did well to beat Juventus 3–2, 0–0 in the quarter-finals. FC Liege provided sterner opposition in the semi-finals. Zaragoza lost 1–0 away, won 2–1 at home and then – again in their own La Romareda – won the play-off 2–0.

Since two Spanish clubs had qualified for the final, and Spain was also playing host that summer to the finals of the European Championship, it was decided to stage a one-off decider in Barcelona. Valencia were favourites but, in front of 50,000 in Nou Camp, Zaragoza won 2–1. The Spanish media nicknamed

their forward line of Canario, Duca, Marcelino, Juan Villa and Carlos Lapetra, the Cincos Magnificos – the Magnificent Five. Indeed, they were magnificent in that era: Canario had been a member of Real Madrid's 1960 Champions Cup-winning side, while Marcelino and Lapetra starred in the Spanish team who won the 1964 European Championship.

By 1964–65, the Fairs Cup had become highly popular. Also, it had nothing to do with industrial trade fairs any longer but formed an opportunity for continental competition for top clubs who had missed out on the right of entry into the other European competitions. For this season, 48 clubs claimed the right of entry which caused chaos as the competition unfolded. The second round involved 24 teams, the third round 12 teams, the quarter-finals six ... thus Juventus and Atletico Madrid drew byes into the semi-finals. It should be noted it was this season's competition, with its extended draw, which pushed the Fairs Cup rapidly down the expansionist path which led, for years, to the Fairs, then UEFA Cup boasting one more round than the other European competitions.

The financial options available proved highly attractive. As far on as 1998, Stuttgart were consoling themselves – after their defeat by Chelsea in the Cup-winners Cup Final – that at least their guaranteed fallback place in the following season's UEFA Cup would prove more lucrative than a Cup-winners' defence.

Manchester United's Scotland star Denis Law was top scorer in the 1964–65 Fairs Cup with eight goals, but that did not prove quite good enough against Hungary's Ferencvaros in the semi-finals. United, who had beaten Djurgarden of Sweden, Borussia Dortmund and Strasbourg, won 3–2 at home, lost 1–0 away then went down again 2–1 in the play-off, in Budapest.

In the final, Ferencvaros had to play a Juventus side who had scored more than one goal only once (and then they scored only twice) in their seven games up to the semi-finals. Here they exerted themselves to beat Atletico Madrid 3–1 in a play-off, in Turin. But the one-off final against Ferencvaros, also in Turin, proved a disaster. Juventus lost 1–0 in front of their own fans. A goal from Dr Mate Fenyvesi, Ferencvaros' outstanding and long-serving left-winger, turned the Hungarians into eastern Europe's first trophy winners in any of the three club competitions.

In 1965–66, the Fairs Cup organizing committee got the system right. Once again, 48 clubs entered but this time all the byes necessary were handed out in the first round so as to produce an even knock-out system from the second round. The fact the competition was organized under UEFA auspices, but not by UEFA, meant a number of disciplinary flashpoints were not being dealt with properly –leading to an increasing number of incidences of violence on the pitch and terraces.

Spain v England was the theme of the semi-finals with Leeds United drawn against Zaragoza and Chelsea matched with Barcelona. Leeds, managed by Don Revie, were building the

Chelsea's Peter Osgood heads for goal against Milan at Stamford Bridge. Chelsea won 2–1 to take the tie to a replay

reputation for hard-edged success which would earn them so much respect but so little love. They lost only 1–0 in Zaragoza, won "only" 2–1 at home but remained favourites after winning the toss of the coin for the play-off. Zaragoza rose to the occasion gloriously, however, winning 3–1 at Elland Road thanks to a spell of three goals in 13 unlucky – for Leeds –minutes.

Chelsea also fell after a play-off. This was harsh, but then luck had smiled on them in the third round when the toss of a coin went their way after they drew 1–1 with Milan in a San Siro play-off. Chelsea then beat 1860 Munich in the quarter-finals to earn the duel with Barcelona. Each club won their home leg 2–0 but Barcelona, with French midfield general Lucien Muller outstanding, thrashed the Londoners 5–0 in the play-off in Spain.

This time, despite the all-Spanish nature of the final and despite it being World Cup year, Zaragoza and Barcelona decided against a one-off game. The two-leg final was postponed to September when Barcelona lost 1–0 at home to a strike from Canario. They appeared dead and buried at 2–0 down in the second leg but stormed back to lead 3–2 after the completion of the regulation 90 minutes. Striker Pujol then completed his hat-trick 30 seconds before the end of extra time and Barcelona thus clinched their third Fairs Cup success 4–3 on aggregate.

Not that Barcelona's reign was a long one. Little more than six weeks after beating Zaragoza their defence was over – ended by Dundee United who won 2–1 in Barcelona and 2–0 in Scotland. Nor did the other Spanish challengers put up a better fight. Valencia made the furthest progress, but were eliminated in the third round. Seville and Athletic Bilbao went out in the first round.

No-one enjoyed their successes for long. Dundee United's joy at beating Barcelona was quickly brought to a halt by Juventus who then succumbed to their East European jinx as they fell to Dinamo Zagreb. The Yugoslavs appeared to be on their way out when they crashed 3–0 at Eintracht Frankfurt in the first leg of the semi-final but recovered to win the return 4–0 and enter the final against Leeds United.

Neutral ground

Leeds had put eight goals past DWS Amsterdam in the second round, beaten former holders Valencia 3–1 overall in the third round, squeezed past Italy's Bologna on the toss of a coin in the quarter-finals and easily defeated Kilmarnock 4–2 on aggregate in the semis. But the final, again, had to be postponed until the start of the following season and, by then, Leeds had gone off the boil. They lost the first, away leg by 2–0 and could only draw 0–0 at home.

That defeat only spurred Leeds on the following season. They fired 16 goals past Spora of Luxembourg in the first round then beat Partizan Belgrade, Hibernian, Rangers and Dundee to return to the final. Dundee had progressed by a comfortable route past DWS Amsterdam, FC Liege and FC Zurich. They put up brave resistance against Leeds but were held 1–1 at home and lost 1–0 at Elland Road.

Ferencvaros, the 1965 winners, beat Liverpool and Bilbao among others to reach the semi-finals where they met Bologna, whose reward for beating holders Dinamo Zagreb in the second round had been a third round bye. Bologna were just past their peak but remained a dangerous attacking unit courtesy of the skills of West German inside forward Helmut Haller. It was the more subtle skills of Hungarian Florian Albert which triumphed in the semi-final however – Ferencvaros winning 3–2, 2–2.

Yet again, the competition had dragged on for so long there was no time to fit the final into the end of the 1967–68 season so it was postponed to the start of the following term. Leeds determined that, this time, they would not be caught flat. The first leg was played on August 7, before the start of the English season and Leeds won by the narrowest of margins thanks to a goal from Mick Jones. By the time the return was played in Budapest, the Leeds defence had a month to settle into their stone-wall ways and confidently secured a goalless draw. Leeds manager Don Revie, at last, had his hands on a European trophy.

The conclusion of the Fairs Cup in 1968–69, also saw an Anglo-Hungarian tussle, between Newcastle United and Ujpest Dozsa. The Hungarians took revenge for Ferencvaros by defeating holders Leeds in the quarter-finals. They had no problems then reaching the final by defeating Goztepe Izmir 8–1 on aggregate.

Ujpest then faced another side who were newcomers to the European final stage in Newcastle. The Geordies had beaten the likes of Sporting Lisbon (previous winners of the Cup-winners Cup) and Zaragoza (previous winners of the Fairs Cup) on their way to a tension-packed semi-final against Rangers. The previous season, Rangers had been furious at losing to Leeds in the quarter-finals and did not take kindly to defeat by Newcastle, either. Newcastle forced a goalless draw at Ibrox then won 2–0 at home where angry Rangers fans ran amok towards the end of the game and forced a brief suspension of play. Newcastle went on to the final; for Rangers it was a sign of things to come.

The final was remarkable for the leadership example of Newcastle's Scotland left-half and captain Bobby Moncur. He had not scored in top-level competition for the club before, but in the first leg against Ujpest he netted twice to inspire a 3–0 win. Not only that, but Moncur forged forward to decisive effect in the return leg. Ujpest were 2–0 up and threatening to level

the aggregate when Moncur beat Hungary's World Cup keeper Antal Szantimihaly for a goal which punctured Hungarian ambition and inspired Newcastle's recovery for a 3–2 win. Newcastle manager Joe Harvey thus completed a remarkable cup double: he had captained the club to their 1951 FA Cup victory over Blackpool.

That victory was a historic one for another reason: the following season, the competition was formally renamed the Inter-Cities Fairs Cup, removing the "Industrial" label to bring some sort of honesty into the concept. The English command was not, however, to be shaken with Arsenal beating Belgium's Anderlecht in the final to collect their first major honour in 17 years.

Arsenal's emergence on the modern European club competition was long overdue since the club had been European pioneers back in the days of Herbert Chapman in the early 1930s. In 1930, for example, Chapman had very nearly become the first English club manager to buy a foreign professional. His target was Rudi Hiden, goalkeeper of Austria's so-called "Wunderteam", but the Ministry of Labour refused a work permit.

Arsenal into Europe... again

Thus Arsenal had to wait until the Fairs Cup season of 1969–70 to make their first successful "splash" in Europe. Bertie Mee was now manager of a team built around the talents of goalkeeper Bob Wilson, defenders Frank McLintock, Peter Simpson and Bob McNab and European survivors from 1963 such as Jon Sammels and George Graham in midfield plus John Radford, Charlie George and winger George Armstrong in attack.

Arsenal opened up with a 3–0 win over Northern Ireland's Glentoran. Goals from Graham (two) and future Wales manager Bobby Gould brought Highbury its first sight of a victorious Arsenal in European competition. Arsenal went on to win 3–1 on aggregate, dispose of Sporting Lisbon 3–0 overall in the second round, Rouen of France 1–0 in the third round and Dinamo Bacau of Romania 9–1 to reach the semi-finals and a duel with Ajax.

The previous season, Ajax had finished runners-up in the Champions Cup. Their prodigious, slimline centre-forward Johan Cruyff was attracting rave notices everywhere he appeared. His day against Arsenal would come – but not yet. Two goals in the last 13 minutes of the first leg from George and Sammels earned a 3–0 win at Highbury. Arsenal conceded an early strike to Gerrie Muhren in Amsterdam but their increasingly fearsome defence held tight for the rest of the 90 minutes.

In the final, Anderlecht were the neutrals' favourites. They had been competing in Europe since the mid-1950s and had, for much of the 1960s, provided the backbone of an excellent Belgian national team. Forward Paul Van Himst would ultimately be hailed as the greatest Belgian player of all time.

The first leg went according to the neutrals' plan. Dutchmen Jan Devrindt and Jan Mulder (twice) shot their Belgian employers into a 3–0 lead by the 76th minute. Then Mee gambled by introducing the young tyro, Ray Kennedy, as substitute for the tiring Graham. Within five minutes he had pulled one goal back – and a crucial goal it proved.

A 52,000 crowd packed Highbury to bursting for the return. Eddie Kelly, tireless in attack and defence, cracked the opening goal after 25 minutes. Radford scored a second and Sammels the aggregate winner in the 71st minute.

Arsenal, uncrowned kings of Europe under Chapman in the 1930s, had at last claimed an international trophy – 40 years on. More than that, they had forged the team spirit and confidence which would lift them, a year later, to win the prized English double of League and FA Cup.

Four in a row for England

In 1970–71, however, the pressure of a domestic fixture pile-up proved fatal to Arsenal's hopes of retaining the Fairs Cup. After overcoming Lazio – whose players set upon Arsenal's stars after the match – Sturm Graz and Belgium's Beveren, they fell to Cologne on away goals in the quarter-finals. Cologne were then well beaten – 3–1 on aggregate – by Juventus. The other semi-final was an all-English affair in which Leeds United defeated Liverpool 1–0, 0–0. Liverpool, remarkably, conceded only one goal in 10 matches – but that goal was scored by Leeds skipper Billy Bremner at Elland Road.

Leeds went on to beat Juventus in the final to secure England's fourth successive victory in the Fairs Cup. The first leg, in Turin, had to be abandoned after 60 minutes following torrential rain. No goals had been scored and the replay, two days later, also ended all-square, at 2–2. Roberto Bettega (future Juventus chief executive) and Fabio Capello (future Champions Cup-winning coach of Milan) scored for Juventus with play-anywhere Paul Madeley and Mick Bates responding for Leeds. The return also ended in a draw, Pietro Anastasi scoring for Juventus and Allan Clarke for Leeds who thus took the cup on away goals.

Now, belatedly, UEFA decided to exert its authority and take over over full control of the event from the Fairs Cup committee. The original trophy, named after Noel Beard, was put up for competition between first winners Barcelona and last winners Leeds. Three-times victors Barcelona, appropriately, won 2–1.

Confusion over entry regulations – the trade fair idea had quickly gone out of the window – and over disciplinary control had contributed towards the demise of the Fairs Cup in its old form. The European governing body's formal adoption of the event produced a new trophy and a new title – the UEFA Cup. Now entry was specifically allocated to highest-placed clubs who did not qualify for the Champions or Cup-winners Cup. In due

course, further checks and balances were introduced into the event. Clubs from the same country were barred from meeting one another until the quarter-finals until the late 1990s, when that was changed to the third round. Also, the 1990s saw the use of the UEFA coefficient to seed clubs and thus even out the draw.

The coefficient was created by adding together all notional points gained by clubs from one country in European competition over the previous five years (two for a win, one for a draw with bonus points for appearances in quarter-finals, semi-finals and finals) then dividing the total by the number of matches played. Countries could thus be ranked in terms of club success and the number of entry places into the UEFA Cup allocated accordingly. The most successful countries, such as Italy and Germany, receive four places while the minnows, such as Finland and Iceland, get one.

An expansion of the UEFA Cup to 100-plus clubs took place in the mid-1990s because of the additional pressure of demand from those in the countries created by the collapse of the Soviet Union and the former Yugoslavia. The redeveloped UEFA Cup also permitted the entry of three clubs through the pools-based summer competition, the Intertoto Cup. Further places were awarded, as a bonus, to the three nations whose teams had the best fair-play record in European international competition. England was a notable beneficiary of this concession, regularly gaining an extra UEFA Cup place to lift its representation from three to four.

The new UEFA Cup was formally launched in 1971–72 and brought no obvious change in the balance of power. English clubs not only maintained their grip on the prize but enhanced their right to be considered Europe's No 1 at club level by providing both finalists in Tottenham Hotspur and Wolverhampton Wanderers.

Spurs defeated Keflavik of Iceland, 15–1 on aggregate, Nantes of France, Rapid and UT Arad of Romania, then Milan in the semi-finals. The tie against Keflavik was notable for the one and only appearance in a Spurs shirt for a homesick teenager named Graeme Souness who, shortly afterwards, abandoned London to make his way in the game at Middlesbrough.

Wolves' fans were thrilled to see their team successful once more in Europe where the club had blazed a trail in its famous floodlit friendlies of the early 1950s against Honved, Moscow Spartak and Real Madrid and in its early Champions Cup adventures. Old heroes such as Billy Wright, Peter Broadbent and Jimmy Murray had been succeeded by the likes of Derek Dougan and Mike Bailey – Dougan finishing top scorer in the 1972–73 UEFA Cup with nine goals.

Wolves opened up by defeating Academica Coimbra of Portugal then Ado Den Haag of Holland. Both victories were by 7–1 on aggregate and the success over the Dutchmen was notable for the fact Den Haag conceded three own goals at Molineux – one by Dick Advocaat who later went on to earn more respectable fame as manager of the Dutch national side who reached the 1994 World Cup quarter-finals. Carl Zeiss Jena fell in the third round then Juventus of Italy in a controversial quarter-final.

Wolves did well to force a 1–1 draw in Turin, in the first leg, after which Juventus lost interest. They were neck and neck with neighbours Torino in the race for the Italian League and considered that much more important than the UEFA Cup. Thus they fielded a weakened team in the return yet still lost only 2–1, largely thanks to the inspirational performance of veteran German Helmut Haller, recalled from the substitutes' bench. The end, incidentally, did ultimately justify the means as far as Juventus were concerned since they did win the Italian title a few months later ... finishing one point clear of Milan and Torino.

As for Wolves, they beat Ferencvaros of Hungary 2–2, 2–1 in the semi-finals to set up the all-English final.

The first leg was at Molineux where Spurs gambled on skipper Alan Mullery, who had missed half the season through injury, to vital effect. He gave a typically dominating display in midfield, England leader Martin Chivers scored twice and Spurs drove home through the night with a 2–1 victory to celebrate. Left-winger David Wagstaffe opened the scoring in the return to keep Wolves in the tie, but Mullery – with a spectacular diving header – pulled Spurs back on terms and ahead on aggregate. Tottenham thus won a second European trophy, to add to the Cup-winners Cup they had collected in 1963.

English clubs had won the Fairs/UEFA Cup for five successive years and Liverpool made it six in 1973. But, along the way, came a warning of a turn in the club tide from West Germany and, specifically, from Borussia Mönchengladbach. Theorist coach Hennes Weisweiler had started building a team using a tactic called "pressing" which lifted the level of technical pace within a game and placed much higher demands on the need not only to possess the ball but to possess space. Weisweiler wanted

Bill Shankly's reward for his 1973 UEFA Cup gamble

players who could be considered football intellectuals and it was thus surely no accident that Berti Vogts went on to become Germany's European Championship-winning coach, Rainer Bonhof his highly-regarded assistant, Gunter Netzer a formidable manager and agent and Jupp Heynckes the Champions Cup-winning coach of Real Madrid.

Not that they did not suffer a number of defeats in gaining the necessary experience, one of the most painful being at the hands of Liverpool in final of the 1972–73 UEFA Cup.

Liverpool, managed by Bill Shankly with the wise assistance of Bob Paisley and further bootroom support of Joe Fagan and Ronnie Moran, were approaching the peak of their powers with the complementary talents of Kevin Keegan and John Toshack the key to their attacking success. Not that Shankly considered Toshack a regular first-choice. Indeed, for the first leg of the final he left him on the sidelines. But the match had to be abandoned because of a waterlogged pitch and that proved disastrous for Borussia. Shankly saw how vulnerable they looked in the air and brought in Toshack for the replay, the next day. Toshack's height caused chaos, Keegan scored twice and Liverpool won 3–0.

The advantage proved decisive. Borussia, using the Rheinstadion in Düsseldorf as their home ground for big matches rather than their own restrictive Bokelberg, played superbly ... but won "only" 2–0 with both goals falling to Heynckes. Liverpool had collected their first UEFA Cup and would repeat their victory over Borussia four years later on the even more prestigious stage of the Champions Cup Final itself, in Rome.

Liverpool did not return to defend the UEFA Cup in 1972–73. They had won the English league title the previous season and thus abandoned the UEFA Cup for the challenge of the Champions Cup. In their absence, English football lost its grip on the trophy after five long, happy years. Tottenham did reach the final for the second time in three seasons but the occasion did not provide happy memories – quite the reverse.

This was the season when Real Madrid, then six-times former champions of Europe, made their debut in the UEFA Cup. It was not an auspicious one since they lost to Bobby Robson's Ipswich Town, one of the up-and-coming forces of the European scene. Ipswich went on to beat Lazio – amid more bad-tempered Italian provocation – and Holland's Twente Enschede. They then lost to Lokomotive Leipzig – and the East Germans were duly beaten by Tottenham.

In the final, Spurs faced Feyenoord of Rotterdam, back in a European final for the second time in four seasons. Feyenoord brought serious pedigree to the event since they had, in 1970, become the first Dutch club to win the Champions Cup. Their midfield general, Wim Van Hanegem, had steered them to that success and was their outstanding figure in the first leg against Spurs – supported as he was by the hard-working Theo De Jong and Wim Jansen.

Spurs went ahead twice but each time Feyenoord levelled.

Wales centre-half Mike England scored first, only for Van Hanegem to equalise with a strike from outside the penalty box. In the second half, Van Daele put through his own net then De Jong equalised. Spurs were up against it going to the Rotterdam stadium even though Van Hanegem was ruled out by suspension. But it was not only Spurs' players who could not cope – neither could their fans. The match score finished 2–0, with defender Wim Rijsbergen and right-winger Peter Ressel scoring for Feyenoord; the arrests score finished at 70 with 200 fans hurt.

Spurs fans were blamed from all quarters for starting a riot during the game despite pleas over the public address system for calm from chairman Sydney Wale before the kick-off and from manager Bill Nicholson at half-time. Nicholson told the crowd: "You hooligans are a disgrace to Tottenham Hotspur and a disgrace to England. This is a football game – not a war." Unfortunately, his words went unheeded, in Rotterdam and down the succeeding decade.

UEFA Cup to World Cup

As for Feyenoord's heroes, a few weeks later Van Hanegem, Rijsbergen, De Jong and Jansen were all starring in the Dutch side who reached the World Cup Final in Munich.

The West German side who won the World Cup in 1974 had been built around a nucleus from Bayern Munich and Borussia Mönchengladbach who carried off the Champions Cup and UEFA Cup respectively the following season, 1974–75. England, hitherto so dominant in the competition, this time managed to provide only one team in the third round. Ipswich, Stoke and Wolves all crashed out at the first hurdle, leaving Derby County. The Rams defeated Servette of Geneva and Atletico Madrid, the previous season's Champions Cup runners-up, before falling to Velez Mostar of Yugoslavia.

Ipswich lost on away goals to little-known Dutch side Twente Enschede, from whom they would later buy two of the finest players in their history, midfielders Arnold Muhren and Frans Thijssen. Twente may have been fortunate but their momentum took them all the way to the final via further successes against Belgium's RWD Molenbeek, the Czechoslovak army side Dukla Prague, Velez Mostar and then, best of all, Juventus. Remarkably, Twente beat Juventus both home and away but that achievement failed to intimidate Borussia Mönchengladbach in the final.

Weisweiler's men had beaten Innsbruck, Lyon, Zaragoza, Banik Ostrava and Cologne. They were now missing Gunter Netzer in midfield after his transfer to Real Madrid in the summer of 1974. But Weisweiler felt they were all the better for that since Netzer had, he felt, tended to hold up play. It did not look like it in the first leg of the final, in Düsseldorf, when Twente held the Germans goalless. But the return in Holland was a different matter. Heynckes scored a hat-trick, taking his total to 11 for the campaign, and the brilliant little Dane, Allan Simonsen, grabbed two more. Borussia won 5–1 and Weisweiler, about to leave for an ill-fated spell at Barcelona, was carried in triumph on his players' shoulders.

Liverpool brought English football back to the fore in 1975–76 after a superb season in which they also won the English League as the springboard for Champions Cup success. Oddly, Liverpool beat Club Brugge in the final just as they would beat them in the 1978 Champions Cup Final. Similarly, of course, they beat Borussia Mönchengladbach in the final of both competitions.

Bob Paisley's men got off to bad start, losing at Hibernian but they recovered happily enough at Anfield thanks to a hat-trick from Wales centre forward John Toshack. They then saw off Real Sociedad, Slask Wroclaw of Poland and Dynamo Dresden and, in the semi-finals, met up with old rival Hennes Weisweiler again, this time in his role as coach of Barcelona. The Catalans had achieved a curious victory over Lazio of Italy in the second round – the Italians losing 4–0 at home then refusing to travel to Spain for the return, fearing political demonstrations.

In the semi-final, Keegan created the only goal of the game for Toshack in the first leg in Nou Camp and Weisweiler duly paid for defeat with his job. Without him, Barcelona forced a 1–1 draw at Anfield in the return but it was not enough.

Brugge were waiting in the final – having recovered brilliantly from being three-down in an earlier round against Ipswich and having squeezed past Hamburg 1–1, 1–0 in the semi-finals.

The Belgians took the first half of the final, at Anfield, by the scruff of the neck. Liverpool were not used to teams attacking them in front of their own fans and found themselves two-down within the opening 15 minutes to strikes from veteran spearhead Raoul Lambert and midfielder Julien Cools. Liverpool turned on their own brand of magic in the second half to score through Ray Kennedy, substitute Jimmy Case and Kevin Keegan, to win the match 3–2. Lambert scored again in the 11th minute of the second leg to pull Brugge level on aggregate and ahead on away goals. But four minutes later, Keegan struck back and Liverpool, with England's Ray Clemence superb in goal, held out for the 1–1 draw and 4–3 overall success.

Rare Italian victory

It was an odd feature of the history of the Fairs/UEFA Cup that almost the first two decades of the competition had seen only one Italian victory, and that was achieved by Roma back in the event's early years in 1961. All that changed in 1976–77, when Juventus took the prize which they had been denied on away goals in the last year of the old Fairs Cup in 1971. In a neat reversal of fortunes, they won it by the same method.

Liverpool were absent and the English representation enjoyed a mixed time of it. Both Manchester clubs qualified but in the first round, whereas United knocked out Ajax, City fell to Juventus – who then beat United. Queens Park Rangers, with Stan Bowles scoring 10 times, ran up a remarkable 23 goals in the first three rounds before losing to AEK Athens – who also eliminated Derby County.

Juventus coach Giovanni Trapattoni was putting together the nucleus of a team which would dominate Italian and, to a lesser extent, European football for much of the next 10 years. Dino Zoff was in goal, Claudio Gentile and Gaetano Scirea sealed up the heart of defence, Marco Tardelli and Franco Causio provided workrate and wisdom in midfield while Roberto Boninsegna and Roberto Bettega scored the goals. Apart from their Manchester double, they beat Shakhtyor Donctsk, Magdeburg and AEK on their way to the final against Athletic Bilbao.

This was the first time Bilbao had appeared in a European final and they were delighted to escape from Turin after the first leg with a 1–0 defeat, Tardelli having struck the decisive goal.

The Basque country was tense for the return. The political balance was changing in Spain and, after years of repression, the Basques were starting to demonstrate their independent spirit. The Bilbao football club was the heart of nationalist feeling and the security dared not challenge any longer the playing of the Basque anthem before matches and the display by the goalkeeper, Jose Iribar, of the Basque nationalist symbol on his jersey.

To reach the final, Bilbao had beaten Ujpest Dozsa, Basle, AC Milan and Johan Cruyff's Barcelona 2–1, 2–2 in the quarter-finals. Goals from international forwards Churruca and Dani earned Bilbao victory in their own "Catedral" of San Mames in the first leg; international midfielder Javier Irureta headed both their goals in the drawn return in Nou Camp.

In the semi-finals, they beat RWD Molenbeek of Belgium on away goals, drawing 1–1 in Belgium – Churruca again – and 0–0 at home. They were confident of overturning Juve's slender advantage in the second leg of the final. But luck turned against them after only nine minutes when Bettega scored in Juve's first attack. Experienced Austrian referee Erich Linemayr waved away Bilbao complaints that Bettega had been offside. Irureta and Carlos subsequently scored the goals which won the game for Bilbao – but they were not enough to win the tie.

The 1977–78 edition of the UEFA Cup was notable for the fact that neither finalist – French club Bastia from the Mediterranean island of Corsica or Holland's PSV Eindhoven – had appeared previously in a European club final. Bastia surprised their fellow Frenchmen as much as they surprised the rest of the Europe by winning both home and away against Sporting of Lisbon, Newcastle United and Torino of Italy in the first three rounds. Their hero was Dutch World Cup striker Johnny Rep whose pace on the break frightened the life out of opposition defenders. Having got thus far, Bastia duly benefited from the luck of the easier draw with the opportunities to beat

Carl Zeiss Jena of East Germany and Grasshopper of Switzerland in the quarter and semi-finals.

As for the other finalists, PSV Eindhoven, they were the fourth club from Holland to reach a European final – after Ajax, Feyenoord and Twente Enschede. They had signed Twente's star twins Willy and Rene Van der Kerkhof and, with skipper Willy Van der Kuylen outstanding in attacks, scored 29 goals on their way to the final. Here, veteran coach Kees Rijvers took no chances. Bastia's home ground of Furiani held only 15,000 fans but was notoriously intimidating. PSV sat in defence and held out for a goalless draw. Back in Holland, Bastia sank without trace, beaten 3–0. Four of PSV's key men – defenders Ernie Brandts and Jan Poortvliet as well as the Van der Kerkhofs – were World Cup runners-up with Holland in Argentina, a few weeks later.

UEFA coefficients

The 1978–79 season was the first in which UEFA introduced its coefficients system to help organize seeding. This had long been demanded by the big clubs who had grown impatient with the quirks of a lottery draw which often paired them against fellow "grandees" in the early rounds and thus allowed the minnows to make what they felt to be undeserved progress.

No such accusations could be levelled at the UEFA Cup this time round, as two class acts in Red Star Belgrade and Borussia Mönchengladbach reached the final. Borussia had maintained their success rate despite a modest budget which meant they had been unable to prevent the departures of stars such as Uli Stielike and Henning Jensen to Real Madrid. They managed, nevertheless, to complete the campaign unbeaten, defeating the likes of Benfica and a Manchester City reinforced by Poland's Kaziu Deyna along the way. In the semi-finals, Borussia overwhelmed fellow Germans MSV Duisburg 6–3 on aggregate with three goals from Simonsen.

As for Red Star, they beat Arsenal along the way with a last-minute goal from Savic at Highbury then defeated Hertha of West Berlin in the semi-finals, on away goals. The showdown was a disappointment despite being Borussia's fourth European final of the 1970s and the first by a Yugoslav team in a final since Dinamo Zagreb's 1967 Fairs Cup success. The first leg in Belgrade ended 1–1. In Düsseldorf, Borussia, already ahead on away goals, confirmed their victory with a penalty converted by European Footballer of the Year Simonsen.

West German success in the UEFA Cup meant it was represented by a record five clubs in 1979–80. Four of them reached the semi-finals, the only comparative failures being Kaiserslautern, eliminated in the quarter-finals by Bayern Munich. Borussia Mönchengladbach saw off Stuttgart in one semi-final while Eintracht Frankfurt thrashed Bayern out of the sight in the other. This Bayern was a mere shadow of the side who had won the Champions Cup three times in a row in the mid-1970s. There was no Sepp Maier in goal, no Beckenbauer or Schwarzenbeck in central defence, no Gerd Müller in attack. Uli Hoeness and Paul Breitner remained from the great days and they scored the goals which earned Bayern a 2–0 victory in the first, home leg. But Frankfurt were unstoppable in the return. Their inspiration was attacking sweeper Bruno Pezzey, the "Austrian Beckenbauer." He opened the scoring in the 31st minute then levelled the tie in the 87th minute, forcing extra time. Here, Frankfurt ran away with the match, to win 5–1 on the night.

No such drama in the other tie where Borussia lost 2–1 at Stuttgart then won 2–0 at home. Lothar Matthäus scored Borussia's first goal in the second leg and was on target again from midfield when Borussia beat Frankfurt 3–2 in the first leg of the final. Borussia appeared on course for yet another UEFA Cup celebration when they held Frankfurt goalless for most of the second leg. Then, in the 77th minute, Frankfurt coach Friedel Rausch sent on young international Fred Schaub as substutite for East German midfielder Norbert Nachtweih.

It was a gamble. Schaub was barely fit. He had missed the first half of the season through injury and had been banned for 10 weeks from domestic competition after a red card. But after just three minutes on the pitch, Schaub struck the only goal and Frankfurt took the Cup on away goals. The club whose greatest fame was earned in losing 7–3 to Real Madrid in the 1960 Champions Cup Final, had a European trophy of their own.

After two seasons of German rule, it was back to England for the UEFA Cup in 1980–81. Ipswich Town, a homespun team who had achieved improbable things under the managements of (later Sir) Alf Ramsey in the early 1960s, then Bobby Robson, collected the trophy after eight years on a European learning curve. Ipswich proved prolific marksmen, scoring five goals against Aris of Salonika, three against Bohemians of Prague, three against St Etienne and two – one home, one away – in the semi-finals against a Cologne side who had surprisingly beaten Barcelona 4–0 in Spain in the third round. Scotland midfielder John Wark was Ipswich's hero, scoring a then record 14 goals.

Opponents AZ'67 Alkmaar were similar to Ipswich, a small provincial club who had achieved success through shrewd coaching and scouting on the foundations of sensible business practices. They had an easier path to the final, beating Red Boys of Luxembourg, Levski Spartak Sofia, Radnicki Nis, of Yugoslavia, Belgium's Lokeren and Sochaux of France.

Two goals from Arnold Muhren and another from England striker Paul Mariner presented Ipswich with a 3–0 home victory in the first leg of the final. Alkmaar fought back courageously in the return, inspired by midfield general Johnny Metgod, who would later play in English football. But a 4–2 victory was not quite enough; Ipswich had got their hands on their one and only European prize.

Ipswich's success was proof of a general tightening of European football standards. The traditional big clubs no longer had things their own way. Any club which used its money sensibly, bought wisely, and invested in a thoughtful coach, could make not merely national but Continental progress. It was not only Ipswich and Alkmaar who proved the point but IFK Gothenburg who, in 1982, became the first Swedish club to win a European trophy when they landed the UEFA Cup.

IFK starred a number of players who went on to earn international reputations including central defender Glenn Hysen, Tord and Tommy Holmgren and Torbjorn Nilsson who was the UEFA Cup's nine-goal top scorer in 1981–82. They were welded into an exceptionally self-confident unit by coach Sven-Goran Eriksson who would later go on to greater things with Benfica, Roma, Fiorentina and Lazio.

Eriksson steered IFK not merely past the awkward hurdle of the Scandinavian winter shutdown but past Finland's Valkeakosken Haka, Austria's Sturm Graz, Dinamo Bucharest, Valencia and Kaiserslautern in the semi-finals. Waiting for IFK in the final were another West German side, Hamburg, former winners of the Cup-winners Cup and clear favourites.

Beckenbauer back

Hamburg had enjoyed a comparatively easy run to the final. Their squad included the veteran Franz Beckenbauer, who had returned from New York Cosmos for one last European season. Beckenbauer had hoped, with Hamburg, to complete a hat-trick since he had, with Bayern Munich, won the Champions and Cup-winners Cup. But he was out of luck. Not only did injury keep him out of the final against IFK but Hamburg lost it – 1–0 in Sweden and, most remarkably, 3–0 in front of their own fans.

IFK's success made coach Eriksson an instant target and he was immediately lured to Benfica, with whom he reached the UEFA Cup Final again the following season, 1982–83. Benfica had not appeared in a European final since losing to Manchester United in the Champions Cup at Wembley, in 1968. They were fortunate to beat Romania's Universitatea Craiova on away goals in the semi-finals but were favoured to beat Belgium's Anderlecht in the final. Eriksson and his men remained confident after losing only 1–0 at the Heysel stadium; Danish striker Kenneth Brylle scored the only goal after half an hour. But, back in Lisbon, Benfica lacked the necessary cutting edge and finished runners-up after being held 1–1.

Anderlecht returned to the final the following season – losing on penalties to Tottenham Hotspur – but were later the subject of the worst scandal to engulf the UEFA Cup. It was a scandal which would pursue the club, and inevitably the competition, for more than a decade.

The subject of controversy was Anderlecht's semi-final victory over English club Nottingham Forest.

In February 1997, Anderlecht's former president Constant Vanden Stock admitted having paid a total of around £350,000 to two agents to keep to themselves allegations that, on the club's behalf, one of them had bribed Spaniard Emilio Guruceta Muro, who refereed the second leg of the 1984 semi-final against Nottingham Forest. Anderlecht, who had lost 2–0 in Nottingham, won the return leg 3–0 after a controversial penalty brought them level on aggregate and a disallowed Forest goal.

It emerged Anderlecht had reported the blackmail matter in 1991 to the Belgian police and the Belgian federation. A report was sent to UEFA by Belgian federation president Michel D'Hooghe only to vanish, mysteriously. Only when the allegations of blackmail surfaced in the Belgian media, in 1997, did UEFA set up a commission of inquiry which eventually banned the club from European competition for a year.

Forest's Dutch goalkeeper at the time, Hans Van Breukelen, said: "I was always convinced we were cheated and that it was that Spanish referee who kept us out of the final. He was Anderlecht's 12th man."

Former Forest full back Kenny Swain, said: "I think there were about three minutes to go, the semi was tied 2–2 on aggregate and one of their players got in behind me. I turned to challenge, hardly made a contact and he went down like a ton of bricks. The referee gave a penalty and I couldn't believe it. Then, in the next minute, Paul Hart had a goal disallowed. I'll never forget it. Anderlecht were a good team on the night but those two late incidents stuck in our craw. "I can remember our manager Brian Clough having a moan about Spanish referees before the game and when we were getting changed for the match he insisted on our dressing-room door being kept open so he could check whether anybody paid a visit to the referee before the kick-off."

Central defender Hart, said: "I was convinced at the time and have never changed my mind that the referee was fixed for that game. We always suspected something, but could never prove it. Some of the decisions he gave against us – including disallowing my late goal that would have put us through to the final – were unbelievable."

When the matter emerged in the media, Anderlecht manager Michel Verschueren denied the club had tried to arrange for the referee to be bribed. He claimed Vanden Stock had been approached directly by Elst who told him the referee faced financial problems. Verschueren said: "He asked him if there was a way to help him." Two years later, Vanden Stock started paying the hush money out of his own personal account after he had been threatened with tape recordings of phone conversations. Anderlecht claimed the recordings had been rigged with remarks taken out of context.

Later, Elst claimed that in addition to the semi-final between Anderlecht and Forest, Anderlecht had also given him 100,000 Belgian francs with which to bribe the referee of a second-round tie in the UEFA Cup that season against Banik Ostrava. Anderlecht won 4–2 on aggregate, winning 2–0 and drawing 2–2. But Elst insisted his bribe attempt was rebuffed, saying: "The referee made it clear to me that Anderlecht should consider itself lucky that he would not report this request to UEFA."

No claim or inquiry could be laid against referee Guruceta, since he had been killed in a car crash in 1987. But Nottingham Forest joined their former players in a legal attempt to pursue compensation payments against Anderlecht for loss of revenue. Anderlecht protested that UEFA had flouted its own 10-year statute of limitations in taking disciplinary action and appealed to the Court of Arbitration for Sport in Lausanne.

In May 1998, in its first ruling on a major soccer dispute, the CAS overturned UEFA's ban on the grounds that "the UEFA executive committee was not competent to make a decision on the case." Instead, "considering the statutes and rules of UEFA, corruption matters should be dealt with by UEFA's legal committees."

Tottenham make it two

Back in 1984, the only club who thought memories of the UEFA Cup Final would linger on down the years were Tottenham, who won the competition for the second time by defeating Anderlecht in a penalty shoot-out at White Hart Lane. Spurs's unlikely hero – considering all the international keepers who had starred for them down the years, such as Ted Ditchburn, Bill Brown and Pat Jennings – was 21-year-old Tony Parks. Both legs had ended 1–1 and Graham Roberts scored with Spurs's first penalty attempt. Parks then handed Spurs the advantage by stopping Anderlecht's opener from veteran Dane, Morten Olsen. Mark Falco, Gary Stevens and Steve Archibald converted for Spurs; De Groote, Enzo Scifo and Frankie Vercauteren replied for the Belgians. Danny Thomas had the chance to win it for Spurs but nerves got the better of him, he shot weakly and Jacques Munaron saved. Spurs still led 4–3 as Iceland's Arnor

Juventus win at last – in 1977

Gudjohnsen prepared to take Anderlecht's last kick. He shot to the goalkeeper's right, Parks also guessed right and pushed the ball away. Spurs thus had another of their "glory, glory" European nights to celebrate.

This appeared to be the beginning of a great new era for Spurs. In fact, it was the beginning of the end. Manager Keith Burkinshaw had already signalled his intention to leave and ambitious chairman Irving Scholar's brave new world was soon to be swallowed up in controversy and financial problems. The following season, 1984–85, Spurs lost their grip on the UEFA Cup and a proud record of never having lost a European tie at White Hart Lane when they went down 1–0 in the quarter-finals to Real Madrid. A Steve Perryman own goal did the damage.

Real went on to win the UEFA Cup that season and the next. The 1985 success was their first European trophy since their sixth Champions Cup victory in 1966 at the tail-end of their most glorious era. The new generation of player of the mid-1980s came not from overseas – with the notable exception of free-scoring Mexican Hugo Sanchez – but from their own youth system. The so-called Quinta del Butre – the Vulture's Pack – housed striker Emilio Butragueno, midfielders Michel and Rafael Martin Vazquez and centre-back Manuel Sanchis. Add German sweeper Uli Stielike, Argentine forward Jorge Valdano and veteran spearhead Carlos Santillana and it was no wonder Real lorded it in the UEFA Cup for two years.

In the 1985 final, they beat Videoton of Hungary 3–1 on aggregate. Goals from Michel, Santillana and Valdano produced a 3–0 win in the first leg in Hungary. Oddly, Madrid lost the return in front of their own fans 1–0 but Lajos Majer's late goal went virtually unnoticed as the balloons and fireworks soared in delight over the Estadio Bernabeu.

Real's success in 1986 was the first time a UEFA/Fairs Cup-winner had successfully defended the crown since Valencia in 1963. Runners-up this time, in their first European final, were Cologne. Klaus Allofs became the competition's top scorer by netting his ninth goal of the campaign in the first leg of the final in Madrid, but keeper Toni Schumacher was beaten five times at the other end. Two goals in the last six minutes by Valdano and Santillana made all the difference between a reasonable defeat and a thrashing. Crowd trouble meant Cologne were barred from staging the return in the Mungersdorfer stadium so they took it to West Berlin's old Olympic stadium. Real lost 2–0 but carried off the trophy 5–3 on aggregate.

There was never any prospect of Real emulating their five-year command of the Champions Cup, in the UEFA Cup. As well as retaining the crown in 1986, they regained possession of the Spanish League and thus abdicated their UEFA Cup throne in 1986–87. Barcelona's bid to succeed their rivals failed when they lost, surprisingly, to Dundee United in the quarter-finals. The Scots overcame other former champions in the shape of Borussia Mönchengladbach in the semi-finals only to fall to IFK

Gothenburg in the final. Stefan Pettersson gave IFK a narrow advantage from the first leg in Sweden and Dundee United believed they were poised to join Celtic, Rangers and Aberdeen on Scotland's European role of honour. Instead, they were held 1–1 in front of their own fans at Tannadice and IFK carried the day 2–1 on aggregate. Dundee United's consolation was that their fans, generous in defeat, earned one of FIFA's prestigious annual fair play awards.

In 1988, for only the third time in the UEFA Cup, both finalists were new to such a rarefied stage of a European event. Bayer Leverkusen, supported by the Bayer chemical company, reached the final in undefeated style by defeating FK Austria, Toulouse, Feyenoord, Barcelona and Werder Bremen. Espanyol – the other Barcelona club – lost only once on their way to the final. Their victims included four former European club finalists in Borussia Mönchengladbach, both Milan teams plus Club Brugge.

Remarkably, Espanyol – coached by future Spain boss Javier Clemente – swamped Leverkusen in the first leg of the final in their own Sarria stadium. Three goals in five minutes either side of half-time appeared to have tied up what would have been a ninth Spanish success in the UEFA/Fairs Cup. Everything was going according to plan when Espanyol held Leverkusen goalless in the first half of the second leg back in West Germany. But then their Cameroon goalkeeper, Thomas Nkono, lost the plot. Leverkusen scored twice in six minutes early in the second half and their South Korean, Cha Bum-kun, shot them level on aggregate nine minutes from time.

For only the second time in the competition's history, the final had to be decided on penalties. The home fans groaned when Alonso converted the first Espanyol kick and Ralf Falkenmayer missed for Leverkusen. Job and Rolff were each successful in the second round but then Espanol's Urquiaga, Zuniga and Losada were all out-psyched by German keeper Rudi Völlborn. Leverkusen took the contest 3–2.

Italian property

Only three times in the subsequent decade did foreign clubs break the monopoly, Ajax in 1992, Bayern Munich in 1996 and Schalke in 1997. Even then, Ajax overcame Italian opposition in Torino only on away goals and Schalke defeated Internazionale on penalties.

Napoli, in 1989, provided Argentine superstar Diego Maradona with only European trophy. Juventus defeated Fiorentina in the 1990 final and then further enraged Florence fans by buying their favourite, Roberto Baggio, for a world record £8 million, a week after the final. In 1991, Internazionale won another all-Italian final by defeating Roma thanks largely to the influence of their German World Cup-winning triumvirate of Andy Brehme, Lothar Matthäus and Jürgen Klinsmann.

Ajax beat Torino on the away goals rule in 1992

After Torino let the Italian side down, comparatively, in 1992, neighbours Juventus restored local and national pride by walking all over Borussia Dortmund in 1993. Juve won 3–1 in Germany and 3–0 at home. Their inspiration was their own German midfielder, Andy Möller. Ironically, Möller would then return home to inspire Dortmund's vengeful victory over Juventus in the 1997 Champions Cup Final. Internazionale regained the UEFA Cup in 1994 with narrow home-and-away victories over Austria Salzburg and were duly succeeded in 1995 by Parma. The final was an all-Italian affair for the third time in seven seasons. This time Juventus were on the losing end. Parma won at home and drew in Turin. Both their goals were scored by midfielder Dino Baggio.

Bayern Munich and Bordeaux provided a rare commercial break for the strengths of German and French football when they reached the 1996 final. Bordeaux had been playing for almost a year since they had earned entry to the UEFA Cup only through success in the Intertoto Cup, in the summer of 1995. No wonder star forwards Zinedine Zidane and Christophe Dugarry were too tired to produce their best either against Bayern or in the subsequent finals of the European Championship for France. Veteran sweeper Matthäus proved an inspirational leader for Bayern, above all in the semi-final when, after being held 2–2 at home by Barcelona, they recovered to win 2–1 in Nou Camp.

Bordeaux proved less testing and Bayern won 2–0 at home and 3–1 in France. Most notable moment in the second leg occurred 13 minutes from time when Klinsmann scored what was not only Bayern's third goal but his 15th of the competition that season, a record for a single-season European campaign.

The UEFA Cup remained in German hands in 1997, Schalke winning their first European trophy by defeating Internazionale on penalties after each club had won their home leg 1–0. But Inter came up with a trump card the following season when they won the UEFA Cup for the third time in eight seasons thanks to a match-winning display by Brazil's new superstar, Ronaldo, against fellow Italians Lazio in the Parc des Princes, Paris.

Format changes again

History was made since this was the first single-leg UEFA Cup Final. The Fairs Cup had twice opted for a single-match in the mid-1960s but that was more through force of circumstances. Now, UEFA wanted to raise the prestige of the event while easing fixture pressure in an over-crowded season's end.

None of the players or fans appeared to resent travelling so far for a domestic occasion. Inter president Massimo Moratti had never been to the Parc before and travelled with his family via Disneyland. Lazio owner Sergio Cragnotti was just delighted that not only had his club reached their first European final but had done so to coincide with the club's stock market launch.

The coaches were not quite as relaxed. Inter's Gigi Simoni was still puzzling over a poor weekend draw against Piacenza, praying his men would make amends for the previous year's shoot-out defeat by Schalke and aware that, if they did not, his job might be on the line. As for Lazio's Sven-Goran Eriksson, he admitted to feeling more relaxed than when he faced Milanese opposition the last time in a European final – as Benfica boss against AC Milan in the Champions Cup decider in 1980.

Lazio claimed the better team, albeit minus the injured Alen Boksic; Inter claimed the better individuals, right down to their prospective match-winner Ronaldo, whose duel with Alessandro Nesta was expected to decide the match. Instead it was Inter's other South American striker, Chile's Ivan Zamorano, who achieved the decisive breakthrough in the fifth minute. Diego Simeone's long through ball caught Lazio flat. Zamorano took off like a greyhound and was already two yards clear of the defence by the time the pass arrived. Keeper Luca Marchegiani made it easier by hesitating in anticipation of an unforthcoming offside flag and Zamorano flicked the ball beyond him. Although possession was shared, Inter were more dangerous and might have increased their lead in the 25th minute when Javier Zanetti and Youri Djorkaeff provided Ronaldo with the chance to smack a 25-yarder against the angle of post and crossbar.

Inter had correctly identified Diego Fuser, wide on the right, as the source of most of Lazio's attacking inspiration and Zanetti's ultimate mastery of him was not the least of his contributions to Inter's success.

While there was only one goal in it, Lazio were still in the final. The introduction of Matyas Almeyda into midfield shortly after the interval promised briefly to help make the difference. He brought an Inter-type of physical commitment to Lazio's midfield and offered a more direct service to Casiraghi and Roberto Mancini. Unfortunately, Almeyda also displayed a penchant for those ugly old tendencies which scarred the reputation of Argentine football: first he was booked for nagging referee Antonio Lopez Nieto over a free-kick then he swung a boot in frustration at Ronaldo as the Brazilian turned Lazio inside out yet again. Lopez Nieto appreciated it was not the most malicious of kicks by extracting only the yellow card. Thus it was the orginal, silly, sin of dissent which, in effect, got Almeyda sent off. Inter's Taribo West was also sent off – for tussling with Casiraghi.

By the time West went, however, the match was over as a contest with Inter already leading 3–0. First Zamorano turned back a long cross from Ronaldo and Zanetti thumped a 25-yarder beyond a stunned Marchegiani and just inside the angle. Then the Lazio defence stopped, misled by the flicker of a linesman's flag, as Ronaldo strode through all alone onto to Benoit Cauet's pass to score the third.

"It was the first goal that did it," said Eriksson afterwards. "We did not expect to concede a goal so quickly. After that we were always chasing the match and they caught us on the classic counter-attack. The longer the match went on the more risks we had to take and the more space we left them. Inter are a strong side, I take my hat off to them. They deserved to win – but not by 3–0."

Simoni agreed with Eriksson's asssessment, saying: "We were very keen to score the first goal – that's why I started with, in effect, three forwards. Scoring after four or five minutes gave us the opportunity to dictate the game. The longer the match went on the stronger we looked. Lazio did not have the same physical edge as us. But then, they have had the Italian Cup to distract them. They got a great result there but maybe they paid the penalty against us."

The history of the UEFA/Fairs Cup is full of clubs who have used it as a springboard to victory in the Champions Cup. No fewer than 14 clubs (Barcelona, Roma, Juventus, Leeds United, Liverpool, Borussia Mönchengladbach, Club Brugge, PSV Eindhoven, Red Star Belgrade, Hamburg, Benfica, Real Madrid, Ajax and Borussia Dortmund) followed up a place in the Fairs/UEFA Cup Final with a subsequent victory or runners-up spot in the senior competition.

Entrance to the UEFA Cup continues to be obtained on a multiple-entry system, based on a ranking list of success rates of a country's clubs in European competitions. The hidden twist in the coefficient tale is that the more clubs entered by a country, the better its chances of maintaining a high coefficient and a high entry rate. This played a significant role in assisting the Italian command of the UEFA Cup in the 1990s. They were helped also by the post-Heysel ban imposed on English entry. By the time English clubs returned to the UEFA Cup, technical and tactical developments meant there was a lot of catching-up to do.

A handful of countries had long been permitted to enter the winners of their League Cup. But UEFA, in a heavy-handed attempt to persuade countries to ease fixture pressure, has been threatening to scrap this right for all countries which operate a top division comprising more than 18 clubs.

In an odd way though, the dispute this provoked merely went on to demontrate how successful the UEFA Cup had become ... albeit far removed from the original concept that was envisaged by its founders in the mid-1950s.

UEFA/FAIRS CUP RESULTS

INDUSTRIAL INTER-CITIES FAIRS CUP

1955–58

SEMI-FINALS

Barcelona bt Birmingham City 3–4, 1–0, 2–1
(play-off, 4–4 agg)
London Select XI bt Lausanne 1–2, 2–0
(3–2 agg)

FINAL

1st leg: Mar 5 (Stamford Bridge, London)
London Select XI 2 (Greaves 10, Langley 88 pen)
Barcelona 2 (Tejada 7, Martinez 35)
HT: 12. Att: 45,466. Ref: Dusch (WG)
LONDON: Kelsey, Sillett, Langley, Blanchflower, Norman, Coote, Groves, Greaves, Smith, Haynes, Robb.
BARCELONA: Estrems, Olivella, Segarra, Gracia, Gensana, Ribelles, Basora, Evaristo, Martinez, Villaverde, Tejada.

2nd leg: May 1 (Nou Camp, Barcelona)
Barcelona 6 (Suarez 6 8, Evaristo 52 75, Martinez 43, Verges 63)
London Select XI 0
HT: 3–0. Att: 62,000. Ref: Dusch (WG)
BARCELONA: Ramallets, Olivella, Segarra, Verges, Brugue, Gensana, Tejada, Evaristo, Martinez, Suarez, Basora.
LONDON: Kelsey, Wright, Cantwell, Blanchflower, Brown, Bowen, Medwin, Groves, Smith, Bloomfield, Lewis.
Winners: Barcelona, 8–2 agg

1958–60

SEMI-FINALS

Barcelona bt Belgrade 3–1, 1–1
(4–2 agg)
Birmingham City bt Union St Gilloise 4–2, 4–2
(8–4 agg)

FINAL

1st leg: Mar 29 (St Andrew's, Birmingham)
Birmingham City 0
Barcelona 0
HT: 0–0. Att: 40,000. Ref: Van Nuffel (Bel)
BIRMINGHAM: Schofield, Farmer, Allen, Watts, Smith, Neal, Astall, Gordon, Weston, Orritt, Hooper.
BARCELONA: Ramallets, Olivella, Gracia, Segarra, Rodri, Gensana, Coll, Kocsis, Martinez, Ribelles, Villaverde.

2nd leg: May 4 (Nou Camp, Barcelona)
Barcelona 4 (Martinez 3, Czibor 6, 48, Coll 78)
Birmingham City 1 (Hooper 82)
HT: 2–0. Att: 70,000. Ref: Van Nuffel (Bel)
BARCELONA: Ramallets, Olivella, Gracia, Verges, Rodri, Segarra, Coll, Ribelles, Martinez, Kubala, Czibor.
BIRMINGHAM: Schofield, Farmer, Allen, Watts, Smith, Neal, Astall, Gordon, Weston, Murphy, Hooper.
Winners: Barcelona, 4–1 agg

1960–61

SEMI-FINALS

Roma bt Hibernian 2–2, 3–3, 6–0
(play-off, 5–5 agg)
Birmingham City bt Internazionale 2–1, 2–1
(4–2 agg)

FINAL

1st leg: Sep 27 (St Andrew's, Birmingham)
Birmingham City 2 (Hellawell 78, Orritt 85)
Roma 2 (Manfredini 30 56)
HT: 0–1. Att: 21,000. Ref: Davidson (Sco)
BIRMINGHAM: Schofield, Farmer, Sissons, Hennessy, Foster, Beard, Hellawell, Bloomfield, Harris, Orritt, Auld.
ROMA: Cudicini, Fontana, Corsini, Giuliano, Losi, Carpanesi, Orlando, Da Costa, Manfredini, Angelillo, Menichelli.

2nd leg: Oct 11 (Olimpico, Rome)
Roma 2 (Farmer og 56, Pestrin 90)
Birmingham City 0
HT: 0–0. Att: 60,000. Ref: Schwinte (Fra)
ROMA: Cudicini, Fontana, Corsini, Carpanesi, Losi, Pestrin, Orlando, Angelillo, Manfredini, Lojacono, Menichelli.
BIRMINGHAM: Schofield, Farmer, Sissons, Hennessy, Smith, Beard, Hellawell, Bloomfield, Harris, Singer, Orritt.
Winners: Roma, 4–2 agg

1961–62

SEMI-FINALS

Valencia bt MTK Budapest 3–0, 7–3
(10–3 agg)
Barcelona bt Red Star Belgrade 2–0, 4–1
(6–1 agg)

FINAL

1st leg: Aug 9 (Luis Casanova, Valencia)
Valencia 6 (Yosu 14 42, Guillot 35 54 67, Nunez 74)
Barcelona 2 (Kocsis 4 20)
HT: 3–2. Att: 65,000. Ref: Barberan (Fra)
VALENCIA: Zamora, Piquer, Mestre, Sastre, Quincoces, Chicao, Nunez, Ribelles, Waldo, Guillot, Yosu.
BARCELONA: Pesudo, Benitez, Rodri, Olivella, Verges, Gracia, Cubilla, Kocsis, Re, Villaverde, Camps.

2nd leg: Sep 9 (Nou Camp, Barcelona)
Barcelona 1 (Kocsis 46)
Valencia 1 (Guillot 87)
HT: 0–0. Att: 60,000. Ref: Campanati (Ita)
BARCELONA: Pesudo, Benitez, Garay, Fuste, Verges, Gracia, Cubilla, Kocsis, Goyvaerts, Villaverde, Camps.

VALENCIA: Zamora, Piquer, Mestre, Sastre, Quincoces, Chicao, Nunez, Urtiago, Waldo, Guillot, Yosu.
Winners: Valencia, 7–3 agg

1962–63

SEMI-FINALS

Valencia bt Roma 3–0, 1–1
(4 1 agg)
Dinamo Zagreb bt Ferencvaros 1–0, 2–1
(3–1 agg)

FINAL

1st leg: Jun 12 (Zagreb)
Dinamo Zagreb 1 (Zambata 13)
Valencia 2 (Waldo 64, Urtiaga 67)
HT: 1–0. Att: 40,000. Ref: Adami (Ita)
DINAMO: Skoric, Belin, Braun, Biscam, Markovic, Perusic, Kobesnac, Zambata, Knez, Matus, Lamza.
VALENCIA: Zamora, Piquer, Chicao, Paquito, Quincoces, Sastre, Mano, Sanchez Lage, Waldo, Ribelles, Urtiaga.

2nd leg: Jun 26 (Luis Casanova, Valencia)
Valencia 2 (Mano 68, Nunez 78)
Dinamo Zagreb 0
HT: 0–0. Att: 55,000. Ref: Howley (Eng)
VALENCIA : Zamora, Piquer, Chicao, Paquito, Quincoces, Sastre, Mano, Sanchez Lage, Waldo, Ribelles, Nunes.
DINAMO: Skoric, Belin, Braun, Matus, Markovic, Perusic, Kobesnac, Lamza, Raus, Zambata, Knez.
Winners: Valencia, 4–1 agg

1963–64

SEMI-FINALS

Real Zaragoza bt FC Liege 0–1, 2–1, 2–0
(play-off, 2–2 agg)
Valencia bt FC Köln 4–1, 0–2
(4–3 agg)

FINAL

Jun 25 (Nou Camp, Barcelona)
Real Zaragoza 2 (Villa 40, Marcelino 83)
Valencia 1 (Urtiaga 41)
HT: 1–1. Att: 50,000. Ref: Campos (Por)
ZARAGOZA: Yarza, Cortizo, Santamaria, Reija, Isasi, Pais, Canario, Duca, Marcelino, Villa, Lapetra.
VALENCIA: Zamora, Arnal, Videgany, Paquito, Quincoces, Roberto, Suco, Guillot, Waldo, Urtiaga, Ficha.

1964–65

SEMI-FINALS

Ferencvaros bt Manchester United 2–3, 1–0, 2–1
(in play-off, 3–3 agg)
Juventus bt Atletico Madrid 1–3, 3–1, 3–1
(play-off, 4–4 agg)

FINAL

June 23 (Comunale, Turin)
Ferencvaros 1 (Fenyvesi 74)
Juventus 0
HT: 0–0. Att: 25,000. Ref: Dienst (Swi)
FERENCVAROS: Geczi, Novak, Horvath, Juhasz,
Matrai, Orosz, Karaba, Varga, Albert, Rakosi,
Fenyvesi.
JUVENTUS: Anzolin, Gori, Sarti, Bercellino,
Castano, Leoncini, Stacchini, Del Sol, Combin,
Mazzia, Menichelli.

1965–66

SEMI-FINALS

Barcelona bt Chelsea 2–0, 0–2, 5–0
(play-off, 2–2 agg)
Real Zaragoza bt Leeds Utd 1–0, 1–2, 3–1
(play-off, 2–2 agg)

FINAL

1st leg: Sep 14 (Nou Camp, Barcelona)
Barcelona 0
Real Zaragoza 1 (Canario 30)
HT: 0–1. Att: 70,000. Ref: Zsolt (Hun)
BARCELONA: Sadurni, Benitez, Eladio, Montesios,
Gallego, Torres, Zaballa, Muller, Zaldua, Fuste,
Vidal.
ZARAGOZA: Yarza, Irusquieta, Reija, Pais,
Santamaria, Violeta, Canario, Santos, Marcelino,
Villa, Lapetra.

2nd leg: Sep 21 (La Romareda, Zaragoza)
Real Zaragoza 2 (Marcelino 24 87)
Barcelona 4 (Pujol 3 86 119, Zaballa 89)
*HT: 1–1. 90min: 2–3. After extra time. Att: 70,000. Ref:
Lo Bello (Ita)*
ZARAGOZA: Yarza, Irusquieta, Reija, Pais,
Santamaria, Violeta, Canario, Santos, Marcelino,
Villa, Lapetra.
BARCELONA: Sadurni, Foncho, Eladio, Montesios,
Gallego, Torres, Zaballa, Mas, Zaldua, Fuste, Pujol.
Winners: Barcelona, 4–3 agg

1966–67

SEMI-FINALS

**Dinamo Zagreb bt Eintracht Frankfurt 0–3,
4–0**
(4–3 agg)
Leeds United bt Kilmarnock 4–2, 0–0
(4–2 agg)

FINAL

1st leg: Aug 30 (Dinamo Stadion, Zagreb)
Dinamo Zagreb 2 (Cercek 39 59)
Leeds United 0
HT: 1–0. Att: 40,000. Ref: Bueno Perales (Spa)
DINAMO: Skoric, Gracanin, Brncic, Belin, Ramljak,
Blaskovic, Cercek, Piric, Zambata, Gucmirtl, Rora.
LEEDS: Sprake, Reaney, Cooper, Bremner,
Charlton, Hunter, Bates, Lorimer, Belfitt, Gray,
OGrady.

2nd leg: Sep 6: (Elland Road, Leeds)
Leeds United 0
Dinamo Zagreb 0
HT: 0–0. Att: 35,000. Ref: Lo Bello (Ita)
Winners: Dinamo Zagreb, 2–0 on agg

LEEDS: Sprake, Bell, Cooper, Bremner, Charlton,
Hunter, Reaney, Belfitt, Greenhoff, Giles,
O'Grady.
DINAMO: Skoric, Gracanin, Brncic, Belin, Ramljak,
Blaskovic, Cercek, Piric, Zambata, Gucmirtl, Rora.

1967–68

SEMI-FINALS

Leeds United bt Dundee 1–1, 1–0
(2–1 agg)
Ferencvaros bt Bologna 3–2, 2–2
(5–4 agg)

FINAL

1st leg: Sep 7 (Elland Road, Leeds)
Leeds United 1 (Jones 41)
Ferencvaros 0
HT: 1–0. Att: 25,000. Ref: Scheurer (Swi)
LEEDS: Sprake, Reaney, Cooper, Bremner,
Charlton, Hunter, Lorimer, Madeley, Jones
(Belfitt), Giles (Greenhoff), E Gray.
FERENCVAROS: Geczi, Novak, Pancsics, Havasi,
Juhasz, Szucs, Szoke, Varga, Albert, Rakosi,
Fenyvesi (Balint)

Sep 11 (Nep, Budapest) 2nd leg
Ferencvaros 0
Leeds United 0
HT: 0–0. Att: 25,000. Ref: Schulenburg (WG)
FERENCVAROS: Geczi, Novak, Pancsics, Havasi,
Juhasz, Szucs, Rakosi, Szoke (Karaba), Varga,
Albert, Katona.
LEEDS: Sprake, Reaney, Cooper, Bremner,
Charlton, Hunter, O'Grady, Lorimer, Jones,
Madeley, Hibbitt (Bates)
Winners: Leeds, 1–0 agg

1968–69

SEMI-FINALS

Newcastle United bt Rangers 0–0, 2–0
(2–0 agg)
Ujpest Dozsa bt Goztepe Ismir 4–1, 4–0
(8–1 agg)

FINAL

1st leg: May 29 (St James Park, Newcastle)
Newcastle United 3 (Moncur 63 72, Scott 83)
Ujpest Dozsa 0
HT: 0–0. Att: 60,000. Ref: Hannet (Fra)
NEWCASTLE: McFaul, Craig, Clark, Gibb, Burton,
Moncur, Scott, Robson, Davies, Arentoft, Sinclair
(Foggon, 75)
UJPEST: Szentmihalyi, Kaposzta, Solymosi, Bankuti,
Nosko, E Dunai, Fazekas, Gorocs, Bene, A Dunai,
Zambo.

2nd leg: Jun 11 (Nep, Budapest)
Ujpest Dozsa 2 (Bene 31, Gorocs 44)
Newcastle United 3 (Moncur 46, Arentoft 50,
Foggon 74)
HT: 2–0. Att: 37,000. Ref: Heymann (Swi)
UJPEST: Szentmihalyi, Kaposzta, Solymosi, Bankuti,
Nosko, E Dunai, Fazekas, Gorocs, Bene, A Dunai,
Zambo.
NEWCASTLE: McFaul, Craig, Clark, Giles, Burton,
Moncur, Scott (Foggon, 76), Arentoft, Robson,
Davies, Sinclair.
Winners: Newcastle, 6–2 agg

1969–70

SEMI-FINALS

Arsenal bt Ajax 3–0, 0–1
(3–1 agg)
Anderlecht bt Internazionale 0–1, 2–0
(2–1 agg)

FINAL

1st leg: Apr 22 (Parc Astrid, Brussels)
Anderlecht 3 (Devrindt 25, Mulder 30 74)
Arsenal 1 (Kennedy 82)
HT: 2–0. Att: 37,000. Ref: Scheurer (Swi)
ANDERLECHT: Trappeniers, Heylens, Velkeneers,
Kialunda, Cornelis (Peeters, 68), Nordahl,
Desanghere, Puis, Devrindt, Van Himst, Mulder.
ARSENAL: Wilson, Storey, McNab, Kelly,
McLintock, Simpson, Armstrong, Sammels,
Radford, George (Kennedy, 77), Graham.

2nd leg: Apr 28 (Highbury, London)
Arsenal 3 (Kelly 25, Radford 75, Sammels 76)
Anderlecht 0
HT: 1–0. Att: 37,000. Ref: Scheurer (Swi)
ARSENAL: Wilson, Storey, McNab, Kelly,
McLintock, Simpson, Armstrong, Sammels,
Radford, George, Graham.
ANDERLECHT: Trappeniers, Heylens, Velkeneers,
Kialunda, Martens, Nordahl, Desanghere, Puis,
Devrindt, Mulder, Van Himst.
Winners: Arsenal, 4–3 agg

1970–71

SEMI-FINALS

Leeds United bt Liverpool 1–0, 0–0
(1–0 agg)
Juventus bt FC Köln 1–1, 2–0
(3–1 agg)

FINAL

1st leg: May 26 (Comunale, Turin)
Juventus 0
Leeds United 0
Att: 65,000. Ref: Van Ravens (Hol)
Abandoned 57 mins, waterlogged pitch
JUVENTUS: Piloni, Spinosi, Marchetti, Furino,
Morini, Salvadore, Haller, Causio, Anastasi,
Capello, Bettega.
LEEDS: Sprake, Reaney, Charlton, Hunter, Cooper,
Bremner, Giles, Clarke, M Jones, Lorimer,
Madeley.

1st leg replay: May 28 (Comunale, Turin)
Juventus 2 (Bettega 27, Capello 55)
Leeds United 2 (Madeley 48, Bates 77)
HT: 1–0. Att: 65,000. Ref: Van Ravens (Hol)
JUVENTUS: Piloni, Spinosi, Salvadore, Marchetti,
Furino, Morini, Haller, Capello, Causio, Anastasi
(Novellini, 72), Bettega.
LEEDS: Sprake, Reaney, Cooper, Bremner,
Charlton, Hunter, Lorimer, Clarke, Jones (Bates,
72), Giles, Madeley.

2nd leg: Jun 3 (Elland Road, Leeds)
Leeds United 1 (Clarke 12)
Juventus 1 (Anastasi 20)
HT: 1–1. Att: 42,000. Ref: Glckner (EG)
LEEDS: Sprake, Reaney, Cooper, Bremner,
Charlton, Hunter, Lorimer, Clarke, Jones, Giles,
Madeley (Bates, 56)
JUVENTUS: Tancredi, Spinosi, Salvadore,

Marchetti, Furino, Morini, Haller, Capello, Causio, Anastasi, Bettega.
Winners: Leeds on away goals, 3–3 agg

The Fairs Cup was fully taken over by UEFA and a new trophy, the UEFA Cup, provided. A one-off, single-leg match was organized between the first and last winners of the Fairs Cup. Barcelona, as first winners, were granted home advantage.

Sep 22, 1971 (Nou Camp, Barcelona)
Barcelona 2 (Duenas 51, 83)
Leeds United 1 (Jordan 53)
HT: 0–0. Att: 35,000. Ref: Zsolt (Hun)
BARCELONA: Sadurni, Rife, Gallego, Torres, Eladio, Costas, Juan Carlos, Rexach, Marcial, Duenas, Asensi (Fuste 46)
LEEDS: Sprake, Reaney, Charlton, Hunter, Darey, Bremner, Giles, Belfitt, Lorimer, Jordan, Galvin.

UEFA CUP

1971–72

SEMI-FINALS

Tottenham Hotspur bt Milan 2–1, 1–1
(3–2 agg)
Wolverhampton Wanderers bt Ferencvaros 2–2, 2–1
(4–3 agg)

FINAL

1st leg: May 3 (Molineux, Wolverhampton)
Wolverhampton Wanderers 1 (McCalliog 72)
Tottenham Hotspur 2 (Chivers 57 87)
HT: 0–0. Att: 38,000. Ref: Bakhramov (SU)
WOLVES: Parkes, Shaw, Taylor, Hegan, Munro, McAlle, McCalliog, Hibbitt, Richards, Dougan, Wagstaffe.
TOTTENHAM: Jennings, Kinnear, Knowles, Mullery, England, Beal, Gilzean, Perryman, Chivers, Peters, Coates (Pratt, 68)

2nd leg: May 17 (White Hart Lane, London)
Tottenham Hotspur 1 (Mullery 30)
Wolverhampton Wanderers 1 (Wagstaffe 41)
HT: 1–1. Att: 54,000. Ref: Van Ravens (Hol)
TOTTENHAM: Jennings, Kinnear, Knowles, Mullery, England, Beal, Gilzean, Perryman, Chivers, Peters, Coates.
WOLVES: Parkes, Shaw, Taylor, Hegan, Munro, McAlle, McCalliog, Hibbitt (Bailey, 55), Richards, Dougan (Curran, 84), Wagstaffe.
Winners: Tottenham Hotspur, 3–2 agg

1972–73

SEMI-FINALS

Liverpool bt Tottenham Hotspur 1–0, 1–2
(away goals, 2–2 agg)
Borussia Mönchengladbach bt Twente Enschede 3–0, 2–1
(5–1 agg)

FINAL

1st leg: May 9 (Anfield, Liverpool)
Liverpool 0
Borussia Mönchengladbach 0
Att: 44,900. Ref: Linemayr (Aut)
Abandoned 27 mins, waterlogged pitch
LIVERPOOL: Clemence, Lawler, Lindsay, Lloyd, Smith, Hughes, Keegan, Cormack, Heighway, Hall, Callaghan.
BORUSSIA: Kleff, Vogts, Michallik, Netzer, Bonhof, Danner, Wimmer, Kulik, Jensen, Rupp, Heynckes.
final
1st leg replay: May 10 (Anfield, Liverpool)
Liverpool 3 (Keegan 21, 32, Lloyd 61)
Borussia Mönchengladbach 0
HT: 2–0. Att: 41,000. Ref: Linemayr (Aut)
LIVERPOOl: Clemence, Lawler, Lindsay, Smith, Lloyd, Hughes, Keegan, Cormack, Toshack, Heighway (Hall 83), Callaghan.
BORUSSIA: Kleff, Michallik, Netzer, Bonhof, Vogts, Wimmer, Danner, Kulik, Jensen, Rupp (Simonsen 82), Heynckes.

May 23 (Bokelberg, Mönchengladbach) 2nd leg
Borussia Mönchengladbach 2 (Heynckes 29 40)
Liverpool 0
HT: 2–0. Att: 35,000. Ref: Kasakov (SU)
BORUSSIA: Kleff, Surau, Netzer, Bonhof, Vogts, Wimmer, Danner, Kulik, Jensen, Rupp, Heynckes.
LIVERPOOL: Clemence, Lawler, Lindsay, Smith, Lloyd, Hughes, Keegan, Cormack, Heighway (Boersma, 77), Toshack, Callaghan.
Winners: Liverpool, 3–2 agg

1973–74

SEMI-FINALS

Feyenoord bt Stuttgart 2–1, 2–2
(4–3 agg)
Tottenham Hotspur bt Lokomotive Leipzig 2–1, 2–0
(4–1 agg)

FINAL

1st leg: May 21 (White Hart Lane, London)
Tottenham Hotspur 2 (England 39, Van Daele og 64)
Feyenoord 2 (Van Hanegem 43, De Jong 85)
HT: 2–1. Att: 46,000. Ref: Scheurer (Swi)
TOTTENHAM: Jennings, Evans, Naylor, Pratt, England, Beal (Dillon, 79), McGrath, Perryman, Peters, Chivers, Coates.
FEYENOORD: Treytel, Rijsbergen, Van Daele, Israel, Vos, De Jong, Jansen, Van Hanegem, Ressel, Schoenmaker, Kristensen.

2nd leg: May 29 (Feyenoord, Rotterdam)
Feyenoord 2 (Rijsbergen 43, Ressel 84)
Tottenham Hotspur 0
HT: 1–0. Att: 59,000. Ref: Lo Bello (Ita)
FEYENOORD: Treytel, Rijsbergen (Boskamp, 76; Wery, 86), Van Daele, Israel, Vos, Ramljak, Jansen, De Jong, Ressel, Schoenmaker, Kristensen.
TOTTENHAM: Jennings, Evans, Naylor, Pratt (Holder, 77), England, Beal, McGrath, Perryman, Peters, Chivers, Coates.
Winners: Feyenoord, 4–2 agg

1974–75

SEMI-FINALS

Borussia Mönchengladbach bt FC Köln 3–1, 1–0
(4–1 agg)
Twente Enschede bt Juventus 3–1, 1–0
(4–1 agg)

FINAL

1st leg: May 7 (Rheinstadion, Düsseldorf)
Borussia Mönchengladbach 0
Twente Enschede 0
HT: 0–0. Att: 21,000. Ref: Palotai (Hun)
BORUSSIA: Kleff, Wittkamp, Stielike, Vogts, Surau, Bonhof, Wimmer, Danner (Del'Haye, 75), Kulik (Schäffer, 78), Simonsen, Jensen.
TWENTE: Gross, Drost, Van Iersel, Overweg, Oranen, Thijssen, Palhplatz, Van der Vall, Bos, Jeuring (Achterberg, 86), Zuidema.

2nd leg: May 21 (Diekman, Enschede)
Twente Enschede 1 (Drost 76)
Borussia Mönchengladbach 5 (Simonsen 2 86, Heynckes 9 50 60)
HT: 2–0. Att: 21,000. Ref: Schiller (Aut)
TWENTE: Gross, Drost, Van Iersel, Overweg, Oranen, Bos (G. Muhren, 53), Thijssen, Pahlplatz (Achterberg, 75), Van der Vall, Jeuring, Zuidema.
BORUSSIA: Kleff, Wittkamp, Vogts, Surau (Schffer, 13), Klinkhammer, Bonhof, Wimmer (Kppel, 75), Danner, Simonsen, Jensen, Heynckes.
Winners: Borussia, 5–1 agg

1975–76

SEMI-FINALS

Liverpool bt Barcelona 1–0, 1–1
(2–1 agg)
Club Brugge bt Hamburg 1–1, 1–0
(2–1 agg)

FINAL

1st leg: Apr 28 (Anfield, Liverpool)
Liverpool 3 (Kennedy 59, Case 61, Keegan 65)
Club Brugge 2 (Lambert 5, Cools 15)
HT: 0–2. Att: 49,000. Ref: Biwersi (Aut)
LIVERPOOL : Clemence, Smith, Neal, Thompson, Hughes, Keegan, Kennedy, Callaghan, Fairclough, Heighway, Toshack (Case, 46)
BRUGGE: Jensen, Bastijns, Krieger, Leekens, Volders, Cools, Vandereycken, Decubber, Van Gool, Lambert, Lefevre.

2nd leg: May 19 (Olympiastadion, Bruges)
Club Brugge 1 (Lambert 11)
Liverpool 1 (Keegan 15)
HT: 1–1. Att: 32,000. Ref: Glckner (EG)
BRUGGE: Jensen, Bastijns, Kriger, Leekens, Volders, Cools, Vandereycken, Decubber (Hinderyckx, 68), Van Gool, Lambert (Sanders, 75), Lefevre.
LIVERPOOL: Clemence, Smith, Neal, Thompson, Hughes, Keegan, Kennedy, Callaghan, Case, Heighway, Toshack (Fairclough, 62)
Winners: Liverpool, 4–3 agg

1976–77

SEMI-FINALS

Juventus bt AEK Athens 4–1, 1–0
(5–1 agg)
Athletic Bilbao bt RWD Molenbeek 1–1, 0–0
(away goals, 1–1 agg)

FINAL

1st leg: May 4 (Comunale, Turin)
Juventus 1 (Tardelli 15)
Athletic Bilbao 0
HT: 1–0. Att: 75,000. Ref: Corver (Hol)
JUVENTUS: Zoff, Cuccureddu, Gentile, Scirea, Morini, Tardelli, Furino, Benetti, Causio, Boninsegna (Gori, 39), Bettega.
ATHLETIC: Iribar, Onaederra, Escalza, Goicoechea, Guisasola, Villar, Irureta, J A Rojo, Churruca, Dani, J F Rojo.

2nd leg: May 18 (San Mames, Bilbao)
Athletic Bilbao 2 (Churruca 11, Carlos 78)
Juventus 1 (Bettega 7)
HT: 1–1. Att: 43,000. Ref: Linemayr (Aut)
ATHLETIC: Iribar, Lasa (Carlos, 63), Guisasola, Alexanco, Escalza, Villar, Churruca, Irureta, Amorrortu, Dani, JF Rojo.
JUVENTUS: Zoff, Cuccureddu, Morini, Scirea, Gentile, Causio, Tardelli, Furino, Benetti, Boninsegna (Spinosi, 59), Bettega.
Winners: Juventus on away goals, 2–2 agg

1977–78

SEMI-FINALS

PSV Eindhoven bt Barcelona 3–0, 1–3
(4–3 agg)
Bastia bt Grasshopper 2–3, 1–0
(away goals, 3–3 agg)

FINAL

1st leg: Apr 26 (Furiani, Bastia)
Bastia 0
PSV Eindhoven 0
HT: 0–0. Att: 15,000. Ref: Maksimovic (Yug)
BASTIA: Hiard, Burkhard, Guesdon, Orlanducci, Cazes, Papi, Lacuesta (Felix, 56), Larios, Rep, Krimau, Mariot.
PSV: Van Beveren, Van Kraay, Krijgh, Stevens, Brandts, Poortvliet, Van der Kuijlen, W Van der Kerkhof, Deijkers, R Van der Kerkhof, Lubse.

2nd leg: May 9 (Philips, Eindhoven) 2nd leg
PSV Eindhoven 3 (W Van der Kerkhof 24, Deijkers 67, Van der Kuijlen 69)
Bastia 0
HT: 1–0. Att: 27,000. Ref: Rainea (Rom)
PSV: Van Beveren, Krijgh, Stevens, Van Kraay (Deacy, 79), Brandts, W Van der Kerkhof, Poortvliet, Van der Kuijlen, Lubse, Deijkers, R Van der Kerkhof.
BASTIA: Hiard (Weller, 75), Marchioni, Orlanducci, Guesdon, Cazes, Lacuesta, Larios, Papi, Rep, Krimau, Mariot (De Zerbi, 67).
Winners: PSV, 3–0 agg

1978–79

SEMI-FINALS

Borussia Mönchengladbach bt MSV Duisburg 2–2, 4–1
(6–3 agg)
Red Star Belgrade bt Hertha Berlin 1–0, 1–2
(away goals, 2–2 agg)

FINAL

1st leg: May 9 (Red Star, Belgrade)
Red Star Belgrade 1 (Sestic 21)
Borussia Mönchengladbach 1 (Jurisic og 60)
HT: 1–0. Att: 87,000. Ref: Foote (Eng)
RED STAR: Stojanovic, Jovanovic, Miletovic, Jurisic, Jovin, Muslin (Krmpotic, 88), Petrovic, Blagojevic, Milosavljevic (Milovanovic, 88), Savic, Sestic.
BORUSSIA: Kneib, Vogts, Hannes, Schäffer, Ringels, Schäfer, Kulik, Nielsen (Danner, 75), Wohlers (Gores, 80), Simonsen, Lienen.

2nd leg: May 23 (Rheinstadion, Düsseldorf) 2nd leg
Borussia Mönchengladbach 1 (Simonsen 15)
Red Star Belgrade 0
HT: 1–0. Att: 45,000. Ref: Michelotti (Ita)
BORUSSIA: Kneib, Vogts, Hannes, Schäffer, Ringels, Schäfer, Kulik (Köppel, 58), Gorcs, Wohlers, Simonsen, Lienen.
RED STAR: Stojanovic, Jovanovic, Miletovic, Jurisic, Jovin, Muslin, Petrovic, Blagojevic, Milovanovic (Sestic, 46), Savic, Milosavljevic.
Winners: Borussia, 2–1 agg

1979–80

SEMI-FINALS

Eintracht Frankfurt bt Bayern Munich 0–2, 5–1
(5–3 agg)
Borussia Mönchengladbach bt Stuttgart 1–2, 2–0
(3–2 agg)

FINAL

1st leg: May 7 (Bokelberg, Mönchengladbach)
Borussia Mönchengladbach 3 (Kulik 44 88, Matthäus 76)
Eintracht Frankfurt 2 (Karger 37, Hlzenbein 71)
HT: 1–1. Att: 25,000. Ref: Guruceta (Spa)
BORUSSIA: Kneib, Hannes, Schäfer, Schäffer, Ringels, Matthäus, Kulik, Nielsen (Thychosen, 86), Del'Haye (Bodaker, 72), Nickel, Lienen.
EINTRACHT: Pahl, Pezzey, Neuberger, Korbel, Ehrmanntraut, Lorant, Hölzenbein (Nachtweih, 79), Borchers, Nickel, Cha Bum-kun, Karger (Trapp, 81)

2nd leg: May 21 (Waldstadion, Frankfurt)
Eintracht Frankfurt 1 (Schaub 81)
Borussia Mönchengladbach 0
HT: 0–0. Att: 59,000. Ref: Ponnet (Bel)
EINTRACHT: Pahl, Pezzey, Neuberger, Korbel, Ehrmanntraut, Lorant, Holzenbein, Borchers, Nickel, Cha Bum-kun, Nachtweih (Schaub, 77).
BORUSSIA: Kneib, Bodecker, Hannes, Schäfer, Ringels, Matthäus (Thychosen, 86), Fleer, Kulik, Nielsen (Del'Haye, 68), Nickel, Lienen.
Winners: Eintracht on away goals, 3–3 agg

1980–81

SEMI-FINALS

Ipswich Town bt FC Köln 1–0, 1–0
(2–0 agg)
AZ67 Alkmaar bt Sochaux 1–1, 3–2
(4–3 agg)

FINAL

1st leg: May 6 (Portman Road, Ipswich)
Ipswich Town 3 (Wark 28, Thijssen 46, Mariner 56)
AZ Alkmaar 0
HT: 1–0. Att: 27,000. Ref: Prokop (EG)
IPSWICH: Cooper, Mills, Osman, Butcher, McCall, Thijssen, Wark, Muhren, Mariner, Brazil, Gates.
ALKMAAR: Treytel, Van der Meer, Spelbos, Metgod, Hovenkamp, Peters, Arntz, Jonker, Nygaard (Welzl, 75), Tol, Kist.

2nd leg: May 20 (Alkmaar)
AZ Alkmaar 4 (Welzl 7, Metgod 25, Tol 40, Jonker 74)
Ipswich Town 2 (Thijssen 4, Wark 32)
HT: 3–2. Att: 28,500. Ref: Eschweiler (WG)
ALKMAAR: Treytel, Reinders, Spelbos, Metgod, Hovenkamp, Peters, Arntz, Jonkers, Nygaard, Welzl (Talan, 79), Tol (Kist, 46)
IPSWICH: Cooper, Mills, Osman, Butcher, McCall, Thijssen, Wark, Muhren, Mariner, Brazil, Gates.
Winners: Ipswich, 5–4 agg

1981–82

SEMI-FINALS

IFK Gothenburg bt Kaiserslautern 1–1, 2–1
(3–2 agg)
Hamburg bt Radnicki Nis 1–2, 5–1
(6–3 agg)

FINAL

1st leg: May 5 (Nya Ullevi, Gothenburg)
IFK Gothenburg 1 (Tord Holmgren 87)
Hamburg 0
HT: 0–0. Att: 42,000. Ref: Carpenter (Ire)
IFK: Wernersson, Svensson, Hysen, C Karlsson, Fredriksson, Tord Holmgren, J Karlsson, Stromberg, Corneliussen, Nilsson (Sandberg, 19), Tommy Holmgren (Schiller, 46)
HAMBURG: Stein, Kaltz, Hieronymus, Groh, Wehmeyer, Hartwig, Jakobs, Magath, Von Heesen (Memering, 82), Hrubesch, Bastrup.

2nd leg: May 19 (Volksparkstadion, Hamburg)
Hamburg 0
IFK Gothenburg 3 (Nilsson 6, Corneliusson 26, Fredriksson 63)
HT: 0–2. Att: 60,000. Ref: Courtney (Eng)
HAMBURG: Stein, Kaltz (Hidien, 75), Hieronymus, Groh, Wehmeyer, Hartwig, Memering, Magath, Von Heesen, Hrubesch, Bastrup.
IFK: Wernersson, Svensson, Hysen (Schiller, 19), C Karlsson, Fredriksson, Tord Holmgren, Stromberg, Karlsson, Corneliussen (Sandberg, 68), Nilsson, Tommy Holmgren.
Winners: Gothenburg 4–0 agg

1982–83

SEMI-FINALS

Anderlecht bt Bohemians Prague 1–0, 3–1
(4–1 agg)
Benfica bt Universitatea Craiova 0–0, 1–1
(away goals, 1–1 agg)

FINAL

1st leg: May 4 (Heysel, Brussels)
Anderlecht 1 (Brylle 29)
Benfica 0
HT: 1–0. Att: 55,000. Ref: Dochev (Bul)
ANDERLECHT: Munaron, Hofkens, Peruzovic, Olsen, De Groot, Frimann, Coeck, Vercauteren, Lozano, Vandenbergh (Czerniatynski, 78), Brylle.
BENFICA: Bento, Pietra, Alvaro, Humberto Coelho, Jose Luis, Sheu (A Bastos Lopes, 78), Frederico, Carlos Manuel, Chalana (Nene, 68), Diamantino, Filipovic.

2nd leg: May 18 (Benfica, Lisbon)
Benfica 1 (Sheu 36)
Anderlecht 1 (Lozano 38)
HT: 1–1. Att: 80,000. Ref: Corver (Hol)
BENFICA: Bento, Pietra, Humberto Coelho, Bastos Lopes, Veloso (Alves, 62), Carlos Manuel, Stromberg, Sheu (Filipovic, 50), Chalana, Nene, Diamantino.
ANDERLECHT: Munaron, Peruzovic, De Gref, Broos, Olsen, De Groot, Frimann, Lozano, Coeck, Vercauteren, Vandenbergh (Brylle, 78).
Winners: Anderlecht 2–1 agg

1983–84

SEMI-FINALS

Tottenham Hotspur bt Hajduk Split 1–2, 1–0
(away goals, 2–2 agg)
Anderlecht bt Nottingham Forest 0–2, 3–0
(3–1 agg)

FINAL

1st leg: May 9 (Parc Astrid, Brussels)
Anderlecht 1(Olsen 85)
Tottenham Hotspur 1 (Miller 57)
HT: 0–0. Att: 35,000. Ref: Galler (Swi)
ANDERLECHT: Munaron, Grun, De Greef, M Olsen, De Groot, Hofkens, Vandereycken, Scifo, Brylle, Vandenbergh (Arnesen, 81), Czerniatynski (Vercauteren, 85).
TOTTENHAM: Parks, Thomas, Roberts, Hughton, Perryman, Miller, Stevens (Mabbutt, 80), Hazard, Galvin, Archibald, Falco.

2nd leg: May 23 (White Hart Lane, London)
Tottenham Hotspur 1 (Roberts 84)
Anderlecht 1 (Czerniatynski 60)
HT: 0–0. 90 min: 1–1. After extra time. Tottenham 4–3 on pens. Att: 46,000. Ref: Roth (WG)
TOTTENHAM: Parks, Thomas, Hughton, Roberts, Miller (Ardiles, 78), Mabbutt (Dick, 74), Hazard, Stevens, Galvin, Archibald, Falco.
ANDERLECHT: Munaron, Hofkens, Grun, De Greef, M Olsen, De Groot, Arnesen (Gudjohnsen, 77, Vercauteren, Scifo, Czerniatynski (Brylle, 103), Vandereycken.

1984–85

SEMI-FINALS

Real Madrid bt Internazionale 0–2, 3–0
(3–2 agg)
Videoton bt Zeljeznicar Sarajevo 3–1, 1–2
(4–3 agg)

FINAL

1st leg: May 8 (Sostol, Szekesfehervar)
Videoton 0
Real Madrid 3 (Michel 31, Santillana 77, Valdano 89)
HT: 0–1. Att: 30,000. Ref: Vautrot (Fra)
VIDEOTON: P Disztl, Borsanyi, L Disztl, Csushay, Horvath, Palkovics, Vegh, Wittman, Vadasz, Novath (Gyenti, 62), Burcsa.
REAL: Miguel Angel, Chendo, Sanchis, Stielike, Camacho, San Jose, Michel, Gallego, Butragueno (Juanito, 80), Santillana (Salguero, 86), Valdano.

2nd leg: May 22 (Santiago Bernabeu, Madrid)
Real Madrid 0
Videoton 1 (Majer 86)
HT: 0–0. Att: 90,000. Ref: Ponnet (Bel)
REAL: Miguel Angel, Chendo, Sanchis, Stielike, Camacho, San Jose, Michel, Gallego, Butragueno, Santillana, Valdano (Juanito, 57)
VIDEOTON: P Disztl, Csushay, L Disztl, Vegh, Horvath, Burcsa, Csongradi (Wittman, 57), Vadasz, Szabo, Majer, Novath (Palkovics, 51)
Winners: Real Madrid, 3–1 agg

1985–86

SEMI-FINALS

Real Madrid bt Internazionale 1–3, 5–1
(6–4 agg)
FC Köln bt Waregem 4–0, 3–3
(7–3 agg)

FINAL

1st leg: Apr 30 (Santiago Bernabeu, Madrid)
Real Madrid 5 (Sanchez 38, Gordillo 42, Valdano 51 84, Santillana 89)
FC Köln 1 (K Allofs 29)
HT: 2–1. Att: 85,000. Ref: Courtney (Eng)
REAL: Agustin, Salguero, Solana, Camacho, Martin Vazquez (Santillana, 83), Michel, Juanito, Gordillo, Butragueno, Sanchez, Valdano.
KÖLN: Schumacher, Geils, Gielchen, Steiner, Prestin, Geilenkirchen, Hönerbach, Bein (Hässler, 71), Janssen, Littbarski (Dickel, 84), K Allofs.

2nd leg: May 6 (Olympiastadion, Berlin)
FC Köln 2 (Bein 22, Geilenkirchen 72)
Real Madrid 0
HT: 1–0. Att: 15,000. Ref: Valentine (Sco)
KÖLN: Schumacher, Prestin, Gielchen, Geils (Schmitz, 82), Geilenkirchen, Steiner, Bein, Hönerbach, Janssen (Pisanti, 51), Littbarski, K Allofs.
REAL MADRID: Agustin, Chendo, Maceda, Solana, Camacho, Michel, Gallego, Valdano, Gordillo, Butragueno (Juanito, 88), Sanchez (Santillana, 20)
Winners: Real Madrid, 5–3 agg

1986–87

SEMI-FINALS

IFK Gothenburg bt Tirol Innsbruck 4–1, 1–0
(5–1 agg)
Dundee Utd bt Borussia Mönchengladbach 0–0, 2–0
(2–0 agg)

FINAL

1st leg: May 6 (Nya Ullevi, Gothenburg)
IFK Gothenburg 1 (Pettersson 38)
Dundee United 0
HT: 1–0. Att: 50,000. Ref: Kirschen (EG)
IFK: Wernersson, C Karlsson, Hysen, Larsson, Fredriksson, Jonsson (R Nilsson, 68), Tord Holmgren (Zetterlund, 89), Andersson, Tommy Holmgren, Pettersson, L Nilsson.
DUNDEE UNITED: Thompson, Malpas, Narey, Hegarty (Clark, 55), Holt, McInally, Kirkwood, Bowman, Bannon, Sturrock (Beaumont 89), Redford.

2nd leg: May 20 (Tannadice Park, Dundee)
Dundee United 1 (Clark 60)
IFK Gothenburg 1 (Nilsson 22)
HT: 0–1. Att: 21,000. Ref: Igna (Rom)
DUNDEE UNITED: Thompson, Malpas, Clark, Narey, Holt (Hegarty, 46), McInally, Ferguson, Kirkwood, Sturrock, Redford (Bannon, 72), Gallacher.
IFK: Wernersson, C Karlsson, Hysen, Larsson, Fredriksson, R Nilsson (Johansson, 78), Tord Holmgren, Andersson, Tommy Holmgren (Mordt, 70), Pettersson, L Nilsson.
Winners: IFK Gothenburg, 2–1 agg

1987–88

SEMI-FINALS

Bayer Leverkusen bt Werder Bremen 1–0, 0–0
(1–0 agg)
Espanol bt Club Brugge 0–2, 3–0
(3–2 agg)

FINAL

1st leg: May 4 (Sarria, Barcelona)
Espanol 3 (Losada 45 56, Soler 49)
Bayer Leverkusen 0
HT: 1–0. Att: 42,000. Ref: Krchnak (Cze)
ESPANOL: N'Kono, Job, Miguel Angel, Gallart, Soler, Orejuela (Golobart, 66), Urquiaga, Iaki, Valverde, Pichi Alonso (Lauridsen, 71), Losada.
BAYER: Vollborn, Rolff, De Kayser, A Reinhardt, Hinterberger, Cha Bum-kun (Götz, 18), Tita, Buncol, Falkenmayer (K Reinhardt, 78), Waas, Tauber.

2nd leg: May 18 (Haberland Stadion, Leverkusen)
Bayer Leverkusen 3 (Tita 57, Götz 63, Cha Bum-kun 81)
Espanol 0
HT: 0–0. 90min: 3–0. After extra time. Bayer Leverkusen 3–2 on pens. Att: 22,000. Ref: Keizer (Hol)
BAYER: Vollborn, Rolff, Seckler, A Reinhardt, K Reinhardt, Schreier, (Waas, 46), Buncol, Falkenmayer, Cha Bum-kun, Götz, Tita (Tuber, 62)
ESPANOL: N'Kono, Miguel Angel, Golobart (Zuniga, 73), Urquiaga, Job, Orejuela (Zubillaga, 67), Iaki, Soler, Pichi Alonso, Gallart, Losada.

1988–89

SEMI-FINALS

Napoli bt Bayern Munich 2–0, 2–2
(4–2 agg)
Stuttgart bt Dynamo Dresden 1–0, 1–1
(2–1 agg)

FINAL

1st leg: May 3 (San Paolo, Naples)
Napoli 2 (Maradona 68, Careca 87)
Stuttgart 1 (Gaudino 17)
HT: 0–1. Att: 83,000. Ref: Germanakos (Gre)
NAPOLI: Giuliani, Renica, Ferrara, Francini, Corradini (Crippa, 46), Alemo, Fusi, De Napoli, Careca, Maradona, Carnevale.
STUTTGART: Immel, Allgöwer, N Schmäler, Hartmann, Buchwald, Schäfer, Katanec, Sigurvinsson, Schröder, Walter (Zietsch, 75), Gaudino.

2nd leg: May 17 (Neckarstadion, Stuttgart)
Stuttgart 3(Klinsmann 27, De Napoli og 70, O Schmäler 89)
Napoli 3 (Alemo 18, Ferrara 39, Careca 62)
HT: 1–2. Att: 67,000. Ref: Sanchez Arminio (Spa)
STUTTGART: Immel, Allgöwer, N Schmäler, Hartmann, Schäffer, Katanec, Sigurvinsson, Schröder, Walter (O Schmäler,77), Klinsmann, Gaudino.
NAPOLI: Giuliani, Renica, Ferrara, Francini, Corradini, Alemo (Carranante, 31), Fusi, De Napoli, Careca (Bigliardi, 70), Maradona, Carnevale.
Winners: Napoli, 5–4 agg

1989–90

SEMI-FINALS

Juventus bt FC Köln 3–2, 0–0
(3–2 agg)
Fiorentina bt Werder Bremen 1–1, 0–0
(away goals, 1–1 agg)

FINAL

1st leg: May 2 (Comunale, Turin)
Juventus 3 (Galia 3, Casiraghi 59, De Agostini 73)
Fiorentina 1 (Buso 10)
HT: 1–1. Att: 45,000. Ref: Soriano Aladren (Spa)
JUVENTUS: Tacconi, Napoli, De Agostini, Galia, Brio (Alessio, 46), Bonetti, Aleinikov, Barros, Marocchi, Casiraghi, Schillaci.
FIORENTINA: Landucci, Dell'Oglio, Volpecina, Pin, Battistini, Dunga, Nappi, Kubik (Malusci, 46), R Baggio, Buso, Di Chiara.

2nd leg: May 16 (Partenio, Avellino) 2nd leg
Fiorentina 0
Juventus 0
Att: 32,000. Ref: Schmidhuber (WG)
FIORENTINA: Landucci, Dell'Oglio, Volpecina, Pin, Battistini, Dunga, Nappi (Zironelli, 72), Kubik, R Baggio, Buso, Di Chiara.
JUVENTUS: Tacconi, Napoli, De Agostini, Galia, Bruno, Alessio, Aleinikov, Barros (Avallone, 72), Marocchi, Casiraghi (Rosa, 78), Schillaci.
Winners: Juventus, 3–1 agg

1990–91

SEMI-FINALS

Internazionale bt Sporting Lisbon 0–0, 2–0
(2–0 agg)
Roma bt Bronbyernes 0–0, 2–1
(2–1 agg)

FINAL

1st leg: May 8 (Giuseppe Meazza, Milan)
Internazionale 2 (Matthäus 55, Berti 67)
Roma 0
HT: 0–0. Att: 75,000. Ref: Spirin (SU)
INTER: Zenga, Bergomi, Brehme, Battistini, Ferri, Paganin (G Baresi, 64), Bianchi, Berti, Matthäus, Klinsmann, Serena (Pizzi, 89)
ROMA: Cervone, Tempestilli, Nela, Berthold, Aldair (Carboni, 72), Comi (Muzzi, 74), Gerolin, Di Mauro, Giannini, Völler, Rizzitelli.

2nd leg: May 22 (Olimpico, Rome)
Roma 1 (Rizzitelli 81)
Internazionale 0
HT: 0–0. Att: 71,000. Ref: Quiniou (Fra)
ROMA: Cervone, Tempestelli (Salsano, 56), Gerolin, Berthold, Aldair, Nela, Desideri (Muzzi, 69), Di Mauro, Giannini, Völler, Rizzitelli.
INTER: Zenga, Bergomi, Brehme, Battistini, Ferri, Paganin, Bianchi, Berti, Matthaus, Klinsmann, Pizzi (Mandorlini, 66)
Winners: Inter 2–1 agg

1991–92

SEMI-FINALS

Ajax bt Genoa 3–2, 1–1
(4–3 agg)
Torino bt Real Madrid 1–2, 2–0
(3–2 agg)

FINAL

1st leg: Apr 29 (Delle Alpi, Turin)
Torino 2 (Casagrande 65 82)
Ajax 2 (Jonk 17, Pettersson 73)
HT: 0–1. Att: 65,000. Ref: Worrall (Eng)
TORINO: Marchegiani, Bruno, Annoni, Cravero (Bresciani, 77), Mussi (Sordo, 80), Benedetti, Scifo, Martin Vasquez, Venturin, Lentini, Casagrande.
AJAX: Menzo, Silooy, Blind, Jonk, F De Boer, Winter, Kreek, Bergkamp, Van't Schip, Pettersson, Roy (Groenendijk, 83)

2nd leg: May 13 (Olympisch Stadion, Amsterdam)
Ajax 0
Torino 0
HT: 0–0. Att: 42,000. Ref: Petrovic (Yug)
AJAX: Menzo, Silooy, Blind, Jonk, F De Boer, Winter, Kreek (Vink, 80), Alflen, Van't Schip, Pettersson, Roy (Van Loen, 65)
TORINO: Marchegiani, Mussi, Cravero (Sordo, 58), Benedetti, Fusi, Policano, Martin Vazquez, Scifo (Bresciani, 62), Veturin, Casagrande, Lentini.
Winners: Ajax on away goals, 2–2 agg

1992–93

SEMI-FINALS

Juventus bt Paris Saint-Germain 2–1, 1–0
(3–1 agg)
Borussia Dortmund bt Auxerre 2–0, 0–2
(6–5 on pens, 2–2 agg)

FINAL

1st leg: May 5 (Westfalenstadion, Dortmund)
Borussia Dortmund 1 (M Rummenigge 2)
Juventus 3 (D Baggio 27, R Baggio 31 74)
HT: 1–2. Att: 37,000. Ref: Puhl (Hun)
BORUSSIA: Klos, Grauer, Reuter, Schmidt, Lusch, Frank (Mill, 46), Zorc (Karl, 75), M Rummenigge, Poschner, K Reinhardt, Chapuisat.
JUVENTUS: Peruzzi, Julio Cesar, Carrera, Kohler, De Marchi, Conti, D Baggio, R Baggio (Di Canio, 80), Marocchi, Vialli, Möller (Galia, 86)

2nd leg: May 19 (Delle Alpi, Turin)
Juventus 3 (D Baggio 5 40, Möller 65)
Borussia Dortmund 0
HT: 20. Att: 60,000. Ref: Blankenstein (Hol)
JUVENTUS: Peruzzi, Carrera, Torricelli (Di Canio, 66), De Marchi, Kohler, Julio Cesar, Mller, D Baggio, R Baggio, Vialli (Ravanelli, 79), Marocchi.
DORTMUND: Klos, Reinhardt, Schmidt, Schulz, Zelic, Poscher, Reuter (Lusch, 65), Karl, Mill, M Rummenigge (Frank, 43), Sippel.
Winners: Juventus, 6–1 agg

1993–94

SEMI-FINALS

Internazionale bt Cagliari 2–3, 3–0
(5–3 agg)
Casino Austria Salzburg bt Karlsruhe 0–0, 1–1
(away goals, 1–1 agg)

FINAL

1st leg: Apr 26 (Ernst-Happel-Stadion, Vienna)
Austria Salzburg 0
Internazionale 1 (Berti 35)
HT: 0–1. Att: 47,000. Nielsen (Den)
SALZBURG: Konrad, Lainer, Weber, Winklhofer (Steiner, 61), Fürstaller, Aigner, Amerhauser (Muzek, 64), Artner, Marquinho, Pfeifenberger, Stadler.
INTER: Zenga, A Paganin, Orlando, Jonk, Bergomi, Battistini, Bianchi, Manicone, Berti, Bergkamp (Dell'Anno, 89), Sosa (Ferri, 74)

2nd leg: May 11 (Giuseppe Meazza, Milan)
Internazionale 1 (Jonk 63)
Austria Salzburg 0
HT: 0–0. Att: 80,000. Ref: McCluskey (Sco)
INTER: Zenga, A Paganin, Fontolan (Ferri 23), Jonk, Bergomi, Battistini, Orlando, Manicone, Berti, Bergkamp (M Paganin, 90) Sosa.
SALZBURG: Konrad, Winklhofer (Amerhauser, 68), Lainer, Weber, Fürstaller, Aigner, Jurcevic, Artner (Steiner), Hütter, Marquinho, Feicrsinger.
Winners: Inter, 2–0 agg

1994–95

SEMI-FINALS

Parma bt Bayer Leverkusen 2–1, 3–0
(5–1 agg)

Juventus bt Borussia Dortmund 2–2, 2–1
(4–3 agg)

FINAL

1st leg: May 3 (Tardini, Parma)

Parma 1 (D Baggio 5)

Juventus 0

HT: 1–0. Att: 22,000. Ref: Lopez Nieto (Spa)
PARMA: Bucci, Benarrivo (Mussi, 8), Minotti, Apolloni, Fernando Couto, Di Chiara, Pin, D Baggio, Sensini, Zola (Fiore, 89), Asprilla.
JUVENTUS: Rampulla, Fusi (Del Piero, 72), Tacchinardi, Carrera (Marocchi, 46), Jarni, Paulo Sousa, Di Livio, Deschamps, Vialli, R Baggio, Ravanelli.

2nd leg: May 17 (Giuseppe Meazza, Milan) 2nd leg

Juventus 1 (Vialli 33)

Parma 1 (D Baggio 54)

HT: 1–0. Att: 80,000. Ref: Van der Wijngaert (Bel)
JUVENTUS: Peruzzi, Ferrara, Porrini, Torricelli, Jarni, Paulo Sousa, Di Livio (Carrera, 80), Marocchi (Del Piero, 73), R Baggio, Vialli, Ravanelli.
PARMA: Bucci, Benarrivo (Mussi, 46), Susic, Minotti, Di Chiara (Castellini, 79), Fernando Couto, Fiore, D Baggio, Crippa, Zola, Asprilla.
Winners: Parma, 2–1 agg

1995–96

SEMI-FINALS

Bayern Munich bt Barcelona 2–2, 2–1
(4–3 agg)

Bordeaux bt Slavia Prague 1–0, 1–0
(2–0 agg)

FINAL

1st leg: May 1 (Olympia, Munich)

Bayern Munich 2 (Helmer 35, Scholl 60)

Bordeaux 0

HT: 1–0. Att: 62,500. Ref: Mühmenthaler (Swi)
BAYERN: Kahn, Matthäus (Frey 53), Babbel, Ziege, Kreuzer, Helmer, Hamann, Scholl, Sforza, Klinsmann, Papin (Witeczek 70).
BORDEAUX: Huard, Grenet, Lizarazu, Friis-Hansen, Dogon, Lucas, Croci, Dutuel, Tholot (Anselin 89), Richard Witschge, Bancarel.

2nd leg: May 15 (Bordeaux)

Bordeaux 1(Dutuel 75)

Bayern Munich 3 (Scholl 53, Kostadinov 65, Klinsmann 79)

HT: 00. Att: 36,000. Ref: Zhuk (Blr)
BORDEAUX: Huard, Bancarel, Lizarazu (Anselin 32), Friis-Hansen, Dogon, Lucas (Grenet 79), Zidane, Croci (Dutuel 57), Tholot, Richard Witschge, Dugarry.
BAYERN: Kahn, Babbel, Ziege, Strunz, Helmer, Frey (Zickler 60), Scholl, Sforza, Klinsmann, Matthäus, Kostadinov (Witeczek 75).
Winners: Bayern, 5–1 agg

1996–97

SEMI-FINALS

Internazionale bt Monaco 3–1, 0–1
(3–2 agg)

Schalke bt Tenerife 0–1, 2–0
(2–1 agg)

FINAL

1st leg: May 7 (Gelsenkirchen)

Schalke 1 (Wilmots 70)

Internazionale 0

HT: 0–0. Att: 57,000. Ref: Batta (Fra)
SCHALKE: Lehmann, De Kock, Thon, Linke, Eigenrauch, Müller, Nemec, Anderbrugge, Buskens (Max 67), Latal, Wilmots.
INTER: Pagliuca, Bergomi, M Paganin, Galante, Pistone, Zanetti, Fresi (Berti 61), Sforza, Winter, Zamorano, Ganz.

2nd leg: May 21 (Giuseppe Meazza, Milan)

Internazionale 1 (Zamorano 84)

Schalke 0

HT: 0–0. 90min: 1–0. After extra time. Schalke 4–1 on pens. Att: 81,675. Ref: Garcia Aranda (Spa)
INTER: Pagliuca, Bergomi (Angloma 71), M Paganin, Fresi, Pistone, Zanetti (Berti 119), Ince, Sforza (Winter 90), Djorkaeff, Zamorano, Ganz.
SCHALKE: Lehmann, De Kock, Thon, Linke, Latal (Held 111), Eigenrauch, Nemec, Müller (Anderbrugge 97), Buskens, Max, Wilmots.

1997–98

SEMI-FINALS

Lazio bt Atletico Madird 1–0, 0–0
(1–0 on agg)

Internazionale bt Spartak Moscow 2–1, 2–1
(4–2 on agg)

FINAL

May 6 (Parc des Princes, Paris)

Lazio 0

Internazionale 3 (Zamorano 5, Zanetti 60, Ronaldo 70)

HT: 0–1. Att: 45,000. Ref: Nieto (Spa)
LAZIO: Marchegiani, Grandoni (Gottardi 55), Nesta, Negro, Favalli, Fuser, Venturin (Almeyda 49), Jugovic, Nedved, Casiraghi, Mancini. Coach: Eriksson.
INTER: Pagliuca, Colonnese, West, Fresi, Zanetti, Winter (Cauet 69) Ze Elias, Simeone, Djorkaeff (Moriero 69), Zamorano (Sartor 74), Ronaldo. Coach: Simoni.

EUROPEAN SUPERCUP

The European Supercup is the youngest of UEFA's mainstream club events and is competed for each season by the winners of the previous season's Champions Cup and Cup-winners Cup.

Just as the Paris newspaper, *L'Equipe*, provided the initiative for the original Champion Clubs' Cup, so it was the Dutch newspaper *De Telegraaf* which helped bring the Supercup to life.

Telegraaf's proposal filled a competitive need which had arisen because directors of Ajax, newly-crowned European club champions in 1971, had been so horrified by events at the previous year's clash between their fellow Dutchmen from Feyenoord and Estudiantes de La Plata, the champions of South America. Accordingly, they refused to play the world club tie and found Rangers, holders of the Cup-winners Cup, ready to launch a European club play-off between holders of the two top titles.

The Dutch, then at their "total football" zenith under the inspiration of Johan Cruyff, won in Holland and Scotland, then thrashed Milan the following year, even though Cruyff had by then been sold to Barcelona. The tie was played over two legs – home and away – as have been the majority of Supercup meetings. Ajax won 3–1 in Amsterdam and 3–2 in Glasgow.

The event has always suffered from fixture date difficulties. The reasons are obvious: very few midweek dates are free once allowances have been made for European club competitions and qualifying matches in national team tournaments such as the World Cup and European Championship. The upshot has been that the event has generally been staged in the year following the teams' European club victories. Thus, the Supercup for the 1997 European club winners was played in 1998.

A consequence of the fixture problems has seen the Supercup ties being played in January or February, at a time when weather conditions are hardly conducive to the attractive football which might enhance the event's image.

Further, staging the match beyond the halfway point of the following season means that, often, the participants have already been eliminated from their European events. The Supercup is thus often perceived as a consolation or second-class event and of little significance beyond the immediate participating clubs.

The Supercup has never been a major crowd-puller, the two-leg matches usually being squashed into mid-season. On three occasions. the clubs involved could find space in their crowded calendars for only a single-match event. Juventus defeated Liverpool in Turin in 1984, Steaua Bucharest saw off Kiev Dynamo the following year then Manchester United squeezed a victory over Red Star Belgrade in 1991. Political problems confused the meeting between United and Red Star; UEFA judged it too risky for United to travel to the capital of the violently-unravelling former Yugoslavia.

Typical of the interest taken in it was the remark in January 1997 of Bernard Lama, goalkeeper of Paris Saint-Germain, that the Supercup "is just a piece of business for the club." Bad business, as it turned out, for Paris, 1996 winners of the Cup-winners Cup, were duly thrashed 6–1 at home and 3–1 away by Juventus. Indeed, Juventus had to take the second leg to Palermo to lure a decent crowd for the second leg. The soccer-saturated public of Turin would have ignored the event had it gone ahead, as scheduled, in their own Delle Alpi stadium.

So far, then, the Champions Cup holders, as befits their superior status, lead 14–8 overall (discounting the 1993 event when Milan substituted for European champions Marseille, who had been barred in the interim after match-fixing revelations).

UEFA has wanted for some time to upgrade the sporting and financial status of the Supercup by switching it to a single match final at a neutral venue. It had been hoped to make the change in 1997–98, but problems arose in finding a suitable, available venue in mid-season.

Milan and Ajax Amsterdam, as befits the founders, have won the Supercup on more occasions – three – than any other clubs.

EUROPEAN SUPERCUP RESULTS

1972

1st leg: Jan 16, 1973 (Glasgow)
Rangers 1 (MacDonald 39)
Ajax 3 (Rep 31, Cruyff 43, Haan 44)
HT: 1-3. Att: 57,000. Ref: Mackenzie (Sco)

2nd leg: Jan 24 (Amsterdam)
Ajax 3 (Haan 9, G Muhren 39, Cruyff 78)
Rangers 2 (MacDonald 7, 26)
HT: 2-2. Att: 37,000. Ref: Weyland (WG)
Winners: Ajax, 6-3 agg

1973

1st leg: Jan 9, 1974 (Milan)
Milan 1 (Chiarugi 77)
Ajax 0
HT: 0-0. Att: 15,000. Ref: Scheurer (Swi)

2nd leg: Jan 16, 1974 (Amsterdam)
Ajax 6 (Mulder 26, Keizer 35, Neeskens 71, Rep 81, Muhren 84, Haan 87)
Milan 0
HT: 2-0. Att: 40,000. Ref: Glockner (EG)
Winners: Ajax, 6-1 agg

1974

Not contested

1975

1st leg: Sep 9 (Munich)
Bayern Munich 0
Kiev Dynamo 1 (Blokhin 66)
HT: 0-0. Att: 30,000. Ref: Gonella (Ita)

2nd leg: Oct 6 (Kiev)
Kiev Dynamo 2 (Blokhin 40, 53)
Bayern Munich 0
HT: 1-0. Att: 100,000. Ref: Babacan (Tur)
Winners: Kiev Dynamo, 3-0 agg

1976

1st leg: Aug 17 (Munich)
Bayern Munich 2 (Müller 58 88)
Anderlecht 1 (Haan 16)
HT: 0-1. Att: 41,000. Ref: Burns (Eng)

2nd leg: Aug 30 (Brussels)
Anderlecht 4 (Rensenbrink 20 82, Van der Elst 25, Haan 59)
Bayern Munich 1 (Müller 63)
HT: 2-0. Att: 35,000. Ref: Schiller (Aut)
Winners: Anderlecht, 5-3 agg

1977

1st leg: Nov 22 (Hamburg)
Hamburg 1 (Keller 29)
Liverpool 1 (Fairclough 65)
HT: 1-0. Att: 16,000. Ref: Garrido (Por)

2nd leg: Dec 6 (Liverpool)

Liverpool 6 (Thompson 21, McDermott 40 56 57, Fairclough 84, Dalglish 88)
Hamburg 0
HT: 2-0. Att: 34,931. Ref: Eriksson (Swe)
Winners: Liverpool, 7-1 agg

1978

1st leg: Dec 4 (Brussels, Parc Astrid)
Anderlecht 3 (Vercauteren 18, Van der Elst 38, Resenbrink 87)
Liverpool 1 (Case 27)
HT: 2-1. Att: 35,000. Ref: Palotai (Hun)

2nd leg: Dec 19 (Liverpool)
Liverpool 2 (Hughes 13, Fairclough 85)
RSC Anderlecht 1 (Van der Elst 71)
HT: 1-0. Att: 23,598. Ref: Rainea (Rom)
Winners: Anderlecht, 4-3 agg

1979

1st leg: Jan 30, 1980 (Nottingham)
Nottingham Forest 1 (George 9)
Barcelona 0
HT: 1-0. Att: 23,807. Ref: Prokop (EG)

2nd leg: Feb 5, 1980 (Barcelona)
Barcelona 1 (Roberto 25)
Nottingham Forest 1 (Burns 42)
HT: 1-1. Att: 80,000. Ref: Eschweiler (WG)
Winners: Nottingham Forest, 2-1 agg

1980

1st leg: Nov 25 (Nottingham)
Nottingham Forest 2 (Bowyer 57 89)
Valencia 1 (Felman 47)
HT: 0-0. Att: 12,463. Ref: Ponnet (Bel)

2nd leg: Dec 17 (Valencia)
Valencia 1 (Morena 51)
Nottingham Forest 0
HT: 0-0. Att: 45,000. Ref: Wohrer (Aus)
Winners: Nottingham Forest, away goals, agg 2-2

1981

Not contested

1982

1st leg: Jan 19, 1983 (Barcelona)
Barcelona 1 (Marcos 52)
Aston Villa 0
HT: 0-0. Att: 50,000. Ref: Galler (Swi)

2nd leg: Jan 26, 1983 (Birmingham)
Aston Villa 3 (Shaw 80, Cowans 99, McNaught 104)
Barcelona 0
HT: 0-0. 90min: 1-0. After extra time. Att: 32,570. Ref: Ponnet (Bel)
Winners: Villa 3-1 agg

1983

1st leg: Nov 22 (Hamburg)
Hamburg 0
Aberdeen 0
Att: 12,000. Ref: Christov (Cze)

2nd leg: Dec 20 (Aberdeen)
Aberdeen 2 (Simpson 47, McGhee 65)

Hamburg 0
HT: 0-0. Att: 24,000. Ref: Brummeier (Aut)
Winners: Aberdeen 2-0 agg

1984

Jan 16, 1984 (Turin)
Juventus 2 (Boniek 39 79)
Liverpool 0
HT: 1-0. Att: 60,000. Ref: Pauly (WG)

1985

Not contested

1986

Feb 24, 1986 (Monte Carlo)
Steaua Bucharesti 1 (Hagi 44)
Kiev Dynamo 0
HT: 1-0. Att: 8,456. Ref: Agnolin (Ita)

1987

1st leg: Nov 24 (Amsterdam)
Ajax 0
FC Porto 1 (Rui Barros 5)
HT: 0-1. Att: 27,000. Ref: Valentine (Sco)

2nd leg: Jan 13, 1988 (Oporto)
FC Porto 1 (Sousa 70)
Ajax 0
HT: 0-0. Att: 50,000. Ref: Schmidhuber (WG)
Winners: Porto, 2-0 agg

1988

1st leg: Feb 1, 1989 (Mechelen)
Mechelen 3 (Bosman 16 50, De Wilde 17)
PSV Eindhoven 0
HT: 2-0. Att: 7,000. Ref: Kirschen (EG)

2nd leg: Feb 8, 1989 (Eindhoven)
PSV Eindhoven 1 (Gilhaus 78)
Mechelen 0
HT: 0-0. Att: 17,100. Ref: Fredriksson (Swe)
Winners: Mechelen, 3-1 agg

1989

1st leg: Nov 23 (Barcelona)
Barcelona 1 (Amor 67)
Milan 1 (Van Basten 44)
HT: 0-1. Att: 70,000. Ref: Quiniou (Fra)

2nd leg: Dec 7 (Milan)
Milan 1 (Evani 55)
Barcelona 0
HT: 0-0. Att: 50,000. Ref: Kohl (Aut)
Winners: Milan, 2-1 agg

1990

1st leg: Oct 10 (Genoa)
Sampdoria 1 (Mikhailichenko 31)
Milan 1 (Evani 40)
HT: 1-1. Att: 25,000. Ref: Rosa dos Santos (Por)

2nd leg: Nov 29 (Milan)
Milan 2 (Gullit 44, Rijkaard 77)
Sampdoria 0
HT: 1-0. Att: 25,000. Ref: Petrovic (Yug)
Winners: Milan, 3-1 on agg

1991

Nov 19 (Manchester)
Manchester United 1 (McClair 67)
Red Star Belgrade 0
HT: 0–0. Att: 22,110. Ref: Van der Ende (Hol)

1992

1st leg: Feb 10, 1993 (Bremen)
Werder Bremen 1 (Allofs 87)
Barcelona 1 (Salinas 37)
HT: 0–1. Att: 22,098. Ref: Nielsen (Den)

2nd leg: Mar 10, 1993 (Barcelona)
Barcelona 2 (Stoichkov 32, Goikoetxea 48)
Werder Bremen 1 (Rufer 41)
HT: 1–1. Att: 75,000. Ref: Karlsson (Swe)
Winners: Barcelona, 3–2 agg

1993

1st leg: Jan 12, 1994 (Parma)
Parma 0
Milan 1 (Papin 43)
HT: 0–1. Att: 8,083. Ref: Diaz Vega (Spa)

2nd leg: Feb 2, 1994 (Milan)
Milan 0
Parma 2 (Sensini 23, Crippa 95)
HT: 0–1. 90min: 0–1. After extra time. Att: 24,074. Ref: Rothlisberger (Swi)
Winners: Parma, 2–1 agg

1994

1st leg: Feb 1, 1994 (Highbury, London)
Arsenal 0
Milan 0
Att: 38,044. Ref: Van der Ende (Hol)

2nd leg: Feb 8, 1994 (Milan)
Milan 2 (Boban 41, Massaro 66)
Arsenal 0
HT: 1–0. Att: 23,953. Ref: Krug (Ger)
Winners: Milan, 2–0 agg

1995

1st leg: Feb 6, 1966 (Zaragoza)
Real Zaragoza 1 (Aguado 28)
Ajax 1 (Kluivert 71)
HT: 1–0. Att: 23,000. Ref: Harrel (Fra)

2nd leg: Feb 28, 1996 (Amsterdam)
Ajax 4 (Bogarde 41, George 53, Blind 63pen, 68pen)
Real Zaragoza 0
HT: 1–0. Att: 22,000. Ref: Mottram (Sco)
Winners: Ajax, 5–1 agg

1996

1st leg: Jan 15, 1997 (Paris, Parc des Princes)
Paris Saint-Germain 1 (Rai 52 pen)
Juventus 6 (Porrini 5, Padovano 21 40, Ferrara 34, Lombardo 83, Amoruso 89)
HT: 0–4. Att: 29,519. Ref: Levnikov (Rus)

2nd leg: Feb 5, 1996 (Palermo)
Juventus 3 (Del Piero 36 70, Vieri 90)
Paris Saint-Germain 1 (Rai 65 pen)
HT: 1–0. Att: 35,100. Ref: Muhmenthaler (Swi)
Winners: Juventus, 9–2 agg

1997

1st leg: Jan 8, 1998 (Barcelona)
Barcelona 2 (Luis Enrique 8, Rivaldo 61 pen)
Borussia Dortmund 0
HT: 1–0. Att: 50,000. Ref: Elleray (Eng)

2nd leg: Mar 11, 1998 (Dortmund)
Borussia Dortmund 1 (Heinrich 64)
Barcelona 1 (Giovanni 8)
HT: 0–1. Att: 32,500. Ref: Ceccarini (Ita)
Winners: Barcelona, 3–1 agg

Paris St-Germain and Juventus, during the Italians' 6–1 victory in Paris in 1996

MITROPA CUP

The Mitropa Cup was the brainchild, in the inter-war years of the 1920s and 1930s, of Austrian football pioneer Hugo Meisl. It was an enormous success. Attempts were made to fix League matches because a place was so important. For this was the true forerunner of today's Champions League, Cup-winners Cup and UEFA Cup.

Meisl's idea was a knock-out competition for club teams of central Europe (hence the name Mitropa – a contraction of the German term Mittel Europa, or Central Europe).

The delicate son of a wealthy Jewish banking family, Meisl showed little interest in the family firm, but plenty in football. For several years, his father tried to separate him from his sports administration but eventually had to give in, and in the late 1920s Meisl became secretary of the Austrian federation as well as manager of the national team. Meisl it was who cleared the way for open professionalism in 1924, and with neighbours Hungary and Czechoslovakia on the brink of accepting paid football, first suggested the Mitropa Cup in 1924.

Meisl came up with the two-leg knock-out formula now so familiar and, with the visits of leading British clubs such as Arsenal, Huddersfield and Rangers in mind, envisaged that one day the Mitropa would extend across Europe.

The mid-1920s were important years for football. For example, in 1925, the offisde law was altered, professionalism became accepted, and at last in July 1927 the concerned football authorities agreed to set up a Mitropa Cup committee and put Meisl's ideas into practice.

Indeed, the competition began that year, with Austria, Czechoslovakia, Hungary and Yugoslavia each putting forward two teams. They could be the champions and runners-up or champions and cup winners. So eight clubs entered the first edition of a competition which would soon draw spectators from neutral countries, a competition which boasted – in the mid-1930s – the first live broadcast of football on the continent, a competition whose popularity and importance would be underlined by the unfortunate incidents which have smeared the game's reputation over the years.

The competition began in August and ended in November and there were, naturally, teething problems. No-one had seriously envisaged that teams might finish level after two games. But in the semi-finals, Hungaria of Budapest (later Voros LobogoRed Banner, then MTK) drew 2–2, 0–0 with Sparta Prague and it was on the toss of a coin that the Czechs went into the final against Rapid Vienna. The Hungarians were furious, though the coin provided a form of rough justice, since their ruthless tactics in the second leg – a 0–0 draw in Vienna – had incensed Austrian fans, who pelted the visitors with rubbish at the end of the game.

Sparta had been founded in 1893 and were the winners of the first Czech championship in 1919. If they had been lucky to reach the final, there was no doubting the value of their win over Rapid. The Czechs won 6–2 in Prague, losing narrowly 2–1 in Vienna, where their rough tackling provoked a hail of stones, fruit and bottles from the crowd. Centre-half Kada had to be carried off after being struck on the head by a missile and the demonstrations which continued long after the game soured Austro-Czech football relations for some time.

From that tentative beginning, the competition caught fire. Sparta and Slavia from Prague were, together with FK Austria and Rapid from Vienna, and FTC (now Ferencvaros) from Hungary, the great clubs of the inter-war Mitropa Cup. In 1929, Italy came on board, with Juventus and Genoa competing – though both crashed in the first round.

The matches aroused enormous passion. In 1930, Rapid Vienna beat Sparta in the two-leg final. Fans at the second leg in Vienna were so incensed by the Czechoslovaks' rugged tackling they pelted the Sparta players with rubbish. Police were so worried about security they refused to allow Dr Gero, president of the Mitropa committee, to make the trophy presentation on the pitch.

In 1932, Bologna became the first Italian winners amid controversy. They had a walkover victory in the final because Juventus and Slavia were disqualified after brutal incidents on and off the pitch in their semi-final.

Another Italian club, Ambrosiana-Inter, reached the final in 1933 but without Bologna's luck. Ambrosiana won 2–1 at home against FK Austria and lost 3–1 in Vienna. The great, tragic, Matthias Sindelar scored a classic solo winner for the Austrians in the dying seconds.

The political and military reorganisation of Europe after the Second World War helped kill off the Mitropa. The Iron Curtain separated the old rivals and the competition disappeared until 1951. Travel and visa problems dissuaded the champion clubs from competing. Four years later, and the launch of the Champions Cup signalled the beginning of the end. From 1980, entry was restricted to Second Division clubs until the competition died off in 1991. Italy's Torino were the last winners.

MITROPA CUP RESULTS

1927

Semi-finals
Sparta bt Hungaria 2–2, 0–0
 (3–2 in play-off, 2–2 agg)
Rapid bt Slavia 2–2, 2–1
 (4–3 agg)

Final
Sparta bt Rapid 6–4, 1–2
 (7–3 agg)

1928

Semi-finals
Rapid bt Viktoria Zizkov 3–4 , 3–2,
 (3–1 in play-off, 6–6 agg)
Ferencvaros bt Admira 2–1, 1–0
 (3–1 agg)

Final
Ferencvaros bt Rapid 7-1, 3–5
 (10–6 agg)

1929

Semi-finals
Slavia bt Vienna 2–3, 4–2
 (6–5 agg)
Ujpest bt Rapid 2–1, 2–3,
 (3–1 in play-off, 4–4 agg)

Final
Ujpest bt Slavia 5–1, 2–2
 (7–3 agg)

1930

Semi-finals
Sparta bt Ambrosiana 2–2, 6–1
 (8–3 agg)
Rapid bt Ferencvaros 5–1, 0–1
 (5–2 agg)

Final
Rapid bt Sparta 2-0, 3–2
 (5–2 agg)

1931

Semi-finals
Vienna bt Roma 3–2, 3–1
 (6–3 agg)
WAC Vienna bt Sparta 2–3, 4–3
 (2–0 in play-off, 6–6 agg)

Final
1st FC Vienna bt WAC Vienna 3–2, 2–1
 (5–3 agg)

1932

Semi-finals
Bologna bt Vienna 2–0, 0–1
 (2–1 agg)
Slavia bt Juventus 4–0, 0–2
 (4–2 agg, both clubs banned)

Final
Bologna walkover

1933

Semi-finals
Ambrosiana bt Sparta 4–1, 2–2
 (6–3 agg)
Austria bt Juventus 3–0, 1–1
 (4–1 agg)

Final
Austria bt Ambrosiana 1–2, 3–1
 (4–3 agg)

1934

Semi-finals
Bologna bt Ferencvaros 1–1, 5–1
 (6–2 agg)
Admira bt Juventus 3–1, 1–2
 (4–3 agg)

Final
Bologna bt Admira 2–3, 4–1
 (6–4 agg)

1935

Semi-finals
Sparta bt Juventus 2–0, 1–3
 (5–1 play-off, 3–3 agg)
Ferencvaros bt FK Austria 4–2, 2–3
 (6–5 agg)

Final
Sparta bt Ferencvaros 1–2, 3–0
 (3–2 agg)

1936

Semi-finals
Sparta bt Ambrosiana 5–3, 3–2
 (8–5 agg)
FK Austria bt Ujpest 2–1, 5–2
 (7–3 agg)

Final
Sparta bt FK Austria 0–0, 1–0
 (1–0 agg)

1937

Semi-finals
Ferencvaros bt FK Austria 1–4, 6–1
 (7–5 agg)
Lazio walkover

Final
Ferencvaros bt Lazio 4–2, 5–4
 (9–6 agg)

1938

Semi-finals
Slavia bt Genova 2–4, 4–0
 (6–4 agg)
Ferencvaros bt Juventus 2–3, 2–0
 (4–3 agg)

Final
Slavia bt Ferencvaros 2–2, 2–0
 (4–2 agg)

1939

Semi-finals
Ferencvaros bt Bologna 1–3, 4–1
 (5–4 agg)
Ujpest bt Beogradski 2–4, 7–1
 (9–5 agg)

Final
Ujpest bt Ferencvaros 4–1, 2–2
 (6–3 agg)

1955

Semi-finals
Voros Lobogo bt Honved 2-5, 5–1
 (7–6 agg)
UDA Prague bt Slovan 0–0, 2–2
 (2–1 in play-off, 2–2 agg)

Final
Voros Lobogo bt UDA Prague 6–0, 2–1
 (8–1 agg)

1956

Semi-finals
Rapid bt Voros Lobogo 3–3, 4–3
 (7–6 agg)
Vasas bt Partizan 0–1, 6–1
 (6-2 agg)

Final
Vasas bt Rapid 3–3, 1–1
 (9–2 play-off, 4–4 agg)

1957

Semi-finals
Vasas bt Red Star 3–1, 3–2
 (6–3 agg)
Vojvodina bt Rapid 0–3, 4–1
 (Rapid withdrew, 4–4 agg)

Final
Vasas bt Vojvodina 4-0, 1–2
 (5–2 agg)

1958

No competition

1959

Semi-finals
Honved bt Partizan 3–3, 2–2
 (Honved on toss of coin, 5–5 agg)
MTK bt Vojvodina 0–0, 2–1
 (2–1 agg)

Final
Honved bt MTK 4–3, 2–2
 (6–5 agg)

1960

Winners: Hungary (based on clubs representation system)

1961

Semi-finals
Bologna bt Kladno 1–0, 2–1
  (3–1 agg)
Nitra bt Udinese 4–3, 1–1
  (5–4 agg)

Final
Bologna bt Nitra 3–2, 3–0
  (6–2 agg)

1962

Semi-finals
Vasas bt Atalanta 0–1, 3–1
  (3–2 agg)
Bologna bt Dinamo Zagreb 1–1, 2–1
  (3–2 agg)

Final
Vasas bt Bologna 5–1, 1–2
  (6–3 agg)

1963

Semi-finals
Vasas bt Torino 5–1, 1–2
  (6–3 agg)
MTK bt Zeljeznicar 1–1, 1–0
  (2–1 agg)

Final
TK bt Vasas 2–1, 1–1
  (3–2 agg)

1964

Semi-finals
Sparta bt Bologna 3–0, 2–2
  (5–2 agg)
Slovan Bratislava bt Vasas 2–0, 1–1
  (3–1 agg)

Final
Sparta bt Slovan Bratislava 0–0, 2–0
  (2–0 agg)

1965

Semi-finals
Vasas bt Sparta 5–4
  after extra time
Fiorentina bt Rapid 3–0

Final
Vasas bt Fiorentina 1–0

1966

Semi-finals
Fiorentina bt Wiener SK 4–2
Trencin bt Vasas 1–0

Final
Fiorentina bt Trencin 1–0

1967

Semi-finals
Trnava bt Fiorentina 2-0, 1–2
  (3–2 agg)
Ujpest bt FK Austria 3–0, 1–2
  (4–2 agg)

Final
Trnava bt Ujpest 2–3, 3–1
  (5-4 agg)

1968

Semi-finals
Red Star bt Ujpest 0–1, 4–1
  (4–2 agg)
Trnava bt Vardar Skopje 4–1, 2–2
  (6–3 agg)

Final
Red Star bt Trnava 0–1, 4–1
  (4–2 agg)

1969

Semi-finals
Inter Bratislava bt Vasas 2–2, 1–0
  (3–2 agg)
Union Teplice bt Zeljeznicar 1–1, 2–1
  (3–2 agg)

Final
Inter Bratislava bt Union Teplice 4–1, 0–0
  (4–1 agg)

1970

Semi-finals
Vasas bt Slavia Prague 1–1, 1–0
  (2–1 agg)
Internazionale bt Honved 1–0, 2–1
  (3–1 agg)

Final
Vasas bt Internazionale 1–2, 4–1
  (5–3 agg)

1971

Semi-finals
Salzburg bt Csepel 0–2, 4–1
  (4–3 agg)
Zenica bt MTK 1–0, 1–1
  (2–1 agg)

Final
Zenica bt Salzburg 3–1

From 1972, the Mitropa Cup was further reduced in size with the introduction of experimental mini-league systems

1972

Winners: Zenica

1973

Winners: Tatabanya

1974

Winners: Tatabanya

1975

Winners: Swarowski Wacker Innsbruck

1976

Winners: Swarowski Wacker Innsbruck

1977

Winners: Vojvodina Novisad

1978

Winners: Partizan Belgrade

1979

Not contested

1980

Winners: Udinese

1981

Winners: Tatran Presov

1982

Winners: Milan

1983

Winners: Vasas Budapest

1984

Winners: Eisenstadt

1985

Winners: Iskra

1986

Winners: Pisa

1987

Winners: Ascoli

1988

Winners: Pisa

1989

Winners: Banik Ostrava

1990

Winners: Bari

1991

Winners: Torino

LATIN CUP

When historians dig deep into the football archives in search of the beginnings of European club competition, they should not overlook the contribution of the Latin Cup.

Launched by the federations of Spain and Portugal, it brought together the champion clubs of the Latin European nations, and encompassed Italy and France. It was not a season-long knock-out event – international travel was still a developing arena. Instead, the event was played over three days in one city between the national champion clubs of those respective four countries.

The system used was the one which later became hugely popular for the annual pre-season tournaments in Spain: two knock-out semi-finals followed by a third place play-off and a final. If two teams finished level after extra time, a replay was staged the following day – no such thing in those days as penalty shoot-outs. However, the Latin Cup's international competitive status owed everything to the way in which success was calculated: clubs represented their country in a very precise manner. The winning club each year gained four points for their country, the runners-up three, third-placed club two and last-placed club one. The points gained were added together every four years to produce a winning nation.

FIRST SERIES 1949–52 RESULTS

1949 BARCELONA

SEMI-FINALS

Sporting 3	Torino 1
Barcelona 5	Reims 0

THIRD PLACE PLAY-OFF

Torino 5 Reims 3

FINAL

Barcelona 2	Sporting 1

1950 LISBON

SEMI-FINALS

Bordeaux 4	Atletico Madrid 2
Benfica 3	Lazio 0

THIRD PLACE PLAY-OFF

Atletico Madrid 2	Lazio 1

FINAL

Benfica 3	Bordeaux 3

Replay:

Benfica 2	Bordeaux 1

1951 MILAN

SEMI-FINALS

Milan 4	Atletico Madrid 1
Lille 1	Sporting 1

Replay:

Lille 6	Sporting 4

THIRD PLACE PLAY-OFF

Atletico Madrid 3	Sporting 1

FINAL

Milan 5	Lille 0

1952 PARIS

SEMI-FINALS

Barcelona 4	Juventus 2
Nice 4	Sporting 2

THIRD PLACE PLAY-OFF

Juventus 3	Sporting 2

FINAL

Barcelona 1	Nice 0

1949–52 final table*

Country	1949	1950	1951	1952	Total
Spain	4	2	2	4	12
France	1	3	3	3	10
Italy	2	1	4	2	9
Portugal	3	4	1	1	9

*4pts for first place; 3pts for runners-up; 2pts for third place; 1pt for fourth place.

SECOND SERIES 1953–57 RESULTS

1953 LISBON

SEMI-FINALS

Milan 4	Sporting 3
Reims 2	Valencia 1

THIRD PLACE PLAY-OFF

Sporting 4	Valencia 1

FINAL

Reims 3	Milan 0

1955 PARIS

SEMI-FINALS

Real Madrid 2	Belenenses 0
Reims 3	Milan 2

THIRD PLACE PLAY-OFF

Milan 3	Belenenses 1

FINAL

Real Madrid 2	Reims 0

1956 MILAN

SEMI-FINALS

Bilbao 2	Nice 0
Milan 4	Benfica 2

THIRD PLACE PLAY-OFF

Benfica 2	Nice 1

FINAL

Milan 3 Bilbao 1

1957 MADRID

SEMI-FINALS

Real Madrid 5	Milan 1
Benfica 1	St-Etienne 0

THIRD PLACE PLAY-OFF

Milan 4	St-Etienne 3

FINAL

Real Madrid 1	Benfica 0

1953–57 series, final table

Country	1949	1950	1951	1952	Total
Spain	1	4	3	4	12
Italy	3	2	4	2	11
France	4	3	1	1	9
Portugal	2	1	2	3	8

*4pts for first place; 3pts for runners-up; 2pts for third place; 1pt for fourth place.

CONCACAF CHAMPIONS CUP

Football has faced a major international challenge in its development in the Central and North American region. On the one hand, the game has always been hugely popular in Mexico and the rest of Central America.

On the other, it has struggled to make progress in the United States and Canada, and took a long time to take off in the Carribean where it first had to contest the sports popularity stakes with cricket and, in the last few years, with American sports such as basketball.

Also, for many years, there was no formal authority to govern soccer in the region. The confederation itself was founded only comparatively recently, in 1961. Previously, football at international level had been administered by various regional bodies. The first such authority was the Central American Sports Congress, launched during the 1924 Olympics with the aim of organizing a regional, scaled-down equivalent of the Games themselves.

It included a football tournament whose organization was later taken over by the Central American and Carribean Confederation, founded in 1938. Later still, Mexico joined the United States and Canada in forming a North American Football Confederation. But it was only after FIFA, under Sir Stanley Rous, enforced the merger of two bodies in 1961 that CONCACAF emerged.

The launch of a regional club competition was the first major test of CONCACAF, two years after its foundation. The European club cups had set a precedent which had been taken up in South America three years earlier. Of course, the lack of funds and geography of the CONCACAF region created its own problems. Thus, the early rounds of the Campeonato Norte-Centroamericano y del Caribe de Futbol Mayor de Campeones have been organised within the regions with two-leg knock-out rounds for the closing stages.

Not everything has gone smoothly over the years. The different regions, for climatic and other reasons, run their football seasons at varying times of the year. Fitting in with domestic demands has been one problem, coping with the financial loss incurred by high travel costs another. CONCACAF later negotiated a supposedly annual match for its champions with the winners of South America's Libertadores Cup, to create an Inter-American Club Championship. But this meant little to the South Americans and fell by the wayside.

Mexican clubs, not surprisingly given the country's pre-eminence within the region, have dominated the CONCACAF Champions Cup. But winning the event has never carried the sort of kudos available to winners of its European and South American equivalents. Entry is generally available to the champions and runners-up of each country. Eight clubs took part in the first tournament in 1962, when Mexico's Guadalajara were the winners.

In 1963, Guadalajara could not be bothered to fly to Haiti for the final against Racing Club who thus took the cup on a walkover. The championships of 1964 and 1965 were not completed and 1966 did not even start. Alianza of El Salvador successfully negotiated all the problems to win in 1967, but a final was impossible in 1968 when Mexico's Toluca won on a walkover. Since then, however, the competition has been staged regularly and, in latter years, demonstrating the progress of football within CONCACAF, the Mexicans have not had it all their own way.

The gradual increase in prestige of the competition meant that, by the mid-1990s, entry levels had multiplied to 32 (compared with the original eight), the final was played at the conclusion of a four-team tournament in the United States and a Cup-winners Cup had been launched.

CONCACAF CHAMPIONS CUP RESULTS

1962
Final
Guadalajara (Mex) bt Comunicaciones (Gua) 1–0, 5–0
(6–0 agg)

1963
Final
Racing Club (Haiti) walkover vs. Guadalajara (Mex)

1964–66
Not completed

1967
Final
Alianza (ESv) bt Jong Colombia (Antigua) 1–2, 3–0,
(3–3 agg, 5–0 play-off)

1968
Final
Toluca (Mex) walkover

1969
Final
Cruz Azul (Mex) bt Comunicaciones (Gua) 0–0, 1–0
(1–0 agg)

1970
Final: Cruz Azul walkover

1971
Final
Cruz Azul (Mex) bt Liga Deportiva Alajuelense (CR) 5–1
*Play-off after Cruz Azul and LDA finished level on points after league format finals tournament.

1972
Final
Olimpia (Hon) bt Robin Hood (Sur) 0–0, 2–0
(2–0 agg)

1973
Final: Transvaal (Sur) walkover

1974
Final
Municipal (Gua) bt Transvaal (Sur) 2–0, 2–0
(4–0 agg)

1975
Final:
Atletico Espanol (Mex) bt Transvaal (Sur) 3–0, 2–1
(5–1 agg)

1976
Final: Aguila (ESv walkover)

1977
Final
America (Mex) bt Robin Hood (Sur) 1–0, 0–0
(1–0 agg)

1978
UAG Guadalajara (Mex) and Defence Force (Tri) joint champions

1979
Final
Deportivo FAS (ESv) bt Jong Colombia (Atg) 1–0, 8–0
(9–0 agg)

1980
Final league tournamnet: 1 UNAM (Mex)

1981
Final
Transvaal (Sur) bt Atletico Marte (ESv) 1–0, 1–1
(2–1 agg)

1982
Final
UNAM (Mex) bt Robin Hood (Sur) 0–0, 2–1
(2–1 agg)

1983
Final
Atlante (Mex) bt Robin Hood (Sur) 1–1, 5–0
(6–1 agg)

1984
Final: Violette (Hai) walkover

1985
Final
Defence Force (Tri) bt Olimpia (Ho) 2–0, 0–1
(2–1 agg)

1986
Final
Liga Deportiva Alajuelense (CR) bt Transvaal (Sur) 4–1, 1–1
(5–2 agg)

1987
Final
America (Mex) bt Defence Force (Tri) 1–1, 2–0
(3–1 agg)

1988
Final
Olimpia (Hon) bt Defence Force (Tri) 2–0, 2–0
(4–0 agg)

1989
Final
UNAM (Mex) bt Pinar del Rio (Cub) 1–1, 3–1
(4–2 agg)

1990
Final
America (Mex) bt Pinar del Rio (Cub) 2–2, 6–0
(8–2 agg)

1991
Final
Puebla (Mex) bt Police FC (Tri) 3–1, 1–1
(4–2 agg)

1992
Final: (Santa Ana, Mexico)
America (Mex) bt Liga Deportiva Alajuelense (CR) 1–0

1993
Final league tournament: Deportivo Saprissa (CR)

1994
Final (San Jose, California, USA):
CS Cartagines (CR) bt Atlante (Mex) 2–1

1995
Final league tournament: Deportivo Saprissa (CR)

1996
Not completed

1997
Final: (Washington, USA)
Cruz Azul (Mex) bt Los Angeles Galaxy 5–3

1998
Final: (Washington, USA)
DC United bt Tolnca (Mex) 1–0

CONCACAF CUP-WINNERS CUP RESULTS

1992
Winners: Atletico Marte (ESv)

1993
Final league tournament: Monterrey (Mex)

1994
Final
Necaxa (Mex) bt Aurora (Gua) 3–0

1995
Final
Univ Autonoma Guadalajara (Mex) bt LA Firpo (ESv) 2–1

AFRICAN CHAMPIONS CUP

Every major club competition has been given breath by one particular team taking a grip on the early years and offering everyone else something – and someone – to aim at.

In the European Champions Cup it was Real Madrid, in South America it was Penarol. In the case of the African Champions Cup, it meant Tout Puissant Englebert of Zaire.

But African football, the sporting flagship of a rapidly changing and developing continent, has reflected the problems associated with change. Thus, Zaire is now the Democratic Republic of Congo and, long before then, Englebert was renamed Mazembe so the club had to change names.

Given the problems which many African nations still have in financing their qualifying campaigns in the World Cup and African Nations Cup, it is remarkable the club competitions have developed as strongly as they have with a high number of entries each year. This may owe much to the strength of support gained from local business. But the power of the clubs has also been revealed in recent years in the development of a Champions League competition with television and sponsorship support.

The African Champions Cup was launched in 1964 in the wake of the increasing success of the Nations Cup. This was a reversal of events in Europe where the championship for national teams had followed the explosive success of the club competition.

By the mid-1960s, the African confederation's membership was increasing rapidly as more countries gained independence and confidence. The club competition was a natural progression with the propulsive force of the Ghanaian association being recognised by its presentation of the Kwame Nkrumah trophy for the winners. The first event featured 14 clubs who played off on a knock-out basis for the right to reach a finals tournament in the Ghanaian capital of Accra.

The first finals

The finals were played over three days with hosts Real Republicans, to the disappointment of the home fans, losing 2–1 to Oryx Douala in the semi-finals. (Two years later, following the overthrow of Nkrumah, the Real Republicans club was dissolved). In the other semi-final, Stade Malien of Mali defeated Cotton Club of Ethiopia 3–1. The presence of the Ethiopian club serves as a reminder of the significant role that Ethiopia – in particular through federation president Tessema – took in the development of the African game.

In the final itself, Oryx Douala beat Stade Malien 2–1. But a thin crowd was a disappointment, and disputes over the best way to develop the competition meant it was not held in 1965. The "thinking time" helped concentrate minds on the best way forward, which meant copying the European model further with

a straight knock-out formula through to the semi-finals. Only the final was different – that, too, being staged as a two-legged, home and away affair.

The event is now held during a calendar year, with the preliminary round in February and March and the final in late November and early December.

Cup-winners Cup

This competition pattern was copied when a Cup-winners Cup was introduced in 1975 and in 1992, for the CAF Cup. This was named after the African confederation, just as the UEFA Cup fulfilled the same role in Europe for top clubs who were runners-up in their national championships.

The first decade of the Champions Cup was dominated by clubs from the sub-Saharan regions of Africa, with the North Africans getting the upper hand from the 1980s onwards.

Kumasi Asante Kotoko were perhaps the first great club of the Champions Cup. They were the most famous team in Africa in the 1960s and 1970s – having been founded by a local taxi driver in the 1920s under the name Titanics. Later, a local witch doctor suggested changing the name to Kotoko – which means porcupine. Asante came from the adoption of the club by the Asanthene tribe in the 1930s.

They won the League in 1959 and again in 1963, 1964 and 1965. That earned them entry into the second Champions Cup, where they lost to Stade Abidjan of Ivory Coast in the final. Asante Kotoko reached the final again in 1967, against TP Englebert of Zaire. The clubs drew 1–1 in Ghana and 2–2 in Lumbumbashi. Away goals did not count double in those days or Asante would have been proclaimed champions. Instead, the African confederation ordered a play-off. Asante objected to the choice of dates and the cup was awarded to their Zairean opponents.

The same clubs returned to the final in 1970. The first leg in Ghana ended 1–1, but Asante Kotoko were leading 2–1 in the second leg with only minutes remaining, when TP were awarded a controversial penalty. Asante players threatened to walk off but, when peace was restored, goalkeeper Robert Mensah retrieved the ball himself and placed it on the spot before stalking defiantly to his goal-line. When the resulting kick sailed aimlessly over the bar, Mensah was the hero of all Ghana.

Asante Kotoko beat Canon of Cameroon to retain the cup in 1971 then suffered their second defeat in the final, against AS Vita of Zaire in 1973. They lost to Al Ahly of Egypt in the 1982 final but took revenge over the same opponents the following year with star forward Upoku Nti scoring the only goal of the 180 minutes. But the balance of power was clearly swinging heavily in favour of North African football, Egypt in particular. Asante returned to the final in 1993, only to lose 7–6 in a penalty shoot-out to Zamalek of Cairo after both legs of the showdown had ended goalless.

The first Egyptian success at club level was that of Al Ismaili, who beat TP Englebert 5–3 on aggregate in the 1969 Champions Cup Final. But that was a mere flash in the pan. It was not until the early 1980s the Egyptian clubs got serious, thanks largely to better organization and administration and a financial power which rivalled that of many big clubs in Europe. Zamalek and Al Ahly (National), traditionally Egypt's top clubs and bitter rivals, shared the glory. But they were not alone. The Arab Contractors club, funded by Osman Ahmed Osman, owner of the construction giant of the same name, also made their mark on the African scene. In 1982 and 1983, under the management of Englishman Mike Everitt, they won the African Cup-winners Cup.

Al Ahly reached their first African Champions final in 1982, under the coaching of Mahmoud Al Gohari, who would later take Egypt to the 1990 World Cup finals. Star forward was Al Khatib, African Footballer of the Year in 1983, whose achievements helped Al Ahly establish a claim to be the most popular club team in the Arab world. Their domestic dominance was impressive: Al Ahly were League champions from 1949 to 1962 with only one interruption by Zamalek in 1959–60. They also established a record unbeaten run between 1974 and 1977. But that dominance was stripped away in the African club competitions.

Politics plays its part

In the 1982 Champions final, Al Ahly beat Asante Kotoko but the Ghanaians took revenge the following year. Al Ahly won the crown again in 1987 by defeating Al Hilal of Sudan and added four victories in the African Cup-winners Cup – 1984, 1985, 1986 and 1993. The 1984 campaign was a memorable and controversial one. Al Ahly beat Egyptian rivals – and holders – Arab Contractors in the semi-finals and were due to face their namesakes, Al Ahly of Libya, in the final.

Politics intervened, however. The Libyans refused to travel to Cairo for the away leg and demanded a neutral venue. When this request was rejected by the African confederation, the Libyans withdrew. Canon Yaounde, of Cameroon, whom the Libyans had beaten in the semi-finals, were then resurrected as finalists. Al Ahly won 1–0 at home, lost 1–0 away and won the ensuing penalty shoot-out. It was their first success in the secondary competition and the launch of an unprecedented hat-trick.

Rivals Zamalek had been founded as an Anglo-Egyptian club in 1925, named originally after King Faruk. No wonder such bitter rivalry existed later, in the 1950s, after President Nasser became honorary president of Al Ahly! The continental arena did, however, provide a stage in which Zamalek could rival, and even out-achieve Al Ahly. In 1976, they reached the quarter-finals of the African Champions Cup and the semi-finals of the Cup-winners Cup. In 1984, they went a step better by winning the Champions Cup. In an exciting semi-final, they overcame the Algerian club JET Tizi-ouzou, and climaxed their greatest season by defeating Shooting Stars of Nigeria home and away in the final. Zamalek won the Champions Cup again in 1986 – squeezing to victory over Africa Sports of the Ivory Coast on penalties – then in 1993 and 1996.

South Africa awakes

The mid-1990s saw a further shift in the balance of African club power, from far north to far south, after the return of South Africa to the international and continental fold following the collapse of the apartheid regime. Orlando Pirates became the first South African club to win a continental prize when they defeated ASEC of Ivory Coast in the Champions Cup Final. Pirates' hero was central defender Mark Fish, steady as a rock in the second, away leg in Abidjan – when Pirates snatched victory with a breakaway goal from Sikosama.

Pirates followed up by beating Algeria's Jeunesse Sportive of Kabyle 1–0 to win the Supercup which, again following the European example, is played each year between the winners of the Champions Cup and the Cup-winners Cup.

AFRICAN CHAMPIONS CUP RESULTS

1964

Oryx Douala (Cam) bt Stade Malien (Mali) 2–1 in Accra, Ghana

1965

Not organized

1966

Real Bamako (Mali) 3
Stade Abidjan (IC) 1

Stade Abidjan 4
Real Bamako 1
Winners: Stade Abidjan, 5–4 agg

1967

Asante Kotoko (Gha) 1
Tout Puissant Englebert (Zai) 1

TP Englebert 2
Asante Kotoko 2
Winners: TP Englebert after Asante Kotoko refused play-off

1968

TP Englebert (Zai)
5 Etoile Filante (Tog) 0

Etoile Filante 4
TP Englebert 1
Winners: TP Englebert, 6–4 agg

1969

TP Englebert (Zai) 2
Al Ismaili (Egy) 2

Al Ismaili 3
TP Englebert 1
Winners: Al Ismaili, 5–3 agg

1970

Asante Kotoko (Gha) 1
TP Englebert (Zai) 1

TP Englebert 1
Asante Kotoko 2
Winners: Asante Kotoko, 3–2 agg

1971

Asante Kotoko (Gha) 3
Canon (Cam) 0

Canon 2
Asante Kotoko 0
Winners: Asante Kotoko 3–2 agg

1972

Hafia Conakry (Gui) 4
Simba FC (Uga 2

Simba FC 2
Hafia 3
Winners: Hafia Conakry, 7–4 agg

1973

Asante Kotoko (Gha) 4
AS Vita (Zai) 2

AS Vita 3
Asante Kotoko 0
Winners: AS Vita, 5–4 agg

1974

CARA Brazzaville (Con) 4
Mehalla (Egy) 2

Mehalla 1
CARA Brazzaville 2
CARA Brazzaville 6–3 agg

1975

Hafia Conakry (Gui) 1
Enugu Rangers (Nig) 0

Enugu Rangers 1
Hafia Conakry 2
Winners: Hafia Conakry, 3–1 agg

1976

Hafia Conakry (Gui) 3
Mouloudia Chalia (Alg) 0

Mouloudia Chalia 3
Hafia Conakry 0
Winners: 3–3 agg, Mouloudia Chalia, 4–1 on pens

1977

Hearts of Oak (Gha) 0
Hafia Conakry (Gui) 1

Hafia Conakry 3
Hearts of Oak 2
Winners: Hafia, 4–2 agg

1978

Hafia Conakry (Gui) 0
Canon (Cam) 0

Canon 2
Hafia 0
Winners: Canon, 2–0 on agg

1979

Hearts of Oak (Gha) 1
Union Douala (Cam) 0

Union Douala 1
Hearts of Oak 0
Winners: Union Douala 5–3 on pens, 1–1 agg

1980

Canon (Cam) 2
AS Bilima (Zai) 2

AS Bilima 0
Canon 3
Winners: Canon 5–2 agg

1981

Jeunesse Electronique Tizi-Ouzou (Alg) 4
AS Vita Club Kinshasa (Con) 0

AS Vita Club 0
JET 1
Winners: JET, 5–0 agg

1982

Al Ahly (Egy) 3
Asante Kotoko (Gha) 0

Asante Kotoko
1 Al Ahly 1
Winners: Al Ahly, 4–1 agg

1983

Al Ahly (Egy) 0
Asante Kotoko (Gha) 0

Asante Kotoko 1
Al Ahly 0
Winners: Asante Kotoko 1–0 agg

1984

Zamalek (Egy) 2
Shooting Stars (Nig) 0

Shooting Stars 0
Zamalek 0
Winners: Zamalek, 2–0 agg

1985

Forces Armees Rabat (Mor) 5
AS Bilima (Zai) 2

AS Bilima 1
FAR 1
Winners: FAR, 6–3 agg

1986

Zamalek (Egy) 2
Africa Sports (IC) 0

Africa Sports 2
Zamalek 0
Winners: Zamalek 4–2 on pens, 2–2 agg

1987

Al Hilal (Sud) 0
Al Ahly (Egy) 0

Al Ahly 2
Al Hilal 0
Winners: Al Ahly, 2–0 agg

1988

Iwuanyanwu Owerri (Nig) 1
Entente Plasticiens (Alg) 0

Entente Plasticiens 4
Iwuanyanwu Owerri 0
Winners: Entente Plasticiens, 4–1 agg

1989

Raja Casablanca (Mor) 1
Mouloudia Oran (Alg) 0

Mouloudia Oran 1
Raja 0
Winners: Raja 4–2 on pens, 1–1 agg

1990

Jeunesse Sportive Kabyle (Alg) 1
Nkana Red Devils (Zam) 0

Nkana Red Devils 1
Jeunesse Sportive Kabyle 0
Winners: Jeunesse Sportive Kabyle 5–3 on pens, 1–1 agg

1991

Club Africain (Tun) 5
Nakivubo Villa (Uga) 1

Nakivubo Villa 1
Club Africain 1
Winners: Club Africain, 6–2 agg

1992

Wydad Casablanca (Mor) 2
El Hilal (Sud) 0

El Hilal 0
Wydad Casablanca 0
Winners: Wydad, 2–0 agg

1993

Asante Kotoko (Gha) 0
Zamalek (Egy) 0

Zamalek 0
Asante Kotoko 0
Winners: Zamalek 7–6 on pens, 0–0 agg

1994

Zamalek (Egy) 0
Esperance Sportive (Tun) 0

Esperance Sportive 3
Zamalek 1
Winners: Esperance Sportive, 3–1 agg

1995

Orlando Pirates (SA) 2
ASEC (IC) 2

ASEC 0
Orlando Pirates 1
Winners: Orlando Pirates, 3–2 agg

1996

Shooting Stars (Nig) 2
Zamalek (Egy) 1

Zamalek 2
Shooting Stars 1
Winners: Zamalek 5–4 on pens, 2–2 agg

1997

Goldfields (Gha) 1
Raja Casablanca (Mor) 0

Raja Casablanca 1
Goldfields 0
Winners: Raja 5–4 on pens, 1–1 agg

AFRICAN CUP-WINNERS CUP RESULTS

1975

Stella Abidjan (IC) 0
Tonnerre (Cam) 1

Tonnerre 4
Stella Abidjan 1
Winners: Tonnerre 5–1, agg

1976

Shooting Stars (Nig) 4
Tonnerre (Cam) 1

Tonnerre 1
Shooting Stars 0
Winners: Shooting Stars, 4–2 agg

1977

Enugu Rangers (Nig) 4
Canon (Cam) 1

Canon 1
Enugu Rangers 1
Winners: Enugu Rangers, 5–2 agg

1978

Milaha Athletic Hussein Dey (Alg) 1
Horoya AC (Gui) 3

Horoya AC 2 MA
Hussein Dey 1
Winners: Horoya AC, 5–2 agg

1979

Gor Mahia (Ken) 0
Canon (Cam) 2

Canon 6
Gor Mahia 0
Winners: Canon, 8–0 agg

1980

Africa Sports (IC) 1
Tout Puissant Mazembe (Zai) 3

TP Mazembe 1
Africa Sports 0
Winners: TP Mazembe, 4–1 agg

1981

Union Douala (Cam) 0
Stationery Stores (Nig) 0

Stationery Stores 1
Union Douala 2
Winners: Union Douala, 2–1 agg

1982

Power Dynamos (Zam) 0
Arab Contractors (Egy) 2

Arab Contractors 2
Power Dynamos 0
Winners: Arab Contractors, 4–0 agg

1983

Agaza Lome (Tog) 0
Arab Contractors (Egy) 1

Arab Contractors 0
Agaza Lome 0
Winners: Arab Contractors, 1–0 agg

1984

Al Ahly (Egy) 1
Canon (Cam) 0

Canon 1
Al Ahly 0
Winners: Al Ahly 4–2 on pens, 1–1 agg

1985

Al Ahly (Egy) 2
Leventis United (Nig) 0

Leventis Utd 1
Al Ahly 0
Winners: Al Ahly, 2–1 agg

1986

Al Ahly (Egy) 3
AS Sogara (Gab) 0

AS Sogara 2
Al Ahly 0
Winners: Al Ahly, 3–2 agg

1987

Esperance Sportive (Tun) 2
Gor Mahia (Ken) 2

Gor Mahia 1
Esperance Sportive 1
Winners: Gor Mahia on away goals, 3–3 agg

1988

Ranchers Bees (Nig) 0
CA Bizerte (Tun) 0

CA Bizerte 1
Ranchers Bees 0
Winners: CA Bizerte, 1–0 agg

1989

Al Merreikh (Sud) 1
Bendel United (Nig) 0

Bendel United 0
Al Merreikh 0
Winners: Al Merreikh, 1–0 agg

1990

BCC Lions (Nig) 3
Club Africain (Tun) 0

Club Africain 1
BCC Lions 1
Winners: BCC Lions, 4–1 agg

1991

BCC Lions (Nig) 3
Power Dynamos (Zam) 2

Power Dynamos 3
BCC Lions 1
Winners: Power Dynamos, 5–4 agg

1992

Vital'o (Bur) 1
Africa Sports (IC) 1

Africa Sports 4
Vital'o 0
Winners: Africa Sports, 5–1 agg

1993

Africa Sports (IC) 1
Al Ahly (Egy) 1

Al Ahly 1
Africa Sports 0
Winners: Al Ahly, 2–1 agg

1994

Daring Club (Zai) 2
Kenya Breweries (Ken) 2

Kenya Breweries 0
Daring Club 3
Winners: Daring Club, 5–2 agg

1995

Julius Berger (Nig) 1
JS Kabyle (Alg) 1

JS Kabyle 2
Julius Berger 1
Winners: JS Kabyle, 3–2 agg

1996

Sodigraf (Zai) 0
Arab Contractors (Egy) 0

Arab Contractors 4
Sodigraf 0
Winners: Arab Contractors, 4–0 agg

1997

Etoile Sahel (Tun) 2
FAR (Mor) 0

FAR 1
Etoile Sahel 0
Winners: Etoile Sahel, 2–1 agg

CAF CUP RESULTS

1992

Nakivuba Villa (Uga) 0
Shootings Stars (Nig) 0

Shooting Stars 3
Nakivubo Villa 0
Winners: Shooting Stars, 3–0 agg

1993

Stella Club (IC) 0
SC Simba (Tan) 0

SC Simba 0
Stella Club 2
Winners: Stella Club, 2–0 agg

1994

Primeiro de Maio (Ang) 1
Bendel Insurance (Nig) 0

Bendel Insurance 3
Primeiro de Maio 0
Winners: Bendel Insurance, 3–1 agg

1995

AS Kaloum (Gui) 0
Etoile Sahel (Tun) 0

Etoile Sahel 2
AS Kaloum 0
Winners: Etoile Sahel, 2–0 agg

1996

Etoile Sahel (Tun) 3
KAC Marrakesh (Mor) 1

KAC Marrakesh 2
Etoile Sahel 0
Winners: KAC Marrakesh on away goals, 3–3 agg

1997

Petro Atletico (Ang) 1
Esperance Sportive (Tun) 0
Esperance Sportive 2
Petro Atletico 0
Winners: Esperance Sportive, 2–1 agg

AFRICAN SUPER CUP RESULTS

1992–93

Africa Sports (IC) 2
Wydad Casablanca (Mor) 2
Winners: Africa Sports, 5–3 on pens
(Abidjan, Ivory Coast)

1993–94

Zamalek (Egy) 1
Al Ahly (Egy) 0
(Johannesburg, South Africa)

1994–95

Esperance Sportive (Tun) 3
Daring Club (Zai) 0
(Alexandria, Egypt)

1995–96

Orlando Pirates (SA) 1
JS Kabyle (Alg) 0
(Johannesburg, South Africa)

1996–97

Zamalek (Egy) 0
Arab Contractors (Egy) 0
Winners: Zamalek, 4–2 on pens
(Cairo, Egypt)

Wydad Casablanca's captain holds the African Champions Cup as Sudan's head of state looks on

TRIES

EUROPE (UEFA)

Albania

Federata Shqiptare e Futbollit
Founded: *1930*
Joined FIFA: *1932*

Albania have never qualified for the finals of either the World Cup or the European Championship. Even the country's recent return to comparatively normal international relations with the rest of Europe brought no immediate respite for a national team who have ranked consistently among the minnows of European football.

Indeed, the speed with which all of Albania's best players headed off into the more lucrative distance, notably Greece, exacerbated the federation's problems in rebuilding a national image tarnished through years of self-imposed political and sporting isolation.

For instance, the national team once went five years without playing any internationals against European rivals because they could not find "politically compatible" opponents. And when Celtic had to play a European club tie in Tirana, the Albanian authorities authorized only nine visas for players! It took a protest to UEFA and an expulsion threat to get a full team in.

In essence, more than half-a-century of sporting potential was lost, since football had been organized at the start of the 1900s. The introductions, of course, had been made by foreign residents. A fledgling club named Independencia was launched in Shkoder but the first championship – exclusively organized among the foreigners – collapsed in chaos at the outbreak of World War One.

It took the influence of various occupying forces in the 1920s to reintroduce the game and this time the locals were encouraged to join in. In 1928 King Zog came to the throne and sports activities were, for the first time, recognized as a legitimate area of governmental concern. In 1930, a Sports Ministry was set up and this spawned, two years later, a quasi-autonomous football federation.

A national league was dominated initially by SK Tirana, and Albania even went as far as to join FIFA in 1932. Unfortunately political unrest in the Balkans meant that it was not until 1946 that the national team made their debut, against neighbouring Yugoslavia.

Several outstanding players – Riza Lushta, Loro Borici and Naim Krieziu – played in Italy after Albania's annexation in the early 1940s. But the country's finest all-round players have been Panajot Pano, a star of the 1950s and early 1960s whose son also became an international, and, more recently, Sulejman Demollari.

CHAMPIONS

1930 SK Tirana
1931 SK Tirana
1932 SK Tirana
1933 Skenderbeu Korce
1934 SK Tirana
1935 Not played
1936 SK Tirana
1937 SK Tirana
1938–44 Not played
1945 Vllaznia Shkoder
1946 Vllaznia Shkoder
1947 Partizani Tirana
1948 Partizani Tirana
1949 Partizani Tirana
1950 Dinamo Tirana
1951 Dinamo Tirana
1952 Dinamo Tirana
1953 Dinamo Tirana
1954 Partizani Tirana
1955 Dinamo Tirana
1956 Dinamo Tirana
1957 Partizani Tirana
1958 Partizani Tirana
1959 Partizani Tirana
1960 Dinamo Tirana
1961 Partizani Tirana
1962 Not played
1963 Partizani Tirana
1964 Partizani Tirana
1965 17 Nentori Tirana
1966 17 Nentori Tirana
1967 Dinamo Tirana
1968 17 Nentori Tirana
1969 Not played
1970 17 Nentori Tirana
1971 Partizani Tirana
1972 Vllaznia Shkoder
1973 Dinamo Tirana
1974 Vllaznia Shkoder
1975 Dinamo Tirana
1976 Dinamo Tirana
1977 Dinamo Tirana
1978 Vllaznia Shkoder
1979 Partizani Tirana
1980 Dinamo Tirana
1981 Partizani Tirana
1982 17 Nentori Tirana
1983 Vllaznia Shkoder
1984 Labinoti Elbasen
1985 17 Nentori Tirana
1986 Dinamo Tirana
1987 Partizani Tirana
1988 17 Nentori Tirana
1989 17 Nentori Tirana
1990 Dinamo Tirana
1991 Flamurtari Vlore
1992 Vllaznia Shkoder
1993 Partizani Tirana
1994 Teuta Durres
1995 SK Tirana
1996 SK Tirana
1997 SK Tirana

CUP WINNERS

1948 Partizani Tirana
1949 Partizani Tirana
1950 Dinamo Tirana
1951 Dinamo Tirana
1952 Dinamo Tirana
1953 Dinamo Tirana
1954 Dinamo Tirana
1955–56 Not played
1957 Partizani Tirana
1958 Partizani Tirana
1959 Not played
1960 Dinamo Tirana
1961 Partizani Tirana
1962 Not played
1963 17 Nentori Tirana
1964 Partizani Tirana
1965 Vllaznia Shkoder
1966 Partizani Tirana
1967 Not played
1968 Partizani Tirana
1969 Not played
1970 Partizani Tirana
1971 Dinamo Tirana
1972 Vllaznia Tirana
1973 Partizani Tirana
1974 Dinamo Tirana
1975 Labinoti Elbasen
1976 17 Nentori Tirana
1977 17 Nentori Tirana
1978 Dinamo Tirana
1979 Vllaznia Tirana
1980 Partizani Tirana
1981 Vllaznia Tirana
1982 Dinamo Tirana
1983 17 Nentori Tirana
1984 17 Nentori Tirana
1985 Flamurtari Vlore
1986 17 Nentori Tirana
1987 Vllaznia Tirana
1988 Flamurtari Vlore
1989 Dinamo Tirana
1990 Dinamo Tirana
1991 Partizani Tirana
1992 SK Elbasini
1993 Partizani Tirana
1994 SK Tirana
1995 Teuta Durres
1996 Teuta Durres
1997 Partizani Tirana
1998 Apolonia Fier

Andorra

Federation Football d'Andorre
Founded: *1994*
Joined FIFA: *1996*

Andorra, a tiny mountainous country best known for skiing and duty-free shopping, became Europe's latest football nation in the summer of 1996…with only 300 registered players. The local championship was then formally relaunched. First champions of the legitimised Andorra league were Principat, a club founded originally by local supporters of Real Madrid and who had initially named their club after their meeting place: Charlie's Bar. It was later felt that something a little formal was necessary if the club were to compete – albeit briefly – in European competition.

CHAMPIONS

1997 Principat
1998 Principat

Armenia

Football Federation of Armenia
Founded: *1992*
Joined FIFA: *1992*

Armenia achieved independence after the Soviet Union's collapse. Leading club Ararat Yerevan had featured regularly in the old Soviet top division. Star player was midfielder Khoren Oganesyan who became the first national coach of Armenia.

CHAMPIONS	CUP WINNERS
1992 Homenetman Yerevan	1992 Banants Abovyan
1993 Ararat Yerevan	1993 Ararat Yerevan
1994 Shirak Gyumri	1994 Ararat Yerevan
1995 Shirak Gyumri	1995 Ararat Yerevan
1996 Pyunic Yerevan	1996 Pyunic Yerevan
1997 Pyunic Yerevan	1997 Pyunic Yerevan
1998 Pyunic Yerevan	1998 Tsement Ararat

Austria's Rapid Vienna take on Paris Saint Germain of France

Austria

Osterreichischer Fussball-Bund
Founded: *1904*
Joined FIFA: *1905*

Austria's greatest days remain the inter-war years which were dominated by the legendary "Wunderteam" – created by one of international football's outstanding early legislators, Hugo Meisl.

Son of a Viennese banking family, Meisl ran the youthful Austrian federation in the early years of the century, brought in legendary English coach, Jimmy Hogan, and signed the famous Konrad brothers, from MTK Budapest, on behalf of FK Austria. They duly became continental Europe's first full-time professionals, inspirations for the man who was to become perhaps the country's greatest-ever player, Matthias Sindelar.

Nicknamed "Der Papierene" (The Man of Paper) because he was so slim, centre forward Sindelar was a superstar almost half-a-century before the term was coined. He led FK Austria to success in the Mitropa Cup and Austria to fourth place at the 1934 World Cup before tragically committing suicide after the German Anschluss of 1938.

After World War Two, Austrian football rebuilt quickly. There were more fine players, such as Ernst Ocwirk – nicknamed "Clockwork" – who was the last of the attacking centre halves, and Gerhardt Hanappi, renowned as a great all-rounder.

Austria had been the first continental team to beat Scotland, gave England a real fright at Stamford Bridge in 1929 – the hosts scraped a 4–3 win – were semi-finalists at the 1934 World Cup and played again at the finals of 1954 and 1958. But, in the 1960s, Austrian football hit a slump. Crowds fell and many clubs were forced into mergers to stay alive.

Even FK Austria had to merge with the Wiener Athletik Club and rely on tobacco sponsorship to stay solvent. But they recovered and, in 1978, became the first Austrian club to reach a European final – losing 4–0 to Anderlecht in the Cup-winners Cup Final in Paris. That same year marked Austria's return to the World Cup finals for the first time in 20 years. They were present again in Spain in 1982, in Italy in 1990 and in France in 1998.

In the meantime, Rapid Vienna followed FK Austria's example in the Cup-winners Cup, finishing runners-up to Everton in 1985 and to Paris Saint Germain in 1996.

CHAMPIONS

1912 Rapid Vienna	1918 Floridsdorfer
1913 Rapid Vienna	1919 Rapid Vienna
1914 Wiener AC	1920 Rapid Vienna
1915 Wiener AC	1921 Rapid Vienna
1916 Rapid Vienna	1922 Wiener Sport-Club
1917 Rapid Vienna	1923 Rapid Vienna
	1924 Amateure
	1925 Hakoah Wien

1926 Amateure
1927 Admira Wien
1928 Admira Wien
1929 Rapid Vienna
1930 Rapid Vienna
1931 First Vienna
1932 Admira Wien
1933 First Vienna
1934 Admira Wien
1935 Rapid Vienna
1936 Admira Wien
1937 Admira Wien
1938 Rapid Vienna
1939 Admira Wien
1940 Rapid Vienna
1941 Rapid Vienna
1942 First Vienna
1943 First Vienna
1944 First Vienna
1945 Not played
1946 Rapid Vienna
1947 Wacker Wien
1948 Rapid Vienna
1949 FK Austria
1950 FK Austria
1951 Rapid Vienna
1952 Rapid Vienna
1953 FK Austria
1954 Rapid Vienna
1955 First Vienna
1956 Rapid Vienna
1957 Rapid Vienna
1958 Wiener Sport-Club
1959 Wiener Sport-Club
1960 Rapid Vienna
1961 FK Austria
1962 FK Austria
1963 FK Austria
1964 SK Rapid
1965 Linzer ASK
1966 Admira Wien
1967 Rapid Vienna
1968 Rapid Vienna
1969 FK Austria
1970 FK Austria
1971 Wacker Innsbruck
1972 Wacker Innsbruck
1973 Wacker Innsbruck
1974 SK Voest
1975 Wacker Innsbruck
1976 FK Austria
1977 Wacker Innsbruck
1978 FK Austria
1979 FK Austria
1980 FK Austria
1981 FK Austria
1982 Rapid Vienna
1983 Rapid Vienna
1984 FK Austria
1985 FK Austria
1986 FK Austria
1987 Rapid Vienna
1988 Rapid Vienna
1989 FC Tirol
1990 FC Tirol
1991 FK Austria

1992 FK Austria
1993 FK Austria
1994 Austria Salzburg
1995 Austria Salzburg
1996 Rapid Vienna
1997 Austria Salzburg
1998 Sturm Graz

CUP WINNERS

1919 Rapid Vienna
1920 Rapid Vienna
1921 Amateure
1922 Wiener AC
1923 Wiener Sport-Club
1924 Amateure
1925 Amateure
1926 Rapid Vienna
1927 Rapid Vienna
1928 Admira Wien
1929 First Vienna
1930 First Vienna
1931 Wiener AC
1932 Admira Wien
1933 FK Austria
1934 Admira Wien
1935 FK Austria
1936 FK Austria
1937 First Vienna
1938 Wiener AC
1939–45 Not played
1946 Rapid Vienna
1947 Wacker Wien
1948 FK Austria
1949 FK Austria
1950–58 Not played
1959 Wiener AC
1960 FK Austria
1961 Rapid Vienna
1962 FK Austria
1963 FK Austria
1964 Admira Wien
1965 Linzer ASK
1966 Admira Wien
1967 FK Austria
1968 Rapid Vienna
1969 Rapid Vienna
1970 Wacker Innsbruck
1971 FK Austria
1972 Rapid Vienna
1973 Wacker Innsbruck
1974 FK Austria
1975 Wacker Innsbruck
1976 Rapid Vienna
1977 FK Austria
1978 Wacker Innsbruck
1979 Wacker Innsbruck
1980 FK Austria
1981 Grazer AK
1982 FK Austria
1983 Rapid Vienna
1984 Rapid Vienna
1985 Rapid Vienna
1986 FK Austria
1987 Rapid Vienna
1988 Kremser SC
1989 FC Tirol

1990 FK Austria	1995 Rapid Vienna
1991 SV Stockerau	1996 Sturm Graz
1992 FK Austria	1997 Sturm Graz
1993 Wacker Innsbruck	1998 Ried
1994 FK Austria	

Azerbaijan

Association of Football Federations of Azerbaijian

Founded: *1992*
Joined FIFA: *1994*

Azerbaijan made their independent international debut in the 1996 European Championship but were forced, because of civil war, to play their home games in Turkey.

CHAMPIONS	CUP WINNERS
1992 Neftchi Baku	1992 Ishaatchi Baku
1993 Karabakh Agdam	1993 Karabakh Agdam
1994 Turan Tauz	1994 Kapaz Ganja
1995 Kapaz Ganja	1995 Neftchi Baku
1996 Neftchi Baku	1996 Neftchi Baku
1997 Karabakh Agdam	1997 Kapaz Ganja
1998 Kapaz Ganja	1998 Kapaz Ganja

Belgium legend Jan Ceulemans

Belarus

Football Federation of the Republic of Belarus

Founded: *1989*
Joined FIFA: *1992*

Belarus attained independence after the Soviet Union's collapse. Minsk Dynamo are their most successful club and Petr Kachouro – who had a spell in England with Sheffield United – their most outstanding player of modern times.

CHAMPIONS	CUP WINNERS
1992 Minsk Dynamo	1992 Minsk Dynamo
1993 Minsk Dynamo	1993 Neman Grodno
1994 Minsk Dynamo	1994 Minsk Dynamo
1995 Minsk Dynamo	1995 Dynamo '93
1996 MPKC Mozyr	1996 MPKC Mozyr
1997 Minsk Dynamo	1997 Belshina Bobruisk

Belgium

Belgische Voetballbond/Union Royale Belge des Societes de Football Association

Founded: *1895*
Joined FIFA: *1904*

Belgium are assured of their place at the finals of the 2000 European Championship thanks to their status as joint hosts. But, even though the national team have been in the doldrums for much of the 1990s, failing to qualif for the second round of France '98, they remain dangerous opponents for any nation.

The potential is evidenced by the past. Belgium were runners-up at the 1980 European Championship then fourth at the 1986 World Cup after developing a generation of players worthy to lace the boots of previous heroes. Indeed, that campaign sparked a run of seven successive World Cups in which Belgium were always present at the finals.

In the inter-war years the old heroes were led by Raymond Braine whose sharp-shooting talents from the wing earned a transfer to the 1930s financial power, Czecho-Slovakia – as that nation was then known. Then, the late 1950s and early 1960s saw the explosive emergence of Paul Van Himst who began as a centre forward and then moved to inside left to exploit his wide range of creative skills in and around the penalty box. Those creative skills were reborn, some 20 years later, in Enzo Scifo, son of Italian immigrant workers.

Belgium were one of the founders of FIFA, the world governing body in 1904. But it took more than 50 years for professionalism to take root and transform the country's football standards and international status. That achievement was emphasized by the international renown achieved by clubs such as Anderlecht and Mechelen (who both won the European Cup-winners Cup) and Standard Liege, Club Brugge and Antwerp (who were all European runners-up). A strong Anderlecht have, down the years, been the key to a successful national team.

At national level Belgium were one of only four European nations to attend the first World Cup finals in Uruguay in 1930. They were eliminated in the first round then, in 1934, in 1938 and, again, in 1954.

Braine and Stanley Van den Eynde were among the continent's leading players in the 1930s. In the 1950s they were succeeded by powerful centre forwards Jef Mermans and Rik Coppens and then – after Van Himst – came the likes of record international Jan Ceulemans, a central figure in the World Cup efforts of the 1980s and 1990.

Sadly, Belgium has also gone down in football history for all the wrong reasons. The Heysel stadium in Brussels – since redeveloped and renamed the King Baudouin stadium – was the scene of the 1985 tragedy in which 39 Juventus fans died before the Champions Cup Final against Liverpool.

CHAMPIONS

1896 FC Liege	1938 Beerschot
1897 Racing CB	1939 Beerschot
1898 FC Liege	1940–41 Not played
1899 FC Liege	1942 Lierse SK
1900 Racing CB	1943 KV Mechelen
1901 Racing CB	1944 Royal Antwerp
1902 Racing CB	1945 Not played
1903 Racing CB	1946 KV Mechelen
1904 Union St Gilloise	1947 RSC Anderlecht
1905 Union St Gilloise	1948 KV Mechelen
1906 Union St Gilloise	1949 RSC Anderlecht
1907 Union St Gilloise	1950 RSC Anderlecht
1908 Racing CB	1951 RSC Anderlecht
1909 Union St Gilloise	1952 Lierse SK
1910 Union St Gilloise	1953 FC Liege
1911 Cercle Brugge	1954 RSC Anderlecht
1912 Daring CB	1955 RSC Anderlecht
1913 Union St Gilloise	1956 RSC Anderlecht
1914 Daring CB	1957 Royal Antwerp
1915–19 Not contested	1958 Standard Liege
1920 Club Brugge	1959 RSC Anderlecht
1921 Daring CB	1960 Lierse SK
1922 Beerschot	1961 Standard Liege
1923 Union St Gilloise	1962 RSC Anderlecht
1924 Beerschot	1963 Standard Liege
1925 Beerschot	1964 RSC Anderlecht
1926 Beerschot	1965 RSC Anderlecht
1927 Cercle Brugge	1966 RSC Anderlecht
1928 Beerschot	1967 RSC Anderlecht
1929 Royal Antwerp	1968 RSC Anderlecht
1930 Cercle Brugge	1969 Standard Liege
1931 Royal Antwerp	1970 Standard Liege
1932 Lierse	1971 Standard Liege
1933 Union St Gilloise	1972 RSC Anderlecht
1934 Union St Gilloise	1973 Club Brugge
1935 Union St Gilloise	1974 RSC Anderlecht
1936 Daring CB	1975 RWD Molenbeek
1937 Daring CB	1976 Club Brugge
	1977 Club Brugge
	1978 Club Brugge

1979 SK Beveren	1965 RSC Anderlecht
1980 Club Brugge	1966 Standard Liege
1981 RSC Anderlecht	1967 Standard Liege
1982 Standard Liege	1968 Club Brugge
1983 Standard Liege	1969 Lierse SK
1984 SK Beveren	1970 Club Brugge
1985 RSC Anderlecht	1971 Beerschot
1986 RSC Anderlecht	1972 RSC Anderlecht
1987 RSC Anderlecht	1973 RSC Anderlecht
1988 RSC Anderlecht	1974 KSV Waregem
1989 RSC Anderlecht	1975 RSC Anderlecht
1990 Club Brugge	1976 RSC Anderlecht
1991 RSC Anderlecht	1977 Club Brugge
1992 Club Brugge	1978 SK Beveren
1993 RSC Anderlecht	1979 Beerschot
1994 RSC Anderlecht	1980 Waterschei THOR
1995 RSC Anderlecht	1981 Standard Liege
1996 Club Brugge	1982 Waterschei THOR
1997 Lierse SK	1983 SK Beveren
1998 Club Brugge	1984 AA Gent
	1985 Cercle Brugge
	1986 Club Brugge

CUP WINNERS

1912 Racing CB	1987 KV Mechelen
1913 Union St Gilloise	1988 RSC Anderlecht
1914 Union St Gilloise	1989 RSC Anderlecht
1915–26 Not played	1990 FC Liege
1927 Cercle Brugge	1991 Club Brugge
1928–53 Not played	1992 Royal Antwerp
1954 Standard Liege	1993 Standard Liege
1955 Royal Antwerp	1994 RSC Anderlecht
1956 Racing Tournai	1995 Club Brugge
1957–63 Not played	1996 Club Brugge
1964 AA Gent	1997 Germinal Ekeren
	1998 Ghent

Bosnia-Herzegovina

Bosnia and Herzegovina Football Federation

Founded: *1991*
FIFA: *1992*

Bosnia made history, on eventual admittance following independence, as UEFA's 50th member nation. At first UEFA delayed a decision on membership because three different organizations claimed to be the "real" federation. The dispute went to FIFA for resolution.

CHAMPIONS

1994 Celik Zenica
1995 Celik Zenica
1996 Celik Zenica
1997 Rudar Ugljevik
1998 Zeljeznicar

CUP WINNERS

1997 Sloga Trn
1998 Sarajevo

Bulgaria

Bulgarski Futbolen Soius
Founded: *1923*
Joined FIFA: *1924*

Bulgaria reached their peak of international achievement by finishing fourth at the 1994 World Cup finals in the USA. Decisive influences were star striker Hristo Stoichkov, midfielders Yordan Lechkov and Krasimir Balakov and goalkeeper Borislav (Bobby) Mihailov.

Their 2–1 quarter-final victory over Cup-holders Germany has gone down as Bulgaria's single most outstanding match. It was the high point, to be followed by defeats at the hands of Italy in the semi-finals and Sweden in the third-place play-off.

Bulgaria's success owed much to the transfer freedom which had followed the collapse of communist-imposed restrictions. The likes of Stoichkov and Lechkov went abroad to hone their talent and brought technical, tactical and psychological lessons back to the national team structure.

Before the 1994 World Cup, Bulgaria had competed in the World Cup finals on five occasions, playing 16 matches, never winning a game, and progressing beyond the first round on only one occasion (in Mexico in 1986). Fourth-place "success" in the USA duly punctured the image of Bulgaria as a nation of footballers with admirable discipline and physical commitment, but a lack of fantasy. However, in the 1998 finals in France, an ageing team was again eliminated in the first round.

Bulgaria was one of the first Balkan states to take to football in the late 19th century. A British university team, engaged on a central European tour, staged the first exhibition of the game in Bulgaria in 1884. It took until 1909, however, before the first formal Bulgarian club was set up and another 14 years before the federation was created to run the competitive game. The following year, 1924, saw Bulgaria play their first international: a 6–0 defeat by Austria in Vienna. FIFA membership was granted in the same year and the first league championship launched in 1925.

International headway had to wait until after World War Two and the communist takeover in 1946. The new regime dismantled all the old sports organizations and created mostly new clubs – notably the army team, CDNA (later CSKA) – on the "state amateur" basis.

Inside forward Ivan Kolev, the so-called "Pocket Puskas" was the finest Bulgarian footballer of the 1950s, but death in a car crash cut short the highly promising career of 1960s centre forward Georgi Asparoukhov. World Cup stalwarts in the 1960s and 1970s such as Dimitar Penev, Ivan Vutsov and Hristo Bonev went on to become World Cup coaches in the 1980s and 1990s.

CHAMPIONS

1925 Vladislav Varna
1926 Vladislav Varna and Slavia Sofia
1927 not contested
1928 Slavia Sofia
1929 Botev Plovdiv
1930 Slavia Sofia
1931 AC 23 Sofia
1932 Shipenski Sokol
1933 Levski Sofia
1934 Vladislav Varna
1935 SC Sofia
1936 Slavia Sofia
1937 Levski Sofia
1938 Ticha Varna
1939 Slavia Sofia
1940 JSK Sofia
1941 Slavia Sofia
1942 Levski Sofia
1943 Slavia Sofia
1944 not contested
1945 Lokomotiv Sofia
1946 Levski Sofia
1947 Levski Sofia
1948 Septemvri CDW
1949 Levski Sofia
1950 Dinamo Sofia
1951 CDNA Sofia
1952 CDNA Sofia
1953 Dinamo Sofia
1954 CDNA Sofia
1955 CDNA Sofia
1956 CDNA Sofia
1957 CDNA Sofia
1958 CDNA Sofia
1959 CDNA Sofia
1960 CDNA Sofia
1961 CDNA Sofia
1962 CDNA Sofia
1963 Spartak Plovdiv
1964 Lokomotiv Sofia
1965 Levski Sofia
1966 CSKA-CZ Sofia
1967 Botev Plovdiv
1968 Levski Sofia
1969 CSKA Sofia
1970 Levski-Spartak
1971 CSKA Sofia
1972 CSKA Sofia
1973 CSKA Sofia
1974 Levski-Spartak
1975 CSKA Sofia
1976 CSKA Sofia
1977 Levski-Spartak
1978 Lokomotiv Sofia
1979 Levski-Spartak
1980 CSKA Sofia
1981 CSKA Sofia
1982 CSKA Sofia
1983 CSKA Sofia
1984 Levski-Spartak
1985 Trakia Plovdiv
1986 Beroe Stara Zagora
1987 CFKA Sredets
1988 Vitisha Sofia
1989 CFKA Sredets
1990 CSKA Sofia
1991 Etar Veliko Tarnovo
1992 CSKA Sofia
1993 Levski Sofia
1994 Levski Sofia
1995 Levski Sofia
1996 Slavia Sofia
1997 CSKA Sofia
1998 Liteks

CUP WINNERS

1938 FK 13 Sofia
1939 Shipka Sofia
1940 FK 13 Sofia
1941 AC 23 Sofia
1942 Levski Sofia
1943–45 not contested

SOVIET ARMY CUP

1946 Levski Sofia
1947 Levski Sofia
1948 Lokomotiv Sofia
1949 Dinamo Sofia
1950 Dinamo Sofia
1951 CDNA Sofia
1952 Udarnik Sofia
1953 Lokomotiv Sofia
1954 CDNA Sofia
1955 CDNA Sofia
1956 Dinamo Sofia
1957 Levski Sofia
1958 Spartak Plovdiv
1959 Levski Sofia
1960 Septemvri CDW Sofia
1961 CDNA Sofia
1962 Botev Plovdiv
1963 Slavia Sofia
1964 Slavia Sofia
1965 CSKA-CZ Sofia
1966 Slavia Sofia
1967 Levski Sofia
1968 Spartak Sofia
1969 CSKA Sofia
1970 Levski-Spartak
1971 Levski-Spartak
1972 CSKA Sofia
1973 CSKA Sofia
1974 CSKA Sofia
1975 Slavia Sofia
1976 Levski-Spartak
1977 Levski-Spartak
1978 Marek St. Dimitrov
1979 Levski-Spartak
1980 Slavia Sofia
1981 Trakia Plovdiv
1982 Lokomotiv Sofia
1983 Lokomotiv Plovdiv
1984 Levski-Spartak
1985 CSKA Sofia
1986 CFKA Sredets
1987 Vitosha Sofia
1988 Vitosha Sofia
1989 CFKA Sredets

Croatia striker Davor Suker, who won the Golden Boot at France '98, celebrates another international goal

1990 CSKA Sofia
1991 Etar Veliko Tarnovo

BUGARIAN CUP

1981 CSKA Sofia
1982 Levski-Spartak
1983 CSKA Sofia
1984 Levski-Spartak
1985 CSKA Sofia
1986 Vitosha Sofia
1987 CFKA Sredets

1988 CFKA Sredets
1989 CFKA Sredets
1990 Sliven
1991 Levski Sofia
1992 Levski Sofia
1993 CSKA Sofia
1994 Levski Sofia
1995 Lokomotiv Sofia
1996 Slavia Sofia
1997 CSKA Sofia
1998 Levski Sofia

Croatia

Hrvatski Nogomatni Savez
Founded: *1912*
Joined FIFA: *1992*

Croatia, quarter-finalists at Euro 96 and third in the 1998 World Cup finals, are not, in fact, total newcomers to international football. The country existed as an independent political and football entity in the 1940s. The Croats organized their own league championship and their own national team. But, under direction from Berlin, they played against only other Axis-aligned nations such as Germany, Italy, Bulgaria and Romania.

Croatia remained a significant source of football strength and talent within the former Yugoslavia after the war. Dinamo Zagreb (now known as FC Croatia) and Hajduk Split built impressive records in European club competitions – which they have extended since Croatia's independent re-emergence in 1990. The first match of the new era was a 2–1 win over the USA on October 17, 1990.

Outstanding players at France '98 included striker Davor Suker (who won the Golden Boot with seven goals) and midfield general and captain Zvonimir Boban.

CHAMPIONS

1941 Gradanski Zagreb
1942 Gradanski Zagreb
1943 Gradanski Zagreb
1944 Gradanski Zagreb
1945–91 No independent Croatia
1992 Hajduk Split
1993 Croatia Zagreb
1994 Hajduk Split
1995 Hajduk Split
1996 Croatia Zagreb
1997 Croatia Zagreb
1998 Croatia Zagreb

CUP WINNERS

1992 Inker Zapresic
1993 Hajduk Split
1994 Croatia Zagreb
1995 Hajduk Split
1996 Croatia Zagreb
1997 Croatia Zagreb
1998 Croatia Zagreb

Cyprus

Kipriaki Omospondia Podosferu
Founded: *1934*
Joined FIFA: *1948*

Cypriot football hit the international headlines for all the wrong reasons in early 1997 when it was revealed that a number of national team players had been allegedly involved in a betting scam on their World Cup qualifying match against Bulgaria in December, 1996.

Cyprus lost 3–1 – not a surprise in itself – but the federation was disturbed by reports of huge sums being gambled on a precise scoreline and a parliamentary inquiry was set up to try to get to the truth.

It all went to prove that, although Cyprus may be considered one of the Europe's minnow nations, the game is followed with enormous passion and intensity. Such passion can be channelled into the wrong areas and this was not the first time that corruption allegations had been raised.

Generally, Cyprus has been considered on a par with the likes of Iceland, Malta, Finland and Luxembourg as European minnows. But the Cypriot national team have rarely been a pushover when playing at home, which says much for the determination of the game on an island split between the Greek and breakaway Turkish communities.

Football control, however, has stayed in the hands of the Greek community and though some of the old Turkish-based clubs remain in domestic league and cup competition they do so only because they moved during the 1974–76 insurrection.

Soccer was played in Cyprus as early as the 1870s by British soldiers and sailors. British troops played the game there during World War One and British residents helped found the Cyprus FA, the league and the cup in 1934.

In 1948, with the island under British control, the Cyprus FA became affiliated to the Football Association in London yet managed to obtain independent membership of FIFA. On July 30, 1949, Cyprus played their first international, losing 3–1 to Israel in Tel Aviv. The international story since then has been mostly of defeats with one of the most controversial arising in the 1988 European Championship qualifying competition.

In October 1987, playing Holland in Rotterdam, Cyprus goalkeeper Andreas Haritou was felled by a smoke bomb thrown from the crowd. For half-an-hour Cyprus refused to play on. When they did so, with a substitute goalkeeper, they lost 8–0. The match had to be replayed but many observers felt Holland were fortunate to stay in a competition…which they went on to win with such style in Germany a year later.

By now the bigger clubs could afford to import foreign players and coaches. British managers included Tommy Cassidy, Ian Moores, Peter Cormack, Alan Dicks and Richie Barker. An increasing number of Bulgarian and Yugoslav players arrived on the playing scene.

The most famous home-grown player remains Sotiris Kaiafas who, in 1975–76, scored 39 league goals to collect the Golden Boot as Europe's top marksman.

CHAMPIONS

1935 Trust AC
1936 Apoel Nicosia
1937 Apoel Nicosia
1938 AEL Limassol
1939 Apoel Nicosia
1940 Apoel Nicosia
1941 AEL Limassol
1942–44 Not played
1945 Apoel Limassol
1946 EPA Larnaca
1947 Apoel Nicosia
1948 Apoel Nicosia
1949 Apoel Nicosia
1950 Anorthosis Famagusta
1951 LTSK Nicosia
1952 Apoel Nicosia
1953 AEL Limassol
1954 Pezoporikos Larnaca
1955 AEL Limassol
1956 AEL Limassol
1957 Anorthosis Famagusta
1958 Anorthosis Famagusta
1959 Not played
1960 Anorthosis Famagusta
1961 Omonia Nicosia
1962 Anorthosis Famagusta
1963 Anorthosis Famagusta
1964 Not played
1965 Apoel Nicosia
1966 Omonia Nicosia
1967 Olympiakos Nicosia
1968 AEL Limassol
1969 Olympiakos Nicosia
1970 EPA Lanarca
1971 Olympiakos Nicosia
1972 Omonia Nicosia
1973 Apoel Nicosia
1974 Omonia Nicosia
1975 Omonia Nicosia
1976 Omonia Nicosia
1977 Omonia Nicosia
1978 Omonia Nicosia
1979 Omonia Nicosia
1980 Apcol Nicosia
1981 Omonia Nicosia
1982 Omonia Nicosia
1983 Omonia Nicosia
1984 Omonia Nicosia
1985 Omonia Nicosia
1986 Apoel Nicosia
1987 Omonia Nicosia
1988 Pezoporikos Larnaca
1989 Omonia Nicosia
1990 Apoel Nicosia
1991 Apollon Limassol
1992 Omonia Nicosia
1993 Omonia Nicosia
1994 Apollon Limassol
1995 Omonia Nicosia
1996 Apoel Nicosia
1997 Anorthosis
1998 Anorthosis

CUP WINNERS

1935 Trust AC
1936 Trust AC
1937 Apoel Nocosia
1938 Trust AC
1939 AEL Limassol
1940 AEL Limassol
1941 Apoel Limassol
1942–44 Not played
1945 EPA Larnaca
1946 EPA Larnaca
1947 Apoel Nicosia
1948 AEL Limassol
1949 Anorthosis Famagusta
1950 EPA Larnaca
1951 Apoel Nicosia
1952 Chetin Kaya
1953 EPA Larnaca
1954 Chetin Kaya
1955 EPA Larnaca
1956–61 Not played
1962 Anorthosis Famagusta
1963 Apoel Nicosia
1964 Not played
1965 Omonia Nicosia
1966 Apollon Limassol
1967 Apollon Limassol
1968 Apoel Nicosia
1969 Apoel Nicosia
1970 Pezoporikos Larnaca
1971 Anorthosis Nicosia
1972 Omonia Nicosia
1973 Apoel Nicosia
1974 Omonia Nicosia
1975 Anorthosis Nicosia
1976 Olympiakos Nicosia
1977 Apocl Nicosia
1978 Apoel Nicosia
1979 Apoel Nicosia
1980 Omonia Nicosia
1981 Omania Nicosia
1982 Omonia Nicosia
1983 Omania Nicosia
1984 Apoel Nicosia
1985 AEL Limassol
1986 Apollon Limassol
1987 AEL Limassol
1988 Omonia Nicosia
1989 AEL Limassol
1990 NEA Salamina Famugusta
1991 Omonia Nicosia
1992 Apollon Limassol
1993 Apoel Nicosia
1994 Omonia Nicosia
1995 Apoel Nicosia
1996 Apoel Nicosia
1997 Apoel Nicosia
1998 Anorhosis

Czech Republic

Ceskomoravsky Fotbalovy Svaz
Founded: *1901/1993*
Joined FIFA: *1907*

The Czech Republic took part for the first time, formally, in international competition in the 1996 European Championship. They marked the occasion by surprising most observers and reaching the Final, which they lost to Germany 2–1 via the controversial golden goal rule. They also revealed three new international stars in winger Karel Poborsky and midfielders

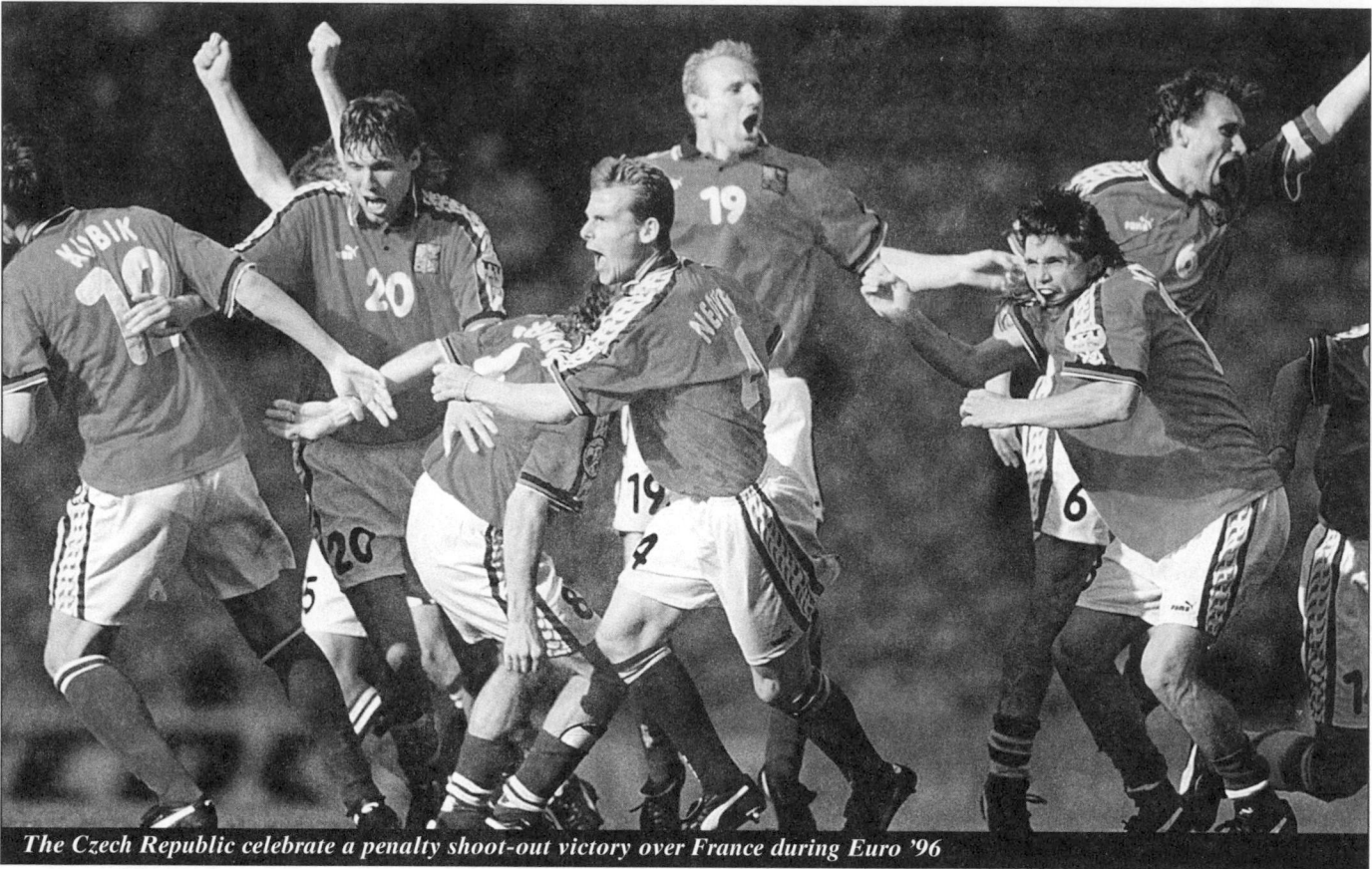

The Czech Republic celebrate a penalty shoot-out victory over France during Euro '96

Patrik Berger and Radek Bejbl.

Previously, of course, the Czechs had played international football as part of the former Czechoslovakia, in one of several politically-dictated changes over the course of the years.

Football began before Czechoslovakia had even been founded in the years before World War One when central Europe was dominated by the Hapsburg empire. The game was launched separately in both what was then Bohemia and Slovakia.

Sports clubs had already been created on a German-inspired model and it was Slavia of Prague who, in the 1880s, were the first to add football to their curriculum. However it was traditional rivals Sparta who won the first Bohemia championship in 1912. Slavia took revenge a year later before the region was engulfed in World War One which, ultimately, led to the creation of a new national identity.

The football federation of the fledgling Czecho-Slovakia (as it was originally styled) was one of the first not merely to accept but welcome professionalism. Thus the Czechs were among Europe's leading football nations throughout the inter-war years. Sparta and Slavia dominated the Mitropa Cup – the forerunner of the present European club tournaments – and the national team finished runners-up to the hosts, Italy in extra-time in the 1934 World Cup Final in Rome. Goalkeeper Frantisek Planicka and forwards Oldrich Nejedly and Antonin Puc were among the great heroes of their day.

Of course, Hitler's greed sliced into Czechoslovakia, late in 1938, and though Sparta and Slavia retained their identities in the Nazi Sudetenland football competition, they were made to pay after the war when the Communists took over. Both clubs had to change their names and saw their best players enrolled into the armed services so they could play for the new army team, Dukla Prague.

Dukla, with a great left back in Ladislav Novak and two wonderful, complementary wing halves in Svatopluk Pluskal and Josef Masopust, provided the foundation for a revived national team which reached the World Cup finals in 1954, 1958 and 1962. In 1954 and 1958, they fell in the first round – albeit eliminated in a play-off by Northern Ireland in 1958. But in 1962 they were runners-up in the Final to Brazil – even taking the lead through Masopust before losing 3–1 in Santiago, Chile.

Czechoslosovakia never again really threatened to repeat that World Cup effort. However, they were among the most successful contenders in the European Championship – winning a thrilling Final in 1976 and finishing third in 1980. Each time they owned their status to penalties – beating West Germany in a shoot-out in the 1976 Final in Belgrade and then Italy (by 9–8) after a goalless draw in the third-place play-off in 1980 in Naples.

A quarter-final appearance at the 1990 World Cup in Italy proved to be the old Czechoslovakia's international swansong. The 1996 European Championship then proved that the Czechs had suffered little from the football split with Slovakia.

CHAMPIONS

1896 FC Kickers shared with DFC
    Prague
1897 Slavia Prague
1898 Slavia Prague
1899 Slavia Prague
1899–1901 Not played
1902 CAFC Vinohrady
1903–11 Not played
1912 Sparta Prague
1913 Slavia Prague
1914–16 Not played
1917 Sparta Prague
1918 Slavia Prague
1919 Sparta Prague
1920 Sparta Prague
1921 Sparta Prague
1922 Sparta Prague
1923 Sparta Prague
1924 Slavia Prague
1925 Slavia Prague
1926 Sparta Prague
1927 Sparta Prague
1928 Viktoria Zizkov
1929 Slavia Prague
1930 Slavia Prague
1931 Slavia Prague
1932 Sparta Prague
1933 Slavia Prague
1934 Slavia Prague
1935 Slavia Prague
1936 Sparta Prague
1937 Slavia Prague
1938 Sparta Prague
1939–45 Not played
1946 Sparta Prague
1947 Slavia Prague
1948 Dynamo Slavia
1949 NV Bratislava
1950 NV Bratislava
1951 NV Bratislava
1952 Sparta Sokolovo
1953 UDA Prague
1954 Sparta Sokolovo
1955 Slovan Bratislava
1956 Dukla Prague
1957 Not played
1958 Dukla Prague
1959 CH Bratislava
1960 Spartak Hradec Kralove
1961 Dukla Prague
1962 Dukla Prague
1963 Dukla Prague
1964 Dukla Prague
1965 Sparta Prague
1966 Dukla Prague
1967 Sparta Prague
1968 Spartak Trnava
1969 Spartak Trnava
1970 Slovan Bratislava
1971 Spartak Trnava
1972 Spartak Trnava
1973 Spartak Trnava
1974 Slovan Bratislava
1975 Slovan Bratislava

1976 Banik Ostrava
1977 Dukla Prague
1978 Zbrojovka Brno
1979 Dukla Prague
1980 Banik Ostrava
1981 Banik Ostrava
1982 Dukla Prague
1983 Bohemians Prague
1984 Sparta Prague
1985 Sparta Prague
1986 Tj Vitkovice
1987 Sparta Prague
1988 Sparta Prague
1989 Sparta Prague
1990 Sparta Prague
1991 Sparta Prague
1992 Slovan Bratislava
1993 Sparta Prague
1994 Sparta Prague
1995 Sparta Prague
1996 Slavia Prague
1997 Sparta Prague
1998 Sparta Prague

CUP WINNERS

1961 Dukla Prague
1962 Slovan Bratislava
1963 Slovan Bratislava
1964 Sparta Sokolovo
1965 Dukla Prague
1966 Dukla Prague
1967 Spartak Trnava
1968 Slovan Bratislava
1969 Dukla Prague
1970 Tj Gottwaldov
1971 Spartak Trnava
1972 Sparta Prague
1973 Banik Ostrava
1974 Slovan Bratislava
1975 Spartak Trnava
1976 Sparta Prague
1977 Lokomotiva Kosice
1978 Banik Ostrava
1979 Lokomotiva Kosice
1980 Sparta Prague
1981 Dukla Prague
1982 Slovan Bratislava
1983 Dukla Prague
1984 Sparta Prague
1985 Dukla Prague
1986 Spartak Trnava
1987 DAC Dunajska Streda
1988 Sparta Prague
1989 Sparta Prague
1990 Dukla Prague
1991 Banik Ostrava
1992 Sparta Prague
1993 1FC Kosice
1994 Viktoria Zizkov
1995 Hradec Kralove
1996 Sparta Prague
1997 Slavia Prague
1998 Jablonec

Denmark

Dansk Boldspil Union
Founded: *1889*
Joined FIFA: *1904*

Denmark's victory in the 1992 European Championship was one of the great international fairytales of modern football times. They should not, for one thing, have been attending the finals in Sweden at all. Manager Richard Moller Nielsen was decorating his kitchen when UEFA decided to send for the Danes only a matter of weeks before the opening match.

The Danes gained their wild-card call-up because of the increasingly fragile conditions in the Balkans and fear over security aspects of Yugoslavia's presence in the finals. The Slavs were barred and Denmark, who had finished runners-up in their qualifying group, stepped in.

They were popular competitors from Peter Schmeichel in goal to Kim Vilfort in midfield and Brian Laudrup in attack. Moller Nielsen had refined Sepp Piontek's "Danish Dynamite" team of the 1980s by adding a bomb-proof defence.

Denmark hardly looked like Europe-beaters in the first round but their ultimate victory against the odds – against Holland in the semi-final and Germany in the Final – proved hugely popular.

Those observers who registered shock over Denmark's success were ignoring the lessons of football history since the Danes had been among the giants of European football in the amateur, pre-first world war days.

Denmark was one of the very first "foreign" lands to be invaded by football-carrying Britons in the 1860s. British residents carried on playing in Copenhagen and a national team played in an exhibition tournament at the first modern Olympic Games in Athens in 1896. Nils Middleboe – the most remarkable son of a famous football family – was English football's first foreign import when he played for Chelsea between 1913 and 1920.

The amateur tradition held Denmark back at international level as professionalism took over elsewhere during and after the inter-war years. The depth of natural talent available was evident however when Denmark finished runner-ups at the 1960 Olympics in Rome and third at the 1964 European Championship finals. But then, the Danes had needed to beat only Malta, Albania and Luxembourg (in a play-off!) along the qualifying path.

Denmark did not reach the finals again until 1984, now under the leadership of former German international full back Sepp Piontek. This was an exciting new team built unashamedly around exiled professionals such as Michael Laudrup and Preben Elkjaer. They overcame England, Greece, Hungary and Luxembourg (again) in the qualifiers then lost to Spain in the semi-finals only after a penalty shoot-out.

Brian Laudrup leads Denmark to victory against Saudi Arabia during the 1998 World Cup finals

Spain defeated Denmark again in the second round of the 1986 World Cup. But the foundations for 1992 had been effectively laid. "Our secret is that we are friends," said skipper Martin Olsen.

The Danis team spirit also shone at France '98, where they reached the quarter-finals before losing narrowly 3–2 to Brazil.

CHAMPIONS

1913 KB Kobenhavn
1914 KB Kobenhavn
1915 Not played
1916 B93 Kobenhavn
1917 KB Kobenhavn
1918 KB Kobenhavn
1919 Akademisk
1920 B1903 Kobenhavn
1921 Akademisk
1922 KB Kobenhavn
1923 Frem Kobenhavn
1924 B1903 Kobenhavn
1925 KB Kobenhavn
1926 B1903 Kobenhavn
1927 B93 Kobenhavn
1928 B93 Kobenhavn
1929 B93 Kobenhavn
1930 B93 Kobenhavn
1931 Frem Kobenhavn
1932 KB Kobenhavn
1933 Frem Kobenhavn
1934 B93 Kobenhavn
1935 B93 Kobenhavn
1936 Frem Kobenhavn
1937 Akademisk
1938 B1903 Kobenhavn
1939 B93 Kobenhavn
1940 KB Kobenhavn
1941 Frem Kobenhavn
1942 B93 Kobenhavn
1943 Akademisk
1944 Frem Kobenhavn
1945 Akademisk
1946 B93 Kobenhavn
1947 Akademisk
1948 KB Kobenhavn
1949 KB Kobenhavn
1950 KB Kobenhavn
1951 Akademisk
1952 Akademisk
1953 KB Kobenhavn
1954 Koge BK
1955 AGF Aarhus
1956 AGF Aarhus
1957 AGF Aarhus
1958 Vejle BK
1959 B1909 Odense
1960 AGF Aarhus
1961 Esbjerg FB
1962 Esbjerg FB
1963 Esbjerg FB
1964 B1909 Odense
1965 Esbjerg FB
1966 Hvidovre BK
1967 Akademisk
1968 KB Kobenhavn
1969 B1903 Kobenhavn
1970 B1903 Kobenhavn
1971 Vejle BK
1972 Vejle BK
1973 Hvidovre BK
1974 KB Kopenhavn
1975 Koge BK
1976 B1903 Kobenhavn
1977 OB Odense
1978 Vejle BK
1979 Esbjerg FB
1980 KB Kobenhavn
1981 Hvidovre BK
1982 OB Odense
1983 Lyngby BK
1984 Vejle BK
1985 Brondbyernes
1986 AGF Aarhus
1987 Brondbyernes
1988 Brondbyernes
1989 OB Odense
1990 Brondbyernes
1991 Brondbyernes
1992 Lyngby BK
1993 FC Kobenhavn
1994 Silkeborg IF
1995 AAB Aalborg
1996 Brondbyernes
1997 Brondbyernes
1998 Brondbyernes

CUP WINNERS

1955 AGF Aarhus
1956 Frem Kobenhavn
1957 AGF Aarhus
1958 Vejle BK
1959 Vejle BK
1960 AGF Aarhus
1961 AGF Aarhus
1962 B1909 Odense
1963 B1913 Odense
1964 Esbjerg FB
1965 AGF Aarhus
1966 AAB Aalborg
1967 Randers Freja
1968 Randers Freja
1969 KB Kobenhavn
1970 AAB Aalborg
1971 B1909 Odense
1972 Vejle BK
1973 Randers Freja
1974 Vanlose BK
1975 Vejle BK

1976 Esbjerg FB	1989 Brondbyernes
1977 Vejle BK	1990 Lyngby BK
1978 Frem Kobenhavn	1991 OB Odense
1979 B1903 Kobenhavn	1992 AGF Aarhus
1980 Hvidovre BK	1993 OB Odense
1981 Vejle BK	1994 Brondbyernes
1982 B93 Kobenhavn	1995 FC Kobenhavn
1983 OB Odense	1996 AGF Aarhus
1984 Lyngby BK	1997 FC Kobenhavn
1985 Lyngby BK	1998 FC Kobenhavn
1986 B1903 Kobenhavn	
1987 AGF Aarhus	
1988 AGF Aarhus	

England

The Football Association
Founded: *1863*
Joined FIFA: *1905*

England regained much of their international prestige at the finals of the 1996 European Championship – and grabbed headlines again at France 98 following a dramatic and controversial second-round clash against Argentina.

In 1996, under the imaginative guidance of Terry Venables, they reached the semi-finals to demonstrate that they remained competitive in the international aren.

On top of that, the peaceful exuberance among the fence-free crowds provided a spectacular stage. FIFA observers were so impressed they immediately launched a campaign to try to achieve the removal of all football pitch fences worldwide.

England came so close to achieving, also, their first trophy success since 1966. Alan Shearer was the tournament's five-goal top scorer, his success earning him third place in both the FIFA and European player of the year polls and raising his value to a world record £15million when he transferred from Blackburn Rovers to Newcastle United a matter of weeks after the finals.

The theme of the finals – "Football's Coming Home" – underlined England's status as the Mother of Football.

And the national enthusiasm for the finals was carried on in 1998 when England, who had topped their qualification group ahead of mighty Italy, only went out of the World Cup after losing on penalties to Argentina. The second-round clash ended 2–2, with teenager Michael Owen scoring arguably the goal of the tournament and launching himself on the world stage in some style England also had David Beckham controversially sent off, a goal disallowed and a penalty claim turned down.

It was in England, in the mid-1800s, that the public schools and universities first codified the modern game. The Football Association (not, note, the English Football Association) was set up in 1863, the FA Challenge Cup launched in 1871 and the Football League in 1888; in between England played Scotland in the world's first international match in 1872. The basic form of the English game then stood the test of time and set a structural standard for the rest of the world. The league championship is the competitive bulwark of the worldwide game and the knock-out cup concept still dominates.

In 1904 England stood aloof from the foundation of FIFA. Later they deigned to join, only to split away in the 1920s in a dispute over broken-time payments for amateurs. That dispute proved critical to the development of the English game. Being outside FIFA, England were excluded from the World Cup, and potentially vital international competitive experience, until the 1950s. Later that political, technical and tactical isolation could be seen to have cost England a decade of development time.

England rejoined FIFA after World War Two, entered the World Cup for the first time in 1950 in Brazil and wished they had not when they lost devastatingly, by 1–0, to the United States in Belo Horizonte. That result was considered a simple – if embarrassing – freak. Not until 1953, when Hungary won 6–3 at Wembley, was the domestic audience provided with a painful lesson about the lost years.

England produced great players such as Stanley Matthews, Tommy Lawton, Tom Finney and Billy Wright. But it took Manchester United's defiance of domestic authority, as the 1950s Busby Babes entered the European Champions Cup, to bring English football into contact with the world game.

Within a decade, lessons were learned. By Brazilian standards England, in 1966, were not one of the greatest World Cup teams, but Bobby Moore, Bobby Charlton, Geoff Hurst and their team-mates could do no more than beat all-comers. Hurst became the only man to score a World Cup Final hat-trick in the 4–2 extra-time victory over West Germany at Wembley.

Tottenham, West Ham and Manchester United provided victorious breakthroughs in European club competitions, while Liverpool, Aston Villa and Nottingham Forest carried it on until the hooliganism epidemic – which reached a tragic peak with the Heysel disaster of 1985 – forced a five-year exile.

Other domestic crowd tragedies, such as Bradford and Hillsborough, led to a reappraisal of facilities. The Taylor Report enforced all-seater stadia and the higher costs of spectating changed the demography of football crowds. Television, sponsorship, and commercial exploitation provided English football with a fashionably acceptable new face. The big clubs took greater control of their own affairs by creating the Premier League and, England regained its status as a football leader.

CHAMPIONS

1889 Preston NE	1897 Aston Villa
1890 Preston NE	1898 Sheffield U
1891 Everton	1899 Aston Villa
1892 Sunderland	1900 Aston Villa
1893 Sunderland	1901 Liverpool
1894 Aston Villa	1902 Sunderland
1895 Sunderland	1903 The Wednesday
1896 Aston Villa	1904 The Wednesday
	1905 Newcastle U

1906 Liverpool
1907 Newcastle U
1908 Manchester U
1909 Newcastle U
1910 Aston Villa
1911 Manchester U
1912 Blackburn R
1913 Sunderland
1914 Blackburn R
1915 Everton
1916–19 Not played
1920 West Bromwich A
1921 Burnley
1922 Liverpool
1923 Liverpool
1924 Huddersfield T
1925 Huddersfield T
1926 Huddersfield T
1927 Newcastle U
1928 Everton
1929 Sheffield W
1930 Sheffield W
1931 Arsenal
1932 Everton

1933 Arsenal
1934 Arsenal
1935 Arsenal
1936 Sunderland
1937 Manchester C
1938 Arsenal
1939 Everton
1940–1946 Not played
1947 Liverpool
1948 Arsenal
1949 Portsmouth
1950 Portsmouth
1951 Tottenham H
1952 Manchester U
1953 Arsenal
1954 Wolverhampton W
1955 Chelsea
1956 Manchester U
1957 Manchester U
1958 Wolverhampton W
1959 Wolverhampton W
1960 Burnley
1961 Tottenham H
1962 Ipswich T

1963 Everton
1964 Liverpool
1965 Manchester U
1966 Liverpool
1967 Manchester U
1968 Manchester C
1969 Leeds U
1970 Everton
1971 Arsenal
1972 Derby Co
1973 Liverpool
1974 Leeds U
1975 Derby Co
1976 Liverpool
1977 Liverpool
1978 Nottingham F
1979 Liverpool
1980 Liverpool
1981 Aston Villa
1982 Liverpool
1983 Liverpool
1984 Liverpool
1985 Everton
1986 Liverpool

1987 Everton
1988 Liverpool
1989 Arsenal
1990 Liverpool
1991 Arsenal
1992 Leeds U
1993 Manchester U
1994 Manchester U
1995 Blackburn R
1996 Manchester U
1997 Manchester U
1998 Arsenal

FA CUP WINNERS

1872 Wanderers
1873 Wanderers
1874 Oxford University
1875 Royal Engineers
1876 Wanderers
1877 Wanderers
1878 Wanderers
1879 Old Etonians
1880 Clapham R
1881 Old Carthusians

England's Alan Shearer celebrates a goal against Holland at Euro '96 with teammate Steve McManaman

1882 Blackburn Olympic	1957 Aston Villa	1983 Liverpool	1992 Manchester U
1883 Blackburn R	1958 Bolton W	1984 Liverpool	1993 Arsenal
1884 Blackburn R	1959 Nottingham F	1985 Norwich C	1994 Aston Villa
1885 Blackburn R	1960 Wolverhampton W	1986 Oxford U	1995 Liverpool
1886 Blackburn R	1961 Tottenham H	1987 Arsenal	1996 Aston Villa
1887 Aston Villa	1962 Tottenham H	1988 Luton T	1997 Leicester City
1888 West Bromwich A	1963 Manchester U	1989 Nottingham F	1998 Chelsea
1889 Preston NE	1964 West Ham U	1990 Nottingham F	
1890 Blackburn R	1965 Liverpool	1991 Sheffield W	
1891 Blackburn R	1966 Everton		
1892 West Bromwich A	1967 Tottenham H		
1893 Wolverhampton W	1968 West Bromwich A		
1894 Notts Co	1969 Manchester C		
1895 Aston Villa	1970 Chelsea		
1896 Sheffield W	1971 Arsenal		
1897 Aston Villa	1972 Leeds U		
1898 Nottingham F	1973 Sunderland		
1899 Sheffield U	1974 Liverpool		
1900 Bury	1975 West Ham U		
1901 Manchester C	1976 Southampton		
1902 Aston Villa	1977 Manchester U		
1903 Bury	1978 Ipswich T		
1904 Manchester C	1979 Arsenal		
1905 Aston Villa	1980 West Ham U		
1906 Everton	1981 Tottenham H		
1907 Sheffield W	1982 Tottenham H		
1908 Wolverhampton W	1983 Manchester U		
1909 Manchester U	1984 Everton		
1910 Newcastle U	1985 Manchester U		
1911 Bradford C	1986 Liverpool		
1912 Barnsley	1987 Coventry C		
1913 Aston Villa	1988 Wimbledon		
1914 Burnley	1989 Liverpool		
1915 Sheffield U	1990 Manchester U		
1920 Aston Villa	1991 Tottenham H		
1921 Tottenham H	1992 Liverpool		
1922 Huddersfield T	1993 Arsenal		
1923 Bolton W	1994 Manchester U		
1924 Newcastle U	1995 Everton		
1925 Sheffield U	1996 Manchester U		
1926 Bolton W	1997 Chelsea		
1927 Cardiff C	1998 Arsenal		
1928 Blackburn R			
1929 Bolton W	**LEAGUE CUP WINNERS**		
1930 Arsenal	1961 Aston Villa		
1931 West Bromwich A	1962 Norwich C		
1932 Newcastle U	1963 Birmingham C		
1933 Everton	1964 Leicester C		
1934 Manchester C	1965 Chelsea		
1935 Sheffield W	1966 West Bromwich A		
1936 Arsenal	1967 QPR		
1937 Sunderland	1968 Leeds U		
1938 Preston NE	1969 Swindon T		
1939 Portsmouth	1970 Manchester C		
1940–1945 Not played	1971 Tottenham H		
1946 Derby Co	1972 Stoke C		
1947 Charlton Ath	1973 Tottenham H		
1948 Manchester U	1974 Wolverhampton W		
1949 Wolverhampton W	1975 Aston Villa		
1950 Arsenal	1976 Manchester C		
1951 Newcastle U	1977 Aston Villa		
1952 Newcastle U	1978 Nottingham F		
1953 Blackpool	1979 Nottingham F		
1954 West Bromwich A	1980 Wolverhampton W		
1955 Newcastle U	1981 Liverpool		
1956 Manchester C	1982 Liverpool		

Estonia

Eesti Jalgpalli Liit
Founded: 1921
Joined FIFA: 1923

Estonia, Latvia and Lithuania make up the Baltic states who appeared briefly on the international football map in the 1920s and 1930s, disappeared following the Soviet expansion of the 1940s and then reappeared again at the start of the 1990s with political independence.

Of the three, Estonia were the busiest in footballing terms in the years between the two wars. They played most of their matches against their Baltic neighbours, but also contested nearly 50 matches against nations from further afield and appeared in the World Cup qualifying competitions of 1934 and 1938.

The collapse of the Soviet empire at the start of the 1990s allowed Estonia to reclaim their sporting identity. FIFA bent the World Cup rules to permit their inclusion in the qualifying competition for 1994 which helped raised badly-needed revenue for an impoverished federation.

Flora Tallinn have provided most of Estonia's international players while the first national coach of the modern era was Uno Piir, a local footballing hero in the 1950s with Kalev Tallinn and who was later a member of the Soviet coaching staff at the 1966 World Cup finals.

All emergent federations make mistakes, however, and Estonia committed a major blunder in the autumn of 1996 over a World Cup qualifying match against Scotland. Complications over TV coverage, kick-off times and floodlighting, produced the so-called "Match that Never Was." Scotland turned up for the kick-off of their tie in Tallinn while Estonia's squad remained at their training camp 60 miles away.

FIFA, perhaps generously as far as Estonia were concerned, ordered the match to be replayed in Monte Carlo. Not turning out had put the Estonians in danger of World Cup expulsion which would have been a devastating blow.

CHAMPIONS

1922 LFLS Kaunas	1925 Tallinn
1922 Sport Tallinn	1926 Sport Tallinn
1923 Kalev Tallinn	1927 Tallinn JK
1924 Sport Tallinn	1928 Tallinn
	1929 Sport Tallinn
	1930 Sport Tallinn

1931 Sport Tallinn
1932 Sport Tallinn
1933 Sport Tallinn
1934 Estonia Tallinn
1935 Estonia Tallinn
1936 Estonia Tallinn
1937 Not played
1938 Estonia Tallinn
1939 Estonia Tallinn
1940 Olumpia Tartu
1941 Not played
1942 PSR Tartu
1943 Estonia Tallinn
1944 Not played
1945 Dunamo Tallinn
1946 BL Tallinn
1947 Dunamo Tallinn
1948 BL Tallinn
1949 Dunamo Tallinn
1950 Dunamo Tallinn
1951 BL Tallinn
1952 BL Tallinn
1953 Dunamo Tallinn
1954 Dunamo Tallinn
1955 Kalev Tallinn
1956 BL Tallinn
1957 Ulemiste Kalev Tallinn
1958 Ulemiste Kalev Tallinn
1959 Ulemiste Kalev Tallinn
1960 BL Tallinn
1961 Kopli Kalev Tallinn
1962 Ulemiste Kalev Tallinn
1963 Tempo Tallinn
1964 Norma Tallinn
1965 BL Tallinn
1966 BL Tallinn
1967 Norma Tallinn
1968 Dvigatel Tallinn
1969 Dvigatel Tallinn
1970 Norma Tallinn
1971 Tempo Tallinn
1972 BL Tallinn
1973 Kreenholm Narva
1974 Baltika Narva
1975 Baltika Narva
1976 Dvigatel Tallinn
1977 Baltika Narva
1978 Dunamo Tallinn
1979 Norma Tallinn
1980 Dunamo Tallinn
1981 Dunamo Tallinn
1982 Tempo Tallinn
1983 Dunamo Tallinn
1984 Estonia Johvi
1985 KK Parnu
1986 Zvezda Tallinn
1987 Tempo Tallinn
1988 Tempo Tallinn
1989 Norma Tallinn
1990 VMV Tallinn
1991 VMV Tallinn
1992 Norma Tallinn
1993 Norma Tallinn
1994 Flora Tallinn
1995 Flora Tallinn
1996 Lantana Tallinn
1997 Lantana Tallin
1998 Flora Tallin

CUP WINNERS

1938 Sport Tallinn
1939 JK Tallinn
1940 JK Tallinn
1941 Not played
1942 Sport Tallinn
1943 PSR Tartu
1944–45 Not played
1946 Dunamo Tallinn
1947 Dunamo Tallinn
1948 VVS Tallinn
1949 Dunamo Tallinn
1950 BL Tallinn
1951 BL Tallinn
1952 BL Tallinn
1953 Dunamo Tallinn
1954 VVS Tallinn
1955 BL Tallinn
1956 BL Tallinn
1957 Spartak Vijandi
1958 Ulemiste Kalev Tallinn
1959 Ulemiste Kalev Tallinn
1960 BL Tallinn
1961 Ulemiste Kalev Tallinn
1962 Norma Tallinn
1963 Kreenholm Narva
1964 Ulemiste Kalev Tallinn
1965 Norma Tallinn
1966 Start Tallinn
1967 BL Tallinn
1968 BL Tallinn
1969 Dvigatel Tallinn
1970 Start Tallinn
1971 Norma Tallinn
1972 Kopli Dunamo Tallinn
1973 Norma Tallinn
1974 Norma Tallinn
1975 Baltika Narva
1976 SK Aseri
1977 Kalev Silamae
1978 Kalev Silamae
1979 Baltika Narva
1980 Dunamo Tallinn
1981 KK Parnu
1982 KK Parnu
1983 Dunamo Tallinn
1984 Tempo Tallinn
1985 Estonia Johvi
1986 Estonia Johvi
1987 Estonia Johvi
1988 KK Parnu
1989 Norma Tallinn
1990 KK Parnu
1991 VMV Tallinn
1992 VMV Tallinn
1993 Nikol Tallinn
1994 Norma Tallinn
1995 Flora Tallinn
1996 Sadam Tallinn
1997 Sadam Tallinn
1998 Lantana

Faroe Islands

Fotboltssamband Foroya

Founded: *1979*
Joined FIFA: *1988*

In the autumn of 1990, the Faroe Islands arrived on the competitive international scene with a victory which made headlines around the world.

The match was a European Championship qualifying tie against Austria, who had been finalists a few months earlier in the World Cup in Italy. Even though the Faroes had to play hosts in Landskrona, Sweden, they scored a 1–0 success – a football miracle for an islands nation whose federation was then only 11 years old.

The Faroes' domestic championship boasted only 20 clubs, 4,500 registered players and 118 referees. All bar one of the players were amateurs, an image enhanced by the bobble-hat worn, picturesquely, by goalkeeper Jens Knudsen.

The only full-time professional was striker Jan Allan Muller and even he was given a free transfer by the Dutch second division club, Go Ahead Eagles of Deventer, not long after the historic defeat of Austria.

Problems with the weather meant that the Faroes were restricted in the months they could play internationally and they lacked any decent natural pitches. One happy consequence, then, of their explosive emergence onto the international scene was the sponsorship funds to create a "proper" pitch in their 8,000-capacity national stadium at Toftir.

CHAMPIONS

1942 KI Klaksvik
1943 TB Tvoroyri
1944 Not played
1945 TB Tvoroyri
1946 TB Tvoroyri
1947 Sl Sorvag
1948 B'36 Torshavn
1949 TB Tvoroyri
1950 B'36 Torshavn
1951 TB Tvoroyri
1952 KI Klaksvik
1953 KI Klaksvik
1954 KI Klaksvik
1955 HB Torshavn
1956 KI Klaksvik
1957 KI Klaksvik
1958 KI Klaksvik
1959 B'36 Torshavn
1960 HB Torshavn
1961 KI Klaksvik
1962 B'36 Torshavn
1963 HB Torshavn
1964 HB Torshavn
1965 HB Torshavn
1966 KI Klaksvik
1967 KI Klaksvik
1968 KI Klaksvik
1969 KI Klaksvik
1970 KI Klaksvik
1971 HB Torshavn
1972 KI Klaksvik
1973 HB Torshavn
1974 HB Torshavn
1975 HB Torshavn
1976 TB Tvoroyri
1977 TB Tvoroyri
1978 HB Torshavn
1979 IF Fugafjordur
1980 TB Torshavn
1981 TB Torshavn
1982 HB Torshavn
1983 GI Gotu
1984 B'68 Toftir
1985 B'68 Toftir
1986 GI Gotu
1987 GI Gotu
1988 HB Torshavn
1989 B'71 Sandur
1990 HB Torshavn
1991 KI Klaksvik
1992 B'68 Toftir
1993 GI Gotu
1994 GI Gotu

1995 GI Gotu
1996 GI Gotu
1997 HB Thorshavn

CUP WINNERS

1967 KI Klaksvik
1968 HB Torshavn
1969–72 Not played
1970 HB Torshavn
1971 VB Vagur
1972 HB Torshavn
1973 HB Torshavn
1974 VB Vagur
1975 HB Torshavn
1976 HB Torshavn
1977 TB Tvoroyri
1978 TB Tvoroyri
1979 TB Tvoroyri
1980 TB Tvoroyri

1981 HB Torshavn
1982 HB Torshavn
1983 GI Gotu
1984 HB Torshavn
1985 GI Gotu
1986 NSI Runavik
1987 HB Torshavn
1988 HB Torshavn
1989 HB Torshavn
1990 KI Klaksvik
1991 B'36 Torshavn
1992 HB Torshavn
1993 B'71 Sandur
1994 KI Klaksvik
1995 HB Torshavn
1996 GI Gotu
1997 GI Gotu

Finland

Suomen Palloliitto (Finlands Bollforbund)
Founded: *1907*
Joined FIFA: *1908*

Football is not the top sport in Finland. That honour belongs, understandably, to the snow-driven winter sports. Thus problems over facilities and the climate means the best players all go abroad to turn professional while the domestic game remains part-time at the top level and amateur below.

Not, of course, that clubs in Holland, Belgium and Germany have objected. All have benefited by buying Finnish players cheap and, frequently, selling them on at a profit. The most successful export has been forward Jari Litmanen who became, with Ajax Amsterdam in 1995, the first Finnish player to secure a Champions Cup-winners medal.

His most noted predecessors in the emigration stakes were winger Juhani Peltonen and centre back Arto Tolsa in the 1960s. The longest-serving expatriate has been midfielder or central defender Kari Ukkonen who spent more than a decade in Belgium, latterly with Anderlecht.

The arrival of football is an old story: English businessmen and workers imported the game in 1890, initially in the capital, Helsinki. In 1907 the Finnish federation was set up, to be followed by a national championship a year later. In 1911 Finland played their first international, losing 5–2 at home to neighbours Sweden.

Finland were also quickly into the international competitive arena, playing at the 1912 Stockholm Olympic Games. But, after defeating Italy 3–2 and Czarist Russia 2–1 they fell 4–0 to Great Britain and were thrashed 9–0 by Holland. Finland's national side have never reached the finals of the World Cup or European Championship and none of their clubs have ever progressed beyond the quarter-finals of any of the European competitions.

CHAMPIONS

1908 Unitas Helsinki
1909 PUS Helsinki
1910 Abo IFK
1911 HJK Helsinki
1912 HJK Helsinki
1913 KIF Helsinki
1914 Not played
1915 KIF Helsinki
1916 KIF Helsinki
1917 HJK Helsinki
1918 HJK Helsinki
1919 HJK Helsinki
1920 Abo IFK
1921 HPS Helsinki
1922 HPS Helsinki
1923 HJK Helsinki
1924 Abo IFK
1925 HJK Helsinki
1926 HJK Helsinki
1927 HPS Helsinki
1928 TPS Turku
1929 HPS Helsinki
1930 HIFK Helsinki
1931 HIFK Helsinki
1932 HPS Helsinki
1933 HIFK Helsinki
1934 HPS Helsinki
1935 HPS Helsinki
1936 HJK Helsinki
1937 HIFK Helsinki
1938 HJK Helsinki
1939 TPS Turku
1940 Sudet Kouvola
1941 TPS Turku
1942 Helsinki Toverit
1943 Not played
1944 IFK Vaasa
1945 VPS Vaasa
1946 IFK Vaasa
1947 HIFK Helsinki
1948 VPS Vaasa
1949 TPS Turku
1950 Ilves Kisssat
1951 KTP Kotka
1952 KTP Kotka
1953 IFK Vaasa
1954 Pyrkiva Turku
1955 KIF Helsinki
1956 KuPS Kuopio
1957 HPS Helsinki
1958 KuPS Kuopio
1959 HIFK Helsinki
1960 Haka Valkeakoski
1961 HIFK Helsinki
1962 Haka Valkeakoski
1963 Reipas Lahti
1964 HJK Helsinki
1965 Haka Valkeakoski
1966 KuPS Kuopio
1967 Reipas Lahti
1968 TPS Turku
1969 KPV Kokkola
1970 Reipas Lahti
1971 TPS Turku

1972 TPS Turku
1973 HJK Helsinki
1974 KuPS Kuopio
1975 TPS Turku
1976 KuPS Kuopio
1977 Haka Valkeakoski
1978 HJK Helsinki
1979 OPS Oulu
1980 OPS Oulu
1981 HJK Helsinki
1982 Kuusysi Lahti
1983 Ilves Tampere
1984 Kuusysi Lahti
1985 HJK Helsinki
1986 Kuusysi Lahti
1987 HJK Helsinki
1988 HJK Helsinki
1989 Kuusysi Lahti
1990 HJK Helsinki
1991 Kuusysi Lahti
1992 HJK Helsinki
1993 FC Jazz
1994 TPV Tampere
1995 Haka
1996 FC Jazz
1997 HJK Helsinki

CUP WINNERS

1955 Haka Valkeakoski
1956 PP Voikka
1957 Drott
1958 KTP Kotka
1959 Haka Valkeakoski
1960 Haka Valkeakoski
1961 KTP Kotka
1962 HPS Helsinki
1963 Haka Valkeakoski
1964 Reipas Lahti
1965 Abo IFK
1966 HJK Helsinki
1967 KTP Kotka
1968 KuPS Kuopio
1969 Haka Valkeakoski
1970 MP Mikkell
1971 MP Mikkell
1972 Reipas Lahti
1973 Reipas Lahti
1974 Reipas Lahti
1975 Reipas Lahti
1976 Reipas Lahti
1977 Haka Valkeakoski
1978 Reipas Lahti
1979 Ilves Tampere
1980 KTP Kotka
1981 HJK Helsinki
1982 Haka Valkeakoski
1983 Kuusysi Lahti
1984 HJK Helsinki
1985 Haka Valkeakoski
1986 RoPS Rovaniemi
1987 Kuusysi Lahti
1988 Haka Valkeakoski
1989 KuPS Kuopio
1990 Ilves Tampere

1991 TPS Turku
1992 MyPa
1993 HJK Helsinki
1994 TPS Turku
1995 HJK Helsinki
1996 HJK Helsinki
1997 Haka U

France

Federation Francais de Football

Founded: *1919*
Joined FIFA: *1904*

France staged, and won, the 1998 World Cup finals in the sure confidence that they deserved host rights as a reward for their achievements both on the pitch and in the corridors of power.

On the field, France competed at the first World Cup finals in 1930; they hosted the first Champions Cup Final in 1956; they were European champions on home soil in 1984; and Just Fontaine holds the 13-goal record as top scorer in the finals of a World Cup (in 1958). Off the pitch it was Robert Guerin who was elected first president of FIFA, the international federation, in 1904; Jules Rimet, also FIFA president for more than 20 years, was instrumental in creating the World Cup; Henri Delaunay was the moving spirit behind the European Championship; Jacques Georges was president of UEFA, and the Paris sports newspaper, L'Equipe, set off the chain of events which created the vastly successful European club competitions.

All that history was overtaken, however, in 1998 when France beat Brazil 3–0 in the World Cup final to become world champions for the first time in their history.

Up until then, their best had been third place at the World

French star Jean Tigana, in action for Marseille

Cup finals in 1958 and 1986 and fourth in 1982. But they also won the European Championship in 1984 the Olympic Games that same year.

French clubs have played their part in spreading the gospel of a style of football which mixes physical commitment with skill and pace. Reims reached the European Champions Cup Final in 1956 and again in 1959, only to lose to Spain's all-conquering Real Madrid on both occasions. Reims later slid down through the leagues and went bankrupt, but Saint Etienne followed them to the Champions Cup Final in 1976, only to lose 1–0 to West Germany's Bayern Munich at Hampden Park.

A decade later, controversial, millionaire businessman Bernard Tapie arrived on the French football scene. He spent a fortune bringing Marseille through from the second division to the peak of European football. They were runners-up – after a penalty shoot-out – to Red Star Belgrade in the 1991 Champions Cup Final in Bari, then defeated Milan two years later in Munich. All the gloss and glory which surrounded this first French victory in the Champions Cup swiftly tarnished when it emerged that Marseille had been engaged in a formalized match-rigging exercise both at home and abroad.

It took Paris Saint Germain's victory in the Cup-winners Cup Final in 1996 – they beat Rapid Vienna 1–0 in Brussels – to start filling-in the credibility cracks which the Marseille scandal had created around the French game.

The strength of the French domestic game has rested more on the provincial clubs than in Paris, but that has not upset the steady flow of great players. Forward Lucien Laurent scored the first goal in World Cup history against Mexico in Uruguay in 1930 and Just Fontaine terrorized World Cup keepers in the 1950s thanks to the inspirational promptings of the great Raymond Kopa. Kopa also was the first Frenchman to win a European Champions Cup medal, after transferring from Reims to Real Madrid in 1956.

The 1960s brought a financial crisis which bankrupted many of the great old clubs, but the 1970s brought a renaissance accompanied by a flood of new talent. Manager Michel Hidalgo, a Champions Cup Final loser in 1956, used his international expertise to build a thrilling national team which reached a glorious peak in winning the 1984 European Championship. The foundations were provided by midfielder Alain Giresse, Jean Tigana, Luis Fernandez and defender Max Bossis while skipper Michel Platini established himself as the greatest French footballer of all time.

Platini, who took his talents to Italy with Juventus, was three times European Footballer of the Year before turning to management. He guided the national team to the finals of the 1992 European Championship and then changed career course again as joint president of the French organizing committee for the 1998 World Cup finals which ended in ultimate glory for his country.

CHAMPIONS

1933 Olympique Lille
1934 FC Sete
1935 FC Sochaux
1936 Racing Club
1937 Olympique Marseille
1938 FC Sochaux
1939 FC Sete
1940–45 Not played
1946 OSC Lille
1947 CO Roubaix
1948 Olympique Marseille
1949 Stade de Reims
1950 Bordeaux
1951 OGC Nice
1952 OGC Nice
1953 Stade de Reims
1954 OSC Lille
1955 Stade de Reims
1956 OGC Nice
1957 AS Saint Etienne
1958 Stade de Reims
1959 OGC Nice
1960 Stade de Reims
1961 Monaco
1962 Stade de Reims
1963 Monaco
1964 AS Saint Etienne
1965 FC Nantes
1966 FC Nantes
1967 AS Saint Etienne
1968 AS Saint Etienne
1969 AS Saint Etienne
1970 AS Saint Etienne
1971 Olympique Marseille
1972 Olympique Marseille
1973 FC Nantes
1974 AS Saint Etienne
1975 AS Saint Etienne
1976 AS Saint Etienne
1977 FC Nantes
1978 Monaco
1979 Strasbourg
1980 FC Nantes
1981 AS Saint Etienne
1982 Monaco
1983 FC Nantes
1984 Bordeaux
1985 Bordeaux
1986 Paris Saint Germain
1987 Girondins Bordeaux
1988 Monaco
1989 Olympique Marseille
1990 Olympique Marseille
1991 Olympique Marseille
1992 Olympique Marseille
1993 Olympique Marseille (title revoked for match-fixing)
1994 Paris Saint Germain
1995 FC Nantes
1996 Auxerre
1997 Monaco
1998 Lens

CUP WINNERS

1918 Olympique de Pantin
1919 CAS Generaux
1920 CA Paris
1921 Red Star Paris
1922 Red Star Paris
1923 Red Star Paris
1924 Olympique Marseille
1925 CAS Generaux
1926 Olympique Marseille
1927 Olympique Marseille
1928 Red Star Paris
1929 SO Montpellier
1930 FC Sete
1931 Club Francais
1932 AS Cannes
1933 Excelsior Roubaix
1934 FC Sete
1935 Olympique Marseille
1936 Racing Club Paris
1937 FC Sochaux
1938 Olympique Marseille
1939 Racing Club Paris
1940 Racing Club Paris
1941 Bordeaux
1942 Red Star Paris
1943 Olympique Marseille
1944 Nancy Lorraine XI
1945 Racing Club Paris
1946 OSC Lille
1947 OSC Lille
1948 OSC Lille
1949 Racing Club Paris
1950 Stade Rennais
1951 Strasbourg
1952 OGC Nice
1953 OGC Lille
1954 OGC Nice
1955 OSC Lille
1956 FC Sedan
1957 FC Toulouse
1958 Stade de Reims
1959 Le Havre AC
1960 Monaco
1961 FC Sedan
1962 AS Saint Etienne
1963 Monaco
1964 Olympique Lyon
1965 Stade Rennais
1966 Strasbourg
1967 Olympique Lyon
1968 AS Saint Etienne
1969 Olympique Marseille
1970 AS Saint Etienne
1971 Stade Rennais
1972 Olympique Marseille
1973 Olympique Lyon
1974 AS Saint Etienne
1975 AS Saint Etienne
1976 Olympique Marseille
1977 AS Saint Etienne
1978 AS Nancy Lorraine
1979 FC Nantes
1980 Monaco
1981 SEC Bastia

1982 Paris Saint Germain
1983 Paris Saint Germain
1984 FC Metz
1985 Monaco
1986 Bordeaux
1987 Bordeaux
1988 FC Metz
1989 Olympique Marseille
1990 SCP Montpellier
1991 Monaco
1992 Not completed (after stadium disaster in Bastia at semi-final)
1993 Paris Saint Germain

1994 Auxerre
1995 Paris Saint Germain
1996 Auxerre
1997 Nice
1998 Paris Saint Germain

LEAGUE CUP WINNERS

1995 Paris Saint Germain
1996 Metz
1997 Strasbourg
1998 Paris Saint Germain

Georgia

Football Federation of Georgia
Founded: *1990*
Joined FIFA: *1992*

The quality of Georgian football first became seriously evident when Tbilisi Dynamo won the European Cup-winners Cup in 1981.

Tbilisi played football with a great deal more flair and technical skill than the northern, Moscow clubs from the Russian republic. That is why Georgia was known, in football, as the "Soviet Italy." Tbilisi Dynamo also won the Soviet championship twice thanks to the ability of players such as Alexander Chivadze in defence, David Kipiani in midfield and Ramaz Shengelia in attack.

Around 30 Georgian players won caps for the Soviet Union, the most successful having been central defender Murtaz Khurtsilava, who scored six goals in 67 internationals between 1976 and 1973 and who played in the 1966 World Cup finals. Kakhi Asatiani, a midfielder who scored five goals in 16 internationals for the Soviet Union and played in the 1970 World Cup finals in Mexico, later became Minister of Sport.

At the end of 1989, however, the Georgian federation withdrew from the Soviet federation. This meant that all Georgian clubs dropped out of the Soviet league and were lost to international sight until after the collapse of the rest of the USSR.

CHAMPIONS

1990 Iberiya Tbilisi
1991 Iberiya Tbilisi
1992 Iberiya Tbilisi
1993 Tbilisi Dinamo
1994 Tbilisi Dinamo
1995 Tbilisi Dinamo
1996 Tbilisi Dinamo
1997 Tbilisi Dinamo
1998 Tbilisi Dinamo

CUP WINNERS

1990 Guriya Lanchkhuti
1991 Not played
1992 Iberiya Tbilisi
1993 Tbilisi Dinamo
1994 Tbilisi Dinamo
1995 Tbilisi Dinamo
1996 Tbilisi Dinamo
1997 Tbilisi Dinamo
1998 Batumi

Germany sweeper Matthias Sammer

Germany

Deutscher Fussball-Bund
Founded: *1900*
Joined FIFA: *1904*

Germany, three times World Cup-winners and current European champions, lay just claim to being the most consistent national team force in Europe in the last 30 years. German clubs, oddly, have under-performed by comparison. But, at the highest level, there can never be any doubting which nation is most dangerous contender for world and European prizes.

The German success rate may be gauged not so much from listing the prizes but the few failures. For example, Germany have been absent from the finals of the World Cup on only two occasions: in 1930 and 1950, and then only because they did not enter. As for the European Championship, Germany did not enter in 1960 and 1964 and failed to qualify for the finals in 1968. Since then, however, they have always been there.

In the summer of 1996 they became the first nation to win the European Championship three times when they defeated the Czech Republic 2–1 at Wembley with the golden goal strike of Oliver Bierhoff in extra time. But they failed to emulate the German team of two decades earlier who held both European and World Cup crowns simultaneously, losing in the quarter-finals of France '98 to Croatia.

Nothing has been allowed to interfere with the single-minded pursuit of footballing excellence, however politicians twisted the country's borders. They were third in their first World Cup attempt in 1934 (as Germany), first-round failures in 1938 (as Greater Germany, having swallowed Austria and its footballers), then winners (as West Germany) for the first time in 1954. In Bern's Wankdorf Stadium they achieved one of the greatest of international upsets with a 3–2 defeat of the legendary Hungarians of Ferenc Puskas.

German international prospects were only strengthened when the old part-time regional-league system was scrapped in the early 1960s in favour of full-time professional football and a unified top division. The historical circle was finally closed in the early 1990s with the return to the national fold of the former East Germany – complete with outstanding players such as Matthias Sammer, Ulf Kirsten, Thomas Doll and Andreas Thom.

Their arrival was icing on the cake of success: in 1966, World Cup runners-up; in 1970, third in the World Cup; European champions for the first time – under Franz Bezckenbauer's captaincy – in 1972; World Cup-winners on home soil, again starring Beckenbauer, in 1974; European runners-up only after a penalty shoot-out in 1976; World Cup second round finalists in 1978; European champions for a second time in 1980; World Cup runners-up for a third time in 1986; European championship semi-finalists in 1988 then runners-up in 1992; World Cup winners again in 1990; quarter-finalists in 1994; European champions in 1996.

Bayern Munich won the European Champions Cup three times in a row in the mid-1970s, also collecting the World Club Cup along the way. They had won the Cup-winners Cup in 1967 and added the UEFA Cup in 1996 – joining Ajax, Barcelona and Juventus as the only clubs to have won all three European trophies. Hamburg and Borussia Dortmund have also won the Champions and Cup-winners Cups. There have been further European laps of honour for Werder Bremen in the Cup-winners Cup and for Borussia Mönchengladbach (twice), Eintracht Frankfurt and Bayer Leverkusen in the UEFA Cup.

A new chapter opened at the start of the 1990s following reunification with the eastern sector of Germany. This had been split away by the Soviet occupying forces after World War Two.

While, in the West, the old German federation, the DFB, carried on its business as usual, an independent East German federation was created (the DFV) with a debut international played on September 21, 1952. The result was a 3–0 defeat at the hands of Poland in Warsaw.

In fact, the East Germans achieved little in international football. The GDR systems created – in a suspiciously secretive manner – a host of medal-winning and record-breaking track and field athletes. But there was no potion powerful enough to conquer team sports. Only once did East Germany reach the finals of a major competition and that was the 1974 World Cup. The venue was West Germany, against whom East Germany recorded a unique 1–0 victory before sinking without a trace in the second round of the finals. Jürgen Sparwasser scored the historic goal turning him into a national hero of East Germany…until several years later, that is, when he defected.

That was also the year in which East Germany collected their only international club success when Magdeburg surprisingly defeated holders Milan 2–0 in a Cup-winners Cup Final played before a mere 4,000 in Rotterdam.

At home, East German football was dominated by the clubs of the political institutions. First, the army club Vorwärts; then the police team, Dynamo Dresden; finally, the club which operated under the aegis of the hated "Stasi" secret police, Dynamo Berlin. They won a "fixed" championship for a world-record 10 years in a row, but once their communist protectors had gone, the club collapsed into the amateur abyss opened up by football reunification.

CHAMPIONS

(Regional league with play-offs for the championship from 1903; unified league began in 1993–1964)

1903 VfB Leipzig
1904–Not played
1905 Union 92 Berlin
1906 VfB Leipzig
1907 SC Freiburg
1908 Viktoria Berlin
1909 Phoenix Karlsruhe
1910 Karlsruher FV
1911 Viktoria Berlin
1912 Holstein Kiel
1913 Vfb Berlin
1914 SPVgg Furth
1915–19 Not played
1920 1FC Nurnberg
1921 1FC Nurnberg
1922 Not played
1923 Hamburger SV
1924 1FC Nurnberg
1925 1FC Nurnberg
1926 SPVgg Furth
1927 1FC Nurnberg
1928 Hamburger SV
1929 SPVgg Furth
1930 Hertha BSC Berlin
1931 Hertha BSC Berlin
1932 Bayern Munich
1933 Fortuna Dusseldorf
1934 FC Schalke 04
1935 FC Schalke 04
1936 1FC Nurnberg
1937 FC Schalke 04
1938 Hannover 96
1939 FC Schalke 04
1940 FC Schalke 04
1941 Rapid Wien
1942 FC Schalke 04
1943 Dresdner SC
1944 Dresdner SC
1945–47 Not Played
1948 1FC Nurnberg
1949 VfR Mannheim
1950 VfB Stuttgart
1951 1FC Kaiserslautern
1952 VfB Stuttgart
1953 1FC Kaiserslautern
1954 Hannover 96
1955 Rot-Weiss Essen
1956 Borussia Dortmund
1957 Borussia Dortmund

1958 FC Schalke 04
1959 Eintracht Frankfurt
1960 Hamburger SV
1961 1FC Nurnberg
1962 1FC Koln
1963 Borussia Dortmund
1964 1FC Koln
1965 Werder Bremen
1966 TSV Munich 1860
1967 Eintracht Braunschweig
1968 1FC Nurnberg
1969 Bayern Munich
1970 Borussia Mönchengladbach
1971 Borussia Mönchengladbach
1972 Bayern Munich
1973 Bayern Munich
1974 Bayern Munich
1975 Borussia Mönchengladbach
1976 Borussia Mönchengladbach
1977 Borussia Mönchengladbach
1978 1FC Koln
1979 Hamburger SV
1980 Bayern Munich
1981 Bayern Munich
1982 Hamburger SV
1983 Hamburger SV
1984 VfB Stuttgart
1985 Bayern Munich
1986 Bayern Munich
1987 Bayern Munich
1988 Werder Bremen
1989 Bayern Munich
1990 Bayern Munich
1991 1FC Kaiserslautern
1992 VfB Stuttgart
1993 Werder Bremen
1994 Bayern Munich
1995 Borussia Dortmund
1996 Borussia Dortmund
1997 Bayern Munich
1998 Kaiserslautern

CUP WINNERS

1935 1FC Nurnberg
1936 VfB Stuttgart
1937 Schalke 04
1938 Rapid Wien
1939 1FC Nurnberg
1940 Dresdner SC
1941 Dresdner SC
1942 TSV Munich 1860
1943 First Vienna
1944 Rot-Weiss Essen
1945 VfB Stuttgart
1946–52 Not Played
1953 Rot-Weiss Essen
1954 VfB Stuttgart
1955 Karlsruher SC
1956 Karlsruher SC
1957 Bayern Munich
1958 VfB Stuttgart
1959 Schwarz-Weiss Essen
1960 Borussia Mönchengladbach
1961 Werder Bremen
1962 1FC Nurnberg
1963 Hamburger SV

1964 TSV Munich 1860
1965 Borussia Dortmund
1966 Bayern Munich
1967 Bayern Munich
1968 1FC Koln
1969 Bayern Munich
1970 Kickers Offenbach
1971 Bayern Munich
1972 FC Schalke 04
1973 Borussia Mönchengladbach
1974 Eintracht Frankfurt
1975 Eintracht Frankfurt
1976 Hamburger SV
1977 1FC Koln
1978 1FC Koln
1979 Fortuna Dusseldorf
1980 Fortuna Dusseldorf
1981 Eintracht Frankfurt
1982 Bayern Munich
1983 1FC Koln
1984 Bayern Munich
1985 Bayer Uerdingen
1986 Bayern Munich
1987 Hamburger SV
1988 Entracht Frankfurt
1989 Borussia Dortmund
1990 1FC Kaiserslautern
1991 Werder Bremen
1992 Hannover 96
1993 Bayer Leverkusen
1994 Werder Bremen
1995 Borussia Mönchengladbach
1996 Borussia Mönchengladbach
1997 Kaiserslautern
1998 Bayern Munich

EAST GERMANY

1948 SG Planitz
1949 ZSG Halle
1950 Horch Zwickau
1951 Chemie Leipzig
1952 Turbine Halle
1953 Dynamo Dresden
1954 Turbine Erfurt
1955 Turbine Erfurt
1956 Wismut KMS
1957 Wismut KMS
1958 Vorwarts Berlin
1959 Wismut KMS
1960 Vorwarts Berlin
1961 Not played
1962 Vorwarts Berlin
1963 Mot Jena
1964 Chemie Leipzig
1965 Vorwarts Berlin
1966 Vorwarts Berlin
1967 FC Karl-Marx-Stadt
1968 Carl-Zeiss Jena
1969 Vorwarts Berlin
1970 Carl-Zeiss Jena
1971 Dynamo Dresden
1972 FC Magdeburg
1973 Dynamo Dresden
1974 FC Magdeburg
1975 FC Magdeburg
1976 Dynamo Dresden

1977 Dynamo Dresden
1978 Dynamo Dresden
1979 Dynamo Berlin
1980 Dynamo Berlin
1981 Dynamo Berlin
1982 Dynamo Berlin
1983 Dynamo Berlin
1984 Dynamo Berlin
1985 Dynamo Berlin
1986 Dynamo Berlin
1987 Dynamo Berlin
1988 Dynamo Berlin
1989 Dynamo Dresden
1990 Dynamo Dresden
1991 Hansa Rostock

CUP WINNERS

1949 Waggonbau Dessau
1950 EHW Thale
1951 Not played
1952 VP Dresden
1953 Not played
1954 Vorwarts Berlin
1955 Wismut KMS
1956 Chemie Halle
1957 SC Lokomotiv Leipzig
1958 Einheit Dresden
1959 Dynamo Berlin
1960 Motor Jena
1961 Not played

1962 Chemie Halle
1963 Motor Zwickau
1964 Aufbau Magdeburg
1965 Aufbau Magdeburg
1966 Chemie Leipzig
1967 Motor Zwickau
1968 FC Union Berlin
1969 FC Magdeburg
1970 Vorwarts Berlin
1971 Dynamo Dresden
1972 Carl Zeiss Jena
1973 FC Magdeburg
1974 Carl-Zeiss Jena
1975 Sachsenrign Zwickau
1976 Lokomotiv Leipzig
1977 Dynamo Dresden
1978 FC Magdeburg
1979 FC Magdeburg
1980 Carl-Zeiss Jena
1981 Lokomotiv Leipzig
1982 Dynamo Dresden
1983 FC Magdeburg
1984 Dynamo Dresden
1985 Dynamo Dresden
1986 Lokomotiv Leipzig
1987 Lokomotov Leipzig
1988 Dynamo Berlin
1989 Dynamo Berlin
1990 Dynamo Dresden
1991 Hansa Rostock

Greece

Eliniki Podosferiki Omospondia
Founded: 1926
Joined FIFA: 1927

The excitement of the moment has long been the key to Greek football. For example, the Greeks were the first nation to introduce three points for a win in league play. That was in the 1950s and was a disciplinary measure.

Teams who won a match were awarded three points, teams who drew a match were awarded two points each and teams who lost but stayed on the pitch to the end of the full 90 minutes (!) were awarded one point. Teams, of course, which lost a match and stormed off in anger before the final whistle got nothing.

Clubs such as Panathinaikos and AEK of Athens and Olympiakos from the nearby port of Piraeus are traditionally considered among the richest in Europe. But the very power of the big clubs worked, for many years, contrary to the interests of the national team. The clubs were reluctant to release their players for internationals and a lack of preparation was reflected in regular failure in the qualifying competitions for both World Cup and European Championship.

The breakthrough came when Greece reached the finals of the European Championship in Italy in 1980 under manager

Altekas Panagulias. They opened their European finals campaign with a narrow 1–0 defeat by Holland, lost 3–1 to defending title-holders Czechoslovakia and finished up with a goalless draw against the West Germans. Four years later Greece reached the final of the European under-21 championship. Their hero was goalscorer Nikols Nioplias who went on to become one of the stars of the senior national team who qualified for the World Cup finals for the first time in 1994.

At club level, Olympiakos are the most successful with 25 championships and 19 cup victories. But Panathianaikos, 2–0 losers to Ajax Amsterdam in the 1971 Champions Cup, remain the only Greek side to have reached a European club final.

CHAMPIONS

1928 Aris Salonica	1980 Olympiakos
1929 Not played	1981 Olympiakos
1930 Panathinaikos	1982 Olympiakos
1931 Olympiakos	1983 Olympiakos
1932 Aris Salonica	1984 Panathinaikos
1933 Olympiakos	1985 PAOK Salonica
1934 Olympiakos	1986 Panathinaikos
1935 Not played	1987 Olympiakos
1936 Olympiakos	1988 Larissa
1937 Olympiakos	1989 AEK Athens
1938 Olympiakos	1990 Panathinaikos
1939 AEK Athens	1991 Panathinaikos
1940 AEK Athens	1992 AEK Athens
1941–45 Not played	1993 AEK Athens
1946 Aris Salonica	1994 AEK Athens
1947 Olympiakos	1995 Panathinaikos
1948 Olympiakos	1996 Panathinaikos
1949 Panathinaikos	1997 Olympiakos
1950 Not played	1998 Olympiakos
1951 Olympiakos	
1952 Not played	
1953 Panathinaikos	

CUP WINNERS

1954 Olympiakos	1932 AEK Athens
1955 Olympiakos	1933 Ethnikos Piraeus
1956 Olympiakos	1934–38 Not played
1957 Olympiakos	1939 AEK Athens
1958 Olympiakos	1940 Panathinaikos
1959 Olympiakos	1941–46 Not played
1960 Panathinaikos	1947 Olympiakos
1961 Panathinaikos	1948 Panathinaikos
1962 Panathinaikos	1949 AEK Athens
1963 AEK Athens	1950 AEK Athens
1964 Panathinaikos	1951 Olympiakos
1965 Panathinaikos	1952 Olympiakos
1966 Olympiakos	1953 Olympiakos
1967 Olympiakos	1954 Olympiakos
1968 AEK Athens	1955 Panathinaikos
1969 Panathinaikos	1956 AEK Athens
1970 Panathinaikos	1957 Olympiakos
1971 AEK Athens	1958 Olympiakos
1972 Panathinaikos	1959 Olympiakos
1973 Olympiakos	1960 Olympiakos
1974 Olympiakos	1961 Olympiakos
1975 Olympiakos	1962 Not played
1976 PAOK Salonica	1963 Olympiakos
1977 Panathinaikos	1964 Not played
1978 AEK Athens	1965 Olympiakos
1979 AEK Athens	1966 AEK Athens
	1967 Panathinaikos
	1968 Olympiakos

1969 Panathinaikos	1984 Panathinaikos
1970 Aris Salonica	1985 Larissa
1971 Aris Salonica	1986 Panathinaikos
1972 PAOK Salonica	1987 OFI Crete
1973 Olympiakos	1988 Panathinaikos
1974 PAOK Salonica	1989 Panathinaikos
1975 Olympiakos	1990 Olympiakos
1976 Iraklis	1991 Panathinaikos
1977 Panathinaikos	1992 Olympiakos
1978 AEK Athens	1993 Panathinaikos
1979 Panionios	1994 Panathinaikos
1980 Kastoria	1995 Panathinaikos
1981 Olympiakos	1996 AEK Athens
1982 Panathinaikos	1997 AEK Athens
1983 AEK Athens	1998 Panionios

Holland

Koninklijke Nederlandsche Voetbalbond

Founded: *1889*

Joined FIFA: *1904*

Holland may be one of the smaller nations in terms of square kilometres. But they are one of the giants of world football – a status which owes everything to the remarkable flowering of talent as bright as the tulips in the country's famous bulb fields.

Dutch football was strictly amateur for more than half of the century, although they qualified for the World Cup finals in 1934 and 1938 – losing each time in the first round.

The 1940s brought war so it was not until the 1950s that conflict of a different sort arose between the amateurs and the impatient would-be professionals. In 1953 a breakaway professional championship was launched. It proved the catalyst for reorganization, for progress towards football reality: a vital step down the path which would lead to "total football" and the great days of the 1970s.

Feyenoord, not Ajax, were Holland's first international winners. Under the guidance of Austrian coach Ernst Happel, they beat Celtic in the 1970 Champions Cup Final, then Estudiantes de La Plata for the World Club Cup. But Feyenoord's achievement was bettered by the sheer spell-binding style with which Ajax – under Rinus Michels then Stefan Kovacs – conquered and entertained Europe for the next three years.

Inspirational superstar Johan Cruyff was sold to Barcelona for a then world record £922,000, but recreated his partnership with Michels to lead the national team to the 1974 World Cup. Holland, beaten 2–1 by hosts West Germany in Munich, finished runners-up. They did so again in 1978, despite Cruyff's decision to abandon the national team six months in advance of the trip to finals. In the Final it was the hosts again, this time Argentina, who beat Holland 3–1 after extra time.

Third in the European championship in 1976, the Dutch magic began to fade in the 1980 European finals when Rudi Krol, Arie

Holland legend Johan Cruyff in action for Ajax in a European Cup tie against Benfica

Haan and the rest failed to progress beyond the first round. Then they failed to qualify for the 1982 World Cup finals. "I think," said Krol, by then starring for Napoli in Italy, "that this may be the end. One great generation of players like that cannot be expected to be matched for maybe a century."

Yet events proved Krol's understandable logic to have been happily flawed. Within a very few years, with Michels back in charge, the Dutchmen were flying again. Michels looked for his team to Ajax who, with Cruyff as coach, had won the Cup-winners Cup in 1987. Marco Van Basten, as young captain, had collected the winning goal against Lokomotiv Leipzig in Athens, to revive the memories and inspiration of the glory days. Simultaneously PSV Eindhoven, one of Europe's richest clubs thanks to their Philips owners, took up the European challenge and won the 1988 Champions Cup in a remarkable summer, climaxed by the European Championship triumph.

Holland beat the Soviet Union 2–0 in the Final in Munich. Skipper Ruud Gullit scored the first goal and Van Basten volleyed a wonderful second.

Gullit, Van Basten and Frank Rijkaard went off to turn Italy's Milan into the dominant club force of the 1990s. Meanwhile, another wave of talent burst through in their wake and Ajax duly regained the Champions Cup in 1995. Then the Dutch took the 1998 World Cup finals by storm – and although they lost on penalties to Brazil in the semi-final in France, many regarded them as the most talented team of the tournament.

CHAMPIONS

1898 RAP Amsterdam	1911 Sparta Rotterdam
1899 RAP Amsterdam	1912 Sparta Rotterdam
1900 HVV Den Haag	1913 Sparta Rotterdam
1901 HVV Den Haag	1914 HVV Den Haag
1902 HVV Den Haag	1915 Sparta Rotterdam
1903 HVV Den Haag	1916 Willen II Tilburg
1904 HBS Den Haag	1917 Go Ahead Deventar
1905 HVV Den Haag	1918 Ajax
1906 HBS Den Haag	1919 Ajax
1907 HVV Den Haag	1920 Be Quick Groningen
1908 Quick Den Haag	1921 NAC Breda
1909 Sparta Rotterdam	1922 Go Ahead Deventer
1910 HVV Den Haag	1923 RCH Haarlem
	1924 Feyenoord
	1925 HBS Den Haag

1926 SC Enschende
1927 Heracles Almelo
1928 Feyenoord
1929 PSV Eindhoven
1930 Go Ahead Deventer
1931 Ajax
1932 Ajax
1933 Go Ahead Deventer
1934 Ajax
1935 PSV Eindhoven
1936 Feyenoord
1937 Ajax
1938 Feyenoord
1939 Ajax
1940 Feyenoord
1941 Heracles Almelo
1942 ADA Den Haag
1943 ADO Den Haag
1944 De Volewijckers
1945 Not played
1946 Haarlem
1947 Ajax
1948 BVV Hertogenbosch
1949 SVV Schieden
1950 Limburg
1951 PSV Eindhoven
1952 Willem II Tilburg
1953 RCH Haarlem
1954 Eindhoven 8 DOS
1955 Willem II Tilburg
1956 Rapid JC Heerlen
1957 Ajax
1958 DOS Atrecht
1959 Sparta Rotterdam
1960 Ajax
1961 Feyenoord
1962 Feyenoord
1963 PSV Eindhoven
1964 DWS Amsterdam
1965 Feyenoord
1966 Ajax
1967 Ajax
1968 Ajax
1969 Feyenoord
1970 Ajax
1971 Feyenoord
1972 Ajax
1973 Ajax
1974 Feyenoord
1975 PSV Eindhoven
1976 PSV Eindhoven
1977 Ajax
1978 PSV Eindhoven
1979 Ajax
1980 Ajax
1981 AZ 67 Alkmaar
1982 Ajax
1983 Ajax
1984 Feyenoord
1985 Ajax
1986 PSV Eindhoven
1987 PSV Eindhoven
1988 PSV Eindhoven
1989 PSV Eindhoven

1990 Ajax
1991 PSV Eindhoven
1992 PSV Eindhoven
1993 Feyenoord
1994 Ajax
1995 Ajax
1996 Ajax
1997 PSV Eindhoven
1998 Ajax

CUP WINNERS

1899 RAP Amsterdam
1900 Velocitas Breda
1901 HBS Den Haag
1902 Haarlem
1903 HVV Den Haag
1904 HFC Haarlem
1905 VOC Rotterdam
1906 Concordia
1907 VOC Rotterdam
1908 HBS Den Haag
1909 Quick Den Haag
1910 Quick Den Haag
1911 Haarlem
1912 Haarlem
1913 HFC Haarlem
1914 DFC Dordrecht
1915 HFC Haarlem
1916 Quick Den Haag
1917 Ajax
1918 RCH Haarlem
1919 Not played
1920 CVV
1921 Schoten
1922–24 Not played
1925 ZFC
1926 LONGA Lichtenvoorde
1927 VUC Den Haag
1928 RCH Haarlem
1929 Not played
1930 Feyenoord
1931 Not played
1932 DFC Dordrecht
1933 Not played
1934 Velocitas Groningen
1935 Feyenoord
1936 Roermond
1937 Eindhoven
1938 VSV Velsen
1939 Wageningen
1940–42 Not played
1943 Ajax
1944 Willem II Tilburg
1945–47 Not played
1948 Wageningen
1949 Quick Nijmegen
1950 PSV Eindhoven
1951–56 Not played
1957 Fortuna '54 Geleen
1958 Sparta Rotterdam
1959 VVV Venlo
1960 Not played
1961 Ajax
1962 Sparta Rotterdam

1963 Willem II Tilburg
1964 Fortuna '54 Geleen
1965 Feyenoord
1966 Sparta Rotterdam
1967 Ajax
1968 Feyenoord
1969 Ajax
1970 Ajax
1971 Ajax
1972 Ajax
1973 NAC Breda
1974 PSV Eindhoven
1975 FC Den Haag
1976 PSV Eindhoven
1977 FC Twente Enschende
1978 AZ 67 Alkmaar
1979 Ajax
1980 Feyenoord

1981 AZ 67 Alkmaar
1982 AZ 67 Alkmaar
1983 Ajax
1984 Feyenoord
1985 FC Utrecht
1986 Ajax
1987 Ajax
1988 PSV Eindhoven
1989 PSV Eindhoven
1990 PSV Eindhoven
1991 Feyenoord
1992 Feneyoord
1993 Ajax
1994 Feyenoord
1995 Feyenoord
1996 PSV Eindhoven
1997 PSV Eindhoven
1998 Ajax

Hungary

Magyar Labdarugo Szovetseg

Founded: 1901
Joined FIFA: 1906

Football was taken to Hungary by English students in 1870s. Yet, some 80 years later, the tables were turned and it was the Hungarians who were handing out a football lesson to the English. Ferenc Puskas was the captain and headmaster of the legendary team of the 1950s whose fame and reputation has intimidated, overshadowed and stifled every other Hungarian team to this day.

The foundations were well laid. Even before the turn of the century, three of the most powerful domestic clubs had been formed in MTK, Ferencvaros and Ujpest. In 1916 the legendary English coach Jimmy Hogan arrived at MTK, discovered the country's first great individual footballer in Gyorgy Orth, and prepared Hungarian football for the advance of professionalism in the 1920s and 1930s.

This era reached a climax in 1938 when Hungary progressed to the World Cup Final in Paris. Their inspiration came from the academic centre forward or centre half Gyorgy Sarosi. Hungary lost 4–2 in the Final to Italy but the disappointment was as nothing compared with the shock waves which went through the world game in 1954. Here again Hungary lost the World Cup Final, by 3–2 to West Germany in Switzerland.

This was the team built around goalkeeper Gyula Grosics, right half Jozsef Bozsik and the inside forward trio of Sandor Kocsis, Nandor Hidegkuti and Puskas. They had won the 1952 Olympic title; they had ended England's record of invincibility against continental opposition, winning 6–3 at Wembley; they had remained unbeaten four years…only to then lose the one match which mattered the most.

It was the beginning of the end. Two years later came the

Hungarian Revolution. Honved, the top club which provided the nucleus for the national team, were touring abroad at the time. Some of the players decided to go home; some to stay in exile, including Puskas, Kocsis and left winger Zoltan Czibor.

Hungary's national team have never been the same though they have reached the finals of the World Cup on six occasions and, in the European Championship, were third in 1964 and fourth in 1972.

The only occasion on which they have seriously threatened to break loose was at the 1966 World Cup finals in England. Then a fine side (managed by Lajos Baroti and starring Florian Albert and Ferenc Bene) scored a memorable 3–1 victory over Brazil only to fall to the Soviet Union in the quarter-finals because of goalkeeping errors.

Twice since then Puskas, the old hero, has been recalled as national manager. But the collapse of communism condemned the domestic game to penury. Star players go abroad as soon as they can. The national team comes bottom of the priority list. Now Hungary are one of eastern Europe's weakest teams.

CHAMPIONS

1901 Budapest	1941 Ferencvaros
1902 Budapest	1942 Csepel
1903 Ferencvaros	1943 Csepel
1904 MTK Budapest	1944 Nagyvaradi
1905 Ferencvaros	1945 Ujpest
1906 Not played	1946 Ujpest
1907 Ferencvaros	1947 Ujpest
1908 MTK Budapest	1948 Csepel
1909 Ferencvaros	1949 Ferencvaros
1910 Ferencvaros	1950 Honved
1911 Ferencvaros	1951 Bastya Budapest
1912 Ferencvaros	1952 Honved
1913 Ferencvaros	1953 Voros Lobogo
1914 MTK Budapest	1954 Honved
1915–16 Not played	1955 Honved
1917 MTK Budapest	1956 Not completed
1918 MTK Budapest	1957 Vasas Budapest
1919 MTK Budapest	1958 MTK Budapest
1920 MTK Budapest	1959 Csepel
1921 MTK Budapest	1960 Ujpest
1922 MTK Budapest	1961 Vasas Budapest
1923 MTK Budapest	1962 Ferencvaros
1924 MTK Budapest	1963 spring championship: Gyor
1925 MTK Budapest	Vasas
1926 Ferencvaros	1964 Ferencvaros
1927 Ferencvaros	1965 Vasas
1928 Ferencvaros	1966 Vasas
1929 Hungaria	1967 Ferencvaros
1930 Ujpest	1968 Ferencvaros
1931 Ujpest	1969 Ujpest Dozsa
1932 Ferencvaros	1970 Ujpest Dozsa
1933 Ujpest	1971 Ujpest Dozsa
1934 Ferencvaros	1972 Ujpest Dozsa
1935 Ujpest	1973 Ujpest Dozsa
1936 Hungaria	1974 Ujpest Dozsa
1937 Hungaria	1975 Ujpest Dozsa
1938 Ferencvaros	1976 Ferencvaros
1939 Ujpest	1977 Vasas
1940 Ferencvaros	1978 Ujpest Dozsa
	1979 Ujpest Dozsa

1980 Honved	1943 Ferencvaros
1981 Ferencvaros	1944 Ferencvaros
1982 Raba ETO Gyor	1945–51 Not played
1983 Raba ETO Gyor	1952 Bastya Budapest
1984 Honved	1953–54 Not played
1985 Honved	1955 Vasas Budapest
1986 Honved	1956 Ferencvaros
1987 MTK-VM Budapest	1957–63 Not played
1988 Honved	1964 Honved
1989 Honved	1965 Vasas ETO Gyor
1990 Ujpest Dozsa	1966 Vasas ETO Gyor
1991 Honved	1967 Vasas ETO Gyor
1992 Ferencvaros	1968 MTK Budapest
1993 Kispest-Honved	1969 Ujpest Dozsa
1994 Vac Samsung	1970 Ujpest Dozsa
1995 Ferencvaros	1971 Not played
1996 Ferencvaros	1972 Ferencvaros
1997 MTK-VM Budapest	1973 Vasas Budapest
1998 Ujest Dozsa	1974 Ferencvaros
	1975 Ujpest Dozsa
	1976 Ferencvaros
	1977 Diosgyori VTK

CUP WINNERS

1910 MTK Budapest	1978 Ferencvaros
1911 MTK Budapest	1979 Raba ETO Gyor
1912 MTK Budapest	1980 Diosgyori VTK
1913 Ferencvaros	1981 Vasas Budapest
1914 MTK Budapest	1982 Ujpest Dozsa
1915–21 Not played	1983 Ujpest Dozsa
1922 Ferencvaros	1984 Siofoki Banyasz
1923 MTK Budapest	1985 Honved
1924 Not played	1986 Vasas Budapest
1925 MTK Budapest	1987 Ujpest Dozsa
1926 Kispest AC	1988 Bekescsaba
1927 Ferencvaros	1989 Honved
1928 Ferencvaros	1990 Pecsi MSC
1929 Not played	1991 Ferencvaros
1930 Bocskai Debrecen	1992 Ujpest TE
1931 III Kerulet TVE	1993 Ferencvaros
1932 Hungaria	1994 Ferencvaros
1933 Ferencvaros	1995 Ferencvaros
1934 Soroksar	1996 Kispest-Honved
1935 Ferencvaros	1997 MTK-VM Budapest
1936–40 Not played	1998 MTK-VM Budapest
1941 Szolnoki MAV	
1942 Ferencvaros	

Iceland

Knattspymusamband Islands
Founded: *1929*
Joined FIFA: *1947*

Iceland do not expect to be seen at the finals of the World Cup or European Championship. But their fans do expect more sophisticated and ambitious opponents to work hard for points and goals against their favourites.

Once considered Europe's last amateurs, Iceland have exported dozens of players south to the professional world with success. The national team have also numbered the likes of Wales, Northern Ireland and East Germany among their victims.

Their most successful national manager was probably Englishman Tony Knapp though many other of his countrymen – among them George Kirby – have worked with great domestic success at Icelandic clubs.

Football in Iceland can be traced back to 1894 when it was apparently introduced by James Ferguson, a Scottish printer and bookseller. An Athletic Union and championship were set up in 1912. This was run on a knock-out basis and the first winners were KR Reykjavik. It was not until 1925 that a proper home-and-away league was set up. First winners – again – were KR.

Iceland's first international was played on July 17, 1946, and ended in a 3–0 defeat in Reykjavik by Denmark – the country from which Iceland had achieved independence only two years earlier. The first World Cup campaign was the 1958 competition. Iceland's qualifying debut was a match to forget: they lost 8–0 to a French side which would finish third. Playing inside left that day was Albert Gudmundsson, for years rated Iceland's finest player and later a senior figure in both federation and government.

1990 Fram Reykjavik	1975 IBK Keflavik
1991 Vikingur Reykjavik	1976 Valur Reykjavik
1992 IA Akranes	1977 Valur Reykjavik
1993 IA Akranes	1978 IA Akranes
1994 IA Akranes	1979 Fram Reykjavik
1995 IA Akranes	1980 Fram Reykjavik
1996 IA Akranes	1981 IBV Vestmannaeyjar
1997 IBV	1982 IA Akranes
	1983 IA Akranes

CUP WINNERS

	1984 IA Akranes
1960 KR Reykjavik	1985 Fram Reykjavik
1961 KR Reykjavik	1986 IA Akranes
1962 KR Reykjavik	1987 Fram Reykjavik
1963 KR Reykjavik	1988 Valur Reykjavik
1964 KR Reykjavik	1989 Fram Reykjavik
1965 Valur Reykjavik	1990 Valur Reykjavik
1966 KR Reykjavik	1991 Valur Reykjavik
1967 KR Reykjavik	1992 Valur Reykjavik
1968 IBV Vestmannaeyjar	1993 IA Akranes
1969 IBA Akureyri	1994 KR Reykjavik
1970 Fram Reykjavik	1995 KR Reykjavik
1971 Vikingur Reykjavik	1996 IBV
1972 IBV Vestmannaeyjar	1997 IBK Keflavik
1973 Fram Reykjavik	
1974 Valur Reykjavik	

CHAMPIONS

1912 KR Reykjavik	1951 IA Akranes
1913 Fram Reykjavik	1952 KR Reykjavik
1914 Fram Reykjavik	1953 IA Akranes
1915 Fram Reykjavik	1954 IA Akranes
1916 Fram Reykjavik	1955 KR Reykjavik
1917 Fram Reykjavik	1956 Valur Reykjavik
1918 Fram Reykjavik	1957 IA Akranes
1919 KR Reykjavik	1958 IA Akranes
1920 Vikingur Reykjavik	1959 KR Reykjavik
1921 Fram Reykjavik	1960 IA Akranes
1922 Fram Reykjavik	1961 KR Reykjavik
1923 Fram Reykjavik	1962 Fram Reykjavik
1924 Vikingur Rekjavik	1963 KR Reykjavik
1925 KR Reykjavik	1964 IBK Keflavik
1926 KR Reykjavik	1965 KR Reykjavik
1927 KR Reykjavik	1966 Valur Rekjavik
1928 KR Reykjavik	1967 Valur Rekjavik
1929 KR Reykjavik	1968 KR Reykjavik
1930 Valur Reykjavik	1969 IBK Keflavik
1931 KR Reykjavik	1970 IA Akranes
1932 KR Reykjavik	1971 IBK Keflavik
1933 Valur Reykjavik	1972 Fram Reykjavik
1934 KR Reykjavik	1973 IBK Keflavik
1935 Valur Reykjavik	1974 IA Akranes
1936 Valur Reykjavik	1975 IA Akranes
1937 Valur Reykjavik	1976 Valur Reykjavik
1938 Valur Reykjavik	1977 IA Akranes
1939 Fram Reykjavik	1978 Valur Reykjavik
1940 Valur Reykjavik	1979 IBV Vestmannaeyjar
1941 KR Reykjavik	1980 Valur Reykjavik
1942 Valur Reykjavik	1981 Vikingur Reykjavik
1943 Valur Reykjavik	1982 Vikingur Reykjavik
1944 Valur Reykjavik	1983 IA Akranes
1945 Valur Reykjavik	1984 IA Akranes
1946 Fram Reykjavic	1985 Valur Reykjavik
1947 Fram Reykjavik	1986 Fram Reykjavik
1948 KR Reykjavik	1987 Valur Reykjavik
1949 KR Reykjavik	1988 Fram Reykjavik
1950 KR Reykjavik	1989 KA Akureyri

Israel

Israel Football Association

Founded: *1928*

Joined FIFA: *1929*

Israel have reached the final stages of the World Cup only once, in 1970, but since being admitted to UEFA in 1991, they have made great progress. Proof was their 3–2 win over France in Paris in the World Cup qualifying competition in November, 1993.

Israel are the only country in the world to have played World Cup qualifiers on all five continents, a legacy of an era in which the Jewish state, which is geographically part of Asia, was kicked out of the Asian federation and regularly forced to compete in the Oceania group with play-offs against South American or European nations.

Now everything has changed. The collapse of the Soviet Union removed the bar to Israeli inclusion in Europe. Israeli teams now compete in all three European club competitions.

The development of Israeli football at international level has been helped by the steady exodus of players – including English-based Ronny Rosenthal and Eyal Berkovic – to European clubs since the mid-1980s. They have learned the game at the highest level and that knowledge has rubbed off on home-based players in the national squad.

CHAMPIONS

1932 British Police	1935 Hapoel Tel Aviv
1933 Not played	1936 Hapoel Tel Aviv
1934 Hapoel Tel Aviv	1937 Maccabi Tel Aviv
	1938 Hapoel Tel Aviv

1939 Maccabi Tel Aviv	1932 British Police
1940 Hapoel Tel Aviv	1933 Maccabi Tel Aviv
1941 Maccabi Tel Aviv	1934 Hapeol Tel Aviv
1942 Not played	1935 Maccabi Petah Tikva
1943 Hapoel Tel Aviv	1936 Not played
1944–46 Not played	1937 Hapoel Tel Aviv
1947 Maccabi Tel Aviv	1938 Hapoel Tel Aviv
1948 Not played	1939 Hapoel Tel Aviv
1949 Maccabi Tel Aviv	1940 Beitar Tel Aviv
1950 Maccabi Tel Aviv	1941 Maccabi Tel Aviv
1951 Not played	1942 Beitar Tel Aviv
1952 Maccabi Tel Aviv	1943–45 Not played
1953 Not played	1946 Macabi Tel Aviv
1954 Maccabi Tel Aviv	1947 Maccabi Tel Aviv
1955 Hapoel Petak Tikva	1948–51 Not played
1956 Maccabi Tel Aviv	1952 Maccabi Petah Tikva
1957 Hapoel Tel Aviv	1953 Not played
1958 Maccabi Tel Aviv	1954 Maccabi Tel Aviv
1959 Hapoel Petah Tivva	1955 Maccabi Tel Aviv
1960 Hapoel Petah Tivva	1956 Not played
1961 Hapoel Petah Tivva	1957 Hapoel Petak Tikva
1962 Hapoel Petah Tivva	1958 Maccabi Tel Aviv
1963 Hapoel Petah Tivva	1959 Maccabi Tel Aviv
1964 Hakoah Ramat Gan	1960 Hapoel Tel Aviv
1965 Hakoah Ramat Gan	1961 Not played
1966 Hapoel Tel Aviv	1962 Maccabi Haifa
1967 Maccabi Tel Aviv	1963 Hapoel Haifa
1968 Maccabi Tel Aviv	1964 Maccabi Tel Aviv
1969 Hapoel Tel Aviv	1965 Maccabi Tel Aviv
1970 Maccabi Tel Aviv	1966 Hapoel Haifa
1971 Maccabi Netanya	1967 Maccabi Tel Aviv
1972 Maccabi Tel Aviv	1968 Briei Yehuda
1973 Hakoah Ramat Gan	1969 Hakoah Ramat Gan
1974 Maccabi Netanya	1970 Maccabi Tel Aviv
1975 Hapoel Beer Sheva	1971 Hakoah Ramat Gan
1976 Hapoel Beer Sheva	1972 Hapoel Tel Aviv
1977 Maccabi Tel Aviv	1973 Hapoel Jerusalem
1978 Maccabi Netanya	1974 Hapoel Haifa
1979 Maccabi Tel Aviv	1975 Hapoel Kfar Sava
1980 Maccabi Netanya	1976 Beitar Jerusalem
1981 Hapoel Tel Aviv	1977 Maccabi Tel Aviv
1982 Hapoel Kfar Sava	1978 Maccabi Netanya
1983 Maccabi Netanya	1979 Beitar Jerusalem
1984 Maccabi Haifa	1980 Hapoel Kfar Sava
1985 Maccabi Haifa	1981 Bnei Yehuda
1986 Hapoel Tel Aviv	1982 Bnei Yehuda
1987 Beitar Jerusalem	1983 Hapoel Tel Aviv
1988 Hapoel Tel Aviv	1984 Hapoel Lod
1989 Maccabi Haifa	1985 Beitar Jerusalem
1990 Bnei Yehuda	1986 Beitar Jerusalem
1991 Maccabi Haifa	1987 Maccabi Tel Aviv
1992 Maccabi Tel Aviv	1988 Maccabi Tel Aviv
1993 Beitar Jerusalem	1989 Beitar Jerusalem
1994 Maccabi Haifa	1990 Hapoel Kfar Sava
1995 Maccabi Tel Aviv	1991 Maccabi Haifa
1996 Maccabi Tel Aviv	1992 Hapoel Petah Tikvah
1997 Beitar Jerusalem	1993 Maccabi Haifa
1998 Beitar Jerusalem	1994 Maccabi Tel Aviv
	1995 Maccabi Haifa
	1996 Maccabi Tel Aviv
CUP WINNERS	1997 Hapoel Ber Sheva
	1998 Maccabi Haifa
1928 Hapoel Tel Aviv	
1929 Maccabi Tel Aviv	
1930 Maccabi Tel Aviv	
1931 Not played	

Italy

Federazione Italiana Gioco Calcio

Founded: *1898*

Joined FIFA: *1905*

Two gunmen once held up a ticket bureau in Naples, but it was not money they wanted. Instead their desperate demand was for tickets to see Argentina's Diego Maradona make his first home appearance after joining the local club from Barcelona for a then world record £5million.

This exemplifies the mad passion which turned Italy into world football's El Dorado from the 1930s until the 1990s, when the television revolution offered big clubs in England and Spain financial parity in terms of transfer funds and pay rates. All the world's transfer records between Barcelona's £922,000 capture of Johan Cruyff in 1973 and Newcastle's £15million acquisition of Alan Shearer in 1996 saw Italian clubs making the payments. Even then it was only a year before Internazionale, paying £19.5million for Ronaldo from Barcelona, had reclaimed Italy's primacy in the expenditure stakes.

The power of the Italian game is illustrated again by glancing through the European club competition record books. Italian clubs have won the World Club Cup on seven occasions, the European Champions Cup on nine occasions, the Cup-winners Cup six times, the UEFA Cup nine times also and the European Supercup six times. All of those Italian victories depended to a significant extent on the extra qualities imported by Frenchmen, Argentines, Brazilians and Germans.

Imports have always played a central role in Italian football, right back to the closing years of the 19th century when English, Scottish and Swiss engineers and students and sailors imported the game.

In 1898 the first Italian championship featured just four teams and was all over and completed in just one day. By 1921 eight regions were involved and a professional, nationwide top division was launched in 1929. Only Internazionale and Juventus can boast of never having been relegated – Juventus having won the championship a record 24 times.

Along the way Juventus joined the handful of clubs to have won all three European club trophies. In nine remarkable months from May 1996, they won the Champions Cup, the World Club Cup and the European Supercup.

The power of calcio is demonstrated most clearly in World Cup history. Italy was the first nation in Europe to host the finals and the first European nation to win the game's greatest prize three times.

In 1934 Italy, managed by the legendary Vittorio Pozzo, took advantage of their status as hosts. Pozzo included three Argentine stars – centre half Luisito Monti and wingers Enrico Guaita and Raimundo Orsi – in the team who defeated

Czechoslovakia 2–1 after extra time in the Final in Rome in front of delighted dictator Benito Mussolini. Ruthless Pozzo rebuilt his team entirely for the World Cup defence in France in 1938. Only the inside forwards Giuseppe Meazza and Giovanni Ferrari survived in the team who defeated Hungary 4–2 in the Final.

Disaster struck as Italy prepared to defend their crown in Brazil in the post-war world of 1950. Just over 12 months before the opening of the finals, the entire first-team squad of Italian champions Torino were wiped out in an air crash, including national captain Valentino Mazzola. The consequence, in World Cup terms, was first-round elimination.

The big clubs spent ever more lavishly on foreign stars and the small clubs responded by perfecting the catenaccio defensive system. The Azzurri – as the team is known to the tifosi (fans) – paid the penalty in terms of World Cup failure. Italy were

Italy captain Paolo Maldini, in action for AC Milan

beaten in the first round of the finals in 1954 and then, humiliatingly, by Northern Ireland in the 1958 qualifying competition. In Chile in 1962 Italy fell in the first round after an infamously violent match against their hosts; in 1966 they were eliminated, notoriously, by North Korea.

Even as European Championship hosts in 1968, Italy struggled to capitalize on home advantage. They beat the Soviet Union in the semi-finals on the toss of a coin and defeated Yugoslavia in the Final only after a replay. The nucleus of that team, under the managership of Ferruccio Valcareggi, went on to finish runners-up to a magnificent Brazil in the World Cup in Mexico two years later.

Valcareggi took Italy through to first-round elimination in Germany in 1974 and was replaced by veteran coach Fulvio Bernardini. He, in turn, gave way to assistant Enzo Bearzot, who steered Italy to fourth place in 1978 in Argentina and then to victory in Spain in 1982, thus achieving Europe's first World Cup hat-trick. Bearzot's men were past their best in Mexico in 1986 and his successor, Azeglio Vicini, was short on luck when Italy played hosts again in 1990 and went out to Argentina in the semi-finals in a penalty shoot-out.

More penalty pain followed four years later when Italy, having scraped through to the Final courtesy of the face-saving goals of Roberto Baggio, lost to Brazil in a penalty shoot-out in Pasadena. Failure to build on that achievement at Euro 96, where Italy crashed out in the first round, led to the departure of controversial theorist coach Arrigo Sacchi. His replacement was the former under-21 coach, Cesare Maldini, father of Paolo. But he also suffered penalty nightmares when Italy lost to France in the quarter-finals of the 1998 World Cup finals on spot-kicks.

Italy's stuttering results and performances on the international scene were in stark contrast to the manner in which Milan dominated European club football. But then, while Italy and Milan shared star defenders Franco Baresi and Paolo Maldini, the national team had no-one quite like Ruud Gullit, Marco Van Basten, Dejan Savicevic and George Weah in attack.

CHAMPIONS

1898 Genoa	1915 Genoa declared winners
1899 Genoa	1916–19 Not played
1900 Genoa	1920 Internazionale
1901 Milan	1921 Pro Vercelli
1902 Genoa	1922 Novese
1903 Genoa	1923 Genoa
1904 Genoa	1924 Genoa
1905 Juventus	1925 Bologna
1906 Milan	1926 Juventus
1907 Milan	1927 Torino
1908 Pro Vercelli	1928 Torino
1909 Pro Vercelli	1929 Bologna
1910 Internazionale	1930 Ambrosiana-Inter
1911 Pro Vercelli	1931 Juventus
1912 Pro Vercelli	1932 Juventus
1913 Pro Vercelli	1933 Juventus
1914 Casale	1934 Juventus
	1935 Juventus

1936 Bologna
1937 Bologna
1938 Ambrosiana-Inter
1939 Bologna
1940 Ambrosiana-Inter
1941 Bologna
1942 Roma
1943 Torino
1944–45 Not played
1946 Torino
1947 Torino
1948 Torino
1949 Torino
1950 Juventus
1951 Milan
1952 Juventus
1953 Internazionale
1954 Internazionale
1955 Milan
1956 Fiorentina
1957 Milan
1958 Juventus
1959 Milan
1960 Juventus
1961 Juventus
1962 Milan
1963 Internazionale
1964 Bologna
1965 Internazionale
1966 Internazionale
1967 Juventus
1968 Milan
1969 Fiorentina
1970 Cagliari
1971 Internazionale
1972 Juventus
1973 Juventus
1974 Lazio
1975 Juventus
1976 Torino
1977 Juventus
1978 Juventus
1979 Milan
1980 Internazionale
1981 Juventus
1982 Juventus
1983 Roma
1984 Juventus
1985 Hellas-Verona
1986 Juventus
1987 Napoli
1988 Milan
1989 Internazionale
1990 Napoli
1991 Sampdoria
1992 Milan
1993 Milan
1994 Milan
1995 Juventus

1996 Milan
1997 Juventus
1998 Juventus

CUP WINNERS

1922 Vado
1923–35 Not played
1936 Torino
1937 Genoa
1938 Juventus
1939 Ambrosiana-Inter
1940 Fiorentina
1941 Venezia
1942 Juventus
1943 Torino
1944–57 Not played
1958 Lazio
1959 Juventus
1960 Juventus
1961 Fiorentina
1962 Napoli
1963 Atalanta
1964 Roma
1965 Juventus
1966 Fiorentina
1967 Milan
1968 Torino
1969 Roma
1970 Bologna
1971 Torino
1972 Milan
1973 Milan
1974 Bologna
1975 Fiorentina
1976 Napoli
1977 Milan
1978 Internazionale
1979 Juventus
1980 Roma
1981 Roma
1982 Internazionale
1983 Juventus
1984 Roma
1985 Sampdoria
1986 Roma
1987 Napoli
1988 Sampdoria
1989 Sampdoria
1990 Juventus
1991 Roma
1992 Parma
1993 Torino
1994 Sampdoria
1995 Juventus
1996 Fiorentina
1997 Vicenza
1998 Lazio

Latvia

Latvian Football Federation
Founded: *1921*
Joined FIFA: *1922*

Latvia stand, alongside Lithuania and Estonia, among the Baltic states who regained their political independence in the early 1990s after 50 years "on ice."

The collapse of the Soviet empire allowed Latvia to reclaim their sporting identity. FIFA duly bent the World Cup rules to permit their late inclusion in the draw for the qualifying competition for 1994. Those matches helped raise badly-needed funds for an impoverished federation. Latvia were independent between the wars, their international experience including a modest record victory by 4–1 over Sweden in 1932 in Riga. Their most notable result of that era was, however, a defeat. In Vienna, in 1937, Latvia lost only 2–1 in a World Cup qualifying tie to an Austrian side who were then one of the giants of the era.

CHAMPIONS

1922 Kaiserwood Riga
1923 Kaiserwood Riga
1924 RFK Riga
1925 RFK Riga
1926 RFK Riga
1927 Olimpija Liepaja
1928 Olimpija Liepaja
1929 Olimpija Liepaja
1930 RFK Riga
1931 RFK Riga
1932 SKA Riga
1933 Olimpija Riga
1934 RFK Riga
1935 RFK Riga
1936 Olimpija Liepaja
1937 Not played
1938 Olimpija Liepaja
1939 Olimpija Liepaja
1940 RFK Riga
1941 Not played
1942 SKA Riga
1943 SKA Riga
1944 SKA Riga
1945 Dinamo Riga
1946 Daugava Liepaja
1947 Daugava Liepaja
1948 Komanda Zhmyleva
1949 Sarkanajs Metalurgs Liepaja
1950 ODO Riga
1951 Sarkanajs Metalurgs Liepaja
1952 ODO Riga
1953 Sarkanajs Metalurgs Liepaja
1954 Sarkanajs Metalurgs Liepaja
1955 Trudovye Reservy Riga
1956 Sarkanajs Metalurgs Liepaja
1957 Sarkanajs Metalurgs Liepaja
1958 Sarkanajs Metalurgs Liepaja
1959 REZ Riga
1960 SKA Riga

1961 SKA Riga
1962 SKA Riga
1963 SKA Riga
1964 SKA Riga
1965 SKA Riga
1966 Energija Riga
1967 Energija Riga
1968 Start Brotseny
1969 Venta Ventspils
1970 VEF Riga
1971 VEF Riga
1972 Jurnieks Riga
1973 VEF Riga
1974 VEF Riga
1975 VEF Riga
1976 Energija Riga
1977 Energija Riga
1978 Khimik Daugavpils
1979 Elektron Riga
1980 Khimik Daugavpils
1981 Elektron Riga
1982 Elektron Riga
1983 VEF Riga
1984 Torpedo Riga
1985 Alfa Riga
1986 Torpedo Riga
1987 Torpedo Riga
1988 RAF Jelgava
1989 RAF Jelgava
1990 Gauja Valmeira
1991 Skonto Riga
1992 Skonto Riga
1993 Skonto Riga
1994 Skonto Riga
1995 Skonto Riga
1996 Skonto Riga
1997 Skonto Riga
1998 Skonto Riga

CUP WINNERS

1945 Daugava Liepaja
1946 Daugava Liepaja
1947 Daugava Liepaja
1948 Sarkanajs Metalurgs Liepaja
1949 Sarkanajs Metalurgs Liepaja
1950 ODO Riga
1951 ODO Riga
1952 ODO Riga
1953 Sarkanajs Metalurgs Liepaja
1954 Sarkanajs Metalurgs Liepaja
1955 Sarkanajs Metalurgs Liepaja
1956 VEF Riga
1957 Dinamo Riga
1958 REZ Riga
1959 SKA Riga
1960 SKA Riga
1961 Start Brotseny
1962 Selmash Liepaja
1963 Selmash Liepaja
1964 Vulkan Kuldiga
1965 Baltija Liepaja
1966 SKA Riga
1967 Venta Ventspils
1968 Start Brotseny
1969 Elektron Riga
1970 Jurnieks Riga
1971 VEF Riga
1972 Jurnieks Riga
1973 Pilot Riga
1974 Elektron Riga
1975 Lijelupe Jurmala
1976 Khimik Daugavpils
1977 Elektron Riga
1978 Elektron Riga
1979 Khimik Daugavpils
1980 Elektron Riga
1981 Elektron Riga
1982 Energija Riga
1983 Elektron Riga
1984 Celtnieks Riga
1985 Celtnieks Riga
1986 Celtnieks Riga
1987 VEF Riga
1988 RAF Jelgava
1989 Torpedo Riga
1990 Daugava Riga
1991 Celtnieks Daugavpils
1992 Skonto Riga
1993 RAF Jelgava
1994 Olimpija Riga
1995 Skonto Riga
1996 RAF Jelgava
1997 Skonto Riga
1998 Liepaja

CUP WINNERS

1946 FC Triesen
1947 FC Triesen
1948 FC Triesen
1949 FC Vaduz
1950 FC Triesen
1951 FC Triesen
1952 FC Vaduz
1953 FC Vaduz
1954 FC Vaduz
1955 FC Schaan
1956 FC Vaduz
1957 FC Vaduz
1958 FC Vaduz
1959 FC Vaduz
1960 FC Vaduz
1961 FC Vaduz
1962 FC Vaduz
1963 FC Schaan
1964 FC Balzers
1965 FC Triesen
1966 FC Vaduz
1967 FC Vaduz
1968 FC Vaduz
1969 FC Vaduz
1970 FC Vaduz
1971 FC Vaduz
1972 FC Triesen
1973 FC Balzers
1974 FC Vaduz
1975 FC Triesen
1976 USV Eschen/Mauren
1977 USV Eschen/Mauren
1978 USV Eschen/Mauren
1979 FC Balzers
1980 FC Vaduz
1981 FC Balzers
1982 FC Balzers
1983 FC Balzers
1984 FC Balzers
1985 FC Vaduz
1986 FC Vaduz
1987 USV Eschen/Mauren
1988 FC Vaduz
1989 FC Balzers
1990 FC Vaduz
1991 FC Balzers
1992 FC Vaduz
1993 FC Balzers
1994 FC Schaan
1995 FC Vaduz
1996 FC Vaduz
1997 FC Balzers
1998 FC Vaduz

Liechtenstein

Liechtensteiner Fussball-Verband
Founded: *1974*
Joined FIFA: *1974*

Liechtenstein have no national championship but that did not stop them entering the World Cup for the first time in 1990.

On the eve of the draw in New York in December, 1991, however, their officials got cold feet and pulled out at the last minute. When they did eventually make their World Cup debut, they were beaten 3–0 by Macedonia in Skopje in the qualifying competition in April, 1996.

Liechtenstein has an autonomous federation but its main clubs all compete in the Swiss regional leagues. The main Liechtenstein competition is the knock-out cup whose winners now enter the European Cup-winners Cup regularly.

Liechtenstein's first outing at any sort of serious international level was in the President's Cup in South Korea in 1981, However, not all of the players that they used in that tournament – in which they drew 1–1 with Malta and beat Indonesia 3–2 – were Liechtenstein nationals and thus properly qualified for international status.

Lithuania

Lithuanian Football Federation
Founded: *1922*
Joined FIFA: *1923/1992*

As with Latvia and Estonia, so with Lithuania. They were independent during the inter-war years and competed, unsuccessfully, in the World Cup qualifying tournaments. After being reintegrated into international life, Lithuania began their football rehabilitation in the 1994 World Cup qualifying competition.

CHAMPIONS

1922 LFLS Kaunas
1923 LFNS Kaunas
1924 Kovas Kaunas
1925 Kovas Kaunas
1926 Kovas Kaunas
1927 LFNS Kaunas
1928 KSS Klaipeda
1929 KSS Klaipeda
1930 KSS Klaipeda
1931 KSS Klaipeda
1932 LFNS Kaunas
1933 Kovas Kaunas
1934 MSK Kaunas
1935 Kovas Kaunas
1936 Kovas Kaunas
1937 KSS Klaipeda
1938 KSS Klaipeda
1939 LGSF Kaunas
1940 Not played
1941 Not played
1942 LFNS Kaunas
1943 Tauras Kaunas
1944 Not played
1945 Spartak Kaunas
1946 Dinamo Kaunas
1947 Lokomotiv Kaunas
1948 Elnias Siauliai
1949 Elnias Siauliai
1950 Inkaras Kaunas
1951 Inkaras Kaunas
1952 Saliutas Vilnius
1953 Elnias Siauliai
1954 Inkaras Kaunas
1955 Lima Kaunas
1956 Linu Audiniai Plunge

1957 Elnias Siauliai
1958 Elnias Siauliai
1959 Raud Zhvaigzhde Vilnius
1960 Elnias Siauliai
1961 Elnias Siauliai
1962 Atletas Kaunas
1963 Statyba Panevzys
1964 Inkaras Kaunas
1965 Inkaras Kaunas
1966 Nevezis Kedainiai
1967 Saliutas Vilnius
1968 Statyba Panevzys
1969 Statybininkas Siauliai
1970 Atletas Kaunas
1971 Pazanga Vilnius
1972 Nevezis Kedainiai
1973 Nevezis Kedainiai
1974 Tauras Siauliai
1975 Dainava Alytus
1976 Atmosfera Mazeikiai
1977 Statybininkis Siauliai
1978 Granitas Klaipeda
1979 Atmosfera Mazeikiai
1980 Granitas Klaipeda
1981 Granitas Klaipeda
1982 Pazanga Vilnius
1983 Pazanga Vilnius
1984 Granitas Klaipeda
1985 Granitas Klaipeda
1986 Banga Kaunas
1987 Tauras Taurage
1988 SRT Vilnius
1989 Banga Kaunas
1990 Sirijus Klaipeda
1991 Zalgiris Vilnius
1992 Zalgiris Vilnius
1993 Ekranas Panevezys
1994 ROMAR Mazeikiai
1995 Inkaras Kaunas
1996 Inkaras Kaunas
1997 Kareda
1998

CUP WINNERS

1947 Lokomotiv Kaunas
1948 Inkaras Kaunas
1949 Inkaras Kaunas
1950 Elnias Siauliai

1951 Inkaras Kaunas
1952 Karinky Vilnius
1953 Lima Kaunas
1954 Inkaras Kaunas
1955 Politechnikos Kaunas
1956 Raudonasis Spalis Kaunas
1957 Elnias Siauliai
1958 Spartak Vilnius
1959 Elnias Siauliai
1960 Komanda Panemunes
1961 Cementininkas Akmenes
1962 Kima Kaunas
1963 Saliutas Vilnius
1964 Minja Krentingos
1965 Inkaras Kaunas
1966 Zalgiris Vilnius
1967 Nevizis Kedainiai
1968 Nevizis Kedainiai
1969 Inkaras Kaunas
1970 Nevezis Kedainiai
1971 Pazanga Vilnius
1972 Nevezis Kedainiai
1973 Nevezis Kedainiai
1974 Statybininkas Siauliai
1975 Vienybe Ukmerges
1976 Kelininkas Kaunas
1977 Granitas Klaipeda
1978 Kelininkas Kaunas
1979 Kelininkas Kaunas
1980 Kelininkas Kaunas
1981 Granitas Klaipeda
1982 Pazanga Vilnius
1983 Granitas Klaipeda
1984 SRT Vilnius
1985 Ekranas Panevzys
1986 Granitas Klaipeda
1987 SRT Vilnius
1988 Sirijus Klaipeda
1989 Not played
1990 Not played
1991 Not played
1992 Lietuvos Vilnius
1993 Zalgiris Vilnius
1994 Zalgiris Vilnius
1995 Inkaras Kaunas
1996 Kareda
1997 Zalgiris

Luxembourg

Luxembourgeoise de Football

Founded: *1908*
Joined FIFA: *1910*

The Grand Duchy are European football's original minnows. Luxembourg had a federation, league, cup and national team structure all firmly in place long before the likes of Cyprus, Malta, Iceland (and of course the Faroes and San Marino) dipped their first toe in the international mainstream. The federation was

founded in 1908, just four years after FIFA, the first championship organized in 1910 and the first domestic cup in 1922. In 1956–57 Spora entered the second edition of the Champions Cup. They almost upset West German champions Borussia Dortmund in the first round. Spora lost 4–3 away, won 2–1 at home but then crashed 7–0 in the play-off in Dortmund (the away goals rule was then undreamed of).

They have also shared some less impressive records. Chelsea beat Jeunesse Hautcharage 21–0 on aggregate in the Cup-winners Cup in 1971–72 and US Rumelange crashed by the same overall margin to Feyenoord of Holland in the UEFA Cup in 1972–73 (Feyenoord's 12–0 win in Luxembourg in that tie remains a record away win in Europe).

The national team compete regularly in the World Cup and European Championship. Their most historic result was in 1961, in the World Cup qualifiers, when they scored a 4–2 victory over a Portugal side for whom Eusebio was making his debut.

CHAMPIONS

1910 Racing Club
1911 Sporting Club
1912 US Hollerich
1913 Not played
1914 US Hollerich
1915 US Hollerich
1916 US Hollerich
1917 US Hollerich
1918 Fola Esch
1919 Sporting Club
1920 Fola Esch
1921 Jeunesse Esch
1922 Fola Esch
1923 Red Boys
1924 Fola Esch
1925 AC Spora
1926 Red Boys
1927 Union Luxembourg
1928 AC Spora
1929 AC Spora
1930 Fola Esch
1931 Red Boys
1932 Red Boys
1933 Red Boys
1934 AC Spora
1935 AC Spora
1936 AC Spora
1937 Jeunesse Esch
1938 AC Spora
1939 Stade Dudelange
1940 Stade Dudelange
1941–44 Not played
1945 Stade Dudelange
1946 Stade Dudelange
1947 Stade Dudelange
1948 Stade Dudelange
1949 AC Spora
1950 Stade Dudelange
1951 Jeunesse Esch
1952 National Schifflange
1953 Progres Niedercorn
1954 Jeunesse Esch

1955 Stade Dudelange
1956 AC Spora
1957 Stade Dudelange
1958 Jeunesse Esch
1959 Jeunesse Esch
1960 Jeunesse Esch
1961 AC Spora
1962 Union Luxembourg
1963 Jeunesse Esch
1964 Aris Bonnevole
1965 Stade Dudelange
1966 Aris Bonnevole
1967 Jeunesse Esch
1968 Jeunesse Esch
1969 Avenir Beggen
1970 Jeunesse Esch
1971 Union Luxembourg
1972 Aris Bonnevole
1973 Jeunesse Esch
1974 Jeunesse Esch
1975 Jeunesse Esch
1976 Jeunesse Esch
1977 Jeunesse Esch
1978 Progres Niedercorn
1979 Red Boys
1980 Jeunesse Esch
1981 Progres Niedercorn
1982 Avenir Beggen
1983 Jeunesse Esch
1984 Avenir Beggen
1985 Jeunesse Esch
1986 Avenir Beggen
1987 Jeunesse Esch
1988 Jeunesse Esch
1989 AC Spora
1990 Union Luxembourg
1991 Union Luxembourg
1992 Union Luxembourg
1993 Avenir Beggen
1994 Avenir Beggen
1995 Jeunesse Esch
1996 Jeunesse Esch

1997 Jeunesse Esch
1998 Jeunesse Esch

CUP WINNERS

1922 Racing Club
1923 Fola Esch
1924 Fola Esch
1925 Red Boys
1926 Red Boys
1927 Red Boys
1928 AC Spora
1929 Red Boys
1930 Red Boys
1931 Red Boys
1932 AC Spora
1933 Progres Niedercorn
1934 Red Boys
1935 Jeunesse Esch
1936 Red Boys
1937 Jeunesse Esch
1938 Stade Dudelange
1939 US Dudelange
1940 AC Spora
1941–44 Not played
1945 Progres Niedercorn
1946 Jeunesse Esch
1947 Union Luxembourg
1948 Stade Dudelange
1949 Stade Dudelange
1950 AC Spora
1951 SC Tetange
1952 Red Boys
1953 Red Boys
1954 Jeunesse Esch
1955 Fola Esch
1956 Stade Dudelange
1957 AC Spora
1958 Red Boys
1959 Union Luxembourg
1960 National Schifflange
1961 Alliance Dudelange

1962 Alliance Dudelange
1963 Union Luxembourg
1964 Union Luxembourg
1965 AC Spora
1966 AC Spora
1967 Aris Bonnevole
1968 US Rumelange
1969 Union Luxembourg
1970 Union Luxembourg
1971 Jeunesse Hautcharage
1972 Red Boys
1973 Jeunesse Esch
1974 Jeunesse Esch
1975 US Rumelange
1976 Jeunesse Esch
1977 Progres Niedercorn
1978 Progres Niedercorn
1979 Red Boys
1980 AC Spora
1981 Jeunesse Esch
1982 Red Boys
1983 Avenir Beggen
1984 Avenir Beggen
1985 Red Boys
1986 Union Luxembourg
1987 Avenir Beggen
1988 Jeunesse Esch
1989 Union Luxembourg
1990 Swift Hesperange
1991 Union Luxembourg
1992 Avenir Beggen
1993 Avenir Beggen
1994 Avenir Beggen
1995 CS Grevenmacher
1996 Union Luxembourg
1997 Jeunesse Esch
1998 Grevenmacher

Macedonia (Former Yugoslav Republic of)

Fudbalski Sojuz Makedonija
Founded: *1992*
Joined FIFA: *1994*

This is the country officially known as the Former Yugoslav Republic of Macedonia as a compromise to meet Greek complaints that this is not the "real" Macedonia of legend, from which Alexander the Great emerged.

It is one of the four states to have gained independence from the bloody fragmentation in the Balkans. Like Slovenia, the separation of Macedonia was comparatively peaceful when compared with events in Croatia and Bosnia.

The national stadium, the Gradski, has a capacity of 25,000, though the volatile nature of the local fans meant it was shut for two matches by UEFA as punishment for hooliganism during the 1996 European Championship qualifying competition.

Vardar Skopje are the oldest and most successful of Macedonian teams, having competed in Europe three times as representatives of the former Yugoslavia. They also won the first three independent Macedonian championships in 1993, 1994 and 1995.

It was in 1993 that Macedonia played their first formal international, beating Slovenia 4–1.

CHAMPIONS

1993 Vardar Skopje
1994 Vardar Skopje
1995 Vardar Skopje
1996 Sileks Kratovo
1997 Sileks Kratovo
1998 Sileks Kratovo

CUP WINNERS

1993 Vardar Skopje
1994 Sileks Kratovo
1995 Vardar Skopje
1996 Sloga Slugomagnat
1997 Sileks Kratovo
1998 Vardar Skopje

Malta

Malta Football Association
Founded: *1900*
Joined FIFA: *1959*

Malta has a special place in football history for it was on the George Cross island that the first referee's whistle was heard. That was in 1886, in a 1–1 draw between soldiers of the Shropshire Regiment and locals from Cospicua St Andrew's.

Thus Maltese football history most clearly stretches back before FIFA – the game having been imported by British servicemen under the Governorship of Sir Arthur Borton. Early records describe matches played in stockinged feet on rough ground.

The original Malta FA was set up in 1900 and a league championship in 1901. These competitions were soon followed by the MFA Cup, the Cousis Shield and the Cassar Charity Shield. The FA Trophy, later to become one of the most prestigious domestic contests, was launched in 1934–35.

Clubs from mainland Europe were invited on guest tours in the mid-1920s, but the first official international was not played until February 24, 1957 when Malta lost 3–2 at home to Austria. Even the status of this match remains in question because Malta had yet to join FIFA.

For years, all important matches were played on the notorious Gzira stadium whose sand, grit and stones intimidated many a visiting team. Later, however, after a great deal of political confusion, Maltese football took possession of the superb new Ta'Qali national stadium complex.

What the national team and clubs such as Sliema Wanderers, Floriana, Valetta and Hibernians lost in home advantage they gained in prestige from the facilities available.

CHAMPIONS

1910 Floriana
1911 Not played
1912 Floriana
1913 Floriana
1914 Hamrun Spartans
1915 Valletta United
1916 Not played
1917 St George's
1918 Hamrun Spartans
1919 KOMR Militia
1920 Sliema Wanderers
1921 Floriana
1922 Floriana
1923 Sliema Wanderers
1924 Sliema Wanderers
1925 Floriana
1926 Sliema Wanderers
1927 Floriana
1928 Floriana
1929 Floriana
1930 Sliema Wanderers
1931 Floriana
1932 Valletta United
1933 Sliema Wanderers
1934 Sliema Wanderers
1935 Floriana
1936 Sliema Wanderers
1937 Floriana
1938 Sliema Wanderers
1939 Sliema Wanderers
1940 Sliema Wanderers
1941–44 Not played
1945 Valletta
1946 Valletta
1947 Hamrun Spartans
1948 Valletta
1949 Sliema Wanderers
1950 Floriana
1951 Floriana
1952 Floriana
1953 Floriana
1954 Sliema Wanderers
1955 Floriana
1956 Sliema Wanderers
1957 Sliema Wanderers
1958 Floriana
1959 Valletta
1960 Valletta
1961 Hibernians
1962 Floriana
1963 Valletta
1964 Sliema Wanderers
1965 Sliema Wanderers
1966 Sliema Wanderers
1967 Hibernians
1968 Floriana
1969 Hibernians
1970 Floriana
1971 Sliema Wanderers
1972 Sliema Wanderers
1973 Floriana
1974 Valletta
1975 Floriana
1976 Sliema Wanderers

1977 Floriana
1978 Valletta
1979 Hibernians
1980 Valletta
1981 Hibernians
1982 Hibernians
1983 Hamrun Spartans
1984 Valletta
1985 Rabat Ajax
1986 Rabat Ajax
1987 Hamrun Spartans
1988 Hamrun Spartans
1989 Sliema Wanderers
1990 Valletta
1991 Hamrun Spartans
1992 Valletta
1993 Floriana
1994 Hibernians
1995 Hibernians
1996 Sliema Wanderers
1997 Valletta
1998 Valletta

CUP WINNERS

1935 Sliema Wanderers
1936 Sliema Wanderers
1937 Sliema Wanderers
1938 Floriana
1939 Melita St Julians
1940 Sliema Wanderers
1941–44 Not played
1945 Floriana
1946 Sliema Wanderers
1947 Floriana
1948 Sliema Wanderers
1949 Floriana
1950 Floriana
1951 Sliema Wanderers
1952 Sliema Wanderers
1953 Floriana
1954 Floriana
1955 Floriana
1956 Sliema Wanderers
1957 Floriana
1958 Floriana
1959 Sliema Wanderers
1960 Valletta
1961 Floriana
1962 Hibernians
1963 Sliema Wanderers
1964 Valletta
1965 Sliema Wanderers
1966 Floriana
1967 Floriana
1968 Sliema Wanderers
1969 Sliema Wanderers
1970 Hibernians
1971 Hibernians
1972 Floriana
1973 Gzira United
1974 Sliema Wanderers
1975 Valletta
1976 Floriana
1977 Valletta
1978 Valletta
1979 Sliema Wanderers

1980 Hibernians
1981 Floriana
1982 Hibernians
1983 Hamrun Spartans
1984 Hamrun Spartans
1985 Zurrieq
1986 Rabat Ajax
1987 Hamrun Spartans
1988 Hamrun Spartans
1989 Hamrun Spartans

1990 Sliema Wanderers
1991 Valletta
1992 Hamrun Spartans
1993 Floriana
1994 Floriana
1995 Valletta
1996 Valletta
1997 Valletta
1998 Hibernian

Moldova

Federatia Moldoveneasca de Fotbal

Founded: *1990*
Joined FIFA: *1994*

Moldova gained independence with the fragmentation of the old Soviet Union. Various ethnic groups expected it to be moulded into either Romania or Ukraine. Instead, the people decided to go their own way – refusing in their haste even to go through the route out offered to the old Soviet provinces by the halfway house of the Commonwealth of the Independent States.

The main stadium in the capital, now known as Chisinau, is the Republic Stadium with a capacity of 20,000, and the country's most famous footballing son is the Russian and former Soviet international, Igor Dobrovolski. He was born in Ukraine but was brought up in Moldova before being "discovered" and lured away as a teenager by Moscow Dynamo.

In the pre-independence days, Moldovan clubs competed in the regional structure of the old Soviet Supreme Championship. Zimbru became the first Moldovan club to compete in European club competition when they were allowed into the Champions Cup in 1993–94. Moldova's national team entered international competition in the 1996 European Championship qualifiers and opened sensationally by defeating Georgia 1–0 in Tbilisi and then Wales 3–2 in Chisinau.

CHAMPIONS

1992 Zimbru Chisinau
1993 Zimbru Chisinau
1994 Zimbru Chisinau
1995 Zimbru Chisinau
1996 Zimbru Chisinau
1997 Constructorul Chisinau
1998 Zimbru Chisinau

CUP WINNERS

1992 Bugeac Camrat
1993 Tiligul Tiraspol
1994 Tiligul Tiraspol
1995 Tiligul Tiraspol
1996 Constructorul Chisinau
1997 Zimbru Chisanau
1998 Constructorol Chisinau

Northern Ireland

Irish Football Association Ltd.

Founded: *1880*
Joined FIFA: *1911*

Football was launched in the days of an Ireland united under British rule. The Irish Football Association was set up in 1880 and the first recorded match was a friendly in Belfast between Scottish clubs Caledonian FC and Queen's Park.

The immediate consequence was the formation of a locally based Ulster FC and then Cliftonville in Ballyclare at the instigation of JM McAlery, the so-called "Father of Irish Football." Belfast Celtic were founded in 1881 and Linfield in 1887.

Within two years of that first match, international fixtures were being undertaken. Initial signs were not promising. First came a 13–0 defeat by England in Belfast and then a 7–1 thrashing by Wales in Wrexham, both within seven days in 1882.

In due course, political developments cast a long shadow across

Moldova's Serghei Stroenco challenges Wales midfielder Mark Pembridge in a European Championship qualifier

the Irish game. A number of matches were marred by politically-influenced crowd disturbances in the run-up to partition. Ultimately, the Irish FA's influence was reduced to the Six Counties of Ulster or Northern Ireland. Up until the mid-1980s, however, its international achievements belied its size.

Northern Ireland shared the Home International Championship titles in 1956, 1958 and 1959 and achieved a historic first win over England at Wembley in 1957. Danny Blanchflower was the inspirational captain and right half who then led the Irish to a shock victory over Italy in the 1958 World Cup qualifying competition. A spirited team managed by Peter Doherty and spearheaded in attack by Aston Villa's Peter MacParland reached the quarter-finals in Sweden before – weakened by injury, fatigue and a lack of players – they went out 4–0 to the France of Just Fontaine and Raymond Kopa.

Northern Ireland have appeared in the finals on a further two occasions but, sadly, their greatest-ever player, George Best, never appeared on the World Cup finals stage. By the time Northern Ireland returned to the finals tournament, in Spain in 1982 and in Mexico in 1986, Best's meteoric career had already burned out.

The mantle of leadership had fallen instead to players such as midfielder Sammy McIlroy and goalkeeper Pat Jennings who, in the 1986 finals in Mexico, set a world record 119 caps.

Northern Ireland's Sammy McIlroy

CHAMPIONS

1891 Linfield	1926 Celtic	1966 Linfield
1892 Linfield	1927 Celtic	1967 Glentoran
1893 Linfield	1928 Celtic	1968 Glentoran
1894 Glentoran	1929 Celtic	1969 Linfield
1895 Linfield	1930 Linfield	1970 Glentoran
1896 Distillery	1931 Glentoran	1971 Linfield
1897 Glentoran	1932 Linfield	1972 Glentoran
1898 Linfield	1933 Celtic	1973 Crusaders
1899 Distillery	1934 Linfield	1974 Coleraine
1900 Celtic	1935 Linfield	1975 Linfield
1901 Distillery	1936 Celtic	1976 Crusaders
1902 Linfield	1937 Celtic	1977 Glentoran
1903 Distillery	1938 Celtic	1978 Linfield
1904 Linfield	1939 Celtic	1979 Linfield
1905 Glentoran	1940 Celtic	1980 Linfield
1906 Cliftonville	1941–47 Not played	1981 Glentoran
1907 Linfield	1948 Celtic	1982 Linfield
1908 Linfield	1949 Linfield	1983 Linfield
1909 Linfield	1950 Linfield	1984 Linfield
1910 Cliftonville	1951 Glentoran	1985 Linfield
1911 Linfield	1952 Glentoran	1986 Linfield
1912 Glentoran	1953 Glentoran	1987 Linfield
1913 Glentoran	1954 Linfield	1988 Glentoran
1914 Linfield	1955 Linfield	1989 Linfield
1915 Celtic	1956 Linfield	1990 Portadown
1916–19 Not played	1957 Glenavon	1991 Portadown
1920 Celtic	1958 Ards	
1921 Glentoran	1959 Linfield	
1922 Linfield	1960 Glenavon	
1923 Linfield	1961 Linfield	
1924 Queen's Island	1962 Linfield	
1925 Glentoran	1963 Distillery	
	1964 Glentoran	
	1965 Derry City	

1992 Glentoran
1993 Linfield
1994 Linfield
1995 Crusaders
1996 Portadown
1997 Crusaders
1998 Cliftonville

CUP WINNERS

1881 Moyola Park
1882 Queen's Island
1883 Cliftonville
1884 Distillery
1885 Distillery
1886 Distillery
1887 Ulster
1888 Cliftonville
1889 Distillery
1890 Gordon Highlanders
1891 Linfield
1892 Linfield
1893 Linfield
1894 Distillery
1895 Linfield
1896 Distillery
1897 Cliftonville

1898 Linfield	1949 Derry City	
1899 Linfield	1950 Linfield	
1900 Cliftonville	1951 Glentoran	
1901 Cliftonville	1952 Ards	
1902 Linfield	1953 Linfield	
1903 Distillery	1954 Derry City	
1904 Linfield	1955 Dundela	
1905 Distillery	1956 Distillery	
1906 Shelbourne	1957 Glenavon	
1907 Cliftonville	1958 Ballymena U	
1908 Bohemians	1959 Glenavon	
1909 Cliftonville	1960 Linfield	
1910 Distillery	1961 Glenavon	
1911 Shelbourne	1962 Linfield	
1912 Linfield	1963 Linfield	
1913 Linfield	1964 Derry City	
1914 Glentoran	1965 Coleraine	
1915 Linfield	1966 Glentoran	
1916 Linfield	1967 Crusaders	
1917 Glentoran	1968 Crusaders	
1918 Celtic	1969 Ards	
1919 Linfield	1970 Linfield	
1920 Shelbourne	1971 Distillery	
1921 Glentoran	1972 Coleraine	
1922 Linfield	1973 Glentoran	
1923 Linfield	1974 Ards	
1924 Queen's Island	1975 Coleraine	
1925 Distillery	1976 Carrick Rangers	
1926 Celtic	1977 Coleraine	
1927 Ards	1978 Linfield	
1928 Willowfield	1979 Cliftonville	
1929 Ballymena U	1980 Linfield	
1930 Linfield	1981 Ballymena U	
1931 Linfield	1982 Linfield	
1932 Glentoran	1983 Glentoran	
1933 Glentoran	1984 Ballymena U	
1934 Linfield	1985 Glentoran	
1935 Glentoran	1986 Glentoran	
1936 Linfield	1987 Glentoran	
1937 Celtic	1988 Glentoran	
1938 Celtic	1989 Ballymena U	
1939 Linfield	1990 Glentoran	
1940 Ballymena U	1991 Portadown	
1941 Celtic	1992 Glenavon	
1942 Linfield	1993 Bangor	
1943 Celtic	1994 Linfield	
1944 Celtic	1995 Linfield	
1945 Linfield	1996 Glentoran	
1946 Linfield	1997 Glenavon	
1947 Celtic	1998 Glentoran	
1948 Linfield		

Norway

Norges Fotballforbund

Founded: 1902
Joined FIFA: 1908

Norway were once considered a sort of inferior Sweden – a Scandinavian side with strength and commitment but lacking in finesse. All that has changed now. Norway can boast having twice out-thought, outplayed and beaten England in World Cup qualifying ties, reached the 1994 and 1998 World Cup finals, sold a string of players to English clubs and seen champions Rosenborg (of Trondheim) knock mighty Milan out of the 1996–97 UEFA Champions League.

Until the turn of the 1980s, Norwegian football's greatest exploit required a football history book. In the 1936 Berlin Olympic Games they caused a historic upset, beating their German hosts in front of an enraged Adolf Hitler. Italy took Axis revenge but even the ultimate gold medal-winners defeated Norway only 2–1 in the semi-finals. Two years later Italy defeated Norway again, this time in the first round of the 1938 World Cup finals in France. Norway lost 3–1 in the Velodrome in Marseille, but not until they had taken Italy to extra time.

Soccer was introduced to the ports of Oslo and Bergen by students in the 1880s. The oldest surviving club are Odds BK, founded in Skien in 1894, but they have long been out of the running for the major prizes. The club scene has been dominated more recently by Moss, Brann Bergen, Viking Stavanger – where Tony Knapp proved one of the many Britons to work successfully in Norway – and Rosenborg.

Ambitious players had to build their reputations in club football abroad. For goalkeeper Erik Thorstvedt that meant with Tottenham in England, which duly welcomed many other compatriots such as Henning Berg, Oyvind Leonhardsen, Steffen Iversen, Stig-Inge Bjornebye and Alf-Inge Haland. Sweeper Rune Bratseth, a cornerstone of the Norwegian side which, in 1994, reached the World Cup finals for only the second time, starred in Germany with Werder Bremen. He was voted best sweeper in the Bundesliga.

In 1998, Norway reached the World Cup finals again and beat Brazil before going out to Italy in the second round.

CHAMPIONS

1938 Fredrikstad FK	1967 Rosenborg
1939 Fredrikstad FK	1968 SOFK Lyn Oslo
1940–47 Not played	1969 Rosenborg
1948 Freidig SK	1970 IF Stromgodset
1949 Fredrikstad FK	1971 Rosenborg
1950 Fram Larvik	1972 Viking FK Stavanger
1951 Fredrikstad FK	1973 Viking FK Stavanger
1952 Fredrikstad FK	1974 Viking FK Stavanger
1953 Larvik Turn IF	1975 Viking FK Stavanger
1954 Fredrikstad FK	1976 Lillestrom SK
1955 Larvik Turn IF	1977 Lillestrom SK
1956 Larvik Turn IF	1978 Start Kristiansand
1957 Fredrikstad FK	1979 Viking FK Stavanger
1958 Viking FK Stavanger	1980 Start Kristiansand
1959 Lillestrom SK	1981 Valerengens
1960 Fredrikstad FK	1982 Viking FK Stavanger
1961 Fredrikstad FK	1983 Valerengens
1962 SK Brann Bergen	1984 Valerengens
1963 SK Brann Bergen	1985 Rosenberg
1964 SOFK Lyn Oslo	1986 Lillestrom SK
1965 Valerengens IF Oslo	1987 Moss FK
1966 FDK Skeid Oslo	1988 Rosenborg
	1989 Lillestrom SK
	1990 Rosenborg

Norwegian side Rosenborg take on Juventus in the European Champions League

1991 Viking FK Stavanger
1992 Rosenborg
1993 Rosenborg
1994 Rosenborg
1995 Rosenborg
1996 Rosenborg
1997 Rosenborg

CUP WINNERS

1902 Grane Nordstrand
1903 Odd SK Skien
1904 Odd SK Skien
1905 Odd SK Skien
1906 Odd SK Skien
1907 Mercantile
1908 SOFK Lyn Oslo
1909 SOFK Lyn Oslo
1910 SOFK Lyn Oslo
1911 SOFK Lyn Oslo
1912 Mercantile
1913 Odd SK Skien
1914 Frigg SK Oslo
1915 Odd SK Skien
1916 Frigg SK Oslo
1917 FK Sarpsborg
1918 Kvik Halden

1919 Odd SK Skien
1920 Orn FK Horten
1921 Frigg SK Oslo
1922 Odd SK Skien
1923 SK Brann Bergen
1924 Odd SK Skien
1925 SK Brann Bergen
1926 Odd SK Skien
1927 Orn FK Horten
1928 Orn FK Horten
1929 FK Sarpsborg
1930 Orn FK Horten
1931 Odd SK Skien
1932 Fredrikstad FK
1933 Mjondalen IF
1934 Mjondalen IF
1935 Fredrikstad FK
1936 Fredrikstad FK
1937 Mjondalen IF
1938 Fredrikstad FK
1939 FK Sarpsborg
1940 Fredrikstad FK
1941–44 Not played
1945 SOFK Lyn Oslo
1946 SOFK Lyn Oslo
1947 FK Skeid Oslo

1948 FK Sarpsborg
1949 FK Sarpsborg
1950 Fredrikstad FK
1951 FK Sarpsborg
1952 Sparta Sarpsborg
1953 Viking FK Stavanger
1954 FK Skeid Oslo
1955 FK Skeid Oslo
1956 FK Skeid Oslo
1957 Fredrikstad FK
1958 FK Skeid Oslo
1959 Viking FK Stavanger
1960 Rosenborg
1961 Fredrikstad FK
1962 Gjovik Lyn
1963 FK Skeid Oslo
1964 Rosenborg
1965 FK Skeid Oslo
1966 Fredrikstad FK
1967 SOFK Lyn Oslo
1968 SOFK Lyn Oslo
1969 IF Stromgodset
1970 IF Stromgodset
1971 Rosenborg
1972 SK Brann Bergen
1973 IF Stromgodset

1974 FK Skeid Oslo
1975 SOFK Bode-Glimt
1976 SK Brann Bergen
1977 Lillestrom SK
1978 Lillestrom SK
1979 Viking FK Stavanger
1980 Valerengens IF Oslo
1981 Lillestrom SK
1982 SK Brann Bergen
1983 Moss FK
1984 Fredrikstad FK
1985 Lillestrom SK
1986 Tromse IL
1987 Bryne IL Stavanger
1988 Rosenborg
1989 Viking FK Stavanger
1990 Rosenborg
1991 IF Stromgodset
1992 Rosenborg
1993 FK Bode/Glimt
1994 Molde FK
1996 Rosenborg
1997 Tromso
1998 Valerengens

Poland

Polski Zwiazek Noznij
Founded: *1919*
Joined FIFA: *1923*

Poland, in both political and consequently sporting terms, was a creation of the fall-out from World War One. Football was popular from the turn of the century, but a formal Polish federation had to wait until 1919, the first international followed in 1921 – a 1–0 defeat by Hungary in Budapest – FIFA membership in 1923 and a national league championship in 1927.

Poland made brief headlines at the 1938 World Cup finals, when Ernst Wilimowski scored all four goals in a remarkable 5–4 defeat by Brazil, but the country had to wait until the 1970s to come of age in world football terms.

Polish clubs were involved, almost from the start, in the development of the European competitions in the late 1950s, when Ernst Pol emerged as Poland's next great player. But it was 1970 which was the watershed year. That was when the miners club from Silesia, Gornik Zabrze, became the first (and, so far, only) Polish club to reach a European final.

A 2–0 defeat by Manchester City in the rain in the Cup-winners Cup Final in Vienna was disappointing in itself, but it signalled great things to come. Thus, in 1972, Poland won the Olympic title in Munich and, two years later, the nucleus of that team – Kazimierz Deyna, Robert Gadocha and Jerzy Gorgon – guided Poland to third place in the World Cup finals in West Germany. Along the way they beat England in the qualifiers.

Poland finished third again in Spain in 1982, when the conveyor belt which had produced so many outstanding players in such a comparatively short time came up with the best of all in Zbigniew Boniek. "Zibi" later became the most expensive eastern European player when he joined Italy's Juventus for £1million in 1982, on his way to winning just short of 80 caps for his country.

Perhaps the greatest of Boniek's talents was the ability to rise to the occasion, such as the World Cup second round tie in 1982, when Solidarity union banners were unfurled on the Nou Camp terraces in Barcelona, and Boniek responded with a thrilling hat-trick against Belgium.

Boniek also scored Juventus' winner against FC Porto in the 1984 Cup-winners Cup Final and it was his pace which led to the controversial penalty from which Michel Platini won the tragic 1985 Champions Cup Final against Liverpool in Brussels.

CHAMPIONS

1921 Cracovia	1926 Pogon Lwow
1922 Pogon Lwow	1927 Wisla Krakow
1923 Pogon Lwow	1928 Wisla Krakow
1924 Not played	1929 Warta Poznan
1925 Pogon Lwow	1930 Cracovia
	1931 Garbarnia

1932 Cracovia	1993 Lech Poznan
1933 Ruch Chorzow	1994 Legia Warsaw
1934 Ruch Chorzow	1995 Legia Warsaw
1935 Ruch Chorzow	1996 Widzew Lodz
1936 Ruch Chorzow	1997 Widzew Lodz
1937 Cracovia	1998 LKS Lodz
1938 Ruch Chorzow	
1939–45 Not played	
1946 Polonia Warsaw	
1947 Warta Poznan	
1948 Cracovia	

CUP WINNERS

1949 Gwardia Krakow	1926 Wisla Krakow
1950 Gwardia Krakow	1927–50 Not played
1951 Gwardia Krakow	1951 Unia Chorzow
1952 Unia Chorzow	1952 Kolejarz Warsaw
1953 Unia Chorzow	1953 Not played
1954 Ogniwo Bytom	1954 Gwardia Warsaw
1955 CWKS Warsaw	1955 CWKS Warsaw
1956 CWKS Warsaw	1956 CWKS Warsaw
1957 Gornik Zabrze	1957 LKS Lodz
1958 LKS Lodz	1958–61 Not played
1959 Gornik Zabrze	1962 Zaglebie Sosnowiec
1960 Ruch Chorzow	1963 Zaglebie Sosnowiec
1961 Gornik Zabrze	1964 Legia Warsaw
1962 Polonia Bytom	1965 Gornik Zabrze
1963 Gornik Zabrze	1966 Legia Warsaw
1964 Gornik Zabrze	1967 Wisla Krakow
1965 Gornik Zabrze	1968 Gornik Zabrze
1966 Gornik Zabrze	1969 Gornik Zabrze
1967 Gornik Zabrze	1970 Gornik Zabrze
1968 Ruch Chorzow	1971 Gornik Zabrze
1969 Legia Warsaw	1972 Gornik Zabrze
1970 Legia Warsaw	1973 Legia Warsaw
1971 Gornik Zabrze	1974 Ruch Chorzow
1972 Gornik Zabrze	1975 Stal Rzeszow
1973 Stal Mielec	1976 Slask Wroclaw
1974 Ruch Chorzow	1977 Zaglebie Sosnowiec
1975 Ruch Chorzow	1978 Zaglebie Sosnowiec
1976 Stal Mielec	1979 Arka Gdynia
1977 Slask Wroclaw	1980 Legia Warsaw
1978 Wisla Krakow	1981 Legia Warsaw
1979 Ruch Chorzow	1982 Lech Poznan
1980 Szombierki Bytom	1983 Lechia Gdansk
1981 Widzew Lodz	1984 Lech Poznan
1982 Widzew Lodz	1985 Widzew Lodz
1983 Lech Poznan	1986 GKS Katowice
1984 Lech Poznan	1987 Slask Wroclaw
1985 Gornik Zabrze	1988 Lech Poznan
1986 Gornik Zabrze	1989 Legia Warsaw
1987 Gornik Zabrze	1990 Legia Warsaw
1988 Gornik Zabrze	1991 GKS Katowice
1989 Ruch Chorzow	1992 Miedz Legnica
1990 Lech Poznan	1993 GKS Katowice
1991 Zaglebie Lubin	1994 Legia Warsaw
1992 Lech Poznan	1995 Legia Warsaw
	1996 Ruch Chorzow
	1997 Legia Warsaw
	1998 Amica Wronkl

Portugal

Federacao Portuguesa de Futebol
Founded: *1914*
Joined FIFA: *1923*

Portugal owe their introduction to football to the British, but it is to Brazil, who share their language, that officials, coaches, players and fans look for their style. Sadly, Portuguese football has also suffered from the sort of administrative confusion which has also been a hallmark of the Brazilian game.

Benfica, FC Porto and Sporting are among the most famous clubs in the world, and Portugal are among the most popular senior national teams and most successful junior teams. Yet all have been held back in recent years by underlying structural problems. For example, it was clearly unsatisfactory that, in the mid-1990s, Porto president Jorge Pinto da Costa was also president of the league and heading up the referees commission.

Simultaneously, the domestic game was awash with rumours of match-fixing which undermined its credibility and drove away the fans. It was all very sad, especially after the Portuguese national team had brought a flair and technical vigour to Euro 96 which deserved better than their quarter-final defeat by the Czech Republic.

The first officially recorded club match in Portugal was played in 1888, Benfica were founded in 1904, Sporting two years later, a league was set up in 1909, the federation in 1914 and the national team made their debut in 1921.

Portugal first entered the World Cup in 1934 and have entered every European Championship since the continental event was launched in 1959–60. In all that time their successes have been few and far between. Portugal's finest World Cup was 1966, when they reached the finals for the first time and finished third.

A team inspired by the attacking power of Eusebio scored a memorable quarter-final victory over North Korea – hitting back from 3–0 down – before losing 2–1 to England in a glorious semi-final. A Eusebio penalty in the closing minutes provided victory against the Soviet Union in the third-place play-off.

Portugal's team was built around the attack of Benfica – European club champions in 1961 and 1962 – plus the defence of Sporting – Cup-winners Cup winners in 1962. Apart from Eusebio, players such as midfield general Mario Coluna, wingers Jose Augusto and Simoes and centre forward Jose Aguas and Jose Torres wrote their names into the history books.

In 1984 Portugal enjoyed their finest European Championship campaign. Once again, the semi-final was as far as they went, before Spain beat them in a penalty shoot-out. Two years later, they were first-round failures in the World Cup finals but amends were made shortly afterwards. Under Carlos Queiros, Portugal were twice world youth champions with budding teenage superstars from goalkeeper Vitor Baia to

midfielders Rui Costa and Paulo Sousa and striker Joao Vieira Pinto.

CHAMPIONS

1935 FC Porto	1958 Sporting
1936 Benfica	1959 FC Porto
1937 Benfica	1960 Benfica
1938 Benfica	1961 Benfica
1939 FC Porto	1962 Sporting
1940 FC Porto	1963 Benfica
1941 Sporting	1964 Benfica
1942 Benfica	1965 Benfica
1943 Benfica	1966 Sporting
1944 Sporting	1967 Benfica
1945 Benfica	1968 Benfica
1946 OS Belenenses	1969 Benfica
1947 Sporting	1970 Sporting
1948 Sporting	1971 Benfica
1949 Sporting	1972 Benfica
1950 Benfica	1973 Benfica
1951 Sporting	1974 Sporting
1952 Sporting	1975 Benfica
1953 Sporting	1976 Benfica
1954 Sporting	1977 Benfica
1955 Benfica	1978 FC Porto
1956 FC Porto	1979 FC Porto
1957 Benfica	1980 Sporting
	1981 Benfica

Portugal's FC Porto lift the European Cup

1982 Sporting
1983 Benfica
1984 Benfica
1985 FC Porto
1986 FC Porto
1987 Benfica
1988 FC Porto
1989 Benfica
1990 FC Porto
1991 Benfica
1992 FC Porto
1993 FC Porto
1994 Benfica
1995 FC Porto
1996 FC Porto
1997 FC Porto
1998 FC Porto

CUP WINNERS

1922 FC Porto
1923 Sporting
1924 SC Olhanense
1925 FC Porto
1926 CS Maritimo
1927 OS Belenenses
1928 Carcavelinhos
1929 OS Belenenses
1930 Benfica
1931 Benfica
1932 FC Porto
1933 OS Belenenses
1934 Sporting
1935 Benfica
1936 Sporting
1937 FC Porto
1938 Sporting
1939 Academica Coimbra
1940 Benfica
1941 Sporting
1942 OS Belenenses
1943 Benfica
1944 Benfica
1945 Sporting
1946 Sporting
1947 Not played
1948 Sporting
1949 Benfica
1950 Not played

1951 Benfica
1952 Benfica
1953 Benfica
1954 Sporting
1955 Benfica
1956 FC Porto
1957 Benfica
1958 FC Porto
1959 Benfica
1960 OS Belenenses
1961 Leixoes SC
1962 Benfica
1963 Sporting
1964 Benfica
1965 Vitoria Setubal
1966 Sporting Braga
1967 Vitoria Setubal
1968 FC Porto
1969 Benfica
1970 Benfica
1971 Sporting
1972 Benfica
1973 Sporting
1974 Sporting
1975 Boavista FC
1976 Benfica
1977 Benfica
1978 Sporting
1979 Boavista FC
1980 Benfica
1981 Benfica
1982 Sporting
1983 Benfica
1984 FC Porto
1985 Benfica
1986 Benfica
1987 Benfica
1988 FC Porto
1989 OS Belenenses
1990 Estrela da Amadora
1991 FC Porto
1992 Boavista FC
1993 Benfica
1994 FC Porto
1995 Sporting CP
1996 Benfica
1997 Boavista
1998 Braga

Republic Of Ireland

Football Association of Ireland
Founded: *1921*
Joined FIFA: *1923*

Football was launched in Ireland in the late 1870s, but the formal history of Irish Republic football began following the political division of 1921 and the establishment of the Football Association of Ireland.

Not bounded by the xenophobia which kept the four British associations out of the international football family, the Irish can boast a proud record of having entered all except the very first World Cup competition. Indeed, in the 1934 event, Paddy Moore became the first player to score four goals in a single qualifying match. His feat was accomplished in a 4–4 draw with Belgium in Dublin.

Throughout the post-war years, footballers from the Irish Republic contributed in significant numbers to top clubs in the English Football League. These ranged from defender Johnny Carey to midfield general Johnny Giles, just two of the considerable number of outstanding talents to shine for Manchester United.

It took an English manager, Jack Charlton, to harness Irish potential at international level. Charlton first took the Republic to the finals of the 1988 European Championship, where they opened with a memorable 1–0 victory over England. This was not the first time the Republic had beaten England: the most notable previous success was by 2–0 at Goodison Park, Liverpool, in 1949. Thus Ireland, rather than Hungary, became the first foreign team to win on English soil.

As for Charlton, England's World Cup-winning centre back in 1966, his ultimate managerial achievement followed in the World Cup. He guided the Republic to the quarter-finals in 1990 and the second round in 1994 before being succeeded by his one-time captain, Mick McCarthy.

CHAMPIONS

1922 St James Gate
1923 Shamrock Rovers
1924 Bohemians
1925 Shamrock Rovers
1926 Shelbourne
1927 Shamrock Rovers
1928 Bohemians
1929 Shelbourne
1930 Bohemians
1931 Shelbourne
1932 Shamrock Rovers
1933 Dundalk
1934 Bohemians
1935 Dolphin
1936 Bohemians
1937 Sligo Rovers
1938 Shamrock Rovers
1939 Shamrock Rovers
1940 St James Gate
1941 Cork United
1942 Cork United
1943 Cork United
1944 Shelbourne
1945 Cork United
1946 Cork United
1947 Shelbourne
1948 Drumcondra
1949 Drumcondra
1950 Cork Athletic
1951 Cork Athletic
1952 St. Patrick's Athletic

1953 Shelbourne
1954 Shamrock Rovers
1955 St Patrick's Athletic
1956 St Patrick's Athletic
1957 Shamrock Rovers
1958 Drumcondra
1959 Shamrock Rovers
1960 Limerick FC
1961 Drumcondra
1962 Shelbourne
1963 Dundalk
1964 Shamrock Rovers
1965 Drumcondra
1966 Waterford
1967 Dundalk
1968 Waterford
1969 Waterford
1970 Waterford
1971 Cork Hibernians
1972 Waterford
1973 Waterford
1974 Cork Celtic
1975 Bohemians
1976 Dundalk
1977 Sligo Rovers
1978 Bohemians
1979 Dundalk
1980 Limerick United
1981 Athlone Town
1982 Dundalk
1983 Athlone Town
1984 Shamrock Rovers
1985 Shamrock Rovers

Denis Irwin takes on Italy for the Republic Of Ireland

1986 Shamrock Rovers
1987 Shamrock Rovers
1988 Dundalk
1989 Derry City
1990 St Patrick's Athletic
1991 Dundalk
1992 Shelbourne
1993 Cork City
1994 Shamrock Rovers
1995 Dundalk
1996 St Patrick's Athletic
1997 Derry City
1998 St Patrick's Athletic

CUP WINNERS

1922 St James Gate
1923 Alton United
1924 Athlone Town
1925 Shamrock Rovers
1926 Fordsons
1927 Drumcondra
1928 Bohemians
1929 Shamrock Rovers
1930 Shamrock Rovers
1931 Shamrock Rovers
1932 Shamrock Rovers
1933 Shamrock Rovers
1934 Cork FC
1935 Bohemians
1936 Shamrock Rovers
1937 Waterford
1938 St James Gate
1939 Shelbourne

1940 Shamrock Rovers
1941 Cork United
1942 Dundalk
1943 Drumcondra
1944 Shamrock Rovers
1945 Shamrock Rovers
1946 Drumcondra
1947 Cork United
1948 Shamrock Rovers
1949 Dundalk
1950 Transport
1951 Cork Athletic
1952 Dundalk
1953 Cork Athletic
1954 Drumcondra
1955 Shamrock Rovers
1956 Shamrock Rovers
1957 Drumcondra
1958 Dundalk
1959 St Patrick's Athletic
1960 Shelbourne
1961 St Patrick's Athletic
1962 Shamrock Rovers
1963 Shelbourne
1964 Shamrock Rovers
1965 Shamrock Rovers
1966 Shamrock Rovers
1967 Shamrock Rovers
1968 Shamrock Rovers
1969 Shamrock Rovers
1970 Bohemians
1971 Limerick FC
1972 Cork Hibernians
1973 Cork Hibernians

1974 Finn Harps
1975 Home Farm
1976 Bohemians
1977 Dundalk
1978 Shamrock Rovers
1979 Dundalk
1980 Waterford
1981 Dundalk
1982 Limerick United
1983 Sligo Rovers
1984 University College
1985 Shamrock Rovers
1986 Shamrock Rovers

1987 Shamrock Rovers
1988 Dundalk
1989 Derry City
1990 Bray Wanderers
1991 Galway United
1992 Bohemians
1993 Shelbourne
1994 Sligo Rovers
1995 Derry City
1996 Shelbourne
1997 Shelbourne
1998 Cork City

Romania

Federatia Romana de Fotbal

Founded: *1909*

Joined FIFA: *1930*

Romania secured a place in soccer history as one of the four European nations who competed at the inaugural World Cup finals in Uruguay in 1930. They did so thanks to the enthusiasm and generosity of King Carol, who offered to pay the wages of the leading players while they were away. His regal gesture was rewarded, however, only by first-round elimination and Romania struggled for 50 years before shining on the world stage – and reaching the finals of the 1984 European Championship.

The nucleus of that team came from the army club, Steaua Bucharest, who became eastern Europe's first European club champions when, in 1986, they beat Barcelona on penalties in Seville. Outstanding players were strikers Dudu Georgescu and Rodion Camataru, both of whom won the Golden Boot awarded annually to Europe's top league goalscorer. Georgescu won with 47 goals in 1977; Camataru with 44 a decade later.

Steaua's coach, Emerich Jenei, was later appointed manager of the national team and steered Romania to the finals of the 1990 World Cup. Here a team inspired in attack by Gheorghe Hagi – the "Maradona of the Carpathians" – and Marius Lacatus reached the second round, only to lose in a penalty shoot-out to the Republic of Ireland.

Four years later they went one round better, defeating Argentina in the second round before again going out on penalties, to Sweden in the quarter-finals. But at Euro '96 they were out of luck, having a potentially vital goal disallowed against France because Danish referee Peter Mikkelsen did not see the ball bounce down from the bar, behind the goal-line and then back into play.

In the 1998 World Cup finals, Romania (still led by veteran Hagi) won their group ahead of much-fancied England and beat Glenn Hoddle's men 2–1. But having qualified they went out in the second round to Croatia, who eventually took third place in the tournament.

CHAMPIONS

1910 Olimpia Bucharest
1911 Olimpia Bucharest
1912 United Ploiesti
1913 Colentina Bucharest
1914 Colentina Bucharest
1915 Romano-Americana
1916 Prahova Ploiesti
1917–19 Not played
1920 Venus Bucharest
1921 Venus Bucharest
1922 Chinezul Timisoara
1923 Chinezul Timisoara
1924 Chinezul Timisoara
1925 Chinezul Timisoara
1926 Chinezul Timisoara
1927 Chinezul Timisoara
1928 Coltea Brasov
1929 Venus Bucharest
1930 Juventus Bucharest
1931 UDR Resita
1932 Venus Bucharest
1933 Ripensia Timisoara
1934 Venus Bucharest
1935 Ripensia Timisoara
1936 Ripensia Timisoara
1937 Venus Bucharest
1938 Ripensia Timisoara
1939 Venus Bucharest
1940 Venus Bucharest

1941 Unirea Tricolor
1942–46 Not played
1947 IT Arad
1948 IT Arad
1949 ICO Oradea
1950 Flamura Rosie
1951 CCA Bucharest
1952 CCA Bucharest
1953 CCA Bucharest
1954 Flamura Rosie
1955 Dinamo Bucharest
1956 CCA Bucharest
1957 Not played
1958 Petrolul Ploiesti
1959 Petrolul Ploiesti
1960 CCA Bucharest
1961 CCA Bucharest
1962 Dinamo Bucharest
1963 Dinamo Bucharest
1964 Dinamo Bucharest
1965 Dinamo Bucharest
1966 Dinamo Bucharest
1967 Rapid Bucharest
1968 Steaua Bucharest
1969 UT Arad
1970 UT Arad
1971 Dinamo Bucharest
1972 FC Arges Pitesti
1973 Dinamo Bucharest
1974 Universitatea Craiova
1975 Dinamo Bucharest

1976 Steau Bucharest
1977 Dinamo Bucharest
1978 Steaua Bucharest
1979 FC Arges Pitesti
1980 Universitatea Craiova
1981 Universitatea Craiova
1982 Dinamo Bucharest
1983 Dinamo Bucharest
1984 Dinamo Bucharest
1985 Steaua Bucharest
1986 Steaua Bucharest
1987 Steaua Bucharest
1988 Steaua Bucharest
1989 Steaua Bucharest
1990 Dinamo Bucharest
1991 Universitatea Craiova
1992 Dinamo Bucharest
1993 Steaua Bucharest
1994 Steaua Bucharest
1995 Steaua Bucharest
1996 Steaua Bucharest
1997 Steaua Bucharest
1998 Steaua Bucharest

CUP WINNERS

1934 Ripensia Timisoara
1935 CFR Bucharest
1936 Ripensia Timisoara
1937 Rapid Bucharest
1938 Rapid Bucharest
1939 Rapid Bucharest
1940 Rapid Bucharest
1941 Rapid Bucharest
1942 Rapid Bucharest
1943 Tirnu Severin
1944–47 Not played
1948 IT Arad
1949 CCA Bucharest
1950 CCA Bucharest
1951 CCA Bucharest
1952 CCA Bucharest
1953 Flamura Rosie
1954 Metalul Resita
1955 CCA Bucharest

1956 Progresul Oradea
1957 Not played
1958 Stinta Timisoara
1959 Dinamo Bucharest
1960 Ariesul Turda
1961 Progresul Oradea
1962 Steaua Bucharest
1963 Petrolul Ploiesti
1964 Dinamo Bucharest
1965 Stinta Cluj
1966 Steaua Bucharest
1967 Steaua Bucharest
1968 Dinamo Bucharest
1969 Steaua Bucharest
1970 Steaua Bucharest
1971 Steaua Bucharest
1972 Rapid Bucharest
1973 Chimea Vilcea
1974 Jiul Petrosani
1975 Rapid Bucharest
1976 Steaua Bucharest
1977 Universitatea Craiova
1978 Universitatea Craiova
1979 Steaua Bucharest
1980 Politehnica Timisoara
1981 Universitatea Craiova
1982 Dinamo Bucharest
1983 Universitatea Craiova
1984 Dinamo Bucharest
1985 Steaua Bucharest
1986 Dinamo Bucharest
1987 Steaua Bucharest
1988 Steaua Bucharest
1989 Steaua Bucharest
1990 Dinamo Bucharest
1991 Universitatea Craiova
1992 Steaua Bucharest
1993 Universitatea Craiova
1994 Gloria Bistrita
1995 Petrolul Ploesti
1996 Steaua Bucharest
1997 Steaua Bucharest
1998 Rapid Bucharest

Romanian legend Gheorghe Hagi

Russia

Rossiiski Futbolnyi Soyuz
Founded: *1912*
Joined FIFA: *1992*

The story of Russian football is a tale of political complexity. Popularly, football is recorded as having been introduced to Czarist Russia in 1887 by Britons Clement and Harry Charnock, whose family managed cotton mills in Orekhovo Zuyevo some 50 miles east of Moscow. Simultaneously, however, students were coming home to St Petersburg from Britain with the new craze and teams were launched there in schools and military academies.

A Moscow league was formed in 1901 and, in the succeeding

few years, regional leagues sprang up throughout the territory and major cities of what would duly become, after all the revolutionary upheavals, the Soviet Union. Russia even entered a team at the 1912 Olympic Games in Stockholm.

In the turmoil of the 1920s, Russian or Soviet sports teams were barred from international contact. But that same decade saw the creation of clubs such as Moscow Dynamo, Spartak, Torpedo and CSKA, which would become pillars of the communist recreational structures. A national league was set up in 1936 but it was not until a decade later, in the wake of World War Two, that Soviet soccer finally came in from the cold.

The Soviet Union won the Olympic title in Melbourne in 1956, reached the quarter-finals two years later on their first tilt at the World Cup and won the inaugural European Championship in 1960. They were European runners-up in 1964, 1972 and 1988 and fourth in 1968. As for the World Cup, despite all their power and pretensions, their best finish was fourth in 1966.

In the 1970s and 1980s the Soviets turned away from the more physical Russian game to embrace the technical bravado of Ukraine's Kiev Dynamo, twice winners of the Cup-winners Cup. But that, ultimately, produced no better results because the weight of fixtures wore down even stars such as European Footballer of the Year Oleg Blokhin.

After the communist collapse, the Soviet Union materialized as the Commonwealth of Independent States at the 1992 European Championship finals. Then the newly-independent Russian federation assumed the Soviet Union's place in the international game. It also took over all those current international players from the other republics who wished to be Russian for, at least, professional purposes. Results were no better, however, as Russia made first-round exits in the finals of both USA 94 and Euro 96 and failed to reach the World Cup finals in 1998.

CHAMPIONS

1992 Moscow Spartak	1941–44 Not played
1993 Moscow Spartak	1945 Moscow Dynamo
1994 Moscow Spartak	1946 CDKA Moscow
1995 Alania-Spartak Vladikavkaz	1947 CDKA Moscow
1996 Moscow Spartak	1948 CDKA Moscow
1997 Moscow Spartak	1949 Moscow Dynamo
	1950 CDKA Moscow
	1951 CDSA Moscow

CUP WINNERS

1993 Moscow Torpedo	1952 Moscow Spartak
1994 Moscow Spartak	1953 Moscow Spartak
1995 Moscow Dynamo	1954 Moscow Dynamo
1996 Lokomotiv Moscow	1955 Moscow Dynamo
1997 Lokomotiv Moscow	1956 Moscow Spartak
	1957 Moscow Dynamo
	1958 Moscow Spartak
	1959 Moscow Dynamo

FORMER SOVIET UNION

1936 spring Moscow Dynamo	1960 Moscow Torpedo
1937 autumn Moscow Spartak	1961 Kiev Dynamo
1938 Moscow Spartak	1962 Moscow Spartak
1939 Moscow Spartak	1963 Moscow Dynamo
1940 Moscow Dynamo	1964 Tbilisi Dynamo
	1965 Moscow Torpedo
1966 Kiev Dynamo	
1967 Kiev Dynamo	
1968 Kiev Dynamo	
1969 Moscow Spartak	
1970 CSKA Moscow	
1971 Kiev Dynamo	
1972 Zarya Voroshilovgrad	
1973 Ararat Yerevan	
1974 Kiev Dynamo	
1975 Kiev Dynamo	
1976 spring Moscow Dynamo	
1976 autumn Moscow Dynamo	
1977 Kiev Dynamo	
1978 Tbilisi Dynamo	
1979 Moscow Spartak	
1980 Kiev Dynamo	
1981 Kiev Dynamo	
1982 Minsk Dynamo	
1983 Dnepr Dnepropetrovsk	
1984 Zenit Leningrad	
1985 Kiev Dynamo	
1986 Kiev Dynamo	
1987 Moscow Spartak	
1988 Dnepr Dnepropetrovsk	
1989 Moscow Spartak	
1990 Kiev Dynamo	
1991 CSKA Moscow	

CUP WINNERS

1936 Lokomotiv Moscow	1952 Moscow Torpedo
1937 Moscow Dynamo	1953 Moscow Dynamo
1938 Moscow Spartak	1954 Kiev Dynamo
1939 Moscow Spartak	1955 CDSA Moscow
1940–43 Not played	1956 Not played
1944 Zenit Leningrad	1957 Lokomotiv Moscow
1945 CDKA Moscow	1958 Moscow Spartak
1946 Moscow Spartak	1959 Not played
1947 Moscow Spartak	1960 Moscow Torpedo
1948 CDKA Moscow	1961 Shakhtyor Donetsk
1949 Moscow Torpedo	1962 Moscow Spartak
1950 Moscow Spartak	1963 Moscow Spartak
1951 CDSA Moscow	1964 Kiev Dynamo
	1965 Moscow Spartak
	1966 Kiev Dynamo
	1967 Moscow Dynamo
	1968 Moscow Torpedo
	1969 Karpaty Lvov
	1970 Moscow Dynamo
	1971 Moscow Spartak
	1972 Moscow Torpedo
	1973 Ararat Yerevan
	1974 Kiev Dynamo
	1975 Ararat Yerevan
	1976 Tbilisi Dynamo
	1977 Moscow Torpedo
	1978 Kiev Dynamo
	1979 Tbilisi Dynamo
	1980 Shakhtyor Donetsk
	1981 SKA Rostov
	1982 Kiev Dynamo
	1983 Shakhtyor Donetsk
	1984 Moscow Dynamo
	1985 Kiev Dynamo
	1986 Moscow Torpedo
	1987 Kiev Dynamo
	1988 Metallist Karkov
	1989 Dnepr Dnepropetrovsk
	1990 Kiev Dynamo
	1991 CSKA Moscow
	1992 Moscow Spartak

San Marino

Federazione Sanmarinese Gioco Calcio

Founded: *1931*
Joined FIFA: *1988*

San Marino, Liechtenstein and Andorra are Europe's weakest three nations. Indeed, San Marino is not so much a nation, rather it is an enclave within Italy, some 15 miles from the Adriatic seaside resort of Rimini.

The principality's history dates back to the 10th century, but a football federation was set up little more than 60 years ago. Even then it was not until after the election of Giorgio Crescenti as president in 1985 that the possibility of full international independence was realized.

Scotland's Pat Nevin shoots past San Marino captain William Guerra in a European Championship qualifier in 1995

UEFA and FIFA membership ultimately followed in the summer of 1988. The first official match played by San Marino was a friendly against the Danish club, Odense BK. This was staged in the 7,000-capacity San Marino "national stadium" at Serravalle, in 1985 and ended in a 1–1 draw.

San Marino has produced only one top-class footballer: Massimo Bonini, a Champions Cup-winning midfielder with Juventus in 1985 who later became San Marino's national coach.

CHAMPIONS	CUP WINNERS
1986 Faetano	1986 La Fiorita
1987 La Fiorita	1987 Libertas
1988 Tre Fiori	1988 Domagnano
1989 Domagnano	1989 Libertas
1990 La Fiorita	1990 Domagnano
1991 Faetano	1991 Libertas
1992 Montevito	1992 Domagnano
1993 Tre Fiori	1993 Faetano
1994 Tre Fiori	1994 Faetano
1995 Tre Fiori	1995 Cosmos
1996 Cosmos	1996 Libertas
1997 Folgore	1997 Murata

Scotland

Scottish Football Association
Founded: *1873*
Joined FIFA: *1910*

Scottish football has always been, at international level, long on pride but comparatively short on achievement. The national team have regularly attended the World Cup finals – though they missed 1994 – and have been present at the last two European Championship finals tournaments. But they have never progressed beyond the first round – a jinx which struck again at France '98 when they crashed out following a humiliating 3–0 defeat against Morocco.

At club level, Celtic are the only Scottish team to have won the European Cup (in 1967). Rangers, for all their European league ambitions, won only the Cup-winners Cup in 1972. Aberdeen also won the Cup-winners Cup once. Yet Rangers and Celtic are two of the most famous clubs in the world and Scottish football has produced a string of stars from Alex James to Paul McStay via Jim Baxter, Dave Mackay, Jock Stein, Denis Law, Kenny Dalglish, Graeme Souness and Ally McCoist.

Scotland's general international path has matched that of

Scotland's midfield hard-man, Graeme Souness

England. They started together in the world's very first international (a 0–0 draw) in 1872, quit FIFA and the international competitive scene together in the 1920s over broken-time payments to amateurs, then returned in 1946.

They might also have travelled, along with England, to the 1950 World Cup finals in Brazil. The Home International Championship was the qualifying event and the top two nations had the right to go to the finals. For reasons never sensibly explained, Scotland insisted that they would go if they finished top of the group. In the event, they finished runners-up.

Even when they qualified, controversy pursued them, as in 1978, when Scotland winger Willie Johnston faileda drugs test in Argentina. Ally MacLeod's managerial reputation never quite recovered from that. But Jock Stein, Alex Ferguson, Andy Roxburgh and Craig Brown made good the damage in the years which followed – culminating in Scotland's appearances at the European finals of 1992 and in 1996, where they were unlucky to lose a dramatic Wembley showdown with England.

CHAMPIONS

1891 Dumbarton
1892 Dumbarton
1893 Celtic
1894 Celtic
1895 Heart of Midlothian
1896 Celtic
1897 Heart of Midlothian
1898 Celtic
1899 Rangers
1900 Rangers
1901 Ramgers
1902 Rangers
1903 Hibernian
1904 Third Lanark
1905 Celtic
1906 Celtic
1907 Celtic
1908 Celtic
1909 Celtic
1910 Celtic
1911 Rangers
1912 Rangers
1913 Rangers
1914 Celtic
1915 Celtic
1916 Celtic
1917 Celtic
1918 Rangers
1919 Celtic
1920 Rangers
1921 Rangers
1922 Celtic
1923 Rangers
1924 Rangers
1925 Rangers
1926 Celtic
1927 Rangers
1928 Rangers
1929 Rangers
1930 Rangers
1931 Rangers
1932 Motherwell
1933 Rangers
1934 Rangers
1935 Rangers
1936 Celtic
1937 Rangers
1938 Celtic
1939 Rangers
1940–46 Not played
1947 Rangers
1948 Hibernian
1949 Rangers
1950 Rangers
1951 Hibernian
1952 Hibernian
1953 Rangers
1954 Celtic
1955 Aberdeen
1956 Rangers
1957 Rangers
1958 Heart of Midlothian
1959 Rangers
1960 Heart of Midlothian
1961 Rangers
1962 Dundee
1963 Rangers
1964 Rangers
1965 Kilmarnock
1966 Celtic
1967 Celtic
1968 Celtic
1969 Celtic
1970 Celtic
1971 Celtic
1972 Celtic
1973 Celtic
1974 Celtic
1975 Rangers
1976 Rangers
1977 Celtic
1978 Rangers
1979 Celtic
1980 Aberdeen
1981 Celtic
1982 Celtic
1983 Dundee U
1984 Aberdeen
1985 Aberdeen
1986 Celtic
1987 Rangers
1988 Celtic
1989 Rangers
1990 Rangers
1991 Rangers
1992 Rangers
1993 Rangers
1994 Rangers
1995 Rangers
1996 Rangers
1997 Rangers
1998 Celtic

CUP WINNERS

1874 Queen's Park
1875 Queen's Park
1876 Queen's Park
1877 Vale of Levan
1878 Vale of Levan
1879 Vale of Levan
1880 Queen's Park
1881 Queen's Park
1882 Queen's Park
1883 Dumbarton
1884 Queen's Park
1885 Renton
1886 Queen's Park
1887 Hibernian
1888 Renton
1889 Third Lanark
1890 Queen's Park
1891 Heart of Midlothian
1892 Celtic
1893 Queen's Park
1894 Rangers
1895 St Bernard's
1896 Heart of Midlothian
1897 Rangers
1898 Rangers
1899 Celtic
1900 Celtic
1901 Heart of Midlothian
1902 Hibernian
1903 Rangers
1904 Celtic
1905 Third Lanark
1906 Heart of Midlothian
1907 Celtic
1908 Celtic
1909 Cup withheld
1910 Dundee
1911 Celtic
1912 Celtic

1913 Falkirk	1989 Celtic
1914 Celtic	1990 Aberdeen
1915–19 Not played	1991 Motherwell
1920 Kilmarnock	1992 Rangers
1921 Partick Thistle	1993 Rangers
1922 Morton	1994 Dundee U
1923 Celtic	1995 Celtic
1924 Airdieonians	1996 Rangers
1925 Celtic	1997 Kilmarnock
1926 St Mirren	1998 Hearts
1927 Celtic	
1928 Rangers	

LEAGUE CUP WINNERS

1929 Kilmarnock	1947 Rangers
1930 Rangers	1948 East Fife
1931 Celtic	1949 Rangers
1932 Rangers	1950 East Fife
1933 Celtic	1951 Motherwell
1934 Rangers	1952 Dundee
1935 Rangers	1953 Dundee
1936 Rangers	1954 East Fife
1937 Celtic	1955 Hearts
1938 East Fife	1956 Aberdeen
1939 Clyde	1957 Celtic
1940–46 Not played	1958 Celtic
1947 Aberdeen	1959 Hearts
1948 Rangers	1960 Hearts
1949 Rangers	1961 Rangers
1950 Rangers	1962 Rangers
1951 Celtic	1963 Hearts
1952 Motherwell	1964 Rangers
1953 Rangers	1965 Rangers
1954 Celtic	1966 Celtic
1955 Clyde	1967 Celtic
1956 Heart of Midlothian	1968 Celtic
1957 Falkirk	1969 Celtic
1958 Clyde	1970 Celtic
1959 St Mirren	1971 Rangers
1960 Rangers	1972 Partick Thistle
1961 Dumferline Athletic	1973 Hibernian
1962 Rangers	1974 Dundee
1963 Rangers	1975 Celtic
1964 Rangers	1976 Rangers
1965 Celtic	1977 Aberdeen
1966 Rangers	1978 Rangers
1967 Celtic	1979 Rangers
1968 Dumferline Athletic	1980 Dundee U
1969 Celtic	1981 Dundee U
1970 Aberdeen	1982 Rangers
1971 Celtic	1983 Celtic
1972 Celtic	1984 Rangers
1973 Rangers	1985 Rangers
1974 Celtic	1986 Aberdeen
1975 Celtic	1987 Rangers
1976 Rangers	1988 Rangers
1977 Celtic	1989 Rangers
1978 Rangers	1990 Aberdeen
1979 Rangers	1991 Rangers
1980 Celtic	1992 Hibernian
1981 Rangers	1993 Rangers
1982 Aberdeen	1994 Rangers
1983 Aberdeen	1995 Raith Rovers
1984 Aberdeen	1996 Aberdeen
1985 Celtic	1997 Rangers
1986 Aberdeen	1998 Celtic
1987 St Mirren	
1988 Celtic	

Slovakia

Football Association of Slovak Republic
Founded: *1990*
Joined FIFA: *1994*

Slovakia were always poor relations in football terms before the split from the Czech Republic, though Slovan Bratislava did once win the European Cup-winners Cup in the 1960s. Slovakia made their international competitive debut in the 1996 European Championship and were unlucky to find themselves drawn in a group dominated by outstanding Romanian and French teams. In such company, third place added up to a promising start.

CHAMPIONS	CUP WINNERS
1994 Slovan Bratislava	1994 Slovan Bratislava
1995 Slovan Bratislava	1995 Inter Bratislava
1996 Slovan Bratislava	1996 Chemlon Humenne
1997 1FC Kosice	1997 Slovan Bratislava
1998 1FC Kosice	1998 Spartak Trnava

Slovenia

Nogometna Zveza Slovenija
Founded: *1920*
Joined FIFA: *1992*

Slovenia, the first state to break free of the former Yugoslavia, finished a disappointing fifth (out of six countries) in their Euro 96 qualifying group on their competitive debut.

CHAMPIONS	CUP WINNERS
1992 Olimpija Ljubljana	1992 Branik Maribor
1993 Olimpija Ljubljana	1993 Olimpia Ljubljana
1994 Olimpija Ljubljana	1994 Maribor Branik
1995 Olimpija Ljubljana	1995 Mura Murska Sobota
1996 Olimpija Ljubljana	1996 Olimpija Ljubljana
1997 Branik Maribor	1997 Primorje
1998 Branik Maribor	1998 Rudar Velenje

Spain

Real Federacion Espanola de Futbol
Founded: *1913*
Joined FIFA: *1904*

The big clubs, rather than the national team, hold responsibility for Spain's intimidating reputation as a football nation.

The European club scene in the 1950s was dominated by Real Madrid and Barcelona. Madrid won the Champions Cup five

Spain's Raul Gonzalez celebrates a goal against Nigeria

times in a row and Barcelona collected the old Fairs Cup (precursor of the UEFA Cup) twice. Along the way various of their foreign signings were pressed into service for Spain – such as Madrid's Alfredo Di Stefano and Hector Rial (ex-Argentina), Jose Santamaria (ex-Uruguay) and even Ferenc Puskas (ex-Hungary). In later years economic realism compelled a greater concentration on youth and nursery team schemes. Thus Madrid's "second generation" for Spain were not imported but home-grown, such as Emilio Butragueno, Michel, Ricardo Gallego and Rafael Martin Vazquez.

That trend continues, despite the virtual collapse of foreign player restrictions, in the wake of the Bosman ruling, and the multi-million TV investment which has permitted the Madrids and Barcelonas to buy up just about anything which moves.

Yet, for all the club domination, the Spanish national team often fail to achieve their potential – as in the World Cup finals of 1998 when they went out in the first round. A 3–2 defeat against Nigeria cost Spain dear and although they showed their true colours by thrashing Bulgaria 6–1, it was all too lae.

The national side have had their moments, though. It was Spain, in Madrid on May 15, 1929, who were the first continental team ever to defeat England. They also won the European Championship in 1964 (also in Madrid) and the 1992 Olympic Games title in Barcelona. But World Cup level, Spain's best remains fourth place in Brazil in 1950.

Spain boasts some of the finest football stadia in the world and some of the most fanatical fans. Football in Spain served as a political vehicle, too. The number of clubs boasting the prefix Real (or Royal) stemmed from the support the sport gained from King Alfonso XIII in the early years of the century.

After the Spanish Civil War, football offered people in the regions such as Catalunya and Vizcaya their only opportunity for protest and tacit opposition to the dictatorship of General Francisco Franco. Thus the traditional rivalry between Barcelona and Real Madrid is more than merely a sporting contest.

The clubs compete against each other in the transfer market – sometimes having even signed players not because they wanted them but to stop their rivals buying them. Very few players have lined up for both clubs. Notable exceptions to the rule in the past 40 years have included Spain forwards Luis Enrique and Justo Tejada, Brazilian centre forward Evaristo de Macedo, French midfielder Lucien Muller, Belgian wing half Ferdinand Goyvaerts and the temperamental German, Bernd Schuster.

CHAMPIONS

1929 Barcelona	1959 Barcelona
1930 Athletic Bilbao	1960 Barcelona
1931 Athletic Bilbao	1961 Real Madrid
1932 Real Madrid	1962 Real Madrid
1933 Real Madrid	1963 Real Madrid
1934 Athletic Bilbao	1964 Real Madrid
1935 Real Betis	1965 Real Madrid
1936 Athletic Bilbao	1966 Atletico Madrid
1937–39 Not played	1967 Real Madrid
1940 Atletico Aviacion	1968 Real Madrid
1941 Atletico Aviacion	1969 Real Madrid
1942 Valencia	1970 Atletico Madrid
1943 Atheltic Bilbao	1971 Valencia
1944 Valencia	1972 Real Madrid
1945 Barcelona	1973 Atletico Madrid
1946 Seville	1974 Barcelona
1947 Valencia	1975 Real Madrid
1948 Barcelona	1976 Real Madrid
1949 Barcelona	1977 Atletico Madrid
1950 Atletico Madrid	1978 Real Madrid
1951 Atletico Madrid	1979 Real Madrid
1952 Barcelona	1980 Real Madrid
1953 Barcelona	1981 Real Sociedad
1954 Real Madrid	1982 Real Sociedad
1955 Real Madrid	1983 Athletic Bilbao
1956 Athleltic Bilbao	1984 Atheltic Bilbao
1957 Real Madrid	1985 Barcelona
1958 Real Madrid	1986 Real Madrid
	1987 Real Madrid
	1988 Real Madrid

1989 Real Madrid	1946 Real Madrid
1990 Real Madrid	1947 Real Madrid
1991 Barcelona	1948 Seville
1992 Barcelona	1949 Valencia
1993 Barcelona	1950 Athletic Bilbao
1994 Barcelona	1951 Barcelona
1995 Real Madrid	1952 Barcelona
1996 Atletico Madrid	1953 Barcelona
1997 Real Madrid	1954 Valencia
1998 Barcelona	1955 Athletic Bilbao
	1956 Athletic Bilbao

CUP WINNERS

1902 Vizcaya Bilbao	1957 Barcelona
1903 Athletic Bilbao	1958 Athletic Bilbao
1904 Athletic Bilbao	1959 Barcelona
1905 Real Madrid	1960 Atletico Madrid
1906 Real Madrid	1961 Atletico Madrid
1907 Real Madrid	1962 Real Madrid
1908 Real Madrid	1963 Barcelona
1909 Ciclista San Sebastian	1964 Real Zaragoza
*1910 Athletic Bilbao	1965 Atletico Madrid
*1910 Barcelona	1966 Real Zaragoza
*rival competitions	1967 Valencia
1911 Athletic Bilbao	1968 Barcelona
1912 Barcelona	1969 Athletic Bilbao
1913 Racing Irun	1970 Real Madrid
1914 Athletic Bilbao	1971 Barcelona
1915 Athletic Bilbao	1972 Atletico Madrid
1916 Athletic Bilbao	1973 Atletico Madrid
1917 Real Madrid	1974 Real Madrid
1918 Red Union Irun	1975 Real Madrid
1919 Arenas Guecho Bilbao	1976 Atletico Madrid
1920 Barcelona	1977 Real Betis
1921 Athletic Bilbao	1978 Barcelona
1922 Barcelona	1979 Valencia
1923 Athletic Bilba	1980 Real Madrid
1924 Real Union Irun	1981 Barcelona
1925 Barcelona	1982 Real Madrid
1926 Barcelona	1983 Barcelona
1927 Real Union Irun	1984 Athletic Bilbao
1928 Barcelona	1985 Atletico Madrid
1929 RCD Espanol	1986 Real Zaragoza
1930 Athletic Bilbao	1987 Real Sociedad
1931 Athletic Bilbao	1988 Barcelona
1932 Athletic Bilbao	1989 Real Madrid
1933 Athletic Bilbao	1990 Barcelona
1934 Real Madrid	1991 Atletico Madrid
1935 Seville	1992 Atletico Madrid
1936 Real Madrid	1993 Real Madrid
1937–38 Not played	1994 Real Zaragoza
1939 Seville	1995 Deportivo La Coruna
1940 RCD Espanol	1996 Atletico Madrid
1941 Valencia	1997 Barcelona
1942 Barcelona	1998 Barcelona
1943 Athletic Bilbao	
1944 Athletic Bilbao	
1945 Athletic Bilbao	

Sweden

Svenska Fotboliforbundet

Founded: 1904

Joined FIFA: 1904

Football was brought to Sweden through the ports and it is the provincial centres of Gothenburg and Malmo which have generally proved more dynamic soccer centres than the capital, Stockholm.

Remarkably Sweden, a country whose domestic game has never been anything more than part-time, have a proud World Cup record which says much for the talent and pragmatism of players and coaches.

They reached the quarter-finals of the World Cup in 1934 and finished fourth in 1938. After the war they won the 1948 Olympic Games in London to launch themselves upon further success at top level.

Managed by Englishman George Raynor, the Swedes boasted a host of great players who were quickly lured away to Italy. The inside forward trio of Gunnar Gren, Gunnar Nordahl and Nils Liedholm became legendary with Milan as the "Grenoli" trio.

Raynor rebuilt his team for the 1950 World Cup where Sweden finished third. That success helped clinch for Sweden the right to stage the 1958 finals, when Raynor was allowed by the federation to recall the Italy-based mercenaries such as Liedholm and Gren and wingers Kurt Hamrin and Lennart "Nacka"

Tomas Brolin after scoring against Germany at Euro 92

Skoglund. Sweden reached the Final before losing 5–2 in Stockholm to Pele's incomparable Brazilians.

In the European Championship, Sweden did not reach the finals for the first time until 1992 – and then only courtesy of their right as hosts. However, under Tommy Svensson, they proved worthy of the status and reached the semi-finals. Svensson used a simple tactical framework while concentrating his players' minds on doing the simple things well.

Solid defending, perceptive midfield control from Jonas Thern and Stefan Schwarz plus the attacking skills of Tomas Brolin then took Sweden on to third place at the 1994 World Cup.

That this was no fluke was underlined by the manner in which IFK Gothenburg, twice winners of the UEFA Cup in the 1980s, became virtual ever-presents in the UEFA Champions League.

CHAMPIONS

1896 Orgryte	1941 Helsingborg
1897 Orgryte	1942 IFK Gothenburg
1898 Orgryte	1943 IFK Norrkoping
1899 Orgryte	1944 Malmo FF
1900 AIK Stockholm	1945 IFK Norrkoping
1901 AIK Stockholm	1946 IFK Norrkoping
1902 Orgryte	1947 IFK Norrkoping
1903 Gothenburg IF	1948 IFK Norrkoping
1904 Orgryte	1949 Malmo FF
1905 Orgryte	1950 Malmo FF
1906 Orgryte	1951 Malmo FF
1907 Orgryte	1952 IFK Norrkoping
1908 IFK Gothenburg	1953 Malmo FF
1909 Orgryte	1954 GAIS Goteborg
1910 IFK Gothenburg	1955 Djurgardens
1911 AIK Stockholm	1956 IFK Norrkoping
1912 Djurgardens	1957 IFK Norrkoping
1913 Orgryte	1958 IFK Gothenburg
1914 AIK Stockholm	1959 Djurgardens
1915 Djurgardens	1960 IFK Norrkoping
1916 AIK Stockholm	1961 IF Elfsborg
1917 Djurgardens	1962 IFK Norrkoping
1918 IFK Gothenburg	1963 IFK Norrkoping
1919 GAIS Goteborg	1964 Djurgardens
1920 Djugardens	1965 Malmo FF
1921 IFK Eskilstuna	1966 Djurgardens
1922 GAIS Goteborg	1967 Malmo FF
1923 AIK Stockholm	1968 Osters IF Vaxjo
1924 Fassbergs	1969 IFK Gothenburg
1925 Brynas IF Gavele	1970 Malmo FF
1926 Orgryte	1971 Malmo FF
1927 GAIS Goteborg	1972 Atvidabergs FF
1928 Orgryte	1973 Atvidabergs FF
1929 Helsingborg	1974 Malmo FF
1930 Helsingborg	1975 Malmo FF
1931 GAIS Goteborg	1976 Halmstad BK
1932 AIK Stockholm	1977 Malmo FF
1933 Helsingborg	1978 Osters IF Vaxjo
1934 Helsingborg	1979 Halmstad BK
1935 IFK Gothenburg	1980 Osters IF Vaxjo
1936 IF Elfsborg	1981 Osters IF Vaxjo
1937 AIK Stockholm	1982 IFK Gothenburg
1938 IK Elfsborg	1983 IFK Gothenburg
1939 IF Elfsborg	1984 IFK Gothenburg
1940 IF Elfsborg	1985 Orgryte
	1986 Malmo FF
	1987 IFK Gothenburg
1988 Malmo FF	
1989 IFK Norrkoping	
1990 IFK Gothenburg	
1991 IFK Gothenburg	
1992 AIK Stockholm	
1993 IFK Gothenburg	
1994 IFK Gothenburg	
1995 IFK Gothenburg	
1996 IFK Gothenburg	
1997 Halmstad BK	

CUP WINNERS

1941 Helsingborg	1970 Atvidabergs FF
1942 GAIS Goteborg	1971 Atvidabergs FF
1943 IFK Norrkoping	1972 Landskrona BoIS
1944 Malmo FF	1973 Malmo FF
1945 IFK Norrkoping	1974 Malmo FF
1946 Malmo FF	1975 Malmo FF
1947 Malmo FF	1976 AIK Stockholm
1948 Raa IF Helsingborg	1977 Osters IF Vaxjo
1949 AIK Stockholm	1978 Malmo FF
1950 AIK Stockholm	1979 IFK Gothenburg
1951 Malmo FF	1980 Malmo FF
1952 Not played	1981 Kalmar FF
1953 Malmo FF	1982 IFK Gothenburg
1954–66 Not played	1983 IFK Gothenburg
1967 Malmo FF	1984 Malmo FF
1968 Not played	1985 AIK Stockholm
1969 IFK Norrkoping	1986 Malmo FF
	1987 Kalmar FF
	1988 IFK Norrkoping
	1989 Malmo FF
	1990 Djurgardens
	1991 IFK Norrkoping
	1992 IFK Gothenburg
	1993 Degerfors
	1994 IFK Norrkoping
	1995 Halmstad BK
	1996 AIK Stockholm
	1997 Halmstad BK

Switzerland

Schweizerische Fussball-Verband

Founded: *1895*
Joined FIFA: *1904*

Switzerland were effective secondary pioneers in spreading the football gospel at the start of the 20th century. They took to the game in the 1860s, then helped carry it south to Milan and Genoa as well as south-west where a Swiss émigré, Hans Gamper, founded Spanish giants Barcelona.

Grasshopper, the best known Swiss club on account of their picturesque name, were founded by the English in 1886, and represent the dominant power of the Swiss-German "school" of soccer. Only Servette, from "French" Geneva, have challenged that supremacy with much success. And the "Italian" clubs have achieved next to nothing.

In 1924, Switzerland reached the Olympic Games Final in Paris only to lose 3–0 to the emergent Uruguayans. Their clubs took part sporadically in the Mitropa Cup – the 1930s forerunner of today's European tournaments – and in 1934 and 1938 Switzerland reached the finals of the World Cup in Italy and France.

Switzerland owed much of their success either side of the Second World War to an Austrian, Karl Rappan, a shrewd manager and tactician who devized the "Swiss bolt" defensive

Switzerland's Ciriaco Sforza lets fly against Norway in a World Cup qualifier

system. This was the foundation through which they reached the 1950 World Cup finals then reached the quarter-finals as hosts in 1954. An astonishing 7–5 defeat by Austria ended their dreams of success.

Switzerland fell in the first round of the finals in 1962 and 1966 and then were largely missing from the international top table until Englishman Roy Hodgson took over the national team in the 1990s. Hodgson built a cohesive unit which brought the best out of a bright new generation of players led by midfielder Ciri Sforza and striker Stephane Chapuisat.

Hodgson took Switzerland to the second round of the World Cup finals in 1994 and secured qualification for Euro 96 before his success encouraged an impossible-to-refuse offer from Italian club Internazionale.

Whatever the fluctuations of the national team's form, Switzerland has never been far from the centre of the international action: its status as home to the headquarters of world governing body FIFA (in Zurich) and the European confederation UEFA (in Nyon, near Geneva) has seen to that. The importance attached by the Swiss to their leading role in international sport was underlined early in 1998 when the Sports Ministry publicly urged Sepp Blatter, the Swiss general secretary of FIFA, to run – successfully – for president on the retirement of Joao Havelange.

CHAMPIONS

1898 Grasshopper-Club
1899 Anglo-American
1900 Grasshopper-Club
1901 Grasshopper-Club
1902 FC Zurich
1903 Young Boys
1904 FC St Gallen
1905 Grasshopper-Club
1906 FC Winterhur
1907 Servette
1908 FC Winterhur
1909 Young Boys
1910 Young Boys
1911 Young Boys
1912 FC Aarau
1913 Montriond Lausanne
1914 FC Aarau
1915 Bruhl St Gallen
1916 Cantonal Neuchatel
1917 FC Winterhur
1918 Servette
1919 Et. Chaux-de-Fonds
1920 Young Boys
1921 Grasshopper-Club
1922 Servette
1923 FC Bern
1924 FC Zurich
1925 Servette
1926 Servette
1927 Grasshopper-Club
1928 Grasshopper-Club
1929 Young Boys
1930 Servette
1931 Grasshopper-Club
1932 Lausanne-Sports
1933 Servette
1934 Servette
1935 Lausanne-Sports
1936 Lausanne-Sports
1937 Grasshopper-Club
1938 FC Lugano
1939 Grasshopper-Club
1940 Servette
1941 FC Lugano
1942 Grasshopper-Club
1943 Grasshopper-Club
1944 Lausanne-Sports
1945 Grasshopper-Club
1946 Servette
1947 FC Biel
1948 AC Bellinzona
1949 FC Lugano
1950 Servette
1951 Lausanne-Sports
1952 Grasshopper-Club
1953 FC Basel
1954 La Chaux-de-Fonds
1955 La Chaux-de-Fonds
1956 Grasshopper-Club
1957 Young Boys
1958 Young Boys

1959 Young Boys	1941 Grasshopper-Club
1960 Young Boys	1942 Grasshopper-Club
1961 Servette	1943 Grasshopper-Club
1962 Servette	1944 Lausanne-Sports
1963 FC Zurich	1945 Young Boys
1964 La Chaux-de-Fonds	1946 Grasshopper-Club
1965 Lausanne-Sports	1947 FC Basel
1966 FC Zurich	1948 La Chaux-de-Fonds
1967 FC Basel	1949 Servette
1968 FC Zurich	1950 Lausanne-Sports
1969 FC Basel	1951 La Chaux-de-Fonds
1970 FC Basel	1952 Grasshopper-Club
1971 Grashopper-Club	1953 Young Boys
1972 FC Basel	1954 La Chaux-de-Fonds
1973 FC Basel	1955 La Chaux-de-Fonds
1974 FC Zurich	1956 Grasshopper-Club
1975 FC Zurich	1957 La Chaux-de-Fonds
1976 FC Zurich	1958 Young Boys
1977 FC Basel	1959 FC Grendchen
1978 Grasshopper-Club	1960 FC Luzern
1979 Servette	1961 La Chaux-de-Fonds
1980 FC Basel	1962 Lausanne-Sports
1981 FC Zurich	1963 FC Basel
1982 Grasshopper-Club	1964 Lausanne-Sports
1983 Grasshopper-Club	1965 FC Sion
1984 Grasshopper-Club	1966 FC Zurich
1985 Servette	1967 FC Basel
1986 Young Boys	1968 FC Lugano
1987 Neuchatel Xamax	1969 FC St Gallen
1988 Neuchatel Xamax	1970 FC Zurich
1989 FC Luzern	1971 Servette
1990 Grasshopper-Club	1972 FC Zurich
1991 Grasshopper-Club	1973 FC Zurich
1992 FC Sion	1974 FC Sion
1993 FC Aarau	1975 FC Basel
1994 Servette	1976 FC Zurich
1995 Grasshopper-Club	1977 Young Boys
1996 Grasshopper-Club	1978 Servette
1997 Sion	1979 Servette
1998 Grasshopper-Club	1980 FC Sion
	1981 Lausanne-Sports

CUP WINNERS

1926 Grasshopper-Club	1982 FC Sion
1927 Grasshopper-Club	1983 Grasshopper-Club
1928 Servette	1984 Servette
1929 Urania Geneve	1985 FC Aarau
1930 Young Boys	1986 FC Sion
1931 FC Lugano	1987 Young Boys
1932 Grasshopper-Club	1988 Grasshopper-Club
1933 FC Basel	1989 Grasshopper-Club
1934 Grasshopper-Club	1990 Grasshopper-Club
1935 Lausanne-Sports	1991 FC Sion
1936 Young Fellows Zurich	1992 FC Luzern
1937 Grasshopper-Club	1993 FC Lugano
1938 Grasshopper-Club	1994 Grasshopper-Club
1939 Lausanne-Sports	1995 FC Sion
1940 Grasshopper-Club	1996 FC Sion
	1997 FC Sion
	1998 Lausanne

Turkey

Turkiye Futbol Federasyonu

Founded: *1923*

Joined FIFA: *1923*

Turkish football has improved by leaps and bounds in the 1990s. The point was made emphatically, at club level, when Galatasaray once eliminated Manchester United from the European Champions Cup and then again when the national team reached the finals of the 1996 European Championship.

They were eliminated in the first round but they did not disgrace themselves against Portugal, Denmark and Croatia. Anyway, as coach Fatih Terim, insisted: "What is important is getting to the finals. This will do wonders for our players' confidence."

Football was first played, in secret, in the early years of the century, when such westernized team sports were considered undesirable. But the climate of opinion changed rapidly and the early years of the century saw the creation of the three Istanbul clubs which still dominate Turkish football today: Galatasaray, Besiktas and Fenerbahce.

A "proper" national championship had to wait until 1960, and it was not long before foreign coaches and then players were hired in droves to help improve domestic standards. One such pioneer was George Dick, a Scottish inside forward who played for five English clubs in the 1940s and early 1950s. British successors, with varying degrees of success, included Brian Birch, Don Howe, Malcolm Allison and Gordon Milne. Later the Turks turned to Germany and imported the likes of Sepp Piontek and Jupp Derwall.

Turkey have reached the World Cup finals on one occasion so far. That was in 1954, when they reached the finals after a play-off against Spain in Rome ended all-square and a blind boy, drawing lots, pulled their name out of the hat.

Two years later, Turkey made headlines again, this time beating the Hungary of Ferenc Puskas, 3–1 in Istanbul. It was only the Hungarians' second defeat in five years and 49 matches. Turkey's stars were goalkeeper Turgay and two-goal winger Kucukandonyadis Lefter. They remained the two most famous Turkish footballers until the recent goal-scoring exploits of Hakan Sukur provided fans with a modern-day hero.

CHAMPIONS

1924 Besiktas	1933 Fenerbahce
1925 Galatasaray	1934 Besiktas
1926 Galatasaray	1935 Fenerbahce
1927 Galatasaray	1936 Fenerbahce
1928 Not played	1937 Fenerbahce
1929 Galatasaray	1938 Gunes
1930 Fenerbahce	1939 Besiktas
1931 Galatasaray	1940 Besiktas
1932 Istanbulsor	1941 Besiktas
	1942 Besiktas
	1943 Besiktas

1944 Fenerbahce	1966 Besiktas	1988 Galatasaray	1971 Eskisehispor
1945 Besiktas	1967 Besiktas	1989 Fenerbahce	1972 MKE Ankaragucu
1946 Besiktas	1968 Fenerbahce	1990 Besiktas	1973 Galatasaray
1947 Fenerbahce	1969 Galatasaray	1991 Besiktas	1974 Fenerbahce
1948 Fenerbahce	1970 Fenerbahce	1992 Besiktas	1975 Besiktas
1949 Galatasaray	1971 Galatasaray	1993 Galatasaray	1976 Galatasaray
1950 Besiktas	1972 Galatasaray	1994 Galatasaray	1977 Trabzonspor
1951 Besiktas	1973 Galatasaray	1995 Besiktas	1978 Trabzonspor
1952 Besiktas	1974 Fenerbahce	1996 Fenerbahce	1979 Fenerbahce
1953 Fenerbahce	1975 Fenerbahce	1997 Galatasaray	1980 Altay Izmir
1954 Besiktas	1976 Trabzonspor	1998 Galatasaray	1981 MKE Ankaraguci
1955 Galatasaray	1977 Trabzonspor		1982 Galatasaray
1956 Galatasaray	1978 Fenerbahce	**CUP WINNERS**	1983 Fenerbahce
1957 Galatasaray	1979 Trabzonspor	1963 Galatasaray	1984 Trabzonspor
1958 Galatasaray	1980 Trabzonspor	1964 Galatasaray	1985 Galatasaray
1959 Fenerbahce	1981 Trabzonspor	1965 Galatasaray	1986 Bursaspor
1960 Besiktas	1982 Besiktas	1966 Galatasaray	1987 Genclerbirligi
1961 Fenerbahce	1983 Fenerbahce	1967 Altay Izmir	1988 Sakaryaspor
1962 Galatasaray	1984 Trabzonspor	1968 Fenerbahce	1989 Besiktas
1963 Galatasaray	1985 Fenerbahce	1969 Goztepe Izmir	1990 Besiktas
1964 Fenerbahce	1986 Besiktas	1970 Goztepe Izmir	1991 Galatasaray
1965 Fenerbahce	1987 Galatasaray		1992 Trazonspor

Turkey's Sergen Yalcin is challenged by Robert Prosinecki of Croatia

1993 Galatasaray
1994 Besiktas
1995 Trabzonspor
1996 Galatasaray

1997 Trabzonspor
1998 Besiktas

Ukraine

Federatsija Futbola Ucrainy
Founded: *1991*
Joined FIFA: *1992*

Kiev Dynamo had been one of Europe's top clubs, yet Ukraine's international competitive debut after the Soviet collapse was disappointing. They offered little threat to Croatia and Italy in the Euro 96 qualifying tournament.

Mafia attempts to infiltrate the domestic game did not help, nor did Kiev's expulsion from European competition for trying to bribe Spanish referee Antonio Lopez Nieto before a Champions League tie. Indeed, Ukraine football was in such a parlous state that UEFA later quashed Kiev's three-year suspension on what might be termed "compassionate grounds."

CHAMPIONS	CUP WINNERS
1992 Tavria Simferopol	1992 Chernomorets Odessa
1993 Kiev Dynamo	1993 Kiev Dynamo
1994 Kiev Dynamo	1994 Chernomorets Odessa
1995 Kiev Dynamo	1995 Shachter Donetsk
1996 Kiev Dynamo	1996 Kiev Dynamo
1997 Kiev Dynamo	1997 Schachter Donetsk
1998 Keiv Dynamo	1998 CSCA Kiev

Wales

Football Association of Wales
Founded: *1876*
Joined FIFA: *1910*

Nowadays Wales appear very much as the poor relations of British football. The national team have qualified for the World Cup finals only once and it is nearly 40 years since Cardiff City appeared in the top division.

The sporting image of Wales remains more strongly identified with rugby union even though the National Stadium is used internationally now by both football codes. Certainly, the image of Welsh domestic football was not helped by the wrangling over the creation of a national league championship.

Cardiff stayed in the English league system but remain the most famous Welsh club – though their greatest years were the 1920s. They missed out once on a League Championship only on goal average (the division of home goals by away goals) and then became the only club ever to take the FA Cup out of England

thanks to a famous Wembley victory over favourites Arsenal.

The country's only World Cup finals appearance was in 1958, after they won a lucky losers' play-off against Israel to reach Sweden. Their outstanding players of the time included Arsenal goalkeeper Jack Kelsey, Ivor and Len Allchurch in attack and the great John Charles – at the height of his "Gentle Giant" powers with Italy's Juventus. Wales reached the quarter-finals before losing only 1–0 to Brazil, for whom the 17-year-old Pele scored the decisive goal.

CHAMPIONS

1993 Cwmbran Town	
1994 Bangor City	
1995 Bangor City	
1996 Barry Town	
1997 Barry Town	
1998 Barry Town	

CUP WINNERS

1878 Wrexham	1924 Wrexham
1879 Newtown	1925 Wrexham
1880 Druids	1926 Ebbw Vale
1881 Druids	1927 Cardiff City
1882 Druids	1928 Cardiff City
1883 Wrexham	1929 Connah's Quay
1884 Oswestry	1930 Cardiff City
1885 Druids	1931 Wrexham
1886 Druids	1932 Swansea Town
1887 Chirk	1933 Chester City
1888 Chirk	1934 Bristol City
1889 Bangor City	1935 Tranmere Rovers
1890 Chirk	1936 Crewe Alexandra
1891 Shrewsbury Town	1937 Crewe Alexandra
1892 Chirk	1938 Shrewsbury Town
1893 Wrexham	1939 South Liverpool
1894 Chirk	1940–46 Not played
1895 Newtown	1947 Chester City
1896 Bangor City	1948 Lovell's Athletic
1897 Wrexham	1949 Methyr Tydfil
1898 Druids	1950 Swansea Town
1899 Druids	1951 Methyr Tydfil
1900 Aberystwyth Town	1952 Rhyl
1901 Oswestry	1953 Rhyl
1902 Wellington	1954 Flint
1903 Wrexham	1955 Barry Town
1904 Druids	1956 Cardiff City
1905 Wrexham	1957 Wrexham
1906 Wellington	1958 Wrexham
1907 Oswestry	1959 Cardiff City
1908 Chester City	1960 Wrexham
1909 Wrexham	1961 Swansea Town
1910 Wrexham	1962 Bangor City
1911 Wrexham	1963 Borough United
1912 Cardiff City	1964 Cardiff City
1913 Swansea Town	1965 Cardiff City
1914 Wrexham	1966 Swansea Town
1915 Wrexham	1967 Cardiff City
1916–19 Not played	1968 Cardiff City
1920 Cardiff City	1969 Cardiff City
1921 Wrexham	1970 Cardiff City
1922 Cardiff City	1971 Cardiff City
1923 Cardiff City	1972 Wrexham
	1973 Cardiff City
	1974 Cardiff City
	1975 Wrexham
	1976 Cardiff City
	1977 Shrewsbury Town
	1978 Wrexham
	1979 Shrewsbury Town
	1980 Newport County
	1981 Swansea City
	1982 Swansea City

1983 Swansea City
1984 Shrewsbury Town
1985 Shrewsbury Town
1986 Wrexham
1987 Methyr Tydfil
1988 Cardiff City
1989 Swansea City
1990 Hereford United
1991 Swansea City
1992 Cardiff City
1993 Cardiff City
1994 Barry Town
1995 Wrexham

1996 Llansantffraid
1997 Barry Town
1998 Bangor City

LEAGUE CUP WINNERS

1993 Caersws
1994 Afan Lido
1995 Llansanttfraid
1996 Connah's Quay
1997 Barry Town
1998 Barry Town

Yugoslavia

Fudbalski Savez Jugoslavije
Founded: *1919*
Joined FIFA: *1919*

Yugoslavia's appearance at the finals of the 1998 World Cup, in which they reached the second round, sealed their return to the international scene after a four-year "freeze" imposed in the early 1990s because of security concerns following the outbreak of the civil war which led to independence for Slovenia, Macedonia, Croatia and Bosnia-Herzegovina. What was left for the new Yugoslavia were the republics of Serbia (capital Belgrade) and Montenegro.

The war increased the flight of players and coaches to western Europe from a region which had always been Europe's leader in the talent export business. That image was first fostered back in 1930, when Yugoslavia were one of only four European nations to brave the Atlantic sea crossing and attend the first World Cup finals in Uruguay. Exports then included inside forward Ivan Beck, who played for Sete in France. He scored one goal in a 2–1 defeat of Brazil which put Yugoslavia in the semi-finals. Other key players were forwards Alexander Tirnanic and Barne Sekulic – both later national managers.

Yugoslavia returned to the World Cup finals in 1950 with a squad full of future managerial talent, including Ivica Horvat, Zlatko Cajkowski, Bernard Vukas, Stjepan Bobek and Rajko Mitic. Luck was against them. Before the match against Brazil Mitic cut his head on a steel rail in the players' tunnel. By the time he had been bandaged up and joined the game, the Slavs were already a goal down. Beaten in the quarter-finals by West Germany in both 1954 and 1958, they achieved their best finish in 1962, when they finished fourth in Chile.

In the European Championship, Yugoslavia were runners-up in 1960 and 1968 and top club Red Star Belgrade won both the UEFA Cup and then the Champions Cup before the eruption of fighting in the early 1990s. Yugoslavia had been among the favourites to win the 1992 European Championship in Sweden, but security concerns caused to their expulsion.

CHAMPIONS

1923 Gradanski Zagreb
1924 Jugoslavia Belgrade
1925 Jugoslavia Belgrade
1926 Gradanski Zagreb
1927 Hajduk Split
1928 Gradanski Zagreb
1929 Hajduk Split
1930 Concordia Zagreb
1931 BSK Belgrade
1932 Concordia Zagreb
1933 BSK Belgrade
1934 Not played
1935 BSK Belgrade
1936 BSK Belgrade
1937 Gradanski Zagreb
1938 HASK Zagreb
1939 BSK Belgrade
1940 Gradanski Zagreb
1941–46 Not played
1947 Partizan Belgrade
1948 Dinamo Zagreb
1949 Partizan Belgrade
1950 Hajduk Split
1951 Crvena Zvezda
1952 Hajduk Split
1953 Red Star (Crvena Zvezda)
1954 Dinamo Zagreb
1955 Hajduk Split
1956 Red Star (Crvena Zvezda)
1957 Red Star (Crvena Zvezda)
1958 Dinamo Zagreb
1959 Red Star (Crvena Zvezda)
1960 Red Star (Crvena Zvezda)
1961 Partizan Belgrade
1962 Partizan Belgrade
1963 Partizan Belgrade
1964 Red Star (Crvena Zvezda)
1965 Partizan Belgrade
1966 Vojvodina Novi Sad
1967 FK Sarajevo
1968 Red Star (Crvena Zvezda)
1969 Red Star (Crvena Zvezda)
1970 Red Star (Crvena Zvezda)
1971 Hajduk Split
1972 Zeljeznicar Sarajevo
1973 Red Star (Crvena Zvezda)
1974 Hajduk Split
1975 Hajduk Split
1976 Partizan Belgrade
1977 Red Star (Crvena Zvezda)
1978 Partizan Belgrade
1979 Hajduk Split
1980 Crvena Split
1981 Crvena Split
1982 Dinamo Zagreb
1983 Partizan Belgrade
1984 Red Star (Crvena Zvezda)
1985 FK Sarajevo
1986 Partizan Belgrade
1987 Partizan Belgrade
1988 Red Star (Crvena Zvezda)
1989 Vojvodina Novi Sad

1990 Red Star (Crvena Zvezda)
1991 Red Star (Crvena Zvezda)
1992 Red Star (Crvena Zvezda)
1993 Partizan Belgrade
1994 Partizan Belgrade
1995 Red Star (Crvena Zvezda)
1996 Partizan Belgrade
1997 Partizan Belgrade
1998 Obilic Belgrade

CUP WINNERS

1947 Partizan Belgrade
1948 Red Star (Crvena Zvezda)
1949 Red Star (Crvena Zvezda)
1950 Red Star (Crvena Zvezda)
1951 Dinamo Zagreb
1952 Partizan Belgrade
1953 BSK Belgrade
1954 Partizan Belgrade
1955 BSK Belgrade
1956 Not played
1957 Partizan Belgrade
1958 Red Star (Crvena Zvezda)
1959 Red Star (Crevena Zvezda)
1960 Dinamo Zagreb
1961 Varda Skopje
1962 OFK Belgrade
1963 Dinamo Zagreb
1964 Red Star (Crvena Zvezda)
1965 Dinamo Zagreb
1966 OFK Belgrade
1967 Hajduk Split
1968 Red Star (Crvena Zvezda)
1969 Dinama Zagreb
1970 Red Star (Crvena Zvezda)
1971 Red Star (Crvena Zvezda)
1972 Hajduk Split
1973 Dinamo Zagreb
1974 Hajduk Split
1975 Hajduk Split
1976 Hajduk Split
1977 Hajduk Split
1978 NK Rijeka
1979 NK Rijeka
1980 Dinamo Zagreb
1981 Velez Mostar
1982 Red Star (Crvena Zvezda)
1983 Dinamo Zagreb
1984 Hajduk Split
1985 Red Star (Crvena Zvezda)
1986 Velez Mostar
1987 Hajduk Split
1988 Borac Banja Luka
1989 Partizan Belgrade
1990 Red Star (Crvena Zvezda)
1991 Hajduk Split
1992 Partizan Belgrade
1993 Red Star (Crvena Zvezda)
1994 Partizan Belgrade
1995 Red Star (Crvena Zvezda)
1996 Red Star (Crvena Zvezda)
1997 Vojvodina
1998 Partizan Belgrade

SOUTH AMERICA (CONMEBOL)

Argentina

Asociacion del Futbol Argentino
Founded: 1893
Joined FIFA: 1912

Of all South American nations, Argentina may claim to have been the most consistently successful across all the international competitive strata.

Football was brought to Argentina by the British in the 1860s, and although, at first, it was exclusive to the British residents in Buenos Aires, by the turn of the century numerous clubs had been formed.

The Argentine Football Association was founded in 1891 by an Englishman, Alexander Hutton, and a league was formed the same year. Although the championship was not a truly national competition – it contained only clubs from Buenos Aires, La Plata, Rosario and Santa Fé – the intense rivalry of the clubs in Buenos Aires ensured that Argentina had a vibrant domestic scene from the outset.

The national side also made an early start, and in 1901 a representative side played neighbouring Uruguay, in the first international match to be staged outside Great Britain. The seeds were sown for a rivalry which has grown into one of the most enduring and intense derby matches in the world.

Professionalism was adopted in 1931, and River Plate and Boca Juniors soon emerged as dominant forces in the new pro league. River's side of the 1940s was the greatest of them all, containing a forward line of Munoz, Moreno, Pedernera, Labruna and Loustau which became known as "La Maquina" – "The Machine."

The national side were runners-up, to Uruguay, in the 1928 Olympics and met their deadly rivals again two years later in the 1930 World Cup Final. Although they lost 4–2, the impressive Argentine side was plundered by Italian agents – starting a draining process which continues today. To avoid a repeat of this poaching, a third-rate side went to the 1934 tournament, and Argentina did not make a serious attempt on the World Cup again until the 1950s.

Indeed, the 1950s saw the birth of an exceptional side, with another famous forward line of Corbatta, Maschio, Angelillo, Sivori and Cruz. They won the South American Championship twice during the 1950s and then made an unsuccessful bid to host the 1958 World Cup. Little progress was made in the 1960s and 1970s, despite Independiente and Estudiantes dominating the Copa Libertadores, and Argentina had to wait until 1978 for her first success in the World Cup.

On home soil, and with a side containing only one overseas-based player, Mario Kempes, Argentina deservedly won the tournament. They did so again in Mexico in 1986, when the side was led by Diego Maradona – who ranks as one of the greatest players the world has ever seen. In fact, Argentina featured in the final of three of the four World Cups from 1978 to 1990, they won the first two South American Championships of the 1990s, and they continue to produce extremely gifted footballers. The captain of the 1978 World Cup winning team, Daniel Passarella, became national coach in 1995 and took them to the 1998 World Cup finals, where they reached the last eight.

Argentina's Diego Maradona takes on Belgium

CHAMPIONS

Amateur League
1891 Saint Andrews
1892 Not played

1893 Lomas Athletic
1894 Loman Athletic
1895 Lomas Athletic
1896 Lomas Academy
1897 Lomas Athletic
1898 Lomas Athletic

1899 Belgrano Athletic	1959 San Lorenzo	
1900 English High School	1960 Independiente	
1901 Alumni	1961 Racing Club	
1902 Alumni	1962 Boca Juniors	
1903 Alumni	1963 Independiente	
1904 Belgrano Athletic	1964 Boca Juniors	
1905 Alumni	1965 Boca Juniors	
1906 Alumni	1966 Racing Club	
1907 Alumni	1967 Estudiantes	
1908 Belgrano Athletic	1968 San Lorenzo	
1909 Alumni	1969 Chacarita Juniors	
1910 Alumni	1970 Independiente	
1911 Quilmes	1971 Independiente	
1912 CA Porteno	1972 San Lorenzo	
1913 Racing Club	1973 Huracan	
1914 CA Porteno	1974 Newell's Old Boys	
1915 Racing Club	1975 River Plate	
1916 Racing Club	1976 Boca Juniors	
1917 Racing Club	1977 River Plate	
1918 Racing Club	1978 Quilmes	
1919 Boca Juniors	1979 River Plate	
1920 River Plate	1980 River Plate	
1921 Huracan	1981 Boca Juniors	
1922 Independiente	1982 Estudiantes	
1923 Boca Juniors	1983 Independiente	
1924 San Lorenzo	1984 Argentinos Juniors	
1925 Huracan	1985 Not played	
1926 Boca Juniors	1986 River Plate	
1927 San Lorenzo	1987 Rosario Central	
1928 Huracan	1988 Newell's Old Boys	
1929 Gimnasia	1989 Independiente	
1930 Boca Juniors	1990 River Plate	
1931 Estudiantil Porteno	1991 Newell's Old Boys	
1932 Sportivo Barracas	1992 River Plate	
1933 Sportivo Dock Sud	1993 Boca Juniors	
1934 Estudiantil Porteno	1994 River Plate	
	1994 Independiente	
	1995 Clausura: River Plate	

Professional League

1931 Boca Juniors	*Apertura: San Lorenzo*
1932 River Plate	1996 Clausura: Velez Sarsfield
1933 San Lorenzo	Apertura: River Plate
1934 Boca Juniors	1997 Clausura: River Plate
1935 Boca Juniors	Apertura: River Plate
1936 River Plate	1998 Clausura: Velez Sarsfield
1937 River Plate	
1938 Independiente	*National Championship*
1939 Independiente	1967 Independiente
1940 Boca Juniors	1968 Velez Sarsfield
1941 River Plate	1969 Boca Juniors
1942 River Plate	1970 Boca Juniors
1943 Boca Juniors	1971 Rosario Central
1944 Boca Juniors	1972 San Lorenzo
1945 River Plate	1973 Rosario Central
1946 San Lorenzo	1974 San Lorenzo
1947 River Plate	1975 River Plate
1948 Independiente	1976 Boca Juniors
1949 Racing Club	1977 Independiente
1950 Racing Club	1978 Independiente
1951 Racing Club	1979 River Plate
1952 Racing Club	1980 Rosario Central
1953 Racing Club	1981 River Plate
1954 Boca Juniors	1982 Ferrocarril Oeste
1955 River Plate	1983 Estudiantes
1956 River Plate	1984 Ferrocarril Oeste
1957 River Plate	1985 Argentinos Juniors
1958 Racing Club	

Bolivia

Federacion Boliviana de Futbol

Founded: *1925*

Joined FIFA: *1926*

Since their first international outing in 1926, Bolivia had been the perennial whipping boys of South American football – until recent years. In the 1994 World Cup qualifiers they finished a close second in Group B to qualify for the finals for the first time in forty years, recording a notable 2–0 victory over Brazil along the way and knocking out Uruguay and Ecuador in the process. In 1997 they not only hosted the Copa America but reached the final before losing to Brazil. Prior to that, apart from World Cup qualification in 1930 and 1950, the 1963 South American Championship victory, played at home, was the only success of note.

CHAMPIONS

La Paz League	1959 Jorge Wilsterman
1914 The Strongest	1960 Jorge Wilsterman
1915 Colegio Militar	1961 Deportivo Municipal
1916 The Strongest	1962 Not played
1917 The Strongest	1963 Aurora
1918–21 Not played	1964 The Strongest
1922 The Strongest	1965 Deportivo Municipal
1923 The Strongest	1966 Bolivar
1924 The Strongest	1967 Jorge Wilsterman
1925 The Strongest	1968 Bolivar
1926 Not played	1969 Universitario La Paz
1927 Nimbles Sport	1970 Chaco Petrolero
1928 Deportivo Militar	1971 Oriente Petrolero
1929 Universitario La Paz	1972 Jorge Wilsterman
1930 The Strongest	1973 Jorge Wilsterman
1931 Nibles Rail	1974 The Strongest
1932 Bolivar	1975 Guabira
1933–34 Not played	1976 Bolivar
1935 The Strongest	
1936 Ayacucho	*Liga Professional*
1937 Bolivar	1977 The Strongest
1938 The Strongest	1978 Bolivar
1939 Bolivar	1979 Oriente Petrolero
1940 Bolivar	1980 Jorge Wilsterman
1941 Bolivar	1981 Jorge Wilsterman
1942 Bolivar	1982 Bolivar
1943 The Strongest	1983 Bolivar
1944 Ferroviario	1984 Blooming
1945–49 Not played	1985 Bolivar
1950 Bolivar	1986 The Strongest
1951 Always Ready	1987 Bolivar
1952 The Strongest	1988 Bolivar
1953 Bolivar	1989 The Strongest
	1990 Oriente Petrolero
Torneo Integrada (La Paz, Cochabamba and Oruro)	1991 Bolivar
	1992 Bolivar
1954 Litoral	1993 The Strongest
1955 San Jose Oruno	1994 Bolivar
1956 Bolivar	1995 San Jose Oruro
1957 Always Ready	1996 Bolivar
	1997 Bolivar
Torneo Nacional	
1958 Jorge Wilsterman	

Brazil's 1970 World Cup side – viewed by many as the greatest football team of all time

Brazil

Confederacao Brasileira de Futebol
Founded: *1914*
Joined FIFA: *1923*

Brazilian football has a romantic air about it that sets it apart from other nations. Between 1958 and 1970 they won the World Cup three times with a team packed full of star players, including arguably the greatest in history – Pele. Brazil remains the only country to have played in every World Cup finals tournament and the only four-time winner.

Brazilian football developed at the end of the 19th century, prompted by migrant British workers, and leagues were established in Rio de Janeiro and Sao Paulo by the turn of the century. The vast size of Brazil meant that a national league was impractical and until the 1970s these leagues dominated domestic football. The "classic" Rio derbies between Flamengo, Fluminense, Botafogo and Vasco da Gama regularly attracted massive crowds to the 200,000-capacity Maracana Stadium.

The national team were a little slower out of the blocks, and their first real international was not played until 1914 with a visit to Buenos Aires. In 1916 Brazil entered the South American Championship, but this event has not been a rewarding one for the Brazilians, who have won it only four times – three of them on home soil.

The World Cup, however, is another matter. The first attempt on the trophy was made in 1930, when they went out in the first round. The 1934 campaign was equally bad, despite the presence of such fine players as Leonidas da Silva and Artur Friedenreich. In 1938, however, they showed the first signs of what was to come by reaching the semi-finals, where they lost to Italy.

The golden age of Brazilian football was between 1950 and 1970, and it is the sides of this era that stick in the memory. In 1950 they were runners-up as Uruguay pipped them for the title in the deciding match. In 1954, with Nilton and Djalma Santos established at the back and Didi running the midfield, they reached the quarter-finals in Switzerland, where they lost to Hungary's "Magical Magyars."

In 1958 Brazil finally won the honour the nation craved. With a forward line consisting of Garrincha, Vava, Zagalo and the 17-year-old Pele, they stormed to victory in Sweden, beating the hosts 5–2 in the Final. In Chile in 1962, an almost identical team – minus the injured Pele – triumphed again, beating Czechoslovakia 3–1 in the Final in Santiago.

In 1966, in England, the side was being rebuilt and Brazil fell in the first round. But the newcomers Tostao, Gerson and Jairzinho were present in Mexico four years later when Brazil clinched a hat-trick of World Cups, earning them the right to keep the Jules Rimet Trophy in perpetuity.

The 1970 side has been described as the best ever seen, and with some justification. The defence, marshalled by Carlos Alberto, was not all that strong, but this did not matter as the Brazilian approach at this time was all-out attack. This was football with a flourish and the global TV audience loved it. In attack, Pele was back to his best and he was superbly assisted by Jairzinho, Rivelinho and Tostao.

After 1970, it was 24 years before the national side again scaled such heights by winning the 1994 World Cup – albeit thanks to a penalty shoot-out. Their best showing along the way was in the 1982 World Cup, when a side containing Zico, Socrates, Junior and Falcao should have gone further than the second round in Spain, where they lost to the eventual winners Italy.

At club level, Brazilian football is in a poor state, with too many meaningless competitions and games against mismatched opponents and continual rows between the various regional governing bodies. Brazil, having won the 1994 World Cup on a penalty shoot-out, then lost to Uruguay in the 1995 Copa America Final by the same method.

The legacy of the Pele years continues to weigh heavily. Any Brazil side, regardless of its capabilities, is expected to play what Pele himself called "the beautiful game." The pressure certainly got to world player of the year Ronaldo when they reached the 1998 World Cup Final against hosts France. The youngster was controversially chosen to play despite suffering a convulsive fit on the morning of the match and did himself no justice as the Brazilians were crushed 3–0.

CHAMPIONS

Sao Paulo Tournament

1937 Atletico Mineiro
1950 Corinthians
1951 Palmeiras
1952 Portuguesa
1953 Corinthians
1954 Corinthians
1955 Portuguesa
1956 Not played
1957 Fluminense
1958 Vasco Da Gama
1959 Santos
1960 Fluminense
1961 Flamengo
1962 Botafogo
1963 Santos
1964 Santos
1965 Palmeiras
1966 Corinthians

Roberto Gomez Pedrosa Tournament

1967 Palmeiras
1968 Santos
1969 Palmeiras
1970 Fluminense

Brazilian National Championship

1971 Atletico Mineiro
1972 Palmeiras
1973 Palmeiras
1974 Vasco Da Gama
1975 Internacional PA
1976 Internacional PA
1977 Sao Paulo
1978 Guarani Campinas
1979 Internacional PA
1980 Flamengo
1981 Gremio
1982 Flamengo
1983 Flamengo
1984 Fluminense
1985 Coritiba FC
1986 Sao Paulo
1987 Flamengo
1988 EC Bahia
1989 Vasco da Gama
1990 Corinthians
1991 Sao Paulo
1992 Flamengo
1993 Palmeiras
1994 Palmeiras
1995 Botafogo
1996 Gremio
1997 Vasco da Gama

CUP WINNERS

1959 Bahia
1960 Palmeiras
1961 Santos
1962 Santos
1963 Santos
1964 Santos
1965 Santos
1966 Cruzeiro
1967 Palmeiras
1968 Not played
1969 Botafogo
1970–88 Not played
1989 Gremio
1990 Flamengo
1991 Criciuma
1992 Internacional PA
1993 Cruzeiro
1994 Gremio
1995 Corinthians
1996 Cruzeiro
1997 Gremio
1998 Palmeiras

Rio De Janeiro State Championship

1906 Fluminense
1907 Fluminense/Botafogo
1908 Fluminense
1909 Fluminense
1910 Botafogo
1911 Fluminense
1912 Paissandu
1913 America FC
1914 Flamengo
1915 Flamengo
1916 America FC
1917 Fluminense
1918 Fluminense
1919 Fluminense
1920 Flamengo
1921 Flamengo
1922 America FC
1923 Vasco da Gama
1924 Vasco da Gama
1925 Flamengo
1926 Sao Cristovao
1927 Flamengo
1928 America FC
1929 Vasco da Gama
1930 Botafogo
1931 America FC
1932 Botafogo
1933 Bangu
1934 Vasco da Gama
1935 America FC
1936 Fluminense
1937 Fluminense
1938 Fluminense
1939 Flamengo
1940 Fluminense
1941 Fluminense
1942 Flamengo
1943 Flamengo
1944 Flamengo
1945 Vasco da Gama
1946 Fluminense
1947 Vasco da Gama
1948 Botafogo
1949 Vasco da Gama
1950 Vasco da Gama
1951 Fluminense
1952 Flamengo
1953 Flamengo
1954 Flamengo
1955 Flamengo
1956 Vasco da Gama
1957 Botafogo
1958 Vasco da Gama
1959 Fluminense
1960 America FC
1961 Botafogo
1962 Botafogo
1963 Flamengo
1964 Fluminense
1965 Flamengo
1966 Bangu
1967 Botafogo
1968 Botafogo
1969 Fluminense
1970 Vasco da Gama
1971 Fluminense
1972 Flamengo
1973 Fluminense
1974 Flamengo
1975 Fluminense
1976 Fluminense
1977 Fluminense
1978 Flamengo
1979 Flamengo
1980 Fluminense
1981 Flamengo
1982 Vasco da Gama
1983 Fluminense
1984 Fluminense
1985 Fluminense
1986 Flamengo
1987 Vasco da Gama
1988 Vasco da Gama
1989 Botafogo
1990 Botafogo
1991 Flamengo
1992 Vasco da Gama
1993 Vasco da Gama
1994 Vasco da Gama
1995 Fluminense
1996 Flamengo

Sao Paulo State Championship

1902 Sao Paulo Athletic
1903 Sao Paulo Athletic
1904 Sao Paulo Athletic
1905 Paulistano
1906 Germania

1907 Internacional Sao Paulo	1952 Corinthians
1908 Paulistano	1953 Sao Paulo
1909 AA das Palmeiras	1954 Corinthians
1910 AA das Palmeiras	1955 Santos
1911 Sao Paulo Athletic	1956 Santos
1912 Americano	1957 Sao Paulo
1913 Americano	1958 Santos
1914 Corinthians	1959 Palmeiras
1915 Germania	1960 Santos
1916 Corinthians	1961 Santos
1917 Paulistano	1962 Santos
1918 Paulistano	1963 Palmeiras
1919 Paulistano	1964 Santos
1920 Palestra Italia	1965 Santos
1921 Paulistano	1966 Palmeiras
1922 Corinthians	1967 Santos
1923 Corinthians	1968 Santos
1924 Corinthians	1969 Santos
1925 Sao Bento	1970 Sao Paulo
1926 Palestra Italia	1971 Sao Paulo
1927 Palestra Italia	1972 Palmeiras
1928 Corinthians	1973 Santos
1929 Corinthians	1974 Palmeiras
1930 Corinthians	1975 Sao Paulo
1931 Sao Paulo	1976 Palmeiras
1932 Palestra Italia	1977 Corinthians
1933 Palestra Italia	1978 Santos
1934 Palestra Italia	1979 Corinthians
1935 Santos	1980 Sao Paulo
1936 Palestra Italia	1981 Sao Paulo
1937 Corinthians	1982 Corinthians
1938 Corinthians	1983 Corinthians
1939 Corinthians	1984 Santos
1940 Palestra Italia	1985 Sao Paulo
1941 Corinthians	1986 Internacional Limeira
1942 Palmeiras	1987 Sao Paulo
1943 Sao Paulo	1988 Corinthians
1944 Palmeiras	1989 Sao Paulo
1945 Sao Paulo	1990 Bragantino
1946 Sao Paulo	1991 Sao Paulo
1947 Palmeiras	1992 Sao Paulo
1948 Sao Paulo	1993 Palmeiras
1949 Sao Paulo	1994 Palmeiras
1950 Palmeiras	1995 Palmeiras
1951 Corinthians	1996 Corinthians

Chile

Federacion de Futbol de Chile
Founded: *1895*
Joined FIFA: *1912*

Until Colo Colo's Copa Libertadores triumph in 1991, no Chilean side had ever won a major honour, and Chile have often been seen as the "nearly men" of South American football.

Chile qualified for six of the 12 post-war World Cups, but have only twice progressed beyond the first round, in 1962, when they reached the semi-finals on home soil, and 1998 when they lost to Brazil. Their best performances in the South American Championship came in 1979 and 1987, when they were runners-up. Chile, like many of its neighbours, is continually drained of

its best players by European clubs, and it will be tough for them to improve on their third place in the 1962 World Cup.

CHAMPIONS

1933 Magallanes	1947 Colo Colo
1934 Magallanes	1948 Auxax Italiano
1935 Magallanes	1949 Universidad Catolica
1936 Audax Italiano	1950 Everton
1937 Colo Colo	1951 Union Espanola
1938 Magallanes	1952 Everton
1939 Colo Colo	1953 Colo Colo
1940 Universidad de Chile	1954 Universidad Catolica
1941 Colo Colo	1955 Palestino
1942 Santiago Morning	1956 Colo Colo
1943 Union Espanola	1957 Audax Italiano
1944 Colo Colo	1958 Wanderers
1945 Green Cross	1959 Universidad de Chile
1946 Audax Italiano	1960 Colo Colo
	1961 Universidad Catolica
	1962 Universidad de Chile

Chile's exciting striker Marcelo Salas

1963 Colo Colo	1997 Univversidad Catolica
1964 Universidad de Chile	1998 Colo Colo
1965 Universidad de Chile	
1966 Universidad Catolica	**CUP WINNERS**
1967 Universidad de Chile	1958 Colo Colo
1968 Wanderers	1959 Wanderers Valparaiso
1969 Universidad de Chile	1960 Not played
1970 Colo Colo	1961 Wanderers Valparaiso
1971 Union San Felipe	1962–73 Not played
1972 Colo Colo	1974 Colo Colo
1973 Union Espanola	1975 Palestino
1974 Huachipato	1976 Not played
1975 Union Espanola	1977 Palestino
1976 Everton	1978 Not played
1977 Union Espanola	1979 Universidad de Chile
1978 Palestino	1980 Deportivo Iquique
1979 Colo Colo	1981 Colo Colo
1980 Cobreloa	1982 Colo Colo
1981 Colo Colo	1983 Universidad Catolica
1982 Cobreloa	1984 Everton
1983 Colo Colo	1985 Colo Colo
1984 Universidad Catolica	1986 Cobreloa
1985 Cobreloa	1987 Cobresal
1986 Colo Colo	1988 Colo Colo
1987 Universidad Catolica	1989 Colo Colo
1988 Cobreloa	1990 Colo Colo
1989 Colo Colo	1991 Universidad Catolica
1990 Colo Colo	1992 Union Espanola
1991 Colo Colo	1993 Union Espanola
1992 Cobreloa	1994 Colo Colo
1993 Colo Colo	1995 Universidad Catolica
1994 Universidad de Chile	1996 Colo Colo
1995 Universidad de Chile	1997 Not held
1996 Colo Colo	1998 Universidad Catolica

Colombia

Federacion Colombiana de Futbol
Founded: *1924*
Joined FIFA: *1936*

Colombia's veteran midfielder, Carlos Valderrama

Colombia's poor showing in the 1998 World Cup finals, in which they went out in the first round, was symptomatic of a country plagued by internal disputes – on and off the football field.

The most notorious incident came in 1950, shortly after professionalism was introduced, when a break-away league outside FIFA jurisdiction, the DiMayor, was formed and Colombian sides began importing players from all over South America, and from Britain. The huge salaries on offer led to the four years of its existence being known as the "El Dorado" period. The bubble burst in 1954, when Colombia were readmitted to FIFA and the league collapsed, leaving many clubs in despcrate financial trouble.

The national side made its debut as late as 1938, and results at first were poor. Between 1949 and 1957 no internationals were played at all, and thereafter outings were infrequent. It was a huge surprise, then, when Colombia qualified for the 1962 World Cup in Chile, although to do so they only had to beat Peru.

However, the best they managed on their World Cup debut was a 4–4 draw with the USSR. In 1965 another breakaway federation was formed and confusion reigned once more. FIFA had to intervene and effectively ran Colombian football up until 1971, when the present administration was installed. A new league structure was introduced in 1968, careful controls on the number of foreign imports were implemented, and the national side soon benefited. In 1989 Nacional Medellin won the Copa Libertadores, the country's only victory, and a year later the national side, coached by Francisco Maturana qualified for the 1990 World Cup finals.

But the best – and the worst – followed. In the 1994 World Cup qualifiers, Argentina were thrashed 5–0 by Colombia in Buenos Aires and consigned to a play-off. This performance led a number of people to consider the Colombians a good bet to win the whole competition.

At USA 94, Colombia's efforts foundered on poor morale, not helped by death threats against players and coach Maturana. Worst of all came after their surprise first-round elimination. Defender Andres Escobar – who had scored an own-goal in the shock 2–1 defeat by the USA – was shot dead in Medellin. That kind of controversy continues to dog the Colombians even four years on.

CHAMPIONS

1948 Independiente Santa Fe	1973 At. Nacional Medellin
1949 Millonarios	1974 Deportivo Cali
1950 Deportes	1975 Independiente Santa Fe
1951 Millonarios	1976 At. Nacional Medellin
1952 Millonarios	1977 Atletico Junior
1953 Millonarios	1978 Millonarios
1954 At. Nacional Medellin	1979 America Cali
1955 Independiente	1980 Atletico Junior
1956 Atletico Quindo	1981 At. Nacional Medellin
1957 Independiente Medellin	1982 America Cali
1958 Independiente	1983 America Cali
1959 Millonarios	1984 America Cali
1960 Independiente	1985 America Cali
1961 Millonarios	1986 America Cali
1962 Millonarios	1987 Millonarios
1963 Millonarios	1988 Millonarios
1964 Millonarios	1989 Not played
1965 Deportivo Cali	1990 America Cali
1966 Independiente	1991 At. Nacional Medellin
1967 Deportivo Cali	1992 America Cali
1968 Union Magdalena	1993 Atletico Junior
1969 Deportivo Cali	1994 Atletico Nacional
1970 Deportivo Cali	1995 Atletico Nacional
1971 Independiente Santa Fe	1996 Deportivo Cali
1972 Millonarios	1997 America Cali

Ecuador

Asociacion Ecuatoriana de Futbol

Founded: 1925

Joined FIFA: 1926

Ecuador are one of South America's weakest nations, and they have yet to qualify for any major tournament. The closest they have gone to reaching the World Cup finals was in 1966, when they lost a play-off to Chile.

Between 1938 and 1975 the national side managed only eight wins, but there are signs of improvement. In 1990, Barcelona of Guayaquil were runners-up in the Copa Libertadores, and the semi-final in which they impressively beat River Plate is surely the country's proudest moment.

CHAMPIONS

1957 Emelec	1977 Nacional Quito
1958–59 Not played	1978 Nacional Quito
1960 Barcelona	1979 Emelec
1961 Emelec	1980 Barcelona
1962 Everest	1981 Barcelona
1963 Barcelona	1982 Nacional Quito
1964 Deportivo Quito	1983 Nacional Quito
1965 Emelec	1984 Nacional Quito
1966 Barcelona	1985 Barcelona
1967 Nacional Quito	1986 Nacional Quito
1968 Deportivo Quito	1987 Barcelona
1969 Liga Deportiva Universitaria	1988 Emelec
1970 Barcelona	1989 Barcelona
1971 Barcelona	1990 Liga Deportivo Universitaria
1972 Emelec	1991 Barcelona
1973 Nacional Quito	1992 Nacional Quito
1974 Liga Deportivo Universitaria	1993 Emelec
1975 Liga Deportivo Universitaria	1994 Emelec
1976 Nacional Quito	1995 Barcelona
	1996 Emelec
	1997 Barcelona

Paraguay

Liga Paraguaya de Futbol

Founded: 1906

Joined FIFA: 1921

Asuncion dominates Paraguayan football, and Olimpia dominate Asuncion. They are the country's most successful side and have won the Copa Libertadores twice, in 1979 and 1990, and have been runners-up three times. The national side has also done well, for such a small and impoverished country. They won the South American Championship in 1953 and again in 1979 – a year in which Paraguayan teams won every trophy available to them. Paraguay have reached the World Cup finals five times, most recently in 1998 thanks to the inspiration of goalscoring goalkeeper Jose Luis Chilavert. He is the only Paraguayan player to have been voted South American Footballer of the Year.

CHAMPIONS

1906 Guarani	1925 Olimpia
1907 Guarani	1926 Nacional Asuncion
1908 Not played	1927 Olimpia
1909 Nacional Asuncion	1928 Olimpia
1910 Not played	1929 Olimpia
1911 Nacional Asuncion	1930 Libertad
1912 Olimpia	1931–34 Not played
1913 Cerro Porteno	1935 Cerro Porteno
1914 Olimpia	1936 Olimpia
1915 Cerro Porteno	1937 Olimpia
1916 Olimpia	1938 Olimpia
1917 Libertad	1939 Cerro Porteno
1918 Cerro Porteno	1940 Cerro Porteno
1919 Cerro Porteno	1941 Cerro Porteno
1920 Libertad	1942 Nacional Asuncion
1921 Guarani	1943 Libertad
1922 Not played	1944 Cerro Porteno
1923 Guarani	1945 Libertad
1924 Nacional Asuncion	1946 Nacional Asuncion

Paraguay celebrate qualifying for France '98 following a 1–1 draw against Argentina

1947 Olimpia
1948 Olimpia
1949 Guarani
1950 Cerro Porteno
1951 Sportivo Luqueno
1952 Presidente Hayes
1953 Sportivo Luqueno
1954 Cerro Porteno
1955 Libertad
1956 Olimpia
1957 Olimpia
1958 Olimpia
1959 Olimpia
1960 Olimpia
1961 Cerro Porteno
1962 Olimpia

1963 Cerro Porteno
1964 Guarani
1965 Olimpia
1966 Cerro Porteno
1967 Guarani
1968 Olimpia
1969 Olimpia
1970 Cerro Porteno
1971 Olimpia
1972 Cerro Porteno
1973 Cerro Porteno
1974 Cerro Porteno
1975 Olimpia
1976 Libertad
1977 Cerro Porteno
1978 Olimpia

1979 Olimpia
1980 Olimpia
1981 Olimpia
1982 Olimpia
1983 Olimpia
1984 Guarani
1985 Olimpia
1986 Sol de America
1987 Cerro Porteno
1988 Olimpia
1989 Olimpia
1990 Cerro Porteno
1991 Sol de America
1992 Cerro Porteno
1993 Olimpia
1994 Cerro Porteno

1995 Olimpia
1996 Cerro Porteno
1997 Olimpia
1998 Olimpia

CUP WINNERS

1990 Atletico Colegiales
1991 Cerro Porteno
1992 Olimpia
1993 Cerro Cora Campo Grande
1994 Not played
1995 Cerro Porteno

Peru

Federacion Peruana de Futbol
Founded: *1922*
Joined FIFA: *1924*

Football in Peru has always been dominated by Lima, and the national association was founded there in 1922.

The local Lima League was the strongest in the country and, until a national championship was introduced in 1966, the winners were considered national champions. Lima's clubs, Alianza, Universitario and Sporting Cristal, have dominated at home, but none have achieved success in the Copa Libertadores. Sadly, the eyes of the world were focused on Peru in 1964, when 300 spectators died in a riot, and in 1988, when the Alianza team was wiped out in a plane crash.

Peru's international debut came in the South American Championship of 1927, and they won the event at home in 1939. The World Cup record was poor, however, until the 1970s, when a generation of notable players came together and made the decade the country's most successful ever.

Stars of the 1970s side were the highly eccentric and entertaining goalkeeper Ramon "El Loco" Quiroga, Hector Chumpitaz and midfield maestro Teofilo Cubillas, the greatest Peruvian player of all time. Coached by Brazilian World Cup winner Didi, this side reached the quarter-finals of the 1970 World Cup, won the 1975 South American Championship, and qualified for the 1978 World Cup, where they fell in the second round.

Peru qualified for the World Cup again in 1982, but the side were past its best and went out in the first round. Since then, Peru have slipped back into their familiar role of the "middle men" of South American football. Political problems in the country have not helped.

Peru's World Cup finals side of 1982 line up before a match against Italy

CHAMPIONS

1926 CS Progreso	1962 Alianza
1927 Alianza	1963 Alianza
1928 Alianza	1964 Universitario
1929 Universitario	1965 Alianza
1930 Atletico Chalcao	1966 Universitario
1931 Alianza	1967 Universitario
1932 Alianza	1968 Sporting Cristal
1933 Alianza	1969 Universitario
1934 Universitario	1970 Sporting Cristal
1935 Sport Boys	1971 Universitario
1936 Not played	1972 Sporting Cristal
1937 Sport Boys	1973 Defensor Lima
1938 Deportivo Municipal	1974 Universitario
1939 Universitario	1975 Alianza
1940 Deportivo Municipal	1976 Union Huaral
1941 Universitario	1977 Alianza
1942 Sport Boys	1978 Alianza
1943 Deportivo Municipal	1979 Sporting Cristal
1944 Mariscal Sucre	1980 Sporting Cristal
1945 Universitario	1981 Mariano Melgar
1946 Universitario	1982 Universitario
1947 Atletico Chalcao	1983 Sporting Cristal
1948 Alianza	1984 Sport Boys
1949 Universitario	1985 Universitario
1950 Deportivo Municipal	1986 Colegio San Augustin
1951 Sport Boys	1987 Universitario
1952 Alianza	1988 Sporting Cristal
1953 Mariscal Sucre	1989 Union Huaral
1954 Alianza	1990 Universitario
1955 Alianza	1991 Sporting Cristal
1956 Sporting Cristal	1992 Universitario
1957 Centro Iqueno	1993 Universitario
1958 Sport Boys	1994 Sporting Cristal
1959 Universitario	1995 Sporting Cristal
1960 Universitario	1996 Sporting Cristal
1961 Sporting Cristal	1997 Alianza
	1998 Universitario

Uruguay

Asociacion Uruguaya de Futbol

Founded: *1900*

Joined FIFA: *1923*

Before World War Two, Uruguay were undoubtedly the best team in the world, effectively winning three World Championships. Today they are no longer a world power, but they have a proud history and can still be dangerous opponents. Montevideo dominates the domestic scene and, as it is located just across the River Plate estuary from Buenos Aires, the two cities can claim to be the centre of South American football.

Montevideo's two great clubs, Penarol and Nacional, have dominated Uruguayan football, winning more than 80 championships between them. The clubs are fierce rivals and have both enjoyed great success in the Copa Libertadores; Penarol winning it five times, Nacional three. Both clubs have also won the World Club Cup.

The national side dominated world football in the first half of this century but has faded since the 1950s. Early successes in the South American Championship were followed by victory in the 1924 Olympics in Amsterdam, at a time when the Olympic winners could justifiably claim to be world champions. Having amazed Europe with their skill at the 1924 Olympics, Uruguay repeated the trick in 1928 and two years later, as the host nation, swept to victory in the first World Cup.

The side of the 1920s and 1930s contained many of Uruguay's all-time greats: skipper Jose Nasazzi, the midfield "Iron Curtain" of Jose Andrade, Lorenzo Fernandez and Alvarez Gestido, and outstanding forwards Hector Castro, Pedro Cea and Hector Scarone.

In 1950 Uruguay pulled off one of the biggest World Cup finals shocks in history, coming from a goal down to beat Brazil 2–1 in the deciding match…in Brazil. The side contained forwards Juan Schiaffino, Uruguay's greatest player, and Omar Miguez, Victor Andrade, nephew of Jose, Roque Maspoli in goal and Obdulio Varela in defence. In Switzerland in 1954, the defence of their crown ended with a 4–2 semi-final defeat by Hungary in one of the best World Cup games ever.

Since then, Uruguay have enjoyed regular success in the South American Championship, but in the World Cup they have failed to matched their feats of the 1930s and 1950s. They finished fourth in the 1970, but elimination by Bolivia in the 1994 qualifiers showed just how far they had slipped.

Uruguay still produces outstanding players, like Enzo Francescoli and Carlos Aguilera, but they often go to Europe to further their careers. With so many foreign-based players, Uruguay developed a schizophrenic approach to the World Cup and South American Championship, often entering wildly different teams for tournaments staged less than a year apart. This unpredictability was shown in 1995, when Uruguay won the Copa America, beating 1994 World Cup winners Brazil after a penalty shoot-out in the Final.

CHAMPIONS

Amateur League	
1900 Penarol	1920 Nacional
1901 Penarol	1921 Penarol
1902 Nacional	1922 Nacional
1903 Nacional	1923 Wanderers
1904 Not played	1924 Penarol
1905 Penarol	1925 Not played
1906 Wanderers	1926 Penarol
1907 Penarol	1927 Rampla Juniors
1908 River Plate	1928 Rampla Juniors
1909 Wanderers	1929 Penarol
1910 River Plate	1930 Not played
1911 Penarol	1931 Wanderers
1912 Nacional	
1913 River Plate	*Professional League*
1914 River Plate	1932 Penarol
1915 Nacional	1933 Nacional
1916 Nacional	1934 Nacional
1917 Nacional	1935 Penarol
1918 Penarol	1936 Penarol
1919 Nacional	1937 Penarol
	1938 Penarol

Uruguay players celebrate a Copa America victory over Brazil in 1995

1939 Nacional	1954 Penarol	1969 Nacional	1984 Central Espanol
1940 Nacional	1955 Nacional	1970 Nacional	1985 Penarol
1941 Nacional	1956 Nacional	1971 Nacional	1986 Nacional
1942 Nacional	1957 Nacional	1972 Nacional	1987 Defensor
1943 Nacional	1958 Penarol	1973 Penarol	1988 Danublo
1944 Penarol	1959 Penarol	1974 Penarol	1989 Progreso
1945 Penarol	1960 Penarol	1975 Penarol	1990 Bella Vista
1946 Nacional	1961 Penarol	1976 Defensor	1991 Defensor
1947 Nacional	1962 Penarol	1977 Nacional	1992 Nacional
1948 Not played	1963 Nacional	1978 Penarol	1993 Penarol
1949 Penarol	1964 Penarol	1979 Penarol	1994 Penarol
1950 Nacional	1965 Penarol	1980 Nacional	1995 Penarol
1951 Penarol	1966 Nacional	1981 Penarol	1996 Penarol
1952 Nacional	1967 Penarol	1982 Penarol	1997 Penarol
1953 Penarol	1968 Penarol	1983 Nacional	

Venezuela

Federacion Venezolana de Futbol
Founded: *1926*
Joined FIFA: *1952*

Venezuela are the weakest of the 10 South American countries, but this is hardly surprising because the national sport is baseball. Originally members of CONCACAF, they made their international debut in 1938 and switched to CONMEBOL in 1958. The national record is awful, with just one match won in the South American Championship and only a handful more in World Cup qualifiers, even though they have entered both regularly.

The clubs are weak, too, and three Copa Libertadores semi-finals are the best they have managed. A professional league was finally set up in 1956, but Venezuela have a long way to go if they are even to catch up with the other South American minnows.

CHAMPIONS

1921 America	1934 Union SC	1967 Deportivo Portugues
1922 Centro Atletico	1935 Union SC	1968 Union Dep. Canarias
1923 America	1936 Dos Caminos SC	1969 Galicia FC
1924 Centro Atletico	1937 Dos Caminos SC	1970 Galicia FC
1925 Loyola SC	1938 Dos Caminos SC	1971 Valencia
1926 Centro Atletico	1939 Union SC	1972 Deportivo Italia
1927 Venzoleo FC	1940 Union SC	1973 PortuguesA
1928 Deportivo Venezuela	1941 Union SC	1974 Galicia FC
1929 Deportivo Venezuela	1942 Dos Caminos SC	1975 Portuguesa
1930 Centro Atletico	1943 Loyola SC	1976 Portuguesa
1931 Deportivo Venezuela	1944 Loyola SC	1977 Portuguesa
1932 Union SC	1945 Dos Caminos SC	1978 Portuguesa
1933 Deportivo Venezuela	1946 Deportivo Espanol	1979 Tachira
	1947 Union SC	1980 Estudiantes Merida
	1948 Loyola SC	1981 Tachira
	1949 Dos Caminos SC	1982 Atletico San Cristobal
	1950 Union SC	1983 ULA Merida
	1951 Universidad Central	1984 Tachira
	1952 Le Salle	1985 Estudiantes Merida
	1953 Universidad Centra	1986 Tachira
	1954 Deportivo Vasco	1987 Maritimo
	1955 Le Salle	1988 Maritimo
	1956 Banco Obrero	1989 Mineros de Guyana
	1957 Universidad Central	1990 Maritimo
	1958 Deportivo Portugues	1991 ULA Merida
	1959 Deportivo Espanol	1992 Caracas FC
	1960 DepOrtivo Portugues	1993 Sport Maritimo
	1961 Deportivo Italia	1994 Caracas FC
	1962 Deportivo Portugues	1995 Caracas FC
	1963 Deportivo Italia	1996 Mineros Puerto Ord
	1964 Galicia FC	1997 Caracas FC
	1965 Deportivo Lara	1998 Atletico Zulia
	1966 Deportivo Italia	

AFRICA (CAF)

FIFA has grown from the seven original members of 1904 through 73 in 1950 to more than 200 nations (including associate members). Africa is the largest of the regional confederations with 51 full members and one associate member state.

In the past 20 years FIFA has concentrated millions of dollars in educational programmes for coaches, referees, administrators and players in the developing world. Progress has been measured by World Cup finals entry: three African nations were present, for the first time, at USA '94, thanks to the feats of her entrants in 199 and at France '98, Nigeria, Cameroon, South Africa and Morocco were all there after the tournament was enlarged from 24 teams to 32.

Algeria

Fédération Algérienne de Football

Founded:	*1962*
Joined FIFA:	*1963*
African Nations Cup:	*1990*

The French brought football to Algeria in the late 1900s, and by the 1930s several Muslim Algerian clubs had been formed. The earliest was Mouloudia Challia (1920), and they won the African Champions Cup in 1976 at the first attempt.

Algeria gained independence in 1962, and since then the national side has improved considerably. In 1980 they reached the final of the African Nations Cup, where they lost 3–0 to hosts Nigeria, and two years later qualified for the World Cup finals in Spain. At the 1982 finals the Algerians pulled off one of the biggest World Cup shocks when they beat West Germany 2–1, and had it not been for a contrived result between the Germans and Austria, Algeria would have reached the second round. Rabah Madjer and Lakhdar Belloumi were the goalscorers against West Germany and they remain Algeria's greatest players. Madjer won a European Cup-winners' Cup medal with FC Porto in 1987, when he was also voted African Footballer of the Year.

Algeria were semi-finalists in the African Nations Cup in 1984 and 1988, and in between qualified for the 1986 World Cup finals. Then, in 1990 they won the African Nations Cup for the first time. In 1993 they qualified for the African Nations Cup finals, but were expelled for fielding an ineligible player in a qualifying game.

Algerian clubs have done well in African competitions, with MC Algiers (1976), J.S Kabylie (1981 and 1990) and ES Setif (1988), all winning the African Champions Cup.

ALGIERS LEAGUE CHAMPIONS

1920	FC Blideen
1921	FC Blideen
1922	FC Blideen
1923	FC Blideen
1924	AS Boufarik
1925	US Blideen
1926	GS d'Orleansville
1927	Gallia Sports
1928	FC Blideen
1929	AS Saint Eugene
1930	AS Boufarik
1931	Gallia Sports
1932	Racing Universitaire
1934	Racing Universitaire
1935	AS Saint Eugene
1936	Gallia Sports
1937	AS Boufarik
1938	AS Boufarik
1939	Not played
1940	Not played
1941	AS Boufarik
1942	AS Saint Eugene
1943	AS Saint Eugene
1944	AS Saint Eugene & Mouloudia Algiers
1945	Racing Universitaire
1946	Gallia Sports
1947	Olympique Hussein-Dey
1948	Olympique Hussein-Dey
1949	Olympique Hussein-Dey

CONSTANTINE LEAGUE CHAMPIONS

1922	AS Bonoise
1923	US Constantine
1924	US Constantine
1925	US Constantine
1926	JS Philippeville
1927	Racing Philippeville
1928	Stade Olympique Setif
1929	AS Bônoise
1930	Stade Olympique Setif
1931	Racing Philippeville
1932	JS Guelmoise
1933	JS Guelmoise
1934	JS Guelmoise
1935	Jeunesse Bône AC
1936	Not played
1937	Jeunesse Bône AC
1938	Jeunesse Bône AC
1939	MO Constantine
1940–44	Not played
1945	USM Setif
1946	USM Bône
1947	JS Jijeli
1948	MO Constantine
1949	AS Bône
1950	USM Setif

ORAN LEAGUE CHAMPIONS

1920	AS Maritime
1921	SC Bel Abbés
1922	SC Bel Abbés
1923	SC Bel Abbés
1924	SC Bel Abbés
1925	SC Bel Abbés
1926	SC Bel Abbés
1927	SC Bel Abbés
1928	AS Maritime
1929	Club Joyeusetes
1930	Gallia Club Oran
1931	Club Joyeusetes
1932	USM Oran
1933	Club Joyeusetes
1934	Not played
1935	Gallia Club Oran
1936	Club Joyeusetes
1937	Club Joyeusetes
1938	Club Joyeusetes
1939	Not played
1940	AS Maritime
1941	Club Joyeusetes
1942	USM Oran
1943	USM Oran
1944	USM Oran
1945	USM Oran
1946	SC Bel Abbés
1947	FC Oran
1948	USM Oran
1949	USM Oran
1950	GC Mascara

NATIONAL LEAGUE CHAMPIONS

1963	USM Algiers
1964	USM Annaba
1965	CR Belcourt
1966	CR Belcourt
1967	NA Hussein-Dey
1968	Entente Setif
1969	CR Belcourt
1970	CR Belcourt
1971	Mouloudia d'Oran
1972	Mouloudia d'Algiers
1973	JS Kabylie
1974	JS Kabylie
1975	Mouloudia d'Algiers
1976	Mouloudia d'Algiers
1977	JS Kawkabi
1978	Mouloudia d'Algiers
1979	Mouloudia d'Algiers
1980	JE Tizi-Ouzou
1981	RS Kouba
1982	JE Tizi-Ouzou
1983	JE Tizi-Ouzou
1984	GCR Mascara
1985	JE Tizi-Ouzou
1986	JE Tizi-Ouzou

1987 Entente Setif
1988 Moloudia d'Oran
1989 JE Tizi-Ouzou
1990 KS Kabylie
1991 MO Constantine
1992 Mouloudia d'Oran
1993 Mouloudia d'Oran
1994 US Chaouia
1995 JS Kabylie
1996 USM Alger
1997 CS Constantine
1998 USM El Harrach

CUP WINNERS

1963 Entente Setif
1964 Entente Setif
1965 MC Saida
1966 CR Belcourt
1967 Entente Setif
1968 Entente Setif
1969 CR Belcourt
1970 CR Belcourt
1971 Mouloudia d'Algiers
1972 Hamra-Annaba
1973 Mouloudia d'Algiers
1974 USM Maison Carrée

1975 Mouloudia d'Oran
1976 Mouloudia d'Algiers
1977 JS Kawkabi
1978 CM Belcourt
1979 MS Hussein-Dey
1980 Entente Setif
1981 USK Algiers
1982 DNC Algiers
1983 Mouloudia d'Algiers
1984 Mouloudia d'Oran
1985 Mouloudia d'Oran
1986 JE Tizi-Ouzou
1987 USM El-Harrach
1988 USK Algiers
1989 Not played
1990 Entente Setif
1991 USM Bel Abbés
1992 JS Kabylie
1993 Not played
1994 JS Kabylie
1995 CR Belouizdad
1996 USM Alger
1997 USM Alger
1998 WA Tlemoen

Angola

Federacao Angolana de Futebol

Founded: *1977*
Joined FIFA: *1980*

CHAMPIONS

1979 Primeiro de Agosto
1980 Primeiro de Agosto
1981 Primeiro de Agosto
1982 Petro Atletico
1983 Primeiro de Maio
1984 Petro Atletico
1985 Primeiro de Maio
1986 Petro Atletico
1987 Petro Atletico
1988 Petro Atletico
1989 Petro Atletico
1990 Petro Atletico
1991 Primeiro de Agosto
1992 Primeiro de Agosto
1993 Petro Atletico
1994 Petro Atletico
1995 Petro Atletico
1996 Primeiro de Agosto

CUP WINNERS

1980 Nacional Benguela
1981 TAAG Luanda
1982 Primeiro de Maio
1984 Primeiro de Agosto
1985 Ferroviaro Huila
1986 Inter Club Luanda
1987 Ferroviario Lubango
1988 Sagrada Esperanca
1989 Ferroviario Lubango
1990 Primeiro de Agosto
1991 Primeiro de Agosto
1992 Petro Atletico
1993 Not played
1994 Petro Atletico
1995 Independiente
1996 Petro Atletico

Benin

Fédération Beninoise de Football

Founded: *1968*
Joined FIFA: *1969*

CHAMPIONS

1969 FAD
1970 AS Porto Novo
1971 AS Cotonou
1972 AS Porto Novo
1973 AS Porto Novo
1974 Etoile Sportive Porto Novo
1975–77 Not played
1978 Dragons de l'Ouème
1979 Dragons de l'Ouème
1980 Buffles de Borgou
1981 Adjidjas FAP
1982 Dragons de l'Ouème
1983 Dragons de l'Ouème
1984 Lions de l'Atakory
1985 Requins de l'Atlantique
1986 Dragons de l'Ouème
1987 Requins de l'Atlantique
1988 Not played
1989 Dragons de l'Ouème
1990 Requins de l'Atlantique
1991 Postel Sport
1992 Buffles de Borgou
1993 Not played
1994 Dragons de l'Ouème
1995 TOFFA
1996 Mogas '90
1997 Mogas '90

CUP WINNERS

1978 Requins de l'Atlantique
1979 Buffles de Borgou
1980 Not played
1981 Requins de l'Atlantique
1982 Buffles de Borgou
1983 Requins de l'Atlantique
1984 Dragons de l'Ouème
1985 Dragons de l'Ouème
1986 Dragons de l'Ouème
1987 Not played
1988 Requins de l'Atlantique
1989 Requins de l'Atlantique
1990 Dragons de l'Ouème
1991 Not played
1992 Mogas '90
1993 Locomotive
1994 Mogas '90
1995 Mogas '90
1996 Université Nationale

Botswana

Botswana Football Association

Founded: *1970*
Joined FIFA: *1976*

CHAMPIONS

1978 FC Notwane
1979 Township Rollers
1980 Township Rollers
1981 Defence Force (BDF XI)
1982 Township Rollers
1983 Township Rollers
1984 Township Rollers
1985 Township Rollers
1986 Gaborone United
1987 Township Rollers
1988 Defence Force
1989 Defence Force
1990 Gaborone United
1991 Defence Force (BDF XI)
1992 Extension Gunners
1993 Extension Gunners
1994 Extension Gunners
1995 Township Rollers
1996 Notwane
1997 Notwane

Burkina Faso

Fédération Burkinabe de Football

Founded: *1960*
Joined FIFA: *1964*

1965 Etoile Filante	1980 Silures
1966 AS Fonctionnaires	1981 Silures
Ouagadougou	1982 Not played
1967 US Ouagadougou	1983 US Ouagadougou
1968 USFERAN	1984 ASFA Ouagadougou
1969 AS Fontionnaries	1985 Etoile Filante
Ouagadougou	1986 Not played
1970 ASFA Ouagadougou	1987 Not played
1971 ASFA Ouagadougou	1988 Etoile Filante
1972 Jeanne d'Arc	1989 ASFA Yennega
1973 Jeanne d'Arc	1990 Etoile Filante
1974 Silures	1991 Etoile Filante
1975 Silures	1992 Etoile Filante
1976 Silures	1993 Etoile Filante
1977 Silures	1994 Etoile Filante
1978 Silures	1995 ASFA Yennega
1979 Silures	1996 R.Bobo Dloulasso

Burundi

Fédération de Football du Burundi

Founded: *1948*
Joined FIFA: *1972*

CHAMPIONS

1972 Sports Dynamic	1986 Inter FC
1973 Sports Dynamic	1987 Inter FC
1974 Inter FC	1988 Inter FC
1975-8 Not played	1989 Inter FC
1979 Vital'O	1990 Vital'O
1980 Not played	1991 Inter Star
1981 Prince Louis	1992 Vital'O
1982 Fantastique	1993 Vital'O
1983 Vital'O	1994 Fantastique
1984 Vital'O	1995 Fantasique
1985 Inter FC	1996 Fantasique
	1997 Fantasique

Cameroon

Fédération Camerounaise de Football

Founded: *1960*
Joined FIFA: *1962*
African Nations Cup: *1984, 1988.*

Of all the African nations to have reached the World Cup finals, Cameroon have made by far the biggest impact. In 1982, in Spain, they drew all three of their first round games – against Italy (eventual winners), Poland (third) and Peru – but went out at that stage. They qualified again in 1990, beat reigning champions Argentina in the opening match and reached the quarter-finals, losing narrowly to England. As a result of these performances FIFA agreed to grant Africa a third berth at the 1994 finals. This time, the `Indomitable Lions' were a major disappointment, torn apart by internal strife and they also went out in the first round of France '98.

Cameroon's greatest player is undoubtedly striker Roger Milla, who played in the 1982, 1990 and 1994 World Cup teams. In 1994, he became the oldest player to appear in the finals. Milla was voted African Footballer of the Year in 1976 and again in 1990, and delighted fans at Italia '90 with his goals and his celebratory wiggle which usually followed. Other Cameroon players to have won the award include Theophile Abega (1984), goalkeeper Thomas N'Kono, who played in Spain, (1979 and 1982) and Jean Onguene (1980).

Cameroon also won the African Nations Cup twice to confirm their status as the top side of the 1980s. Cameroon clubs have enjoyed success in African competitions: with five wins in the Champions Cup and three in the Cup Winners' Cup.

CHAMPIONS

1961 Oryx Douala	1996 Unisport
1962 Caiman Douala	1997 Cotonsport
1963 Oryx Douala	
1964 Oryx Douala	
1965 Oryx Douala	### CUP WINNERS
1966 Diamant Yaoundé	1956 Oryx Douala
1967 Oryx Douala	1957 Canon Yaoundé
1968 Caiman Douala	1958 Tonnerre Yaoundé
1969 Union Douala	1959 Not played
1970 Canon Yaoundé	1960 Lions Yaoundé
1971 Aigle Nkongsamba	1961 Union Douala
1972 Leopards Douala	1962 Lions Yaoundé
1973 Leopards Douala	1963 Oryx Douala
1974 Canon Yaoundé	1964 Diamant Yaoundé
1975 Caiman Douala	1965 Lions Yaoundé
1976 Union Douala	1966 Lions Yaoundé
1977 Canon Yaoundé	1967 Canon Yaoundé
1978 Union Douala	1968 Oryx Yaoundé
1979 Canon Yaoundé	1969 Union Douala
1980 Canon Yaoundé	1970 Not played
1981 Tonnerre Yaoundé	1971 Diamant Yaoundé
1982 Canon Yaoundé	1972 Diamant Yaoundé
1983 Tonnerre Yaoundé	1973 Canon Yaoundé
1984 Tonnerre Yaoundé	1974 Tonnerre Yaoundé
1985 Canon Yaoundé	1975 Canon Yaoundé
1986 Canon Yaoundé	1976 Canon Yaoundé
1987 Tonnerre Yaoundé	1977 Canon Yaoundé
1988 Tonnerre Yaoundé	1978 Canon Yaoundé
1989 Racing Bafoussam	1979 Dynamo Douala
1990 Union Douala	1980 Union Douala
1991 Canon Yaoundé	1981 Dynamo Douala
1992 Racing Bafoussam	1982 Dragons Yaoundé
1993 Racing Bafoussam	1983 Canon Yaoundé
1994 Aigle Nkongsamba	1984 Dihep de Nkam
1995 Racing Bafoussam	1985 Union Douala
	1986 Canon Yaoundé
	1987 Tonnerre Yaoundé

1988 Panthère Bangangte
1989 Tonnerre Yaoundé
1990 Prevoyance FC Yaoundé
1991 Tonnerre Yaoundé
1992 L'Olympic Mvolyé
1993 Canon Yaoundé

1994 L'Olympic Mvolyé
1995 Canon Yaoundé
1996 -
1997 Union Douala

Cape Verde

Federacao Cabo-Verdiana de Futebol

Founded:	*1982*
Joined FIFA:	*1986*

Central African Republic

Fédération Centrafricaine de Football

Founded:	*1937*
Joined FIFA:	*1963*

CHAMPIONS

1973 Olympique Real
1974 ASDR Fatima
1975 Olympique Real
1976 AS Tempete Mocaf
1977 SCAF Tocages
1978 ASDR Fatima
1979 Olympique Real
1980 USCA Bangui
1981 Sporting Moura
1982 Olympique Real
1983 ASDR Fatima
1984 AS Tempete Mocaf

1985 SCAF Tocages
1986 Sporting Moura
1987 Not played
1988 ASDR Fatima
1989 SCAF Tocages
1990 AS Tempete Mocaf
1991 FACA FC
1992 USCA Bangui
1993 AS Tempete Mocaf
1994 -
1995 FACA FC

Chad

Fédération Tchadienne de Football

Founded:	*1962*
Joined FIFA:	*1988*

Congo

Fédération Congolaise de Football

Founded:	*1962*
Joined FIFA:	*1962*
African Nations Cup:	*1972*

CHAMPIONS

1965 Diables Noirs
1966 Abeilles FC
1967 Etoile du Congo
1968 Patronage
1969 CARA Brazzaville
1970 Victoria Club Mokanda
1971 CARA Brazzaville
1972 CARA Brazzaville
1973 CARA Brazzaville
1974 CARA Brazzaville
1975 CARA Brazzaville
1976 Diables Noirs
1977 Inter Club
1978 Etoile du Congo
1979 Etoile du Congo
1980 Etoile du Congo
1981 Etoile du Congo
1982 CARA Brazzaville
1983 Kotoko Mfoa
1984 CARA Brazzaville
1985 Etoile du Congo
1986 Patronage
1987 Etoile du Congo
1988 Inter Club
1989 Etoile du Congo
1990 Inter Club

1991 Diables Noirs
1992 Etoile du Congo
1993 Not played
1994 Etoile du Congo
1995 Etoile du Congo
1996 Etoile du Congo
1997 Muisport

CUP WINNERS

1982 AS Cheminots
1983 Etoile du Congo
1984 AS Cheminots
1985 Inter Club
1986 CARA Brazzaville
1987 Inter Club
1988 Patronage
1989 Diables Noirs
1990 Diables Noirs
1991 Elecsport
1992 CARA Brazzaville
1993 Not played
1994 EPB
1995 EPB
1996 EPB
1997 EPB

Djibouti

Federation Djiboutienne de Football

Founded:	*1977*
Joined FIFA:	*1994*

Egypt

All Ettihad el Masri Li Korat el Kadam

Founded:	*1921*
Joined FIFA:	*1923*
African Nations Cup:	*1957, 1959, 1986, 1998*

Egypt were one of the four founder members of the Confédération Africaine de Football and were the first Africans to join FIFA, in 1923. Given this 20-year start on most of her neighbours, it is no surprise that Egypt became one of the great African powers, winning the first two Nations Cups in 1957 and 1959.

Egypt finished fourth in the 1928 Olympics and entered the World Cup in 1934. Having beaten Palestine in a qualifying play-off, they lost 4–2 to Hungary in the first round. Olympic semi-finalists again in 1964, Egypt entered only one of the World Cups played between 1938 and 1970.

A revival in the 1970s saw them finish third in the African Nations Cup in 1970 and 1974, fourth in 1976 and reach the Olympic quarter-finals in 1984. Two years later, as hosts, they won the African Nations Cup for the third time, and then qualified for the 1990 World Cup finals, where they did well to hold Holland and the Republic of Ireland to draws.

Failure to qualify for the 1998 World Cup was a disappointment, though some consolation came in winning the 1998 African Nations Cup in Burkino Faso, defeating holders South African 2-0 in the final.

Allied to this success at national level, Egyptian clubs are among the most powerful in Africa. Well organized, wealthy and well supported, Egypt's clubs have won the African Champions Cup and the African Cup Winners' Cup ten times. Al Ahly, the most successful, have won the former twice and the latter thrice – in consecutive years from 1984 to 1986.

Al-Titsh, who played for Al Ahly in the 1920s, was one of Egypt's finest players, and Ahly's stadium still bears his name. Other great Egyptian players include Mahmoud Al Khatib, Ibrahim Youssef and Abu Zeid, Egypt's best striker during the 1980s.

CHAMPIONS

1949 Al Ahly	1984 Zamalek
1950 Al Ahly	1985 Al Ahly
1951 Al Ahly	1986 Al Ahly
1952 Not played	1987 Al Ahly
1953 Al Ahly	1988 Zamalek
1954 Al Ahly	1989 Al Ahly
1955 Not played	1990 Al Ahly
1956 Al Ahly	1991 Ismaili
1957 Al Ahly	1992 Zamalek
1958 Al Ahly	1993 Zamalek
1959 Al Ahly	1994 Zamalek
1960 Zamalek	1995 Al Ahly
1961 Al Ahly	1996 Al Ahly
1962 Al Ahly	1997 Al Ahly
1963 Al Tersana	1998 Al Ahly
1964 Zamalek	
1965 Zamalek	
1966 Olympic	## CUP WINNERS
1967 Ismaili	
1968-72 Not played	1922 Cairo International SC
1973 Mehalla Al Kubra	1923 Cairo International SC
1974 Not played	1924 Al Ahly
1975 Al Ahly	1925 Al Ahly
1976 Al Ahly	1926 Al Ittihad
1977 Al Ahly	1927 Al Ahly
1978 Zamalek	1928 Al Ahly
1979 Al Ahly	1929 Al Tersana
1980 Al Ahly	1930 Al Ahly
1981 Al Ahly	1931 Al Ahly
1982 Al Ahly	1932 Zamalek
1983 Al Mokaouloum	1933 Olympic
	1934 Olympic

1935 Zamalek	1965 Al Tersana
1936 Al Ittihad	1966 Al Ahly
1937 Al Ahly	1967 Al Tersana
1938 Zamalek	1968-72 Not played
1939 Al Teram SC	1973 Al Ittihad
1940 Al Ahly	1974 Not played
1941 Zamalek	1975 Zamalek
1942 Al Ahly	1976 Al Ittihad
1943 Al Ahly & Zamalek	1977 Zamalek
1944 Zamalek	1978 Al Ahly
1945 Al Ahly	1979 Zamalek
1946 Al Ahly	1980 Not played
1947 Al Ahly	1981 Al Ahly
1948 Al Ittihad	1982 Not played
	1983 Al Ahly
## CUP WINNERS	1984 Al Ahly
	1985 Al Ahly
1949 Al Ahly	1986 Al Tersana
1950 Al Ahly	1987 Zamalek
1951 Al Ahly	1988 Zamalek
1952 Zamalek	1989 Zamalek
1953 Al Ahly	1990 Al Mokaouloum
1954 Al Tersana	1991 Al Ahly
1955 Zamalek	1992 Al Ahly
1956 Al Ahly	1993 Al Ahly
1957 Zamalek	1994 Not played
1958 Zamalek & Al Ahly	1995 Al Mokaouloum
1959 Zamalek	1996 Al Ahly
1960 Zamalek	1997 Al Ahly
1961 Al Ahly	
1962 Zamalek	
1963 Al Ittihad	
1964 Suez Canal	

Equatorial Guinea

Federacion Equatoguineana de Futbol

Founded:	1976
FIFA:	1986

CHAMPIONS

1979 Real Rebola	1988 CD Ela Nguema
1980 FC Mongomo	1989 CD Ela Nguema
1981 Atletico Malabo	1990 CD Ela Nguema
1982 Atletico Malabo	1991 CD Ela Nguema
1983 FC Dragons	1992 Akonangui FC
1984 CD Ela Nguema	1996 Cafe Bond Sportif
1985 CD Ela Nguema	1997 Cafe Bond Sportif
1986 CD Ela Nguema	
1987 CD Ela Nguema	

Ethiopia

Yeithiopia Football Federechin

Founded: 1943
Joined FIFA: 1953
African Nations Cup: 1962

CHAMPIONS

1965 Ethio-cement
1966 St. Georges
1967 St. Georges
1968 St. Georges
1969 Tele Asmara
1970 Tele Asmara
1971 St. Georges
1972 Tele Asmara
1973 Tele Asmara
1974 Embassoria
1975 St. Georges
1976 Mechal Army
1977 Medr Babur
1978 Ogaden Anbassa
1979-83 Not played
1984 Ground Forces
1985 Brewery Jimma
1986 Brewery Jimma
1987-9 Not played
1990 Brewery Addis
1991 St. Georges
1992 St. Georges
1993 Electric Sports
1995 St George
1996 St George
1997 St George

Gabon

Fédération Gabonaise de Football

Founded: 1962
Joined FIFA: 1963

CHAMPIONS

1968 Olympique Sportif
1969 Aigle Royal
1970 Aigle Royal
1971 AS Solidarite
1972 Olympique Sportif
1973 AS Police
1974 Zalang COC
1975 Petrosports FC
1976 Vautour Club Mangoungou
1977 Vautour Club Mangougou
1978 FC 105
1979 Anges ABC
1980 US Mbila Nzambi
1981 US Mbila Nzambi
1982 FC 105
1983 FC 105
1984 AS Sogara
1985 FC 105
1986 FC 105
1987 FC 105
1988 US Mbila Nzambi
1989 AC Sogara
1990 JAC Port Gentil
1991 AS Sogara
1992 AS Sogara
1993 AS Sogara
1994 AS Sogara
1995 AS Sogara
1996 AS Sogara

Gambia

Gambia Football Association

Founded: 1952
Joined FIFA: 1966

CHAMPIONS

1973 Ports Authority
1974 Wallidan
1975 Real Banjul
1976 Not played
1977 Wallidan
1978 Real Banjul
1979 Wallidan
1980 Starlight
1981 Starlight
1982 Ports Authority
1983 Real Banjul
1984 Ports Authority
1985 Wallidan
1986 Wallidan
1987 Wallidan
1988 Wallidan
1989 Wallidan
1990 Wallidan
1991 Wallidan
1992 Wallidan
1993 Hawks
1994 Wallidan
1995 Wallidan
1996 Wallidan
1997 Wallidan

Ghana

Ghana Football Association

Founded: 1957
Joined FIFA: 1958
African Nations Cup: 1963, 1965, 1978, 1982

Ghana achieved independence in 1957 and the "Black Stars" quickly established themselves as a powerful force in African football. They won the African Nations Cup in 1963, at their first attempt, retained the trophy two years later and in the following two events, 1968 and 1970, were beaten finalists. Ghana is the only nation to win the trophy four times.

In club football, Asante Kotoko have won the African Champions Cup twice and Ghana have produced some outstanding players. Mohamed Ahmed Polo and Adolf Armah were stars in the 1970s; Ibrahim Sunday, African footballer of the year in 1971, played for Werder Bremen in the German League; Abedi Pele won many trophies with Marseille in the 1980s; and Nii Lamptey, of PSV Eindhoven, led Ghana to victory in the 1991 World Youth Championship. Nevertheless, Ghana have yet to qualify for the World Cup finals.

CHAMPIONS

1957 Hearts of Oak
1958 Hearts of Oak
1959 Asante Kotoko
1960 Eleven Wise FC
1961 Not played
1962 Hearts of Oak
1963 Asante Kotoko
1964 Asante Kotoko
1965 Asante Kotoko
1966 Real Republicans
1967 Asante Kotoko
1968 Cape Coast Dwarfs
1969 Asante Kotoko
1970 Asante Kotoko
1971 Great Olympics
1972 Asante Kotoko
1973 Hearts of Oak
1974 Great Olympics
1975 Asante Kotoko
1976 Hearts of Oak

1977 Hearts of Oak
1978 Hearts of Oak
1979 Hearts of Oak
1980 Asante Kotoko
1981 Asante Kotoko
1982 Asante Kotoko
1983 Asante Kotoko
1984 Hearts of Oak
1985 Hearts of Oak
1986 Asante Kotoko
1987 Asante Kotoko
1988 Not played
1989 Asante Kotoko
1990 Hearts of Oak
1991 Asante Kotoko
1992 Asante Kotoko
1993 Asante Kotokp
1994 Goldfields
1995 Goldfields
1996 Goldfields
1997 Hearts of Oak

CUP WINNERS

1958 Asante Kotoko
1959 Cornerstones
1960 Asante Kotoko
1961 Not played
1962 Real Republicans
1963 Real Republicans
1964 Real Republicans

1965 Real Republicans
1966-8 Not played
1969 Cape Coast Dwarfs
1970-2 Not played
1973 Hearts of Oak
1974 Hearts of Oak
1975 Great Olympics
1976 Asante Kotoko
1977 Not played
1978 Asante Kotoko
1979 Hearts of Oak
1980 Not played
1981 Hearts of Oak
1982 Eleven Wise FC
1983 Great Olympics
1984 Asante Kotoko
1985 Sekondi Hasaacas
1986 Okwahu United
1987 Hearts of Oak
1988 Not played
1989 Hearts of Oak
1990 Hearts of Oak
1991 Not played
1992 Voradep
1993 Goldfields
1994 Hearts of Oak
1997 Ghaoha Readers

Guinea

Fédération Guinéenne de Football

Founded:	*1959*
Joined FIFA:	*1961*

CHAMPIONS

1965 Conakry I
1966 Conakry II
1967 Conakry II
1968 Conakry II
1969 Conakry I
1970 Conakry I
1971 Hafia FC
1972 Hafia FC
1973 Hafia FC
1974 Hafia FC
1975 Hafia FC
1976 Hafia FC
1977 Hafia FC
1978 Hafia FC
1979 Hafia FC
1980 Kaloum Star

1981 Kaloum Star
1982 Hafia FC
1983 Hafia FC
1984 Kaloum Star
1985 Hafia FC
1986 Horoya AC
1987 Kaloum Star
1988 Horoya AC
1989 Horoya AC
1990 Horoya AC
1991 Horoya AC
1992 Horoya AC
1993 Kaloum Star
1994 Horoya AC
1995 Horoya AC
1996 ASK Kaloum
1997 CI Kamsar

Guinea-Bissau

Federacao de Football da Guinea-Bissau

Founded:	*1974*
Joined FIFA:	*1986*

CHAMPIONS

1975 Balantes
1976 UDIB Bissau
1977 Benfica
1978 Not played
1979 Benfica
1980 Benfica
1981 Not played
1982 Benfica
1983 Sporting Clube Bissau
1984 Sporting Clube Bissau
1985 UDIB Bissau
1986 Sporting Clube Bissau

1987 Sporting Clube Bissau
1988 Benfica
1989 Benfica
1990 Sporting Clube Bissau
1991 Not played
1992 Sporting Clube Bissau
1993 Not played
1994 Porto FC
1995 Porto FC
1996 Porto FC
1997 Porto FC

Ivory Coast

Fédération Ivoirienne de Football

Founded:	*1960*
Joined FIFA:	*1960*
African Nations Cup:	*1992*

The Ivory Coast are one of Africa's great footballing enigmas. Of the field, they have a stable government and a healthy economy; on it the Ivory Coast has a well-organized league – advantages which many African countries do not enjoy – and yet success at international level eluded them until 1992. In that year 'The Elephants' won the African Nations Cup in Senegal, defeating Ghana on penalties in the final. They had previously been semi-finalists three times without going further.

The 1992 success confirmed the Ivorians as favourites to qualify for the 1994 World Cup finals for the first time ever, but they faded badly in the final round and finished second behind Nigeria.

CHAMPIONS

1960 Onze Freres
1961 Not played
1962 Stade Abidjan
1963 Stade Abidjan
1964 ASEC Abidjan
1965 Stade Abidjan
1966 Stade Abidjan
1967 Africa Sports
1968 Africa Sports
1969 Stade Abidjan
1970 ASEC Abidjan
1971 Africa Sports

1972 ASEC Abidjan
1973 ASEC Abidjan
1974 ASEC Abidjan
1975 ASEC Abidjan
1976 SC Gagnoa
1977 Africa Sports
1978 Africa Sports
1979 Stella Club
1980 ASEC Abidjan
1981 Stella Club
1982 Africa Sports
1983 Africa Sports
1984 Stella Club
1985 Africa Sports

1986 Africa Sports
1987 Africa Sports
1988 Africa Sports
1989 Africa Sports
1990 ASEC Abidjan
1991 ASEC Abidjan
1992 ASEC Abidjan
1993 ASEC Abidjan
1994 ASEC Abidjan
1995 ASEC Abidjan
1996 Africa Sports
1997 ASEC Abidjan

CUP WINNERS

1960 Espoir de Man
1961 Africa Sports
1962 ASEC Abidjan
1963 Jeunesse
1964 Africa Sports
1965 Not played
1966 Not played
1967 ASEC Abidjan
1968 ASEC Abidjan
1969 ASEC Abidjan
1970 ASEC Abidjan
1971 Stade Abidjan
1972 ASEC Abidjan

1973 ASEC Abidjan
1974 Stella Club
1975 Stella Club
1976 Stade Abidjan
1977 Africa Sports
1978 Africa Sports
1979 Africa Sports
1980 Reveil Daloa
1981 Africa Sports
1982 Africa Sports
1983 ASEC Abidjan
1984 Stade Abidjan
1985 Africa Sports
1986 Africa Sports
1987 ASC Bouake
1988 ASI Abengouron
1989 Africa Sports
1990 SC Gagnoa
1991 Africa Sports
1992 ASEC Abidjan
1993 Africa Sports
1994 Stade Abidjan
1995 ASEC Abidjan
1996 Soa
1997 ASEC Abidjan

Kenya

Kenya Football Federation
Founded: 1932
Joined FIFA: 1960

CHAMPIONS

1963 Nakuru All Stars
1964 Luo Union
1965 Liverpool
1966 Abaluhya United
1967 Abaluhya United
1968 Not played
1969 Gor Mahia
1970 Abuluhya United
1971 Not played
1972 Kenya Breweries
1973 Abaluyha
1974 Gor Mahia
1975 Luo Union
1976 Gor Mahia
1977 Kenya Breweries
1978 Kenya Breweries
1979 Gor Mahia
1980 Abaluyha
1981 AFC Leopards
1982 AFC Leopards
1983 Gor Mahia
1984 Gor Mahia
1985 Gor Mahia
1986 AFC Leopards
1987 Shabana Kissi
1988 AFC Leopards

1989 AFC Leopards
1990 Gor Mahia
1991 Gor Mahia
1992 AFC Leopards
1993 Gor Mahia
1994 Kenya Breweries
1995 Gor Mahia
1996 Kenya Breweries
1997 Utali

CUP WINNERS

1986 Gor Mahia
1987 Gor Mahia
1988 Gor Mahia
1989 Kenya Breweries
1990 Rivatex
1991 AFC Leopards
1992 Kenya Breweries
1993 Kenya Breweries
1994 AFC Leopards
1995 Gor Mahia
1996 Mumais Sugar
1997 Eldoret KCC

Lesotho

Lesotho Sports Council
Founded: 1932
Joined FIFA: 1964

CHAMPIONS

1970 Maseru United
1971 Majantja
1972 Police
1973 Linare
1974 Matlama
1975 FC Maseru
1976 Maseru United
1977 Matlama
1978 Matlama
1979 Linare
1980 Linare
1981 Maseru Brothers
1982 Matlama
1983 LPF Maseru

1984 LPF Maseru
1985 Lioli Teyateyaneng
1986 Matlama
1987 RLDF Maseru
1988 Matlama
1989 Arsenal
1990 RLDF Maseru
1991 Arsenal
1992 Matlama
1993 Arsenal
1994 RLDF Maseru
1995 RLDF Mascru
1996 RLDF Maseru
1997 Rovers

Liberia

Liberia Football Association
Founded: 1936
Joined FIFA: 1962

CHAMPIONS

1965 Invincible Eleven
1966 Invincible Eleven
1967 Mighty Barolle
1968-71 Not played
1972 Mighty Barolle
1973 Mighty Barolle
1974 Mighty Barolle
1975 Not played
1976 St. Joseph
1977 Not played
1978 St. Joseph
1979 St. Joseph
1980 Invincible Eleven
1981 Invincible Eleven
1982 Not played

1983 Invincible Eleven
1984 Invincible Eleven
1985 Invincible Eleven
1986 Mighty Barolle
1987 Invincible Eleven
1988 Mighty Barolle
1989 Mighty Barolle
1990 Not played
1991 LPRC Oilers
1992 LPRC Oilers
1993 Mighty Barolle
1994 NPA Anchors
1997 Junior Professional

Libya

Libyan Arab Jamahiriya Football Federation

Founded: 1962
Joined FIFA: 1963

CHAMPIONS

1964 Al Ahly Tripoli
1965 Al Ittihad
1966 Not played
1967 Al Tahaddy
1968 Not played
1969 Al Ittihad
1970 Al Ahly Benghazi
1971 Al Ahly Tripoli
1972 Al Ahly Benghazi
1973 Al Ahly Tripoli
1974 Al Ahly Tripoli
1975 Al Ahly Benghazi
1976 Al Medina
1977 Al Tahaddy
1978 Al Ahly Tripoli
1979 Not played
1980 Al Ahly Tripoli
1981 Not played
1982 Al Ahly Tripoli
1983 Al Medina
1984 Al Ahly Tripoli
1985 Al Adhara
1986 Al Ahly Tripoli
1987 Al Nasr
1988 Al Ittihad
1989 Al Ittihad
1990 Al Ittihad
1991 Al Ittihad
1992 Al Ahly Benghazi
1993 Al Ahly Tripoli
1994 Al Ahly Tripoli
1995 Al Ahly Tripoli
1996 Al Ahly Tripoli
1997 Al Ahly Tripoli

Madagascar

Fédération Malagasy de Football

Founded: 1961
Joined FIFA: 1962

CHAMPIONS

1968 Fitarikandro
1969 US Fontionnaires
1970 MMM Tamatave
1971 AS St. Michael
1972 Fortior Mahajanga
1973 Antalaha
1974 Corps Enseignant
1975 Corps Enseignant
1976 Not played
1977 Corps Enseignant
1978 AS St. Michael
1979 Fortior Mahajanga
1980 MMM Tamatave
1981 AS Somasud
1982 Dinamo Fima
1983 Dinamo Fima
1984 Not played
1985 AC Sotema
1986 BTM Antananarivo
1989 AC Sotema
1990 ASF Fianarantsoa
1991 AC Sotema
1992 AC Sotema
1993 BTM
1993 BTM
1995 Fobar
1996 FC BFV
1997 FC BFV

Malawi

Football Association of Malawi

Founded: 1966
Joined FIFA: 1967

Mali

Fédération Malienne de Football

Founded: 1960
Joined FIFA: 1962

CHAMPIONS

1980 AS Real Bamako
1981 AS Real Bamako
1982 Djoliba
1983 AS Real Bamako
1984 Stade Malien
1985 Djoliba
1986 AS Real Bamako
1987 Stade Malien
1988 Djoliba
1989 Stade Malien
1990 Djoliba
1991 Real Bamako
1992 Djoliba
1993 Stade Malien
1994 Not played
1995 Stade Malien
1996Djoliba

CUP WINNERS

1961 Stade Malien
1962 Real Bamako
1963 Stade Malien
1964 Real Bamako
1965 Djoliba
1966 Real Bamako
1967 Real Bamako
1968 Real Bamako
1969 Real Bamako
1970 Stade Malien
1971 Djoliba
1972 Stade Malien
1973 Djoliba
1974 Djoliba
1975 Djoliba
1976 Djoliba
1977 Djoliba
1978 Djoliba
1979 Djoliba
1980 Real Bamako
1981 Djoliba
1982 Stade Malien
1983 Djoliba
1984 Stade Malien
1985 Stade Malien
1986 Stade Malien
1987 Sigui Kayes
1988 Stade Malien
1989 Real Bamako
1990 Stade Malien
1991 Real Bamako
1992 Stade Malien
1993 Djoliba
1994 Stade Malien
1995 Stade Malien
1996 Stade Malien
1997 Djoliba

Mauritania

Fédération de Football de la République de Mauritanie

Founded: 1961
Joined FIFA: 1964

CHAMPIONS

1976 ASC Garde Nationale
1977 ASC Garde Nationale
1978 ASC Garde Nationale
1979 ASC Garde Nationale
1980 Not played
1981 AS Police
1982 AS Police
1983 AS Ksar
1984 ASC Garde Nationale
1985 AS Ksar
1986 AS Police
1987 AS Police
1988 AS Police
1989 Not played
1990 AS Police
1991 AS Police
1992 AS Sonader Ksar
1993 AS Sonader Ksar
1994 ASC Garde Nationale
1995 ASC Sonalec

1982 Police Club	1991 Sunrise SC
1983 Fire Brigade	1992 Sunrise SC
1984 Fire Brigade	1993 Fire Brigade
1985 Fire Brigade	1994 Fire Brigade
1986 Tamil Cadets	1995 Sunrise SC
1987 Sunrise SC	1996 Sunrise SC
1988 Fire Brigade	1997 Sunrise SC
1989 Sunrise SC	1998 Scouts Club
1990 Sunrise SC	

Salaheddine Bassir, one of Morocco's stars

Mauritius

Mauritius Football Association
Founded: 1952
Joined FIFA: 1962

CHAMPIONS

1970 FC Dodo
1971 Police Club
1972 Police Club
1973 Fire Brigade
1974 Fire Brigade
1975 Hindu Cadets
1976 Muslim Scouts
1977 Hindu Cadets
1978 Racing Club
1979 Hindu Cadets
1980 Fire Brigade
1981 Police Club

Morocco

Fédération Royale Marocaine de Football
Founded: 1955
Joined FIFA: 1956
African Nations Cup: 1976

Morocco qualified for the World Cup finals in 1970 – the first African side to do so – and have made steady progress since, even applying to host the finals in 1984 and 1998. In those 1970 finals they held Bulgaria to a draw and gave West Germany a terrible fright before losing 2–1. They qualified again in 1986 and won their first round group ahead of England, Poland and Portugal. In the second round they lost to the Germans again, but only through an unfortunate free-kick in the last minute. The side contained an outstanding goalkeeper, Zaki, and Mohammed Timoumi and Aziz Bouderbala were fine ball players in midfield. In 1976 they won the African Nations Cup for the only time and their presence at their third and fourth World Cup finals in 1994 and 1998 (in which striker Mustapha Hadji proved himself world class) confirmed them, along with Cameroon, as one of the leading soccer nations of Africa.

Moroccan domestic football is untypical of Africa, inasmuch as the clubs are well spread throughout the country, rather than concentrated in one city. They have also been very successful. FAR Rabat won the Champions Cup in 1985, as did Raja in 1989, followed by Wydad Casablanca in 1992.

Morocco has also provided several stars of French football. Probably the greatest was Larbi Ben Barek, the "Black Pearl", who won 17 French caps and had a distinguished career with Marseille and Stade Français in the inter-war years. Another French star born in Morocco was Just Fontaine, whose 13 goals in the 1958 World Cup finals remains a record.

CHAMPIONS

1916 CA Casablanca
1917 US Marocaine
1918 US Marocaine
1919 US Marocaine
1920 Olympique Marocaine
1921 Olympique Marocaine
1922 Olympique Marocaine
1923 US Fès
1924 Olympique Marocaine
1925 US Fès
1926 US Athletique
1927 Stade Marocaine
1928 Not played
1929 US Athletique
1930 Stade Marocaine
1931 US Marocaine
1932 US Marocaine
1933 US Marocaine
1934 US Marocaine
1935 US Marocaine

1936 Olympique Marocaine
1937 Olympique Marocaine
1938 US Marocaine
1939 US Marocaine
1940 US Marocaine
1941 US Marocaine
1942 US Marocaine
1943 US Marocaine
1944 Stade Marocaine
1945 Racing Avant-Garde
1946 US Marocaine
1947 US Athletique
1948 WAC Casablanca
1949 WAC Casablanca
1950 WAC Casablanca
1951 WAC Casablanca
1952-6 Not played
1957 WAC Casablanca
1958 KAC Marrakech
1959 EJS Casablanca
1960 KAC Kenitra
1961 FAR Rabat
1962 FAR Rabat
1963 FAR Rabat
1964 FAR Rabat
1965 MAS Fès
1966 WAC Casablanca
1967 FAR Rabat
1968 FAR Rabat
1969 WAC Casablanca
1970 FAR Rabat
1971 RS Settat
1972 ADM Casablanca
1973 KAC Kenitra
1974 RBM Beni Mellal
1975 MC Oujda
1976 WAC Casablanca
1977 WAC Casablanca
1978 WAC Casablanca
1979 MAS Fès
1980 Chebab Mohammedia
1981 KAC Kenitra
1982 KAC Kenitra
1983 MAS Fes
1984 FAR Rabat
1985 MAS Fes
1986 WAC Casablanca
1987 FAR Rabat
1988 Raja Casablanca
1989 FAR Rabat
1990 WAC Casablanca
1991 WAC Casablanca

1992 KAC Marrakech
1993 WAC Casablanca
1994 Olympic Casablanca
1995 COD Meknes
1996 Raja Casablanca
1997 Raja Casablanca
1998 Raja Casablanca

CUP WINNERS

1957 MC Oujda
1958 MC Oujda
1959 FAR Rabat
1960 MC Oujda
1961 KAC Kenitra
1962 MC Oujda
1963 KAC Marrakech
1964 KAC Marrakech
1965 KAC Marrakech
1966 COD Meknes
1967 FUS Rabat
1968 Raja Casablanca
1969 RS Settat
1970 WAC Casablanca
1971 FAR Rabat
1972 Chabab Mohammedia
1973 FUS Rabat
1974 Raja Casablanca
1975 Chabab Mohammedia
1976 FUS Rabat
1977 Raja Casablanca
1978 WAC Casablanca
1979 WAC Casablanca
1980 MAS Fes
1981 WAC Casablanca
1982 Raja Casablanca
1983 CLAS Casablanca
1984 FAR Rabat
1985 FAR Rabat
1986 FAR Rabat
1987 KAC Marrakech
1988 Not played
1989 WAC Casablanca
1990 Not played
1991 Not played
1992 Olympic Casablanca
1993 WAC Casablanca
1995 FAR Rabat
1996 Raja Casablanca
1997 WAC Casablanca

1980 Costa do Sol
1981 Textil Pungue Beira
1982 Ferroviario Maputo
1983 Grupo Desportivo Maputo
1984 Maxaquene
1985 Maxaquene
1986 Maxaquene
1987 Matchedje
1988 Grupo Desportivo Maputo
1989 Ferroviario Maputo

1990 Matchadje
1991 Costa do Sol
1992 Costa do Sol
1993 Costa do Sol
1994 Costa do Sol
1995 Costa do Sol
1996 Costa do Sol
1997 Ferraviario

Namibia

Namibia Football Federation

Founded:	*1992*
Joined FIFA:	*1992*

Niger

Fédération Nigérienne de Football

Founded:	*1967*
Joined FIFA:	*1967*

CHAMPIONS

1966 Secteur 6
1967 Secteur 6
1968 Secteur 6
1969 Secteur 6
1970 Secteur 6
1971 ASFAN Niamey
1972 Not played
1973 Secteur 7
1974 Olympic FC
1975 ASFAN Niamey
1976 Olympic FC
1977 Olympic FC
1978 Olympic FC
1979 Not played
1980 AS Niamey
1981 AS Niamey

1982 AS Niamey
1983 Djan-Gorzo Maradi
1984 Espoir FC Zinder
1985 Zumunta AC
1986 Not played
1987 Sahel SC
1988 Zumunta AC
1989 Olympic FC
1990 Olympic FC
1991 Sahel SC
1992 Sahel SC
1993 Zumunta AC
1994 Sahel SC
1997 Sahel SC

Mozambique

Federacao Moçambicana de Futebol

Founded:	*1975*
Joined FIFA:	*1978*

CHAMPIONS

1976 Textafrica

1977 Grupo Desportivo Maputo
1978 Grupo Desportivo Maputo
1979 Costa do Sol

Nigeria

Nigeria Football Association

Founded:	*1945*
Joined FIFA:	*1959*
Olympic Games:	*1996*
African Nations Cup:	*1980, 1994*

Nigeria, with a huge population and over 500 registered clubs, emerged at last in the 1990s as one of the most powerful nations in Africa. Nigeria's youngsters had already proved well capable of winning trophies, and this continues to bode well for the future

Nigeria's Sunday Oliseh celebrates the goal that beat Spain 3–2 in the 1998 World Cup Finals

of the national side. In 1985 Nigeria won the World Under-17 Championship, becoming the first African side to win a FIFA world tournament at any level, beating West Germany 2–0 in the final; in 1989, Nigeria were runners-up in the World Under-20 Youth Championship; and in 1993 the "Green Eaglets" won their second Under-17 title in only the event's fifth staging.

A World Cup breakthrough came in 1994 when Nigeria nearly sprang one of the greatest of all upsets. They topped their first-round group, ahead of Argentina, Bulgaria and Greece, and only narrowly went out to eventual finalists Italy in the second round.

Sadly, political problems prevented Nigeria from defending their African Nations title in South Africa in 1996. But they more than atoned later in the year by becoming the first African nation to win the Olympic tournament – beating favourites Brazil in the semi-final and Argentina in the final.

At France '98, Nigeria made an instant impact by beating Spain 3-2 in a first-round thriller and the players talked of becoming world champions. But, having topped their group, Nigeria crashed 4-1 to Denmark in the second round. The finals saw the emotional return of striker Nwankwo Kanu, who only two years earlier had been told his career was over because of a heart defect.

CHAMPIONS

1972 Mighty Jets
1973 Bendel Insurance
1974 Enugu Rangers
1975 Enugu Rangers
1976 IICC Shooting Stars
1977 Enugu Rangers
1978 Racca Rovers
1979 Bendel Insurance
1980 IICC Shooting Stars
1981 Enugu Rangers
1982 Enugu Rangers
1983 IICC Shooting Stars
1984 Enugu Rangers
1985 New Nigeria Bank
1986 Leventis United
1987 Iwuanyanwu Owerri
1988 Iwuanyanwu Owerri
1989 Iwuanyanwu Owerri
1990 Iwuanyanwu Owerri
1991 Julius Berger
1992 Stationery Stores
1993 Iwuanyanwu Owerri
1994 BCC Lions
1995 HCC Shooting Stars
1996 Udoji United Aura
1997 Eagle Cement

CUP WINNERS

1945 Marine
1946 Lagos Railways
1947 Marine
1948 Lagos Railways
1949 Lagos Railways
1950 GO Urion
1951 Lagos Railways
1952 Lagos Railways
1953 Kano
1954 Calabar
1955 Port Harcourt
1956 Lagos Railways
1957 Lagos Railways
1958 Port Harcourt
1959 Ibadan Lions
1960 Lagos EDN
1961 Ibadan Lions
1962 Police
1963 Port Harcourt
1964 Lagos Railways
1965 Lagos EDN
1966 Ibadan Lions
1967 Stationery Stores
1968 Stationery Stores
1969 Ibadan Lions
1970 Lagos EDN
1971 IICC Shooting Stars

1972 Bendel Insurance
1973 Not played
1974 Enugu Rangers
1975 Enugu Rangers
1976 Enugu Rangers
1977 IICC Shooting Stars
1978 Bendel Insurance
1979 IICC Shooting Stars
1980 Bendel Insurance
1981 Enugu Rangers
1982 Stationery Stores
1983 Enugu Rangers
1984 Leventis United
1985 Abiola Babes

1986 Leventis United
1987 Abiola Babes
1988 Iwuanyanwu Owerri
1989 BCC Lions
1990 Stationery Stores
1991 El Kanemi Warriors
1992 El Kanemi Warriors
1993 BCC Lions
1994 BCC Lions
1995 Shooting Stars
1996 Julius Berger

Reunion

Ligue de la Réunion
Founded: 1985
Joined FIFA: *Associate member*

Rwanda

Fédération Rwandaise de Football Amateur
Founded: 1972
Joined FIFA: 1976

CHAMPIONS

1981 Rayon Sports
1982 Not played
1983 Kiyovou Sports
1984 Pantheres Noires
1985 Pantheres Noires
1986 Pantheres Noires
1987 Pantheres Noires
1988 Mukungwa Ruhengeri

1989 Mukungwa Ruhengeri
1990 Not played
1991 Not played
1992 Kiyovou Sports
1993 Kiyovou Sports
1994 -
1995 APR

Sao Tome And Principe

Federacion Santomense de Futebol
Founded: 1975
Joined FIFA: 1986

CHAMPIONS

1977 Vitoria Riboque
1978 Vitoria Riboque
1979 Vitoria Riboque
1980 Desportivo Guadelupe
1981 Desportivo Guadelupe
1982 Praia Cruz
1983 Not played
1984 Andorinhas
1985 Praia Cruz

1986 Vitoria Riboque
1987 Not played
1988 6 de Septembro
1989 Vitoria Riboque
1990 OS Operacios
1991 Santana
1992 OS Operacios
1996 Santana
1997 Santana

Senegal

Fédération Sénégalaise de Football
Founded: 1960
Joined FIFA: 1962

CHAMPIONS

1970 ASC Diaraf
1971 ASFA Dakar
1972 ASFA Dakar
1973 ASC Jeanne d'Arc
1974 ASFA Dakar
1975 ASC Diaraf
1976 ASC Diaraf
1977 ASC Diaraf
1978 US Goreé
1979 AS Police
1980 SEIB Diourbel
1981 US Goreé
1982 ASC Diaraf
1983 SEIB Diourbel
1984 US Goreé
1985 ASC Jeanne d'Arc
1986 ASC Jeanne d'Arc
1987 SEIB Diourbel
1988 ASC Jeanne d'Arc
1989 ASC Diaraf
1990 Port Autonome
1991 Port Autonome
1992 Ndiambour
1993 AS Douanes
1994 Ndiambour
1995 ASC Diaraf

CUP WINNERS

1961 Espoir St. Louis
1962 ASC Jeanne d'Arc
1963 US Rail
1964 US Ouakam
1965 US Goreé

1966 AS St. Louisienne
1967 Foyer France-Senegal
1968 Foyer France-Senegal
1969 ASC Jeanne d'Arc
1970 ASC Diaraf
1971 ASC Linguère
1972 US Goreé
1973 ASC Diaraf
1974 ASC Jeanne d'Arc
1975 ASC Diaraf
1976 ASF Police
1977 Saltigue
1978 ASF Police
1979 Casa Sport
1980 ASC Jeanne d'Arc
1981 ASF Police
1982 ASC Diaraf
1983 ASC Diaraf
1984 ASC Jeanne d'Arc
1985 ASC Diaraf
1986 AS Douanes
1987 ASC Jeanne d'Arc
1988 ASC Linguère
1989 US Ouakam
1990 ASC Linguère
1991 ASC Diaraf
1992 US Goreé
1993 ASC Diaraf
1994 ASC Diaraf
1995 Diardf
1996 Sonacos
1997 AS Dohanes

Seychelles

Seychelles Football Federation
Founded: 1976
Joined FIFA: 1986

CHAMPIONS

1986 St. Louis
1987 St. Louis
1988 St. Louis
1988 St. Louis
1989 St. Louis
1990 St. Louis

1991 St. Louis
1992 St. Louis
1993 -
1994 -
1995 Sunshine
1996 -
1997 S. Michel United

Sierra Leone

Sierra Leone Amateur Football Association

Founded: 1923
Joined FIFA: 1967

CHAMPIONS

1978 Mighty Blackpool
1979 Mighty Blackpool
1980 East End Lions
1981 Real Republicans
1982 Sierra Fisheries
1983 Real Republicans
1984 Real Republicans
1985 East End Lions
1986 Sierra Fisheries
1987 Sierra Fisheries
1988 Mighty Blackpool
1989 Freetown United
1990 Old Edwardians
1991 Mighty Blackpool
1992 Not played
1993 East End Lions
1994 Mighty Blackpool
1995 Mighty Blackpool
1996 Mighty Blackpool
1997 Mighty Blackpool

Somalia

Somalia Football Federation

Founded: 1951
Joined FIFA: 1961

CHAMPIONS

1967 Somali Police
1968 Hoga Mogadishu
1969 Lavori Publici
1970 Lavori Publici
1971 Lavori Publici
1972 Horsed
1973 Horsed
1974 Horsed
1975 Mogadishu Municipality
1976 Horsed
1977 Horsed
1978 Horsed
1979 Horsed
1980 Horsed
1981 Lavori Publici
1982 Wagad
1983 Printing Agency
1984 Marine Club
1985 Wagad
1986 Mogadishu Municipality
1987 Wagad
1988 Wagad
1989 Mogadishu Municipality
1990 Jadidka
1991 -
1992 -
1993 -
1994 Morris Supplies
1995 Alba

Johannesburg, South Africa: home to the 1996 African Nations Cup Final which was won by the hosts

South Africa

South African Football Association

Founded:	*1892*
Joined FIFA:	*1952 (suspended 1964–76), 1992*
African Nations Cup:	*1996*

Football is the sport of the masses in South Africa, but for 30 years the top clubs, such as the Kaiser Chiefs and Orlando Pirates, were football outcasts in Africa, until the collapse of apartheid. Returning to the fold in 1992, South Africa not only hosted the 1996 African Nations Cup but shocked the world by winning it. But, despite the emergence of new scoring sensation Benni McCarthy, they failed to defend it in 1998, losing 2-0 to Egypt in the final in Burkina Faso. South Africa made their World Cup finals debut in France the same year, going out in the first round.

CHAMPIONS

1971 Orlando Pirates
1972 AmaZulu
1973 Orlando Pirates
1974 Kaizer Chiefs
1975 Orlando Pirates
1976 Kaizer Chiefs
1977 Kaizer Chiefs
1978 Lusitano
1979 Kaizer Chiefs
1980 Highlands Park
1981 Kaizer Chiefs
1982 Durban City
1983 Durban City
1984 Kaizer Chiefs
1985 Bush Bucks
1986 Rangers
1987 Jomo Cosmos
1988 Mamelodi Sundowns
1989 Kaizer Chiefs
1990 Mamelodi Sundowns
1991 Kaizer Chiefs
1992 Kaizer Chiefs
1993 Mamelodi Sundowns
1994 Orlando Pirates
1995 Cape Town Spurs
1996 Cape Town Spurs
1997 Manning Rangers
1998 Mamelodi Sundowns

CUP WINNERS

1978 Wits University
1979 Kaizer Chiefs
1980 Orlando Pirates
1981 Kaizer Chiefs
1982 Kaizer Chiefs
1983 Moroka Swallows
1984 Kaizer Chiefs
1985 Bloemfontein Celtic
1986 Mamelodi Sundowns
1987 Kaizer Chiefs
1988 Orlando Pirates
1989 Moroka Swallows
1990 Jomo Cosmos
1991 Moroka Swallows
1992 Kaizer Chiefs
1993 Witbank Aces
1994 Vaal Professionals
1995 -
1996 Orlando Pirates

Sudan

Sudan Football Federation

Founded:	*1936*
Joined FIFA:	*1948*
African Nations Cup:	*1970*

CHAMPIONS

1964 Al Hilal
1965 Al Hilal
1966 Al Hilal
1967 Al Hilal
1968 Al Mourouda
1969 Burri
1970 Al Merreikh
1971 Al Merreikh
1972 Al Merreikh
1973 Al Merreikh
1974 Al Hilal
1975 Al Merreikh
1976 Not played
1977 Al Merreikh
1978 Al Merreikh
1979 Not played
1980 Not played
1981 Al Hilal
1982 Al Merreikh
1983 Al Hilal
1984 Al Hilal
1985 Al Merreikh
1986 Al Hilal
1987 Al Hilal
1988 Al Hilal
1989 Al Hilal
1990 Al Merreikh
1991 Al Hilal
1992 Al Hilal
1993 Al Merreikh
1994 Al Hilal
1995 Al Hilal
1996 Al Hilal
1997 Al Hilal

Swaziland

National Football Association of Swaziland

Founded:	*1964*
Joined FIFA:	*1976*

CHAMPIONS

1980 Mbabane Highlanders
1981 Peacemakers
1982 Mbabane Highlanders
1983 Manzini Wanderers
1984 Mbabane Highlanders
1985 Manzine Wanderers
1986 Mbabane Highlanders
1987 Manzini Wanderers
1988 Mbabane Highlanders
1989 Denver Sundowns
1990 Denver Sundowns
1991 Mbabane Highlanders
1992 Mbabane Highlanders
1993 Mbabane Swallows
1994 Eleven Men In Flight
1995 Mbabane Highlanders
1996 Elven Men In Flight
1997 Mbabane Highlanders
1998 Mbabane Highlanders

Tanzania

Football Association of Tanzania

Founded:	*1930*
Joined FIFA:	*1964*

CHAMPIONS

1965 Dar Sunderland
1966 Dar Sunderland
1967 Cosmopolitans
1968 Young Africans
1969 Young Africans
1970 Young Africans
1971 Young Africans
1972 SC Simba
1973 SC Simba
1974 Young Africans
1975 Mseto
1976 SC Simba
1977 SC Simba
1978 SC Simba
1979 SC Simba
1980 SC Simba
1981 Young Africans
1982 Pan African
1983 Young Africans
1984 KMKM Zanzibar
1985 Maji Maji
1986 Maji Maji
1987 Young Africans
1988 Pan African
1989 Malindi
1990 Pamba SC
1991 Young Africans
1992 Malindi
1993 SC Simba
1994 Young Africans
1995 SC Simba
1996 SC Simba
1997 Young Africans

Togo

Fédération Togolaise de Football

Founded:	*1960*
Joined FIFA:	*1962*

CHAMPIONS

1965 Etoile Filante
1966 Modele Lomé
1967 Etoile Filante
1968 Etoile Filante
1969 Modele Lomé
1970 Dynamic Lomé
1971 Dynamic Lomé
1972 Modele Lomé
1973 Modele Lomé
1974 Lomé I
1975 Lomé I
1976 Lomé I
1977 Not played
1978 Not played
1979 Semassi Sokode
1980 Agaza Lomé

1981 Semassi Sokode
1982 Semassi Sokode
1983 Semassi Sokode
1984 Agaza Lomé
1985 ASFOSA
1986 ASFOSA
1987 Doumbe Sausanne-Mango
1988 ASKO Kara
1989 ASKO Kara
1990 Ifodje Atakpame
1991 Not played
1992 Etoile Filante
1993 Semassi Sokodé
1994 Semassi Sokodé
1995 Semassi Sokodé
1996 Asko Kara
1997 Dynamic Lomé
1998 Dynamic Lomé

Tunisia

Fédération Tunisienne de Football

Founded:	*1956*
Joined FIFA:	*1960*

CHAMPIONS

1921 Racing Club
1922 Stade Gauloise
1923 Stade Gauloise
1924 Racing Club
1925 Sporting Club
1926 Stade Gauloise
1927 Sporting Club
1928 Avant Garde
1929 US Tunisienne
1930 US Tunisienne
1931 Italia de Tunis
1932 US Tunisienne
1933 Sfax Railway
1934 Italia de Tunis
1935 Italia de Tunis
1936 Italia de Tunis
1937 Savoia de la Goulette
1938 CS Gabesien
1939 Not played
1940 Not played
1941 Esperance Tunis
1942 Not played
1943 Not played
1944 CA Bizerte
1945 CA Bizerte
1946 Club Africain
1947 Club Africain

1948 CA Bizerte
1949 Etoile du Sahel
1950 CS Hammam-Lif
1951-5 Not played
1956 CS Hammam-Lif
1957 Stade Tunisien
1958 Etoile du Sahel
1959 Esperance Tunis
1960 Esperance Tunis
1961 Stade Tunisien
1962 Stade Tunisien
1963 Etoil du Sahel
1964 Club Africain
1965 Stade Tunisien
1966 Etoile du Sahel
1967 Club Africain
1968 Sfax Railway
1969 CS Sfax
1970 Esperance Tunis
1971 CS Sfax
1972 Etoile du Sahel
1973 Club Africain
1974 Club Africain
1975 Esperance Tunis
1976 Esperance Tunis
1977 JS Kairouan
1978 CS Sfax
1979 Club Africain

Sami Trabelsi of Tunisia takes on England's Paul Scholes

1980 Club Africain
1981 CS Sfax
1982 Esperance Tunis
1983 CS Sfax
1984 CA Bizerte
1985 Esperance Tunis
1986 Etoile du Sahel
1987 Etoile du Sahel
1988 Esperance Tunis
1989 Esperance Tunis
1990 Club Africain
1991 Esperancc Tunis
1992 Club Africain
1993 Esperance Tunis
1994 Esperance Tunis
1995 CS Sfax
1996 Club Africain
1997 Esperance Tunis

1998 Esperance Tunis

CUP WINNERS

1922 Avant Garde
1923 Racing Club
1924 Stade Gauloise
1925 Sporting Club
1926 Stade Gauloise
1927 Not played
1928 Not played
1929 US Tunisiene
1930 US Tunisiene
1931 Racing Club
1932 US Tunisiene
1933 US Tunisiene
1934 US Tunisiene
1935 Italia de Tunis
1936 Stade Gauloise

1937 Sporting Club
1938 Esperance Tunis
1939 Not played
1940 Not played
1941 US Ferryville
1942 Not played
1943 Not played
1944 Olympique Tunis
1945 Patrie FC Bizerte
1946 CS Hammam-Lif
1947 CS Hammam-Lif
1948 CS Hammam-Lif
1949 CS Hammam-Lif
1950 CS Hammam-Lif
1951-5 Not played
1956 Stade Tunisien
1957 Etoile de Tunis
1958 Stade Tunisien
1959 Etoile du Sahel
1960 Stade Tunisien
1961 AS Marsa
1962 Stade Tunisien
1963 Etoile du Sahel
1964 Esperance Tunis
1965 Club Africain
1966 Stade Tunisien
1967 Club Africain
1968 Club Africain
1969 Club Africain

1970 Club Africain
1971 CS Sfax
1972 Club Africain
1973 Club Africain
1974 Etoile du Sahel
1975 Etoile du Sahel
1976 Club Africain
1977 AS Marsa
1978 Not played
1979 Esperance Tunis
1980 Esperance Tunis
1981 Etoile du Sahel
1982 CA Bizerte
1983 Etoile du Sahel
1984 AS Marsa
1985 CS Hammam-Lif
1986 Esperance Tunis
1987 CA Bizerte
1988 COT Tunis
1989 Club Africain
1990 AS Marsa
1991 Etoile du Sarhel
1992 Club Africain
1993 Olympique Beja
1994 AS Marsa
1995 CS Sfaxien
1996 Etoile du Sahel
1997 Esperance Tunis

Uganda

Federation of Uganda Football Associations

Founded:	1924
Joined FIFA:	1959

CHAMPIONS

1966 Express FC
1967 Bitumastic
1968 Not played
1969 Prisons FC
1970 Coffee FC
1971 Simba FC
1972 Simba FC
1973 Simba FC
1974 Express FC
1975 Express FC
1976 Kampala CC
1977 Kampala CC
1978 Kampala CC
1979 Commercial Bank
1980 Nile FC
1981 Kampala CC

1982 Nakivubo Villa
1983 Kampala CC
1984 Nakivubo Villa
1985 Kampala CC
1986 Kampala CC
1987 Nakivubo Villa
1988 Express FC
1989 Express FC
1990 Nakivubo Villa
1991 Kampala CC
1992 Nakivubo Villa
1993 Express FC
1994 Nakivubo Villa
1995 Express Red Eagles
1996 Express Red Eagles
1997 City Council SC

Zaire

Fédération Zaireoise de Football-Association

Founded:	1919
Joined FIFA:	1964
African Nations Cup:	1968, 1974

Zaire won their second African Nations Cup in 1974, the year in which they also became the first black African side to qualify for the World Cup finals. But the gulf in experience between the `Leopards' and their European and South American opponents was cruelly exposed. Since then, their best performances have been in the African Nations Cup.

CHAMPIONS

1990 FC Lupopo
1991 Mikishi
1992 US Bilombe
1993 AS Vita Club
1994 AS Vita Club
1995 AS Vita Club
1996 AS Vita Club
1997 Motemba Pembe

CUP WINNERS

1964 Daring Club Motema Pembe
1965 Dragond Kinshasa
1966 Toute Puissant Englebert
1967 Toute Puissant Englebert
1968 St. Eloi
1969 Not played
1970 Not played
1971 AS Vita Club
1972 AS Vita Club

1973 AS Vita Club
1974 CS Imana
1975 AS Vita Club
1976 Toute Puissant Englebert
1977 AS Vita Club
1978 CS Imana
1979 AS Bilima
1980 AS Vita Club
1981 FC Lupopo
1982 AS Bilima
1983 Sanga Balende
1984 AS Bilima
1985 US Tshinkunku Kalamu
1986 FC Lupopo
1987 Daring Club Motema Pembe
1988 AS Vita Club
1989 Daring Club Motema Pembe
1995 AC Sodigraf
1996 AC Sodigraf
1997 AC Sodigraf

Zambia

Football Association of Zambia

Founded:	1929
Joined FIFA:	1964

Zambia's national side have been semi-finalists in the African Nations Cup three times since 1974, and pulled off a remarkable victory over Italy in the 1988 Olympics in Seoul. The star was Kalusha Bwalya, who became a top professional with PSV Eindhoven in Holland.

Sadly, Zambia will always now be remembered for the plane crash in April 1993 which wiped out the entire national squad – bar the five overseas-based professionals who were not travelling with the rest to a World Cup qualifier in Senegal. Astonishingly, the Zambians rebuilt their squad around their five exports, and went on to reach the 1994 African Nations Cup Final. They reached to the second round of the African World Cup qualifiers but missed clinching a place in the finals losing the last game, 1–0 in Morocco.

Zambian clubs are also beginning to do well in the African club competitions. Nkana Red Devils were runners-up in the 1990 Champions Cup, and Power Dynamos won the 1991 Cup-winners' Cup.

CHAMPIONS

1962 Roan United
1963 Mufulira Wanderers
1964 City of Lusaka
1965 Mufulira Wanderers
1966 Mufulira Wanderers
1967 Mufulira Wanderers
1968 Kabwe Warriors
1969 Mufulira Wanderers
1970 Kabwe Warriors
1971 Kabwe Warriors
1972 Kabwe Warriors
1973 Zambia Army
1974 Zambia Army
1975 Green Buffaloes
1976 Mufulira Wanderers
1977 Green Buffaloes
1978 Mufulira Wanderers
1979 Green Buffalocs
1980 Nchanga Rangers
1981 Green Buffaloes
1982 Nkana Red Devils
1983 Nkana Red Devils
1984 Power Dynamos
1985 Nkana Red Devils
1986 Nkana Red Devils
1987 Kabwe Warriors
1988 Nkana Red Devils
1989 Nkana Red Devils
1990 Nkana Red Devils
1991 Power Dynamos
1992 Nkana Red Devils
1993 Nkana FC
1994 Power Dynamos
1995 Power Dynamos
1996 Power Dynamos
1997 Power Dynamos

CUP WINNERS

1962 Bulawayo Rovers
1963 Salisbury Callies
1964 Not played
1965 Salisbury City Wanderers
1966 Mangula
1967 Salisbury Callies
1968 Arcadia United
1969 Arcadia United
1970 Wankie
1971 Chibuku
1972 Mangula
1973 Wankie
1974 Chibuku
1975 Salisbury Callies
1976 Dynamos
1977 Zimbabwe Saints
1978 Zisco Steel
1979 Zimbabwe Saints
1980 CAPS United
1981 CAPS United
1982 CAPS United
1983 CAPS United
1984 Black Rhinos
1985 Dynamos
1986 Highlanders
1987 CAPS United
1988 Dynamos
1989 Dynamos
1990 Highlanders
1991 Dynamos
1992 Wankie
1993 Tanganda Mutare
1994 Blackpool
1995 Blackpool
1996 Blackpool
1997 Blackpool

Zimbabwe

Zimbabwe Football Association	
Founded:	*1950*
Joined FIFA:	*1965*

Zimbabwe won independence as recently as 1983 and have been making steady progress ever since. They went within one game of reaching the 1994 World Cup finals, but lost the last group match 3–1 in Cameroon. Their emergence owed much to former Liverpool goalkeeper Bruce Grobbelaar, and another English based player, Peter Ndlovu.

CHAMPIONS

1962 Bulawayo Rovers
1963 Dynamos
1964 St. Pauls
1965 Dynamos
1966 St. Pauls
1967 Tornados
1968 Sables
1969 Sables
1970 Dynamos
1971 Arcadia United
1972 Sables
1973 Metal Box
1974 Sables
1975 Chibuku
1976 Dynamos
1977 Zimbabwe Saints
1978 Dynamos
1979 CAPS United
1980 Dynamos
1981 Dynamos
1982 Dynamos
1983 Dynamos
1984 Black Rhinos
1985 Dynamos
1986 Dynamos
1987 Black Rhinos
1988 Zimbabwe Saints
1989 Dynamos
1990 Highlanders
1991 Dynamos
1992 Black Aces
1993 Bulawayo Highlanders
1994 Dynamos
1995 Dynamos
1996 Caps United
1997 Dynamos
1998 Dynamos

The Zambia national team train before spectators

ASIA (AFC)

Sheer geography makes Asia the most awkward of FIFA's regional confederations. The varied time zones and climates between Lebanon in the west, the former Soviet republics in the north, Japan in the east and India in the south long hindered the development of credible international tournaments.

A signal that Asian football has come of age was evident when FIFA awarded Japan and South Korean rights to – uniquely – co-host the 2002 World Cup finals. It will be the first time the game's top event has been staged in Asia.

Although it is probably many years away, the time will come when an Asian nation – whether it is a current power such as South Korea or Saudi Arabia, or a new force such as Japan or China – wins the World Cup.

Afghanistan

The Football Federation of the National Olympic Committee

Founded:	*1922*
Joined FIFA:	*1948*

Bahrain

Bahrain Football Association

Founded:	*1951*
Joined FIFA:	*1966*

CHAMPIONS

1957 Muharraq	1977 Al Ahly
1958 Muharraq	1978 Bahrain Club
1959 As Nasr	1979 Al Hala
1960 Muharraq	1980 Muharraq
1961 Muharraq	1981 Bahrain Club
1962 Muharraq	1982 West Riffa
1963 Muharraq	1983 Muharraq
1964 Muharraq	1984 Muharraq
1965 Muharraq	1985 Bahrain Club
1966 Muharraq	1986 Muharraq
1967 Muharraq	1987 West Riffa
1968 Bahrain Club	1988 Muharraq
1969 Al Ahly	1989 Bahrain Club
1970 Muharraq	1990 West Riffa
1971 Muharraq	1991 Muharraq
1972 Al Ahly	1992 Muharraq
1973 Muharraq	1993 West Riffa
1974 Muharraq	1994 East Riffa
1975 Al Arabi	1995 Muharraq
1976 Muharraq	1996 Muharraq
	1997 Al Hilal

Bangladesh

Bangladesh Football Federation

Founded:	*1972*
Joined FIFA:	*1974*

CHAMPIONS

1948 Victoria Sporting	1973 Bangladesh IDC
1949 East Pakistan Gymkhana	1974 Abahani Krira Chakra
1950 Dhaka Wanderers	1975 Mohammedan Sporting
1951 Dhaka Wanderers	1976 Mohammedan Sporting
1952 Bengal Government Press	1977 Abahani Krira Chakra
1953 Dhaka Wanderers	1978 Mohammedan Sporting
1954 Dhaka Wanderers	1979 Bangladdesh Jute Mill Corp
1955 Dhaka Wanderers	1980 Mohammedan Sporting
1956 Dhaka Wanderers	1981 Abahani Krira Chakra
1957 Mohammedan Sporting	1982 Mohammedan Sporting
1958 Azad Sporting	1983 Abahani Krira Chakra
1959 Mohammedan Sporting	1984 Abahani Krira Chakra
1960 Dhaka Wanderers	1985 Abahani Krira Chakra
1961 Mohammedan Sporting	1986 Mohammedan Sporting
1962 Victoria Sporting	1987 Mohammedan Sporting
1963 Mohammedan Sporting	1988 Mohammedan Sporting
1964 Victoria Sporting	1989 Mohammedan Sporting
1965 Mohammedan Sporting	1990 Abahni Krira Chakra
1966 Mohammedan Sporting	1991 Not played
1967 East Pakistan IDC	1992 Abahani Krira Chakra
1968 East Pakistan IDC	1993 Abahani Krira Chakra
1969 Mohammedan Sporting	1994 Abahini Krira Chakra
1970 East Pakistan IDC	1995 Abahini Krira Chakra
1971–72 Not played	1996 Mohammedan SC
	1997 Muktijoddha SKC
	1998 Muktijoddha SKC

Bhutan

Bhutan Football Federation

Founded:	*1960*
Joined FIFA:	*Associate member*

Brunei Darussalam

Brunei Amateur Football Association

Founded:	*1959*
Joined FIFA:	*1969*

Cambodia

Federation Khmere De Football Association

Founded:	*1933*
Joined FIFA:	*1953*

China

Football Association of the People's Republic of China

Founded: 1924
FIFA: 1931–58, 1979

China took part in the first international match played on Asian soil, when they met the Philippines, in Manila, in February 1913, in the Far Eastern Games. But progress was thwarted because of the Taiwan issue. A side containing only Hong Kong players took part in the 1954 Asian Games, calling themselves China. The Chinese Association protested that they were the controlling body and subsequently withdrew from FIFA in 1958.

Despite being the most populous country on earth, success has utterly eluded China. Their greatest achievement to date is a runners-up spot in the 1984 Asian Cup.

Efforts to improve the game are now being made, with the launch of a professional league backed by multi-national sponsorship, but China are still some way short of their Asian rivals – as disappointing qualifying round exits in the 1994 and 1998 World Cup qualifiers illustrated.

CHAMPIONS

1926 South China	Institute
1927 South China	1965 Jilin
1928 East China	1966–72 Not played
1929 East China	1973 Beijing
1930 South China	1974 Army
1931 East China	1975 Guangxi
1932 Not played	1976 Beijing
1933 East China	1977 Army
1934–46 Not played	1978 Liaoning
1947 Tung Hwa and East China	1979 Guangdong
1948 East China and Tsing Peh	1980 Tianjin
1949 Tsing Peh	1981 Army
1950 Not played	1982 Beijing
1951 North East China	1983 Shanghai
1952 Not played	1984 Beijing
1953 Army	1985 Liaoning
1954 North East China	1986 Army
1955 Central Institute of Physical	1987 Guangdong
Culture	1988 Liaoning
1956 Not played	1989 Liaoning
1957 Tianjin	1990 Liaoning
1958 Beijing	1991 Liaoning
1959 Army	1992 Liaoning
1960 Tianjin	1993 Liaoning
1961 Shanghai	1994 Dalian
1962 Shanghai	1995 Shanghai
1963 Beijing Youth	1996 Dalian
1964 Beijing Physical Culture	1997 Dalian

Chinese Tapei

Chinese Tapei Football Association

Founded: 1936
Joined FIFA: 1954

Guam

Guam Soccer Association

Founded: 1975
FIFA: Associate member

Hong Kong

Hong Kong Football Association

Founded: 1914
FIFA: 1954

Football has been played in Hong Kong since the 1880s. The Hong Kong Shield – an early knock-out competition – was launched in 1896, a football association was founded in 1913 and affiliated to the Football Association in London a year later.

The sport reached its peak in the colony in the 1970s. The league's top clubs became fully professional and imported a string of veteran players from England and continental Europe. South China were one of the last clubs to turn pro, by which time sponsorship had arrived with powerful teams organized by the Seiko and Bulova corporations.

The national team have competed regularly in international events – having first entered the World Cup in vain in 1974. It was thought that football independence might disappear when the colony was handed back to China in 1997 but FIFA decided, following the lead of the International Olympic Committee, that Hong Kong could remain an independent sporting "nation."

CHAMPIONS

1946 Royal Air Force	1963 Yuen Long
1947 Sing Tao	1964 Kitchee
1948 Kitchee	1965 Happy Valley
1949 South China	1966 South China
1950 Kitchee	1967 Kowloon Motor Bus Co
1951 South China	1968 South China
1952 South China	1969 South China
1953 South China	1970 Jardines
1954 Kowloon Motor Bus Co	1971 Rangers
1955 South China	1972 South China
1956 Eastern	1973 Seiko
1957 South China	1974 South China
1958 South China	1975 Seiko
1959 South China	1976 South China
1960 South China	1977 South China
1961 South China	1978 South China
1962 South China	1979 Seiko
	1980 Seiko

1981 Seiko
1982 Seiko
1983 Seiko
1984 Seiko
1985 Seiko
1986 South China
1987 South China
1988 South China
1989 Happy Valley
1990 South China
1991 South China
1992 South China
1993 Eastern
1994 Eastern
1995 Eastern

CUP WINNERS

1975 Seiko
1976 Seiko
1977 Rangers
1978 Seiko
1979 Yuen Long
1980 Seiko

1981 Seiko
1982 Bulova
1983 Bulova
1984 Eastern
1985 South China
1986 Seiko
1987 South China
1988 South China
1989 Lei Sun
1990 South China
1991 South China
1992 Ernest Borel
1993 Eastern
1994 Eastern
1995 Rangers
1996 Eastern
1997 South China

India

All India Football Federation	
Founded:	*1937*
Joined FIFA:	*1948*

India's only successes at international level have come in the Asian Games, which they won in 1951 and 1962. They finished third at the 1956 Olympics, but since then the national side's record has been poor, despite massive enthusiasm for football in this huge heavily-populated country.

The annual Nehru Cup tournament, featuring guest European and South American national sides or selections, is a popular event, though India have never won it. The Calcutta League – the best in the country – is dominated by India's most famous clubs, Mohammedan Sporting, East Bengal and Mohun Bagan.

Originally brought to India by the British in the late 1800s (the Gloucestershire Regiment were the first Calcutta champions), football is now rapidly gaining popularity in a country where cricket has always been the top sport.

CALCUTTA CHAMPIONS

1898 Gloucestershire Regiments
1899 Calcutta Football Club
1900 Royal Irish Rifles
1901 Royal Irish Rifles
1902 King's Own Scottish
    Borderers
1903 93rd Highlanders
1904 King's Own Regiment
1905 King's Own Regiment

1906 Highland Light Infantry
1907 Calcutta Football Club
1908 Gordon Light Infantry
1909 Gordon Light Infantry
1910 Dalhousi
1911 70th Company RGA
1912 Black Watch
1913 Black Watch
1914 91st Highlanders
1915 10th Middlesex Regiment
1916 Calcutta Football Club
1917 Lincolnshire Regiment

1918 Calcutta Football Club
1919 12th Special Service Battalion
1920 Calcutta Football Club
1921 Dalhousi
1922 Calcutta Football Club
1923 Calcutta Football Club
1924 Cameron Highlanders
1925 Calcutta Football Club
1926 North Staffordshire Regiment
1927 North Staffordshire Regiment
1928 Dalhousi
1929 Dalhousi
1930 Not played
1931 Durham Light Infantry
1932 Durham Light Infantry
1933 Durham Light Infantry
1934 Mohammedan Sporting
1935 Mohammedan Sporting
1936 Mohammedan Sporting
1937 Mohammedan Sporting
1938 Mohammedan Sporting
1939 Mohun Bagan
1940 Mohammedan Sporting
1941 Mohammedan Sporting
1942 East Bengal
1943 Mohun Bagan
1944 Mohun Bagan
1945 East Bengal
1946 East Bengal
1947 Not played
1948 Mohammedan Sporting
1949 East Bengal
1950 East Bengal
1951 Mohun Bengal
1952 East Bengal
1953 Not played
1954 Mohun Bagan
1955 Mohun Bagan
1956 Mohun Bagan
1957 Mohammedan Sporting
1958 Eastern Railway
1959 Mohun Bagan
1960 Mohun Bagan
1961 East Bengal
1962 Mohun Bagan
1963 Mohun Bagan
1964 Mohun Bagan
1965 Mohun Bagan
1966 East Bengal
1967 Mohammedan Sporting
1968 Not played
1969 Mohun Bagan
1970 East Bengal
1971 East Bengal

1972 Est Bengal
1973 East Bengal
1974 East Bengal
1975 East Bengal
1976 Mohun Bagan
1977 East Bengal
1978 Mohun Bagan
1979 Mohun Bagan
1980 Not played
1981 Mohammedan Sporting
1982 East Bengal
1983 Mohun Bagan
1984 Mohun Bagan
1985 East Bengal
1986 Mohun Bagan
1987 East Bengal
1988 East Bengal
1989 East Bengal
1990 Monhan Bagan
1991 East Bengal
1992 Mohun Bagan
1993 East Bengal
1994 Mohun Bagan
1995 Mohun Bagan
1996 East Bengal
1997 Churchill
1998 Mohun Bagan

CUP WINNERS

1977 ITI Banglalore
1978 East Bengal/Mohun Bagan
1979 BSF Jullundur
1980 Mohun Bagan/East Bengal
1981 Mohun Bagan
1982 Mohun Bagan
1983 Mohammedan Sporting
1984 Mohammedan Sporting
1985 East Bengal
1986 Mohun Bagan
1987 Mohun Bagan
1988 Salgacor
1989 Salgacor
1990 Kerala Police
1992 Mohun Bagan
1993 Mohun Bagan
1994 Mohun Bagan
1995 Jagatif Cotton and Textile (JCT)
1996 East Bengal
1997 Salgaocar

Indonesia

All Indonesia Football Federation

Founded: 1930
Joined FIFA: 1952

CHAMPIONS

1980 Warna Agung
1981 Not played
1982 NIAC Mitra
1983 NIAC Mitra
1984 Yanita Utama Bogor
1984 Yanita Utama Bogor
1985 Tiga Berlian
1986 Tiga Berlian
1987 Not played
1988 NIAC Mitra
1989 Pelita Jaya
1990 Pelita Jaya
1991 Not played
1992 Arseto
1993 Arema
1994 Pelita Jaya
1995 Persia Bandung
1996 Matrans Bandung Raya
1997 Persebaya Surbaya

CUP WINNERS

1985 Arseto
1986 Makassar Utama
1987 Tiga Berlian
1988 Tiga Berlian
1989 Tiga Berlian
1990 Not played
1991 Not played
1992 Semen Padang
1993 Not played
1994 Gelora Dewata
1995–98 Not played

Iran

Football Federation of the Islamic Republic of Iran

Founded: 1920
Joined FIFA: 1948
Asian Championship: 1968, 1972, 1976
Asian Games: 1974, 1990

Iran emerged as a major Asian power in the 1960s, and in the 1970s they were the continent's most successful national side. They took a hat-trick of Asian Championships, in 1968, 1972 and 1976, won the gold medal at the 1974 Asian Games and then qualified for the 1978 World Cup finals in Argentina. There, they shocked Scotland, holding them to a 1–1 draw, and the Scots goal was an own goal!

The Asian Championship hat-trick was remarkable because Iran won every game they played in the tournament between 1968 and 1976. Since then, they have reached the semi-finals in each of the three subsequent tournaments that have been played, and almost qualified for the 1994 World Cup finals in the United States. They did qualify for the finals in 1998 – setting a World Cup record along the way when they beat Maldives 17–0 in a qualifying tie in June 1997.

Iranian teams have twice won the Asian Champions Cup – Taj Club in 1970 and Esteghlal SC in 1990.

CHAMPIONS

1974 Persepolis
1975 Taj
1976 Persepolis
1977 Persepolis
1978 Pas
1979 Shahbaz
1980 Persepolis
1981–85 Not played
1986 Malavan SC
1987 Not played
1988 Pirouzi
1989 Shanin FC
1990 Esteghlal SC
1991 Not played
1992 Pas
1993 Pas
1994 Saipa
1995 Pirouzi
1996 Pirouzi
1997 Pirouzi

Iraq

Iraqi Football Association

Founded: 1948
Joined FIFA: 1951
Asian Games: 1982

The 1970s witnessed a shift in the balance of power in Asian football towards the Arab states, and Iraq have been at the forefront of this movement. They won the Asian Games gold medal in 1982 and four years later qualified for the World Cup finals in Mexico, where they put up creditable performances.

Iraq have huge resources at their disposal, and this should ensure that the national side will remain strong for many years to come. Iraq were thrown out of FIFA and suspended from international football in 1991 because of the invasion of Kuwait, but have since been re-admitted to the international fold. They almost qualified for the 1994 World Cup finals. Iraq's most noted player was striker Ahmed Radhi.

CHAMPIONS

1974 Al Tayeran
1975 Al Tayeran
1976 Al Zewra
1977 Al Zewra
1978 Al Mena
1979 A l Zewra
1980 Al Schurta
1981 Al Talaba
1982 Al Talaba
1983 Sal-el-Deen
1984 Al Jaische
1985 Al Rasheed
1986 Al Talaba
1987 Al Rasheed
1988 Al Rasheed
1989 Al Rasheed
1990 Al Rasheed
1991 Al Zewra
1992 Not played
1993 Not played
1994 Not played
1995 Al Zewra
1996 Al Zewra
1997 Al Zewra

Japan

The Football Association of Japan

Founded: 1921
Joined FIFA: 1929–45, 1950
Asian Championship: 1992

One victory in the Asian Cup – in 1992 – is the sum total of Japan's efforts on the international scene. But that could soon change

Japan's Akira Narahashi takes on Jamaica's Fitzroy Simpson at the 1998 World Cup finals in France

in the wake of the success of the JFA's ambitious programme to put the country firmly on the international football map.

In 1993 a professional league, the J League, was introduced, and the corporate-backed teams used their wealth to attract numerous star veterans including England's Gary Lineker, Brazil's Dunga, Leonardo and Zico, Italy's Toto Schillaci and Germany's Guido Buchwald and Pierre Littbarski. The league has proved to be very successful with many teams drawing huge and fanatical crowds on a regular basis.

Simultaneously, the Japanese put together an impressive bid for the hosting rights to the 2002 World Cup. Japan undoubtedly had the stadiums, communications and facilities to stage the event alone but, ultimately, political considerations within FIFA meant they were assigned to share host rights with South Korea.

Japan almost qualified for the 1994 World Cup finals. Going into the final game of the qualifiying tournament they needed a victory to qualify, but they missed out when in the last minute of the match against Iraq, they conceded a soft equaliser. No such mistake was made next time around when Japan qualified for the finals in 1998 for the first time – although, disappointingly, they returned home without having won a match.

Several Japanese players have made an impact alongside the imported stars in the J. League, notably national team striker Kazuyoshi Miura, known as "Kazu," who had a brief spell with Genoa of Italy's Serie A in 1994. He was surprisingly dropped from the national squad just before the 1998 World Cup finals. But already, by then, his mantle as the most popular Japanese footballer had been taken over by midfielder Hidetoshi Nakata.

CHAMPIONS

1965 Toyo Kogyo	1973 Mitsubishi
1966 Togo Kogyo	1974 Yanmar Diesel
1967 Togo Kogyo	1975 Yanmar Dieselk
1968 Togo Kogyo	1976 Furukawa
1969 Mitsubishi	1977 Fujita
1970 Toyo Kogyo	1978 Mitsubishi
1971 Yanmar Diesel	1979 Fujita
1972 Hitachi	1980 Yanmar Diesel
	1981 Fujita

1982 Mitsubishi
1983 Yomiuri
1984 Yomiuri
1985 Furukawa
1986 Furukawa
1987 Yomiuri
1988 Yamaha
1989 Nissan
1990 Nissan
1991 Yomiuri
1992 Yomiuri

J-LEAGUE

1993 Verdy Kawasaki
1994 Verdy Kawasaki
1995 Yokohama Marinos
1996 Kashima Antlers
1997 Juilo Iwata

CUP WINNERS

1921 Tokyo FC
1922 Nagoya FC
1923 Astra
1924 Rijyo Club
1925 Rijyo Club
1926 Not played
1927 Kobe High School
1928 Waseda University
1929 Kansei Gakuin University
1930 Kansei Gakuin University
1931 Tokyo Imperial University
1932 Keio Club
1933 Tokyo OB
1934 Not played
1935 All Keijyo FC
1936 Keio BRB
1937 Keio University
1938 Waseda University
1939 Keio BRB
1940 Keio BRB
1941–45 Not played
1946 Tokyo University
1947–48 Not played
1949 Tokyo University
1950 All Kansei Gakuin
1951 Keio BRB

1952 All Keio
1953 All Kansei Gakuin
1954 Keio BRB
1955 All Kansei Gakuin
1956 Keio BRB
1957 Cho University
1958 Kansei Gakuin Club
1959 Kansei Gakuin Club
1960 Furukawa Electric
1961 Furukawa Electric
1962 Chuo University
1963 Not played
1964 Waseda University
1965 Yawata Steel
1966 Toyo Kogyo
1967 Waseda University
1968 Toyo Kogyo
1969 Yanmar Diesel
1970 Toyo Kogyo
1971 Yanmar Diesel
1972 Mitsubishi
1973 Hitachi
1974 Mitsubishi
1975 Yanmar Diesel
1976 Hitachi
1977 Furukawa
1978 Fujita
1979 Mitsubishi
1980 Fujita
1981 Mitsubishi
1982 Nippon Kokan
1983 Yamaha
1984 Nissan
1985 Yomiuir
1986 Nissan
1987 Yomiuri
1988 Yomiuri
1989 Nissan
1990 Nissan
1991 Matsushita
1992 Nissan
1993 Nissan
1994 Yokohama Flugels
1995 Bellamre Hiratsuka
1996 Verdy Kawasaki
1997 Kashima Antlers

1973 Al Faisaly
1974 Al Faisaly
1975 Al Faisaly
1976 Al Faisaly
1977 Al Faisaly
1978 Al Ahly
1979 Al Ahly
1980 Al Wehdat
1981 Al Ramta
1982 Al Ramta
1983 Al Faisaly
1984 Amman Club
1985 Al Faisaly
1986 Al Faisaly
1987 Al Deffatain
1988 Al Wehdat
1989 Al Ramta
1990 Al Faisaly
1991 Al Faisaly
1992 Al Wehdat
1993 Al Faisaly
1994 Al Faisaly
1995 Al Wehdat
1996 Al Wehdat

1997 Al Wehdat
1998 Al Wehdat

CUP WINNERS

1981 Al Faisaly
1982 Al Faisaly
1983 Al Wehdat
1984 Al Faisaly
1985 Al Jazira
1986 Al Wehdat
1987 Al Arabi
1988 Al Faisaly
1989 Al Wehdat
1990 Al Faisaly
1991 Al Ramta
1992 Al Ramta
1993 Al Faisaly
1994 Al Faisaly
1995 Al Faisaly
1996 Al Faisaly
1997 Al Wahdat

Kampuchea

Federation Khmere de Football Association

Founded:	*1953*
FIFA:	*1953*

Kazakhstan

Football Association of theRepublic of Kazakhstan

Founded:	*1914*
FIFA:	*1994*

Kuwait

Kuwait Football Association

Founded:	*1952*
FIFA:	*1962*
Asian Championship:	*1980*

Jordan

Jordan Football Association

Founded:	*1949*
Joined FIFA:	*1958*

CHAMPIONS

1959 Al Faisaly
1960 Al Faisaly
1961 Al Faisaly
1962 Al Faisaly
1963 Al Faisaly
1964 Al Faisaly

1965 Al Faisaly
1966 Al Faisaly
1967 Not played
1968 Al Faisaly
1969 Al Faisaly
1970 Al Faisaly
1971 Al Faisaly
1972 Al Faisaly

CHAMPIONS

1962 Al Arabi
1963 Al Arabi
1964 Al Arabi
1965 Al Kuwait
1966 Al Arabi
1967 Al Arabi
1968 Al Kuwait
1969 Al Qadisiyah
1970 Al Arabi

1971 Al Qadisiyah
1972 Al Kuwait
1973 Al Qadisiyah
1974 Al Kuwait
1975 Al Qadisiyah
1976 Al Qadisiyah
1977 Al Kuwait
1979 Al Kuwait
1980 Al Arabi
1981 Al Salmiyah
1982 Al Arabi

1983 Al Arabi
1984 Al Arabi
1985 Al Arabi
1986 Al Kazmah
1987 Al Kazmah
1988 Al Arabi
1989 Al Arabi
1990 Al Jabaa
1991 Not played
1992 Al Qadisiyah
1993 Al Arabi
1994 Al Kazmah
1995 Al Salmiyah
1996 Al Salmiyah
1997 Al Arabi

CUP WINNERS

1962 Al Arabi
1963 Al Arabi
1964 Al Arabi
1965 Al Qadisiyah
1966 Al Arabi
1967 Al Qadisiyah
1968 Al Qadisiyah
1969 Al Arabi
1970 Al Yarmouk
1971 Al Arabi
1972 Al Qadisiyah

1973 Not played
1974 Al Qadisiyah
1975 Al Qadisiyah
1976 Al Kuwait
1977 Al Kuwait
1978 Al Kuwait
1979 Al Qadisiyah
1980 Al Kuwait
1981 Al Arabi
1982 Al Kazmah
1983 Al Arabi
1984 Al Kazmah
1985 Al Kuwait
1986 Al Fheyheel
1987 Al Kuwait
1988 Al Kuwait
1989 Al Qadisiyah
1990 Al Kazmah
1991 Not played
1992 Al Arabi
1993 Al Salmiyah
1994 Al Qadisiyah
1995 Al Arabi
1996 Al Kazmah
1997 Al Kazmah

Kyrgysztan

Football Association of Kyrgyzstan

Founded: 1992
Joined FIFA: 1994

CHAMPIONS

1992 Alga Bishkek
1993 Alga-RIIF Bishkek
1994 Kant Oil
1995 Kant Oil
1996 Metallurg Kadanjay
1997 Dinamo Bishek

CUP WINNERS

1992 Alga Bishkek
1993 Alga-RIIF Bishkek
1994 Ak-Maral Tokmak
1995 Semetei Kyzyl-Kiya
1996 AIK Bishkek
1997 Alga PVO Bishkek

Laos

Fédération de Foot-Ball Lao

Founded: 1951
Joined FIFA: 1952

Lebanon

Fédération Libanaise de Football

Founded: 1933
Joined FIFA: 1935

CHAMPIONS

1934 Al Nahda
1935 American University
1936 Sika
1937 American University
1938 American University
1939 Sika
1940 Not played
1941 Sika
1942 Al Nahda
1943 Al Nahda
1944 Homentmen
1945 Homentmen
1946 Homentmen
1947 Al Nahda
1948 Homentmen
1949 Al Nahda
1950 Not played
1951 Homentmen
1952 Not played
1953 Not played
1954 Homentmen
1955 Homentmen
1956 Racing
1957 Homentmen
1958–60 Not played
1961 Homentmen

1962 Not played
1963 Homentmen
1964 Not played
1965 Racing
1966 Not played
1967 Chabiba Mazraa
1968 Not played
1969 Homentmen
1970 Racing
1971 Not played
1972 Not played
1973 Al Nejmeh
1974 Not played
1975 Al Nejmeh
1976–87 Not played
1988 Al Ansar
1989 Al Ansar
1990 Al Ansar
1991 Al Ansar
1992 Al Ansar
1993 Al Ansar
1994 Al Ansar
1995 Al Ansar
1996 Al Ansar
1997 Al Ansar
1998 Al Ansar

Macao

Associacao de Futebol de Macau

Founded: 1939
Joined FIFA: 1976

Malaysia

Persuatuan Bolasepak Malaysia

Founded: 1933
Joined FIFA: 1956

CUP WINNERS

1921 Singapore
1922 Selangor
1923 Singapore
1924 Singapore
1925 Singapore
1926 Perak

1927 Selangor
1926 Perak
1927 Selangor
1928 Singapore and Selangor
1929 Singapore and Selangor
1930 Singapore
1931 Perak
1932 Singapore

1933 Singapore
1934 Singapore
1935 Selangor
1936 Selangor
1937 Singapore
1938 Selangor
1939 Singapore
1940 Singapore
1941–47 Not played
1948 Negri Sembrian
1949 Selangor
1950 Singapore
1951 Singapore
1952 Singapore
1953 Penang
1954 Penang
1955 Singapore
1956 Selangor
1957 Perak
1958 Penang
1959 Selangor
1960 Singapore
1961 Selangor
1962 Selangor
1963 Selangor
1964 Singapore
1965 Singapore
1966 Selangor
1967 Perak
1968 Selangor
1969 Selangor

1970 Perak
1971 Selangor
1972 Selangor
1973 Selangor
1974 Penang
1975 Selangor
1976 Selangor
1977 Singapore
1978 Selangor
1979 Selangor
1980 Singapore
1981 Selangor
1982 Selangor
1983 Pahang
1984 Selangor
1985 Johore
1986 Selangor
1987 Kuala Lumpur
1988 Kuala Lumpur
1989 Kuala Lumpur
1990 Kuala Lumpur
1991 Kedah
1992 Pahang
1993 Kedah
1994 Singapore
1995 Pahang
1996 Sabah
1997 Sarawak

Maldives

Football Association of Maldives

Founded: 1983
Joined FIFA: 1986

CHAMPIONS

1983 Valencia
1984 Valencia
1985 Valencia
1986 Victory SC
1987 Victory SC
1988 Victory SC
1989 Club Lagoons

Myanmar

Myanmar Football Federation

Founded: 1947
Joined FIFA: 1947
Asian Games: 1966, 1970

Nepal

All Nepal Football Association

Founded: 1951
Joined FIFA: 1970

CHAMPIONS

1985 New Road Team
1986 Manang Marsyangdi
1987 Kathmandu SC
1988 Kathmandu SC
1989 Ranipokhari
1997 Mahendara Police Clubs

North Korea

Football Association of the Democratic People's Republic of Korea

Founded: 1945
Joined FIFA: 1958
Asian Games: 1978

North Korea's national side has consistently lived in the shadow of more successful neighbours from the South, but in 1966 the North made headlines around the world. At the 1966 World Cup finals in England, the North Koreans stunned Italy in the first round, winning 1–0. Pak Do Ik will be remembered for ever as the man who scored the most famous goal in North Korean football history. Then, in an incredible quarter-final against Portugal, the Koreans went 3–0 ahead after 22 minutes. But the dream faded almost as dramatically, as Portugal won 5–3. North Korea has failed to qualify for the World Cup since then.

Their South Korea neighbours have suggested that North Korea may be offered the opportunity to stage several matches in the 2002 World Cup finals, which the South Koreans share with Japan.

Oman

Oman Football Association

Founded: 1978
Joined FIFA: 1980

Pakistan

Pakistan Football Federation

Founded: 1948
Joined FIFA: 1948

CHAMPIONS

1948 Karachi Red
1949 Not played
1950 Baluchistan
1951 Not played
1952 Punjab
1953 Punjab
1954 Punjab
1955 Punjab
1956 Baluchistan
1957 Punjab
1958 Punjab Blue
1959 Baluchistan
1960 Dacca
1961 Dacca
1962 Dacca
1963 Karachi
1964 Karachi
1965 Not played
1966 Karachi
1967 Not played
1968 Peshawar
1969 Pakistan Railways
1970 Chittagong
1971 Pakistan International Airlines
1972 Pakistan International Airlines
1973 Karachi Yellow
1974 Pakistan International Airlines
1975 Sind Red
1976 Pakistan International Airlines
1977 Not played
1978 Pakistan International Airlines
1979 Karachi Red
1980 Karachi Red
1981 Pakistan International Airlines
1982 Habib Bank
1983 WAPDA
1984 Pakistan Railways
1985 Quetta
1986 Pakistan Air Force
1987 Not played
1988 Not played
1989 Punjab Red
1990 Punjab Red
1991 WAPDA
1992 WAPDA
1993 Defence Lahore
1994 Pakistan Army
1995 Crescent Mills
1996 Crescent Mills
1997 Allied Bank Limited

Qatar

Qatar Football Association

Founded: 1960
Joined FIFA: 1970

CHAMPIONS	CUP WINNERS
1973 Al Estekdal	1973 Al Ahly
1974 Al Saad	1974 Al Estekdal
1975 Not played	1975 Al Saad
1976 Al Rayyan	1976 Al Estekdal
1977 Al Estekdal	1977 Al Saad
1978 Al Rayyan	1978 Al Arabi
1979 Al Saad	1979 Al Arabi
1980 Al Saad	1980 Al Arabi
1981 Al Saad	1981 Al Ahly
1982 Al Rayyan	1982 Al Saad
1983 Al Arabi	1983 Al Arabi
1984 Al Rayyan	1984 Al Arabi
1985 Al Arabi	1985 Al Saad
1986 Al Rayyan	1986 Al Saad
1987 Al Saad	1987 Al Ahly
1988 Al Saad	1988 Al Saad
1989 Al Saad	1989 Al Arabi
1990 Al Rayyan	1990 Al Arabi
1991 Al Arabi	1991 Al Ahly
1992 Al Itahad	1992 Al Ahly
1993 Al Arabi	1993 Al Arabi
1994 Al Arabi	1994 Al Saad
1995 Al Rayyan	1995 Al Rayyan
1996 Al Rayyan	1996 Al Ittihad
1997 Al Rayyan	1997 Al Ittihad

Palestine

Palestinian Football Federation

Founded: 1994
Joined FIFA: 1995 (provisional member)

Philippines

Philippine Football Federation

Founded: 1907
Joined FIFA: 1928

Saudi Arabia

Saudi Arabian Football Federation

Founded: 1959
Joined FIFA: 1959
Asian Championship: 1984, 1988

Saudi Arabia are one of the emergent nations of Asian football, and with untold oil-based wealth at their disposal, they could come to dominate the region's football as the Koreans and the Iranians have. Saudi Arabia's first honours came in the 1980s, when they won the 1984 and 1988 Asian Championships. The work continued with progress to the second round of the 1994 World Cup finals and to the finals again in 1998.

The Saudi Arabians are also developing their infrastructure and organization. Many foreign coaches have been employed and the magnificent King Fahd stadium in Riyadh is one of the best in the world.

They were the first hosts of the Intercontinental Cup in 1993 (a competition for the five continental champions), and the event is to become a regular feature of the FIFA calendar. Playing against the best nations in the world can only further strengthen Saudi Arabian football and their international standing.

CHAMPIONS

1977 Al Hilal	1967 Al Wehda
1978 Al Ahly	1968 Al Ittihad
1979 Al Hilal	1969 Al Ittifaq
1980 Al Nasr	1970 Al Ahly
1981 Al Nasr	1971 Al Ahly
1982 Al Ittihad	1972 Al Ahly
1983 Al Ittafaq	1973 Al Ahly
1984 Al Ahly	1974 Al Ahly
1985 Al Hilal	1975 Not played
1986 Al Hilal	1976 Al Nasr
1987 Al Ittafaq	1977 Al Nasr
1988 Al Hilal	1978 Al Ahly
1989 Al Nasr	1979 Al Ahly
1990 Al Hilal	1980 Not played
1991 Al Shabab	1981 Al Nasr
1992 Al Shabab	1982 Not played
1993 Al Shabab	1983 Al Ahly
1994 Al Nasr	1984 Not played
1995 Al Nasr	1985 Al Ittifaq
1996 Al Hilal	1986 Al Nasr
1997 Al Ittihad	1987 Al Ittifaq
1998 Al Hilal	1988 Al Ittihad

CUP WINNERS

1958 Al Wehda	1989 Al Hilal
1959 Al Ittihad	1990 Al Nasr
1960 Al Ittihad	1991 Al Ittihad
1961 Not played	1992 Al Qadisiyah
1962 Not played	1993 Al Shabab
1963 Al Ahly	1994 Al Riyadh
1964 Al Ittihad	1995 Al Hilal
1965 Not played	1996 Al Shabab
1966 Al Ahly	1997 Al Ittihad
	1998 Al Ahli

Singapore

Football Association of Singapore	
Founded:	*1892*
FIFA:	*1952*

CHAMPIONS

1975 Geylang International	1986 Singapore Armed Forces
1976 Geylang International	1987 Tiong Bahru
1977 Geylang International	1988 Geylang International
1978 Singapore Armed Forces	1989 Geylang International
1979 Tampines Rovers	1990 Geylang International
1980 Tampines Rovers	1991 Geylang International
1981 Singapore Armed Forces	1992 Geylang International
1982 Farrer Park United	1993 Geylang International
1983 Tiong Bahru	1994 Perth Kangaroos
1984 Tampines Rovers	1995 Not played
1985 Police SA	1996 Geylang United
	1997 Singapore Armed Forces

South Korea

Korea Football Association	
Founded:	*1928*
Joined FIFA:	*1948*
Asian Championship:	*1956, 1960*
Asian Games:	*1970. 1978, 1986*

South Korea has always been the strongest nation in Asian football, and they won the first two Asian Championship tournaments, in 1956 and 1960. Their World Cup record is also the best in Asia, with qualification comingt first in 1954 and then for the four most recent tournaments: 1986, 1990, 1994 and 1998.

In the qualifying tournament for the 1994 World Cup they were undefeated in the first round, but were less impressive in the next stage and only scraped through from the second round group. Once in America, however, they scored two late goals to snatch a draw with Spain in Dallas, then held Bolivia to a goalless draw and lost narrowly to defending champions Germany 3–2.

Cha Bum Kun is probably South Korea's best-known player, having enjoyed a lengthy career in Germany's Bundesliga. In 1988 he helped Bayer Leverkusen win the UEFA Cup, scoring the crucial aggregate-levelling goal in the second leg of the final against Spain's Espanol. Later Cha managed the South Korean national team at the 1998 World Cup finals, where they went out in the first round following a 5–0 defeat against Holland.

In 1993, South Korea, decided to challenge front-runners Japan for the honour of becoming the first Asian hosts for the World Cup. Their competitive pedigree, plus positive memories of Seoul's staging of the 1988 Olympic Games, duly earned the Koreans joint hosting rights, with Japan in 2002.

Sri Lanka

Football Federation of Sri Lanka	
Founded:	*1939*
Joined FIFA:	*1950*

Syria

Association Arabe Syrienne de Football	
Founded:	*1936*
Joined FIFA:	*1937*

CHAMPIONS

1967 Al Ittihad	1972 Not played
1968 Al Ittihad	1973 Al Jaish
1969 Al Majd	1974 Not played
1970 Al Majd	1975 Al Karama
1971 Not played	1976 Al Jaish
	1977 Al Ittihad
	1978 Not played

1979 Al Jaish
1980 Al Shourta
1981 Not played
1982 Teshrin
1983 Al Karama
1984 Al Karama
1985 Al Jaish
1986 Al Jaish
1987 Jabala
1988 Jabala
1989 Jabala
1990 Al Foutoua
1991 Al Foutoua
1992 Al Foutoua
1993 Al Ittihad
1994 Al Horria
1995 Al Ittihad
1996 Karama
1997 Teshrin
1998 Al Jaish

CUP WINNERS

1966 Al Ittihad
1967 Al Shourta
1968 Al Shourta
1969 Al Shourta
1970 Al Mahjazel
1971 Not played
1972 Not played
1973 Al Ittihad
1974 Not played
1975 Not played
1976 Not played
1977 Not played
1978 Al Majd
1979 Not played
1980 Al Shourta
1981 Al Shourta
1982 Al Ittihad
1983 Al Karama
1984 Al Ittihad
1985 Al Ittihad
1986 Al Jaish
1987 Al Karama
1988 Al Foutoua
1989 Al Foutoua
1990 Al Foutoua
1991 Al Foutoua
1992 Al Horria
1993 Al Wahda
1994 Al Ittihad
1995 Al Karama
1996 Al Karama
1997 Al Jaish
1998 Al Jaish

Taiwan

Chinese Taipei Football Association

Founded:	*1936*
Joined FIFA:	*1954*
Asian Games:	*1954, 1958*

Tajikistan

Football Federation of Tajikistan

Founded:	*1991*
Joined FIFA:	*1994*

Thailand

Football Association of Thailand

Founded:	*1916*
Joined FIFA:	*1925*

Turkmenistan

Football Federation of Turkmenistan

Founded:	*1992*
Joined FIFA:	*1994*

United Arab Emirates

United Arab Emirates Football Association

Founded:	*1971*
Joined FIFA:	*1972*

With only 25 registered clubs and 3,400 players, the United Arab Emirates caused a big surprise when they qualified for the 1990 World Cup finals. Brazilian coach Mario Zagalo led them in qualifying, but he was surprisingly sacked just prior to the tournament to be succeeded by compatriot Carlos Alberto Parreira. The UAE were somewhat out of their depth in Italy and were beaten in all three of their first-round matches.

CHAMPIONS

1975 Al Ahly
1976 Al Ahly
1977 Al Ain
1978 Al Nasr
1979 Al Nasr
1980 Al Ahly
1981 Al Ain
1982 Al Wasl
1983 Al Wasl
1984 Al Ain
1985 Al Wasl
1986 Al Nasr
1987 Al Sharjah
1988 Al Wasl
1989 Al Sharjah
1990 Al Shabab
1991 Not played
1992 Al Wasl
1993 Al Ain
1994 Al Sharjah
1995 Al Shabab
1996 Sharjah
1997 Al Wasl
1998 Al Ain

Uzbekistan

Football Federation of Uzbekistan

Founded:	*1946*
Joined FIFA:	*1994*
Asian Games:	*1994*

Uzbekistan gained independence after the collapse of the Soviet Union. The federation gained immediate admittance into the Asian confederation, which they stunned by winning the Asian Games title on their debut.

CHAMPIONS

1992 Neftchi Fergana & Pachtakor
    Tashkent
1993 Neftchi Fergana
1994 Neftchi Fergana
1995 Neftchi Fergana
1996 Novibakhor Namangan
1997 Mhsk Tashkent

CUP WINNERS

1993 Pachtakor Tashkent
1994 Neftchi Fergana
1995 Novbakhor Namangan
1996 Neftchi Fergana
1997 Pachtakor Tashkent

Vietnam

Association de Football de la République du Vietnam

Founded: 1962

Joined FIFA: 1964

CHAMPIONS

1981 Tong Cuc Duong Sat
1982 Cau Lac Bo Quan Doi
1983 Cau Lac Bo Quan Doi
1984 Cong An Hanoi
1985 Cong Nghiep Ham Nam Ninh
1986 Cang Siagon
1987 Cau Lac Bo Quan Doi
1988 Cong An Hanoi
1989 Dong Thap
1990 Not played
1991 Not played
1992 Quang Nam Danang
1993 Quang Nam Danang
1994 Port Saigon
1995 Ho Chi Minh City Police
1996 Ho Chi Minh City Police
1997 Dong Thap

Yemen

Republic of Yemen Football Association

Founded: 1940 (South), 1976 (North)

Joined FIFA: 1967 (South), 1980 (North)

The United Arab Emirates team line up for a game at the World Cup in 1990

NORTH & CENTRAL AMERICA AND THE CARIBBEAN (CONCACAF)

Many central American nations may appear little more than a statistical dot in the world game's atlas. But CONCACAF (North and Central American confederation) is very quickly learning how to capitalize on the commercial value of football. The income is being used profitably for coaching schemes and administrative improvements. 'American' soccer is much more now than merely those nations which have done well in the World Cup: Mexico's double staging of the World Cup finals in 1970 and 1986 proves the point. So, of course, did USA '94...

Anguilla

Anguilla Football Association

Founded:	*n/a*
Joined FIFA:	*1996*

Antigua and Barbuda

The Antigua Football Association

Founded:	*1928*
Joined FIFA:	*1970*

Aruba

Arubaanse Voetbal Bond

Founded:	*1932*
Joined FIFA:	*1988*

The Bahamas

The Bahamas Football Association

Founded:	*1967*
Joined FIFA:	*1968*

Barbados

Barbados Football Association

Founded:	*1910*
Joined FIFA:	*1968*

Belize

Belize National Football Association

Founded:	*1980*
Joined FIFA:	*1986*

Bermuda

The Bermuda Football Association

Founded:	*1928*
Joined FIFA:	*1962*

British Virgin Islands

British Virgin Islands Football Association

Founded:	*n/a*
Joined FIFA:	*1996*

Canada

The Canadian Soccer Association

Founded:	*1912*
Joined FIFA:	*1912*

Football in Canada has struggled to establish itself for two main reasons. First, the enormous size of the country makes a coherent structure difficult to implement and consequently a true, national league was only set up in 1987. Second, the sport trails badly in popularity behind ice hockey, baseball, gridiron and basketball – the big North American sports.

Football took hold in Canada at the turn of the century, and in 1904 Galt FC from Ontario entered the St Louis Olympic Games. Soccer was only a demonstration sport, but Galt won the event, still Canada's only major honour. The national side made a few outings in the 1920s, but went into hibernation until the 1950s when they entered the 1958 World Cup – their first attempt. Success eluded them, however, and even when Montreal hosted the 1976 Olympics, they were eliminated in the first round.

In the 1970s, three Canadian clubs, from Vancouver, Toronto and Edmonton, played in the North American Soccer League – as many of Canada's ice hockey and baseball clubs do. In 1976, Toronto won the NASL Soccer Bowl, as did Vancouver in 1979, and many of the Canadians playing in the NASL formed the backbone of the national side which reached the 1986 World Cup finals, their only appearance to date.

In the 1994 qualifiers Canada, with five British-based professionals in the side, reached a play-off with Oceania winners Australia, but lost on penalties. The side was coached by Bobby Lenarduzzi, who had been a member of the 1986 side.

CHAMPIONS

1987 Calgary Kickers
1988 Vancouver 86ers
1989 Vancouver 86ers
1990 Vancouver 86ers
1991 Vancouver 86ers
1992 Winnipeg Fury

CUP WINNERS

1913 Norwood Wanderers
1914 Norwood Wanderers
1915 Winnipeg Scots
1916–18 Not played
1920 Westinghouse Ontario
1921 Toronto Scots
1922 Hillhurst Calgary
1923 Nanaimo
1924 Weston University
1925 Toronto Ulsters
1926 Weston University
1927 Nanaimo
1928 New Westminster Royals
1929 CNR Montreal
1930 New Westminster Royals
1931 New Westminster Royals
1932 Toronto Scots
1933 Toronto Scots
1934 Werduns Montreal
1935 Aldreds Montreal
1936 New Westminster Royals
1937 Johnston Nationals
1938 North Shore Vancouver
1939 Radials Vancouver
1940–45 Not played
1946 Toronto Ulters
1947 St. Andrews Vancouver
1948 Carsteel Montreal
1949 North Shore Vancouver
1950 Vancouver City
1951 Ulster United Toronto
1952 Steelco Montreal
1953 New Westminster Royals
1954 Scottish Winnipeg
1955 New Westminster Royals
1956 Halecos Vancouver
1957 Ukrainia SC Montreal
1958 New Westminster Royals
1959 Alouetts Montreal
1960 New Westminster Royals
1961 Concordia Montreal
1962 Scottish Winnipeg
1963 Not played
1964 Columbus Vancouver
1965 Vancouver Firefighters
1966 Vancouver Firefighters
1967 Toronto
1968 Toronto Royals
1969 Columbus Vancouver
1970 Manitoba Selects
1971 Eintracht Vancouver
1972 New Westminster Blues
1973 Vancouver Firefighters
1974 Calgary Springer Kickers
1975 London Boxing Club Victoria
1976 Victoria West SC
1977 Columbus Vancouver
1978 Columbus Vancouver
1979 Victoria West SC
1980 St. John Dry Dock
1981 Toronto Ciocario
1982 Victoria West SC
1983 Vancouver Firefighters
1984 Victoria West SC
1985 Vancouver Croatia
1986 Hamilton Steelers
1987 Lucania SC
1988 Holy Cross
1989 Scarborough Azzurri
1990 Vancouver Firefighters
1991 Norvan SC
1992 Norvan SC
1993 West Side Rino
1994 Edmonton Ital-Canadians

Cayman Islands

Cayman Islands Football Association

Founded:	*1966*
Joined FIFA:	*1992*

Costa Rica

Federacion Costarricense de Futbol

Founded:	*1921*
Joined FIFA:	*1921*

CCCF and CONCACAF Championship: 1941, 1946, 1948, 1953, 1955, 1960, 1961, 1963, 1969, 1989

Costa Rica are one of the better teams from Central America, and between 1940 and 1970 they won an impressive nine CONCACAF Championships. Despite this, Costa Rica struggled to make an impact in the World Cup – El Salvador and Honduras both qualified before them – but in 1990 the breakthrough came. Under coach Bora Milutinovic, they not only qualified for the finals, but also defeated Scotland and Sweden to progress into the second round. Costa Rica has a very healthy domestic scene too, and two clubs, Deportivo Saprissa and LD Alajeulense, have both won the CONCACAF Club Championship.

Cuba

Associacion de Futbol de Cuba

Founded:	*1924*
Joined FIFA:	*1932*

Dominica

Dominica Football Association

Joined Founded:	*1970*
FIFA:	*1994*

Dominican Republic

Federacion Dominicana de Futbol

Founded:	*1953*
Joined FIFA:	*1958*

El Salvador

Federacion Salvadorena de Futbol

Founded:	*1935*
Joined FIFA:	*1938*
CCCF Championship:	*1943*

El Salvador's biggest claim to soccer fame is the 1969 'Football War' with Central American neighbours Honduras. The countries met in a World Cup qualifying group and rioting followed both matches, especially after the second game when El Salvador forced a play-off. El Salvador won it and, as tension mounted, the army invaded Honduras on the pretext of protecting expatriate Salvadorean citizens. The World Cup match was more an excuse than a cause for the war, but the conflict cost 3,000 lives before it was settled.

El Salvador have qualified for the World Cup finals twice, losing all three games in 1970 and again in 1982 – which included a 10–1 thrashing by Hungary.

Grenada

Grenada Football Association

Founded:	*1924*
Joined FIFA:	*1976*

Guatemala

Federacion Nacional de Futbol de Guatemala

Founded:	*1926*
Joined FIFA:	*1933*
CONCACAF Championship:	*1967*

Guyana

Guyana Football Association

Founded:	*1902*
Joined FIFA:	*1968*

Haiti

Federation Haitienne de Football

Founded:	*1904*
Joined FIFA:	*1933*
CCCF Championship:	*1957*

Honduras

Federacion Nacional Autonoma de Futbol de Honduras

Founded:	*1935*
FIFA:	*1946*

Honduras, like neighbouring El Salvador, is a country which has been plagued by insurgency and guerrilla warfare. Indeed, the two went to war in 1969, over the outcome of a football match, as described in the entry for El Salvador. Honduras made their sole appearance in the World Cup finals in 1982, when they drew 1–1 with hosts, Spain, and Northern Ireland, before losing 1–0 to Yugoslavia and going out of the tournament.

Honduran clubs have enjoyed some success in the CONCACAF Club Championship, notably Olimpia, who won the event in 1972 and 1988, and were runners-up in 1985.

Jamaica

Jamaica Football Association

Founded:	*1910*
Joined FIFA:	*1962*

Rapid progress was made after the Brazilian Federation loaned Jamaica coach Rene Simoes. Jamaica received a special award as the most improved team in the 1995 FIFA rankings and reached their first ever World Cup finals in 1998. In France they went out in the first round, but scored their first finals victory by beating Japan.

CHAMPIONS

1974 Santos
1975 Santos
1976 Santos
1977 Santos
1978 Arnett Gardens
1979 Not played
1980 Santos
1981 Cavalier FC
1982 Not played
1983 Tivoli Gardens
1984 Boys' Town
1985 JDF
1986 Boys' Town
1987 Seba United
1988 Wadadah
1989 Boys' Town
1990 Reno
1991 Reno
1992 Wadadah
1993 Hazard United
1994 Violent Kickers
1996 Violent Kickers
1997 Seba United
1998 Waterhouse

CUP WINNERS

1992 Seba United
1993 Olympic Gardens
1994 Harbour View FC
1995 Seba United

Mexico

Federacion Mexicana de Futbol Asociacion A. C.

Founded: 1927
Joined FIFA: 1929
CONCACAF Championship: *1965, 1977, 1991, 1993*

Mexico utterly dominate their Central American region, but this has hindered rather than helped their game. With no decent, local opposition for the national side or the clubs, Mexico have enjoyed their greatest moments in the World Cup.

The federation was formed in 1927, and a trip to the Amsterdam Olympics a year later ended after just one match. Two years later they entered the World Cup and have qualified for 10 of the 15 finals tournaments, a record which includes 1990, when they were barred by FIFA for breaches of age regulations in a youth tournament. Mexico's best World Cups were in 1970 and 1986, when they were hosts. They reached the quarter-finals of both and in 1986 only lost on penalties to West Germany.

Star of the 1986 side was Hugo Sanchez, an agile forward who led Real Madrid to many honours in the 1980s. Famous for his exuberant, cartwheeling celebrations when he scored, Sanchez was Mexico's greatest player since Antonio Carbajal, the goalkeeper who created a record by playing in all five World Cup finals tournaments from 1950 to 1966. Mexico won the CONCACAF Championship four times, but were shocked in 1991 when the United States beat them in the semi-finals, though Mexico regained the upper hand in 1993. Many believe Mexico would benefit from joining the South Americans, and in 1993 they, and the USA, were invited to take part in the South American Championship.

Mexico embarrassed their hosts by reaching the final, losing narrowly to Argentina. Mexico then qualified for the 1994 World Cup finals with comparative ease, only to lose to Bulgaria in a second round penalty shoot-out. They also made France '98 but went out in the second round again, to Germany.

Jamaica's Robbie Earle at the 1998 World Cup finals

CHAMPIONS

1903 Orizaba Athletic Club	1943 Marte
1904 Mexico Cricket Club	1944 Asturias
1905 Pachuca Athletic Club	1945 Espana Real Club
1906 Reforma Athletic Club	1946 Veracruz
1907 Reforma Athletic Club	1947 Atlante
1908 British Club	1948 Leon
1909 Reforma Athletic Club	1949 Leon
1910 Reforma Athletic Club	1950 Veracruz
1911 Reforma Athletic Club	1951 Atlas
1912 Reforma Athletic Club	1952 Leon
1913 Club Mexico	1953 Tampico
1914 Espana Club	1954 Marte
1915 Espana Club	1955 Zacatepec
1916 Espana Club	1956 Leon
1917 Espana Club	1957 Guadalajara CD
1918 Pachuca Athletic Club	1958 Zacatepec
1919 Espana Real Club	1959 Guadalajara CD
1920 Espana Real Club	1960 Guadalajara CD
1921 Espana Real Club	1961 Guadalajara CD
1922 Espana Club	1962 Guadalajara CD
1923 Astuirias	1963 Oro Jalisco
1924 Espana Real Club	1964 Guadalajara CD
1925 America	1965 Guadalajara CD
1925 America	1966 America
1926 America	1967 Toluca
1927 America	1968 Toluca
1928 America	1969 Cruz Azul
1929 Marte	1970 Cruz Azul
1930 Espana Real Club	1971 America
1931 Not played	1972 Cruz Azul
1932 Atlante	1973 Cruz Azul
1933 Necaxa	1974 Cruz Azul
1934 Espana Real Club	1975 Toluca
1935 Necaxa	1976 America
1936 Espana Real Club	1977 UNAM
1937 Necaxa	1978 Universidad Nuevo Leon
1938 Necaxa	1979 Cruz Azul
1939 Asturias	1980 Cruz Azul
1940 Espana Real Club	1981 UNAM
1941 Atlante	1982 Universidad Neuvo Leon
1942 Espana Real Club	1983 Puebla
	1984 America
	1985 America

Mexico's Luis Hernandez celebrates a goal against South Korea at the France '98 World Cup finals

1985 America
1986 Monterrey
1987 Guadalajara
1988 America
1989 America
1990 Puebla
1991 UNAM
1992 Leon
1993 Atlante
1994 Univ. Autonoma Guadalajara
1995 Necaxa
1996 Necaxa
1996 (winter) Santos Laguna
1997 (spring) Guadalajara
1997 (winter) Cruz Azul
1998 (summer) Toluca

CUP WINNERS

1908 Pachuca Athletic Club
1909 Reforma Athletic Club
1910 Reforma Athletic Club
1911 British Club
1912 Pachuca Athletic Club
1913 Not played
1914 Club Mexico
1915 Espana Club
1916 Rovers
1917 Espana Club

1918 Espana Club
1919 Espana Club
1920 Not played
1921 Club Mexico
1922 Asturias
1923 Asturias
1924 Asturias
1925 Necaxa
1926 Necaxa
1927–32 Not played
1933 Necaxa
1934 Asturias
1935 Not played
1936 Necaxa
1937 Asturias
1938 America
1939 Asturias
1940 Asturias
1941 Asturias
1942 Atlante
1943 Moctezuma
1944 Espana Real Club
1945 Puebla
1946 Atlas
1947 Moctezuma
1948 Veracruz
1949 Leon
1950 Atlas
1951 Atlante

1952 Atlante
1953 Puebla
1954 America
1955 America
1956 Toluca
1957 Zacatepec
1958 Leon
1959 Zacatepec
1960 Necaxa
1961 Tampico
1962 Atlas
1963 Guadalajara CD
1964 America
1965 America
1966 Necaxa
1967 Leon
1968 Atlas
1969 Cruz Azul
1970 Guadalajara CD

1971 Not played
1972 Leon
1973 Leon
1974 America
1975 UNAM
1976 Universidad Nuevo Leon
1977–87 Not played
1988 Puebla
1989 Toluca
1990 Puebla
1991 Monterrey
1992 Universidad Nuevo Leon
1993 Not played
1994 Not played
1995 Necaxa
1996 Universidad Nueuo Leon
1997 Cruz Azul

Montserrat

Montserrat Football Association

Founded:	*n/a*
FIFA:	*1996*

Netherlands Antilles

Nederlands Antiliaanse Voetbal Unie

Founded: 1921
Joined FIFA: 1932

Nicaragua

Federacion Nicaraguense de Futbol

Founded: 1931
Joined FIFA: 1950

Panama

Federacion Nacional de Futbol de Panama

Founded: 1937
Joined FIFA: 1938
CCCF Championship: 1951

Puerto Rico

Federacion Puertorriquena de Futbol

Founded: 1940
Joined FIFA: 1960

Saint Lucia

St. Lucia National Football Union

Founded: n/a
Joined FIFA: 1988

St Kitts and Nevis

St. Kitts and Nevis Amateur Football Association

Founded: 1932
Joined FIFA: 1992

St Vincent and the Grenadines

St. Vincent and the Grenadines Football Federation

Founded: n/a
Joined FIFA: 1988

Surinam

Surinaamse Voetbal Bond

Founded: 1920
Joined FIFA: 1929

CHAMPIONS

1950 Transvaal	1974 Transvaal
1951 Transvaal	1975 Robin Hood
1952 Voorwaarts	1976 Robin Hood
1953 Robin Hood	1977 Voorwaarts
1954 Robin Hood	1978 Leo Victor
1955 Robin Hood	1979 Robin Hood
1956 Robin Hood	1980 Robin Hood
1957 Voorwaarts	1981 Robin Hood
1958 Not played	1982 Leo Victor
1959 Robin Hood	1983 Robin Hood
1960 Not played	1984 Robin Hood
1961 Robin Hood	1985 Robin Hood
1962 Transvaal	1986 Robin Hood
1963 Leo Victor	1987 Robin Hood
1964 Robin Hood	1988 Robin Hood
1965 Transvaal	1989 Robin Hood
1966 Transvaal	1990 Transvaal
1967 Transvaal	1991 Transvaal
1968 Transvaal	1992 Robin Hood
1969 Transvaal	1993 Robin Hood
1970 Transvaal	1994 Robin Hood
1971 Robin Hood	1995 Transvaal
1972 Not played	1996 Transvaal
1973 Transvaal	1997 Transvaal

Trinidad and Tobago

Trinidad and Tobago Football Association

Founded: 1906
Joined FIFA: 1963

United States

United States Soccer Federation

Founded: 1913
Joined FIFA: 1913
CONCACAF Championship: 1991

The United States is viewed by many as a non-football country, yet US football has a long and interesting history. For example, the Oneida club of Boston was founded in 1862, making it the oldest outside England.

The national side entered the 1924 and 1928 Olympics and then travelled to Uruguay for the first World Cup in 1930 – where they reached the semi-finals. Four years later they were represented at the finals again, but lost to hosts Italy in the first

USA goalkeeper Kasey Keller holds Brazil at bay during the 1998 CONCACAF Gold Cup in Los Angeles

round. In 1950 the US caused one of the biggest World Cup shocks ever when they beat England 1–0, with Haiti-born Joe Gaetjens scoring the winning goal.

Back home, the North American Soccer League was formed in 1967, and featured corporate-backed teams – which enabled the clubs to pay huge wages and attract top foreign stars. such as Pele, Franz Beckenbauer, Johan Cruyff and George Best. But the NASL collapsed in the late 1980s.

With Mexico suspended, the US qualified for the 1990 World Cup finals, but their international naivety was clearly shown, losing all three matches. FIFA, bidding to promote the game world-wide, selected the US to host the 1994 finals. No one doubted that they would be well organized, the fears were all about the hosts' quality of play.

But, under coach Bora Milutinovic, the team became hard to beat and, in 1991 they won the CONCACAF Championship D their only honour to date. The US side, containing a number of players with experience of club football in Europe, then produced one of the shocks of the 1994 World Cup when they defeated dark horses Colombia in the group stage and lost only 1–0 to Brazil in the second round.

The 1995 Copa America, under a new coach Steve Sampson proved this success was not a fluke, as the US reached the semi-finals after defeating Argentina 3–0.

But Sampson resigned after the 1998 World Cup finals in France, where the US finished bottom of their group having suffered three defeats, including a 2–1 reverse against Iran.

Future hopes depend on the success of Major League Soccer, the first outdoor professional league since the demise of NASL, which was formed in 1996. It has already begun to produce some home-grown talent.

CHAMPIONS

WESTERN SOCCER LEAGUE
1985 San Jose Earthquakes
1986 Hollywood Kickers
1987 San Diego Nomads
1988 Seattle Storm
1989 San Diego Nomads
1990 San Francisco Bayhawks

AMERICAN SOCCER LEAGUE
1988 Washington Diplomats
1989 Fort Lauderdale Strikers
1990 Maryland Bays

AMERICAN PROFESSIONAL SOCCER LEAGUE
1989 Fort Lauderdale Strikers
1990 Maryland Bays
1991 San Francisco Bayhawks
1992 Colorado Foxes
1993 Colorado Foxes
1994 Montreal Impact

MAJOR LEAGUE SOCCER
1996 DC United
1997 DC United

CUP WINNERS
1914 Brooklyn Field Club, NY
1915 Bethlehem Steel, Pa
1916 Bethlehem Steel, Pa
1917 Fall River Rovers, Mass
1918 Bethlehem Steel, Pa
1919 Bethlehem Steel, Pa
1920 Ben Millers, Mo
1921 Robins Dry Dock, NY
1922 Scullin Steel, Mo
1923 Paterson, NJ
1924 Fall River, Mass
1923 Paterson, NJ
1924 Fall River, Mass
1925 Shawsheen, Mass
1926 Bethlehem Steel, Pa
1927 Fall River, Mass
1928 New York Nationals
1929 Hokoah All Stars, NY
1930 Fall River, Mass
1931 Fall River, Mass
1932 New Bedford, Mass
1933 Stix, Baer and Fuller, Mo
1934 Stis, Baer and Fuller, Mo
1935 Central Breweries, Mo
1936 German-American, Pa
1937 New York Americans
1938 Sparta ABA Chicago
1939 St. Mary's Celtic, NY
1940 Sparta ABA Chicago
1941 Pawtucket, RI
1942 Gallatin Pittsburgh
1943 Brooklyn Hispano
1944 Brooklyn Hispano
1945 Brookhattan, NY
1946 Chicago Vikings
1947 Ponta Delgada, Mass
1948 Simpkins-Ford, Mo
1949 Morgan Pittsburgh
1950 Simpkins-Ford, Mo
1951 German-Hungarian, NY
1952 Harmarville, Pa
1953 Chicago Falcons
1954 New York Americans
1955 Eintracht SC, NY
1956 Harmarville, Pa
1957 Kutis SC, Mo
1958 Los Angeles Kickers
1959 Canvasbacks, Ca
1960 Ukrainian Nationals, Pa
1961 Ukrainian Nationals, Pa
1962 New York Hungaria
1963 Ukrainian Nationals, Pa
1964 Los Angeles Kickers
1965 New York Ukrainians
1966 Ukrainian Nationals
1967 Greek-Americans, NY
1968 Greek-Americans, NY
1969 Greek-Americans, NY
1970 Elizabeth, NJ
1971 New York Horta
1972 Elizabeth, NJ
1973 Maccabee Los Angeles
1974 Greek-Americans, NY
1975 Maccabee Los Angeles
1976 Sn Francisco SC
1977 Maccabee Los Angeles
1978 Maccabee Los Angeles
1979 Brooklyn Dodgers
1980 New York Freedoms
1981 Maccabee Los Angeles
1982 New York Freedoms
1983 New York Freedoms
1984 AO Krete, NY
1985 Greek-Americans, Ca
1986 Kutis SC, Mo
1987 Espana Washington
1988 Busch SC, Mo
1989 Kickers St Petersburg
1990 Chicago Eagles
1991 Brooklyn Italians
1992 San Jose Oaks
1993 CD Mexico, Ca
1994 Greek Americans, Ca
1995 Richmond Kickers
1996 DC United
1997 Dalls Burn

OCEANIA

OCEANIA took a major step forward in 1996 when it was finally accepted by FIFA as a fully-fledged regional confederation.

But that was still not enough to earn a guaranteed place for at least one of its nations at the World Cup finals.

The best Oceania nation was still condemned to a qualifying play-off against one of the Asian nations, with Australia narrowly missing out to Iran.

American Samoa

American Samoa Football Association

Founded:　　*1975*

Joined FIFA:　*Associate member*

Australia

Australia Soccer Federation

Founded:　　*1961*

Joined FIFA:　*1963*

Soccer has struggled to gain a foothold in Australia, where cricket, Aussie Rules football and rugby are the most popular sports. The domestic league formed in 1977, has many ethnically linked clubs such as South Melbourne Hellas and Adelaide City Juventus.

Australia's only World Cup finals appearance, in 1974, proved to be a disappointment. In the 1994 World Cup qualifiers, the `Socceroos' as they are known lost to Argentina for the last spot in the finals.

And they suffered a similar fate in 1998 when, under coach Terry Venables, they came agonisingly close to reaching the finals in France. They gave away a two-goal lead against Iran in Melbourne to crash out at the very last hurdle.

CHAMPIONS

1977 Sydney City Hakoah
1978 West Adelaide Hellas
1979 Marconi
1980 Sydney City Hakoah
1981 Sydney City Hakoah
1982 Sydney City Hakoah
1983 St. George Budapest
1984 South Melbourne Hellas
1985 Brunswick Juventus
1986 Adelaide City Juventus
1987 APIA-Leichhardt
1988 Marconi
1989 Marconi
1990 Sydney Olympic
1991 South Melbourne Hellas
1992 Adelaide City Juventus
1993 Marconi
1994 Adelaide City
1995 Melbourne Knights
1996 Melbourne Knights
1997 Brisbane Strikers
1998 South Melbourne Lakers

CUP WINNERS

1977 Brisbane City
1978 Brisbane City
1979 Adelaide City Juventus
1980 Marconi
1981 Brisbane Lions
1982 APIA Leichhardt
1983 Sydney Olympic
1984 Newcastle Rosebud
1985 Sydney Olympic
1986 Sydney City Hakoah
1987 Sydney Croatia
1988 APIA Leichhardt
1989 Adelaide City Juventus
1990 South Melbourne Hellas
1991 Parramatta Melita
1992 Adelaide City Juventus
1993 Heidelberg United
1994 Parramatta Eagles
1995 Melbourne Knights
1996 South Melbourne
1997 Collingwood Warriors

Cook Islands

Cook Islands Football Federation

Founded:　　*1971*

Joined FIFA:　*1994*

Fiji

Fiji Football Association

Founded:　　*1938*

Joined FIFA:　*1963*

New Caledonia

Federation Neo-Caledonienne de Football

Founded:　　*1960*

Joined FIFA:　*Associate member*

New Zealand

New Zealand Football Association

Founded:　　*1938*

Joined FIFA:　*1963*

New Zealand's only World Cup finals appearance was in 1982, when they were eliminated in the first round.

Wynton Rufer was a member of that side, and won a German Championship medal with Werder Bremen in 1992–93 to establish himself as New Zealand's greatest-ever player.

CHAMPIONS

1970 Blockhouse Bay
1971 Eastern Suburbs
1972 Mount Wellington
1973 Christchurch United
1974 Mount Wellington
1975 Christchurch United
1976 Wellington Diamond
United
1977 North Shore United
1978 Christchurch United
1979 Mount Wellington
1980 Mount Wellington
1981 Wellington Diamond
United
1982 Mount Wellington
1983 Manurewa
1984 Gisburne City
1985 Wellington Diamond
United
1986 Mount Wellington
1987 Christchurch United
1988 Christchurch United
1989 Napier City Rovers
1990 Waitakere City
1991 Christchurch United
1992 Napier City Rovers
1993 Waitakere City
1994 North Shore United
1995 Waitakere City
1996 waitakere City
1997 Waitakere City
1998 Napier City Rovers

CUP WINNERS

1923 Seacliff
1924 Auckland Harbour Board
1925 Wellington YMCA
1926 Sunnyside
1927 Ponsonby
1928 Petone
1929 Tramways
1930 Petone
1931 Tramurewa
1932 Wellington Marist
1933 Ponsonby
1934 Auckland Thistle
1935 Wellington Hospital
1936 Western
1937 Not played
1938 Waterside
1939 Waterside
1940 Waterside
1941–44 Not played
1945 Western
1946 Wellington Marist
1947 Waterside
1948 Christchurch Technical

1949 Petone
1950 Eden
1951 Eastern Suburbs
1952 North Shore United and
Western
1953 Eastern Suburbs
1954 Onehunga
1955 Western
1956 Stop Out
1957 Seatoun
1958 Seatoun
1959 Northern
1960 North Shore United
1961 Northern
1962 Hamilton Technical
1963 North Shore United
1964 Mount Roskil
1965 Eastern Suburbs
1966 Eastern Suburbs
1967 North Shore United
1968 Eastern Suburbs
1969 Eastern Suburbs
1970 Blockhouse Bay
1971 Western Suburbs
1972 Christchurch United
1973 Mount Wellington
1974 Christchurch United
1975 Christchurch United
1976 Christchurch United
1977 Nelson United
1978 Manurewa
1979 North Shore United
1980 Mount Wellington
1981 Dunedin City
1982 Mount Wellington
1983 Mount Wellington
1984 Manurewa
1985 Napier City Rovers
1986 North Shore United
1987 Gisburne City
1988 Waikato United
1989 Christchurch United
1990 Mount Wellington
1991 Christchurch United
1992 Miramar
1993 Napier City Rovers
1994 Waitakere City
1995 Waitakere City
1996 Waitakere City
1997 Central United

Papua New Guinea

Papua New Guinea Football Association
Founded: *1962*
Joined FIFA: *1963*

Solomon Islands

Solomon Islands Football Federation
Founded: *1988*
Joined FIFA: *1988*

Tahiti

Lique de Football de Polynesie
Founded: *1938*
Joined FIFA: *1990*

Tonga

Tonga Football Association
Founded: *1965*
Joined FIFA: *1995*

Vanuatu

Vanuatu Football Federation
Founded: *1934*
Joined FIFA: *1988*

Western Samoa

Western Samoa Football Association
Founded: *1968*
Joined FIFA: *1986*

Chapter 5 THE GREAT

CLUBS

EUROPE

Aberdeen

Scotland
Founded: *1903*
Stadium: *Pittodrie (21,634)*
Colours: *Red/white*
Honours: *European Cup-winners Cup 1983; Supercup 1983;*
League 4; Cup 7; League Cup 5

Aberdeen, thanks to their successful years under Alex Ferguson in the early 1980s, are considered the third force in Scottish club football. Events since then, however, have reopened up the significant gap between the club from the Granite City and Glasgow's Rangers and Celtic.

In the 1980s Aberdeen's key role as a centre for the North Sea oil industry was reflected on the football pitch by victory over Real Madrid in the 1983 Cup-winners Cup Final. Ferguson's team deserved to win, maintaining a remarkable tempo in the rain in Gothenburg. Eric Black's early goal was wiped out by a Juanito penalty and only eight minutes remained in extra time when John Hewitt grabbed the winner. To reach the final, Aberdeen had beaten Sion, Dinamo Tirana, Lech Poznan, Bayern and Waterschei, running up a remarkable 23 goals and stealing the European thunder of the Old Firm.

Success in Gothenburg was not the end of the matter. At the end of 1983 Aberdeen faced Champions Cup-winners Hamburg for the Supercup. The first leg was played in West Germany and ended goalless. At Pittodrie it was a different story. Goals from Paul Simpson and Mark McGhee in the first 20 minutes of the second half provided Aberdeen's second European prize inside a year.

Aberdeen followed up with league championship triumphs in 1984 and 1985, including the league and cup Double in 1984. In 1990 they won both Scottish Cup and League Cup. But Ferguson had, by now, been lured away to Manchester United and further European success proved beyond his successors.

Ajax

Amsterdam, Holland
Founded: *1900*
Stadium: *Arena (50,000)*
Colours: *White with a broad red stripe/white*
Honours: *World Club Cup 1972, 1995; European Champions Cup*
1971, 1972, 1973, 1995; Cup-winners Cup 1987; UEFA
Cup 1992; Supercup 1972, 1973, 1995; League 27; Cup 13

Ajax Amsterdam initiated a football revolution when they won the Champions Cup three times in succession in the early 1970s with "total football" – a style in which players of high technical ability, fitness and football intellect inter-changed position at will.

The style was still in its infancy the first time Ajax had reached the Champions Cup Final in 1969, and they crashed 4–1 to Milan, for whom Pierino Prati scored a hat-trick. The foreign player restrictions then in force limited the movement of players across national boundaries and meant this Ajax team, built around the genius of Johan Cruyff, stayed together to mature into a Europe-dominating force in 1971, 1972 and 1973. By today's standards, it seems incredible that six members of that great team were born within two miles of the club. Cruyff himself was born and grew up in a street next to Ajax's old De Meer stadium.

Ajax had shot to international prominence after nearly 70 years of domestic success. The start was a meeting of half a dozen young football enthusiasts and a few interested businessmen in top hats at the East India Restaurant in Kalverstraat, now the Dutch capital's main shopping street, in March 1900.

Two years later the fledgling club was promoted to the Dutch third division, gained entry to the top flight by 1911 and won its first top league titles in 1918 and 1919. During the 1920s the English trainer Jack Reynolds made his mark, founding the side which dominated the Golden 1930s when Ajax won the Dutch title five times in nine years.

The arrival of professional soccer in the mid-1950s revolutionized the Dutch domestic scene and Ajax helped set up the premier league in 1956. Two years later the Amsterdam club entered the Champions Cup for the first time, but fortunes dipped and only the arrival of Rinus Michels – their former centre forward – as coach helped to beat off the impending threat of relegation in 1964–65.

Michels created the all-conquering Ajax side of the 1970s. They won the league in 1966, 1967 and 1968 as the young Cruyff's skills blossomed. In Europe, too, Ajax were becoming a force to be reckoned with, their exploits including a sensational 5–1 Champions Cup win over Liverpool on a famous foggy night in Amsterdam in 1966.

Three years later Ajax became the first Dutch side to reach the Champions Cup Final, crashing to Milan. But they were soon back in the Final to triumph over Panathinaikos (1971), Inter Milan (1972) and Juventus (1973) with a side built around Cruyff, Ruud Krol, Johan Neeskens, Arie Haan, Piet Keizer and Johnny Rep. They went on to be crowned World Club champions by beating South American champions Independiente in 1972.

Neeskens and Cruyff were lured away to Spain, but Ajax replaced them from within their own, highly-refined youth system. This produced a new generation including players

Dutch striking legend Marco Van Basten, in action for Ajax

renowned the world over, for example Frank Rijkaard, Marco Van Basten, John Bosman, Dennis Bergkamp, Bryan Roy and, later, the De Boer twins (Frank and Ronald), Clarence Seedorf and Patrick Kluivert.

Cruyff returned briefly as trainer and, in 1987, Ajax beat Locomotive Leipzig to capture the Cup-winners Cup and then the UEFA Cup in 1992. By now the Ajax youth policy had become world-famous and its master, Louis Van Gaal, was promoted to boss of the first-team – whom he guided to victory in the Champions Cup in 1995. Kluivert, latest product of the Ajax conveyor belt, scored the winner against Milan in Vienna.

To match their high-profile status, Ajax left behind their old De Meer home in the summer of 1996 – although their big nights in Europe were played at the equally old Olympic Stadium – to take over the 50,000-capacity new Arena stadium.

Anderlecht

Brussels, Belgium
Founded: *1908*
Stadium: *Constant Vanden Stock (28,063)*
Colours: *White with mauve/white*
Honours: *European Cup-winners Cup 1976, 1978; UEFA Cup 1983; Supercup 1976, 1978; League 24; Cup 8*

Anderlecht are the most famous club in Belgium with a proud record in European competition which includes two victories in the Cup-winners Cup in 1976 and 1978. Their greatest past players include Paul Van Himst, who later managed the Belgian national team at the 1994 World Cup finals.

The shadow of scandal fell across the club, however, in early

1997 when it was revealed that long-time president Constant Vanden Stock had been the subject of blackmail over claims that Anderlecht had sought to fix matches in their favour in the 1983–84 UEFA Cup campaign.

All of that was unthinkable when Sporting Club Anderlecht were founded in 1908. The club joined the national federation a year later and moved in 1919 to the Parc Astrid – still their home. It took another 16 years to qualify for the top division by which time Anderlecht had been honoured by royal decree with the right to describe themselves as a Societé Royale, allowing them to wear a crown in their club badge.

Albert Roosens and Constant Vanden Stock were members of the team who won promotion to the top division. Roosens later became president of the club, and then general secretary of the Belgian Football Association while brewery boss Vanden Stock became club president.

In 1947 Anderlecht won the championship for the first time, coached by a former Blackburn Rovers goalkeeper, Englishman Bill Gormlie. In the late 1940s and the early 1950s, Anderlecht owed much to their powerful centre forward Jef Mermans. Later it was the subtle skills of bespectacled midfield general Jef Jurion and the great Van Himst upfront which proved decisive.

In the 1960s Anderlecht won the championship five years in a row. Under French coach Pierre Sinibaldi, they practised a highly-effective zone defence system which relied heavily on the offside trap and upset a string of top-rank rivals. Among them were Real Madrid, over whom Anderlecht scored a famous victory in the 1962–63 Champions Cup. When Belgium beat Holland 1–0 in 1964, all the players in the Belgian line-up were from Anderlecht.

"Sporting" had been among the founders of the inaugural Champions Cup in 1955–56. Then, in 1970, they became the first Belgian club to reach a European final, losing 4–3 on aggregate to Arsenal in the Fairs Cup. The following year Vanden Stock succeeded Roosens as president and led the club into new era which brought three successive appearances in the Cup-Winners' Cup Final. Anderlecht defeated West Ham in 1976, lost to Hamburg in 1977, then thrashed FK Austria 4–0 in 1978. Star player was the Dutch World Cup winger Rob Rensenbrink.

In 1980 Michel Verschueren joined the club as general manager to initiate another golden era. The stadium was redeveloped – with the first executive boxes in Belgium – while another European prize was secured. This was the 1983 UEFA Cup which Anderlecht won by defeating Benfica. They reached the Final again the following season, losing to Tottenham after a penalty shoot-out – but amid ultimate controversy.

A decade later it emerged that Vanden Stock had paid more than £300,000 in "hush money" to an agent who claimed to have recorded telephone calls concerning an attempt to fix the semi-final second leg against Nottingham Forest – which Anderlecht won 3–0.

Arsenal's Tony Adams lifts aloft the Premiership trophy

Arsenal

London, England
Founded: *1886*
Stadium: *Highbury (38,500)*
Colours: *Red with white sleeves/white*
Honours: *European Cup-winners Cup 1994; Fairs Cup 1970; League 11; Cup 7; League Cup 2*

Arsenal are one of the most famous clubs in the game – as proved by the number of teams throughout the world who adopted that illustrious title in the hope it might bring them the same glory.

The nickname "Gunners' owes everything to their original foundation in south London, in the vicinity of Woolwich and its naval arsenal. In 1913, however, they moved from south to north London in the search for greater support.

The inter-war years were sensational. Legendary manager Herbert Chapman arrived from Huddersfield Town, where he had created a highly-successful team in the early 1920s, and made all the difference to a club which had until that point never won a major trophy, leading Arsenal to one success after another and laying the foundations for one of the game's enduring legends.

Until the Liverpools and Manchester Uniteds of recent years, no club had dominated a decade in English football as completely as Arsenal in the 1930s. Using the innovative stopper centre half, they won the league championship five times, finished runners-up once, and won the FA Cup twice, again finishing runners-up once. The great players of those days – wingers Joe Hulme and Cliff Bastin, attacking general Alex James and immaculate full back Eddie Hapgood are still, today, legends of British football.

The 1930s aura survived both the premature death of Chapman in early 1934 and World War Two, so that Arsenal, now under the guidance of Tom Whittaker, won the league again in 1948 and 1953. Veteran wing half Joe Mercer was an inspirational captain, unaware of the meaning of fear.

Yet the greatest achievement of all came in 1970–71, when Arsenal became only the second English team of the 20th century to complete the celebrated Double – winning both the league championship and the FA Cup in the same season.

A first European success had come in the Fairs Cup in 1970, when Arsenal beat Belgian club Anderlecht in the two-legged final. The Belgian capital of Brussels was not such a happy venue a decade later, however, when Arsenal lost the Cup-winners Cup Final to Spain's Valencia on a penalty shoot-out.

Great players of the modern era included England's 1966 World Cup-winner Alan Ball, Irishmen Liam Brady, David O'Leary and Frank Stapleton and Northern Ireland's great goalkeeper Pat Jennings. In the early 1970s Arsenal were guided from midfield by George Graham who then returned in 1986 as manager to re-ignite the flames of success.

The most dramatic came in May 1989, when Arsenal became London's first league champions in 18 years thanks to a last-minute, final-match goal scored by Michael Thomas to deny Liverpool – a club he later joined – at a shocked Anfield. Two years later the wing magic of Sweden's Anders Limpar helped inspire another championship success before Graham parted company with the club following a row over transfer "bungs."

Bruce Rioch succeeded Graham but was himself replaced early in the 1996–97 season by Frenchman Arsène Wenger. Under his revolutionary leadership Arsenal turned from being one of the most dour of sides into one of the most entertaining. Wenger used to the full his contacts and knowledge of European football to bring in a string of new signings, most notably Frenchmen Patrick Vieira, Emmanuel Petit and Nicolas Anelka. His reward, with Dutchman Dennis Bergkamp outstanding, was to win the league and cup Double in 1998.

Aston Villa

Birmingham, England
Founded: *1874*
Stadium: *Villa Park (39,341)*
Colours: *Claret with blue sleeves/white*
Honours: *European Champions Cup 1982; Supercup 1982; League 7; Cup 7; League Cup 5*

Aston Villa means Tradition with a capital T. Few clubs anywhere in England, let alone the world, boast a timeline of success which runs right back to the pioneering days of 1874.

In the 1880s and 1890s Villa, founder members of the Football League, won five of their six championships and two of their seven FA Cups. They established a reputation for entertaining, positive football which was enhanced when they set a scoring record for the old First Division by running up no fewer than 128 goals in the 1930–31 league season…yet finished runners-up to Arsenal.

In 1957 Villa won the FA Cup for a then record seventh time when they defeated Manchester United's Busby Babes 2-1 amid controversy at Wembley. United had to play most of the match with 10 men after goalkeeper Ray Wood was felled by a shoulder charge by Villa's top-scoring left winger Peter MacParland.

In the early 1960s Villa drew admirers from far and wide with an attacking team managed by former England wing half Joe Mercer and spearheaded by the England World Cup leader Gerry Hitchens. They were inaugural winners of the Football League Cup in 1961 beating Rotherham United in two-legs.

In the 1970s Villa suffered the humiliation of a slide down into the old Third Division. But Vic Crowe, a wing half stalwart of both Villa and Wales in the 1960s, returned as manager to undertake a rebuilding programme. Steady progress was rewarded with the double glory of league championship success under Ron Saunders in 1981 and then triumph in the Champions Cup a year later under former assistant, Tony Barton.

The greatest moment in Villa's history was achieved with a 1–0 victory over Germany's Bayern Munich. South African-born Peter Withe stabbed home the winner from close range in the Feyenoord stadium in Rotterdam.

Such standards proved impossible to maintain, however, and just five years later they found themselves in division two. Watford manager Graham Taylor was brought to Villa Park with the sole objective of restoring the glory days to the club. He guided them back into the top flight after just one season and in 1989–90 they were runners-up to Liverpool in the championship. Such achievements by Taylor unfortunately attracted the attention of England, and when he was lured away to take charge of the national team, Ron Atkinson stepped into the breach. He took them to Premiership runners-up in 1992–93 and the club's fourth League Cup victory the following season.

Atletico Madrid

Spain
Founded: *1903*
Stadium: *Vicente Calderon (62,000)*
Colours: *Red and white stripes/blue*
Honours: *World Club Cup 1974; Cup-winners Cup 1962; League 9; Cup 9*

Atletico Madrid's star name over the past decade had not been that of a player or coach. Instead, whatever the identity of the coach or the star players, the personality which has dominated the club has been that of president Jesus Gil.

Gil is a millionaire, a builder, and a politician, who has owned Atletico since 1987 and went through more than a dozen team managers in his search for the guru who could depose neighbours Real Madrid as the Spanish capital's top team. Eventually he found his man in Radomir Antic, who guided Atletico to the league and cup Double in 1996.

Such ambition is not new for an Atletico president. It was the driving force behind the club in the late 1950s and early 1960s under a previous president, Vicente Calderon. But somehow, although Atletico won the occasional domestic championship and cup and even the Cup-winners Cup once, they never stayed the pace for long.

That appeared to be the club's destiny. Back in the late 1930s, after the Spanish Civil War, it had taken a merger with the air-force club to keep Atletico in business; in the early 1960s they had to borrow the use of Real's Estadio Bernabeu because Atletico's Metropolitano had been sold to developers before the club's new stadium could be completed.

In 1966, Atletico toppled Real in a thrilling run-in to pip their neighbours to the championship. Yet even then their moment of glory was overshadowed as Real won the Champions Cup.

Atletico spent heavily trying to compete with Real and Barcelona in the domestic transfer market. When, in 1973, the federation eased a ban on import restrictions, Atletico picked up a string of fine players such as the Argentines Ruben Hugo Ayala, Ramon Heredia and Ruben "Panadero" Diaz.

Their reward was the 1973 league title and in 1974 they reached the Champions Cup Final. But, facing Bayern Munich, Atletico were pushed to the brink of glory, then slapped in the face. Goalless at 90 minutes, it seemed the outcome was resolved when inside forward Luis curled a textbook free kick beyond Sepp Maier. But, with seconds remaining, Bayern centre back Hans-Georg Schwarzenbeck tried a low, speculative shot which somehow skimmed into the bottom corner of the net for an equaliser. There was not even time to restart the game. Atletico were well beaten in the replay.

Controversial coach Juan Carlos Lorenzo was dismissed early the next season. As caretaker, the club appointed former midfield star Luis and he led them to victory in the World Club Cup (Bayern having refused to compete).

Luis later returned for two stints as club coach under Gil, who had spent around £130,000 of his private fortune in campaigning to win the presidential election in 1987. New signings swiftly followed. Top of the list was Portuguese star Paulo Futre, who cost £2million plus the yellow Porsche which was Futre's personal dream; Cesar Luis Menotti, Argentina's 1978 World Cup-winning coach was the first of the string of managers; later Gil swooped in spectacular style to sign Bernd Schuster when the controversial German veteran fell out with Real Madrid.

For all that, it took nine years before Atletico finally made his dream come true.

Barcelona

Spain
Founded: *1899*
Stadium: *Camp Nou (115,000)*
Colours: *Blue and red stripes/blue*
Honours: *Champions Cup 1992; Cup-winners Cup 1979, 1982, 1989, 1997; Fairs Cup 1958, 1960, 1966; Supercup 1992, 1997; League 15; Cup 23*

Barcelona are more than a football club. They are the flagship of the Catalan region, and a vast multi-sports organization which caters for a European record 108,000 members and runs its own bank and radio station.

Barcelona have frequently been described, not surprisingly, as the world's richest club. Precise comparisons are awkward because of their "private club" status but such a claim cannot be far from the truth with average attendances hovering around 80,000 – the average even topped 100,000 in the 1981–82 season – and with no need to indulge in such tacky commercialization as shirt advertising.

The club's explosion would have amazed Hans Gamper, the Swiss emigrant who founded the club in 1899 and whose name is perpetuated in the club's prestigious annual pre-season tournament. Barcelona were the first Spanish league champions in 1929 and share with Athletic Bilbao and Real Madrid the honour of never having been relegated.

Their international status was achieved in the 1950s and early 1960s. In 13 years from 1948 Barcelona won the league six times, the cup five times, the Fairs Cup twice and the Latin Cup twice. They were also desperately unlucky to lose 3–2 to Benfica in the 1961 Champions Cup Final in Berne. At one time – long before Bosman! – they boasted 20 internationals from seven countries. Three of the greatest were Hungarians. Ladislav Kubala escaped to Spain in the late 1940s while Sandor Kocsis and Zoltan Czibor fled Hungary after the 1956 Revolution.

Coach in the late 1950s was Helenio Herrera, the charismatic trainer who later went on to win the Champions Cup with Internazionale. Herrera rarely fielded the same line-up for two matches running – often switching inside forwards to wing half for home matches when Barcelona were expected to run up the goals. Apart from a glittering array of foreign players, Herrera's squad also boasted some of Spain's finest in goalkeeper Antonio Ramallets, wing halves Juan Segarra, Jesus Garay and Martin Verges and inside forward Luis Suarez.

In the early 1960s Barcelona had their wings clipped when the Spanish Federation banned imports, but after that barrier was lifted in 1973 the club immediately splashed a world record £922,000 on Holland's Johan Cruyff.

He led them, within six months, from relegation zone to league title in an astonishing revival which included a 5–0 away win over Real Madrid. But for all the talents of Cruyff and later Diego Maradona, it was not until Cruyff had returned as coach that Barcelona attained their long-sought goal of winning the Champions Cup.

An extra-time goal from Ronald Koeman broke down Sampdoria's resistance at Wembley. But Cruyff's touchy relationship with the board deteriorated after a 4–0 thrashing by Milan in the 1994 European final and he was subsequently dismissed among a flurry of fans protests and legal battles.

Barcelona's fanatical supporters in the Nou Camp stadium

Ex-England coach Bobby Robson found putting the pieces back together a thankless task. He guided Barcelona, nevertheless, to the European Cup-winners Cup in his only season in charge but was then moved "upstairs" to make way for Dutchman Louis Van Gaal from Ajax. Ronaldo's acrimonious pre-season departure for Internazionale proved no loss as Barça won the league and cup Double.

Bayer Leverkusen

Germany
Founded: *1904*
Stadium: *Ulrich Haberland (26,500)*
Colours: *Red/white*
Honours: *UEFA Cup 1988; Cup 1*

Bayer Leverkusen made history in 1997–98 when they became one of the first intake of domestic runners-up to be invited into the newly-expanded UEFA Champions League.

Their campaign was ended in the quarter-finals by ultimate winners Real Madrid – but not before Leverkusen had proved their European pedigree. They reminded the rest of Europe that their 1988 UEFA Cup win was no flash in the pan, by finishing second in their group, with only one defeat and equal on points with group winners Monaco. They drew 1–1 at home to Real in the last eight before losing the second leg 3–0.

Leverkusen reached the UEFA Cup final 10 years earlier by defeating FK Austria, Toulouse, Feyenoord, Barcelona and their fellow Germans Werder Bremen. The quarter-final success over Barcelona was notable for the fact that Leverkusen were held 0–0 at home yet won the tie with a 1–0 success in Nou Camp thanks to a goal from Brazilian import Tita.

The final, against Barcelona's "poor" neighbours, Espanol, was a topsy-turvey affair. Leverkusen lost 3–0 in Spain but then won by the same margin in Germany: Tita scored their first goal and South Korea's Cha Bum-Kun their aggregate equaliser. After extra-time proved goal-less, Leverkusen then triumphed 3-2 on penalties.

The victory means Bayer are one of only six German clubs to boast a victory in Europe, and it is perhaps surprising that no further successes have been recorded since then.

The sponsor/owner support of the Bayer chemical corporation led many experts to predict that Leverkusen would take a leading role in German football in the same way as the Philips offshoot, PSV Eindhoven, in Holland.

Leverkusen's comparative failure may have been due, in part, to Bayer's simultaneous support for Bayer Uerdingen (now KSC Uerdingen).

However, in 1995, Bayer decided to concentrate on Leverkusen and the first signs of this policy paying off came with the Champions League adventure in 1997–98.

Bayern Munich

Germany
Founded: *1900*
Stadium: *Olympiastadion (64,000)*
Colours: *All red*
Honours: *World Club Cup 1976; European Champions Cup 1974, 1975, 1976; Cup-winners Cup 1967; UEFA Cup 1996; League 14; Cup 9*

Bayern Munich are Germany's greatest modern football club and the only one to have climbed every peak of the international football mountain: domestic championship and cup, Champions Cup, Cup-winners Cup, UEFA Cup and World Club Cup.

The Bavarian club had achieved little before the introduction of the unifying Bundesliga in 1963. Until then German league competition had been organized on a regional basis with the "local" winners playing off for the national title. Bayern triumphed once in the championship, in 1932, and once in the cup, in 1957.

Their record did not earn Bayern a place in the inaugural Bundesliga, so they had to fight their way up through the promotion play-offs in 1965. Once they had made it into the top flight, however, there was no looking back. In 1966 Bayern won the cup by defeating MSV Duisburg 4—2 to qualify for the Cup-Winners' Cup. The Final was played not far north of Munich, in Nuremberg, where Bayern overcame Rangers 1–0 after extra time.

Already Bayern had the nucleus of the team which would conquer Europe and the world at both club and national team level. Sepp Maier was the goalkeeper, Paul Breitner a left back whose creative talent was so pronounced he later converted into midfield general, Gerd Müller one of the all-time great strikers and Franz Beckenbauer simply one of the greatest footballers of all time.

Beckenbauer played midfield for West Germany in the late 1960s but was already developing, at Bayern, the revolutionary attacking sweeper role from which he captained his country to victory in both the finals of the 1972 European Championship and 1974 World Cup.

That year, 1974, saw Bayern at their most brilliant as they defeated Atletico Madrid 4–0 in a replayed Final to win the Champions Cup for the first time. Müller and Uli Hoeness – later to become general manager – scored two goals apiece. The next year a side battered by injury defeated Leeds 2–0 in a controversial Champions Cup Final in Paris then, in 1975, Bayern squeaked past Saint-Etienne 1–0 at Hampden Park, Glasgow. A 2–0, 0–0 win over Cruzeiro of Brazil brought Bayern the World Club Cup as well.

Then it was time to rebuild. Breitner had already gone to Real Madrid and Beckenbauer went off to New York Cosmos. The new hero of the fans was flying forward Karl-Heinz Rummenigge who led Bayern to two more Champions Cup Finals – and defeats against Aston Villa in 1982, then FC Porto five years later.

As the commercial balance of football changed, so it became obvious that Bayern, financially, were head and shoulders above the rest of German football. Beckenbauer returned, successively, as director, championship-winning coach then club president. Rummenigge joined him on the board in the mid-1990s when Bayern brought Lothar Matthäus back from Italy and Jürgen Klinsmann home from England.

It took another superstar to manage such big egos which is why Beckenbauer himself had to step back in as coach in May 1996 to steer Bayern to victory in the UEFA Cup – making them, along with Ajax, Barcelona and Juventus, one of only four clubs to have won all three major European club prizes.

Benfica

Lisbon, Portugal
Founded: *1904*
Stadium: *Sport Lisboa e Benfica (92,385)*
Colours: *Red/white*
Honours: *European Champions Cup 1961, 1962; League 30; Cup 26*

Benfica, for all the recent success of FC Porto, remain Portugal's most successful and renowned club. A statue of their greatest footballer, Eusebio, stands at the entrance to the largest football stadium in Europe to intimidate each and every rival.

Their story is synonymous with that of Portuguese football since founder Cosme Damiao learned the game from English residents in Lisbon at the turn of the century. It was Damiao who laid down the tradition that Benfica should use only Portuguese citizens. This, of course, included players from the African colonies. The club's victories in the 1961 and 1962 Champions Cup finals would have been unthinkable without the presence of goalkeeper Costa Pereira and centre forward Jose Aguas from Angola as well as schemer Mario Coluna and Eusebio from Mozambique.

Benfica cater, as a club, for two dozen sports, but football is by far the most important and finances the other sections. It was in 1910 that Benfica landed their first title, the Lisbon championship, and from then on they have dominated domestic football. Typically, Benfica have also built the most well-appointed Portuguese stadium, the Estadio da Luz or Stadium of Light. This is the club's fifth permanent home, to which they moved in December 1954, just in time for the European explosion.

Benfica were, perhaps, lucky to win the 1961 Champions Cup Final against Barcelona. But under Hungarian coach Bela Guttmann they well deserved a brilliant 5–3 victory over Real Madrid a year later. However, losses in the World Club Final in both years have been followed by a hat-trick of defeats in the Champions Cup Finals.

With Eusebio winning the domestic goalscorer's title seven times, the club remained the dominating force at home. But despite the emergence of later stars such as goalkeeper Manuel Bento, centre back Humberto Coelho and forwards Nene and Chalana, Benfica have not found it as easy abroad any more.

The African option was ended by the colonies' independence in the mid-1970s. So, in the summer of 1978, Benfica members voted by a majority of two-to-one to break with tradition and enter the foreign market. The fruits could be seen in the team which reached the 1983 UEFA Cup final with the Yugoslav spearhead Zoran Filipovic and the Swedish midfielder Glenn Stromberg.

But further appearance success proved beyond them. An increasing reliance on player imports led to controversy and financial problems which further undermined their resistance to Porto's domestic domination.

Borussia Dortmund

Germany
Founded: *1909*
Stadium: *Westfalenstadion (42,800)*
Colours: *Yellow/black*
Honours: *World Club Cup 1997; European Champions Cup 1997; Cup-winners Cup 1966; League 5; Cup 2*

Borussia hold a particular place in history because they were the first German club to win a European trophy. That was in 1966, when they beat Liverpool 2–1 after extra time in the Final of the Cup-winners Cup in Glasgow.

Pride in that achievement extended almost to superstition when the members of that team were flown by Dortmund to the away leg of their 1993 UEFA Cup semi-final against French club Auxerre. The "lucky charms" paid off again, with Dortmund losing 2–0 but winning the penalty shoot-out 6–5. But the magic proved unrepeatable as Dortmund lost the final 1–3, 0–3 against Juventus. Revenge arrived in style four years later, when Dortmund beat Juventus 3–1 in the Champions Cup Final in Munich. Two goals from Karlheinz Riedle and one from substitute Lars Ricken turned Dortmund into Germany's first European club champions since Hamburg 14 years earlier.

Dortmund have been German champions on a total of five occasions and cup-winners twice, but the 1996 triumph was their first championship since the inception of the Bundesliga in the early 1960s.

The foundations had been laid several years earlier. Evidence was clear when Dortmund finished runners-up in 1992 then, again, in January 1993 when they paid £3million to bring home attacking sweeper Matthias Sammer from Internazionale of Italy.

Stephane Chapuisat of Borussia Dortmund in the 1997 European Cup final against Juventus

The former East German international had been sold to Inter only the previous summer by Stuttgart, but he failed to adapt to football, life and the language in Italy and Dortmund's enterprise in bringing him home was fully rewarded with remarkable success both at home and abroad.

The Westfalenstadion is one of the few modern German stadia which was created primarily for football. There is no athletics track surrounding the pitch and, in player polls, Dortmund is always voted as one of their favourite venues. It was built for the 1974 World Cup finals and was opened on April 2 that year with a Ruhr derby between Dortmund and Schalke 04. Two weeks later the stadium staged a friendly international, between West Germany and Hungary.

Borussia Mönchengladbach

Germany
Founded: *1900*
Stadium: *Bokelberg (34,500)*
Colours: *All white with green trim*
Honours: *UEFA Cup 1975, 1979; League 5; Cup 3*

As they prepare to celebrate the centenary, Borussia Mönchengladbach are struggling to regain the position of pre-eminence they enjoyed not so long ago in both Germany and Europe. They won the West German championship five times between 1970 and 1977, added the German cup in 1995 to two previous successes in the 1960s and 1970s and collected the UEFA Cup in 1975 and 1979.

Those were the years in which all the progressive management of master coach Hennes Weisweiler earned its due reward. Borussia became renowned as a football academy in the same way as West Ham in England – with one difference: Borussia not only played superb football, they were consistently successful at the highest level. Indeed, they very nearly crowned it all with the Champions Cup but were beaten by Liverpool in an outstanding Final in Rome in 1977.

Many of Weisweiler's pupils – most notably Berti Vogts (Germany's 1996 European Championship-winning boss) and Jupp Heynckes (later of Bayern Munich, Bilbao, Eintracht Frankfurt and Real Madrid) – became successful coaches in their own right. Even when Weisweiler himself was tempted away to Spain, to Barcelona, the foundations he had laid proved firm for his successors to build further success.

Borussia were founded on August 1, 1900. They first won the western region German title in 1920. But it was 40 years before they topped that, with a first victory in the West German cup. Under coach Bernd Oles, Borussia beat Karlsruhe 3–2 in the 1960 final, the goals being shared among the inside forward trio of Brulls, Kohn, Muhlhausen.

Albert Brulls was the first major star Borussia ever had. He played 25 times for West Germany and was a member of their World Cup finals squads both in Chile in 1962 and England in 1966 before transferring to Italy's Brescia.

Celtic manager Wim Jansen celebrates his club's 1998 Scottish Premier League triumph

Celtic

Glasgow, Scotland
Founded: *1888*
Stadium: *Celtic Park (47,500)*
Colours: *Green and white hoops/white*
Honours: *Champions Cup 1967; League 36; Cup 30; League Cup 10*

Celtic and Rangers are without question Scottish football's dominant clubs, their financial power having multiplied beyond all expectations following the television and sponsor-driven awakening of the 1990s.

That created its own problems and frustrations. However much the Old Firm invested in high-quality players, they needed the stimulus of top-class competition to stay sharp to achieve matching success in European competition. The greater the power of Celtic and Rangers, the more distance they put between themselves and the rest of the Scottish football – and the more obviously they pined for top-level competition.

Rangers have had the better of the past decade, but Celtic boast the historic achievement of having become the first British club – and, still, the only Scottish club – to have won the Champions Cup in 1967. It was a measure of the way they swept all before them that season that they won everything at home as well: the league, the cup and the league cup. No other team in Europe has ended a season with a 100 per cent record in all four major competitions.

The 1967 "Lisbon Lions" had been assembled shrewdly by manager Jock Stein, a former Celtic player. As well as new Scottish stars he included veterans such as goalkeeper Ronnie Simpson and inside left and schemer Bertie Auld. In the Final in Lisbon they beat former holders Internazionale from Italy by

2–1, with goals from full back Tommy Gemmell and centre forward Steve Chalmers. They did it with dash and style despite having gone behind to an early penalty.

Sadly, Celtic's golden touch did not last long at international level. Only months later they fell to Kiev Dynamo at the start of their Cup defence. They were then dragged down in the infamous World Club Cup final against Racing of Argentina – a clash which saw six players ordered off in a play-off in Montevideo, ultimately won by Racing by 1–0.

Celtic remained a Champions Cup power in the early 1970s. They returned to the final in 1970, in Milan, only to lose 2–1 to Feyenoord in extra time. In 1971 they reached the quarter-finals, losing to eventual winners Ajax, and in 1972 they came within a whisker of a third final appearance – losing on penalties to Internazionale in the semi-finals after two goalless draws. Celtic were beaten semi-finalists again in 1974 before being overtaken both by Rangers and by the destructive force of boardroom uncertainty.

Fergus McCann's seizure of control in the mid-1990s proved a new turning point. Parkhead was redeveloped and manager Tommy Burns was given the financial support to trawl Europe for new faces – Andreas Thom, Pierre Van Hooijdonk, Paolo Di Canio, Henrik Larsson and Jorge Cadete proving among the most successful and popular. In 1998, under Dutch coach Wim Jansen, Celtic halted Rangers' bid for a record-breaking 10th successive league title.

Chelsea

London, England
Founded: *1905*
Stadium: *Stamford Bridge (31,791)*
Colours: *All blue*
Honours: *European Cup-winners Cup 1971, 1998; League 1; Cup 1; League Cup 2*

Chelsea's honours list may be comparatively modest compared with other English sides, but the West London outfit have been one of the most continually fascinating of clubs.

Chelsea should have been England's first competitors in the Champions Cup. They were invited to enter the inaugural competition in 1955–56, but reluctantly withdrew on the orders of the Football League, which feared a fixtures snarl-up. The next year Manchester United did compete and thus, ironically, opened the way for Chelsea to accept an invitation into the 1968–69 Fairs Cup.

They reached the quarter-finals then and went a step further in 1966, reaching the semi-finals – beating Milan on the way in a thriller decided on the toss of a coin after a drawn play-off in San Siro – and Munich 1860 before losing to Barcelona.

Manager Tommy Docherty had brought a wind of change

Chelsea player-boss Gianluca Vialli with the League Cup

blowing through English football with a young team featuring the likes of Peter Osgood, Bobby Tambling and Terry Venables. But it required the more pragmatic approach of Dave Sexton to steer the team to a European title.

Chelsea won the FA Cup in a memorable, if physical, replay against Leeds in 1970, to earn a shot at the Cup-winners Cup. They began with a 6–2 aggregate victory over Aris Salonika, which proved a good omen as the Final was back in Greece. There, they beat Real Madrid after a replay.

Inside 10 years, however, Chelsea were in grave financial difficulties and it took all the business ingenuity new chairman Ken Bates could muster could turn the club around. This he did with such success that, in the mid-1990s, Chelsea had become London's most fashionable club to watch.

Just as in the Swinging Sixties, Chelsea were a glamorous club, attracting high-profile fans who were entertained by an imaginative transfer policy which brought in first Glenn Hoddle as player-manager then, in his wake, Ruud Gullit. The Dutchman took charge after Hoddle's departure for the England job and kept the revolution moving by importing Italy's Gianluca Vialli, Roberto Di Matteo and Gianfranco Zola. Vialli then took over with immediate success after Gullit's controversial departure in the spring of 1998. The Italian had barely been in management more than a few weeks than he was celebrating success in first the League Cup and then the European Cup-winners Cup.

Eintracht Frankfurt

Germany
Founded: *1899*
Stadium: *Waldstadion (61,146)*
Colours: *Black and red stripes/black*
Honours: *UEFA Cup 1980; League 1; Cup 4*

Eintracht Frankfurt hold a very particular place in football legend as the team beaten by Real Madrid in the European Champions Cup Final at Hampden back in 1960. The score was 7-3 to Madrid, but Frankfurt were far from crushed and had proved their class by putting six goals past Glasgow Rangers - both home and away - in the semi-finals.

Frankfurt's team was built on the midfield strength of Dieter Stinka and Jurgen Lindner plus the creative talents of veteran inside left Alfred Pfaff and right winger Richard Kress. Ultimately, however, everything after that legendary defeat by Madrid has been an anti-climax.

Although Frankfurt were founder members of the West German Bundesliga in 1963, they have achieved comparatively little since then. The mid-1980s were taken up with a three-year struggle against relegation - Frankfurt once saving themselves only in the relegation/promotion play-off. Boardroom problems also dogged the club until the businessman Matthias Ohms, took over and appointed Bernd Hölzenbein, World Cup-winner in 1974 and old Frankfurt favourite, as his executive vice- president. Holzenbein put Frankfurt back on a sound financial footing and raised the money to buy in stars such as midfielder Andy Moller (later sold to Juventus) and the brilliant but temperamental Ghanaian striker, Anthony Yeboah (later sold to Leeds). In 1992-93 Frankfurt led the league for much of the season but were pipped at the post by Werder Bremen after the controversial mid-season departure of their charismatic Yugoslav coach, Dragoslav Stepanovic.

Four years later they were relegated for the first time in the Bundesliga's history. Frankfurt's one European success over the years was in winning the UEFA Cup in 1980. They beat their fellow Germans, Borussia Mönchengladbach, on the away goals rule in the Final, losing 3-2 away then showing commendable grit to come back and win 1-0 in the Waldstadion. Hölzenbein had himself scored the all-important second away goal in the first leg that proved so crucial.

Everton

Liverpool, England
Founded: *1878*
Stadium: *Goodison Park (42,200)*
Colours: *Blue/white*
Honours: *European Cup-winners Cup 1985; League 9; Cup 5*

Everton have lived – too long, say their fans – in the domestic and European shadow of neighbours Liverpool. Luck has not always been with them. They hit the European heights themselves in 1985 when they defeated Rapid Vienna 3–1 in Rotterdam in the Cup-winners Cup Final. Sadly, the hooligan horror of Heysel two weeks later – ironically, predominantly the work of barbaric Liverpool supporters – brought a European ban on all English clubs for the next five years. Everton were neither allowed to defend the Cup-winners Cup nor to compete against Juventus in the European Supercup.

The talents at the disposal of manager Howard Kendall were beyond dispute. Gary Lineker was, in 1986, not only top scorer in the World Cup finals in Mexico (with six goals) but leading marksman in the league with 30. Everton finished runners-up, three points behind Liverpool and suffered further agony a few days later in the FA Cup, losing 3–1 – to Liverpool!

Lineker's departure for Barcelona did not weaken Everton one iota. Indeed, they won the league championship for the ninth (and, so far, last) time a year later. But then the Goodison Park faithful had to wait a further eight years, until 1995, for the next celebration – but the delight of FA Cup success was in sharp contrast to simultaneous struggles at the wrong end of the Premiership table.

Despite the fact that Everton are second only to Arsenal in terms of unbroken years in the top flight (they have been in elite division since 1954), for much of the 1990s they have had to stave off relegation to division one. The appointment of former Rangers' manager Walter Smith should certainly help usher in a new era of success to go with the new millennium.

Everton had been league founder members in 1888 and Lineker and £4.4million Duncan Ferguson have been only the more recent in a long line of outstanding attackers to grace the "School of Science." Joe Parker and Bert Freeman were free-scoring forwards in the early years of the century, followed by the record-breaking Bill "Dixie" Dean in the 1920s and 30s. For an outlay of £3,000, Everton secured the 17-year-old who would total 349 league goals – a record 60 in 1927–28.

He was succeeded in the No 9 shirt, in due course, by Tommy Lawton – for many an even greater centre forward – and then Scotland's Alex Young. Subsequent heroes included England's World Cup-winning midfield dynamo Alan Ball, who was bought and sold for then club record fees – £110,00 from Blackpool in 1966 and £225,000 to Arsenal in 1971.

Everton, whose team of the mid-80s brought domestic and European silverware to Goodison Park

FK Austria Vienna

Austria
Founded: *1911*
Stadium: *Horr (10,500) / Prater (62,270)*
Colours: *White with mauve/white*
Honours: *League 21; Cup 22*

The history of the Fussball Klub Austria-Memphis began with a game of cricket. Just as the English exported their industrial knowhow and educational skills around the world in the latter half of the 19th century, they took with them their newly-codified games and sports. Thus the Vienna Cricket and Football Club was founded by the expatriate community in the 1890s. Cricket did not gain universal acceptance. But football was another matter and November 15, 1894 saw the first proper football match ever staged in Austria. The Vienna Cricket and Football Club beat 1st Vienna FC by 4-0 - and they have been winning matches and titles ever since. Changing their name in 1925, FKA's honours list includes runners-up spot in the Cup-winners Cup in 1978, when a team inspired by midfield general Herbert Prohaska became the first Austrian side to reach a modern-day European final. That was long overdue since, in the late 1920s, FK Austria were one of the pioneers of European international

club soccer when the Mitropa Cup drew clubs from Austria, Czechoslovakia, Hungary, Yugoslavia, Switzerland and Italy. FK Austria were triumphant in 1933 and 1936, inspired by the legendary centre-forward Matthias Sindelar. Their delicate style of play known as the "Vienna School" was modelled on the old Scottish close-passing game and had been taught them by Englishman Jimmy Hogan whose coaching genius contributed mightily to the development of the so-called "Wunderteam" which lost unluckily to England, by 4-3, at Stamford Bridge in 1932 and then reached the semi- finals of the 1934 World Cup. The backbone of the team was provided by FK Austria. That tradition has been maintained ever since. Thus no fewer than six FKA stars travelled with the national squad to the 1990 World Cup finals in Italy.

Ferencvaros

Budapest, Hungary
Founded: *1899*
Stadium: *Ulloi ut (17,743)*
Colours: *Green and white stripes/white*
Honours: *Fairs Cup 1965; League 25; Cup 18*

Ferencvaros Club – Athletic Club of Ferencvaros – are the one

Hungarian club who have stood their European ground at a time when the domestic game appears to be falling apart.

But then, Ferencvaros have been defending a reputation and pride built up since their foundation under Dr Ferenc Springer in 1899. Even then the club's colours were green and white, arranged in five green and four white stripes symbolizing the Notn district of Budapest, the Hungarian capital.

The three letters on the emblem refer to the motto of the club which, translated, is: "Strength, Understanding, Morality."

Ferencvaros' football section has its own emblem which dates back to 1928 and features a bronze eagle gripping a football. Also known in the inter-war years as FTC, they are the only club to have taken part in every Hungarian top division championship and their 25 league titles is a record.

The most remarkable season was 1931–32 when Ferencvaros won every game. They were also European competition pioneers and were twice winners of the Mitropa Cup in its heyday of the 1920s and 1930s. Their record in modern international affairs is also a proud one, winning the Fairs Cup in 1965, being runners-up to Leeds in 1968, and losing to Kiev Dynamo in the Cup-winners Cup Final of 1975.

Great players have featured down the years. The first was Imre Schlosser who scored a record 48 goals for Hungary in the early 1900s. Gyorgy Sarosi and Geza Toldi were World Cup heroes in the 1930s; Sarosi scored 613 goals in 607 matches for the club – both records.

Ferenc Deak set a one-season record with 59 goals in 1948–49 while Laszlo Budai, Sandor Kocsis and Zoltan Czibor – members of the great Hungarian national team of the 1950s – first made their names with Ferencvaros. In more recent times Florian Albert became, in 1967, the only Hungarian player so far to win the European Footballer of the Year award, while Tibor Nyilasi was runner-up in 1981.

In 1996–97 Ferencvaros became one of the first teams to play in two different European competitions in the same season.

First, as champions of Hungary they played in the Champions League preliminary round, but lost to IFK Gothenburg of Sweden and were thus relegated into the UEFA Cup; here they were knocked-out in the second round by Newcastle United.

Feyenoord

Rotterdam, Holland
Founded: *1908*
Stadium: *Feyenoord (52,000)*
Colours: *Red and white halves/black*
Honours: *World Club Cup 1970; Champions Cup 1970; UEFA Cup 1974; League 13; Cup 10*

It is Feyenoord, and not Ajax, who hold the honour of having been the first Dutch club to capture the Champions Cup. They

triumphed in 1970 – one year before Ajax won the first of three back-to-back titles.

The Rotterdam club also gained success in the UEFA Cup before hitting financial problems in the late 1980s and early 1990s. Major investment was backed by the signing of former World Cup finalist Arie Haan as coach, and Ronald Koeman returned from Spain to reorganize the defence. But even that was not quite enough to break the Ajax-PSV domination of the league championship – though Feyenoord did finish runners-up in 1997 and thus qualify for the Champions League.

Feyenoord were the first Dutch club to make an international mark in the early 1960s courtesy of the talents of players such as goalkeeper Eddy Pieters Graafland and outside left Coen Moulijn. Later, under Austrian coach Ernst Happel, they won the Champions Cup by defeating Celtic 2–1 in extra time in Milan. Swedish striker Ove Kindall scored the decisive goal and Feyenoord went on to add the World Club Cup by defeating Estudiantes de La Plata.

Sadly Feyenoord's reputation has been tarnished by a hooligan fringe attached to the club. In 1996 Rotterdam's mayor, Bram Peper, demanded that their league match against Ajax should be moved from an evening kick-off to the afternoon so that up to 400 police could control fans.

Six years earlier, a teenage Feyenoord fan had been jailed for hurling a home-made bomb which injured over a dozen rival fans at an Ajax-Feyenoord game. In the spring of 1997 fans from both clubs fought a pitched battle on a motorway near Volendam.

Fiorentina

Florence, Italy
Founded: *1926*
Stadium: *Artemio Franchi (47,350)*
Colours: *All violet*
Honours: *European Cup-winners Cup 1961; League 2; Cup 5*

Fiorentina's reputation over the years has been for skilful, inventive football – thanks to the contributions of the likes of Giancarlo Antognoni, Daniel Bertoni, Kurt Hamrin and Julinho in the ranks – yet they owed their most famous success to an iron defence.

This was the team with which they won their first league title in 1956. Fiorentina conceded a then record of only 20 goals in their 34 league games and remained unbeaten until the last day of the season, when they went down 3–1 to Genoa.

Coach Fulvio Bernardini, a former Italian international, created a water-tight unit at the back. Goalkeeper Giuliano Sarti, left back Sergio Cervato, wing halves Beppe Chiappella and Armando Segato and the inside right Guido Gratton were the Italian foundations on which the outstanding Brazilian right wing Julinho and Chilean inside left Miguel Montuori built the incisive counter-attacks. This team reached the 1957 Champions' Cup Final, but unluckily had to face Real Madrid in the Spanish capital, and lost 2–0. Fiorentina, however, gained the consolation of becoming the first winners of the Cup-Winners' Cup in 1961, and lost to Atletico Madrid only after a replay in the following year's Final.

In the mid-1960s former star Chiappella became coach and built a fine young team which was later guided to the league title by the Swedish manager, Nils Liedholm. A key figure was Brazil's 1962 World Cup star Amarildo while midfielder Giancarlo De Sisti later became coach.

The "Viola" reached a further European final when they lost to Internazionale in the UEFA Cup in 1990. But three years later they suffered the ignominy of relegation for the first time in more than 50 years.

An instant revival owed much to the financial power of film-maker Vittorio Cecchi Gori and the acquisition of international stars such as Portuguese midfielder Rui Costa, Sweden's Stefan Schwarz and Gabriel Batistuta, the record-breaking Argentine centre forward.

Batistuta scored twice as Fiorentina defeated Atalanta 1–0, 2–0 in the 1996 cup final – their first trophy in 21 years.

Hamburg

Germany
Founded: *1887*
Stadium: *Volksparkstadion (61,234)*
Colours: *White/red*
Honours: *Champions Cup 1983; Cup-winners Cup 1977; League 6; Cup 3*

Hamburg are the second most successful German side in Europe after Bayern Munich. They and Borussia Dortmund are the only German clubs to have won two of Europe's three prizes – the Hamburg trophy room boasts replicas of both the Champions Cup (from 1983) and the Cup-winners Cup (from 1977).

The club first made their European mark in the Champions Cup of 1960–61. Those were the days of the great centre forward Uwe Seeler, allied with his brother Dieter at wing half and a fine left-wing partnership in Klaus Sturmer and Gerd Dorfel. They came within a minute of beating Barcelona in the 1961 semi-finals but had to settle instead for a play-off, which they lost 1–0.

Seven years later they reached a European final, but Seeler's men went down 2–0 to Milan in Rotterdam in the Cup-Winners' Cup. Nine years later Hamburg were back. Again the final was in Holland – but in Amsterdam – and this time Hamburg defeated holders Anderlecht 2–0. Their second goal was scored by midfield general Felix Magath, who was also the match-winning hero in 1983 when Hamburg, against all expectations, defeated Michel Platini's Juventus 1–0 in the Champions Cup

Final in the new Olympic stadium in Athens.

"I think I deserved that," said Magath later. He had also been a member of the Hamburg squad which – despite the presence of Kevin Keegan – lost the 1980 Champions Cup Final to Nottingham Forest and then lost the 1982 UEFA Cup Final to IFK Gothenburg.

Remarkably Hamburg have, since then, won only one other trophy the German cup in 1987. Somehow, the club lost their way both on and off the pitch. Not until the second coming of Uwe Seeler in 1995 – this time as president, with Magath as coach – did Hamburg start to pull their weight once more within the Bundesliga.

IFK Gothenburg

Sweden
Founded: *1904*
Stadium: *Gamla Ullevi (18,000)*
Colours: *Blue and white stripes/blue*
Honours: *UEFA Cup 1982, 1987; League 17; Cup 4*

IFK, founded in 1904 by a group of sports enthusiasts gathered at a cafe in Annedal, one of Gothenburg's working-class areas, are the only Swedish club to have won a European prize – the UEFA Cup.

The first members of IFK played not only football but also athletics and winter sports, but it did not take long for IFK to became one of Sweden's leading football clubs. Apart from eight seasons in the second division since the start of the national league, the "Blaavit" (Blue/white) – as the club are nicknamed – have belonged to the elite.

After winning the league in 1969, they were immediately relegated – underlining their reputation for entertaining, if erratic football – and it took them six years to return to the top flight. Once they were back, IFK invested heavily in experience. Ove Kindvall, Bjorn Nordqvist and Ralf Edstrom were all brought back from Holland. Yet this crowd-pleasing team did not win any honours. The turning point came in 1979, when Sven Goran Eriksson was signed from Degerfors as coach. He immediately guided IFK to their first-ever triumph in the Cup – defeating Aatvidaberg 6–1 in the final.

In 1982 IFK, also nicknamed "The Angels", became the first Swedish club to win a European club prize, when they beat Hamburg of Germany both home (1–0) and away (3–0) in the UEFA Cup Final. In 1986 they reached the Champions Cup semi-final, losing only on the dreaded penalty shoot-out to Barcelona. The following year, they once again won the UEFA Cup, beating Dundee United 1–0 in Gothenburg and drawing 1–1 in Scotland.

Many Swedish football legends have played for IFK, including 1950s inside forward Gunnar Gren, 1970s striker Torbjorn

Nilsson, Glenn Stromberg and Glenn Hysen and keeper Thomas Ravelli, the most-capped European player of all time.

IFK play in the Nya Ullevi stadium – sharing with fellow Allsvenska teams Orgryte and GAIS – which was built for the 1958 World Cup finals and hosted Denmark's remarkable victory over Germany in the 1992 European Championship Final.

Internazionale

Milan, Italy
Founded: *1908*
Stadium: *Giuseppe Meazza (85,443)*
Colours: *Blue and black stripes/black*
Honours: *World Club Cup 1964, 1965; Champions Cup 1964, 1965; UEFA Cup 1991, 1994, 1998; League 13; Cup 3*

One of the greatest of inter-city rivalries is that in Milan between Internazionale and AC (Associazione Calcio) Milan – a rivalry which goes back more than 90 years since the Inter club was founded directly because of a dispute within the Milan club. Some 45 members, led by committee man Giovanni Paramithiotti, broke away in protest at the authoritarian way Milan was being run by the powerful Camperio brothers.

That was not the end of the politics. In the 1930s, fascist laws forced Internazionale into a name-change to rid the club of the foreign associations of their title. So they took the name of the city of Milan's patron saint and became Ambrosiana.

Under this title they led the way in continental club competition – being one of the leading lights in the pre-war Mitropa Cup (the 1930s forerunner of today's European competitions).

After the war, the club reverted to the Internazionale name and led the way in a tactical revolution. So many star foreign forwards were being introduced into the Italian league that the old defensive systems were no longer effective. Alfredo Foni, a World Cup-winning full back before the war and Inter's coach after it, devised a new tactical system. He pulled winger Gino Armani back into midfield to help improve the defensive cover – and Inter won the Italian league titles in both 1953 and 1954.

The brilliance of Milan (with Nils Liedholm and Juan Schiaffino) and then Juventus (Omar Sivori and John Charles) overpowered even Inter in the late 1950s and early 1960s. But then Moratti became president and brought in coach Helenio Herrera who, in turn, built an outstanding team around Spanish midfield general Luis Suarez. In defence Herrera constructed the most formidable unit in club football. Goalkeeper Giuliano Sarti – a championship-winner with Fiorentina in 1956 – sweeper Armando Picchi and backs Tarcisio Burgnich, Aristide Guarneri and Giacinto Facchetti were as near watertight as possible.

They were the foundation on which outstanding forwards such as Brazil's Jair da Costa, Spain's Joaquim Peiro and Italy's own

Sandro Mazzola built success. Inter won the European and World Club Cups in both 1964 and 1965 – beating Real Madrid and Benfica in Europe, and Argentina's Independiente twice for the world crown.

But even they could not soak up pressure indefinitely. In 1966 Real Madrid toppled Inter in the Champions Cup semi-finals and Celtic repeated the trick a year later in a memorable Final in Lisbon.

Moratti retired and Herrera was lured away to Roma. But the elegant Mazzola remained in attack to lead Inter back to the Champions' Cup final in 1972, when they lost 2–0 to Ajax in Rotterdam – Johan Cruyff scoring both goals.

The Italian federation's ban on foreign players restricted Inter's ambitions for the rest of the 1970s. But the 1980 championship triumph coincided with the reopening of the borders and the following season Austrian midfielder Herbert Prohaska guided them to the Champions Cup semi-finals. Later, in the ranks of illustrious foreigners, came West German midfield general Hansi Muller, then Ireland's Liam Brady, before Lothar Matthäus drove Inter to their 1989 league title and a fine 1991 UEFA Cup triumph.

The "third" European trophy dominated Inter's international ambitions in the 1990s. They won it three times – adding victories in 1994 and 1998 to their 1991 success – and were runners-up in 1997, after losing a penalty shoot-out to Germany's Schalke.

The 1998 victory was notable because Inter's inspiration was Brazilian centre-forward Ronaldo – providing the first returns on the then world record £19.5million fee Inter had splashed out on him a year earlier.

Juventus

Turin, Italy
Founded: *1897*
Stadium: *Delle Alpi (71,012)*
Colours: *Black and white stripes/white*
Honours: *World Club Cup 1985, 1996; European Champions Cup 1985, 1996: Cup-winners Cup 1984: UEFA Cup 1977, 1990, 1993; Supercup 1984, 1996; League 25: Cup 9*

Juventus were founded by a group of Italian students who decided originally to adopt red as the colour for their shirts. However in 1903, when the club was six years old, one of the committee members was so impressed on a trip to England by Notts County's black-and-white stripes that he bought a set of shirts to take home to Turin.

In the 1930s Juventus laid the foundations for their legend, winning the Italian league championship five times in a row. Simultaneously they also reached the semi-finals of the Mitropa Cup on four occasions and supplied Italy's World Cup-winning teams with five players in 1934 and three in 1938. Goalkeeper

French superstar Michel Platini, in action for Italian giants Juventus

Gianpiero Combi, from Juventus, was Italy's Cup-lifting captain in 1934 just as another Juve keeper, Dino Zoff, would be in 1982.

After the war the "Zebras" (after the colours of their shirts) scoured the world for talent to battle the import-led foreign contingent. First came the Danes, John and Karl Hansen, then the Argentine favourite Omar Sivori and Wales' "Gentle Giant" John Charles, followed by Spanish inside forward Luis Del Sol and French inspiration Michel Platini. In 1971 they lost the Fairs Cup Final to Leeds United on the away goals rule but, six years later, it was the same regulation which brought Juventus victory over Athletic Bilbao in the UEFA Cup Final.

In 1982 no fewer than six Juve players featured in Italy's World Cup-winning line-up and the likes of Antonio Cabrini, Marco Tardelli, Gaetano Scirea, Claudio Gentile and Paolo Rossi went on to help Juve win the 1984 Cup-winners Cup and the 1985 Champions Cup. Seeking new magic, Juventus paid huge fees for Italy's Roberto Baggio and Gianluca Vialli who helped Juve secure a record 23rd league title – before Baggio was transferred to Milan.

Without him Juventus won the Champions Cup – beating Ajax on penalties in Rome – and then ripped up their team again by bringing in French midfielder Zinedine Zidane and Croatian striker Alen Boksic, while shipping out both Vialli and fellow striker Fabrizio Ravanelli. Despite these wholesale changes, Juventus reached the Champions Cup Final again in successive years – 1997 and 1998 – only to lose on each occasion. Both times Juve failed to live up to their favourites' billing against Borussia Dortmund in Munich in 1997 and then against Real Madrid in Amsterdam in 1998.

Kiev Dynamo

Ukraine

Founded: *1927*

Stadium: *Republican (100,169)*

Colours: *White/blue*

Honours: *European Cup-winners Cup 1975, 1986: Supercup 1975: League 18 (5 Ukraine, 13 USSR); Cup 11 (2 Ukraine, 9 USSR)*

Ukraine is now an independent nation with Dynamo Kiev acknowledged as the top team. Originally the club was formed as a subsidiary of police organizations which inaugurated the USSR-wide network of Dynamo clubs in the late 1920s.

Kiev Dynamo were founded in 1927 but quickly earned recognition as one of the best in the Soviet Union. A national league was introduced in 1936, with Kiev founding members of the top division. They were never relegated.

In 1961, Dynamo became the first club from outside Moscow to win the national championship. In 1975, they went on to become the first Soviet side to win a European prize, when they defeated Ferencvaros of Budapest 3–0 in the Cup-winners Cup Final in Basle. Later that year, Dynamo beat Bayern Munich in the European Super Cup, which helped earn success for left winger Oleg Blokhin in the European Footballer of the Year poll.

Valeri Lobanovski was the head coach then and he was still the boss when Dynamo regained the Cup-winners Cup in 1986, this time defeating Atletico Madrid 3–0 in front of a 40,000 crowd in Lyon and millions of television viewers throughout Europe. Experts described the performance as "football of the next century" and Igor Belanov followed in Blokhin's footsteps as European Footballer of the Year.

Kiev's skilled, thoughtful and entertaining approach was a breath of fresh air compared with the unimaginative, stereotyped teams which had been coming out of the Soviet Union for many years. Unfortunately the Soviet federation tried to make too much of a good thing.

It turned Dynamo Kiev into the national team, and the combined weight of domestic and international fixtures took the sparkle from their play. They might, otherwise, have won more European trophies. Dynamo won the Soviet Supreme Championship 13 times (a record) and were runners-up 11 times. They also won the Cup nine times before the dissolution of the USSR and the foundation of the independent state of Ukraine.

Life in independent Ukraine was not easy. Football fought a long battle to try to resist mafia infiltration. In 1995 Kiev were expelled from the Champions League after a clumsy attempt to bribe Spanish referee Antonio Lopez Nieto on the eve of their tie against Panathinaikos of Greece.

Kiev were barred from Europe, initially, for three years. But UEFA, considering the financial pressures on the Ukraine game, later took pity and allowed them back in to the Champions League the following season.

Leeds United

England
Founded: *1919*
Stadium: *Elland Road (39,775)*
Colours: *All white*
Honours: *Fairs Cup 1968, 1971; League 3; Cup 1; League Cup 1*

Leeds United attained a reputation for the ultimate in disciplined, effective English football in the late 1960s and early 1970s under the managership of Don Revie, a former England inside forward. He instilled these qualities, plus an immense pride, which made Leeds feared opponents at home and abroad.

Yet the extent to which Leeds set the agenda in English football is hardly demonstrated by the trophies they won. Leeds were more often runners-up than winners: five times in the league, three times in the FA Cup, once each in the Champions

Cup (in 1975), Cup-winners Cup (in 1973) and Fairs Cup (in 1967).

Later, after Revie's spell as England manager had ended amid controversy, it became fashionable to carp at the dossiers on opponents, at the organized games of carpet bowls for the players. But few "teachers" inspired so many pupils to go into football management – among them Billy Bremner, Eddie Gray, Norman Hunter, Allan Clarke, Johnny Giles and, most notably, Jack Charlton.

Leeds first earned international headlines in 1957 when they sold Welshman John Charles to Juventus for a then British record £57,000. The club itself did not enter Europe until 1965 in the Fairs Cup – a competition they won after Finals against Ferencvaros in 1968 and Juventus in 1971. They were permanent fixtures then in Europe until the UEFA-imposed suspension in 1975 after rioting Leeds fans ripped out seats in the Champions Cup Final in Paris. Leeds had lost 2–0 against an injury-weakened Bayern Munich. By then Revie had already gone to the England job and Jimmy Armfield was manager. It was a sad end to an era.

Relegation followed in 1982 and Leeds stayed down eight long years before Howard Wilkinson not only brought them back up but turned them – thanks to the fleeting inspiration of Eric Cantona – into league champions once more.

Don Revie was Leeds' all-powerful manager

Manchester United manager Alex Ferguson celebrates his league and cup Double in 1996

Liverpool

England
Founded: *1892*
Stadium: *Anfield (41,210)*
Colours: *All red*
Honours: *Champions Cup 1977, 1978, 1981, 1984; UEFA Cup 1973,*
1976; Supercup 1977; League 18; Cup 5; League Cup 5

Successful sportsmen the world over tell the same tale: reaching the top is tough, but not as tough as staying at the top. The enormous pressures generated by success even wore down the cogs of the Liverpool machine in the end – but only after a phenomenal 28 years of unprecedented achievement.

The modern adventure began in 1954 when Liverpool, with a proud history behind them, slipped into the old second division. They remained there for eight years until Bill Shankly's unrivalled enthusiasm and football insight guided them back to the top division in 1962. Shankly had arrived in 1959, just after the club had reached its nadir, an exit from the FA Cup at the hands on Southern League Worcester City.

In 1964 – surfing the waves of Beatlemania – Liverpool won the first of their modern championships. In the next 26 years, they were to win the league 13 times (adding up to a record 18 in all), the FA Cup five times, the League Cup four times and the league and cup Double once.

Such drive proved relentlessly successful in Europe. Shankly and successors Bob Paisley and Joe Fagan managed to create a style which incorporated the physically-based strengths of the English game with the more technically thoughtful school of the best continental sides. It worked like a dream. Four times Liverpool won the Champions Cup and twice the UEFA Cup. They were runners-up in the Champions Cup once and the Cup-winners Cup once. The only occasion on which Liverpool were put to the sword on a mainline occasion was the 1981 World Club Cup final in Tokyo. Zico's Flamengo, from Brazil, were well-deserved 3–0 winners.

Borussia Mönchengladbach and Brugge suffered worst from Liverpool. Borussia were the victims of Liverpool's first UEFA Cup triumph, and the victims again in Rome in 1977 when Kevin Keegan bowed out of the Anfield scene with the club's first Champions Cup secured. Brugge were beaten by Liverpool in both the UEFA Cup Final in 1976 and the Champions Cup final at Wembley in 1978. The winning goal second time around was scored by Kenny Dalglish, who had arrived from Celtic to fill – seamlessly – the gap left by Keegan's departure for Hamburg.

Dalglish, wherever his career may subsequently have taken him, will always be considered – at least in England – as a legend of Anfield. He took over as manager in the awful wake of the Heysel tragedy in 1985 and later had to bear the burden of pain of the city after the 1989 Hillsborough disaster. At Heysel, 39 Juventus fans died; at Hillsborough 96 Liverpool fans were crushed to death.

In between, Dalglish became the only player-manager to have guided his team to the league and cup Double in 1986 and there were further honours. The league title trophy returned in 1988 and 1990 and the FA Cup in 1989 before Dalglish stepped out from beneath the combined stress of triumph and tragedy.

Successor Graeme Souness won "only" the FA Cup before Liverpool went back to the old Boot Room regime and promoted long-time servant Roy Evans to the manager's chair. A League Cup win in 1995 and the emergence of new heroes such as Steve McManaman, Robbie Fowler and Michael Owen promised an imminent return to the glory days...but did nothing to quell growing impatience among the fans. In 1998 Liverpool appointed Frenchman Gerard Houllier as co-manager alongside Evans in a bid to challenge for honours once more.

Manchester United

England
Founded: *1878*
Stadium: *Old Trafford (55,800)*
Colours: *Red/white*
Honours: *European Champions Cup 1968; Cup-winners Cup 1991;*
Supercup 1991; League 11; Cup 9; League Cup 1

Matt Busby may stand as the most charismatic of Manchester United managers. But even Sir Matt's record of achievement cannot compare with that of Alex Ferguson in the 1990s which saw United – a commercial as well as footballing monolith – hailed as the richest club in the world.

United had been founded in 1878 as Newton Heath by employees of the Lancashire and Yorkshire Railway Company. Ironically, considering events of 90 years later, Newton Heath went bankrupt in 1902 and it was out of that commercial failure that a new club, entitled Manchester United, was formed.

The club floated in and out of the top division between the wars but it was the 1948 Cup Final victory which provided the spark for the future. United twice hit back from a goal down to defeat Stanley Matthews's Blackpool 4–2 in what remains considered one of the great FA Cup Finals.

This was the first outstanding team built by manager Busby, who had played before the war for neighbour Manchester City. His second outstanding team were the so-called "Busby Babes" of the mid-1950s. United defied establishment orders and entered the European Champions Cup in 1956–57. They opened with a 10–0 thrashing of Belgium's Anderlecht and never looked back – not even in the bleak days of February 1958, after eight players, including England internationals Roger Byrne, Tommy Taylor and Duncan Edwards, died in the Munich air disaster.

It took United 10 years to recover, in international terms. Thus it was in May, 1968 that United's European quest was rewarded as they defeated Benfica 4–1 in extra time at Wembley. Bobby Charlton, a Munich survivor along with defender Bill Foulkes and manager Busby, scored twice to secure the club's most emotional triumph. Foulkes himself had scored the match-winner in a dramatic semi-final against Real Madrid.

The club became synonymous with entertaining, attacking soccer as epitomized by the talents of Charlton, Denis Law and the wayward but mesmeric Northern Irishman, George Best. Later came England's long-serving skipper Bryan Robson, who was still in harness in 1993 when United, under Alex Ferguson, regained the English league title for the first time in 26 years.

Ferguson, brought south from Aberdeen, had managed on a knife-edge in his early days. Victory in the European Cup-winners Cup in 1991 – United were first back, appropriately, after the five-year post-Heysel ban – proved that Ferguson was on the right lines. Events in the next five years underlined the point. Between 1993 and 1996 United won the league title three times in four seasons, including an unprecedented "double Double" of league and FA Cup in 1994 and 1996. Danish goalkeeper Peter Schmeichel and French forward Eric Cantona contributed the cosmopolitan icing to the most successful English club recipe of the 1990s.

Marseille

France
Founded: *1898*
Stadium: *Velodrome (46,000)*
Colours: *All white*
Honours: *European Champions Cup 1993; League 9 (1993 revoked); Cup 10*

September 6, 1993, was the blackest day in the history of Olympique Marseille. That was the date on which UEFA decided to bar Marseille from defending the Champions Cup – won against Milan just over three months earlier – and opened up the path for an avalanche of match-fixing revelations which scandalized French football. To compound their humiliation, Marseille were later stripped of the Champions Cup.

Some 16 days later, the French federation stripped Marseille of their league title and suspended former secretary Jean-Pierre Bernes and three of the four players involved in the bribery scandal – Jean-Jacques Eydelie and Valenciennes' Christophe Robert and Argentine international Jorge Burruchaga. No action was taken immediately against Marseille president Bernard Tapie, but in due course he too stood trial in court for match-fixing and was imprisoned for corruption. Marseille had played Valenciennes in May 1993, just before their Champions Cup Final against Milan, and by winning 2–0 had claimed the title, or so they thought.

European exclusion cost Marseille an estimated £14million and they were duly punished by the French federation with enforced relegation. Only in 1996 did Marseille, now under the direction of new owners led by Adidas boss Robert Louis-Dreyfus, regain top division status.

All of this was a sad comedown for a club which had been renowned as one of the richest in France, with perhaps the most loyal and fanatical fans. Marseille are one of the oldest of French clubs, but their history has been chequered with controversy. Their 1971 and 1972 league championship successes were tarnished after they had lured away top goalkeeper Georges Carnus and defender Bernard Bosquier from closest rivals Saint Etienne in mid-season.

Marseille boasted other great players such as Yugoslav striker Josip Skoblar, who was the league's top scorer for three years in a row, but their most enduring talent has proved to be one for courting controversy.

Mechelen

Belgium
Founded: *1904*
Stadium: *Achter de Kazerne (14,131)*
Colours: *Yellow with thin red stripes/black*
Honours: *European Cup-winners Cup 1988; Supercup 1988; League 4; Cup 1*

Mechelen won the Belgian championship – when the domestic game was amateur – on three occasions in the 1940s but were unrated as an international force when they shocked Europe in general and Ajax Amsterdam in particular to win the 1988 Cup-winners Cup.

The previous season they had won the Belgian cup for the first time to earn their first-ever European qualification and they reached the Final in Strasbourg without having lost a game. Dinamo Bucharest were beaten 1–0 home and 2–0 away, St Mirren 2–0 away, Dynamo Minsk 1–0 at home and Italy's Atalanta 2–1 both home and away in the semi-finals.

Ajax were holders of the Cup-winners Cup and overwhelming favourites to become the first club to retain the trophy. But defender Danny Blind was sent off after 17 minutes and Mechelen, coached by Dutchman Aad de Mos, won with a 53rd-minute goal from Den Boer. Mechelen midfielder Erwin Koeman, yet another Dutchman, set up a rare family double that year because, two weeks after his triumph, Erwin's brother Ronald collected a winner's medal in the Champions Cup with PSV Eindhoven.

Mechelen, with whom goalkeeper Michel Preud'homme was resurrecting his career after an earlier match-fixing scandal while with Standard Liege, won the championship in 1989 but lost their grip on the Cup-winners Cup in the semi-final against Sampdoria.

Milan

Italy

Founded: *1899*

Stadium: *Giuseppe Meazza (85,443)*

Colours: *Red and black stripes/black*

Honours: *World Club Cup 1969, 1989, 1990; Champions Cup 1963, 1969, 1989, 1990, 1994; Cup-winners Cup 1968, 1973; Supercup 1989, 1990, 1995: League 15; Cup 4*

Milan were the dominant club in Europe for a decade from the late 1980s. The era began when the club signed Holland's Ruud Gullit and Marco Van Basten in 1987. The next year they won the Italian championship and then, two years in a row, the Champions Cup. In 1993 Milan lost 1–0 in the final to Marseille, defeated Barcelona in thrilling style by 4–0 in 1994, then lost to Ajax by 1–0 in Vienna in 1995.

Milan's reign was constructed on a futuristic commercial blueprint laid down by the media magnate Silvio Berlusconi. He had come to the rescue in 1986 – investing £20million to save Milan from bankruptcy and turn the club into a key player in his commercial empire. Milan had been one of the founders of the Italian championship back in 1898 but most of the pre-World War Two years were spent in the shadows of neighbours Internazionale – or Ambrosiana as they were then called. After the war Milan achieved spectacular success thanks to their forays into the international transfer market – at that stage virtually uncontrolled by the Italian league authorities.

Sweden had won the 1948 Olympic title thanks to the inside forward skills of Gunnar Gren, Gunnar Nordahl and Nils Liedholm, so Milan signed them en bloc and then followed up by paying a then world record £72,000 for Juan Schiaffino – hero

Ruud Gullit inspired the re-emergence of Milan in the late 1980s

of Uruguay's shock World Cup victory in 1950.

Milan were the first major rivals to Real Madrid in the new European Champions Cup – losing to the Spanish club in the 1956 semi-finals, then only after extra-time in the 1958 Final. That was also the year Milan discovered the teenager Gianni Rivera, whose inside forward genius inspired Milan to their first Champions Cup victory in 1963.

His partnership with Brazilian centre forward Jose Altafini destroyed Benfica in the Final and skipper and sweeper Cesare Maldini held the Cup aloft at Wembley – where he would later enjoy another significant success, this time as manager of Italy, in the 1998 World Cup qualifying event.

Rivera was Milan's figurehead in the 1960s and early 1970s, winning the Champions Cup again in 1969 and the Cup-winners Cup. But even his charisma could not save the club from the scandals and financial disasters inflicted by a string of disastrous presidents.

That was where Berlusconi came in, providing the money and the men – coaches Arrigo Sacchi and Fabio Capello, Dutch superstars Ruud Gullit, Marco Van Basten, Frank Rijkaard as well as Italy's Franco Baresi and Paolo Maldini (son of Cesare) – for a "new media" football club for the 21st century.

Moscow Dynamo

Russia
Founded: *1923*
Stadium: *Dynamo (51,000)*
Colours: *White/blue*
Honours: *League 11 (USSR 11); 7 (Russia 1; USSR 6)*

Dynamo are probably the most famous of Russian clubs, having been the first Soviet side to venture beyond the Iron Curtain in the 1940s and 1950s. Also, they were fortunate enough to possess, in goalkeeper Lev Yashin, one of the greatest personalities in the modern game – a show-stopper wherever he went. Yet Dynamo's origins go back to the start of soccer in Russia, introduced by the Charnock brothers at their cotton mills towards the end of last century. The team won successive Moscow championships under the name Morozovsti and, after the Russian Revolution, were taken over by first the electrical trades union and then the police.

Thus 1923 marks the formal setting-up of Moscow Dynamo rather than the foundation of the original club. In the years immediately after the end of the second world war, Dynamo established a legend as a result of a four-match British tour. They drew 3–3 with Chelsea and 2–2 with Rangers, thrashed Cardiff 10–1 and beat a reinforced Arsenal 4–3 in thick fog. Inside forward Constantin Beskov later became national manager but it was goalkeeper Alexei "Tiger" Khomich whose reputation lasted long after he had retired to become a sports press photographer. He was succeeded in the team by an even greater

goalkeeper in Yashin who was to become the first Soviet player honoured as European Footballer of the Year. Given Dynamo's leadership, it was appropriate that, in 1972, they should become the first Soviet side to reach a European final. But their 3–2 defeat by Rangers in Barcelona also stands as the high point of their modern achievement. Back home, Dynamo were pushed back down the ranks by neighbours Moscow Spartak and the fast-rising Kiev Dynamo.

Moscow Spartak

Russia
Founded: *1922*
Stadium: *Lenin/Luzhniki (102,000)*
Colours: *Red and white/white*
Honours: *League 17 (Russia 5; Soviet 12); Cup 11 (Russia 1, USSR 10)*

Moscow Spartak, champions of Russia in five of the first six seasons since the collapse of the Soviet Union, face an enormous challenge in the years ahead. Spartak were a power in the land under the old system but those were the days when players were not allowed to move abroad. Now Spartak must maintain their domestic command and compete effectively in Europe in an "open" transfer society. This is all the more challenging because Spartak had, for years, represented the Party line. They play their home matches in the 103,000- capacity Olympic-Lenin stadium in the Luzhniki suburb of Moscow and their past heroes included such officially-approved characters as 1950s' top scorer Nikita Simonian (holder of a club record 133 goals) and left half Igor Netto (a club record 367 appearances).

Spartak's best season in Europe was 1990-91 when they beat both Napoli and Real Madrid to reach the semi-finals of the Champions Cup before falling 5-1 on aggregate to Marseille. For years the club had been ruled by the most respected members of the managerial old guard in veteran administrator Nikolai Starostin and former 'national coach Constantin Beskov. Starostin, a player in the club's early days, stayed on after the political upheaval but Beskov handed over the coaching mantle to his former pupil and international full back, Oleg Romantsev. Despite the loss of sweeper Vasili Kulkov and midfielders Igor Shalimov and Alexander Mostovoi, Romantsev kept Spartak on top of the table. New heroes were left back and skipper Viktor Onopko, versatile Igor Lediakhov and young forward Mikhail Beschastnikh.

Not only did Spartak win the 1992 and 1993 Russian league titles, they also won - in both 1993 and 1994 - the pre-season CIS Cup competed among the champions of all the former Soviet states. Onopko and Beschastnikh were soon heading for western Europe, however, and Spartak looked to yet another generation, led by Dmitri Alenichev, to maintain their command.

Napoli

Italy

Founded: *1904*

Stadium: *San Paolo (72,810)*

Colours: *Blue/white*

Honours: *UEFA Cup 1989; League 2; Cup 3*

Napoli were, for years, a club with more passion than purpose. The original Naples club – English language style, of course – were founded in 1904 then underwent a series of mergers before taking the present Associazione Calcio Napoli title in 1926. In the further inter-war years they held their place in Serie A but could make little headway against the giants of the era, Juventus, Bologna and Ambrosiana-Inter.

Relegated in the penultimate pre-war season – 1941–42 – Napoli spent much of the first 20 post-war years hopping between divisions. They also collected a string of ground suspensions whenever the passion of their huge following boiled over.

The "new era" began in 1965. Napoli had just regained their Serie A place when the club found new investors able to fund the sensational purchases of Jose Altafini from Milan and Omar Sivori from Juventus.

Both superstars were past their best and had squabbled their way out of their previous clubs. But their presence revolutionized the atmosphere around Fuorigrotta.

In the next decade Napoli established themselves as virtual ever-presents in the league's top four but they had only two Italian cups to show for it. The step up to European achievement demanded a further coup – which president Corrado Ferlaino provided in 1984 when he signed Diego Maradona from Barcelona for a world record £5million.

Within a fortnight of the transfer, Napoli had recouped most of the fee in season-ticket sales. Maradona played to sell-out 85,000 crowds and inspired Napoli to win the league title twice, the UEFA Cup and the Italian cup. The money Napoli made, however, was frittered away. After Maradona's dope-ban exit in 1991, the club collapsed to the brink of bankruptcy and then, in 1998, to relegation to Serie B.

Newcastle United

England

Founded: *1881*

Stadium: *St James' Park (36,610)*

Colours: *Black and white stripes/black*

Honours: *Fairs Cup 1969; League 4; Cup 6*

Newcastle's revival in the 1990s had everything to do with Kevin Keegan. He was given financial carte blanche by chairman Sir John Hall, but far more managers have squandered cash than invested wisely. Keegan's achievement was to breathe life and soul back into an apparently moribund club.

In his first half-season he saved Newcastle from relegation

Newcastle United striker Alan Shearer signs autographs after his £15 million transfer

from the old second division; in his first full season he achieved promotion to the Premiership; in the next he guided Newcastle to third place and into the UEFA Cup; his third full season culminated in sixth place; in 1996 Newcastle finished second. Keegan then splashed a world record £15million on England spearhead Alan Shearer before bailing out in mid-season and handing over to Kenny Dalglish.

The sky appeared to be the limit. The north-east of England had known nothing like it since the Magpies dominated English football in the early years of the century. Then, with such heroes as defender Bill McCracken – the man who forced the offside law change from three defenders to two – they won the league three times and reached the cup final five times (albeit winning only once).

In the early 1950s Newcastle became the first club of the 20th century to win the FA Cup twice in a row – beating Blackpool 2–0 in 1951 then Arsenal 1–0. Centre forward "Wor Jackie" Milburn was one hero, left winger Bobby Mitchell another, tough-tackling right half Jimmy Scoular a third.

After four years in the old second division, Newcastle returned to achieve the feat of winning a European prize at first attempt. This was the 1969 Fairs Cup, which they captured by defeating Hungary's Ujpest Dozsa 3–0 at home then 3–2 away after being 2–0 down. Skipper Bobby Moncur scored three of Newcastle's six goals from wing half – his opener in the first leg of the Final being his first for Newcastle in nine years!

Nottingham Forest

England
Founded: *1865*
Stadium: *City Ground (30,602)*
Colours: *Red/white*
Honours: *European Champions Cup 1979, 1980; Supercup 1979; League 1; Cup 2; League Cup 4*

Nottingham Forest joined illustrious company when they defeated Malmo 1–0 in Munich in 1979 to win the Champions Cup. Only Real Madrid (in the inaugural tournament in 1955–56) and Internazionale (in 1963–64) had ever won Europe's most prestigious club prize at the first attempt. Forest won it again the following year, defeating Hamburg this time by the same minimal margin, in Madrid. This double only further enshrined the legend of Brian Clough in English football folklore, although such was the particular style of the man that his aura made little impression abroad – despite the achievements of his team.

When Clough took over in the mid-1970s, Forest were a famous old club in the middle of what was then the second division and apparently going nowhere. They had never won the league title and had won the FA Cup only twice – in 1898 and then again in 1959, when they beat Luton 2–1 despite losing right

winger Roy Dwight with a broken leg.

Clough had made his managerial name at Derby, with whom he gained his first taste of the Champions Cup, reaching the semi-finals in 1973. With Forest he went one step better. Forest came up into the top division in 1977, won the league a year later then the Champions Cup. Along the way Forest invested some of their new-found riches by turning Trevor Francis, from Birmingham City, into English football's first £1million player.

Francis's European debut for Forest was a dream – the 1979 Champions Cup Final in which he headed the only goal. A year later it was the turn of Scotland's John Robertson to decide matters. Forest were also four-times winners of the League Cup under Clough, who finally stepped down amid the depression of relegation in 1993. Promotion and another relegation followed, but Forest are back in the Premiership now after winning the First Division Championship in 1998.

Paris Saint Germain

France
Founded: *1970*
Stadium: *Parc des Princes (49,000)*
Colours: *Blue with broad red stripe/blue*
Honours: *European Cup-winners Cup 1996: League 2: Cup 5; League Cup 2*

Paris Saint Germain, remarkably, became the very first club from the French capital to win a European prize when they defeated Rapid Vienna 1–0 in the Cup-winners Cup Final in 1996.

Yet PSG had been founded only 26 years earlier – by Parisian fans anxious to fill the gap left by the collapse of professional football in the French capital. They did not turn formally full professional until 1973, by which time they had risen to the brink of promotion to the French top division under the enthusiastic presidency of the couturier, Daniel Hechter. He spent money on players the same way his fashions encouraged women to spend money on clothes, signing Yugoslav goalkeeper Ilija Pantelic and midfielder Safet Susic, record-breaking Argentine centre forward Carlos Bianchi and French World Cup internationals Dominique Rocheteau, Dominique Bathenay and Luis Fernandez. The trophy breakthrough arrived with Paris' French cup successes in 1982 and 1983 and was extended in 1986 when, under former English teacher Gerard Houllier, Paris won their first league title. Amazingly, it was the first time a Paris club had won the national championship since Racing Club exactly 50 years earlier in 1936.

In due course Houllier was spirited away to become assistant and then full manager of the French national team and Paris had to look for new resources and backers. They found them in 1995, in the ambitious television station Canal-Plus. Denisot invested heavily in a string of new star players – such as Liberian George

Weah, Frenchman David Ginola and Brazilians Ricardo, Valdo and Rai – and the results are now plain to see.

PSG reached European semi-finals in four successive seasons: losing in the UEFA Cup in 1993, the Cup-winners Cup in 1994 and the Champions League 1995, but this hurdle was finally cleared in the 1996 Cup-winners Cup. However, their Final victory over Rapid was followed by the departures of coach Luis Fernandez and attacking key Youri Djorkaeff – provoking wide-ranging changes among both playing staff and management. PSG lost in the Cup-winners final to Barcelona the following season, a defeat which ultimately provoked changes in both boardroom and team management with noted broadcaster Charles Bietry taking over as chief executive and ex-international Alain Giresse as coach.

Parma

Italy
Founded: *1913*
Stadium: *Ennio Tardini (29,048)*
Colours: *All white*
Honours: *Cup-winners Cup 1993: UEFA Cup 1995; Supercup 1993; Cup 1*

The town of Parma is world famous for its ham and as the birthplace of the great composer Giuseppe Verdi. Now it is also renowned world-wide as the home of one of European football's fastest-growing clubs. This particular Parma have produced plenty of star names in the past. One was coach Arrigo Sacchi, who took Italy to the 1994 World Cup Final; others include players such as Nicola Berti (later Inter) and Carlo Ancelotti (one-time Milan).

But plenty has changed in a few short years. Now Parma can hold on to their star men if they wish. The financial backing of sponsors Parmalat, the dairy produce company, means Parma have become transfer raiders themselves. In 1990 they bought Sweden's baby-faced World Cup star Tomas Brolin; later came Colombian talent Faustino Asprilla, then Italy's own Gianfranco Zola and Enrico Chiesa as well as Argentina's Hernan Crespo.

Parma were founded on July 27, 1913 – originally under the name of Verdi Foot Ball Club. Five months later the composer disappeared from view as the club committee voted to change titles to Parma Foot Ball Club. Most of the years up until the early 1950s were spent in the fourth, third and second divisions. In the 1950s Parma appeared to establish themselves in the second division but were relegated in 1965 and slipped right on down into the fourth division and had to merge with another local club to survive.

Finally, in 1986, under Sacchi they gained promotion back to Serie B and, four years later, were in Serie A for the first time

in their history. They finished fifth in their first season and earned entry to the UEFA Cup, falling unluckily on the away goals rule in the first round to CSKA Sofia. That same season they beat Juventus 0–1, 2–0 in the Italian cup final, returned to Europe in the Cup-winners Cup and triumphed thanks to a 3–1 victory over Belgian club Antwerp at Wembley. Against Arsenal a year later, Parma narrowly failed to become the first club to retain the Cup-winners Cup. But their European consolation, a year later, was to beat fellow Italians Juventus in the UEFA Cup Final.

FC Porto

Portugal
Founded: *1893*
Stadium: *Das Antas (76,000)*
Colours: *Blue and white stripes/blue*
Honours: *World Club Cup 1987; Champions Cup 1987; Supercup 1987; League 17; Cup 13*

FC Porto had always been always considered the "third club" in the Portuguese football hierarchy until their thrilling Champions Cup victory over Bayern Munich in Vienna in 1987. Events then and since have ensured that Porto, while their trophy count may not yet match that of Benfica and Sporting, are considered an alternative centre of power in the domestic game. Indeed, Porto are now the club in Portugal, having won the league championship eight times in the last decade.

Their basic pattern of tactics and style means that the team can withstand whatever changes may be enforced by the uncertainties of the transfer market. In the summer of 1996, for instance, Porto lost coach Bobby Robson and international goalkeeper Vitor Baia (both to Barcelona), defender Carlos Secretario (to Real Madrid) and Brazilian midfielder Emerson (to Middlesbrough). Yet they went on to complete a hat-trick of league championships with such command that one newspaper wrote of the "Scottishization" of Portuguese football , only Porto, Sporting and Benfica have won the league title since Belenenses in 1945. Certainly, no-one who witnessed the Brazilian-style skill

Filito scores Porto's 1987 winning goal against Bayern

and movement of their national team at Euro 96 can doubt the outstanding quality of the top Portuguese teams.

Foreign imports have always played an important role in Porto football. But that was entirely appropriate since, in the early 1930s, Porto had been pioneers in the international transfer market. They began by bringing in two Yugoslavs, and that ambition was reflected in Porto's initial championship successes in 1938 and 1939. Almost 40 years later, Porto beat Bayern in the Champions Cup Final with a Polish goalkeeper Mlynarczyk, Brazilians Celso and Juary and Algerian winger Rabah Madjer supporting Portugal's own wonderboy, Paulo Futre.

Originally, Porto's home was the old, rundown Campo da Constituciao. Now, as befits a club with European cup-winning pedigree, home is the impressive, 70,000-capacity Estadio das Antas.

PSV Eindhoven

Holland
Founded: *1913*
Stadium: *Philips (30,000)*
Colours: *Red and white stripes/white*
Honours: *European Champions Cup 1988; UEFA Cup 1978;*
League 14; Cup; 7

PSV have gained international kudos not merely as the sporting arm of the Philips electronics corporation but through their own achievements. They have won the Dutch championship 14 times – one more than Feyenoord though 12 fewer than Ajax – and the cup on seven occasions. On five occasions they were domestic cup runners-up while at international level they won the European Champions Cup in 1988 and the UEFA Cup in 1978.

Along the way, PSV have also benefited from the services of some of the most outstanding Dutch footballers of the modern era, including Ruud Gullit and Ronald Koeman.

In the 1960s Feyenoord took the international eye on behalf of Holland, an era which they climaxed by winning the Champions Cup and the World Club Cup in 1970. Then came Ajax Amsterdam's three-year domination of the Champions Cup, and PSV took their cue in style in 1978. They won the UEFA Cup that year with a team built around the intuitive attacking partnership of midfielder Willy Van der Kerkhof and his wing twin, Rene.

Both were regulars in the Dutch national squad at the 1974 and 1978 World Cups while combative defensive midfielders Jan Poortvliet and Ernie Brandts were also among Holland's World Cup stalwarts in Argentina.

It needed a 10-year gap and the development of a new generation of star players before PSV again made headlines in Europe. In 1987–88 they were virtually irresistible at club level. Hans Van Breukelen was an outstanding personality in goal, Ivan

Nielsen a Danish rock at the heart of defence, Jan Heintze a dangerous raiding left back and Soren Lerby – another Dane – a feisty, energetic midfield dynamo. Mix in the power-packed shooting of the young Ronald Koeman and the attacking talent of Wim Kieft and PSV presented a virtually unbeatable force.

It took a penalty shoot-out, however, for PSV to defeat the experienced old campaigners of Portugal's Benfica in the Champions Cup Final in Stuttgart. Weeks later, Van Breukelen, full back Berry Van Aerle, midfielder Gerald Vanenburg and Koeman completed an international double as members of the Dutch team which won the European Championship Final by 2–0 against the Soviet Union in Munich.

At one stage the Philips corporation allowed the sports club to exist almost as an autonomous entity. But as football grew ever more important as a promotional vehicle, so the company invested more money into both the impressive Philips stadium – with, naturally, its state-of-the-art floodlighting system – and the coaching and playing staff.

One of the club's major coups was to sign up Bobby Robson to take over immediately after he had led England to the semi-finals and fourth place in the 1990 World Cup. Robson stayed two years, winning the championship both times, before moving on to Portugal with Sporting of Lisbon.

His star player was the Brazilian striker Romario, whom PSV had picked up at a virtual bargain price after he starred at the 1988 Olympic Games football tournament in South Korea. Romario later transferred to Barcelona – the same path followed in due course by PSV's next highly-profitable Brazilian discovery, the dazzling Ronaldo.

Rangers

Glasgow, Scotland
Founded: *1873*
Stadium: *Ibrox (50,411)*
Colours: *Blue/white*
Honours: *European Cup-winners Cup 1972; League 47; Cup 27;*
League Cup 20

Rangers represent one half – and, in recent years, the more successful half – of the Old Firm. Their rivalry with Glasgow neighbours Celtic has dominated Scottish football for a century. Yet the 'Gers have never been able to extend their power into Europe. Their only prize from virtual non-stop international competition has been the 1972 Cup-Winners' Cup, which they won by defeating Moscow Dynamo in Barcelona.

Not that their history is short on proud moments. One particular era of legend was the 1920s when Rangers' heroes included the legendary "Wee Blue Devil" Alan Morton. His career overlapped with that of Bob McPhail, whose record of 233 goals in 354 league matches was only recently overtaken by

Rangers celebrate another Scottish championship victory - they managed nine in a row from 1989-1997

the flamboyant sharpshooter Ally McCoist.

After World War Two, Rangers' success was built on the so-called "Iron Curtain" defence starring George Young and Willie Woodburn, with the goals created by Willie Waddell for Willie Thornton. But in Europe in the 1960s Rangers were brought down to earth by heavy defeats at the hands of Eintracht Frankfurt, Tottenham and Real Madrid.

The start of the 1970s was a time of mixed emotions: 1971 saw the Ibrox Disaster, when 66 fans died in a stairway crush at the end of a game against Celtic. Less than 18 months later, there was European glory, but the Old Firm's grip was loosened by Aberdeen and Dundee United.

Rangers' upturn began in November, 1985, when Lawrence Marlboro, a Nevada-based businessman and grandson of a previous club chairman, bought control of the club. The following April came stage two, when he brought in Graeme Souness as player-manager. In 1988 steel magnate David Murray bought the club and Souness revolutionized Rangers' image and the transfer market by buying no fewer than 18 English players and smashing the club's traditional Protestant-only ethic with his £1.5million capture of striker Mo Johnston, a Roman Catholic.

Souness' successor, Walter Smith, brought in Denmark's Brian Laudrup and England's Paul Gascoigne to help lift Rangers towards a championship-winning decade. Intriguingly, it was only in the season which was known to be both players' last at Ibrox that Rangers lost their record-equalling nine-year grip on the championship. European success, despite all Rangers' pretensions to a place among the elite, remained as elusive as ever with a series of embarrassing flops in the competition.

Rapid Vienna

Austria
Founded: *1899*
Stadium: *Hanappi (19,600)*
Colours: *Green and white/green*
Honours: *League 30; Cup 14*

Rapid were founded as the 1st Arbeiter-Fussballklub (First Workers Football Club) but, on changing their name, also set about refining the "Vienna School" short-passing style to such great effect that they won the championship eight times between 1912 and 1923. The success story did not end there. In 1930 Rapid became the first Austrian club to win the Mitropa Cup, defeating powerful Sparta Prague 2-0, 2-3 in the Final. Several of Rapid's key players were members of the "Wunderteam", the national side who finished fourth 1934 World Cup under the captaincy of Rapid centre half Pepe Smistik. Four years later Austria was swallowed up into Greater Germany and the Austrian league was incorprated into the Greater German championship. To the mischievous delight of their fans, Rapid not only won the German Cup in 1938 (3- 2 against FSV Frankfurt) but also the German championship in 1941. On a day which has entered football legend Rapid hit back from 3-0 down to defeat an outstanding Schalke side 4-3 before a 90,000 crowd in the Olympic stadium in Berlin. Their hero was centre forward Franz 'Bimbo' Binder whose hat-trick was crowned by the winning goal when he hammered a free kick through the defensive wall. Binder ended a great career with 1,006 goals and later would become club coach. Many of Rapid's old heroes later returned as coaches, among them Karl Rappan (who developed the "Swiss Bolt" system), Edi Fruhwirth and Karl Decker. Great players in the post-war years included wing half Gerhard Hanappi - an architect by profession who laid out the designs for the club stadium - tough-tackling defender Ernst Happel and another prolific centre forward in Hans Krankl. He led Rapid's attack on their first appearance in a European final, the 2-1 defeat by Everton in the 1985 Cup-winners Cup decider in Rotterdam. Rapid were runners-up again, this time to Paris Saint Germain, in 1996.

Real Madrid

Spain
Founded: *1902*
Stadium: *Santiago Bernabeu (105,000)*
Colours: *All white*
Honours: *World Club Cup 1960; European Champions Cup 1956, 1957, 1958, 1959, 1960, 1966, 1998; UEFA Cup 1985, 1986; League 27; Cup 27*

Real Madrid have won it all: they are record seven-times champions of Europe and record 27-times champions of Spain. They also boast one World Club Cup, two UEFA Cups and 17 Spanish cups plus a host of other trophies and awards from around the world. All of which makes Madrid's trophy room one of the wonders of world football.

Madrid were founded by students in 1898 but did not become an official entity until 1902. Their first manager was an Englishman, Arthur Johnson, who was so fanatical about football that he even arranged his wedding for a morning so he could play football for Madrid FC – the Real title, meaning Royal, was later granted by special permission of King Alfonso XIII – in the afternoon.

Madrid were not only among the founders of cup and then league competition of Spain: it was also the Madrid president, Carlos Padros, who represented Spain at the inaugural meeting of FIFA in Paris in 1904. In the late 1920s Madrid launched a policy of buying big. They paid a then Spanish record fee of £2,000 for Ricardo Zamora, still revered as the greatest Spanish goalkeeper of all time.

The Spanish Civil War left Madrid's Chamartin stadium in ruins. The club had no money but boasted one of the greatest visionaries in European football history. He was Santiago Bernabeu, a lawyer who had been, by turn, player, team manager, secretary and now club president. Bernabeu found the funds to build both the great stadium which now bears his name and then a team worthy of it.

Bernabeu scoured Europe and South America for stars. The greatest of these was centre forward Alfredo Di Stefano from Argentina – for many experts the greatest footballer of all time.

He inspired Madrid to victory in the first five Champions Cup Finals and scored in them all. Most notable was the 7–3 demolition of Germany's Eintracht Frankfurt at Hampden Park, Glasgow, in 1960. Di Stefano scored three goals with Madrid's other four being snapped up by another legend of the game, Hungarian Ferenc Puskas.

Of course, the standards those players and that team set, could never be maintained. Outstanding players who have tried include Spanish superstars Pirri and Amancio in the 1960s, Germany's Gunter Netzer and Paul Breitner in the 1970s, Spain's Emilio Butragueno and Michel and Mexico's Hugo Sanchez in the 1980s and most recently Croatia's Davor Suker, Holland's Clarence Seedorf and Brazil's Roberto Carlos.

It is generally accepted that the legacy of the legends is an enormous one to bear. Thus, in 1996, Madrid president Lorenzo Sanz lured Milan coach Fabio Capello to bring some Italian know-how to the challenge of turning the European clock back. Capello returned to his beloved Milan after a year but successor Jupp Heynckes achieved the miracle of guiding Madrid to victory in the Champions League Cup they had not won for more than 30 years. A second-half goal from Yugoslav striker Predrag Mijatovic brought a 1–0 victory over Juventus in the 1998 Final in Amsterdam which restored Madrid to a position of pre-eminence they had not enjoyed since the great days of flying left winger Francisco Gento and co in the 1960s.

Real Zaragoza

Spain
Founded: *1932*
Stadium: *La Romareda (43,554)*
Colours: *Blue and white/blue*
Honours: *European Cup-winners Cup 1995; Fairs Cup 1964; Cup 4*

Zaragoza are proof that football in Spain is about much, much more than Real Madrid and Barcelona.

They have never won the Spanish league – second in 1975 remains their best finish. But they have landed the Spanish Cup on four occasions and twice conquered Europe. The first time was in the 1964 Fairs Cup with a superb forward line known as the Cincos Magnificos (Magnificent Five); the second time was in winning the Cup-winners Cup against Arsenal in Paris in 1995.

Zaragoza were founder members of the Spanish second division in 1928 and took their present full title after a merger with the Iberia Club de Futbol in 1932. They gained access to the top division in 1936 – the year the Civil War put an end to sporting matters for three years. Zaragoza were relegated two seasons after the restart and vacillated between the top divisions before establishing themselves at last after the 1956–57 promotion campaign.

In 1962 new president Waldo Marco shocked the fans by selling star Peruvian forward Juan Seminario to Italy's Fiorentina and midfielder or full back Julio Benitez to Barcelona. But the cash financed the finishing touches to the team of the Magnificent Five forward line: Brazilian right-wing pair Canario and Santos, centre forward Marcelino, Spanish inside left Juan Villa (a Real Madrid cast-off) and left winger Carlos Lapetra.

In 1962 left back Severino Reija became the first Zaragoza player ever capped by Spain. From 1963 to 1966, Zaragoza played in six finals all against native opposition in Spain, but twice in the Fairs Cup. In 1963 and 1965 Zaragoza were Spanish cup runners-up but in 1964 and 1966 its winners. Their first cup victory became a double when they also won the Fairs Cup, beating Valencia 2–1 in a single match final in Barcelona. Zaragoza were runners-up in 1966, losing by 1–0 and 2–4 to Barcelona.

In the middle of all that Marcelino and Lapetra were both members of the Spanish national team which won the 1964 European championship against the Soviet Union.

However defeat by Barcelona in the 1966 Fairs Cup Final sparked a long slide from glory which was not reversed for almost 30 years when Zaragoza achieved Cup-winners success against Arsenal. Midfielder Nayim – who had spent time in England playing for the Gunners' fiercest rivals Tottenham – lobbed an astonishing winning goal from out on the right touchline in the dying moments of extra-time.

Red Star Belgrade

Yugoslavia
Founded: *1945*
Stadium: *Red Star (Crvena Zvezda) (97,422)*
Colours: *Red and white stripes/red*
Honours: *World Club Cup 1991; European Champions Cup 1991; League 20; Cup 16*

The name Crvena Zvezda means next to nothing outside their own country. Instead it is as Red Star that Yugoslavia's greatest club are known in England; as Estrella Roja in Spain; as Stella Rossa in Italy; as Etoile Rouge in France; and as Roter Stern in Germany.

Their achievements really speak for themselves: a record 20 league championships, a record 16 national cups. And then, to top it all off, Red Star won the Champions Cup in 1991, just before the Balkans exploded in the sort of conflict Europe thought it had left behind in the 1940s.

Red Star were among the great clubs who created the glamour and fascination of the Champions Cup in the late 1950s. It was against Red Star that Manchester United played their last match before the Munich air disaster. United won – but not before players such as fierce-shooting Bora Kostic and artistic schemer Dragoslav Sekularac had stamped their seal of quality on the international game.

Red Star Belgrade

Dragan Dzajic was one of the world's greatest left wingers in the 1960s before exporting his talents to France then bringing his experience to bear back with Red Star as general manager.

Dzajic was a senior executive when Red Star achieved their greatest success. They had already reached one European final when they finished runners-up in the UEFA Cup in 1979. Two years later, under coach Ljubko Petrovic, Red Star swept through the Champions Cup with an even finer team. Players such as Vladimir Jugovic, Robert Prosinecki, Dejan Savicevic, Sinisa Mihajlovic and Darko Pancev went on to stardom elsewhere in Europe after defeating Marseille in an amazing Final in a dramatic penalty shoot-out.

The troubles in the Balkans in the 1990s saw Yugoslav clubs, Red Star included, being barred from Europe for four years. International sanctions also cost the club dear in other ways because much of the money Red Star had collected from selling their stars was then frozen in western European banks.

Roma

Italy
Founded: *1927*
Stadium: *Olimpico (82,922)*
Colours: *All burgundy*
Honours: *Fairs Cup 1961; League 2; Cup 7*

All the fuss afforded the clubs of Milan and Turin over the years has obscured the fact that Roma were one of the first two Italians clubs to win a European trophy. That was in 1961 when Roma beat Birmingham City over two legs to win the Fairs Cup; that same year Fiorentina defeated Rangers to land the Cup-winners Cup.

Roma's team included two highly popular Argentine forwards in Pedro Manfredonia and Antonio Valentin Angelillo and an Italian goalkeeper in Fabio Cudicini who later became the first player to collect a winner's medal in all three European club competitions.

Roma came closest to a European prize again in 1984. They were favourites to beat Liverpool in the Champions Cup Final since the venue was their own Stadio Olimpico. But the match ended 1–1 after extra time and Roma proved more nervy in the penalty shoot-out, which they lost 4–2. Brazilian midfielder Paulo Roberto Falcao, one of the outstanding personalities in Italian football in the 1980s, stayed aloof from the shoot-out and his relationship with Roma fans was never quite the same again.

Roma were founded from a merger of four city clubs – Alba, Fortitudo, Roman and Pro Patria. They were members of the inaugural first division in 1929–30, finishing sixth. Runners-up in 1931 and 1936 they rose to surprise championship winners in 1942 – inspired by the goals of Amadeo Amadei.

The club were nearly bankrupted by relegation in 1951 and then again a decade later after miscalculating the high cost of signing German striker Jürgen Schutz and the Italo-Brazilian centre-forward Angelo Benedetto Sormani for a then world record £250,000.

Sampdoria

Genoa, Italy
Founded: *1946*
Stadium: *Luigi Ferraris*
Colours: *Blue/white*
Honours: *Cup-winners Cup 1990; League 1; Cup 4*

Sampdoria have built a reputation, since the take-over by the oil-rich Mantovani family in the early 1980s, as one of Italy's most attractive teams. That has not been reflected in as much success as perhaps they deserved despite having won the Cup-winners Cup once and finished runners-up once in the Champions Cup.

Sampdoria had been founded only in 1946 from the merger of two unsuccessful local clubs, Sampierdaranese and Andrea Doria. Hence the club title, Sampdoria. Where neighbours Genoa were the "establishment" club, Sampdoria resorted to the cheque book as a short cut to success and popularity. One of the biggest early signings was Eddie Firmani, from Charlton Athletic. In 1958 Firmani was second in the Italian scoring charts, behind only John Charles of Juventus.

A string of famous coaches failed to prevent Sampdoria's gradual slide towards relegation in 1966. They bounced straight up at first attempt, but went back down in 1975. Tycoon Paolo Mantovani was then a director, and on becoming president in 1979, he launched a one-man revolution.

His drive steered Sampdoria back to Serie A in 1982. Mantovani also provided the finance to purchase English league stars Liam Brady, Trevor Francis and Graeme Souness as well as Roberto Mancini from Bologna. The first tangible sign of success was a cup victory in 1985, which Samp repeated in 1988

Graeme Souness celebrates scoring for Sampdoria

and 1989. In due course, England's David Platt and Dutch veteran Ruud Gullit, from Milan, would follow an increasingly well-worn path.

The peak of the Mantovani years was Sampdoria's appearance in the Champions Cup Final in 1992. But an extra-time thunderbolt from Barcelona's Ronald Koeman was the only goal of the game. Sampdoria had finished out of the UEFA Cup frame in the Italian league and thus dropped out of the European mainstream.

Slovan Bratislava

Slovakia
Founded: *1919*
Stadium: *Tehelne Pole (32,000)*
Colours: *All blue*
Honours: *European Cup-winners Cup 1969; League 11 (Slovakia 3; Czechoslovakia 8); Cup 7 (Slovakia 2, Czechoslovakia 5)*

Slovan Bratislava are the one major Slovak club from the former Czechoslovakia. Founded in 1919 as S K Bratislava, the club first made an impact after becoming N K Bratislava in the late 1940s. They won the Czechoslovakian championship three years in succession before changing their name yet again to the present form, Slovan.

Financial and logistical support from the town's major chemical works helped Slovan to maintain a high-profile presence in the Czech championship. In 1969, they became the only club from Czechoslovakia (Czech Republic or Slovakia, for that matter) to win a modern European club prize. Sparta and Slavia of Prague had been prime forces in the Mitropa Cup in pre-World War Two days, but that was the end of Czech/Slovak club power in Europe – until 1968–69 when Slovan won the Cup-winners Cup.

Their success was hugely ironic since almost every other Eastern Bloc club had – under Soviet orders – withdrawn from the three European club cups that season. The reason was to protest at the re-drawing of the opening rounds to keep eastern and western European clubs apart for a political cooling-off period following the Warsaw Pact invasion of Czechoslovakia.

Somehow Slovan slipped through the net of anger, defeated Bor (Yugoslavia), Porto, Torino and Dunfermline before defeating odds-on favourites Barcelona 3–2 in the final in Basle.

Sparta Prague

Czech Republic
Founded: *1893*
Stadium: *Letna (36,000)*
Colours: *All red*
Honours: *League 23; Cup 9*

Sparta are the most popular club in what is now the Czech Republic and one of the oldest – founded as King's Vineyard in 1893 and taking the name of Sparta, from one of the Greek heroes of mythology, a year later. They remain one of the game's pre-second world war greats, winning the Mitropa Cup in the inaugural final in 1927 against Rapid Vienna. Victory over Ferencvaros of Hungary followed in 1935 and they were runners-up in 1936. Sparta's team then included the great inside left, Oldrich Nejedly. He was a star in the 1934 World Ciup when Czechoslovakia finished runners-up. Again in 1962, when the Czechs next reached the World Cup Final, there were key places in the team for Sparta men such as right winger Tomas Pospichal and schemer Andrzej Kvasnak. Sparta suffered after the last war, being forced to alter their name to Sparta Bratrstvi and then Spartak Sokolovo. But their loyal fans never called them anything but Sparta and reality was recognised when the present club title was adopted in 1965. That same year they celebrated their first league title in more than a decade. Memories of the glory days of the Mitropa Cup were revived by the club's run to the Cup-winners Cup semi-finals in 1973 and the impressive 1983-84 UEFA Cup campaign during which they scored notable victories over Real Madrid and Widzew Lodz. Sparta's continuing domination of the domestic game in the early 1990s was remarkable because, immediately after the World Cup finals, they lost a string of senior internationals such as goalkeeper Jan Stejskal, defenders Julius Bielik and Michal Bilek, midfield general Ivan Hasek and striker Tomas Skuhravy, second-top scorer at Italia 90 with five goals.

Sporting Clube

Lisbon, Portugal
Founded: *1906*
Stadium: *Jose Alvalade (52,411)*
Colours: *Green and white hoops/green*
Honours: *European Cup-winners Cup 1964; League 16; Cup 16*

Sporting Clube make up, with neighbours Benfica and FC Porto, Portuguese football's "Big Three." Yet remarkably, for all their power and fame and perpetual presence in European competitions, fans have to look back to 1964 for the last time they triumphed in an international final. That was when they won the Cup-winners Cup in a replay against MTK Budapest.

Despite raising their fans hopes time and again, Sporting have never quite managed to regain the pre-eminence at home and abroad of those years. Indeed, their 2–0 victory over Maritimo in the 1995 Portuguese Cup Final was the first trophy they had secured since winning the league and cup Double 13 years earlier under English coach Malcolm Allison.

Back in the 1950s, Sporting rivalled Benfica as the country's top club and took the championship seven times in eight years. The tables were turned for most of the 1960s, with Benfica dominating at home and reaching the Champions Cup Final five times, winning two, losing three. The pressure to match this success drew Sporting into a Barcelona/Manchester United-like syndrome (competing against more successful compatriots Real Madrid and Liverpool respectively) and they spent a great deal of money for comparatively minimal return.

Signs of progress emerged in the early 1990s, however, when Sporting reached the semi-final of the UEFA Cup before losing 0–0, 0–2 to eventual winners Internazionale of Milan.

Top coaches such as ex-England boss Bobby Robson and then Portugal's World Youth Cup-winning manager Carlos Queiros were hired and fired at high speed – their attempts to rebuild a successful team undermined by ongoing financial problems which demanded the regular sale of Sporting's best players.

Steaua

Bucharest, Romania
Founded: *1947*
Stadium: *Steaua (30,000)*
Colours: *Red/blue*
Honours: *European Champions Cup 1986; Supercup 1986; League 20; Cup 20*

Steaua of Bucharest were typical of an entire generation of clubs created or converted in eastern Europe after World War Two. Each country within the Eastern Bloc organized its sports clubs along similar subsidized, "state amateur" lines. The different state sectors had their own teams with the army club being traditionally the strongest.

That meant CSKA Moscow in the Soviet Union itself; CSKW Legia in Poland; CDNA (later CSKA) Sofia in Bulgaria; Dukla in Czechoslovakia; Vorwärts in East Germany; and AS Armata, later CSCA then CCA then, from 1961, Steaua (or Star) in Romania. The club was an umbrella sports body comprising facilities for football, volleyball, rugby, target shooting, athletics, tennis – Ilie Nastase was discovered playing football! – and basketball.

Up until the revolution of Christmas 1989, the balance of power in Romanian football was held between Steaua and Dinamo, the team of the secret police. As time went on, so Steaua got the upper hand thanks largely to the influential support of Valentin Ceaucescu, son of the dictator Nicolae Ceaucescu, who ordered the transfers of the country's best players to the army sports complex to the west of Bucharest.

Coached by Emerich Jenei, Steaua became the first eastern Europe team to win the Champions Cup when, in 1986, they defeated Terry Venables' Barcelona in Seville. A goal-less draw after extra-time was followed by a penalty shoot-out in which Steaua goalkeeper Helmut Ducadam proved unbeatable and the Romanians won 2–0.

Sweeper Miodrag Belodedici and striker Marius Lacatus were among Romania's finest players and Steaua had added midfielder Gheorghe Hagi – the country's greatest player – to their squad by the time they returned to the Champions Cup Final in 1989. Not that his presence did them a lot of good in Barcelona as an out-of-sorts Steaua crashed 4–0 to Milan.

They maintained their domestic domination after the 1989 revolution but lacked the power to hold on to their star players. By the late 1990s officials were seriously considering severing all links with the army and "privatizing" the club.

Tottenham Hotspur

London, England
Founded: *1882*
Stadium: *White Hart Lane (33,083)*
Colours: *White/blue*
Honours: *European Cup-winners Cup 1963; UEFA Cup: 1972, 1984; League 2; Cup 8; League Cup 2*

Since 1984 Tottenham Hotspur have not appeared in a European final, yet it says everything about the enduring romance of European football that Spurs' adventures between 1961 and 1963 should still retain a magical aura.

Danny Blanchflower was Spurs' captain leader from right half; he had guided the team to the first English league and cup Double of the century. A team boasting Scotland left half Dave Mackay, will o'the wisp inside right John White and – later – deadly goalscorer Jimmy Greaves expected the onward march to continue untroubled through Europe.

But, in the first round of the 1961–62 Champions Cup, Spurs nearly came unstuck in Poland. Gornik Zabrze led them 4–0 before goals from Cliff Jones and Terry Dyson hauled Spurs back from the brink. At White Hart Lane it was a different story. Spurs hit eight goals with three coming from Jones.

Feyenoord were beaten 3–1, 1–1 in the second round and Dukla Prague 0–1, 4–1 in the quarter-finals. The away leg in Prague saw Spurs bolster their defence by including defensive wing half Tony Marchi instead of a forward. Manager Bill Nicholson used similar cautious tactics in the first leg of the semi-final away to holders Benfica but could not avert a 3–1 defeat. Spurs won the blood-and-thunder return only 2–1 and narrowly went out.

It actually proved to have been good practice for the following season's Cup-winners Cup campaign, which ended in a triumphant 5–1 victory over Atletico Madrid in Rotterdam. Spurs thus became the first British team to win a European trophy.

Nine years later, at the expense of fellow English club Wolves, they became the first holders of the newly-presented UEFA Cup. They were runners-up to old foes Feyenoord in 1974, but regained the UEFA Cup, after a penalty shoot-out victory over holders Anderlecht in 1984.

Along the way Tottenham electrified English football with an innovative transfer policy which included signing Argentine World Cup-winners Osvaldo Ardiles and Ricardo Villa in the summer of 1978. They both proved tremendous successes with Villa scoring the memorable winning goal in the 1981 FA Cup Final and Ardilles coming back to manage the club in the early 1990s. Domestic favourites such as Glenn Hoddle, Chris Waddle, Paul Gascoigne and Gary Lineker kept the fans' attention, with the winning of the 1991 FA Cup continuing the club's extraordinary tradition of winning the competition when the year ends in a '1' – 1901, 1921, 1961, 1981 and 1991. A series of bitter boardroom skirmishes featuring the likes of Irving Scholar, Terry Venables and computer millionaire Alan Sugar also made sure Tottenham Hotspur was neverfar from the headlines.

It was Sugar who masterminded the signing in 1994 of German striker Jürgen Klinsmann. He made an enormous impact on the English game in just one season, returning in 1998 to help the club escape the humiliation of relegation to the first division, but Tottenham – for all their occasional successes in the FA Cup which they had first won in unique fashion as a non-league team in 1901 – remained as far away as ever from regaining the championship for the first time since the halcyon days of Blanchflower, White and Mackay. A

Tbilisi Dinamo

Georgia
Founded: *1925*
Stadium: *Boris Paichadze (75,000)*
Colours: *All blue*
Honours: *European Cup-winners Cup 1981; League 10 (Georgia 8 USSR 2); Cup 7 (Georgia 6, USSR 2)*

The political fragmentation of the Soviet Union in the early 1990s was felt in many ways other than socio-economic– particularly in eastern European football. One was financial, with the ending of government subsidies; another was qualitative. The rigid police states had been able to prevent players from transferring abroad. Without that protection, many clubs lost significant ground compared to their western European rivals.

Georgia had early warning of these developments, having seceded within the Soviet political and administrative structure two years before the ultimate collapse.

Tbilisi's Dinamo club were both favourites and victims of the systems. In the 1950s and 1960s they travelled abroad frequently to earn hard currency through international friendly matches. Later they formalized that success by winning the European Cup-winners Cup courtesy of a 2–1 victory over East Germany's Carl Zeiss Jena in Dusseldorf.

Players such as centre back Alexander Chivadze, midfielders David Kipiani and Vitali Daraselia and forward Ramaz Shengelia ranked among the finest in their positions in Europe. But Tbilisi could not build on their Dusseldorf foundations. Kipiani suffered a serious leg fracture in a friendly against Real Madrid then Daraselia was killed in a car crash.

Valencia

Spain
Founded: *1919*
Stadium: *Luis Casanova (49,291)*
Colours: *all white*
Honours: *European Cup-winners Cup 1980: Fairs Cup 1962, 1963; Supercup 1980; League 4; Cup 5*

Valencia, in the early 1960s, underlined Spain's status as the top European nation at club level at least. Real Madrid had won the European Champions Cup five times; Barcelona had won the Fairs Cup twice and Valencia stepped straight into their footsteps by reaching the Fairs Cup Final themselves in three consecutive years, 1962–64.

Valencia defeated Barcelona and Dinamo Zagreb respectively in the first two. The 1962 victory over Barcelona was an explosive occasion, Valencia winning the first leg 6–2, with a hat-trick from Spanish international Vicente Guillot, then drawing 1–1 in the Catalan capital. A year later Valencia won both legs against Zagreb – 2–1 away and 2–0 at home. But it was not to be third time lucky for them, losing in the 1964 Final to compatriots Zaragoza.

At domestic level, Valencia gave their fans little to celebrate. They won the league for the fourth time in 1971, then the cup for a fifth time in 1979. A year later Valencia regained European allure by winning the Cup-winners Cup. The final against Arsenal in the Heysel stadium was a disappointment. Even Argentina's 1978 World Cup hero, Mario Kempes, was unable to engineer a breakthrough, but at least Valencia had the consolation of winning on penalties.

In the late 1990s Valencia sought in vain to regain their earlier pre-eminence with the appointment of Italian Claudio Ranieri as coach and the high-cost purchase of superstars such as Brazil's Romario and Argentina's Ariel Ortega.

Werder Bremen

Germany
Founded: *1899*
Stadium: *Weserstadion (29,850)*
Colours: *White/green*
Honours: *European Cup-winners Cup 1992; League 3; Cup 3*

Werder Bremen are one of the least fashionable clubs in

Valencia's Mario Kempes: the 1980 Cup-winners Cup Final

Germany. However, over the years, they have been one of the most consistent.Not for Bremen the big splash in the transfer market or the constant changing of coaches. Otto Rehhagel was boss for a decade before being lured away to Bayern Munich in 1995 and his wife was almost as well-known a figure around the Weserstadion.

Bremen won the cup for the first time in 1961, and then again in 1991 and 1994. As for the league championship, that was taken home to North Germany in 1965, 1988 and 1993.

The 1965 team's strength lay in defence where full backs Horst-Dieter Hottges and Sepp Piontek were members of the West German squad who finished runners-up at the 1966 World Cup. Piontek went on to greater fame as the manager who turned

Denmark's national team, in the 1980s, from an acorn into an oak – reaching the semi-finals of the 1984 European Championship and the second round of the 1986 World Cup finals.

In 1992 Bremen won their first European trophy when they defeated Monaco of France in the Cup-winners Cup Final in the Benfica stadium in Lisbon.

West Ham United

London, England
Founded: *1895*
Stadium: *Upton Park*
Colours: *Claret/blue*
Honours: *European Cup-Winners Cup 1965; FA Cup 3*

West Ham have long been known as the "Football Academy", not only for the class of footballer they turn out but also for the class of football they play. Never was that image better illustrated than on the day they won the Cup-winners Cup at Wembley in 1965. To do it they defeated Munich 1860 by 2–0, both goals arriving from Tony Sealey on a night which was a credit to English football.

Many of West Ham's heroes that night went onto greater things. Manager Ron Greenwood would take up the same post with England and lead them to the finals of both the 1980 European Championship and the 1982 World Cup. Left half Bobby Moore is probably the most famous English footballer the country has ever produced - epitomizing the English sense of 'fair play' so recognized throughout the world. He captained England to victory in the 1966 World Cup Final, supported by Hammers' Martin Peters and Geoff Hurst who, of course, made history as the only man to score a hat-trick in a World Cup Final when he put three past West Germany's Hans Tilkowski.

It is an odd feature of West Ham's career in Europe that they have competed only in the Cup-winners Cup. In 1964–65 they took part as FA Cup holders and the following season as defending champions. However, defeat both home and away at the hands of eventual winners Borussia Dortmund ended their European commitment for nearly a decade.

After winning the FA Cup against Fulham in 1975 – this time with Moore on the losing side – West Ham returned to Europe. They beat Lahden Reipas, Ararat Erevan, Den Haag and Eintracht Frankfurt on their way to the Final against Anderlecht in their home city of Brussels. In the Heysel Stadium, goals by Pat Holland and Keith Robson were not enough. Frank Lampard made a crucial mistake and two goals each from Rob Rensenbrink and François Van der Elst meant the Hammers lost 4–2. Van der Elst later spent two seasons at Upton Park.

Since they won the FA Cup for the third time in 1980, the Hammers have remained trophy-less, but never dull.

SOUTH AMERICA

Atletico Nacional

Colombia
Founded: *1938*
Stadium: *Atanasio Giradot (35,000)*
Colours: *Green and white stripes/white*
Honours: *South American Libertadores Cup 1989; Inter-american Cup 1989; League 4*

Atletico Nacional of Medellin are not the most famous club to come out of Colombia. That honour will always belong to Millonarios, who led the professional, pirate revolution in the early 1950s. But Nacional earned a place in history by becoming the first club to take the Copa Libertadores (the South American Club Cup), across the Andes to the western side of the continent. Nacional, who provided the base of the Colombian World Cup team in 1990, were in 1954 the first champions of Colombia after the rapprochement with FIFA. Yet it was not until 1971 that they first made their debut in the South American Club Cup under Argentine coach Osvaldo Zubeldia. He had earned a fearsome reputation as boss of the rugged Estudiantes de La Plata team which had dominated Argentine and South American club football in the late 1960s. However Zubeldia, without resorting to the cynicism which made Estudiantes hated, turned Nacional into Colombian champions three times in the mid-1970s and early 1980s. He was followed by Luis Cubilla and then, in 1986, at Cubilla's suggestion, Nacionl appointed a former stalwart central defender, Francisco Maturana, as boss. In 1987 and 1988 they finished championship runners-up and then, in 1989, seized the South American club crown.

Unfortunately, their preparations for the world club showdown with Milan the same year were wrecked when the government halted the league season because of incresing violence engendered on the fringes of the game by the drug and betting cartels. Nacional did not emerge with their reputation unscathed. It did not go unnoticed that Medellin was the centre of the drugs trade and that several players were friends of the notorious drugs baron Pablo Escobar. Indeed, when Escobar was eventually killed by security forces, the coffin at his funeral was draped in a Nacional flag.

Maradona in action for Boca Juniors in 1981

Boca Juniors Buenos Aires

Argentina
Founded: *1905*
Stadium: *Bombonera (58,740)*
Colours: *Blue with yellow hoop/blue*
Honours: *World Club Cup 1977; South American Libertadores Club Cup: 1977, 1978; South American Supercup 1989; Inter-american Cup: 1989; League 19*

Boca are the "other" great club in the Argentine capital of Buenos Aires along with old rivals River Plate. They were founded by an Irishman named Patrick MacCarthy and a group of newly-arrived Italian immigrants. They joined the league in 1913 and were immediately caught up in a domestic football "war" which saw two championships being organised for most of the 1920s and early 1930s. Boca bestrode the two eras. They won the last Argentine amateur championship in 1930 and the first unified professional one the following year. Two more titles followed in the next four years thanks to some fine players, including the great Brazilian defender, Domingos da Guia. In the 1940s and 1950s Boca slipped into River Plate's shadow, re-emerging in 1963 when a team fired by the goals of Jose Sanfilippo reached the Final of the South American Club Cup. Winning the title, however, would have to wait until the late 1970s. Then they reached the Final three years in a row – beating Brazil's Cruzeiro in 1977 and Deportivo Cali of Colombia in 1978 before losing to Olimpia of Paraguay in 1979. Boca's rugged style, under Juan Carlos Lorenzo, proved controversial. Not one Boca player figured in the squad with which Cesar Menotti's Argentina won the 1978 World Cup. But Boca had already secured their own world crown, beating West Germany's Borussia Mönchengladbach in the World Club Cup in 1977. Boca rebuilt their team around Diego Maradona in 1981 but wasted the £3million record fee they received from Barcelona for him a year later and plunged into a decade of financial uncertainty.

Colo Colo Santiago

Chile
Founded: *1925*
Stadium: *Colo Colo (50,000)*
Colours: *White/black*
League: *18*
Honours: *South American Libertadores Club Cup 1991; South American Recopa 1991; League 20*

Colo Colo, Chilean nickname for a wildcat, were founded by five angry members of the old Magallanes FC. Even though Chilean football is generally held to lag far behind that of traditional giants Brazil, Argentina and Uruguay, Colo Colo's reputation through the continent is enormous. The club's vision has always stretched before the Andes. Such a tradition was laid down by David Orellano. He was a founder member of Colo Colo and one of the five Magallanes rebels who disagreed over the choice of a new club captain. The choice of the five fell upon Orellano and, within two years of Colo Colo's foundation, they had sent a team off to tour Spain and Portugal. In 1933 Colo Colo were among the founders of a professional league; in 1941 they set another pioneering trend by introducing a foreign coach in the Hungarian, Ferenc Platko; and in 1948 they organised a South American club tournament which can now be seen as a forerunner of the Copa Libertadores, the official South American Club Cup launched in 1960. Record league winners in Chile and the transfer pinnacle for most domestic players, Colo Colo's greatest achievement was in winning the 1991 South American Club Cup. They had been runners-up after a play-off against Independiente of Argentina in 1973. This time they scored a decisive victory over former champions Olimpia of Paraguay. Colo Colo forced a 0–0 draw in Asuncion then won 3–0 back in Santiago.

Flamengo Rio de Janeiro

Brazil
Founded: *1895 as sailing club; 1911 as football club*
Stadium: *Gavea (20,000) and Maracana (130,000)*
Colours: *Black and red hoops/white*
Honours: *World Club Cup 1981; South American Libertadores Club Cup 1981; Rio State League 24; Brazil Championship (including Torneo Rio-Sao Paulo) 5*

Flamengo are the most popular club in Brazil, having been organised by dissident members of the Fluminense club but under the umbrella of the Flamengo sailing club – which now boasts more than 70,000 members. They first competed in the Rio League in 1912, winning the title two years later. In 1915 they regained the crown without having lost a game. A string of great names have graced the red-and-black hoops over the years, among them defenders Domingos Da Guia and the legendary centre-forward Leonidas da Silva. Known as "The Black Diamond", he played for Flamengo from 1936 to 1942, inspiring two state championship triumphs and earning a worldwide reputation through his brilliance in the 1938 World Cup finals in France. Flamengo ran up a Rio State hat-trick in the mid-1950s with their team nicknamed "The Steamroller" but did not reach a pinnacle of success until 1981. Now, riding high on the goals of a new hero in Zico – the so-called "White Pele" – they won both the South American and World Club Cups. The South American Cup campaign was one of the most hostile in memory. Flamengo won a first-round play-off against Atletico Mineiro after their Brazilian opponents had five players sent off, provoking referee Jose Roberto Wright to abandon the game. In the Final, Flamengo beat Cobreloa of Chile in a play-off in Montevideo which saw the expulsion of five players. Fears about the outcome of Flamengo's world showdown against Liverpool proved unfounded. Zico was in a class of his own. Liverpool could not touch him as he created all of Flamengo's goals in a 3–0 win. The players dedicated their success to the memory of Claudio Coutinho, their former coach who had died in a skin-diving accident.

Fluminense Rio de Janeiro

Brazil
Founded: *1902*
Stadium: *Laranjeira (20,000) and Maracana (130,000)*
Colours: *Red, green and white stripes/white*
Honours: *Rio State League 27; Brazil Championship (incl Torneo Rio-Sao Paulo) 4*

Fluminense have yet to win an international trophy but that doesn't affect their status as one of South America's great clubs. "Flu" were founded in 1902 by an Englishman named Arthur Cox. Many of their first players were British residents. The club's wealth and upper-class clientele resulted in the nickname "Po de Arroz" ('Face Powder" after the fashion of the time at the turn of the century). Today the club's fans wear white powder on the faces as a sign of loyalty. In 1905 Flu were founder members of the Rio de Janeiro League and of the Brazilian Confederation; they won the first four Rio (Carioca) championships in 1906–1909; and, in 1932, Flu became the first Brazilian club to go professional. In all this time the Flu-Fla derby (against Flamengo) flourished.

The first clash of the clubs was in 1912. In 1963 their clash drew an official crowd of 177,656 to the Maracana stadium in Rio. This remains a world record for a club game. By 1930 Flu's stadium was the home of the national team and the club had launched a weekly newspaper as well as other schemes. A few years later and Flu were running the game with five Rio titles in a row between 1936 to 1941. Star players were forwards Romeu, Carreiro and Tim – who coached Peru at the 1978 World Cup finals. In the early 1950s Fluminense's star was the World Cup-winning midfield general Didi. In the late 1960s and early 1970s the key player was another World Cup-winner, Brazil's 1970 captain and right back, Carlos Alberto Torres.

In the 1980s the mantle of inspiration-in-chief passed to the Paraguayan Romerito (Julio Cesar Romero). Fluminense won a hat-trick of Rio titles in 1983, 1984 and 1985 with Romero their guiding light. He was rewarded with the award as South American Footballer of the Year in 1985 and later starred at the 1986 World Cup finals.

Independiente Avellaneda

Argentina
Founded: *1904*
Stadium: *Cordero (55,000)*
Colours: *Red/blue*
Honours: *World Club Cup 1973, 1984; South American Libertadores Club Cup 1964, 1965, 1972, 1973, 1974, 1975, 1984; Inter-american cup: 1973, 1974, 1976; League 11*

Independiente are perhaps the most shadowy of club world's great achievers, outside Argentina at least. This is because, despite two lengthy periods of dominance in South American club football, they won the world title only once in five attempts and that at a time when the competition's image was tarnished. Also, Independiente have always relied on team football rather than superstar inspiration. One outstanding player who made his name with the club, however, was Raimundo Orsi. He was the left winger who played for Argentina in the 1930 World Cup Final defeat by Uruguay and then scored Italy's vital equaliser

on their way to victory over Czechoslovakia in the 1934 Final in Rome. Later, the Independiente fans had the great Paraguayan centre forward, Arsenio Erico, to idolise. He was the boyhood hero of Alfredo Di Stefano and, in 1937, set an Argentine first division record of 37 goals in a season. Independiente did not recover their pride until the early 1960s when coach Manuel Giudice imported an Italian-style catenaccio defence which secured the South American Club Cup in both 1964 and 1965. Independiente were the first Argentine team to win the continent's top club prize, but in the World Club Cup final they fell twice to the high priests of catenaccio, Internazionale of Italy.

In the 1970s Independiente's "Red Devils" won the South American Club Cup four times in a row and collected the World Club Cup. It was an odd victory: European champions Hamburg declined to compete so runners-up Juventus took their place on condition that the Final was a one-off match in Italy. Independiente not only agreed, they won it with a single goal from midfield general Ricardo Bochini.

Millonarios Bogota

Colombia
Founded: *1938*
Stadium: *El Campin – Estadio Distrital Nemesio Camacho (57,000)*
Colours: *Blue/white*
Honour: *League 13*

Millonarios remain a legendary name because of the manner in which they led Colombia's fledgling professional clubs into the "El Dorado" rebellion which lured star players from all over the world at the end of the 1940s and in the early 1950s. Many famous names in the game made their reputations there. The then club president, Alfonso Senior, later became president of the Colombian Federation and a highly-respected FIFA delegate. Star player Alfredo Di Stefano used Millonarios as a springboard to greatness with Real Madrid.

Taking massive advantage of an Argentine players' strike, Millonarios led the flight from FIFA and the chase for great players – not only Di Stefano but the acrobatic goalkeeper Julio Cozzi, attacking centre half Nestor Rossi and general Adolfo Pedernera. Nicknamed "The Blue Ballet", they dominated the pirate league and, when an amnesty was negotiated with FIFA, made lucrative "farewell" tours in Europe. Credit for the club's name goes to a journalist, Camacho Montayo.

The club had been founded as an amateur side, Deportivo Municipal, in 1938. But as they pushed for a professional league, so Montayo wrote: "The Municipalistas have become the Millonarios." The name stuck. Millonarios remain a leading club but, despite appearing frequently in the South American Club Cup, the glory days have never been repeated.

Nacional Montevideo

Uruguay
Founded: *1899*
Stadium: *Parque Central (20,000) and Centenario (73,609)*
Colours: *White/blue*
Honours: *World Club Cup 1971, 1980, 1988; South American Libertadores Club Cup 1971, 1980, 1988; South American Recopa 1988; Inter-american Cup 1971; League 35*

Penarol Montevideo

Uruguay
Founded: *1891*
Stadium: *Las Acacias (15,000) and Centenario (73,609)*
Colours: *Black and yellow stripes/black*
Honours: *World Club Cup 1961, 1966, 1982; South American Libertadores Club Cup 1960, 1961, 1966, 1982, 1987; Inter-american Cup 1969; League 44*

Nacional and Penarol are the two great clubs of Uruguay and bitter rivals on both domestic and international stages. Nacional were founded from a merger of the Montevideo Football Club and the Uruguay Athletic Club and were chosen, in 1903, to line up as Uruguay's national team against Argentina in Buenos Aires. Nacional won 3–2 and have enjoyed the international limelight ever since.

Penarol won the first South American Club Cup in 1960 but Nacional soon set about catching up: runners-up three times in the 1960s, they first won the cup by defeating Estudiantes de La Plata in 1981. That led Nacional on to the World Club Cup where they beat Panathinaikos of Greece (European title-holders Ajax having refused to compete). The two decisive goals in Montevideo were scored by Nacional's former Argentine World Cup spearhead, Luis Artime.

It was nine years before Nacional regained their crown. This time they had a new centre forward in Waldemar Victorino who scored the only goal in the South American Cup triumph over Internacional of Brazil then the lone strike which decided the world final against Nottingham Forest in Tokyo.

Victorino later left for Italy just as so many Uruguayan stars had been sold to Europe before and since. Back in the 1930s Nacional sold centre half Michele Andreolo to Italy with whom he won the 1938 World Cup. But Nacional quickly replaced him and, from 1939 to 1943, achieved what is nostalgically described as their "Quinquenio de Oro": their golden five years.

Nacional won the league in each of those seasons with a legendary forward line built around the prolific Argentine marksman Atilio Garcia. He was Uruguay's top scorer eight times and ended his career with a record of 464 goals in 435 games. Under Scottish manager William Reasdale, Nacional also celebrated an 8–0 thrashing of the old enemy from Penarol.

Penarol were the first club to win the World Club Cup three times, but their success is no modern phenomenon. They have been the pre-eminent power in Uruguayan football since its earliest days, providing a host of outstanding players for Uruguay's 1930 and 1950 World Cup-winning teams. Their own international awakening came in 1960 when Penarol won the inaugural South American Club Cup (the Copa Libertadores). They were thrashed by Real Madrid in the World Club Cup but made amends the next year with victory over Benfica. It was no less than the talents of players such as William Martinez, centre half Nestor Goncalves and striker Alberto Spencer deserved. Penarol regained the world club crown in 1966, at the expense of Real Madrid, and then again in 1982 when they beat Aston Villa in Tokyo. By now Penarol had unearthed another superstar in centre forward Fernando Morena. He was the latest in a long line which included the nucleus of the Uruguayan national team which shocked Brazil by winning the 1950 World Cup. Goalkeeper Roque Maspoli – later World Club Cup-winning coach in 1966 – captain and centre half Obdulio Varela, right winger Alcides Ghiggia, centre forward Oscar Miguez, right half Rodriguez Andrade and inside right Juan Schiaffino all came from Penarol. Schiaffino was the greatest of all. Penarol had been founded as the Central Uruguayan Railway Cricket Club in 1891 and changed their name in 1913 as the British influence waned. The railways sidings and offices were near the Italian Pignarolo district – after the landowner Pedro Pignarolo – and so the Spanish style of the name was adopted for the club.

River Plate Buenos Aires

Argentina
Founded: *1901*
Stadium: *Antonio Liberti/Monumental (76,000)*
Colours: *White with red sash/black*
Honours: *World Club Cup 1986; South American Libertadores Club Cup 1986, 1996; Inter-american Cup 1986; League 28*

Ruver Plate are one of the two giants of Argentine football, Boca Juniors being the other. Traditionally the club from the rich side of Buenos Aires, River were founder members of the first

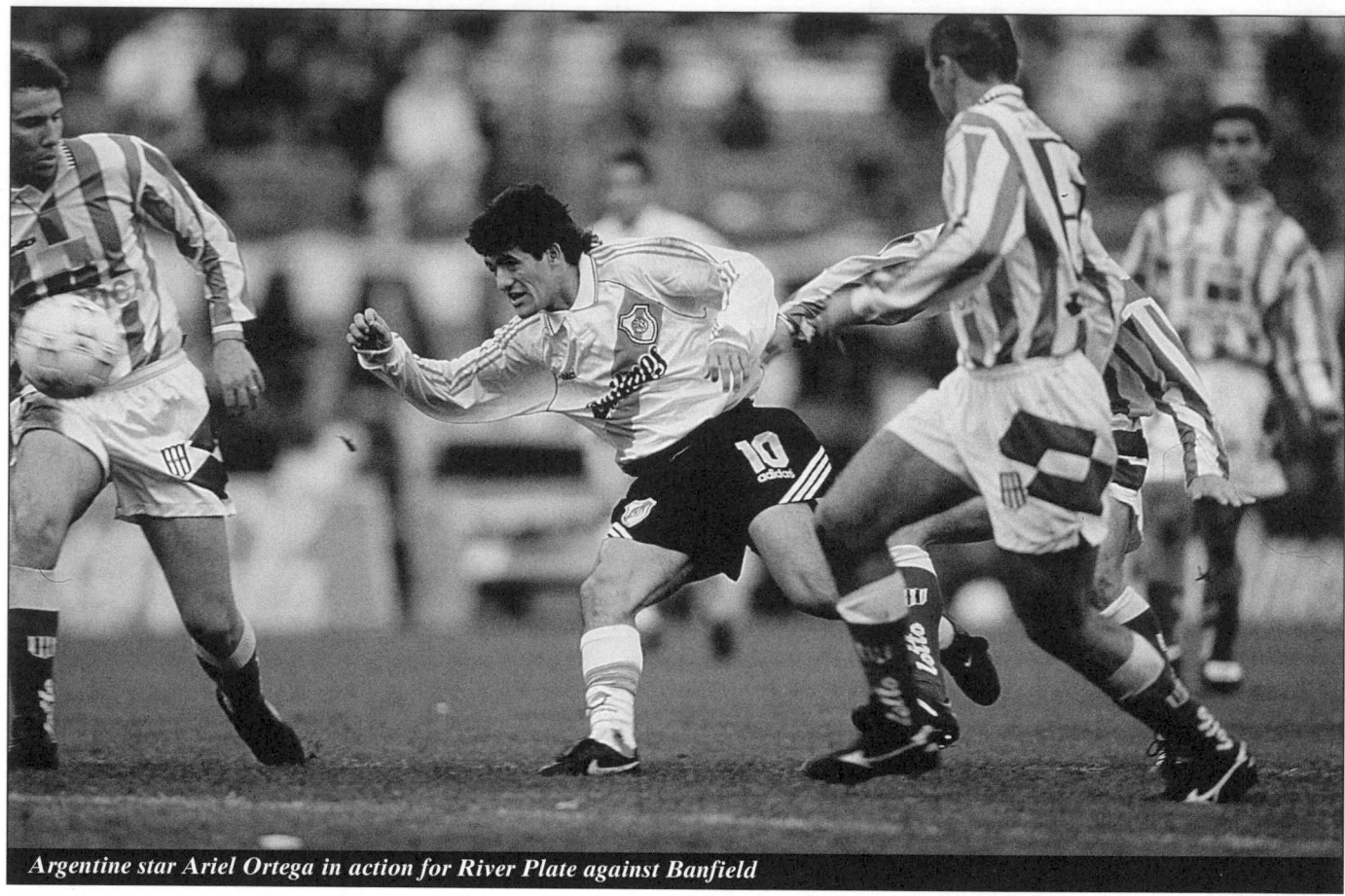

Argentine star Ariel Ortega in action for River Plate against Banfield

division in 1908 then took a leading role in the "war" which accompanied the introduction of professional football in the 1920s. Over the years River have put together some wonderful teams. In the 1930s they boasted Bernabe Ferreyra, a legendary figure in Argentine football; in the late 1940s their high-scoring forward line was so feared and admired they were nicknamed "La Maquina" ("The Machine"). The names of Munoz, Moreno, Pedernera, Labruna and Loustau mean little beyond Argentina today. But in Buenos Aires they inspire the sort of awe aroused in Europe by the great Real Madrid and Hungarian sides. Later River produced more great players: Alfredo Di Stefano, who would one day turn Real Madrid into possibly the greatest team of all time; Omar Sivori, who would form a wonderful partnership with John Charles after joining Italian club, Juventus; and then 1978 World Cup-winners Ubaldo Fillol, Daniel Passarella, Leopoldo Luque and Mario Kempes. In 1986 they were joined in River's Hall of Fame by the likes of goalkeeper Nery Pumpido, centre back Oscar Ruggeri and schemer Norberto Alonso after victory in the South American Club Cup provided River with formal confirmation of their high-prestige status. River really should have succeeded to the crown years earlier but were unlucky runners-up in both 1966 and 1976, first to Penarol of Uruguay, then Cruzeiro of Brazil. In 1986 they made no such mistake, beating America of Colombia over two legs then adding the world club cup after defeating Steaua of

Romania 1–0 in Tokyo. Ten years later River repeated the trick – this time beating America of Colombia 0–1, 2–0 in the final, thanks largely to the veteran inspiration of Enzo Francescoli and the youthful energy of striker Enrico Crespo.

Santos

Brazil

Founded: *1912*

Stadium: *Vila Belmiro (20,000)*

Colours: *All white*

Honours: *World Club Cup: 1962, 1963; South American Libertadores Club Cup 1962, 1963; Sao Paulo State League 15; Brazilian Championship (incl Torneo Rio-Sao Paulo) 5*

The name of Santos will always be synonymous with that of Pele who played all his mainstream career with the club and returned as a director at the end of 1993 to try to lift them out of the depths of a financial and administrative crisis. Santos had been founded by three members of the Americano club, who stayed home in the port of Santos when their club moved to Sao Paulo. Santos joined the Sao Paulo State Championship in 1916, became only the second Brazilian club to take up professionalism in 1933 but did not hit the headlines until the mid 1950s. Then, to organise a host of talented youngsters, they signed the 1950 World Cup veteran, Jair da Rosa Pinto, and discovered the 15-year-old Pele. To say Santos were a one-man team, as it often appeared from the publicity, would be unfair. Santos harvested millions of pounds from whistle-stop friendly match tours around the world and reinvested heavily in surrounding Pele with fine players – World Cup-winners in goalkeeper Gilmar, centre back Mauro and wing half Zito; an outside left with a ferocious shot in Pepe; and the precocious young talents of right winger Dorval, schemer Mengalvio and centre forward Coutinho, Pele's so-called "twin" with whom he established an almost telepathic relationship on the pitch. Santos were more than a football team; they were a touring circus. Sadly, the constant travelling burned out many young players before they had a chance to establish their talent. But not before Santos had scaled the competitive heights as Pele inspired their victories in World and South American Club Cups in both 1962 and 1963. One more year and it was all over. Independiente beat Santos in the 1964 South American Cup semi-finals and the spell had been broken. Santos went on touring and raking in cash, capitalising on Pele's name, for as long as they could. But further competitive achievement was rare and, at the end of it all in the early 1970s, much of the money appeared to have vanished as well.

Sao Paulo

Brazil

Founded: *1935*

Stadium: *Morumbi (150,000)*

Colours: *White with a red and black hoop/white*

Honours: *World Club Cup 1992, 1993; South American Libertadores Club Cup: 1992, 1993; Sao Paulo State League 17; Brazil Championship (incl Torneo Rio-Sao Paulo) 4*

Sao Paulo's victories over Barcelona and Milan in the 1992 and 1993 World Club Cups in Tokyo left no doubt about the finest club side in the world – for all the European hype which had surrounded the Italian champions. Those victories also underlined the depth of talent available to Sao Paulo since their key midfielder, Rai (younger brother of 1986 World Cup star Socrates), had been sold to French club Paris Saint Germain in the summer of 1993. Dual success also enhanced the reputation of coach Tele Santana, Brazil's World Cup manager in 1982 and 1986 and one of the most eloquent and down-to-earth of football analysts. Sao Paulo are, even so, comparative newcomers – having been founded in 1935 at a time when the likes of River Plate, Penarol and the rest were already well-established powers in their own lands. The club was formed of a merger between CA Paulistano and AA Palmeiras. A leading light was Paulo Machado de Carvalho who would later become a senior administrator behind the scenes for Brazil's World Cup hat-trick. Within less than a decade of being founded, Sao Paulo rose to become the strongest team in the country, winning the state title five times in the 1940s. They imported Argentine inside forward Antonio Sastre and the continuing pressure of success led to the construction of the 150,000-capacity Morumbi stadium – the world's largest club-owned sports arena. In the 1960s Sao Paulo had to take a back seat to Santos. In 1974 they reached their first South American Club final (losing to Argentina's Independiente) but it was not until the arrival of Santana, in the late 1980s, that Sao Paulo emerged from the doldrums. Despite the continuing sale of star players – key defender Ricardo Rocha went to Real Madrid – Sao Paulo secured three state league titles in four years, used the cash to strengthen their squad and were duly rewarded at the highest level.

Vasco Da Gama Rio de Janeiro

Brazil

Founded: *1898 as sailing club, 1915 as football club*

Stadium: *Sao Januario (50,000) and Maracana (130,000)*

Colours: *All white with black sash*

Honours: *Rio State League 17; Brazil Championship (incl Torneo Rio-Sao Paulo) 4*

Like Flamengo, one of their long-time Rio de Janeiro rivals, Vasco grew from a sailing club – the impetus for football coming from former members of a controversial outfit called Luzitania FC who had been refused entry to the early Rio de Janeiro State Championship because of their "Portuguese-only" policy. Transformed into Vasco da Gama, however, they were elected to the championship in 1915 and progressed to the top flight by 1923. Support, both vocal and financial, has come to the club over the years from the city's Portuguese community. In spite of their original policies, Vasco quickly became noted for their inclusion of mixed-race players at a time, early in Brazilian football's development, when the game was torn by discrimination of both race and class. Vasco led the way, too, in creating the San Januario stadium which was the first national stadium in Brazil and hosted all major club and national team matches before the building of the Maracana in 1950. In 1958 Vasco supplied Brazil's World Cup-winning team with centre back Luiz Bellini, the captain, and centre forward Vava. They earned a long-awaited consolation for events eight years earlier when no fewer than eight Vasco players had figured in the Brazilian squad pipped to the World Cup by Uruguay. In the 1960s and 1970s Vasco figured, as ever, among the most powerful of challengers to the likes of Fluminense and Flamengo – from whom they controversially signed the popular World Cup striker, Bebeto.

OTHER CLUBS OF THE WORLD

Al-Ahly

Egypt

Al-Ahly are virtually an Egyptian national institution, the red insignia of the club having been described as symbolising "the anti-colonial struggle and Egypt's infitah (opening-up) in 1952." The rivalry between Al-Ahly and Zamalek has dominated Egyptian football at club level. But Al-Ahly have generally had the upper hand. Indeed, Zamalek only broke Al-Ahly's iron grip on the championship once, and the club went unbeaten from 1974 to 1977. Al-Ahly were the first of the two clubs to win the African Champions Cup in 1982, again five years later, and the Cup-winners Cup for three years in succession from 1984 to 1986, and once more in 1993.

Arab Contractors

Egypt

Despite having been founded as recently as 1962, Arab Contractors surprisingly emerged as a major forces in African football during the 1980s, winning the African Cup-winners Cup in 1982 and 1983, the first time any Egyptian side had achieved such a feat. It was actually Al-Ahly who denied them a third consecutive title, defeating them in 1984 on the way to their own Cup-winners Cup hat-trick. Boasting a stadium to match those of Al-Ahly and Zamalek, Arab Contractors still wait for their first Egyptian title.

Asante Kotoko

Ghana

In 1930 the Asante Football Association was founded, and it was Asante Kotoko who quickly emerged as not only Ghana's most formidable club, but one of the biggest and most popular in Africa. A taxi driver from Kumasi, Kwesi Kuma, provided the club's unlikely beginnings, forming the Rainbow Football Club after being inspired by Accra teams, Hearts of Oak and Standfast. By 1931, the team had become known as the Titanics, until a local oracle advised a name-change to Kotoko, meaning porcupine. After the Asanthene, the king of the Asante accepted the club as a gift in 1935, the soon-to-be-famous name Asante Kotoko was confirmed. Kotoko decided to recruit from areas other than Asante, and won their first league championship in 1959. They won

the African Champions Cup in 1970 but lost in the 1971, 1973 and 1982 finals Since then, Kotoko have failed to add to their African titles, but have dominated the Ghanaian championship: the 1993 season saw them clinch their 19th league title.

Cosmos (now defunct)

United States

New York Cosmos possess a glamorous place in football history, thanks to the collection of some of the game's greatest names in the late 1970s. Founded in 1971, immediate success such as the 1972 NASL championship title was not sustained until the sensational signing of Pele in 1975. The next big-name import to Giants Stadium in New Jersey was Franz Beckenbauer and Brazil's 1970 World Cup-winning captain, Carlos Alberto: inevitably, the 1977 NASL championship trophy again found its way to New York, before Pele bowed out of football in a friendly against his only other club, Santos. Cosmos cruised to a third title in 1978, Vladislav Bogicevic and Dennis Tueart having arrived from Red Star Belgrade and Manchester City respectively, to be followed by Dutch duo Wim Rijsbergen and Johan Neeskens, and Brazilian Francisco Marinho in 1979.

DC United

United States

DC United, from Washington, have been one of the success stories of the Major League Soccer project which followed hard on the heels of the American staging of the World Cup finals in 1994. United started the inaugural MLS season in 1996 in confident mood, having secured the services of Bruce Arena as coach. He possessed a rare talent, though, in Bolivian midfielder Marco Etcheverry, one of the shining lights of the MLS in its formative years. Having American captain John Harkes alongside Etcheverry in midfield made DC United a formidable proposition. So it proved, the Washington side swiftly becoming the team to beat, safely securing the first two MLS titles.

Enugu Rangers

Nigeria

The emergence in the 1970s of Enugu Rangers as a major force in Nigerian football was especially satisfying, as the club had risen out of the ravages of civil war. Goalkeeper Emmanuel Okala, voted best goalkeeper in Africa in 1979, and 1980 African Footballer of the Year Christian Chukwu became heroes in Enugu as the Rangers won three Nigerian league titles in three years, and a hat-trick of FA Challenge Cups in the 1970s. The 1980s brought a further two FA Cups and three league titles, but the 1984 Championship trophy was the last silverware to come Enugu's way. Rangers can still boast having had one of Nigeria's greatest players as their captain, however – Godwin Achebe skippering both Enugu and the Nigerian national side.

Esperance

Tunisia

Esperance have always been the most respected of Tunisia's club sides, possessing the largest support and a distinctive gold and red strip which marks them out as characteristically Tunisian. But it was not until the late 1980s and early 1990s that they started to consistently make their mark in both Tunisian and African football. After their first Tunisian league title in 1941, an 18-year wait prefaced their next championship, clinched in 1959 and retained in 1960. Since then, they have taken their tally to 13 league titles – including consecutive successes in 1975 and 1976, 1988 and 1989, and 1993 and 1994 – and three Cup of Tunis triumphs, but their greatest glory came in 1994. Egyptian side Zamelak went into the African Cup Final as the reigning champions, but Esperance won the tie 3–1 on aggregate to become only the second Tunisian side to lift the trophy. The same year, a 3–0 win over Zaire's Motema Pembe brought Esperance the African Supercup.

Etoile Sahel

Tunisia

Etoile Sahel, along with Club Sportif of Sahel, have always stood out in Tunisian football, being based away from the capital Tunis, unlike the three other major clubs Esperance, Club Africain and Stade Tunisien. The most obvious effect of this geographical difference has been more unstable finances, but both clubs have confounded any misgivings about their participation in the national competitions. With seven league titles and seven cup successes to their name, the club have more than proved their worth – even if it took subsidies from the Tunisian federation to support their original entry into African international club competition. The reward finally came in 1995, when they beat AS Kaloum from Guinea, 2–0, to take the African CAF Cup, thanks to a brace of goals from Ben Younis, who went on to play for Tunisia in the 1998 World Cup finals in France.

FAR Rabat

Morocco

Royal Armed Forces (FAR) enjoyed their greatest years in the 1960s, including a spell of four successive Moroccan league titles from 1961 to 1964, and further championships in 1967, 1968 and 1970. Although the club failed to win the league again in the 1970s, cup successes in 1971 helped maintain their position as one of the country's major clubs. In 1985 they won glory by winning the African Champions Cup. FAR were thus the first Moroccan club to win an African title, the highlight of three remarkable years which brought a Moroccan league and cup double in 1984, the African and Moroccan Cups in 1985, and a third successive Moroccan Cup in 1986. The club continued their consistent league performances with national championships in 1987 and 1989, taking their haul to a round 10 league titles.

Gor Mahia

Kenya

Gor Mahia exploded onto the Kenyan football scene by finishing runners-up to Nakuru All Stars only a year after their formation. Since then, Leopards and Gor Mahia have waged an almost yearly battle for dominance: from 1979 to 1986, they were the only two clubs to win the title before Shabana Kissi broke the two-club stranglehold in 1987. During the same period, the two teams dominated the East and Central African Club Cup, Gor Mahia running out winners on three occasions, defeating Leopards themselves in 1980 and 1985. Although both sides have won the Kenyan league 10 times apiece, Gor Mahia can claim the superior position thanks to their three Kenyan Cup triumphs and their African Cup-winners Cup success in 1987, making them the only Kenyan side to win an African trophy.

Hearts of Oak

Ghana

Hearts of Oak were founded in 1911 as one of the country's first football clubs. They have often failed to live up to their reputation, after winning the first national league in 1965. Befitting their position in Ghanaian football history, they were the country's first club to participate in the African Champions Cup in 1972, and reached the final in 1977 and 1979, only losing the latter match in a penalty shoot-out. The most recent additions to their illustrious history include a league and cup double in 1990, their eighth national cup success in 1994 and, in 1997, their 13th Ghanaian league championship.

Kaizer Chiefs

South Africa

Kaizer Chiefs were born in the imagination of Kaizer Motaung – a former Soweto player and once Rookie of the Year in the North American Soccer League – and he turned his dream into reality when his collection of Orlando Pirates team-mates broke away in 1970 and began their own footballing adventure. Within just four years the Chiefs had already won both the South African league championship and the Top Eight Cup, the league success all the more enjoyable since they took the title from the Pirates. Orlando regained their crown in 1975, but once again the Chiefs fought back, to win not only the 1976 championship, but retain the title in 1977. Since then, not only have the club taken their honours list to nine league titles but also added six South African Super Bowl cups, four Coca-Cola League Cups and 11 Top Eight Cups.

Kashima Antlers

Japan

Kashima take their name from the deer of the Kashima Shrine, the Antlers rose to runners-up position in the newly-enlarged championship of 1996, before winning their first title in 1997. Zico having retired, it was the responsibility of fellow Brazilians Jorginho, Mazinho and Bismarck to inspire the club's talented Japanese players, adding the Emperor's Cup to their honours. The presence in attack of Mazinho helped inspire Japanese prodigy Atsushi Yanagisawa, who made his goal-scoring mark as a 19 year-old. The sole black mark came in December 1997 when the crowd stormed the pitch after Kashima lost to Jubilo Iwata in the second leg of the championship play-off.

Kawasaki Verdy

Japan

It was no surprise when Kawasaki Verdy ran out comfortable champions of the inaugural J.League season in 1993, and then retained their title in 1994: they had been overwhelming favourites in the run-up to the J.League, having won the previous year's Soccer League Cup – a trophy they duly defended successfully in both 1993 and 1994. Despite subsequently losing their grip on the championship, Kawasaki ran out comfortable 3–0 winners over Sanfrecce Hiroshima in the 1997 Emperor's Cup final. In the years preceding the launch of the J.League, Verdy – owned by the Yomiuri media empire – had made their mark as the first independent professional football club in Japan.

JSK (formerly JET)

Algeria

Jeunesse Sportive de Kabylie – formerly known as Jeunesse Electronique de Tizi-Ouzou (JET) – are one of only three Algerian sides to have won the African Champions Cup, and the only one to win it twice, in 1981 and 1990. Founded in 1946, JSK firmly emerged as one of Algeria's top sides in the 1970s under the managership of Mahieddine Khalef, before his Polish understudy Ziwotko assumed control. Despite exemplary training and preparational tactics, however, they owed their 1981 African Cup success to a little luck when Egyptian side Al-Ahly pulled out of their semi-final clash. The Algerian side provided a resounding victory in the fina crushing Vita Club of Zaire 5–2 on aggregate. The JET success story continued through the 1980s and 1990s before they reverted to the JSK title in 1990. The 1996 season brought the club their 12th Algerian league title, two years after their third Algerian Cup success.

Leopards

Kenya

AFC Leopards have been the main thorn in the side of deadly rivals Gor Mahia in the struggle for control of Kenyan league football. Leopards can claim the superiority of four Central African titles to Gor Mahia's three, but despite matching their rivals' 10 league titles, they have yet to win an African continental trophy. The club were variously known as Abuluhya FC and Abuluhya United after their formation in 1964, winning their first title in 1970, but their progress was soured in 1973 when a dispute with the KFF precipitated a two-year withdrawal from the league.

Los Angeles Galaxy

United States

Mexican goalkeeper Jorge Campos helped the Galaxy reach the first MLS final, before the superior skills of DC United ended Los Angeles dreams of first-season glory. The enthusiastic Mexican support has helped keep Galaxy attendances way above the MLS average although American stars such as Cobi Jones also proved crowd-pleasers In the Rose Bowl, Galaxy boast one of the USA's game's major venues which had hosted the most games in the 1994 World Cup finals, as well as the most important ties of the 1984 Olympics plus the 1986 FIFA World All-Star Game. Los Angeles, in the NASL days, had been home to the Aztecs, for whom Johan Cruyff starred in 1979.

Mouloudia PA

Algeria

Mouloudia des Petroliers d'Algier (MPA) boast a collection of Algeria records to their name: they are Algeria's oldest club side, they were the first Algerian side to compete in African competition, and in 1976 they won the national league by ammassing a record 73 points. Based at the enormous 5 Juillet Stadium in Algiers, the club was formerly known as Mouloudia Challia, its name change reflecting the controlling influence of the national oil giant, SONATRACH. The club's finest hour came in 1977, when they won the African Champions Cup at their first attempt, mounting an amazing recovery after losing the first leg of the final 3–0 to Hafia, from Guinea. In the return tie in Algiers, Mouloudia won by three goals, before prevailing on a penalty shoot-out.

Nagoya Grampus 8

Japan

In all the hype preceding the launch of the J.League, it was Grampus 8 who achieved perhaps the scoop of the lot, persuading former England captain Gary Lineker the first English player to sample Japanese football. Unfortunately for Lineker and his expectant new fans, it was not the success story anticipated, injury problems curtailing his appearances. It was another Tottenham exile who helped Grampus 8 to their most encouraging successes, former Argentina midfielder Osvaldo Ardiles after he took over as team coach in the mid-1990s. Goals from Fukuda and Yugoslav playmaker Dragan Stojkovic clinched the Xerox Supercup in 1995, as Grampus 8 overcame the challenge of the Yokohama Marinos. Stojkovic went on to be Yugoslavia's midfield playmaker in the 1998 World Cup finals in France. Both the club's name and their badge come from the legend of the killer whales (grampus) which, according to legend, rescued the city from fire by spouting water from the sea.

Raja Casablanca

Morocco

Wydad of Casablanca (WAC) may boast the grander history, but their city rivals, Raja Casablanca (RCA), achieved the greater feat in 1989 by winning the African Champions Cup. Playing their home matches at Morocco's Mohamed V national stadium, the club had only won their first Moroccan league title the previous year, in 1988 – thus making their African Cup glory all the more sensational. Consecutive league triumphs in 1995 and 1996 have seen them cement their recently-acquired status

as one of Morocco's most formidable sides. Their fifth Moroccan Cup title in 1996 completed their first ever league and cup double.

Stade Abidjan

Ivory Coast

Stade Abidjan's first impact came in 1962 when they broke up the dominance of the two clubs, Africa Sport and ASEC, to win their first league championship – followed by three more in the four years that followed. Even more spectacular was the club's first African Champions Cup campaign, when they powered to an 1966 African Cup final victory against Real of Bamako from Mali. Since winning their fifth league title in 1969, the championship has remained off-limits for Stade Abidjan, but they won a hat-trick of Ivory Coast Cup finals from 1994 to 1996, taking their cup tally to six cup victories.

WAC

Morocco

Wydad of Casablanca (WAC) hit their peak in the late 1940s and early 1950s, when the legendary trio of Driss, Chtouki and Abdessalem inspired them to four successive Moroccan league titles from 1948 to 1951. The league championship did not take place from 1952 to 1956 because of civil unrest, but when it resumed in 1957 WAC continued where they left off, securing their fifth title, since when they have taken their tally to 14 league championships and seven Moroccan Cups, the most recent of which came in 1997.

Zamalek

Egypt

Zamalek have spent a large part of their history in the shadow of Cairo rivals Al-Ahly, but the last Egyptian side to win the African Champions Cup is the country's most successful participant in that competition. Zamalek's triumph in 1984 over Nigeria's IICC was perhaps the club's greatest moment. Two years later, Zamalek became the first Egyptian side to win a second African Cup, and clinched their third and fourth titles in 1993 and 1996. They secured the African Supercup in 1997, beating Egyptian rivals Arab Contractors 4–2 on penalties. Founded as an Anglo-Egyptian side in 1925, the club's original name was Faruk, after the then King of Egypt. With 18 Egyptian Cup triumphs to their name, Zamalek are eager to regain their position at the top of the national league to clinch their 10th championship title.

PLAYERS

Ercan **Abdullah**

Country: *Turkey (born December 8, 1971)*
Position: *Midfielder*
Clubs: *Fenerbahce, Trabzonspor*

Abdullah was Turkey's best player in the finals of the 1996 European Championship. He had begun in the Fenerbahce youth sections, but it was thought he would not make the grade and he was transferred to Trabzonspor with whom he made his league debut in 1991. His superb form at Euro 96 attracted numerous scouts from foreign clubs. Abdullah was a gold-medal winner with the Turkish Olympic Under-21 team at the 1993 Mediterranean Games.

Trello **Abegglen**

Country: *Switzerland (born March 7, 1909)*
Position: *Inside forward*
Clubs: *Etoile Rouge, Cantonal, Grasshopper, Sochaux (France), Servette, La Chaux-de-Fonds*

The Abegglen brothers were the first, outstanding internationals in Swiss football history. André and his brother Max, known universally by his name reversal of Xam, filled the inside-forward roles together for the famous Grasshopper-Club of Zürich. Trello scored 30 goals in 52 internationals for Switzerland between 1927 and 1943. He starred at the 1934 and 1938 World Cup finals and won three Swiss championships, two with Grasshopper and one after moving to Servette of Geneva. The elder brother, Max, appeared 68 times for his country between 1923 and 1937, was top scorer at the 1924 Olympic Games soccer tournament and was five times a Swiss champion and six times a cup-winner with Grasshopper.

Tony **Adams**

Country: *England (born October 10, 1966)*
Position: *Central defender*
Clubs: *Arsenal*

Adams made his league debut for Arsenal at 17 and his England debut in 1987 against Spain. He missed the 1990 World Cup finals in Italy, then displayed enormous strength of character to become captain of both Arsenal and England after serving a prison sentence for a motoring offence. He went on to captain Arsenal to three league championships and to victories in the finals of the FA Cup – the 1998 triumph securing the league and cup double – the League Cup and European Cup-winners' Cup. His displays for England during the 1998 World Cup were immense, marking him out as one of the world's great defenders.

Ademir **Marques de Menezes**

Country: *Brazil (born November 8, 1922)*
Position: *Centre forward*
Clubs: *FC Recife, Vasco da Gama, Fluminense, Vasco da Gama*

Brazilian football historians have claimed that Brazilian coaches created the 4–2–4 tactical formation because Ademir's ability forced opposing teams to play with an extra central defender. His niche in history was assured when he was the seven-goal leading scorer at the 1950 World Cup finals, playing centre-forward for Brazil in an inside-forward trio with Zizinho and Jair da Rosa, considered as one of the greatest in Brazil's history. Ademir scored 32 goals in 37 internationals after beginning his career as an outside left. He had a powerful shot in both feet and was six times a Rio state league champion, five times with Vasco da Gama and once with Fluminense.

José Pinto Carvalho dos Santos **Aguas**

Country: *Portugal (born November 9, 1930)*
Position: *Centre forward*
Clubs: *Benfica, FK Austria (Austria)*

Legend has it that Aguas, born in Angola, was a famed local lion-hunter when Benfica convinced him he could enjoy a more lucrative existence hunting goals. He flew to Portugal in 1950 and scored more than 250 goals for Benfica as well as finishing top league scorer five times. Aguas was captain and centre forward of the Benfica side which succeeded Real Madrid as European champions in 1961. In 1960–61 he was also top scorer, with 11 goals, in the Champions Cup. He was winning captain again in 1962, then transferred to FK Austria to wind down his playing career. Later he returned to Portugal to work as a coach.

Mohammed **Al Deayea**

Country: *Saudi Arabia (born August 2, 1972)*
Position: *Goalkeeper*
Club: *Al-Tae*

Al Deayea lays claim to being the finest international goalkeeper yet produced by Middle East football. Goalkeeping talent runs in the family since his elder brother, Abdullah, kept goal in the winning Saudi Arabian teams at the 1984 and 1988 Asian Cups. The younger Al Deayea followed in his brother's footsteps in the victorious Saudi team at the 1996 Asian Cup, where he was voted best goalkeeper. He was the key figure in Saudi Arabia's qualification for the 1998 World Cup finals in France with two penalty saves in crucial matches. Once there, however, Saudi Arabia struggled, finishing bottom of their group.

Saeed **Al Owairan**

Country: *Saudi Arabia (born August 19, 1967)*
Position: *Centre forward*
Clubs: *Al Shabab*

Saeed Al Owairan scored one of the greatest solo goals ever seen in the history of the World Cup when he ran on from deep inside his own half to score against Belgium in Washington in the first round of the 1994 finals. Not surprisingly he was then voted 1994 Asian Footballer of the Year. Al Owairan had first hit the international scene as a member of the Saudi team which finished runners-up to Japan at the 1992 Asian Cup. After the 1994 World Cup he was an unsuccessful transfer target for several European clubs. But in 1995 he was banned for 18 months after being found at an illegal drinks party – an offence under the strict Islamic law – and missed the stunning Saudi success at the 1996 Asian Cup. When the ban ended, he was soon recalled to the national team in December 1997 for a friendly against Iceland, keeping his place for the 1998 Confederations Cup. However, he failed to score a goal in the 1998 World Cup finals as the Saudis failed to win any of their three group matches.

Florian **Albert**

Country: *Hungary (born September 15, 1941)*
Position: *Centre forward*
Clubs: *Ferencvaros*
European Footballer of the Year 1967

When Florian Albert was hailed as the new Hungarian hero in the early 1960s, it was hardly a matter of note. After all, Hungarian football was recognised as one of the most powerful forces in the game – twice World Cup runners-up either side of the war and tactical revolutionaries in the early 1950s. Hindsight, however, has shown that Albert was one of the last products of his country's great flowering of football talent. Only Lajos Detari, of successor generations, has proved worthy to rank with Albert in terms of ability – and Detari never made a mark on the World Cup as Albert did in 1966. The son of a farmer, Albert moved to Budapest while still a boy for the sake of his education. But it was as a sporting talent that he shone as a teenager. At 15 he was signed by Ferencvaros and at 17 he was making his national team debut in a 3–2 win over Sweden in Budapest – within a week of sitting school examinations. Slim and with tight control, Albert was both an outstanding creator and finisher. He made many international goals for team-mates such as veteran Lajos Tichy but was also four times the league's leading marksman. His greatest game was Hungary's 3–1 win over Brazil at the 1966 World Cup finals and he was a popular choice as European Footballer of the Year the following year.

Demetrio **Albertini**

Country: *Italy (born August 23, 1971)*
Position: *Midfielder*
Clubs: *Padova, Milan*

Albertini has proved an exemplary central midfielder both for Italy and for Milan – able to keep command deep in his own territory but find time for the creative passing which offered so many counter-attacking opportunities. He made his league debut for Milan in 1989, and his national team debut in 1991 against Cyprus – in only former Milan coach Arrigo Sacchi's second game in charge. Sacchi called him "the player who makes the side tick over," but he was one of the Italians who missed during the 1998 World Cup penalty shootout with France.

Albertini: Milan's European hero

Alfonso Perez Munoz

Country: *Spain (born September 26, 1972)*
Position: *Centre forward*
Clubs: *Castilla, Real Madrid, Betis, Real Madrid, Betis*

Alfonso has had a more complicated career than had appeared likely when he joined Real Madrid at 13 and later made an instant impact with Castilla, Madrid's nursery team. A powerful, direct striker, he played a starring role in Spain's gold-medal 1992 Olympic campaign. Two months later, he made his full international debut. Three months after that, he scored his first goal for his country when Spain beat Latvia 5–0 in Seville. His career hit a major crisis when he suffered a cruciate ligament injury during Real Madrid's 5–0 defeat in Barcelona in January, 1994. He thus missed the 1994 World Cup finals and, at the start of the following season, suffered an ankle injury which cost him another four months out. Madrid could not wait for him to get fit and bought Chilean striker Ivan Zamorano. When Alfonso was eventually fit, there was no place for him and he was sold to ambitious Betis for £3.5 million in 1995 with a buy-back clause which Madrid duly activated in 1996. He was part of the Spanish side who under-performed massively at the 1998 World Cup Finals, failing to make it through to the second round.

Ivor Allchurch

Country: *Wales (born October 16, 1919)*
Position: *Inside left*
Clubs: *Swansea, Newcastle (England), Cardiff, Swansea*

Allchurch won 68 caps for Wales, spread over 16 years, and scored 23 goals – records which stood until the 1990s. His 251 league goals in nearly 700 appearances emphasised the excellence of his finishing. Slim, elegant and creative, Ivor the Golden Boy had just about everything an inside forward needed in the first quarter-century after World War Two, except luck. He was fated to play in mediocre teams throughout his long career, and even his excellent work for his country went largely to waste apart from the 1958 World Cup. Brother Len was an outside right for Wales.

Luigi Allemandi

Country: *Italy (born November 18, 1903)*
Position: *Left back*
Clubs: *Juventus, Internazionale, Roma*

Allemandi played 25 times for his country at left back and would have made more appearances but for a match-fixing scandal. Allemandi was accused of having accepted a bribe from a director of Torino to fix a match while playing for Juventus in 1927. The matter did not emerge until a year later when Allemandi, despite reports identifying him as one of the best players on the field, was suspended for life. By now he was playing for Internazionale who fought the charge on his behalf and had it quashed. In 1929 Allemandi returned to Italy's team for a match against Czechoslovakia and he went on to win a World Cup medal in 1934. He was certainly one of the outstanding personalities in Calcio in the inter-war years.

Jose Altafini

Country: *Brazil and Italy (born August 27, 1938)*
Position: *Centre forward*
Clubs: *Palmeiras, Sao Paulo, Milan (Italy), Napoli (Italy), Juventus (Italy), Chiasso (Switzerland)*

A direct, aggressive centre-forward, Altafini was a subject of both confusion and admiration throughout his career. He began with Palmeiras of Sao Paulo where he was known by the nickname of Mazzola because of his resemblance to the Italian star of the late 1940s. He played at the 1958 World Cup and was immediately signed by Milan. The Italians insisted on reverting to Altafini's own name and he played for his "new" country at the 1962 World Cup finals. A year later Altafini scored a record 14 goals in Milan's Champions Cup success, including two goals in the final victory over Benfica at Wembley. Later he fell out with Milan, partly for professional and partly for private reasons. He joined Omar Sivori in inspiring a Napoli revival and still later became an influential "super substitute" with Juventus. Altafini is now a popular TV soccer analyst in Italy.

Amancio Amaro Varela

Country: *Spain (born October 12, 1939)*
Position: *Right winger/inside forward*
Clubs: *La Coruna, Real Madrid*

Amancio's outstanding technique and acceleration brought him a string of honours during his illustrious playing career. He played 42 times for Spain between 1964 and 1971, was ten times a Spanish league champion with Madrid and four times a cup-winner. In 1968 he was honoured with selection for a World XI against Brazil, but the highlight of his career was undoubtedly winning the European Nations Championship with Spain in 1964 on his home ground, the Estadio Bernabeu in Madrid. He had joined Real in 1962 when Madrid needed a replacement for Italy-bound Luis del Sol. Amancio was then an outside right with his home-town club, Real Deportivo de La Coruna. Coach Miguel Munoz switched him to inside right.playing first in midfield and then as a striker.

Amarildo Tavares Silveira

Country: *Brazil (born June 29, 1939)*
Position: *Inside left*
Clubs: *Botafogo, Milan (Italy), Fiorentina (Italy)*

Amarildo exploded on the international scene at the 1962 World Cup finals after Pele was injured. An attacking inside left whose slight appearance disguised a wiry frame, he had not expected to play when he was called in to deputise for O Rei in a decisive group match against Spain. Brazil recovered from a goal down to win 2–1 thanks to two late strikes from Amarildo and, in the final against Czechoslovakia, he proved decisive once more – scoring with a snapshot which deceived the goalkeeper on the near post. Milan bought Amarildo a year later and he enjoyed a successful career in Italy, winning the championship with Fiorentina in 1969. He stayed in Italy after retiring and joined Fiorentina's youth coaching staff.

Manuel Amoros

Country: *France (born February 1, 1961)*
Position: *Full back*
Clubs: *Monaco, Marseille*

Born in Nimes of Spanish parents, Amoros was an outstanding teenage exponent of both soccer and rugby. Monaco persuaded him to concentrate on soccer and he played for France at youth and under-21 level before a surprise – and highly successful – promotion to the senior national team at the 1982 World Cup finals in which France finished fourth. Amoros played right and left back in the memorable French national team of the 1980s. He won a European Championship medal in 1984, despite missing most of the tournament after being sent off in the opening match against Denmark. He played most of his club career with Monaco, then joined Marseille and set a French record of 82 caps.

Emmanuel Amunike

Country: *Nigeria (born December 25, 1970)*
Position: *Winger*
Clubs: *Nigerlux, Concord, Julius Berger, Zamalek (Egypt), Sporting (Portugal), Barcelona (Spain)*

Amunike was one of the heroes of the Nigeria explosion of the late 1990s. Originally he played for local clubs Nigerlux, Concord and Julius Berger before joining top Egyptian club Zamalek. MSV Duisburg and Sporting of Portugal both tried to sign him and the transfer dispute had to be settled, eventually, by FIFA. Sporting won the fight – and then transferred Amunike to

Emmanuel Amunike: Nigerian Olympic hero

Barcelona in the summer of 1996. Ironically he then missed most of the 1996–97 season because of serious injury. By then, however, he had established his reputation in helping Nigeria win the Olympic Games in 1996 and the African Nations Cup in 1994. He scored both Nigeria's goals in the 2–1 win over Zambia in the 1994 African Nations Cup – his first game in the tournament. He also scored the winning goal in the 3–2 win over Argentina in the Olympic Games Final in Athens, Georgia. Amunike was voted 1994 African Footballer of the Year.

José Leandro Andrade

Country: *Uruguay (born November 20, 1898)*
Position: *Right half*
Clubs: *Bella Vista, Nacional*

Andrade was a stalwart of the great Uruguayan teams of the 1920s and 1930s, winning the Olympic Games soccer tournament gold medal in both 1924 and 1928. Injury then threatened to end his career but Andrade was recalled, because of his vast experience, for the inaugural World Cup finals which Uruguay won on home ground in 1930. He was an old-fashioned wing-half in the 2–3–5 tactical system which served much of the soccer world for the first half of the century, and he played 41 times for his country before retiring in 1933. Andrade's nephew, Victor Rodriguez Andrade, won the World Cup himself in 1950 and was never once booked or sent off.

Giancarlo **Antognoni**

Country: *Italy (born April 1, 1954)*
Position: *Midfielder*
Clubs: *Fiorentina, Lausanne (Switzerland)*

A graceful, wonderfully intuitive midfield general, Antognoni cost Fiorentina £750,000 as a teenager from fourth division Astimacombi in 1972. He went straight into the Fiorentina team and made the first of his 73 appearances for Italy in the autumn of 1974. Antognoni was a regular transfer target for Italy's richest clubs but remained faithful to Fiorentina until he eventually wound down his career with Lausanne in Switzerland. Sadly, Antognoni missed Italy's victory over West Germany in the 1982 World Cup Final after suffering a gashed ankle in the semi-final defeat of Poland. He was considered by Italian fans the successor to Milan's Gianni Rivera as their golden boy in the 1970s and early 1980s.

Osvaldo **Ardiles**

Country: *Argentina (born August 3, 1952)*
Position: *Midfielder*
Clubs: *Huracan, Tottenham (England), Paris Saint-Germain (France), Tottenham (England), Queens Park Rangers (England)*

Ardiles earned his initial reputation as midfield general of Argentina under the managership of Cesar Luis Menotti. Hardly had he collected his winner's medal at the 1978 World Cup than Ardiles and national team-mate Ricardo Villa were subjects of a remarkable transfer to Tottenham Hotspur. Ardiles cost £300,000, which made him one of the greatest bargains in modern soccer history by the time he had completed an outstanding playing career which included the FA Cup success of 1981 and UEFA Cup triumph of 1984. As a player he had combined legal and soccer studies in the mid-1970s, but he put ideas of a career in law aside when he returned to White Hart Lane as manager in the summer of 1993. He later coached in Japan.

Luis **Artime**

Country: *Argentina (born December 2, 1938)*
Position: *Centre forward*
Clubs: *Atlanta, River Plate, Independiente, Palmeiras (Brazil), Nacional (Uruguay), Fluminense (Brazil)*

Artime scored 47 goals in two teenage seasons with minor Buenos Aires club Atlanta to earn a move to River Plate in 1961, with whom he will always be most closely linked. He played in the traditional mould of Argentine spearheads – powerful, aggressive and prolific. He climaxed a three-year spell, including 66 league goals, with leadership of Argentina's attack at the 1966 World Cup finals. After the finals he was sold to Independiente, scoring 44 goals in 18 months and earning further transfers to Palmeiras, then Nacional of Montevideo , with whom he was top Uruguayan league marksman three years in a row. He also scored 24 goals in all for Argentina.

Aljosa **Asanovic**

Country: *Croatia (born December 14, 1965)*
Position: *Midfielder*
Club: *Hajduk Split, Metz (France), Cannes (France), Montpellier (France), Hajduk Split, Valladolid (Spain), Hajduk Split, Derby County (England), Napoli (Italy)*

Asanovic, a one-time youth, Olympic and full international for the former Yugoslavia, had to wait until his early 30s for recognition of his talents at Euro 96. His first successes were in winning two Croat league championships and national cup competitions with Hajduk Split. He also scored one of modern Croatia's first international goals in a 2–1 win over the United States in Zagreb in 1990 – having chartered a private jet at his own expense to make sure he reached the match in time. He wandered away to France but returned to Hajduk in 1994 even though the club were still, at the time, trying to recover £100,000 they claimed to have been owed under the terms of his original transfer to Metz. Kept moving after Euro 96 – first to Derby County, then to Napoli.

Georgi **Asparoukhov**

Country: *Bulgaria (born May 4, 1943)*
Position: *Centre forward*
Clubs: *Levski Sofia, Botev Plovdiv, Spartak Sofia*

"Gundi" Asparoukhov was a tall, direct centre forward who scored 19 goals in 49 internationals before being killed in a car crash at the age of 28 in 1971, along with fellow Bulgarian international Nikola Kotkov. Their deaths shook the country greatly and marked the beginning of a long period of transition from "state amateurism" to post-communist professionalism. Asparoukhov led Bulgaria's attack in the World Cup finals of 1962, 1966 and 1970 and scored 150 goals in 245 league games for his only senior club, Levski Sofia. The Portuguese club Benfica tried to sign him in 1966 after being impressed with Asparoukhov in a Champions Cup tie. But he was not interested in moving because he had all he wanted in Bulgaria...including his favourite Alfa Romeo sports car which, ultimately, proved the death of him. He remains one of the most outstanding yet tragic players in Bulgaria's history.

Faustino **Asprilla**

Country: *Colombia (born November 10, 1969)*
Position: *Right winger/centre forward*
Clubs: *Cucuta, Nacional, Parma (Italy), Newcastle (England), Parma (Italy), River Plate (Arg)*

Asprilla was overlooked by a string of local professional clubs in Tulua and was attending college when he joined Cucuta, one of Colombia's smaller sides. After 15 games, Nacional picked him up for £100,000 in 1989. Parma paid £2.5 million for him a year later. Asprilla proved a sensation in Italian football, then scored two of Colombia's goals in their historic five-goal thrashing of Argentina in Buenos Aires in the 1994 World Cup qualifiers. But the big occasions have not always gone his way. He missed Parma's 1993 Cup-winners Cup Final victory over Antwerp because of injury and was an overawed disappointment at the

Faustino Asprilla: a courter of controversy

1994 World Cup finals. After a spell with Newcastle United, Asprilla moved back to Parma, and became embroiled in controversy during the 1998 World Cup when he inexplicably walked out on Colombia after only one match.

Dino **Baggio**

Country: *Italy (born July 24, 1971)*
Position: *Midfielder*
Clubs: *Torino, Internazionale, Parma*

Dino Baggio contribution in steadying the midfield, has been crucial since he made his national team debut against Cyprus in 1991. Baggio is predominantly a ball-winner but he can also move forward to effect – as he demonstrated at the 1994 World Cup finals with important goals against Spain and Norway. He turned down the offer of a move from Juventus to Parma in the summer of 1994 – then thought better of it, just in time to prevent the teenaged Alessandro Del Piero being sent to Parma instead! Baggio helped Juventus win the UEFA Cup in 1993 and then won it again with Parma in 1995. He was a prominent member of the Italian team which reached the quarter-finals of the 1998 World Cup.

Roberto **Baggio**

Country: *Italy (born February 18, 1967)*
Position: *Centre forward*
Clubs: *Fiorentina, Juventus, Milan, Bologna*

For a peace-loving Buddhist, Roberto Baggio has provoked a remarkable number of controversies – including street violence and inner-city riots. He made his name originally as a winger with local club Vicenza in the Italian third division as a 15-year-old and was picked up three years later by Fiorentina's much-admired scouting system. In five seasons by the Arno, Baggio developed from provincial nobody to superstar. His finest season was his fifth, in which he scored 17 goals in 32 league games and led Fiorentina to the semi-finals of the UEFA Cup – where they lost to Juventus. Fury then erupted in the Renaissance city when it emerged that Baggio was being sold to none other than Juventus for a world-record £8 million. It needed riot police to quell the protesting Fiorentina fans. Baggio demonstrated a few weeks later just why he was worth such a fee when he scored a marvellous solo goal against Czechoslovakia. Juventus saw him as the successor to Michel Platini. He helped deliver the UEFA Cup in 1993 and the league title in 1995. He was also voted FIFA's World Player of the Year and European Footballer of the Year at the end of 1993. His status as a national hero reached its peak after he scored the goals which took Italy to the 1994 World Cup Final. He played despite having pulling a hamstring in the semi-

Roberto Baggio: star of three World Cups

final. But he missed the decisive penalty in the final shoot-out, and had to endure four years of anguish before scoring two spot-kicks during the 1998 World Cup that expunged the memory.

Krasimir **Balakov**

Country: *Bulgaria (born March 29, 1966)*
Position: *Midfielder*
Clubs: *Etar Veliko Tarnovo, Sporting Clube (Portugal), Stuttgart (Germany)*

Balakov was a boy wonder in Bulgaria where he made his league debut at the age of 16 in 1982 and then his senior international debut against Denmark six years later after overcoming serious injury. Balakov was briefly suspended in 1990 when the Bulgarian Football Union found he had signed for both Etar and CSKA. Etar won the wrangle but almost immediately sold him on to Sporting Lisbon in 1991. Despite his midfield role, he was Sporting's 15-goal top scorer in the 1993–94 season. He and Petar Hubchev were then the only Bulgarians to play right through all their seven matches at the 1994 World Cup finals. Many observers at USA 94 picked Balakov in their "Team of the Tournament," and German club Stuttgart duly took the transfer hint. He led them to the 1998 Cup-winners Cup Final where injury-they lost 1–0 to Chelsea in Stockholm. More disappointment followed with a poor display from Bulgaria during the 1998 World Cup finals in France.

Marcelo **Balboa**

Country: *United States (born August 8, 1967)*
Position: *Central defender*
Clubs: *Leon (Mexico), Colorado Rapids*

Balboa was the defensive anchor around which the United States national team – and American soccer in general – developed throughout the 1990s. He played in the 1990 World Cup finals in Italy and then captained the US as hosts in 1994 to the second round. His dependable display earned a transfer to Mexico's Leon and then back to the US with Colorado on the launch of Major League Soccer. The first American to reach a century of international apperarances, he was honoured with selection in the FIFA All-Stars match for Kobe earthquake victims in 1995. He is the son of a former Argentine professional, Luis Balboa, who emigrated to the United States.

Alan **Ball**

Country: *England (born May 12, 1945)*
Position: *Inside forward/midfielder*
Clubs: *Blackpool, Everton, Arsenal, Southampton*

Ball, son of a former professional player and manager of the same name, was one of the unexpected heroes of England's 1966 World Cup triumph – a red-haired bundle of energy who worked like a Trojan and ran the great Karl-Heinz Schnellinger virtually into the Wembley turf in the final. Ball made his name with Blackpool and collected a league championship medal with Everton in 1970, later moving to Arsenal for what was then a Gunners' record fee of £220,000. Later he moved to Southampton before returning to Blackpool as player-manager. His determination to remain within the game saw him take up a variety of managerial appointments including spells at Stoke City, Manchester City, Southampton and Portsmouth.

Gordon **Banks**

Country: *England (born December 20, 1937)*
Position: *Goalkeeper*
Clubs: *Leicester, Stoke City, Fort Lauderdale Strikers (USA)*

Banks set all kinds of goalkeeping records, including 73 caps, 23 consecutive internationals in a row and seven consecutive clean sheets eventually ended by Eusebio's penalty in the 1966 World Cup semi-final. His late withdrawal from the 1970 quarter-final probably cost England the match from 2–0 up. He was a loser in two FA Cup finals with Leicester (at fault with two goals in the second) and, unluckiest of all, lost an eye in a car crash when he still had years left to play. A product of the prolific

Chesterfield goalkeeper academy, Banks may yet be considered to have been superior to the man who eventually succeeded him with both Leicester and England, Peter Shilton.

Franco **Baresi**

Country: *Italy (born May 8, 1960)*
Position: *Sweeper*
Club: *Milan*

Baresi, who retired in 1997 after a wonderful one-club career, was commonly acknowledged as the best sweeper in the world for much of the 1980s and 1990s. But he was much more than a defender with both club and country. While Dutchmen Ruud Gullit and Marco Van Basten were granted much of the glory at Milan, discerning observers recognised Baresi's enormous influence. Not for him the old static sweeper role: Baresi brought the ball through to launch – and join – attacks and help revolutionise Italian tactical theory. He joined Milan in the summer of 1977 while elder brother Giuseppe joined local rivals Inter. Franco made his Italy debut against Romania in 1982 and was a (non-playing) member of the World Cup-winning squad in Spain that same year. Suspension meant he missed Milan's wonderful Champions Cup Final victory over Barcelona in 1994 but he led the club to all their other modern triumphs in World Club Cup, Champions Cup and European Supercup as well as domestic league championship. He had an incident-packed World Cup in 1994 – undergoing knee surgery in the middle of the finals, yet returning to play superbly in the final 0–0 draw against Brazil. Unfortunately, he was one of the two Italians who missed their penalties in the dramatic shoot-out.

Gordon Banks: 1966 World Cup winner

Mario **Basler**

Country: *Germany (born December 18, 1968)*
Position: *Midfielder*
Clubs: *VfL Neustadt-Weinstrasse, Kaiserslautern, Rot-Weiss Essen, Hertha Berlin, Werder Bremen, Bayern Munich*

Basler may be one of the characters of the German game but he has also proved something of a late developer. Kaiserslautern did not rate him as a youngster and gave him away on a free transfer in 1989. Basler's determination to make the grade eventually paid off when he joined Werder Bremen from Hertha Berlin in 1993 for £850,000. He won the German cup in 1994 at the end of his first season with Bremen. He was then the Bundesliga's joint top-scorer in 1995 – with Heiko Herrlich – on 20 goals. Nicknamed Super Mario, he is a specialist at dead-ball situations. He joined Bayern Munich after the finals of the 1996 European Championship.

Cliff **Bastin**

Country: *England (born March 14, 1912)*
Position: *Centre forward*
Clubs: *Exeter City, Arsenal*

In the days before European trophies beckoned, Bastin was a boy wonder who won the three honours available – England cap, FA Cup and League championship – before he was 21. In 1930, at 18 years and 43 days, he was the youngest finalist in Wembley's then brief history, and that record stood until 1958. He won another Cup Final medal and five in the League in addition to playing 21 times for England. He is remembered as a left winger of abundant pace and scoring ability. "Boy" Bastin's club record of 157 goals in 367 League games stood for 50 years until Ian Wright came along. A combination of increasing deafness and the Second World War ended his career prematurely.

Gabriel Omar **Batistuta**

Country: *Argentina (born February 1, 1963)*
Position: *Centre forward*
Clubs: *Newells Old Boys, River Plate, Boca Juniors, Fiorentina (Italy)*

Batistuta was long under-rated by Argentine fans who are used to centre forwards with a more refined technical style. But he was top scorer with six goals when Argentina won the 1991 South American Championship – a haul which earned him a transfer to Italy and Fiorentina. Nicknamed "Batigol" in Florence, he endeared himself to the fans when he insisted on staying with Fiorentina following their shock relegation in 1992 – and scored

Franz Beckenbauer: revolutionary attacking sweeper

the goals which brought them back up to Serie A at the first attempt. He was one of the few Argentine players to do himself justice at the 1994 World Cup, and did even better in the 1998 tournament, scoring a total of five goals as Argentina reached the quarter-finals.

Bebeto (Full name: José Roberto Gama de Oliveira)

Country: *Brazil (born February 16, 1964)*
Position: *Centre forward*
Clubs: *Flamengo, Vasco da Gama, Deportivo de La Coruna (Spain), Vitoria Bahia, Gremio, Botafogo*

Bebeto could have made an international impact long before the 1994 World Cup but for weak temperament and bad luck with injuries. He was predictably nicknamed the New Zico after exploding with Flamengo in 1982 when the real thing was on World Cup duty. He was outstanding when Flamengo won the Rio de Janeiro championship in 1986 and was the club's top scorer for four years in a row. His transfer to Rio rivals Vasco da Gama in 1989 caused a major sensation which was dissipated in Brazil's 1989 South American championship triumph, in which he scored six goals. Bebeto, who used to keep sheep and goats as pets, moved to Europe with Spain's La Coruna in 1993, then scored three goals in Brazil's World Cup triumph a year later. He repeated that number during the 1998 tournament, but this time Brazil were beaten by France in the final.

Franz Beckenbauer

Country: *West Germany (born September 11, 1945)*
Position: *Midfielder/sweeper*
Clubs: *Bayern Munich, Cosmos New York (USA), Hamburg*

Franz Beckenbauer has always been accompanied by the sort of luck which only a personality of his genius might earn. The smile of fate was on him through an illustrious playing career and on into management when – in his first appointment at any level – he took West Germany to the Final of the World Cup in Mexico in 1986 and followed that up four years later with victory itself in Italy. Thus only Kaiser Franz can boast that he has lifted the World Cup as both captain, in 1974, and manager. But Beckenbauer was, above and beyond that, one of the exclusive group of football players to whom the epithet of 'great' most truly applies. He was the first German to reach a century of international appearances before leaving Bayern Munich for spells with New York Cosmos and then with Hamburg, where he wound down his playing career. His honours degree reveals the World Cup in 1974 (runner-up in 1966), the European championship in 1972 (runner-up 1976), the World Club Cup (1976), the European Champions Cup (1974, 1975, 1976), the Cup-winners Cup (1967), and the West German league and cup. He was also a runner-up in the UEFA Cup with Hamburg and a runner-up in the Supercup with Bayern. With New York Cosmos, he also won the NASL Superbowl in 1977, 1978 and

1980. Twice he was voted European Footballer of the Year, in 1972 and 1976. But achievement is not, in itself, sufficient evidence of true greatness. Beckenbauer's innovative strength was through the revolutionary role of attacking sweeper which, with the encouragement of Bayern Munich coach Tschik Cajkovski, he introduced in the late 1960s. The boy Beckenbauer took his first steps on the football ladder with local club Munich 1906 before he switched to Bayern and was first recognised by West Germany at youth level. Within a year of making his league debut with Bayern, as an outside left, he was promoted into the senior national team. The occasion was one to test the nerve of the most experienced player, never mind a fledgling newcomer: West Germany were away to Sweden in a decisive qualifier for the 1966 World Cup and the odds were against them. Yet they won 2–1. West Germany's place in the World Cup finals was all but secured and Beckenbauer's place in the national team was settled for almost a decade. In due course he was voted German Footballer of the Year and European Footballer of the Year. Out on the pitch he was grace and elegance personified, combining an athlete's physique with a computer-like brain for the game which saw gaps before they had opened and goal opportunities – for himself and his team-mates – for which the opposing defence had not prepared. Beckenbauer spent almost all his senior career with Bayern Munich as attacking sweeper. Many critics said he was wasting his talent. But Beckenbauer, in an increasingly crowded modern game, found that the sweeper role provided him with time and space in which to work his magical influence on a match. Not that he shied away from the attacking opportunity when it presented itself. Indeed, West German manager Helmut Schon maintained him in midfield – from which he scored the goal which inspired West Germany's revival against England in the legendary 1970 World Cup quarter-final – far longer than Bayern had done. Beckenbauer moved forward again into midfield during his four years in New York. Cosmos' management believed that the American public would be too naïve to understand why their latest high-profile superstar played defence. Beckenbauer made many friends and admirers in the United States and was long expected to take a central role in their 1994 World Cup wind-up before other interests distracted him. On retiring, he was in demand as a newspaper and television columnist and it was in inviting him to put his words into deeds that he was offered the post of national manager in succession to Jupp Derwall after the disappointing 1984 European championship. The Germans had always promoted managers from within their system. Beckenbauer was an outsider with no coaching experience: his appointment represented a huge gamble not only with his own golden reputation but by DFB president Hermann Neuberger. Six years later the gamble paid off. Such was Beckenbauer's Midas touch that not only were 'his' West Germany crowned world champions in Rome but Beckenbauer's guiding role earned him that other unique place

in history. He retired after the 1990 World Cup triumph only to return to coaching twice – once, briefly and unsuccessful with Marseille, and then again with Bayern to win a German league title and the UEFA Cup in 1996. Already doubling as a club director, he then became Bayern president.

David **Beckham**

Country: *England (born May 2, 1975)*
Position: *Midfielder*
Club: *Manchester United*

Beckham was the outstanding discovery of the 1996–97 season in England – right from the moment, on the opening day of the season, when he scored an extraordinary goal from his own half against Wimbledon. A hatful of powerful long-range goals won him a place in England's World Cup squad while, simultaneously, Beckham starred in Manchester United's Champions League campaign. Ironically, he had been born in Leytonstone and had been on Tottenham's books as a youth player. Beckham, however, had always wanted to play for United and he turned professional at Old Trafford in 1992. His fortunes, however, took a nosedive when he was sent off during England's crunch 1998 World Cup match with Argentina after a petulant retaliation having been fouled. He was criticized by many for his moment of madness, but if he can control his temperament, then the footballing world is his oyster.

David Beckham: Hot-headed, but brilliant, youngster

Radek **Bejbl**

Country: *Czech Republic (born August 29, 1972)*
Position: *Midfielder*
Clubs: *Slavia Prague, Atletico Madrid (Spain)*

Bejbl was one of the international discoveries of the 1996 European Championship finals in England. He lacked the pace and creativity of team-mate Patrik Berger but offered, by contrast, strength in the tackle and reliability which was a key factor in the Czech Republic's progress to runners-up spot at Euro 96. Having just helped Slavia to win the league title for the first time in 49 years, Bejbl was lured away to Spain by Atletico Madrid's eccentric president, Jesus Gil.

Ivan **Bek**

Country: *Yugoslavia and France (born October 29, 1909)*
Position: *Inside forward*
Clubs: *BSK Belgrade (Yugoslavia), Sète (France)*

A place in history as one of the earliest and most outstanding exports should be granted to Bek. An inside right, he had played only once for Yugoslavia, despite scoring 51 goals in 50 games for BSK Belgrade, when he moved to France with FC Sète in 1927. He proved a hugely popular forward in the French championship and was recalled by Yugoslavia for the 1930 World Cup finals in Uruguay. His professional experience in France proved crucial and he scored three goals in three games before the Slavs' semi-final defeat by Uruguay, Later, now known in his adopted homeland as Beck, he played four times for France between 1935 and 1937. He died in Sète in 1963.

Igor **Belanov**

Country: *Soviet Union (born September 25, 1960)*
Position: *Right winger*
Clubs: *Kiev Dynamo, Borussia Mönchengladbach (Germany)*

Had the magazine *France Football* changed their rules a decade earlier, Igor Belanov would not have become European Footballer of the Year in 1986. If voting had been open among all players of any nationality in Europe, then the 1986 award would have been a walkover for Diego Maradona – then starring with Napoli at club level while inspiring Argentina's World Cup triumph. But Belanov was, that year, the European hit of the finals. In fact, he was lucky to have made the finals at all. Belanov had been called up in the spring of 1986 by Eduard Malofeyev but he was sacked on the eve of the finals and managerial successor Valeri Lobanovski turned the squad upside-down. The fact that Lobanovski worked with Belanov at Kiev tipped the

balance in his favour. He duly repaid Lobanovski with a string of sensational performances. Belanov scored in the initial 6–0 thrashing of Hungary which set the Soviets off towards the top of the group, then scored a superb hat-trick in the dramatic 4–3 extra time defeat by Belgium in the second round. Two years later he helped the Soviets finish runners-up at the 1988 European Championship but his career – and private life – went rapidly downhill after a transfer to Borussia Mönchengladbach.

Miodrag **Belodedici**

Country: *Romania (born May 20, 1964)*
Position: *Sweeper*
Clubs: *Steaua, Crvena Zvezda Beograd [Red Star] (Yugoslavia), Valencia (Spain), Valladolid (Spain), Villarreal (Spain)*

Belodedici became the first man to win the Champions Cup with two clubs – Steaua in 1986 and Red Star in 1991. Born in a small village on the Serbian border, he was brought up in Romania and starred as sweeper in Steaua's 1986 Champions Cup victory over Barcelona. He made his Romania debut against China in 1984 but then sought asylum in Yugoslavia in December, 1988. After diplomatic wrangling he joined Red Star and was duly invited to play again for Romania. He refused in 1990, fearing possible recriminations, but after the collapse of the Ceascescu regime, Belodedici was happy to make a comeback in 1992 He was considered by FIFA's technical commission one of the best sweepers on view at the 1994 World Cup finals when Romania made it through to the quarter-finals, having beaten Argentina 3–2 in the second round, only to cruelly lose on penalties to Sweden.

Ferenc **Bene**

Country: *Hungary (born December 17, 1944)*
Position: *Centre forward*
Clubs: *Kaposzvar, Ujpest Dozsa*

Bene was first capped in 1962 but did not explode on the international scene until two years later when he finished top scorer with 12 goals in Hungary's victory at the Tokyo Olympic Games. A versatile attacker, he played centre forward for Ujpest Dozsa but usually outside right for Hungary because of the presence of Florian Albert. Three times Bene was the Hungarian league's leading scorer and he won the championship four times with Ujpest. In 1966 he was an outstanding member of the Hungarian team which scored a famous 3–1 victory over Brazil at Goodison Park, Liverpool during the World Cup. Hungary lost 2–1 to the Soviet Union in the quarter-finals, but Bene's consolation was having scored once in each of their four matches, including the famous 3–1 win against Brazil.

Patrik **Berger**

Country: *Czech Republic (born November 10, 1973)*
Position: *Midfielder*
Clubs: *Slavia, Sparta, Borussia Dortmund (Germany),*
Liverpool (England)

The greatest natural talent discovered in Czech football in the 1990s, Berger originally played in the youth sections of Sparta Prague, but the club did not offer him a professional contract and he joined old rivals Slavia instead. Twice league championship runner-up with Slavia, he was transferred in the summer of 1995 to Borussia Dortmund and played a key role in 1995–96 as Dortmund reached the quarter-finals of the UEFA Champions League. He scored four times in the Czech Republic's Euro 96 qualifying campaign and also claimed their goal in the Final defeat by Germany. He transferred afterwards to Liverpool but enjoyed only fitful success.

Dennis **Bergkamp**

Country: *Holland (born May 10, 1969)*
Position: *Centre forward*
Clubs: *Wilskracht SNL Amsterdam, Ajax, Internazionale (Italy),*
Arsenal (England)

Named after his father's football hero, Denis Law; (the registrar refused to accept the spelling with one 'n' because it was considered similar to the girl's name, Denise), he made his League debut for Ajax at 17 in a 2–0 home win against Roda in December 1986. His teenage talent was so obvious he made his European club debut for Ajax in a match against Malmö for which he had to fly out on the day of the game after sitting school examinations the previous afternoon. A Dutch cup winner in 1987 and 1993, he won the Cup-winners Cup with Ajax in 1987 and was voted Dutch Young Player of the Year in 1990. Two years later he won the UEFA Cup with Ajax before repeating the feat with Internazionale in 1994. He was a member of the Dutch squad at the finals of the 1992 European Championship and 1994 World Cup. Transferred jointly from Ajax to Inter in 1993 for £8 million, he failed to adapt to the football and lifestyle in Italy and left for Arsenal in the summer of 1995. Three years later he was an inspirational figure in Arsenal's League and Cup double-winning side – although injury kept him out of the decisive last league games and the FA Cup Final victory over Newcastle. Bergkamp was voted 1998 Footballer of the Year by the English Football Writers' Association. Although his injury hadn't fully healed by the time of the World Cup in France, Bergkamp still played an active part in Holland's campaign and, although not firing on all cylinders, he scored the goal of the tournament against Argentina in the quarter-final win.

Dennis Bergkamp: was destined to star in England

Orvar **Bergmark**

Country: *Sweden (born November 16, 1930)*
Position: *Right back*
Clubs: *Orebro, AIK Solna, Roma (Italy)*

Bergmark was one of the great European full-backs of the 1950s and early 1960s. He began with Orebro in 1949 as a centre forward but quickly converted to full-back and made his debut there for Sweden in 1951. He was voted best right back at the 1958 World Cup finals, in which his steady play helped the hosts reach the final against Brazil. Bergmark also had a spell in Italy with Roma before retiring with a then-record 94 caps for his country. He was appointed manager of Sweden in 1966 and guided them to the 1970 World Cup finals. One of his players then was Tommy Svensson, who would emulate him as World Cup boss in 1994.

Vladimir **Beschastnykh**

Country: *Russia (born April 1, 1974)*
Position: *Centre forward*
Clubs: *Moscow Spartak, Werder Bremen (Germany), Santander*

Burst on the scene at 18 with two goals for Spartak in the Russian Cup final against CSKA (one of his first games for Spartak) in 1992 . Became Russian champion with Spartak in 1993 and 1994. He has a twin brother, Mikhail, who was sold by Spartak to Nizhni Novgorod. Vladimir left Spartak for Werder in 1994 and scored ten goals in his first season, but he found it difficult to adapt to the coaching change at Werder Bremen when Otto Rehhagel left. Personal difficulties added to his problems in adapting to both the football and lifestyle in Germany and he transferred to Spain with Santander.

George **Best**

Country:	Northern Ireland (born May 22, 1946)
Position:	Centre forward
Clubs:	Manchester United, Fulham, Hibernian (Scotland), Tampa Bay Rowdies (USA)

George Best is proof that appearances at the World Cup finals are not necessary for greatness to be perceived. It was Best's unfortunate international luck that his great years fell in between Northern Ireland's own finest eras – marked by the World Cups first of 1958, then of 1982 and 1986. Apart from being perhaps the greatest free talent ever to grace the British game, he was also a symbol of a new era. He was nicknamed El Beatle in Spain, in the days when footballers began moving towards pop star popularity with the high-wage incomes denied their predecessors opening the doors to a fast-lane image of smart cars and pretty girls. In a sense, that is unfair to Best who possessed almost unbounded natural talent which could take him nimbly, yet at high speed, through the most disciplined defence. He was twice a League Championship winner with Manchester United – his only club at the top of an explosive career – as well as an inspiration in the Champions Cup win of 1968. Best was twice a League winner with United, also collecting the 1968 European Footballer of the Year award. Within a year, however, the pressures of fame and fortune had begun to wear him down and after a spell at Fulham, he made a string of short-lived comebacks in Scotland and Ireland, before delighting audiences in the ill-fated North American Soccer League. Even into his 50s, however, he found himself the centre of much attention.

Oliver **Bierhoff**

Country:	Germany (born May 1, 1968)
Position:	Centre forward
Clubs:	Essener SG, Schwarz-Weiss Essen, Bayer Uerdingen, Hamburg, Borussia Monchengladbach, Austria Salzburg (Austria), Ascoli (Italy), Udinese (Italy), Milan (Italy)

Germany's golden goal hero in the final of the 1996 European Championship against the Czech Republic, Bierhoff had also scored the Germans' first goal after appearing as a second-half substitute. Previously he had been capped eight times at under-18 level, four times at under-19 and ten times at under-21. Earned selection with his goalscoring successes in Austria and Italy rather than in Germany. His three goals during the 1998 World Cup were not enough to prevent Germany exiting the tournament at the quarter-final stage in a 3–0 defeat against Croatia .

Slaven **Bilic**

Country:	Croatia (born September 11, 1968)
Position:	Central defender
Clubs:	Hajduk Split, Sibenik, Hajduk Split, Karlsruhe (Germany), West Ham United (England), Everton (England)

George Best: the first footballing "pop star"

The only university graduate in the Croatia squad at the 1996 European finals – having qualified as a lawyer – Bilic won one national championship and two national cups while with Hajduk Split. He was appointed captain during his first season with Karlsruhe and was also picked in the German 1994–95 Bundesliga "Team of the Season". Bilic then moved to England to play his football, ending up with Everton. Despite a superb World Cup for Croatia as a whole, Bilic achieved some unwanted notoriety during the finals after a theatrical dive in the semi-final clash with France resulted in French idol Laurent Blanc receiving a red card and a two-match ban, hence ruling him out of the final with Brazil.

Franz "Bimbo" **Binder**

Country: *Austria and Greater Germany (born December 1, 1911)*
Position: *Centre forward/inside forward*
Clubs: *St Polten, Rapid Vienna*

Binder was a prolific marksman from centre or inside forward and is popularly considered to have been the first European player to have topped 1,000 goals in his first-class career. When he retired in 1950 to become manager of his old club, Rapid, he claimed career figures of 1,006 in 756 games. Binder was Rapid's greatest player in the 1930s, playing 20 times for Austria before being selected nine times for Greater Germany after the Anschluss of 1938. Ironically, his greatest achivement for Rapid was in the 1941 Greater German Championship Play-off, when he scored a hat-trick against Schalke in Rapid's 4–3 victory. Later he coached not only Rapid but also the Austrian national team.

Billy **Bingham**

Country: *Northern Ireland (born August 5, 1931)*
Position: *Outside right*
Clubs: *Glentoran, Sunderland (England), Luton (England), Everton (England), Port Vale (England)*

Long before establishing himself as a World Cup manager, Bingham was an outstanding outside right. Fast and clever, he played 56 times for his country, having moved to England in 1950 with Sunderland after a fine display for the Irish League against the Football League. He was a member of the "Bank of England" side at Roker and played more than 200 league games before being sold to Luton, with whom he gained an FA Cup runners-up medal against Nottingham Forest in 1959. Almost 18 months later he moved to Everton before winding down in the Potteries. Bingham duly became national manager of Greece as well as Northern Ireland, for whom he had appeared at the 1958 World Cup finals in Sweden and then managed to the 1982 and 1986 finals in Spain and Mexico respectively.

Joachim **Björklund**

Country: *Sweden (born March 15, 1971)*
Position: *Central defender*
Clubs: *IFK Gothenburg, Brann Bergen, Vicenza, Rangers*

Björklund was a member of the Swedes' under-21 side which lost narrowly to Italy in the 1992 European final (2–1 on aggregate). Quick to cover, firm in the tackle, he earned a place at the heart of Sweden's defence through sheer talent and not because he was the nephew of the then national manager Tommy Svensson. His favourite club as a boy were Leeds United, but when he moved to British football in 1996 it was with Rangers' with whom he won the Scottish league title in 1997.

Laurent **Blanc**

Country: *France (born November 19, 1965)*
Position: *Sweeper*
Clubs: *Ales, Montpellier, Napoli (Italy), Nîmes, Saint Etienne, Auxerre, Barcelona (Spain), Marseille*

One of the most accomplished defenders in Europe after having begun his career as an attacking midfielder – the position in which he made his France debut in 1989 against the Republic of Ireland. His top-scoring season was 1986–87, with 18 goals in 34 games for Montpellier. He made his top division debut in July 1987 and was a European under-21 championship winner with France in 1988. He won the French cup in 1990 with Montpellier, had a spell in Italy, then returned to Auxerre in July 1995 before joining Barcelona after Euro 96. Blanc scored the goal which provided France with an impressive victory over Germany in Stuttgart on the eve of Euro 96, and scored the 114th -minute golden goal against Paraguay in the second round of the 1998 World Cup that kept France's bandwagon on course. Blanc was at his commanding best during the tournament, but was cruelly deprived of playing in the final after being unjustly sent off in the semi-final against Croatia.

Danny **Blanchflower**

Country: *Northern Ireland (born February 10, 1926)*
Position: *Right half*
Clubs: *Barnsley (England), Aston Villa (England), Tottenham (England)*

Blanchflower, who died aged 67 in December 1993, was the brains behind Northern Ireland's remarkable 1958 World Cup success and Tottenham Hotspur's excellent team of the early 1960s. A League and Cup double was followed by another Cup and the Cup-winners Cup, with Blanchflower's cerebral approach blending perfectly with the more robust style of wing half partner

Dave Mackay. In the days when few sportsmen appeared on TV, the loquacious Blanchflower was a media darling, always entertaining and forthright in speech or in print. As so often with gifted players, however, his foray into management, with Chelsea, was an anti-climax.

Danny **Blind**

Country: *Holland (born August 1, 1961)*
Position: *Sweeper*
Clubs: *Racing Club Souburg, Sparta Rotterdam, Ajax*

Experienced central defender who began his career as a right back with Sparta Rotterdam. After his transfer to Ajax, he won 16 titles including Dutch champion five times, cup-winner three times and Dutch Supercup-winner three times. He captained Ajax to victory in the 1995 Champions Cup Final against Milan in Vienna, but was unlucky in the Cup-winners Cup: he missed Ajax's final victory in 1987 against Lokomotiv Leipzig through injury and was sent off in their 1988 defeat by Mechelen. Many considered him fortunate to have been available for the 1995 Champions Cup Final after he was shown only a yellow card for a glaring handball offence in the second semi-final against Bayern Munich. With Ajax he also won the UEFA Cup in 1992, the Champions Cup and World Club Cup in 1995 and the European Supercup in 1996. For many years he was Ronald Koeman's deputy as sweeper in the national team.

Oleg **Blokhin**

Country: *Soviet Union (born November 5, 1952)*
Position: *Left winger*
Clubs: *Kiev Dynamo, Vorwarts Steyr (Austria)*

If Oleg Blokhin had been playing in the 1990s, it is highly unlikely that he would have risen to the achievement level possible during his own playing career. That is the ironic perspective now cast through events more political than sporting. In the mid-1970s Blokhin was the star player for Kiev Dynamo from the Ukraine who were the dominant club force in Soviet football. Kiev provided the Soviet national team virtually *en bloc*, plus the Olympic team. They regularly won the domestic championship and were provided with all the financial subsidies necessary from Moscow to compete on equal terms with the likes of Ajax and Bayern. Blokhin was both their top scorer and their quickest attacking raider – thanks to the training tips of his friend and fellow-Ukrainian Valeri Borzov, the Olympic sprint champion. Blokhin's key role in Kiev's Cup-winners Cup triumph of 1975 earned him the European Footballer of the Year accolade. He went on to play in the World Cups of 1982 and 1986, having by then become the first Soviet player to top a century of

international appearances (he ultimately totalled 39 goals in 109 games). Real Madrid once tried to prise him out of the Soviet game but failed. By the time he was "freed" to move west with Vorwarts Steyr of Austria, he was past his best. He stayed in the West to develop a successful career as a coach in Greece.

Steve **Bloomer**

Country: *England (born January 20, 1874)*
Position: *Inside forward*
Clubs: *Derby County, Middlesbrough, Derby County*

England's most famous player before the First World War, with records lasting much longer. His 352 League goals were not exceeded until the 1930s; his 28 goals for his country, in only 23 games, were not surpassed until the 1950s. Bloomer was of medium height and slightly built, often the target for unscrupulous defenders equipped with heavy boots and desperate intent. But he survived, thanks to agility and a sharp brain, through 22 years until the start of the First World War. He was Derbyshire born and bred, and a Derby County player throughout his career apart from a four-year spell with Middlesbrough. After his retirement in 1914, he took a coaching job in Germany and when war broke out he was interned for the duration - but still managed to play football.

Alen Boksic: Croatian star of Euro 96

Zvonimir **Boban**

Country: *Croatia (born October 8, 1968)*
Position: *Midfielder*
Clubs: *Dinamo Zagreb, Bari (Italy), Milan (Italy)*

A member of the former Yugoslavia national team which won the 1987 World Youth Cup in Chile, he was Dinamo Zagreb's youngest-ever captain at 18. Boban became a national hero after he came to the defence of Croat fans being manhandled by police at a high-tension match in the former Yugoslav league between Dinamo (now FC Croatia) and Crvena Zvezda (Red Star). He was suspended for six months by the former Yugoslav federation. That suspension cost him a place in the former Yugoslavia squad at the 1990 World Cup finals, but he was to avenge the ban eight years later when he captained Croatia to their first-ever World Cup finals. Boban was inspirational as Croatia surpassed all expectations, finishing third and boosting the previously fragile self-esteem of the country's people.

Winston **Bogarde**

Country: *Holland (born October 22, 1970)*
Position: *Left back*
Clubs: *Sparta, Alexandria '66 (Rotterdam), SVV, Excelsior, SVV, Sparta, Ajax, Milan (Italy), Barcelona (Spain)*

Bogarde was a teenage talent who made his league debut at 17 for SVV in a 2–2 draw away to Heracles. He played as a left winger at Sparta, became a defender at Ajax, but had to revert to his old position in the 1995–96 UEFA Champions League because of Marc Overmars's knee injury and the ineligibility of Peter Hoekstra. With Ajax, he was a Dutch league champion in 1995 and 1996 and winner of the Dutch Supercup and European Champion Clubs' Cup in 1995 – the same year he was also a member of the Ajax squad which won the World Club Cup and European Supercup. Bogarde moved to Milan in the summer of 1997 on a free transfer courtesy of the Bosman ruling but did not stay long, soon rejoining his old Ajax mentor, Louis Van Gaal, at Barcelona.

Alen **Boksic**

Country: *Croatia (born January 31, 1970)*
Position: *Centre forward*
Clubs: *Hajduk Split, Cannes (France), Marseille (France), Lazio (Italy), Juventus (Italy), Lazio (Italy)*

Boksic's international career – and ambition to play in Italy – began early. He travelled to Rome at the age of 12 to play for Hajduk in a youth tournament. The only souvenir he bought was a Lazio shirt – the club for whom he later played. He won one Yugoslav cup with Hajduk, scoring the only goal in a 1–0 win over Crvena Zvezda [Red Star] in Belgrade. Spent his first season in France under suspension because of complications in his original transfer to Marseille with whom he later won the French league and cup and Champions Cup. Boksic was Footballer of the Year in Croatia for 1993 when he was also top scorer in France with 23 goals. Transferred to Juventus – as successor to Chelsea-bound Gianluca Vialli – after Euro 96 but returned after only one season to Lazio, helping them to reach the 1998 UEFA Cup Final and win the Italian cup, but missing the World Cup finals because of injury.

Zbigniew **Boniek**

Country: *Poland (born March 3, 1956)*
Position: *Centre forward*
Clubs: *Zawisza Bydgoszcz, Widzew Lodz, Juventus (Italy), Roma (Italy)*

Boniek was the greatest Polish player of all time despite being a member of the generation that followed the outstanding side of the early- to mid-1970s. His talents shone in succeeding World Cups and in European club competition with Juventus. He made his name with Widzew Lodz and his hat-trick against Belgium in the 1982 World Cup finals persuaded Juventus to splash out £1.1 million for his services. Boniek scored Juve's winner in the 1984 Cup-winners Cup Final defeat of FC Porto and was a member of the side which won the Champions Cup a year later against Liverpool in the shadow of the Heysel disaster. He scored 24 goals in 80 internationals.

Giampiero **Boniperti**

Country: *Italy (born July 4, 1928)*
Position: *Centre forward/inside forward*
Club: *Juventus*

Boniperti enjoyed a meteoric rise, being signed by Juventus from minor club Momo in July 1946 and being promoted only four months later to the Italian national team in a 5–1 defeat by Austria in Vienna. Originally a centre-forward, he later switched to inside forward and played right wing for FIFA's World XI against England in 1953 (he scored twice in a thrilling 4–4 draw). Boniperti won five Italian league titles with Juventus, for whom he played a record 444 league games. He was a "father figure" in the Charles/Sivori team of the 1950s and scored eight goals in 38 internationals. He retired to a business career which turned full circle when he became the hugely successful president of Juventus in the 1970s and 1980s under the powerful Agnelli family's patronage.

Maxime **Bossis**

Country: *France (born June 26, 1955)*
Position: *Left back/central defender*
Clubs: *Nantes, Racing Club*

Bossis was an outstanding, no-nonsense left back and later central defender in the French national team which contributed so much entertainment and excitement at international level in the 1980s. Bossis was discovered by Nantes, staying from 1973 until 1985 when he was transferred, amid controversy, to the newly-reformed Racing Club of Paris in the second division. He held his national team place despite self-imposed relegation and led Racing into the top flight in his first season. Bossis also earned an unwanted place in World Cup history as the man who missed the decisive penalty in the semi-final shoot-out against West Germany in Spain in 1982. His consolation was to help win the European Championship on home turf in Paris two years later.

Jozsef **Bozsik**

Country: *Hungary (born September 28, 1929)*
Position: *Right half*
Clubs: *Kispest, Honved*

Right half in the Magical Magyars side of the 1950s, Bozsik rates among the very greatest players of all time. He was a team-mate of Ferenc Puskas with Kispest and then Honved, providing both midfield brains as well as spectacular goals, including one from 30 yards in the historic 6–3 win over England at Wembley in 1953. Bozsik made his debut for Hungary against Bulgaria in 1947, returned home – unlike team-mates Puskas, Kocsis and Czibor – after the 1956 Revolution and combined a career as footballer with that of MP. In 1962 he scored a goal against Uruguay in a friendly to mark his 100th and last game for his country. Bozsik was a member of Hungary's victorious Olympic side at Helsinki in 1952.

Raymond **Braine**

Country: *Belgium (born April 28, 1907)*
Position: *Centre forward*
Clubs: *Beerschot, Sparta Prague (Czechoslovakia), Beerschot*

Not until the advent of Paul Van Himst in the 1960s did Belgium produce a player to rival or emulate Braine in hero status. He was only 15 when he made his league debut for Beerschot and was chosen, that same year, for a Belgian XI against Holland. Clapton Orient of London tried to sign the striker in 1928 but could not obtain a work permit for him to come to England. Braine wanted to turn professional in Belgium but the federation

Branco: feared for his deadly free kicks

refused him permission so he went to Czechoslovakia to play for the great Sparta Prague club instead. The Czechs wanted Braine to take citizenship and play for them in the 1934 World Cup but he preferred to stay Belgian. He appeared at the 1938 World Cup finals with Belgium after returning home to play for Beerschot. His centre forward talents earned him selection for Western Europe against Central Europe in 1938 and then for Europe against England that same year. He won 54 caps for Belgium.

Branco (Full name: Claudio Ibrahim Vaz Leal)

Country: *Brazil (born April 4, 1964)*
Position: *Left back*
Clubs: *Fluminense, Brescia (Italy), FC Porto (Portugal), Genoa (Italy), Fluminense, Flamengo, Middlesbrough (England)*

Branco possessed one of the most fearsome right-foot shots in the world game in the 1980s and 1990s. He made his name with Rio giants Fluminense, then took with both hands the chance offered to play left back for Brazil at the 1986 World Cup. Branco was snapped up by Italy's Brescia, only to leave after two seasons following the club's relegation. He stayed on in Europe, in Portugal and then back in Italy, before returning home to Fluminense ahead of the 1994 World Cup. Lucky, initially, to squeeze into the squad he ended up in the starting line-up for the final against Italy, after the suspension of first-choice Leonardo, and picked up a winners' medal Flirted briefly and surprisingly with English football at Middlesbrough in 1996 in the twilight of his career.

Rune **Bratseth**

Country: *Norway (born March 19, 1961)*
Position: *Central defender*
Clubs: *Rosenborg Trondheim, Werder Bremen (Germany)*

Bratseth, Norway's most complete footballer of all time, was the defensive commander of their 1994 World Cup campaign having previously masterminded Werder Bremen's victory in the 1992 Cup-winners Cup. He began with Rosenborg Trondheim, did not turn even part-time professional until he was 23, then moved to Germany in December, 1986. He cost Bremen only £65,000 but he was twice nominated as the best foreigner in the German league. Bratseth made his Norway debut in a 2–1 win over Grenada in St George's on a Caribbean tour in February, 1986. A trained teacher, he led a Bible-study group in Bremen attended by a number of team-mates and their wives. On retiring from German football, he returned home as manager of Rosenborg.

Andreas **Brehme**

Country: *West Germany (born November 9, 1960)*
Position: *Midfielder/left back*
Clubs: *Kaiserslautern, Bayern Munich, Internazionale (Italy), Zaragoza (Spain), Kaiserslautern*

Brehme earned his niche in football history by converting West Germany's controversial match-winning penalty against Argentina in the 1990 World Cup Final. He retired from the national team after the 1992 European Championships shock final defeat against Denmark, but was persuaded to come back by national manager Berti Vogts in time for the 1994 World Cup finals where Germany struggled in the heat of the USA. Uncompromising in the tackle, Brehme was long considered one of the most effective left backs in the world despite spending much of his time supporting attacking moves. He was already based in Italy, with Inter at the time of the 1990 World Cup. Two years later he left for Zaragoza but fell out with the club in mid-season and returned to Germany with his first club, Kaiserslautern. He aptained them to a remarkable league title triumph in 1998 before retiring.

Paul **Breitner**

Country: *West Germany (born September 5, 1951)*
Position: *Left back/midfielder*
Clubs: *Bayern Munich, Real Madrid (Spain), Eintracht Braunschweig, Bayern Munich*

Breitner was "discovered" for West Germany by Helmut Schon in 1970. An adventurous, skilled left back, he was a key figure in the new era founded on Bayern Munich and also featuring Franz Beckenbauer, Sepp Maier, Uli Hoeness and Gerd Muller. Breitner demonstrated his big-match temperament by nervelessly converting the penalty which brought West Germany level in the 1974 World Cup Final against Holland. A footballing intellectual, he considered he was being stifled at Bayern and moved forward to midfield on transferring to Real Madrid. A personality clash meant he missed the 1978 World Cup, returning in 1982 to score the Germans' consolation goal in their defeat by Italy in the final on his old home ground in Madrid.

Billy **Bremner**

Country: *Scotland (born December 9, 1942)*
Position: *Midfielder*
Clubs: *Leeds (England), Hull (England), Doncaster (England)*

Bremner began as a right winger with Leeds, partnered at inside forward by a man nearly twice his age in Don Revie. A decade later, midfield tiger Bremner and manager Revie were outstanding figures as Leeds came from decades of mediocrity to be a force feared throughout the game. Bremner's fierce tackling, competitive spirit and selfless example made him a merited winner of various medals, though the list of second places was much longer. Not a prolific scorer but a useful one, with the winner in each of three FA Cup semi-finals, he also won 55 caps, including the 1974 World Cup, when Scotland were eliminated after three matches without defeat.

Billy Bremner: a good partnership with Don Revie

Tomas **Brolin**

Country: Sweden (born November 29, 1969)
Position: Centre forward
Clubs: GIF Sundsvall, Parma (Italy), Leeds (England),
FC Zurich (Switzerland), Crystal Palace (England)

Brolin exploded on to the international scene by scoring twice on his Sweden debut in a 4–2 win over Wales in the spring of 1990. He followed up with two more against Finland to earn a late call into Sweden's World Cup team. He was outstanding at Italia 90, though the team were disappointing and were quickly eliminated. His displays alerted Italian clubs and Parma immediately bought him. He starred for Sweden at the 1992 European Championship – scoring a marvellous solo goal against England – and then helped Parma to their first European success in the 1993 Cup-winners Cup. A year later Brolin was one of the major figures at the 1994 World Cup finals, scoring three goals and creating havoc by roaming across the breadth of attack from a nominal role wide on the right in midfield. A serious ankle injury, suffered against Hungary in the 1996 European Championship qualifiers, effectively wrecked his career. He was never the same player again, his reputation scarred by problems with bosses Nevio Scala at Parma and then Howard Wilkinson and George Graham at Leeds United. He was briefly caretaker assistant-manager at London club Crystal Palace in the spring of 1998, but was released after the club's relegation out of the Premier League, having spent most of the season overweight and struggling with the pace of the English Premiership.

Trevor **Brooking**

Country: England (born October 2, 1948)
Position: Midfielder
Club: West Ham (England)

Brooking became an institution in English football – even having a street named after him – first through his loyal service to West Ham United and the England national team, then through his broadcasting work for the BBC. Brooking, an old-school inside left, came up through the West Ham apprentice system and earned representative honours at England junior and League level. West Ham have never been noted for trophy-collecting but Brooking picked up FA Cup-winner medals twice in five years (the club has only won the competition on three occasions) – first against Fulham in 1975, then against overwhelming favourites Arsenal in 1980, when a rare Brooking header provided the winner for the then second division club. He played 47 times for England but injury, sadly, restricted him to only one appearance in the World Cup finals – as a substitute against hosts Spain in the 1982 second round.

Guido **Buchwald**

Country: West Germany (born January 24, 1961)
Position: Central defender/midfielder
Clubs: Stuttgart Kickers, VfB Stuttgart, Urawa Red Diamonds (Japan), Karlsruhe

Buchwald began as an orthodox defender but ended up as midfield "minder" to Andy Möller at the 1994 World Cup finals before winding down his career in Japan. Originally Buchwald, who won 76 caps, progressed up the league ladder with minor clubs SV Wannweil, TSV Pliezhausen and Stuttgart Kickers before moving into the Bundesliga with Stuttgart in 1983. A year later he made his national team debut in the 1–0 win over Italy in Zurich which marked FIFA's 80th anniversary. Injury cost him his place at the 1986 World Cup and 1988 European championship but the 1990 World Cup provided ample consolation when he was hailed by national manager Beckenbauer as "our best player."

Bulent Korkmaz

Country: Turkey (born November 24, 1968)
Position: Central defender
Club: Galatasaray

Bulent was the most consistent Turkish international in the 1990s – having made his national team debut in 1990 against the Republic of Ireland. Domestic honours included multiple league, cup and President's cup successes with Galatasaray, his only club. Earlier he was also an up-and-coming member of the Galatasaray team which reached the Champions Cup semi-finals in 1989.

Emilio **Butragueno**

Country: Spain (born July 22, 1963)
Position: Centre forward
Clubs: Castilla, Real Madrid, Atletico Celaya (Mexico)

Butragueno won the Prix Bravo as Europe's best young player in 1985 and 1986 and made a scoring debut for Spain in a World Cup qualifying victory over Wales in 1984. Yet he was once considered not good enough by Real Madrid's youth coaches. Fortunately, nursery club Castilla had second thoughts and Butragueno became "leader" of Madrid throughout the 1980s. His close control and marksmanship helped Madrid win the UEFA Cup in 1985 and 1986. The same year Butragueno, nicknamed The Vulture, became a World Cup sensation when he scored four times for Spain in a five-goal thrashing of Denmark in the second round of the finals in Mexico. After leaving Real Madrid, he vowed never to play for another Spanish

Emilio Butragueno: penalty box "vulture"

club and went back to Mexico, scene of his 1986 World Cup success, with Atletico Celaya. Became a cult figure before retiring in the spring of 1998.

Roger **Byrne**

Country: *England (born February 8, 1929)*
Position: *Left back*
Club: *Manchester United*

Byrne was captain and left back of the Manchester United "Busby Babes" team which was torn apart in the Munich air disaster of 1958. He was one of eight players killed, a loss not only to his family and friends and club but to his country: Byrne was a fixture at left back for England and was expected to prove a defensive pillar at the World Cup finals a few months further on in Sweden. He had joined United originally as an outside left but quickly switched to defence where he won the first of his 33 caps against Scotland in 1954. He won three league championship medals and captained United in their ill-starred FA Cup Final defeat by Aston Villa in 1957.

Antonio **Cabrini**

Country: *Italy (born October 8, 1957)*
Position: *Left back*
Clubs: *Atalanta, Juventus*

Cabrini was hailed, almost overnight, as the "new Facchetti" when, after having appeared in only 22 games at left back for Juventus, he was selected by national manager Enzo Bearzot for the 1978 World Cup finals in Argentina. Four years later Cabrini made a luckless piece of history when, against West Germany, he became the first man to miss a penalty in a World Cup Final. But he deserves to be remembered for his all-round abilities which saw him established as both an outstanding defender and tackler. He won almost every honour in the game during a decade of service with Juventus.

Jorge Paulo **Cadete**

Country: *Portugal (born August 27, 1968)*
Position: *Centre forward*
Clubs: *Santarem, Sporting Clube, Brescia (Italy), Sporting Clube, Celtic (Scotland), Celta Vigo (Spain)*

Rose to fame at Sporting under the coaching direction of Bobby Robson, who appointed him captain. Cadete was the league's top scorer with 18 goals for Sporting in 1992–93. Played in Italy in 1994–95 but could not save Brescia from relegation. Strangely, he played in only one of Portugal's matches in the 1996 European Championship qualifying competition – appearing as a 66th-minute substitute for Domingos in Portugal's last game – and scored the final goal in the final minute of the 3–0 win over the Irish Republic. He was top scorer for Celtic with 25 goals in 1996–97 before returning to Iberian football with Celta Vigo.

Jose Antonio **Camacho**

Country: *Spain (born June 8, 1955)*
Position: *Full back*
Club: *Real Madrid*

Defence, traditionally, has never been Real Madrid's greatest strength, but Camacho came as near as any of the club's modern defenders to putting that right. A combative left back originally, Camacho was promoted through the youth ranks in the mid-1970s and later served club and country in central defence and also at right back. He was nearly lost to the game after suffering a serious knee ligament injury in training in 1978. The injury cost him a place at the 1978 World Cup finals as well as 18 months out of his career. But he made a remarkable recovery and went on to amass a then-record number of 81 international appearances for Spain. After retiring, he quickly earned a reputation as a disciplinarian coach.

Rodion **Camataru**

Country: *Romania (born June 22, 1958)*
Position: *Centre forward*
Clubs: *Universitatea Craiova, Dinamo Bucharest, Charleroi (Belgium)*

Camataru was a bluff, determined centre forward who, in 1986–87, won the Golden Boot awarded to Europe's top league marksman amid controversial circumstances. He totalled 44 goals but many of them were scored in a string of "easy" matches towards the end of the season and revelations after the collapse of the Communist regime cast doubt on the integrity of the matches. Not that this detracted from Camataru's abilities which were rewarded, even in the twilight of his career, with selection for the 1990 World Cup finals. He scored more than 300 goals in Romanian league football before transferring to Belgium towards the end of his career.

José Luis Perez **Caminero**

Country: *Spain (born November 8, 1967)*
Position: *Midfielder*
Clubs: *Castilla, Valladolid, Atletico Madrid, Valladolid*

Caminero started with Real Madrid but they sold him to Valladolid because his route from nursery side Castilla to the first team was blocked by Michel. He was then converted to sweeper at Valladolid by coach Francisco Maturana before signing for Atletico in a £1 million move in 1993. He made his international debut in September 1993 as a substitute in a 2–0 friendly win over Chile in Alicante and followed it up by scoring Spain's first goal in his next match against Albania. Despite being suspended from the second-round win over Switzerland, he was Spain's three-goal top scorer at the 1994 World Cup.

Jorge **Campos**

Country: *Mexico (born October 15, 1966)*
Position: *Goalkeeper*
Clubs: *UNAM, Atlante, Los Angeles Galaxy (USA), Chicago Fire (USA)*

Campos was one of the great personalities of the 1994 World Cup finals. Formerly a forward, Campos still occasionally plays up front. He was once top scorer for UNAM in the Mexican league and was used as a substitute forward by the national team in the 1993 CONCACAF Gold Cup. His taste for garishly-coloured jerseys has landed him in trouble with the Mexican federation which has several times ordered him to wear more sober attire. Born in Acapulco, he was named the third-best goakeeper in the world in 1993 by a German soccer magazine despite his unorthodox style. On the launch of Major League Soccer he proved a major drawing card for expatriate Mexican fans, first in Los Angeles, then in Chicago. He starred for Mexico during their 1998 World Cup run when they reached the second round before losing in the dying minutes to Germany.

Claudio Paul **Caniggia**

Country: *Argentina (born January 9, 1967)*
Position: *Centre forward*
Clubs: *River Plate, Verona (Italy), Atalanta (Italy), Roma (Italy), Benfica (Portugal), Boca Juniors*

Caniggia was one of the most intriguing stars of the 1994 World Cup, having completed only weeks earlier a 13-month suspension after he tested positive for cocaine abuse in Italy. He marked his return to duty with a goal in a 3–0 friendly win over Israel in Tel Aviv. However, a muscle strain forced him out of the World Cup on the eve of the second-round defeat by Romania. Caniggia began with River Plate, moving to Italy in 1988. His flying pace was one of Argentina's few redeeming features at the 1990 World Cup when he scored the quarter-final winner against Brazil and headed a decisive semi-final equaliser against Italy. Caniggia also collected a second yellow card of the event for hand-ball. Suspension meant he missed the final and, without him, Argentina had nothing to offer in attack. A dope-test failure led to his sudden departure from Roma and he led Benfica's attack in the UEFA Champions League before returning home to Argentina with Boca Juniors.

Eric **Cantona**

Country: *France (born May 24, 1966)*
Position: *Centre forward*
Clubs: *Martigues, Auxerre, Marseille, Bordeaux, Montpellier, Leeds (England), Manchester United (England)*

Cantona will go down as one of football's great paradoxes, his career a mixture of glorious success and disciplinary disaster. Born in Marseille, he was discovered by Auxerre, sold to Marseille for £2 million in 1988 and scored two months later on his international debut against West Germany. Later he was banned for a year from the national team for insulting manager Henri Michel, then bounced controversially to Bordeaux, Montpellier and Nîmes before quitting the game after a shouting match with yet another disciplinary commission. Sheffield Wednesday offered him a trial but it was neighbours Leeds whom

Eric Cantona: a popular Frenchman

he joined. He played a crucial role in their 1992 League title win then repeated the magic twice for Manchester United, whom he captained to their 1996 League and Cup double. Not only that, but Cantona scored the winning goal in the final against Liverpool. He could not stay clear, however, of disciplinary trouble. First he incurred a lengthy European ban for insulting a referee after the final whistle of a Manchester United game against Galatasaray in Turkey. Then he drew a seven-month suspension – plus a criminal sentence – for attacking a fan with a kung-fu kick at Selhurst Park after having been sent off. At one stage Cantona was also captain of France but national coach Aime Jacquet later thought his presence might compromise team spirit. Cantona retired suddenly in the summer of 1997, to launch a new career as an actor. He landed several small parts in French films, but missed the greater chance of glory of being part of the 1998 French team which won the World Cup on home soil.

Antonio **Carbajal**

Country: *Mexico (born June 7, 1929)*
Position: *Goalkeeper*
Clubs: *Espana, Leon*

Carbajal remains a figure of legend and history in Mexico and within the annals of the World Cup. He achieved a record when, at the 1966 World Cup in England, he became the only man to have appeared in no fewer than five finals tournaments. A tall, agile goalkeeper, he played for Mexico in the 1950 finals in Brazil, in Switzerland in 1954, in Sweden in 1958 and in Chile in 1962. The 1966 finals provided an appropriate retirement point, since Carbajal had made his international debut at the 1948 London Olympic Games. On his return he signed professional forms with Leon and played for them until his retirement in 1966. Later he became a respected and popular coach and was presented with FIFA's gold award for services to the world game.

Careca (Full name: Antonio de Oliveira Filho)

Country: *Brazil (born October 5, 1960)*
Position: *Centre forward*
Clubs: *Guarani, Sao Paulo, Napoli (Italy), Hitachi (Japan)*

Careca proved the ideal successor in the Brazilian centre-forward line of Ademir, Vava and Tostao in the 1980s and early 1990s. Born in Brazil's Campinas state, he helped unrated Guarani win the 1987–88 national championship and was later sold to Sao Paulo. He missed the 1982 World Cup after being cruelly injured in training on the eve of the finals. He made superb amends with five goals in Mexico in 1986 and was subsequently voted Brazil's Sportsman of the Year. Careca's performance during Mexico made him the target of several clubs and he was soon transferred to Italy's Napoli. His attacking partnership with Diego Maradona quickly bore fruit and lifted Napoli to new heights, winning the 1989 UEFA Cup and 1990 Italian league championship. Careca quit Brazil's World Cup squad in the spring of 1993 to start a new career in Japan.

Johnny **Carey**

Country: *Republic of Ireland (born February 23, 1919)*
Position: *Full back*
Club: *Manchester United (England)*

Carey was one of the earliest top-class, all-purpose players – at home as full back, wing half, inside forward, even as deputy goalkeeper. A calming influence, who was short on pace but long on perception, his transfer for just £200 from a Dublin junior club to Manchester United was one of the transfer bargains of all time. He captained the fine Manchester United team of the early post-war years, when they won one League and one Cup and narrowly missed several more. During an international career that earned him 37 caps, Carey scored three goals and led the Rest of Europe selection against Great Britain in 1946. He later managed Blackburn (twice), Everton – sacked in the back of a taxi when fifth in the table – Leyton Orient and Nottingham Forest.

Carlos Alberto Torres

Country: *Brazil (born July 17, 1944)*
Position: *Right back*
Clubs: *Fluminense, Santos, Botafogo, Fluminense, Cosmos New York (USA)*

Carlos Alberto – not to be confused with Saudi Arabia's World Cup coach – secured his own place in football legend at the 1970 World Cup finals. Not only was he captain of the Brazilian team which achieved a historic third World Cup triumph, but he put the seal on a glorious achievement with a thrilling fourth and final goal in the 4–1 defeat of Italy in the Estadio Azteca in Mexico City. Carlos Alberto began his professional career in the juniors of Fluminense in Rio de Janeiro – winning his first league title in 1964 when "Flu" broke Botafogo's three-year grip on the Carioca championship. That same year he made his Brazil national team debut in a 5–1 win over England at Maracana. In 1965 he joined Pele at Santos, helping them collect a hat-trick of Sao Paulo league titles, but just missed out on selection for the 1966 World Cup squad. In 1970, however, there was no question that he was not only the best right back in Brazil but the best in the world. He later went on to play for Botafogo and Fluminense again before helping Pele launch the American soccer dream at Cosmos in the mid-1970s.

Amadeo **Carrizo**

Country: *Argentina (born June 12, 1926)*
Position: *Goalkeeper*
Clubs: *River Plate, Alianza (Peru), Millonarios (Colombia)*

Carrizo set a string of longevity records in a goalkeeping career which lasted from the mid-1940s to the mid-1960s. A dominant character with great personality, Carrizo played 520 Argentine league matches over 21 seasons until he was 44. He won five league championships with River Plate in the early 1950s and played in the 1958 World Cup finals in Sweden. Carrizo was blamed for Argentina's 6–1 defeat by Czechoslovakia but was recalled two years later with great success when Argentina beat England and Brazil to win the 1960 "Little World Cup" in Brazil. After ending his career in Argentina he played on in Peru and Colombia before returning home to coach youth teams.

Pierluigi **Casiraghi**

Country: *Italy (born March 4, 1969)*
Position: *Centre forward*
Clubs: *Monza, Juventus, Lazio, Chelsea (England)*

Casiraghi made his international debut in 1991 against Belgium but had to wait to establish himself because of a long-running rivalry with Fabrizio Ravanelli. His height and strength earned him many comparisons with a traditional English centre forward and he ultimately fulfilled his apparent destiny by transferring to Chelsea in the summer of 1998 where he linked up with several compatriots. He learned football under Arrigo Sacchi at Monza in the mid-1980s, moving in 1989 to Juventus with whom he won the UEFA Cup twice and the Italian cup once. Transferred in 1993 to Lazio with whom he won the Italian cup again in 1998 and finished, a few weeks later, as UEFA Cup runner-up.

Cha Bum-kun: Korea's finest footballing export

Carlos **Caszely**

Country: *Chile (born July 5, 1950)*
Position: *Centre forward*
Clubs: *Colo Colo, Levante (Spain), Colo Colo*

Caszely inspired Colo Colo to become the first Chilean club to reach a final of the South American Club Cup. He was an outstanding inside forward in the early 1970s, but his loudly-proclaimed left-wing political beliefs placed him at risk after the revolution which overthrew President Allende in 1973. Thus he moved to Spain with Levante. Caszely played for Chile in the 1974 World Cup finals in West Germany and then again eight years later in Spain. By this time, the political situation had eased back home and he had returned to Chile with Colo Colo

Jan **Ceulemans**

Country: *Belgium (born February 28, 1957)*
Position: *Centre forward/midfielder*
Clubs: *Lierse, Club Brugge*

Ceulemans, who cost Brugge a then-record domestic fee of £250,000 in the summer of 1978, was the backbone of Belgium's national team throughout the 1980s, first as a striker, then as a midfield general. He began with Lierse and in 1980 scored 29 of Brugge's league title-winning 76 goals to earn the accolade of Footballer of the Year for the first time. A year later Ceulemans was poised to join Milan but his mother persuaded him to stay in Belgium, a decision he never regretted. Ceulemans played with distinction in the Belgian team which finished fourth at the 1986 World Cup finals in Mexico. He scored 26 goals in a record 96 internationals for his country.

Cha **Bum-kun**

Country: *South Korea (born May 21, 1953)*
Position: *Left winger/midfielder*
Clubs: *Darmstadt (Germany), Eintracht Frankfurt (Germany), Bayer Leverkusen (Germany)*

Cha ranks as the finest South Korean player for his record at the peak of the European game in the West German Bundesliga. Here he was a popular fixture from 1978, when he arrived at Darmstadt, until his retirement in 1986 after appearing at his first and last World Cup finals. Cha, who won the UEFA Cup with Eintracht Frankfurt in 1980 and with Leverkusen in 1988, was ignored by his country after moving to Germany. Recalling him for duty at Mexico 86 demanded a major diplomatic exercise. Original Korean records claimed an astonishing 141 international appearances for Cha but this was later reduced to the more probable 41. He returned to the World Cup as South Korea's national coach in 1998, but was sacked before the final game, as the team failed to impress.

Stephane **Chapuisat**

Country: *Switzerland (born June 28, 1969)*
Position: *Centre forward*
Clubs: *Red Star Zurich, Lausanne-Sports, Malley, Lausanne-Sports, Bayer Uerdingen (Germany), Borussia Dortmund (Germany)*

Son of a former Swiss international defender, Pierre-Albert Chapuisat, and grandson of a former top division player, Stephane was the first of the new Swiss generation of players to move abroad in 1990. Nicknamed The Little Prince after the leading character of a popular story, he moved to Germany in 1991 with Uerdingen and transferred to Dortmund a year later, helping them reach the 1993 UEFA Cup Final. He was then regarded as the top foreigner in the Bundesliga. He was voted the 1994 Swiss Footballer of the Year in 1994 but a serious knee ligament injury within the same week sidelined him until February 1996. He was, nevertheless, German league champion with Borussia Dortmund in 1995 and 1996, led Switzerland's attack at the 1996 European Championship finals and won the World Club Cup and UEFA Champions League Cup with Dortmund in 1997.

John **Charles**

Country: *Wales (born December 27, 1931)*
Position: *Centre forward/centre half*
Clubs: *Leeds (England), Juventus (Italy), Leeds (England), Roma (Italy), Cardiff (Wales)*

The Gentle Giant set a Leeds record of 42 goals in one season while also playing as a dominant centre defender for his country. He matched great skill with an awesome physique and great presence on the ball and was one of the first British exports to Italy, in 1957. For a long time he could also be considered as having been the best export. The £67,000 fee, a record for a British player, bought Juventus a player who became a legend and helped to win the Serie A title three times in five years, scoring 93 times in 155 games. After some unhappy final seasons he became a non-league manager, publican and shopkeeper.

Bobby **Charlton**

Country: *England (born October 11, 1937)*
Position: *Inside left/outside left/centre forward*
Clubs: *Manchester United, Preston*

A knighthood was the inevitable ultimate reward for Charlton's career at the apex of English international football. He remains probably the most famous English footballer to ever thrill a crowd and his name is synonymous with the highest traditions

Stephane Chapuisat: overcame knee injuries

of sportsmanship and integrity. Long after he had finished playing, his reputation worked wonders in breaking down the tightest security at World Cups and European championships. It only needed a player or manager to glance out and see Charlton arriving for barred doors and gates to be flung open. Football was always in the blood. The Charltons – Bobby and World Cup-winning brother Jackie – were nephews of that great Newcastle United hero of the 1950s, Jackie Milburn. They began their careers in the back streets of Ashington in the north-east of England and Charlton fulfilled every schoolboy's dream when, at just 17, he was signed by Manchester United. Matt Busby had invested more time and determination than any other manager in seeking out the finest young talents in the country. Not only Charlton but Duncan Edwards, Eddie Colman, David Pegg and many more had been singled out for the Old Trafford treatment, turned from boys into young footballing men under the tutelage of assistant Jimmy Murphy and then released to explode into the English First Division. This was the philosophy behind the Busby Babes, the team of youngsters who took the league by storm in the mid-1950s and brought a breath of optimistic fresh air into an austere post-war England. It was that sense of added loss which intensified the national grief when United's airliner crashed in the snow at the end of a runway in Munich on their way home from a European Champions Cup quarter-final in

Bobby Charlton: knighted for services to football

Belgrade in February 1958. Charlton had established his first-team potential the previous season. He was initially an inside right, later switched to outside left with England and finally settled as a deep-lying centre forward, using his pace out of midfield and thunderous shot to score some spectacular goals. One such goal marked his England debut against Scotland; another broke the goalless barrier against Mexico on England's way to winning the 1966 World Cup (and also won him the accolade of European Footballer of the Year). Dozens more of his goals inspired Manchester United's post-Munich revival. The search for the holy grail of the European Champions Cup was finally concluded at Wembley in 1968, when United beat Benfica 4–1 after extra time. Charlton, appropriately, scored two of the goals and carried off the cup as United captain. Then, as now, he was the perfect ambassador for the game, not merely in England but at the highest international level.

Jack **Charlton**

Country: *England (born May 8, 1935)*
Position: *Central defender*
Club: *Leeds United*

The elder brother of Bobby and a total footballing contrast. Where Bobby was a thrilling attacking inspiration, Jack was a no-nonsense central defender. Yet it was not until shortly before his 30th birthday that Charlton was offered his first England cap after injury to Maurice Norman. Once in place, Charlton forged an ideal partnership with Bobby Moore. At club level, Charlton was one of the pillars of Don Revie's controversially successful Leeds United, winning the league, FA Cup, League Cup and Fairs Cup. Charlton retired at 37, went into management at Middlesbrough, Sheffield Wednesday and Newcastle United before returning to the international arena as boss of the Republic of Ireland, and proving a highly successful manager, making the most of their limited resources while guiding them to two successive World Cups in 1990 and 1994.

Stanislav **Cherchesov**

Country: *Russia (born September 2, 1963)*
Position: *Goalkeeper*
Clubs: *Spartak Vladikavkaz, Lokomotiv Moscow, Spartak Moscow, Dynamo Dresden (Germany), Spartak Moscow, Tirol (Austria)*

Cherchesov started with Spartak but became frustrated after four years as reserve to Rinat Dasayev and transferred to Lokomotiv in 1988. Returned to Spartak Moscow in 1989 after Dasayev's sale to Seville and conceded five goals in his first game. A reserve to Dmitri Kharine at the 1992 European Championship finals in Sweden for the Commonwealth of Independent States, he won three national titles with Spartak in 1989, 1992 and 1993. Had a first farewell game organised in his honour when he left Spartak for Dresden in 1993. Returned to Spartak in the summer of 1995 on a six-month loan from Dresden to help his old club win their first-round group in the UEFA Champions League. He was bought from Dresden by Tirol and left Spartak in 1995.

José Luis **Chilavert**

Country: *Paraguay (born July 27, 1965)*
Position: *Goalkeeper*
Clubs: *Sportivo Luqueno, Zaragoza (Spain),*
Velez Sarsfield (Argentina)

Chilavert emerged as one of the most powerful personalities of South American football in the late 1990s, his aggressive approach to goalkeeping carrying his influence way beyond his own penalty area. After playing at home in Paraguay and then in Spain, he achieved his greatest success in Argentina with Velez Sarsfield of Buenos Aires – displaying a remarkable ability to score goals himself from free kicks and penalties. His success in this dual role helped earn him awards as the 1997 South American Footballer of the Year and World Goalkeeper of the Year. He attributes his goalscoring success to the fact that, for a big man, he has small feet. He scored his most famous free-kick goal against Argentina in the 1998 World Cup qualifying competition. Once in France, Chilavert led by example throughout the pool stage, conceding just one goal in three matches as the Paraguans remained unbeaten and made it through to the second round. In a tight, tense affair against the hosts, France, Chilavert inspired his defence to repel the French attacks until, in the 24th minute of extra-time, a golden goal by Laurent Blanc shattered the dreams of Chilavert.

Igor **Chislenko**

Country: *Soviet Union (born January 4, 1939)*
Position: *Centre forward*
Clubs: *Moscow Torpedo, Moscow Dynamo*

Chislenko was only 5ft 7in but, in the 1960s, was one of Europe's most dynamic outside or inside rights. Having started his career with the Moscow Torpedo youth section, he transferred to Dynamo at 17 and played 300 league games, winning two league titles. Chislenko, also a good ice-hockey player, appeared at the World Cups of 1962 and 1966 as well as in the European Nations Championship in between. He was the best Soviet forward in the 1966 World Cup and their prospects of reaching the final disappeared when he was sent off during the semi-final against West Germany.

Hector **Chumpitaz**

Country: *Peru (born April 12, 1944)*
Position: *Central defender*
Club: *Sporting Cristal*

Chumpitaz, an inspirational captain and centre back, was long considered to have held the world record for international appearances with 147 matches to his credit. These claims were later discounted on the grounds that Peru played only 110 matches in his time. But he was a wonderful leader of his country and starred in the World Cup finals of both 1970 and 1978. The first time he was a promising youngster; on the second occasion he was an experienced, resilient organiser of an otherwise fragile defence. Chumpitaz played all his senior career with Sporting Cristal of Lima and appeared around 100 times for his country between his debut in 1966 and the six-goal thrashing by Argentina which ended Peru's 1978 World Cup campaign in controversial fashion.

John **Collins**

Country: *Scotland (born January 31, 1968)*
Position: *Midfielder*
Clubs: *Hibernian, Celtic, Monaco (France), Everton (England)*

Collins's home town of Galashiels in the Scottish Borders is more renowned for producing rugby players, but Collins was a football fanatic and he scored on his debut for Scotland against Saudi Arabia in Riyadh in 1988. Renowned for his "dead ball" striking

John Collins: benefited from Bosman ruling

ability, Collins was the only player to have appeared in all Scotland's matches in the European Championship – in both the qualifying competition and the finals. Afterwards he took advantage of the Bosman ruling moving on a free transfer to Monaco. He scored Scotland's opening goal of the 1998 World Cup, in the 2–1 defeat against Brazil.

Mario Esteves **Coluna**

Country: *Portugal (born August 6, 1935)*
Position: *Inside left/midfielder*
Clubs: *Deportivo Lourenço Marques (Mozambique), Benfica*

Coluna commanded the Portuguese national team which reached the World Cup semi-finals in 1966 and was midfield general of Benfica's outstanding club side in the 1960s. Born in Mozambique, he was the local long-jump record-holder when he was lured away by Benfica to play football in 1954. Originally a centre forward, he was converted to inside left and then midfield by Benfica and won 73 caps for Portugal. In both Benfica's 1961 and 1962 Champions Cup Final victories, he scored with typically spectacular long-range efforts. He later turned to coaching and became Sports Minister in Mozambique.

Gianpiero **Combi**

Country: *Italy (born December 18, 1902)*
Position: *Goalkeeper*
Club: *Juventus*

Considerably pre-dated Dino Zoff (circa 1982) as goalkeeper and captain of the Italian team which won the 1934 World Cup. Indeed, Combi, who also played for Juventus, was considered Italy's best goalkeeper until Zoff came along. He was beaten seven times by Hungary in Budapest in his first international in 1924 and did not regain a regular place in Italy's team until the Paris Olympics of 1928. He was goalkeeper in Juventus' four consecutive league title successes of 1931 to 1934, the year when he retired – immediately after captaining Italy to victory over Czechoslovakia in the World Cup Final in Rome.

Nestor **Combin**

Country: *France (born December 29, 1940, in Argentina)*
Position: *Centre forward*
Clubs: *Lyon, Juventus (Italy), Varese (Italy), Torino (Italy), Milan (Italy), Metz, Red Star Paris*

Combin was born of French emigré parents in Las Rosas, Argentina, where he was discovered by a local scout for French outfit Lyon. They gambled on this unknown and were profitably rewarded. Combin's centre forward play, supplied by the inspiration of Fleury Di Nallo, brought Lyon victory in the 1963 French cup. That success was followed by a call-up for France and a 1964 transfer to Juventus. He was overawed by his new surroundings and could not cope with a tactical squabble between Omar Sivori and coach Heriberto Herrera. In 1969 he joined Milan and collected the World Club Cup – along with a fearsome physical battering at the hands of his original Argentine compatriots from Estudiantes de La Plata.

Bruno **Conti**

Country: *Italy (born March 13, 1955)*
Position: *Right winger/midfielder*
Clubs: *Roma, Genoa, Roma*

Italy's right winger proved a crucial influence in the 1982 World Cup triumph, even though it was the reformed teammate Paolo Rossi who stole the headlines for most of the tournament. Conti's counter-attacking pace helped Italy step up their game to outplay Argentina and Brazil in a frightenly competitive second stage and go on via a semi-final 2–0 stroll past Poland to a 3–1 victory in the final over West Germany. Despite his World Cup winners' medal, Conti had struggled to make an impression in the early years of his career, but was rescued by Swedish coach Nils Liedholm, who brought him back from a loan spell with Genoa and turned him into one of the most consistently effective creative players in Italy. He scored five goals in 47 internationals between his debut against Luxembourg in 1980 and the second-round defeat by France at the 1986 World Cup that marked the end of his international career. One of the lowlights of his career came in the 1984 European Cup Final when his club AS Roma lost to Liverpool on penalties, and he blasted his spot kick high and wide.

Henri "Rik" **Coppens**

Country: *Belgium (born April 29, 1930)*
Position: *Centre forward*
Clubs: *Beerschot, Charleroi, Crossing Molenbeek, Berchem, Tubantia*

Coppens was the "*enfant terrible*" of Belgian football in the 1950s, a centre forward or occasional outside left of great goal-scoring talent who carried his aggression over into his dealings with team-mates, clubs and other officials. He began with Beerschot as a ten-year-old, and scored twice and made Beerschot's two other goals on his debut in a crucial relegation match at 16. Three times he was the league's leading scorer and ended his career with a then-record total of 217 goals. He once scored six goals in one game against Tilleur and played 47 times for Belgium.

Wilf **Copping**

Country: *England (born August 17, 1907)*

Position: *Central defender*

Clubs: *Leeds, Arsenal*

Copping was renowned as the original "Iron Man" because of his strong tackling in the 1930s when he formed a wing half partnership with Jack Crayston which many consider the best in Arsenal's history. A Yorkshire miner, he turned professional with Leeds in 1930 after being turned down by local club Barnsley. He made 159 league appearances before moving to Highbury for £8,000 in 1934, by which time he had already won six England caps. In five seasons at Arsenal he won two championships and the FA Cup. His further 13 England caps included perhaps his finest performance in the 3–2 victory over World Cup-holders Italy on home ground at Highbury in November 1934.

Alberto da **Costa Pereira**

Country: *Portugal (born December 12, 1929)*

Position: *Goalkeeper*

Club: *Benfica*

Costa 'Pereira, with 24 caps, was another of Portugal's great discoveries in the African colonies. He was born in Nacala, Mozambique, and joined Benfica in 1954. He was a tower of strength in their biggest triumphs, though prone to the odd error when the pressure was off. He won seven league titles with Benfica and played in four Champions Cup Finals – the victories of 1961 and 1962 and the defeats of 1963 and 1965. In the latter game, against Internazionale on a quagmire of a pitch in Milan, he was injured early in the game and had to leave the pitch. He retired soon after to take up coaching. Not to be confused with the José Pereira who kept goal at the 1966 World Cup.

Alessandro "Billy" **Costacurta**

Country: *Italy (born April 24, 1966)*

Position: *Central defender*

Clubs: *Monza, Milan*

Italy's key man in the centre of defence after the international retirement of Franco Baresi. Also played a central role in the successes of the great Milan side of the last decade. He made his international debut in Arrigo Sacchi's first game in charge – a 1–1 European Championship draw with Norway in Genoa in November, 1991. Remarkably, suspensions meant he missed both Milan's 1994 Champions Cup Final victory over Barcelona and Italy's 1994 World Cup Final clash with Brazil.

Johan **Cruyff**

Country: *Holland (born April 25, 1947)*

Position: *Centre forward*

Clubs: *Ajax Amsterdam, Barcelona (Spain), Los Angeles Aztecs (USA), Cosmos New York (USA), Levante (Spain), Ajax, Feyenoord*

Johan Cruyff stands as not merely the greatest Dutch footballer but one of the greatest players of all time – a status which owes much to the persistence of his mother. She worked as a cleaner in the offices of the Ajax club and persuaded the coaching staff to take Johan into their youth sections when he was still only 12 years old. The rest is history and a virtually unbroken 25-year succession of trophies and awards as first player and then coach. Cruyff made his first-team debut at 17, his goal-scoring international debut at 19 and went on to inspire Ajax and Holland throughout most of the 1970s, the era of "total football". Nominally he played as a centre-forward, but his perception of the position was as unorthodox as the squad No 14 he wore on his back for most of his career with Ajax. He did turn up at the apex of the attack: but he was also to be found meandering through midfield and out on the wings, using his nimble, coltish pace to unhinge defences from a variety of angles and positions. Single-handed, he not only pulled Internazionale of Italy apart in the 1972 Champions Cup final but scored both goals in Ajax's 2–0 win. The next year he inspired one of the greatest 20-minute spells of football ever seen in Belgrade as Ajax overcame another Italian outfit, Juventus. Already the vultures were gathering. Spain had reopened their borders to foreign players and eventually Barcelona won the transfer race. He cost a then-world record of £922,000 and such was the magnitude of the deal that the federation bent its own regulations so Cruyff could play immediately. When he arrived in Barcelona, the Catalans were struggling down the table. By the end of term they were champions, Cruyff's triumphant progress having included a spectacular 5–0 victory away to deadly rivals Real Madrid. Surprisingly, apart from that league title, Barcelona won little else though Cruyff himself completed the first-ever hat-trick of European Footballer of the Year awards (in 1971, 1973 and 1974). It was at the end of his first season with Barcelona that Cruyff's career reached its international zenith. At the 1974 World Cup finals Holland took their total football through round after round. No-one could follow the mercurial Cruyff who inspired victories over Uruguay and Bulgaria in the first round, then provided two goals to lead the way against Argentina in the second. The last group match – in effect the semi-final – was against Brazil: old masters against the new. Cruyff scored Holland's decisive second goal in a 2–0 victory which signalled a new era. The final, of course, ended in defeat against West Germany and, though Holland reached the final again in

1978, Cruyff had by then retired from the European game and headed to the USA. First he joined the Los Angeles Aztecs in the NASL, winning the Most Valuable Player award, before moving to Washington Diplomats in 1980 and, late in 1981, returned to Holland to win the championship twice more with Ajax and once with old rivals Feyenoord. Cruyff's move into management, typically, aroused new controversy since he had never bothered to obtain the necessary examination qualifications. Not that it mattered. He guided Ajax to the Cup-winners' Cup in 1987. Then, after returning to Barcelona, he repeated the trick with the Catalan giants in 1989, adding four successive Spanish league titles and the European Champions Cup in 1992. His tactical innovations caused as much fuss as the total football concept of his playing days. Although ousted at Barcelona in the spring of 1996, Cruyff ranks one of the game's greatest players, personalities and innovators.

Teofilo **Cubillas**

Country: *Peru (born March 8, 1949)*
Position: *Centre forward*
Clubs: *Alianza, Basel (Switzerland), FC Porto (Portugal), Alianza, Fort Lauderdale Strikers (USA)*

Cubillas was a powerfully-built inside left, who secured an ideal partnership with the more nimble Hugo Sotil in Peru's 1970 World Cup. Eight years later, in the 1978 finals in Argentina, he re-emerged as an attacking director. Cubillas also packed a powerful shot, scoring one memorable goal against Scotland in the 1978 finals. He was not particularly successful in Europe where he grew homesick, but in Peru he remained a living legend after a career which brought 38 goals in 88 internationals and an appearance for the World XI in the 1978 Unicef charity match.

Kenny Dalglish: first Scot to top 100 caps

Zoltan **Czibor**

Country: *Hungary (born August 23, 1929)*
Position: *Outside left*
Clubs: *Ferencvaros, Csepel, Honved (Hungary), Barcelona (Spain), Espanol (Spain)*

Czibor, with natural pace and a powerful shot, was outside left in the great Hungarian team of the early 1950s. He played 43 times for the Magical Magyars – including the 1954 World Cup Final – before taking self-imposed exile in Spain after the Hungarian Revolution of 1956. Czibor and team-mate Sandor Kocsis were persuaded to sign for Barcelona and enjoyed five more years in the international spotlight, reaching a climax when Barcelona, most unluckily, lost to Benfica in the 1961 Champions Cup Final. He had a short spell with neighbours Espanol and eventually returned home in retirement to live in Hungary.

Martin **Dahlin**

Country: *Sweden (born April 16, 1968)*
Position: *Centre forward*
Clubs: *Lund, Malmo, Borussia Mönchengladbach (Germany), Roma (Italy), Borussia Mönchengladbach (Germany), Blackburn Rovers (England)*

Dahlin became the first black player to appear in a senior international for Sweden when he made his debut in the 1–1 draw with Brazil in Stockholm in July, 1991. He followed up with some spectacular goals for club and country but then had his career halted by a broken leg. In the spring of 1992 he was sold to Borussia but found it hard work adapting to higher standards of technique and fitness in Germany. He played a decisive goal-scoring role in Sweden's 1994 World Cup qualification and then in the finals themselves. After being linked with clubs all over Europe, he finally left Borussia for Roma but failed to secure a first-team place and returned briefly to Borussia on his way to trying his luck in England with Blackburn Rovers.

Kenny **Dalglish**

Country: *Scotland (born March 4, 1951)*
Position: *Centre forward*
Clubs: *Celtic, Liverpool (England)*

Hero of Parkhead, Anfield – twice over – and Ewood Park, Dalglish is the most successful personality in the English game. He has won 26 major trophies as player and manager, in addition to 102 caps (a record for Scotland) and 30 goals (joint-top with Denis Law). Dalglish's signing for Celtic was their other coup – aside from their European triumph – in 1967. He inspired the club to more great deeds before joining Liverpool for £440,000 in 1977 as a replacement Kevin Keegan. From being a very good player, he became legendary at Anfield, with initial pace, excellent control and the priceless gift that so few have, appearing to exist in his own cocoon of time and space. He guided them to the league-and-cup double as player-manager in 1986; then, after a brief "retirement," returned to management to guide Blackburn Rovers to their first league title in 81 years. In January 1997 he re-emerged from a second managerial "retirement" to take over the Newcastle challenge in the wake of Kevin Keegan's controversial retirement. Fans and media criticised his more pragmatic approach but he took Newcastle into the 1997–98 UEFA Champions League and to the 1998 FA Cup Final.

Edgar Steven **Davids**

Country: *Holland (born March 13, 1973)*
Position: *Midfielder*
Clubs: *Schellingwoude (Amsterdam), Ajax, Milan (Italy), Juventus (Italy)*

Davids has made good and bad headlines throughout his career since making his Ajax league debut in a remarkable 5–1 win over RKC in September 1991. He was a Dutch league champion with Ajax in 1994 and 1995 as well as Dutch cup winner in 1993 and Supercup winner in 1993, 1994 and 1995. He also helped the Amsterdam club to win the World Club Cup, European Champions Cup and European Supercup in 1995 and the UEFA Cup in 1992. He was beaten to a place in Holland's 1994 World Cup squad by Rob Witschge of Feyenoord but forced his way into the team for the European finals in 1996, and scored the vital goal against Yugoslavia in the 1998 World Cup that took the Dutch into the quarter-finals. Davids had taken advantage of the Bosman ruling to move on a free transfer to Milan but that had been marred when he broke a leg in the spring of 1997. He transferred, in mid-season 1997–98, to Juventus with whom he duly finished UEFA Champions League runner-up.

Frank **De Boer**

Country: *Holland (born May 15, 1970)*
Position: *Central defender*
Clubs: *De Zouaven, Ajax*

Frank De Boer, twin brother of club-mate Ronald, has played more than 300 games for Ajax since making his debut in 1988–89 and has played more than 50 times for his country, including the finals of the 1992 European Championship and the 1994 World Cup. He likes to advance for the occasional goal attempt and has succeeded Ronald Koeman as the national team's free-kick specialist. A late injury ruled him out of the finals of the 1996

Dixie Dean: record unlikely to be beaten

European Championship in England – where Holland missed him greatly – but he was prominent throughout the 1998 World Cup, particularly in the semi-final defeat against Brazil where he was in outstanding form.

Ronald **De Boer**

Country: *Holland (born May 15, 1970)*
Position: *Midfielder*
Clubs: *De Zouaven, Ajax, FC Twente, Ajax*

Twin brother of defender Frank De Boer. The twins' early careers developed in tandem, apart from 18 months when Ronald played for Twente while Frank stayed with their original club, Ajax. He made his league debut in a remarkable 6–4 Ajax victory over Pec Zwolle in November 1987. De Boer was a Dutch league champion with the club in 1990, 1994, 1995, 1996 and 1998, as well as a Dutch cup winner in 1993 and 1998 and winner of the Champions Cup in 1995. He was also a member of the Ajax squad which won the 1995 World Club Cup and European Supercup. Voted Dutch Footballer of the Year in 1994 and 1996, De Boer can play in a variety of positions but prefers right midfield. Former Ajax coach Louis Van Gaal used him as centre forward, right wing, left wing and even, briefly, right back. He enjoyed a fine World Cup in France, scoring twice in the pool matches as Holland reached the semi-final stage.

Dixie **Dean**

Country: *England (born January 22, 1907)*
Position: *Centre forward*
Clubs: *Tranmere, Everton, Notts County*

Dean's achievements are all the more remarkable considering that, as a teenager, he fractured his skull as well as undergoing major abdominal surgery. Yet he then began his international career by scoring two, three, two, two and three goals in consecutive matches which, even in days of lax defence and the old offside rule, earned a place in the Hall of Fame. The curly-topped striker was 20 at the time, and still only 21 when he surpassed the record of Middlesbrough striker George Camsell's 59 goals in a single season. On the last day of the 1927–28 season, he had 57 goals to his credit as Everton faced the visit of Arsenal. The Gunners took the lead after only two minutes, but Dean equalized a minute later and his second before half-time brought him level with Campsell's record. With less than ten minutes of the match remaining, the crowd feared their hero was going to miss out on the record, but in the 82nd minute Dean headed the ball into the net to notch his 60th goal of the season. Overall, he scored 18 goals in 16 England appearances, 47 in 18 other representative matches which were so popular in pre-television days, 28 in 33 cup-ties and 379 in 438 League games.

Alessandro Del Piero: Champions League top-scorer

Marc **Degryse**

Country: *Belgium (born September 4, 1965)*
Position: *Centre forward*
Clubs: *Antwerp, Club Brugge, Anderlecht, Sheffield Wednesday (England), PSV Eindhoven (Holland)*

Degryse is one of Belgium's senior internationals, having won more than 70 caps to add to his earlier appearances at youth, under-21 and Olympic level. He started his top-flight career with Antwerp, moving on to Brugge – where he was voted Players' Player of the Year – and then to Anderlecht for a domestic record £1.5 million in 1989. He repaid them by scoring 50 goals in the next four years. Degryse was an uncapped member of the 1984 European Championship squad but then starred at the 1986 and 1990 World Cup finals. Had an 18-month spell in England with Sheffield Wednesday before joining PSV.

Alessandro **Del Piero**

Country: *Italy (born November 9, 1974)*
Position: *Centre forward/midfielder*
Clubs: *Padova, Juventus*

The new "boy wonder" of Italian soccer made his league debut for Juventus in a 1–1 away draw with Foggia in September 1993 – then marked his first full league season with a hat-trick against Parma. Made his international debut in the 4–1 Euro 96 qualifying win against Estonia on March 25 1995 in Salerno. Has been kept busy ever since in league and cup and UEFA Champions League as well as playing for Italy at senior, under-21 and military level. Scored in each one of Juventus' first five games in their 1995–96 Champions League group and went on to help them win the Cup. He was runner-up then with Juventus in both 1997 and 1998 – when he was the UEFA Champions League top scorer with ten goals. An ankle injury sustained late in the season for Juventus, restricted Del Piero to a bit-part role in the 1998 World Cup finals.

Luis **Del Sol** Cascajares

Country: *Spain (born April 6, 1935)*
Position: *Inside forward*
Clubs: *Betis, Real Madrid, Juventus (Italy), Roma (Italy)*

Del Sol was midfield motor in the legendary Real Madrid side which overwhelmed Eintracht Frankfurt in the 1960 European Champions Cup Final. He was then inside right but, as an aggressive midfielder, had been a wing half at his home-town club, Betis of Seville, when Madrid decided that the great Brazilian Didi was not fitting in well enough alongside Alfredo

Di Stefano. Del Sol was hurriedly bought in the middle of the 1959–60 season, but was sold in 1962 to Juventus to raise the cash for a vain attempt to buy Pele from Santos. Del Sol was a pillar of the Italian league, consistently reliable and inspirational through eight seasons with Juventus and two with Roma before he retired and returned to Spain in 1972.

Denilson

Country: *Brazil (born August 24, 1977)*
Position: *Inside forward*
Clubs: *Sao Paulo, Betis (Spain)*

Denilson exploded on the world scene with his brilliant displays for Brazil in 1997 at the pre-World Cup Tournoi de France – where he made his senior international debut against Italy – and at the Copa America. He had been a highly-rated trainer at the Sao Paulo club from the age of 12, being promoted to the first-team squad at 17 by ex-World Cup coach Tele Santana. In the autumn of 1997, Sao Paulo negotiated his transfer to Betis in Spain for a world record fee of more than £20 million – but to come into effect only after the 1998 World Cup finals.

Marcel **Desailly**

Country: *France (born September 7, 1968)*
Position: *Midfielder*
Clubs: *Nantes, Marseille, Milan (Italy)*

Desailly was born in Accra, Ghana, and moved to France with his mother and brothers when a child. He is the only player to have won the Champions Cup with two different clubs in successive seasons – having triumphed first with Marseille against Milan in 1993, then for Milan against Barcelona a year later. His transfer to Italy was prompted by the financial collapse of Marseille following revelations that the club had been deeply involved in match-fixing. Desailly won the European Supercup with AC Milan in 1994 and the Italian league championship in 1994 and 1996. He was also a Champions Cup runner-up with Milan against Ajax in Vienna in 1995. He had mixed fortunes in the 1998 World Cup, picking up a winners' medal – despite being sent off in the second half of the final against Brazil.

Didier **Deschamps**

Country: *France (born October 15, 1968)*
Position: *Midfielder*
Clubs: *Bayonne, Nantes, Bordeaux, Marseille, Juventus (Italy)*

Deschamps, like Desailly, has won the Champions Cup with French and Italian clubs. But while they were team-mates at Marseille in 1993, Deschamps won his second European prize in 1996 after transferring to Juventus. That success marked his tenth year in top-flight football since Deschamps made his league debut in August 1986. He won French league championship medals with Marseille in 1990 and 1992 and the Italian championship with Juventus in 1995, 1997 and 1998. He joined Juventus in July 1994, winning the Italian league and cup in his first season as well as finishing runner-up in the UEFA Cup. But without doubt the high point of Deschamps career came in the summer of 1998 when he became the first French captain to lift the World Cup – and in front of an ecstatic home crowd – after a memorable 3–0 defeat of Brazil in Paris.

Kazimierz **Deyna**

Country: *Poland (born October 23, 1947)*
Position: *Midfielder*
Clubs: *Starogard, Sportowy Lodz, Legia Warsaw, Manchester City (England), San Diego (USA).*

Deyna earned a domestic reputation in helping army club Legia win the Polish league in 1969 and was promoted into the national squad when Legia coach Kazimierz Gorski was appointed international manager. Poland's emergence as a world power in the early 1970s owed a huge debt to his skills in the centre of midfield. Deyna, assisted by the likes of Maszczyk and Kasperczak, created a host of attacking openings for strikers Lato and Gadocha. He won the 1972 Olympic gold medal with Poland in Munich, then returned to the Olympiastadion two years later to celebrate Poland's best-ever third-place finish at the World Cup. He was never quite the same player after moving abroad, first to England, then to the United States where he died prematurely in a car crash. Deyna scored 38 goals in 102 internationals.

Angelo **Di Livio**

Country: *Italy (born July 26, 1966)*
Position: *Midfielder*
Clubs: *Roma, Reggiana, Nocerina, Perugia, Padova, Juventus*

Di Livio played nine seasons in second, third and fourth division football in Italy before breaking into the Juventus squad comparatively late in his career. Made his Serie A debut in 1993 at the late age of 27 – against Roma, who had given him away on a free transfer in 1985. Nicknamed The Little Soldier at Juventus, an important role in the Turin club's 1995 successes earned him a national team call-up at 29. He won the Italian league title with Juventus in 1995, 1997 and 1998, and also helped them to three successive UEFA Champions League Cup Finals – winning in 1996 and losing in 1997 and 1998.

Roberto Di Matteo

Country: *Italy (born May 29, 1970)*
Position: *Midfielder*
Clubs: *Schaffhausen (Switzerland), Zurich (Switzerland), Aarau (Switzerland), Lazio (Italy), Chelsea (England)*

Di Matteo was born in Switzerland of Italian parents and made his senior league debut in the Swiss championship with Schaffhausen in 1988–89. His dual nationality qualifications made him a priority transfer target for Italian clubs and he eventually chose to go to Lazio in 1993 – making his Serie A debut in a 0–0 home draw against Foggia. Made his international debut as late substitute for Albertini in the surprise 2–1 Euro 96 qualifying defeat by Croatia in Parma in November, 1994. Transferred to English football with Chelsea after being one of the few successes of Italy's campaign at the 1996 European Championship finals. He then made history by scoring the fastest FA Cup Final goal this century in 45 seconds against Middlesbrough in 1997. A year later he collected more winner's medals in the English League Cup and the European Cup-winners Cup.

Alfredo Di Stefano

Country: *Argentina and Spain (born July 4, 1926)*
Position: *Centre forward*
Clubs: *San Lorenzo, River Plate (Argentina), Millonarios Bogota (Colombia), Real Madrid, Espanol (Spain)*

Alfredo Di Stefano may easily be considered the greatest footballer of all. And if Pele's admirers may consider that sacrilege, then the millions who wondered at Di Stefano's awesome majesty as he dominated European football in the 1950s and early 1960s will happily respond. His greatness lay not only in his achievement in leading Madrid to victory in the first five consecutive European Champions Cup finals – and thus inspiring a great breakthrough in international football – but because no other footballer has so effectively combined his individual expertise with an all-embracing ability to organise a team to play to his command. He was born in Barracas, a poor suburb of the Argentine capital of Buenos Aires, and learned his football first in the tough streets of the capital, then out on the family farm. His grandfather had emigrated to Argentina from Capri, while father had played for the leading Buenos Aires club River Plate. To Di Stefano senior football was a recreation, not a means to earn a living. Thus he was not particularly enthusiastic when his sons Alfredo and Tulio launched their own teenage careers with local teams. Eventually he relented and young Alfredo – nicknamed El Aleman, The German, because of his blond hair – made his River Plate debut on August 18, 1944, at outside right. His hero had been Independiente's free-scoring Paraguayan star Arsenio Erico, and he wanted to be a centre-forward himself. He learned his trade while on loan to Huracan, then returned to River in 1947 as successor to another great attack leader, Adolfo Pedernera. River's forward line was nicknamed La Maquina, The Machine, for the monotonous consistency with which they took opposing defences apart. Di Stefano transferred his attacking prowess into the Argentine national team with equal success at the 1947 South American championship. In 1949 Argentine players went on strike over pay and conditions. The clubs locked them out and completed their fixtures with amateur players. Meanwhile, the star professionals were lured away to play in the pirate league which had been set up, beyond FIFA jurisdiction, in Colombia. Di Stefano was the star of stars there, playing for Millonarios of Bogota, the so-called "Blue Ballet." When Colombia was finally reintegrated in FIFA, Millonarios went on one last world tour…where Di Stefano was spotted by Real Madrid after starring in the Spanish club's 50th anniversary tournament. Madrid agreed a fee with Millonarios and thus neatly outflanked rivals Barcelona, who had sealed a deal with Di Stefano's old club, River Plate. A Spanish soccer court ruled that Di Stefano should play one season for Madrid, one season for Barcelona. But after he made a quiet start to the season Barcelona, unimpressed, sold out their share to Madrid. Four days later he scored a hat-trick in a 5–0 win against…Barcelona. A legend had been born. Madrid were champions of Spain in Di Stefano's first two seasons and champions of Europe in his next five. He scored in each of Madrid's victorious European Cup finals, including that hat-trick against Frankfurt in 1960. He was "total football" personified before the term had been invented. One moment he was defending in his own penalty box, the next organising his midfield, the next scoring from the edge of the box at the other end of the pitch. As Miguel Munoz, long-time Madrid colleague first as player and then coach, once said: "The greatness of Di Stefano was that, with him in your side, you had two players in every position." Di Stefano, the European Footballer of the Year in 1957 and 1959, later won the Cup-winners Cup as coach of Valencia in 1980.

Didi (Full name Waldyr Pereira)

Country: *Brazil (born October 8, 1928)*
Position: *Inside right/midfielder*
Clubs: *FC Rio Branco, FC Lencoes, Madureiro, Fluminense, Botafogo, Real Madrid, Valencia (Spain), Botafogo*

Didi's technique was extraordinary. Team-mates said he could "make the ball talk," and drop it on a coin from any distance, any angle. He perfected the "dead leaf" free kick with which he scored a dozen of his 31 goals in 85 appearances for Brazil. He won the World Cup in 1958 and 1962 and counted the only failure of his career as a spell in between with Real Madrid where he failed to settle in alongside Di Stefano and Puskas. The success of Brazil's 4–2–4 system, revealed in all its glory internationally at the 1958 World Cup, rested heavily on Didi's creative talent. He was one of the greatest of midfield generals.

Youri **Djorkaeff**

Country: *France (born March 9, 1968)*
Position: *Midfielder/inside forward*
Clubs: *Grenoble, Strasbourg, Monaco, Paris Saint-Germain, Internazionale (Italy)*

Football runs in the Djorkaeff family, father Jean having played full-back for France at the 1966 World Cup finals. Son Youri first earned international praise as a member of the Monaco side beaten in the 1992 Cup-winners Cup Final by Werder Bremen. He was top-scorer in the top division in 1993–94 with 20 goals and signed for Paris Saint-Germain in 1995 – 25 years to the day after his father signed for the club. Voted 1995 Footballer of the Year by the sports newspaper, *L'Equipe*, he was outstanding in Paris' victory in the 1996 Cup-winners Cup Final. Djorkaeff then transferred to Inter with whom he reached two successive UEFA Cup Finals – losing in 1997 and winning in 1998, the same year he also became a World Cup winner with France.

Jose Paciencia Oliveira **Domingos**

Country: *Portugal (born January 2, 1969)*
Position: *Centre forward*
Club: *FC Porto*

Domingos is a former World Youth Cup-winner who became one of the most dangerous goal-scorers in Europe. He was the second-best Portuguese scorer in 1990–91 with 24 goals but managed only 23 in the next three seasons because of injuries. He recovered to be Porto's top scorer once again in 1994–95 with 19 goals and the best in the entire league with 25 goals in 1995–96. Domingos won the championship with Porto in 1988, 1990, 1992, 1993, 1995 and 1996 and the Portuguese cup in 1988, 1991 and 1994 – making him one of the most successful Portuguese footballers of all time. Former Porto coach Bobby Robson compared his qualities in the penalty box with those of Liberia's George Weah.

Antonio Da Guia **Domingos**

Country: *Brazil (born November 19, 1912)*
Position: *Full back*
Clubs: *Bangu, Vasco da Gama, Boca Juniors (Argentina), Flamengo, Corinthians, Bangu*

Domingos was a full-back of the old school, as much a pivoting central defender as a marker in the original 2–3–5 formation. His talents earned him transfers all round South America and he remains as much of a legend in Uruguay and Argentina as he is in Brazil. The Uruguayans nicknamed him The Divine Master. He made his debut for Brazil in 1931 and was a key member of the team which reached the 1938 World Cup semi-finals. His longevity was remarkable and he did not retire until 1948. By this time he had returned to his original club, Bangu. His contemporary, centre forward Leonidas da Silva, once said no defender ever "read a game" better.

Hans-Jürgen **Dörner**

Country: *East Germany (born January 25, 1951)*
Position: *Sweeper*
Club: *Dynamo Dresden*

Dorner was the greatest defender among the handful of outstanding individual players to emerge during the existence of East Germany between 1950 and 1990. Joachim Streich was a fine centre-forward, Jürgen Sparwasser a dangerous fellow striker, Hans-Jürgen Kreische the most creative inside forward and Dorner a stopper, then sweeper, who commanded the edge of his penalty area with security and gained the respect of both friend and foe. He was a one-club man, playing his entire career with Dynamo Dresden and he totalled exactly 100 internationals between 1969 and 1985, scoring nine goals and winning Olympic Games gold in 1976 in Canada. He was three times Footballer of the Year, five times East German champion and four times cup-winner. After reunification of Germany he was appointed to the coaching staff of the German federation.

Ted **Drake**

Country: *England (born August 16, 1912)*
Position: *Centre forward*
Clubs: *Southampton, Arsenal*

Drake was the greatest centre forward in Arsenal's history and still holds the club record for the most goals in a season (42 in 41 appearances in 1934–35). He scored 48 goals in 72 games for Southampton before joining Arsenal for £6,500 in 1934. In his first full season he set his 42-goal record which included seven hat-tricks. The following season, he created a First Division record by scoring all Arsenal's goals in a 7–1 victory at Aston Villa. At the season's end, though not fully fit after injury, he scored the only goal in Arsenal's 1936 FA Cup Final win over Sheffield United. Among his other honours were two championships and five international caps (six goals) for England. After the war he turned to management and guided Chelsea to their only league title in 1955.

Dunga: captain by word and deed

Dunga (Full name: Carlos Bledorn Verri)

Country: *Brazil (born October 31, 1963)*
Position: *Midfielder*
Clubs: *Vasco da Gama, Pisa (Italy), Fiorentina (Italy), Pescara (Italy), Stuttgart (Germany), Jubilo Iwata (Japan)*

Dunga, one of the most controversial modern Brazilian players, obtained the ultimate revenge over his critics when, as captain, he raised the World Cup after the victory over Italy in the 1994 Final. He encountered consistent criticism because of his style as a defensive midfield player, strong and keen in the tackle but slightly slow and a little clumsy on the ball. But he possessed a strong shot in both feet and 1994 World Cup boss Carlos Alberto Perreira considered Dunga's tactical discipline essential to his campaign strategy. Not surprisingly, perhaps, he proved a success in Germany with Stuttgart and then in Japan with Iwata. His leadership skills were evident in 1998 as he took Brazil to another World Cup final, but this time they lost out to France 3–0.

Dragan Dzajic

Country: *Yugoslavia (born May 30, 1956)*
Position: *Left winger*
Clubs: *Red Star Belgrade, Bastia (France), Red Star Belgrade*

The British press baptised Dzajic the "magic Dragan" after his left-wing skills helped take England apart in the semi-finals of the 1968 European Nations Championship. Dzajic had pace, skill and intelligence and was perhaps the greatest football hero to

have emerged in post-war Yugoslavia. He was five times a national champion, four times a cup-winner and earned selection for a variety of World and European XIs on five different occasions. He remained an outside left throughout a career which brought him 23 goals in 85 internationals, never needing to fade back into midfield like so many wingers who lose the edge of their talent. He retired in 1978 and became general manager of his original club, Red Star.

Duncan Edwards

Country: *England (born October 1, 1936)*
Position: *Left half*
Club: *Manchester United*

A giant still revered by generations who never saw him play, Edwards was a football genius whose bright flame was cruelly extinguished in 1958 when he was killed in the Munich air disaster along with seven other Manchester United players. For three weeks, Edwards lay in a German hospital with terrible injuries, only his immense strength keeping him alive. Ironically, it was against West Germany in 1956 that Edwards had announced himself to the world with a superb goal that helped England defeat the Germans in Berlin. When he finally succumbed to his injuries the news of his death submerged England in a tidal wave of grief. Nicknamed "Boom-Boom" for the power of his kick, Edwards had already scored five international goals in 18 appearances for his country since making his debut against Scotland in 1955. Edwards was *the* "babe" of Manchester United's "Busby Babes", and had his life not been cut short, there is little doubt that he would have played a starring role in the 1958, 1962 and 1966 World Cups, and would also have set a new record for England appearances.

Dieter Eilts

Country: *Germany (born December 10, 1964)*
Position: *Midfielder*
Clubs: *SV Hage, Werder Bremen*

Eilts joined Bremen at the age of 20 and was twice a league championship winner with them, in 1988 and 1993. He was also twice a German cup winner with Bremen in 1991 and 1994 and a key member of Bremen's only European trophy-winning team in the Cup-winners Cup in 1992. He has spent his entire professional career with Werder Bremen, where he became club captain, and is considered the best defensive central midfielder over recent seasons in the Bundesliga. Nicknamed Mr Reliable, he was voted the tournament's best player after helping Germany win the 1996 European Championship with a 2–1 defeat of the Czech Republic in the final.

Mike **England**

Country: *Wales (born December 2, 1941)*
Position: *Central defender*
Clubs: *Blackburn Rovers (England), Tottenham Hotspur (England)*

England was a Welsh international central defender of great strength and presence. Bill Nicholson considered him a man around whom to rebuild the team which had won the League-and-Cup double in 1961. Of course, Spurs could never regain those peaks again, though England helped win the FA Cup (against Chelsea) in his first season. He proved well worth the £95,000 Spurs had paid for him in the summer of 1966 and played more than 300 league games before ending his career back in Wales with Cardiff City. At international level, England played 44 matches for Wales over 13 years after making his debut against Northern Ireland in 1961–62. Later England took over as Wales manager and twice went desperately close to qualifying for World Cup and European Championship finals.

Arsenio **Erico**

Country: *Paraguay (born 1915)*
Position: *Centre forward*
Clubs: *FC Asuncion, Independiente (Argentina), Huracan (Argentina)*

The quality of Erico as a centre forward is best illustrated by the fact that he was the boyhood hero of none other than Alfredo Di Stefano. Born in Paraguay, he went to Buenos Aires at 17 to play for a fund-raising team organised by the Paraguay Red Cross during the war with Bolivia. Directors of Independiente in the crowd were so impressed they signed him immediately after the match in exchange for a donation to the charity. Erico started badly, twice breaking his arm, but once he was fully fit he scored at a prolific rate and set a record with 47 goals in the 1937–38 season. Several times he scored five goals in a game before returning to Paraguay in 1941 after squabbling over terms with Independiente. The Argentines persuaded him to return but knee cartilage trouble forced his early retirement in 1944.

Eusebio da Silva Ferreira

Country: *Portugal (born January 25, 1942)*
Position: *Centre forward*
Clubs: *Benfica, Monterrey (Mexico), Boston Minutemen (USA), Toronto Metros-Croatia (Canada)*

Eusebio was the first great African footballer – he was born and brought up in Mozambique, which was then still one of Portugal's African colonies. The big Portuguese clubs such as Benfica, Sporting and Porto financed nursery teams in Mozambique and neighbouring Angola and unearthed a wealth of talent which they transported into not only league football but the Portuguese national team. The young Eusebio, ironically, was a nursery product not of Benfica but of their great Lisbon rivals, Sporting. But when Sporting summoned him to Lisbon for a trial in 1961, he was virtually kidnapped off the aeroplane by Benfica officials and hidden away until the fuss had died down. Bela Guttmann, a veteran Hungarian, was coach of Benfica and had a high regard for the potential offered by Mozambique and Angola. The nucleus of the Benfica team which he had guided to European Champions Cup victory over Barcelona that year of 1961 came from Africa: goalkeeper Costa Pereira, centre forward and captain Jose Aguas, and inside forwards Joaquim Santana and Mario Coluna. But Eusebio would prove the greatest of all. Guttmann introduced him to the first team at the end of the 1960–61 season. He was a reserve when Benfica went to France to face Santos of Brazil – inspired by Pele – in the famous Paris Tournament. At half-time Benfica were losing 3–0. Guttmann, with nothing to lose, sent on Eusebio. Benfica still lost, but Eusebio scored a spectacular hat-trick and outshone even Pele. He was still only 19. A year later Eusebio scored two cannonball goals in the 5–3 victory Benfica ran up against Real Madrid in the Champions Cup Final in Amsterdam. In 13 seasons he helped

Eusebio: Portuguese football legend

Benfica win the league seven times and the cup twice; he was European Footballer of the Year in 1965; top scorer with nine goals in the 1966 World Cup finals; scorer of 38 goals in 46 internationals; and the league's leading scorer seven times before knee trouble forced his retirement at 32. But football was Eusebio's life. The fledgling North American Soccer League offered him the chance of a lucrative extension to his career so he flew West to play for Boston Minutemen (alongside old Benfica team-mate Antonio Simoes), for Toronto Metros-Croatia, then for Las Vegas Quicksilver. Benfica's faithful had mixed feelings about his self-imposed exile in North America. But controversy was soon forgotten when he returned 'home' to take up various appointments as television analyst, as assistant coach and as the most honoured public face of Benfica. Fans around the world took Eusebio to their hearts not only because of his ability but because of the sportsmanslike way he played the people's game. At Wembley in 1968 Eusebio very nearly won the European Champions Cup Final for Benfica against Manchester United in the closing minutes of normal time, being foiled only by the intuition of Alex Stepney. Wembley stadium played major roles in Eusebio's career. It was at Wembley, in a 2–0 World Cup qualifying defeat by England, that his youthful power first made the international game sit up; it was at Wembley, in 1963, that he scored one of his finest individual goals as consolation in a 2–1 Champions Cup Final defeat by Milan; and it was at Wembley again that Eusebio led Portugal to their best-ever third place in the World Cup, in 1966. The semi-final, in which Portugal lost 2–1 to England, will long be remembered as as exemplary exhibition of great sportsmanship under the greatest pressure. Appropriately, a statue of Eusebio in action now dominates the entrance to the Estadio da Luz. Appropriately, also, a film made about his life was subtitled: *Sua Majestade o Rei* ... His Majesty the King.

Giacinto **Facchetti**

Country: *Italy (born July 18, 1942)*
Position: *Left back/sweeper*
Club: *Trevigliese, Internazionale*

Facchetti ended his career as a long-striding sweeper at the heart of defence for Inter and Italy. But his greatest days were earlier, when he revolutionised full-back play in the 1960s. He had been a centre-forward with his local club in Treviso when he was signed by Inter and converted into a left-back by coach Helenio Herrera. The man-to-man marking system perfected by Herrera permitted Facchetti the freedom, when Inter attacked, to stride upfield in support of his own forwards. Facchetti scored 60 league goals, a record for a full-back in Italy, including ten in the 1965–66 season. But his most important goal was reserved for the 1965 European Cup semi-final when

he scored a decisive winning goal against Liverpool. Later Facchetti converted to sweeper, from which position he captained Italy against Brazil in the 1970 World Cup Final. He finished his career with 94 caps.

Luis **Fernandez**

Country: *France (born October 2, 1959)*
Position: *Midfielder*
Clubs: *Paris Saint-Germain, Racing Club*

France's midfield in their triumphant era of the mid-1980s was ideally balanced between the inspiration of Michel Platini, the guile of Alain Giresse and Jean Tigana and the physical dynamism of Fernandez. He was born in Taziza, Spain, but his family left Andalucia for France when he was a child. He made his international debut in a shock 2–1 away win over Holland in November 1982 and then led rising Paris Saint-Germain to their first-ever league title. Various Spanish clubs were interested in taking Fernandez home, but when he did move on it was to take the controversial short trip across Paris to Racing. He later returned to Paris Saint-Germain as coach, guiding them to victory in the 1996 European Cup-winners Cup, then moved to Spain and Athletic Bilbao.

Fernando Manuel Silva Couto

Country: *Portugal (born August 2, 1969)*
Position: *Defender/midfielder*
Clubs: *FC Porto, Famalicao, Academica Coimbra, Porto, Parma (Italy), Barcelona (Spain)*

Fernando Couto had the height to be an outstanding central defender and the technique to excel in midfield. He joined Porto originally from regional league club Lourosa at the age of 17 but was sent out on loan spells to Famalicao and Academica. He returned to Porto in 1990 and was a league champion with them in 1992 and 1993 as well as Portuguese Cup winner in 1991 and 1994. He transferred to Parma of Italy in 1994 and helped them win the UEFA Cup. He was sold to Barcelona after the 1996 European Championship, helping them to win the Cup-winners Cup in 1997 and Spanish league in 1998.

Giovanni **Ferrari**

Country: *Italy (born December 6, 1907)*
Position: *Inside forward*
Clubs: *Alessandria, Juventus, Internazionale, Bologna*

"Gioanin" Ferrari was one of only two team members – the other was Giuseppe Meazza – retained from Italy's 1934 World Cup-winning side for the 1938 triumph in France. Appropriately, both men made their international debut in the same game against Switzerland in Rome in 1930. Ferrari played then for Alessandria but soon moved to Juventus, with whom he won a record five consecutive league titles. He won further championship honours with Ambrosiana-Inter in 1940 and with Bologna in 1941. He scored 14 goals in 44 internationals and later was manager of Italy at the 1962 World Cup finals in Chile.

Bernabe **Ferreyra**

Country: *Argentina (born 1909)*
Position: *Inside forward*
Clubs: *Tigre, River Plate*

Nicknamed "The Mortar" for his ferocious shooting, Ferreyra was the first great hero of Argentine football. He scored more than 200 goals for Tigre and then River Plate in the 1930s, having joined River after the establishment of professionalism. In his first season with River, 1932–33, he scored a league record 43 goals and was such a regular feature of the weekly scoresheets that one Buenos Aires newspaper offered a gold medal to any goalkeeper who could keep a clean sheet against him. However, Ferreyra played only four internationals before retiring in 1939 and going back to his home town of Rufino. In 1943 he returned to River's front office and, in 1956, was honoured with a testimonial match for his loyalty.

Luis Filipe Madeira Caeiro **Figo**

Country: *Portugal (born November 4, 1972)*
Position: *Midfielder*
Clubs: *Sporting Clube, Barcelona (Spain)*

Figo was a European champion at under-16 level in 1989 and a World Youth Cup-winner in 1991. He was also a member of the Portuguese squad which reached the finals of the European Under-21 Championship in France in the 1993–94 season and a winner of the Portuguese Cup with Sporting Clube in 1995. In the spring of 1995 both Juventus and Parma claimed Figo would be joining them at the season's end. Both clubs later withdrew their interest and Figo was transferred instead to Barcelona. He was an instant success in Spain – helping Barcelona win the European Cup-winners Cup in 1997 and captaining them to the Spanish league title in 1998. His only regret was that the demands of busy Barcelona – in a 22-club league with Spanish cup and European commitments – made it difficult for him to obtain regular release to join the Portuguese national team training sessions, and his absence from some of these sessions certainly hindered the Portuguese team in their unsuccessfyl attempt to qualify for the 1998 World Cup.

Tom **Finney**

Country: *England (born April 5, 1922)*
Position: *Outside right/centre forward/outside left*
Club: *Preston North End*

Finney was famed as the "Preston plumber" after his business interests. But he ranks as one of the very greatest English players of all time despite being modest in height and general appearance. "Grizzly strong" was the description applied to him by Bill Shankly, who played wing half behind Finney at Preston. Finney always had a generous word for opponents as well as a rock-like solidity that belied his frame. Genuinely two-footed, brave as they come, and in his later years a deep-lying centre forward on Hidegkuti lines, a lack of support left him bereft of honours at club level. But a 12-year England career, with 76 caps and a then-record 30 goals, established him at the very top level. In his mid-70s he was, belatedly, knighted for his services to British football.

Just **Fontaine**

Country: *France (born August 18, 1933)*
Position: *Centre forward*
Clubs: *AC Marrakesh (Morocco), USM Casablanca (Morocco), Nice, Reims*

Fontaine remains a World Cup record-holder thanks to the 13 goals he collected for France at the 1958 World Cup finals. Yet he was born in Morocco and had played only twice for France before 1958. Discovered by Nice, he had been bought by Reims as a replacement for Raymond Kopa, who had joined Real Madrid in 1956. He expected to be reserve to Reims team-mate René Bliard at the 1958 World Cup, but Bliard was injured on the eve of the finals and Fontaine took his opportunity in record-breaking style. The majority of his goals he owed to Kopa's creative work alongside him and the partnership was renewed when Kopa returned to Reims in 1959. Sadly Fontaine had to retire in 1961 with a broken leg. He was twice top league scorer and totalled 27 goals in 20 internationals. Later he was president of the French players' union and also, briefly, national manager.

Enzo **Francescoli**

Country: *Uruguay (born November 12, 1961)*
Position: *Centre forward*
Clubs: *Wanderers, River Plate (Argentina), Matra Racing (France), Marseille (France), Cagliari (Italy), Torino (Italy), River Plate (Argentina)*

Francescoli, in the 1980s, became the latest in a long line of

Uruguayan superstars, starting with the heroes of the 1920s and 1930s and continuing through Schiaffino, Goncalves and Rocha. He began with a small club, Wanderers, and River Plate of Argentina outbid both Uruguayan giants Penarol and Nacional for his services. He was top scorer in the Argentine league and voted South American Footballer of the Year before moving to France with Racing in 1986. Sadly, even Francescoli's 32 goals in three seasons were not enough to save the club from sporting and financial failure. He scored 11 goals in 28 games in Marseille's championship season of 1989–90 before transferring, better late than never, to Italy with Cagliari and then Torino. In 1994 he returned to South America for one last Argentine championship-winning hurrah with River Plate.

Arthur **Friedenreich**

Country: *Brazil (born 1892)*
Position: *Centre forward*
Clubs: *Germania, Ipiranga, Americao, Paulistano, Sao Paulo FC, Flamengo*

Friedenreich was the first great Brazilian footballer and the first player officially credited with more than 1,000 goals. His overall total was 1,329. Son of a German father and Brazilian mother, he was also the first coloured player to break through the early racial/cultural barriers in Brazilian soccer. Nicknamed The Tiger, Friedenreich began playing senior football at 17 and did not retire until 1935, when he was 43. He scored eight goals in 17 internationals for Brazil between 1914 and 1930 though his first representative appearance was in a 2–0 win against English club Exeter City on July 21, 1914. Friedenreich did not score in the match, but instead lost two teeth in a painful collision with an Exeter defender.

Paulo **Futre**

Country: *Portugal (born February 28, 1966)*
Position: *Left winger*
Clubs: *Sporting, FC Porto, Atletico Madrid (Spain), Benfica, Marseille (France), Reggiana (Italy), Milan (Italy), West Ham (England), Atletico Madrid (Spain)*

Futre was only 17 when he made his internatioanl debut and his star continued to shine brightly after FC Porto snatched him away from Sporting to inspire their Champions Cup victory of 1987. In the early stages of his career, he drew favourable comparisons with Argentina's Diego Maradona. A few weeks later he was signed by Atletico Madrid as the first major coup in the controversial presidency of Jesus Gil. Futre survived all the tempests at Atletico until the start of 1993 when he forced his sale home to Benfica. However, financing the deal proved

beyond even Benfica. They sold him to Marseille who then had to sell him after only a few months to resolve their own cash crisis. Reggiana of Italy paid £8 million to become Futre's fourth club in a year, only to see him tear knee ligaments after scoring on his Italian league debut. From then on his career began a steady decline as his knee injury refused to heal satisfactorily. He attempted a comeback with Milan in Italy, then moved to West Ham in England in the summer of 1996, but managed only a handful of matches for the London club before he was on the move again –this time with Atletico Madrid in Spain – where he also spent a year as technical director.

Robert **Gadocha**

Country: *Poland (born January 10, 1946)*
Position: *Outside left*
Clubs: *Legia Warsaw, Nantes (France)*

Gadocha was an unorthodox left winger, not particularly quick but intelligent in his use of the ball and an outstanding finisher. He scored 17 goals in 65 internationals between 1967 and 1976 and won Olympic Games gold in 1972 and then a third-place finish at the World Cup back in Germany two years later when Poland were considered by many to be desperately unlucky not to make it to the final, their only defeat in seven matches a narrow 1–0 loss against eventual winners West Germany. Poland's outstanding team of the early 1970s depended as much on him as on Deyna in midfield, Tomaszewski and Gorgon in defence and attacking partner Lato. He was twice Polish champion with Legia in 1969 and 1970 as well as winning the cup when he was a 20-year-old in 1966. He wound down his career in France with Nantes in the late 1970s.

Agustin **Gainza**

Country: *Spain (born May 28, 1922)*
Position: *Outside left*
Club: *Athletic Bilbao*

Spain boasted a string of great outside lefts in the post-war era, at least until both the position and the term fell into disuse. Francisco Gento at Real Madrid, Carlos Lapetra at Zaragoza and Enrique Collar at Atletico Madrid were three who earned fame through domestic and European competition. But the father figure was Gainza, nicknamed Piru. Born in the Basque province, he remained loyal to Bilbao for 40 years as player, youth coach, senior coach and then youth coach again. He earned a big reputation for pace on the wing and opportunism in the penalty box with minor clubs San Fausto and Porron before joining Bilbao at 18. He played 33 times for Spain including the fourth-place finish at the 1950 World Cup.

Garrincha (Full name Manoel Francisco dos Santos)

Country: *Brazil (born October 28, 1933)*
Position: *Outside right*
Clubs: *Pau Grande, Botafogo, Corinthians, Atletico Junior Barranquilla (Colombia), Flamengo, Bangu, Red Star Paris (France), Portuguesa, Olaria*

Garrincha – the nickname means "Little Bird" – rose to greatness despite a childhood illness which left his legs badly twisted. Surgeons who carried out corrective surgery thought he would do well merely to walk, let alone turn out to be perhaps the quickest and most dangerous right winger of all time. Yet now Garrincha is up there alongside Pele and Nilton Santos in the pantheon of Brazilian football for his contributions to the World Cup victories of 1958 and 1962. He was a great practical joker, a fun-loving trait which nearly cost him his place in Brazil's team. It took a players' deputation to persuade manager Vicente Feola to include him in the 1958 World Cup side in Sweden. Once in, he was there to stay. He became the dominant personality at the 1962 finals in Chile after Pele was injured early on, scoring twice in the quarter-final win over England and twice again in the semi-final triumph over hosts Chile. He signed off from the World Cup with a remarkable free-kick goal against Bulgaria in England in 1966. Knee trouble later curtailed his career and he died prematurely in 1983.

Paul Gascoigne

Country: *England (born May 27, 1967)*
Position: *Midfielder*
Clubs: *Newcastle, Tottenham Hotspur, Lazio (Italy), Rangers (Scotland), Middlesbrough*

Gascoigne has been an outstanding talent whose career has been perpetually hampered by injuries and controversy. He cost Tottenham £2 million from Newcastle in 1988, and superb displays, allied to his televised tears as England went out of the World Cup in Italy two years later, helped to make him a national figure. He was carried off with a career-threatening knee injury after fouling an opponent early in the 1991 FA Cup Final; Spurs won and the medal he obtained remains his only English honour. In June 1992 he moved to Lazio for £5.5 million, equalling the British record. Frequent injuries, including a broken leg in a freak training accident, and off-field problems prevented him from inspiring Lazio to meaningful success, and he joined Rangers in 1995 for £4.3 million with a championship-winning impact which earned him the Scottish Footballer of the Year award. He scored a wonderful goal against Scotland in the 1996 European Championship but revelations over his domestic problems cost him a great deal of public sympathy. Having returned to English football in the spring of 1998 to help Middlesbrough back into the Premier League, he was sensationally omitted from Glenn Hoddle's World Cup squad due to fitness problems, stemming from excessive eating and drinking. As with George Best, Gascoigne's sublime talent for football often played second fiddle to his love of the high life.

Tommy Gemmell

Country: *Scotland (born October 16, 1943)*
Position: *Left back*
Clubs: *Celtic, Nottingham Forest (England)*

A big and deceptively awkward-looking full back who became a folk hero because of his goals. He scored eight in European matches for his club – a remarkable record for a so-called defender – and two of them were in Champions Cup Finals. Gemmell crashed one past Internazionale to equalise when Celtic won in 1967, and another against Feyenoord when they

Paul Gascoigne: career unfulfilled

lost three years later. His extrovert style of play was well suited to upsetting foreign defences during Celtic's greatest years, but he also collected a large haul of domestic honours.

Francisco **Gento**

Country: *Spain (born October 22, 1933)*
Position: *Outside left*
Clubs: *Santander, Real Madrid*

Gento, nicknamed "El Supersonico", was as much part of the entertainment in Real Madrid's great team of the 1950s and 1960s as Di Stefano and Puskas. His contribution was tearing holes in opposing defences from outside left. He began with Santander and was considered a player with pace but little else when Madrid signed him in 1953. Fortunately, he found a marvellous inside left partner in Jose Hector Rial. He is the only man to have won six European Champions Cup medals. He was also runner-up in the Champions Cup in 1962 and 1964 and in the Cup-winners Cup in 1971. He scored 256 goals in 800 games for Madrid, with whom he was Spanish champion on 12 occasions.

Alain **Geiger**

Country: *Switzerland (born November 5, 1960)*
Position: *Central defender*
Clubs: *Sion, Servette, Saint Etienne (France), Sion*

Geiger ranks alongside inter-war hero Severino Minelli as one of the greatest Swiss defenders in the country's history, although he also played in midfield in emergency for both clubs and country. He started his career as a left back with Sion and played a starring role in their 1981 cup final triumph over Young Boys before joining Servette of Geneva, with whom he enjoyed more cup final success over the years. He moved to France with Saint Etienne, then returned to Sion in 1991. His total of 113 international appearances included the 1994 World Cup when Switzerland reached the second phase of the tournament. He was also prominent for the Swiss during the 1996 European Championship in England.

Ryan **Giggs**

Country: *Wales (born November 29, 1973)*
Position: *Left winger*
Club: *Manchester United*

Giggs has been called the new George Best – not for his off-field antics but for the ability to leave opposing defenders for dead. The son of a rugby league player, he played for England schoolboys but then decided to opt for his mother's country,

David Ginola: plays football and works for charity

Wales, after his parents split up. United manager Alex Ferguson was fiercely protective of Giggs' talent, keeping the media at bay and vetting the potential sponsors queueing at his door. He was Wales' youngest-ever international when he played against Germany in October 1991 at 17 years and 321 days. With United he has won the league championship four times (in 1993, 1994, 1996 and 1997), the FA Cup twice and one League Cup. He demonstrated his international quality to the full in United's 1996–97 Champions League campaign when he was inspirational in the 4–0 defeat of FC Porto in the quarter-finals.

Johnny **Giles**

Country: *Republic of Ireland (born January 6, 1940)*
Position: *Outside right/inside left/midfielder*
Clubs: *Home Farm, Manchester United (England), Leeds (England), West Brom (England), Vancouver Whitecaps (Canada), Shamrock Rovers (Republic of Ireland)*

Giles was the outstanding figure in Republic of Ireland international football before the advent of Jack Charlton – ironic, since the two were team-mates in the great days of Leeds United in the late 1960s and early 1970s. Born in Dublin, he joined Manchester United originally as an orthodox outside right but converted into a midfield general on moving to Leeds. He was the creative fulcrum of Don Revie's Leeds machine before moving into player-management at West Brom and then returning to Ireland in an ultimately unsuccessful attempt to turn Shamrock Rovers into a major force. He was player-manager of the Irish Republic, but was replaced by Jack Charlton.

David **Ginola**

Country: *France (born January 25, 1967)*
Position: *Left winger*
Clubs: *Toulon, Brest, Paris Saint-Germain, Newcastle (England), Tottenham Hotspur (England)*

A former French Footballer of the Year, Ginola has always been a centre of controversy. Born near Marseille, he made his name with Toulon and Brest. Marseille and Paris both bid for him but Ginola preferred Paris because, he said, playing for Marseille would have been "too easy." He became an instant hero on Tyneside after Kevin Keegan signed him for Newcastle in 1995 but he was reported to be getting homesick even before the arrival of the less-impressed Kenny Dalglish as manager at the start of 1997. He has also enjoyed a mixed national team career. In 1993 he publicly demanded a place in the team alongside Jean-Pierre Papin and Eric Cantona but, when given the chance, he gave away possession fatally in the Paris defeat by Bulgaria which cost France a place in the World Cup finals. Aime Jacquet

Sergio Goycochea: penalty-stopping hero in 1990

ignored Ginola for the finals of both the European Championship in 1996 and the World Cup in 1998, and as his compatriots won the latter, he had to content himself with becoming a world spokesman for a landmine charity that Diana, Princess of Wales had previously represented before her death.

Alain **Giresse**

Country: *France (born September 2, 1952)*
Position: *Midfielder*
Clubs: *Bordeaux, Marseille*

Giresse was one of the smallest of World Cup heroes but had emerged as precisely that at the heart of the French midfield in Spain in 1982. He contributed, among other things, a memorable goal in the dramatic semi-final against West Germany, enhanced his reputation in the 1984 European Championship success, and helped Bordeaux to the Champions Cup semi-finals in 1985 and then France to third place in the World Cup in Mexico the following year. He played more than 500 league games for Bordeaux before transferring, briefly, to Marseille after the 1986 World Cup finals. Ironically Giresse, a few weeks earlier, had scored Bordeaux's extra-time winner in the French cup final against Marseille. Later entered management and was appointed, in the summer of 1998, as coach of Paris Saint-Germain.

Philippe **Gondet**

Country: *France (born May 17, 1942)*
Position: *Centre forward*
Clubs: *Stade Français, Nantes*

French football suffered a major setback in the early 1960s with the enforced premature retirement of Just Fontaine. Into his goalscoring gap stepped "Thunder" Gondet. As a left winger he was given away by Stade Français, then switched to inside forward with Nantes. He took his second chance, scored on his national team debut against Yugoslavia in 1965–66, ended the campaign as top domestic marksman and earned a starting place in the French line-up at the World Cup finals. Unfortunately, like Fontaine himself, he was also a victim of ruthless defenders. He suffered a serious knee injury against Hungary, underwent two major operations but never played seriously again.

Sergio Javier **Goycochea**

Country: *Argentina (born October 17, 1963)*
Position: *Goalkeeper*
Clubs: *River Plate, Millonarios (Colombia), Racing, Brest (France), Cerro Porteno (Paraguay), River Plate, Deportivo Mandiyu*

Goycochea has gone down in World Cup history as the greatest penalty-stopper of them all. His reputation rests largely on his feats at the 1990 World Cup finals when he stepped into the action during Argentina's match against the Soviet Union after Nery Pumpido had broken a leg. Goycochea's heroics in the penalty shoot-out victories over Yugoslavia and Italy took Argentina to the final. Yet he had not played a competitive game over the previous six months because of the domestic unrest in Colombia where he had been contracted to Millonarios of Bogota. After Italia 90 he was signed by the ambitious French provincial club, Brest. Within a few months, however, they had been declared bankrupt. Goycochea looked in England for a club without success before returning to South America.

Jimmy Greaves

Country: England (born February 20, 1940)
Position: Inside forward
Clubs: Chelsea, Milan (Italy), Tottenham, West Ham United

Greaves may later have become a humorous television pundit, but his instinctive talent for putting the ball in the net was no joke for opposing defenders. Despite his lightweight build, he scored 44 goals in 57 full internationals included two fours and four threes, and his 357 in League games (all in the former First Division) included three fives. An unhappy interlude in Italy with Milan (despite nine goals in ten league games) did little to mar his scoring ability, and he gave Tottenham wonderful value for money when he was bought by Bill Nicholson for the then British record transfer fee of £99,999 – Nicholson didn't want to saddle him with the burden of being Britain's first £100,000 player. He finished his days his with West Ham United, but by then drink had taken a grip, and his successful battles to overcome that blight provided inspiration for many others.

Harry Gregg

Country: Northern Ireland (born October 25, 1932)
Position: Goalkeeper
Clubs: Dundalk (N Ireland), Doncaster (England), Manchester United (England), Stoke (England)

Hardly had goalkeeper Gregg left second-division Doncaster for Manchester United than he was a survivor of the Munich air crash. Later that year he performed wonders in helping his club to the FA Cup Final, where they lost 2–0 to Bolton, and then assisted the Irish to the quarter-final of the World Cup in Sweden. Injury kept him out of United's FA Cup-winning side in 1963. Genial and popular, he won his first cap after only nine games for Doncaster, and had barely established himself as Ireland's first choice before the fateful 1957–58 season.

John Greig

Country: Scotland (born September 11, 1942)
Position: Right half/central defender
Club: Rangers

A 16-year spell of hard labour in defence and midfield brought Greig a record 496 League appearances for Rangers and a considerable number of honours, although Celtic were the dominant team in Scotland for a large part of that time. He was Footballer of the Year in 1966, the season in which he scored a spectacular goal against Italy in a World Cup qualifier, and won 44 caps, often as skipper. Greig also played in two Cup-winners Cup finals, losing in 1967 and winning in 1972, and after quitting as a player had a spell as Ibrox manager.

Gunnar Gren

Country: Sweden (born October 31, 1920)
Position: Inside forward
Clubs: IFK Gothenburg, Milan (Italy), Fiorentina (Italy), Orgryte, GAIS Gothenburg

Gren, nicknamed "the Professor", claimed Italian attention when he won the Olympic Games soccer tournament in London in 1948. His nickname stemmed both from his premature baldness and his astute inside forward play. Milan won the transfer race and Gren forged, with fellow Swedes Nordahl and Liedholm, the legendary Grenoli trio which took Italian football by storm. In 1955, after a spell with Fiorentina, he returned home to Sweden and, at 37, helped the hosts to the final of the 1958 World Cup. That was the last of his 57 internationals. Later he returned to his original club, IFK Gothenburg – with whom he had won the Swedish championship in 1942 – as manager of the souvenir shop.

Georges Grun

Country: Belgium (born January 25, 1962)
Position: Central defender/midfielder
Clubs: Anderlecht, Parma (Italy), Anderlecht

Grun has been one of the most versatile defenders in Belgian football history. He began with Anderlecht as a right back, played for his country in central defence, then moved up into midfield after being sold to Italy's Parma – with whom he won the European Cup-winners Cup in 1992. He made his debut in the 2–0 win over Yugoslavia with which Belgium began their European Championship finals campaign in 1984 – owing his place to the en bloc suspension which ruled out Belgium's previous back four after a match-fixing scandal. Grun established himself as a stalwart for the 1986 and 1990 World Cups and would have won even more than his 70-plus international caps had it not been for serious injury.

Josep **Guardiola**

Country: *Spain (born January 18, 1971)*
Position: *Midfielder*
Club: *Barcelona*

Guardiola, a former youth and under-21 international, has been one of the few Spanish players certain of their place with Barcelona throughout the 1990s. One of only a handful of local boys to force his way into the team, he took over the midfield gap left vacant in 1991 by the departure of Luis Milla for Real Madrid. Raised in the Barcelona suburb of Manresa, he was promoted into the Spanish national team after only 20 games for Barcelona. In 1992 he won the Prix Bravo, which is awarded annually to the outstanding under-23 footballer in Europe. But injuries constantly thwarted his attempts to fulfil his potential, one such costing him the chance of playing in the 1998 World Cup finals in France.

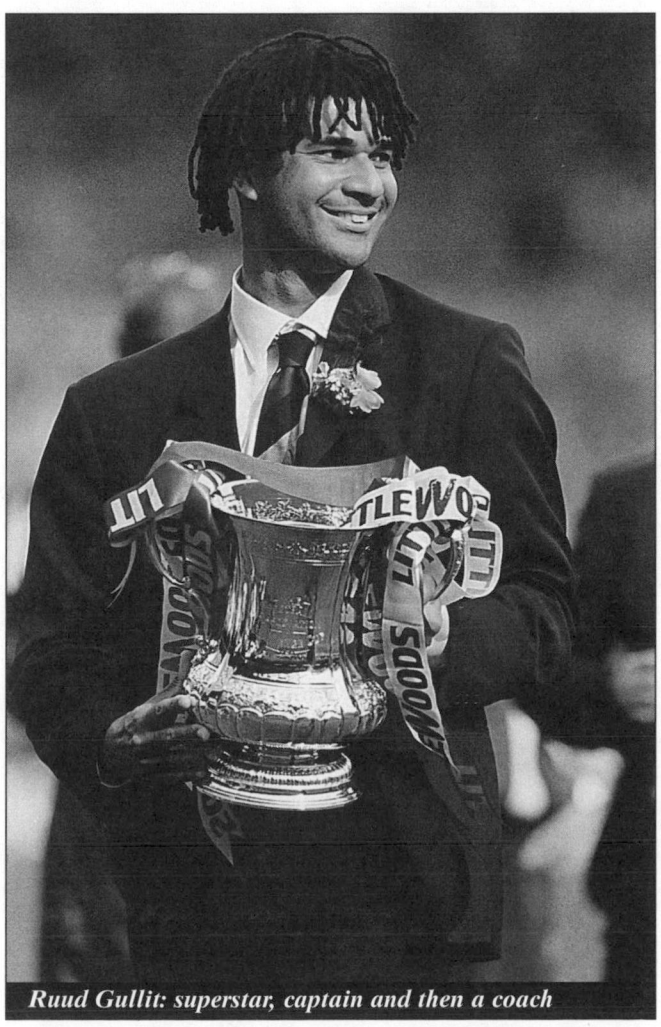

Ruud Gullit: superstar, captain and then a coach

Julen **Guerrero Lopez**

Country: *Spain (born January 7, 1974)*
Position: *Centre forward*
Club: *Athletic Bilbao*

Guerrero is the latest hero of the fiercely independent Basque region in Spain – turning down a stream of lucrative offers to stay with his local Bilbao club. He was given his league debut by coach Jupp Heynckes in 1992 for a 2–1 win over Cadiz. He then became Spain's second-youngest international of all time when he played the first 63 minutes of Spain's 1–1 draw with Mexico in Las Palmas in January 1993. His first two international goals secured a 2–0 victory over Lithuania in Vilnius. At the 1994 World Cup Guerrero played only 45 minutes against South Korea and 90 minutes against Bolivia because coach Javier Clemente preferred the greater experience of Caminero in the linking role. He is under contract at Bilbao until 2007 and the release clause stipulates £7.5 million "compensation".

Ruud **Gullit**

Country: *Holland (born September 1, 1962)*
Position: *Centre forward/sweeper*
Clubs: *Haarlem, Feyenoord, PSV Eindhoven, Milan (Italy), Sampdoria (Italy), Milan (Italy), Chelsea (England)*

Football intelligence has been the hallmark of Gullit's career – from his early days when he was playing sweeper for Barry Hughes at Haarlem, on via Feyenoord to his leadership of the Milan revival in the late 1980s and managerial stardom in England in the late 1990s. Along the way he also demonstrated that footballers can look beyond the narrow confines of the game with his vehement support for the release of Nelson Mandela. He would surely have won the European Footballer accolade more than once had it not been for the cruel knee injuries which interrupted his career. Milan paid a world record £6.5 million for Gullit in 1987 and were rewarded with an Italian championship in his first season and Champions Cups in his second and third. Remarkably, he helped Milan win the second European Cup, against Benfica in Vienna in 1990, despite having been restricted by injury to only two league games all season. His impatience with injuries and with the "overflow" foreigners policy of coach Fabio Capello led to his release on a free transfer to Sampdoria in 1994. He soon returned to Milan, however, before setting off for England to first play for, and then succeed, manager Glenn Hoddle at Chelsea. His Holland career was full of ups and downs. He captained them to European Championship success in 1988 but quit midway through the 1994 World Cup qualifying campaign. A year later he made a one-match comeback before quitting a second time on the eve of the finals. His player-manager reign at Chelsea was short but spectacular. The club won the 1997 FA Cup but his idiosyncratic management style eventually got under the skin of both directors and players and he was ousted in the spring of 1998.

Gheorghe **Hagi**

Country: *Romania (born February 5, 1965)*
Position: *Midfielder*
Clubs: *Constanta, Sportul Studentesc, Steaua, Real Madrid (Spain), Brescia (Italy), Barcelona (Spain), Galatasaray (Turkey)*

Hagi is Romania's greatest-ever player – scoring his first international goal against Northern Ireland in a World Cup qualifier in September 1984 when still only 19. At 15 he was a youth international, at 17 a regular top-flight player and at 18 a fully-fledged international – attending the European Championship finals in 1984. A year later he was 20-goal top league marksman, and again in 1986 when he totalled 31 goals after scoring six in one match. Steaua Bucharest virtually kidnapped him from neighbours Sportul without paying a transfer fee, and three times in a row he was a league-and-cup double-winner. After the 1990 World Cup he transferred with only limited success to Real Madrid before joining Italian side Brescia. At the 1994 World Cup finals, Hagi was considered by many to be the outstanding midfield general on view. Romania reached the quarter-finals, losing on penalties to the Swedes having beaten Argentina in the second phase. After a brief spell at Barcelona, he moved to Galatasaray, with whom he won the Turkish league title in 1997. He played in his third World Cup in 1998 as Romania finished top of their group but went out to the Croatians in the second round.

Hakan Sukur

Country: *Turkey (born September 1, 1971)*
Position: *Centre forward*
Clubs: *Sakaryaspor, Bursaspor, Galatasaray, Torino (Italy), Galatasaray*

Turkey's prospects of international success rest largely on Hakan's shoulders. He joined Galatasary originally from Bursaspor in 1992 and is regularly their leading marksman: 19 goals in 1992–93, 16 goals in 1993–94 and 19 goals in 1994-95. He was also a member of Turkey's gold medal-winning team at the 1993 Mediterranean Games. He impressed Torino officials with a spectacular goal against Switzerland in Berne in the Euro 96 qualifiers and they signed him for £3 million in the summer of 1995. Hakan grew homesick in Italy, however, and was sold back to Galatasaray in November for the same fee.

Helmut **Haller**

Country: *West Germany (born July 21, 1939)*
Position: *Inside forward*
Clubs: *BC Augsburg, Bologna (Italy), Juventus (Italy), BC Augsburg*

Haller was a star of the immediate pre-Bundesliga, pre-full-time professionalism era in German football. An inside forward of great flair, he moved to Italy with Bologna. In 1963 his partnership with Denmark's Harald Nielsen brought them their first league title in more than 20 years. Later Haller played with success for Juventus before returning to his home town of Augsburg. Mostly, he will remembered for his outstanding contribution to West Germany's 1966 World Cup campaign.

Kurt **Hamrin**

Country: *Sweden (born November 19, 1934)*
Position: *Outside right*
Clubs: *AIK Solna, Juventus (Italy), Padova (Italy), Fiorentina (Italy), Milan (Italy), Napoli (Italy), Caserta (Italy)*

Hamrin loved cutting in on goal himself and must be considered close behind Matthews and Garrincha among the great outside rights. He was a quick, darting attacker who ultimately proved one of the most successful goal-grabbers in Italian league history. Hamrin disappointed Juventus in his first season in Italy and they sold him off after only one year. Once he had adjusted, however, he proved an irresistible one-man strike force with Fiorentina with whom he scored 150 goals in nine seasons and won the European Cup-winners Cup in 1961. At the ripe old age of 34 he added a Champions Cup-winner's medal to his impressive collection, with Milan.

Gerhard **Hanappi**

Country: *Austria (born July 9, 1929)*
Position: *Wing half*
Clubs: *Wacker, Rapid Vienna*

Hanappi was one of the world's most versatile footballers in the 1950s. He played mainly wing half or occasionally inside forward for his long-time club, Rapid, but also lined up at centre forward and full-back in the course of winning 93 caps. An architect by profession, he designed a new stadium for Rapid which was, after his premature death, named in his honour. He was an Austrian champion and cup-winner with Wacker, then national champion six times and a cup-winner once again with Rapid. He played for FIFA's World XI against England at Wembley in 1953 which ended in a 4–4 draw.

Alan **Hansen**

Country: *Scotland (born June 13, 1955)*
Position: *Central defender*
Clubs: *Partick Thistle, Liverpool (England)*

Now carving out a second career as a television pundit, Hansen was one of the most elegant central defenders of post-war British football. Bob Paisley paid Partick Thistle £100,000 to take him to Anfield in April 1977, and the fee proved a bargain. He was a European Champions Cup-winner three times with Liverpool and also played on that tragic night in the Heysel stadium in Brussels. In 1985–86, though Kenny Dalglish was by then Liverpool's player-manager, it was Hansen whom he chose to be captain and lift the trophies at the end of a sensational league-and-cup double-winning season. An outstanding all-round sportsman, he represented Scotland at golf and squash.

Eddie **Hapgood**

Country: *England (born September 27, 1908)*
Position: *Left back*
Club: *Arsenal*

A small but teak-tough left back, and an inspiring captain who led England in 21 of his 30 games during the 1930s, with 13 more during the war. He was an amateur with Bristol Rovers in his teens, but was allowed to leave and was with non-league Kettering when Arsenal recruited him. He went on to earn five championship medals and played in three FA Cup finals, winning two. His first international was against Italy in Rome, his first as captain was against Italy on his club ground in the infamous "Battle of Highbury" – when he returned to play on after an opponent's elbow had smashed his nose. He later managed Blackburn and Watford.

Ernst **Happel**

Country: *Austria (born June 29, 1925)*
Position: *Central defender*
Clubs: *Rapid Vienna, 1st FC Vienna, Racing Club Paris (France)*

Happel once scored a Champions Cup hat-trick against Real Madrid with penalties and free kicks though he was not an attacker, rather a full-back or centre back. He made his name with Rapid Vienna before winding down his career in France. He won 51 caps for Austria, his international career reaching a climax at the 1958 World Cup finals. After retiring he became one of Europe's most successful coaches, taking Feyenoord to the World and European Cups in 1970, Hamburg also to the European Champions Cup in 1983 and then Holland to the runners-up spot at the 1978 World Cup finals

Alan Hansen: footballer turned media pundit

Thomas **Hässler**

Country: *Germany (born March 20, 1966)*
Position: *Midfielder*
Clubs: *Meteor O6 Berlin, Reinickendorfer Fuchse, Köln, Juventus (Italy), Roma (Italy), Karlsruhe*

Hässler has been one of the finest German players of the 1990s. He came steadily up the international ladder – playing 12 times for Germany's Olympic team. He was voted Footballer of the Year in both 1989 and 1992, was a World Cup winner in 1990 and a European Championship winner in 1996. He joined Köln as an 18-year-old in 1984 and led them to the semi-finals of the 1990 UEFA Cup. Here they lost to Juventus, but the Italians were sufficiently impressed by Hässler to pay £5.5 million for him that summer. He spent only one season with Juventus before being sold to Roma in 1991 for £5.8 million. A free kick specialist who made his Germany debut in a 4–0 World Cup win over Finland in Helsinki in August 1988, he returned home to Karlsruhe after the 1994 World Cup finals. He was part of an ageing German team that struggled in the 1998 World Cup, and Hässler failed to find the net during the tournament.

Johnny **Haynes**

Country: *England (born October 17, 1934)*
Position: *Inside left*
Club: *Fulham*

Haynes was England's first £100-a-week footballer after the abolition of the maximum wage at the start of the 1960s. He won no major trophies in nearly two decades with one club but was the settled, scheming inside left over a 56-cap international career with England. He came in for a great deal of unjust criticism as he stayed fiercely loyal to Fulham (generally struggling) and England (frequently rampant). His career might have added up differently if Milan had persisted in their bid for him, and if he had escaped serious injury in a car accident in Blackpool that had an affect on his health. He ended his career in South Africa winning a championship medal with Durban City.

Helder Marino Rodrigues Cristovao

Country: *Portugal (born March 21, 1971)*
Position: *Central defender*
Clubs: *Estoril, Praia, Benfica, La Coruna (Spain)*

Helder was a national champion with Benfica in 1994 and Portuguese Cup-winner in 1993. One of the latest African-born players to build an international career in Portugal, he scored his first goal for his adopted country in only his second international, a 1–1 draw against Austria. His performances for quarter-finalists Portugal at the 1996 European Championship earned him a reputation as one of the most dependable and versatile central defenders in Europe.

Thomas Helmer

Country: *Germany (born April 21, 1965)*
Position: *Central defender*
Clubs: *Bad Salzuflen, Arminia Bielefeld, Borussia Dortmund, Bayern Munich*

Helmer, a rugged, courageous centre back, joined Bayern amid controversy in 1992. Dortmund did not want to sell to German rivals so Helmer joined French club Lyon…and then Bayern a month later for £3.2 million. That made him Bayern's then most expensive player. Berti Vogts threatened to drop him from the 1992 European Championship squad because of the distraction the transfer controversy was causing. A winner of both German championship and cup, his preferred position is sweeper though he has played most of his football at top level as a man-marker. He was part of Germany's 1998 World Cup squad in France, but along with many of the team's veteran stars, find age catching up with him under the burning French skies. He was replaced in the first half of the second round match against Mexico, and wasn't selected for the quarter-final tie with Croatia that ended in defeat for the Germans.

Willie Henderson

Country: *Scotland (born January 24, 1944)*
Position: *Outside right*
Clubs: *Rangers, Sheffield Wednesday (England)*

If "Wee Willie" had gone throughout his career as he went through his first few years, he would have been perhaps the best Scottish player ever. Despite persistent foot trouble and imperfect eyesight, he had won all four domestic honours – League, Cup, League Cup and cap – before his 20th birthday. By then Rangers had sold international winger Alex Scott to Everton in order to make room for him. He went on to play in 29 internationals and captivate fans with his wizardry, but his career was marred by discontent and gradually petered out.

Colin Hendry

Country: *Scotland (born December 7, 1965)*
Position: *Central defender*
Clubs: *Keith, Dundee, Blackburn Rovers (England), Manchester City (England), Blackburn Rovers (England), Rangers*

Inspirational central defender who has proved a rock for both clubs and country. Starred twice over with Blackburn – having rejoined the club from Manchester City in 1992 for a fee of £700,000. Won an English league championship medal with Rovers under the management of Kenny Dalglish in 1993–94. A pillar of Scotland's defence in the 1996 European Championship finals, he held his place through to the 1998 World Cup in France, where the Scots once again failed to make it through to the second round of the competition.

Andreas Herzog

Country: *Austria (born September 10, 1968)*
Position: *Midfielder*
Clubs: *First Vienna, Rapid, Werder Bremen (Germany), Bayern Munich (Germany), Werder Bremen (Germany)*

Colin Hendry: Scottish Braveheart

Herzog was a Rapid youth product who did not match his potential until he had been loaned out to neighbouring First Vienna. His fine form earned a national team call-up and Rapid forced Vienna to send him back. Herzog fulfilled his potential when he moved to Germany and inspired Werder Bremen's 1994 championship win. He was then rated the most valuable foreign player in the Bundesliga. He joined Bayern Munich in the summer of 1995 but never settled and soon returned to Bremen. He was a member of Austria's 1998 World Cup squad, and although he scored against Italy, Austria went out in round one.

Harry **Hibbs**

Country: *England (born May 27, 1906)*
Position: *Goalkeeper*
Club: *Birmingham City*

Despite his lack of inches, Hibbs was an outstanding England goalkeeper during the inter-war years. Born in Staffordshire, he joined Birmingham City from Tamworth in the summer of 1924. He quickly earned widespread admiration and secured the first of his 25 caps against Wales at Stamford Bridge in November 1929, when George Camsell scored a hat-trick in England's 6–0 win. Hibbs had a part in several outstanding England performances including a 4–3 victory over the legendary Austrian Wunderteam at Stamford Bridge in December 1932. That match was part of an impressive ten-game unbeaten run which included victories over Scotland (5–0), Germany (6–0 and 5–0), Switzerland (8–1) and Hungary (8–2). For Birmingham City, he played 340 league games between 1929 and 1940. His only major disappointment was the 1931 FA Cup Final defeat by neighbouring West Bromwich Albion, then in the second division.

Fernando Ruiz **Hierro**

Country: *Spain (born March 23, 1968)*
Position: *Central defender*
Clubs: *Malaga, Valladolid, Real Madrid*

Skipper of Real Madrid whom he joined for £1.4 million in 1989 from Valladolid, he contributed seven goals to Madrid's league record of 107 under John Toshack in the 1989–90 season. Hierro made his international debut on September 10,1989, when Luis Suarez sent him on after 24 minutes of a 1–0 win over Poland in La Coruna. He was a non-playing substitute at the 1990 World Cup finals but played in all Spain's games at the 1994 finals and in the finals of the 1996 European Championship. Perhaps Hierro's greatest match was the 1998 UEFA Champions League Cup Final when his sure-footed tackling inspired Madrid to victory.

Uli **Hoeness**

Country: *West Germany (born January 5, 1952)*
Position: *Inside forward*
Clubs: *Ulm, Bayern Munich*

In 1970 West Germany finished third in the World Cup finals and were considered among the favourites to win the 1972 European Championship. They achieved this, but much of the credit was due to two men who in 1970 had barely signed professional forms – Hoeness and Paul Breitner. Hoeness was an attacking inside forward who had proved an overnight sensation at Bayern Munich, with whom he won the European Champions Cup. Knee trouble forced an early end to his career but his thoughtful approach to the game had long since made an impression on Bayern's directors. He stayed with the club in an administrative role and would later become general manager.

Hong **Myung-bo**

Country: *South Korea (born February 12, 1969)*
Position: *Central defender*
Clubs: *Posco Atoms, Bellmare Hiratsuka (Japan)*

Hong was an automatic choice for the South Korean national team in their outstanding 1994 World Cup campaign and one of the most effective performers in their own domestic league championship. He was at once one of Korea's best central defenders and also doubled as a powerful midfield player who could score outstanding long-range goals – such as one against Germany in a dramatic first-round group match in the 1994 finals in Dallas. After first appearing in the 1990 finals, Hong made it three World Cups in France 1998.

Mark **Hughes**

Country: *Wales (born November 1, 1963)*
Position: *Centre forward*
Clubs: *Manchester United (England), Barcelona (Spain), Bayern Munich (Germany), Manchester United (England), Chelsea (England), Southampton (England)*

Hughes has been one of the most combative attack leaders in European football for more than a decade. Welsh-born, he was a product of the Manchester United youth system, scoring in his first full league game against Leicester City in March 1984. Later that year he also scored against England on his first full international appearance for Wales. A year later he was United's top scorer, an FA Cup-winner and hailed as Young Player of the Year by his fellow-professionals. Increasing interest from Europe was confirmed when Barcelona bought Hughes for £2.3 million in 1986 but he never adapted either to the football or life in Spain. After half a season on loan to Bayern Munich, he returned to United in the summer of 1988. He was released in 1996 and joined Chelsea. He collected a record fourth FA Cup-winner's medal with Chelsea in 1997, helped them win the European Cup-winners Cup in 1998, then moved to Southampton in the summer.

Joe **Hulme**

Country: *England (born August 26, 1904)*
Position: *Outside right*
Clubs: *Hull City, Blackburn Rovers, Arsenal, Huddersfield Town*

Hulme was considered the fastest winger in the game in the 1930s when he was outside right for Herbert Chapman's Arsenal. He began with Hull City, joining Blackburn in 1924 and then Arsenal for £3,500 as one of Chapman's first signings. He soon received international recognition, against Scotland in April 1927, the first of nine caps. His speed and accurate crosses created many goals for his team-mates, though his own scoring rate was not far short of Cliff Bastin's. While at Highbury, he won three championships and played in four FA Cup Finals, making a fifth Wembley appearance with Huddersfield Town in 1938. He managed Tottenham from 1945 to 1949.

Geoff **Hurst**

Country: *England (born December 8, 1941)*
Position: *Centre forward*
Clubs: *West Ham, Stoke City*

Still the only man to have scored a hat-trick in a World Cup Final. Strong and deceptively fast, he gave loyal, workmanlike service to West Ham in the league, but generally came up with something exceptional on the big occasions. Hurst scored a record 46 League Cup goals for West Ham and 23 in the FA Cup. Then

Geoff Hurst: waited 32 years for his knighthood

there was also the 1966 World Cup when he appeared virtually from nowhere to put the trophy on the nation's sideboard with his hat-trick in the final against West Germany. He was briefly manager of Chelsea before concentrating on his insurance business. Knighted in 1998.

Masami **Ihara**

Country: *Japan (born September 18, 1967)*
Position: *Central defender*
Club: *Yokohama Marinos*

Ihara has been one of the outstanding Japanese players in the cosmopolitan J League since its launch in 1993. He played for Yokohama Marinos before the League opened up for business and has now totalled more than 200 matches. An outstanding sweeper, he first made an international impression in the Japanese national team which won the Asian Cup in 1992. As far as the World Cup was concerned, 1998 turned out to be third time lucky for Ihara, Japan finally qualifying for the finals for the first time, although they lost all their matches. He had played for Japan in their previous attempts to qualify for the finals of 1990 and '94. He was voted Asian Footballer of the Year in 1995.

Victor **Ikpeba**

Country: *Nigeria (born June 12, 1973)*
Position: *Forward*
Clubs: *Monaco (France)*

Ikpeba has been one of the great successes of Nigerian football in the 1990s. An outstanding attacker who can create and take goals with the best, he was discovered by the now-defunct Belgian club FC Liège. He transferred to Monaco in 1993 and was a member of the Nigerian squad which reached the second round of the 1994 World Cup finals. Disappointingly for Ikpeba, he spent the entire campaign on the substitutes' bench. But he made full amends back in the United States in the summer of 1996 helping Nigeria win Olympic gold – beating Argentina 3–2 in the Final – and scored his first World Cup goal in France 1998 against Bulgaria as Nigeria reached the second phase.

Paul **Ince**

Country: *England (born October 21, 1967)*
Position: *Midfield*
Clubs: *West Ham, Manchester United, Internazionale (Italy), Liverpool*

Ince was outstanding as a youth player with West Ham who received £800,000 for him when he joined Manchester United

Trifon Ivanov: Bulgaria's World Cup foundation

in 1989. Six years later United transferred him to Italy for £7.5 million. While at Old Trafford, Ince helped United win the Premiership twice, the FA Cup twice, the League Cup and the Cup-winners Cup. He became the first black player to captain England against the United States in Boston in 1993. Spent two seasons with Internazionale in Italy before returning home to Liverpool. The "Guv'nor" as he's nicknamed, was one of the star's of England's 1998 World Cup campaign, playing in the tournament despite having sustained a fracture of his ankle just prior to the competition. His splendid defiance in the face of adversity after England had been reduced to ten men in the second round match against Argentina earned him a whole host of new admirers, but came as no surprise to his teammates.

Trifon **Ivanov**

Country: *Bulgaria (born July 27, 1965)*
Position: *Central defender*
Clubs: *Etar Veliko Tarnovo, CSKA Sofia, Betis (Spain), Xamax Neuchatel (Switzerland), CSKA Sofia, Rapid Vienna (Austria), FK Austria (Austria), CSKA Sofia*

Ivanov was an intimidating-looking defender who has wandered imposingly around European football. Not content with taking out opposing strikers, Ivanov enjoys thundering home long-range shots. Ivanov joined Betis of Seville in Spain in the middle of the 1990–91 season, left the club after their relegation to the Spanish second division and moved to Xamax on loan in January 1994. He was a key figure in the Bulgaria side which reached the semi-finals of the 1994 World Cup – missing only the second-round win over Mexico through suspension. Later Ivanov was

a member of the Rapid team which finished runners-up to Paris Saint-Germain in the 1995–96 Cup-winners Cup. He played for Bulgaria in their disappointing 1998 World Cup.

David **Jack**

Country: *England (born April 3, 1899)*
Position: *Inside right*
Clubs: *Plymouth Argyle, Bolton Wanderers, Arsenal*

Jack cost Arsenal what was then a British record transfer fee of £10,890 when the legendary Gunners' manager Herbert Chapman signed him from Bolton in October 1928. The fee was more than repaid as Jack played a key role in Arsenal's domination of the domestic game in the 1930s. His Highbury honours included three championships and a third FA Cup winners' medal (he had already won two with Bolton). An England international before his transfer having won his first cap against Scotland in 1924, Jack eventually won nine in all, although his last appearance for his country wasn't until 1932 against Austria. He was also the first Arsenal player to captain England. Later he moved into management with Southend United, Middlesborough and Shelbourne (Ireland). He secured a place in history with the first-ever goal at Wembley, in the historic 1923 "White Horse" Cup Final.

Jairzinho (Full name Jair Ventura Filho)

Country: *Brazil (born December 25, 1944)*
Position: *Outside right/striker*
Clubs: *Botafogo, Marseille (France), Cruzeiro, Portuguesa (Venezuela)*

Jairzinho moved from his home town of Caxias to sign professional forms with Botafogo at 15 and played in the same Brazil squad as his hero, Garrincha, at the 1966 World Cup when,

Jairzhino: scored in every game at the 1970 World Cup

unfortunately, Brazil failed to impress. Four years later he made history by scoring in every game in every round of the World Cup on the way to a stunning victory. He scored seven goals, including two in Brazil's opening win over Czechoslovakia and one in the final defeat of Italy. He tried his luck in Europe with Marseille but returned home after disciplinary problems to win yet another trophy, the South American Club Cup, with Cruzeiro.

Alex **James**

Country: *Scotland (born September 14, 1901)*
Position: *Inside forward*
Clubs: *Raith, Preston (England), Arsenal (England)*

Eight Scotland caps were meagre reward for the outstanding inside forward of the 1930s. First capped in 1926 against Wales, James began as a fiery attacking player (sent off twice in successive matches at Raith) but changed his style to fit Arsenal manager Herbert Chapman's "W" formation. After he arrived at the London club from Preston North End in 1929 for £9000. He scored only 26 League goals in eight years at Highbury but made countless others with his astute passing from deep to the flying wingers or through the middle to Cliff Bastin (until surpassed by Ian Wright in 1997 the record Arsenal goal-scorer) and Ted Drake, who scored seven in a single game against Aston Villa during the 1934–35 season. Despite his superb display in the 5–1 rout of England by the "Wembley Wizards" of Scotland in 1928 , James was often thought too clever by the selectors, though not by fans who adored the little man who stood only 5ft 5in with his baggy pants and shuffling gait. He became a firm favourite with during the 1930s as Arsenal dominated English football. with four championships and two FA Cups.

Paul **Janes**

Country: *Germany (born March 11, 1912)*
Position: *Full back*
Club: *Fortuna Dusseldorf*

One of the greatest German national teams of all time never won the World Cup or any other trophy. This was the so-called Breslau Team, who took their name from the venue of an 8–0 thrashing of Denmark in 1938. Janes was the defensive cornerstone at right back, approaching his peak in the middle of a international career which spanned a then record 71 appearances. Janes captained Greater Germany in their last game before war forced a halt to football – a 5–2 win over Slovakia in Bratislava on November 22, 1942. He was a one-club player, spending all his senior career with Fortuna Dusseldorf, with whom he won the German championship in 1933.

Robert **Jarni**

Country: *Croatia (born October 26, 1968)*
Position: *Left back*
Clubs: *Hajduk Split, Bari (Italy), Torino (Italy), Juventus (Italy), Betis (Spain)*

Jarni was the quickest sprinter in the Croatia national team in the mid-1990s, having been timed at 100 metres in 11 seconds in boots. A member of the former Yugoslavia national team which won the World Youth Cup in Chile in 1987, he went on to play for Yugoslavia at the 1990 World Cup finals in Italy. His departure from Hajduk Split was followed by a complicated legal dispute over £500,000 he claimed he was due from the transfer to Bari. He won the Italian league and cup with Juventus and the Croat cup twice with Hajduk Split.He was one of the mainstays of the Croatia side that performed so admirably during the 1998 World Cup reaching the semi-finals.

Pat **Jennings**

Country: *Northern Ireland (born June 12, 1945)*
Position: *Goalkeeper*
Clubs: *Newry Town, Watford (England), Tottenham (England), Arsenal (England)*

Jennings quit football in honour as he won his 119th cap on his 41st birthday in the 1986 World Cup finals. Only defeat, by Brazil, marred the occasion. By then he had played well over 1,000 senior matches in a 24-year career, four of them in FA Cup Finals. He won with Tottenham Hotspur in 1967 and with their bitter north London rival, Arsenal, in 1979, and lost with the Gunners in 1978 and 1980. He also scored a goal with a clearance from hand during the 1967 Charity Shield against Manchester United. He remains one of the finest British goalkeepers ever and a great ambassador for the game.

Pat Jennings: more than 1,000 matches

Joao Manuel Vieira Pinto

Country:	*Portugal (born August 19, 1971)*
Position:	*Centre forward*
Clubs:	*Boavista, Oporto, Atletico Madrileno (Spain), Benfica*

Often known as Joao Vieira Pinto to distinguish him from the veteran Porto full back and captain, Joao Pinto. JVP became, in 1991, the only player then to have won the World Youth Cup twice – first in Riyadh, Saudi Arabia, in 1989, and then in Lisbon. He was subsequently sold by Boavista to Atletico Madrid of Spain in season 1990–91, but was loaned out to their second division nursery club and quickly grew homesick. Portugal's Footballer of the Year in 1993 and winner of the Portuguese Cup with Boavista in 1992 and with Benfica in 1993, his greatest club game was in May 1994, when his hat-trick inspired Benfica to win 6–3 away to Sporting to secure the league title and dispel fears of a financial crisis that had plagued the club.

Jimmy Johnstone

Country:	*Scotland (born September 30, 1944)*
Position:	*Outside right*
Clubs:	*Celtic, San Jose (USA), Sheffield United (England), Dundee*

Johnstone was particularly effective in the 1966–67 season when Celtic won every competition they entered, culminating in their magnificent defeat of Internazionale in a bruising Champions Cup Final in Lisbon. He possessed remarkable talents but, like many great players, was infuriatingly inconsistent – his 23 caps were spread over 12 years. An old-style "tanner-ball dribbler" nicknamed The Flea, he won 16 medals with his club – one European Cup, eight League, three Scottish Cup and four League Cup as Celtic dominated Scottish football. Johnstone also earned a reputation for occasional wayward behaviour, on the field and as well as off it.

Robert Jonquet

Country:	*France (born May 3, 1925)*
Position:	*Central defender*
Clubs:	*Reims, Strasbourg*

"Bob" Jonquet is still considered by many as the greatest French central defender ever. He began in Paris with minor clubs Chatenay-Malabry and SS Voltaire. But at 17 he signed for Reims where he achieved great things. Cool under pressure and an astute reader of a game, he made his name with a resolute display as France drew 2–2 with England at Highbury in 1951. His domestic achievements added up to five league titles and two French cups. He was centre back for Reims, whom he also captained for years, in their two Champions Cup final defeats by Real Madrid in 1956 and 1959. A year earlier, it was only after Jonquet had been injured in the 37th minute (in pre-substitute days when ten men had to carry on the fight) that France had gone down to Brazil 5–2 in the World Cup semi-finals.

Jordi (Full name Johan Jordi Cruyff)

Country:	*Holland (born February 9, 1974)*
Position:	*Midfielder*
Clubs:	*Ajax, Barcelona (Spain), Manchester United (England)*

Jordi was the son of the legendary Johan Cruyff, who named his boy after the patron saint of Catalonia. Played in the Ajax youth sections when his father was head coach in the mid-1980s, then moved to Barcelona when Cruyff senior was appointed manager there in 1988. For several years he refused to commit himself to either Holland or Spain so as not to jeopardise his dual nationality qualifications. However, in the spring of 1996, after he had recovered from a career-threatening knee injury, he decided to throw in his lot with Holland for whom he played in the European Championship finals in England when the Dutch failed to click. His father's acrimonious departure as Barcelona coach meant the writing was also on the wall for Jordi and he was duly sold to Manchester United. Unfortunately, since arriving at the English club, Jordi has been plagued by injury which, coupled with his loss of form, restricted his first team appearances for the club.

Jorginho (Full name Jorge Amorin Campos)

Country:	*Brazil (born August 17, 1964)*
Position:	*Right back*
Clubs:	*America FC, Flamengo, Bayer Leverkusen (Germany), Bayern Munich (Germany), Kashime Antlers (Japan)*

Jorginho was considered as the best right back in the world throughout the first half of the 1990s when his career swung from Brazil to Germany. He made his name in Rio de Janeiro with America and then Flamengo. He won the Copa America with Brazil and then the 1994 World Cup. The Final, in Pasadena, ended after only 20 minutes for Jorginho when he was injured and had to substituted. At club level, he gambled on a transfer to Germany with Bayer Leverkusen after playing in the 1990 World Cup finals. He joined Bayern in the summer of 1992, helped them win the 1994 league title, then – to the fans' surprise – transferred to Japan in the middle of Bayern's 1994–95 Champions Cup campaign. A leading adherent of the Athletes of Christ movement, he was also a winner of the FIFA Fair Play award for his charity work

Jose Augusto Pinto de Almeida

Country: *Portugal (born April 13, 1937)*
Position: *Outside right/midfielder*
Clubs: *Barreirense, Benfica*

Jose Augusto was considered, after Frenchman Raymond Kopa, as the best "thinking" right winger in Europe in the late 1950s and early 1960s and appeared in five Champions Cup Finals. He was a winner in 1961 and 1962 and a loser in 1963, 1965 and 1968 against Manchester United, by which time he had been transformed into an attacking midfield player. He was a key member of the Portugal side which finished third at the 1966 World Cup and later, after retiring, coached both Benfica and the Portuguese national team. Augusto was originally a centre forward, a position in which he had already made his debut for Portugal when Benfica bought him from local club Barreirense in 1959 on the recommendation of coach Bela Guttmann – who then converted him, with great success, into an outside right.

Julinho (Full name Julio Botelho)

Country: *Brazil (born August 3, 1929)*
Position: *Outside right*
Clubs: *Portuguesa, Fiorentina (Italy), Palmeiras*

The later emergence of Garrincha tended to overshadow the genius of Julinho on the Brazilian right wing. He was playing for Portuguesa of Sao Paulo when he starred in the Brazil side which fell to Hungary in the quarter-finals of the 1954 World Cup. Fiorentina took Julinho to Italy a year later where he enjoyed a wonderful three seasons, including a keynote contribution to Fiorentina's league title win in 1956 when they lost only once. Playing in Italy cost him a chance of playing for Brazil in the 1958 World Cup. A year later he returned home with Palmeiras but, despite one match-winning display against England, failed to regain his place from Garrincha.

Jef Jurion

Country: *Belgium (born February 4, 1937)*
Position: *Inside right*
Clubs: *Anderlecht, Lokeren (Bel)*

Anderlecht's dominance of Belgian football in the 1950s owed an enormous debt to the commitment and precision of Jurion – one of the few players to have achieved international status despite playing in spectacles. He joined "Sporting" in 1948 as an 11-year-old and stayed to win five league championships, the Belgian cup once and the domestic Footballer of the Year award twice. At first Jurion was a right winger but, after the arrival of

coach Pierre Sinibaldi, he was converted into the midfield general, feeding the attacking threat of Paul Van Himst. He was outstanding in Anderlecht's remarkable Champions Cup victory over Real Madrid in 1962. Jurion played 64 times for the Belgian national team between 1955 and 1967 and captained them on 29 occasions.

Miroslav Kadlec

Country: *Czech Republic (born June 26, 1964)*
Position: *Central defender*
Clubs: *Slavia Uherske Hradiste, RH Cheb, TJ Vitkovice, Kaiserslautern (Germany)*

Kadlec was, for a decade, one of the most resolute of European international defenders after making his debut for the former Czechoslovakia against Wales in 1987. Originally a stopper, he later switched to sweeper with great effect. Joined Vitkovice from Cheb in 1985 and was a major influence in their surprise league championship victory a year later. A member of the Czechoslovakia team which reached the 1990 World Cup quarter-finals in Italy, he transferred to Germany where he won the league title a year later with Kaiserslautern. He was acclaimed as Man of the Match in Kaiserslautern's 1–0 win over Karlsruhe in the 1996 German Cup Final.

Andrei Kanchelskis: difficult winger to pin down

Christian Karembeu: World Cup collecter in 1998

Nwankwo **Kanu**

Country: *Nigeria (born August 1, 1976)*
Position: *Centre forward*
Clubs: *Ajax (Holland), Internazionale (Italy)*

Wonderfully-talented forward who appeared to be enjoying a textbook rise towards superstardom. He first attracted the scouts when he helped Nigeria win the World Under-17 Cup in Japan in 1993. Ajax brought him to Holland where he helped them win the 1994 Dutch league title and then the 1995 UEFA Champions League Cup. Ajax beat Milan 1–0 in the final, Kanu appearing as a second-half substitute. He then moved up the international ladder by orchestrating Nigeria's gold-medal triumph at the 1996 Olympic Games. He scored the only goal in their opening 1–0 win over Hungary and hit two more – including the decisive golden goal – in the dramatic 4–3 semi-final defeat of favourites Brazil. Kanu returned from the Olympics to negotiate a transfer to Italy's Internazionale. Within days of signing, Inter's doctors discovered he was suffering from a congenital heart defect. He underwent open-heart surgery in early 1997 and, remarkably, was fit enough to rejoin Inter's squad for the 1997–98 season. His extraordinary comeback was completed in the summer of 1998 when he was a member of the Nigerian World Cup squad. Although he started the tournament as a subsitute he finished as Victor Ikpeba's striking partner in the second round defeat by the Danes.

Christian **Karembeu**

Country: *France (December 3, 1970)*
Position: *Midfielder*
Clubs: *Nantes, Sampdoria (Italy), Real Madrid (Spain)*

Karembeu may have played all his career in Europe but he was voted Oceania Footballer of the Year in 1995 – having been born and brought up in New Caledonia in the South Seas. He made his league debut in France for Nantes in 1991 and was a national champion in 1995, although his hot temper got him sent off during a 1993 French Cup final defeat by Paris Saint-Germain and then again during France's 0–0 draw with Poland in the 1996 European Championship qualifiers. He later moved to Sampdoria and made a banner protest, at an Italian league match, of his opposition to French nuclear tests in the South Pacific. Karembeu missed the first half of the 1997–98 season because Sampdoria would not submit to his demand that they transfer him to Real Madrid. Eventually the deal went through and he won a Champions League medal in 1998. A few weeks later he won another medal – the one every footballer dreams about – a World Cup winners' medal, as a member of the French team that beat Brazil in the final.

Andrei **Kanchelskis**

Country: *Russia (January 3, 1969)*
Position: *Outside right*
Clubs: *Zvezda Kirovograd, Dynamo Kiev, Shakhtyor Donetsk, Manchester United (England), Everton (England), Fiorentina (Italy), Rangers (Scotland)*

Kanchelskis, for all his talent, was not the easiest player for successive managers to handle. Born to a Lithuanian father and Ukrainian mother, his first transfer was to Shakhtyor Donetsk in 1990 after a short spell with Kiev Dynamo. He played for the Commonwealth of Independent States at the 1992 European Championship finals but then gave up his Ukrainian football citizenship to play for Russia. After moving to England he was Manchester United's top league marksman and a league champion in 1993 and 1994, the latter also the year United won the FA Cup to achieve their first "double". Kanchelskis had moved to Everton whom he left in the spring of 1997 for Fiorentina. But the attractions of Britain lured him back in the summer of 1998 when he arrived in Scotland to play for Glasgow Rangers. A temperamental individual, Kanchelskis missed playing for Russia in the 1994 World Cup finals in the USA because he refused to play under the management of Pavel Sadyrin.

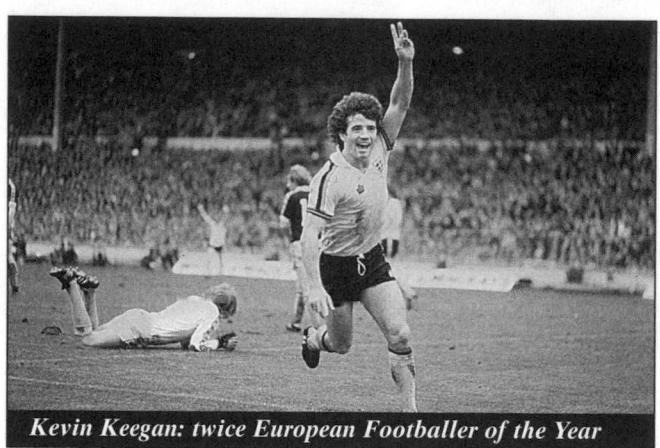

Kevin Keegan: twice European Footballer of the Year

Valeri **Karpin**

Country: *Russia (born February 2, 1969)*
Position: *Midfielder*
Clubs: *Spartak (Tallinn), CSKA Moscow, Fakel (Voronezh), Moscow Spartak, Real Sociedad (Spain), Celta (Spain)*

Karpin earned a place in history by scoring the first goal for the "new" Russia – from a penalty after 61 minutes of a 2–0 win over Mexico in Moscow in August, 1992. He was also considered one of the team's most tactically intelligent players. After winning the 1993 and 1994 Russian league titles with Spartak, he was sold to Real Sociedad in Spain. He is a versatile midfielder who has been used in central midfield by Real Sociedad and then Celta Vigo, but mainly on the right for Russia.

Kevin **Keegan**

Country: *England (born February 14, 1951)*
Position: *Centre forward*
Clubs: *Scunthorpe, Liverpool, Hamburg (West Germany), Southampton, Newcastle United*

European Footballer of the Year in 1978 and 1979, Kevin Keegan was the outstanding England player of the 1970s and early 1980s. By dint of dedication and determination he lifted himself above players with greater natural talent – as his European player accolades prove. In fact, it was a mystery that Keegan did not win the award a year earlier, in 1977, after inspiring Liverpool to their first Champions Cup success. Keegan left immediately afterwards for Hamburg, and he triumphed again – leading them to the German league title and to the 1980 Champions Cup Final (where they lost to Nottingham Forest in Madrid). He was duly voted European Footballer of the Year in 1978 and 1979. The 1982 World Cup should have been the climax of his career. Instead he was kept on the sidelines by injury and played only as a half-fit second-half substitute against Spain in the goalless

draw which brought England's second round elimination. It proved to be his last game for his country. Keegan then invested his enthusiasm in club revivals, first in Southampton, then in Newcastle. In 1984 he retired before returning to Newcastle as manager. He spent heavily, saving them from relegation to the second division and lifting them into the highest reaches of the Premiership. When his cavalier style of football failed to earn rewards, he quit in January 1997. However, he was appointed 'Chief of Operations' at lowly Fulham less than a year later.

Jack **Kelsey**

Country: *Wales (born November 19, 1929)*
Position: *Goalkeeper*
Club: *Arsenal*

"Big Jack" won 43 caps in goal for Wales and played for Britain against the Rest of Europe in 1955. That was a fine record, considering he had been beaten five times on his debut for Arsenal in 1951. Kelsey then went on to be first choice for 11 years until a spinal injury, in a collision with Vava of Brazil, forced him to retire. He remained a familiar figure at Highbury as manager of the club shop. He was powerful enough to withstand the challenges of an age when keepers were not well protected, and agile enough to make many remarkable stops, helped by running chewing gun into his palms. His greatest moment undoubtedly came in the 1958 World Cup finals – the first time Wales had qualified – when he helped them reach the quarter-finals, defeating the mighty Hungary along the way, where they lost 1–0 to the eventual winners, Brazil.

Mario Alberto **Kempes**

Country: *Argentina (born July 15, 1952)*
Position: *Centre forward*
Clubs: *Instituto Cordoba, Rosario Central, Valencia (Spain), River Plate, Hercules (Spain), Vienna (Austria), Austria Salzburg (Austria)*

Kempes was the outstanding individual at the 1978 World Cup finals, though this aggressive striker had gained a first taste of World Cup football in West Germany in 1974. He swiftly earned a transfer to Spain with Valencia and was the only foreign-based player in Cesar Luis Menotti's World Cup squad in 1978. Kempes was the tournament's top scorer with six goals, including two in the 3–1 defeat of Holland in the Final. Strangely, he was never able to scale those heights again, despite playing once more for Argentina in the 1982 finals in Spain, where he should have felt at home. At club level, he won the European Cup-winners Cup in 1980 with Valencia though he missed with his spot-kick in the penalty shoot-out victory over Arsenal in the Final in Brussels.

Dmitri **Kharine**

Country: *Russia (born September 8, 1968)*
Position: *Goalkeeper*
Clubs: *Spartak Moscow, Dynamo Moscow, CSKA Moscow, Chelsea (England)*

Kharine made his top division debut at the age of 16 for Torpedo and his debut in European club competition at 18. At 20 he was Olympic champion in Seoul at the 1988 Games. A year later his career appeared over after he was badly injured, but specialist treatment in Spain put him back between the posts and, after quitting Moscow Dynamo, he was a league champion in 1991 with the army club, CSKA. He played in all three CIS games at the 1992 European Championship finals in Sweden.

Kiko (Full name Francisco Narvaez Machon)

Country: *Spain (born April 26, 1972)*
Position: *Inside forward*
Clubs: *Cadiz, Atletico Madrid*

A tall, rangy, right-side attacker, Kiko made his name by top-scoring for Spain's gold-medal Olympic side in 1992. His five goals included the last-minute winner in the final against Poland. Then he surprisingly fell out of international favour for two years until being recalled for a 3–0 win over FYR

Jürgen Klinsmann: captained Germany to Euro 96 win

Macedonia in November 1995 – when he scored his first goal for Spain. His early club career was a struggle. He joined Cadiz at 13 and spent six years playing decisive roles in two relegation play-offs against Figueras and Malaga. He scored 12 goals in 78 games for Cadiz and was then sold to Atletico Madrid in 1993. He was a member of Spain's 1998 World Cup squad.

Georgi **Kinkladze**

Country: *Georgia (born July 6, 1973)*
Position: *Inside forward*
Clubs: *Tbilisi Dynamo, Manchester City (England), Ajax (Holland)*

Kinkladze has probably been Georgia's finest modern football export. After inspiring Tbilisi to the league-and-cup double in 1995, Kinkladze had a trial with Boca Juniors in Argentina. That was too far away so he returned to Europe in a £2 million transfer to Manchester City. Even his skills could not save them from relegation from the Premier League in 1996 and then from the first division in 1998 – while Kinkladze was negotiating his summer transfer to Ajax. Along the way he scored superb goals both home and away against Wales in the 1996 European Championship qualifying competition.

Sergei **Kiriakov**

Country: *Russia (born January 1, 1970)*
Position: *Centre forward*
Clubs: *Dynamo Moscow, Karlsruhe (Germany)*

Kiriakov became an instant favourite with first Dynamo and then Karlsruhe for his brilliant ball control. Ever the man for an occasion, he marked his Soviet Union debut with a goal against Poland in Lublin, in August 1989. His pace and trickery earned many penalties for Dynamo, yet he scored only nine league goals himself in five years. Joined Karlsruhe in 1992, scoring 11 goals in the first season and nine in the second. He was also a key contributor to Karlsruhe's excellent 1994–95 UEFA Cup campaign in which they reached the semi-finals. Played for the CIS at the 1992 European Championship finals but missed the 1994 World Cup finals.

Jürgen **Klinsmann**

Country: *Germany (September 30, 1964)*
Position: *Centre forward*
Clubs: *Gingen, Geislingen, Stuttgarter Kickers, VfB Stuttgart, Internazionale (Italy), Monaco (France), Tottenham Hotspur (England), Bayern Munich, Sampdoria (Italy), Tottenham Hotspur (England)*

Klinsmann must be the richest striker in the world after a string of highly-paid transfers which has seen him starring in four different countries – Germany, Italy, France and England. "Klinsi" was top scorer in the German league with 19 goals in 1987–88, a UEFA Cup-winner with Internazionale in 1991, with Bayern Munich in 1996 and runner-up with Stuttgart in 1989. He was twice Footballer of the Year in Germany in 1988 and 1994 and also voted Footballer of the Year in England in 1995, on the strength of his first remarkable season with Tottenham Hotspur which featured 20 goals in the league and nine in FA and League Cups. His most memorable international performance was inspiring West Germany to a 2–1 win over Holland in the second round of the 1990 World Cup finals. Klinsmann returned to Germany with Bayern Munich in 1995, after an acrimonious departure from Tottenham, and scored a record 15 goals on their way to UEFA Cup success. He then took over as captain of Germany from injured Lothar Matthaus and led his country – despite injury – to victory in the 1996 European Championship. After a short spell with Sampdoria, he returned to Spurs in 1998 to help save the former giants from humiliating relegation (which he did with four goals on the last day of the season). One of the primary reasons behind his return to England and Spurs – where he was well-received by the fans despite fears he might not be – was a desire to play for Germany in the 1998 World Cup. It is alleged that he had written into his contract at Spurs a clause preventing him from being dropped..But Klinsmann did make the World Cup, scoring three goals as Germany reached the quarter-final stage.

Ronald Koeman: decisive free kicks

Patrick Stephan **Kluivert**

Country: *Holland (September 1, 1976)*
Position: *Centre forward*
Clubs: *Schellingewoude (Amsterdam), Ajax, Milan (Italy)*

Kluivert is, to many experts, the finest natural Dutch talent since Johan Cruyff. A product of the Ajax junior system, he made a sensational debut at 18 in a 3–0 win over old rivals Feyenoord in the 1994 Dutch Supercup. Another Supercup success fell his way in 1995 as well as Dutch league crowns in 1995 and 1996. Above all, he scored the goal which beat Milan in the European Champions Cup Final in Vienna in 1995. He then helped Ajax win the 1995 World Club Cup and the European Supercup. He scored both goals to take Holland to Euro 96 when they beat the Republic of Ireland 2–0 in a play-off at Anfield, Liverpool, in December 1995, but knee surgery the following spring reduced his effectiveness in the finals. Kluivert took advantage of the Bosman ruling to join Milan in the summer of 1997 on a free transfer. He enjoyed a mixed 1998 World Cup finals with Holland, scoring in the semi-final against Brazil, but at other times he looked diffident and hurried.

Sandor **Kocsis**

Country: *Hungary (born September 30, 1929)*
Position: *Inside right*
Clubs: *Ferencvaros, Honved, Young Fellows (Switzerland), Barcelona (Spain)*

Kocsis was one of international football's great strikers, with 75 goals in 68 games. He was also three times the Hungarian league's top scorer and leading marksman, with 11 goals, at the 1954 World Cup finals. In the Honved and Hungary teams of the early 1950s, Kocsis and fellow inside-forward Puskas pushed up while the nominal centre forward withdrew towards midfield, creating gaps for the others to exploit. After the Hungarian Revolution of 1956, he decided to stay abroad and joined Barcelona, winning the Fairs Cup in 1960. A year later he was on the losing side in the Champions Cup Final against Benfica.

Ronald **Koeman**

Country: *Holland (born March 21, 1963)*
Position: *Central defender*
Clubs: *Groningen, PSV Eindhoven, Barcelona (Spain)*

Despite lacking pace, Koeman established himself as one of the world's best sweepers as well as becoming a free-kick expert. It was from a dead-ball opportunity that Koeman thundered the winner for Barcelona in the final of the 1992 Champions Cup, a trophy he also won with PSV Eindhoven in 1988. He was joint top-scorer with three goals in the 1993–94 Champions League, thanks to his free-kicks and ice-cool penalties. Ronald and brother Erwin began with their father's old club, Groningen, and were later members of the Holland side which won the European Championship, beating the Soviet Union 2–0 in 1988, a good year from him as he also won the treble of European Champions Cup, Dutch league and cup in 1988, then moved to Barcelona in 1989 – winning four Spanish league titles and the Champions Cup again in 1992.

Jürgen **Kohler**

Country: *Germany (born October 6, 1965)*
Position: *Central defender*
Clubs: *Jahn Lambsheim, Waldhof-Mannheim, Köln, Bayern Munich, Juventus (Italy), Borussia Dortmund*

Kohler was perhaps the best man-marking stopper in European football in the 1990s. He made his name with Waldhof-Mannheim, then Köln – who sold him to Bayern Munich for £1 million in 1989. He was transferred to Juventus in 1991 for £5 million, then a world record for a defender. A World Cup-winner in 1990, he was, with Juventus, a UEFA Cup winner in 1993 and Italian league champion in 1995. He returned to Germany in the summer of 1995 – yet still ended up playing, with Dortmund, in the same UEFA Champions League group he would have played in for Juventus. He had announced that he would retire from national team football after the 1996 European Championship finals, but he was injured early in the Germans' opening match against the Czech Republic and missed the rest of the tournament. He then decided to postpone his retirement, and was rewarded with a Champions League winners' medal in 1997 when Dortmund beat Juventus; and he also won a place in the 1998 German World Cup squad.

Ivan **Kolev**

Country: *Bulgaria (born November 1, 1930)*
Position: *Inside forward/outside left*
Club: *CDNA/CSKA Sofia*

Kolev was the first great Bulgarian footballer. He was often compared for control and vision with Hungary's Ferenc Puskas, with whom he was a contemporary. Kolev could play outside or inside left and spent all his career with the Bulgarian army club, variously known as CDNA and then as CSKA Sofia. He scored 25 goals in 75 internationals and led Bulgaria on their first appearance at a major soccer tournament in the 1952 Helsinki Olympic Games. With CDNA/CSKA he was champion of Bulgaria on 11 occasions and won the cup four times.

Kalman **Konrad**

Country: *Hungary (born 1895)*
Position: *Inside forward*
Clubs: *MTK Budapest, FK Austria (Austria)*

Konrad was one of the early greats of central European football, first capped for Hungary at inside-forward in 1914, the same year MTK Budapest began a decade-long domination of the domestic game. His skills were hailed as the example followed by successive early stars such as Alfred Schaffer – the original "Football King" – and Gyorgy Orth. Konrad was persuaded to move to FK Austria in the mid-1920s, returned to Hungary to play again for the national team in 1928 and later retired to become a coach in Sweden.

Raymond **Kopa**

Country: *France (born October 13, 1931)*
Position: *Centre-forward/outside-right*
Clubs: *Angers, Reims, Real Madrid (Spain), Reims*

Much of the strength of French football in the 1950s and early 1960s came from the influx of Polish migrant families. Raymond Kopaszewski was the most notable product of that generation. His father had moved to France to work in the mines of Noeux-les-Mines and had expected his son to follow him down the pits. Young Kopa did – but not for long, because of a mining accident in which he damaged a hand. His fortune, literally, was his football talent. He was spotted playing for Noeux-les-Mines by Angers and was sold to Reims in 1950. Kopa wore the No. 9 shirt, but was more creator than finisher and had virtually agreed transfer terms with Spain's Real Madrid before the Spanish club beat Reims in Paris in the first European Champions Cup Final in 1956. Di Stefano was the kingpin at Madrid so Kopa switched to outside right – regaining his old centre forward role with France at the 1958 World Cup finals. Just Fontaine may have scored a record 13 goals but he owed it all to Kopa, who was rewarded with the European Footballer of the Year prize. Kopa returned to Reims in 1959 but his later years were marred by injuries and frequent run-ins with authority over players' rights

Andreas **Köpke**

Country: *Germany (born March 12, 1962)*
Position: *Goalkeeper*
Clubs: *Holstein Kiel, Charlottenburg Berlin, Hertha Berlin, Nürnberg, Eintracht Frankfurt, Marseille (France)*

Köpke turned national hero when he saved Gareth Southgate's penalty in the semi-final shoot-out which followed the European

Championship semi-final against England at Wembley. Yet he had been a regular member of the national squad for seven years – being held in virtually permanent reserve status by the dominance of Bodo Illgner. A member of Germany's World Cup squads in both 1990 and 1994, Köpke was voted Footballer of the Year in 1993. Both Stuttgart and Barcelona bid for him after his displays in the 1996 European Championships, but he eventually ended up joining the Marseille revival in France, where he represented Germany in the 1998 World Cup finals as they reached the quarter-finals.

Emil **Kostadinov**

Country: *Bulgaria (born August 12, 1967)*
Position: *Centre forward*
Clubs: *CSKA Sofia, FC Porto (Portugal),*
Deportivo La Coruna (Spain),
Bayern Munich (Germany), Fenerbahce (Turkey)

Kostadinov made his name with CSKA before joining FC Porto in 1990. That same season he scored vital goals for Bulgaria in European Championship qualifying ties against Scotland and Switzerland. He had twice won the Bulgarian cup with CSKA and added the Portuguese version in 1991, scoring Porto's extra-time winner against Beira Mar. His two late goals in the last match of the 1994 World Cup qualifying campaign – against France in Paris – were crucial. They took Bulgaria to the finals in the United States where they finished a best-ever fourth. Kostadinov went briefly on loan to La Coruna in 1994 before transferring to Bayern Munich – with whom he won the UEFA Cup in 1996 – and then on to the 1998 World Cup finals.

Johannes "Hans" **Krankl**

Country: *Austria (born February 14, 1953)*
Position: *Centre forward*
Clubs: *Rapid Vienna, Barcelona (Spain), 1st FC Vienna,*
Barcelona (Spain), Rapid, Wiener Sportclub

Centre-forward Krankl scored 34 goals in 69 internationals and was top league scorer four times in Austria and once in Spain. The finest year for this son of a Viennese tram driver was 1978 – when he scored 41 goals for Rapid Vienna to win the prestigious Golden Boot as the leading league marksman in Europe and starred for Austria at the World Cup finals in Argentina. Barcelona beat Valencia to his signature and he inspired their victory over Fortuna Dusseldorf in the 1979 Cup-winners-cup' final. Serious injury in a car crash interrupted his career in Spain and he went home to Austria briefly. Later he returned permanently to his original club Rapid, with whom he began a new career in management.

Ladislav **Kubala**

Country: *Czechoslovakia, Hungary and Spain (born June 10, 1927)*
Position: *Inside right*
Clubs: *Ferencvaros (Hungary), Bratislava (Czech), Vasas*
Budapest (Hungary), Barcelona (Spain), Espanol
(Spain), FC Zurich (Switzerland), Toronto Falcons (Can)

Kubala, a devastating attacking inside-right, is the only player confirmed as having gained international recognition with three countries – winning seven caps for Czechoslovakia, three for Hungary and 19 for Spain. Yet one of the ironies of 1950s football was that Hungary created a great team without, in Kubala, one of their very greatest players, after he fled to the West in the late 1940s. In exile in Italy, he formed a refugees team called Pro Patria which played exhibition tours and provided him with the springboard to join Barcelona. Kubala was Spanish champion five times and a Fairs Cup-winner twice. He left the Catalan club after the 1961 Champions Cup Final defeat by Benfica but later returned to coach both Barcelona and the Spanish national team.

Ernst **Kuzorra**

Country: *Germany (born October 16, 1905)*
Position: *Inside forward/centre forward*
Club: *Schalke*

Schalke, from the Ruhr township of Gelsenkirchen, were the dominant German club of the 1930s and early 1940s. They won the national championship six times with Kuzorra at inside or centre forward. In 1934 he scored a courageous winning goal against Nürnberg in the last minute and had to be carried off, injured. He played for Schalke from the age of 15 until his retirement in 1950 when, at 45, he was one of the oldest players ever to appear in the original regionalised league system. Kuzorra was, for years, captain of Schalke. Surprisingly, perhaps, he played only 12 times for Germany, though his international career spanned 11 years between a 2–2 draw against Holland in 1927 and a 1–1 draw against Hungary in 1938.

Angel Amadeo **Labruna**

Country: *Argentina (born September 26, 1918)*
Position: *Inside left*
Clubs: *River Plate, Platense, Green Cross (Chile), Rampla*
Juniors (Uruguay)

Labruna remains one of the greatest Argentine football personalities of all time. Not only was he a great inside left, but he earned longevity records by playing with River Plate for 29 years. At the 1958 World Cup finals in Sweden, he was recalled at the age of 40 to complete an international career which brought him 17 goals in 36 games for Argentina. He began with River Plate when he was 12 and won nine league championships. In the late 1940s he was a member of the legendary "Maquina" forward line. In 1986 Labruna was coach when River won the South American Club Cup.

Marius **Lacatus**

Country: *Romania (born April 5, 1964)*
Position: *Outside right/centre forward*
Clubs: *Steaua Bucharest, Fiorentina (Italy), Oviedo (Spain), Steaua Bucharest*

Lacatus, at first an orthodox outside-right, then an out-and-out striker, was a key figure in the Romanian upsurge of the 1980s. Playing nominally as outside right, he used his pace to great effect and scored his first two goals for Romania in a 3–2 win over Portugal in 1985. Lacatus shot his country to the 1990 World Cup finals, then stayed on in Italy with Fiorentina. Later he moved

to Spain before returning home in the autumn of 1993. He found it hard to readjust to Romanian football and was omitted from the World Cup squad for the United States in 1994. At club level, he won all his country's domestic honours with Steaua. He was also a key member of the Steaua team which became, in 1986, the first eastern European team to win the Champions Cup. He forced his way back in to the Romanian side for France '98.

Alexi **Lalas**

Country: *USA (born June 1, 1970)*
Position: *Central defender*
Clubs: *Rutgers University, USSF (full-time contract), Padova (Italy), New England Revolution, New York/New Jersey MetroStars*

Lalas would never claim to rank among the great technicians of the game, but the American central defender was one of the leading personalities of the 1994 World Cup finals. With his wild hairstyle and goatee beard, he was the high-profile personality the media needed to help promote the finals. Lalas had been a college soccer star at Rutgers University and was then signed up to a full-time contract by the USA federation for the 1994 World Cup preparatory campaign. At the finals he claimed some notable scalps: top strikers such as Switzerland's Stephane Chapuisat, Romania's Florin Raducioiu and Brazil's Romario all ended their duels with Lalas without a goal. Once the finals were over, he made history by becoming, with Padova, the first US professional to play in Italy's Serie A. Returned home on

the launch of Major League Soccer, and was a member of the US side which lost all three matches in the 1998 World Cup.

Bernard **Lama**

Country: *France (born April 7, 1963)*
Position: *Goalkeeper*
Clubs: *Lille, Abbeville, Besancon, Metz, Brest, Lens, Paris Saint-Germain, West Ham Utd (England), Paris Saint-Germain*

Lama is another of the modern generation of goalscoring goalkeepers. Early in his career he scored twice in the French top division, for Lille in 1989 and the second for Lens in 1992. It was Lama's saving rather than scoring abilities, however, which had earned the greatest attention and he was snapped up by Paris Saint-Germain – winning the French cup in his first season. The league championship followed in 1994, the league cup and French cup again in 1995 and the European Cup-winners Cup in 1996. A suspension for failing a dope test in the spring of 1997 and then a contract squabble with PSG upset his career. Lama made a comeback on loan to West Ham in England in the spring of 1998 before returning to France and a place in the Paris Saint-Germain squad.

Alexi Lalas: the first American to star in Italy

Grzegorz Lato

Country: *Poland (born April 8, 1950)*
Position: *Centre forward*
Clubs: *Stal Mielec (Poland), Lokeren (Belgium), Atlante (Mex)*

At the 1974 World Cup finals, Lato was top scorer with seven goals. (In the six World Cup finals since no player has managed to score more than six). It was his goals that helped the Poles to third place after they had beaten Argentina, Italy, Sweden and Brazil along the way (their only loss was a 1–0 defeat to eventual champions West Germany.). He was an outstanding striker who later moved back into midfield and proved equally influential. Lato had made his debut for Poland against Spain in 1971 and was a member of the squad which won the Olympic Games title in Munich a year later. In 1973 he became a fixture in the senior national team after impressing on a tour to the United States and Canada, and he went on to score 46 goals in 104 internationals, a Polish record. After leading Poland's attack at the 1978 World Cup finals in Argentina, he was permitted the "reward" of a transfer to Lokeren in Belgium and ended his career in Mexico.

Brian Laudrup

Country: *Denmark (born February 22, 1969)*
Position: *Inside forward*
Clubs: *Brondby, Bayer Uerdingen (Germany), Bayern Munich (Germany), Fiorentina (Italy), Milan (Italy), Rangers (Scotland), Chelsea (England)*

Brian has carried on the Laudrup footballing dynasty to great effect as the younger brother of Michael and son of former Danish international Finn. His first success was in winning the Danish Cup with Brondby in 1989. He then starred in the 1992 European Championship triumph when brother Michael would not play – ironically after a row with manager Richard Moller Nielsen over which position best suited Brian. He then had brief spells in Germany and Italy where, at Milan, he was a victim of the "turnover" policy when six foreigners were contracted but only three could play. The surprise move to Scotland with Glasgow Rangers re-ignited his career and he thrived in the Premier League as he became the first foreign player to be voted Scotland's Footballer of the Year in his first season as Rangers won their seventh league title in succession. He won two more league titles with Rangers and then transferred to English club Chelsea at the end of the 1997–98 season, shortly before he played a large part (scoring two goals) in helping Denmark reach the quarter-final of the 1998 World Cup finals where they lost 3–2 to Brazil. Brian has been Player of the Year a record three times in Denmark – in 1989, 1992 and 1995.

Michael Laudrup

Country: *Denmark (born June 15, 1964)*
Position: *Midfielder*
Clubs: *Vanlose, KB Copenhagen, Brondby (Denmark), Lazio (Italy), Juventus (Italy), Barcelona (Spain), Real Madrid (Spain), Vissel Kobe (Japan), Ajax (Holland)*

Michael Laudrup may well be considered Denmark's greatest-ever player. He has certainly proved Danish football's greatest achiever. Worldwide acclaim first greeted him at the 1986 World Cup finals in Mexico after he inspired Denmark's 6–1 win over Uruguay in Neza. He then missed the European Championship triumph in 1992 because of a dispute over tactics with coach Moller Nielsen. He would probably have secured well over 100 international appearances but for his self-imposed isolation. As a teenager, all Europe's top clubs wanted him, but he opted for Juventus and was loaned at first to Lazio. In 1985 he was recalled by Juventus to replace Poland's Zbigniew Boniek and within a few months was helping them win the World Club Cup in Tokyo. He won the Champions Cup with Barcelona in 1992 at Wembley against Sampdoria and ended his Spanish stint having won five league titles – four with Barcelona and one with Real Madrid. He joined the Japanese second division club Vissel Kobe after Euro 96 but continued playing for Denmark in the run-up to the 1998 World Cup, where he shined as Denmark reached the quarter-finals. He had returned to European football in 1997 with Ajax.

Denis Law

Country: *Scotland (born February 22, 1940)*
Position: *Inside forward*
Clubs: *Huddersfield, Manchester City (England), Torino (Italy), Manchester United (England), Manchester City (England)*

Many Manchester United fans insist that Denis Law ranked above Bobby Charlton and George Best in terms of all-round football genius. Not for nothing was he nicknamed The King. His father was an engineer on a fishing trawler and, as a boy, there was no spare cash to spend on the luxury of football boots – when he was picked to play left back (!) for his school team he had to borrow a pair from the boy next door. Law was a Rangers fans but it was English club Huddersfield which first spotted his potential and signed him as apprentice. He made his league debut at 16, scored on his Scotland debut at 18 and was sold to Manchester City for a then-record £55,000 when he was 20. It was during his ten months at Maine Road that he achieved the feat of scoring six goals which did not count in an FA Cup tie. City were beating Luton 6–2 after 70 minutes when the match was abandoned. The achievement did not go unnoticed in Italy and Torino swooped, signing both Law

Denis Law: hailed the king of Old Trafford

and Joe Baker. Their season in Turin was not a happy one, however. Law scored ten goals in 27 games before a car crash ended his season and he was transferred back to Manchester – and United. Now the prizes rolled in. Law won two league titles and the 1963 FA Cup, was voted 1964 European Footballer of the Year and ran up 30 goals in 55 internationals. Sadly, he missed United's Champions Cup victory in 1968 through knee trouble. He ended his career back with City…scoring the goal which condemned United to relegation in 1974.

Tommy **Lawton**

Country: *England (born October 6, 1919)*
Position: *Centre forward*
Clubs: *Burnley, Everton, Chelsea, Notts County, Brentford, Arsenal*

Tommy Lawton was one of the first footballers to realise what his market value was, and to work at getting it. Hence his frequent moves, at a time when there was rarely any percentage should a maximum-wage "serf" swap one set of shackles for another. Lawton was a star from his dubbin-smothered toecaps to his glistening centre parting. He scored a hat-trick on his senior debut at 16 before making his name with Everton. He won a First Division title medal at 19, scored 23 goals in 22 full internationals and was still frightening foes deep into his 1930s (he finished top-scorer in both the 1937–38 (28 goals) and 1938–39 (35 goals) seasons. First capped in 1939, his best years were lost to the war.

Leonardo Nascimento de Araujo

Country: *Brazil (born September 5, 1969)*
Position: *Left back/midfielder*
Clubs: *Flamengo, Sao Paulo, Valencia (Spain), Sao Paulo, Kashima Antlers (Japan), Paris Saint-Germain (France), Milan (Italy)*

Remarkable all-rounder Leonardo was a left back when he was a member of the Brazil squad who won the World Cup in 1994. He would have played in the final had he not been suspended after being sent off for a foul on Tab Ramos of the United States in Brazil's second-round victory. A year earlier he had helped Sao Paulo win the South American Club Cup and the unofficial World Club Cup in Tokyo. In 1997 he won the Copa America with Brazil. After spells in Japan, France and then Italy, he linked up with his compatriots for the 1998 World Cup finals.

Leonidas da Silva

Country: *Brazil (born November 11, 1910)*
Position: *Centre forward*
Clubs: *Havanesa, Barroso, Sul Americano, Sirio Libanes, Bomsucesso, Nacional (Uruguay), Vasco da Gama, Botafogo, Flamengo, Sao Paulo*

Leonidas played only 23 times at centre forward for Brazil but that was in the 1930s. He is credited with having invented the overhead bicycle-kick, which was unveiled to the international game when he scored twice on his debut against Uruguay in 1932. The Uruguayans were so impressed he was immediately signed up by top club Nacional. He was eight-goal top scorer at the 1938 World Cup, including four in a 6–5 victory over Poland. Unfortunately, Leonidas was rested in the semi-final against Italy, to keep him fresh for the final…but Brazil lost.

Yordan **Lechkov**

Country: *Bulgaria (born July 9, 1967)*
Position: *Midfielder*
Clubs: *Sliven, CSKA Sofia, Hamburg (Germany), Galatasaray (Turkey)*

Lechkov was one of the surprise heroes of the 1994 World Cup finals. He had begun as a striker with Sliven before being commandeered by the army club, CSKA Sofia. He was their championship-winning leading scorer with 17 goals in 29 league games before moving to Hamburg in 1992. Lechkov then turned the tables on his club hosts by scoring the historic winner for Bulgaria which eliminated holders Germany in Giants Stadium, New Jersey, in the 1994 World Cup quarter-finals.

Billy **Liddell**

Country: *Scotland (born January 10, 1922)*
Position: *Outside right/outside left/centre forward*
Club: *Liverpool*

An accountant, Justice of the Peace and youth worker who allied all these activities to football, Billy Liddell is still revered as among the greatest players in Liverpool history, which is saying a great deal given the club's glorious past. Liddell lost six of what would have been his best years to war service and spent all his career with the one club. Apart from the championship in 1947 and a Cup Final defeat three years later, Liverpool achieved little during his 15 years, but he set club records with 492 League appearances and 216 goals, as well as representing Scotland 28 times and Great Britain in two games against the Rest of Europe. A crowd of more than 40,000 turned out at Anfield for his emotional testimonial.

Gary Lineker: the salute of success

Nils **Liedholm**

Country: *Sweden (born October 8, 1922)*
Position: *Inside forward/sweeper*
Clubs: *Norrkoping, Milan (Italy)*

Liedholm would, in due course, become as outstanding and successful a coach as he had been a player. Initially an inside forward, he later moved back to wing half and was one of the best of sweepers in his veteran years. He began with Norrköping, winning two championship medals and playing 18 times for his country before transferring to Italy after helping Sweden win, from outside left, the 1948 Olympic title. In Italy he formed the Grenoli trio with Gunnar Nordahl and Gunnar Gren and scored 60 goals in 367 league games for Milan. At the end of his career he captained hosts Sweden to the runners-up spot at the 1958 World Cup finals. After retiring as a player, he stayed with Milan as a youth coach and later took charge of the senior team in 1964. He also managed Fiorentina and Roma.

Gary **Lineker**

Country: *England (born November 30, 1960)*
Position: *Centre forward*
Clubs: *Leicester, Everton, Barcelona (Spain), Tottenham, Nagoya Grampus 8 (Japan)*

Lineker went within one of England's 49-goal scoring record, with ten of them in World Cup final stages, led the First Division marksmen with three clubs, scored a hat-trick against Real Madrid and won the FA Cup after missing a penalty, having scored in an earlier final and lost. Along the way all sorts of other records fell to this unassuming son of a market trader, who accepted good and bad with the smiling sincerity that, allied to his skill, made him such a popular figure all over the world. successful spells at Everton, Barcelona and Tottenham Hotspur, where for a while he formed a thrilling understanding with Paul Gascoigne, Lineker ended his playing career as a superb ambassador for the game on its professional launch in Japan. On retiring he launched a new career as a broadcaster.

Pierre **Littbarski**

Country: *West Germany (born April 16, 1960)*
Position: *Outside right*
Clubs: *Hertha Zehlendorf, Köln, Racing Paris (France), Köln, JEF United (Japan)*

Before heading out to Japan to wind down his career, Littbarski described his career ambition as "scoring a goal after beating all ten outfield players, dribbling round the goalkeeper and putting the ball in the net with a backheel." An outside right who later took his dribbling skills back into midfield, he shot to fame by hitting two goals on his debut for West Germany in a World Cup qualifier against Austria in 1981. He joined Köln, the club with which he is most associated, in 1978, played in the 1982 and 1986 World Cup finals and finally won a winners' medal in 1990 when Germany avenged their 1986 final defeat, by beating Argentina 1–0 in the final.

Nat **Lofthouse**

Country:	*England (born August 27, 1925)*
Position:	*Centre forward*
Club:	*Bolton Wanderers*

Nicknamed the Lion of Vienna thanks to the courage and commitment which earned this dashing centre-forward a dramatic goal in an international against Austria. A native of Bolton, he followed Tommy Lawton into the local school side, gaining a first England cap against Yugoslavia in 1951. He was Footballer of the Year in 1953 when Bolton lost to Blackpool in the FA Cup Final. When he did collect an FA Cup-winner's medal, in 1958, it was amid controversy after he shoulder-charged Manchester United keeper Harry Gregg over the goal-line for one of Bolton's two goals. In 1959 he made a remarkable international comeback for England, at the age of 35, against both Wales and the Soviet Union.

Patrice **Loko**

Country:	*France (born February 6, 1970)*
Position:	*Centre forward*
Clubs:	*Nantes, Paris Saint-Germain*

Loko enjoyed the odd experience of making his international debut for France in a "non-match" – a 2–0 win in a goodwill friendly against Sporting Clube of Portugal for the benefit of the Portuguese colony in Paris. He had earned his chance by scoring 22 goals for the Nantes side which won the 1995 league championship. He did not stay for their Champions League campaign, however, transferring during the summer to Paris Saint-Germain. At first he appeared to have made a disastrously wrong choice. Within weeks of the start of the 1995–96 season he was admitted to a psychiatric clinic after suffering a mental breakdown brought on by the mixed pressure of his transfer to PSG and domestic difficulties he was experiencing. The season had a happy ending, however, when Loko fought back from his trauma and returned to duty in time to help Paris beat Rapid Vienna 1–0 to become the first French club to win the European Cup-winners Cup.

Patrice Loko: ongoing battle to beat the pressure

Wlodzimierz **Lubanski**

Country:	*Poland (born February 28, 1947)*
Position:	*Centre forward*
Clubs:	*GKS Gliwice, Gornik Zabrze, Lokeren (Belgium), Valenciennes (France), Quimper (France), Lokeren (Belgium)*

Lubanski emerged with the miners' club, Gornik, in the mid-1960s and took over the mantle of inspiration with both clubs and country from Ernest Pol. He counts among Poland's finest players even though injuries were not kind to him. Lubanski was four times top league marksman in Poland and captained his country to the 1972 Olympic Games victory in Munich. The following year he suffered a serious thigh injury in a World Cup qualifier against England and missed the finals in which Poland finished third. He returned to national team duty at the 1978 finals in Argentina but by now the rest of the team was past its best. He wound down his career in Belgium and France.

Luis Enrique Martinez Garcia

Country:	*Spain (born May 8, 1970)*
Position:	*Full back/midfield/striker*
Clubs:	*Sporting Gijon, Real Madrid, Barcelona*

Not many players transfer between Real Madrid and Barcelona, the twin giants of the Spanish game. Luis Enrique became one of that handful, however, after starring at the finals of the 1996 European Championship. He then demonstrated his mental resilience with a man-of-the-match display on his first return to Madrid's Bernabeu stadium for his new team – even though Barcelona lost 2–0 and he was jeered by 100,000 Madridistas. Oddly, Luis Enrique was rejected by Barcelona after a five-day trial, so he joined Madrid instead for £1.25 million in 1991. A year later he was a key member of Spain's gold-medal side in the Barcelona Olympics and earned promotion to the senior national team. The 1994 World Cup was a painful experience, however, since Luis Enrique ended it with a broken nose from the elbow of Italy's Mauro Tassotti (who was duly suspended for nine international matches). He won the Spanish league with Real Madrid in 1995 and Barcelona in 1998.

Luis Garcia

Country: *Mexico (born June 10, 1969)*
Position: *Midfielder*
Clubs: *UNAM, Atletico Madrid (Spain), Atlante*

Luis Garcia has been portrayed as the successor to Hugo Sanchez as figurehead for the Mexican national team. A quick-thinking, quick-moving forward with an eye for goal, he began with the Pumas of UNAM in Mexico City, then moved to Atletico Madrid in 1989. Club obligations limited his appearances for the national team, but Luis Garcia was Mexico's second-top scorer with four goals in the 1994 World Cup qualifiers and received a Prima award from the Mexican federation for his outstanding contribution to qualification for the finals. He was used both in midfield and as a forward in Mejia Baron's 4–4–2 tactical system. At USA 94 he was two-goal man-of-the-match in the 2–1 win over the Irish Republic, but injury cruelly deprived him of a place in Mexico's team in the 1998 World Cup finals when his skills would have proved invaluable.

Sepp Maier

Country: *West Germany (born February 28, 1944)*
Position: *Goalkeeper*
Clubs: *TSV Haar, Bayern Munich*

Maier made his West Germany debut in 1966, when he was No. 3 goalkeeper in the World Cup squad in England, and was a member of the Germans' European Championship-winning side against the Soviet Union in Brussels in 1972. He won the European Champions Cup three times with Bayern as well as the World Club Cup against Atletico Mineiro of Brazil in 1976. The pinnacle of his career was in 1974 when he first won the European Champions Cup with Bayern Munich and then the World Cup with West Germany. He was noted for his love of tennis and even opened a tennis school thanks to the money he earned in a 19-year career with Bayern. Maier played 473 league matches including a run of 422 consecutive games.

Majid Abdullah Mohammed

Country: *Saudi Arabia (born January 11, 1959)*
Position: *Centre forward*
Club: *Al-Nasr*

Majid was confirmed in the spring of 1995 as the world game's record international with no fewer than 147 senior matches to his credit. He was born, in fact, in Sudan but his family emigrated to Saudi Arabia when he was a child. Saudi Arabia's best-ever player, he was variously nicknamed the "Arab Pele" or the "Pele of the Desert" and was voted 1984 Asian Footballer of the Year. He made his international debut at 17 in 1978 and was the key figure in the Saudis' progress to the 1984 Olympics, scoring six goals in four matches in the qualifiers. That same year he scored a brilliant solo goal in a 2–0 victory over China in the final of the Asian Cup. He also scored the 71st-minute equaliser which earned Saudi Arabia a 2–2 draw with Scotland in Riyadh in 1988. Sadly, the Saudis' 1994 World Cup debut was just too late for the world to see Majid at his best. He played just half a match against both Holland and Belgium.

Paolo Maldini

Country: *Italy (born June 26, 1968)*
Position: *Left back/sweeper*
Club: *Milan*

Sepp Maier: 1974 World Cup winner

Maldini junior, captain of Milan and Italy, has been an automatic choice for most observers' "World XI" throughout the 1990s. His career has seen him emulate the success of his father, Cesare, who was captain of Milan's 1963 European Champions Cup-winning side and more recently national manager. Son Paolo started under his father's tutelage in the Milan youth system and made his league debut as 16-year-old in a 1–1 draw with Udinese in January, 1985. Once asked if his father had favoured him, Paolo replied: "No, quite the opposite. He was much harder on me than on any of the others!" Maldini followed in father's footsteps by winning the Champions Cup in 1989, 1990 and 1993 – the latter success having been achieved as deputy for suspended Franco Baresi in his father's old role as sweeper. Maldini won World Cup medals when Italy finished third in 1990 and as runners-up in 1994, but left France '98 empty-handed after Italy lost in the quarter-finals to the French.

Diego Maradona: greatest player of his generation

Diego **Maradona**

Country: *Argentina (born October 30, 1960)*

Position: *Centre forward*

Clubs: *Argentinos Juniors, Boca Juniors, Barcelona (Spain), Napoli (Italy), Seville (Spain), Newell's Old Boys, Boca J*

Diego Maradona was much more than the world's greatest footballer throughout the 1980s and early 1990s. He was also the most controversial and the most enigmatic, unable to appear in public or on a football pitch without arousing the most contrasting of emotions. His admirers in Argentina, where he enjoyed early glory with Argentinos Juniors and Boca Juniors, considered him little less than a god and the *tifosi* in Italy, where he triumphed with Napoli, worshipped his bootlaces. So did all of Argentina after Maradona reached the zenith of his career, captaining his country to victory in the 1986 World Cup finals in Mexico. English fans still rage over his "Hand of God" goal in the quarter-final in Mexico City. But Argentine fans remember most clearly his other goal in that game when he collected the ball inside his own half and outwitted five defenders and goalkeeper Peter Shilton before gliding home one of the greatest goals in the history of the World Cup. He provided a repeat against Belgium in the semi-finals: another brilliant slalom through the defence but from the left, not the right. Then, in the final against West Germany, it was Maradona who provided the slide-rule pass which sent Jorge Burruchaga away to score the dramatic winner. Maradona's great ability made his subsequent fall all the greater. His love affair with Italian football went sour after the 1990 World Cup when Argentina defeated the hosts on penalties in the semi-final in Maradona's adopted home of Naples. The following spring a dope test showed cocaine traces. He was banned from Italian and then world football for 15 months, returned to Argentina and was arrested there for

cocaine possession. Released on probation, he sought to revive his playing career in Spain but half a season at Seville proved a disaster. Only after he returned once more to Argentina did glimpses emerge of the great footballer he had once been. He even returned to the World Cup stage but that ended in the greatest humiliation of all when he was banished from the 1994 finals in the United States after failing another dope test. Where it may end remains an open question. Where it all began is certain: in the working-class Fiorito suburb of Lanus in the province of Buenos Aires where Maradona began playing for a kids' team named Estrella Roja (Red Star) at the age of nine. Later he and his friends founded a team known as Los Cebollitas (The Little Onions) who were so promising that the whole side was signed up en bloc by unfashionable first division club Argentinos Juniors and turned into one of the club's youth sides. On October 20, 1976, Maradona (wearing No. 16) made his league debut as a 15-year-old substitute against Talleres of

Cordoba and a week later he played his first full match against Newell's Old Boys from Rosario. In February 1977 he made his debut for Argentina as a substitute for Rene Houseman in a 5–1 victory in a friendly against Hungary. It appeared odds-on that Maradona would be a member of the squad with which manager Cesar Luis Menotti planned to win the World Cup for Argentina for the first time in front of their own fanatical fans in 1978. Menotti included Maradona in a preparatory squad of 25 players but he was one of the three players dropped on the eve of the finals. It was months before he would speak to Menotti again, but their eventual peace talk paved the way for the first international success of Maradona's career at the 1979 World Youth Cup in Japan. Boca Juniors bought him for a world record £1 million, then later resold him to Spain's Barcelona for a further record £3 million. Before joining the Catalans he succumbed to the pressures of his World Cup, in Spain in 1982, where he was sent off for an awful lunge at Batista of Brazil. It was the recurring theme of his career: a unique talent for football shadowed by a similarly unique ability to arouse controversy. It says much for the magical technique of his left foot that, despite all the negative vibes, Maradona continued to entrance the game. In 1984 Napoli paid another world record, this time £5 million, to end his injury-battered two-year stay with Barcelona. Napoli president Corrado Ferlaino had all manner of problems raising the money. But he was repaid within weeks as Napoli sold a staggering 70,000 season tickets. Two Italian league championships and one UEFA Cup success were the reward for the fans while souvenir merchants did a roaring trade in Maradona wigs. Seven glorious, roller-coaster years later and the partnership was dissolved. Maradona made his first comeback in Spain with Seville but there even Carlos Bilardo, who had been his World Cup-winning coach in Mexico, grew tired of his stormy ways. Back in Argentina he turned briefly to coach Deportivo Mandiyu, then Racing, before undertaking two more playing comebacks – first with Newell's Old Boys, then with his old love, Boca Juniors.

Roger **Marche**

Country: *France (born March 5, 1924)*
Position: *Left back*
Clubs: *Reims, Racing Paris*

Marche was, for years, the "Old Lion" of French football – a nickname which owed much to the fact that he lost most of his hair in his early 20s. A quick, determined left back, he made his league debut with Reims in 1947, won the championship in 1949 and 1953, the cup in 1950 and the now-defunct Latin Cup in 1953. A year later Reims made the supreme mistake of believing Marche was finished and gave him away to Racing. He did not win any more domestic titles but he extended his international

career, which had begun in 1947, right through to 1959 when he boasted a then-French record 63 international appearances. Marche was a cornerstone in defence for the French national team which finished third at the 1958 World Cup finals.

Marquitos (Full name Marcos Alonso Imaz)

Country: *Spain (born April 16, 1933)*
Position: *Central defender/right back*
Clubs: *Rayo Cantabria, Santander, Real Madrid, Murcia, Calvo Sotelo, Toluca*

Marquitos was a defensive pillar of the Real Madrid team which dominated European and world club football in the 1950s. He was born in Santander and followed the same path to fame and fortune as Francisco Gento and, later, Carlos Santillana. He won the first of only four caps in a 2–1 defeat by France in Madrid in March, 1955, but became a national hero two months later when he scored a crucial solo goal in Madrid's 4–3 victory over Reims in the inaugural European Champions Cup Final. Marquitos played centre back in Madrid's first two Champions Cup victories, then at right back in 1959 and 1960. His last club triumph with Madrid was helping them win the Spanish cup against Seville in 1962.

Silvio **Marzolini**

Country: *Argentina (born October 4, 1940)*
Position: *Left back*
Clubs: *Ferro Carril Oeste, Boca Juniors*

Marzolini was a vastly talented left back who could tackle and intercept with the best of them but also display the technique and virtuoso skill of a forward. Thus he was, to many experts and not only Argentines, the finest full-back of the modern era. At only 13, he won the Buenos Aires youth title with Ferro Carril Oeste and became a first division regular at 19. In 1960 he was bought by Boca Juniors, winning the league title in 1962, 1964 and 1965 and playing in the World Cup finals of 1962 and 1966 – where he rose above all the unpleasant mayhem of the quarter-final defeat by England at Wembley to produce the skills commonly associated with South Americans. After retirement, he enjoyed some success as a TV and film actor before he returned to Boca as coach and took them to the league title in 1981. He was forced to retire because of a heart condition.

Josef **Masopust**

Country: *Czechoslovakia (born February 9, 1931)*
Position: *Left half*
Clubs: *Union Teplice, Dukla Prague, Crossing Molenbeek (Belgium)*

Josef Masopust's reign as the finest Czechoslovak footballer of his generation spanned a time of tactical change within the European game. A tidily-built player with great stamina and strength but also delicate control, he was originally a left-half. His defensive understanding with left back Ladislav Novak and right half Svotopluk Pluskal was the foundation of many a victory for both Czechoslovakia and the army club, Dukla Prague. As time went on, however, so Masopust moved towards the centre of midfield for a controlling role which he performed with enormous success at the 1962 World Cup finals. The Czechoslovaks, against the odds, reached the final and even took the lead – after Masopust ran on to a pass and left-footed the ball past the goalkeeper – before losing 3–1 to Brazil. Still, his contribution earned him the European Footballer of the Year prize. Surprisingly, Czechoslovakia failed to reach the World Cup finals in 1966 and Masopust was allowed, as a reward for his honorable service, a then rare permit to move abroad. He played out his career as a midfield general in Belgium.

Lothar **Matthäus**

Country: *Germany (born March 21, 1961)*
Position: *Midfielder/sweeper*
Clubs: *Borussia Mönchengladbach, Bayern Munich, Internazionale (Italy), Bayern Munich*

Unexpectedly recalled for the 1998 World Cup finals at the grand old age of 37, Matthäus notched up his 25th World Cup finals appearance – four more than any other player – when he played for Germany against Croatia in the quarter final. In addition, he is only the second player to have appeared in five consecutive World Cups (the other being Mexican Antonio Carbajal). Matthäus played his first World Cup match way back in 1982, when Germany was still a divided country and reunification seemed generations away. He skippered his country to triumph in the 1990 World Cup, having finished a World Cup runner-up to Argentina four years earlier when they lost out 3–2 in an epic encounter. He later claimed he did not want to take the slightest chance of letting them off the hook second time around. Matthäus played with success for Borussia Mönchengladbach, Bayern and Inter who then sold him back to Bayern while he was still recovering from the knee injury which had forced him out of the 1992 European Championship finals. He switched back from his midfield role to sweeper but his prospects of emulating Franz Beckenbauer and collecting, as captain, the 1996 European Championship were wrecked by an Achilles tendon injury which kept him out for much of the previous season, as well as a highly-publicised squabble over the national team captaincy with Jurgen Klinsmann. Matthäus won league titles and the UEFA Cup with both Inter and Bayern and was the 1990 European Footballer of the Year.

Lothar Matthäus: appeared in a record five World Cups

Stanley **Matthews**

Country: *England (born February 1, 1915)*
Position: *Outside right*
Clubs: *Stoke City, Blackpool, Stoke City*

Stanley Matthews, the original European Footballer of the Year in 1956, was the first great English footballer of the modern era. There will be cases made for Billy Wright, Tom Finney, Bobby Charlton, Bobby Moore and others, but none dominated their particular era as long as the son of a barber from the Potteries in the English Midlands. He was nicknamed the Wizard of Dribble and the magic of his talent survived right through to the closing days of his career when he returned to his original club, Stoke City, and inspired them to win promotion out of the second division. That achieved, at the climax of the longest first-class career of any player, he decided to retire. He went out in a style befitting one of the great legends of the game after a testimonial match at Stoke which underlined his reputation through the identities of the other great players who turned out to pay homage, including Di Stefano, Puskas and Yashin. Always keen to put back into football as much, if not more, than he had taken out in terms of fame and glory, he became general manager of another Potteries club, Port Vale. But the role was too restrictive for a man who had painted his football on a grand canvas and Matthews left after 18 months to take coaching and exhibition courses around the world, in particular in Africa. Later he lived for many years in Malta before returning to settle again in the England. In the 1930s and 1940s he was without rival as the

Stanley Matthews: legendary Wizard of Dribble

inspiring example for all the youngsters who desired to emulate him. His knighthood was appropriate recognition for a 33-year career completed without a single dismissal or even booking.

Alessandro "Sandro" **Mazzola**

Country: *Italy (born November 7, 1942)*
Position: *Centre forward/midfielder*
Club: *Internazionale*

Sandro Mazzola was only six when his father, Valentino, skipper of Torino and Italy, was killed in the 1949 Superga air disaster. It was to evade comparisons for as long as possible that Sandro ultimately launched his football career with Inter rather than Torino. He made his debut in a 9–1 defeat by Juventus in which Inter fielded their youth team in protest at the federation's decision to order an earlier game to be replayed. In 1962–63 the striking inside forward scored ten goals in 23 games as Inter won the league title. In both 1964 and 1965 he won the European Champions Cup and World Club Cup, scoring decisive goals in both European Final victories over Real Madrid and Benfica. Mazzola helped Italy win the 1968 European Championship and was outstanding when Italy reached the World Cup Final in 1970.

Valentino **Mazzola**

Country: *Italy (born January 26, 1919)*
Position: *Inside left*
Clubs: *Venezia, Torino*

Valentino was born in Milan, where he played for Tresoldi and then the Alfa Romeo works side. In 1939 he was bought by Venezia with whom he struck up a remarkable inside forward partnership with Ezio Loik – the pair moved to Torino in 1942. Mazzola captained and inspired Torino to five consecutive league championship victories in 1943 and 1946–49. Before he could celebrate the fifth title, however, he and 17 of his Torino colleagues had been killed in the 1949 Superga air disaster. Mazzola made his Italy debut against Croatia in Genoa in 1942 and was the league's top scorer in 1947. He scored four goals in just 12 internationals and would certainly have captained Italy's World Cup defence in Brazil in 1950.

Ally **McCoist**

Country: *Scotland (born September 24, 1962)*
Position: *Centre forward*
Clubs: *St Johnstone, Sunderland (England), Rangers*

McCoist reached the peak of his career in 1995–96. First he came back from a long injury absence to score Scotland's winner in a

greatest outside right in the world. Opposing left backs feared their duels with him as Matthews brought the ball towards them, feinted one way and accelerated clear another. His adoring public desperately wanted to see him crown his career with an FA Cup-winner's medal. That dream was denied by Manchester United in 1948. But five years later Matthews tried again. When Blackpool were 3–1 down to Bolton with time running out, it seemed as if he was destined never to claim that elusive prize. But Matthews himself took over, ripping the Bolton defence to shreds and providing not only the inspiration for Blackpool's recovery to 3–3 but the vital pass from which Bill Perry shot the winning goal. Like any footballer, Matthews knew his share of defeats. One of the most remarkable was England's 1–0 upset by the USA at the 1950 World Cup finals in Belo Horizonte, Brazil. But England might have found more consistent if controversy had not been raised now and again over whether Matthews or Preston's Tom Finney was the more effective right winger. Eventually the problem was solved by switching the versatile Finney to outside left – though he played for much of his club career at centre forward. Matthews, by contrast, was always and only an outside right, demonstrating his artistry in a position which was later declared redundant when work rate mechanics took over the game in the mid-1960s. Only much later, when coaches suddenly understood the value of breaking down massed defences by going around the wings, was "old-fashioned" wing play revived. Matthews was a true personality and an decisive European Championship qualifying match against Greece at Hampden Park, Glasgow. Then he became Rangers' all-time highest goalscorer, breaking the long-standing record set by the legendary Bob McPhail. Yet McCoist had started out as a midfield player with St Johnstone. Only fortunate accident saw him switched forward into what would prove his ideal role. The goals vanished during a short spell in England with Sunderland. But, with Rangers, he was back on target – being hailed as Europe's top league marksman in 1991–92 and 1992–93. Although he was used effectively as a sub in qualification, McCoist wasn't selected for the Scotland 1998 World Cup squad.

Paul **McGrath**

Country: *Republic of Ireland (born December 4, 1959)*
Position: *Central defender*
Clubs: *St Patrick's Athletic, Manchester United (England), Aston Villa (England), Derby County (England)*

McGrath became the most-capped Republic international despite a career chequered with injury and occasional vanishing

Ally McCoist: Rangers' record marksman

acts on the eve of big games. He won the first of his 83 caps against Italy in February 1985. Born in Middlesex of Irish parentage, he began with St Patrick's Athletic in the League of Ireland before joining Manchester United for a bargain £30,000 in 1982. He helped them win the FA Cup in 1985 before Ron Atkinson – who took him to United – signed him for Aston Villa with whom he won the League Cup in 1994 and 1996. He continued in the top division with Derby County. Each time his managers thought that knee injuries had virtually finished his career; each time he proved them wrong. McGrath was a rock at the heart of the Irish defence in their historic first appearances at the finals of both the European Championship in 1988 and then the World Cup in 1990 (and 1994).

Jimmy **McGrory**

Country: *Scotland (born April 26, 1904)*
Position: *Centre forward*
Clubs: *Clydebank, Celtic*

McGrory remains one of the legendary centre forwards of Scottish football thanks to a string of marksmanship records which included a British record career aggregate of 550 goals (including a Scottish record 410 in 408 league appearances.) His goals included eight in one game for Celtic against Dunfermline Athletic in January 1928, which still stands as a top division record in Scotland. McGrory also claimed the Scottish league's fastest hat-trick when he scored three in three minutes against Motherwell in March 1936. Born in Glasgow, he retired in 1937, managing Kilmarnock before the war and then Celtic for 20 years from 1945 until Jock Stein's takeover. Incomprehensibly, he played only seven times for Scotland.

Jimmy **McIlroy**

Country: *Northern Ireland (born October 25, 1931)*
Position: *Inside forward*
Clubs: *Glentoran, Burnley (England), Stoke City (England), Oldham Athletic (England)*

Jimmy McIlroy was not far behind Danny Blanchflower in terms of his influence and creative contribution to Northern Ireland's remarkable 1958 World Cup campaign. His unhurried, elegant work at inside forward proved ideal for the team's tactics devised by team manager Peter Doherty. He played 51 other games for his country, as well as those four in Sweden, to go with more than 600 at club level, earning a championship medal with the attractive young Burnley side in 1960 and a runners-up medal in the FA Cup two years later – against Blanchflower's Tottenham. He later had a brief but brilliant combination at Stoke alongside Stanley Matthews.

Sammy McIlroy

Country: *Northern Ireland (born August 1, 1954)*
Position: *Midfielder*
Clubs: *Manchester United (England), Stoke City (England), Manchester City (England)*

Sammy McIlroy's all-action midfield style was ideally suited to the hurly-burly of the modern game and earned him 88 games for his country, spread over 15 years, but only five goals. He also played in three FA Cup finals with Manchester United, losing to Southampton in 1976 and Arsenal in 1979, beating Liverpool in 1977. McIlroy's late equaliser in the last of those three seemed sure to take the game to extra time, but Arsenal snatched the winner straight from the restart.

Steve McManaman

Country: *England (born February 11, 1972)*
Position: *Midfielder*
Club: *Liverpool*

Mexico's coach, Bora Milutinovic, summed up what most opposition managers feel when he scanned England's team sheet before a friendly international at Wembley in March 1997. Pointing to the name of McManaman, he said: "That's one name I could do without seeing." McManaman, though indelibly linked now with Liverpool, had supported neighbours Everton as a schoolboy. As a young newcomer, he was one of the most consistent players at Anfield during the latter part of the turbulent management of Graeme Souness. He won an FA Cup medal before he was 21, against Sunderland in 1992, then returned to Wembley to score a personal triumph – and both goals – against Bolton in the 1994–95 League Cup Final. He collected the Man of the Match award, fittingly, from Sir Stanley Matthews – with whom his dribbling skills had earned comparison. Further praise flowed after the 1996 European Championship when no less a player than Pele praised McManaman as one of the event's outstanding talents.

Billy McNeill

Country: *Scotland (born March 2, 1940)*
Position: *Central defender*
Club: *Celtic*

In both size and style, McNeill was a big man, hub of the Celtic defence during their great days of the 1960s, festooned with domestic medals and, in 1967, the first Briton to collect the European Champions Cup. He was a soldier's son and educated at a rugby-playing school, but made up for a late introduction

to soccer with years of splendid service and a club record of appearances. His international debut was in the 9–3 mauling by England in 1961, but he recovered to gain 28 more caps. Later managed his old club (twice), Aston Villa and Manchester City.

Peter McParland

Country: *Northern Ireland (born April 25, 1934)*
Position: *Outside left*
Clubs: *Dundalk, Aston Villa (England), Wolverhampton Wanderers (England), Plymouth Argyle (England)*

McParland was a goal-scoring left winger, equally popular with fans at Villa Park as he was with those home in Newry. He began with Dundalk, making his Northern Ireland debut against Wales in the Home Championship in 1953–54, a year after joining Villa. He scored 98 league goals in 293 league games for Villa between 1952 and 1961 and was also one of Northern Ireland's stars when they reached the quarter-finals on their remarkable World Cup finals debut in 1958 in Sweden. He also featured in one of the greatest of FA Cup controversies: it was his challenge on Ray Wood which resulted in the Manchester United goalkeeper being carried off with a fractured cheekbone in the 1957 final. He scored one of Villa's goals in their subsequent 2–1 win.

Paul McStay

Country: *Scotland (born October 22, 1964)*
Position: *Midfielder*
Club: *Celtic*

An outstanding product of Hamilton, McStay played for his country as a schoolboy and at youth level before graduating to the under-21 team and so to the full national squad. He made his senior debut against Uruguay in 1983 and had plied his creative midfield trade to such good effect that, until injury got in the way, it appeared Kenny Dalglish's record of 102 caps might possibly be within his reach. McStay's loyalty to Celtic was a welcome change in the modern atmosphere of frequent transfers, and he offered outstanding service in difficult years when his club were largely overshadowed by Rangers. An elegant, classy play-maker with a necessary touch of steel.

Giuseppe Meazza

Country: *Italy (born August 23, 1910)*
Position: *Inside forward*
Clubs: *Internazionale, Milan, Juventus, Varese, Atalanta*

Meazza was considered the most complete inside forward of his generation, equally able to score goals and create them. Born in Milan, he made his debut with Inter at 17 and scored a then-league record 33 goals in 1928–29. He spent a decade with Inter before switching to Milan in 1938, playing wartime football with Juventus and Varese and retiring in 1947 after two seasons with Atalanta. Meazza marked his international debut by scoring twice in a 4–2 win over Switzerland in Rome in 1930 and, later the same year, scored a hat-trick in a 5–0 defeat of Hungary. He was one of only two players who won the World Cup with Italy in both 1934 and 1938: inside forward partner Giovanni Ferrari was the other. Prior to the 1938 final, so the story goes, the Italian players received a telegram from their ruthless dictator, Benito Mussolini, that simply said "Win or die". With motivation like that, perhaps it wasn't surprising that Hungary were beaten 4-2. In all, Meazza scored 33 goals in 53 internationals.

Dave **Meiklejohn**

Country: *Scotland (born December 12, 1900)*
Position: *Right half/central defender*
Club: *Rangers*

Meiklejohn, a right half or old-style attacking centre half, is one of the legendary figures in Rangers' history. He joined from Maryhill Juniors in 1919 and played for the Ibrox giants for 18 years until his retirement in 1937. His achievements in that time included 15 Scotland caps between 1922 and 1934, six appearances for the Scottish League, plus a flood of club honours including 12 championships and five Scottish Cups. Born in the shipyard township of Govan, he was a qualified engineer and brought a rare intensity to both his studies and his football career. He returned to football in 1947 as manager of Partick Thistle, an appointment he held until his death in August 1959.

Joe **Mercer**

Country: *England (born August 9, 1914)*
Position: *Wing half*
Clubs: *Everton, Arsenal*

Mercer was once told, "Your legs wouldn't last a postman his morning round," by the great Dixie Dean. But he played for a quarter of a century on his odd-shaped pins before breaking one of them and going into management. Won a League title with Everton and two with Arsenal after they had "splashed" £7,000 on him when he was 32 and carrying two dodgy knees. He also won a Cup Final with the Gunners in 1950 and lost one two years later, despite his heroic leadership of ten men after Walley Barnes had to retire with an injured knee. He repeated his League and Cup success as manager of Manchester City and had a brief spell as England caretaker, between Sir Alf Ramsey's departure and Don Revie's arrival in the spring of 1974.

Billy **Meredith**

Country: *Wales (born July 30, 1874)*
Position: *Outside right*
Clubs: *Manchester City, Manchester United, Manchester City*

Meredith won his first medal, for a dribbling contest, at the age of 10, and played his last senior game – a losing FA Cup semi-final – when nearly 50. Originally a miner, he was often involved in off-field rows with officialdom. On the field he was rarely in trouble, plying his trade down the right wing with enviable skill and consistency. He won 48 caps (11 goals) spread over 25 years, with five lost to the First World War, and played around 1,000 first-team matches, despite missing a complete season after being involved in a match-fixing scandal.

Henri **Michel**

Country: *France (born October 28, 1947)*
Position: *Midfielder*
Club: *Nantes*

Michel was the finest footballer Aix-en-Provence has produced, probably ahead of the 1960s goalkeeper, Georges Carnus. Nantes persuaded Michel to turn professional and, in due course, he became the midfield general and captain of both club and country in the 1970s. He won the French championship twice, in 1973 and 1977, was twice runner-up in the French cup and made the first of his 47 international appearances against Poland in 1967. Later he was hand-picked as assistant national coach by Michel Hidalgo, whom he succeeded after the 1984 European Championship triumph. Not every player was happy under him – most notably Eric Cantona – but Michel proved his own point by guiding France to success in the 1984 Olympics. He coached three different nations at the World Cup finals: France in 1986, Cameroon in 1994 and Morocco in 1998.

Michel (Full name José Miguel Gonzalez Maria del Campo)

Country: *Spain (born March 23, 1963)*
Position: *Midfielder*
Clubs: *Castilla, Real Madrid, Atletico Celaya (Mexico)*

Michel made his debut with Castilla, the nursery team of Real Madrid, and was promoted to the senior outfit in 1984. A year later he starred in the UEFA Cup Final defeat of Videoton, scoring Madrid's first goal and making the other two in their 3–0 win in the first leg in Hungary. He was one of European football's classic midfield operators throughout the 1980s and early 1990s, – making his Spain debut in 1985. He was unlucky to be denied a goal at the 1986 World Cup finals when his shot was cleared from behind the line against Brazil, but he made starring amends in 1990 in Italy when he claimed a first-round hat-trick against South Korea. Later wound down his career alongside old Madrid team-mate Emilio Butragueno with Mexican club Celaya.

Predrag Mijatovic

Country: *Yugoslavia (born January 19, 1969)*
Position: *Centre forward*
Clubs: *Buducnost, Partizan Belgrade, Valencia (Spain), Real Madrid (Spain)*

Mijatovic arrived late on the international stage as events following the break-up of the former Yugoslavia saw his country barred on security grounds from the World Cup and European Championship in the mid-1990s. In that time he established a reputation as a voracious marksman with first Buducnost and then Partizan Belgrade. In 1993 he moved to Spain with Valencia and then Real Madrid in 1996. He won the Spanish league title a year later and then scored a masterful poacher's goal which won Madrid the UEFA Champions League Cup Final against Juventus in 1998. Earlier he had won the 1993 Yugoslav league title and 1992 Yugoslav cup with Partizan Belgrade. In the 1998 World Cup qualifying competition, he was the European zone top scorer with 14 goals – but failed to find the net when the tournament proper got underway in France even though Yugoslavia put a creditworthy performance making it through to the second phase of the competition before losing 2–1 to the Dutch.

Boris Mikhailov

Country: *Bulgaria (born February 12, 1962)*
Position: *Goalkeeper*
Clubs: *Levski-Spartak Sofia, Belenenses (Portugal), Mulhouse (France), Reading (England), CSKA*

Mikhailov enjoyed a high-profile domestic and international career including a starring role at the 1994 World Cup finals. He was once banned for life by the Bulgarian federation for his part in a cup-final punch-up. He was then amnestied in time to play in the 1986 World Cup in Mexico and was voted Footballer of the Year. As Eastern European transfer barriers came down, he left Levski-Spartak for Portuguese football in 1988. Later, after Belenenses were relegated, he moved to France with Mulhouse where he was playing in the second division when the call came to captain Bulgaria in their 1994 World Cup campaign. He proved a superb choice as leader, steering the Bulgarians to an unforgettable 2–1 defeat of the champions Germany in the quarter-finals, before only an inspired display by Italian star Roberto Baggio denied them a place in the final.

John "Jackie" Milburn

Country: *England (born May 11, 1924)*
Position: *Centre forward/outside right*
Club: *Newcastle United*

Jackie Milburn was a centre forward or winger with lightning pace and a knack of scoring memorable goals – particularly the two he obtained for Newcastle in the 1951 Cup Final. For the first, he outpaced the Blackpool defence in a dash from halfway. For the second, he crashed in a 20-yard left-foot drive as the ball was back-heeled to him. Milburn gained two other winners' medals, in 1952 and 1955, when he headed a first-minute goal against Manchester City. He was born in Ashington and spent all his playing career with Newcastle United (the city later erected a statue in his honour) scoring over 173 league goals in 11 seasons. Although he lost the early part of his career to the Second World War, Milburn still collected a total of 13 caps, scoring ten goals, between his debut in 1949 and 1956. United had no more popular servant than "Wor Jackie".

Predrag Mijatovic: decisive goal in Champions' League

Roger **Milla**

Country: *Cameroon (born May 20, 1952)*
Position: *Centre forward*
Clubs: *Leopard Douala, Tonnerre Yaounde, Valenciennes (France), Monaco (France), Bastia (France), Saint Etienne (France), Montpellier (France)*

Milla – real name Miller – made history as the oldest World Cup finals footballer of all time when he played at USA 94 at the age of 42. Four years earlier he had delighted crowds at the 1990 World Cup with his celebratory dances around the corner flags. His goals, particular his second-round winner against Colombia, turned him into the first player to win the African Footballer of the Year accolade for a second time. Milla played most of his football in France, winning the cup there in 1980 with Monaco and in 1981 with Bastia. He was first voted African Footballer of the Year in 1976. Five years later he scored six goals in the qualifiers to lead Cameroon to the World Cup finals for the first time.

Milos **Milutinovic**

Country: *Yugoslavia (born February 5, 1933)*
Position: *Centre forward*
Clubs: *FK Bor, Partizan, OFK Belgrade, Bayern Munich (Germany), Racing Paris (France), Stade Francais*

Milutinovic, a powerful, aggressive centre-forward, was head of a famous dynasty of footballers which has included Bora Milutinovic, coach to the United States' 1994 World Cup side. Milos began with FK Bor, made his debut for Yugoslavia in 1951 and, the same year, transferred to Belgrade with army club Partizan. He scored 183 goals in 192 games before moving controversially to neighbours OFK, then off to Germany with Bayern Munich, before he settled in France. He proved a huge success with Racing Paris before injury forced his retirement in 1965. He scored 16 goals in 33 matches between 1953 and 1958.

Severino **Minelli**

Country: *Switzerland (born September 6, 1909)*
Position: *Right back*
Clubs: *Kussnacht, Servette, Grasshopper*

Minelli was a steady, reliable right back with great positional sense who played a then-record 79 times for Switzerland during the inter-war years. In 1930 he made his national team debut while simultaneously winning his first league championship medals with Servette of Geneva. In the next 13 years he won another five league medals as well as eight cup finals with

Roger Milla: oldest marksman in World Cup history

Grasshopper-Club of Zurich. Minelli was a key figure in the Bolt or Verrou defence introduced by fellow-countryman Karl Rappan and played with great effect for Switzerland in the World Cups of both 1934 and 1938. One of his finest games was Switzerland's 2–1 defeat of England in Zurich in May, 1938.

Luis **Molowny**

Country: *Spain (born May 12, 1925)*
Position: *Outside right/inside right*
Clubs: *Tenerife, Real Madrid, Las Palmas*

Molowny was the first great Real Madrid star of the post-Spanish Civil War era. At first an inside right, later a creative right winger, he may still count as the greatest player to come out of the Canary Islands. He played as a junior for Tenerife and a variety of other island clubs. At 20 he was taken to the mainland by Real Madrid and won the Spanish cup with them in 1947. Three times in the mid-1950s Molowny won the league championship with Madrid but by then a string of injuries had begun to spoil his talent and self-confidence. Doctors recommended early retirement but after Molowny had gone home to the Canaries he made a brief comeback with Las Palmas. He played seven times only for Spain and was later, briefly, national manager.

Andreas **Möller**

Country: *Germany (born September 2, 1967)*
Position: *Midfielder*
Clubs: *Schwarz-Weiss Frankfurt, Borussia Dortmund, Eintracht Frankfurt, Juventus (Italy), Borussia Dortmund*

Möller's emergence as a key member of the German midfield in the mid-1990s was no surprise to those who had listened to Berti Vogts a decade earlier. Vogts, when in charge of Germany's youth team, had forecast that Möller would one day become the seniors' playmaker. Möller played for his country at every junior level and graduated to become a fringe member of the West German World Cup-winning squad in 1990 and was a first choice at the 1992 European Championship and 1994 World Cup finals. In 1996 it was Möller's penalty which won the European Championship semi-final shoot-out against England. But he celebrated it knowing he would miss the final through suspension after having collected a second yellow card. His early club career was a volatile one. His original transfer from Borussia Dortmund to Eintracht Frankfurt had to be resolved by a civil court case. Möller then spent two years with Juventus, helping them beat Borussia Dortmund in the 1993 UEFA Cup Final. Two years later he was playing for Dortmund when Juventus beat them again, this time in the UEFA Cup semi-finals. He had his revenge over his former Italian employers when he helped Dortmund turn the tables on Juventus in the 1997 UEFA Champions League Cup Final in Munich. Along the way Möller also led Dortmund to the German league title in both 1995 and 1996. Although he was in the German 1998 World Cup squad, he played only a bit part in proceedings.

Luis **Monti**

Country: *Argentina and Italy (born January 15, 1901)*
Position: *Central defender*
Clubs: *Boca Juniors (Argentina), Juventus (Italy)*

Monti was notable for a rugged, ruthless style, but he was also one of the great achievers of the inter-war years. An old-style attacking centre half, he won the Copa America in 1927 and an Olympic Games silver medal in 1928 – when Argentina lost to Uruguay in Amsterdam. He was also on the losing side against the same opponents again at the first World Cup Final two years later. In 1931 Juventus brought Monti to Italy. He looked slow and vastly overweight but a month's lone training brought him back to fitness and, little more than a year later, he made his debut for Italy in a 4–2 win over Hungary in Milan. He was not only a key figure in four successive league title-winning sides for Juventus but won the World Cup – at last – with Italy against Czechoslovakia in 1934.

Bobby **Moore**

Country: *England (born April 12, 1941)*
Position: *Central defender/wing half*
Clubs: *West Ham, Fulham, San Antonio Thunder (USA), Seattle Sounders (USA)*

Moore was the golden boy of English football in the 1960s when he was winning captain three times in a row at Wembley – first with West Ham in 1964, then with the Hammers in the European Cup-winners Cup, then with England in the memorable 1966 World Cup triumph over West Germany at Wembley. But not only through his leadership but through his playing example, Moore lives in the memory as a truly great player and remarkable man. Two FA Cups, one Cup-winners Cup and 108 England caps – 100 of them under the management of Sir Alf Ramsey – represent only part of his value to West Ham and England. Even at 34 he returned to the FA Cup Final as a runner-up with Fulham against his old club, West Ham. Born in Barking in Essex, he played a then-record 18 times for the England youth team before making his senior debut against Peru on the eve of the 1962 World Cup finals. He then missed only ten England matches in the next ten years. Moore was in supreme form during the 1970 World Cup when, against Brazil, he fought out an epic duel with the great Pele. He made 544 league appearances for West Ham between 1958 and 1974 and then another 124 with Fulham before retiring in 1976. He died in 1993 only nine days after revealing to the world that he had cancer. One of his greatest adversaries from his footballing days, Pele, was greatly upset by his friend's premature death, calling him a great ambassador for his sport and his country.

Bobby Moore: Wembley winning skipper in 1966

Kevin **Moran**

Country: *Republic of Ireland (born April 29, 1956)*
Position: *Central defender*
Clubs: *Pegasus, Bohemians, Manchester United (England), Gijon (Spain), Blackburn Rovers (England)*

Moran, the Irish Republic's outstanding central defender in the Jack Charlton era, was also an outstanding Gaelic footballer. He inspired Dublin's All-Ireland victory over Kerry in 1976 but switched allegiance when, in January 1978, he signed for Manchester United. Two years later he made his Republic debut against Switzerland and had totalled another 70 appearances by the time the Irish came home from the 1994 World Cup finals. His physical courage was proved time and again as he defied a string of cuts and bruises to hold defence together for club and country. One unwanted historical note: Moran became the first man to be sent off in an FA Cup Final when he was given his marching orders in United's 1985 win over Everton.

Juan Manuel **Moreno**

Country: *Argentina (born August 3, 1916)*
Position: *Inside right*
Clubs: *River Plate, Espana (Mexico), Universidad Catolica (Chile), Boca Juniors, Defensor (Uruguay), FC Oeste, Medellin (Colombia)*

Some older Argentine connoisseurs of the game still consider Moreno to have been the greatest footballer of all time. An inside right for most of his career, he began with River Plate's youth teams and was a league championship winner in 1936. He won four league titles with River and was a member of the legendary "Maquina" forward line of the late 1940s, which comprised outside right Munoz, centre forward Pedernera, Labruna and Loustau. He played for Espana in Mexico between 1944 and 1946, returned to River for two more years, then wandered off again to Chile, Uruguay and Colombia. He scored 20 goals in 33 internationals.

Max **Morlock**

Country: *West Germany (born May 11, 1925)*
osition: *Inside right*
Clubs: *Eintracht Nürnberg, Nürnberg*

Morlock earned German sporting immortality in 1954 when he scored one of his country's goals in the historic World Cup Final victory over Hungary. But that was merely the peak achievement of a superb career which spanned both the pre- and post-war years. An inside right of the old school, both worker and goal-scorer, he was brought up in Nuremberg and played all his football there. He was twice a German champion with 1st FC Nürnberg, in 1948 and 1961. The second title, when Morlock was already 36, earned him his first accolade as Footballer of the Year. He scored 21 goals in 28 national team games between 1950 and his international retirement after the 1958 World Cup finals.

Stan **Mortensen**

Country: *England (born May 26, 1921)*
Position: *Inside right*
Clubs: *Blackpool, Hull, Southport*

Mortensen was as fast over ten yards as any English forward in the late 1940s and early 1950s, with finishing skill to round off the openings his pace earned. He scored four in a 10–0 win over Portugal (away!) in his first international, and his goal in his last England game was his 23rd in 25 appearances. That was against the 1953 Hungarians, a few months after he had become the first man to score a hat-trick in a Wembley Cup Final: his third, after two defeats. Morty loved the knockout, scoring in Blackpool's first 12 post-war rounds in the tournament and finishing with 28 Cup goals as well as 225 in the League.

Alan **Morton**

Country: *Scotland (born April 24, 1893)*
Position: *Outside left*
Clubs: *Queen's Park, Rangers.*

Morton, the original "Wee Blue Devil", was a left winger with elusive dribbling skill and a waspish shot who had a 20-year career and gained nine championship medals and three for the Scottish Cup. He was a mining engineer who spent several seasons with the amateurs at Queen's Park before becoming the first signing for Rangers by new manager, William Struth, who stayed with the club for 34 years. Morton played well over 500 games for Rangers and is reputed never to have appeared in the reserves. He was always a gentleman, often appearing for matches in a bowler hat and carrying an umbrella.

Coen **Moulijn**

Country: *Holland (born February 15, 1937)*
Position: *Outside left*
Clubs: *Xerxes, Feyenoord*

Moulijn played 38 times for Holland between his debut in a 1–0 defeat by Belgium in Antwerp in 1956 and his last game, a 1–1 World Cup draw against Bulgaria in October 1969. That may have been Moulijn's last international but it was far from his final achievement – the following May his Feyenoord side beat Celtic in the European Champions Cup Final in 1970. He helped Feyenoord go on to beat Estudiantes de La Plata in the World Club Cup and retired in 1972 with five league championships to his name. At the insistence of the Dutch federation, Feyenoord inserted a clause in Moulijn's contract that he should never be sold abroad.

Gerd **Müller**

Country: *West Germany (born November 3, 1945)*
Position: *Centre forward*
Clubs: *TSV Nordlingen, Bayern Munich, Fort Lauderdale Strikers (USA)*

Helmut Schon, West Germany's hugely successful national manager in the 1960s and 1970s, described Müller as "my scorer of little goals." It was not a demeaning comment – merely a statement of fact that Müller possessed a wonderful gift for pouncing on any ball, loose for even one split-second, deep in any penalty box and scoring. His most famous "little goal" was, indeed, the winner in the 1974 World Cup Final when Müller twisted to meet a short cross which Rainer Bonhof appeared to have pulled too far back and stabbed into the Dutch net. For all that, Müller was under-rated as a footballer. Rarely did he have a chance to display the full range of his abilities, but Leeds United were certainly caught out in the 1975 Champions Cup Final when Müller had to drop back into the Bayern Munich midfield because of injuries. Not that everyone found even his goal-scoring talents easy to admire. His first coach at Bayern, Zlatko "Tschik" Cajkovski, thought president Wilhelm Neudecker was joking when he introduced the new, young centre-forward at pre-season. "I'm not putting that little elephant in among my string of thoroughbreds," complained Cajkovski. But he did – and Bayern never looked back. Müller's goals shot them out of the regional league to victory in the Cup-winners Cup glory inside three years. At the end, before trying his luck with ultimately sorry consequences in the North American Soccer League, he had scored well over 600 goals including a record 365 in the Bundesliga and an astonishing 68 in 62 internationals. He was voted European Footballer of the Year in 1970 and awarded FIFA's prestigious Order of Merit for services to the game in 1998.

Jose **Nasazzi**

Country: *Uruguay (born May 24, 1901)*
Position: *Right back*
Clubs: *Lito, Roland Moor, Nacional, Bella Vista*

Gerd Müller (right): triumph in 1974 World Cup

Nasazzi led Uruguay to their victories in the 1924 and 1928 Olympic Games and then to the 1930 World Cup. Not only was he one of the great captains, he was also nicknamed The Marshall for his organisational ability at the heart of defence from right back, though he also played occasionally at centre half and at inside forward. He was also a South American champion on four occasions in his 15-year, 64-game international career and was a key member of the Nacional team which so dominated the league championship in 1934 it became nicknamed The Machine. After retiring Nasazzi was briefly national manager for Uruguay at the unofficial 1945 South American championship.

Zdenek **Nehoda**

Country: *Czechoslovakia (born May 9, 1952)*
Position: *Centre forward*
Clubs: *TJ Hulin, TJ Gottwaldov, Dukla Prague, SV Darmstadt (Germany), Standard Liège (Belgium), FC Grenoble (Switzerland)*

Nehoda, a skilled, mobile general of a centre-forward, was the first – and last – Czechoslovak player to come close to a century of caps. He scored 31 goals in 90 internationals, with the peak of his career being the European Championship victory over West Germany in Belgrade in 1976. He was three times a champion of Czechoslovakia with the army club, Dukla Prague, twice a domestic cup-winner and was twice voted Footballer of the Year in 1978 and 1979. Nehoda's international reputation also earned him selection for a Europe XI against Italy in 1981 before he left Czechoslovakia for a career fade-out in Germany, Belgium and Switzerland.

Johan **Neeskens**

Country: *Holland (born September 15, 1951)*
Position: *Midfield*
Clubs: *Haarlem, Ajax, Barcelona (Spain), Cosmos New York (USA)*

Neeskens provided the steel which supported the more technical gifts of team-mates Cruyff, Keizer and Van Hanegem amid Holland's total football of the 1970s. He scored 17 goals in 49 internationals and earned a place in history by converting the first-ever World Cup Final penalty against West Germany in Munich in 1974. He won hat-tricks with Ajax in the Champions Cup, the Dutch league and the Dutch cup. After moving to Barcelona in 1974 he won the Spanish cup in 1978 and the European Cup-winners Cup in 1979. After a spell in the North American Soccer League he attempted a comeback, in vain, in Switzerland.

Oldrich **Nejedly**

Country: *Czechslovakia (born December 13, 1909)*
Position: *Inside left*
Clubs: *Zebrak, Rakovnik, Sparta Prague*

Nejedly scored 28 goals from inside left for Czechoslovakia in 44 internationals and was chosen for Central Europe against Western Europe in 1937. He starred for the Sparta club which dominated the Mitropa Cup for much of the 1930s and for the Czechoslovak national team which reached the 1934 World Cup Final. His skills were described as "pure as Bohemian crystal," and his partnership with outside left Antonin Puc was one of the best of its kind in Europe in the inter-war years. Nejedly scored twice in the 3–1 defeat of Germany in the semi-finals but could make no headway against Italy in the final. Nevertheless he was the World Cup's top scorer with five goals. A broken leg against Brazil in 1938 ended his dream of revenge over Italy.

Igor **Netto**

Country: *Soviet Union (born September 4, 1930)*
Position: *Left half*
Club: *Moscow Spartak*

Netto captained the Soviet Union to victory in the 1956 Olympic Games in Melbourne. A stylish left half, he led the Soviets by

example, captaining them from 1954 to 1963 and winning what was then a record 57 caps with four goals. However, injury meant he missed all but one match at the 1958 World Cup finals. In 1962 he played in all four games when the Soviets reached the quarter-finals in Chile. Altogether he scored 37 goals in 367 league games for Spartak, winning five Soviet championships. Strangely, after retiring as a player in 1966 he became a coach, not in football but in ice hockey. He stayed with Moscow Spartak throughout his playing career.

Günter **Netzer**

Country: *West Germany (born September 14, 1944)*
Position: *Midfielder*
Clubs: *Borussia Mönchengladbach (Germany), Real Madrid (Spain), Grasshopper (Switzerland)*

Netzer was at his best as midfield schemer of the West German side which won the 1972 European Championship, forging a refined partnership with sweeper Beckenbauer behind him. He lost his place in the national team after transferring to Spain with Real Madrid and never regained it from Wolfgang Overath, though Netzer did make an occasional appearance for West Germany at the 1974 World Cup finals. He was twice German champion with Borussia, twice Spanish champion with Real Madrid and a cup-winner once in each country. He was also once West German Footballer of the Year before retiring to the management role from which he masterminded Hamburg's 1989 German championship.

Yuri **Nikiforov**

Country: *Russia (born September 16, 1970)*
Position: *Sweeper/midfielder*
Clubs: *Kiev Dynamo, SKA Odessa, Chernomorets Odessa, Spartak Moscow, Gijon (Spain)*

As a teenager Nikiforov was once described by the legendary Brazilian Pele as one of the world's most promising young strikers. That was after he had led the Soviet Union to victory in the World Junior (Under-16) Championship. But it was as a skilled, attacking sweeper than he ultimately made his mark at senior level. He made his debut with Kiev in the old Soviet league at the age of 17, then transferred to Moscow Spartak in 1993. He was twice Russian national champion with Spartak as well as the league's highest-scoring defender and won the 1995 Goal of the Year award. He went on to score five times from sweeper in the UEFA Champions league in 1995–96, including two decisive goals against Rosenborg Trondheim. The clean-cut Nikiforov was once voted Russia's most sexy player in a poll among female fans.

Luc **Nilis**

Country: *Belgium (born May 25, 1967)*
Position: *Centre forward*
Clubs: *Winterslag, Anderlecht, PSV Eindhoven (Holland)*

Nilis was one of Belgian football's top domestic strikers in the late 1980s and throughout the 1990s. Yet even though he scored more than 100 goals in six years for Winterslag and Anderlecht before moving to Holland with PSV, he did not claim his first goal for his country until shortly before the 1994 World Cup in a 9–0 win against Zambia. He was established in attack with Belgium for the World Cups of 1994 after being controversially omitted from their squad for the 1990 finals in Italy, and played in the 1998 finals where Belgium under-performed.

Thomas **Nkono**

Country: *Cameroon (born July 20, 1955)*
Position: *Goalkeeper*
Clubs: *Tonnerre Yaounde, Espanol (Spain), Hospitalet (Spain)*

Nkono was once African Footballer of the Year and star of the Cameroon side who first reached the World Cup finals in Spain in 1982, then reached the quarter-finals eight years later in Italy. In between, he became the first Cameroon player to appear in a European club final when he starred in Espanol's run to the 1988 UEFA Cup Final. Played for the World XI against Brazil in the match staged in Milan in October 1993, to celebrate Pele's 50th birthday. Then he turned out for the Italia 90 team in Peter Shilton's testimonial at White Hart Lane the following December. He joined the Cameroon squad at USA 94 but did not play.

Gunnar **Nordahl**

Country: *Sweden (born October 19, 1921)*
Position: *Centre forward*
Clubs: *Degerfors, Norrkoping, Milan (Italy), Roma (Italy)*

Nordahl was the most famous of five first division brothers. He was born in Hornefors in Northern Sweden and scored 77 goals in 58 games with local Degerfors. Next came 93 goals in 92 games which brought Norrkoping four championships in a row. A fireman by training, he gave that up in 1948 when, after Sweden's Olympic Games victory in London, he was lured away to Milan. He formed the central spearhead of the Grenoli trio (with Gunnar Gren and Nils Liedholm). Five times he was the Italian league's leading scorer, having totalled 225 goals in 257 Italian league matches by the time he retired in 1957.

Bjorn **Nordqvist**

Country: *Sweden (born October 6, 1942)*
Position: *Central defender*
Clubs: *IFK Hallsberg, Norrkoping, PSV Eindhoven (Holland), IFK Gothenburg, Minnesota Kicks (USA), Orgryte*

Nordqvist was, at one time, the world record international – having won 115 caps in the 1970s and early 1980s. He also played in three World Cups, in 1970, 1974 and 1978, and, with Norrköping, was twice champion of Sweden and once cup-winner. Having taken the plunge to turn full-time professional in 1974, he immediately won the Dutch league championship with PSV Eindhoven and later tried his luck briefly with Minnesota in the North American Soccer League. Surprisingly, considering his century of caps, he had to wait a year between his Sweden debut – against Finland in 1963 – and his second appearance against Norway in September 1964.

Ernst **Ocwirk**

Country: *Austria (born March 7, 1926)*
Position: *Central defender/midfielder*
Clubs: *FK Austria, Sampdoria (Italy)*

Ocwirk, nicknamed "Clockwork" by the British for his consistent creativity in midfield, was the last of the old-fashioned attacking centre halves. He began with FK Austria of Vienna, made his debut for his country in 1947 and appeared at the 1948 Olympic Games in London. Three years later he was back at Wembley, captaining an Austrian side which well deserved a 2–2 draw against England. In 1953 the stopper centre back had taken over throughout Europe and Ocwirk was selected at wing half in the Rest of the World team which drew 4–4 with England to celebrate the 90th anniversary of the Football Association. In 1956, at the advanced age of 30, he undertook the Italian adventure with Sampdoria with whom he spent five seasons before returning for one last campaign with FK Austria. Later he coached FKA to league titles in 1969 and 1970.

Viktor **Onopko**

Country: *Russia (born October 14, 1969)*
Position: *Left back/sweeper/midfielder*
Clubs: *Stakhanovets, Kiev Dynamo, Shakhtyor Donetsk, Moscow Spartak, Oviedo (Spain)*

First a left-back, then an all-controlling left-side midfielder, Onopko emerged as an international figure just as Russian football was going through its biggest-ever upheaval. In one 12-

month period he played international football for the Soviet Union, in late 1991, then for the Commonwealth of Independent States in the 1992 European Championship finals, and finally for the newly-independent Russian national team in the 1994 World Cup. He was a former youth and under-21 international and made his senior debut as a substitute in a 2–2 draw against England in Moscow in 1992. He earned international plaudits for the way he played Ruud Gullit to a standstill at the 1992 European Championship in Sweden. Onopko was Russia's Footballer of the Year in 1992 and 1993 and won Russian league titles with Spartak in 1992, 1993 and 1994. Oviedo just beat Spanish rivals Atletico Madrid in the race to sign him in 1995.

Raimundo **Orsi**

Country: *Argentina and Italy (born December 2, 1901)*
Position: *Outside left*
Clubs: *Independiente (Argentina), Juventus (Italy)*

Orsi played outside left for Argentina in the 1928 Olympic Final against Uruguay before switching, amid controversy, to Juventus. He spent six months kicking his heels before finally making his Juventus debut. Within four months he was playing for Italy and

Ariel Ortega: tipped as a new "Maradona"

scoring twice on his debut in a 6–1 win over Portugal in November, 1929. Vittorio Pozzo, Italy's manager in the 1920s and 1930s, had no hesitation in picking imported South Americans such as Orsi for his team. As Pozzo said: "If they can die for Italy, they can play football for Italy." Orsi was one of the exceptional players who won five successive league titles with Juventus in the early 1930s. For good measure, he scored Italy's all-important equaliser on the way to an extra-time victory over Czechoslovakia in the 1934 World Cup Final.

Ariel Arnaldo **Ortega**

Country: *Argentina (born March 4, 1974)*
Position: *Centre forward*
Clubs: *River Plate, Valencia (Spain)*

Ortega emerged in the early 1990s with River Plate and had to carry the weight of the label as a "new Maradona." Destiny pushed him further along that particular path when he was called up as deputy for the newly-disgraced Maradona during the 1994 World Cup finals in the United States. Displaying outstanding ball control, playmaking skills and an eye for goal, he did not let manager Alfio Basile down with his performances. He transferred to Spanish club Valencia for £8 million in 1997 but did not see eye-to-eye with Italian coach Claudio Ranieri and failed, initially, to do his talent justice. Ortega did, however, redeem himself with Argentina in the 1998 World Cup qualifiers. He missed only one of Argentina's 16 matches and was their five-goal top-scorer. The mercurial Argentine showed both sides of his character in the finals themselves, scoring twice against Jamaica in a pool match, the first a stunning piece of fancy footwork, but he was later shown a red card in the quarter-final against Holland for a clear headbutt on the Dutch goalkeeper.

Wolfgang **Overath**

Country: *West Germany (born September 29, 1943)*
Position: *Midfielder*
Club: *Köln*

Overath was one of the most admired members of the West German sides which featured in starring roles at the World Cups of 1966, 1970 and 1974. He played all his senior club career for Köln and scored 17 goals in 81 internationals between 1963 and 1974. An old-style inside left, then left-footed midfield general, he was a World Cup runner-up in 1966, scored the goal against Uruguay which earned West Germany third place in 1970 and won a personal duel to oust Gunter Netzer as midfield commander for the World Cup victory of 1974. He then retired from the national team, though he was selected for the World XI which played Brazil in Rio de Janeiro in 1968.

Marc **Overmars**

Country: *Holland (born March 29, 1973)*
Position: *Winger*
Clubs: *Go Ahead Eagles, Willem II, Ajax, Arsenal (England)*

Overmars has been a highly successful anachronism in 1990s football. Thirty years after Sir Alf Ramsey was thought to have killed off wingers, he was still using his pace and skill to take on full-backs – on either right or left wing – head for the byline and cross to devastating effect. Ajax signed him from Willem II in 1992 and he scored his first international goal after just four minutes with the first kick of his debut against Turkey in February 1993. Two months later he scored twice in Ajax's 6–2 victory over Heerenveen in the Dutch cup final. He took England apart in a World Cup qualifier at Wembley in 1993 that killed their dreams of USA '94 and did the same to Real Madrid – twice – in the UEFA Champions League 18 months later. Overmars transferred to Arsenal in 1997 and climaxed his first season in England by helping inspire the club to the League and FA Cup double; the goal he scored in the 1–0 win against Manchester United at Old Trafford was arguably the most important goal of that season, even more than the one he scored at Wembley in the FA Cup Final. He was sadly plagued by injury during France '98 and never shone in the World Cup.

Michael **Owen**

Country: *England (born December 14, 1979)*
Position: *Centre forward*
Clubs: *Liverpool*

Prior to the 1998 World Cup, all the talk was about Brazilian superstar Ronaldo. But before the competition had even reached the quarter-final stage, the name on everyone's lips was Michael Owen. Only 18 years old, the Englishmen scored a truly magnificent goal against Argentina in the second round, to follow on from the one he scored against Romania in his first full World Cup match. Incredibly, he had only made his full international debut earlier in the year against Chile, becoming the youngest Englishman to represent his country this century (he was 18 years and 59 days). When he scored against Morocco in a pre-World Cup friendly, he also became the goal-scorer for England this century. Having been a prolific scorer at youth level, Owen played his first senior match for Liverpool against Wimbledon at the end of the 1996–97 season and, not surprisngly, scored. Level-headed and modest, the teenager possesses all the attributes to become a world-class star, and it is a comforting thought to all England fans that, barring injury, Owen will be in his prime for the next three World Cup finals

Antonin **Panenka**

Country: *Czechoslovakia (born December 2, 1948)*
Position: *Midfielder*
Clubs: *Bohemians Prague, Rapid Vienna (Austria)*

Panenka spent most of his career in the Czech shadows with Bohemians until national manager Vaclav Jezek rescued him for the 1976 European Championship finals. He was influential in midfield and struck the decisive blow in the Final when his penalty shot, stroked so deliberately past Sepp Maier, brought Czechoslovakia their shoot-out triumph against the much-fancied West Germans. Later he spent several successful years in Austria with Rapid Vienna. His 65 caps included helping Czechoslovakia finish third, this time after a penalty shoot-out against Italy, in the 1980 European championship. In many respects, Panenka was a throwback in style to another era: a languid, skilled dreamer of a midfield general who might have appeared more at home in the central European game of the 1930s than in the increasing hurly-burly of international football in the 1970s and early 1980s.

Jean-Pierre **Papin**

Country: *France (born November 5, 1963)*
Position: *Centre forward*
Clubs: *Valenciennes, Club Brugge (Belgium), Marseille, Milan (Italy), Bayern Munich (Germany), Bordeaux*

In the autumn of 1996, Papin had just returned to his native France from Bayern Munich to play for Bordeaux at a time when the French league had confirmed the introduction of squad numbers and names on the backs of shirts. Every other player had their name across their shoulders. It was enough, however, for Papin to have the initials "J P P". He started out with his native Valenciennes and played in Belgium with Brugge before returning to France to become the captain and attacking inspiration of Marseille. In the now-notorious regime under Bernard Tapie, he was top scorer in the French league for four successive seasons before joining Milan in the summer of 1992. A year later he found himself appearing as a substitute for Milan against Marseille in the Champions Cup Final which the French club won 1–0. That was Papin's second European Final defeat – having been on the losing side in a penalty shoot-out when Red Star Belgrade beat Marseille in Bari in 1991. His consolation was to be voted European Footballer of the Year seven months later but he never really adjusted to football either in Italy or later Germany. His comparative failures to set alight either Milan or Munich cost him a place in the France squad at Euro 96. He was voted European Footballer of the Year in 1991.

Daniel Passarella: national team captain, then coach

Daniel **Passarella**

Country: *Argentina (born May 25, 1953)*
Position: *Central defender*
Clubs: *Sarmiento, River Plate, Fiorentina (Italy), Internazionale (Italy)*

Passarella returned to the hub of international football when, after the 1994 World Cup finals, he was appointed Argentina's new national coach in succession to Alfio Basile. Earlier he gained membership of that small band of heroes who can claim to have received the World Cup as winning captain. His moment of triumph came in the River Plate stadium – his own home club ground – in 1978. Passarella had guided, controlled and commanded Argentina from central defence. Time and again he powered up into midfield to serve Ardiles and Kempes; then again, Passarella's vicious free kicks and strength in the air at corners added to the pressure on opposing defences. He was three players in one and later enjoyed outstanding success as a goal-grabbing defender with Fiorentina and Inter in Italy before returning home to River Plate as coach.

Paulo **Manuel Carvalho Sousa**

Country: *Portugal (born August 13, 1970)*
Position: *Midfielder*
Clubs: *Academica Viseu, Benfica, Sporting Clube, Juventus (Italy), Borussia Dortmund (Germany)*

The son of a car mechanic in Viseu, Paulo Sousa had planned to become a teacher until football took over his life. He began with his local youth team, Repesesc, rising to become a member of the Portuguese squad which won the 1989 World Youth Cup in Saudi Arabia before joining Benfica. He quit the Stadium of Light in 1994 in a dispute over wages and joined Sporting Clube – moving on again after only one year to Juventus. Paulo Sousa may now be considered to have been the most successful Portuguese export to Italy – winning the league and cup double with Juventus in 1995 and the European Champions Cup in 1996. He starred at Euro 96 and was then sold, surprisingly, to Borussia Dortmund. He complained that the pressures at Juventus had forced him to play on when unfit and aggravate a serious knee problem. He took remarkable revenge by helping Dortmund defeat Juventus in the 1997 UEFA Champions League Cup Final. That made him only the second player, after Marcel Desailly, to win the Champions Cup with different clubs in two successive seasons.

Stuart **Pearce**

Country: *England (born April 24, 1962)*
Position: *Left back*
Clubs: *Coventry City, Nottingham Forest, Newcastle United*

Pearce, nicknamed Psycho for his single-minded concentration on his job, was a late developer. He was an outstanding amateur with Wealdstone and did not make his full league debut until he was nearly 22. He made his first England appearance less than four years later, against Brazil at Wembley, having joined Nottingham Forest for a bargain £200,000 in June 1985. Later he became the 999th player to win a full England cap. He missed a famous shoot-out penalty against Germany in the 1990 World Cup semi-final but made glorious amends with shoot-out conversions against both Spain and Germany in the closing stages of the 1996 European Championship. Never afraid of responsibility, he stepped up as player-manager to lead Forest's bid to escape relegation from the Premier League in 1996–97. He then enjoyed an Indian summer with Newcastle United.

Adolfo **Pedernera**

Country: *Argentina (born November 15, 1918)*
Position: *Centre forward*
Clubs: *River Plate, Atlanta, Huracan, Millonarios (Colombia)*

Pedernera was a great centre forward-turned-revolutionary. He made his debut for River Plate in 1936 and won five league championships in 11 years. He also played 21 times for Argentina, winning the Copa America in 1941 and 1942. In the late 1940s he led the legendary "Maquina" attack with Munoz,

Moreno, Labruna and Loustau. River sold him, perhaps prematurely, to Atlanta and he joined Huracan just before the famous Argentine footballers' strike of 1948. Millonarios of Bogota, from the pirate Colombian league, signed up Pedernera not merely as a player but as "liaison" officer to lure away other top Argentines, including his centre forward successor at River Plate, Alfredo Di Stefano. Later he returned to Argentina as coach of the national team (1969–70) and of clubs Gimnasia y Esgrima, Boca Juniors, Huracan and Independiente. He coached Colombia on their first appearance at the World Cup finals in Chile in 1962.

Joaquin **Peiro**

Country: *Spain (born January 29, 1936)*
Position: *Inside left/inside forward*
Clubs: *Murcia, Atletico Madrid, Torino (Italy), Internazionale (Italy), Roma (Italy)*

Peiro was inside left in the Atletico team which challenged neighbours Real for supremacy in capital, country and even Europe in the late 1950s. Born in Madrid, he played for a string of junior clubs before Atletico beat Real to his signature in 1954, when he was 18. A year later he was making his debut for Spain and, in 1961, he was sold to Italy's Torino. It was not until after moving to Inter, however, that Peiro earned the accolades he deserved. He was not always a first-choice at Inter because of the two-foreigners restriction. But that did not apply in Europe. He led Inter's Champions Cup-winning attack in 1964–65 with enormous panache – including a notoriously cheeky goal in the semi-final against Liverpool. In Spain he had won the cup with Atletico in 1960 and 1961.

Pele (Full name Edson Arantes do Nascimento)

Country: *Brazil (born October 23, 1940)*
Position: *Inside left/inside forward*
Clubs: *Santos, Cosmos New York (USA)*

Pele remains one of those great examples of the world's culture: a poor boy whose talent lifted him to the peaks of achievement, fame and fortune...yet who, amidst all that, retained his innate sense of sportsmanship and the respect of team-mates and opponents alike. His father Dondinho has been a useful footballer himself in the 1940s, but his career had been ended prematurely by injury. He was his son's first coach and his first supporter. Most Brazilian footballers are known by nicknames. Pele does not know the origin of his own tag. He recalled only that he did not like it and was in trouble at school for fighting with class mates who called him Pele. Later, of course, it became the most famous name in world sport. His teenage exploits as

Pele: the greatest ever

a player earned him a transfer at only 15 to Santos. Rapidly he earned national and then international recognition. At 16 he was playing for Brazil, at 17 he was winning a World Cup. Yet it took pressure from some of his senior team-mates to persuade national manager Vicente Feola to throw him into the action in Sweden in 1958. Santos were not slow to recognise the potential he offered. The directors created a circus, touring the world, playing two and three times a week for lucrative match fees which, in turn, gave the club the financial leverage to buy a supporting cast which helped turn Santos into World Club champions in 1962 and 1963. The pressure on Pele was reflected in injuries, one of which restricted him to only a peripheral role at the 1962 World Cup finals. He scored a marvellous solo goal against Mexico in the first round but pulled a muscle and missed the rest of the tournament. Brazil, even without him, went on to win the Jules Rimet Trophy again. In 1966 Pele led Brazil in England. But referees were unprepared to give players of skill and creativity the necessary protection. One of the saddest images of the tournament was Pele, a raincoat around his shoulders, leaving the pitch after being kicked out of the tournament by Portugal. Brazil, this time, did not possess such alternative resources as in 1962, and crashed out. Four years later Pele took his revenge in the most glorious way. As long as the game is played, the 1970 World Cup finals will be revered as the apotheosis of a great player, not only at his very best, but achieving the rewards his talent deserved. It says everything about Pele's transcending genius that he was the one man able to set light to the soccer vision launched in the United States in the 1970s. The North American Soccer League eventually collapsed amid financial confusion. But soccer was firmly established as a grass roots American sport and, without Pele's original allure, the capture of host rights for the 1994 finals would never have been possible. In the late 1990s he accepted an appointment as Brazil's Sports Minister. In the teeth of fierce opposition from top club directors, he drove through the so-called "Pele Law" which promised to reform the hitherto chaotic organisation of Brazilian domestic football.

Martin **Peters**

Country: *England (born November 8, 1943)*
Position: *Midfielder*
Clubs: *West Ham, Tottenham Hotspur, Norwich City, Sheffield United*

Peters was the World Cup-winning midfielder whose versatility earned the controversial comment by manager Sir Alf Ramsey that he was "ten years ahead of his time." His ability to fill a number of roles with equal success threatened to hold him back early in his career but once he had established himself as a World Cup hero he settled in midfield and became English football's first £200,000 footballer when he moved to Tottenham in the summer of 1970. Peters won the Cup-winners Cup with West Ham in 1965 and the UEFA Cup with Tottenham in 1972. He also scored England's second goal in the 1966 triumph over West Germany. But for Weber's 90th-minute equaliser, he would have gone down as the man who won the World Cup.

Roger **Piantoni**

Country: *France (born December 26, 1931)*
Position: *Inside left*
Clubs: *Nancy, Reims*

Piantoni was one of the last great European inside forwards, before the "old" positions were wiped out by the advent of 4–2–4 and 4–3–3 with their new roles and terminology. Piantoni built his reputation with Nancy and transferred to Reims in 1957 in time to play in the World Cup finals of 1958 – when France finished third – and in the European Champions Cup Final of 1959 (which Reims lost to Real Madrid). He played 38 times for France, having made a scoring debut in a 1–1 draw against the Irish Republic in Dublin in 1952. Nine years later, against Finland, he scored in his last international. His left-wing partnership, for Reims and France, with outside left Jean Vincent was famed throughout the continent.

Pichichi (Full name Rafael Moreno Aranzadi)

Country: *Spain (born 1892)*
Position: *Centre forward/inside forward*
Clubs: *Colegio de los Escolapios de Bilbao, Athletic Bilbao*

Pichichi remains one of the legends of Spanish football. Born in the Basque province, his fame was earned and secured in Bilbao. He played for a foundling college team, the Colegio de los Escolapios de Bilbao, and then with Athletic Bilbao. He was an obvious choice at inside left for Spain's very first national team selection, the 1–0 win over Denmark in Brussels in the 1920 Olympic Games. Sadly, Pichichi died just two years later but by then his goal-scoring feats had earned legendary status. His fame lives on in the name of the annual award presented each year to the leading goalscorer in the Spanish championship.

Silvio **Piola**

Country: *Italy (born September 29, 1913)*
Position: *Centre forward*
Clubs: *Pro Vercelli, Lazio, Torino, Juventus, Novara*

Piola scored 30 goals in 24 internationals between his debut against Austria in 1935 and his last game against England in 1952. A tall, aggressive centre forward, he was a World Cup-winner in 1938 when he scored twice in the 4–2 final defeat of Hungary. He would have collected more goals and caps had it not been for the war years. As it was, he played on until he was 43 in a prolific career which included his fair share of controversy – such as the goal he later admitted he punched against England, nearly 50 years before Maradona's Hand of God repetition. Piola scored six goals in Pro Vercelli's 7–2 win over Fiorentina in 1933–34.

Pirri (Full name Jose Martinez Sanchez)

Country: *Spain (born March 11, 1945)*
Position: *Inside forward/midfielder/central defender*
Club: *Real Madrid*

For 15 years, between 1964 and 1979, Pirri epitomised the spirit of Spanish football in an extraordinary career with Real Madrid. He began as a goal-grabbing inside forward, then shifted back successively to midfielder and central defender in a glittering career which brought honours flooding in – eight Spanish championships, three Spanish cups and the European Champions Cup in 1966. He played 44 times for Spain between 1966 and 1978 and was twice selected for Europe XIs, first against Benfica in 1970, then against South America in 1973. After retiring he completed his studies to qualify as a doctor and was appointed to the Real Madrid medical staff.

Michel Platini: France's finest footballer

at home in France, as the No. 1 sports personality of his generation. Platini set out on the road to superstardom at the Montreal Olympics and stepped up a gear at the 1978 World Cup in Argentina. Four years later he inspired France to fourth place in Spain after being voted man of the match in the dramatic semi-final shoot-out defeat by West Germany in Seville. After the finals he was sold to Juventus with whom he was three times the Italian league's top scorer and converted the penalty kick which brought Juve their long-awaited European Champions Cup victory in 1985 (albeit overshadowed in the midst of the Heysel tragedy). At national team level, he scored 41 goals in 72 internationals and led by example when France won the 1984 European Championship on home soil. He was not only their captain but their top scorer with nine goals including hat-tricks against Belgium and Yugoslavia and the first goal in the 2–0 victory over Spain in the final. Platini was, simply, the greatest football achiever of his generation and the only player voted European Footballer of the Year three years in succession. After retiring he concentrated briefly on commercial interests and TV work until he was persuaded to become national manager and took France to the finals of the 1992 European Championship. France disappointed but Platini moved up to an even more prestigious role as co-president of the domestic Organizing Committee for the 1998 World Cup finals.

Frantisek **Planicka**

Country: *Czechoslovakia (born June 2, 1904)*
Position: *Goalkeeper*
Clubs: *Slovan Prague, Bubenec, Slavia Prague*

Planicka played 74 times in goal for Czechoslovakia between 1925 and 1938. He was the finest goalkeeper of his era in central Europe, as well as an outstanding and courageous player in the World Cups of both 1934 – when Czechoslovakia lost the final 2–1 to Italy – and 1938. In the latter competition, he played the last half of the quarter-final draw against Brazil despite the pain of a broken arm, in the days long before substitutes. He was a domestic league champion nine times with the great Slavia club, won the cup six times and the Mitropa Cup – forerunner of today's European club competitions – in 1938.

Michel **Platini**

Country: *France (born June 21, 1955)*
Position: *Inside forward/midfielder*
Clubs: *Nancy Lorraine, Saint Etienne, Juventus (Italy)*

Few footballers have made a greater global impact than Platini. Within a few weeks in the spring of 1997 he was voted, in Italy, as the greatest player ever to have lined up for Juventus and,

David **Platt**

Country: *England (born June 10, 1966)*
Position: *Midfielder*
Clubs: *Manchester United, Crewe, Aston Villa, Bari (Italy), Juventus (Italy), Sampdoria (Italy), Arsenal (England)*

Platt, an England cornerstone and ultimately captain in the first half of the 1990s, was one who got away from Manchester United: they gave him a free transfer. He spent four years with Crewe before bringing them their then-record fee, £200,000, on his sale to Aston Villa in 1988. He was then sold four more times for a reported total of £22 million – £5.5 million from Villa to Bari in 1991, £6.5 million from Bari to Juventus a year later, £5.2 million from Juventus to Sampdoria in 1993, and £4.8 million from Sampdoria to Arsenal in 1995. The moves to and from Bari both broke the record fee for a British player. A busy midfielder, Platt chose a most dramatic moment to open his scoring account for England – the last minute of extra-time in the 1990 World Cup second-round tie against Belgium in Bologna. He ranks joint sixth in the all-time England goal-scorers' list. Impeccable in attitude both on and off the pitch, he was an obvious choice to become England captain under Terry Venables. Injuries then spoiled his England prospects though he remained a valued member of the Arsenal squad, helping win the league and cup double in 1998, before announcing his retirement.

Ernst **Pol**

Country: *Poland (born November 3, 1932)*
Position: *Inside forward*
Clubs: *Legia Warsaw, Gornik Zabrze*

It was the ill-fortune of Pol, the first great Polish footballer of the post-war era, that eastern European players were barred from transfer abroad during the 1950s. He played centre or inside forward, scored a then-record 40 goals in 49 internationals between 1950 and 1966 and totalled a then-record 186 goals in league games. Pol won the Polish championship twice with the army club Legia, then five times with Gornik, the Silesian miners' club. He scored five goals once in an international against Tunisia in 1960 and had the consolation of scoring a marvellous individual strike for Gornik in their 8–1 thrashing by Tottenham in the European Champions Cup in 1961.

Anton "Toni" **Polster**

Country: *Austria (born March 10, 1964)*
Position: *Centre forward*
Clubs: *Simmering, FK Austria, Torino (Italy), Ascoli (Italy), Seville (Spain), Logrones (Spain), Rayo Vallecano (Spain), Köln (Germany)*

Polster has been one of European football's most outstanding league marksmen for a decade and with eight clubs in four different countries. He was once described as a "poor man's Klinsmann." He first made his mark when he was runner-up in the Golden Boot competition for Europe's top league goalscorer in 1986–87: he scored 39 goals for FK Austria only to find his total overtaken, amid controversy, by the Romanian spearhead, Rodion Camataru (Camataru's goalscoring achievements are generally believed to have been 'fixed' by the notorious Romanian regime). Polster then moved to Italy with Torino and Ascoli before rediscovering his shooting boots in Spain with Seville, Logrones and Rayo Vallecano, then moving on to Germany.

Gheorghe "Gica" **Popescu**

Country: *Romania (born October 9, 1967)*
Position: *Central defender*
Clubs: *Steaua, Universitatea Craiova, PSV Eindhoven (Holland), Tottenham Hotspur (England), Barcelona (Spain), Galatasaray (Turkey)*

Popescu is one of Europe's most versatile defensive midfielders. He played sweeper for Romania at the 1990 World Cup finals, then as a defensive midfielder in 1994. Starred in all five of Romania's games at USA 94 through to the quarter-final shoot-out defeat by Sweden. He played as a junior for Steaua but made his name in Romania with Craiova. He joined PSV Eindhoven in Holland originally as a replacement in the centre of defence for Barcelona-bound Ronald Koeman – whom he later followed to the Catalan capital. He spent one season in England with Tottenham in 1994–95, but was overshadowed by German team-mate Jürgen Klinsmann and did not enjoy the frenetic pace of the football. Four times Romanian Footballer of the Year – in 1990, 1991, 1992 and 1993. He was again involved with Romania in the 1998 finals, helping his side reach the second round of the World Cup, including a defeat of England, before losing 1–0 to Croatia in the second round.

Michel **Preud'homme**

Country: *Belgium (born January 24, 1959)*
Position: *Goalkeeper*
Clubs: *Standard Liège, Mechelen, Benfica (Portugal)*

A figure first of controversy, then admiration. Preud'homme began with Standard Liège, made his national debut in a goalless draw against Austria in May 1979, but missed the 1984 European championships and 1986 World Cup after his involvement in a match-fixing scandal. He enjoyed an excellent World Cup in Italy despite worrying then-manager Guy Thys with nerves which prevented him eating on match days. Preud'homme was hailed as one of the finest keepers on view at the 1994 World Cup, when Belgium reached the second round, after which he finally decided to take the long-considered plunge and move abroad with Portuguese champions Benfica.

Robert Prosinecki: World Cup marksman for Croats

Robert **Prosinecki**

Country: *Croatia (born January 12, 1969)*
Position: *Midfielder*
Clubs: *Dinamo Zagreb, Crvena Zvezda [Red Star] Belgrade, Real Madrid (Spain), Oviedo (Spain), Barcelona (Spain) FC Croatia Zagreb*

Prosinecki promised, at one time, to become the outstanding European player of his generation. A string of niggling injuries scarred his career, however, after he had moved to Real Madrid in what should have been the keynote transfer of his career. He first starred with the former Yugoslavia squad which won the World Youth Cup in 1987. He was voted Player of the Tournament even though he missed the final – a penalty shoot-out victory over West Germany – because of suspension. Miroslav Blazevic, later Croatia national coach, let him leave Dinamo for Red Star, doubting whether he would establish himself as a professional player, but he went on to win three Yugoslav championships while in Belgrade – plus the European Champions Cup in 1991. After moving to Spain he became one of the handful of players to have appeared for both Real Madrid and Barcelona. His family background is mixed Croatian and Serbian and he was wanted by both countries. Finally he declared himself a Croat, played for them in the 1996 European Championships when they performed well in a tough competition. However, Prosinecki reached new heights along with his countrymen in the 1998 World Cup finals in France. Croatia were playing in the competition for the first time, yet they still managed to reach the semi-finals (they eventually beat Holland in the third place play-off), with Prosinecki scoring two goals along the way.

Ferenc **Puskas**

Country: *Hungary and Spain (born April 2, 1927)*
Position: *Inside left*
Clubs: *Kispest (Hungary), Honved (Hungary), Real Madrid (Spain)*

Ferenc Puskas remains one of the greatest players of all time – a symbol of the Magical Magyars who dominated European football in the early 1950s. Football had been brought to Hungary by English students in the 1870s and was refined after the first world war by the legendary English coach Jimmy Hogan. It was an era which reached a grand climax in 1938 when Hungary reached the World Cup Final in Paris with a team inspired by the academic centre forward or centre half Gyorgy Sarosi. Hungary lost 4–2 to Italy – a huge disappointment for Puskas, then an 11-year-old in Budapest. His father was a player and later coach with the local club, Kispest. At 16 Ferenc was a regular at inside left, terrorising opposing goalkeepers with the power of his shooting. He never used his right foot, but then his left was so lethal he never needed it. At 18 he was in the national team, his brilliance having much to do with the decision to convert Kispest into a new army sports club named Honved. That team formed the basis of a national side which swept all before it. For four years the team built around goalkeeper Gyula Grosics, right half Jozsef Bozsik and the inside forward trio of Sandor Kocsis, Nandor Hidegkuti amd Puskas crushed all opposition. They also introduced a new tactical concept. The inside forwards, Kocsis and Puskas, formed the spearhead of their attack, with Hidegkuti a revolutionary deep-lying centre forward. Hungary won the 1952 Olympic title before ending England's record of invincibility against continental opposition with a stunning 6–3 triumph at Wembley. They also thrashed England 7–1 in Budapest early the following year. No wonder they were overwhelming favourites to win the 1954 World Cup in Switzerland. But Puskas presented a problem. He had been injured in an early round game against West Germany and was a hobbling spectator at training before the final, against the Germans, in Berne. Could his great left foot withstand the strain? Puskas thought so and decided to play. After only 12 minutes the gamble appeared to be paying off when Hungary led 2–0. But ultimately they lost 3–2: the end of an era in the one match which mattered most. It was eight long years before Puskas would return to the World Cup finals. Then, in Chile in 1962, his trusty left foot was doing duty for Spain because he had, in the meantime, joined Real Madrid. Honved had been abroad when the Hungarian Revolution of 1956 erupted. Puskas and several team-mates decided to stay in the West. He tried to sign for several Italian clubs, but they thought him too old. How wrong they were was underlined when Puskas developed, at Madrid, a new career to emulate his first in brilliance. Four times he was the Spanish league's top scorer and his partnership with the Argentine centre-forward, Alfredo Di Stefano, was one of the greatest of all time. They hit perfection together on the famous night when Madrid thrashed Eintracht Frankfurt 7–3 in the European Champions' Cup Final before a record 135,000 crowd at Hampden Park. Di Stefano scored three goals, Puskas scored four. The Spanish fans loved him. In his Hungarian army club days at Honved, Puskas had been known as the Galloping Major. Now the aficionados called him 'Canoncito' – the little cannon. In 1966 he finally retired. His future was secure thanks to business investments which included a sausage factory near Madrid. He tried his hand at coaching without a great deal of success – save for one remarkable year when he took Panathinaikos of Athens to the European Cup Final. Eventually the relaxation of years allowed him to visit his native Hungary, where he was celebrated once more as a national hero. Hardly surprising. After all, how many players can boast 83 goals in 84 games for their country.

Helmut **Rahn**

Country: *West Germany (born August 16, 1929)*
Position: *Outside right*
Clubs: *Altenessen, Olde 09, Sportfreunde Katernberg, Rot-Weiss Essen, Köln, Enschede (Holland), Meiderich SV Duisburg*

Outside right Rahn's shooting power was immense – as Hungary found to their cost in the 1954 World Cup Final. He struck the equaliser at 2–2 and then the winner with only minutes remaining. Yet Rahn, enfant terrible of the German game, might not have even been in Europe: shortly before the finals he had been on a South American tour with Rot-Weiss and was in negotiations with Nacional of Uruguay when national coach Sepp Herberger sent a telegram to summon him home. Rahn, far from either his best form or his best playing weight, could not repeat the World Cup miracle in 1958. He scored 21 goals in 40 internationals.

Rai (Full name Raimundo Souza Vieira de Oliveira)

Country: *Brazil (born May 15, 1965)*
Position: *Midfielder*
Clubs: *Sao Paulo, Paris Saint-Germain (France), Sao Paulo*

Rai, former South American Footballer of the Year, was one of the younger brothers of the 1980s Brazilian superstar Socrates. He followed his brother into the national team's midfield and also emulated him by becoming captain. He won Brazilian, South American and world club honours with Sao Paulo under the guidance of Tele Santana, then transferred to PSG in the summer of 1993. He was expected to take French football by storm but, like Socrates in Italy in the 1980s, he took time to adapt both on and off the field. He lost form to such an extent that he was even dropped in the middle of Brazil's 1994 World Cup-winning campaign. He starred in Paris Saint-Germain's triumphant 1995–96 European Cup-winners Cup campaign, then returned to his original club, Sao Paulo, in the spring of 1998. He was offered a chance to play his way back into World Cup favour but made his return in a warm-up defeat by Argentina – and was promptly dropped again.

Tabare "Tab" **Ramos**

Country: *United States (born September 21, 1966)*
Position: *Midfielder*
Clubs: *United States Federation, Figueras (Spain), Betis (Spain), Tigre (Mexico), New York/New Jersey MetroStars*

Ramos was the most gifted American player of his generation, as befitted the son of a former Uruguayan professional. In the early 1990s his technical talent shone out in an American national squad built more on stamina than skill. His ability attracted offers from Spain and Mexico and he justified all the hype when he played a key role in the USA's defeat of England at the 1993 US Cup. A year later, in the World Cup finals, he created Ernie Stewart's decisive goal against Colombia in the first round. But in the second he was the victim of a touchline assault by Brazilian defender Leonardo which left him with a badly broken jaw. He took some time to recover confidence and then his form. One of a handful of American players to take part in the World Cup finals in 1990, 1994 and 1998, the latter ending in bitter disappointment as the US failed to win a game, and suffered the indignity of losing to Iran.

Antonio **Rattin**

Country: *Argentina (born May 16, 1937)*
Position: *Central defender*
Club: *Boca Juniors*

Rattin earned notoriety in the 1966 World Cup finals when he was sent off, amid chaos and controversy, in the quarter-final against England at Wembley. Yet that image did not do justice to a midfield pillar with club and country in the 1950s and 1960s. He made his league debut in 1956 and played 14 inspiring seasons with Boca Juniors, amassing a club record 357 league appearances and winning five championships. Rattin was also a key figure in the Boca side – along with Silvio Marzolini and Angel Rojas – which lost narrowly to Pele's Santos in the final of the South American club cup in 1963. He played 37 times for Argentina, including the 1966 World Cup quarter-final when Rattin's refusal to accept expulsion by German referee Kreitlein very nearly provoked a walk-off by the entire Argentine team.

Raul Gonzalez Blanco

Country: *Spain (born June 27, 1977)*
Position: *Centre forward*
Clubs: *Atletico Madrid, Real Madrid*

Raul was the Spanish soccer sensation of the 1990s. Originally he played for Atletico Madrid's youth teams. But when president Jesus Gil cut back the juniors as a cash-saving measure, he was snatched by neighbours Real. Thrust into the first team by coach Jorge Valdano at 17 – Madrid's youngest-ever league player – he scored six goals in his first 11 games and kept such veteran internationals as Emilio Butragueno and Rafael Martin Vazquez on the bench. Ironically, Raul made his debut against his old club, Atletico, scoring one superb goal and making another. He scored six goals in the 1995–96 Champions League, including a hat-trick against Hungary's Ferencvaros and a quarter-final match-winner

Tomas Ravelli: Europe's record international

against Juventus. Fans clamoured for him to be called up by Spain for Euro 96 but coach Javier Clemente preferred, perhaps mistakenly with hindsight, to save him for the Olympic tournament. Raul then established himself in the national team in time for the World Cup finals in 1998, although he didn't live up to hype, failing to spark as Spain became the only seeded team not to make the second round. The same year he also helped Real Madrid lay the ghost of history by defeating Juventus 1–0 in Amsterdam to win the UEFA Champions League Cup Final.

Fabrizio **Ravanelli**

Country: *Italy (born December 11, 1968)*
Position: *Centre forward*
Clubs: *Perugia, Avellino, Reggiana, Juventus, Middlesbrough (England), Marseille (France)*

The summer of 1996 was a remarkable one for Ravanelli: one moment he was a Champions Cup-winning hero with Juventus,

the next he was – to his own surprise – on his way to joining Middlesbrough, an English provincial club of whom he had never heard. Ravanelli knuckled down to lead Boro' to the League Cup Final and the FA Cup Final. He was also their top scorer with 31 goals in league and cups. Middlesbrough's relegation, however, persuaded him that he been mistaken to move to England and – after a sulky few months – he secured a transfer to French football with Marseille. Surprisingly, he had not made his Italian Serie A debut until shortly before his 24th birthday. He made his international debut in the 4–1 Euro 96 qualifying win over Estonia in 1995, after scoring more than a century of goals in ten seasons of top, second, third and fourth division football. Nicknamed The White Feather because of his prematurely grey hair, he ended the 1995–96 season by scoring Juventus' all-important goal in their UEFA Champions League Cup Final triumph over Ajax in Rome, and began the next season with a hat-trick against Liverpool for Middlesbrough.

Tomas **Ravelli**

Country: *Sweden (born August 13, 1959)*
Position: *Goalkeeper*
Clubs: *Oster Vaxjo, IFK Gothenburg, Tampa Bay Mutiny (USA)*

Ravelli became the most-capped European footballer of all time when he chalked up 138 international appearances between 1981 and 1997. He took the honour on overtaking Peter Shilton's old world goalkeeping record of 125 caps in 1994. His father was an Austrian who emigrated to Sweden where Thomas and twin brother Andreas – an international midfielder – were born. Both became youth and under-21 internationals, and Thomas went on to a century of caps and the accolade of Footballer of the Year in 1981. The high point of his international career was 1994 when he was voted one of the top goalkeepers at the World Cup in the United States, where Sweden took third place. He joined IFK Gothenburg in the spring of 1989 as replacement for Tottenham-bound Erik Thorstvedt, and transferred to Major League Soccer in the US at the start of 1998 with Tampa Bay.

Fernando Carlos **Redondo**

Country: *Argentina (born June 6, 1969)*
Position: *Midfielder*
Clubs: *Argentinos Juniors, Tenerife (Spain), Real Madrid (Spain)*

Redondo, with his trademark long hair, followed in the Argentine tradition of pivotal midfield directors such as Nestor Rossi, Antonio Rattin and Sergio Daniel Batista. He was born in Buenos Aires, began with Argentinos Juniors and was sold to Spain's Tenerife in 1990 when he refused a call to play for

Argentina at the World Cup finals because he did not like coach Carlos Bilardo's safety-first approach. Redondo's superb play for Tenerife then earned a £3 million transfer to Real Madrid, along with coach Jorge Valdano, after the 1994 World Cup finals – in which Redondo did agree to play for Alfio Basile. He fell out with Basile's successor Daniel Passarella, however, and was thus absent again from the World Cup in 1998. His consolation, a few weeks before the finals, was to play a key role in Real Madrid's UEFA Champions League Cup triumph over Juventus.

Jose Hector **Rial**

Country: *Argentina and Spain (born October 14, 1928)*
Position: *Inside forward/centre forward*
Clubs: *San Lorenzo (Argentina), Independiente (Colombia), Nacional (Uruguay), Real Madrid (Spain), Union Espanola (Chile), Espanol (Spain), Marseille (France)*

Rial, four times a European Champions Cup-winner with Real Madrid, was one of the finest yet most under-rated players of the 1950s. A centre forward or inside left, he was considered the virtual equal of Di Stefano when he fled Argentine football at the end of the 1940s to star in the pirate El Dorado of Colombia. After the Colombian collapse, he played briefly in Uruguay before joining Madrid just after Di Stefano. Heavily-built but technically nimble and highly astute, he scored twice in Madrid's inaugural Champions Cup Final victory over Reims in 1956. Perhaps equally as important, his guiding influence enabled Madrid to get the best out of the flying left winger, Francisco Gento. As veteran manager and commentator José Villalonga once said: "Rial was the man who made Gento play."

Frank **Rijkaard**

Country: *Holland (born September 30, 1962)*
Position: *Midfielder/central defender*
Clubs: *Ajax Amsterdam, Sporting (Portugal), Zaragoza (Spain), Milan (Italy), Ajax*

Rijkaard turned professional under Johan Cruyff at Ajax in 1979 and made his Holland debut at 19 despite the club's protests that he was "too young." In 1987 he fell out with Cruyff and had brief spells in Portugal and Spain before committing the key years of his career to Milan with whom he won the World Club and European Champions Cups twice apiece. He developed as one of the most universally-admired and versatile players in the world game. Rijkaard played in midfield for Milan but in central defence as a member of the Dutch national side with whom he won the 1988 European Championship. He returned to Ajax after the 1993 Champions Cup Final defeat by Marseille – helping Ajax, ironically, beat Milan in the 1995 Final in Vienna.

Luigi "Gigi" **Riva**

Country: *Italy (born November 7, 1944)*
Position: *Centre forward*
Club: *Cagliari*

Riva, orphaned in early childhood, was adopted by all Italy after shooting the national team to the 1970 World Cup Final. He had built a teenage reputation with third division Legnano as a left winger and was signed by second division Sardinian club Cagliari in 1963. A formidable left foot and eye for goal sent Cagliari rocketing out of the shadows and to ultimate league championship success in 1970. Riva was top league marksman three times, including the 1969–70 season when he scored 21 goals in 28 games. His 35 goals in 42 internationals meant Riva carried much of the weight of responsibility for Italy's World Cup challenge in 1970. He scored three times in the quarter- and semi-final victories over Mexico and West Germany on the way to Italy's runners-up finish. Complications stemming from two broken legs ultimately forced a premature retirement.

Roberto **Rivelino**

Country: *Brazil (born January 1, 1946)*
Position: *Outside left/midfielder*
Clubs: *Corinthians, Fluminense, Al Hilal (Saudi Arabia)*

Rivelino was not particularly quick but was possessed of a superb technique which made him a perpetual danger with his banana-bending of free kicks and corners. He was also the deep-lying left winger who filled the Zagallo role for Brazil's 1970 World Cup victory. He later moved into central midfield as Brazil's general in succession to Gerson and was influential in the third-place finish of 1978. He is credited unofficially with the fastest goal in football history: scored in three seconds with a direct shot from the kick-off after he noticed the opposing goalkeeper still concentrating on his pre-match prayers.

Gianni **Rivera**

Country: *Italy (born August 18, 1943)*
Position: *Centre forward/midfielder*
Clubs: *Alessandria, Milan*

Rivera was the great enigma of Italian football in the 1960s and early 1970s. His glorious talents and achievements were beyond reproach. Yet the Bambino d'Oro, the Golden Boy, was never quite at home playing for his country and successive managers struggled to find a way to get the best out of him. Intellect was not the problem, for Rivera was one of the brainiest inside forwards of his day and went on to become, briefly, president of Milan and later a Member of Parliament. The mystery long outlived a career which began amid headlines and controversy when Milan paid his first club, Alessandria, what was then an amazing £65,000 for a half-share in him, at the age of 15! Milan signed him "for real" at just about the time, in 1961, that they bought Englishman Jimmy Greaves. Rivera was considered the apprentice. But within half a season the homesick Greaves had returned to England and Rivera was established as the new Boy Wonder of Italian football. In 16 years with the *rossoneri* he was twice a winner of the World Club Cup, the Champions Cup and the Italian league as well as three times an Italian cup-winner and once European Footballer of the Year, in 1969. But his national team career brought only 14 goals in 60 games and reached a painful nadir at the 1970 World Cup when Rivera had to alternate in the team with Sandro Mazzola before being "granted" a substitute's last six minutes of thefinal defeat by Brazil.

Roberto Carlos da Silva

Country: *Brazil (April 10, 1973)*
Position: *Left back*
Clubs: *Union San Joao de Araras, Palmeiras, Internazionale (Italy), Real Madrid (Spain)*

Roberto Carlos quickly established a ferocious reputation in the late 1990s as one of the great free kick exponents. He came into the Brazilian national team after the 1994 World Cup, starring in the 1995 Panamerican Games and Umbro Tournament in England, then staying in Europe after transferring to

Roberto Carlos: Brazilian free-kick wizard

Internazionale of Milan. In 1996 he was sold to Real Madrid with whom he won the Spanish league in his first season and the UEFA Champions League Cup in his second. He caused a sensation with one remarkable goal from a direct free kick for Brazil against France in Le Tournoi de France in the summer of 1997. It helped raise Roberto Carlos to runner-up behind friend and Brazilian team-mate Ronaldo in the FIFA World Footballer of the Year poll. He finished runner-up again, the following year, this time in the 1998 World Cup Final.

Bryan Robson

Country: *England (born January 11, 1957)*
Position: *Midfielder*
Clubs: *West Brom, Manchester United, Middlesbrough*

Robson appeared possessed of a season-ticket to surgery in the 1980s but his courage and physical commitment were second to none. He broke his leg twice as a teenager with West Brom but later left the club for Manchester United for a then-British record £1.5 million and ended his career with an impressive string of honours to his name. He won 90 England caps (often as captain), three FA Cup-winning medals, the Cup-winners Cup in 1991 - and the championship with Manchester United in the first season of the Premiership. He was an inspiring, driving force in midfield, with a good scoring record, and a believer in the value of an early strike: three of his England goals were claimed in the first minute including his 27-second goal against France in Bilbao in the 1982 World Cup finals. Robson later carved out an impressive career as a manager with Middlesbrough whom he twice took up into the Premier League and for whom he created enormous interest with his imaginative, and expensive, purchases of players such as Brazilians Juninho, Branco and Emerson, Italy's Fabrizio Ravanelli and Denmark's Mikkel Beck.

Pedro Rocha

Country: *Uruguay (born December 3, 1942)*
Position: *Inside forward*
Clubs: *Penarol, Sao Paulo (Brazil)*

Rocha was a statuesque inside left of great skill. Fans considered him slow but opponents described him as deceptively quick. He joined Penarol of Montevideo at 17 and, seven times in the next nine seasons, was a champion of Uruguay as well as inspiring Penarol to victory both home and away over Real Madrid in the 1966 World Club Cup final. He captained Uruguay into the 1970 World Cup finals but was injured in the first match and missed the rest of the event. Fit again, he moved to Brazil and led Sao Paulo to debut season victory in the Paulista state championship. Rocha won 62 caps for Uruguay.

Romario da Souza Faria

Country: *Brazil (born January 29, 1966)*
Position: *Centre forward*
Clubs: *Vasco da Gama, PSV Eindhoven (Holland), Barcelona (Spain), Flamengo, Valencia (Spain), Flamengo*

Romario has been arguably the finest attacker in the world game in the 1990s. Discovered by Vasco da Gama, he was still a teenager when he began to establish a reputation for controversy after being banished from Brazil's World Youth Cup squad for flouting a hotel curfew. After starring at the Seoul Olympics, when Brazil finished runners-up in 1988, he transferred to PSV Eindhoven. He clashed with coaches and team-mates, yet still totalled 98 league goals in five seasons to earn a £3 million sale to Barcelona in 1993. Simultaneously, he was recalled by Brazil after a year in the wilderness and scored the two goals which beat Uruguay and sent Brazil to the 1994 World Cup finals – where he collected a winner's medal plus five goals. Romario grew restless at Barcelona, particularly with the close attention given by the media to his private life. He returned home in the spring of 1995 to Flamengo, returned briefly to Spain in 1996 with Valencia and then went back to Flamengo yet again. For much of this time he was ignored by national coach Mario Zagallo. But then, when Romario indicated he was putting the playboy lifestyle to one side, Zagallo recalled him for the run-up to France 98, but injury ruled him out of the final squad.

Ronaldo Luis Nazario

Country: *Brazil (born September 22, 1976)*
Position: *Centre forward*
Clubs: *Cruzeiro, PSV Eindhoven (Holland), Barcelona (Spain), Internazionale (Italy)*

FIFA's World Player of the Year in both 1996 and 1997 – the first footballer to collect the award twice - Ronaldo was discovered as a teenager by Brazil's 1970 World Cup hero Jairzinho, who took him to Cruzeiro. He scored 58 goals in 60 matches to earn enormous interest and a lucrative transfer to Holland's PSV Eindhoven as successor to Brazil-bound Romario. Brazil manager Carlos Alberto Parreira took Ronaldo, then only 17, to the 1994 World Cup finals but kept him on the subs' bench, telling him: "You are here only to learn. Your turn will come later." Barcelona paid PSV £12.9 million for Ronaldo in 1996 and he had a sensational season in Spain – scoring the penalty goal which won the European Cup-winners Cup and collecting the Golden Boot as Europe's top league marksman after scoring 34 goals. Barcelona, Ronaldo and his agents then fell out over an improved contract and he forced his sale to Internazionale in the summer of 1997 for a then-world record £19.5 million.

Ronaldo: world No. 1 in the late 1990s

Ronaldo ended his first Italian season as Inter's top scorer with 25 goals and inspired their UEFA Cup Final victory over Lazio in Paris. Yet the most dramatic chapter of the Ronaldo story emerged in the aftermath of Brazil's World Cup final thrashing against France. Ronaldo looked a shadow of the player who had scored four goals up to that point, and it later transpired he had suffered a fit only a few hours before the match. He clearly wasn't fit to play and why he did has never been fully explained.

Paolo **Rossi**

Country: *Italy (born September 23, 1956)*
Position: *Centre forward*
Clubs: *Prato, Juventus, Como, Lanerossi Vicenza, Perugia, Juventus, Milan*

Rossi's progress from villain to hero was accomplished in less than a year. He began 1982 still under a two-year suspension for his alleged role in a match-fixing scandal organised in Italy by underworld betting gangs. The suspension expired in April of 1982 when Rossi resumed his playing career with Juventus, who had bought him during the ban. Rossi played the last three games of the season, then went to Spain to lead Italy's attack in the World Cup finals. After a slow start, he scored a sensational second-round hat-trick against Brazil, followed up with two goals against Poland in the semi-final and one more against West Germany in Italy's 3–1 win in the final. He was the competition's top scorer with six goals and duly collected the European Footballer of the year prize. It was a second remarkable turn to Rossi's career. The earlier one concerned his teenage years. He had been given away on a free transfer by Juventus because of knee trouble before he had ever played a league game. Fortunately other coaches had more faith in Rossi, who burst on to the international scene at the 1978 World Cup finals. Juventus tried to buy him back but were outbid by Perugia. But finding the world record £3.5 million fee virtually bankrupted the provincial club who were relegated and had no option but to sell Rossi – suspended by now – to Juve at a huge loss. Sadly, his earlier injuries caught up with him and he retired aged 29.

Rui Manuel Cesar Costa

Country: *Portugal (March 29, 1972)*
Position: *Midfielder*
Clubs: *Fafe, Benfica, Fiorentina (Italy)*

Rui Costa realised how far he had come in his career when the oldest youth tournament in Portugal – organised by minor club Centre Cultural da Pontinha – was renamed in his honour as the Torneo Rui Costa. He had been an outstanding youth player himself – as a World Youth Cup-winner against Brazil in Lisbon in 1991 and as a member of the Portuguese team which reached the finals of the 1994 European Under-21 Championship in France. He began with second division Fafe, then moved to Benfica with whom he won the Portuguese cup in 1993 and league title in 1994. He was then sold to the Italian club Fiorentina, for whom he played a starring role in their 1996–97 Cup-winners Cup campaign.

Karl-Heinz Rummenigge: goal in the 1986 World Cup

Karl-Heinz Rummenigge

Country: *West Germany (born September 25, 1955)*
Position: *Centre forward*
Clubs: *Lippstadt, Bayern Munich, Internazionale (Italy), Servette (Switzerland)*

Karl-Heinz Rummenigge was Bayern Munich's leading player in the immediate post-Beckenbauer era. They narrowly overlapped, Rummenigge's first Champions Cup Final in 1976 being Beckenbauer's last. Initially a right winger, he later moved inside to a role he preferred, linking midfield with attack, and he would have played even more than 95 times (with 45 goals) for West Germany had it not been for injuries. Rummenigge was working as a bank clerk in his teens while playing part-time for Borussia Lippstadt. He turned professional when Bayern came in with an offer, and he cost the Munich club a mere £4,500 – which must count as one of the bargains of modern German football since they sold him later to Italy's Internazionale for £2 million. He had first impressed Inter with a World Cup hat-trick against Mexico in 1978 and followed up at international level by captaining his country to a European Championship victory in 1980. Injuries reduced his effectiveness in the early 1980s and controversy lingered over whether West German manager Jupp Derwall was right to play him from the start in the losing 1982 World Cup Final against Italy in Madrid, when he looked slow and off the pace. Rummenigge, European Footballer of the Year in 1980 and 1981, ended his playing career with Servette in Switzerland before returning home to become a vice-president of Bayern Munich.

Oscar Ruggeri

Country: *Argentina (born January 26, 1962)*
Position: *Central defender*
Clubs: *Velez Sarsfield, Boca Juniors, River Plate, Logrones (Spain), Real Madrid (Spain), Ancona (Italy), America (Mexico), San Lorenzo*

Ruggeri was the heart of the Argentine defence in the 1980s, winner of a record 89 caps and successor to Diego Maradona as national captain. He was a World Cup-winner in Mexico in 1986 and one of few Argentine players to have lined up for both the big Buenos Aires rivals, Boca Juniors and River Plate. He left for Spain after the 1986 World Cup with Logrones and then transferred to Real Madrid, but left again after one unsettled season. His honours included the 1989 South American Championship – even though he was sent off twice in the tournament. Later he transferred to Italy and Mexico where his ruthless tackling and iron-willed command of his fellow defenders established him as one of Argentina's most successful modern exports.

Ian **Rush**

Country:	*Wales (born October 20, 1961)*
Position:	*Centre forward*
Clubs:	*Chester, Liverpool (England), Juventus (Italy), Liverpool (England), Leeds (England), Newcastle (England), Sheffield United (England), Newcastle (England)*

Rush ranks among the finest Welsh players of all and among the greatest trophy winners in English football. Liverpool signed him for just £300,000 from Chester in 1980 and he stayed loyal to Anfield for 16 years – with one year "out" for a season in Italy with Juventus. Rush totalled 229 league goals for Liverpool, second only in the club's history to Roger Hunt's aggregate of 245. He won the league championship five times, the Football League Cup five times, the FA Cup three times and the European Cup once – against Roma in Rome in 1984. Later he gave loyal service to Leeds and Newcastle. At international level for Wales, he never had the chance of playing in the World Cup or European Championship finals. But in more than 70 internationals he easily outstripped the previous Wales scoring record of 23 goals held jointly by Trevor Ford and Ivor Allchurch.

Marcelo Salas: two-year rise to superstardom

Marcelo **Salas**

Country:	*Chile (December 24, 1974)*
Position:	*Centre forward*
Clubs:	*Universidad de Chile, River Plate (Argentina), Lazio (Italy)*

Salas was merely a supporting artist when Chile set out on the 1998 World Cup qualifying road. By the time they reached the finals he had laid claim to being one of the game's modern-day superstars. His 99 goals for Universidad de Chile earned a 1996 transfer to River Plate with whom he won three successive Argentine championships and the South American Supercup. In between he still found time to play in Chile's marathon 1998 World Cup qualifying campaign, where his tally of 11 goals included hat-tricks against both Colombia and Peru. He then put his talents on show for a European audience, scoring one of the most spectacular goals ever seen at Wembley stadium in Chile's 2–0 win in early 1998. He scored four goals in the 1998 World Cup finals, including one in the 4–1 defeat by Brazil.

Oleg **Salenko**

Country:	*Russia (born October 25, 1969)*
Position:	*Centre forward*
Clubs:	*Kiev Dynamo (Soviet Union), Logrones (Spain), Valencia (Spain), Rangers (Scotland), Istanbulspor (Turkey)*

Salenko made World Cup history when he scored five goals for Russia against Cameroon in the 1994 finals in the United States. It was the finest exhibition of one-man markmanship in the competition's history. Yet Salenko was not Russian by birth, having been born and brought up in the Ukraine in the years before it gained independence following the collapse of the USSR. He then took up the option to continue his international career with Russia, not his native Ukraine, precisely so he could play in USA 94. Salenko's sometimes awkward personality otherwise restricted his international opportunities and he was dropped by Russia again immediately after his historic match.

Matthias **Sammer**

Country:	*Germany (born September 5, 1967)*
Position:	*Sweeper*
Clubs:	*Grodlitz, Einheit Dresden, Dynamo Dresden (all East Germany), Stuttgart, Internazionale (Italy), Borussia Dortmund*

Matthias Sammer made history in December 1996 when he became the first player from the former East Germany to win the treasured Golden Ball as European Footballer of the Year.

His father, Klaus, had been a midfield general with Dresden and the East German national team. He had barely retired before son Matthias was making his own reputation with Dresden and the national team. In 1986 young Sammer guided East Germany from midfield to the European youth title. He was promoted almost immediately into the senior national squad, helped Dresden win the GDR championship in 1989 and then the league and cup double a year later. That summer also brought the collapse of the Berlin Wall – and Sammer was immediately brought west by Stuttgart. It was in his new home of the Neckarstadion that he became, the following December, the first East German to play for a unified Germany in a 4–0 defeat of Switzerland. The 1992 European Championship was not a happy memory for Sammer. He failed to find a spark of form in the shock final defeat against Denmark and was substituted at half-time. It was the start of a dismal nine months. A transfer to Internazionale proved a disaster as he failed to adjust to either the lifestyle or the football, and Dortmund brought him home in mid-season. The fee, reported to have been a record paid by a German club of £4 million, was ridiculed at the time. But two league championships plus the 1997 UEFA Champions League Cup vindicated Dortmund's judgment – along with Sammer's key role in Germany's triumph at Euro 96.

Erwin **Sanchez**

Country: *Bolivia (born October 19, 1969)*
Position: *Midfielder*
Clubs: *Bolivar, Albacete (Spain), Benfica (Portugal), Boavista*

Sanchez has proved an outstanding graduate of Bolivia's world-famous Tahuichi youth academy. He starred at the 1989 South American championship, then moved to Portugal less than a year later to join Benfica – thus becoming the first Bolivian to play in Europe. In his teenage years, his ability to score incredible goals, plus his habit of playing with his shirt out and his socks rolled down, earned him the nickname "Platini". Sanchez scored a hat-trick against Venezuela in Bolivia's opening match of the 1994 World Cup qualifiers and never looked back as his country made it to the finals after 44 years. In 1994 he had the satisfaction of winning a cup medal in Portugal with Boavista.

Hugo **Sanchez**

Country: *Mexico (born June 11, 1958)*
Position: *Striker*
Clubs: *UNAM, Atletico Madrid (Spain), Real Madrid (Spain), America, Rayo Vallecano (Spain)*

Each one of Sanchez's goals was followed by a celebratory somersault, taught originally by a sister who was a gymnast in Mexico's team for the 1976 Olympics in Montreal – at which brother Hugo made his football debut on the international stage. Five seasons in a row in the late 1980s and early 1990s he was top league goalscorer in Spain . His 230-plus goals in Spain left him second overall behind Bilbao's Telmo Zarra and underlined his claim to be considered one of the great strikers of the modern game. In fact, despite a World Cup finals debut as far back as 1978, Sanchez totalled only around 50 games for Mexico – either because of club commitments in Spain or because of disputes with Mexican soccer bureaucracy.

Leonel **Sanchez**

Country: *Chile (born April 25, 1936)*
Position: *Outside left*
Club: *Universidad de Chile*

Sanchez was a star of the Chilean side which finished third as hosts in the 1962 World Cup, though he also featured in controversy: earlier in the tournament he somehow escaped punishment from the referee for a punch which flattened Humberto Maschio in the so-called Battle of Santiago against Italy. He was the outstanding left winger in South America in the late 1950s and early 1960s – perhaps not as hard-shooting as Pepe of Brazil or as hard-working and intelligent as Mario Zagallo but more forceful when it came to making his presence felt in the penalty box. Sanchez played 106 times for Chile, although of that number only 62 counted as full internationals, theothers being non-cap matches.

José Emilio **Santamaria**

Country: *Uruguay and Spain (born July 31, 1929)*
Position: *Central defender*
Clubs: *Nacional (Uruguay), Real Madrid (Spain)*

Santamaria was a World Club Cup and triple European champion with Real Madrid and later managed hosts Spain at the 1982 World Cup finals in front of their home crowd. A ruthless and uncompromising centre back, his finest years were spent at Real Madrid in the 1950s and early 1960s, closing down the defensive gaps left by great attacking colleagues such as Di Stefano, Puskas and Gento. He was first called up at 20 by Uruguay but missed the 1950 World Cup finals because his club, Nacional, refused to let him accept the inside forward spot allocated to him in the squad bound for Brazil. Four years later Santamaria was one of the stars of the 1954 World Cup finals, this time in his traditional place in the centre of defence. Madrid brought him to Europe in 1957 and, having played 35 times for Uruguay, he collected another 17 caps in the service of Spain including the 1962 World Cup.

Djalma **Santos**

Country: *Brazil (born February 27, 1929)*
Position: *Right back*
Clubs: *Portuguesa, Palmeiras, Atletico Curitiba*

Djalma Santos – no relation to international full back partner Nilton Santos – became the first Brazilian player to reach an official century of international appearances though he was well past his best when recalled – to even his own surprise – by manager Vicente Feola for the 1966 World Cup finals in England. He played for the World XI against England in 1963 in the match which celebrated the 100th anniversary of the FA. Santos was considered a cornerstone of the Brazil side which won the World Cup in 1958 and 1962 and lost it in 1966. Yet in Sweden in 1958 he was brought in only for the final itself because Feola considered his acute football brain and positional sense would be more effective against Swedish left-winger Skoglund than regular right back Nilton Da Sordi.

Nilton dos Reis **Santos**

Country: *Brazil (born May 16, 1925)*
Position: *Left back*
Club: *Botafogo*

Nilton Santos was Brazil's inspirational World Cup-winning left back in 1958 and 1962 – no relation to full-back partner Djalma Santos, yet even more outstanding. Nilton Santos played 82 times for his country between 1949 and 1963, having made his Brazil debut just a year after signing for his only club, Botafogo of Rio. He loved nothing more than powering forward in support of attack – a tactic which surprised the opposition and owed everything to the new freedom afforded "wing backs" by the advent of 4–2–4. Santos was first called up by Brazil for the Copa America in 1949. He was a member of the luckless World Cup squad in 1950 but did not play. In 1954 he helped Brazil to the quarter-finals of the World Cup in Switzerland and progressed to World Cup-winner in 1958 and 1962. He was immensely respected by team-mates and officials. He led the player delegation which, in Sweden in 1958, crucially persuaded coach Vicente Feola to call up his match-winning Botafogo team-mate and right winger Garrincha. Santos was as sharp as ever at the 1962 World Cup in Chile, despite being then 37. He retired the following year.

Dimitris **Saravakos**

Country: *Greece (born July 27, 1961)*
Position: *Centre forward*
Club: *Panathinaikos*

Greece's success in reaching the finals of the World Cup for the first time in 1994 marked a career peak for their finest modern players – and for striker Saravakos in particular as he closed in on Nikos Anastopoulos's record of 74 international appearances. Saravakos, despite having been a prolific goalscorer at national championship level for top club Panathinaikos, was never as successful a marksman for the national team. Injuries had upset his international career in later seasons but he remained, in the words of World Cup coach Altekas Panagulias, "one of the best players in Greek football history – both for his own abilities and the way he inspires those around him to play above themselves."

Gyorgy **Sarosi**

Country: *Hungary (born September 12, 1912)*
Position: *Centre forward/central defender*
Club: *Ferencvaros*

Sarosi was one of the world's greatest footballers between the wars, playing both centre forward and centre half for FTC (Ferencvaros) and scoring 349 goals in 383 games. He won the Hungarian championship eight times, the cup once and the Mitropa Cup once. Sarosi scored 42 goals in 75 internationals, captaining Hungary to the 1938 World Cup Final. Doctor, lawyer and magistrate, he made his debut for Hungary in a 3–2 defeat by Italy in Turin in November, 1931. He fled Hungary on the communist takeover in 1947, moving to Italy where he coached Padova, Lucchese, Bari, Juventus (winners of the 1952 championship), Genoa, Roma, Bologna and Brescia. He also coached Lugano in Switzerland before retiring to Genoa.

Dejan **Savicevic**

Country: *Yugoslavia (born September 15, 1966)*
Position: *Midfielder/inside forward*
Clubs: *Buducnost Titograd, Crvena Zvezda [Red Star] Belgrade, AC Milan (Italy)*

Savicevic was one of Europe's outstanding attackers of the 1990s. After starring at the 1990 World Cup he helped Red Star win the European Champions Cup and then the World Club Cup (albeit he was sent off in the victory over Chile's Colo Colo in Tokyo). With Yugoslavia descending into crisis, Savicevic "escaped" to the west courtesy of a £3.5 million transfer to Milan. However, he spent as much time on the sidelines as on the pitch because of foreign player restrictions and knee trouble. Eventually, he was able to express his talent to the full in inspiring Milan's brilliant 4–0 victory over Barcelona in the 1994 European Champions Cup Final. He helped Yugoslavia reach the 1998 World Cup finals, where he appeared as a substitute.

Dejan Savicevic: Euro champion with Red Star

Hector **Scarone**

Country: *Uruguay (born June 21, 1898)*
Position: *Inside forward*
Clubs: *Sportsman, Nacional, Barcelona (Spain), Ambrosiana-Internazionale (Italy), Palermo (Italy)*

Scarone was Uruguay's inspiring inside forward in their greatest era of the 1920s and early 1930s. He won the Olympic Games title in Paris in 1924 and in Amsterdam in 1928 (playing in between for Barcelona), was top scorer at both the 1926 and 1927 South American championships, then led Uruguay to victory at the inaugural World Cup finals on home soil in Montevideo in 1930. Inevitably, his talents drew more offers from Europe, but he insisted on waiting until after the 1930 World Cup before returning, this time to Italy with Ambrosiana-Inter. Later he returned to Spain in the early 1950s as coach to Real Madrid, then made a playing comeback in Uruguay with Nacional – retiring finally at the age of 55, a South American record.

Juan Alberto **Schiaffino**

Country: *Uruguay and Italy (born July 28, 1925)*
Position: *Inside forward/centre forward/midfielder*
Clubs: *Penarol, Milan (Italy), Roma (Italy)*

In World Cup terms, "Pepe" Schiaffino peaked in 1950 when he scored Uruguay's equaliser at 1–1 on the way to their shock victory over Brazil. After starring again at the finals in 1954, he was sold to Milan for a world record £72,000. He counts among the greatest of players to have graced Italian football, winding down his career with Roma after failing narrowly to lead Milan to victory over Real Madrid in the 1958 Champions Cup Final. They lost 3–2 despite Schiaffino's fine solo goal. As a boy, he had always wanted to play centre forward but youth coaches with Penarol of Montevideo, his first club, considered him too thin and fragile. They switched him to inside forward and, at 20, he was playing for Uruguay at the South American championship and top-scoring with 19 goals in Penarol's league-winning side.

Salvatore **Schillaci**

Country: *Italy (born December 1, 1964)*
Position: *Centre forward*
Clubs: *Messina, Juventus, Internazionale, Jubilo Iwata (Japan)*

"Toto" Schillaci was Italy's out-of-the-blue hero at the 1994 World Cup when he only just squeezed into the squad, then came off the substitutes' bench to become the tournament's six-goal top scorer. Yet the previous season had been his first in Serie A after joining Juventus from the minor Sicilian club Messina. He made his Italy debut in a 1–0 win over Switzerland shortly before the World Cup began. But his form lost its edge after the World Cup and he started to regain confidence only after being sold at a knock-down price to Internazionale. Domestic problems did not help Schillaci's concentration on his game and, in the summer of 1994, he became the first top-name Italian player to try his luck in Japan's J League.

Peter **Schmeichel**

Country: *Denmark (born November 18, 1963)*
Position: *Goalkeeper*
Clubs: *Hvidovre, Brondbye, Manchester United (England)*

Schmeichel's very demeanour in a match speaks volumes about his will to win. That dedication carried him through his difficult early years in Danish football when he played part-time and took various jobs, including running a shop for the World Wildlife Fund and working as a newspaper advertising salesman. Everything paid off ultimately with his £750,000 move to Manchester United in 1991. Schmeichel had come to international prominence in the 1988 European Championships when he replaced Troels Rasmussen in Denmark's final match. He has been voted Denmark's player of the year on two occasions and was immense in the Danes' 1992 European Championship triumph. His honours with Manchester United include four league titles and two FA Cups. He played for his country during the 1998 World Cup finals in France.

Karl-Heinz **Schnellinger**

Country: *West Germany (born March 31, 1939)*
Position: *Central defender*
Clubs: *Duren, Köln, Mantova (Italy), Roma (Italy), Milan (Italy)*

Schnellinger stood out in the 1960s not merely for his blond hair and bulky frame but for his power, pace and will-to-win – mostly expressed from left back, though occasionally from midfield. He made his World Cup finals debut at 19 in Sweden and was a quarter-finalist (1962), runner-up (1966) and third-placed (1970) over the next 12 years. Roma took him to Italy but had to sell him to Milan to overcome a cash crisis. Their loss was Milan's gain as Schnellinger's steel lifted them to victory in the 1969 European Champions Cup. This was the peak of a career which also earned success in German and Italian championships and Italian cup, three selections for World XIs and four for Europe Selects. He was West German Footballer of the Year in 1962.

Harald "Toni" **Schumacher**

Country: *West Germany (born March 6, 1954)*
Position: *Goalkeeper*
Clubs: *Köln, Fenerbahce (Turkey), Bayern Munich*

Schumacher was as controversial a personality as he was inspirational as a goalkeeper in West Germany's international campaigns of the 1980s, when he was a World Cup runner-up

Gaetano Scirea: Italy's most skilful sweeper

in both 1982 and 1986. However, it was a disgraceful foul by Schumacher against France in the 1982 semi-final that earned him worldwide notoriety. His club career was spent almost entirely with Köln. Schumacher was twice voted Footballer of the Year and earned various selections for World and Europe selections. He was banished from German football, however, after writing a controversial autobiography lifting the lid on internal dissent within the national squad and making various allegations regarding dope-taking. After a short spell in Turkey he returned as standby goalkeeper for Bayern Munich.

Enzo **Scifo**

Country: *Belgium (born February 19, 1966)*
Position: *Midfielder*
Clubs: *Anderlecht, Internazionale (Italy), Bordeaux (France), Montpellier (France), Torino (Italy), Monaco (France), Anderlecht*

Scifo was born of Italian parents in Belgium. He was a prolific goalscorer in youth football with La Louvierè while still at school and was signed by Anderlecht. In 1984 he opted to take up Belgian citizenship and played in the European Championship finals in France – as well as in the controversial UEFA Cup semi-final against Nottingham Forest and losing final against Tottenham. A football prodigy, he was taken "home" to Italy by Internazionale but was overcome by the pressure and was loaned to Bordeaux and Montpellier in France. He returned to Italy with Torino after the 1990 World Cup and helped them to reach the 1992 UEFA Cup Final. Torino's financial problems led to Scifo being sold to Monaco in 1993. He then returned home in 1997 to Anderlecht in time to reach the World Cup finals for the fourth time, although Belgium and Scifo lacked flair.

Gaetano **Scirea**

Country: *Italy (born May 25, 1953)*
Position: *Sweeper*
Clubs: *Atalanta, Juventus*

Scirea's central defensive partnership with Claudio Gentile was one of the most effective in the international game, as they proved at the heart of Italy's World Cup-winning defence in Spain in 1982. He was a skilled, graceful performer very different to the sort of ruthless "killers" employed by many Italian clubs of that era. Scirea began with Atalanta as an inside forward and later became the defensive cornerstone of the all-conquering Juventus side of the 1980s. His long-lasting brilliance – he was seven times Italian champion with Juventus in 11 years –restricted the international ambitions of Franco Baresi. Sadly, he was killed in a car crash shortly after his retirement.

David Seaman

Country: *England (born September 19, 1963)*
Position: *Goalkeeper*
Clubs: *Leeds, Peterborough United, Birmingham City, Queens Park Rangers, Arsenal*

Seaman, like many goalkeepers, proved a late developer. Despite around 700 appearances in various competitions, his top-grade career did not fully 'take off' until he joined Arsenal in May 1990 for £1.3 million, then a record for an English goalkeeper. With Arsenal he has won the league championship twice, FA Cup twice, League Cup and European Cup-winners Cup. The peak of his club career was in winning the league and cup double in under French manager Arsène Wenger in 1998, although he had won an array of medals under George Graham. At international level, Seaman established himself as first-choice for England in 1994 after waiting patiently in line behind Peter Shilton and Chris Woods. Outstanding at Euro 96, with a decisive penalty-defying performances in England's victory over Spain, he played in all his country's 1998 World Cup matches.

Uwe Seeler

Country: *West Germany (born November 5, 1936)*
Position: *Centre forward*
Club: *Hamburg*

German fans used Seeler's name, "Uwe, Uwe," as their chant at international matches in the 1960s. The son of a former Hamburg player, he played for Hamburg all his career from 1952 to 1971, making his full senior debut for West Germany in a 3–1 defeat by England at Wembley in 1954 when still only 18. Seeler captained West Germany in their World Cup Final defeat at Wembley in 1966 but gained a measure of revenge by scoring a remarkable back-headed goal when Germany won 3–2 in extra-time in a dramatic 1970 quarter-final in Leon. Seeler rejected a string of lucrative offers from Italy and Spain to stay loyal to Hamburg. He scored 43 goals in 72 internationals.

Clarence Clyde Seedorf

Country: *Holland (born April 1, 1976)*
Position: *Midfielder*
Clubs: *AS '80, Real Almere, AS '80, Ajax, Sampdoria (Italy), Real Madrid (Spain)*

Almost every competition Seedorf has graced has brought success. With Ajax he was voted Young Player of the Year in Holland in 1993 and 1994, winning the championship in 1994 and 1995, the cup in 1993, the Dutch supercup in 1993 and 1994 and

then the ultimate prize – the European Champions Cup in 1995. That proved one of his last matches for the club since he rejected advice to stay another year or two in Amsterdam and decided to try his luck in Italy with Sampdoria. He admitted later that he had been perhaps too young and inexperienced for the Italian challenge. But he learned fast and regained his status as one of Europe's outstanding creative forces after transferring to Real Madrid in the summer of 1996. Seedorf found instant success with his won the Spanish league title in his first season and the UEFA Champions League Cup – again – in his second – beating Juventus 1–0 in the final – and he also featured for the Dutch, mainly as an effective substitute, in their 1998 World Cup campaign that ended in defeat against Brazil.

Juan Segarra

Country: *Spain (born November 15, 1927)*
Position: *Left back/left half*
Club: *Barcelona*

Spain played comparatively few internationals in the 1950s, which is why Segarra appeared only 28 times for his country. He was, nevertheless, a Spanish football stalwart throughout the 1950s – one of the handful of great Barcelona players who were actually born and brought up in the Catalan capital. Segarra joined Barcelona from a minor local club, Villafranca, in 1950, and ended the season with a Spanish cup medal as well as having made his international debut. He was originally a left back but later moved up to left half where his powerful stride and strong tackle were ideally employed. He was later captain of Barcelona, retiring with five cup medals between 1951 and 1963, four league titles and two Fairs Cup medals.

Dragoslav Sekularac

Country: *Yugoslavia (born November 10, 1937)*
Position: *Inside forward*
Clubs: *Red Star Belgrade, TSV 1860 Munich (Germany), Karlsruhe (Germany), St Louis (USA), OFK Belgrade*

"Sekki" was one of the creative geniuses of European football in the late 1950s and early 1960s. His dribbling talents and eye-of-the-needle passing created goal upon goal for attacking partners such as Bora Kostic, and he was a star member of the Red Star side which jousted so memorably with Manchester United on the eve of the Munich air disaster. Sekularac's Achilles heel was a quick temper which brought him into repeated conflict with match officials, administrators and team-mates. After wandering to the United States and back he turned to coaching, first in Yugoslavia, then later in Central and South America.

Alan Shearer: five-goal top scorer at Euro 96

Internazionale in 1996. After Hodgson left, so did Sforza – returning to Kaiserslautern whom he helped win the German league title in sensational fashion in 1998. Never before had a newly-promoted club won the Bundesliga.

Alan **Shearer**

Country: *England (born August 31, 1970)*
Position: *Centre forward*
Clubs: *Southampton, Blackburn Rovers, Newcastle United*

Shearer brought the world transfer record back to England for the first time in 60 years when he was the subject of a £15 million move from Blackburn Rovers to his home-town club, Newcastle United, in the summer of 1996. He had just proved his pedigree by finishing as five-goal top scorer in the European Championship finals and was about to be installed as new captain of England by national coach Glenn Hoddle. A Geordie spotted by Southampton in 1988, he was spirited down south to start his career as a trainee at The Dell. His League career began in truly sensational style: at the age of 17 years and 240 days he scored three goals against Arsenal, the club with traditionally the meanest defence in the English league, in only his fourth senior appearance, thus becoming the youngest player ever to hit a Football League hat-trick. Transferred to Blackburn in July 1992 for a record £3.3 million, his 34 goals in 1994–95 led Blackburn to their first modern league championship. Early in 1996 he became the first man to score 100 goals in the Premiership. After suffering a terrible ankle injury in the summer of 1997, Shearer was out for six months before returning to football. Yet he lacked his previous sparkle and never looked on top of his game during the 1998 World Cup finals.

Ciriaco **Sforza**

Country: *Switzerland (born March 2, 1970)*
Position: *Midfielder*
Clubs: *Villkomen Wohlen, Grasshopper, Aarau, Grasshopper, Kaiserslautern (Germany), Bayern Munich (Germany), Internazionale (Italy), Kaiserslautern (Germany)*

Sforza, despite coming from unfashionable Switzerland, is acknowledged as one of the most resilient anchor-man midfielders in continental football. Italian by birth, he always considered himself Swiss and took up formal citizenship in 1990. Less than a year later he made his national team debut against Czechoslovakia. Sforza starred initially for Grasshopper, winning the cup in 1988 and the championship in 1991. He was Footballer of the Year in 1993 and played in all his country's four matches in the 1994 World Cup finals and then in all 11 qualifying and finals matches in the 1996 European Championship. A powerful shot also helped make him a favourite with Switzerland manager Roy Hodgson – who was instrumental in Sforza's transfer to

Peter **Shilton**

Country: *England (born September 18, 1949)*
Position: *Goalkeeper*
Clubs: *Leicester, Stoke City, Nottingham Forest, Southampton, Derby County, Plymouth Argyle, Leyton Orient*

Shilton set a world record when, at 41, he made his 125th and last appearance in the third-place play-off at the 1990 World Cup finals. That was his 17th game in such competitions, a record for a Briton. Having made his senior England debut at 20, he conceded only 80 international goals, every one of them a dreadful blow to a perfectionist. Shilton's awesome pursuit of personal fitness and elimination of error were renowned throughout the game. He played a losing FA Cup Final with Leicester (who were relegated as well) when 19, but never in another: only when he got to Nottingham Forest, and their brief dominance of England and Europe, did club honours flow.

Allan Simonsen: European Footballer of the Year

Nikita **Simonian**

Country: *Soviet Union (born October 12, 1926)*
Position: *Centre forward*
Clubs: *Kirilia Sovietov, Moscow Spartak*

Simonian was small for a centre forward but skilful and quick – talents which saw him shoot a then-record 142 goals in 265 league matches in the 1950s. Three times he was leading scorer in the Soviet Supreme league, including 34 in 1950 – a record not overtaken until the emergence of Oleg Protasov in the 1980s. Simonian began his career on Georgia's Black Sea Coast, moved to Moscow with "Wings of the Soviet" and, three years later in 1949, joined Spartak. He won the league four times, the cup twice and scored 12 goals in 23 internationals before retiring. Later he was coach to Spartak, then joint manager of the Soviet national team at the 1982 World Cup finals in Spain.

Allan **Simonsen**

Country: *Denmark (born December 15, 1952)*
Position: *Centre forward*
Clubs: *Vejle, Mönchengladbach (Germany), Barcelona (Spain), Charlton Athletic (England), Vejle*

Allan Simonsen was the pint-sized forward who inspired Denmark's emergence in the early 1980s that inspired the likes of the Laudrup brothers – Brian and Michael – as well Manchester United goalkeeper, Peter Schmeichel. Sadly, he broke an ankle in the opening match of the 1984 European Championship finals against France and never quite regained the same form for the rest of his career. He played successfully for the Danish club Vejle, then in Germany with Borussia Mönchengladbach where he proved to be very successful. He was three times champion of Germany, once German cup-winner and twice UEFA Cup-winner with Borussia. He also inspired them to reach the 1977 European Champions Cup Final where they lost to Liverpool in a memorable clash. Later, after moving to Spain, he continued his collection of European medals when he won the Spanish cup and the European Cup-winners Cup with Barcelona. Simonsen was happy in Barcelona while master coach Hennes Weisweiler, his mentor previously at Borussia, was in charge. But Weisweiler fell foul of club politics and his abrupt exit left the writing on the wall for Simonsen. English club Charlton Athletic managed to persuade him to join them but the experiment soon turned sour. He scored nine goals in only 16 games in England before returning home to Vejle. Simonsen played 54 times for Denmark, scoring 20 goals, and was voted 1977 European Footballer of the Year. The most important of his international goals was probably the penalty with which the Danes beat England at Wembley in the 1984 European Championship qualifiers. Simonsen returned to the international scene in the 1990s as national coach to the tiny Faroe Islands.

Agne **Simonsson**

Country: *Sweden (born October 19, 1935)*
Position: *Centre forward*
Clubs: *Orgryte (Sweden), Real Madrid (Spain), Real Sociedad (Spain), Orgryte*

Foreign-based veterans were very important to the Swedish team which reached the 1958 World Cup Final on home soil losing 5–2 to Brazil, but they also depended for energy and vigour on Simonsson, their blond good-looking centre forward from the Gothenburg club of Orgryte. Simonsson enhanced his reputation by leading Sweden to victory over England at Wembley in 1959 and was signed the following summer by Spanish giants Real Madrid. They envisaged Simonsson becoming the successor to ageing Alfredo Di Stefano. But, on the one hand, Simonsson failed to adjust to life and football in Spain while, on the other, Di Stefano was not ready to go. Simonsson returned to Orgryte and played again for Sweden, but he never quite recovered his early-career spark.

Matthias **Sindelar**

Country: *Austria (born February 18, 1903)*
Position: *Centre forward*
Clubs: *FC Hertha Vienna, FK Austria*

Sindelar was the very spirit of the Austrian Wunderteam of the 1930s. Born in Czechoslovakia, he was discovered by a minor Viennese club, Hertha, in 1920, and joined neighbouring giants FK Austria a year later. Twice he won the Mitropa Cup – the inter-war forerunner of the European Champions Cup – with FK Austria in the 1930s and added 27 goals in 43 internationals to his list of honours. Those 27 included two hat-tricks against Hungary in 1928 and the two goals which beat Italy in the newly-built Prater Stadium in Vienna in 1932. Sindelar scored in both Austria's matches against England in 1932 and 1936 and led Austria to the World Cup semi-finals of 1934. Depressed by the 1938 Anschluss, he and his girlfriend committed suicide in 1939.

Omar Enrique **Sivori**

Country: *Argentina and Italy (born October 2, 1935)*
Position: *Inside left*
Clubs: *River Plate (Argentina), Juventus (Italy), Napoli (Italy)*

In 1957 Argentina won the South American Championship almost by a walkover thanks to the brilliance of an inside forward trio of Humberto Maschio, Antonio Valentin Angelillo and Omar Sivori. Success lifted them among the favourites for the 1958 World Cup finals. Yet that potential was never realised because, within a year, all three players had been sold to Italian clubs and axed from the national team as punishment for disloyalty. Sivori, who cost Juventus a world record £91,000 from River Plate, was the most outrageous personality of the three. He was an attacking inside left who loved nothing better than humiliating his marker with a nutmeg, but he was also an outstanding team player and dovetailed perfectly with the pragmatic and powerful Welshman, John Charles. Under Sivori's leadership, Juventus won the league title three times in four years at the turn of the 1960s. Sivori and Charles provided 140 of their title-winning goals. Sivori was nicknamed "Cabezon" – Big Head – by his admirers in Argentina and Italy and his self-confidence eventually led to a major confrontation with coach Heriberto Herrera and, ultimately, transfer to Napoli. The rapturous reception Sivori gained at Napoli foreshadowed the atmosphere on the arrival, years later, of fellow Argentine Diego Maradona. Sivori played 18 times for Argentina, nine times for Italy – including the controversial 1962 World Cup – and was voted European Footballer of the Year in 1961. He also scored the solitary goal which, in the spring of 1962, condemned Real Madrid to their first-ever home defeat in the Champions Cup.

Tomas **Skuhravy**

Country: *Czechoslovakia (born September 7, 1965)*
Position: *Centre forward*
Clubs: *Sparta Prague, Genoa (Italy), Sporting (Portugal), Genoa (Italy)*

Skuhravy was the five-goal second-top scorer at the 1990 World Cup finals. He began with a hat-trick in the Czechoslovaks' 6–1 defeat of the USA and finished the tournament with a lucrative new contract from Genoa in his pocket. Skuhravy's partnership there with the Uruguayan Carlos Aguilera brought Genoa some measure of success in league and UEFA Cup before a succession of injuries took their toll. Skuhravy, who invested his money in an old prince's castle in Italy, always insisted that he would prefer to have starred in Formula One grand prix motor racing rather than in football.

Graeme **Souness**

Country: *Scotland (born May 6, 1953)*
Position: *Midfielder*
Clubs: *Tottenham (England), Middlesbrough (England), Liverpool (England), Sampdoria (Italy), Rangers (Scotland)*

Souness did appear once for Tottenham in a European tie in Iceland but grew homesick and returned north. Later he made his name with Middlesbrough, developing into a world-class midfielder, winning 54 caps and a string of honours with Liverpool, where he was an influential player and captain. Souness later became a great favourite in Italy before returning to British football as player-manager of Rangers. His huge revivalist spending ensured a string of titles for the club. He also reversed a traditional transfer trend by importing a host of English players from south of the border. Souness proved unable to repeat such success during a short-lived and controversial managerial return to Anfield, where he succeeded his old friend Kenny Dalglish. Later coached Galatasaray in Turkey and Torino in Italy before being appointed in late 1997 by Portugal's Benfica.

Neville **Southall**

Country: *Wales (born September 16, 1958)*
Position: *Goalkeeper*
Clubs: *Bury (England), Everton (England), Port Vale (England), Everton*

A fiery character who played Welsh League football at 14 and worked as a dish-washer, hod-carrier and dustman before joining Bury. He was then 21, and was soon signed by Everton. A moderate start and a brief loan period were forgotten after his return, when he suddenly hit the form that established him as one of the world's top goalkeepers. He won two title medals, one FA Cup and one Cup-winners' Cup, and was voted Footballer of the Year in 1985. After passing the Welsh record of 73 caps, he ironically made an expensive error in the defeat that prevented Wales from qualifying for the 1994 World Cup.

Jürgen **Sparwasser**

Country:	*East Germany (born June 14, 1948)*
Position:	*Centre forward*
Club:	*Magdeburg*

A fine attacking midfielder, Sparwasser scored the historic goal in Hamburg which beat World Cup hosts West Germany in the first and last meeting between the two states at senior level. Along with Joachim Streich, Hans-Jürgen Kreische and Hans-Jurgen Dorner, he was one of the handful of outstanding footballers produced by East Germany in its 40 years of independent football existence. Sparwasser's career featured 15 goals in 77 internationals and a Cup-winners Cup medal after Magdeburg's victory over Milan in Rotterdam in 1974. Later he fled East Germany by taking advantage of his selection for a veterans' tournament in West Germany.

Hristo **Stoichkov**

Country:	*Bulgaria (born August 2, 1966)*
Position:	*Midfielder/centre forward*
Clubs:	*Maritza Plovdiv, Hebros Harmanli, CSKA Sofia (Bulgaria), Barcelona (Spain), Parma (Italy), Barcelona (Spain), CSKA Sofia (Bulgaria)*

Hristo Stoichkov was furious when he was placed second to Roberto Baggio in the European Footballer poll in 1993 – and his indignation provoked his superb form in the 1994 World Cup when his top-scoring six goals took Bulgaria to the semi-finals for the first time in their history. His career had always been volatile. As a 19-year-old he was banned for a year after a player brawl at the Bulgarian cup final. He was voted Footballer of the Year for four successive years from 1989 to 1992 and was three times league champion with CSKA. The goals flowed at home and abroad. Stoichkov was joint winner with Real Madrid's Hugo Sanchez of the 1989–90 Golden Boot as top league scorer in Europe with 38 goals and was duly signed by Barcelona on coach Johan Cruyff's personal recommendation. Stoichkov and Cruyff were not always so friendly even though, together, they celebrated four successive Spanish championships and victory in the 1992 Champions Cup. In 1994 he was not only – finally – voted European Footballer of the Year but became only the

second Bulgarian footballer to be voted national Sportsman of the Year (after the late Georgi Asparoukhov). By that time, Stoichkov and Cruyff were not speaking and the Bulgarian was sold to Parma. Italian club discipline was not, however, to his liking and he returned a year later to Barcelona. He returned on loan to his original club, CSKA, in the spring of 1998, and played in the World Cup finals the same summer.

Joachim **Streich**

Country:	*East Germany (born April 13, 1951)*
Position:	*Centre forward*
Clubs:	*Hansa Rostock, Magdeburg*

Streich was one of two East Germans to achieve a century of international appearances during the state's 40-year lifetime – the other having been Hans-Jürgen Dorner. He was a forceful centre forward with great resilience and strength under pressure which meant he completed his career without ever suffering major problems with injury. Streich played 102 times for East Germany between his debut as a substitute in a 1–1 draw against Iraq in 1969 and 1984, scoring 55 goals. He led the East German attack on their historic appearance in the World Cup finals in West Germany in 1974, was three times East German cup-winner and twice the domestic Footballer of the Year in 1979 and 1983.

Luis **Suarez**

Country:	*Spain (born May 2, 1935)*
Position:	*Inside left*
Clubs:	*Deportivo de La Coruna, Barcelona (Spain), Inter (Italy)*

Hristo Stoichkov: temperamental Bulgarian

Spain's greatest players have, in general, been foreign imports – the likes of Di Stefano, Kubala, Puskas, Cruyff and Ronaldo. Long before the Bosman judgment which destroyed controls on imports, the Spanish game was awash with foreign players. That explains the enormous pride generated around home-grown products who proved they could live, internationally, with the best. Goalkeeper Ricardo Zamora, the superstar of the 1920s and 1930s, was acknowledged as Spain's greatest discovery until the emergence of Luis Suarez in the 1950s. Born and brought up in La Coruna, in the north-west corner of Spain, Suarez made an instant impact on his debut for La Coruna away to Barcelona. La Coruna lost but the Catalan crowd gave Suarez a standing ovation and Barcelona officials insisted on agreeing transfer terms immediately after the match. It says everything about Suarez's talent that he establishing himself as a playmaking inside left in a Barcelona squad overflowing with international attacking genius including not only Kubala but fellow Hungarians Sandor Kocsis and Zoltan Czibor, Paraguay's Ramon Villaverde and Eulogio Martinez and Brazil's Evaristo de Macedo. Coach Helenio Herrera insisted on taking Suarez with him after moving to Internazionale and it was around Suarez's organisational ability that Herrera built a team to dominate world club football in the mid-1960s. Suarez's ability to turn defence into attack with one pinpoint pass suited Inter's hit-and-hold tactics admirably. Later Suarez, who had been voted 1960 European Footballer of the Year, spent many years on the Inter coaching staff – twice being handed charge of the senior side – and he also managed Spain at the 1990 World Cup finals.

Davor **Suker**

Country: *Croatia (born January 1, 1968)*
Position: *Centre forward*
Clubs: *Osijek, FC Zagreb, Seville (Spain), Real Madrid (Spain)*

Suker, for all the riches which international football success has brought him, has remained a down-to-earth character. He starred first in the Yugoslavia squad which won the World Youth Cup in 1987. He then became top league marksman with 18 goals while with Osijek to earn selection for the 1990 World Cup finals, but did not play. After the civil war in the Balkans he declared himself for Croatia and was the overall top scorer in the Euro 96 qualifying competition with 12 goals in ten matches. At the finals Suker scored a memorable goal against Denmark, chipping goalkeeper Peter Schmeichel. He held a leading role within the national squad – negotiating with the federation and potential sponsors on all matters concerned with pay, commercial rights, etc. He won the Spanish league in 1997, then the UEFA Champions League Cup in 1998, both with Real Madrid, and then emerged as the new Croatian hero during the 1998 World Cup, finishing as leading goal-scorer with a total of six.

Davor Suker: top scorer at the 1998 World Cup

Frank **Swift**

Country: *England (born December 26, 1913)*
Position: *Goalkeeper*
Club: *Manchester City*

Swift was a personality among goalkeepers, enjoying a joke with opponents and referees, yet deadly serious at stopping shots. "Big Frank" stood in the crowd and watched Manchester City lose the 1933 FA Cup Final, then played for them when they won a year later, fainting at the finish as nervous exhaustion overcame him. During the war his entertainment value became even greater, and he won 19 caps while in his 30s – only twice on the losing side. After his retirement from the sport he became a well-respected journalist, and was one of those killed in the Munich air crash in 1958 while travelling, ironically with City's local rivals, Manchester United.

Friedrich "Fritz" **Szepan**

Country: *Germany (born September 2, 1907)*
Position: *Inside forward/central defender*
Club: *Schalke*

Szepan, the greatest German international of the 1930s, came from a Polish background but was born and brought up in the Ruhr and starred for local team Schalke. He played his entire career for them, switching between inside forward and new-style defensive centre half. Szepan was the mastermind of Schalke's six German championship successes between 1934 and 1942. He played 34 times for Germany between 1929 and 1939 and was a member of the team which finished third at the 1934 World Cup finals in Italy. Years later a veteran commentator, trying to explain Szepan's influence, described him as "like Franz Beckenbauer and Gunter Netzer rolled into one."

Claudio Andre Mergen **Taffarel**

Country: *Brazil (born May 8, 1966)*
Position: *Goalkeeper*
Clubs: *Crissiuma, Internacional Porto Alegre, Parma (Italy), Reggiana (Italy), Palmeiras, Atletico Mineiro*

Taffarel first gained attention in Brazil's 1985 World Youth Cup winning side which beat Spain 1–0 in the final. He began with Crissiuma and was later bought by Internacional of Porto Alegre and starred at the finals of the 1988 Olympic Games. He saved three penalties in the semi-final against West Germany – one during the match and two in the penalty shoot-out. After the 1990 World Cup, he was bought by Parma of Italy but his form faded after two seasons and he was sold to Reggiana. Brazil boss Carlos Alberto Parreira believed, however, that Taffarel was as good as ever and he was a World Cup winner in 1994, retaining his place in 1998, as he saved more penalties in a semi-final shoot-out against Holland, although Brazil lost the final to France.

Marco **Tardelli**

Country: *Italy (born September 24, 1954)*
Position: *Midfielder*
Clubs: *Pisa, Como, Juventus, Internazionale*

Tardelli scored six goals in 81 appearances for Italy and was voted official Man of the Match at the end of the 1982 World Cup Final defeat of West Germany in Madrid. A utility defender or midfielder, he was seen to best effect playing for Juventus and Italy in the first half of the 1980s. With both club and country he succeeded the more overtly physical Romeo Benetti in midfield, though his Azzurri debut, against Portugal in Turin in 1976, was in fact at right back. He is one of the very few players to have won every major prize the modern domestic and European game had to offer, from the 1982 World Cup with Italy to the 1985 Champions Cup with Juventus.

Tommy **Taylor**

Country: *England (born January 29, 1932)*
Position: *Centre forward*
Clubs: *Barnsley, Manchester United*

Taylor was the centre forward who cost United £29,999 from Barnsley in March 1953 because manager Matt Busby did not want him saddled with the pressure of being a "£30,000 player." Taylor had a fierce shot in each foot and was outstanding in the air. Wolves, Sheffield Wednesday and Derby County were all beaten by United in the transfer race and he scored 112 goals in 168 first division appearances before the Munich air disaster, when he was one of eight United players killed on their way back from a European Champions Cup quarter-final tie against Red Star Belgrade in 1958. He would have been England's first-choice centre forward at the subsequent World Cup finals in Sweden. As it was, he scored 16 goals in his 19 international appearances.

Jonas **Thern**

Country: *Sweden (born March 20, 1967)*
Position: *Midfielder*
Clubs: *Malmö, Benfica (Portugal), Napoli (Italy), Roma (Italy), Rangers (Scotland)*

Thern captained Sweden through their outstanding revivalist era in the early 1990s and was praised by manager Tommy Svensson as "our No. 1 footballer." He made his name with Malmö and joined Benfica for £800,000 in 1989. He had already made his presence felt on the international scene by then – having scored a fine goal and then been sent off in the 2–2 draw against Tunisia with which Sweden began their Olympic Games campaign in Seoul in 1988. Thern made his senior Sweden debut in a 1–1 draw with West Germany in Gelsenkirchen in October 1987. He moved to Italy with Napoli and transferred in 1994 to Roma who appointed him captain and then moved on to Rangers in 1997.

John **Thomson**

Country: *Scotland (born January 18, 1908)*
Position: *Goalkeeper*
Clubs: *Ayr United, Celtic*

An assortment of Scottish goalkeepers have, in recent years, established a popular notoriety for unreliability, but that was never the case with Thomson, even in a short career which ended with his tragic death at 23 after an accident in an Old Firm derby against Rangers in September, 1931. Thomson, born in Buckhaven, Fife, joined Celtic in the 1926–27 season. Within a few months he was a first-team regular and winning a Scottish Cup medal. He had played four times for the Scottish League and made four senior appearances for Scotland by the time he was fatally injured, diving to save at the feet of Rangers' Sam English. Thomson's funeral in Fife was attended by 3,000 mourners, two special trains having been put on to bring at least 2,000 from Glasgow.

Jean Amadou **Tigana**

Country: *France (born June 23, 1955)*
Position: *Midfielder*
Clubs: *Toulon, Lyon, Bordeaux*

Tigana was a late developer who owed an enormous debt to the talent-spotting of long-serving coach Aime Jacquet (later French national manager). Born in Mali, he came to France as a child with his family of nine brothers and sisters. On leaving school he found work first in a spaghetti factory, then as a postman to supplement his part-time earnings from football. Toulon signed him at 20 but gave him a free transfer, and Jacquet stepped in to "rescue" Tigana for Lyon. It was not until he moved to high-profile Bordeaux in 1981 that Tigana's international career took off. He was a regular starter for France in midfield in the World Cups of 1982 and 1986 as well as the European Championship-winning campaign in between. He later coached Monaco to the French league title in 1997 and to the UEFA Champions League semi-finals the following season.

Tostao (Full name Eduardo Goncalves Andrade)

Country: *Brazil (born January 25, 1947)*
Position: *Centre forward*
Clubs: *Cruzeiro, Vasco da Gama*

Tostao, a small, nimble centre forward, was already nicknamed the "White Pele" when he made his World Cup debut for Brazil at the 1966 finals in England. He scored Brazil's consolation goal in their 3–1 defeat by Hungary and that threatened to become his first and last World Cup-tie when, in 1969, he suffered a detached retina. The injury occured in a South American cup-tie against Millonarios in Bogota. Tostao underwent specialist surgery in Houston and recovered to become one of the heroes of Brazil's World Cup victory in Mexico a year later. However Tostao, a qualified doctor, recognised that the longer he played on, the more he risked permanent injury and retired at 26 in197 to become an eye specialist.

Marius Tresor

Country: *France (born January 15, 1950)*
Position: *Central defender*
Clubs: *Ajaccio, Marseille, Bordeaux*

Tresor played locally for Juventus of Saint-Anne before being brought to the French championship by the Corsican club Ajaccio. He played both stopper and sweeper for the national team just too early to be a part of the European title-winning experience in 1984. Powerful in the tackle but technically gifted as well, he led France by example in the World Cup finals tournaments of both 1978 – defying painful muscle injuries to do so – and 1982. In Spain he captained France in the third-place play-off (which they lost, narrowly, to Poland). The core of his club career was spent with Marseille between 1972 and 1980 when, after relegation, he transferred to bitter rivals Bordeaux.

Toni Turek

Country: *West Germany (born January 18, 1919)*
Position: *Goalkeeper*
Clubs: *Duisburg, Ulm, Eintracht Frankfurt, Fortuna Dusseldorf, Borussia Mönchengladbach*

Turek was a World Cup-winning hero in 1954, not merely for his presence in the German team but for the reflexes which helped hold the legendary Hungarian team at bay during the first half of the Final. He was then, remarkably, 35 years old and had already demonstrated his abilities with a match-saving performance against Yugoslavia in the quarter-finals. His form was a surprise to foreign observers but not to his fellow Germans. Yet Turek had not made his international debut until he was 31, playing in goal for Germany in the 1–0 win over Switzerland in Dusseldorf which marked their return to the international scene in 1950. Clearly, without the war he would have won far more than his 20 internationals.

Jorge Valdano

Country: *Argentina (born October 4, 1955)*
Position: *Centre forward*
Clubs: *Newell's Old Boys, Alaves (Spain), Zaragoza (Spain), Real Madrid (Spain)*

Valdano proved a rare personality in the world game: an author, poet, polemicist, coach and World Cup-winning player. Born in Las Parejas, he left Argentina for political reasons as a teenager and built his playing career in Spain. His success in winning the UEFA Cup twice in the mid-1980s with Real Madrid earned him selection for Argentina and his positional and tactical nous were influential in the 1986 World Cup win. Originally an outside left, he was converted by Argentine coach Carlos Bilardo into a roving link between midfield and attack. Unfortunately he was later struck down by hepatitis, struggled in vain to make a World Cup comeback in 1990 and retired to become a journalist, analyst and then a successful coach with Tenerife and later back with Real Madrid.

Carlos Valderrama

Country: *Colombia (born September 2, 1961)*
Position: *Midfielder*
Clubs: *Santa Marta, Millonarios, Atletico Nacional, Montpellier (France), Valladolid (Spain), Medellin, Atletico Junior Barranquilla, Tampa Bay Mutiny, Miami Fusion (USA)*

The combination of frizzy hairstyle and all-round skill earmarked Valderrama as a character as he shared South American Cup glory with Atletico Nacional before trying his luck in Europe with Montpellier of France and Valladolid of Spain. In neither country could he adapt – rediscovering his touch only after returning to Colombia in 1992. But the manner in which he masterminded Colombia's sensational World Cup qualifying campaign in 1994 earned him a second award as South American Footballer of the Year. The Colombians, however, flopped at the 1994 World Cup, as they did four years later in France.

Marco **Van Basten**

Country: *Holland (born October 31, 1964)*
Position: *Centre forward*
Clubs: *Ajax Amsterdam (Holland), Milan (Italy)*

Van Basten was the last player to have secured the European Footballer award three times. He might even have qualified for a fourth success had it not been for the ankle injuries which brought his career to a sadly premature halt in 1995. Tall and angular, he first earned international acclaim at the 1983 World Youth Cup. By then he had already been discovered in Holland by Ajax and it was as a substitute for his mentor Johan Cruyff that he made his competitive debut. In all, Van Basten scored 128 league goals for Ajax before joining Milan for a mere £1.5 million in 1987. With Ajax he had won not just domestic prizes and the Cup-winners Cup but also the European Golden Boot – awarded to Europe's top league marksman – with 37 goals in season 1985–86. At Milan he picked up winner's medals for the World and European Champions Club Cups, plus individual honours including the FIFA World Footballer of the Year trophy. Milan looked to a half-fit Van Basten in the 1993 Champions Cup Final against Marseille in Munich but he had played only 15 intermittent league games all season and the challenge proved beyond him. He never played again. At least he left a wonderful legacy for football's memory – one of the all-time great international goals when he volleyed home a long, looping cross to shoot Holland 2–0 ahead against the Soviet Union in the 1988 European Championship Final in Munich.

Franky **Van Der Elst**

Country: *Belgium (born April 30, 1961)*
Position: *Midfielder*
Clubs: *Blauw-Wit, Brugge*

Van der Elst, a central defender or midfielder, began his career with Blauw-Wit from his home town of Lombeek. He was discovered there by RWD Molenbeek and spent three years with the suburban Brussels club before joining Club Brugge in 1983. Almost immediately he was rushed into the national team for the 1984 European Championship finals in France after the entire back four were suspended following league match-fixing allegations. Van der Elst (no relation to François Van der Elst, once of Anderlecht, Cosmos and West Ham) was a pillar at the heart of the national team for the next decade. After playing 69 times for Belgium, he retired from the national team after a European qualifying defeat by Spain in the autumn of 1994 but was persuaded to make a comeback for the 1998 World Cup.

Paul **Van Himst**

Country: *Belgium (born October 2, 1943)*
Position: *Centre forward*
Clubs: *Anderlecht, RWD Molenbeek, Eendracht Aalst*

Van Himst is still regarded as his country's greatest player. He joined Anderlecht at the age of nine and, by 16, was playing centre forward in the first team. He was to be Belgian champion eight times, cup-winner four times, league top scorer three times and was four times Footballer of the Year. He scored 31 goals

Marco Van Basten: injuries forced early retirement

in 81 internationals between 1960 and 1979, which included the 1970 World Cup finals and a third-place finish as hosts at the 1972 European Championship. Later he coached Anderlecht to victory in the UEFA Cup before being appointed manager of Belgium after the qualifying failure in the 1992 European Championship. Van Himst managed Belgium to the second round of the World Cup finals in 1994.

Odbulio **Varela**

Country: *Uruguay (born September 20, 1917)*
Position: *Central defender*
Clubs: *Wanderers, Penarol*

Varela was an old-style attacking centre half. He was also captain by example of the Uruguayan team which shocked Brazil by beating their hosts in the Maracana stadium in Rio de Janeiro in the 1950 World Cup Final. Varela had made his league debut with Wanderers at 21 and had already played for Uruguay before joining local giants Penarol in 1942. Twice he won the South American championship with Uruguay but the 1950 World Cup saw him at his zenith, driving his team forward with every confidence even after Uruguay went 1–0 down early on. He was outstanding again, even at 37, in the 1954 World Cup finals in Switzerland. He retired immediately afterwards and was briefly coach to Penarol before quitting the game.

Vava (Full name Edvaldo Izidio Neto)

Country: *Brazil (born November 12, 1934)*
Position: *Inside forward/centre forward*
Clubs: *Recife, Vasco, Atletico Madrid, Palmeiras, Botafogo*

Originally an inside left, Vava was switched to the centre of attack by Brazil at the 1958 World Cup to accomodate Pele. He scored twice in the 5–2 final victory over Sweden to earn a transfer to Spain with Atletico Madrid. He was successful and hugely popular in Spain, but his family grew homesick and he returned home in time to regain his Brazil place for the World Cup defence in Chile in 1962 when he scored another of his typically vital goals in the 3–1 final victory over the Czechs. Vava scored 15 goals in 22 internationals spread over 12 years between 1952 and 1964.

Martin **Verges**

Country: *Spain (born March 8, 1934)*
Position: *Wing half*
Club: *Barcelona*

Barcelona, in the late 1950s, possessed one of the most outstanding squad of players boasted by any European club in the modern era. In attack, midfield and defence they mixed technical skill with power and pure talent. Verges, a right half admired sometimes more by opponents than by Catalans, was a key figure in purveying the ball out of defence up to great forwards such as Kubala, Kocsis and Suarez. He played 16 times for Spain and won two leagues, two cups and two Fairs Cups. He was discovered by Barcelona playing for his local team, Vidreras, was sent on loan to Espana Industrial and recalled to the first-team squad in 1956.

Christian **Vieri**

Country: *Italy (born July 12, 1973)*
Position: *Centre forward*
Clubs: *Prato, Torino, Pisa, Ravenna, Venezia, Atalanta, Juventus, Atletico Madrid (Spain)*

A late developer, Vieri is the son of a former Torino midfield player, and was brought up in Australia. On returning to Italy, he joined Prato in Serie C, aged 15. He moved to his father's old club Torino in 1990 but played only seven matches in three seasons and moved on via Pisa, Ravenna, Venezia and Atalanta before returning to Turin with Juventus. Injury to Alen Boksic gave Vieri his chance to become first-choice with Juventus in 1996–97 when he scored eight goals in only 15 games. He was a UEFA Champions League Cup runner-up with Juventus in 1997 against Borussia Dortmund. Transferred in 1997 to Atletico Madrid he ended his first season as the league's 24-goal top scorer, and was also on song in the 1998 World Cup with five goals in the tournament for Italy.

Vitor Manuel Martins Baia

Country: *Portugal (born October 15, 1969)*
Position: *Goalkeeper*
Clubs: *FC Porto, Barcelona (Spain)*

Vitor Baia, considered by many as Europe's finest keeper, became a professional almost by accident. His family were fans of Benfica when he went for a trial with Porto as a teenager just to keep another hopeful company. Porto immediately recognised his potential and would not let him go. He was promoted to the first team in emergency in 1988–89 after injury to Polish keeper Jozsef Mlynarczyk while Portuguese international Ze Beto was suspended. Later he became captain of the national team. He was national champion with Porto in 1990, 1992, 1993, 1995 and 1996 and winner of the Portuguese Cup in 1991 and 1994. Vitor Baia was acclaimed Footballer of the Year in 1992 after setting a domestic record by not conceding a goal for more than 1,000 minutes of play. He was awarded Europe's top goalkeeper prize by ESM (European Sports

Magazines) in 1996, and he followed coach Bobby Robson from Porto to Spain's Barcelona in the summer of 1996, winning the European Cup-winners Cup in his first season as the Spanish club defeated French club and holders Paris Saint-Germain 1–0 in the final in Rotterdam.

Rudi **Völler**

Country: *Germany (born April 13, 1960)*
Position: *Centre forward*
Clubs: *1860 Munich, Werder Bremen, Roma (Italy), Marseille (France), Bayer Leverkusen*

Völler, with 47 goals in 90 games, was one of Germany's most competitive international players in the 1980s and 1990s, although he didn't always endure himself to opposition fans with his theatrical dives and ability to feign sudden injury in an attempt to win a free-kick or penalty. He appeared to great effect in the World Cup finals events of 1986, 1990 and – after being persuaded by manager Berti Vogts to rescind a "retirement" decision – in 1994. Völler made his name with TSV 1860 Munich, joined Werder Bremen in 1982 and, in his first season, was league top scorer with 23 goals, won the Footballer of the Yea award and was awarded his first cap as a substitute for Lothar Matthäus against Northern Ireland. Voller was a World Cup runner-up in 1986 and a winner four years later against Argentina. But his luck broke, along with his left arm, against the Commonwealth of Independent States (ex-Soviet Union) in Germany's first match in the 1992 European Championship finals.

Fritz **Walter**

Country: *West Germany (born October 31, 1920)*
Position: *Inside left*
Club: *Kaiserslautern*

Walter scored a hat-trick on his Germany debut in his favourite position of inside left in a 9–2 thrashing of Romania in July 1940. His career was cut in half by the war when he was called up as a paratrooper and his war-time experiences led him to refuse to fly to games in peacetime years. On the resumption of German international football, he was restored as captain by long-time admirer and manager Sepp Herberger. Consequently, Walter and centre forward brother Ottmar were World Cup-winners together against hot favourites Hungary in the 1954 final in Berne, Switzerland. Walter retired from the national team but played on with his only club, Kaiserslautern. He was then persuaded by Herberger to return to duty in 1958 when, now 37, he led West Germany to the semi-finals. Walter, who scored 33 goals in his 61 internationals, later wrote a string of successful football books.

George **Weah**

Country: *Liberia (born October 1, 1966)*
Position: *Centre forward*
Clubs: *Young Survivors, Bongrang, Mighty Barolla, Tonnerre (Cameroon), Monaco (France), Paris SG (France), Milan (Italy)*

Weah made history in 1995, becoming the first winner of the European Footballer poll after the change of rules which opened the award up to players of any nationality. Yet, although a Liberian international, he was in fact a French citizen – having taken citizenship after his years of residence while playing for Monaco and Paris Saint-Germain. Born in the Liberian capital of Monrovia, he played in Cameroon with Tonnerre before moving to France with Monaco in 1988. He rose to stardom under the guidance of Arsene Wenger to win the league championship in 1991 then moved to Paris a year later. In 1994 he joined Milan for £3.5million. The price looks very cheap now considering Weah's status in the world game and his ability to score goals of breathtaking brilliance. He has put his multi-million earnings to sensible use. His wife and children live in New York while he has re-invested thousands of pounds in football in his native Liberia. Without the money Weah provided, Liberia could not have fielded their national team in the qualifying competitions for the 1998 African Nations Cup or World Cup.

Taribo **West**

Country: *Nigeria (born March 26, 1974)*
Position: *Central defender*
Clubs: *Port Harcourt Sharks, Enugu Rangers, Julius Berger, Auxerre (France), Internazionale (Italy)*

West is a no-nonsense utility defender who has earned a cult following in France and Italy since first arriving in Europe with his bus fare and little else in his pocket in 1993. He found life at Auxerre tough as he struggled to learn both the language and the football. He made great strides to become a key member of the Olympic Games in 1996 with Nigeria and was transferred a year later to Inter. One blemish on his 1998 UEFA Cup success with Inter was his sending off. He represented Nigeria during the 1998 World Cup, helping them to the second round.

John **White**

Country: *Scotland (born April 28, 1937)*
Position: *Inside right*
Clubs: *Alloa Athletic, Falkirk, Tottenham Hotspur (England)*

White was an inside right of delicate creative skill who earned a place in football legend as a key member of the Tottenham

George Weah: invested in Liberian football

team which won the English league and cup double in 1961. His positional and passing skills complemented the inspirational abilities of wing halves Danny Blanchflower and Dave Mackay. White, who cost Spurs a mere £20,000 in October 1959, should have been a central figure at White Hart Lane throughout the 1960s, but died tragically after being struck by lightning on a golf course on July 21, 1964. He played 22 times for Scotland, collected representative appearances at League and under-23 level and won the Cup-winners Cup with Spurs in 1963.

Norman **Whiteside**

Country: *Northern Ireland (born May 7, 1965)*
Position: *Midfielder*
Clubs: *Manchester United, Everton*

The youngest World Cup player in history at only 17 in 1982, when he made his debut after only two League appearances, one

as a substitute. He later became the youngest-ever FA Cup Final and League Cup Final scorer, against Brighton (won) and Liverpool (lost), and curled a splendid winner into the Everton net to earn another FA medal in 1985. By then his muscular work in attack had altered to a more painstaking approach through midfield, partially brought about by the amount of damage he had sustained at the sharp end. Everton later bought him, but yet another injury ended his career before he was 30.

Ernst **Wilimowski**

Country: *Poland (born June 23, 1916)*
Position: *Centre forward*
Clubs: *Ruch Chorzow, PSV Chemnitz (Germany), TSV 1860 Munich (Germany), Hameln 07 (Germany), BC Augsburg (Germany), Singen 04 (Germany), VfR Kaiserslautern (Germany)*

Ironically, considering what would later happen, Wilimowski made his Poland debut against Germany in 1934. He then wrote his name into World Cup history when he scored four goals against Brazil in a first-round tie in France in 1938, yet still finished on the losing side after a 6–5 extra-time defeat. He totalled 21 goals in 22 games for Poland, where he won five league titles with Ruch Chorzow. Yet for years his name was omitted from Polish sports records – because Wilimowski, after the German invasion, continued his career with German clubs and scored a further 13 goals in eight internationals for Greater Germany. In 1942 he scored 1860 Munich's first goal in their 2–0 defeat of Schalke in the Greater German Cup Final. After the war he played on with a string of regional league clubs before retiring at 37 in 1953.

Billy **Wright**

Country: *England (born February 6, 1924)*
Position: *Wing half/central defender*
Club: *Wolverhampton Wanderers*

A lively wing half who moved into the centre of defence and – by reading play superbly, timing tackles well and leaping to remarkable heights for a smallish man – he extended his career for years and years. Two League titles and one FA Cup went his way, plus the little matter of 105 caps in 13 seasons (out of a possible 108). He was world football's first cap centurion when he led England to victory over Scotland in 1959, and was an inspirational player for both country and Wolves. Away from pitch he was a charismatic character, and his marriage to one of the glamorous 'Beverley Sisters' – the Spice Girls of their day – made him a darling with the media. He later managed Arsenal without much success and then became a TV executive.

Ian **Wright**

Country: *England (born November 3, 1963)*
Position: *Centre forward*
Clubs: *Crystal Palace, Arsenal, West Ham*

In a little corner of north London, the name Ian Wright will be revered for years to come. Although he started his rollercoaster career in south London with Crystal Palace, having not become a professional until the comparatively late age of 21, it will always be Arsenal which is inextricably linked with Ian Wright. In September 1997 he surpassed Cliff Bastin's club goal-scoring record that had stood since the 1940s. His hat-trick against Bolton took him past the 178 goals of Bastin and established Wright as the greatest goalscorer in the history of the famous club. Already an FA Cup, League Cup and European Cup-winners' Cup winner with the Gunners, in 1998 Wright picked up his first championship-winners' medal, and another FA Cup one, as Arsenal won a rare league and cup double, under French manager Arsène Wenger. Despite first playing for England against Cameroon in 1991, his international days looked to be over when he was omitted from the 1996 European Championships. But the indefatigable Wright forced his way back during the World Cup qualifiying matches, impressing new coach Glenn Hoddle with his boundless enthusiasm, playing a great game alone up front against Italy in Rome in 1997. Desperate to play in the 1998 World Cup – in a live television interview immediately after the Rome game when England had secured their place in France he begged Hoddle to pick him – he looked to have recovered from a mid-season hamstring injury that had kept him out of the Arsenal side for four months but, having been picked in the initial squad, he suffered a recurrence of the injury in a pre-season friendly and was devastated to be ruled out of the finals. But he quickly recovered from the disappointment, and a move to West Ham United – this time in the East of London – in the summer of 1998 provided a happy place to see out his great career.

Lev **Yashin**

Country: *Soviet Union (born October 22, 1929)*
Position: *Goalkeeper*
Club: *Moscow Dynamo*

In South America they called Yashin the Black Spider; in Europe the Black Panther. Portugal's Eusebio described him as "the peerless goalkeeper of the century." Yet he very nearly gave up soccer altogether in favour of ice hockey. That was in 1953. He was growing tired of standing in as reserve at Moscow Dynamo to the legendary Alexei "Tiger" Khomich. He was, after all, 23, and Dynamo's ice hockey coaches were pleading with him to

Lev Yashin: greatest goalkeeper of them all

commit himself to their cause. Then Khomich was injured. Dynamo coach Arkady Cherenyshev called on the impatient reserve and Yashin took over to such outstanding effect that, a year later, he was making his debut for the Soviet Union in a 3–2 win over Sweden. Two years later, in 1956, Yashin kept goal for the Soviet side which won the Olympic Games title in Melbourne, Australia. In 1960 he was goalkeeper for the Soviet side which won the inaugural European Championship. In the first seven years after his debut for the Soviet Union he missed only two internationals, ending his career with a then-record 78 caps. For Dynamo, he played 326 Supreme League matches and won the league title six times and the Soviet cup twice and was European Footballer of the Year in 1963. On his death in 1990, the official news agency, Tass, described him as "the most famous Soviet sportsman ever." Yashin's fame had spread throughout the world not merely for his ability as a goalkeeper to stop the shots no-one else could reach, but as an outstanding sportsman and ambassador for the game. Appropriately, in 1963 he became the first Soviet and/or Russian player to be crowned as European Footballer of the Year by the French magazine, *France Football*.

To this day, he remains the only goalkeeper to have received the award. The World Cups of 1958, 1962 and 1966 saw Yashin at work and he was in Mexico, too, in 1970, though only as a reserve because of his value of his experience behind the scenes. In 1965 he was outstanding in the Stanley Matthews Retirement Match at Stoke when a British XI lost narrowly to a World XI. One of his saves that night – diving full-length across the face of his goal to grip a shot from Jimmy Greaves – will live for ever in the memory of those present. Yashin is reputed to have saved more than 150 penalties during his career. One of the few which got past him was struck by Eusebio in the third place play-off at the 1966 World Cup finals at Wembley. The Soviets finished fourth but, with Yashin in goal, that remained their best finish in the competition. He remained in sport after his retirement, not as a coach or trainer but as head of the Ministry of Sport's football department and then as a vice-president of the national association. Towards the end of his career, he was honoured by the Soviet government with the Order of Lenin. Of course, Lenin's reputation has gone into steep decline in subsequent years: something that could never be said for Lev Yashin.

Rashidi **Yekini**

Country: *Nigeria (born October 23, 1963)*
Position: *Centre forward*
Clubs: *Kaduna, Vitoria Setubal (Portugal), Olympiakos Pireus (Greece), Gijon (Spain), FC Zurich (Switzerland)*

Yekini was, more than any other player, responsible for Nigeria's sensational 1994 World Cup. He had made his international debut ten years earlier yet, did not become a regular until the 1992 African Nations Cup when he scored four goals in a qualifier against Burkina Faso, then the winner in the third-place play-off against Cameroon. Yekini was eight-goal top scorer in the African qualifiers of the 1994 World Cup, then top-scored again with five goals at the 1994 African Nations finals. The 1993 African Footballer of the Year, he made history when he scored – against Bulgaria – Nigeria's first-ever goal in the World Cup finals. He then left Setubal for an odyssey through European club football but ran out of luck – regaining form only just in time to challenge for a World Cup return in France.

George **Young**

Country: *Scotland (born October 27, 1922)*
Position: *Central defender*
Club: *Rangers*

George Young was a dominant figure in the 1940s and 1950s, nearly 15 stones of muscle and a keen brain as well. He was equally adept at right back and centre half, and played in 53 of Scotland's first 62 post-war internationals. Of those, he was skipper a remarkable 48 times. Young was remarkably clever on the ball for such a huge man, an inspiring captain and a dead shot with a penalty. He scored twice from the spot in the 1949 Scottish Cup Final and acted as deputy goalkeeper in the 1953 match, helping to ensure a replay that Rangers won to give him his fourth medal. He also gained six championship medals and two for the League Cup, and had a spell as Scotland national manager before going into business. Despite his huge frame, Young remains one of the few men in Scottish football never to have been sent off or even cautioned during his playing career.

Ricardo **Zamora**

Country: *Spain (born January 21, 1901)*
Position: *Goalkeeper*
Clubs: *Espanol, Real Madrid, Nice (France)*

Zamora was a legendary goalkeeper who helped Spain become the first foreign side to beat England when they triumphed by 4–3 in Madrid in 1929. Conversely, one of the worst moments in Zamora's career was Spain's seven-goal thrashing in the revenge fixture at Highbury, London, two years later. In the 1934 World Cup quarter-finals, he brilliantly and courageously defied a rugged Italian attack as Spain clung on for a 1–1 extra-time draw in Florence. Unfortunately, he took such a battering he was not fit enough for the replay, which Spain lost. In 1936, when Spanish football was shut down by the civil war, Zamora moved to France to play two further years with Nice before returning home to coach. He played 46 times for Spain and his transfer in 1929 from Espanol to Real Madrid set a Spanish record...equivalent to £2,000.

Ivan **Zamorano**

Country: *Chile (born January 18, 1968)*
Position: *Centre forward*
Clubs: *Cobresal, Bologna (Italy), St Gallen (Switzerland), Seville (Spain), Real Madrid (Spain), Internazionale (Italy)*

Zamorano was one of the most dangerous marksmen in European club football in the 1990s but only reached the World Cup stage with Chile in 1998 in France – and failed to find the net. He was largely responsible for his country's qualifying success, having contributed 12 goals to the campaign. At club level, he moved to Europe at 21 with Bologna but moved almost immediately to Swiss club St Gallen. His goal-scoring exploits earned a transfer to Seville and then Real Madrid. He became top scorer in the Spanish league before transferring to Inter in 1996. With Inter he was UEFA Cup runner-up in 1997 and then winner in 1998.

Zico (Full name Artur Antunes Coimbra)

Country: *Brazil (born March 3, 1953)*

Position: *Centre forward*

Clubs: *Flamengo (Brazil), Udinese (Italy), Flamengo (Brazil), Kashima Antlers (Japan)*

It took special diets and weight training to turn the teenage waif Zico into the wiry attacker who scored with one of his speciality free kicks on his Brazil debut against Uruguay in 1975. Injury and tactical disagreements spoiled the 1978 and 1986 World Cups for him and he was thus seen at his best only in Spain in 1982. After winning all three pool matches, putting four past both Scotland and New Zealand, Zico and Brazil met Italy and Argentina in the second phase. They disposed of the Argentinians, the holders, 3–1, before an epic 3–2 defeat against the Italians eliminated the Brazilians from the competition. The

1986 finals were particularly galling for Zico for, in another thrilling World Cup clash, Brazil drew 1–1 with France in the quarter-final, and in the ensuing penalty shoot-out, Zico missed from the spot and France were through. At club level he inspired Flamengo's victory in the 1981 South American Club Cup and their subsequent demolition of Liverpool in Tokyo in the World Club final. That was the start of Zico's mutual love affair with Japan which was resumed when, after a brief spell as Brazil's Minister of Sport, he joined Kashima Antlers to lead the adventurous launch of the professional J League in the spring of 1993.

Zinedine Zidane

Country: *France (born June 23, 1972)*

Position: *Midfielder*

Clubs: *Cannes, Bordeaux, Juventus (Italy)*

Zidane took over from Eric Cantona, in the late 1990s, as the top French footballer, but thankfully minus the rebellious streak that restricted Cantona's international progress. Zidane's rise had been rapid. He made his top division debut in May 1989, joined Bordeaux in 1992 and was voted Young Player of the Year in 1992. He marked a sensational national team debut by scoring both France's goals in the closing stages to rescue a 2–2 draw against the Czech Republic. He played more games than any other player in France during 1995–96: 57 including league, European club and international appearances. Not surprisingly, he was then too tired to do himself justice in the 1996 European Championship. But that did not dissuade Juventus from signing him he was inspirational in their runs to the UEFA Champions League Finals of 1997 and 1998. Despite these successes with Juventus, Zidane's finest few hour came during the 1998 World Cup, staged in France, when he discovered the vagaries of sport. In France's second match of the tournament, he was shown the red card, many said unjustly, after treading on an opponent during the 4–0 defeat of Saudi Arabia. Suspended for two games, France struggled without their inspirational playmaker, but they were still in the competition when he returned for the quarter-final clash with Italy. France won that match on penalties, then disposed of Croatia in the semi-final before meeting holders Brazil in front of 75,000 raucous Parisians. Zidane rose to the occasion magnificently, as well as rising to two corners that he headed into the back of the Brazilian net to give his side a 2–0 half-time lead. France extended that scoreline to 3–0 in the dying minutes to secure a famous victory that sent the country wild.. Zidane, born in Marseille in the south of France, but the son of Algerian parents, seemed to symbolize the new-found racial harmony that had enveloped the French nation during the World Cup finals. As the streets of Paris thronged with celebrating French, Zidane was the new hero.

Zico: hero in Brazil and Japan

Zinedine Zidane: two goals in the World Cup Final

Dino **Zoff**

Country: *Italy (born February 28, 1942)*
Position: *Goalkeeper*
Clubs: *Udinese, Mantova, Napoli, Juventus*

Zoff's story is a remarkable one which has seen him touch every level of the game – and with great success. First he became Italy's record international, with 112 appearances to his credit of which the 106th was the World Cup Final defeat of West Germany in Madrid in 1982. Zoff secured a remarkable double that day, becoming the second Juventus goalkeeper to receive the World Cup after 1934 skipper Gianpiero Combi. He played his way steadily up Italian football's hierarchy. After spells with Udinese and Mantova, transferring to Napoli provided him with the springboard to national team recognition in time to help win the 1968 European Nations Championship. In 1973–74 he set a record of 1,143 international minutes without conceding a goal. By now he had moved on to Juventus with whom he won the league, cup and European Cup-winners Cup. Later Zoff turned to coaching with Juventus and guided them to UEFA Cup success in 1990 before moving to Lazio, where he duly graduated from coach to the ultimate power of president, one of his first investments being English star Paul Gascoigne.

Andoni **Zubizarreta**

Country: *Spain (born October 23, 1961)*
Position: *Goalkeeper*
Clubs: *Bilbao, Barcelona, Valencia*

Zubizarreta was probably the finest product of the remarkable Basque school of goalkeeping which produced internationals such as Carmelo, Iribar, Artola and Arconada. He made his league debut with Bilbao in 1981 and his international debut as a substitute for fellow-Basque Luis Arconada in a 3–1 win over Finland in Alicante in 1985. Successive national managers made "Zubi" their first-choice keeper at the finals of the 1986, 1990 and 1994 World Cups. In the summer of 1986 he cost Barcelona a then-world record fee for a goalkeeper of £1.2 million. He won two league titles and one cup at Bilbao; four leagues, two cups, the European Champions Cup, Cup-winners Cup and European Supercup with Barcelona. He missed Barcelona's 1991 Cup-winners Cup Final defeat by Manchester United through suspension. Worse still, he was given a free transfer by Barcelona after their 4–0 Champions Cup Final defeat by Milan in 1994, yet subsequently regained his footballing touch with Valencia and became the first Spanish player to reach a century of international appearances, although he blotted his copybook with an own goal against Nigeria in the 1998 World Cup finals that cost his side the match.

Gianfranco **Zola**

Country: *Italy (born July 5, 1966)*
Position: *Inside forward*
Clubs: *Nuorese, Torres, Napoli, Parma, Chelsea (England)*

Zola learned his trade in the shadow of Diego Maradona at Napoli – picking up all the Argentine superstar's good technical habits and none of his less fortunate personal ones. Above all, he achieved a remarkable success-rate with direct free kicks. But it was not until after his transfer to Parma that he was fully appreciated as an intuitive, creative attacker in his own right. Zola had an unfortunate time at Euro 96, missing a penalty after having been brought down in the decisive group match against Germany. Ironically, he regained all his old confidence thanks to a transfer to England, to Chelsea, midway through the 1996–97 season. He proved that his marksmanship had not deserted him at international level when he scored Italy's winner against England at Wembley in a World Cup qualifier in February 1997. Just over a year later he appeared as substitute to strike a brilliant winning goal for Chelsea in the 1998 European Cup-winners Cup Final against Stuttgart.

COACHES

Radomir (Raddy) Antic

Born: *November 22, 1949 (Yugoslavia)*

Antic, born in Zitiste, Yugoslavia, played wing-half for Sloboda Tuzla, Partizan, Fenerbahce of Istanbul, Zaragoza and Luton Town – whom he once saved, famously, from relegation with a last-ditch goal. Played five times in midfield for Yugoslavia. Started his coaching career in the Partizan youth section in 1984 and returned to Spain as boss of Zaragoza in 1988. Moved to Real Madrid in 1990 and had them eight points clear at the top of the table in January 1991 when he was sacked. Spent three seasons with Oviedo and was then appointed by Atletico Madrid in 1995 – guiding them to the League and Cup double in his first season. Left Atletico in 1998 after a record employment stint under the presidency of the unpredictable Jesus Gil.

Artur Jorge Braga Melo Teixeira

Born: *February 13, 1946 (Portugal)*

Outstanding reputation on the international scene. Artur Jorge played his club football entirely in Portugal with FC Porto, Academica Coimbra, Benfica and Belenenses. He then moved into coaching with Vitoria Guimaraes (as assistant), Belenenses, Portimonense, FC Porto, Matra Racing Paris, Paris Saint-Germain and Benfica. He was twice national coach of Portugal and managed Switzerland at the 1996 European Championship finals. Artur Jorge's greatest successs was in guiding FC Porto to victory in the 1987 European Champions Cup. Both champion and cup-winner in France with Paris Saint-Germain. Doctor of Philosophy and German studies who also speaks French, English, Spanish and Italian. Author of a book of poetry. Made a remarkably quick return to his coaching appointment with Benfica after undergoing emergency surgery to remove a brain tumour in the autumn of 1994.

Fulvio Bernardini

Born: *January 1, 1906 (Italy); died 1984*

Bernardini was an outstanding attacking centre-half in the 1930s with Lazio and Ambrosiana Inter at a time when national coach Vittorio Pozzo preferred the new third-back tactic for his World Cup-winning national team. Bernardini, who played 26 times for Italy between 1925 and 1932, turned to coaching after the war. He managed Roma, Lazio and Sampdoria and turned both Fiorentina in 1956 and Bologna in 1964 into League champions, cracking the title hegemony of the rich Turin and Milan clubs. His Fiorentina lost only one game in 1955–56, the last of the season. But Bologna needed a play-off to beat Internazionale

after a stormy season in which Bernardini had to defend his players against dope-test allegations. In 1974, Bernardini was brought out of retirement to start rebuilding Italy's team after their poor showing at the World Cup finals in West Germany.

Konstantin Beskov

Born: *November 18, 1920 (Soviet Union)*

Beskov was a goal-scoring inside forward with the Moscow Dynamo who toured Britain in the winter of 1945. He won six championships and one cup with Dynamo before retiring to their coaching staff. He was also subsequently twice appointed national coach – most notably when the Soviet Union reached the second round of the 1982 World Cup finals.

Carlos Bilardo

Born: *March 16, 1938 (Argentina)*

Bilardo learned his football under the ruthless Osvaldo Zubeldia at Estudiantes de La Plata when they won the Copa Libertadores three years in a row, in the late 1960s. Bilardo was in the team which beat Manchester United to win the 1968 World Club Cup while simultaneously qualifying as a children's doctor. Managed Colombia in the 1982 World Cup qualifiers, then took Estudiantes to the Argentine title before being appointed national coach in 1983. In Mexico, in 1986, Bilardo joined the illustrious group of managers who can say they have won the World Cup. Unfortunately, Bilardo's football style, coloured by the Estudiantes years, depended on the disciplined and pragmatic rather than the colourful and extravagant. It was by applying precisely these principles that Argentina, under Bilardo, finished runners-up in 1990.

Miroslav Blazevic

Born: *February 10, 1935 (Yugoslavia)*

Guided Croatia to the quarter-finals of the 1996 European Championship and then surpassed all expectations by taking them to the semi-final of the 1998 World Cup finals in France. He achieved that despite having, simultaneously, to fight off allegations linking him to the Marseille match-fixing scandal of the early 1990s. After a successful career as a right-winger for several Yugoslav teams and Swiss sides Sion and Vevey in the 1960s, Blazevic stayed on in Switzerland to coach Grasshopper to a national championship. On returning to Yugoslavia, he became a Croat national hero when he won the title with Dinamo Zagreb in 1982. Blazevic also worked for Nantes in France and PAOK Salonika in Greece. When Croatia declared independence from Yugoslavia, Blazevic returned to his "first love", Dinamo, now Croatia Zagreb. He became a major shareholder in the club and steered them to the League title in 1994. In March 1994, he became coach of the national team on a personal appeal from "my friend" President Franjo Tudjman, and four years later came his finest hour.

Craig **Brown**

Born:	*July 1, 1940 (Scotland)*

Brown, national manager of Scotland at the 1996 European Championship and 1998 World Cup, had played originally for Rangers, Dundee and Falkirk before his career was ended prematurely by a knee injury. He then pursued a career in education as head teacher and then college lecturer. Became assistant manager at Motherwell (1972–77) and then manager of Clyde. In 1986, he became assistant national coach to Andy Roxburgh whom he succeeded in 1993 when Roxburgh was appointed to head UEFA's coaching directorate.

Marton **Bukovi**

Born:	*1904 (Hungary)*

Bukovi was an attacking centre-half with Ferencvaros (FTC), then with Sochaux and Racing in France. He played 11 times for Hungary between 1926 and 1930 and, in 1929, was a member of the FTC side which beat Olympic champions Uruguay in front of their own fans in Montevideo. After the war, Bukovi became coach of the MTK/Red Banner side which helped Honved form the backbone of the "Magical Magyars" national team. The great, withdrawn centre-forward Nandor Hidegkuti was one of his star pupils.

Matt **Busby**

Born:	*May 26, 1909 (Scotland); died January 20, 1994*

Scotland wing-half who played pre-war for Liverpool and Manchester City and took over Manchester United in 1945 when air raid damage had reduced Old Trafford to near-rubble. Such was his gift for management that, within three years, he had created the first of three memorable teams. His 1948 side won the FA Cup, his Busby Babes of the mid-1950s went twice to the Champions Cup semi-finals before being wrecked by the Munich air disaster and his third team completed the European quest with victory over Benfica in 1968. He retired in 1971 and became a club director. Busby's love of entertaining football inspired some of British football's greatest talents –Johnny Carey, Duncan Edwards, Bobby Charlton, Denis Law and George Best.

Zlatko "Tschik" **Cajkovski**

Born:	*November 24, 1923 (Yugoslavia)*

Was an outstanding, ebullient wing-half who captained Yugoslavia at the 1950 and 1954 World Cups. Played ten years with Partizan Belgrade before retiring in 1955. Then he coached in Israel, Turkey and West Germany, where he took over at Bayern Munich. It was under Cajkovski that the youthful Franz Beckenbauer developed his ideas about an attacking sweeper's role on the way to winning the 1967 European Cup-winners Cup. Cajkovski later coached Dinamo Zagreb and Nuremberg.

Fabio **Capello**

Born:	*June 18, 1946 (Italy)*

Former Italian international midfielder who scored the historic goal with which Italy beat England at Wembley in 1973. That was one of Capello's eight goals in 32 appearances for his country during an outstanding playing career which took him to Spal, Roma, Juventus and Milan. After retiring, he joined the Milan coaching staff and was appointed first-team boss when Arrigo Sacchi became national manager in 1991. Capello, more pragmatic than Sacchi, guided Milan to four League titles and one European Champions Cup. In 175 League matches as coach

Matt Busby: The European Cup at last

of Milan, his team lost just 17 times with eight defeats coming in the 1994–95 season. In 1991–92, his debut season as coach, Milan were unbeaten. Capello finally left Milan in 1996 for Real Madrid whom he steered to the 1997 Spanish League title – laying the disciplinary and selection foundations of the team which won the UEFA Champions League the following year. By then, Capello had returned to Milan but was not allowed the time he felt he needed to rebuild the team.

Carlos Alberto Gomes Parreira

Born: *March 25, 1943 (Brazil)*

Succeeded Paulo Roberto Falcao as Brazil boss in September 1991 and guided them to World Cup success less than three years later. No relation to the Carlos Alberto Torres who captained the 1970 World Cup winners; no relation either to the Carlos Alberto da Silva who coached Brazil in the late 1980s and, briefly, at Porto in Portugal. Parreira coached junior clubs in Rio before being seconded to help the Ghana federation in Africa in 1967. He returned to top jobs in Brazil. In 1970 and 1974, he was a member of Mario Zagallo's World Cup coaching squad. He combined this with top jobs in charge of Vasco da Gama and Fluminense, whom he guided to the 1974 Rio de Janeiro state championship. In 1976, Carlos Alberto first travelled out to the Middle East as aide to Zagallo in Kuwait. When Zagallo left, in 1978, Carlos Alberto was handed full control. In 1982, he was rewarded with a first-ever appearance at the World Cup finals. That success brought 1983's appointment as manager of Brazil, but he left after a year following defeat by Uruguay in the final of the South American championship. Returning to the club world, Carlos Alberto took Fluminense to the Rio League title in 1984. He then returned to the Middle East. Saudi Arabia appointed him manager in 1988 and held on to him so tightly that at the start of 1989 Carlos Alberto could not take up the post of Brazil manager (Sebastiao Lazaroni was second choice). After the Saudis' World Cup qualifying failure, Carlos Alberto was snapped up by the United Arab Emirates and managed them at the 1990 World Cup finals. In 1998, Carlos Alberto – now with Saudi Arabia – and Bora Milutinovic became the first men to coach four different nations at the World Cup finals.

Herbert Chapman

Born: *1873 (England); died 1934*

Proved the first great innovative manager in world football in the nine years between his appointment at Arsenal in 1925 and his death from pneumonia. It was Chapman who changed the club's name from 'The Arsenal' to simply 'Arsenal' so as to move to the top of the Football League's alphabetical ladder; proposed

shirt numbers and floodlit matches; persuaded London Electric Railway to change the name of the local underground station from Gillespie Road to Arsenal; signed Charlie Buchan in a payment-by-results deal which would not be out of place today (£2,000 down and £100 per goal); and pulled the centre half back into the centre of defence to form the classic WM shape. Chapman also tried to sign a foreign goalkeeper in Austria's Rudi Hiden but could not obtain a work permit. Chapman did sign "greats" such as Alex James and Cliff Bastin and his Arsenal won the League three times and the FA Cup once. Before arriving at Highbury, Chapman played for Tottenham and Northampton Town where he became player-manager; he was also manager at Leeds City and Huddersfield Town.

Javier Clemente

Born: *March 12, 1950 (Spain)*

Basque by birth and nature, played for home-town team Barakaldo as a teenage midfielder and was signed by Bilbao. Apparently had a long, successful career ahead of him when he was struck down by injury at 23. Three years and seven operations later he was forced to retire and, like all good ex-Bilbao pros, was offered a post on the club coaching staff. Spread his wings with minor Basque clubs Arenas Guecho and Basconia before returning to Bilbao as youth coach. Was appointed first-team boss in 1980 and guided them twice to the League title, once to the double. But his down-to-earth, hard-working demands were not universally popular and he was forced out by player power in 1986. Espanyol signed him and were rewarded with a run to the UEFA Cup Final in 1988. Later, Clemente had a brief spell with Atletico Madrid. Not afraid to call a spade a spade, Clemente was once hauled before the federation's disciplinary committee after a public slanging match with his predecessor as Atletico coach, Argentina's Cesar Luis Menotti. Clemente had commented "the only thing Menotti ever won had to be bought for him by the President of Argentina..." Clemente was appointed national coach in 1992, making his debut with a 1–0 win over Graham Taylor's England in Santander. Building a club "feel" into his squad, Clemente took Spain to the quarter-finals of the 1994 World Cup and the 1996 European Championship.

Brian Clough

Born: *March 21, 1935 (England)*

Clough was the maverick manager who established himself as one of the outstanding personalities in English football even though his reputation did not "translate" easily further afield. A goal-hungry centre-forward with Middlesbrough in the 1950s,

Brian Clough: unique style proved successful

into the first Swedish club to win a European trophy when they lifted the UEFA Cup in 1982 – as well as the Swedish League and cup double all in the same year. He later won three Portuguese league titles in two spells with Benfica who under his management were also Champions Cup runners-up to Milan in 1989. In Italy Eriksson coached Roma, Fiorentina and Sampdoria before moving to Lazio in 1997 – after having first agreed to take over Blackburn Rovers. In 1998, Eriksson guided Lazio to victory in the Italian Cup and the runners-up spot in the UEFA Cup.

Vicente **Feola**

Born: *November 1, 1909 (Brazil); died November 6, 1975*

Feola was coach of the Brazil team who made history by winning the 1958 World Cup on the "wrong" continent. He played for Palmeiras and Americano in the 1930s but quit to take up coaching when only 28. Feola had two successul spells with Sao Paulo before being appointed to the national team coaching staff in 1958, shortly before the finals. Famously, it took a deputation of senior players to persuade him to play Pele and Garrincha, but it says much for Feola that he was not too proud to take their advice. Brazil's success helped earn Feola a lucrative club contract with Boca Juniors, whom he guided to success in the Argentine championship in the spring of 1962. He was then summoned home to manage Brazil's World Cup defence in Chile, but was taken ill and could not travel. His 1958 assistant, Aimore Moreira, stepped up successfully in his place. Feola returned as manager of Brazil at the 1966 finals in England but by then his team was over the hill.

Alex **Ferguson**

Born: *December 31, 1941 (Scotland)*

After a slow start, Ferguson proved the ideal successor to fellow Scot Matt Busby at Manchester United. Ferguson was no great star in his playing days at Rangers, Queen's Park and Dunfermline, but after starting in management with East Stirling and St Mirren in the 1970s he achieved phenomenal success with Aberdeen in the 1980s. Having broken Celtic and Rangers' grip on the Scottish championship in 1980, he took the Dons to four Scottish Cups and two more League titles as well as the European Cup-winners Cup in 1983. After a brief caretaker role with Scotland at the 1986 World Cup, he began his reign at Old Trafford where he transformed United from under-achievers to the most successful club in Britain. A down-to-earth approach, tinged with occasional outbreaks of gamesmanship, brought Ferguson four English League championships, three FA Cups and one European Cup-winners Cup.

Clough was forced to retire by knee trouble after having played only once for England. In 1965 he became at 30, the youngest manager in the English Football League with Hartlepool and worked his way up the ladder. He took Derby County out of the doldrums and to the League title in 1972 and to the Champions Cup semi-finals a year later. Had a notorious 44-day spell as boss of Leeds before building his masterpiece at Nottingham Forest – whom he galvanised into winning the Champions Cup in 1979 and 1980. An outspoken personality, Clough retired in 1993.

Sven-Goran **Eriksson**

Born: *February 9, 1948 (Sweden)*

Eriksson made his name with IFK Gothenburg, turning them

Raymond Goethals

Born: *October 17, 1921 (Belgium)*

Goethals was one of the most enigmatic, but also most successful, of Belgian coaches. He played originally in goal for minor town club Hanut, near Brussels, then for Racing and Daring. He also played twice for Belgium but found his true *metier* only after turning to coaching with Waregem and St Trond, whom he joined in 1959. He took them, against all the odds, to the Belgian League title in 1966, then managed Belgium at the 1970 World Cup finals. In 1978 Goethals took Anderlecht to victory in the European Cup-winners Cup but could not quite repeat the trick four years later with Standard Liège, which lost the final to Barcelona. Consolation followed in the shape of the 1982 and 1983 League titles. Goethals developed a reputation as the man for an emergency – in Brazil with Sao Paulo, in Portugal with Vitoria Guimaraes and in France with Bordeaux, then Marseille. Goethals was hired by Marseille's president, Bernard Tapie, in the spring of 1991 when the appointment of Franz Beckenbauer had run into trouble. Goethals took Marseille to the Champions Cup Final where they lost on penalties to Red Star Belgrade. He steered Marseille to two championships in 1991 and 1992, then retired – only to be brought back in November 1992. The following May, Goethals had become the oldest man to coach a European Champions Cup-winning team. Goethals was never implicated in the Marseille match-fixing scam but was suspended by the Belgian authorities after evidence that Standard had fixed a decisive match at the end of the 1981–82 League title-winning season.

Bela Guttman

Born: *1900 (Hungary); died 1981*

Guttmann was a dancing master by profession and a top-level amateur player, first with MTK, then with Hakoah of Vienna and the New York Giants. He played for Hungary at the 1924 Olympics, won four caps, then turned to coaching in the late 1930s. He started with Enschede (Holland) in 1937–38, then won the Hungarian championship with Ujpest Dozsa in 1939. After the war, he coached Dinamo Bucharest (1945), Vasas Budapest (1946) and had a spell as boss of Ferenc Puskas's developing Honved side. Coached in Italy with Padova, Triestina and Milan, then moved to Portugal. Coached Porto in 1958–59 before being lured to Lisbon by Benfica. He converted them back from 4–2–4 to WM and they thus overwhelmed Barcelona in the 1961 Champions Cup Final in Berne. Guttman moved to Uruguay with Penarol, returned to Benfica for a season in 1965–66 and had short spells with Servette, Panathinaikos and FK Austria before retiring. Had League title success as coach in Hungary (with Ujpest), Italy (Milan), Portugal (Benfica and Porto) and Uruguay (Penarol).

Josef "Sepp" Herberger

Born: *March 28, 1897 (Germany); died April 28, 1977*

Herberger was the founder of a German management dynasty. An inside forward who played three times for Germany between 1921 and 1925, he became assistant national manager to Dr Otto Nerz in 1932 and succeeded him after the disastrous defeat by Norway at the 1936 Berlin Olympics. Herberger travelled widely to keep abreast of the world game and astutely managed his players and tactics to maximum effect, above all at the 1954 World Cup. There he took the bold step of fielding his reserves for a first-round match against Hungary. He was unfazed by the 8–3 defeat, knowing that his fresh first team could still reach the later stages and go on, as they did, to beat Hungary 3–2 in the final. He retired in 1963 and handed over to his hand-picked assistant, Helmut Schön.

Helenio Herrera

Born: *April 17, 1916 (Argentina); died November 9, 1997*

One of the world's most innovative and single-minded coaches. Herrera, born in Argentina, was brought up in Morocco and played in France. He then enjoyed a meteoric rise to coaching superstardom with spells at Red Star Paris, Stade Français (France), Atletico Madrid, Valladolid, Sevilla (Spain), Belenenses (Portugal), Barcelona (Spain), Internazionale and Roma (Italy); also the Spanish and Italian national teams. Herrera amazed fans at Barcelona in the 1950s by using inside-forwards at wing-half to turn "easy" matches into goal sprees. His attacking tactics proved ineffective at Inter so Herrera developed, instead, the most ruthlessly-disciplined *catenaccio*. Herrera demanded total obedience, insisting his players place their hands on the ball and swear loyalty to each other before going out for a match. Stars who baulked at such rituals were sold, however popular or successful. Inter won the World and Champions Cups twice each before Herrera's career went into decline at Roma.

Jupp Heynckes

Born: *May 9, 1945 (West Germany)*

Heynckes has gone down in football history as the man who put Real Madrid back on top of the European mountain in 1998. As a player, Heynckes was a prolific striker with Borussia Mönchengladbach. He was also in the West German team which won the 1972 European Championship and the squad which won the World Cup in 1974, though he did not play in the final. He won the West German League five times, the Cup once and the UEFA Cup once. Heynckes's coaching career took him back to Borussia Mönchengladbach before he twice guided Bayern Munich to the League title. Heynckes, perhaps then too outspoken in public, was dismissed in 1991 and took over Athletic Bilbao in 1992. He stayed two years, went back to Germany for a troubled season with Eintracht Frankfurt, then returned to Spain with Tenerife. He was appointed coach to Real Madrid in 1997, guiding them to the UEFA Champions League Cup in 1998 before – remarkably – being dismissed.

Ottmar **Hitzfeld**

Born: *January 12, 1949 (Switzerland)*

Hitzfeld was originally a workmanlike midfielder who played for a number of minor German clubs, then for Basle (Switzerland), Stuttgart (Germany) and Lugano and Lucerne (Switzerland). But he turned into an outstanding coach. Hitzfeld started coaching work in Switzerland with Zug. Later, he managed FA Aarau and Grasshopper Zurich – winning the Swiss championship twice and the domestic cup three times. In July 1991, he took over from Horst Koppel as Borussia Dortmund coach. Here, he won the German League in 1995 and 1996 and the UEFA Champions League Cup against Juventus in 1997, in Munich where he returned in the summer of 1998 as new coach of Bayern in succession to Giovanni Trapattoni.

Roy **Hodgson**

Born: *August 9, 1947 (England)*

Hodgson may lay claim to being the most successful English coach anywhere in the world in the 1990s – with the single exception of Bobby Robson. He was on Crystal Palace's books as a youngster but failed to make the grade and played non-league instead with Maidstone. Later, Hodgson went to South Africa, playing for Berea Park, where he first met Bob Houghton. In the mid-1970s Houghton helped Hodgson make a coaching start in Europe, in Sweden. He bossed Halmstad from 1976 to 1980, spent two years as aide to Houghton at Bristol City, then returned to Sweden with Orebro before trying his luck in Switzerland with Neuchatel Xamax. Hodgson was an instant hit, taking Xamax to the League runners-up spot in 1991 and 1992, then being appointed Switzerland's national manager. In 1994, Hodgson took the Swiss to the World Cup finals for the first time in 30 years, then steered them to the finals of Euro 96. Switzerland went without Hodgson who had, by that time, been lured to Internazionale, with whom he was UEFA Cup runner-

up in 1997. Took up his first major English post a few weeks later with Blackburn and achieved a fair amount of success in the 1997–98 season, guiding them to sixth position in the Premier League and a spot in the UEFA Cup.

Guus **Hiddink**

Born: *November 8, 1946 (Holland)*

Hiddink played in the 1960s for a variety of Dutch clubs (Sport Varsseveld, De Graafschap, PSV Eindhoven and NEC Nijmegen) before moving into the North American Soccer League (Washington Diplomats and San José Earthquakes). He then returned to a four-year stint as youth coach with De Graafschap. Became assistant at PSV Eindhoven for three years before taking over the senior team from Hans Kraay in 1986. In 1988 he guided PSV to victory in the European Champions Cup. Moved to Spain with Valencia before succeeding Dick Advocaat as national coach in the autumn of 1994. Took Holland to the quarter-finals of the 1996 European Championship and the semi-final of the 1998 World Cup before returning to Spain with Real Madrid.

Jimmy **Hogan**

Born: *1888 (England); died 1974*

Hogan was the one man, more than any other, who "taught" skilled modern football to the countries of central Europe. Hogan, second of 13 children of an Irish Catholic millworker in Colne, Lancashire, played for Nelson, Swindon, Fulham, Burnley and Bolton. His first foreign coaching venture was to Holland, in the early years of the century, with Dordrecht. He returned frequently to work in Britain with the likes of Fulham, Aston Villa, Brentford and Celtic. But his most devoted pupils were on the continent – above all in Austria, until he was interned during the First World War. Hogan was released only on condition that he continue his coaching work in Hungary and report regularly to the police. He did such a good job in Hungary that he was handed much of the credit by the Hungarians after their sensational 6–3 victory over England at Wembley in 1953.

Anghel **Iordanescu**

Born: *May 4, 1950 (Romania)*

Took over from sacked Cornel Dinu in mid-1993 as national team coach after spending most of his long and successful career with Steaua Bucharest. As a player he was capped 64 times for the national team, scoring 26 goals, and won several national championships with the club. Iordanescu was player-assistant coach when Steaua beat Barcelona in the 1986 European Champions Cup Final in Seville. Between 1990 and 1992, he coached Cypriot team Anorthosis Famagusta before returning to Steaua in 1992 – winning two League titles before being appointed national manager. Known as "The General" – and also holds that rank in the Romanian armed forces. Took the national team to their greatest-ever success in the World Cup, reaching the quarter-finals in 1994 before losing to Sweden in a penalty shoot-out. Iordanescu frequently took advantage of his "untouchable" status in Romania to speak out publicly against corruption and financial maladministration within the domestic game.

Tomislav **Ivic**

Born: *June 30, 1933 (Yugoslavia)*

One of the most experienced and widely-travelled of Europe's leading coaches, Ivic worked originally with his home-town club, Hajduk Split. In 1982, he moved abroad for the first time with Anderlecht, then worked in quick succession at a record number of clubs in a record number of countries: Galatasaray in Turkey, Avellino (Italy), Panathinaikos, Dinamo Zagreb (then Yugoslavia), FC Porto, Paris Saint-Germain, Ajax, Anderlecht, Atletico Madrid, Marseille and Benfica. In the spring of 1998, he was appointed national coach of World Cup finalists Iran, only to be dismissed on orders from Tehran – while he was running a training camp in France! – three weeks before the finals.

Aime **Jacquet**

Born: *November 27, 1941 (France)*

Jacquet was awarded the *Legion d'Honneur* in the summer of 1998 after he had steered France to their first ever World Cup win. Jacquet, who retired after the ultimate footballing triumph, had endured months of criticism by the French press because of his coaching methods and team selections, yet his style paid off as France defeated, among others, Italy, Croatia and in the final Brazil 3–0. As a teenager, he worked on a factory assembly line until he was talent-spotted by St Etienne with whom he won five league championships and three domestic cups. Jacquet, a hard-working midfielder, played twice for France. He moved into coaching after a knee injury ended his career. Won three French titles, two French Cups and reached European Champion Clubs Cup and Cup-winners Cup semi-finals as coach of Bordeaux in 1980s. Sacked in 1989 for being "too honest" by president Claude Bez who was himself later jailed for fraud. Joined national coaching staff in July 1992 and was appointed national coach in December 1993 in succession to Gèrard Houllier, after France's failure to reach 1994 World Cup finals.

Marcello **Lippi**

Born: *April 11, 1948 (Italy)*

Lippi was for many years sweeper with Sampdoria, but it was as coach to Juventus in the mid-1990s that he earned greatest respect and success. His coaching career had begun with the youth sections of Sampdoria followed by stints with minor clubs such as Pontedra, Siena, Pistoia and Carrara. His first Serie A job was with Cesena but his reward for saving them from relegation was the sack. Appointments with Atalanta and Napoli followed before Lippi was handed the job of running Juventus in 1994. The first thing he did was visit his father's tomb in his home town of Viareggio. Salvatore Lippi had died three years previously, after Marcello had been fired by Cesena. The younger Lippi said: "I know that you never liked this team (Juventus) because you considered it the symbol of power. But wait and see. You will be pleased by the signature I made today." So were Juventus. In his first season, Lippi took Juventus to the League title, Italian Cup and UEFA Cup Final; in his second, they won the European Champions Cup and Italian Supercup; in his third they won the League and the World Club Cup and were European runners-up; and in his fourth they retained the championsip and were again Champions Cup runners-up. "Lippismo," the secret of his success, has been defined as a subtle mixture of patience, pragmatism and a mastery of team psychology.

Valeri **Lobanovski**

Born: *January 6, 1939 (Ukraine)*

Lobanovski, more than any other coach, gained outstanding results from applying the theories of "scientific soccer" with Kiev Dynamo and the Soviet Union national team. Lobanovski played outside left for Chernomorets Odessa, Shakhtor Donetsk and Kiev Dynamo. He won two caps for the Soviet Union. Lobanovski then coached Dnepr from 1969 to 1973, when he began his long coaching association with Kiev. Lobonovski reduced football to a science in which tactics and pitch discipline were as important as physical fitness and mental discipline. The application of his football formulae by players of the natural talent of Oleg Blokhin and Alexander Zavarov was intimidating. Kiev won the 1986 Cup-winners Cup with a cold brilliance which shattered Atletico Madrid. Two years later, Lobanovski's Soviet team reached the final of the European Championship in West Germany. It says everything about Lobanovski's programmed approach that the suspension of stopper Oleg Kuznetsov from the final upset the balance of the team and they lost 2–0 to Holland. That was the third of Lobanovski's spells in charge of the Soviet national team, having been appointed this time around just three weeks before the start of the 1986 World Cup finals. Since half the squad came from his own Kiev team, that did not raise as many problems as it would have for another manager.

Juan Carlos **Lorenzo**

Born: *October 22, 1922 (Argentina)*

A useful centre or inside-forward in the 1940s, Lorenzo played in France before retiring. A great admirer of the "British way of football," Lorenzo was one of the first foreign coaches to come to England to sit for his FA coaching badge under the tutelage of Walter Winterbottom. That was particularly ironic in view of subsequent events. After coaching in Spain and Peru, Lorenzo was appointed boss of Argentina at the 1966 World Cup. The trademark ruthlessness he encouraged in all his teams was in evidence not only during the infamous quarter-final defeat by England at Wembley, but in the preceding group matches – notably against West Germany. Later, Lorenzo was appointed coach of Atletico Madrid whose will-to-win caused similar storms. They had no fewer than three players sent off against Celtic in one leg of the 1974 Champions Cup semi-final. Lorenzo then returned to his native Argentina to take over Boca Juniors. They won the Copa Libertadores twice under Lorenzo but it said everything about his philosophy that not one of his players was included by Cesar Menotti in Argentina's 1978 World Cup-winning squad.

Cesare **Maldini**

Born: *February 5, 1932 (Italy)*

Maldini, father of 1990s star Paolo, was an outstanding defender in his own right. He played full-back for Milan against Real Madrid in the 1958 Champions Cup Final, then turned into a sweeper of great class. It was as sweeper that Maldini captained Milan to victory over Benfica at Wembley in the Champions Cup, in 1963. Maldini played only 16 times for Italy but this included two appearances at the 1962 World Cup finals in Chile. After retiring, Maldini joined the Milan coaching set-up, then the Italian federation's coaching staff. He was No. 2 to Enzo Bearzot in Italy's 1982 World Cup-winning campaign and later, in his own right, guided Italy to victory three times in the European Under-21 championship. Maldini took over an Italian national team in crisis in the middle of the 1998 World Cup qualifying campaign. But in his first competitive match, he guided Italy to a 1–0 win against England, at Wembley. Although they stumbled a couple of times during the qualifying matches, Italy made it to France and the 1998 World Cup, where they met lost to the French in the quarter-final courtesy of the dreaded penalty shoot-out.

Francis **Maturana**

Born: *February 15, 1949 (Colombia)*

Maturana, for working so many nerveless years at the heart of Colombian fooball, may be considered one of the most courageous coaches in the world. A former defender who represented Colombia at various levels, he gained six caps in 1981. Spent most of his ten-year playing career with Nacional Medellin, later moving to Bucaramanga, Deportivo Cali and Tolima before retiring in 1983. A central defender, he played for Colombia in the qualifying tournaments for the World Cups of 1978 and 1982 as well as in the Panamerican Games and Olympic preliminaries. His last international was a 2–0 defeat by Peru in a World Cup qualifying tie in August, 1981. Was preparing to set up his own dental practice in 1983 before he received a call to coach Nacional's youth side. In 1986, he took over the professional side Cristal Caldas, then Nacional, and Colombia in 1987. Playing the short-passing game, Nacional won the 1989 Copa Libertadores, and the Colombians qualified for the 1990 World Cup. After that, Maturana joined America Cali, and duly won his first League title with them before taking the national side back to the World Cup for the ill-fated finals of 1994 when Colombia under-performed, and an own goal by defender Escobar against the USA, culminated in his murder when he returned home.

Hugo **Meisl**

Born: *November 16, 1881 (Austria); died February 17, 1937*

Meisl was the errant son of a Viennese banking family who was too infatuated with football in central Europe in the early years of the century to want to enter the business. Meisl was playing inside-forward for FK Austria when he met the English coach Jimmy Hogan, whom he persuaded to come and work in Vienna. Later, Meisl became involved with neighbours Admira and then became secretary of the Austrian federation from 1906 until his death in 1937. Simultaneously, he was national manager, and his partnership with Hogan led to the rise of the legendary Austrian "Wunderteam" of the 1920s and early 1930s. Meisl and Vittorio Pozzo were the two dominant figures in pre-war continental football.

Cesar Luis **Menotti**

Born: *November 5, 1938 (Argentina)*

Menotti was the football romantic who masterminded Argentina's original World Cup triumph in front of their own fanatical followers in 1978. Menotti, one of the game's most notorious chain-smokers, played centre-half originally for Rosario Central, then in the United States for New York Generals, for whom he scored a hat-trick against Pele's touring Santos. The Brazilian club were so impressed they signed Menotti and he stayed a year before ending his career with Juventus of Sao Paulo. Returning home to Argentina, Menotti was appointed assistant coach to Newell's Old Boys, then took Huracan to the League title in 1973. That earned him the task of national coach in succession to Vladislao Cap. Menotti's football philosophy clashed virulently with the ruthless approach of Juan Carlos Lorenzo, who was then coach of Argentina's top club, Boca Juniors. It was no accident that Boca, even though reigning South American club champions, did not supply one player to Menotti's World Cup-winning squad. He was even self-confident enough to leave a prodigiously-talented 17-year-old out of the squad – Diego Maradona. Menotti was justified by results – just as his ultimate departure was justified by Argentina's failure to hold on to the World Cup in Spain, in 1982. Always in demand, Menotti coached all Argentina's top clubs such as River Plate, Boca Juniors and Independiente.

Marinus "Rinus" Michels

Born: *February 9, 1928 (Holland)*

Michels, a Dutch international centre forward in the early 1950s, led a revolution in the late 1960s when he developed the "total football" philosophy at Ajax. Much of Michels's coaching career linked with the presence, as leader on the pitch, of Johan Cruyff. Michels went to Barcelona after winning the Champions Cup with Ajax in 1971, went back to Ajax to sign Cruyff and the pair were partners again when Holland finished runners-up at the 1974 World Cup. "Iron Rinus" was never afraid to take tactical risks, such as when he guided Holland to European Championship success in 1988 by using Ruud Gullit as a static, right-side attacker. Nor was Michels ever afraid of stating his opinions, however blunt. His other coaching appointments included stints with Bayer Leverkusen in Germany and Los Angeles Aztecs in the North American Soccer League.

Velibor "Bora" Milutinovic

Born: *September 7, 1944 (Yugoslavia)*

One of three Serbian brothers who played for Partizan Belgrade in the 1960s. A midfielder, Milutinovic also played in France and Switzerland, before moving in 1972 to Mexico where he settled – playing for, and later coaching, top club UNAM. Holds, jointly with Carlos Alberto Parreira, the record of having managed four different nations at the World Cup finals – Mexico as hosts in 1986, Costa Rica in 1990, the United States as hosts in 1994 and

"Bora" Milutinovic: sharp-dressed manager

Nigeria in 1998. Achieved success with an idiosyncratic mixture combining tactical awareness with a close attention to player psychology and group motivation.

Miguel Munoz

Born: *1922 (Spain)*

Munoz played inside-forward and then right-half for Logrones, Racing Santander and Celta Vigo before transferring to Real Madrid in 1948. He became Real's captain and scored their first goal in European club competition against Servette of Geneva in the inaugural Champions Cup of 1955–56. Munoz captained Real to their European victories in 1956 and 1957. He retired in 1958, being granted the proceeds of a testimonial against Pele's Santos. Munoz became coach of nursery club Plus Ultra and was then appointed Real Madrid's first team coach shortly before the 1960 thrashing of Eintracht Frankfurt. Munoz stayed a further 13 years, winning everything. He then had two brief spells as national manager before returning to the club milieu with Hercules, Seville and Las Palmas. Under Munoz, Spain's national team were runners-up in the 1984 European Championship and reached the finals of the 1986 World Cup.

Egil **Olsen**

Born: *April 22, 1942 (Norway)*

Marxist-Leninist nicknamed "Drillo" who guided Norway to the 1994 and 1998 World Cup finals. In the latter tournament, Norway progressed to the second round where they lost 1–0 to Italy. Olsen used to wear wellington boots (because of an old back injury) on the bench and boasted he had made more money out of poker than football. Olsen played 16 times for his country in the 1960s at outside or inside right but never scored a goal. After retiring, he became a lecturer in physical education while coaching part-time. He brought famous old Lyn Oslo back up from the third division, then successively managed the national under-21 side, the Olympic team and the under-21s again. In October 1990, he was appointed senior national manager. Olsen is a great advocate of videos to study the opposition and his own team. He claims, thanks to video, to have counted every pass made at the 1990 World Cup finals (36,300).

Joseph "Sepp" **Piontek**

Born: *March 5, 1940 (Germany/Poland)*

Piontek brought about the Danish national team revolution. Born in what is now Wroclaw, Poland, he was brought up near Bremen and was Werder's first-choice right back throughout the 1960s. He played 203 Bundesliga games as well as six times for West Germany. Piontek retired in 1972 and coached Fortuna Düsseldorf and the Haiti national team before earning international acclaim for his work with Denmark. Piontek took them to the semi-finals of the 1984 European Championship, the second round of the 1986 World Cup and the finals of the 1988 European Championship before returning to the club game.

Vittorio **Pozzo**

Born: *March 12, 1886 (Italy); died December 21, 1968*

Pozzo was a giant figure in Italian football history. He "found" football when he came to England as a student before the First World War. His admiration for Manchester United, their centre-half Charlie Roberts and football in general led to his refusing family orders to come home, until he was sent a return ticket. In 1912, Pozzo managed Italy's team at the Olympic Games in Stockholm, where he met Hugo Meisl. He later became an admirer of Herbert Chapman. At club level Pozzo was long associated with Torino and he was manager and psychologist of the Italian team which won the World Cup in 1934 and 1938 and the Olympic Games tournament in 1936. Appointed in 1932, Pozzo retired in 1948 and put his insight into the game to use in newspaper columns.

Carlos Manuel Brito Leal **Queiros**

Born: *March 1, 1953 (Mozambique, then Portuguese colony)*

Queiros was the first coach to accompany successful youth players through to the big-time at international level. Born in Africa in Mozambique, he went to Portugal originally to pursue a low-key career as a goalkeeper. Queiros earned consideration as one of the leading coaches in Europe after twice leading Portugal to surprise victory in the World Youth Cup. Later, using many of those youth players, he was senior manager of the Portuguese national side which was pipped by Switzerland and Italy to a place at the 1994 World Cup finals in the United States of America. Within a month of the completion of the qualifying tournament, he had been snapped up by Sporting Lisbon as a replacement for Bobby Robson. Later worked with New York/New Jersey MetroStars in the United States and with Nagoya Grampus 8 in Japan.

(Sir) Alf **Ramsey**

Born: *January 22, 1920 (England)*

Ramsey earned a knighthood for managing England to World Cup victory over West Germany at Wembley in 1966, the peak of a double international career as player and administrator. As a player, Ramsey was a creative and intelligent right back with Southampton and Tottenham Hotspur and an integral member of Spurs's push-and-run team which won the Second and First Division titles in successive seasons in 1950 and 1951. On retiring in 1955, Ramsey became manager of Ipswich and his success in taking the unfashionable East Anglian club from the Third Division to the First Division title in seven years earned his appointment in 1963 as England's first "proper" manager with sole responsibility for team selection. He won the affection of every Englishman by bringing the trophy to the founding country of the game. He was dismissed after the World Cup qualifying failure against Poland a decade later, but he remained very much in the public affection in later life.

Otto **Rehhagel**

Born: *August 9, 1938 (Germany)*

Rehhagel was a pioneering professional in the early years of the Bundesliga in the early 1960s. He played for Rot-Weiss Essen, Hertha Berlin and Kaiserslautern before turning to coaching with Saarbrücken. Rehhagel's originally outspoken style of management mellowed during successive appointments with Kickers Offenbach, Werder Bremen (saving them from relegation in 1976), Borussia Dortmund, Arminia Bielefeld and Fortuna Düsseldorf. Rehhagel returned to Bremen in April 1981 when coach Otto Knefler was hurt in a car crash. He stayed 14 years, winning the German League and the European Cup-winners Cup. After one embattled year at Bayern Munich in 1995–96, Rehhagel took over the challenge of rebuilding the fallen giants of Kaiserslautern. He brought them out of the Second Division in 1997 and turned them into League champions a year later – the first time a promoted side had won the championship at the first attempt.

Bobby **Robson**

Born: *February 18, 1933 (England)*

Robson earned greater fame as a manager than as a player but he had also been an international in his own right. Robson made his name at inside forward with Fulham, who turned down a then-record £25,000 offer from Newcastle before eventually selling him to West Bromwich Albion. Robson was a member of England's World Cup squads in 1958 and 1962, his career having gained a second wind when he and Johnny Haynes became the pivotal midfielders as manager Walter Winterbottom abandoned England's traditional WM formation in favour of 4-2-4. After retiring, Robson was hugely successful as manager of unfashionable Ipswich Town, winning the FA Cup with them in 1978 against the favourites Arsenal, finishing runners-up in the first division in both 1981 and 1982 and, the crowning glory, guiding them to UEFA Cup success in 1981. He then left to take over as England boss in the summer of 1982. He finished on a "high" with fourth place at the 1990 World Cup, after losing on penalties to West Germany in the semi-final, before returning to the club world with PSV Eindhoven. Dutch fans and media were scathing on his appointment, but Robson won them over by winning the championship in each of his two seasons there. He then moved to Portugal with Sporting Lisbon before twice winning the championship there, too, with FC Porto. In 1996, Robson achieved a managerial ambition when he was appointed by Barcelona. He won the Cup-winners Cup and Spanish Cup with them in 1997 before being pushed sideways by the arrival of Louis Van Gaal, and returned to PSV in the summer of 1998.

Nereo **Rocco**

Born: *1912 (Italy)*

Tough and rugged coach who was born and brought up in Triestina and played first for the local club. His Italy experience covered just half a match in 1934. In the early 1950s, Rocco, now coaching at Padova, devised a defensive formation in which one of the wingers slipped back into midfield. It proved successful enough to be copied slavishly by coaches of all the smaller clubs in Serie A as protection against the skills of the expensively-imported stars of the big clubs. Rocco himself became a big-club coach in due course with Milan, whom he guided to the League title in 1962 and a European Champions Cup win in 1963. Rocco won the Champions Cup again in 1969 and the Cup-winners Cup in 1968. It was entirely in keeping with his style that, for the 1963 final, he made a late change to include a midfield policeman – Gino Pivatelli – instead of winger Paolo Barison. Pivatelli's job was to hunt down Benfica playmaker Mario Coluna, which he did with crippling effect.

Arrigo **Sacchi**

Born: *April 1, 1946 (Italy)*

Sacchi was never a top-level player and once famously met criticism by saying: "A jockey does not have to have been a horse to be successful." In fact, he was working in a shoe factory when he began his coaching career in charge of the Cesena youth team in 1977. He qualified from the Coverciano coaching centre that same year and was appointed to his first senior post with third division Rimini in 1982. In 1985 he took over Parma, who had just been relegated to the Third Division. They were promoted back at the first attempt. Then, at the start of the 1986–87 season, Parma surprisingly knocked out Milan in the Italian Cup. The now-disgraced Milan president Silvio Berlusconi decided Sacchi was "The Man" to lead Milan in the future and he succeeded Roma-bound Nils Liedholm in 1987. A year later, this "unknown" had guided a team overflowing with the egos of players such as Ruud Gullit and Marco Van Basten to the Italian championship. Sacchi was a prime mover in bringing positive attitudes back to the Italian game as he won one Italian league title, two European Champions Cups and two World Club Cups before being appointed national coach in 1991. Sacchi took Italy to the 1994 World Cup finals where they experienced a turbulent opening few matches, losing to Ireland and needing extra-time to see off the threat of Nigeria. But, they survived and made it to the final where they lost to Brazil. After a disappointing 1996 European Championships, Sacchi returned briefly to Milan for half a season in 1996–97, before taking a year's sabbatical. Returned to work with Atletico Madrid in 1998.

Tele **Santana**

Born:	*July 26, 1933 (Brazil)*

Santana was an outside-right with Fluminense in the early 1950s, but never good enough to challenge Julinho or Garrincha in Brazil's World Cup teams. Instead, he reached the World Cup finals in 1982 and 1986 as manager of Brazil. Santana's insistence on attacking football was criticised as naïve after Brazil's failures in, respectively, the second round and quarter-finals. But Santana had the last laugh when he won the World Club Cup twice as boss of Sao Paulo in 1992 and 1993. Simultaneously, Santana was not afraid to pinpoint high levels of corruption in the Brazilian game as well as poor refereeing for the failure to regain World Cup primacy in the 1980s and early 1990s. His coaching experience included appointments with Atletico Mineiro, Gremio, Flamengo, Fluminense, Palmeiras, Al Ahly (Saudi Arabia) and Sao Paulo.

Helmut **Schön**

Born:	*September 15, 1915 (Germany); died February 23, 1996*

Schön scored 17 goals in 16 internationals for Germany between 1937 and 1941, when he was a star inside forward with the famous Dresden SC. After the war, he played in Berlin for a while and then became national coach to the briefly independent Federation of the Saar. In 1955, Schön was appointed No. 2 to Sepp Herberger as manager of West Germany and succeeded him, with enormous success, in 1963. Schön took West Germany to the World Cup runners-up spot in 1966 against hosts England, third place in 1970 and finally to victory in 1974 on home soil against the Dutch. Under Schön, Germany were also European champions in 1972 and runners-up in 1976. He retired after the 1978 World Cup in Argentina.

Gusztav **Sebes**

Born:	*June 21, 1906 (Hungary); died January 30, 1986*

Sebes was a successful player in the 1920s with Vasas and MTK Budapest, but is best-known for the creation of the "Magic Magyars" of the late 1940s and 1950s. The Communist takeover allowed the Hungarian federation to transfer Hungary's top players into the two top clubs, Honved and Red Banner (formerly MTK) and Sebes fused their talents for the national team, built around the tactic of the withdrawn centre-forward. Hungary won the 1952 Olympic title but lost the 1954 World Cup Final, against all the odds, to West Germany. Sebes resigned following the loss of many star players who fled abroad after the 1956 Revolution.

Bill **Shankly**

Born:	*September 2, 1913 (Scotland); died September 29, 1981*

Shankly played for Carlisle, Preston and Scotland in the 1930s and returned to Carlisle to begin his managerial career. After spells with Grimsby, Workington and Huddersfield – where he launched the teenage career of Denis Law – he took over a faded Liverpool in the Second Division, in December 1959. There was no stopping either him or the club once promotion had been achieved in 1962. Shankly's dry humour struck a chord with Anfield fans. He brought them League, FA Cup and League championship again in successive seasons, signed some of the club's greatest servants and laid foundations for further success on and off the pitch. Shankly had an eye for youthful talent – which he squirrelled away in the reserves until they were ready – and for managerial expertise. Highly-successful managerial successors such as Bob Paisley and Joe Fagan came out of Shankly's fabled "boot room."

Jock **Stein**

Born:	*October 5, 1922 (Scotland); died September 10, 1985*

Stein remains the most successful of all Scottish managers. He played centre-half for Albion Rovers in the late 1940s, moved to the Welsh League with Llanelli, then returned to Scotland when Celtic were seeking a reserve centre-half. Stein forced his way into the first team, became captain and led Celtic to the 1954 League and Cup double. In 1960, he entered management with Dunfermline, beating Celtic of all teams to win the Scottish Cup. In 1964, Stein took over Hibernian but left within a year for the Celtic job to succeed Jimmy McGrory. This was Celtic's most glorious era. They won the championship nine years in a row and became the first British side to win the European Champions Cup by defeating Internazionale in Lisbon in 1967. That was a sensational season in which Celtic won everything available – including the League, League Cup and the Scottish Cup. Later, Stein became Scotland manager, steering them to the 1986 finals in Mexico. He did not go with his team – having collapsed with a heart attack in the closing minutes of the concluding qualifying match against Wales.

Tommy **Svensson**

Born:	*March 4, 1945 (Sweden)*

Svensson played 700 League and Cup matches with Oster Vaxjo in the 1970s as well as two years in Belgium, in midfield for Standard Liège. His 40 caps for Sweden included appearances at the 1970 World Cup finals in Mexico and he was once voted

Footballer of the Year before retiring to coaching. Svensson played eight times for Sweden at under-23 level and six times at youth level. He made his senior debut on May 17, 1967, in a 1–0 home defeat against East Germany. After retiring, Svensson worked successfully at his old club Oster, then for two years with Tromsö in Norway before being appointed to succeed Olle Nordin after Sweden's disastrous showing at the 1990 World Cup finals. Svensson's cool, undemonstrative but highly-competent approach worked wonders with a domestic game in the doldrums. Svensson was then duly hailed as a national hero after taking Sweden, as hosts, to the semi-finals of the 1992 European Championship and third place at the 1994 World Cup.

Giovanni **Trapattoni**

Born: *March 17, 1939 (Italy)*

Trapattoni was a wing-half in the late 1950s and early 1960s whose sure tackling and football brain earned him a reputation as the only man who could play Pele out of a game, by fair means rather than foul. After winning two Champions Cups with Milan, Trapattoni retired to a post on the youth coaching staff. In time he became first-team caretaker, guiding Milan to a controversial victory over Leeds United in the 1973 Cup-winners Cup Final. Later, he switched to Juventus with whom he became the most successful Italian club coach of all time. Inside eight years, Trapattoni guided Juve to the World Club Cup, Champions Cup, Cup-winners Cup, UEFA Cup, European Supercup, seven Italian championships and two domestic cups. Later, he won the League and UEFA Cup with Internazionale before taking a major career gamble by moving to Bayern Munich. Despite struggling notoriously with the German language, Trapattoni was rewarded with Bundesliga success in 1997. Had two spells at Bayern, and a brief unsuccessful spell with Cagliari in Italy sandwiched in between.

Louis **Van Gaal**

Born: *August 8, 1951 (Holland)*

Van Gaal was a respected player in the 1970s with Ajax, Antwerp, Telstar, Sparta and AZ 67 Alkmaar. He returned to Ajax as youth coach and worked his way up to become assistant to first-team boss Leo Beenhakker. Van Gaal then took over the top job in 1991 when Beenhakker returned to Real Madrid. Van Gaal wasted no time in promoting his youth team and bringing a fresh approach. Under Van Gaal, Ajax won the UEFA Cup in 1992, Dutch Cup in 1993, League in 1994, League and Champions Cup in 1995 and League and Campions Cup runners-up placings in 1996. In 1997, he left Ajax for Barcelona whom he turned into Spanish champions in his first season.

Terry **Venables**

Born: *January 6, 1943 (England)*

Venables has enjoyed a high-profile career, no matter what twists and turns that has meant. As a player he was inside forward and then midfielder with Chelsea, Tottenham, Queens Park Rangers and Crystal Palace. He played for England at every level, from schoolboy, through amateur, youth and under-23 to the senior national side. His outstanding coaching career began in London with QPR and Palace and reached its first peak with a Spanish championship at Barcelona in 1985. Under Venables, they were then runners-up the following season in the European Champions Cup. Returned to London with Tottenham but the partnership with Alan Sugar ended acrimoniously before Venables was appointed England coach, in succession to Graham Taylor, in January 1994. Venables took England to the semi-finals of the 1996 European Championship before leaving, controversially, on the expiry of his contract. He then became part-owner and chief executive of Portsmouth while simultaneously guiding Australia's national team to within a matter of minutes of a place at the 1998 World Cup finals, being edged out by Iran in a play-off. Away from the coaching ground, Venables has dabbled in a number of ventures, including television script-writing, London night clubs and a regular role as a football pundit on British television. A lovable Cockney rogue, the secret of Venables' success has been his 'matey' relationship with the sometimes vicious British newspapers.

Berti **Vogts**

Born: *December 30, 1946 (West Germany)*

Vogts' appointment in 1990, to succeed Franz Beckenbauer after the World Cup victory, maintained the tradition that every manager of Germany since the war has been an international (Sepp Herberger, Helmut Schön, Jupp Derwall, Beckenbauer and Vogts). Vogts' international experience began with appearances in the 1965 European youth championship. That same year he joined Borussia Mönchengladbach and, two years later, made the first of 96 senior appearances in defence for West Germany. Vogts played 419 League games (scoring 33 goals) in 14 years with Borussia, won the World Cup in 1974, two UEFA Cups, five West German championships and the German Cup once. He was a member of the West German team which finished runners-up on penalties to Czechoslovakia in the 1976 European finals. Twice he was Footballer of the Year before joining the German federation coaching staff in 1979. He guided Germany to the European Championship Final in 1992, the World Cup quarter-finals in 1994, the European Championship triumph in 1996 and the 1998 World Cup quarter-finals in France.

Mario Zagallo: Familiar with World Cup success

Arsène **Wenger**

Born: *October 22, 1949 (France)*

Frenchman Wenger arrived from Grampus 8 of Japan to take over Arsenal on September 30, 1996. It took him less than two years to make history as the first foreign coach to win the championship – and not only that, but to achieve the League and FA Cup double. Wenger played for Strasbourg before becoming their youth coach in 1981. He later held coaching posts with Cannes and Nancy before hitting the big time with Monaco, whom he guided to the 1988 French title – with the on-field help of George Weah. Monaco finished runners-up in the European Cup-winners Cup in 1992, before Wenger left for Grampus 8 in 1995. He turned them from relegation candidates into J League runners-up before moving to Highbury and turning the club into one of the most exciting sides in England.

Mario Lobo **Zagallo**

Born: *August 9, 1931 (Brazil)*

Zagallo was outside-left in the Brazil side which won the World Cup in 1958 and 1962 (in the 1958 final against Sweden he scored one of Brazil's goals in the 5–2 win). As a left winger with America, Flamengo and Botafogo, Zagallo's work rate earned him the nickname "Formiguinha" (little ant). After his retirement as a player, he turned his hand to coaching with great success, guiding Brazil to their third World Cup in 1970, when former teammate Pele was in inspired form. Zagallo returned to the national side coaching set-up in 1994 as assistant to Carlos Alberto Parreira, and became the first man in football history to be involved in four World Cup triumphs when Brazil beat Italy. By the time of the 1998 finals, Zagallo was head coach and came close to a fifth success, losing to France in the final.

Chapter 8

GREAT BRITAIN

AND IRELAND
INTERNATIONAL
RESULTS

INTERNATIONAL RESULTS – ENGLAND

KEY TO ABBREVIATIONS			
WCQ = *World Cup Qualifier*		USBT = *United States Bicentenniel Tournament*	
ECQ = *European Championship Qualifier*		USC = *United States Cup*	
WCF = *World Cup Finals*		UT = *Umbro Trophy*	
ECF = *European Championship Finals*		TDF = *Tournoi de France*	
BT = *Brazilian Tournament*		KHT = *King Hussein tournament*	

Date	Opponents	Venue	Score	Date	Opponents	Venue	Score
30/11/1872	Scotland	Glasgow	0–0	12/3/94	Wales	Wrexham	5–1
8/3/73	Scotland	Kennington Oval	4–2	7/4/94	Scotland	Glasgow	2–2
7/3/74	Scotland	Glasgow	1–2	9/3/95	Ireland	Derby	9–0
6/3/75	Scotland	Kennington Oval	2–2	18/3/95	Wales	Queen's Club, London	1–1
4/3/76	Scotland	Glasgow	0–3	6/4/95	Scotland	Goodison Park	3–0
3/3/77	Scotland	Kennington Oval	1–3	7/3/96	Ireland	Belfast	2–0
2/3/78	Scotland	Glasgow	2–7	16/3/96	Wales	Cardiff	9–1
18/1/79	Wales	Kennington Oval	2–1	4/4/96	Scotland	Glasgow	1–2
5/4/79	Scotland	Kennington Oval	5–4	20/2/97	Ireland	Nottingham	6–0
13/3/80	Scotland	Glasgow	4–5	29/3/97	Wales	Sheffield	4–0
15/3/80	Wales	Wrexham	3–2	3/4/97	Scotland	Crystal Palace	1–2
26/2/81	Wales	Blackburn	0–1	5/3/98	Ireland	Belfast	3–2
12/3/81	Scotland	Kennington Oval	1–6	28/3/98	Wales	Wrexham	3–0
18/2/82	Ireland	Belfast	13–0	2/4/98	Scotland	Glasgow	3–1
11/3/82	Scotland	Glasgow	1–5	18/2/99	Ireland	Sunderland	13–2
13/3/82	Wales	Wrexham	3–5	20/3/99	Wales	Bristol	4–0
3/2/83	Wales	Kennington Oval	5–0	8/4/99	Scotland	Birmingham	2–1
24/2/83	Ireland	Liverpool	7–0	17/3/1900	Ireland	Dublin	2–0
10/3/83	Scotland	Sheffield	2–3	26/3/00	Wales	Cardiff	1–1
25/2/84	Ireland	Belfast	8–1	7/4/00	Scotland	Glasgow	1–4
15/3/84	Scotland	Glasgow	0–1	9/3/01	Ireland	Southampton	3–0
17/3/84	Wales	Wrexham	4–0	18/3/01	Wales	Newcastle	6–0
28/2/85	Ireland	Manchester	4–0	30/3/01	Scotland	Crystal Palace	2–2
14/3/85	Wales	Blackburn	1–1	3/3/02	Wales	Wrexham	0–0
21/3/85	Scotland	Kennington Oval	1–1	22/3/02	Ireland	Belfast	1–0
13/3/86	Ireland	Belfast	6–1	3/5/02	Scotland	Birmingham	2–2
29/3/86	Wales	Wrexham	3–1	14/2/03	Ireland	Wolverhampton	4–0
31/3/86	Scotland	Glasgow	1–1	2/3/03	Wales	Portsmouth	2–1
5/2/87	Ireland	Sheffield	7–0	4/4/03	Scotland	Sheffield	1–2
26/2/87	Wales	Kennington Oval	4–0	29/2/04	Wales	Wrexham	2–2
19/3/87	Scotland	Blackburn	2–3	12/3/04	Ireland	Belfast	3–1
4/2/88	Wales	Crewe	5–1	9/4/04	Scotland	Glasgow	1–0
17/3/88	Scotland	Glasgow	5–0	25/2/05	Ireland	Middlesbrough	1–1
31/3/88	Ireland	Belfast	5–1	27/3/05	Wales	Liverpool	3–1
23/2/89	Wales	Stoke	4–1	1/4/05	Scotland	Crystal Palace	1–0
2/3/89	Ireland	Everton	6–1	17/2/06	Ireland	Belfast	5–0
13/4/89	Scotland	Kennington Oval	2–3	19/3/06	Wales	Cardiff	1–0
15/3/90	Wales	Wrexham	3–1	7/4/06	Scotland	Glasgow	1–2
15/3/90	Ireland	Belfast	9–1	16/2/07	Ireland	Goodison Park	1–0
5/4/90	Scotland	Glasgow	1–1	18/3/07	Wales	Fulham	1–1
7/3/91	Wales	Sunderland	4–1	6/4/07	Scotland	Newcastle	1–1
7/3/91	Ireland	Wolverhampton	6–1	15/2/08	Ireland	Belfast	3–1
6/4/91	Scotland	Blackburn	2–1	16/3/08	Wales	Wrexham	7–1
5/3/92	Wales	Wrexham	2–0	4/4/08	Scotland	Glasgow	1–1
5/3/92	Ireland	Belfast	2–0	6/6/08	Austria	Vienna	6–1
2/4/92	Scotland	Glasgow	4–1	8/6/08	Austria	Vienna	11–1
25/2/93	Ireland	Birmingham	6–1	10/6/08	Hungary	Budapest	7–0
13/3/93	Wales	Stoke	6–0	13/6/08	Bohemia	Prague	4–0
1/4/93	Scotland	Richmond	5–2	13/2/09	Ireland	Bradford	4–0
1/3/94	Ireland	Belfast	2–2	15/3/09	Wales	Nottingham	2–0

Date	Opponents	Venue	Score
3/4/09	**Scotland**	Crystal Palace	2–0
29/5/09	**Hungary**	Budapest	4–2
31/5/09	**Hungary**	Budapest	8–2
1/6/09	**Austria**	Vienna	8–1
12/2/10	**Ireland**	Belfast	1–1
14/3/10	**Wales**	Cardiff	1–0
2/4/10	**Scotland**	Glasgow	0–2
11/2/11	**Ireland**	Derby	2–1
13/3/11	**Wales**	Millwall	3–0
1/4/11	**Scotland**	Goodison Park	1–1
10/2/12	**Ireland**	Dublin	6–1
11/3/12	**Wales**	Wrexham	2–0
23/3/12	**Scotland**	Glasgow	1–1
15/2/13	**Ireland**	Belfast	1–2
17/3/13	**Wales**	Bristol	4–3
5/4/13	**Scotland**	Stamford Bridge	1–0
14/2/14	**Ireland**	Middlesbrough	0–3
16/3/14	**Wales**	Cardiff	2–0
4/4/14	**Scotland**	Glasgow	1–3
25/10/19	**Ireland**	Belfast	1–1
15/3/20	**Wales**	Highbury	1–2
10/4/20	**Scotland**	Sheffield	5–4
23/10/20	**Ireland**	Sunderland	2–0
14/3/21	**Wales**	Cardiff	0–0
9/4/21	**Scotland**	Glasgow	0–3
21/5/21	**Belgium**	Brussels	2–0
22/10/21	**Ireland**	Belfast	1–1
13/3/22	**Wales**	Anfield	1–0
8/4/22	**Scotland**	Birmingham	0–1
21/10/22	**Ireland**	West Bromwich	2–0
5/3/23	**Wales**	Cardiff	2–2
19/3/23	**Belgium**	Highbury	6–1
14/4/23	**Scotland**	Glasgow	2–2
10/5/23	**France**	Paris	4–1
21/5/23	**Sweden**	Stockholm	4–2
24/5/23	**Sweden**	Stockholm	3–1
20/10/23	**Ireland**	Belfast	1–2
1/11/23	**Belgium**	Antwerp	2–2
3/3/24	**Wales**	Blackburn	1–2
12/4/24	**Scotland**	Wembley	1–1
17/5/24	**France**	Paris	3–1
22/10/24	**Ireland**	Anfield	3–1
8/12/24	**Belgium**	West Bromwich	4–0
28/2/25	**Wales**	Swansea	2–1
4/4/25	**Scotland**	Glasgow	0–2
21/5/25	**France**	Paris	3–2
24/10/25	**Ireland**	Belfast	0–0
1/3/26	**Wales**	Selhurst Park	1–3
17/4/26	**Scotland**	Manchester	0–1
24/4/26	**Belgium**	Antwerp	5–3
20/10/26	**Ireland**	Anfield	3–3
12/2/27	**Wales**	Wrexham	3–3
2/4/27	**Scotland**	Glasgow	2–1
11/5/27	**Belgium**	Brussels	9–1
21/5/27	**Luxembourg**	Luxembourg	5–2
26/5/27	**France**	Paris	6–0
22/10/27	**Ireland**	Belfast	0–2
28/11/27	**Wales**	Burnley	1–2
31/3/28	**Scotland**	Wembley	1–5
17/5/28	**France**	Paris	5–1
19/5/28	**Belgium**	Antwerp	3–1

Date	Opponents	Venue	Score
22/10/28	**Ireland**	Anfield	2–1
17/11/28	**Wales**	Swansea	3–2
13/4/29	**Scotland**	Glasgow	0–1
9/5/29	**France**	Paris	4–1
11/5/29	**Belgium**	Brussels	5–1
15/5/29	**Spain**	Madrid	3–4
19/10/29	**Ireland**	Belfast	3–0
20/11/29	**Wales**	Stamford Bridge	6–0
5/4/30	**Scotland**	Wembley	5–2
10/5/30	**Germany**	Berlin	3–3
14/5/30	**Austria**	Vienna	0–0
20/10/30	**Ireland**	Sheffield	5–1
22/11/30	**Wales**	Wrexham	4–0
28/3/31	**Scotland**	Glasgow	0–2
14/5/31	**France**	Paris	2–5
16/5/31	**Belgium**	Brussels	4–1
17/10/31	**Ireland**	Belfast	6–2
18/11/31	**Wales**	Anfield	3–1
9/12/31	**Spain**	Highbury	7–1
9/4/32	**Scotland**	Wembley	3–0
17/10/32	**Ireland**	Blackpool	1–0
16/11/32	**Wales**	Wrexham	0–0
7/12/32	**Austria**	Stamford Bridge	4–3
1/4/33	**Scotland**	Glasgow	1–2
13/5/33	**Italy**	Rome	1–1
20/5/33	**Switzerland**	Berne	4–0
14/10/33	**Ireland**	Belfast	3–0
15/11/33	**Wales**	Newcastle	1–2
6/12/33	**France**	White Hart Lane	4–1
14/4/34	**Scotland**	Wembley	3–0
10/5/34	**Hungary**	Budapest	1–2
16/5/34	**Czechoslovakia**	Prague	1–2
29/9/34	**Wales**	Cardiff	4–0
14/11/34	**Italy**	Highbury	3–2
6/2/35	**Ireland**	Goodison Park	2–1
6/4/35	**Scotland**	Glasgow	0–2
18/5/35	**Holland**	Amsterdam	1–0
19/10/35	**Ireland**	Belfast	3–1
4/12/35	**Germany**	White Hart Lane	3–0
5/2/36	**Wales**	Wolverhampton	1–2
4/4/36	**Scotland**	Wembley	1–1
6/5/36	**Austria**	Vienna	1–2
9/5/36	**Belgium**	Brussels	2–3
17/10/36	**Wales**	Cardiff	1–2
18/11/36	**Ireland**	Stoke	3–1
2/12/36	**Hungary**	Highbury	6–2
17/4/37	**Scotland**	Glasgow	1–3
14/5/37	**Norway**	Oslo	6–0
17/5/37	**Sweden**	Stockholm	4–0
20/5/37	**Finland**	Helsinki	8–0
23/10/37	**Ireland**	Belfast	5–1
17/11/37	**Wales**	Middlesbrough	2–1
1/12/37	**Czechoslovakia**	White Hart Lane	5–4
9/4/38	**Scotland**	Wembley	0–1
14/5/38	**Germany**	Berlin	6–3
21/5/38	**Switzerland**	Zurich	1–2
26/5/38	**France**	Paris	4–2
22/10/38	**Wales**	Cardiff	2–4
26/10/38	**FIFA**	Highbury	3–0
9/11/38	**Norway**	Newcastle	4–0
16/11/38	**Ireland**	Manchester	7–0

Date	Opponents	Venue	Score
15/4/39	Scotland	Glasgow	2–1
13/5/39	Italy	Milan	2–2
18/5/39	Yugoslavia	Belgrade	1–2
24/5/39	Romania	Bucharest	2–0
28/9/46	N Ireland	Belfast	7–2
30/9/46	Rep of ireland	Dublin	1–0
19/10/46	Wales	Maine Road	3–0
27/11/46	Holland	Huddersfield	8–2
12/4/47	Scotland	Wembley	1–1
3/5/47	France	Highbury	3–0
18/5/47	Switzerland	Zurich	0–1
27/5/47	Portugal	Lisbon	10–0
21/9/47	Belgium	Brussels	5–2
18/10/47	Wales	Cardiff	3–0
5/11/47	N Ireland	Goodison Park	2–2
19/11/47	Sweden	Highbury	4–2
10/4/48	Scotland	Glasgow	2–0
16/5/48	Italy	Turin	4–0
26/9/48	Denmark	Copenhagen	0–0
9/10/48	N Ireland	Belfast	6–2
10/11/48	Wales	Villa Park	1–0
1/12/48	Switzerland	Highbury	6–0
9/4/48	Scotland	Wembley	1–3
13/5/49	Sweden	Stockholm	1–3
18/5/49	Norway	Oslo	4–1
22/5/49	France	Paris	3–1
21/9/49	Rep of Ireland	Goodison Park	0–2
15/10/49	Wales	Cardiff	4–1 (WCQ)
16/11/49	N Ireland	Maine Road	9–2 (WCQ)
30/11/49	Italy	White Hart Lane	2–0
15/4/50	Scotland	Glasgow	1–0 (WCQ)
14/5/50	Portugal	Lisbon	5–3
18/5/50	Belgium	Brussels	4–1
15/6/50	Chile	Rio de Janeiro	2–0 (WCF)
29/6/50	USA	Belo Horizonte	0–1 (WCF)
2/7/50	Spain	Rio de Janeiro	0–1 (WCF)
7/10/50	N Ireland	Belfast	4–1
15/11/50	Wales	Sunderland	4–2
22/11/50	Yugoslavia	Highbury	2–2
14/4/51	Scotland	Wembley	2–3
9/5/51	Argentina	Wembley	2–1
9/5/51	Portugal	Goodison Park	5–2
3/10/51	France	Highbury	2–2
20/10/51	Wales	Cardiff	1–1
14/11/51	N Ireland	Villa Park	2–0
28/11/51	Austria	Wembley	2–2
5/4/52	Scotland	Glasgow	2–1
18/5/52	Italy	Florence	1–1
25/5/52	Austria	Vienna	3–2
28/5/52	Switzerland	Zurich	3–0
4/10/52	N Ireland	Belfast	2–2
12/11/52	Wales	Wembley	5–2
26/11/52	Belgium	Wembley	5–0
18/4/53	Scotland	Wembley	2–2
17/5/53	Argentina (abandoned after 21 minutes)	Buenos Aires	0–0
24/5/53	Chile	Santiago	2–1
31/5/53	Uruguay	Montevideo	1–2
8/6/53	USA	New York	6–3
10/10/53	Wales	Cardiff	4–1 (WCQ)
21/10/53	Rest of Europe	Wembley	4–4

Date	Opponents	Venue	Score
11/11/53	N Ireland	Goodison Park	3–1 (WCQ)
25/11/53	Hungary	Wembley	3–6
3/4/54	Scotland	Glasgow	4–2 (WCQ)
16/5/54	Yugoslavia	Belgrade	0–1
23/5/54	Hungary	Budapest	1–7
17/6/54	Belgium	Basle	4–4* (WCF)
20/6/54	Switzerland	Berne	2–0 (WCF)
26/6/54	Uruguay	Basle	2–4 (WCF)
2/10/54	N Ireland	Belfast	2–0
10/11/54	Wales	Wembley	3–2
1/12/54	W Germany	Wembley	3–1
2/4/55	Scotland	Wembley	7–2
18/5/55	France	Paris	0–1
18/5/55	Spain	Madrid	1–1
22/5/55	Portugal	Oporto	1–3
2/10/55	Denmark	Copenhagen	5–1
22/10/55	Wales	Cardiff	1–1
2/11/55	N Ireland	Wembley	3–0
30/11/55	Spain	Wembley	4–1
14/4/56	Scotland	Glasgow	1–1
9/5/56	Brazil	Wembley	4–2
16/5/56	Sweden	Stockholm	0–0
20/5/56	Finland	Helsinki	5–1
26/5/56	West Germany	Berlin	3–1
6/10/56	N Ireland	Belfast	1–1
14/11/56	Wales	Wembley	3–1
28/11/56	Yugoslavia	Wembley	3–0
5/12/56	Denmark	Wolverhampton	5–2 (WCQ)
6/4/57	Scotland	Wembley	2–1
8/5/57	Rep of Ireland	Wembley	5–1 (WCQ)
15/5/57	Denmark	Copenhagen	4–1 (WCQ)
19/5/57	Rep of Ireland	Dublin	1–1 (WCQ)
19/10/57	Wales	Cardiff	4–0
6/11/57	N Ireland	Wembley	2–3
27/11/57	France	Wembley	4–0
19/4/58	Scotland	Glasgow	4–0
7/5/58	Portugal	Wembley	2–1
11/5/58	Yugoslavia	Belgrade	0–5
18/5/58	USSR	Moscow	1–1
8/6/58	USSR	Gothenburg	2–2 (WCF)
11/6/58	Brazil	Gothenburg	0–0 (WCF)
15/6/58	Austria	Boras	2–2 (WCF)
17/6/58	USSR	Gothenburg	0–1 (WCF)
4/10/58	N Ireland	Belfast	3–3
22/10/58	USSR	Wembley	5–0
26/11/58	Wales	Villa Park	2–2
11/4/59	Scotland	Wembley	1–0
6/5/59	Italy	Wembley	2–2
13/5/59	Brazil	Rio de Janeiro	0–2
17/5/59	Peru	Lima	1–4
24/5/59	Mexico	Mexico City	1–2
28/5/59	USA	Los Angeles	8–1
17/10/59	Wales	Cardiff	1–1
28/10/59	Sweden	Wembley	2–3
18/11/59	N Ireland	Wembley	2–1

1960

Date	Opponents	Venue	Score
19/4	**Scotland**	Glasgow	1–1
11/5	**Yugoslavia**	Wembley	3–3
15/5	**Spain**	Madrid	0–3
22/5	**Hungary**	Budapest	0–2
8/10	**N Ireland**	Belfast	5–2
19/10	**Luxembourg**	Luxembourg	9–0 (WCQ)
26/10	**Spain**	Wembley	4–2
23/11	**Wales**	Wembley	5–1

1961

Date	Opponents	Venue	Score
15/4	**Scotland**	Wembley	9–3
10/5	**Mexico**	Wembley	8–0
21/5	**Portugal**	Lisbon	1–1 (WCQ)
24/5	**Italy**	Rome	3–2
27/5	**Austria**	Vienna	1–3
28/9	**Luxembourg**	Highbury	4–1 (WCQ)
14/10	**Wales**	Cardiff	1–1
25/10	**Portugal**	Wembley	2–0 (WCQ)
22–11	**N Ireland**	Wembley	1–1

1962

Date	Opponents	Venue	Score
4/4	**Austria**	Wembley	3–1
14/4	**Scotland**	Glasgow	0–2
9/5	**Switzerland**	Wembley	3–1
20/5	**Peru**	Lima	4–0
31/5	**Hungary**	Rancagua	1–2 (WCF)
2/6	**Argentina**	Rancagua	3–1 (WCF)
7/6	**Bulgaria**	Rancagua	0–0 (WCF)
10/6	**Brazil**	Vina del Mar	1–3 (WCF)
3/10	**France**	Hillsborough	1–1 (ECQ)
20/10	**N Ireland**	Belfast	3–1
21/11	**Wales**	Wembley	4–0

1963

Date	Opponents	Venue	Score
27/2	**France**	Paris	2–5 (ECQ)
6/4	**Scotland**	Wembley	1–2
8/5	**Brazil**	Wembley	1–1
20/5	**Czechoslovakia**	Bratislava	4–2
2/6	**East Germany**	Leipzig	2–1
5/6	**Switzerland**	Basle	8–1
12/10	**Wales**	Cardiff	4–0
23/10	**Rest of World**	Wembley	2–1
20/11	**N Ireland**	Wembley	8–3

1964

Date	Opponents	Venue	Score
11/4	**Scotland**	Glasgow	0–1
6/5	**Uruguay**	Wembley	2–1
17/5	**Portugal**	Lisbon	4–3
24/5	**Rep of Ireland**	Dublin	3–1
27/5	**USA**	New York	10–0
30/5	**Brazil**	Rio de Janeiro	1–5 (BT)
4/6	**Portugal**	Sao Paulo	1–1 (BT)
6/6	**Argentina**	Rio de Janeiro	0–1 (BT)
3/10	**N Ireland**	Belfast	4–3
21/10	**Belgium**	Wembley	2–2
18/11	**Wales**	Wembley	2–1
9/12	**Holland**	Amsterdam	1–1

1965

Date	Opponents	Venue	Score
10/4	**Scotland**	Wembley	2–2
5/5	**Hungary**	Wembley	1–0
9/5	**Yugoslavia**	Belgrade	1–1
12/5	**W Germany**	Nuremberg	1–0
16/5	**Sweden**	Gothenburg	2–1
2/10	**Wales**	Cardiff	0–0
20/10	**Austria**	Wembley	2–3
10/11	**N Ireland**	Wembley	2–1
8/12	**Spain**	Madrid	2–0

1966

Date	Opponents	Venue	Score
5/1	**Poland**	Anfield	1–1
23/2	**W Germany**	Wembley	1–0
2/4	**Scotland**	Glasgow	4–3
4/5	**Yugoslavia**	Wembley	2–0
26/6	**Finland**	Helsinki	3–0
29/6	**Norway**	Oslo	6–1
3/7	**Denmark**	Copenhagen	2–0
5/7	**Poland**	Chorzow	1–0
11/7	**Uruguay**	Wembley	0–0 (WCF)
16/7	**Mexico**	Wembley	2–0 (WCF)
20/7	**France**	Wembley	2–0 (WCF)
23/7	**Argentina**	Wembley	1–0 (WCF)
26/7	**Portugal**	Wembley	2–1 (WCF)
30/7	**W Germany**	Wembley	4–2* (WCF)
22/10	**N Ireland**	Belfast	2–0 (ECQ)
2/11	**Czechoslovakia**	Wembley	0–0
16/11	**Wales**	Wembley	5–1 (ECQ)

1967

Date	Opponents	Venue	Score
15/4	**Scotland**	Wembley	2–3 (ECQ)
24/5	**Spain**	Wembley	2–0
27/5	**Austria**	Vienna	1–0
21/10	**Wales**	Cardiff	3–0 (ECQ)
22/11	**N Ireland**	Wembley	2–0 (ECQ)
6/12	**USSR**	Wembley	2–2

1968

Date	Opponents	Venue	Score
24/2	Scotland	Glasgow	1–1 (ECQ)
3/4	Spain	Wembley	1–0 (ECQ)
8/5	Spain	Madrid	2–1 (ECQ)
22/5	Sweden	Wembley	3–1
1/6	W Germany	Hanover	0–1
5/6	Yugoslavia	Florence	0–1 (ECF)
8/6	USSR	Rome	2–0 (ECF)
6/11	Romania	Bucharest	0–0
11/12	Bulgaria	Wembley	1–1

1969

Date	Opponents	Venue	Score
15/1	Romania	Wembley	1–1
12/3	France	Wembley	5–0
3/5	N Ireland	Belfast	3–1
7/5	Wales	Wembley	2–1
10/5	Scotland	Wembley	4–1
1/6	Mexico	Mexico City	0–0
8/6	Uruguay	Montevideo	2–1
12/6	Brazil	Rio de Janeiro	1–2
5/11	Holland	Amsterdam	1–0
10/12	Portugal	Wembley	1–0

1970

Date	Opponents	Venue	Score
14/1	Holland	Wembley	0–0
25/2	Belgium	Brussels	3–1
18/4	Wales	Cardiff	1–1
21/4	N Ireland	Wembley	3–1
25/4	Scotland	Glasgow	0–0
20/5	Colombia	Bogota	4–0
24/5	Ecuador	Quito	2–0
2/6	Romania	Guadalajara	1–0 (WCF)
7/6	Brazil	Guadalajara	0–1 (WCF)
11/6	Czechoslovakia	Guadalajara	1–0 (WCF)
14/6	W Germany	Leon	2–3* (WCF)
25/11	E Germany	Wembley	3–1

1971

Date	Opponents	Venue	Score
3/2	Malta	Valletta	1–0 (ECQ)
21/4	Greece	Wembley	4–0 (ECQ)
12/5	Malta	Wembley	5–0 (ECQ)
15/5	N Ireland	Belfast	1–0
19/5	Wales	Wembley	0–0
22/5	Scotland	Wembley	3–1
13/10	Switzerland	Basle	3–2 (ECQ)
10/11	Switzerland	Wembley	1–1 (ECQ)
1/12	Greece	Athens	2–0 (ECQ)

1972

Date	Opponents	Venue	Score
29/4	W Germany	Wembley	1–3 (ECQ)
13/5	W Germany	Berlin	0–0 (ECQ)
20/5	Wales	Cardiff	3–0
23/5	N Ireland	Wembley	0–1
27/5	Scotland	Glasgow	1–0
11/10	Yugoslavia	Wembley	1–1
15/11	Wales	Cardiff	1 0 (WCQ)

1973

Date	Opponents	Venue	Score
24/1	Wales	Wembley	1–1 (WCQ)
14/2	Scotland	Glasgow	5–0
12/5	N Ireland	Anfield	2–1
15/5	Wales	Wembley	3–0
19/5	Scotland	Wembley	1–0
27/5	Czechoslovakia	Prague	1–1
6/6	Poland	Chorzow	0–2 (WCQ)
10/6	USSR	Moscow	2–1
14/6	Italy	Turin	0–2
26/9	Austria	Wembley	7–0
17/10	Poland	Wembley	1–1 (WCQ)
14/11	Italy	Wembley	0–1

1974

Date	Opponents	Venue	Score
3/4	Portugal	Lisbon	0–0
11/5	Wales	Cardiff	2–0
15/5	N Ireland	Wembley	1–0
18/5	Scotland	Glasgow	0–2
22/5	Argentina	Wembley	2–2
29/5	East Germany	Leipzig	1–1
1/6	Bulgaria	Sofia	1–0
5/6	Yugoslavia	Belgrade	2–2
30/10	Czechoslovakia	Wembley	3–0 (ECQ)
20/11	Portugal	Wembley	0–0 (ECQ)

1975

Date	Opponents	Venue	Score
12/3	W Germany	Wembley	2–0
16/4	Cyprus	Wembley	5–0 (ECQ)
11/5	Cyprus	Limassol	1–0 (ECQ)
17/5	N Ireland	Belfast	0–0
21/5	Wales	Wembley	2–2
24/5	Scotland	Wembley	5–1
3/9	Switzerland	Basle	2–1
30/10	Czechoslovakia	Bratislava	1–2 (ECQ)
19/11	Portugal	Lisbon	1–1 (ECQ)

1976

Date	Opponents	Venue	Score
24/3	Wales	Wrexham	2–1
8/5	Wales	Cardiff	1–0

1976 *continued*

Date	Opponents	Venue	Score
11/5	**N Ireland**	Wembley	4–0
15/5	**Scotland**	Glasgow	1–2
23/5	**Brazil**	Los Angeles	0–1 (USBT)
28/5	**Italy**	New York	3–2 (USBT)
13/6	**Finland**	Helsinki	4–1 (WCQ)
8/9	**Rep of Ireland**	Wembley	1–1
13/10	**Finland**	Wembley	2–1 (WCQ)
17/11	**Italy**	Rome	0–2 (WCQ)

1977

Date	Opponents	Venue	Score
9/2	**Holland**	Wembley	0–2
30/3	**Luxembourg**	Wembley	5–0 (WCQ)
28/5	**N Ireland**	Belfast	2–1
31/5	**Wales**	Wembley	0–1
4/6	**Scotland**	Wembley	1–2
8/6	**Brazil**	Rio de Janeiro	0–0
12/6	**Argentina**	Buenos Aires	1–1
15/6	**Uruguay**	Montevideo	0–0
7/9	**Switzerland**	Wembley	0–0
12/10	**Luxembourg**	Luxembourg	2–0 (WCQ)
16/11	**Italy**	Wembley	2–0 (WCQ)

1978

Date	Opponents	Venue	Score
22/2	**W Germany**	Munich	1–2
19/4	**Brazil**	Wembley	1–1
13/5	**Wales**	Cardiff	3–1
16/5	**N Ireland**	Wembley	1–0
20/5	**Scotland**	Glasgow	1–0
24/5	**Hungary**	Wembley	4–1
20/9	**Denmark**	Copenhagen	4–3 (ECQ)
25/10	**Rep of Ireland**	Dublin	1–1 (ECQ)
29/11	**Czechoslovakia**	Wembley	1–0

1979

Date	Opponents	Venue	Score
7/2	**N Ireland**	Wembley	4–0 (ECQ)
19/5	**N Ireland**	Belfast	2–0
23/5	**Wales**	Wembley	0–0
26/5	**Scotland**	Wembley	3–1
6/6	**Bulgaria**	Sofia	3–0 (ECQ)
10/6	**Sweden**	Stockholm	0–0
13/6	**Austria**	Vienna	3–4
12/9	**Denmark**	Wembley	1–0 (ECQ)
17/10	**N Ireland**	Belfast	5–1 (ECQ)
22/11	**Bulgaria**	Wembley	2–0 (ECQ)

1980

Date	Opponents	Venue	Score
6/2	**Rep of Ireland**	Wembley	2–0 (ECQ)
26/3	**Spain**	Barcelona	2–0

1980 *continued*

Date	Opponents	Venue	Score
13/5	**Argentina**	Wembley	3–1
17/5	**Wales**	Wrexham	1–4
20/5	**N Ireland**	Wembley	1–1
24/5	**Scotland**	Glasgow	2–0
31/5	**Australia**	Sydney	2–1
12/6	**Belgium**	Turin	1–1 (ECF)
15/6	**Italy**	Turin	0–1 (ECF)
18/6	**Spain**	Naples	2–1 (ECF)
10/9	**Norway**	Wembley	4–0 (WCQ)
15/10	**Romania**	Bucharest	1–2 (WCQ)
19/11	**Switzerland**	Wembley	2–1 (WCQ)

1981

Date	Opponents	Venue	Score
25/3	**Spain**	Wembley	1–2
29/4	**Romania**	Wembley	0–0 (WCQ)
12/5	**Brazil**	Wembley	0–1
20/5	**Wales**	Wembley	0–0
23/5	**Scotland**	Wembley	0–1
30/5	**Switzerland**	Basle	1–2 (WCQ)
6/6	**Hungary**	Budapest	3–1 (WCQ)
9/9	**Norway**	Oslo	1–2 (WCQ)
18/11	**Hungary**	Wembley	1–0 (WCQ)

1982

Date	Opponents	Venue	Score
23/2	**N Ireland**	Wembley	4–0
25/5	**Holland**	Wembley	2–0
29/5	**Scotland**	Glasgow	1–0
2/6	**Iceland**	Reykjavik	1–1
3/6	**Finland**	Helsinki	4–1
16/6	**France**	Bilbao	3–1 (WCF)
20/6	**Czechoslovakia**	Bilbao	2–0 (WCF)
25/6	**Kuwait**	Bilbao	1–0 (WCF)
29/6	**W Germany**	Madrid	0–0 (WCF)
5/7	**Spain**	Madrid	0–0 (WCF)
22/9	**Denmark**	Copenhagen	2–2 (ECQ)
13/10	**W Germany**	Wembley	1–2
17/11	**Greece**	Salonika	3–0 (ECQ)
15/12	**Luxembourg**	Wembley	9–0 (ECQ)

1983

Date	Opponents	Venue	Score
23/2	**Wales**	Wembley	2–1
30/3	**Greece**	Wembley	0–0 (ECQ)
27/4	**Hungary**	Wembley	2–0 (ECQ)
28/5	**N Ireland**	Belfast	0–0
1/6	**Scotland**	Wembley	2–0
12/6	**Australia**	Sydney	0–0
15/6	**Australia**	Brisbane	1–0
19/6	**Australia**	Melbourne	1–1
21/9	**Denmark**	Wembley	0–1 (ECQ)
12/10	**Hungary**	Budapest	3–0 (ECQ)
16/11	**Luxembourg**	Luxembourg	4–0 (ECQ)

1984

Date	Opponents	Venue	Score
29/2	France	Paris	0–2
4/4	N Ireland	Wembley	1–0
2/5	Wales	Wrexham	0–1
26/5	Scotland	Glasgow	1–1
2/6	USSR	Wembley	0–2
10/6	Brazil	Rio de Janeiro	2–0
13/6	Uruguay	Montevideo	0–2
17/6	Chile	Santiago	0–0
12/9	E Germany	Wembley	1–0
17/10	Finland	Wembley	5–0 (WCQ)
14/11	Turkey	Istanbul	8–0 (WCQ)

1985

Date	Opponents	Venue	Score
27/2	N Ireland	Belfast	1–0 (WCQ)
26/3	Rep of Ireland	Wembley	2–1
1/5	Romania	Bucharest	0–0 (WCQ)
22/5	Finland	Helsinki	1–1 (WCQ)
25/5	Scotland	Glasgow	0–1
6/6	Italy	Mexico City	1–2
9/6	Mexico	Mexico City	0–1
12/6	W Germany	Mexico City	3–0
16/6	USA	Los Angeles	5–0
11/9	Romania	Wembley	1–1 (WCQ)
16/10	Turkey	Wembley	5–0 (WCQ)
13/11	N Ireland	Wembley	0–0 (WCQ)

1986

Date	Opponents	Venue	Score
29/1	Egypt	Cairo	4–0
26/2	Israel	Ramat Gan	2–1
26/3	USSR	Tbilisi	1–0
23/4	Scotland	Wembley	2–1
17/5	Mexico	Los Angeles	3–0
24/5	Canada	Burnaby	1–0
3/6	Portugal	Monterrey	0–1 (WCF)
6/6	Morocco	Monterrey	0–0 (WCF)
11/6	Poland	Monterrey	3–0 (WCF)
18/6	Paraguay	Mexico City	3–0 (WCF)
22/6	Argentina	Mexico City	1–2 (WCF)
10/9	Sweden	Stockholm	0–1
15/10	N Ireland	Wembley	3–0 (ECQ)
12/11	Yugoslavia	Wembley	2–0 (ECQ)

1987

Date	Opponents	Venue	Score
10/2	Spain	Madrid	4–2
1/4	N Ireland	Belfast	2–0 (ECQ)
29/4	Turkey	Izmir	0–0 (ECQ)
19/5	Brazil	Wembley	1–1
23/5	Scotland	Glasgow	0–0
9/9	W Germany	Düsseldorf	1–3
14/10	Turkey	Wembley	8–0 (ECQ)
11/11	Yugoslavia	Belgrade	4–1 (ECQ)

1988

Date	Opponents	Venue	Score
17/2	Israel	Tel Aviv	0–0
23/3	Holland	Wembley	2–2
27/4	Hungary	Budapest	0–0
21/5	Scotland	Wembley	1–0
24/5	Colombia	Wembley	1–1
28/5	Switzerland	Lausanne	1–0
12/6	Rep of Ireland	Stuttgart	0–1 (ECF)
15/6	Holland	Düsseldorf	1–3 (ECF)
18/6	USSR	Frankfurt	1–3 (ECF)
14/9	Denmark	Wembley	1–0
19/10	Sweden	Wembley	0–0 (WCQ)
16/11	Saudi Arabia	Riyadh	1–1

1989

Date	Opponents	Venue	Score
8/2	Greece	Athens	2–1
8/3	Albania	Tirana	2–0 (WCQ)
26/4	Albania	Wembley	5–0 (WCQ)
23/5	Chile	Wembley	0–0
27/5	Scotland	Glasgow	2–0
3/6	Poland	Wembley	3–0 (WCQ)
7/6	Denmark	Copenhagen	1–1
6/9	Sweden	Stockholm	0–0 (WCQ)
11/10	Poland	Katowice	0–0 (WCQ)
15/11	Italy	Wembley	0–0
13/12	Yugoslavia	Wembley	2–1

1990

Date	Opponents	Venue	Score
28/3	Brazil	Wembley	1–0
25/4	Czechoslovakia	Wembley	4–2
15/5	Denmark	Wembley	1–0
22/5	Uruguay	Wembley	1–2
2/6	Tunisia	Tunis	1–1
11/6	Rep of Ireland	Cagliari	1–1 (WCF)
16/6	Holland	Cagliari	0–0 (WCF)
21/6	Egypt	Cagliari	1–0 (WCF)
26/6	Belgium	Bologna	1–0 (WCF)
1/7	Cameroon	Naples	3–2 (WCF)
4/7	W Germany (England lost 3–4 on penalties)	Turin	1–1* (WCF)
7/7	Italy	Bari	1–2 (WCF)
12/9	Hungary	Wembley	1–0
17/10	Poland	Wembley	2–0 (ECQ)
14/11	Rep of Ireland	Dublin	1–1 (ECQ)

1991

Date	Opponents	Venue	Score
6/2	Cameroon	Wembley	2–0
27/3	Rep of Ireland	Wembley	1–1 (ECQ)
1/5	Turkey	Izmir	1–0 (ECQ)
21/5	USSR	Wembley	3–1
25/5	Argentina	Wembley	2–2
1/6	Australia	Sydney	1–0

1991 *continued*

Date	Opponents	Venue	Score
3/6	**New Zealand**	Auckland	1–0
8/6	**New Zealand**	Wellington	2–0
12/6	**Malaysia**	Kuala Lumpur	4–2
11/9	**Germany**	Wembley	0–1
16/10	**Turkey**	Wembley	1–0 (ECQ)
13/11	**Poland**	Poznan	1–1 (ECQ)

1992

Date	Opponents	Venue	Score
19/2	**France**	Wembley	2–0
25/3	**Czechoslovakia**	Prague	2–2
29/4	**CIS**	Moscow	2–2
12/5	**Hungary**	Budapest	1–0
17/5	**Brazil**	Wembley	1–1
3/6	**Finland**	Helsinki	2–1
11/6	**Denmark**	Malmo	0–0 (ECF)
14/6	**France**	Malmo	0–0 (ECF)
17/6	**Sweden**	Stockholm	1–2 (ECF)
9/9	**Spain**	Santander	0–1
14/10	**Norway**	Wembley	1–1 (WCQ)
18/11	**Turkey**	Wembley	4–0 (WCQ)

1993

Date	Opponents	Venue	Score
17/2	**San Marino**	Wembley	6–0 (WCQ)
31/3	**Turkey**	Izmir	2–0 (WCQ)
28/4	**Holland**	Wembley	2–2 (WCQ)
29/5	**Poland**	Katowice	1–1 (WCQ)
2/6	**Norway**	Oslo	0–2 (WCQ)
9/6	**USA**	Boston	0–2 (USC)
13/6	**Brazil**	Washington	1–1 (USC)
19/6	**Germany**	Detroit	1–2 (USC)
8/9	**Poland**	Wembley	3–0 (WCQ)
13/10	**Holland**	Rotterdam	0–2 (WCQ)
17/11	**San Marino**	Bologna	7–1 (WCQ)

1994

Date	Opponents	Venue	Score
9/3	**Denmark**	Wembley	1–0
17/5	**Greece**	Wembley	5–0
22/5	**Norway**	Wembley	0–0
7/9	**United States**	Wembley	2–0
16/11	**Nigeria**	Wembley	1–0

1995

Date	Opponents	Venue	Score
15/2	**Rep of Ireland** (abandoned after 21 minutes)	Dublin	0–1
29/3	**Uruguay**	Wembley	0–0
3/6	**Japan**	Wembley	2–1 (UT)
8/6	**Sweden**	Leeds	3–3 (UT)
11/6	**Brazil**	Wembley	1–3 (UT)

1995 *continued*

Date	Opponents	Venue	Score
6/9	**Colombia**	Wembley	0–0
11/10	**Norway**	Oslo	0–0
15/11	**Switzerland**	Wembley	3–1
12/12	**Portugal**	Wembley	1–1

1996

Date	Opponents	Venue	Score
27/3	**Bulgaria**	Wembley	1–0
24/4	**Croatia**	Wembley	0–0
18/5	**Hungary**	Wembley	3–0
23/5	**China**	Beijing	3–0
8/6	**Switzerland**	Wembley	1–1 (ECF)
15/6	**Scotland**	Wembley	2–0 (ECF)
18/6	**Holland**	Wembley	4–1 (ECF)
22/6	**Spain** (England won 4–2 on penalties)	Wembley	0–0 (ECF)
26/6	**Germany** (England lost 5–6 on penalties)	Wembley	1–1 (ECF)
1/9	**Moldova**	Chisinau	3–0 (WCQ)
9/10	**Poland**	Wembley	2–1 (WCQ)
9/11	**Georgia**	Tbilisi	2–0 (WCQ)

1997

Date	Opponents	Venue	Score
12/2	**Italy**	Wembley	0–1 (WCQ)
29/3	**Mexico**	Wembley	2–0
30/4	**Georgia**	Wembley	2–0 (WCQ)
24/5	**South Africa**	Old Trafford	2–1
31/5	**Poland**	Chorzow	2–0 (WCQ)
4/6	**Italy**	Nantes	2–0 (TDF)
7/6	**France**	Montpellier	1–0 (TDF)
10/6	**Brazil**	Paris	0–1 (TDF)
10/9	**Moldova**	Wembley	4–0 (WCQ)
11/10	**Italy**	Rome	0–0 (WCQ)
15/11	**Cameroon**	Wembley	2–0

1998

Date	Opponents	Venue	Score
11/2	**Chile**	Wembley	0–2
25/3	**Switzerland**	Berne	1–1
22/4	**Portugal**	Wembley	3–0
23/5	**Saudi Arabia**	Wembley	0–0
27/5	**Morocco**	Casablanca	2–0 (KHT)
29/5	**Belgium** (Belgium won 4–3 on penalties)	Casablanca	0–0 (KHT)
15/6	**Tunisia**	Marseille	2–0 (WCF)
22/6	**Romania**	Toulouse	1–2 (WCF)
26/6	**Colombia**	Lens	2–0 (WCF)
30/6	**Argentina** (Argentina won 4–3 on penalties)	St.Etienne	2–2 (WCF)

INTERNATIONAL RESULTS – SCOTLAND

KEY TO ABBREVIATIONS	
WCQ =	*World Cup Qualifier*
ECQ =	*European Championship Qualifier*
WCF =	*World Cup Finals*
ECF =	*European Championship Finals*

Date	Opponents	Venue	F–A
30/11/1872	England	Glasgow	0–0
8/3/73	England	London	2–4
7/3/74	England	Glasgow	2–1
6/3/75	England	London	2–2
4/3/76	England	Glasgow	3–0
25/3/76	Wales	Glasgow	4–0
3/3/77	England	London	3–1
5/3/77	Wales	Wrexham	2–0
2/3/78	England	Glasgow	7–2
23/3/78	Wales	Glasgow	9–0
7/4/79	Wales	Wrexham	3–0
5/4/79	England	London	4–5
13/3/80	England	Glasgow	5–4
27/3/80	Wales	Glasgow	5–1
12/3/81	England	London	6–1
14/3/81	Wales	Wrexham	5–1
11/3/82	England	Glasgow	5–1
25/3/82	Wales	Glasgow	5–0
10/3/83	England	Sheffield	3–2
12/3/83	Wales	Wrexham	3–0
26/1/84	Ireland	Belfast	5–0
15/3/84	England	Glasgow	1–0
29/3/84	Wales	Glasgow	4–1
14/3/85	Ireland	Glasgow	8–2
21/3/85	England	London	1–1
23/3/85	Wales	Wrexham	8–1
20/3/86	Ireland	Belfast	7–2
31/3/86	England	Glasgow	1–1
10/4/86	Wales	Glasgow	4–4
19/2/87	Ireland	Glasgow	4–1
19/3/87	England	Blackburn	3–2
21/3/87	Wales	Wrexham	2–0
10/3/88	Wales	Edinburgh	5–1
17/3/88	England	Glasgow	0–5
24/3/88	Ireland	Belfast	10–2
9/3/89	Ireland	Glasgow	7–0
13/4/89	England	London	3–2
15/4/89	Wales	Wrexham	0–0
22/3/90	Wales	Glasgow	5–0
29/3/90	Ireland	Belfast	4–1
5/4/90	England	Glasgow	1–1
21/3/91	Wales	Wrexham	4–3
28/3/91	Ireland	Glasgow	2–1
6/4/91	England	Blackburn	1–2
19/3/92	Ireland	Belfast	3–2
26/3/92	Wales	Edinburgh	6–1
2/4/92	England	Glasgow	1–4
18/3/93	Wales	Wrexham	8–0
25/3/93	Ireland	Glasgow	6–1
1/4/93	England	Richmond	2–5

Date	Opponents	Venue	F–A
24/3/94	Wales	Kilmarnock	5–2
31/3/94	Ireland	Belfast	2–1
7/4/94	England	Glasgow	2–2
23/3/95	Wales	Wrexham	2–2
30/3/95	Ireland	Glasgow	3–1
6/4/95	England	Liverpool	0–3
21/3/96	Wales	Dundee	4–0
28/3/96	Ireland	Belfast	3–3
4/4/96	England	Glasgow	2–1
20/3/97	Wales	Wrexham	2–2
27/3/97	Ireland	Glasgow	5–1
3/4/97	England	London	2–1
19/3/98	Wales	Motherwell	5–2
26/3/98	Ireland	Belfast	3–0
2/4/98	England	Glasgow	1–3
18/3/99	Wales	Wrexham	6–0
25/3/99	Ireland	Glasgow	9–1
8/4/99	England	Birmingham	1–2

1900–1959

Date	Opponents	Venue	F–A
3/2/00	Wales	Aberdeen	5–2
3/3/00	Ireland	Belfast	3–0
7/4/00	England	Glasgow	4–1
23/2/01	Ireland	Glasgow	11–0
2/3/01	Wales	Wrexham	1–1
30/3/01	England	London	2–2
1/3/02	Ireland	Belfast	5–1
15/3/02	Wales	Greenock	5–1
3/5/02	England	Birmingham	2–2
9/3/03	Wales	Cardiff	1–0
21/3/03	Ireland	Glasgow	0–2
4/4/03	England	Sheffield	2–1
12/3/04	Wales	Dundee	1–1
26/3/04	Ireland	Dublin	1–1
9/4/04	England	Glasgow	0–1
6/3/05	Wales	Wrexham	1–3
18/3/05	Ireland	Glasgow	4–0
1/4/05	England	London	0–1
3/3/06	Wales	Edinburgh	0–2
17/3/06	Ireland	Dublin	1–0
7/4/06	England	Glasgow	2–1
4/3/07	Wales	Wrexham	0–1
16/3/07	Ireland	Glasgow	3–0
6/4/07	England	Newcastle	1–1
7/3/08	Wales	Dundee	2–1
14/3/08	Ireland	Dublin	5–0
4/4/08	England	Glasgow	1–1

Date	Opponents	Venue	F–A
1/3/09	**Wales**	Wrexham	2–3
15/3/09	**Ireland**	Glasgow	5–0
3/4/09	**England**	London	0–2
5/3/10	**Wales**	Kilmarnock	1–0
19/3/10	**Ireland**	Belfast	0–1
2/4/10	**England**	Glasgow	2–0
6/3/11	**Wales**	Cardiff	2–2
18/3/11	**Ireland**	Glasgow	2–0
1/4/11	**England**	Liverpool	1–1
2/3/12	**Wales**	Edinburgh	1–0
16/3/12	**Ireland**	Belfast	4–1
23/3/12	**England**	Glasgow	1–1
3/3/13	**Wales**	Wrexham	0–0
15/3/13	**Ireland**	Dublin	2–1
5/4/13	**England**	Stamford Bridge	0–1
28/2/14	**Wales**	Glasgow	0–0
14/3/14	**Ireland**	Belfast	1–1
4/4/14	**England**	Glasgow	3–1
26/2/20	**Wales**	Cardiff	1–1
13/3/20	**Ireland**	Glasgow	3–0
10/4/20	**England**	Sheffield	4–5
12/2/21	**Wales**	Aberdeen	2–1
26/2/21	**Ireland**	Belfast	2–0
9/4/21	**England**	Glasgow	3–0
4/2/22	**Wales**	Wrexham	1–2
4/3/22	**Ireland**	Glasgow	2–1
8/4/22	**England**	Birmingham	1–0
3/3/23	**Ireland**	Belfast	1–0
17/3/23	**Wales**	Glasgow	2–0
14/4/23	**England**	Glasgow	2–2
16/2/24	**Wales**	Cardiff	0–2
1/3/24	**Ireland**	Glasgow	2–0
12/4/24	**England**	Wembley	1–1
14/2/25	**Wales**	Edinburgh	3–1
28/2/25	**Ireland**	Belfast	3–0
4/4/25	**England**	Glasgow	2–0
31/10/25	**Wales**	Cardiff	3–0
27/2/26	**Ireland**	Glasgow	4–0
17/4/26	**England**	Manchester	1–0
30/10/26	**Wales**	Glasgow	3–0
26/2/27	**Ireland**	Belfast	2–0
2/4/27	**England**	Glasgow	1–2
29/10/27	**Wales**	Wrexham	2–2
25/2/28	**Ireland**	Glasgow	0–1
31/3/28	**England**	Wembley	5–1
27/10/28	**Wales**	Glasgow	4–2
23/2/29	**Ireland**	Belfast	7–3
13/4/29	**England**	Glasgow	1–0
26/5/29	**Norway**	Bergen	7–3
1/6/29	**Germany**	Berlin	1–1
4/6/29	**Holland**	Amsterdam	2–0
26/10/29	**Wales**	Cardiff	4–2
22/2/30	**Ireland**	Glasgow	3–1
5/4/30	**England**	Wembley	2–5
18/5/30	**France**	Paris	2–0
25/10/30	**Wales**	Glasgow	1–1
21/2/31	**Ireland**	Belfast	0–0
28/3/31	**England**	Glasgow	2–0
16/5/31	**Austria**	Vienna	0–5
20/5/31	**Italy**	Rome	0–3
24/5/31	**Switzerland**	Geneva	3–2

Date	Opponents	Venue	F–A
19/9/31	**Ireland**	Glasgow	3–1
31/10/31	**Wales**	Wrexham	3–2
9/4/32	**England**	Wembley	0–3
8/5/32	**France**	Paris	3–1
19/9/32	**Ireland**	Belfast	4–0
26/10/32	**Wales**	Edinburgh	2–5
1/4/33	**England**	Glasgow	2–1
16/9/33	**Ireland**	Glasgow	1–2
4/10/33	**Wales**	Cardiff	2–3
29/11/33	**Austria**	Glasgow	2–2
14/4/34	**England**	Wembley	0–3
20/10/34	**Ireland**	Belfast	1–2
21/11/34	**Wales**	Aberdeen	3–2
6/4/35	**England**	Glasgow	2–0
5/10/35	**Wales**	Cardiff	1–1
13/11/35	**Ireland**	Edinburgh	2–1
4/4/36	**England**	Wembley	1–1
14/10/36	**Germany**	Glasgow	2–0
31/10/36	**Ireland**	Belfast	3–1
2/12/36	**Wales**	Dundee	1–2
17/4/37	**England**	Glasgow	3–1
9/5/37	**Austria**	Vienna	1–1
22/5/37	**Czechoslovakia**	Prague	3–1
30/10/37	**Wales**	Cardiff	1–2
10/11/37	**Ireland**	Aberdeen	1–1
8/12/37	**Czechoslovakia**	Glasgow	5–0
9/4/38	**England**	Wembley	1–0
21/5/38	**Holland**	Amsterdam	3–1
8/10/38	**Ireland**	Belfast	2–0
9/11/38	**Wales**	Edinburgh	3–2
7/12/38	**Hungary**	Glasgow	3–1
15/4/39	**England**	Glasgow	1–2
19/10/46	**Wales**	Wrexham	1–3
27/11/46	**N Ireland**	Glasgow	0–0
12/4/47	**England**	Wembley	1–1
18/5/47	**Belgium**	Brussels	1–2
24/5/47	**Luxembourg**	Luxembourg	6–0
4/10/47	**N Ireland**	Belfast	0–2
12/11/47	**Wales**	Glasgow	1–2
10/4/48	**England**	Glasgow	0–2
28/4/48	**Belgium**	Glasgow	2–0
17/5/48	**Switzerland**	Berne	1–2
23/5/48	**France**	Paris	0–3
23/10/48	**Wales**	Cardiff	3–1
17/11/48	**N Ireland**	Glasgow	3–2
9/4/49	**England**	Wembley	3–1
27/4/49	**France**	Glasgow	2–0
1/10/49	**N Ireland**	Belfast	8–2 (WCQ)
9/11/49	**Wales**	Glasgow	2–0 (WCQ)
15/4/50	**England**	Glasgow	0–1 (WCQ)
26/4/50	**Switzerland**	Glasgow	3–1
25/5/50	**Portugal**	Lisbon	2–2
27/5/50	**France**	Paris	1–0
21/10/50	**Wales**	Cardiff	3–1
1/11/50	**N Ireland**	Glasgow	6–1
13/12/50	**Austria**	Glasgow	0–1
14/4/51	**England**	Wembley	3–2
12/5/51	**Denmark**	Glasgow	3–1
16/5/51	**France**	Glasgow	1–0
20/5/51	**Belgium**	Brussels	5–0
27/5/51	**Austria**	Vienna	0–4

Date	Opponents	Venue	F–A
6/10/51	**N Ireland**	Belfast	3–0
28/11/51	**Wales**	Glasgow	0–1
5/4/52	**England**	Glasgow	1–2
30/4/52	**USA**	Glasgow	6–0
25/5/52	**Denmark**	Copenhagen	2–1
30/5/52	**Sweden**	Stockholm	1–3
15/10/52	**Wales**	Cardiff	2–1
5/11/52	**N Ireland**	Glasgow	1–1
18/4/53	**England**	Wembley	2–2
6/5/53	**Sweden**	Glasgow	1–2
3/10/53	**N Ireland**	Belfast	3–1 (WCQ)
4/11/53	**Wales**	Glasgow	3–3 (WCQ)
3/4/54	**England**	Glasgow	2–4 (WCQ)
5/5/54	**Norway**	Glasgow	1–0
19/5/54	**Norway**	Oslo	1–1
25/5/54	**Finland**	Helsinki	2–1
16/6/54	**Austria**	Zurich	0–1 (WCF)
19/6/54	**Uruguay**	Basle	0–7 (WCF)
16/10/54	**Wales**	Cardiff	1–0
3/11/54	**N Ireland**	Glasgow	2–2
8/12/54	**Hungary**	Glasgow	2–4
2/4/55	**England**	Wembley	2–7
16/5/55	**Portugal**	Glasgow	3–0
15/5/55	**Yugoslavia**	Belgrade	2–2
19/5/55	**Austria**	Vienna	4–1
29/5/55	**Hungary**	Budapest	1–3
8/10/55	**N Ireland**	Belfast	1–2
9/11/55	**Wales**	Glasgow	2–0
14/4/56	**England**	Glasgow	1–1
2/5/56	**Austria**	Glasgow	1–1
20/10/56	**Wales**	Cardiff	2–2
7/11/56	**N Ireland**	Glasgow	1–0
21/11/56	**Yugoslavia**	Glasgow	2–0
6/4/57	**England**	Wembley	1–2
8/5/57	**Spain**	Glasgow	4–2 (WCQ)
19/5/57	**Switzerland**	Basle	2–1 (WCQ)
22/5/57	**W Germany**	Stuttgart	3–1
26/5/57	**Spain**	Madrid	1–4 (WCQ)
5/10/57	**N Ireland**	Belfast	1–1
6/11/57	**Switzerland**	Glasgow	3–2 (WCQ)
13/11/57	**Wales**	Glasgow	1–1
19/4/58	**England**	Glasgow	0–4
7/5/58	**Hungary**	Glasgow	1–1
1/6/58	**Poland**	Warsaw	2–1
8/6/58	**Yugoslavia**	Vasteras	1–1 (WCF)
11/6/58	**Paraguay**	Norrköping	2–3 (WCF)
15/6/58	**France**	Örebro	1–2 (WCF)
18/10/58	**Wales**	Cardiff	3–0
5/11/58	**N Ireland**	Glasgow	2–2
11/4/59	**England**	Wembley	0–1
6/5/59	**W Germany**	Glasgow	3–2
27/5/59	**Holland**	Amsterdam	2–1
3/6/59	**Portugal**	Lisbon	0–1
3/10/59	**N Ireland**	Belfast	4–0
14/11/59	**Wales**	Glasgow	1–1

1960

Date	Opponents	Venue	F–A
9/4/60	**England**	Glasgow	1–1
4/5/60	**Poland**	Glasgow	2–3
29/5/60	**Austria**	Vienna	1–4
5/6/60	**Hungary**	Budapest	3–3
8/6/60	**Turkey**	Ankara	2–4
22/10/60	**Wales**	Cardiff	0–2
9/11/60	**N Ireland**	Glasgow	5–2

1961

Date	Opponents	Venue	F–A
15/4/61	**England**	Wembley	3–9
3/5/61	**Rep of Ireland**	Glasgow	4–1 (WCQ)
7/5/61	**Rep of Ireland**	Dublin	3–0 (WCQ)
14/5/61	**Czechoslovakia**	Bratislava	0–4 (WCQ)
26/9/61	**Czechoslovakia**	Glasgow	3–2 (WCQ)
7/10/61	**N Ireland**	Belfast	6–1
8/11/61	**Wales**	Glasgow	2–0
29/11/61	**Czechoslovakia**	Brussels	2–4 (WCQ)

1962

Date	Opponents	Venue	F–A
14/4/62	**England**	Glasgow	2–0
2/5/62	**Uruguay**	Glasgow	2–3
20/10/62	**Wales**	Cardiff	3–2
7/11/62	**N Ireland**	Glasgow	5–1

1963

Date	Opponents	Venue	F–A
6/4/63	**England**	Wembley	2–1
8/5/63	**Austria**	Glasgow	4–1
4/6/63	**Norway**	Bergen	3–4
9/6/63	**Rep of Ireland**	Dublin	0–1
13/6/63	**Spain**	Madrid	6–2
12/10/63	**N Ireland**	Belfast	1–2
7/11/63	**Norway**	Glasgow	6–1
20/11/63	**Wales**	Glasgow	2–1

1964

Date	Opponents	Venue	F–A
11/4/64	**England**	Glasgow	1–0
12/5/64	**W Germany**	Hanover	2–2
3/10/64	**Wales**	Cardiff	2–3
21/10/64	**Finland**	Glasgow	3–1 (WCQ)
25/11/64	**N Ireland**	Glasgow	3–2
10/4/65	**England**	Wembley	2–2

1965

Date	Opponents	Venue	F–A
8/5/65	**Spain**	Glasgow	0–0
23/5/65	**Poland**	Chorzow	1–1 (WCQ)
27/5/65	**Finland**	Helsinki	2–1 (WCQ)
2/10/65	**N Ireland**	Belfast	2–3
13/10/65	**Poland**	Glasgow	1–2 (WCQ)
9/11/65	**Italy**	Glasgow	1–0 (WCQ)
24/11/65	**Wales**	Glasgow	4–1
7/12/65	**Italy**	Naples	0–3 (WCQ)

1966

Date	Opponents	Venue	F–A
2/4/66	**England**	Glasgow	3–4
11/5/66	**Holland**	Glasgow	0–3
18/6/66	**Portugal**	Glasgow	0–1
25/6/66	**Brazil**	Glasgow	1–1
22/10/66	**Wales**	Cardiff	1–1 (ECQ)
16/11/66	**N Ireland**	Glasgow	2–1 (ECQ)

1967

Date	Opponents	Venue	F–A
15/4/67	**England**	Wembley	3–2 (ECQ)
10/5/67	**USSR**	Glasgow	0–2
21/10/67	**N Ireland**	Belfast	0–1 (ECQ)
22/11/67	**Wales**	Glasgow	3–2 (ECQ)

1968

Date	Opponents	Venue	F–A
24/2/68	**England**	Glasgow	1–1 (ECQ)
30/5/68	**Holland**	Amsterdam	0–0
16/10/68	**Denmark**	Copenhagen	1–0
6/11/68	**Austria**	Glasgow	2–1 (WCQ)
11/12/68	**Cyprus**	Nicosia	5–0 (WCQ)

1969

Date	Opponents	Venue	F–A
16/4/69	**W Germany**	Glasgow	1–1 (WCQ)
3/5/69	**Wales**	Wrexham	5–3
6/5/69	**N Ireland**	Glasgow	1–1
10/6/69	**England**	Wembley	1–4
12/5/69	**Cyprus**	Glasgow	8–0 (WCQ)
21/9/69	**Rep of Ireland**	Dublin	1–1
22/10/69	**W Germany**	Hamburg	2–3 (WCQ)
5/11/69	**Austria**	Vienna	0–2 (WCQ)

1970

Date	Opponents	Venue	F–A
18/4/70	**N Ireland**	Belfast	1–0
22/4/70	**Wales**	Glasgow	0–0

1970 *continued*

Date	Opponents	Venue	F–A
25/4/70	**England**	Glasgow	0–0
11/11/70	**Denmark**	Glasgow	1–0 (ECQ)

1971

Date	Opponents	Venue	F–A
3/2/71	**Belgium**	Liège	0–3 (ECQ)
21/4/71	**Portugal**	Lisbon	0–2 (ECQ)
15/5/71	**Wales**	Cardiff	0–0
18/5/71	**N Ireland**	Glasgow	0–1
22/5/71	**England**	Wembley	1–3
9/6/71	**Denmark**	Copenhagen	0–1 (ECQ)
14/6/71	**USSR**	Moscow	0–1
13/10/71	**Portugal**	Glasgow	2–1 (ECQ)
10/11/71	**Belgium**	Aberdeen	1–0 (ECQ)
1/12/71	**Holland**	Rotterdam	1–2

1972

Date	Opponents	Venue	F–A
26/4/72	**Peru**	Glasgow	2–0
20/5/72	**N Ireland**	Glasgow	2–0
24/5/72	**Wales**	Glasgow	1–0
27/5/72	**England**	Glasgow	0–1
29/6/72	**Yugoslavia**	Belo Horizonte	2–2
2/7/72	**Czechoslovakia**	Porto Alegre	0–0
5/7/72	**Brazil**	Rio de Janeiro	0–1
18/10/72	**Denmark**	Copenhagen	4–1 (WCQ)
15/11/72	**Denmark**	Glasgow	2–0 (WCQ)

1973

Date	Opponents	Venue	F–A
14/2/73	**England**	Glasgow	0–5
12/5/73	**Wales**	Wrexham	2–0
16/5/73	**N Ireland**	Glasgow	1–2
19/5/73	**England**	Wembley	0–1
22/6/73	**Switzerland**	Berne	0–1
30/6/73	**Brazil**	Glasgow	0–1
26/9/73	**Czechoslovakia**	Glasgow	2–1 (WCQ)
17/10/73	**Czechoslovakia**	Bratislava	0–1 (WCQ)
14/11/73	**W Germany**	Glasgow	1–1

1974

Date	Opponents	Venue	F–A
27/3/74	**W Germany**	Frankfurt	1–2
11/5/74	**N Ireland**	Glasgow	0–1
14/5/74	**Wales**	Glasgow	2–0
18/5/74	**England**	Glasgow	2–0
2/6/74	**Belgium**	Brussels	1–2
6/6/74	**Norway**	Oslo	2–1
14/6/74	**Zaïre**	Dortmund	2–0 (WCF)
18/6/74	**Brazil**	Frankfurt	0–0 (WCF)
22/6/74	**Yugoslavia**	Frankfurt	1–1 (WCF)

1974 *continued*

Date	Opponents	Venue	F–A
30/10/74	E Germany	Glasgow	3–0
20/11/74	Spain	Glasgow	1–2 (ECQ)

1975

Date	Opponents	Venue	F–A
5/2/75	Spain	Valencia	1–1 (ECQ)
16/4/75	Sweden	Gothenburg	1–1
13/5/75	Portugal	Glasgow	1–0
17/5/75	Wales	Cardiff	2–2
20/5/75	N Ireland	Glasgow	3–0
24/5/75	England	Wembley	1–5
1/6/75	Romania	Bucharest	1–1 (ECQ)
3/9/75	Denmark	Copenhagen	1–0 (ECQ)
29/10/75	Denmark	Glasgow	3–1 (ECQ)
17/12/75	Romania	Glasgow	1–1 (ECQ)

1976

Date	Opponents	Venue	F–A
7/4/76	Switzerland	Glasgow	1–0
6/5/76	Wales	Glasgow	3–1
8/5/76	N Ireland	Glasgow	3–0
15/5/76	England	Glasgow	2–1
8/9/76	Finland	Glasgow	6–0
13/10/76	Czechoslovakia	Prague	0–2 (WCQ)
17/11/76	Wales	Glasgow	1–0 (WCQ)

1977

Date	Opponents	Venue	F–A
27/4/77	Sweden	Glasgow	3–1
28/5/77	Wales	Wrexham	0–0
1/6/77	N Ireland	Glasgow	3–0
4/6/77	England	Wembley	2–0
15/6/77	Chile	Santiago	4–2
18/6/77	Argentina	Buenos Aires	1–1
23/6/77	Brazil	Rio de Janeiro	0–2
7/9/77	E Germany	E Berlin	0–1
21/9/77	Czechoslovakia	Glasgow	3–1 (WCQ)
12/10/77	Wales	Liverpool	2–0 (WCQ)

1978

Date	Opponents	Venue	F–A
22/2//78	Bulgaria	Glasgow	2–1
13/5/78	N Ireland	Glasgow	1–1
17/5/78	Wales	Glasgow	1–1
20/5/78	England	Glasgow	0–1
3/6/78	Peru	Cordoba	1–3 (WCF)
7/6/78	Iran	Cordoba	1–1 (WCF)
11/6/78	Holland	Mendoza	3–2 (WCF)
20/9/78	Austria	Vienna	2–3 (ECQ)
25/10/78	Norway	Glasgow	3–2 (ECQ)
29/11/78	Portugal	Lisbon	0–1 (ECQ)

1979

Date	Opponents	Venue	F–A
19/5/79	Wales	Cardiff	0–3
22/5/79	N Ireland	Glasgow	1–0
26/5/79	England	Wembley	1–3
2/6/79	Argentina	Glasgow	1–3
7/6/79	Norway	Oslo	4–0 (ECQ)
12/9/79	Peru	Glasgow	1–1
17/10/79	Austria	Glasgow	1–1 (ECQ)
21/11/79	Belgium	Brussels	0–2 (ECQ)
19/12/79	Belgium	Glasgow	1–3 (ECQ)

1980

Date	Opponents	Venue	F–A
26/3	Portugal	Glasgow	4–1 (ECQ)
16/5	N Ireland	Belfast	0–1
21/5	Wales	Glasgow	1–0
24/5	England	Glasgow	0–2
28/5	Poland	Poznan	0–1
31/5	Hungary	Budapest	1–3
10/9	Sweden	Stockholm	1–0 (WCQ)
15/10	Portugal	Glasgow	0–0 (WCQ)

1981

Date	Opponents	Venue	F–A
25/2	Israel	Tel Aviv	1–0 (WCQ)
25/3	N Ireland	Glasgow	1–1 (WCQ)
28/4	Israel	Glasgow	3–1 (WCQ)
16/5	Wales	Swansea	0–2
19/5	N Ireland	Glasgow	2–0
23/5	England	Wembley	1–0
9/9	Sweden	Glasgow	2–0 (WCQ)
14/10	N Ireland	Belfast	0–0 (WCQ)
18/11	Portugal	Lisbon	1–2 (WCQ)

1982

Date	Opponents	Venue	F–A
24/2	Spain	Valencia	0–3
23/3	Holland	Glasgow	2–1
28/4	N Ireland	Belfast	1–1
24/5	Wales	Glasgow	1–0
29/5	England	Glasgow	0–1
15/6	New Zealand	Malaga	5–2 (WCF)
18/6	Brazil	Seville	1–4 (WCF)
22/6	USSR	Malaga	2–2 (WCF)
13/10	E Germany	Glasgow	2–0 (ECQ)
17/11	Switzerland	Berne	0–2 (ECQ)
15/12	Belgium	Brussels	2–3 (ECQ)

1983

Date	Opponents	Venue	F–A
30/3	Switzerland	Glasgow	2–2 (ECQ)
24/5	N Ireland	Glasgow	0–0

1983 *continued*

Date	Opponents	Venue	F–A
28/5	**Wales**	Cardiff	2–0
1/6	**England**	Wembley	0–2
12/6	**Canada**	Vancouver	2–0
16/6	**Canada**	Edmonton	3–0
20/6	**Canada**	Toronto	2–0
21/9	**Uruguay**	Glasgow	2–0
12/10	**Belgium**	Glasgow	1–1 (ECQ)
16/11	**E Germany**	Halle	1–2 (ECQ)
13/12	**N Ireland**	Belfast	0–2

1984

Date	Opponents	Venue	F–A
28/2	**Wales**	Glasgow	2–1
26/5	**England**	Glasgow	1–1
1/6	**France**	Marseille	0–2
12/9	**Yugoslavia**	Glasgow	6–1
17/10	**Iceland**	Glasgow	3–0 (WCQ)
14/11	**Spain**	Glasgow	3–1 (WCQ)

1985

Date	Opponents	Venue	F–A
27/2	**Spain**	Seville	0–1 (WCQ)
27/3	**Wales**	Glasgow	0–1 (WCQ)
25/5	**England**	Glasgow	1–0
28/5	**Iceland**	Reykjavik	1–0 (WCQ)
10/9	**Wales**	Cardiff	1–1 (WCQ)
16/10	**E Germany**	Glasgow	0–0
20/11	**Australia**	Glasgow	2–0 (WCQ)
4/12	**Australia**	Melbourne	0–0 (WCQ)

1986

Date	Opponents	Venue	F–A
28/1	**Israel**	Tel Aviv	1–0
26/3	**Romania**	Glasgow	3–0
23/4	**England**	Wembley	1–2
29/4	**Holland**	Eindhoven	0–0
4/6	**Denmark**	Nezahualcoyotl	0–1 (WCF)
8/6	**W Germany**	Queretaro	1–2 (WCF)
13/6	**Uruguay**	Nezahualcoyotl	0–0 (WCF)
10/9	**Bulgaria**	Glasgow	0–0 (ECQ)
15/10	**Rep of Ireland**	Dublin	0–0 (ECQ)
12/11	**Luxembourg**	Glasgow	3–0 (ECQ)

1987

Date	Opponents	Venue	F–A
18/2	**Rep of Ireland**	Glasgow	0–1 (ECQ)
1/4	**Belgium**	Brussels	1–4 (ECQ)
6/5	**Brazil**	Glasgow	0–2
23/5	**England**	Glasgow	0–0
9/9	**Hungary**	Glasgow	2–0
14/10	**Belgium**	Glasgow	2–0 (ECQ)

1987 *continued*

Date	Opponents	Venue	F–A
11/11	**Bulgaria**	Sofia	1–0 (ECQ)
2/12	**Luxembourg**	Esch	0–0 (ECQ)

1988

Date	Opponents	Venue	F–A
17/2	**Saudi Arabia**	Riyadh	2–2
22/3	**Malta**	Valletta	1–1
27/4	**Spain**	Madrid	0–0
17/5	**Colombia**	Glasgow	0–0
21/5	**England**	Wembley	0–1
14/9	**Norway**	Oslo	2–1 (WCQ)
19/10	**Yugoslavia**	Glasgow	1–1 (WCQ)
22/12	**Italy**	Perugia	0–2

1989

Date	Opponents	Venue	F–A
8/2	**Cyprus**	Limassol	3–2 (WCQ)
8/3	**France**	Glasgow	2–0 (WCQ)
26/4	**Cyprus**	Glasgow	2–1 (WCQ)
27/5	**England**	Glasgow	0–2
30/5	**Chile**	Glasgow	2–0
6/9	**Yugoslavia**	Zagreb	1–3 (WCQ)
11/10	**France**	Paris	0–3 (WCQ)
15/11	**Norway**	Glasgow	1–1 (WCQ)

1990

Date	Opponents	Venue	F–A
28/3	**Argentina**	Glasgow	1–0
25/4	**E Germany**	Glasgow	0–1
19/5	**Poland**	Glasgow	1–1
28/5	**Malta**	Valletta	2–1
11/6	**Costa Rica**	Genoa	0–1 (WCF)
16/6	**Sweden**	Genoa	2–1 (WCF)
20/6	**Brazil**	Turin	0–1 (WCF)
12/9	**Romania**	Glasgow	2–1 (ECQ)
17/10	**Switzerland**	Glasgow	2–1 (ECQ)
14/11	**Bulgaria**	Sofia	1–1 (ECQ)

1991

Date	Opponents	Venue	F–A
6/2	**USSR**	Glasgow	0–1
27/3	**Bulgaria**	Glasgow	1–1 (ECQ)
1/5	**San Marino**	Serravalle	2–0 (ECQ)
11/9	**Switzerland**	Berne	2–2 (ECQ)
16/10	**Romania**	Bucharest	0–1 (ECQ)
13/11	**San Marino**	Glasgow	4–0 (ECQ)

1992

Date	Opponents	Venue	F–A
25/3	Finland	Glasgow	1–1
17/5	USA	Denver	1–0
21/5	Canada	Toronto	3–1
3/6	Norway	Oslo	0–0
12/6	Holland	Gothenburg	0–1 (ECF)
15/6	Germany	Gothenburg	0–2 (ECF)
18/6	CIS	Norrkoping	3–0 (ECF)
9/9	Switzerland	Berne	1–3 (WCQ)
14/10	Portugal	Glasgow	0–0 (WCQ)
18/11	Italy	Glasgow	0–0 (WCQ)

1993

Date	Opponents	Venue	F–A
17/2	Malta	Glasgow	3–0 (WCQ)
24/3	Germany	Glasgow	0–1
28/4	Portugal	Lisbon	0–5 (WCQ)
19/5	Estonia	Tallinn	3–0 (WCQ)
2/6	Estonia	Aberdeen	3–1 (WCQ)
8/9	Switzerland	Glasgow	1–1 (WCQ)
13/10	Italy	Rome	1–3 (WCQ)
17/11	Malta	Sliema	2–0 (WCQ)

1994

Date	Opponents	Venue	F–A
23/3	Holland	Glasgow	0–1
20/4	Austria	Vienna	2–1
27/5	Holland	Utrecht	1–3
7/9	Finland	Helsinki	2–0 (ECQ)
12/10	Faroe Islands	Glasgow	5–1 (ECQ)
16/11	Russia	Glasgow	1–1 (ECQ)
19/12	Greece	Athens	0–1 (ECQ)

1995

Date	Opponents	Venue	F–A
29/3	Russia	Moscow	0–0 (ECQ)
26/4	San Marino	Serravalle	2–0 (ECQ)
21/5	Japan	Hiroshima	0–0
24/5	Ecuador	Toyama, Japan	2–1
7/6	Faroe Islands	Toftir	2–0 (ECQ)
16/8	Greece	Glasgow	1–0 (ECQ)
6/9	Finland	Glasgow	1–0 (ECQ)
11/10	Sweden	Stockholm	0–2
15/11	San Marino	Glasgow	5–0 (ECQ)

1996

Date	Opponents	Venue	F–A
27/3	Australia	Glasgow	1–0
24/4	Denmark	Copenhagen	0–2
26/5	United States	New Britain, Conn	1–2
29/5	Colombia	Miami	0–1
10/6	Holland	Birmingham	0–0 (ECF)
15/6	England	Wembley	0–2 (ECF)
18/6	Switzerland	Birmingham	1–0 (ECF)
31/8	Austria	Vienna	0–0 (WCQ)
5/10	Latvia	Riga	2–0 (WCQ)
9/10	Estonia	Tallinn	0–0 (WCQ)
(abandoned because Estonia did not arrive)			
10/11	Sweden	Glasgow	1–0 (WCQ)

1997

Date	Opponents	Venue	F–A
11/2	Estonia	Monaco	0–0 (WCQ)
29/3	Estonia	Kilmarnock	2–0 (WCQ)
2/4	Austria	Glasgow	2–0 (WCQ)
30/4	Sweden	Gothenburg	1–2 (WCQ)
27/5	Wales	Kilmarnock	0–1
1/6	Malta	Valletta	3–2
8/6	Belarus	Minsk	1–0 (WCQ)
7/9	Belarus	Aberdeen	4–1 (WCQ)
11/10	Latvia	Glasgow	2–0 (WCQ)
12/11	France	St Etienne	1–2

1998

Date	Opponents	Venue	F–A
25/3	Denmark	Glasgow	0–1
22/4	Finland	Edinburgh	1–1
23/5	Colombia	New Jersey	2–2
30/5	United States	Washington	0–0
10/6	Brazil	St Denis	1–2 (WCF)
16/6	Norway	Bordeaux	1–1 (WCF)
23/6	Morocco	St Etienne	0–3 (WCF)

INTERNATIONAL RESULTS –
NORTHERN IRELAND (Including Ireland results up to 1926)

KEY TO ABBREVIATIONS			
WCQ = *World Cup Qualifier*		WCF = *World Cup Finals*	
ECQ = *European Championship Qualifier*		ECF = *European Championship Finals*	

Date	Opponents	Venue	F-A
18/2/1882	**England**	Belfast	0–13
25/2/82	**Wales**	Wrexham	1–7
24/2/83	**England**	Liverpool	0–7
17/3/83	**Wales**	Belfast	1–1
26/1/84	**Scotland**	Belfast	0–5
9/2/84	**Wales**	Wrexham	0–6
23/2/84	**England**	Belfast	1–8
28/2/85	**England**	Manchester	0–4
14/3/85	**Scotland**	Glasgow	2–8
11/4/85	**Wales**	Belfast	2–8
27/2/86	**Wales**	Wrexham	0–5
13/3/86	**England**	Belfast	1–6
20/3/86	**Scotland**	Belfast	2–7
5/2/87	**England**	Sheffield	0–7
19/2/87	**Scotland**	Glasgow	1–4
12/3/87	**Wales**	Belfast	4–1
3/3/88	**Wales**	Wrexham	0–11
24/3/88	**Scotland**	Belfast	2–10
7/4/88	**England**	Belfast	1–5
2/3/89	**England**	Liverpool	1–6
9/3/89	**Scotland**	Glasgow	0–7
27/4/89	**Wales**	Belfast	1–3
8/2/90	**Wales**	Shrewsbury	2–5
15/3/90	**England**	Belfast	1–9
29/3/90	**Scotland**	Belfast	1–4
7/2/91	**Wales**	Belfast	7–2
7/3/91	**England**	Wolverhampton	1–6
28/3/91	**Scotland**	Glasgow	1–2
27/2/92	**Wales**	Bangor	1–1
5/3/92	**England**	Belfast	0–2
19/3/92	**Scotland**	Belfast	2–3
25/2/93	**England**	Birmingham	1–6
25/3/93	**Scotland**	Glasgow	1–6
5/4/93	**Wales**	Belfast	4–3
24/2/94	**Wales**	Swansea	1–4
3/3/94	**England**	Belfast	2–2
31/3/94	**Scotland**	Belfast	1–2
9/3/95	**England**	Derby	0–9
16/3/95	**Wales**	Belfast	2–2
30/3/95	**Scotland**	Glasgow	1–3
29/2/96	**Wales**	Wrexham	1–6
7/3/96	**England**	Belfast	0–2
28/3/96	**Scotland**	Belfast	3–3
20/2/97	**England**	Nottingham	0–6
6/3/97	**Wales**	Belfast	4–3
27/3/97	**Scotland**	Glasgow	1–5
19/2/98	**Wales**	Llandudno	1–0
5/3/98	**England**	Belfast	2–3
26/3/98	**Scotland**	Belfast	0–3
18/299	**England**	Sunderland	2–13

Date	Opponents	Venue	F-A
4/3/99	**Wales**	Belfast	1–0
25/3/99	**Scotland**	Glasgow	1–9
24/2/1900	**Wales**	Llandudno	0–2
3/3/00	**Scotland**	Belfast	0–3
17/3/00	**England**	Dublin	0–2
23/2/01	**Scotland**	Glasgow	0–11
9/3/01	**England**	Southampton	0–3
23/3/01	**Wales**	Belfast	0–1
22/2/02	**Wales**	Cardiff	3–0
1/3/02	**Scotland**	Belfast	1–3
22/3/02	**England**	Belfast	0–1
14/2/03	**England**	Wolverhampton	0–4
21/3/03	**Scotland**	Glasgow	2–0
28/3/03	**Wales**	Belfast	2–0
12/3/04	**England**	Belfast	1–3
21/3/04	**Wales**	Bangor	1–0
26/3/04	**Scotland**	Dublin	1–1
25/2/05	**England**	Middlesbrough	1–1
18/3/05	**Scotland**	Glasgow	0–4
8/4/05	**Wales**	Belfast	2–2
17/2/06	**England**	Belfast	0–5
17/3/06	**Scotland**	Dublin	0–1
2/4/06	**Wales**	Wrexham	4–4
16/2/07	**England**	Liverpool	0–1
23/2/07	**Wales**	Belfast	2–3
16/3/07	**Scotland**	Glasgow	0–3
15/2/08	**England**	Belfast	1–3
14/3/08	**Scotland**	Dublin	0–5
11/4/08	**Wales**	Aberdare	1–0
13/2/09	**England**	Bradford	0–4
15/309	**Scotland**	Glasgow	0–5
20/3/09	**Wales**	Belfast	2–3
12/2/10	**England**	Belfast	1–1
19/3/10	**Scotland**	Belfast	1–0
11/4/10	**Wales**	Wrexham	1–4
28/1/11	**Wales**	Belfast	1–2
11/2/11	**England**	Derby	1–2
18/3/11	**Scotland**	Glasgow	0–2
10/2/12	**England**	Dublin	1–6
16/3/12	**Scotland**	Belfast	1–4
13/4/12	**Wales**	Cardiff	3–2
18/1/13	**Wales**	Belfast	0–1
15/2/13	**England**	Belfast	2–1
15/3/13	**Scotland**	Dublin	1–2
19/1/14	**Wales**	Wrexham	2–1
14/2/14	**England**	Middlesbrough	3–0
14/3/14	**Scotland**	Belfast	1–1
25/10/19	**England**	Belfast	1–1
14/2/20	**Wales**	Belfast	2–2
13/3/20	**Scotland**	Glasgow	0–3

Date	Opponents	Venue	F–A
23/10/20	England	Sunderland	0–2
26/2/21	Scotland	Belfast	0–2
9/4/21	Wales	Swansea	1–2
22/10/21	England	Belfast	1–1
4/3/22	Scotland	Glasgow	1–2
1/4/22	Wales	Belfast	1–1
21/10/22	England	West Bromwich	0–2
3/3/23	Scotland	Belfast	0–1
14/4/23	Wales	Wrexham	3–0
20/10/23	England	Belfast	2–1
1/3/24	Scotland	Glasgow	0–2
15/3/24	Wales	Belfast	0–1
22/10/24	England	Liverpool	1–3
28/2/25	Scotland	Belfast	0–3
18/4/25	Wales	Wrexham	0–0
24/10/25	England	Belfast	0–0
13/226	Wales	Belfast	3–0
27/2/26	Scotland	Glasgow	0–4
20/10/26	England	Liverpool	3–3
26/2/27	Scotland	Belfast	0–2
19/4/27	Wales	Cardiff	2–2
22/10/27	England	Belfast	2–0
4/2/28	Wales	Belfast	1–2
25/2/28	Scotland	Glasgow	1–0
22/10/28	England	Liverpool	1–2
2/2/29	Wales	Wrexham	2–2
23/2/29	Scotland	Belfast	3–7
19/10/29	England	Belfast	0–3
1/2/30	Wales	Belfast	0–7
22/2/30	Scotland	Glasgow	1–3
20/10/30	England	Sheffield	1–5
21/2/31	Scotland	Belfast	0–0
22/4/31	Wales	Wrexham	2–3
19/9/31	Scotland	Glasgow	1–3
17/10/31	England	Belfast	2–6
5/12/31	Wales	Belfast	4–0
12/9/32	Scotland	Belfast	0–4
17/10/32	England	Blackpool	0–1
7/12/32	Wales	Wrexham	1–4
16/9/33	Scotland	Glasgow	2–1
14/10/33	England	Belfast	0–3
4/11/33	Wales	Belfast	1–1
20/10/34	Scotland	Belfast	2–1
6/2/35	England	Liverpool	1–2
27/3/35	Wales	Wrexham	1–3
19/10/35	England	Belfast	1–3
13/11/35	Scotland	Edinburgh	1–2
11/3/36	Wales	Belfast	3–2
31/10/36	Scotland	Belfast	1–3
18/11/36	England	Stoke–on–Trent	1–3
17/3/37	Wales	Wrexham	1–4
23/10/37	England	Belfast	1–5
10/11/37	Scotland	Aberdeen	1–1
16/3/38	Wales	Belfast	1–0
8/11/38	Scotland	Belfast	0–2
16/11/38	England	Manchester	0–7
15/3/39	Wales	Wrexham	1–3
28/9/40	England	Belfast	2–7
27/11/40	Scotland	Glasgow	0–0
16/4/47	Wales	Belfast	2–1
4/10/47	Scotland	Belfast	2–0

Date	Opponents	Venue	F–A
5/11/47	England	Everton	2–2
10/3/48	Wales	Wrexham	0–2
9/10/48	England	Belfast	2–6
17/11/48	Scotland	Glasgow	2–3
9/3/49	Wales	Belfast	0–2
1/10/49	Scotland	Belfast	2–8 (WCQ)
6/11/49	England	Manchester	2–9 (WCQ)
8/3/50	Wales	Wrexham	0–0 (WCQ)
7/10/50	England	Belfast	1–4
1/11/50	Scotland	Glasgow	1–6
7/3/51	Wales	Belfast	1–2
12/5/51	France	Belfast	2–2
6/10/51	Scotland	Belfast	0–3
20/11/51	England	Villa Park	0–2
19/3/52	Wales	Swansea	0–3
4/10/52	England	Belfast	2–2
5/11/52	Scotland	Glasgow	1–1
11/11/52	France	Paris	1–3
15/4/53	Wales	Belfast	2–3
3/10/53	Scotland	Belfast	1–3 (WCQ)
11/11/53	England	Everton	1–3 (WCQ)
31/3/54	Wales	Wrexham	2–1 (WCQ)
2/10/54	England	Belfast	0–2
3/11/54	Scotland	Glasgow	2–2
20/4/55	Wales	Belfast	2–3
8/10/55	Scotland	Belfast	2–1
2/11/55	England	Wembley	0–3
11/4/56	Wales	Cardiff	1–1
6/10/56	England	Belfast	1–1
7/11/56	Scotland	Glasgow	0–1
16/1/57	Portugal	Lisbon	1–1 (WCQ)
10/4/57	Wales	Belfast	0–0
25/4/57	Italy	Rome	0–1 (WCQ)
1/5/57	Portugal	Belfast	3–0 (WCQ)
5/10/57	Scotland	Belfast	1–1
6/11/57	England	Wembley	3–2
4/12/57	Italy	Belfast	2–2
15/1/58	Italy	Belfast	2–1 (WCQ)
16/4/58	Wales	Cardiff	1–1
8/10/58	Czechoslovakia	Halmstad	1–0 (WCF)
11/6/58	Argentina	Halmstad	1–3 (WCF)
15/6/58	West Germany	Malmo	2–2 (WCF)
17/6/58	Czechoslovakia	Malmo	2–1 (WCF)
19/6/58	France	Norrkoping	0–4 (WCF)
4/10/58	England	Belfast	3–3
15/10/58	Spain	Madrid	2–6
5/11/58	Scotland	Glasgow	2–2
22/4//59	Wales	Belfast	4–1
3/10/59	Scotland	Belfast	0–4
18/11/59	England	Wembley	1–2

1960

Date	Opponents	Venue	F–A
6/4	**Wales**	Wrexham	2–3
8/10	**England**	Belfast	2–5
26/10	**W Germany**	Belfast	3–4 (WCQ)
9/11	**Scotland**	Glasgow	2–5

1961

Date	Opponents	Venue	F–A
12/4	**Wales**	Belfast	1–5
25/4	**Italy**	Bologna	2–3
3/5	**Greece**	Athens	1–2 (WCQ)
10/5	**W Germany**	Berlin	1–2 (WCQ)
7/10	**Scotland**	Belfast	1–6
17/10	**Greece**	Belfast	2–0 (WCQ)
22/11	**England**	Wembley	1–1

1962

Date	Opponents	Venue	F–A
11/4	**Wales**	Cardiff	0–4
9/5	**Holland**	Rotterdam	0–4
10/10	**Poland**	Katowice	2–0 (ECQ)
20/10	**England**	Belfast	1–3
7/11	**Scotland**	Glasgow	1–5
28/11	**Poland**	Belfast	2–0 (ECQ)

1963

Date	Opponents	Venue	F–A
3/4	**Wales**	Belfast	1–4
30/5	**Spain**	Bilbao	1–1
12/10	**Scotland**	Belfast	2–1
30/10	**Spain**	Belfast	0–1
20/11	**England**	Wembley	3–8

1964

Date	Opponents	Venue	F–A
15/4	**Wales**	Swansea	3–2
29/4	**Uruguay**	Belfast	3–0
3/10	**England**	Belfast	3–4
14/10	**Switzerland**	Belfast	1–0 (WCQ)
14/11	**Switzerland**	Lausanne	1–2 (WCQ)
25/11	**Scotland**	Glasgow	2–3

1965

Date	Opponents	Venue	F–A
17/3	**Holland**	Belfast	2–1 (WCQ)
31/3	**Wales**	Belfast	0–5
7/4	**Holland**	Rotterdam	0–0 (WCQ)
7/5	**Albania**	Belfast	4–1 (WCQ)
2/10	**Scotland**	Belfast	3–2

1965 *continued*

Date	Opponents	Venue	F–A
10/11	**England**	Wembley	1–2
24/11	**Albania**	Tirana	1–1 (WCQ)

1966

Date	Opponents	Venue	F–A
30/3	**Wales**	Cardiff	4–1
7/5	**W Germany**	Belfast	0–2
22/6	**Mexico**	Belfast	4–1
22/10	**England**	Belfast	0–2 (ECQ)
16/11	**Scotland**	Glasgow	1–2

1967

Date	Opponents	Venue	F–A
12/4	**Wales**	Belfast	0–0 (ECQ)
21/10	**Scotland**	Belfast	1–0
22/11	**England**	Wembley	0–2 (ECQ)

1968

Date	Opponents	Venue	F–A
28/2	**Wales**	Wrexham	0–2 (ECQ)
10/9	**Israel**	Jaffa	3–2
23/10	**Turkey**	Belfast	4–1 (WCQ)
11/12	**Turkey**	Istanbul	3–0 (WCQ)

1969

Date	Opponents	Venue	F–A
3/5	**England**	Belfast	1–3
6/5	**Scotland**	Glasgow	1–1
10/5	**Wales**	Belfast	0–0
10/9	**USSR**	Belfast	0–0 (WCQ)
22/10	**USSR**	Moscow	0–2 (WCQ)

1970

Date	Opponents	Venue	F–A
18/4	**Scotland**	Belfast	0–1
21/4	**England**	Wembley	1–3
25/4	**Wales**	Swansea	0–1
11/11	**Spain**	Seville	0–3 (ECQ)

1971

Date	Opponents	Venue	F–A
3/2	**Cyprus**	Nicosia	3–0 (ECQ)
21/4	**Cyprus**	Belfast	5–0 (ECQ)
15/5	**England**	Belfast	0–1
18/5	**Scotland**	Glasgow	1–0
22/5	**Wales**	Belfast	1–0

1971 *continued*

Date	Opponents	Venue	F–A
22/9	USSR	Moscow	0–1 (ECQ)
13/10	USSR	Belfast	1–1 (ECQ)

1972

Date	Opponents	Venue	F–A
16/2	Spain	Hull	1–1 (ECQ)
20/5	Scotland	Glasgow	0–2
23/5	England	Wembley	1–0
27/5	Wales	Wrexham	0–0
18/10	Bulgaria	Sofia	0–3 (WCQ)

1973

Date	Opponents	Venue	F–A
14/2	Cyprus	Nicosia	0–1 (WCQ)
28/3	Portugal	Coventry	1–1 (WCQ)
8/5	Cyprus	London	3–0 (WCQ)
12/5	England	Liverpool	1–2
16/5	Scotland	Glasgow	2–1
19/5	Wales	Liverpool	1–0
26/9	Bulgaria	Hillsborough	0–0 (WCQ)
14/11	Portugal	Lisbon	1–1 (WCQ)

1974

Date	Opponents	Venue	F–A
11/5	Scotland	Glasgow	1–0
15/5	England	Wembley	0–1
18/5	Wales	Wrexham	0–1
4/9	Norway	Oslo	1–2 (ECQ)
30/10	Sweden	Solna	2–0 (ECQ)

1975

Date	Opponents	Venue	F–A
16/3	Yugoslavia	Belfast	1–0 (ECQ)
17/5	England	Belfast	0–0
20/5	Scotland	Glasgow	0–3
23/5	Wales	Belfast	1–0
3/9	Sweden	Belfast	1–2 (ECQ)
29/10	Norway	Belfast	3–0 (ECQ)
19/11	Yugoslavia	Belgrade	0–1 (ECQ)

1976

Date	Opponents	Venue	F–A
24/3	Israel	Tel Aviv	1–1
8/5	Scotland	Glasgow	0–3
11/5	England	Wembley	0–4
14/5	Wales	Swansea	0–1
13/10	Holland	Rotterdam	2–2 (WCQ)
10/11	Belgium	Liège	0–2 (WCQ)

1977

Date	Opponents	Venue	F–A
27/4	W Germany	Cologne	0–5
28/5	England	Belfast	1–2
1/6	Scotland	Glasgow	0–2
3/6	Wales	Belfast	1–1
11/6	Iceland	Reykjavik	0–1 (WCQ)
21/9	Iceland	Belfast	2–0 (WCQ)
12/10	Holland	Belfast	0–1 (WCQ)
16/11	Belgium	Belfast	3–0 (WCQ)

1978

Date	Opponents	Venue	F–A
13/5	Scotland	Glasgow	1–1
16/5	England	Wembley	0–1
19/5	Wales	Wrexham	0–1
20/9	Rep of Ireland	Dublin	0–0 (ECQ)
25/10	Denmark	Belfast	2–1 (ECQ)
29/11	Bulgaria	Sofia	2–0 (ECQ)

1979

Date	Opponents	Venue	F–A
7/2	England	Wembley	0–4 (ECQ)
2/5	Bulgaria	Belfast	2–0 (ECQ)
19/5	England	Belfast	0–2
22/5	Scotland	Glasgow	0–1
25/5	Wales	Belfast	1–1
6/6	Denmark	Copenhagen	0–4 (ECQ)
17/10	England	Belfast	1–5 (ECQ)
21/11	Rep of Ireland	Belfast	1–0 (ECQ)

1980

Date	Opponents	Venue	F–A
26/3	Israel	Tel Aviv	0–0 (WCQ)
16/5	Scotland	Belfast	1–0
20/5	England	Wembley	1–1
23/5	Wales	Cardiff	1–0
11/6	Australia	Sydney	2–1
15/6	Australia	Melbourne	1–1
18/6	Australia	Adelaide	2–1
15/10	Sweden	Belfast	3–0 (WCQ)
19/11	Portugal	Lisbon	0–1 (WCQ)

1981

Date	Opponents	Venue	F–A
25/3	Scotland	Glasgow	1–1 (WCQ)
29/4	Portugal	Belfast	1–0 (WCQ)
19/5	Scotland	Glasgow	0–2
3/6	Sweden	Stockholm	0–1 (WCQ)
14/10	Scotland	Belfast	0–0 (WCQ)
18/11	Israel	Belfast	1–0 (WCQ)

1982

Date	Opponents	Venue	F–A
23/2	**England**	Wembley	0–4
24/3	**France**	Paris	0–4
28/4	**Scotland**	Belfast	1–1
27/5	**Wales**	Wrexham	0–3
17/6	**Yugoslavia**	Zaragoza	0–0 (WCF)
21/6	**Honduras**	Zaragoza	1–1 (WCF)
25/6	**Spain**	Valencia	1–0 (WCF)
1/7	**Austria**	Madrid	2–2 (WCF)
4/7	**France**	Madrid	1–4 (WCF)
13/10	**Austria**	Vienna	0–2 (ECQ)
17/11	**W Germany**	Belfast	1–0 (ECQ)
15/12	**Albania**	Tirana	0–0 (ECQ)

1983

Date	Opponents	Venue	F–A
30/3	**Turkey**	Belfast	2–1 (ECQ)
27/4	**Albania**	Belfast	1–0 (ECQ)
24/5	**Scotland**	Glasgow	0–0
28/5	**England**	Belfast	0–0
31/5	**Wales**	Belfast	0–I
21/9	**Austria**	Belfast	3–1 (ECQ)
12/10	**Turkey**	Ankara	0–1 (ECQ)
16/11	**W Germany**	Hamburg	1–0 (ECQ)
13/12	**Scotland**	Belfast	2–0

1984

Date	Opponents	Venue	F–A
4/4	**England**	Wembley	0–1
22/5	**Wales**	Swansea	1–1
27/5	**Finland**	Pori	0–1 (WCQ)
12/9	**Romania**	Belfast	3–2 (WCQ)
16/10	**Israel**	Belfast	3–0
14/11	**Finland**	Belfast	2–1 (WCQ)

1985

Date	Opponents	Venue	F–A
27/2	**England**	Belfast	0–1 (WCQ)
27/3	**Spain**	Palma	0–0
1/5	**Turkey**	Belfast	2–0 (WCQ)
11/9	**Turkey**	Izmir	0–0 (WCQ)
16/10	**Romania**	Bucharest	1–0 (WCQ)
13/11	**England**	Wembley	0–0 (WCQ)

1986

Date	Opponents	Venue	F–A
26/2	**France**	Paris	0–0
26/3	**Denmark**	Belfast	1–1
23/4	**Morocco**	Belfast	2–1
3/6	**Algeria**	Guadalajara	1–1 (WCF)
7/6	**Spain**	Guadalajara	1–2 (WCF)
12/6	**Brazil**	Guadalajara	0–3 (WCF)

1986 *continued*

Date	Opponents	Venue	F–A
15/10	**England**	Wembley	0–3 (ECQ)
12/11	**Turkey**	Izmir	0–0 (ECQ)

1987

Date	Opponents	Venue	F–A
18/2	**Israel**	Tel Aviv	1–1
1/4	**England**	Belfast	0–2 (ECQ)
29/4	**Yugoslavia**	Belfast	1–2 (ECQ)
14/10	**Yugoslavia**	Sarajevo	0–3 (ECQ)
11/11	**Turkey**	Belfast	1–0 (ECQ)

1988

Date	Opponents	Venue	F–A
17/2	**Greece**	Athens	2–3
23/3	**Poland**	Belfast	1–1
27/4	**France**	Belfast	0–0
21/5	**Malta**	Belfast	3–0 (WCQ)
14/9	**Rep of Ireland**	Belfast	0–0 (WCQ)
19/10	**Hungary**	Budapest	0–1 (WCQ)
21/12	**Spain**	Seville	0–4 (WCQ)

1989

Date	Opponents	Venue	F–A
8/2	**Spain**	Belfast	0–2 (WCQ)
26/4	**Malta**	Valletta	2–0 (WCQ)
26/5	**Chile**	Belfast	0–1
6/9	**Hungary**	Belfast	1–2 (WCQ)
11/10	**Rep of Ireland**	Dublin	0–3 (WCQ)

1990

Date	Opponents	Venue	F–A
27/3	**Norway**	Belfast	2–3
18/5	**Uruguay**	Belfast	1–0
12/9	**Yugoslavia**	Belfast	0–2 (ECQ)
17/10	**Denmark**	Belfast	1–1 (ECQ)
14/11	**Austria**	Vienna	0–0 (ECQ)

1991

Date	Opponents	Venue	F–A
5/2	**Poland**	Belfast	3–1
27/3	**Yugoslavia**	Belgrade	1–4 (ECQ)
1/5	**Faeroes**	Belfast	1–1 (ECQ)
11/9	**Faeroes**	Landskrona	5–0 (ECQ)
16/10	**Austria**	Belfast	2–1 (ECQ)
13/11	**Denmark**	Odense	1–2 (ECQ)

1992

Date	Opponents	Venue	F–A
28/4	**Lithuania**	Belfast	2–2 (WCQ)
2/6	**Germany**	Bremen	1–1
9/9	**Albania**	Belfast	3–0 (WCQ)
14/10	**Spain**	Belfast	0–0 (WCQ)
18/11	**Denmark**	Belfast	0–1 (WCQ)

1993

Date	Opponents	Venue	F–A
17/2	**Albania**	Tirana	2–1 (WCQ)
31/3	**Rep of Ireland**	Dublin	0–3 (WCQ)
28/4	**Spain**	Seville	1–3 (WCQ)
25/5	**Lithuania**	Vilnius	1–0 (WCQ)
2/6	**Latvia**	Riga	2–1 (WCQ)
8/9	**Latvia**	Belfast	2–0 (WCQ)
13/10	**Denmark**	Copenhagen	0–1 (WCQ)
17/11	**Rep of Ireland**	Belfast	1–1 (WCQ)

1994

Date	Opponents	Venue	F–A
20/4	**Liechtenstein**	Belfast	4–1 (ECQ)
3/6	**Colombia**	Boston	0–2
12/6	**Mexico**	Miami	0–3
7/9	**Portugal**	Belfast	1–2 (ECQ)
12/10	**Austria**	Vienna	2–1 (ECQ)
16/11	**Rep of Ireland**	Belfast	0–4 (ECQ)

1995

Date	Opponents	Venue	F–A
29/3	**Rep of Ireland**	Dublin	1–1 (ECQ)
26/4	**Latvia**	Riga	1–0 (ECQ)
22/5	**Canada**	Edmonton	0–2
25/5	**Chile**	Edmonton	1–2
7/6	**Latvia**	Belfast	1–2 (ECQ)
26/4	**Latvia**	Riga	1–0 (ECQ)
3/9	**Portugal**	Lisbon	1–1 (ECQ)
11/10	**Liechtenstein**	Eschen	4–0 (ECQ)
15/11	**Austria**	Belfast	5–3 (ECQ)

1996

Date	Opponents	Venue	F–A
27/3	**Norway**	Belfast	0–2
24/4	**Sweden**	Belfast	1–2
29/5	**Germany**	Belfast	1–1
31/8	**Ukraine**	Belfast	0–1 (WCQ)
5/10	**Armenia**	Belfast	1–1 (WCQ)
9/11	**Germany**	Nüremburg	1–1 (WCQ)
14/12	**Albania**	Belfast	2–0 (WCQ)

1997

Date	Opponents	Venue	F–A
29/3	**Portugal**	Belfast	0–0 (WCQ)
2/4	**Ukraine**	Kiev	1–2 (WCQ)
30/4	**Armenia**	Yerevan	0–0 (WCQ)
21/5	**Thailand**	Bangkok	0–0
20/8	**Germany**	Belfast	1–3 (WCQ)
10/9	**Albania**	Zurich	0–1 (WCQ)
11/10	**Portugal**	Lisbon	0–1 (WCQ)

1998

Date	Opponents	Venue	F–A
25/3	**Slovakia**	Belfast	1–0
22/4	**Switzerland**	Belfast	1–0

INTERNATIONAL RESULTS – WALES

KEY TO ABBREVIATIONS	
WCQ =	*World Cup Qualifier*
ECQ =	*European Championship Qualifier*
WCF =	*World Cup Finals*
ECF =	*European Championship Finals*

Date	Opponents	Venue	F-A
25/3/76	Scotland	Glasgow	0–4
5/3/77	Scotland	Wrexham	0–2
23/3/78	Scotland	Glasgow	0–9
18/1/79	England	London	1–2
7/4/79	Scotland	Wrexham	0–3
15/3/80	England	Wrexham	2–3
27/3/80	Scotland	Glasgow	1–5
26/2/81	England	Blackburn	1–0
14/3/81	Scotland	Wrexham	1–5
25/2/82	Ireland	Wrexham	7–1
15/3/82	England	Wrexham	5–3
25/3/82	Scotland	Glasgow	0–5
3/2/83	England	London	0–5
12/3/83	Scotland	Wrexham	0–3
17/3/83	Ireland	Belfast	1–1
9/2/84	Ireland	Wrexham	6–0
17/3/84	England	Wrexham	0–4
29/3/84	Scotland	Glasgow	1–4
14/3/85	England	Blackburn	1–1
23/3/85	Scotland	Wrexham	1–8
11/4/85	Ireland	Belfast	8–2
27/2/86	Ireland	Wrexham	5–0
29/3/86	England	Wrexham	1–3
10/4/86	Scotland	Glasgow	1–4
26/2/87	England	London	0–4
12/3/87	Ireland	Belfast	1–4
21/3/87	Scotland	Wrexham	0–2
4/2/88	England	Crewe	1–5
3/3/88	Ireland	Wrexham	11–0
10/3/88	Scotland	Edinburgh	1–5
23/2/89	England	Stoke	1–4
15/4/89	Scotland	Wrexham	0–0
27/4/89	Ireland	Belfast	3–1
8/2/90	Ireland	Shrewsbury	5–2
15/3/90	England	Wrexham	1–3
22/3/90	Scotland	Glasgow	0–5
7/2/91	Ireland	Belfast	2–7
7/3/91	England	Sunderland	1–4
21/3/91	Scotland	Wrexham	3–4
27/2/92	Ireland	Bangor	1–1
5/3/92	England	Wrexham	0–2
26/3/92	Scotland	Edinburgh	1–6
13/3/93	England	Stoke–on–Trent	0–6
18/3/93	Scotland	Wrexham	0–8
5/4/93	Ireland	Belfast	3–4
24/2/94	Ireland	Swansea	4–1
12/3/94	England	Wrexham	1–5
24/3/94	Scotland	Kilmarnock	2–5
16/3/95	Ireland	Belfast	2–2
18/3/95	England	London	1–1

Date	Opponents	Venue	F-A
23/3/95	Scotland	Wrexham	2–2
29/2/96	Ireland	Wrexham	6–1
16/3/96	England	Cardiff	1–9
21/3/96	Scotland	Dundee	0–4
6/3/97	Ireland	Belfast	3–4
20/3/97	Scotland	Wrexham	2–2
29/3/97	England	Sheffield	0–4
19/2/98	Ireland	Llandudno	0–1
19/3/98	Scotland	Motherwell	2–5
28/3/98	England	Wrexham	0–3
4/3/99	Ireland	Belfast	0–1
18/3/99	Scotland	Wrexham	0–6
20/3/99	England	Bristol	0–4

1900–1959

Date	Opponents	Venue	F-A
3/2/00	Scotland	Aberdeen	2–5
24/2/00	Ireland	Llandudno	2–0
26/3/00	England	Cardiff	1–1
2/3/01	Scotland	Wrexham	1–1
18/3/01	England	Newcastle	0–6
23/3/01	Ireland	Belfast	1–0
22/2/02	Ireland	Cardiff	0–3
3/3/02	England	Wrexham	0–0
15/3/02	Scotland	Greenock	1–5
2/3/03	England	Portsmouth	1–2
9/3/03	Scotland	Cardiff	0–1
28/3/03	Ireland	Belfast	0–2
29/2/04	England	Wrexham	2–2
12/3/04	Scotland	Dundee	1–1
21/3/04	Ireland	Bangor	0–1
6/3/05	Scotland	Wrexham	3–1
27/3/05	England	Liverpool	1–5
8/4/05	Ireland	Belfast	2–2
3/3/06	Scotland	Edinburgh	2–0
19/3/06	England	Cardiff	0–1
2/4/06	Ireland	Wrexham	4–4
23/2/07	Ireland	Belfast	3–2
4/3/07	Scotland	Wrexham	1–0
18/3/07	England	Fulham	1–1
7/3/08	Scotland	Dundee	1–2
16/3/08	England	Wrexham	1–7
11/4/08	Ireland	Aberdare	0–1
1/3/09	Scotland	Wrexham	3–2
15/3/09	England	Nottingham	0–2
20/3/09	Ireland	Belfast	3–2
5/3/10	Scotland	Kilmarnock	0–1
14/3/10	England	Cardiff	0–1

Date	Opponents	Venue	F–A
11/4/10	**Ireland**	Wrexham	4–1
28/1/11	**Ireland**	Belfast	2–1
6/3/11	**Scotland**	Cardiff	2–2
13/3/11	**England**	London	0–3
2/3/12	**Scotland**	Edinburgh	0–1
11/3/12	**England**	Wrexham	0–2
13/4/12	**Ireland**	Cardiff	2–3
18/1/13	**Ireland**	Belfast	1–0
3/3/13	**Scotland**	Wrexham	0–0
17/3/13	**England**	Bristol	3–4
19/1/14	**Ireland**	Wrexham	1–2
28/2/14	**Scotland**	Glasgow	0–0
16/3/14	**England**	Cardiff	0–2
14/2/20	**Ireland**	Belfast	2–2
26/2/20	**Scotland**	Cardiff	1–1
15/3/20	**England**	London	2–1
12/2/21	**Scotland**	Aberdeen	1–2
16/3/21	**England**	Cardiff	0–0
9/4/21	**Ireland**	Swansea	2–1
4/2/22	**Scotland**	Wrexham	2–1
13/3/22	**England**	Liverpool	0–1
1/4/22	**Ireland**	Belfast	1–1
5/3/23	**England**	Cardiff	2–2
17/3/23	**Scotland**	Glasgow	0–2
14/4/23	**Ireland**	Wrexham	0–3
16/2/24	**Scotland**	Cardiff	2–0
3/3/24	**England**	Blackburn	2–1
15/3/24	**Ireland**	Belfast	1–0
14/2/25	**Scotland**	Edinburgh	1–3
28/2/25	**England**	Swansea	1–2
18/4/25	**Ireland**	Wrexham	0–0
31/10/25	**Scotland**	Cardiff	0–3
13/2/26	**Ireland**	Belfast	0–3
1/3/26	**England**	London	3–1
30/10/26	**Scotland**	Glasgow	0–3
14/2/27	**England**	Wrexham	3–3
9/4/27	**Ireland**	Cardiff	2–2
29/10/27	**Scotland**	Wrexham	2–2
28/11/27	**England**	Burnley	2–1
4/2/28	**Ireland**	Belfast	2–1
27/10/28	**Scotland**	Glasgow	2–4
17/11/28	**England**	Swansea	2–3
2/2/29	**Ireland**	Wrexham	2–2
26/10/29	**Scotland**	Cardiff	2–4
20/11/29	**England**	London	0–6
1/2/30	**Ireland**	Belfast	0–7
25/10/30	**Scotland**	Glasgow	1–1
22/11/30	**England**	Wrexham	0–4
22/4/31	**Ireland**	Wrexham	3–2
31/10/31	**Scotland**	Wrexham	2–3
18/11/31	**England**	Liverpool	1–3
5/12/31	**Ireland**	Belfast	0–4
26/10/32	**Scotland**	Edinburgh	5–2
16/11/32	**England**	Wrexham	0–0
7/12/32	**Ireland**	Wrexham	4–1
25/5/33	**France**	Paris	1–1
4/10/33	**Scotland**	Cardiff	3–2
4/11/33	**Ireland**	Belfast	1–1
15/11/33	**England**	Newcastle	2–1
29/9/34	**England**	Cardiff	0–4
21/11/34	**Scotland**	Aberdeen	2–3

Date	Opponents	Venue	F–A
27/3/35	**Ireland**	Wrexham	3–1
5/10/35	**Scotland**	Cardiff	1–1
5/2/36	**England**	Wolverhampton	2–1
11/3/36	**Ireland**	Belfast	2–3
17/10/36	**England**	Cardiff	2–1
2/12/36	**Scotland**	Dundee	2–1
17/3/37	**Ireland**	Wrexham	4–1
30/10/37	**Scotland**	Cardiff	2–1
17/11/37	**England**	Middlesbrough	1–2
16/3/38	**Ireland**	Belfast	0–1
22/10/38	**England**	Cardiff	4–2
9/11/38	**Scotland**	Edinburgh	2–3
15/3/39	**Ireland**	Wrexham	3–1
20/5/39	**France**	Paris	1–2
19/10/46	**Scotland**	Wrexham	3–1
13/11/46	**England**	Manchester	0–3
16/4/47	**N Ireland**	Belfast	1–2
18/10/47	**England**	Cardiff	0–3
12/11/47	**Scotland**	Glasgow	2–1
10/3/48	**N Ireland**	Wrexham	2–0
23/10/48	**Scotland**	Cardiff	1–3
10/11/48	**England**	Villa Park	0–1
9/3/49	**N Ireland**	Belfast	2–0
15/5/49	**Portugal**	Lisbon	2–3
23/5/49	**Belgium**	Liege	1–3
26/5/49	**Switzerland**	Berne	0–4
15/10/49	**England**	Cardiff	1–4 (WCQ)
9/11/49	**Scotland**	Glasgow	0–2 (WCQ)
23/11/49	**Belgium**	Cardiff	5–1
8/3/50	**N Ireland**	Wrexham	0–0 (WCQ)
21/10/50	**Scotland**	Cardiff	1–3
15/11/50	**England**	Sunderland	2–4
7/3/51	**N Ireland**	Belfast	2–1
12/5/51	**Portugal**	Cardiff	2–1
16/5/51	**Switzerland**	Wrexham	3–2
20/10/51	**England**	Cardiff	1–1
20/11/51	**Scotland**	Glasgow	1–0
5/12/51	**Rest of UK**	Cardiff	3–2
19/3/52	**N Ireland**	Swansea	3–0
18/10/52	**Scotland**	Cardiff	1–2
12/11/52	**England**	Wembley	2–5
15/4/53	**N Ireland**	Belfast	3–2
14/5/53	**France**	Paris	1–6
21/5/53	**Yugoslavia**	Belgrade	2–5
10/10/53	**England**	Cardiff	1–4 (WCQ)
4/11/53	**Scotland**	Glasgow	3–3 (WCQ)
31/3/54	**N Ireland**	Wrexham	1–2 (WCQ)
9/5/54	**Austria**	Vienna	0–2 (ECQ)
22/9/54	**Yugoslavia**	Cardiff	1–3
16/10/54	**Scotland**	Cardiff	0–1
10/11/54	**England**	Wembley	2–3
20/4/55	**N Ireland**	Belfast	3–2
22/10/55	**England**	Cardiff	2–1
9/11/55	**Scotland**	Glasgow	0–2
23/11/55	**Austria**	Wrexham	1–2 (ECQ)
11/4/56	**N Ireland**	Cardiff	1–1
20/10/56	**Scotland**	Cardiff	2–2
14/11/56	**England**	Wembley	1–3
10/4/57	**N Ireland**	Belfast	0–0
1/5/57	**Czechoslovakia**	Cardiff	1–0 (WCQ)
19/5/57	**E Germany**	Leipzig	1–2 (WCQ)

Date	Opponents	Venue	F–A
26/5/57	**Czechoslovakia**	Prague	0–2 (WCQ)
25/9/57	**E Germany**	Cardiff	4–1 (WCQ)
19/10/57	**England**	Cardiff	0–4
13/11/57	**Scotland**	Glasgow	1–1
15/1/58	**Israel**	Tel Aviv	2–0 (WCQ)
5/2/58	**Israel**	Cardiff	2–0 (WCQ)
16/4/58	**N Ireland**	Cardiff	1–1
8/6/58	**Hungary**	Sandviken	1–1 (WCF)
11/6/58	**Mexico**	Stockholm	1–1 (WCF)
15/6/58	**Sweden**	Stockholm	0–0 (WCF)
17/6/58	**Hungary**	Stockholm	2–1 (WCF)
19/6/58	**Brazil**	Gothenburg	0–1 (WCF)
18/10/58	**Scotland**	Cardiff	0–3
26/11/58	**England**	Villa Park	2–2
22/4/59	**N Ireland**	Belfast	1–4
17/10/59	**England**	Cardiff	1–1
4/11/59	**Scotland**	Glasgow	1–1

1960

Date	Opponents	Venue	F–A
6/4/60	**N Ireland**	Wrexham	3–2
28/9/60	**Rep of Ireland**	Dublin	3–2
22/10/60	**Scotland**	Cardiff	2–0
23/11/60	**England**	Wembley	1–5

1961

Date	Opponents	Venue	F–A
12/4/61	**N Ireland**	Belfast	5–1
19/4/61	**Spain**	Cardiff	1–2 (WCQ)
18/5/61	**Spain**	Madrid	1–1 (WCQ)
28/5/61	**Hungary**	Budapest	2–3
14/10/61	**England**	Cardiff	1–1
8/11/61	**Scotland**	Glasgow	0–2

1962

Date	Opponents	Venue	F–A
11/4/62	**N Ireland**	Cardiff	4–0
12/5/62	**Brazil**	Rio de Janeiro	1–3
16/5/62	**Brazil**	São Paulo	1–3
22/5/62	**Mexico**	Mexico City	1–2
20/10/62	**Scotland**	Cardiff	2–3
7/11/62	**Hungary**	Budapest	1–3 (ECQ)
21/11/62	**England**	Wembley	0–4

1963

Date	Opponents	Venue	F–A
20/3/63	**Hungary**	Cardiff	1–1 (ECQ)
3/4/63	**N Ireland**	Belfast	4–1
12/10/63	**England**	Cardiff	0–4
20/11/63	**Scotland**	Glasgow	1–2

1964

Date	Opponents	Venue	F–A
15/4/64	**N Ireland**	Swansea	2–3
3/10/64	**Scotland**	Cardiff	3–2
21/10/64	**Denmark**	Copenhagen	0–1 (WCQ)
18/11/64	**England**	Wembley	1–2
9/12/64	**Greece**	Athens	0–2 (WCQ)

1965

Date	Opponents	Venue	F–A
17/2/65	**Greece**	Cardiff	4–1 (WCQ)
31/3/65	**N Ireland**	Belfast	5–0
1/5/65	**Italy**	Florence	1–4
30/5/65	**USSR**	Moscow	1–2 (WCQ)
2/10/65	**England**	Cardiff	0–0
27/10/65	**USSR**	Cardiff	2–1 (WCQ)
24/11/65	**Scotland**	Glasgow	1–4 (ECQ)
1/12/65	**Denmark**	Wrexham	4–2 (WCQ)

1966

Date	Opponents	Venue	F–A
30/3/66	**N Ireland**	Cardiff	1–4
14/5/66	**Brazil**	Rio de Janeiro	1–3
18/5/66	**Brazil**	Belo Horizonte	0–1
22/5/66	**Chile**	Santiago	0–2
22/10/66	**Scotland**	Cardiff	1–1 (ECQ)
16/11/66	**England**	Wembley	1–5 (ECQ)

1967

Date	Opponents	Venue	F–A
12/4/67	**N Ireland**	Belfast	0–0 (ECQ)
21/10/67	**England**	Cardiff	0–3 (ECQ)
22/11/67	**Scotland**	Glasgow	2–3

1968

Date	Opponents	Venue	F–A
28/2/68	**N Ireland**	Wrexham	2–0 (ECQ)
8/5/68	**W Germany**	Cardiff	1–1
23/10/68	**Italy**	Cardiff	0–1 (WCQ)

1969

Date	Opponents	Venue	F–A
26/3/69	**W Germany**	Frankfurt	1–1
16/4/69	**E Germany**	Dresden	1–2 (WCQ)
3/5/69	**Scotland**	Wrexham	3–5
7/5/69	**England**	Wembley	1–2
10/5/69	**N Ireland**	Belfast	0–0
28/7/69	**Rest of UK**	Cardiff	0–1
22/10/69	**E Germany**	Cardiff	1–3 (WCQ)
4/11/69	**Italy**	Rome	1–4 (WCQ)

1970

Date	Opponents	Venue	F–A
18/4/70	England	Cardiff	1–1
22/4/70	Scotland	Glasgow	0–0
25/4/70	N Ireland	Swansea	1–0
11/11/70	Romania	Cardiff	0–0 (ECQ)

1971

Date	Opponents	Venue	F–A
21/4/71	Czechoslovakia	Swansea	1–3 (ECQ)
15/5/71	Scotland	Cardiff	0–0
18/5/71	England	Wembley	0–0
22/5/71	N Ireland	Belfast	0–1
26/5/71	Finland	Helsinki	1–0 (ECQ)
13/10/71	Finland	Swansea	3–0 (ECQ)
27/10/71	Czechoslovakia	Prague	0–1 (ECQ)
24/11/71	Romania	Bucharest	0–2 (ECQ)

1972

Date	Opponents	Venue	F–A
20/5/72	England	Cardiff	0–3
24/5/72	Scotland	Glasgow	0–1
27/5/72	N Ireland	Wrexham	0–0
15/11/72	England	Cardiff	0–1 (WCQ)

1973

Date	Opponents	Venue	F–A
24/1/73	England	Wembley	1–1 (WCQ)
28/3/73	Poland	Cardiff	2–0 (WCQ)
12/5/73	Scotland	Wrexham	0–2
15/5/73	England	Wembley	0–3
19/5/73	N Ireland	Liverpool	0–1
26/9/73	Poland	Chorzow	0–3 (WCQ)

1974

Date	Opponents	Venue	F–A
11/5/74	England	Cardiff	0–2
14/5/74	Scotland	Glasgow	0–2
18/5/74	N Ireland	Wrexham	1–0
4/9/74	Austria	Vienna	1–2 (ECQ)
30/10/74	Hungary	Cardiff	2–0 (ECQ)
20/11/74	Luxembourg	Swansea	5–0 (ECQ)

1975

Date	Opponents	Venue	F–A
16/4/75	Hungary	Budapest	2–1 (ECQ)
1/5/75	Luxembourg	Luxembourg	3–1 (ECQ)
17/5/75	Scotland	Cardiff	2–2
21/5/75	England	Wembley	2–2
23/5/75	N Ireland	Belfast	0–1
19/11/75	Austria	Wrexham	1–0 (ECQ)

1976

Date	Opponents	Venue	F–A
24/3/76	England	Wrexham	1–2
24/4/76	Yugoslavia	Zagreb	0–2 (ECQ)
6/5/76	Scotland	Glasgow	1–3
8/5/76	England	Cardiff	0–1
14/5/76	N Ireland	Swansea	1–0
22/5/76	Yugoslavia	Cardiff	1–1 (ECQ)
6/10/76	W Germany	Cardiff	0–2
17/11/76	Scotland	Glasgow	0–1 (WCQ)

1977

Date	Opponents	Venue	F–A
30/3/77	Czechoslovakia	Wrexham	3–0 (WCQ)
28/5/77	Scotland	Wrexham	0–0
31/5/77	England	Wembley	1–0
3/6/77	N Ireland	Belfast	1–1
6/9/77	Kuwait	Wrexham	0–0
20/9/77	Kuwait	Kuwait	0–0
12/10/77	Scotland	Liverpool	0–2 (WCQ)
16/11/77	Czechoslovakia	Prague	0–1 (WCQ)
14/12/77	W Germany	Dortmund	1–1

1978

Date	Opponents	Venue	F–A
18/4/78	Iran	Teheran	1–0
13/5/78	England	Cardiff	1–3
17/5/78	Scotland	Glasgow	1–1
19/5/78	N Ireland	Wrexham	1–0
25/10/78	Malta	Wrexham	7–0 (ECQ)
29/11/78	Turkey	Wrexham	1–0 (ECQ)

1979

Date	Opponents	Venue	F–A
2/5/79	W Germany	Wrexham	0–2 (ECQ)
19/5/79	Scotland	Cardiff	3–0
23/5/79	England	Wembley	0–0
25/5/79	N Ireland	Belfast	1–1
2/6/79	Malta	Valetta	2–0 (ECQ)
11/9/79	Rep of Ireland	Swansea	2–1
17/10/79	W Germany	Koln	1–5 (ECQ)
21/11/79	Turkey	Izmir	0–1 (ECQ)

1980

Date	Opponents	Venue	F–A
17/5	England	Wrexham	4–1
21/5	Scotland	Glasgow	0–1
23/5	N Ireland	Cardiff	0–1
2/6	Iceland	Reykjavik	4–0 (WCQ)
15/10	Turkey	Cardiff	4–0 (WCQ)
19/11	Czechoslovakia	Cardiff	1–0 (WCQ)

1981

Date	Opponents	Venue	F–A
24/2	**Rep of Ireland**	Dublin	3–1
25/3	**Turkey**	Ankara	1–0 (WCQ)
16/5	**Scotland**	Swansea	2–0
20/5	**England**	Wembley	0–0
30/5	**USSR**	Wrexham	0–0 (WCQ)
9/9	**Czechoslovakia**	Prague	0–2 (WCQ)
14/10	**Iceland**	Swansea	2–2 (WCQ)
18/11	**USSR**	Tbilisi	0–3 (WCQ)

1982

Date	Opponents	Venue	F–A
24/3	**Spain**	Valencia	1–1
27/4	**England**	Cardiff	0–1
24/5	**Scotland**	Glasgow	0–1
27/5	**N Ireland**	Wrexham	3–0
2/6	**France**	Toulouse	1–0
22/9	**Norway**	Swansea	1–0 (ECQ)
15/12	**Yugoslavia**	Titograd	4–4 (ECQ)

1983

Date	Opponents	Venue	F–A
23/2	**England**	Wembley	1–2
27/4	**Bulgaria**	Wrexham	1–0 (ECQ)
28/5	**Scotland**	Cardiff	0–2
31/5	**N Ireland**	Belfast	1–0
12/6	**Brazil**	Cardiff	1–1
21/9	**Norway**	Oslo	0–0 (ECQ)
12/10	**Romania**	Wrexham	5–0
16/11	**Bulgaria**	Sofia	0–1 (ECQ)
14/12	**Yugoslavia**	Cardiff	1–1 (ECQ)

1984

Date	Opponents	Venue	F–A
28/2	**Scotland**	Glasgow	1–2
2/5	**England**	Wrexham	1–0
22/5	**N Ireland**	Swansea	1–1
6/6	**Norway**	Trondheim	0–1
10/6	**Israel**	Tel Aviv	0–0
12/9	**Iceland**	Reykjavik	0–1 (WCQ)
17/10	**Spain**	Seville	0–3 (WCQ)
14/11	**Iceland**	Cardiff	2–1 (WCQ)

1985

Date	Opponents	Venue	F–A
26/2	**Norway**	Wrexham	1–1
27/3	**Scotland**	Glasgow	1–0 (WCQ)
30/4	**Spain**	Wrexham	3–0 (WCQ)
5/6	**Norway**	Bergen	2–4
10/9	**Scotland**	Cardiff	1–1 (WCQ)
16/10	**Hungary**	Cardiff	0–3

1986

Date	Opponents	Venue	F–A
25/2	**Saudi Arabia**	Dhahran	2–1
26/3	**Rep of Ireland**	Dublin	1–0
21/4	**Uruguay**	Cardiff	0–0
10/5	**Canada**	Toronto	0–2
20/5	**Canada**	Vancouver	3–0
10/9	**Finland**	Helsinki	1–1 (ECQ)

1987

Date	Opponents	Venue	F–A
18/2	**USSR**	Swansea	0–0
1/4	**Finland**	Wrexham	4–0 (ECQ)
29/4	**Czechoslovakia**	Wrexham	1–1 (ECQ)
9/9	**Denmark**	Cardiff	1–0 (ECQ)
14/10	**Denmark**	Copenhagen	0–1 (ECQ)
11/11	**Czechoslovakia**	Prague	0–2 (ECQ)

1988

Date	Opponents	Venue	F–A
23/3	**Yugoslavia**	Swansea	1–2
27/4	**Sweden**	Stockholm	1–4
1/6	**Malta**	Valletta	3–2
4/6	**Italy**	Brescia	1–0
14/9	**Holland**	Amsterdam	0–1 (WCQ)
19/10	**Finland**	Swansea	2–2 (WCQ)

1989

Date	Opponents	Venue	F–A
8/2	**Israel**	Tel Aviv	3–3
26/4	**Sweden**	Wrexham	0–2
31/5	**W Germany**	Cardiff	0–0 (WCQ)
6/9	**Finland**	Helsinki	0–1 (WCQ)
11/10	**Holland**	Wrexham	1–2 (WCQ)
15/11	**W Germany**	Kohn	1–2 (WCQ)

1990

Date	Opponents	Venue	F–A
28/3	**Rep of Ireland**	Dublin	0–1
25/4	**Sweden**	Stockholm	2–4
20/5	**Costa Rica**	Cardiff	1–0
1/9	**Denmark**	Copenhagen	0–1
17/10	**Belgium**	Cardiff	3–1 (ECQ)
14/11	**Luxembourg**	Luxembourg	1–0 (ECQ)

1991

Date	Opponents	Venue	F–A
6/2	**Rep of Ireland**	Wrexham	0–3
27/3	**Belgium**	Brussels	1–1 (ECQ)
1/5	**Iceland**	Cardiff	1–0
29/5	**Poland**	Radom	0–0

1991 *continued*

Date	Opponents	Venue	F–A
5/6	**W Germany**	Cardiff	1–0 (ECQ)
11/9	**Brazil**	Cardiff	1–0
16/10	**W Germany**	Nuremburg	1–4 (ECQ)
13/11	**Luxembourg**	Cardiff	1–0 (ECQ)

1992

Date	Opponents	Venue	F–A
19/2	**Rep of Ireland**	Dublin	1–0
29/4	**Austria**	Vienna	1–1
20/5	**Romania**	Bucharest	1–5 (WCQ)
30/5	**Holland**	Utrecht	0–4
3/6	**Argentina**	Tokyo	0–1
7/6	**Japan**	Matsuyama	1–0
9/9	**Faeroes**	Cardiff	6–0 (WCQ)
14/10	**Cyprus**	Limassol	1–0 (WCQ)
18/11	**Belgium**	Brussels	0–2 (WCQ)

1993

Date	Opponents	Venue	F–A
17/2	**Rep of Ireland**	Dublin	1–2
31/3	**Belgium**	Cardiff	2–0 (WCQ)
28/4	**Czechoslovakia**	Ostrava	1–1 (WCQ)
6/6	**Faeroes**	Toftir	3–0 (WCQ)
8/9	**RCS***	Cardiff	2–2 (WCQ)
* Representation of Czechs & Slovaks (was Czechoslovakia).			
13/10	**Cyprus**	Cardiff	2–0 (WCQ)
17/11	**Romania**	Cardiff	1–2 (WCQ)

1994

Date	Opponents	Venue	F–A
9/3	**Norway**	Cardiff	1–3
20/4	**Sweden**	Wrexham	0–2
23/5	**Estonia**	Tallinn	2–1
7/9	**Albania**	Cardiff	2–0 (ECQ)
12/10	**Moldova**	Chislau	2–3 (ECQ)
16/11	**Georgia**	Tbilisi	0–5 (ECQ)
14/12	**Bulgaria**	Cardiff	0–3 (ECQ)
7/9	**Albania**	Cardiff	2–0 (ECQ)

1995

Date	Opponents	Venue	F–A
29/3	**Bulgaria**	Sofia	1–3 (ECQ)
26/4	**Germany**	Düsseldorf	1–1 (ECQ)
7/6	**Georgia**	Cardiff	0–1 (ECQ)
6/9	**Moldova**	Cardiff	1–0 (ECQ)
11/10	**Germany**	Cardiff	1–2 (ECQ)
15/11	**Albania**	Tirana	1–1 (ECQ)

1996

Date	Opponents	Venue	F–A
24/1	**Italy**	Terni	0–3
24/4	**Switzerland**	Lugano	0–2
2/6	**San Marino**	Sarravalle	5–0 (WCQ)
31/8	**San Marino**	Cardiff	6–0 (WCQ)
5/10	**Holland**	Cardiff	1–3 (WCQ)
9/11	**Holland**	Eindhoven	1–7 (WCQ)
14/12	**Turkey**	Cardiff	0–0 (WCQ)

1997

Date	Opponents	Venue	F–A
11/2	**Rep of Ireland**	Cardiff	0–0
29/3	**Belgium**	Cardiff	1–2 (WCQ)
27/5	**Scotland**	Kilmarnock	1–0
20/8	**Turkey**	Istanbul	4–6 (WCQ)
11/10	**Belgium**	Brussels	2–3 (WCQ)
11/11	**Brazil**	Brasilia	0–3

1998

Date	Opponents	Venue	F–A
25/3	**Jamaica**	Cardiff	0–0
6/6	**Tunisia**	Tunis	0–4

INTERNATIONAL RESULTS – REPUBLIC OF IRELAND

KEY TO ABBREVIATIONS			
WCQ	= World Cup Qualifier	WCF	= World Cup Final
ECQ	= Euro Championship Qualifier	ECF	= Euro Championship Final

Date	Opponents	Venue	F–A
21/3/26	Italy	Turin	0–3
23/4/27	Italy	Dublin	1–2
12/2/28	Belgium	Liège	4–2
30/4/29	Belgium	Dublin	4–0
11/5/30	Belgium	Brussels	3–1
26/4/31	Spain	Barcelona	1–1
13/12/31	Spain	Dublin	0–5
8/5/32	Holland	Amsterdam	2–0
25/2/34	Belgium	Dublin	4–4 (WCQ)
8/4/34	Holland	Amsterdam	2–5 (WCQ)
15/12/34	Hungary	Dublin	2–4
5/5/35	Switzerland	Basle	0–1
8/5/35	Germany	Dortmund	1–3
8/12/35	Holland	Dublin	3–5
17/3/36	Switzerland	Dublin	1–0
3/5/36	Hungary	Budapest	3–3
9/5/36	Luxembourg	Luxembourg	5–1
17/10/36	Germany	Dublin	5–2
6/12/36	Hungary	Dublin	2–3
17/5/37	Switzerland	Berne	1–0
23/5/37	France	Paris	2–0
10/10/37	Norway	Oslo	2–3 (WCQ)
7/11/37	Norway	Dublin	3–3 (WCQ)
18/5/38	Czechoslovakia	Prague	2–2
22/5/38	Poland	Warsaw	0–6
18/9/38	Switzerland	Dublin	4–0
13/11/38	Poland	Dublin	3–2
19/3/39	Hungary	Cork	2–2
18/5/39	Hungary	Budapest	2–2
23/5/39	Germany	Bremen	1–1
16/6/46	Portugal	Lisbon	1–3
23/6/46	Spain	Madrid	1–0
30/9/46	England	Dublin	0–1
2/3/47	Spain	Dublin	3–2
4/5/47	Portugal	Dublin	0–2
23/5/48	Portugal	Lisbon	0–2
30/5/48	Spain	Barcelona	1–2
5/12/48	Switzerland	Dublin	0–1
24/4/49	Belgium	Dublin	0–2
22/5/49	Portugal	Dublin	1–0
2/6/49	Sweden	Stockholm	1–3 (WCQ)
12/6/49	Spain	Dublin	1–4
8/9/49	Finland	Dublin	3–0 (WCQ)
21/9/49	England	Everton	2–0
9/10/49	Finland	Helsinki	1–1 (WCQ)
13/11/49	Sweden	Dublin	1–3 (WCQ)
10/5/50	Belgium	Brussels	1–5
26/11/50	Norway	Dublin	2–2
13/5/51	Argentina	Dublin	0–1
30/5/51	Norway	Oslo	3–2

Date	Opponents	Venue	F–A
17/10/51	W Germany	Dublin	3–2
4/5/52	W Germany	Cologne	0–3
7/5/52	Austria	Vienna	0–6
1/6/52	Spain	Madrid	0–6
25/3/53	Austria	Dublin	4–0
4/10/53	France	Dublin	3–5 (WCQ)
28/10/53	Luxembourg	Dublin	4–0 (WCQ)
25/11/53	France	Paris	0–1 (WCQ)
7/3/54	Luxembourg	Luxembourg	1–0 (WCQ)
8/11/54	Norway	Dublin	2–1
1/5/55	Holland	Dublin	1–0
25/5/55	Norway	Oslo	3–1
28/5/55	W Germany	Hamburg	1–2
19/9/55	Yugoslavia	Dublin	1–4
27/11/55	Spain	Dublin	2–2
10/5/56	Holland	Rotterdam	4–1
3/10/56	Denmark	Dublin	2–1 (WCQ)
25/11/56	W Germany	Dublin	3–0
8/5/57	England	Wembley	1–5 (WCQ)
19/5/57	England	Dublin	1–1 (WCQ)
2/10/57	Denmark	Copenhagen	2–0 (WCQ)
14/3/58	Austria	Vienna	1–3
11/5/58	Poland	Katowice	2–2
5/10/58	Poland	Dublin	2–2
5/4/59	Czechoslovakia	Dublin	2–0 (ECQ)
10/5/59	Czechoslovakia	Bratislava	0–4 (ECQ)
1/11/59	Sweden	Dublin	3–2

1960

Date	Opponents	Venue	F–A
30/3/60	Chile	Dublin	2–0
11/5/60	W Germany	Düsseldorf	1–0
18/5/60	Sweden	Malmö	1–4
28/9/60	Wales	Dublin	2–3
6/11/60	Norway	Dublin	3–1

1961

Date	Opponents	Venue	F–A
3/5/61	Scotland	Glasgow	1–4 (WCQ)
7/5/61	Scotland	Dublin	0–3 (WCQ)
8/10/61	Czechoslovakia	Dublin	1–3 (WCQ)
29/10/61	Czechoslovakia	Prague	1–7 (WCQ)

1962

Date	Opponents	Venue	F–A
8/4/62	**Austria**	Dublin	2–3
12/8/62	**Iceland**	Dublin	4–2 (ECQ)
2/9/62	**Iceland**	Reykjavik	1–1 (ECQ)

1963

Date	Opponents	Venue	F–A
9/6/63	**Scotland**	Dublin	1–0
25/9/63	**Austria**	Vienna	0–0 (ECQ)
13/10/63	**Austria**	Dublin	3–2 (ECQ)

1964

Date	Opponents	Venue	F–A
11/3/64	**Spain**	Seville	1–5 (ECQ)
8/4/64	**Spain**	Dublin	0–2 (ECQ)
10/5/64	**Poland**	Cracow	1–3
13/5/64	**Norway**	Oslo	4–1
24/5/64	**England**	Dublin	1–3
25/10/64	**Poland**	Dublin	3–2

1965

Date	Opponents	Venue	F–A
24/3/65	**Belgium**	Dublin	0–2
5/5/65	**Spain**	Dublin	1–0 (WCQ)
27/10/65	**Spain**	Seville	1–4 (WCQ)
10/11/65	**Spain**	Paris	0–1 (WCQ)

1966

Date	Opponents	Venue	F–A
4/5/66	**W Germany**	Dublin	0–4
22/5/66	**Austria**	Vienna	0–1
25/5/66	**Belgium**	Liège	3–2
23/10/66	**Spain**	Dublin	0–0 (ECQ)
16/11/66	**Turkey**	Dublin	2–1 (ECQ)
7/12/66	**Spain**	Valencia	0–2 (ECQ)

1967

Date	Opponents	Venue	F–A
22/2/67	**Turkey**	Ankara	1–2 (ECQ)
21/5/67	**Czechoslovakia**	Dublin	0–2 (ECQ)
22/11/67	**Czechoslovakia**	Prague	2–1 (ECQ)

1968

Date	Opponents	Venue	F–A
15/5/68	**Poland**	Dublin	2–2
30/10/68	**Poland**	Katowice	0–1
10/11/68	**Austria**	Dublin	2–2

1968 *continued*

Date	Opponents	Venue	F–A
4/12/68 (abandoned after 51 minutes)	**Denmark**	Dublin	1–1 (WCQ)

1969

Date	Opponents	Venue	F–A
4/5/69	**Czechoslovakia**	Dublin	1–2 (WCQ)
27/5/69	**Denmark**	Copenhagen	0–2 (WCQ)
8/6/69	**Hungary**	Dublin	1–2 (WCQ)
21/9/69	**Scotland**	Dublin	1–1
7/10/69	**Czechoslovakia**	Prague	0–3 (WCQ)
15/10/69	**Denmark**	Dublin	1–1 (WCQ)
5/11/69	**Hungary**	Budapest	0–4 (WCQ)

1970

Date	Opponents	Venue	F–A
6/5/70	**Poland**	Dublin	1–2
9/5/70	**W Germany**	Berlin	1–2
23/9/70	**Poland**	Dublin	0–2
14/10/70	**Sweden**	Dublin	1–1 (ECQ)
28/10/70	**Sweden**	Malmö	0–1 (ECQ)

1971

Date	Opponents	Venue	F–A
8/12/71	**Italy**	Rome	0–3 (ECQ)
10/5/71	**Italy**	Dublin	1–2 (ECQ)
30/5/71	**Austria**	Dublin	1–4 (ECQ)
10/10/71	**Austria**	Linz	0–6 (ECQ)

1972

Date	Opponents	Venue	F–A
18/6/72	**Iran**	Recife	2–1
19/6/72	**Ecuador**	Natal	3–2
21/6/72	**Chile**	Recife	1–2
25/6/72	**Portugal**	Recife	1–2
18/10/72	**USSR**	Dublin	1–2 (WCQ)
15/11/72	**France**	Dublin	2–1 (WCQ)

1973

Date	Opponents	Venue	F–A
13/5/73	**USSR**	Moscow	0–1 (WCQ)
16/5/73	**Poland**	Wroclaw	0–2
19/5/73	**France**	Paris	1–1 (WCQ)
6/6/73	**Norway**	Oslo	1–1
21/10/73	**Poland**	Dublin	1–0

1974

Date	Opponents	Venue	F–A
8/5/74	**Uruguay**	Montevideo	0–2
12/5/74	**Chile**	Santiago	2–1
30/10/74	**USSR**	Dublin	3–0 (ECQ)
20/11/74	**Turkey**	Izmir	1–1 (ECQ)

1975

Date	Opponents	Venue	F–A
1/3/75 (+ W Germany 'B' side)	**W Germany**	Dublin	1–0 +
11/5/75	**Switzerland**	Dublin	2–1 (ECQ)
18/5/75	**USSR**	Kiev	1–2 (ECQ)
29/10/75	**Turkey**	Dublin	4–0 (ECQ)

1976

Date	Opponents	Venue	F–A
24/3/76	**Norway**	Dublin	3–0
26/5/76	**Poland**	Prosjan	2–0
8/9/76	**England**	Wembley	1–1
13/10/76	**Turkey**	Ankara	3–3
17/11/76	**France**	Paris	0–2 (WCQ)

1977

Date	Opponents	Venue	F–A
9/2/77	**Spain**	Dublin	0–1
30/3/77	**France**	Dublin	1–0 (WCQ)
24/4/77	**Poland**	Dublin	0–0
1/6/77	**Bulgaria**	Sofia	1–2 (WCQ)
12/10/77	**Bulgaria**	Dublin	0–0 (WCQ)

1978

Date	Opponents	Venue	F–A
5/4/78	**Turkey**	Dublin	4–2
12/4/78	**Poland**	Lodz	0–3
21/5/78	**Norway**	Oslo	0–0
24/5/78	**Denmark**	Copenhagen	3–3 (ECQ)
20/9/78	**N Ireland**	Dublin	0–0 (ECQ)
25/10/78	**England**	Dublin	1–1 (ECQ)

1979

Date	Opponents	Venue	F–A
2/5/79	**Denmark**	Dublin	2–0 (ECQ)
19/5/79	**Bulgaria**	Sofia	0–1 (ECQ)
22/5/79	**W Germany**	Dublin	1–3
11/9/79	**Wales**	Swansea	1–2
26/9/79	**Czechoslovakia**	Prague	1–4
17/10/79	**Bulgaria**	Dublin	3–0 (ECQ)
29/10/79	**USA**	Dublin	3–2
21/11/79	**N Ireland**	Belfast	0–1 (ECQ)

1980

Date	Opponents	Venue	F–A
6/2/80	**England**	Wembley	0–2 (ECQ)
26/3/80	**Cyprus**	Nicosia	3–2 (WCQ)
30/4/80	**Switzerland**	Dublin	2–0
16/5/80	**Argentina**	Dublin	0–1
10/9/80	**Holland**	Dublin	2–1 (WCQ)
15/10/80	**Belgium**	Dublin	1–1 (WCQ)
28/10/80	**France**	Paris	0–2 (WCQ)
19/11/80	**Cyprus**	Dublin	6–0 (WCQ)

1981

Date	Opponents	Venue	F–A
24/2/81	**Wales**	Dublin	1–3
25/3/81	**Belgium**	Brussels	0–1 (WCQ)
29/4/81	**Czechoslovakia**	Dublin	3–1
21/5/81 (W Germany 'B' side)	**W Germany**	Bremen	0–3
23/5/81	**Poland**	Bydgoszcz	0–3
9/9/81	**Holland**	Rotterdam	2–2 (WCQ)
14/10/81	**France**	Dublin	3–2 (WCQ)

1982

Date	Opponents	Venue	F–A
22/5/82	**Chile**	Santiago	0–1
27/5/82	**Brazil**	Vberlandia	0–7
30/5/82	**Trinidad & Tobago**	Port Of Spain	1–2
22/9/82	**Holland**	Rotterdam	1–2 (ECQ)
17/11/82	**Spain**	Dublin	3–3 (ECQ)

1983

Date	Opponents	Venue	F–A
30/3/83	**Malta**	Valletta	1–0 (ECQ)
27/4/83	**Spain**	Zaragoza	0–2 (ECQ)
12/10/83	**Holland**	Dublin	2–3 (ECQ)
16/11/83	**Malta**	Dublin	8–0 (ECQ)

1984

Date	Opponents	Venue	F–A
4/4/84	**Israel**	Tel Aviv	0–3
23/5/84	**Poland**	Dublin	0–0
3/6/84	**China**	Sapporo	1–0
8/8/84	**Mexico**	Dublin	0–0
12/9/84	**USSR**	Dublin	1–0 (WCQ)
17/10/84	**Norway**	Oslo	0–1 (WCQ)
14/11/84	**Denmark**	Copenhagen	0–3

1985

Date	Opponents	Venue	F–A
5/2/85	**Italy**	Dublin	1–2

1985 *continued*

Date	Opponents	Venue	F-A
26/3/85	**England**	Wembley	1–2
1/5/85	**Norway**	Dublin	0–0 (WCQ)
21/5/85	**Israel**	Tel Aviv	0–0
26/5/85	**Spain**	Cork	0–0 (WCQ)
2/6/85	**Switzerland**	Dublin	3–0 (WCQ)
11/9/85	**Switzerland**	Berne	0–0 (WCQ)
16/10/85	**USSR**	Moscow	0–2 (WCQ)
13/11/85	**Denmark**	Dublin	1–4 (WCQ)

1986

Date	Opponents	Venue	F-A
26/3/86	**Wales**	Dublin	0–1
23/4/86	**Uruguay**	Dublin	1–1
25/5/86	**Iceland**	Reykjvik	2–1
27/5/86	**Czechoslovakia**	Reykjvik	1–0
10/9/86	**Belgium**	Brussels	2–2 (ECQ)
15/10/86	**Scotland**	Dublin	0–0 (ECQ)
12/11/86	**Poland**	Warsaw	0–1

1987

Date	Opponents	Venue	F-A
18/2/87	**Scotland**	Glasgow	1–0 (ECQ)
1/4/87	**Bulgaria**	Sofia	1–2 (ECQ)
29/4/87	**Belgium**	Dublin	0–0 (ECQ)
23/5/87	**Brazil**	Dublin	1–0
28/5/87	**Luxembourg**	Luxembourg	2–0 (ECQ)
9/9/87	**Luxembourg**	Dublin	2–1 (ECQ)
14/10/87	**Bulgaria**	Dublin	2–0 (ECQ)
10/11/87	**Israel**	Dublin	5–0

1988

Date	Opponents	Venue	F-A
23/3/88	**Romania**	Dublin	2–0
27/4/88	**Yugoslavia**	Dublin	2–0
22/5/88	**Poland**	Dublin	3–1
1/6/88	**Norway**	Oslo	0–0
12/6/88	**England**	Stuggart	1–0 (ECF)
15/6/88	**USSR**	Hanover	1–1 (ECF)
18/6/88	**Holland**	Gelsenkirchen	0–1 (ECF)
14/9/88	**N Ireland**	Belfast	0–0 (WCQ)
19/10/88	**Tunisia**	Dublin	4–0
16/11/88	**Spain**	Seville	0–2 (WCQ)

1989

Date	Opponents	Venue	F-A
7/2/89	**France**	Dublin	0–0
8/3/89	**Hungary**	Budapest	0–0 (WCQ)
26/4/89	**Spain**	Dublin	1–0 (WCQ)
28/5/89	**Malta**	Dublin	2–0 (WCQ)
4/6/89	**Hungary**	Dublin	2–0 (WCQ)
6/9/89	**W Germany**	Dublin	1–1

1989 *continued*

Date	Opponents	Venue	F-A
11/10/89	**N Ireland**	Dublin	3–0 (WCQ)
15/11/89	**Malta**	Valetta	2–0 (WCQ)

1990

Date	Opponents	Venue	F-A
12/1	**Morocco**	Dublin	1–0
28/3	**Wales**	Dublin	1–0
25/4	**USSR**	Dublin	1–0
16/5	**Finland**	Dublin	1–1
27/5	**Turkey**	Izmir	0–0
3/6	**Malta**	Valetta	3–0
11/6	**England**	Cagliari	1–1 (WCF)
17/6	**Egypt**	Palermo	0–0 (WCF)
21/6	**Holland**	Palermo	1–1 (WCF)
25/6	**Romania**	Genoa	0–0 (WCF)
(Rep of Ireland won on penalties: 5–4)			
30/6	**Italy**	Rome	0–1 (WCF)
17/10	**Turkey**	Dublin	5–0 (ECQ)
14/11	**England**	Dublin	1–1 (ECQ)

1991

Date	Opponents	Venue	F-A
6/2	**Wales**	Wrexham	3–0
27/3	**England**	Wembley	1–1 (ECQ)
1/5	**Poland**	Dublin	0–0 (ECQ)
22/5	**Chile**	Dublin	1–1
2/6	**USA**	Foxboro	1–1
11/9	**Hungary**	Gyor	2–1
16/10	**Poland**	Poznan	3–3 (ECQ)
13/11	**Turkey**	Istanbul	3–1 (ECQ)

1992

Date	Opponents	Venue	F-A
19/2	**Wales**	Dublin	0–1
25/3	**Switzerland**	Dublin	2–1
29/4	**USA**	Dublin	4–1
26/5	**Albania**	Dublin	2–0 (WCQ)
30/5	**USA**	Washington	1–3
4/6	**Italy**	Foxboro	0–2
7/6	**Portugal**	Foxboro	2–0
9/9	**Latvia**	Dublin	4–0 (WCQ)
14/10	**Denmark**	Copenhagen	0–0 (WCQ)
18/11	**Spain**	Seville	0–0 (WCQ)

1993

Date	Opponents	Venue	F-A
17/2	**Wales**	Dublin	2–1
31/3	**N Ireland**	Dublin	3–0 (WCQ)
28/4	**Denmark**	Dublin	1–1 (WCQ)
26/5	**Albania**	Tirana	2–1 (WCQ)
2/6	**Latvia**	Riga	2–1 (WCQ)

1993 *continued*

Date	Opponents	Venue	F–A
16/6	**Lithuania**	Vilnius	1–0 (WCQ)
8/9	**Lithuania**	Dublin	2–0 (WCQ)
13/10	**Spain**	Dublin	1–3 (WCQ)
17/11	**N Ireland**	Belfast	1–1 (WCQ)

1994

Date	Opponents	Venue	F–A
23/3	**Russia**	Dublin	0–0
20/4	**Holland**	Tilburg	1–0
24/5	**Bolivia**	Dublin	1–0
29/5	**Germany**	Hanover	2–0
4/6	**Czech Republic**	Dublin	1–3
18/6	**Italy**	New York	1–0 (WCF)
24/6	**Mexico**	Orlando	1–2 (WCF)
28/6	**Norway**	New York	0–0 (WCF)
4/7	**Holland**	Orlando	0–2 (WCF)
7/9	**Latvia**	Riga	3–0 (ECQ)
12/10	**Liechtenstein**	Dublin	4–0 (ECQ)
16/11	**N Ireland**	Belfast	4–0 (ECQ)

1995

Date	Opponents	Venue	F–A
15/2 (abandoned after 21 minutes)	**England**	Dublin	1–0
29/3	**N Ireland**	Dublin	1–1 (ECQ)
26/4	**Portugal**	Dublin	1–0 (ECQ)
3/6	**Liechtenstein**	Vaduz	0–0 (ECQ)
11/6	**Austria**	Dublin	1–3 (ECQ)
6/9	**Austria**	Vienna	1–3 (ECQ)
11/10	**Latvia**	Dublin	2–1 (ECQ)
15/11	**Portugal**	Lisbon	0–3 (ECQ)
13/12	**Holland**	Liverpool	0–2 (ECQ)

1996

Date	Opponents	Venue	F–A
27/3	**Russia**	Dublin	0–2
24/4	**Czech Republic**	Prague	0–2
29/5	**Portugal**	Dublin	0–1
31/8	**Liechtenstein**	Vaduz	5–0 (WCQ)
9/10	**FYR Macedonia**	Dublin	3–0 (WCQ)
10/11	**Iceland**	Dublin	0–0 (WCQ)

1997

Date	Opponents	Venue	F–A
11/2	**Wales**	Cardiff	0–0
2/4	**FYR Macedonia**	Skopje	2–3 (WCQ)
30/4	**Romania**	Bucharest	0–1 (WCQ)
21/5	**Liechtenstein**	Dublin	5–0 (WCQ)
20/8	**Lithuania**	Dublin	0–0 (WCQ)
10/9	**Lithuania**	Vilnius	2–1 (WCQ)
11/10	**Romania**	Dublin	1–1 (WCQ)

1997 *continued*

Date	Opponents	Venue	F–A
29/10	**Belgium**	Dublin	1–1 (WCQ)
15/11	**Belgium**	Brussels	1–2 (WCQ)

1998

Date	Opponents	Venue	F–A
25/3	**Czech Republic**	Olomouc	1–2
22/4	**Argentina**	Dublin	0–2
23/5	**Mexico**	Dublin	0–0

Chapter 9

GREAT BRITAIN

AND IRELAND
INTERNATIONAL
PLAYER RECORDS

BRITISH INTERNATIONAL PLAYERS' RECORDS

This is the full list of total number of appearances and goals by British and Irish internationals from the first official international in 1872 to the 1998 World Cup finals. The player's club(s) and season(s) when he won his caps are in brackets and total caps come before total goals.

England

Abbott, W (Everton, 1902): 1/0
A'Court, A (Liverpool, 1958–9): 5/1
Adams, T A (Arsenal, 1987–98): 55/4
Adcock, H (Leicester, 1929–30): 5/1
Alcock, C W (Wanderers, 1875): 1/1
Alderson, J T (C Palace, 1923): 1/0
Aldridge, A (WBA, Walsall Town Swifts, 1888–9): 2/0
Allen, A (Stoke, 1960): 3/0
Allen, A (A Villa, 1888): 1/3
Allen, C (QPR, Tottenham, 1984–88): 5/0
Allen, H (Wolves, 1888–90): 5/0
Allen, J P (Portsmouth, 1934): 2/0
Allen, R (WBA, 1952–5): 5/0
Alsford, W J (Tottenham, 1935): 1/0
Amos, A (Old Carthusians, 1885–6): 2/0
Anderson, R D (Old Etonians, 1879): 1/0
Anderson, S (Sunderland, 1962): 2/0
Anderson, V (Notts Forest, Arsenal, Man Utd, 1979–88): 30/2
Anderton, D R (Tottenham, 1994–98): 22/6
Angus, J (Burnley, 1961): 1/0
Armfield, J C (Blackpool, 1959–66): 43/0
Armitage, G H (Charlton, 1926): 1/0
Armstrong, D (Middlesbrough, Southampton, 1980–4): 3/0
Armstrong, K (Chelsea, 1955): 1/0
Arnold, J (Fulham, 1933): 1/0
Arthur, J W H (Blackburn, 1885–7): 7/0
Ashcroft, J (Arsenal, 1906): 3/0
Ashmore, G S (WBA, 1926): 1/0
Ashton, C T (Corinthians, 1926): 1/0
Ashurst, W (Notts Co, 1923–5): 5/0
Astall, G (Birmingham, 1956): 2/1
Astle, J (WBA, 1969–70): 5/0
Aston, J (Man Utd, 1949–51): 17/0
Athersmith, W C (A Villa, 1892–1900): 12/3
Atyeo, P J W (Bristol C, 1956–7): 6/5
Austin, S W (Man City, 1926): 1/0
Bach, P (Sunderland, 1899): 1/0
Bache, J W (A Villa, 1903–11): 7/4
Baddeley, T (Wolves, 1903–4): 7/0
Bagshaw, J J (Derby, 1920): 1/0
Bailey, G R (Man Utd, 1985): 2/0
Bailey, H P (Leicester Fosse, 1908): 5/0
Bailey, M A (Charlton, 1964–5): 2/0
Bailey, N C (Clapham Rovers, 1878–87): 19/2
Baily, E F (Tottenham, 1950–3): 9/5
Bain, J (Oxford University, 1887): 1/0
Baker, A (Arsenal, 1928): 1/0
Baker, B H (Everton, Chelsea, 1921–6): 2/0

Baker, J H (Hibernian, Arsenal, 1960–6): 8/3
Ball, A J (Blackpool, Everton, Arsenal, 1965–75): 72/8
Ball, J (Bury, 1928): 1/0
Balmer, W (Everton, 1905): 1/0
Bamber, J (Liverpool, 1921): 1/0
Bambridge, A L (Swifts, 1881–4): 3/1
Bambridge, E C (Swifts, 1979–87): 18/12
Bambridge, E H (Swifts, 1876): 1/0
Banks, G (Leicester, Stoke, 1963–72): 73/0
Banks, H E (Millwall, 1901): 1/0
Banks, T (Bolton, 1958–9): 6/0
Bannister, W (Burnley, Bolton, 1901–2): 2/0
Barclay, R (Sheff Utd, 1932–6): 3/2
Barham, M (Norwich, 1983): 2/0
Barkas, S (Man City, 1936–8): 5/0
Barker, J (Derby, 1935–7): 11/0
Barker, R (Herts Rangers, 1872): 1/0
Barker, R R (Casuals, 1895): 1/0
Barlow, R J (WBA, 1955): 1/0
Barmby, N J (Tottenham, Middlesbrough, Everton 1995–7): 10/3
Barnes, J (Watford, Liverpool, 1983–96): 79/11
Barnes, P S (Man City, WBA, Leeds, 1978–82): 22/4
Barnet, H H (Royal Engineers, 1882): 1/0
Barrass, M W (Bolton, 1952–3): 3/0
Barrett, A F (Fulham, 1930): 1/0
Barrett, E D (Oldham, 1991–3): 3/0
Barrett, J W (West Ham, 1929): 1/0
Barry, L (Leicester, 1928–9): 5/0
Barson, F (A Villa, 1920): 1/0
Barton, J (Blackburn, 1890): 1/1
Barton, P H (Birmingham, 1921–5): 7/0
Barton, W D (Wimbledon, Newcastle, 1995): 3/0
Bassett, W I (WBA, 1888–96): 16/7
Bastard, S R (Upton Park, 1880): 1/0
Bastin, C S (Arsenal, 1932–8): 21/12
Batty, D (Leeds, Blackburn, Newcastle, 1991–8): 35/0
Baugh, R (Stafford Road, Wolves, 1886–90): 2/0
Bayliss, A E J M (WBA, 1891): 1/0
Baynham, R L (Luton, 1956): 3/0
Beardsley, P A (Newcastle, Liverpool, Newcastle 1986–96): 59/9
Beasant, D J (Chelsea, 1990): 2/0
Beasley, A (Huddersfield, 1939): 1/1
Beats, W E (Wolves, 1901–2): 2/0
Beattie, T K (Ipswich, 1975–8): 9/1
Beckham, D R J (Man Utd, 1997–8): 18/1
Becton, F (Preston, Liverpool, 1895–7): 2/2
Bedford, H (Blackpool, 1923–5): 2/1
Bell, C (Man City, 1968–76): 48/9

Bennett, W (Sheff Utd, 1901): 2/0
Benson, R W (Sheff Utd, 1913): 1/0
Bentley, R T F (Chelsea, 1949–55): 12/9
Beresford, J (A Villa, 1934): 1/0
Berry, A (Oxford University, 1909): 1/0
Berry, J J (Man Utd, 1953–6): 4/0
Bestall, J G (Grimsby, 1935): 1/0
Betmead, H A (Grimsby, 1937): 1/0
Betts, M P (Old Harrovians, 1877): 1/0
Betts, W (Sheff Wed, 1889): 1/0
Beverley, J (Blackburn, 1884): 3/0
Birkett, R H (Clapham Rovers, 1879): 1/0
Birkett, R J E (Middlesbrough, 1936): 1/0
Birley, F H (Oxford University, Wanderers, 1874–5): 2/0
Birtles, G (Nottingham Forest, 1980–1): 3/0
Bishop, S M (Leicester, 1927): 4/1
Blackburn, F (Blackburn, 1901–4): 3/1
Blackburn, G F (A Villa, 1924): 1/0
Blenkinsop, E (Sheff Wed, 1928–33): 26/0
Bliss, H (Tottenham, 1921): 1/0
Blissett, L (Watford, Milan, 1983–4): 14/3
Blockley, J P (Arsenal, 1973): 1/0
Bloomer, S (Derby, Middlesbrough, 1895–1907): 23/28
Blunstone, F (Chelsea, 1955–7): 5/0
Bond, R (Preston, Bradford, 1905–10): 8/2
Bonetti, P P (Chelsea, 1966–70): 7/0
Bonsor, A G (Wanderers, 1873–5): 2/1
Booth, F (Man City, 1905): 1/0
Booth, T (Blackburn, Everton, 1898–1903): 2/0
Bould, S A (Arsenal, 1994): 2/0
Bowden, E R (Arsenal, 1935–7): 6/1
Bower, A G (Corinthians, 1924–7): 5/0
Bowers, J W (Derby, 1934): 3/2
Bowles, S (QPR, 1974–7): 5/1
Bowser, S (WBA, 1920): 1/0
Boyer, P J (Norwich, 1976): 1/0
Boyes, W (WBA, 1935–9): 3/0
Boyle, T W (Burnley, 1913): 1/0
Brabrook, P (Chelsea, 1958–60): 3/0
Bracewell, P W (Everton, 1985–6): 3/0
Bradford, G R W (Bristol R, 1956): 1/1
Bradford, J (Birmingham, 1924–31): 12/7
Bradley, W (Man Utd, 1959): 3/2
Bradshaw, F (Sheff Wed, 1908): 1/3
Bradshaw, T H (Liverpool, 1897): 1/0
Bradshaw, W (Blackburn, 1910–3): 4/0
Brann, G (Swifts, 1886–91): 3/0
Brawn, W F (A Villa, 1904): 2/0
Bray, J (Man City, 1935–7): 6/0
Brayshaw, E (Sheff Wed, 1887): 1/0
Bridges, B J (Chelsea, 1965–6): 4/1
Bridgett, A (Sunderland, 1905–9): 11/3

Brindle, T (Darwen, 1880): 2/1
Brittleton, J T (Sheff Wed, 1912–4): 5/0
Britton, C S (Everton, 1935–7): 9/1
Broadbent, P F (Wolves, 1958–60): 7/2
Broadis, I A (Man City, Newcastle, 1952–4): 14/8
Brockbank, J (Cambridge University, 1872): 1/0
Brodie, J B (Wolves, 1889–91): 3/1
Bromilow, T G (Liverpool, 1921–6): 5/0
Bromley–Davenport, W E (Oxford University, 1884): 2/2
Brook, E F (Man City, 1930–8): 18/10
Brooking, T D (West Ham, 1974–82): 47/5
Brooks, J (Tottenham, 1957): 3/2
Broome, F H (A Villa, 1938–9): 7/3
Brown, A (A Villa, 1882): 3/4
Brown, A S (Sheff Utd, 1904–6): 2/1
Brown, A (WBA, 1971): 1/0
Brown, G (Huddersfield, A Villa, 1927–33): 9/5
Brown, J (Blackburn, 1881–5): 5/3
Brown, J H (Sheff Wed, 1927–30): 6/0
Brown, K (West Ham, 1960): 1/0
Brown, W (West Ham, 1924): 1/1
Bruton, J (Burnley, 1928–9): 3/0
Bryant, W I (Clapton, 1925): 1/0
Buchan, C M (Sunderland, 1913–24): 6/4
Buchanan, W S (Clapham Rovers, 1876): 1/0
Buckley, F C (Derby, 1914): 1/0
Bull, S G (Wolves, 1989–91): 13/4
Bullock, F E (Huddersfield, 1921): 1/0
Bullock, N (Bury, 1923–7): 3/2
Burgess, H (Man City, 1904–6): 4/4
Burgess, H (Sheff Wed, 1931): 4/4
Burnup, C J (Cambridge University, 1896): 1/0
Burrows, H (Sheff Wed, 1934–5): 3/0
Burton, F E (Nottingham Forest, 1889): 1/0
Bury, L (Cambridge University, Old Etonians, 1877–9): 2/0
Butcher, T (Ipswich, Rangers, 1980–90): 77/3
Butler, J D (Arsenal, 1925): 1/0
Butler, W (Bolton, 1924): 1/0
Butt, N (Man Utd, 1997–8): 6/0
Byrne, G (Liverpool, 1963–6): 2/0
Byrne, J J (C Palace, West Ham, 1962–5): 11/8
Byrne, R W (Man Utd, 1954–8): 33/0
Callaghan, I R (Liverpool, 1966–78): 4/0
Calvey, J (Nottingham Forest, 1902): 1/0
Campbell, A F (Blackburn, Huddersfield, 1929–32): 8/0
Campbell, S (Tottenham, 1996–8): 20/0
Camsell, G H (Middlesbrough, 1929–36): 9/18
Capes, A J (Stoke, 1903): 1/0
Carr, J (Middlesbrough, 1920–3): 2/0
Carr, J (Newcastle, 1905–7): 2/0
Carr, W H (Owlerton, Sheffield, 1875): 1/0
Carter, H S (Sunderland, Derby, 1934–47): 13/7
Carter, J H (WBA, 1926–9): 3/4
Catlin, A E (Sheff Wed, 1937): 5/0
Chadwick, A (Southampton, 1900): 2/0
Chadwick, E (Everton, 1891–7): 7/3
Chamberlain, M (Stoke, 1983–5): 8/1
Chambers, H (Liverpool, 1921–4): 8/5
Channon, M R (Southampton, Man City, 1973–8): 46/21
Charles, G A (Nottingham Forest, 1991): 2/0
Charlton, J (Leeds, 1965–70): 35/6
Charlton, R (Man Utd, 1958–70): 106/49

Charnley, R O (Blackpool, 1963): 1/0
Charsley, C C (Small Heath, 1893): 1/0
Chedgzoy, S (Everton, 1920–5): 8/0
Chenery, C J (C Palace, 1872–4): 3/1
Cherry, T J (Leeds, 1976–80): 27/0
Chilton, A (Man Utd, 1951–2): 2/0
Chippendale, H (Blackburn, 1894): 1/0
Chivers, M (Tottenham, 1971–4): 24/13
Christian, E (Old Etonians, 1879): 1/0
Clamp, E (Wolves, 1958): 4/0
Clapton, D R (Arsenal, 1959): 1/0
Clare, T (Stoke, 1889–94): 4/0
Clarke, A J (Leeds, 1970–6): 19/10
Clarke, H A (Tottenham, 1954): 1/0
Clay, T (Tottenham, 1920–2): 4/0
Clayton, R (Blackburn, 1956–60): 35/0
Clegg, J C (Sheff Wed, 1872): 1/0
Clegg, W E (Sheff Wed, Sheff Albion, 1873–9): 2/0
Clemence, R N (Liverpool, Tottenham, 1973–84): 61/0
Clement, D T (QPR, 1976–7): 5/0
Clough, B H (Middlesbrough, 1960): 2/0
Clough, N H (Nottingham Forest, 1989–93): 14/0
Coates, R (Burnley, Tottenham, 1970–1): 4/0
Cobbold, W N (Cambridge University, Old Carthusians, 1883–7): 9/7
Cock, J G (Huddersfield, Chelsea, 1920): 2/2
Cockburn, H (Man Utd, 1947–52): 13/0
Cohen, G R (Fulham, 1964–8): 37/0
Cole, A (Man Utd, 1995–7): 2/0
Coleclough, H (C Palace, 1914): 1/0
Coleman, E H (Dulwich Hamlet, 1921): 1/0
Coleman, J (Arsenal, 1907): 1/0
Collymore, S V (Nottingham Forest, A Villa, 1995–8): 3/0
Common, A (Sheff Utd, Middlesbrough, 1904–6): 3/2
Compton, L H (Arsenal, 1951): 2/0
Conlin, J (Bradford, 1906): 1/0
Connelly, J M (Burnley, Man Utd, 1960–6): 20/7
Cook, T E R (Brighton, 1925): 1/0
Cooper, C T (Nottingham Forest, 1995): 2/0
Cooper, N C (Cambridge University, 1893): 1/0
Cooper, T (Derby, 1928–35): 15/0
Cooper, T (Leeds, 1969–75): 20/0
Coppell, S J (Man Utd, 1978–83): 42/7
Copping, W (Leeds, Arsenal, Leeds 1933–9): 20/0
Corbett, B O (Corinthians, 1901): 1/0
Corbett, R (Old Malvernians, 1903): 1/0
Corbett, W S (Birmingham, 1908): 3/0
Corrigan, J T (Man City, 1978–82): 9/0
Cottee, A R (West Ham, Everton, 1987–9): 7/0
Cotterill, G H (Cambridge University, Old Brightonians, 1891–3): 4/2
Cottle, J R (Bristol C, 1909): 1/0
Cowan, S (Man City, 1926–31): 3/0
Cowans, G (A Villa, Bari, A Villa, 1983–91): 10/2
Cowell, A (Blackburn, 1910): 1/0
Cox, J (Liverpool, 1901–3): 3/0
Cox, J D (Derby, 1892): 1/0
Crabtree, J W (Burnley, A Villa, 1894–1902): 14/0
Crawford, J F (Chelsea, 1931): 1/0

Crawford, R (Ipswich, 1962): 2/1
Crawshaw, T H (Sheff Wed, 1895–1904): 10/1
Crayston, W J (Arsenal, 1936–8): 8/1
Creek, F N S (Corinthians, 1923): 1/1
Cresswell, W (South Shields, Sunderland, Everton, 1921–30): 7/0
Crompton, R (Blackburn, 1902–14): 41/0
Crooks, S D (Derby, 1930–7): 26/7
Crowe, C (Wolves, 1963): 1/0
Cuggy, F (Sunderland, 1913): 2/0
Cullis, S (Wolves, 1938–9): 12/0
Cunliffe, A (Blackburn, 1933): 2/0
Cunliffe, D (Portsmouth, 1900): 1/0
Cunliffe, J N (Everton, 1936): 1/0
Cunningham, L (WBA, Real Madrid, 1979–80): 6/0
Curle, K (Man City, 1992): 3/0
Currey, E S (Oxford University, 1890): 2/2
Currie, A W (Sheff Utd, Leeds, 1890): 17/3
Cursham, A W (Notts Co, 1876–83): 6/2
Cursham, H A (Notts Co, 1880–4): 8/5
Daft, H B (Notts Co, 1889–92): 5/3
Daley, A M (A Villa, 1992): 7/0
Danks, T (Nottingham Forest, 1885): 1/0
Davenport, P (Nottingham Forest, 1985): 1/0
Davenport, J K (Bolton, 1885–90): 2/2
Davis, G (Derby, 1904): 2/1
Davis, H (Sheff Utd, 1903): 3/1
Davison, J E (Sheff Wed, 1922): 1/0
Dawson, J (Burnley, 1922): 2/0
Day, S H (Old Malvernians, 1906): 3/2
Dean, W R (Everton, 1927–33): 16/18
Deane, B C (Sheff Utd, 1991–3): 3/0
Deeley, N V (Wolves, 1959): 2/0
Devey, J H G (A Villa, 1892–4): 2/1
Devonshire, A (West Ham, 1980–4): 8/0
Dewhurst, F (Preston, 1886–9): 9/11
Dewhurst, G P (Liverpool Ramblers, 1895): 1/0
Dickinson, J W (Portsmouth, 1949–57): 48/0
Dimmock, J H (Tottenham, 1921–6): 3/0
Ditchburn, E G (Tottenham, 1949–57): 6/0
Dix, R W (Derby, 1939): 1/1
Dixon, J A (Notts Co, 1885): 1/0
Dixon, K M (Chelsea, 1985–7): 8/4
Dixon, L M (Arsenal, 1990–4): 21/1
Dobson, A T C (Notts Co, 1882–4): 4/0
Dobson, C F (Notts Co, 1886): 1/0
Dobson, J M (Burnley, Everton, 1974–5): 5/0
Doggart, A G (Corinthians, 1924): 1/0
Dorigo, A E (Chelsea, Leeds, 1990–4): 15/0
Dorrell, A R (A Villa, 1925–6): 4/0
Douglas, B (Blackburn, 1958–63): 36/11
Downs, R W (Everton 1921): 1/0
Doyle, M (Man City, 1976–7): 5/0
Drake, E J (Arsenal, 1935–8): 5/6
Ducat, A (Arsenal, A Villa, 1910–21): 6/1
Dublin, D (Coventry, 1998): 3/0
Dunn, A T B (Cambridge University, Old Etonians, 1883–92): 4/2
Duxbury, M (Man Utd, 1984–5): 10/0
Earle, S G J (Clapton, West Ham, 1924–8): 2/0
Eastham, G (Arsenal, 1963–6): 19/2
Eastham, G R (Bolton, 1935): 1/0
Eckersley, W (Blackburn, 1950–4): 17/0
Edwards, D (Man Utd, 1955–8): 18/5
Edwards, J H (Shropshire Wanderers, 1874): 1/0

Edwards, W (Leeds, 1926–30): 16/0
Ehiogu, U (A Villa, 1996): 1/0
Ellerington, W (Southampton, 1949): 2/0
Elliott, G W (Middlesbrough, 1913–20): 3/0
Elliott, W H (Burnley, 1952–3): 5/3
Evans, R E (Sheff Utd, 1911–2): 4/1
Ewer, F H (Casuals, 1924–5): 2/0
Fairclough, P (Old Foresters, 1878): 1/0
Fairhurst, D (Newcastle, 1934): 1/0
Fantham, J (Sheff Wed, 1962): 1/0
Fashanu, J (Wimbledon, 1989): 2/0
Felton, W (Sheff Wed, 1925): 1/0
Fenton, M (Middlesbrough, 1938): 1/0
Fenwick, T (QPR, Tottenham, 1984–88): 20/0
Ferdinand, R (West Ham, 1998): 3/0
Ferdinand, L (QPR, Newcastle, Tottenham, 1993–8): 17/5
Field, E (Clapham Rovers, 1876–81): 2/0
Finney, T (Preston, 1947–59): 76/30
Fleming, H J (Swindon, 1909–14): 11/9
Fletcher, A (Wolves, 1889–90): 2/0
Flowers, R (Wolves, 1955–66): 49/10
Flowers, T D (Southampton, Blackburn, 1993–8): 11/0
Forman, Frank (Nottingham Forest, 1898–1903): 9/1
Forman, F R (Nottingham Forest, 1899): 3/3
Forrest, J H (Blackburn, 1884–90): 11/0
Fort, J (Millwall, 1921): 1/0
Foster, R E (Oxford University, Corinthians, 1900–2): 5/3
Foster, S (Brighton, 1982): 3/0
Foulke, W J (Sheff Utd, 1897): 1/0
Foulkes, W A (Man Utd, 1955): 1/0
Fowler, R B (Liverpool, 1996–7): 7/2
Fox, F S (Millwall, 1925): 1/0
Francis, G C J (QPR, 1975–6): 12/3
Francis, T (Birmingham, Nottingham Forest, Man City, Sampdoria, 1977–86): 52/12
Franklin, C F (Stoke, 1947–50): 27/0
Freeman, B C (Everton, Burnley, 1909–12): 5/3
Froggatt, J (Portsmouth, 1950–3): 13/2
Froggatt, R (Sheff Wed, 1953): 4/2
Fry, C B (Corinthians, 1901): 1/0
Furness, W I (Leeds, 1933): 1/0
Galley, T (Wolves, 1937): 2/1
Gardner, T (A Villa, 1934–5): 2/0
Garfield, B (WBA, 1898): 1/0
Garratty, W (A Villa, 1903): 1/0
Garrett, T (Blackpool, 1952–4): 3/0
Gascoigne, P J (Tottenham, Lazio, Rangers, Middlesbrough, 1989–98): 57/10
Gates, E (Ipswich, 1981): 2/0
Gay, L H (Cambridge University, Old Brightonians, 1893–4): 3/0
Geary, F (Everton, 1890–1): 2/3
Geaves, R L (Clapham Rovers, 1875): 1/0
Gee, C W (Everton, 1932–7): 3/0
Geldard, A (Everton, 1933–8): 4/0
George, C (Derby, 1977): 1/0
George, W (A Villa, 1902): 3/0
Gibbins, W V T (Clapton, 1924–5): 2/3
Gidman, J (A Villa, 1977): 1/0
Gillard, I T (QPR, 1975–6): 3/0
Gilliat, W E (Old Carthusians, 1893): 1/3
Goddard, P (West Ham, 1982): 1/1

Goodall, F R (Huddersfield, 1926–34): 25/0
Goodall, J (Preston, 1888–98): 14/12
Goodhart, H C (Old Etonians, 1883): 3/0
Goodwyn, A G (Royal Engineers, 1873): 1/0
Goodyer, A C (Nottingham Forest, 1879): 1/1
Gosling, R C (Old Etonians, 1892–5): 5/2
Gosnell, A A (Newcastle, 1906): 1/0
Gough, H C (Sheff Utd, 1921): 1/0
Goulden, L A (West Ham, 1937–9): 14/4
Graham, L (Millwall, 1925): 2/0
Graham, T (Nottingham Forest, 1931–2): 2/0
Grainger, C (Sheff Utd, Sunderland, 1956–7): 7/3
Gray, A A (C Palace, 1992): 1/0
Greaves, J (Chelsea, Tottenham, 1959–67): 57/44
Green, F T (Wanderers, 1876): 1/0
Green, G H (Sheff Utd, 1925–8): 8/0
Greenhalgh, E H (Notts Co, 1872–3): 2/0
Greenhoff, B (Man Utd, Leeds, 1976–80): 18/0
Greenwood, D H (Blackburn, 1882): 2/0
Gregory, J (QPR, 1983–4): 6/0
Grimsdell, A (Tottenham, 1920–3): 6/0
Grosvenor, A T (Birmingham, 1934): 3/2
Gunn, W (Notts Co, 1884): 2/1
Gurney, R (Sunderland, 1935): 1/0
Hacking, J (Oldham, 1929): 3/0
Hadley, N (WBA, 1903): 1/0
Hagan, J (Sheff Utd, 1949): 1/0
Haines, J T W (WBA, 1949): 1/2
Hall, A E (A Villa, 1910): 1/0
Hall, G W (Tottenham, 1934–9): 10/9
Hall, J (Birmingham, 1956–7): 17/0
Halse, J H (Man Utd, 1909): 1/2
Hammond, H E D (Oxford University, 1889): 1/0
Hampson, J (Blackpool, 1931–3): 3/5
Hampton, H (A Villa, 1913–4): 4/2
Hancocks, J (Wolves, 1949–51): 3/2
Hapgood, E (Arsenal, 1933–9): 30/0
Hardinge, H T W (Sheff Utd, 1910): 1/0
Hardman, H P (Everton, 1905–8): 4/1
Hardwick, G F M (Middlesbrough, 1947–8): 13/0
Hardy, H (Stockport, 1925): 1/0
Hardy, S (Liverpool, A Villa, 1907–20): 21/0
Harford, M G (Luton, 1988–9): 2/0
Hargreaves, F W (Blackburn, 1880–2): 3/0
Hargreaves, J (Blackburn, 1881): 2/0
Harper, E C (Blackburn, 1926): 1/0
Harris, G (Burnley, 1966): 1/0
Harris, P P (Portsmouth, 1950–4): 2/0
Harris, S S (Cambridge University, Old Westminsters, 1904–6): 6/2
Harrison, A H (Old Westminsters, 1893): 2/0
Harrison, G (Everton, 1921–2): 2/0
Harrow, J H (Chelsea, 1923): 2/0
Hart, E (Leeds, 1929–34): 8/0
Hartley, F (Oxford C, 1923): 1/0
Harvey, A (Wednesbury Strollers, 1881): 1/0
Harvey, J C (Everton, 1971): 1/0
Hassall, H W (Huddersfield, Bolton, 1951–4): 5/4
Hateley, M (Portsmouth, Milan, Monaco, Rangers, 1984–92): 32/9
Haworth, G (Accrington, 1887–90): 5/0
Hawtrey, J P (Old Etonians, 1881): 2/0

Hawkes, R M (Luton, 1907–8): 5/0
Haygarth, E B (Swifts, 1875): 1/0
Haynes, J N (Fulham, 1955–62): 56/18
Healless, H (Blackburn, 1925–8): 2/0
Hector, K J (Derby, 1974): 2/0
Hedley, G A (Sheff Utd, 1901): 1/0
Hegan, K E (Corinthians, 1923–4): 4/4
Hellawell, M S (Birmingham, 1963): 2/0
Henfrey, A G (Cambridge University, Corinthians, 1891–6): 5/2
Henry, R P (Tottenham, 1963): 1/0
Heron, F (Wanderers, 1876): 1/0
Heron, G H H (Uxbridge, Wanderers, 1873–8): 5/0
Hibbert, W (Bury, 1910): 1/0
Hibbs, H E (Birmingham, 1930–6): 25/0
Hill, F (Bolton, 1963): 2/0
Hill, G A (Man Utd, 1976–8): 6/0
Hill, J H (Burnley, Newcastle, 1925–9): 11/0
Hill, R (Luton, 1983–6): 3/0
Hill, R H (Millwall, 1926): 1/0
Hillman, J (Burnley, 1899): 1/0
Hills, A F (Old Harrovians, 1879): 1/0
Hilsdon, G R (Chelsea, 1907–9): 8/14
Hinchcliffe, A G (Everton, Sheff Wed, 1997–8): 6/0
Hine, E W (Leicester, 1929–32): 6/4
Hinton, A T (Wolves, Nottingham Forest, 1963–5): 3/0
Hirst, D E (Sheff Wed, 1991–2): 3/1
Hitchens, G A (A Villa, Inter, 1961–2): 7/5
Hobbis, H H F (Charlton, 1936): 2/1
Hoddle, G (Tottenham, Monaco, 1980–8): 53/8
Hodge, S B (A Villa, Tottenham, Nottingham Forest, 1986–91): 24/0
Hodgetts, D (A Villa, 1888–94): 6/1
Hodgkinson, A (Sheff Utd, 1957–61): 5/0
Hodgson, G (Liverpool, 1931): 3/1
Hodkinson, J (Blackburn, 1913–20): 3/0
Hogg, W (Sunderland, 1902): 3/0
Holdcroft, G H (Preston, 1937): 2/0
Holden, A D (Bolton, 1959): 5/0
Holden, G H (Wednesbury OA, 1881–4): 4/0
Holden–White, C (Corinthians, 1888): 2/0
Holford, T (Stoke, 1903): 1/0
Holley, G H (Sunderland, 1909–13): 10/8
Holliday, E (Middlesbrough, 1960): 3/0
Hollins, J W (Chelsea, 1967): 1/0
Holmes, R (Preston, 1888–95): 7/0
Holt, J (Everton, Reading, 1890–1900): 10/0
Hopkinson, E (Bolton, 1958–60): 14/0
Hossack, A H (Corinthians, 1892–4): 2/0
Houghton, W E (A Villa, 1931–3): 7/5
Houlker, A E (Blackburn, Portsmouth, Southampton, 1902–6): 5/0
Howarth, R H (Preston, Everton, 1887–94): 5/0
Howe, D (WBA, 1958–60): 23/0
Howe, J R (Derby, 1948–9): 3/0
Howell, L S (Wanderers, 1873): 1/0
Howell, R (Sheff Utd, Liverpool, 1895–9): 2/1
Howey, S N (Newcastle, 1995–6): 4/0
Hudson, A A (Stoke, 1975): 2/0
Hudson, J (Sheffield, 1883): 1/0
Hudspeth, F C (Newcastle, 1926): 1/0
Hufton, A E (West Ham, 1924–9): 6/0
Hughes, E W (Liverpool, Wolves, 1970–80): 62/1

Hughes, L (Liverpool, 1950): 3/0
Hulme, J H A (Arsenal, 1927–33): 9/4
Humphreys, P (Notts Co, 1903): 1/0
Hunt, G S (Tottenham, 1933): 3/1
Hunt, Rev K R G (Leyton, 1911): 2/0
Hunt, R (Liverpool, 1962–9): 34/18
Hunt, S (WBA, 1984): 2/0
Hunter, J (Sheffield Heeley, 1878–82): 7/0
Hunter, N (Leeds, 1966–75): 28/2
Hurst, G C (West Ham, 1966–72): 49/24
Ince, P E C (Man Utd, Internazionale, Liverpool, 1993–8): 43/2
Iremonger, J (Nottingham Forest, 1901–2): 2/0
Jack, D N B (Bolton, Arsenal, 1924–33): 9/3
Jackson, E (Oxford University, 1891): 1/0
James, D B (Liverpool, 1997): 1/0
Jarrett, B G (Cambridge University, 1876–8): 3/0
Jefferis, F (Everton, 1912): 2/0
Jezzurd, B A G (Fulham, 1954–6): 2/0
Johnson, D E (Ipswich, Liverpool, 1975–80): 8/6
Johnson, E (Saltley College, Stoke, 1880–4): 2/2
Johnson, J A (Stoke, 1937): 5/2
Johnson, T C F (Man City, Everton, 1926–33): 5/5
Johnson, W H (Sheff Utd, 1900–3): 6/1
Johnston, H (Blackpool, 1947–54): 10/0
Jones, A (Walsall Swifts, Great Lever, 1882–3): 3/0
Jones, H (Blackburn, 1927–8): 6/0
Jones, H (Nottingham Forest, 1923): 1/0
Jones, M D (Sheff Utd, Leeds, 1965–70): 3/0
Jones, R (Liverpool, 1992–5): 8/0
Jones, W (Bristol C, 1901): 1/0
Jones, W H (Liverpool, 1950): 2/0
Joy, B (Casuals, 1936): 1/0
Kail, E I L (Dulwich Hamlet, 1929): 3/2
Kay, A H (Everton, 1963): 1/1
Kean, F W (Sheff Wed, Bolton, 1923–9): 9/0
Keegan, J K (Liverpool, Hamburg, Southampton, 1973–82): 63/21
Keen, E R L (Derby, 1933–7): 4/0
Kelly, R (Burnley, Sunderland, Huddersfield, 1920–8): 14/8
Kennedy, A (Liverpool, 1984): 2/0
Kennedy, R (Liverpool, 1976–80): 17/3
Kenyon–Slaney, W S (Wanderers, 1873): 1/2
Keown, M R (Everton, Arsenal, 1992–8): 18/3
Kevan, D T (WBA, 1957–61): 14/8
Kidd, B (Man Utd, 1970): 2/1
King, R S (Oxford University, 1882): 1/0
Kingsford, R K (Wanderers, 1874): 1/1
Kingsley, M (Newcastle, 1901): 1/0
Kinsey, G (Wolves, Derby, 1892–6): 4/0
Kirchen, A J (Arsenal, 1937): 3/2
Kirton, W J (A Villa, 1922): 1/1
Knight, A E (Portsmouth, 1920): 1/0
Knowles, C (Tottenham, 1968): 4/0
Labone, B L (Everton, 1963–70): 26/0
Lampard, F R G (West Ham, 1973–80): 2/0
Langley, E J (Fulham, 1958): 3/0
Langton, R (Blackburn, Preston, Bolton, 1947–51): 11/1
Latchford, R D (Everton, 1978–9): 12/5
Latheron, E G (Blackburn, 1913–4): 2/1
Lawler, C (Liverpool, 1971–2): 4/1
Lawton, T (Everton, Chelsea, Notts Co,

1939–49): 23/22
Leach, T (Sheff Wed, 1931): 2/0
Leake, A (A Villa, 1904–5): 5/0
Lee, E A (Southampton, 1904): 1/0
Lee, F H (Man City, 1969–72): 27/10
Lee, J (Derby, 1951): 1/1
Lee, R M (Newcastle, 1995–8): 18/2
Lee, S (Liverpool, 1983–4): 14/2
Leighton, J E (Nottingham Forest, 1886): 1/0
Le Saux, G P (Blackburn, Chelsea, 1994–8): 29/1
Le Tissier, M P (Southampton, 1994–7): 8/0
Lilley, H E (Sheff Utd, 1892): 1/0
Linacre, H J (Nottingham Forest, 1905): 2/0
Lindley, T (Cambridge University, Nottingham Forest, 1886–91): 13/15
Lindsay, A (Liverpool, 1974): 4/0
Lindsay, W (Wanderers, 1877): 1/0
Lineker, G (Leicester, Everton, Barcelona, Tottenham, 1984–92): 80/48
Lintott, E H (QPR, Bradford, 1908–9): 7/0
Lipsham, H B (Sheff Utd, 1902): 1/0
Little, B (A Villa, 1975): 1/0
Lloyd, L V (Liverpool, Nottingham Forest, 1971–80): 4/0
Lockett, A (Stoke, 1903): 1/0
Lodge, L V (Cambridge University, Corinthians, 1894–6): 5/0
Lofthouse, J M (Blackburn, Accrington, Blackburn, 1885–90): 7/3
Lofthouse, N (Bolton, 1951–9): 33/30
Longworth, E (Liverpool, 1920–3): 5/0
Lowder, A (Wolves, 1889): 1/0
Lowe, E (A Villa, 1947): 3/0
Lucas, T (Liverpool, 1922–6): 3/0
Luntley, E (Nottingham Forest, 1880): 2/0
Lyttleton, Hon A (Cambridge University, 1877): 1/1
Lyttleton, Hon E (Cambridge University, 1878): 1/0
McCall, J (Preston, 1913–21): 5/1
McDermott, T (Liverpool, 1978–82): 25/3
McDonald, C A (Burnley, 1958–9): 8/0
McFarland, R L (Derby, 1971–7): 28/0
McGarry, W H (Huddersfield, 1954–6): 4/0
McGuiness, W (Man Utd, 1959): 4/0
McInroy, A (Sunderland, 1927): 1/0
McMahon, S (Liverpool, 1988–91): 17/0
McManaman, S (Liverpool, 1995–8): 22/0
McNab, R (Arsenal, 1969): 4/0
McNeal, R (WBA, 1914): 2/0
McNeil, M (Middlesbrough, 1961–2): 9/0
Mabbutt, G (Tottenham, 1983–92): 16/1
Macauley, R H (Cambridge University, 1881): 1/0
Macdonald, M (Newcastle, 1972–6): 14/6
Macrae, S (Notts Co, 1883–4): 6/0
Maddison, F B (Oxford University, 1872): 1/0
Madeley, P E (Leeds, 1971–7): 24/0
Magee, T P (WBA, 1923–5): 5/0
Makepeace, H (Everton, 1906–12): 4/0
Male, C G (Arsenal, 1935–9): 19/0
Mannion, W J (Middlesbrough, 1947–52): 26/11
Mariner, P (Ipswich, Arsenal, 1977–85): 35/13
Marsden, J T (Darwen, 1891): 1/0
Marsden, W (Sheff Wed, 1930): 3/0
Marsh, R W (QPR, Man City, 1972–3): 9/1

Marshall, T (Darwen, 1880–1): 2/0
Martin, A (West Ham, 1981–7): 17/0
Martin, H (Sunderland, 1914): 1/0
Martyn, A N (C Palace, Leeds, 1992–8): 7/0
Marwood, B (Arsenal, 1989): 1/0
Maskrey, H M (Derby, 1908): 1/0
Mason, C (Wolves, 1887–90): 3/0
Matthews, R D (Coventry, 1956–7): 5/0
Matthews, S (Stoke, Blackpool, 1935–57): 54/11
Matthews, V (Sheff Utd, 1928): 2/1
Maynard, W J (1st Surrey Rifles, 1872–6): 2/0
Meadows, J (Man City, 1955): 1/0
Medley, L D (Tottenham, 1951–2): 6/1
Meehan, T (Chelsea, 1924): 1/0
Melia, J (Liverpool, 1963): 2/1
Mercer, D W (Sheff Utd, 1923): 2/1
Mercer, J (Everton, 1939): 5/0
Merrick, G H (Birmingham, 1952–4): 23/0
Merson, P C (Arsenal, Middlesbrough, 1992–8): 19/2
Metcalfe, V (Huddersfield, 1951): 2/0
Mew, J W (Man Utd, 1921): 1/0
Middleditch, B (Corinthians, 1897): 1/0
Milburn, J E T (Newcastle, 1949–56): 13/10
Miller, B G (Burnley, 1961): 1/0
Miller, H S (Charlton, 1923): 1/1
Mills, G R (Chelsea, 1938): 3/3
Mills, M D (Ipswich, 1973–82): 42/0
Milne, G (Liverpool, 1963–5): 14/0
Milton, C A (Arsenal, 1952): 1/0
Milward, A (Everton, 1891–7): 4/3
Mitchell, C (Upton Park, 1880–5): 5/5
Mitchell, J F (Man City, 1925): 1/0
Moffat, H (Oldham, 1913): 1/0
Molyneux, G (Southampton, 1902–3): 4/0
Moon, W R (Old Westminsters, 1888–91): 7/0
Moore, H T (Notts Co, 1883–5): 2/0
Moore, J (Derby, 1923): 1/1
Moore, R F (West Ham, 1962–74): 108/2
Moore, W G B (West Ham, 1923): 1/2
Mordue, J (Sunderland, 1912–3): 2/0
Morice, C J (Barnes, 1872): 1/0
Morley, A (A Villa, 1982–3): 6/0
Morley, H (Notts Co, 1910): 1/0
Morren, T (Sheff Utd, 1898): 1/1
Morris, F (WBA, 1920–1): 2/1
Morris, J (Derby, 1949–50): 3/3
Morris, W W (Wolves, 1939): 3/0
Morse, H (Notts Co, 1879): 1/0
Mort, T (A Villa, 1924–6): 3/0
Morten, A (C Palace, 1873): 1/0
Mortensen, S H (Blackpool, 1947–54): 25/23
Morton, J R (West Ham, 1938): 1/1
Mosforth, W (Sheff Wed, Sheff Albion, Sheff Wed, 1877–82): 9/3
Moss, F (Arsenal, 1934–5): 4/0
Moss, F (A Villa, 1922–4): 5/0
Mosscrop, E (Burnley, 1914): 2/0
Mozley, B (Derby, 1950): 3/0
Mullen, J (Wolves, 1947–54): 12/6
Mullery, A P (Tottenham, 1965–72): 35/1
Neal, P G (Liverpool, 1976–84): 50/5
Needham, E (Sheff Utd, 1894–1902): 16/3
Neville, G A (Man Utd, 1995–8): 30/0
Neville, P J (Man Utd, 1996–8): 12/0
Newton, K R (Blackburn, Everton, 1966–70):

27/0

Nicholls, J (WBA, 1954): 2/1
Nicholson, W E (Tottenham, 1951): 1/1
Nish, D J (Derby, 1973–4): 5/0
Norman, M (Tottenham, 1962–5): 23/0
Nuttall, H (Bolton, 1928–9): 3/0
Oakley, W J (Oxford University, Corinthians, 1895–1901): 16/0
O'Dowd, J P (Chelsea, 1932–3): 3/0
O'Grady, M (Huddersfield, Leeds, 1963–9): 2/3
Ogilvie, R A M M (Clapham Rovers, 1874): 1/0
Oliver, L F (Fulham, 1929): 1/0
Olney, B A (A Villa, 1928): 2/0
Osborne, F R (Fulham, Tottenham, 1923–6): 4/3
Osborne, R (Leicester, 1928): 1/0
Osgood, P L (Chelsea, 1970–4): 4/0
Osman, R (Ipswich, 1980–4): 11/0
Ottaway, C J (Oxford University, 1872–4): 2/0
Owen, J R B (Sheffield, 1874): 1/0
Owen, M (Liverpool, 1998): 9/3
Owen, S W (Luton, 1954): 3/0
Page, L A (Burnley, 1927–8): 7/1
Paine, T L (Southampton, 1963–6): 19/7
Pallister, G A (Middlesbrough, Man Utd, 1988–97): 22/0
Palmer, C L (Sheff Wed, 1992–4): 18/1
Pantling, H H (Sheff Utd, 1924): 1/0
Paravacini, P J de (Cambridge University, 1883): 3/0
Parker, P A (QPR, Man Utd, 1989–94): 19/0
Parker, T R (Southampton, 1925): 1/0
Parkes, P B (QPR, 1974): 1/0
Parkinson, J (Liverpool, 1910): 2/0
Parr, P C (Oxford University, 1882): 1/0
Parry, E H (Old Carthusians, 1879–82): 3/1
Parry, R A (Bolton, 1960): 2/1
Patchitt, B C A (Corinthians, 1923): 2/0
Pawson, F W (Cambridge University, Swifts, 1883–5): 2/1
Payne, J (Luton, 1937): 1/2
Peacock, A (Middlesbrough, Leeds, 1962–6): 6/3
Peacock, J (Middlesbrough, 1937): 3/0
Pearce, S (Nottingham Forest, 1987–97): 76/4
Pearson, H F (WBA, 1932): 1/0
Pearson, J H (Crewe, 1892): 1/0
Pearson, J S (Man Utd, 1976–8): 15/5
Pearson, S C (Man Utd, 1948–52): 8/5
Pease, W H (Middlesbrough, 1927): 1/0
Pegg, D (Man Utd, 1957): 1/0
Pejic, M (Stoke, 1974): 4/0
Pelly, F R (Old Foresters, 1893–4): 3/0
Pennington, J (WBA, 1907–20): 25/0
Pentland, F B (Middlesbrough, 1909): 5/0
Perry, C (WBA, 1890–3): 3/0
Perry, T (WBA, 1898): 1/0
Perry, W (Blackpool, 1956): 3/2
Perryman, S (Tottenham, 1982): 1/0
Peters, M (West Ham, Tottenham, 1966–74): 67/20
Phelan, M C (Man Utd, 1990): 1/0
Phillips, L H (Portsmouth, 1952–5): 3/0
Pickering, F (Everton, 1964–5): 3/5
Pickering, J (Sheff Utd, 1933): 1/0
Pickering, N (Sunderland, 1983): 1/0
Pike, T M (Cambridge University, 1886): 1/0
Pilkington, B (Burnley, 1955): 1/0

Plant, J (Bury, 1900): 1/0
Platt, D (A Villa, Bari, Juventus, Sampdoria, Arsenal, 1990–6): 62/27
Plum, S L (Charlton, 1923): 1/0
Pointer, R (Burnley, 1962): 3/2
Porteous, T S (Sunderland, 1891): 1/0
Priest, A E (Sheff Utd, 1900): 1/0
Prinsep, J F M (Clapham Rovers, 1879): 1/0
Puddefoot, S C (Blackburn, 1926): 2/0
Pye, J (Wolves, 1950): 1/0
Pym, R H (Bolton, 1925–6): 3/0
Quantrill, A (Derby, 1920–1): 4/1
Quixall, A (Sheff Wed, 1954–5): 5/0
Radford, J (Arsenal, 1969–72): 2/0
Raikes, G B (Oxford University, 1895–6): 4/0
Ramsey, A E (Southampton, Tottenham, 1949–54): 32/3
Rawlings, A (Preston, 1921): 1/0
Rawlings, W E (Southampton, 1922): 2/0
Rawlinson, J F P (Cambridge University, 1882): 1/0
Rawson, H E (Royal Engineers, 1875): 1/0
Rawson, W S (Oxford University, 1875–7): 2/0
Read, A (Tufnell Park, 1921): 1/0
Reader, J (WBA, 1894): 1/0
Reaney, P (Leeds, 1969–71): 3/0
Redknapp, J F (Liverpool, 1996–7): 8/0
Reeves, K (Norwich, Man City, 1980): 2/0
Regis, C (WBA, Coventry, 1982–8): 5/0
Reid, P (Everton, 1985–8): 13/0
Revie, D G (Man City, 1955–7): 6/4
Reynolds, J (WBA, A Villa, 1892–7): 8/3
Richards, C H (Nottingham Forest, 1898): 1/0
Richards, G H (Derby, 1909): 1/0
Richards, J P (Wolves, 1973): 1/0
Richardson, J R (Newcastle, 1933): 2/2
Richardson, K (A Villa, 1994): 1/0
Richardson, W G (WBA, 1935): 1/0
Rickaby, S (WBA, 1954): 1/0
Rigby, A (Blackburn, 1927–8): 1/3
Rimmer, E J (Sheff Wed, 1930–2): 4/2
Rimmer, J J (Arsenal, 1976): 1/0
Ripley, S E (Blackburn, 1993–7): 2/0
Rix, G (Arsenal, 1981–4): 17/0
Robb, G (Tottenham, 1954): 1/0
Roberts, C (Man Utd, 1905): 3/0
Roberts, F (Man City, 1925): 4/0
Roberts, G (Tottenham, 1983–4): 6/0
Roberts, H (Arsenal, 1931): 1/1
Roberts, H (Millwall, 1931): 1/1
Roberts, R (WBA, 1887–90): 3/0
Roberts, W T (Preston, 1924): 2/4
Robinson, J (Sheff Wed, 1937–9): 4/3
Robinson, J W (Derby, New Brighton Tower, Southampton, 1897–1901): 11/0
Robson, B (WBA, Man Utd, 1980–92): 90/26
Robson, R (WBA, 1958–62): 20/4
Rocastle, D (Arsenal, 1989–92): 14/0
Rose, W C (Wolves, Preston, Wolves, 1884–91): 5/0
Rostron, T (Darwen, 1881): 2/0
Rowe, A (Tottenham, 1934): 1/0
Rowley, J F (Man Utd, 1949–52): 6/6
Rowley, W (Stoke, 1889–92): 2/0
Royle, J (Everton, Man City, 1971–77): 6/2
Ruddlesdin, H (Sheff Wed, 1904–5): 3/0

Ruddock, N (Liverpool, 1995): 1/0
Ruffell, J W (West Ham, 1926–30): 6/0
Rutherford, J (Newcastle, 1904–8): 11/3
Sadler, D (Man Utd, 1968–71): 4/0
Sagar, C (Bury, 1900–2): 2/1
Sagar, E (Everton, 1936): 4/0
Salako, J A (C Palace, 1991–2): 5/0
Sandford, E A (WBA, 1933): 1/0
Sandilands, R R (Old Westminsters, 1892–6): 5/2
Sands, J (Nottingham Forest, 1880): 1/0
Sansom, K (C Palace, Arsenal, 1979–88): 86/1
Saunders, F E (Swifts, 1888): 1/0
Savage, A H (C Palace, 1876): 1/0
Sayer, J (Stoke, 1887): 1/0
Scales, J R (Liverpool, 1995): 3/0
Scattergood, E (Derby, 1913): 1/0
Schofield, J (Stoke, 1892–5): 3/1
Scholes, P (Man Utd, 1997–8): 11/4
Scott, L (Arsenal, 1947–9): 17/0
Scott, W R (Brentford, 1937): 1/0
Seaman, D A (QPR, Arsenal, 1989–98): 44/0
Seddon, J (Bolton, 1923–9): 6/0
Seed, J M (Tottenham, 1921–5): 5/1
Settle, J (Bury, Everton, 1899–1903): 6/6
Sewell, J (Sheff Wed, 1952–4): 6/3
Sewell, W R (Blackburn, 1924): 1/0
Shackleton, L F (Sunderland, 1949–55): 5/1
Sharp, J (Everton, 1903–5): 2/1
Sharpe, L S (Man Utd, 1991–4): 8/0
Shaw, G E (WBA, 1932): 1/0
Shaw, G L (Sheff Utd, 1959–63): 5/0
Shea, D (Blackburn, 1914): 2/0
Shearer, A (Southampton, Blackburn, Newcastle, 1992–8): 43/20
Shellito, K J (Chelsea, 1963): 1/0
Shelton, A (Notts Co, 1889–92): 6/0
Shelton, C (Notts Rangers, 1888): 1/0
Shepherd, A (Bolton, Newcastle, 1906–11): 2/2
Sheringham, E P (Tottenham, Man Utd, 1993–8): 35/9
Shilton, P L (Leicester, Stoke, Nottingham Forest, Southampton, Derby, 1971–90): 125/0
Shimwell, E (Blackpool, 1949): 1/0
Shutt, G (Stoke, 1886): 1/0
Silcock, J (Man Utd, 1921–3): 3/0
Sillett, R P (Chelsea, 1955): 3/0
Simms, E (Luton, 1922): 1/0
Simpson, J (Blackburn, 1911–4): 8/1
Sinton, A (QPR, Sheff Wed, 1992–4): 12/0
Slater, W J (Wolves, 1955–60): 12/0
Smalley, T (Wolves, 1937): 1/0
Smart, T (A Villa, 1921–30): 5/0
Smith, A (Nottingham Forest, 1891–3): 3/0
Smith, A K (Oxford University, 1872): 1/0
Smith, A M (Arsenal, 1989–92): 13/2
Smith, B (Tottenham, 1921–2): 2/0
Smith, C E (C Palace, 1876): 1/0
Smith, G O (Oxford University, Old Carthusians, Corinthians, 1893–1901): 20/12
Smith, H (Reading, 1905–6): 4/0
Smith, J (WBA, 1920–3): 2/1
Smith, J (Bolton, 1913–20): 5/2
Smith, J C R (Millwall, 1939): 2/0
Smith, J W (Portsmouth, 1932): 3/4
Smith, L (Brentford, 1939): 1/0

Smith, L (Arsenal, 1951–3): 6/0
Smith, R A (Tottenham, 1961–4): 15/13
Smith, S (A Villa, 1895): 1/1
Smith, S C (Leicester, 1936): 1/0
Smith, T (Birmingham, 1960): 2/0
Smith, T (Liverpool, 1971): 1/0
Smith, W H (Huddersfield, 1922–8): 3/0
Sorby, T H (Thursday Wanderers, 1879): 1/1
Southgate, G (A Villa, 1996–8): 27/0
Southworth, J (Blackburn, 1889–92): 3/3
Sparks, F J (Herts Rangers, Clapham Rovers, 1879–80): 3/3
Spence, J W (Man Utd, 1926–7): 2/1
Spence, R (Chelsea, 1936): 2/0
Spencer, C W (Newcastle, 1924–5): 2/0
Spencer, H (A Villa, 1897–1905): 6/0
Spiksley, F (Sheff Wed, 1893–8): 7/5
Spilsbury, B W (Cambridge University, 1885–6): 3/5
Spink, N (A Villa, 1983): 1/0
Spouncer, W A (Nottingham Forest, 1900): 1/0
Springett, R D G (Sheff Wed, 1960–6): 33/0
Sproston, B (Leeds, Tottenham, Man City, 1937–9): 11/0
Squire, R T (Cambridge University, 1886): 3/0
Stanbrough, M H (Old Carthusians, 1895): 1/0
Staniforth, R (Huddersfield, 1954–5): 8/0
Starling, R W (Sheff Wed, A Villa, 1933–7): 2/0
Statham, D (WBA, 1983): 3/0
Steele, F C (Stoke, 1937): 6/8
Stein, B (Luton, 1984): 1/0
Stephenson, C (Huddersfield, 1924): 1/0
Stephenson, G T (Derby, Sheff Wed, 1928–31): 3/2
Stephenson, J E (Leeds, 1938–9): 2/0
Stepney, A C (Man Utd, 1968): 1/0
Sterland, M (Sheff Wed, 1989): 1/0
Steven, T M (Everton, Rangers, Marseille, 1985–92): 36/4
Stevens, G A (Tottenham, 1985–6): 7/0
Stevens, M G (Everton, 1985–92): 46/0
Stewart, J (Sheff Wed, Newcastle, 1907–11): 3/2
Stewart, P A (Tottenham, 1992): 3/0
Stiles, N P (Man Utd, 1965–70): 28/1
Stoker, J (Birmingham, 1933–4): 3/0
Stone, S B (Nottingham Forest, 1996): 9/2
Storer, H (Derby, 1924–8): 2/1
Storey, P E (Arsenal, 1971–3): 19/0
Storey–Moore, Ian (Nottingham Forest, 1970): 1/0
Strange, A H (Sheff Wed, 1930–4): 20/0
Stratford, A H (Wanderers, 1874): 1/0
Streten, B (Luton, 1950): 1/0
Sturgess, A (Sheff Utd, 1911–4): 2/0
Summerbee, M G (Man City, 1968–73): 8/1
Sunderland, A (Arsenal, 1980): 1/0
Sutcliffe, J W (Bolton, Millwall, 1893–1903): 5/0
Sutton, C (Blackburn, 1997): 1/0
Swan, P (Sheff Wed, 1960–2): 19/0
Swepstone, H A (Pilgrims, 1880–3): 6/0
Swift, F V (Man City, 1947–9): 19/0
Tait, G (Birmingham Excelsior, 1881): 1/0
Talbot, B (Ipswich, 1977–80): 6/0
Tambling, R V (Chelsea, 1963–6): 3/1
Tate, J T (A Villa, 1931–3): 3/0
Taylor, E (Blackpool, 1954): 8/0

Taylor, E H (Huddersfield, 1923–6): 8/0
Taylor, J G (Fulham, 1951): 2/0
Taylor, P H (Liverpool, 1948): 3/0
Taylor, P J (C Palace, 1976): 4/2
Taylor, T (Man Utd, 1953–8): 19/16
Temple, D W (Everton, 1965): 1/0
Thickett, H (Sheff Utd, 1899): 2/0
Thomas, D (Coventry, 1983): 2/0
Thomas, D (QPR, 1975–6): 8/0
Thomas, G R (C Palace, 1991–2): 9/0
Thomas, M L (Arsenal, 1989–90): 2/0
Thompson, P (Liverpool, 1964–70): 16/0
Thompson, P B (Liverpool, 1976–83): 42/1
Thompson, T (A Villa, Preston, 1952–7): 2/0
Thomson, R A (Wolves, 1964–5): 8/0
Thornewell, G (Derby, 1923–5): 4/1
Thornley, I (Man City, 1907): 1/0
Tilson, S F (Man City, 1934–6): 4/6
Titmuss, F (Southampton, 1922–3): 2/0
Todd, C (Derby, 1972–7): 27/0
Toone, G (Notts Co, 1892): 2/0
Topham, A G (Casuals, 1894): 1/0
Topham, R (Wolves, Casuals, 1893–4): 2/0
Towers, M A (Sunderland, 1976): 3/0
Townley, W J (Blackburn, 1889–90): 2/2
Townrow, J E (Clapham Orient, 1925–6): 2/0
Tremelling, D R (Birmingham, 1928): 1/0
Tresadern, J (West Ham, 1923): 2/0
Tueart, D (Man City, 1975–7): 6/2
Tunstall, F E (Sheff Utd, 1923–5): 7/0
Turnbull, R J (Bradford, 1920): 1/0
Turner, A (Southampton, 1900–1): 2/0
Turner, H (Huddersfield, 1931): 2/0
Turner, J A (Bolton, Stoke, Derby, 1893–8): 3/0
Tweedy, G J (Grimsby, 1937): 1/0
Ufton, D G (Charlton, 1954): 1/0
Underwood, A (Stoke, 1891–2): 2/0
Unsworth, D G (Everton, 1995): 1/0
Urwin, T (Middlesbrough, Newcastle, 1923–6): 4/0
Utley, G (Barnsley, 1913): 1/0
Vaughton, O H (A Villa, 1882–4): 5/6
Veitch, C C M (Newcastle, 1906–9): 6/0
Veitch, J G (Old Westminsters, 1894): 1/3
Venables, T F (Chelsea, 1965): 2/0
Venison, B (Newcastle, 1995): 2/0
Vidal, R W S (Oxford University, 1873): 1/0
Viljoen, C (Ipswich, 1975): 2/0
Viollet, D S (Man Utd, 1960–2): 2/1
Von Donop (Royal Engineers, 1873–5): 2/0
Wace, H (Wanderers, 1878–9): 3/0
Waddle, C R (Newcastle, Tottenham, Marseille, 1985–92): 62/6
Wadsworth, S J (Huddersfield, 1922–7): 9/0
Wainscoat, W R (Leeds, 1929): 1/0
Waiters, A K (Blackpool, 1964–5): 5/0
Walden, F I (Tottenham, 1914–22): 2/0
Walker, D S (Nottingham Forest, Sampdoria, Sheff Wed, 1989–94): 59/0
Walker, I M (Tottenham, 1996–7): 3/0
Walker, W H (A Villa, 1921–33): 18/9
Wall, G (Man Utd, 1907–13): 7/2
Wallace, C W (A Villa, 1913–20): 3/0
Wallace, D L (Southampton, 1986): 1/1
Walsh, P (Luton, 1983–4): 5/1
Walters, A M (Cambridge University, Old

Carthusians, 1885–90): 9/0
Walters, K M (Rangers, 1991): 1/0
Walters, P M (Oxford University, Old Carthusians, 1885–90): 13/0
Walton, N (Blackburn, 1890): 1/0
Ward, J T (Blackburn Olympic, 1885): 1/0
Ward, P (Brighton, 1980): 1/0
Ward, T V (Derby, 1948–9): 2/0
Waring, T (A Villa, 1931–2): 5/4
Warner, C (Upton Park, 1878): 1/0
Warren, B (Derby, Chelsea, 1906–11): 22/2
Waterfield, G S (Burnley, 1927): 1/0
Watson, D (Norwich, Everton, 1984–8): 12/0
Watson, D V (Sunderland, Man City, Werder Bremen, Southampton, Stoke, 1974–82): 65/4
Watson, V M (West Ham, 1923–30): 5/4
Watson, W (Burnley, 1913–20): 3/0
Watson, W (Sunderland, 1950–1): 4/0
Weaver, S (Newcastle, 1932–3): 3/0
Webb, G W (West Ham, 1911): 2/1
Webb, N J (Nottingham Forest, Man Utd, 1911): 26/4
Webster, M (Middlesbrough, 1930): 3/0
Wedlock, W J (Bristol C, 1907–14): 26/2
Weir, D (Bolton, 1889): 2/2
Welch, R de C (Wanderers, Harrow Chequers, 1872–4): 2/0
Weller, K (Leicester, 1974): 4/1
Welsh, D (Charlton, 1938–9): 3/1
West, G (Everton, 1969): 3/0
Westwood, R W (Bolton, 1935–7): 6/0

Whateley, O (A Villa, 1883): 2/2
Wheeler, J E (Bolton, 1955): 1/0
Wheldon, G F (Bolton, 1897–8): 1/6
White, D (Man City, 1993): 1/0
White, T A (Everton, 1933): 1/0
Whitehead, J (Accrington, Blackburn, 1893–4): 2/0
Whitfield, H (Old Etonians, 1879): 1/1
Witham, M (Sheff Utd, 1892): 1/0
Whitworth, S (Leicester, 1975–6): 7/0
Whymark, T J (Ipswich, 1978): 1/0
Widdowson, S W (Nottingham Forest, 1880): 1/0
Wignall, F (Nottingham Forest, 1965): 2/2
Wilcox, J M (Blackburn, 1996): 1/0
Wilkes, A (A Villa, 1901–2): 5/1
Wilkins, R G (Chelsea, Man Utd, Milan, 1976–87): 84/3
Wilkinson, B (Sheff Utd, 1904): 1/0
Wilkinson, L R (Oxford University, 1891): 1/0
Williams, B F (Wolves, 1949–56): 24/0
Williams, O (Clapton Orient, 1923): 2/0
Williams, S (Southampton, 1983–5): 6/0
Williams, W (WBA, 1897–9): 6/0
Williamson, E C (Arsenal, 1923): 2/0
Williamson, R G (Middlesbrough, 1905–13): 7/0
Willingham, C K (Huddersfield, 1937–9): 12/1
Willis, A (Tottenham, 1952): 1/0
Wilshaw, D J (Wolves, 1954–7): 12/10
Wilson, C P (Hendon, 1884): 2/0
Wilson, C W (Oxford University, 1879–81): 2/0
Wilson, G (Sheff Wed, 1921–4): 12/0
Wilson, G P (Corinthians, 1900): 2/1
Wilson, R (Huddersfield, Everton, 1960–8): 63/0
Wilson, T (Huddersfield, 1928): 1/0

Winckworth, W N (Old Westminsters, 1892–3): 2/1

Windridge, J E (Chelsea, 1908–9): 8/7

Wingfield–Stratford, C V (Royal Engineers, 1877): 1/0

Winterburn, N (Arsenal, 1990–3): 2/0

Wise, D F (Chelsea, 1991–6): 12/1

Withe, P (A Villa, 1981–5): 11/1

Wollaston, C H R (Wanderers, 1874–80): 4/1

Wolstenholme, S (Everton, Blackburn, 1904–5): 3/0

Wood, H (Wolves, 1890–6): 3/1

Wood, R E (Man Utd, 1955–6): 3/0

Woodcock, A S (Nottingham Forest, Kohn, Arsenal, 1978–86): 42/16

Woodger, G (Oldham, 1911): 1/0

Woodhall, G (WBA, 1888): 2/1

Woodley, V R (Chelsea, 1937–9): 19/0

Woods, C C E (Norwich, Rangers, Sheff Wed, 1985–93): 43/0

Woodward, V J (Tottenham, Chelsea, 1903–11): 23/29

Woosnam, M (Man City, 1922): 1/0

Worrall, F (Portsmouth, 1935–7): 2/2

Worthington, F S (Leicester, 1974–5): 8/2

Wreford–Brown, C (Oxford University, Old Carthusians, 1889–98): 4/0

Wright, E G D (Cambridge University, 1906): 1/0

Wright, I E (C Palace, Arsenal, 1991–8): 31/9

Wright, J D (Newcastle, 1939): 1/0

Wright, M (Southampton, Derby, Liverpool, 1984–96): 45/1

Wright, T J (Everton, 1968–70): 11/0

Wright, W A (Wolves, 1947–59): 105/3

Wylie, J G (Wanderers, 1878): 1/1

Yates, J (Burnley, 1889): 1/3

York, R E (A Villa, 1922–6): 2/0

Young, A (Huddersfield, 1933–9): 9/0

Young, G M (Sheff Wed, 1965): 1/0

Scotland

Adams, J (Hearts, 1889–93): 3/0

Agnew, W B (Kilmarnock, 1907–8): 3/0

Aird, J (Burnley, 1954): 4/0

Aitken, A (Newcastle, Middlesbrough, Leicester Fosse, 1901–11): 14/0

Aitken, G G (East Fife, Sunderland, 1949–54): 8/0

Aitken, R (Dumbarton, 1886–8): 2/0

Aitken, R (Celtic, Newcastle, St Mirren, 1980–92): 57/1

Aitkenhead, W A C (Blackburn, 1912): 1/2

Albiston, A (Man Utd, 1982–6): 14/0

Alexander, D (East Stirlingshire, 1894): 2/1

Allan, D S (Queen's Park, 1885–6): 3/4

Allan, G (Liverpool, 1897): 1/0

Allan, H (Hearts, 1902): 1/0

Allan, J (Queen's Park, 1887): 2/2

Allan, T (Dundee, 1974): 2/0

Ancell, R F D (Newcastle, 1937): 2/0

Anderson, A (Hearts, 1933–9): 23/0

Anderson, F (Clydesdale, 1874): 1/1

Anderson, G (Kilmarnock, 1901): 1/0

Anderson, H A (Raith, 1914): 1/0

Anderson, J (Leicester, 1954): 1/0

Anderson, W (Queen's Park, 1882–5): 6/4

Andrews, P (Eastern, 1875): 1/1

Archibald, A (Rangers, 1921–32): 8/1

Archibald, S (Aberdeen, Tottenham, Barcelona, 1980–6): 27/4

Armstrong, M W (Aberdeen, 1936–7): 3/0

Arnott, W (Queen's Park, 1883–93): 14/0

Auld, J R (Third Lanark, 1887 9): 3/0

Auld, R (Celtic, 1959–60): 3/0

Baird, A (Queen's Park, 1892–4): 2/0

Baird, D (Hearts, 1890–2): 3/2

Baird, H (Airdrieonians, 1956): 1/0

Baird, J C (Vale of Leven, 1876–80): 3/2

Baird, S (Rangers, 1957–8): 7/2

Baird, W U (St Bernard, 1897): 1/0

Bannon, E (Dundee Utd, 1980–6): 11/1

Barbour, A (Renton, 1885): 1/1

Barker, J B (Rangers, 1893–4): 2/4

Barrett, F (Dundee, 1894–5): 2/0

Battles, B (Celtic, 1901): 3/0

Battles, B junior (Hearts, 1931): 1/1

Bauld, W (Hearts, 1950): 3/2

Baxter, J C (Rangers, Sunderland, 1961–8): 34/3

Baxter, R D (Middlesbrough, 1939): 3/0

Beattie, A (Preston, 1937–9): 7/0

Beattie, R (Preston, 1939): 1/0

Begbie, I (Hearts, 1890–4): 4/0

Bell, A (Man Utd, 1912): 1/0

Bell, J (Dumbarton, Everton, Celtic, 1890–1900): 10/5

Bell, M (Hearts, 1901): 1/0

Bell, W J (Leeds, 1966): 2/0

Bennett, A (Celtic, Rangers, 1904–13): 11/2

Bennie, R (Airdrieonians, 1925–6): 3/0

Bernard, P R J (Oldham, 1995): 2/0

Berry, D (Queen's Park, 1894–9): 3/1

Berry, W H (Queen's Park, 1888–91): 4/0

Bett, J (Rangers, Lokeren, Aberdeen, 1982–90): 25/1

Beveridge, W W (Glasgow University, 1879–80): 3/1

Black, A (Hearts, 1938–9): 3/3

Black, D (Hurlford, 1889): 1/1

Black, E (Metz, 1988): 2/0

Black, I H (Southampton, 1948): 1/0

Blackburn, J E (Royal Engineers, 1873): 1/0

Blacklaw, A S (Burnley, 1963–6): 3/0

Blackley, J (Hibernian, 1974–7): 7/0

Blair, D (Clyde, A Villa, 1929–33): 8/0

Blair, J (Sheff Wed, Cardiff, 1920–4): 8/0

Blair, J (Motherwell, 1934): 1/0

Blair, J A (Blackpool, 1947): 1/0

Blair, W (Third Lanark, 1896): 1/0

Blessington, J (Celtic, 1894–6): 4/0

Blyth, J A (Coventry, 1978): 2/0

Bone, J (Norwich, 1972–3): 2/1

Booth, S (Aberdeen, Borussia Dortmund, 1993–8): 16/5

Bowie, J (Rangers, 1920): 2/0

Bowie, W (Linthouse, 1891): 1/0

Bowman, D (Dundee Utd, 1992–4): 6/0

Bowman, G A (Montrose, 1892): 1/0

Boyd, J M (Newcastle, 1934): 1/0

Boyd, R (Mossend Swifts, 1889–91): 2/2

Boyd, T (Motherwell, Celtic, 1991–8): 55/1

Boyd, W G (Clyde, 1931): 2/1

Brackenbridge, T (Hearts, 1888): 1/1

Bradshaw, T (Bury, 1928): 1/0

Brand, R (Rangers, 1961–2): 8/8

Branden, T (Blackburn, 1896): 1/0

Brazil, A (Ipswich, Tottenham, 1980–3): 13/1

Bremner, D (Hibernian, 1976): 1/0

Bremner, W J (Leeds, 1965–76): 54/3

Brennan, F (Newcastle, 1947–54): 7/0

Breslin, B (Hibernian, 1897): 1/0

Brewster, G (Everton, 1921): 1/0

Brogan, J (Celtic, 1971): 4/0

Brown, A (Middlesbrough, 1904): 1/0

Brown, A (St Mirren, 1890–1): 2/0

Brown, A D (East Fife, Blackpool, 1950–4): 14/6

Brown, G C P (Rangers, 1931–7): 19/0

Brown, H (Partick, 1947): 3/0

Brown, J (Cambuslang, 1890): 1/0

Brown, J B (Clyde, 1939): 1/0

Brown, J G (Sheff Utd, 1975): 1/0

Brown, R (Dumbarton, 1884): 2/0

Brown, R (Rangers, 1947–52): 3/0

Brown, R junior (Dumbarton, 1885): 1/0

Brown, W D F (Dundee, Tottenham, 1958–66): 28/0

Browning, J (Celtic, 1914): 1/0

Brownlie, J (Hibernian, 1971–6): 7/0

Bruce, D (Vale of Leven, 1890): 1/0

Bruce, R F (Middlesbrough, 1934): 1/0

Buchan, M M (Aberdeen, Man Utd, 1972–9): 34/0

Buchanan, J (Cambuslang, 1889): 1/0

Buchanan, J (Rangers, 1929–30): 2/0

Buchanan, P S (Chelsea, 1938): 1/1

Buchanan, R (Abercorn, 1891): 1/1

Buckley, P (Aberdeen, 1954–5): 3/1

Buick, A (Hearts, 1902): 2/2

Burley, C W (Chelsea, Celtic, 1995–8): 25/1

Burley, G (Ipswich, 1979–82): 11/0

Burns, F (Man Utd, 1970): 1/0

Burns, K (Birmingham, Nottingham Forest, 1974–81): 20/1

Burns, T (Celtic, 1981–88): 8/0

Busby, M W (Man Utd, 1934): 1/0

Cairns, T (Rangers, 1920–5): 8/1

Calderhead, D (Queen of the South, 1889): 1/0

Calderwood, C (Tottenham, 1995–8): 28/1

Calderwood, R (Cartvale, 1885): 3/2

Caldow, E (Rangers, 1957–63): 40/4

Callaghan, P (Hibernian, 1900): 1/0

Callaghan, W (Dunfermline, 1970): 2/0

Cameron, J (Rangers, 1886): 1/0

Cameron, J (Queen's Park, 1896): 1/0

Cameron, J (St Mirren, Chelsea, 1904–9): 2/0

Campbell, C (Queen's Park, 1874–86): 13/1

Campbell, H (Renton, 1889): 1/0

Campbell, Jas (Sheff Wed, 1913): 1/0

Campbell, J (South Western, 1880): 1/0

Campbell, J (Kilmarnock, 1891–2): 2/0

Campbell, J (Celtic, 1893–1903): 12/5

Campbell, J (Rangers, 1899–1901): 4/4

Campbell, K (Liverpool, Partick, 1920–2): 8/0

Campbell, P (Rangers, 1878–9): 2/2

Campbell, P (Morton, 1898): 1/0

Campbell, R (Falkirk, Chelsea, 1947–50): 5/1
Campbell, W (Morton, 1947–8): 5/0
Carabine, J (Third Lanark, 1938–9): 3/0
Carr, W M (Coventry, 1970–3): 6/0
Cassidy, J (Celtic, 1921–4): 4/1
Chalmers, S (Celtic, 1965–7): 5/3
Chalmers, W (Rangers, 1885): 1/0
Chalmers, W S (Queen's Park, 1929): 1/0
Chambers, T (Hearts, 1894): 1/1
Chaplin, G D (Dundee, 1908): 1/0
Cheyne, A G (Aberdeen, 1929–30): 5/4
Christie, A J (Queen's Park, 1898–9): 3/1
Christie, R M (Queen's Park, 1884): 1/0
Clark, J (Celtic, 1966–7): 4/0
Clark, R B (Aberdeen, 1968–73): 17/0
Clarke, S (Chelsea, 1988–94): 6/0
Cleland, J (Royal Albert, 1891): 1/0
Clements, R (Leith Ath, 1891): 1/0
Clunas, W L (Sunderland, 1924–6): 2/1
Collier, W (Raith, 1922): 1/0
Collins, J (Hibernian, Celtic, Monaco, 1988–98): 49/10
Collins, R Y (Celtic, Everton, Leeds, 1951–65): 31/10
Collins, T (Hearts, 1909): 1/0
Colman, D (Aberdeen, 1911–3): 4/0
Colquhoun, E P (Sheff Utd, 1972–3): 9/0
Colquhoun, J (Hearts, 1988): 1/0
Combe, J R (Hibernian, 1948): 3/1
Conn, A (Hearts, 1956): 1/0
Conn, A (Tottenham, 1975): 2/1
Connachan, E D (Dunfermline, 1962): 2/0
Connelly, G (Celtic, 1974): 2/0
Connolly, J (Everton, 1973): 1/0
Connor, J (Airdrieonians, 1886): 1/0
Connor, J (Sunderland, 1930–5): 4/0
Connor, R (Dundee, Aberdeen, 1986–91): 5/0
Cook, W L (Bolton, 1934–5): 3/0
Cooke, C (Dundee, Chelsea, 1966–75): 16/0
Cooper, D (Rangers, Motherwell, 1980–90): 22/6
Cormack, P B (Hibernian, Nottingham Forest, 1966–72): 9/0
Cowan, J (A Villa, 1896–8): 3/0
Cowan, J (Morton, 1948–52): 25/0
Cowan, W D (Newcastle, 1924): 1/0
Cowie, D (Dundee, 1953–8): 20/0
Cox, C J (Hearts, 1948): 1/0
Cox, S (Rangers, 1949–54): 24/0
Craig, A (Motherwell, 1929–32): 3/0
Craig, J (Celtic, 1977): 1/1
Craig, J P (Celtic, 1968): 1/0
Craig, T (Rangers, 1927–30): 8/1
Craig, T B (Newcastle, 1976): 1/0
Crapnell, J (Airdrieonians, 1929–33): 9/0
Crawford, D (St Mirren, 1894–1900): 3/0
Crawford, J (Queen's Park, 1932–3): 5/0
Crawford, S (Raith, 1995): 1/1
Crerand, P T (Celtic, Man Utd, 1961–6): 16/0
Cringan, W (Celtic, 1920–3): 5/0
Crosbie, J A (Ayr, Birmingham, 1920–2): 2/0
Croal, J A (Falkirk, 1913–4): 3/0
Cropley, A J (Hibernian, 1972): 2/0
Cross, J H (Third Lanark, 1903): 1/0
Cruickshank, J (Hearts, 1964–76): 6/0
Crum, J (Celtic, 1936–9): 2/0
Cullen, M J (Luton, 1956): 1/0

Cumming, D S (Middlesbrough, 1938): 1/0
Cumming, J (Hearts, 1955–60): 9/0
Cummings, G (Partick, A Villa, 1935–9): 9/0
Cunningham, A N (Rangers, 1920–7): 12/5
Cunningham, W C (Preston, 1954–5): 8/0
Curran, H P (Wolves, 1970): 5/1
Dailly, C (Derby, 1997–8): 9/1
Dalglish, K (Celtic, Liverpool, 1972–87): 102/30
Davidson, D (Queen's Park, 1878–81): 5/1
Davidson, J A (Partick, 1954–55): 8/1
Davidson, S (Middlesbrough, 1921): 1/0
Dawson, A (Rangers, 1980–3): 5/0
Dawson, J (Rangers, 1935–8): 14/0
Deans, J (Celtic, 1975): 2/0
Delaney, J (Celtic, Man Utd, 1936–48): 13/3
Devine, A (Falkirk, 1910): 1/1
Dewar, G (Dumbarton, 1888–9): 2/1
Dewar, N (Third Lanark, 1932–3): 3/4
Dick, J (West Ham, 1959): 1/0
Dickie, M (Rangers, 1897–1900): 3/0
Dickson, W (Dumbarton, 1888): 1/0
Dickson, W (Kilmarnock, 1970–1): 5/4
Divers, J (Celtic, 1895): 1/1
Divers, J (Celtic, 1939): 1/1
Docherty, T H (Preston, Arsenal, 1952–9): 25/1
Dodds, D (Dundee Utd, 1984): 2/1
Dodds, J (Celtic, 1914): 3/0
Dodds, W (Aberdeen, 1997–8): 4/0
Doig, J E (Arbroath, Sunderland, 1887–1903): 5/0
Donachie, W (Man City, 1972–9): 35/0
Donaldson, A (Bolton, 1914–22): 6/4
Donnachie, J (Oldham, 1913–4): 3/1
Donnelly, S (Celtic, 1997): 7/0
Dougall, C (Birmingham, 1947): 1/0
Dougall, J (Preston, 1939): 1/1
Dougan, R (Hearts, 1950): 1/0
Douglas, A (Chelsea, 1911): 1/0
Douglas, J (Renfrew, 1880): 1/0
Dowds, P (Celtic, 1892): 1/0
Downie, R (Third Lanark, 1892): 1/0
Doyle, D (Celtic, 1892–8): 8/0
Doyle, J (Ayr, 1976): 1/0
Drummond, J (Falkirk, Rangers, 1892–1903): 14/2
Dunbar, M (Cartvale, 1886): 1/1
Duncan, A (Hibernian, 1975–6): 6/0
Duncan, D (Derby, 1933–8): 14/7
Duncan, D M (East Fife, 1948): 3/1
Duncan, J (Alexandra Ath, 1878–82): 2/1
Duncan, J (Leicester, 1926): 1/1
Duncanson, J (Rangers, 1947): 1/0
Dunlop, J (St Mirren, 1890): 1/0
Dunlop, W (Liverpool, 1906): 1/0
Dunn, J (Hibernian, Everton, 1925–9): 6/2
Durie, G S (Chelsea, Tottenham, Rangers, 1988–98): 39/7
Durrant, I (Rangers, 1988–94): 11/0
Dykes, J (Hearts, 1938–9): 2/0
Easson, J F (Portsmouth, 1931–4): 3/1
Elliott, M (Leicester, 1997–8): 3/0
Ellis, J (Mossend Swifts, 1892): 1/1
Evans, A (A Villa, 1982): 4/0
Evans, R (Celtic, Chelsea, 1949–60): 48/0
Ewart, J (Bradford, 1921): 1/0

Ewing, T (Partick, 1958): 2/0
Farm, G N (Blackpool, 1953–9): 10/0
Ferguson, D (Rangers, 1988): 2/0
Ferguson, D (Dundee Utd, Everton, 1992–7): 7/0
Ferguson, I (Rangers, 1989–97): 9/0
Ferguson, J (Vale of Leven, 1974–8): 6/6
Ferguson, R (Kilmarnock, 1966–7): 7/0
Fernie, W (Celtic, 1954–8): 12/1
Findlay, R (Kilmarnock, 1898): 1/0
Fitchie, T T (Arsenal, Queen's Park, 1905–7): 4/1
Flavell, R (Airdrieonians, 1947): 2/2
Fleck, R (Norwich, 1990–1): 4/0
Fleming, C (East Fife, 1954): 1/2
Fleming, J W (Rangers, 1929–30): 3/3
Fleming, R (Morton, 1886): 1/0
Forbes, A R (Sheff Utd, Arsenal, 1947–52): 14/0
Forbes, J (Vale of Leven, 1884–7): 5/0
Ford, D (Hearts, 1974): 3/0
Forrest, J (Rangers, Aberdeen, 1966–71): 5/0
Forsyth, A (Partick, Man Utd, 1972–6): 10/0
Forsyth, C (Kilmarnock, 1964–5): 4/0
Forsyth, T (Motherwell, Rangers, 1971–8): 22/0
Foyers, R (St Bernards, 1893–4): 2/0
Fraser, D M (WBA, 1968–9): 2/0
Fraser, J (Moffat, 1891): 1/0
Fraser, J (Dundee, 1907): 1/0
Fraser, M J E (Queen's Park, 1880–3): 5/4
Fraser, W (Sunderland, 1955): 2/0
Fulton, W (Abercorn, 1884): 1/0
Fyfe, J H (Third Lanark, 1895): 1/0
Gabriel, J (Everton, 1961–4): 2/0
Gallacher, H K (Airdrieonians, Newcastle, Chelsea, Derby, 1924–35): 20/23
Gallacher, K W (Dundee Utd, Coventry, Blackburn, 1988–98): 36/8
Gallacher, P (Sunderland, 1935): 1/1
Galloway, M (Celtic, 1992): 1/0
Galt, J H (Rangers, 1908): 2/1
Gardiner, I (Motherwell, 1958): 1/0
Gardner, D R (Third Lanark, 1897): 1/0
Gardner, R (Queen's Park, 1872–8): 5/0
Gemmell, T (St Mirren, 1955): 2/1
Gemmell, T (Celtic, 1966–71): 18/1
Gemmill, A (Derby, Nottingham Forest, Birmingham, 1971–81): 43/8
Gemmill, S (Nottingham Forest, 1995–8): 13/0
Gibb, W (Clydesdale, 1873): 1/1
Gibson, D W (Leicester, 1963–5): 7/3
Gibson, J D (Partick, A Villa, 1926–30): 8/2
Gibson, N (Rangers, Partick, 1895–1905): 14/1
Gilchrist, J E (Celtic, 1922): 1/0
Gilhooley, M (Hull, 1922): 1/0
Gillespie, G (Rangers, Queen's Park, 1880–91): 7/0
Gillespie, G T (Liverpool, 1988–91): 13/0
Gillespie, J (Third Lanark, 1898): 1/3
Gillespie, J (Queen's Park, 1896): 1/0
Gillespie, R (Queen's Park, 1927–33): 4/0
Gillick, T (Everton, 1937–9): 5/3
Gilmour, J (Dundee, 1931): 1/0
Gilzean, A J (Dundee, Tottenham, 1964–71): 22/12
Glavin, R (Celtic, 1977): 1/0
Glen, A (Aberdeen, 1956): 2/0

Glen, R (Renton, Hibernian, 1895–1900): 3/0

Goram, A L (Oldham, Hibernian, Rangers, 1986–98): 43/0

Gordon, J E (Rangers, 1912–20): 10/0

Gossland, J (Rangers, 1884): 1/2

Goudie, J (Abercorn, 1884): 1/1

Gough, C R (Dundee Utd, Tottenham, Rangers, 1983–93): 61/6

Gourlay, J (Cambuslang, 1886–8): 2/1

Govan, J (Hibernian, 1948–9): 6/0

Gow, D R (Rangers, 1888): 1/0

Gow, J J (Queen's Park, 1885): 1/0

Gow, J R (Rangers, 1888): 1/0

Graham, A (Leeds, 1978–81): 10/2

Graham, G (Arsenal, Man Utd, 1972–3): 12/3

Graham, J (Annbank, 1884): 1/0

Graham, J A (Arsenal, 1921): 1/0

Grant, J (Hibernian, 1959): 2/0

Grant, P (Celtic, 1989): 2/0

Gray, A (Hibernian, 1903): 1/0

Gray, A M (A Villa, Wolves, Everton, 1976–85): 20/7

Gray, D (Rangers, 1929–33): 10/0

Gray, E (Leeds, 1969–77): 12/3

Gray, F T (Leeds, Nottingham Forest, Leeds, 1976–83): 32/1

Gray, W (Pollokshields Ath, 1886): 1/0

Green, A (Blackpool, Newcastle, 1971–2): 6/0

Greig, J (Rangers, 1964–65): 44/3

Groves, W (Hibernian, Celtic, 1888–90): 3/5

Guilliland, W (Queen's Park, 1891–5): 4/0

Gunn, B (Norwich, 1990–4): 6/0

Haddock, H (Clyde, 1955–8): 6/0

Haddow, D (Rangers, 1894): 1/0

Haffey, F (Celtic, 1960–1): 2/0

Hamilton, A W (Dundee, 1962–6): 24/0

Hamilton, G (Aberdeen, 1947–54): 5/4

Hamilton, G (Port Glasgow Ath, 1906): 1/0

Hamilton, J (Queen's Park, 1892–3): 3/3

Hamilton, J (St Mirren, 1924): 1/0

Hamilton, R C (Rangers, Dundee, 1899–1911): 11/14

Hamilton, T (Hurlford, 1891): 1/0

Hamilton, T (Rangers, 1932): 1/0

Hamilton, W M (Hibernian, 1965): 1/0

Hannah, A B (Renton, 1888): 1/0

Hannah, J (Third Lanark, 1889): 1/0

Hansen, A D (Liverpool, 1979–87): 26/0

Hansen, J (Partick, 1972): 2/0

Harkness, J D (Queen's Park, Hearts, 1927–34): 12/0

Harper, J M (Aberdeen, Hibernian, Aberdeen, 1973–8): 4/2

Harper, W (Hibernian, Arsenal, 1923–6): 11/0

Harris, J (Partick, 1921): 2/0

Harris, N (Newcastle, 1924): 1/0

Harrower, W (Queen's Park, 1882–6): 3/5

Hartford, R A (WBA, Man City, Everton, Man City, 1972–82): 50/4

Harvey, D (Leeds, 1973–77): 16/0

Hastings, A C (Sunderland, 1936–8): 2/0

Haughney, M (Celtic, 1954): 1/0

Hay, D (Celtic, 1970–4): 27/0

Hay, J (Celtic, Newcastle, 1905–14): 11/0

Hegarty, P (Dundee Utd, 1979–83): 8/0

Heggie, C (Rangers, 1886): 1/5

Henderson, G H (Rangers, 1904): 1/0

Henderson, J G (Portsmouth, Arsenal, 1953–9): 7/1

Henderson, W (Rangers, 1963–71): 29/5

Hendry, E C J (Blackburn, 1993–8): 31/1

Hepburn, J (Alloa, 1891): 1/0

Hepburn, R (Ayr, 1932): 1/0

Herd, A C (Hearts, 1935): 1/0

Herd, D G (Arsenal, 1959–61): 5/4

Herd, G (Clyde, 1958–61): 5/0

Heriot, J (Birmingham, 1969–70): 8/0

Hewie, J D (Charlton, 1956–60): 19/2

Higgins, A (Kilmarnock, 1885): 1/4

Higgins, A (Newcastle, 1910–1): 4/1

Highet, T C (Queen's Park, 1875–8): 4/1

Hill, D (Rangers, 1881–2): 3/0

Hill, D A (Third Lanark, 1906); 1/0

Hill, F R (Aberdeen, 1930–1): 3/0

Hill, J (Ayr, 1922): 1/0

Hogg, R M (Celtic, 1937): 1/0

Holm, A H (Queen's Park, 1882–3): 3/0

Holt, D D (Hearts, 1963–4): 5/0

Holton, J A (Man Utd, 1973–5): 15/2

Hope, R (WBA, 1968–9): 2/0

Hopkin, D (C Palace, Leeds, 1997–8): 4/2

Houliston, W (Queen of the South, 1949): 3/2

Houston, S M (Man Utd, 1976): 1/0

Howden, W (Partick, 1905): 1/0

Howie, J (Newcastle, 1905–80): 3/2

Howie, H (Hibernian, 1949): 1/1

Howieson, J (St Mirren, 1927): 1/0

Hughes, J (Celtic, 1965–70): 8/1

Hughes, W (Sunderland, 1975): 1/0

Humphries, W (Motherwell, 1952): 1/0

Hunter, A (Kilmarnock, Celtic, 1972–4): 4/0

Hunter, J (Dundee, 1909): 1/0

Hunter, J (Third Lanark, Eastern, Third Lanark, 1874–7): 4/0

Hunter, R (St Mirren, 1890): 1/0

Hunter, W (Motherwell, 1960–1): 3/1

Husband, J (Partick, 1947): 1/0

Hutchison, T (Coventry, 1974–6): 17/1

Hutton, J (Aberdeen, Blackburn, 1923–7): 10/1

Hyslop, T (Stoke, Rangers, 1896–7): 2/1

Imlach, J J S (Nottingham Forest, 1958): 4/0

Imrie, W N (St Johnstone, 1929): 2/1

Inglis, J (Kilmarnock Ath, 1884): 1/0

Inglis, J (Rangers, 1883): 2/0

Irons, J H (Queen's Park, 1900): 1/0

Irvine, B (Aberdeen, 1991–4): 9/0

Jackson, A (Cambuslang, 1886–8): 2/0

Jackson, A (Aberdeen, Huddersfield, 1925–30): 17/8

Jackson, C (Rangers, 1975–6): 8/1

Jackson, D (Hibernian, Celtic, 1995–8): 24/4

Jackson, J (Partick, Chelsea, 1931–5): 8/0

Jackson, T A (St Mirren, 1904–7): 6/0

James, A W (Preston, Arsenal, 1926–33): 8/3

Jardine, A (Rangers, 1971–80): 38/1

Jarvie, A (Airdrieonians, 1971): 3/0

Jenkinson, T (Hearts, 1887): 1/1

Jess, E (Aberdeen, 1993–8): 14/1

Johnston, L H (Clyde, 1948): 2/1

Johnston, M (Watford, Celtic, Nantes, Rangers, 1984–92): 38/14

Johnston, R (Sunderland, 1938): 1/0

Johnston, W (Rangers, 1966–78): 22/0

Johnstone, D (Rangers, 1973–80): 14/2

Johnstone, J (Abercorn, 1888): 1/0

Johnstone, J (Celtic, 1965–75): 23/4

Johnstone, J (Kilmarnock, 1894): 1/1

Johnstone, J A (Hearts, 1930–3): 3/0

Johnstone, R (Hibernian, Man City, 1951–6): 17/9

Johnstone, W (Third Lanark, 1887–90): 3/1

Jordan, J (Leeds, Man Utd, Milan, 1973–82): 52/11

Kay, J L (Queen's Park, 1880–4): 6/5

Keillor, A (Montrose, Dundee, 1891–7): 6/3

Keir, L (Dumbarton, 1885–8): 5/0

Kelly, H T (Blackpool, 1952): 1/0

Kelly, J (Renton, Celtic, 1888–96): 8/1

Kelly, J C (Barnsley, 1949): 2/0

Kelso, R (Renton, Dundee, 1885–98): 8/1

Kelso, T (Dundee, 1914): 1/1

Kennaway, J (Celtic, 1934): 1/0

Kennedy, A (Eastern, Third Lanark, 1875–84): 6/0

Kennedy, J (Celtic, 1964–5): 6/0

Kennedy, J (Hibernian, 1897): 1/0

Kennedy, S (Aberdeen, 1978–82): 8/0

Kennedy, S (Partick, 1905): 1/0

Kennedy, S (Rangers, 1975): 5/0

Ker, G (Queen's Park, 1880–2): 5/10

Ker, W (Granville, Queen's Park, 1872–3): 2/0

Kerr, A (Partick, 1955): 2/0

Kerr, P (Hibernian, 1924): 1/0

Key, G (Hearts, 1902): 1/0

Key, W (Queen's Park, 1907): 1/0

King, A (Hearts, Celtic, 1896–9): 6/1

King, J (Hamilton, 1933–4): 2/0

King, W S (Queen's Park, 1929): 1/0

Kinloch, J D (Partick, 1922): 1/0

Kinnaird, A F (Wanderers, 1872): 1/0

Kinnear, D (Rangers, 1938): 1/1

Lambert, P (Motherwell, Borussia Dortmund, Celtic, 1995–8): 12/0

Lambie, J A (Queen's Park, 1886–8): 3/0

Lambie, W A (Queen's Park, 1892–7): 9/5

Lamont, D (Pilgrims, 1885): 1/0

Lang, A (Dumbarton, 1880): 1/0

Lang, J J (Clydesdale, Third Lanark, 1876–8): 2/1

Latta, A (Dumbarton, 1888–9): 2/0

Law, D (Huddersfield, Man City, Torino, Man Utd, Man City, 1959–74): 55/30

Law, G (Rangers, 1910): 3/0

Law, T (Chelsea, 1928–30): 2/0

Lawrence, J (Newcastle, 1911): 1/0

Lawrence, T (Liverpool, 1963–9): 3/0

Lawson, D (St Mirren, 1923): 1/0

Leckie, R (Queen's Park, 1872): 1/0

Leggat, G (Aberdeen, Fulham, 1956–60): 18/8

Leighton, J (Aberdeen, Man Utd, Hibernian, 1983–98): 86/0

Lennie, W (Aberdeen, 1908): 2/1

Lennox, R (Celtic, 1967–70): 10/3

Leslie, L G (Airdrieonians, 1961): 5/0

Levein, C (Hearts, 1990–95): 16/0

Liddell, W (Liverpool, 1947–56): 28/6

Liddle, D (East Fife, 1931): 3/0

Lindsay, D (St Mirren, 1903): 1/0

Lindsay, J (Dumbarton, 1880–6): 8/6
Lindsay, J (Renton, 1888–93): 3/0
Linwood, A B (Clyde, 1950): 1/1
Little, R J (Rangers, 1953): 1/0
Livingstone, G T (Man City, Rangers, 1906–7): 2/0
Lochhead, A (Third Lanark, 1889): 1/0
Logan, J (Ayr, 1891): 1/1
Logan, T (Falkirk, 1913): 1/0
Logie, J T (Arsenal, 1953): 1/0
Loney, W (Celtic, 1910): 2/0
Long, H (Clyde, 1947): 1/0
Longair, W (Dundee, 1894): 1/0
Lorimer, P (Leeds, 1970–6): 21/4
Love, A (Aberdeen, 1931): 3/1
Low, A (Falkirk, 1934): 1/0
Low, T P (Rangers, 1897): 1/0
Low, W L (Newcastle, 1911–20): 5/0
Lowe, J (Cambuslang, 1891): 1/1
Lowe, J (St Bernards, 1887): 1/1
Lundie, J (Hibernian, 1886): 1/0
Lyall, J (Sheff Wed, 1905): 1/0
McAdam, J (Third Lanark, 1880): 1/1
McAllister, B (Wimbledon, 1997): 3/0
McAllister, G (Leicester, Leeds, Coventry, 1990–7): 56/5
McArthur, D (Celtic, 1895–9): 3/0
McAtee, A (Celtic, 1913): 1/0
McAulay, J (Dumbarton, Arthurlie, 1882–4): 2/1
McAulay, J (Dumbarton, 1883–7): 8/0
McAuley, R (Rangers, 1932): 2/0
McAvennie, F (West Ham, Celtic, 1986–8): 5/1
McBain, E (St Mirren, 1894): 1/0
McBain, N (Man Utd, Everton, 1922–4): 3/0
McBride, J (Celtic, 1967): 2/0
McBride, P (Preston, 1904–9): 6/0
McCall, J (Renton, 1886–90): 5/1
McCall, S M (Everton, Rangers, 1990–8): 40/1
McCalliog, J (Sheff Wed, Wolves, 1967–71): 5/1
McCallum, N (Renton, 1888): 1/1
McCann, R J (Motherwell, 1959–61): 5/0
McCartney, W (Hibernian, 1902): 1/0
McClair, B (Celtic, Man Utd, 1987–93): 30/2
McClory, A (Motherwell, 1927–35): 3/0
McCloy, P (Ayr, 1924–5): 2/0
McCloy, P (Rangers, 1973): 4/0
McCoist, A (Rangers, 1986–97): 58/19
McColl, A (Renton, 1888): 1/0
McColl, I M (Rangers, 1950–8): 14/0
McColl, R S (Queen's Park, Newcastle, Queen's Park, 1896–1908): 13/13
McColl, W (Renton, 1895): 1/0
McCombie, A (Sunderland, Newcastle, 1903–5): 4/0
McCorkindale, J (Partick, 1891): 1/0
McCormick, R (Abercorn, 1886): 1/0
McCrae, D (St Mirren, 1929): 2/0
McCreadie, A (Rangers, 1893–4): 2/0
McCreadie, E G (Chelsea, 1965–9): 23/0
McCulloch, F (Hearts, Brentford, Derby, 1935–9): 7/13
MacDonald, A (Rangers, 1976): 1/0
McDonald, J (Edinburgh University, 1886): 1/0
McDonald, J (Sunderland, 1956): 2/0
MacDougall, E J (Norwich, 1975–6): 7/3
McDougall, J (Liverpool, 1931): 2/4

McDougall, J (Airdrieonians, 1926): 1/0
McDougall, J (Vale of Leven, 1877–9): 5/0
McFadyen, W (Motherwell, 1934): 2/2
Macfarlane, A (Dundee, 1904–11): 5/1
McFarlane, R (Greenock Morton, 1896): 1/0
McGarr, E (Aberdeen, 1970): 2/0
McGarvey, F P (Liverpool, Celtic, 1979–84): 7/0
McGeoch, A (Dumbreck, 1876–7): 4/0
McGhee, J (Hibernian, 1886): 1/0
McGhee, M (Aberdeen, 1983–4): 4/2
McGinlay, J (Bolton, 1994–7): 13/4
McGonagle, W (Celtic, 1933–5): 6/0
McGrain, D (Celtic, 1973–82): 62/0
McGregor, J C (Vale of Leven, 1877–80): 4/1
McGrory, J E (Kilmarnock, 1965–6): 3/0
McGrory, J (Celtic, 1928–34): 7/6
McGuire, W (Beith, 1881): 2/1
McGurk, F (Birmingham, 1934): 1/0
McHardy, H (Rangers, 1885): 1/0
McInally, A (A Villa, Bayern Munich, 1989–90): 8/3
McInally, J (Dundee Utd, 1987–93): 10/0
McInally, T B (Celtic, 1926–7): 2/0
McInnes, T (Cowlairs, 1926–7): 2/2
McIntosh, W (Third Lanark, 1905): 1/0
McIntyre, A (Vale of Leven, 1878–82): 2/0
McIntyre, H (Rangers, 1880): 1/0
McIntyre, J (Rangers, 1884): 1/0
McKay, D C (Hearts, Tottenham, 1957–66): 22/4
Mackay, G (Hearts, 1988): 4/1
McKay, J (Blackburn, 1924): 1/0
McKay, R (Newcastle, 1928): 1/0
McKean, R (Rangers, 1976): 1/0
McKenzie, D (Brentford, 1938): 1/0
Mackenzie, J A (Partick, 1954–6): 9/1
McKeown, M (Celtic, 1889–90): 2/0
McKie, J (East Stirlingshire, 1898): 1/2
McKillop, T R (Rangers, 1938): 1/0
McKimmie, S (Aberdeen, 1989–96): 40/1
McKinlay, D (Liverpool, 1922): 2/0
McKinlay, T (Celtic, 1996–8): 19/0
McKinlay, W (Dundee Utd, Blackburn, 1994–8): 25/4
McKinnon, A (Queen's Park, 1874): 1/1
McKinnon, R (Rangers, 1966–71): 28/0
McKinnon, R (Motherwell, 1994–5): 3/1
MacKinnon, W (Dumbarton, 1883–4): 4/1
McKinnon, W W (Queen's Park, 1872–1879): 9/5
McLaren, A (St Johnstone, 1929–33): 5/0
McLaren, A (Preston, 1947–8): 4/4
McLaren, A (Hearts, Rangers, 1992–6): 24/4
McLaren, J (Hibernian, Celtic, 1888–90): 3/0
McLean, A (Celtic, 1926–7): 4/1
McLean, D (St Bernards, 1896–7): 2/0
McLean, D (Sheff Wed, 1912): 1/0
McLean, G (Dundee, 1968): 1/0
McLean, T (Kilmarnock, 1969–71): 6/1
McLeish, A (Aberdeen, 1980–93): 77/0
McLeod, D (Celtic, 1905–6): 4/0
McLeod, J (Dumbarton, 188–93): 5/0
MacLeod, J M (Hibernian, 1961): 4/0
MacLeod, M (Celtic, Borussia Dortmund, Hibernian, 1985–91): 20/1
McLeod, W (Cowlairs, 1886): 1/0
McLintock, A (Vale of Leven, 1875–80): 3/0
McLintock, F (Leicester, Arsenal, 1963–71): 9/1

McLuckie, J S (Man City, 1934): 1/0
McMahon, A (Celtic, 1892–1902): 6/6
McMenemy, J (Celtic, 1905–20): 12/5
McMenemy, J (Motherwell, 1934): 1/0
McMillan, J (St Bernards, 1897): 1/0
McMillan, I L (Airdrieonians, Rangers, 1952–61): 6/2
McMillan, T (Dumbarton, 1887): 1/0
McMullan, J (Partick, Man City, 1920–9): 16/0
McNab, A (Morton, 1921): 2/0
McNab, A (Sunderland, WBA, 1937–9): 2/0
McNab, C D (Dundee, 1931–2): 6/0
McNab, J S (Liverpool, 1923): 1/0
McNair, A (Celtic, 1906–20): 15/0
McNamara, J (Celtic, 1997–8): 7/0
McNaught, W (Raith, 1951–5): 5/0
McNeil, H (Queen's Park, 1874–81): 10/5
McNeil, M (Rangers, 1876–80): 2/0
McNeill, W (Celtic, 1961–72): 29/3
McPhail, J (Celtic, 1950–4): 5/3
McPhail, R (Airdrieonians, Rangers, 1927–38): 17/7
McPherson, D (Kilmarnock, 1892): 1/0
McPherson, D (Hearts, Rangers, 1989–93): 27/0
McPherson, J (Clydesdale, 1875): 1/0
McPherson, J (Vale of Leven, 1879–85): 8/8
McPherson, J (Kilmarnock, Cowlairs, Rangers, 1888–97): 9/8
McPherson, J (Hearts, 1891): 1/0
McPherson, R (Arthurlie, 1882): 1/1
McQueen, G (Leeds, Man Utd, 1974–81): 30/5
McQueen, M (Leith Ath, 1890–1): 2/0
McRorie, D M (Morton, 1931): 1/0
McSpadyen, A (Partick, 1939): 2/0
McStay, P (Celtic, 1984–97): 76/9
McStay, W (Celtic, 1921–8): 13/0
McTavish, J (Falkirk, 1910): 1/0
McWhattie. G C (Queen's Park, 1901): 2/0
McWilliam, P (Newcastle, 1905–11): 8/0
Macari, L (Celtic, Man Utd, 1972–8): 24/5
Macauley, A R (Brentford, Arsenal, 1947–8): 7/0
Madden, J (Celtic, 1893): 2/5
Main, F R (Rangers, 1938): 1/0
Main, J (Hibernian, 1909): 1/0
Maley, W (Celtic, 1893): 2/0
Malpas, M (Dundee Utd, 1984–93): 55/0
Marshall, G (Celtic, 1992): 1/0
Marshall, H (Celtic, 1899–1900): 2/1
Marshall, J (Middlesbrough, Llanelly, 1921–4): 7/1
Marshall, J (Third Lanark, 1885–7): 4/1
Marshall, J (Rangers, 1932–4): 3/1
Marshall, R W (Rangers, 1892–4): 2/0
Martin, B (Motherwell, 1995): 2/0
Martin, F (Aberdeen, 1954–5): 6/0
Martin, N (Hibernian, Sunderland, 1965–6): 3/0
Martis, J (Motherwell, 1961): 1/0
Mason, J (Third Lanark, 1949–51): 7/4
Massie, A (Hearts, A Villa, 1932–8): 18/1
Masson, D S (QPR, Derby, 1976–8): 17/5
Mathers, D (Partick, 1954): 1/0
Maxwell, W S (Stoke, 1898): 1/0
May, J (Rangers, 1906–9): 5/0
Meechan, P (Celtic, 1896): 1/0
Meiklejohn, D D (Rangers, 1922–34): 15/3
Menzies, A (Hearts, 1906): 1/0

Mercer, R (Hearts, 1912–3): 2/0
Middleton, R (Cowdenbeath, 1930): 1/0
Millar, A (Hearts, 1939): 1/0
Millar, J (Rangers, 1897–8): 3/2
Millar, J (Rangers, 1963): 2/0
Miller, J (St Mirren, 1931–4): 5/0
Miller, P (Dumbarton, 1882–3): 3/0
Miller, T (Liverpool, Man Utd, 1920–1): 3/2
Miller, W (Third Lanark, 1876): 1/0
Miller, W (Celtic, 1947–8): 6/1
Miller, W (Aberdeen, 1975–90): 65/1
Mills, W (Aberdeen, 1936–7): 3/0
Milne, J V (Middlesbrough, 1938–9): 2/0
Mitchell, D (Rangers, 1890–4): 5/0
Mitchell, J (Kilmarnock, 1908–10): 3/0
Mitchell, R C (Newcastle, 1951): 2/1
Mochan, N (Celtic, 1954): 3/0
Moir, W (Bolton, 1950): 1/0
Moncur, R (Newcastle, 1968–72): 16/0
Morgan, H (St Mirren, Liverpool, 1898–9): 2/0
Morgan, W (Burnley, Man Utd, 1968–74): 21/1
Morris, D (Raith, 1923–5): 6/1
Morris, H (East Fife, 1950): 1/3
Morrison, T (St Mirren, 1927): 1/0
Morton, A L (Queen's Park, Rangers, 1920–32): 31/5
Morton, H A (Kilmarnock, 1929): 2/0
Mudie, J K (Blackpool, 1957–8): 17/9
Muir, W (Dundee, 1907): 1/0
Muirhead, T A (Rangers, 1922–30): 8/0
Mulhall, G (Aberdeen, Sunderland, 1960–4): 3/1
Munro, A D (Hearts, Blackpool, 1937–8): 3/1
Munro, F M (Wolves, 1971–5): 9/0
Munro, I (St Mirren, 1979–80): 7/0
Munro, N (Abercorn, 1888–9): 2/1
Murdoch, J (Motherwell, 1931): 1/0
Murdoch, R (Celtic, 1966–70): 12/5
Murphy, F (Celtic, 1938): 1/1
Murray, J (Renton, 1895): 1/0
Murray, J (Hearts, 1958): 5/1
Murray, J W (Vale of Leven, 1890): 1/0
Murray, P (Hibernian, 1896–7): 2/0
Murray, S (Aberdeen, 1972): 1/0
Mutch, G (Preston, 1938): 1/0
Napier, C E (Celtic, Derby, 1932–7): 5/3
Narey, D (Dundee Utd, 1977–89): 35/1
Neil, R G (Hibernian, Rangers, 1900): 2/2
Neill, R W (Queen's Park, 176–80): 5/0
Neilles, P (Hearts, 1914): 2/0
Nelson, J (Cardiff, 1925–30): 4/0
Nevin, P K F (Chelsea, Everton, Tranmere, 1986–96): 28/5
Niblo, T D (A Villa, 1904): 1/0
Nibloe, J (Kilmarnock, 1929–32): 11/0
Nicholas, C (Celtic, Arsenal, Aberdeen, 1983–9): 20/5
Nicol, S (Liverpool, 1985–92): 27/0
Nisbet, J (Ayr, 1929): 3/2
Niven, J B (Moffatt, 1885): 1/0
O'Donnell, F (Preston, Blackpool, 1937–8): 6/2
O'Donnell, P (Motherwell, 1994): 1/0
Ogilvie, D H (Motherwell, 1934): 1/0
O'Hare, J (Derby, 1970–2): 13/5
O'Neil, B (Celtic, 1996): 1/0
Ormond, W F (Hibernian, 1954–9): 6/1
O'Rourke, F (Airdrieonians, 1907): 1/1

Orr, J (Kilmarnock, 1892): 1/0
Orr, R (Newcastle, 1902–4): 2/1
Orr, T (Morton, 1952): 2/1
Orr, W (Celtic, 1900–4): 3/0
Orrock, R (Falkirk, 1913): 1/0
Oswald, J (Third Lanark, St Bernards, Rangers, 1889–97): 3/1
Parker, A H (Falkirk, Everton, 1955–8): 15/0
Parlane, D (Rangers, 1973–7): 12/1
Parlane, R (Vale of Leven, 1878–9): 3/0
Paterson, G D (Celtic, 1939): 1/0
Paterson, J (Leicester, 1920): 1/0
Paterson, J (Cowdenbeath, 1931): 3/0
Paton, A (Motherwell, 1952): 2/0
Paton, D (St Bernards, 1896): 1/0
Paton, M (Dumbarton, 1883–6): 5/0
Paton, R (Vale of Leven, 1879): 2/0
Patrick, J (St Mirren, 1897): 2/0
Paul, H (Queen's Park, 1909): 3/2
Paul, W (Partick, 1888–90): 3/6
Paul, W (Dykebar, 1891): 1/0
Pearson, T (Newcastle, 1947): 2/0
Penman, A (Dundee, 1966): 1/0
Pettigrew, W (Motherwell, 1976–7): 5/2
Phillips, J (Queen's Park, 1877–8): 3/0
Plenderleith, J B (Man City, 1961): 1/0
Porteous, W (Hearts, 1903): 1/0
Pringle, C (St Mirren, 1921): 1/0
Provan, D (Rangers, 1964–6): 5/1
Provan, D (Celtic, 1980–2): 10/1
Pursell, P (Queen's Park, 1914): 1/0
Quinn, J (Celtic, 1905–12): 11/7
Quinn, P (Motherwell, 1961–2): 4/1
Rae, J (Third Lanark, 1889–90): 2/0
Raeside, J S (Third Lanark, 1906): 1/0
Raisbeck, A G (Liverpool, 1900–7): 8/0
Rankin, G (Vale of Leven, 1890–1): 2/2
Rankin, R (St Mirren, 1929): 3/2
Redpath, W (Motherwell, 1949–52): 9/0
Reid, J G (Airdrieonians, 1914–24): 3/0
Reid, R (Brentford, 1938): 2/0
Reid, W (Rangers, 1911–4): 9/4
Reilly, L (Hibernian, 1949–57): 38/22
Rennie, H G (Hearts, Hibernian, 1900–8): 13/0
Renny–Tailyour, H W (Royal Engineers, 1873): 1/1
Rhind, A (Queen's Park, 1872): 1/0
Richmond, A (Queen's Park, 1906): 1/0
Richmond, J T (Clydesdale, Queen's Park, 1877–82): 3/1
Ring, T (Clyde, 1953–8): 12/2
Rioch, B D (Derby, Everton, Derby, 1974–8): 24/6
Ritchie, A (East Stirlingshire, 1891): 1/0
Ritchie, H (Hibernian, 1923–8): 2/0
Ritchie, J (Queen's Park, 1897): 1/1
Ritchie, W (Rangers, 1962): 1/0
Robb, D T (Aberdeen, 1971): 5/0
Robb, W (Rangers, Hibernian, 1926–8): 2/0
Robertson, A (Clyde, 1955–8): 5/2
Robertson, D (Rangers, 1992–4): 3/0
Robertson, G (Motherwell, Sheff Wed, 1910–3): 4/0
Robertson, H (Dundee, 1962): 1/0
Robertson, J (Dundee, 1931): 2/2
Robertson, J (Hearts, 1991–6): 16/2

Roberston, J N (Nottingham Forest, Derby, 1978–84): 28/9
Robertson, J G (Tottenham, 1965): 1/0
Robertson, J T (Everton, Southampton, Rangers, 1898–1905): 16/2
Robertson, P (Dundee, 1903): 1/0
Robertson, T (Queen's Park, 1889–92): 4/1
Robertson, T (Hearts, 1898): 1/1
Robertson, W (Dumbarton, 1887): 2/1
Robinson, R (Dundee, 1974–5): 4/0
Rough, A (Partick, Hibernian, 1976–86): 53/0
Rougvie, D (Aberdeen, 1984): 1/0
Rowan, A (Caledonian, Queen's Park, 1880–2): 2/0
Russell, D (Hearts, Celtic, 1895–1901): 6/1
Russell, J (Cambuslang, 1890): 1/0
Russell, W F (Airdrieonians, 1924–5): 2/0
Rutherford, E (Rangers, 1948): 1/0
St John, I (Motherwell, Liverpool, 1959–65): 21/9
Sawers, W (Dundee, 1895): 1/0
Scarff, P (Celtic, 1931): 1/0
Schaedler, E (Hibernian, 1974): 1/0
Scott, A S (Rangers, Everton, 1957–65): 21/5
Scott, J (Hibernian, 1966): 1/0
Scott, J (Dundee, 1971): 2/0
Scott, M (Airdrieonians, 1898): 1/0
Scott, R (Airdrieonians, 1894): 1/0
Scoular, J (Portsmouth, 1951–3): 9/0
Sellar, W (Battlefield, Queen's Park, 1885–93): 9/4
Semple, W (Cambuslang, 1886): 1/0
Shankly, W (Preston, 1938–9): 5/0
Sharp, G M (Everton, 1985–8): 12/1
Sharp, J (Dundee, Arsenal, Fulham, 1904–9): 5/0
Shaw, D (Hibernian, 1947–9): 8/0
Shaw, F W (Pollokshields Ath, 1884): 2/1
Shaw, J (Rangers, 1961): 4/0
Shearer, D (Aberdeen, 1994–6): 7/2
Shearer, R (Rangers, 1961): 4/0
Sillars, D C (Queen's Park, 1891–5): 5/0
Simpson, J (Third Lanark, 1895): 3/1
Simpson, J (Rangers, 1935–8): 14/1
Simpson, N (Aberdeen, 1983–8): 4/0
Simpson, R C (Celtic, 1967–9): 5/0
Sinclair, G L (Hearts, 1910–2): 3/0
Sinclair, J W E (Leicester, 1966): 1/0
Skene, L H (Queen's Park, 1904): 1/0
Sloan, T (Third Lanark, 1904): 1/0
Smellie, R (Queen's Park, 1887–93): 6/0
Smith, A (Rangers, 1898–1911): 20/5
Smith, D (Aberdeen, Rangers, 1966–80): 2/0
Smith, G (Hibernian, 1947–57): 18/4
Smith, H G (Hearts, 1988–92): 3/0
Smith, J (Rangers, 1935–8): 2/1
Smith, J (Ayr, 1924): 1/1
Smith, J (Aberdeen, Newcastle, 1968–74): 4/0
Smith, J E (Celtic, 1959): 2/0
Smith, J (Queen's Park, 1872): 1/1
Smith, J (Mauchline, Edinburgh University, Queen's Park, 1877–84): 10/12
Smith, N (Rangers, 1897–1902): 12/0
Smith, R (Queen's Park, 1872–3): 2/0
Smith, T M (Kilmarnock, Preston, 1934–8): 2/0
Somers, P (Celtic, 1905–9): 4/0
Somers, W S (Third Lanark, Queen's Park,

1879–80): 3/0

Somerville, G (Queen's Park, 1886): 1/1

Souness, G J (Middlesbrough, Liverpool, Sampdoria, 1975–86): 54/3

Speedie, D R (Chelsea, Coventry, 1985–89): 10/0

Speedie, F (Rangers, 1903): 3/2

Speirs, J H (Rangers, 1908): 1/0

Spencer, J (Chelsea, QPR, 1995–7): 14/0

Stanton, P (Hibernian, 1966–74): 16/0

Stark, J (Rangers, 1909): 2/0

Steel, W (Morton, Derby, Dundee, 1947–53): 30/12

Steele, D M (Huddersfield, 1923): 3/0

Stein, C (Rangers, Coventry, 1969–73): 21/10

Stephen, J F (Bradford, 1947–8): 2/0

Stevenson, G (Motherwell, 1928–35): 12/4

Stewart, A (Queen's Park, 1888–9): 2/0

Stewart, A (Third Lanark, 1894): 1/0

Stewart, D (Dumbarton, 1888): 1/0

Stewart, D (Queen's Park, 1893–7): 3/0

Stewart, D S (Leeds, 1978): 1/0

Stewart, G (Hibernian, Man City, 1906–7): 4/0

Stewart, J (Kilmarnock, Middlesbrough, 1977–9): 2/0

Stewart, R (West Ham, 1981–7): 10/1

Stewart, W E (Queen's Park, 1898–1900): 2/1

Storrier, D (Celtic, 1899): 3/0

Strachan, G (Aberdeen, Man Utd, Leeds Utd, 1980–92): 50/5

Sturrock, P (Dundee Utd, 1981–7): 20/3

Sullivan, N (Wimbledon, 1997–8): 3/0

Summers, W (St Mirren, 1926): 1/0

Symon, J S (Rangers, 1939): 1/0

Tait, T S (Sunderland, 1911): 1/0

Taylor, J (Queen's Park, 1872–6): 6/0

Taylor, J D (Dumbarton, St Mirren, 1892–5): 4/1

Taylor, W (Hearts, 1892): 1/0

Telfer, W (Motherwell, 1933–4): 2/0

Telfer, W D (St Mirren, 1954): 1/0

Templeton, R (A Villa, Newcastle, Arsenal, Kilmarnock, 1902–13): 11/1

Thomson, A (Arthurlie, 1886): 1/1

Thomson, A (Third Lanark, 1889): 1/1

Thomson, A (Airdrieonians, 1909): 1/1

Thomson, A (Celtic, 1926–33): 3/1

Thomson, C (Hearts, Sunderland, 1904–14): 21/4

Thomson, C (Sunderland, 1937): 1/0

Thomson, D (Dundee, 1920): 1/0

Thomson, J (Celtic, 1930–1): 4/0

Thomson, J J (Queen's Park, 1872–4): 3/0

Thomson, J R (Everton, 1933): 1/0

Thomson, R (Celtic, 1932): 1/1

Thomson, R W (Falkirk, 1927): 1/0

Thomson, S (Rangers, 1884): 2/0

Thomson, W (Dumbarton, 1892–8): 4/1

Thomson, W (Dundee, 1896): 1/1

Thomson, W (St Mirren, 1980–4): 7/0

Thornton, W (Rangers, 1947–52): 7/1

Toner, W (Kilmarnock, 1959): 2/0

Townsley, T (Falkirk, 1926): 1/0

Troup, A (Dundee, Everton, 1920–6): 5/0

Turnbull, E (Hibernian, 1948–58): 8/0

Turner, T (Arthurlie, 1884): 1/0

Turner, W (Pollokshields Ath, 1885–6): 2/0

Ure, J F (Dundee, Arsenal, 1962–8): 11/0

Urquhart, D (Hibernian, 1934): 1/0

Vallance, T (Rangers, 1877–81): 7/0

Venters, A (Cowdenbeath, Rangers, 1936–9): 3/0

Waddell, T S (Queen's Park, 1891–5): 6/1

Waddell, W (Rangers, 1947–55): 17/6

Wales, H M (Motherwell, 1933): 1/0

Walker, A (Celtic, 1988–95): 3/0

Walker, F (Third Lanark, 1922): 1/0

Walker, G (St Mirren, 1930–1): 4/0

Walker, J (Hearts, Rangers, 1895–1904): 5/2

Walker, J (Swindon, 1911–3): 9/2

Walker, J N (Hearts, Partick, 1993–6): 2/0

Walker, R (Hearts, 1900–13): 29/7

Walker, T (Hearts, 1935–9): 20/9

Walker, W (Clyde, 1909–10): 2/0

Wallace, I A (Coventry, 1978–9): 3/1

Wallace, W S B (Hearts, Celtic, 1965–9): 7/0

Wardhaugh, J (Hearts, 1955–7): 2/0

Wark, J (Ipswich, Liverpool, 1979–85): 29/7

Watson, A (Queen's Park, 1881–2): 3/0

Watson, J (Sunderland, Middlesbrough, 1903–9): 6/0

Watson, J (Motherwell, Huddersfield, 1948–54): 2/0

Watson, J A K (Rangers, 1878): 1/1

Watson, P R (Blackpool, 1934): 1/0

Watson, R (Motherwell, 1971): 1/0

Watson, W (Falkirk, 1898): 1/0

Watt, F (Kilbirnie, 1889–91): 4/2

Watt, W W (Queen's Park, 1887): 1/1

Waugh, W (Hearts, 1938): 1/0

Weir, A (Motherwell, 1959–60): 6/1

Weir, D G (Hearts, 1997–8): 5/0

Weir, J (Third Lanark, 1887): 1/0

Weir, J B (Queen's Park, 1872–8): 4/2

Weir, P (St Mirren, Aberdeen, 1980–4): 6/0

White, J (Albion Rovers, Hearts, 1922–3): 2/0

White, J A (Falkirk, Tottenham, 1959–64): 22/3

White, W (Bolton, 1907–8): 2/0

Whitelaw, A (Vale of Leven, 1887–90): 2/0

Whyte, D (Celtic, Middlesbrough, 1988–98): 11/0

Wilson, A (Sheff Wed, 1907–14): 6/2

Wilson, A (Portsmouth, 1954): 1/0

Wilson, A N (Dunfermline, Middlesbrough, 1920–2): 12/13

Wilson, D (Queen's Park, 1900): 1/2

Wilson, D (Oldham, 1913): 1/0

Wilson, D (Rangers, 1961–5): 22/9

Wilson, G W (Hearts, Everton, Newcastle, 1904–9): 6/0

Wilson, H (Newmilns, Sunderland, Third Lanark, 1890–1904): 4/1

Wilson, I A (Leicester, Everton, 1987–8): 5/0

Wilson, J (Vale of Leven, 1888–91): 4/0

Wilson, P (Celtic, 1926–33): 4/0

Wilson, P (Celtic, 1975): 1/0

Wilson, R P (Arsenal, 1972): 2/0

Wiseman, W (Queen's Park, 1927–30): 2/0

Wood, G (Everton, Arsenal, 1979–82): 4/0

Woodburn, W A (Rangers, 1947–52): 24/0

Wotherspoon, D N (Queen's Park, 1872–3): 2/0

Wright, K (Hibernian, 1992): 1/0

Wright, S (Aberdeen, 1993): 2/0

Wright, T (Sunderland, 1953): 3/0

Wylie, T G (Rangers, 1890): 1/1

Yeats, R (Liverpool, 1965–6): 2/0

Yorston, B C (Aberdeen, 1931): 1/0

Yorston, H (Aberdeen, 1955): 1/0

Young, A (Hearts, Everton, 1960–6): 8/5

Young, A (Everton, 1905–7): 2/0

Young, G L (Rangers, 1947–57): 53/0

Young, J (Celtic, 1906): 1/0

Younger, T (Hibernian, Liverpool, 1955–8): 24/0

Northern Ireland

Aherne, T (Belfast C, Luton, 1947–50): 4/0

Alexander, A (Cliftonville, 1895): 1/0

Allen, C A (Cliftonville, 1936): 1/0

Allen, J (Limavady, 1887): 1/0

Anderson, T (Man Utd, Swindon, Peterborough, 1973–9): 22/4

Anderson, W (Linfield, 1898–9): 4/0

Andrews, W (Glentoran, Grimsby, 1908–13): 3/0

Armstrong, G (Tottenham, Watford, Real Mallorca, WBA, Chesterfield, 1977–86): 63/12

Baird, G (Distillery, 1896): 3/0

Baird, H (Huddersfield, 1939): 1/0

Balfe, J (Shelbourne, 1909–10): 2/0

Bambrick, J (Linfield, Chelsea, 1929–38): 11/12

Banks, S J (Cliftonville, 1937): 1/0

Barr, H H (Linfield, Coventry, 1962–3): 3/1

Barron, H (Cliftonville, 1894–7): 7/3

Barry, H (Bohemians, 1900): 1/0

Baxter, R A (Cliftonville, 1887): 2/0

Bennett, L V (Dublin University, 1889): 1/0

Berry, J (Cliftonville, 1888–9): 3/0

Best, G (Man Utd, Fulham, 1964–78): 37/9

Bingham, W L (Sunderland, Luton, Everton, Port Vale, 1951–64): 56/10

Black, J (Glentoran, 1901): 1/0

Black, K (Luton, Nottingham Forest, 1988–94): 30/1

Blair, H (Portadown, Swansea, 1931–4): 3/0

Blair, J (Cliftonville, 1907–8): 5/0

Blair, R V (Oldham, 1975–6): 5/0

Blanchflower, R D (Barnsley, A Villa, Tottenham, 1950–63): 56/2

Blanchflower, J (Man Utd, 1954–80): 12/1

Bookman, L O (Bradford, Luton, 1914–22): 4/0

Bothwell, A W (Ards, 1926–7): 5/0

Bowler, G C (Hull, 1950): 3/0

Boyle, P (Sheff Utd, 1901–4): 5/0

Braithwaite, R S (Linfield, Middlesbrough, 1962–5): 10/0

Breen, T (Belfast C, Man Utd, 1935–9): 9/0

Brennan, B (Bohemians, 1912): 1/1

Brennan, R A (Luton, Birmingham, Fulham, 1949–51): 5/1

Briggs, W R (Man Utd, Swansea, 1962–5): 2/0

Brisby, D (Distillery, 1891): 1/0

Brolly, T (Millwall, 1937–9): 4/0

Brookes, E A (Shelbourne, 1920): 1/0

Brotherston, N (Blackburn, 1980–5): 27/3

Brown, J (Glenavon, Tranmere, 1921–4): 3/1

Brown, J (Wolves, Coventry, Birmingham, 1935–9): 10/1

Brown, W G (Glenavon, 1926): 1/0

Brown, W M (Limavady, 1887): 1/0

Browne, F (Cliftonville, 1887–8): 5/2

Browne, R J (Leeds, 1936–9): 6/0

Bruce, W (Glentoran, 1961–7): 2/0

Buckle, H (Cliftonville, 1882): 1/0

Buckle, H R (Sunderland, Bristol R, 1904–8): 2/0

Burnett, J (Distillery, Glentoran, 1894–5): 5/0

Burnison, J (Distillery, 1901): 2/0

Burnison, S (Distillery, Bradford, Distillery, 1908–13): 8/0

Burns, J (Glenavon, 1923): 1/0

Butler, M P (Blackpool, 1939): 1/0

Campbell, A C (Crusaders, 1963–5): 2/0

Campbell, D A (Nottingham Forest, Charlton, 1986–8): 10/0

Campbell, J (Cliftonville, Distillery, Cliftonville, 1896–1904): 15/1

Campbell, J P (Fulham, 1951): 2/0

Campbell, R (Bradford, 1982): 2/0

Campbell, W G (Dundee, 1968–70): 6/1

Carey, J J (Man Utd, 1947–9): 7/0

Carroll, E (Glenavon, 1925): 1/0

Carroll, R E (Wigan, 1997): 1/0

Casey, T (Newcastle, Portsmouth, 1955–9): 12/2

Cashin, M (Cliftonville, 1898): 1/0

Caskey, W (Derby, Tulsa R, 1979–82): 7/1

Cassidy, T (Newcastle, Burnley, 1971–82): 24/1

Caughey, M (Linfield, 1986): 2/0

Chambers, J (Distillery, Bury, Nottingham Forest, 1921–32): 12/3

Chatton, H A (Partick, 1925–6): 3/0

Christian, J (Linfield, 1889): 1/0

Clarke, C J (Bournemouth, Southampton, QPR, Portsmouth, 1986–93): 38/13

Clarke, R (Belfast C, 1901): 2/0

Cleary, J (Glentoran, 1982–5): 5/0

Clements, D (Coventry, Sheff Wed, Everton, New York Cosmos, 1965–76): 48/2

Clugston, J (Cliftonville, 1888–93): 14/0

Cochrane, D (Leeds, 1939–50): 12/0

Cochrane, M (Distillery, Leicester Fosse, 1898–1901): 8/0

Cochrane, T (Coleraine, Burnley, Middlesbrough, Gillingham, 1976–84): 26/1

Collins, F (Celtic, 1922): 1/0

Condy, J (Distillery, 1882–6): 3/1

Connell, T (Coleraine, 1978): 1/0

Connor, J (Glentoran, Belfast C, 1901–11): 13/0

Connor, M J (Brentford, Fulham, 1903–4): 3/1

Cook, W (Celtic, Everton, 1933–9): 15/0

Cooke, S (Belfast YMCA, Cliftonville, 1889–90): 3/0

Coulter, J (Belfast C, Everton, Grimsby, Chelmsford C, 1934–9): 11/1

Cowan, J (Newcastle, 1970): 1/0

Cowan, T S (Queen's Island, 1925): 1/0

Coyle, F (Coleraine, Nottingham Forest): 1956–8): 4/0

Coyle, L (Derry C, 1989): 1/0

Coyle, R I (Sheff Wed, 1973–4): 5/0

Craig, A B (Rangers, Morton, 1908–14); 9/0

Craig, D J (Newcastle, 1967–75): 25/0

Crawford, S (Distillery, Cliftonville, 1889–93): 7/0

Croft, T (Queen's Island, 1924): 1/1

Crone, R (Distillery, 1889–90): 4/0

Crone, W (Distillery, 1882–90): 12/1

Crooks, W (Man Utd, 1922): 1/0

Crossan, E (Blackburn, 1950–5): 3/0

Crossan, J A (Sparta Rotterdam, Sunderland, Man City, Middlesbrough, 1960–8): 24/1

Crothers, C (Distillery, 1907): 1/0

Cumming, L (Huddersfield, Oldham, 1929–30): 3/0

Cunningham, R (Ulster, 1892–3): 4/0

Cunningham, W E (St Mirren, Leicester, Dunfermline, 1951–62): 30/0

Curran, S (Belfast C, 1926–8): 3/2

Curran, J J (Glenavon, Pontypridd, Glenavon, 1922–4): 4/0

Cush, W W (Glenavon, Leeds, Portadown, 1951–62): 26/5

Dalton, W (YMCA, Linfield, 1888–94): 11/6

D'Arcy, S D (Chelsea, Brentford, 1952–3): 5/1

Darling, J (Linfield, 1897–1912); 21/1

Davey, H H (Reading, Portsmouth, 1926–8): 5/1

Davis, T L (Oldham, 1937): 1/1

Davison, A J (Bolton, Bradford, 1996–7): 3/0

Davison, J R (Cliftonville, 1882–5): 8/0

Dennison, R (Wolves, 1988–97): 18/0

Devine, J (Glentoran, 1990): 1/0

Devine, W (Limavady, 1886–8): 4/0

Dickson, D (Coleraine, 1970–3): 4/0

Dickson, T A (Linfield, 1957): 1/0

Dickson, W (Chelsea, Arsenal, 1951–5): 12/0

Diffin, W (Belfast, 1931): 1/0

Dill, A H (Knock and Down Ath, Cliftonville, 1882–5): 9/1

Doherty, I (Belfast C, 1901): 1/0

Doherty, J (Cliftonville, 1933): 2/0

Doherty, L (Linfield, 1985–8): 2/1

Doherty, M (Derry, 1938): 1/0

Doherty, P D (Blackpool, Man City, Derby, Huddersfield, Doncaster, 1935–51): 16/3

Donaghy, M (Luton, Man Utd, Chelsea, 1980–94): 91/0

Donnelly, L (Distillery, 1913): 1/0

Doran, J F (Brighton, 1921–2): 3/0

Dougan, A D (Portsmouth, Blackburn, A Villa, Leicester, Wolves, 1958–73): 43/8

Douglas, J P (Belfast C, 1947): 1/0

Dowd, H O (Glenavon, Sheff Wed, 1974–5): 3/0

Dowie, I (Luton, West Ham, Southampton, C Palace, West Ham, QPR, 1990–98): 48/11

Duggan, H A (Leeds, 1930–6): 8/0

Dunlop, G (Linfield, 1985–90): 4/0

Dunne, J (Sheff Utd, 1928–33): 7/4

Eames, W L E (Dublin U, 1885): 3/0

Eglington, T J (Everton, 1947–9): 6/0

Elder, A R (Burnley, Stoke, 1960–70): 40/1

Elleman, A R (Cliftonville, 1889–90): 2/0

Elwood, J H (Bradford, 1929–30): 2/0

Emerson, W (Glentoran, Burnley, 1920–4): 11/1

English, S (Rangers, 1933): 2/1

Enright, J (Leeds C, 1912): 1/0

Falloon, E (Aberdeen, 1931–3): 2/0

Farquharson, T G (Cardiff, 1923–5): 7/0

Farrell, P (Distillery, 1901): 2/0

Farrell, P (Hibernian, 1938): 1/0

Farrell, P D (Everton, 1947–9): 7/0

Feeney, J M (Linfield, Swansea, 1947–50): 2/0

Feeney, W (Glentoran, 1976): 1/0

Ferguson, W (Linfield, 1966–7): 2/1

Ferris, J (Belfast C, Chelsea, Belfast C, 1920–8): 5/1

Ferris, R O (Birmingham, 1950–2): 3/1

Fettis, A (Hull, Nottingham Forest, 1992–8): 21/0

Finney, T (Sunderland, Cambridge, 1975–80): 14/2

Fitzpatrick, J C (Bohemians, 1896). 2/0

Flack, H (Burnley, 1929): 1/0

Fleming, J G (Nottingham Forest, Man City, Barnsley, 1987–95): 31/0

Forbes, G (Limavady, Distillery, 1888–91): 3/0

Forde, J T (Ards, 1959–61): 4/0

Foreman, T A (Cliftonville, 1899): 1/0

Forsyth, J (YMCA, 1888): 2/0

Fox, W (Ulster, 1887): 2/0

Fulton, R P (Belfast C, 1930–8): 20/0

Gaffikin, J (Linfield Ath, 1890–5): 15/5

Galbraith, W (Distillery, 1890): 1/0

Gallagher, P (Celtic, Falkirk, 1920–7): 11/0

Gallogly, C (Huddersfield, 1951): 2/0

Gara, A (Preston, 1902): 3/3

Gardiner, A (Cliftonville, 1930–2): 5/0

Garrett, J (Distillery, 1925): 1/0

Gaston, R (Oxford U, 1969): 1/0

Gaukrodger, G (Linfield, 1895): 1/2

Gaussen, A W (Moyola Park, 1884–9): 6/0

Geary, J (Glentoran, 1931–2): 2/0

Gibb, J T (Wellington Park, 1884–9): 10/2

Gibb, T J (Cliftonville, 1936): 1/1

Gibson, W K (Cliftonville, 1894–1902): 13/1

Gillespie, K R (Man Utd, Newcastle, 1995–8): 21/1

Gillespie, R (Hertford, 1886–7): 6/0

Gillespie, W (Sheff Utd, 1913–31): 25/12

Gillespie, W (West Down, 1889): 1/0

Goodall, A L (Derby, 1899–1904): 10/2

Goodbody, M F (Dublin University, 1889–91): 2/0

Gordon, H (Linfield, 1891–6): 11/0

Gordon, T (Linfield, 1894–5): 2/0

Gorman, W C (Brentford, 1947–8): 4/0

Gowdy, J (Glentoran, Queen's Island, Falkirk, 1920–7): 6/0

Gowdy, W A (Hull, Sheff Wed, Linfield, Hibernian, 1932–6): 6/0

Graham, W G (Doncaster, 1951–9): 14/0

Gray, P (Luton, Sunderland, Nancy, 1993–7): 20/5

Greer, W (QPR, 1909): 3/0

Gregg, H (Doncaster, Man Utd, 1954–64): 25/0

Griffin, D J (St Johnstone, 1996–7): 7/0

Hall, G (Distillery, 1897): 1/0

Halligan, W (Derby, Wolves, 1911–2): 2/1

Hamill, M (Man Utd, Belfast C, Man City, 1912–21): 7/1

Hamilton, B (Linfield, Ipswich, Everton, Millwall, Swindon, 1969–80): 50/4

Hamilton, J (Knock, 1882): 2/0

Hamilton, R (Distillery, 1908): 1/0

Hamilton, R (Rangers, 1928–32): 5/0

Hamilton, W (QPR, Burnley, Oxford, 1978–86): 41/5

Hamilton, W D (Dublin Association, 1885): 1/0
Hamilton, W J (Dublin Association, 1885): 1/0
Hampton, H (Bradford, 1911–4): 9/0
Hanna, D R A (Portsmouth, 1899): 1/0
Hanna, J (Nottingham Forest, 1912): 2/0
Hannon, D J (Bohemians, 1908–13): 6/1
Harkin, J T (Southport, Shrewsbury, 1968–71): 5/2
Harland, A I (Linfield, 1923): 1/0
Harris, J (Cliftonville, 1921): 1/0
Harris, V (Shelbourne, Everton, 1906–14): 20/0
Harvey, M (Sunderland, 1961–71): 34/3
Hastings, J (Knock, 1882–6): 7/0
Hatton, S (Linfield, 1963): 2/0
Hayes, W E (Huddersfield, 1938–9): 4/0
Healy, F (Coleraine, Glentoran, 1982–3): 4/0
Hegan, D (WBA, Wolves, 1970–3): 7/0
Hehir, J C (Bohemians, 1910): 1/0
Henderson, A W (Ulster, 1885): 3/0
Hewison, G (Moyola Park, 1885): 2/0
Hill, C F (Sheff Utd, Leicester, 1990–8): 26/1
Hill, M J (Norwich, 1959–64): 7/0
Hinton, E (Fulham, Millwall, 1947–51): 7/0
Hopkins, J (Brighton, 1926): 1/0
Horlock, K (Swindon, Man City, 1995–7): 12/0
Houston, J (Linfield, Everton, 1912–4): 6/0
Houston, W (Linfield, 1933): 1/0
Houston, W G (Moyola Park, 1885): 2/0
Hughes, A (Newcastle, 1998): 2/0
Hughes, M E (Man City, Strasbourg, West Ham, 1992–8): 41/3
Hughes, P (Bury, 1987): 3/0
Hughes, W (Bolton, 1951): 1/0
Humphries, W (Ards, Coventry, Swansea, 1962–5): 14/1
Hunter, A (Distillery, Belfast C, 1905–9): 8/1
Hunter, A (Blackburn, Ipswich, 1970–80): 53/1
Hunter, B V (Wrexham, Reading, 1995–7): 11/1
Hunter, R J (Cliftonville, 1884): 3/0
Hunter, V (Coleraine, 1962–4): 2/0
Irvine, R J (Linfield, 1962–5): 8/0
Irvine, R W (Everton, Portsmouth, Connah's Quay, Derry C, 1922–32): 15/3
Irvine, W J (Burnley, Preston, Brighton, 1962–72): 23/8
Irving, S J (Dundee, Cardiff, Chelsea, 1923–31): 18/0
Jackson, T (Everton, Nottingham Forest, Man Utd, 1969–77): 35/0
Jamison, J (Glentoran, 1976): 1/0
Jenkins, I (Chester, 1997–8): 3/0
Jennings, P A (Watford, Tottenham, Arsenal, Tottenham, 1964–86): 119/0
Johnston, H (Portadown, 1927): 1/2
Johnston, R (Old Park, 1885): 2/0
Johnston, S (Distillery, 1882–6): 4/2
Johnston, S (Linfield, 1890–4): 4/2
Johnston, S (Distillery, 1905): 1/2
Johnston, W C (Glenavon, Oldham, 1962–6): 2/1
Jones, J (Linfield, Glenavon, 1930–8): 23/0
Jones, J (Glenavon, 1956–7): 3/1
Jones, S (Distillery, Blackpool, 1934): 2/1
Jordan, T (Linfield, 1895): 2/0
Kavanagh, P J (Celtic, 1930): 1/0
Keane, T R (Swansea, 1949): 1/0

Kearns, A (Distillery, 1900–2): 6/0
Kee, P V (Oxford, 1990–5): 9/0
Keith, R M (Newcastle, 1958–62): 23/0
Kelly, H R (Fulham, Southampton, 1950–1): 4/0
Kelly, J (Glentoran, 1896): 1/0
Kelly, J (Derry, 1932–7): 11/4
Kelly, P (Man City, 1921): 1/0
Kelly, P M (Barnsley, 1950): 1/0
Kennedy, A L (Arsenal, 1923–5): 2/0
Kernaghan, N (Belfast C, 1936–8): 3/2
Kirkwood, H (Cliftonville, 1904): 1/0
Kirwan, J (Tottenham, Chelsea, Clyde, 1900–9): 17/2
Lacey, W (Everton, Liverpool, New Brighton, 1909–25): 23/3
Lawther, W I (Sunderland, Blackburn, 1960–2): 4/0
Leatham, J (Belfast C, 1939): 1/0
Ledwidge, J J (Shelbourne, 1906): 2/0
Lemon, J (Glentoran, Belfast YMCA, 1886–9): 3/2
Lennon, N F (Crewe, Leicester, 1994–8): 20/1
Leslie, W (YMCA, 1887): 1/0
Lewis, J (Glentoran, Distillery, 1899–1900): 4/0
Little, J (Glentoran, 1898): 1/0
Lockhart, H (Rossall School, 1884): 1/0
Lockhart, N (Linfield, Coventry, A Villa, 1947–56): 8/3
Lomas, S M (Man City, West Ham, 1994–98): 26/2
Lowther, R (Glentoran, 1888): 2/0
Loyal, J (Clarence, 1891): 1/0
Lutton, R J (Wolves, West Ham, 1970–4): 6/0
Lyner, D (Glentoran, Man Utd, Kilmarnock, 1920–3): 6/0
McAdams, W J (Man City, Bolton, Leeds, 1954–62): 15/7
McAlery, J M (Cliftonville, 1882): 2/0
McAlinden, J (Belfast C, Portsmouth, Southend, 1938–49): 4/0
McAllen, J (Linfield, 1898–1902): 9/1
McAlpine, W J (Cliftonville, 1901): 1/0
McArthur, A (Distillery, 1886): 1/0
McAuley, J L (Huddersfield, 1911–3): 6/1
McAuley, P (Belfast, 1900): 1/0
McBride, S (Glenavon, 1991–2): 4/0
McCabe, J J (Leeds, 1949–54): 6/0
McCabe, W (Ulster, 1891): 1/0
McCambridge, J (Ballymena, Cardiff, 1930–2): 4/0
McCandless, J (Bradford, 1912–21): 5/3
McCandless, W (Linfield, Rangers, 1920–9): 9/0
McCann, P (Belfast C, Glentoran, 1910–3): 7/0
McCarthy, J D (Port Vale, 1996–8): 6/0
McCashin, J (Cliftonville, 1896–9): 4/0
McCavana, W T (Coleraine, 1955–6): 3/0
McCaw, D (Distillery, 1882): 1/0
McCaw, J H (Linfield, 1927–31): 5/1
McClatchey, J (Distillery, 1886): 3/0
McClatchey, R (Distillery, 1882): 1/0
McCleary, J W (Cliftonville, 1955): 1/0
McCleery, W (Linfield, 1930–3): 9/0
McClelland, J (Arsenal, Fulham, 1961–6): 6/1
McClelland, J (Mansfield, Rangers, Watford, Leeds, 1980–90): 53/1
McCluggage, A (Bradford, Burnley, 1924–31):

12/2
McClure, G (Cliftonville, Distillery, 1907–9): 4/0
McConnell, E (Cliftonville, Glentoran, Sunderland, Sheff Wed, 1904–10): 12/0
McConnell, P (Doncaster, Southport, 1928–32): 2/0
McConnell, W G (Bohemians, 1912–4): 6/0
McConnell, W H (Reading, 1925–8): 8/0
McCourt, F J (Man City, 1952–3): 6/0
McCoy, J (Distillery, 1896): 1/0
McCoy, R (Coleraine, 1987): 1/0
McCracken, R (C Palace, 1921–2): 4/0
McCracken, W (Distillery, Newcastle, Hull, 1902–23): 15/1
McCreery, D (Man Utd, QPR, Tulsa R, Newcastle, Hearts, 1976–90): 67/0
McCrory, S (Southend, 1958): 1/1
McCullough, K (Belfast C, Man City, 1935–7): 5/0
McCullough, W J (Arsenal, Millwall, 1961–7): 10/0
McCurdy, C (Linfield, 1980): 1/1
McDonald, A (QPR, 1986–96): 52/3
McDonald, R (Rangers, 1930–2): 2/0
McDonnell, J (Bohemians, 1911–3): 4/0
McElhinney, G (Bolton, 1984–5): 6/0
McFaul, W S (Linfield, Newcastle, 1967–74): 6/0
McGarry, J K (Cliftonville, 1951): 3/1
McGaughey, M (Linfield, 1985): 1/0
McGee, G (Wellington Park, 1885): 3/0
McGibbon, P C G (Man Utd, 1995–7): 6/0
McGrath, R C (Tottenham, Man City, 1974–9): 21/4
McGregor, S (Glentoran, 1921): 1/0
McGrillen, J (Clyde, Belfast C, 1924–7): 2/0
McGuire, E (Distillery, 1907): 1/0
McIlroy, H (Cliftonville, 1906): 1/0
McIlroy, J (Burnley, Stoke, 1952–63): 55/10
McIlroy, S B (Man Utd, Stoke, Man City, 1972–87): 88/5
McIlvenny, J (Distillery, 1890–1): 2/0
McIlvenny, P (Distillery, 1924): 1/0
McKeag, W (Glentoran, 1968): 2/0
McKee, F W (Cliftonville, Belfast C, 1906–14): 5/0
McKelvie, H (Glentoran, 1901): 1/0
McKenna, J (Huddersfield, 1950–2): 7/0
McKenzie, H (Distillery, 1923): 1/0
McKenzie, R (Airdrieonians, 1967): 1/0
McKeown, H (Linfield, 1892–4): 7/0
McKie, H (Cliftonville, 1895): 3/0
McKinney, V J (Falkirk, 1966): 1/0
McKnight, A (Celtic, West Ham, 1988–9): 10/0
McKnight, J (Preston, Glentoran, 1912–3): 2/2
McLaughlin, J C (Shrewsbury, Swansea, 1962–6): 12/6
McLean, T (Limavady, 1885): 1/0
McMahon, G J (Tottenham, Stoke, 1995–7): 17/2
McMahon, J (Bohemians, 1934): 1/0
McMaster, G (Glentoran, 1897): 3/0
McMichael, A (Newcastle, 1950–60): 40/0
McMillan, G (Distillery, 1903–5): 2/0
McMillan, S (Man Utd, 1963): 2/0
McMillen, W S (Man Utd, Chesterfield, 1934–9): 7/0

McMordie, A S (Middlesbrough, 1969–73): 21/3

McMorran, E J (Belfast C, Barnsley, Doncaster, 1947–56): 15/04

McMullan, D (Liverpool, 1926–7): 3/0

McNally, B A (Shrewsbury, 1986–8): 5/0

McNinch, J (Ballymena, 1931–2): 3/0

McParland, P J (A Villa, Wolves, 1954–62): 34/10

McShane, J (Cliftonville, 1899–1900): 4/0

McVickers, J (Glentoran, 1888–9): 2/0

McWha, W B R (Knock, Cliftonville, 1882–5): 7/1

Macartney, A (Ulster, Linfield, Everton, Belfast C, Glentoran, 1903–9): 1915/0

Mackie, J (Arsenal, Portsmouth, 1923–35): 3/0

Madden, O (Norwich, 1938): 1/0

Magill, E J (Arsenal, Brighton, 1962–66): 26/0

Magilton, J (Oxford, Southampton, Sheff Wed, 1991–7): 38/5

Maginnis, H (Linfield, 1900–4): 8/0

Maguire, E (Distillery, 1907): 1/0

Mahood, J (Belfast C, Ballymena, 1926–34): 9/2

Manderson, R (Rangers, 1920–6): 5/0

Mansfield, J (Dublin Freebooters, 1901): 1/0

Martin, C J (Glentoran, Leeds, A Villa, 1947–50): 6/0

Martin, C (Bo'ness, 1925): 1/0

Martin, D C (Cliftonville, 1882–3): 3/0

Martin, D K (Belfast C, Wolves, Nottingham Forest, 1934–9): 10/3

Mathieson, A (Luton, 1921–2): 2/0

Maxwell, J (Linfield, Glentoran, Belfast C, 1902–7): 7/7

Meek, H L (Glentoran, 1925): 1/0

Mehaffy, J A C (Queen's Island, 1922): 1/0

Meldon, P A (Dublin Freebooters, 1899): 2/1

Mercer, H V A (Linfield, 1908): 1/0

Mercer, J T (Distillery, Linfield, Distillery, Derby, 1898–1905): 11/1

Millar, W (Barrow, 1932–3): 2/1

Miller, J (Middlesbrough, 1929–30): 3/0

Milligan, D (Chesterfield, 1939): 1/1

Milne, R G (Linfield, 1894–1906): 27/2

Mitchell, E J (Cliftonville, Glentoran, 1933–4): 2/0

Mitchell, W (Distillery, Chelsea, 1932–8): 15/0

Molyneux, T B (Ligoniel, Cliftonville, 1883–8): 11/1

Montgomery, F J (Coleraine, 1955): 1/0

Moore, C (Glentoran, 1949): 1/0

Moore, J (Linfield Ath, 1891): 3/0

Moore, P (Aberdeen, 1933): 1/0

Moore, T (Ulster, 1887): 2/0

Moore, W (Falkirk, 1923): 1/0

Moorhead, F W (Dublin University, 1885): 1/0

Moorhead, G (Linfield, 1923–9): 3/0

Moran, J (Leeds C, 1912): 1/0

Moreland, V (Derby, 1979–80): 6/1

Morgan, F G (Linfield, Nottingham Forest, 1923–9): 7/0

Morgan, S (Port Vale, A Villa, Brighton, Sparta Rotterdam, 1972–9): 18/3

Morrison, J (Linfield Ath, 1891): 2/0

Morrison, T (Glentoran, Burnley, 1895–1902): 7/0

Morrogh, E (Bohemians, 1896): 1/0

Morrow, S J (Arsenal, QPR, 1990–8): 31/1

Morrow, W J (Moyola Park, 1883–4): 3/1

Muir, R (Oldpark, 1885): 2/0

Mullan, G (Glentoran, 1983): 4/0

Mulholland, S (Celtic, 1906): 2/0

Mulligan, J (Man City, 1921): 1/0

Mulryne, P P (Man Utd, 1997): 4/1

Murphy, J (Bradford, 1910): 3/0

Murphy, N (QPR, 1905): 3/1

Murray, J M (Motherwell, Sheff Wed, 1910): 3/0

Napier, R J (Bolton, 1966): 1/0

Neill, W J T (Arsenal, Hull, 1961–73): 59/2

Nelis, P (Nottingham Forest, 1923): 1/0

Nelson, S (Arsenal, Brighton, 1970–82): 51/1

Nicholl, C J (A Villa, Southampton, Grimsby, 1975–84): 51/3

Nicholl, H (Belfast C, 1902–5): 3/0

Nicholl, J M (Man Utd, Toronto B, Sunderland, Toronto B, Rangers, Toronto B, WBA): 1976–86): 73/2

Nicholson, J J (Man Utd, Huddersfield, 1961–72): 41/6

Nixon, R (Linfield, 1914): 1/0

Nolan, I R (Sheff Wed, 1997): 7/0

Nolan–Whelan, J V (Dublin Freebooters, 1901–2): 4/0

O'Boyle, G (Dunfermline, St Johnstone, 1994–8): 12/1

O'Brien, M T (QPR, Leicester, Hull, Derby, 1921–7): 10/0

O'Connell, P (Sheff Wed, Hull, 1912–4): 5/0

O'Doherty, A (Coleraine, 1970): 2/0

O'Driscoll, J F (Swansea, 1949): 3/0

O'Hagan, C (Tottenham, Aberdeen, 1905–9): 11/2

O'Hagan, W (St Mirren, 1920): 2/0

O'Kane, W J (Nottingham Forest, 1970–5): 20/1

O'Mahoney, M T (Bristol R, 1939): 1/0

O'Neill, C (Motherwell, 1989–91): 3/0

O'Neill, J (Leicester, 1980–6): 39/1

O'Neill, J (Sunderland, 1962): 1/1

O'Neill, M A (Newcastle, Dundee Utd, Hibernian, Coventry, 1988–97): 31/4

O'Neill, M H (Distillery, Nottingham Forest, Norwich, Man City, Norwich, Notts Co, 1972–85): 64/8

O'Reilly, H (Dublin Freebooters, 1901–4): 3/0

Parke, J (Linfield, Hibernian, Sunderland, 1964–8): 14/0

Patterson, D J (C Palace, Luton, 1994–8): 11/1

Peacock, R (Celtic, Coleraine, 1952–62): 31/2

Peden, J (Linfield, Distillery, Linfield, 1887–99): 24/7

Penney, S (Brighton, 1985–9): 17/2

Percy, J C (Belfast YMCA, 1889): 1/0

Platt, J A (Middlesbrough, Ballymena U, Coleraine, 1976–86): 23/0

Ponsonby, J (Distillery, 1895–9): 8/0

Potts, R M C (Cliftonville, 1883): 2/0

Priestley, T J (Coleraine, Chelsea, 1933–4): 2/0

Pyper, J (Cliftonville, 1897–1900): 7/2

Pyper, J (Cliftonville, 1897–1902): 9/1

Pyper, M (Linfield, 1932): 1/0

Quinn, J M (Blackburn, Swindon, Leicester, Bradford, West Ham, Bournemouth, Reading, 1985–96): 46/12

Quinn, S J (Blackpool, 1996–8): 12/1

Rafferty, P (Linfield, 1980): 1/0

Ramsey, P (Leicester, 1984–9): 14/0

Rankine, J (Alexander, 1883): 2/0

Raper, E O (Dublin University, 1886): 1/0

Rattray, D (Avoniel, 1882–3): 3/0

Rea, B (Glentoran, 1901): 1/0

Redmond, J (Cliftonville, 1884): 1/0

Reid, G H (Cardiff, 1923): 1/0

Reid, J (Ulster, 1883–90): 6/0

Reid, S F (Derby, 1934–6): 3/0

Reid, W (Hearts, 1931): 1/0

Reilly, M M (Portsmouth, 1900–2): 2/0

Renneville, W T (Leyton, A Villa, 1910–11): 4/0

Reynolds, J (Distillery, Ulster, 1890–1): 5/1

Reynolds, R (Bohemians, 1905): 1/0

Rice, P J (Arsenal, 1969–80): 49/0

Roberts, F C (Glentoran, 1931): 1/0

Robinson, P (Distillery, Blackburn, 1921): 2/0

Robinson, S (Bournemouth, 1997): 1/0

Rigan, A (Celtic, Sunderland, Millwall, 1988–97): 18/0

Rollo, D (Linfield, Blackburn, 1912–27): 16/0

Rosbotham, A (Cliftonville, 1887–9): 7/0

Ross, W E (Newcastle, 1969): 1/0

Rowland, K (West Ham, 1995–7): 12/0

Rowley, R W M (Southampton, Tottenham, 1929–32): 6/2

Russell, A (Linfield, 1947): 1/0

Russell, S R (Bradford, Derry, 1930–2): 3/0

Ryan, R A (WBA, 1950): 1/0

Sanchez, L P (Wimbledon, 1987–9): 3/0

Scott, E (Liverpool, Belfast C, 1920–36): 31/0

Scott, J (Grimsby, 1958): 2/0

Scott, J E (Cliftonville, 1901): 1/0

Scott, L J (Dublin University, 1895): 2/0

Scott, P W (Everton, York, Aldershot, 1975–9): 10/0

Scott, T (Cliftonville, 1894–1900): 13/0

Scott, W (Linfield, Everton, Leeds City, 1903–13): 25/0

Scraggs, M J (Glentoran, 1921–2): 2/0

Seymour, H C (Bohemians, 1914): 1/0

Seymour, J (Cliftonville, 1907–9): 2/0

Shanks, T (Arsenal, Brentford, 1903–5): 3/0

Sharkey, P (Ipswich, 1976): 1/0

Sheehan, Dr G (Bohemians, 1899–1900): 3/0

Sheridan, J (Everton, Stoke, 1903–5): 6/2

Sherrard, J (Limavady, 1885–8): 3/1

Sherrard, W (Cliftonville, 1895): 3/0

Sherry, J J (Bohemians, 1906–7): 2/0

Shields, J (Southampton, 1957): 1/0

Silo, M (Belfast YMCA, 1888): 1/0

Simpson, W J (Rangers, 1954–9): 12/5

Sinclair, J (Knock, 1882): 2/0

Slemin, J C (Bohemians, 1909): 1/0

Sloan, A S (London Caledonians, 1925): 1/0

Sloan, D (Oxford, 1969–71): 2/0

Sloan, H A de B (Bohemians, 1903–9): 8/4

Sloan, J W (Arsenal, 1947): 1/0

Sloan, T (Cardiff, Linfield, 1926–31): 11/0

Sloan, T (Man Utd, 1979): 3/0

Small, J (Clarence, 1887): 1/0

Small, J M (Cliftonville, 1893): 3/0

Smith, E E (Cardiff, 1921–4): 4/0

Smith, J (Distillery, 1901): 2/0

Smith, R H (Dublin University, 1886): 1/0
Smyth, S (Wolves, Stoke, 1948–52): 9/5
Smyth, W (Distillery, 1949–54): 4/0
Snape, A (Airdrieonians, 1920): 1/0
Spence, D W (Bury, Blackpool, Southend, 1975–82): 29/3
Spencer, S (Distillery, 1883–4): 5/0
Spiller, E A (Cliftonville, 1883–4): 5/0
Stanfield, O M (Distillery, 1887–97): 30/9
Steele, A (Charlton, Fulham, 1926–9): 4/0
Stevenson, A E (Rangers, Everton, 1934–48): 17/5
Stewart, A (Glentoran, Derby, 1967–9): 17/0
Stewart, D C (Hull, 1978): 1/0
Stewart, I (QPR, Newcastle, 1982–7): 31/2
Stewart, R H (St Columb's Court, Cliftonville, 1890–4): 11/0
Stewart, T C (Linfield, 1961): 1/0
Swan, S (Linfield, 1899): 1/0
Taggart, G P (Barnsley, Bolton, 1990–7): 44/6
Taggart, J (Walsall, 1899): 1/0
Thompson, F W (Cliftonville, Bradford, Linfield, Clyde, 1910–14): 12/2
Thompson, J (Belfast Ath, 1889): 1/0
Thunder, P J (Bohemians, 1911): 1/0
Todd, S J (Burnley, Sheff Wed, 1966–71): 11/0
Toner, J (Arsenal, St Johnstone, 1922–7): 8/0
Torrans, R (Linfield, 1893): 1/0
Torrans, S (Linfield, 1889–1901): 26/0
Trainor, D (Crusaders, 1967): 1/0
Tully, C P (Celtic, 1949–59): 10/3
Turner, E (Cliftonville, 1896): 2/1
Turner, W (Cliftonville, 1886–8): 3/0
Twoomey, J F (Leeds, 1938–9): 2/0
Uprichard, W N M C (Swindon, Portsmouth, 1952–9): 18/0
Vernon, J (Belfast C, WBA, 1947–52): 17/0
Waddell, T M R (Cliftonville, 1906): 1/0
Walker, J (Doncaster, 1955): 1/1
Walker, T (Bury, 1911): 1/0
Walsh, D J (WBA, 1947–50): 9/5
Waring, W (Man City, 1948–9): 5/0
Warren, P (Shelbourne, 1913): 2/0
Watson, J (Ulster, 1883–9): 9/0
Watson, P (Distillery, 1971): 1/0
Watson, T (Cardiff, 1926): 1/0
Wattle, J (Distillery, 1899): 1/0
Webb, C G (Brighton, 1909–11): 3/0
Weir, E (Clyde, 1939): 1/0
Welsh, E (Carlisle, 1966–7): 4/1
Whiteside, N (Man Utd, Everton, 1982–90): 38/9
Whiteside, T (Distillery, 1891): 1/1
Whitfield, E R (Dublin University, 1886): 1/0
Whitley, J (Man City, 1997): 2/0
Williams, J R (Ulster, 1886): 2/1
Williams, P A (WBA, 1991): 1/0
Williamson, J (Cliftonville, 1890–3): 3/1
Willigham, T (Burnley, 1933–4): 2/0
Willis, G (Linfield, 1906–12): 4/0
Wilson, D J (Brighton, Luton, Sheff Wed, 1987–92): 24/1
Wilson, H (Linfield, 1925): 1/0
Wilson, K J (Ipswich, Chelsea, Notts Co, Walsall, 1987–95): 42/6
Wilson, M (Distillery, 1884): 3/0
Wilson, R (Cliftonville, 1888): 1/0

Wilson, S J (Glenavon, Falkirk, Dundee, 1962–8): 12/7
Wilton, J M (St Columb's Court, Cliftonville, St Columb's Court, 1888–93): 7/2
Wood, T J (Walsall, 1996): 1/0
Worthington, N (Sheff Wed, Leeds, Stoke, 1984–97): 66/0
Wright, J (Cliftonville, 1906–7): 6/0
Wright, T J (Newcastle, Nottingham Forest, Man City, 1989–97): 29/0
Young, S (Linfield, Airdrie, Linfield, 1907–14): 9/2

Wales

Adams, H (Berwyn R, Druids, 1882–3): 4/0
Aizlewood, M (Charlton, Bradford, Bristol C, Cardiff, 1986–95): 39/0
Allchurch, I J (Swansea T, Newcastle, Swansea T, 1951–66): 68/23
Allchurch, L (Swansea T, Sheff Utd, 1955–64): 11/0
Allen, B W (Coventry, 1951): 2/0
Allen, M (Watford, Norwich, Millwall, Newcastle, 1986–94): 14/3
Arridge, S (Bootle, Everton, New Brighton Tower, 1892–9): 8/0
Astley, D J (Charlton, A Villa, Derby, Blackpool, 1931–9): 13/12
Atherton, R W (Hibernian, Middlesbrough, 1899–1905): 9/2
Bailiff, W E (Llanelly, 1913–20): 4/0
Baker, C W (Cardiff, 1958–62): 7/0
Baker, W G (Cardiff, 1948): 1/0
Bamford, T (Wrexham, 1931–3): 5/1
Barnard, D (Barnsley, 1998): 1/0
Barnes, W (Arsenal, 1948–55): 22/1
Bartley, T (Glossop NE, 1898): 1/0
Bastock, A M (Shrewsbury, 1892): 1/0
Beadles, G H (Cardiff, 1925): 2/0
Bell, W S (Shrewsbury Engineers, Crewe, 1881–6): 5/0
Bellamy, C (Watford, 1998): 1/0
Bennion, S R (Man Utd, 1926–32): 10/0
Berry, G F (Wolves, 1979–83): 5/0
Blackmore, C G (Man Utd, Middlesbrough, 1985–97): 39/1
Blake, N A (Sheff Utd, Bolton, 1994–6): 7/2
Blew, H (Wrexham, 1899–1910): 22/0
Boden, T (Wrexham, 1880): 1/0
Bodin, P J (Swindon, C Palace, Swindon, 1990–5): 23/3
Boulter, L M (Brentford, 1939): 1/1
Bowdler, H E (Shrewsbury, 1893): 1/0
Bowdler, J C H (Shrewsbury, Wolves, Shrewsbury, 1890–4): 4/3
Bowen, D L (Arsenal, 1955–9): 19/1
Bowen, E (Druids, 1880–3): 2/0
Bowen, J P (Swansea, Birmingham, 1994–7): 2/0
Bowen, M R (Tottenham, Norwich, 1986–97): 41/3
Bowsher, S J (Burnley, 1929): 1/0
Boyle, T C (C Palace, 1981): 2/1
Britten, T J (Parkgrove, Presteigne, 1878–80): 2/0

Brookes, S J (Llandudno, 1900): 2/0
Brown, A I (Aberdare Ath, 1926): 1/0
Browning, M T (Bristol R, 1996–7): 5/0
Bryan, T (Oswestry, 1886): 2/1
Buckland, T (Bangor, 1899): 1/0
Burgess, W A R (Tottenham, 1947–54): 32/1
Burke, T (Wrexham, Newton Heath, 1883–8): 8/1
Burnett, T B (Ruabon, 1877): 1/0
Burton, A D (Norwich, Newcastle, 1963–72): 9/0
Butler, J (Chirk, 1893): 3/1
Butler, W T (Druids, 1900): 2/1
Cartwright, L (Coventry, Wrexham, 1974–9): 7/0
Challen, J B (Corinthians, Wellingborough GS, 1887–90): 4/0
Chapman, T (Newtown, Man City, 1894–7): 7/2
Charles, J M (Swansea, QPR, Oxford, 1981–7): 19/1
Charles, M (Swansea, Arsenal, Cardiff, 1955–63): 31/6
Charles, W J (Leeds, Juventus, Leeds, Cardiff, 1955–65): 38/15
Clarke, R J (Man City, 1949–56): 22/5
Coleman, C (C Palace, Blackburn, Fulham, 1992–8): 17/4
Collier, D J (Grimsby, 1921): 1/1
Collins, W S (Llanelly, 1931): 1/0
Conde, C (Chirk, 1884): 3/0
Cook, F C (Newport, Portsmouth, 1925–32): 8/0
Cornforth, J M (Swansea, 1995): 2/0
Coyne, D (Tranmere, 1996): 1/0
Crompton, W (Wrexham, 1931): 3/0
Cross, E A (Wrexham, 1876–7): 2/0
Cross, K (Druids, 1879–81): 3/1
Crossley, M G (Nottingham Forest, 1997): 1/0
Crowe, V H (A Villa, 1959–63): 16/0
Cumner, R H (Arsenal, 1939): 3/1
Curtis, A (Swansea, Leeds, Swansea, Southampton, Cardiff, 1976–87): 35/6
Curtis, E R (Cardiff, Birmingham, 1928–34): 3/3
Daniel, R W (Arsenal, Sunderland, 1951–7): 21/0
Darvell, S (Oxford University, 1897): 2/0
Davies, A (Man Utd, Newcastle, Swansea, Bradford, 1983–90): 11/0
Davies, A (Wrexham, 1876–7): 2/0
Davies, A (Druids, Middlesbrough, 1904–5): 2/0
Davies, A O (Barmouth, Swifts, Wrexham, Crewe, 1885–90): 9/0
Davies, A T (Shrewsbury, 1891): 1/0
Davies, C (Brecon, Hereford, 1899–1900): 2/0
Davies, C (Charlton, 1972): 1/0
Davies, D (Bolton, 1904–8): 3/0
Davies, D C (Brecon, Hereford, 1899–1900): 2/0
Davies, D W (Treharris, Oldham, 1912–3): 2/1
Davies, E L (Stoke, Northampton, 1904–14): 16/1
Davies, E R (Newcastle, 1953–8): 6/0
Davies, G (Fulham, Man City, 1980–6): 16/2
Davies, Rev H (Wrexham, 1928): 1/0
Davies, I (Liverpool Marine, 1923): 1/0
Davies, J E (Oswestry, 1885): 1/0
Davies, J (Wrexham, 1878): 1/0
Davies, J (Wrexham, 1879): 1/0
Davies, J (Newton Heath, Wolves, 1888–93): 7/0

Davies, J (Everton, Chirk, Ardwick, Sheff Utd, Man City, Millwall, Reading, 1889–1900): 11/0

Davies, J P (Druids, 1883): 2/0

Davies, L (Wrexham, Everton, Wrexham, 1907–14): 13/0

Davies, L S (Cardiff, 1922–30): 23/6

Davies, O (Wrexham, 1890): 1/0

Davies, R (Wrexham, 1883–5): 3/0

Davies, R (Druids, 1885): 1/0

Davies, R O (Wrexham, 1892): 2/0

Davies, R T (Norwich, Southampton, Portsmouth, 1964–74): 29/8

Davies, R W (Bolton, Newcastle, Man City, Man Utd, Blackpool, 1964–74): 34/7

Davies, S I (Man Utd, 1996): 1/0

Davies, S (Preston, Everton, WBA, Rotherham, 1920–30): 18/5

Davies, T (Oswestry, 1886): 1/0

Davies, T (Druids, 1903–4): 4/0

Davies, W (Wrexham, 1884): 1/0

Davies, W (Swansea T, Cardiff, Notts Co, 1924–30): 17/6

Davies, W (Wrexham, Blackburn, 1903–12): 11/5

Davies, W C (C Palace, WBA, C Palace, 1908–14): 4/0

Davies, W D (Everton, Wrexham, Swansea C, 1975–83): 52/0

Davies, W H (Oswestry, 1876–80): 4/1

Davies, W O (Millwall Ath, 1913–4): 5/1

Davis, G (Wrexham, 1978): 3/0

Day, A (Tottenham, 1934): 1/0

Deacy, N (PSV Eindhoven, Beringen, 1977–9): 12/4

Dearson, D J (Birmingham, 1939): 3/0

Derrett, S C (Cardiff, 1969–71): 4/0

Dewey, F T (Cardiff Corinthians, 1931): 2/0

Dibble, A (Luton, Man City, 1986–9): 3/0

Doughty, J (Druids, Newton Heath, 1886–90): 8/6

Doughty, R (Newton Heath, Druids, 1888): 2/2

Durban, A (Derby, 1966–72): 27/2

Dwyer, P (Cardiff, 1978–80): 10/2

Edwards, C (Wrexham, 1878): 1/0

Edwards, C N H (Swansea C, 1996–8): 3/0

Edwards, G (Birmingham, Cardiff, 1947–50): 12/2

Edwards, H (Wrexham Civil Service, 1878–87): 7/0

Edwards, J H (Wanderers, 1876): 1/0

Edwards, J H (Oswestry, 1895–7): 3/0

Edwards, J H (Aberystwyth, 1898): 1/0

Edwards, L T (Charlton, 1957): 2/0

Edwards, R I (Chester, Wrexham, 1978–80): 4/4

Edwards, T (Linfield, 1932): 1/0

Egan, W (Chirk, 1892): 1/0

Ellis, B (Motherwell, 1932–7): 6/0

Ellis, E (Nunhead, Oswestry, 1931–2): 3/0

Emanuel, W J (Bristol C, 1973): 2/0

England, H M (Blackburn, Tottenham, 1962–75): 44/3

Evans, B C (Swansea, Hereford, 1972–4): 7/0

Evans, D G (Reading, Huddersfield, 1926–9): 4/0

Evans, H P (Cardiff, 1922–4): 6/0

Evans, I (C Palace, 1976–8): 13/1

Evans, J (Oswestry, 1893–4): 3/1

Evans, J (Cardiff, 1912–23): 8/1

Evans, J H (Southend, 1922–3): 4/0

Evans, L (Aberdare Ath, Cardiff, Birmingham, 1927–34): 4/0

Evans, M (Oswestry, 1884): 1/0

Evans, R (Clapton, 1902): 1/0

Evans, R E (Wrexham, A Villa, Sheff Utd, 1906–10): 10/2

Evans, R O (Wrexham, Blackburn, Coventry, 1902–12): 10/0

Evans, R S (Swansea T, 1964): 1/0

Evans, T J (Clapton Orient, Newcastle, 1927–8): 4/0

Evans, W (Tottenham, 1933–6): 6/1

Evans, W A W (Oxford University, 1876–7): 2/0

Evans, W G (Bootle, A Villa, 1890–2): 3/0

Evelyn, E C (Crusaders, 1887): 1/0

Eyton–Jones, J A (Wrexham, 1883–4): 4/1

Farmer, G (Oswestry, 1885): 2/0

Felgate, D (Lincoln, 1984): 1/0

Finnigan, R J (Wrexham, 1930): 1/0

Flynn, B (Burnley, Leeds, Burnley, 1975–84): 66/7

Ford, T (Swansea, A Villa, Sunderland, Cardiff, 1947–57): 38/23

Foulkes, H E (WBA, 1932): 1/0

Foulkes, W I (Newcastle, 1952–4): 11/1

Foulkes, W T (Oswestry, 1884–5): 2/0

Fowler, J (Swansea, 1925–9): 6/3

Garner, J (Aberystwyth, 1896): 1/0

Giggs, R J (Man Utd, 1991–8): 21/5

Giles, D (Swansea, C Palace, 1980–3): 12/2

Gillam, S G (Wrexham, Shrewsbury, Clapton, 1889–94): 5/0

Glascodine, G (Wrexham, 1879): 1/0

Glover, E M (Grimsby, 1932–9): 7/7

Godding, G (Wrexham, 1923): 2/0

Godfrey, B C (Preston, 1964–5): 3/2

Goodwin, U (Ruthin, 1881): 1/0

Goss, J (Norwich, 1991–6): 9/0

Gough, R T (Oswestry White Star, 1883): 1/0

Gray, A (Oldham, Man City, Manchester Central, Tranmere, Chester, 1924–37): 24/0

Green, A W (A Villa, Notts Co, Nottingham Forest, 1901–8): 8/3

Green, C R (Birmingham, 1965–9): 15/0

Green, G H (Charlton, 1938–9): 4/0

Green, R (Wolves, 1998): 2/0

Grey, Dr W (Druids, 1876–8): 2/0

Griffiths, A T (Wrexham, 1971–7): 17/6

Griffiths, F J (Blackpool, 1900): 2/0

Griffiths, G (Chirk, 1887): 1/0

Griffiths, J H (Swansea, 1953): 1/0

Griffiths, L (Wrexham, 1902): 1/0

Griffiths, M W (Leicester, 1947–54): 11/2

Griffiths, P (Chirk, 1884–91): 6/0

Griffiths, P H (Everton, 1932): 1/0

Griffiths, S (Wrexham, 1902): 1/0

Griffiths, T P (Everton, Bolton, Middlesbrough, A Villa, 1927–37): 21/3

Hall, G D (Chelsea, 1988–92): 9/0

Hallam, J (Oswestry, 1889): 1/0

Hanford, H (Swansea T, Sheff Wed, 1934–9): 7/0

Harrington, A C (Cardiff, 1956–62): 11/0

Harris, C S (Leeds, 1976–82): 24/1

Harris, W C (Middlesbrough, 1954–8): 6/0

Harrison, W C (Wrexham, 1899–1901): 5/0

Hartson, J (Arsenal, West Ham, 1995–8): 12/1

Haworth, S O (Cardiff, 1997–8): 3/0

Hayes, A (Wrexham, 1890–4): 2/0

Hennessey, W T (Birmingham, Nottingham Forest, Derby, 1962–73): 39/0

Hersee, A M (Bangor, 1886): 2/0

Hersee, R (Llandudno, 1886): 1/1

Hewitt, R (Cardiff, 1958): 5/1

Howitt, T J (Wrexham, Chelsea, South Liverpool, 1911–4): 8/0

Heywood, D (Druids, 1879): 1/0

Hibbott, H (Newtown Excelsior, Newtown, 1880–5): 3/0

Higham, G G (Oswestry, 1878–9): 2/0

Hill, M R (Ipswich, 1972): 2/0

Hockey, T (Sheff Utd, Norwich, A Villa, 1972–4): 9/1

Hoddinott, T F (Watford, 1921): 2/0

Hodges, G (Wimbledon, Newcastle, Watford, Sheff Utd, 1984–96): 18/2

Hodgkinson, A V (Southampton, 1908): 1/0

Holden, A (Chester, 1984): 1/0

Hole, B C (Cardiff, Blackburn, A Villa, Swansea, 1963–71): 30/0

Hole, W J (Swansea T, 1921–9): 9/1

Hollins, D M (Newcastle, 1962–6): 11/0

Hopkins, I J (Brentford, 1935–9): 12/2

Hopkins, J (Fulham, C Palace, 1983–90): 16/0

Hopkins, M (Tottenham, 1956–63): 34/0

Horne, B (Portsmouth, Southampton, Everton, Birmingham, 1988–97): 59/2

Howell, E G (Builth, 1888–91): 3/3

Howells, R G (Cardiff, 1954): 2/0

Hugh, A R (Newport 1930): 1/0

Hughes, A (Rhos, 1894): 2/0

Hughes, A (Chirk, 1907): 1/0

Hughes, C M (Luton, Wimbledon, 1992–7): 8/0

Hughes, E (Everton, Tottenham, 1899–1907): 14/0

Hughes, E (Wrexham, Nottingham Forest, Wrexham, Man City, 1906–14): 16/0

Hughes, F W (Northwich Victoria, 1882–4): 6/0

Hughes, I (Luton, 1951): 4/0

Hughes, J (Cambridge University, Aberystwyth, 1877–9): 2/0

Hughes, J (Liverpool, 1905): 3/0

Hughes, J I (Blackburn, 1905): 3/0

Hughes, L M (Man Utd, Barcelona, Man Utd, Chelsea, 1984–97): 66/16

Hughes, P W (Bangor, 1887–9): 3/0

Hughes, W (Bootle, 1891–2): 3/0

Hughes, W A (Blackburn, 1949): 5/0

Hughes, W M (Birmingham, 1934–47): 10/0

Humphreys, J V (Everton, 1947): 1/0

Humphreys, R (Druids, 1888): 1/0

Hunter, A H (FA of Wales Secretary, 1887): 1/0

Jackett, K (Watford, 1983–8): 31/0

Jackson, W (St Helens Rec, 1899): 1/0

James, E (Chirk, 1893–9): 8/2

James, E G (Blackpool, 1966–71): 9/0

James, L (Burnley, Derby, Burnley, Swansea, Sunderland, 1972–83): 54/10

James, R M (Swansea, Stoke, QPR, Leicester, Swansea, 1979–88): 47/8

James, W (West Ham, 1931–2): 2/0
Jarrett, R H (Ruthin, 1889–90): 2/3
Jarvis, A L (Hull, 1967): 3/0
Jenkins, E (Lovell's Ath, 1925): 1/0
Jenkins, J (Brighton, 1924–7): 8/0
Jenkins, R W (Rhyl, 1902): 1/0
Jenkins, S R (Swansea, Huddersfield, 1996–8): 10/0
Jenkyns, C A L (Small Heath, Arsenal, Newton Heath, Walsall, 1892–8): 8/1
Jennings, W (Bolton, 1914–29): 11/0
John, R F (Arsenal, 1923–37): 15/0
John, W R (Walsall, Stoke, Preston, Sheff Utd, Swansea, 1931–9): 14/0
Johnson, M G (Swansea, 1964): 1/0
Jones, A (Port Vale, Charlton, 1987–90): 6/1
Jones, A F (Oxford University, 1877): 1/0
Jones, A T (Nottingham Forest, Notts Co, 1905–6): 2/0
Jones, B (Wolves, Arsenal, 1935–49): 17/6
Jones, B S (Swansea, Plymouth, Cardiff, 1963–9): 15/2
Jones, C (Nottingham Forest, Arsenal, 1926–33): 8/0
Jones, C (Swansea, Tottenham, Fulham, 1954–69): 59/15
Jones, C W (Birmingham, 1935–9): 2/1
Jones, D (Chirk, Bolton, Man City, 1888–1900): 14/0
Jones, D E (Norwich, 1976–80): 8/1
Jones, D O (Leicester, 1934–7): 7/0
Jones, E (Chelsea, Oldham, Bolton, 1910–4): 7/1
Jones, F R (Bangor, 1885–6): 3/0
Jones, F W (Small Heath, 1893): 1/0
Jones, G P (Wrexham, 1907): 2/0
Jones, H (Aberaman, 1902): 1/1
Jones, H (Bangor, Queen's Park, East Stirlingshire, Queen's Park, 1885–91): 14/0
Jones, I (Swansea, WBA, 1920–6): 10/1
Jones, J (Llandrindod Wells, 1908–10): 3/0
Jones, J (Druids, 1876): 1/0
Jones, J (Berwyn Rangers, 1883–4): 3/0
Jones, J (Wrexham, 1925): 1/0
Jones, J L (Sheff Utd, Tottenham, 1895–1904): 21/0
Jones, J L (Stoke, Middlesbrough, 1906–10): 2/0
Jones, J O (Bangor, 1901): 1/1
Jones, J P (Liverpool, Wrexham, Chelsea, Huddersfield, 1976–86): 72/1
Jones, J T (Stoke, C Palace, 1912–2): 15/0
Jones, K (A Villa, 1950): 1/0
Jones, L J (Cardiff, Coventry, Arsenal, 1933–9): 11/1
Jones, P L (Liverpool, Tranmere, 1997): 2/0
Jones, P S (Stockport, Southampton, 1997–8): 4/0
Jones, P W (Bristol R, 1971): 1/0
Jones, R (Bangor, Crewe, 1887–90): 3/0
Jones, R (Leicester Fosse, 1898): 1/0
Jones, R (Druids, 1899): 1/0
Jones, R (Bangor, 1900): 2/0
Jones, R (Millwall, 1906): 2/0
Jones, R A (Druids, 1884–5): 4/2
Jones, R A (Sheff Wed, 1994): 1/0
Jones, R S (Everton, 1894): 1/0
Jones, S (Wrexham, Chester, 1887–90): 2/0

Jones, S (Wrexham, Burton Swifts, Druids, 1893–9): 6/0
Jones, T (Man Utd, 1926–30): 4/0
Jones, T D (Aberdare, 1908): 1/0
Jones, T G (Everton, 1938–50): 17/0
Jones, T J (Sheff Wed, 1932–3): 2/0
Jones, V P (Wimbledon, 1995–7): 9/0
Jones, W E A (Swansea T, Tottenham, 1947–9): 4/0
Jones, W J (Aberdare, West Ham, 1901–2): 4/0
Jones, W L (Man City, Southend, 1905–20): 20/6
Jones, W P (Druids, Wynstay, 1889–90): 4/0
Jones, W R (Aberystwyth, 1897): 1/0
Keenor, F C (Cardiff, Crewe, 1920–33): 32/2
Kelly, F C (Wrexham, Druids, 1899–1902): 3/0
Kelsey, A J (Arsenal, 1954–62): 41/0
Kenrick, S L (Druids, Oswestry, Shropshire Wanderers, 1876–81): 5/0
Ketley, C F (Druids, 1882): 1/0
King, J (Swansea, 1955): 1/0
Kinsey, N (Norwich, Birmingham, 1951–6): 7/0
Knill, A R (Swansea, 1989): 1/0
Krzywicki, R L (WBA, Huddersfield, 1970–2): 8/1
Lambert, R (Liverpool, 1947–9): 5/0
Latham, G (Liverpool, Southport Central, 1905–13): 10/0
Law, B J (QPR, 1990): 1/0
Lawrence, E (Clapton Orient, Notts Co, 1930–2): 2/0
Lawrence, S (Swansea T, 1932–6): 8/0
Lea, A (Wrexham, 1889–93): 4/0
Leary, P (Bangor, 1889): 1/0
Leek, K (Leicester, Newcastle, Birmingham, Northampton, 1961–5): 13/5
Legg, A (Birmingham, 1996–7): 4/0
Lever, A R (Leicester, 1953): 1/0
Lewis, B (Chester, Wrexham, Middlesbrough, Wrexham, 1891–5): 10/3
Lewis, D (Arsenal, 1927–30): 3/0
Lewis, D (Swansea, 1983): 1/0
Lewis, D J (Swansea, 1933): 2/0
Lewis, D M (Bangor, 1890): 2/0
Lewis, J (Bristol R, 1906): 1/1
Lewis, J (Cardiff, 1926): 1/1
Lewis, T (Wrexham, 1881): 2/0
Lewis, W (Bangor, Crewe, Chester, Man City, Chester, 1885–98): 27/10
Lewis, W L (Swansea, Huddersfield, 1927–30): 6/2
Lloyd, B W (Wrexham, 1976): 3/0
Lloyd, J W (Wrexham, Newtown, 1879–85): 2/0
Lloyd, R A (Ruthin, 1891–5): 2/0
Lockley, A (Chirk, 1898): 1/0
Lovell, S (C Palace, Millwall, 1982–6): 6/1
Lowrie, G (Coventry, Newcastle, 1948–9): 4/2
Lowndes, S (Newport, Millwall, Barnsley, 1983–8): 10/0
Lucas, P M (Leyton Orient, 1962–3): 4/0
Lucas, W H (Swansea, 1949–51): 7/0
Lumberg, A (Wrexham, Wolves, 1929–32): 4/0
McCarthy, T P (Wrexham, 1899): 1/0
McMillan, R (Shrewsbury Engineers, 1881): 2/0
Maguire, G T (Portsmouth, 1900–2): 7/0
Mahoney, J F (Stoke, Middlesbrough, Swansea, 1968–83): 51/1

Mardon, P J (WBA): 1/0
Marriott, A (Wrexham, 1996–7): 4/0
Martin, T J (Newport, 1930): 1/0
Marustik, C (Swansea, 1982–3): 6/0
Mates, J (Chirk, 1891–7): 3/0
Mathews, R W (Liverpool, Bristol C, Bradford, 1921–6): 3/0
Matthews, W (Chester, 1905–8): 2/0
Matthias, J S (Brymbo, Shrewsbury, Wolves, 1896–9): 5/0
Matthias, T J (Wrexham, 1914–23): 12/0
Mays, A W (Wrexham, 1929): 1/1
Medwin, T C (Swansea, Tottenham, 1953–63): 30/6
Melville, A K (Swansea, Oxford, Sunderland, 1990–7): 32/3
Meredith, S (Chirk, Stoke, Leyton, 1900–7): 8/0
Meredith, W H (Man City, Man Utd, 1895–1920): 48/11
Mielczarek, R (Rotherham, 1971): 1/0
Millership, J (Rotherham Co, 1920–1): 6/0
Millington, A H (WBA, C Palace, Peterborough, Swansea T, 1963–72): 21/0
Mills, T J (Clapham Orient, Leicester, 1934–5): 4/1
Mills–Roberts, R H (St Thomas' Hospital, Llanberis, 1885–92): 8/0
Moore, G (Cardiff, Chelsea, Man Utd, Northampton, Charlton, 1960–71): 21/1
Morgan, J R (Cambridge University, Swansea T, Derby School Staff, Swansea T, 1877–83): 10/2
Morgan, J T (Wrexham, 1905): 1/0
Morgan–Owen, H (Oxford University, Welshpool, 1901–7): 5/1
Morgan–Owen, M M (Oxford University, Corinthians, 1897–1907): 12/2
Morley, E J (Swansea T, Clapton Orient, 1925–9): 4/0
Morris, A G (Aberystwyth, Swindon, Nottingham Forest, 1896–1912): 21/9
Morris, C (Chirk, Derby, Huddersfield, 1900–11): 28/0
Morris, E (Chirk, 1893): 3/0
Morris, H (Sheff Utd, Man City, Grimsby, 1894–7): 3/2
Morris, J (Oswestry, 1887): 1/0
Morris, J (Chirk, 1898): 1/0
Morris, R (Chirk, Shrewsbury, 1900–3): 6/1
Morris, R (Druids, Newtown, Liverpool, Leeds C, Grimsby, Plymouth, 1902–8): 11/1
Morris, S (Birmingham, 1937–9): 5/0
Morris, W (Burnley, 1947–52): 5/0
Moulsdale, J R B (Corinthians, 1925): 1/0
Murphy, J P (WBA, 1933–8): 15/0
Nardiello, D (Coventry, 1978): 2/0
Neal, J E (Colwyn Bay, 1931): 2/0
Neilson, A B (Newcastle, Southampton, 1992–7): 5/0
Newnes, J (Nelson, 1926): 1/0
Newton, L F (Cardiff Corinthians, 1912): 1/0
Nicholas, D S (Stoke, Swansea, 1927): 3/0
Nicholas, P (C Palace, Arsenal, C Palace, Luton, Aberdeen, Chelsea, Watford, 1979–92): 73/2
Nicholls, J (Newport, Cardiff, 1924–5): 4/0
Niedzwiecki, E A (Chelsea, 1985–8): 2/0

Nock, W (Newtown, 1897): 1/0
Nogan, L M (Watford, Reading, 1992–6): 2/0
Norman, A J (Hull, 1986–8): 5/0
Nurse, M T G (Swansea T, Middlesbrough, 1960–4): 12/0
O'Callaghan, E (Tottenham, 1929–35): 11/3
Oliver, A (Blackburn, Bangor, 1905): 2/0
O'Sullivan, P A (Brighton, 1973–9): 3/1
Oster, J (Everton, 1997–8): 3/0
Owen, D (Oswestry, 1879): 1/0
Owen, E (Ruthin Grammar School, 1884): 3/0
Owen, G (Chirk, Newtown Heath, 1888–93): 4/2
Owen, J (Newtown Heath, 1892): 1/0
Owen, T (Crewe, 1899): 2/0
Owen T (Oswestry, 1879): 1/0
Owen, W (Chirk, 1884–93): 16/4
Owen, W P (Ruthin, 1880–4): 12/6
Owens, J (Wrexham, 1902): 1/0
Page, M E (Birmingham, 1971–9): 28/0
Page, R J (Watford, 1997): 5/0
Palmer, D (Swansea, 1957–8): 3/3
Parris, J E (Bradford, 1932): 1/0
Parry, B J (Swansea T, 1951): 1/0
Parry, C (Everton, Newtown, 1891–8): 13/0
Parry, E (Liverpool, 1922–6): 5/0
Parry, M (Liverpool, 1901–9): 16/0
Parry, T D (Oswestry, 1900–2): 7/3
Parry, W (Newtown, 1895): 1/0
Pascoe, C (Swansea, Sunderland, 1984–92): 10/0
Paul, R (Swansea T, Man City, 1949–56): 33/1
Peake, E (Aberystwyth, Liverpool, 1908–14): 11/1
Peers, E J (Wolves, Port Vale, 1914–23): 12/0
Pembridge, M A (Luton, Derby, Sheff Wed, 1992–8): 26/4
Perry, E (Doncaster, 1938): 3/1
Perry, J (Cardiff, 1994): 1/0
Phennah, E (Civil Service, 1878): 1/0
Phillips, C (Wolves, A Villa, 1931–8): 13/5
Phillips, D (Plymouth, Man City, Coventry, Norwich, Nottingham Forest, 1984–96): 62/2
Phillips, L (Cardiff, A Villa, Swansea, Charlton, 1971–82): 58/0
Phillips, T J S (Chelsea, 1973–8): 4/0
Phoenix, H (Wrexham, 1882): 1/0
Poland, G (Wrexham, 1939): 2/0
Pontin, K (Cardiff, 1980): 2/0
Powell, A (Leeds, Everton, Birmingham, 1947–51): 8/1
Powell, D (Wrexham, Sheff Utd, 1968–71): 11/1
Powell, I V (QPR, A Villa, 1947–51): 8/0
Powell, J (Druids, Bolton, Newton Heath, 1878–88): 15/0
Powell, S (WBA, 1885–92): 7/0
Price, H (A Villa, Burton U, Wrexham, 1907–9): 5/0
Price, J (Wrexham, Druids, 1877–83): 12/4
Price, P (Luton, Tottenham, 1980–4): 25/1
Pring, K D (Rotherham, 1966–7): 3/0
Pritchard, H K (Bristol C, 1985): 1/0
Pryce–Jones, A W (Newtown, 1895): 1/0
Pryce–Jones, W E (Cambridge University, 1887–90): 5/3
Pugh, A (Rhostyllen, 1889): 1/0
Pugh, D H (Wrexham, Lincoln, 1896–1901): 7/2
Pugsley, J (Charlton, 1930): 1/0

Pullen, W J (Plymouth, 1926): 1/0
Rankmore, F E J (Peterborough, 1966): 1/0
Ratcliffe, K (Everton, Cardiff, 1981–93): 59/0
Rea, J C (Aberystwyth, 1894–8): 9/0
Ready, K (QPR, 1997): 3/0
Reece, G I (Sheff Utd, Cardiff, 1966–75): 29/2
Reed, W G (Ipswich, 1955): 2/0
Rees, A (Birmingham, 1984): 1/0
Rees, J M (Luton, 1992): 1/0
Rees, R R (Coventry, WBA, Nottingham Forest, 1965–72): 39/3
Rees, W (Cardiff, Tottenham, 1949–50): 4/0
Richards, A (Barnsley, 1932): 1/0
Richards, D (Wolves, Brentford, Birmingham, 1931–9): 21/0
Richards, G (Druids, Oswestry, Shrewsbury, 1899–1905): 6/0
Richards, R W (Wolves, West Ham, Mold, 1920–6): 9/1
Richards, S V (Cardiff, 1947): 1/0
Richards, W E (Fulham, 1933): 1/0
Roach, J (Oswestry, 1885): 1/2
Robbins, W W (Cardiff, Huddersfield, Leicester, 1990–5): 7/4
Roberts, J (Chirk, 1898): 1/1
Roberts, J (Wrexham, 1913): 2/1
Roberts, J (Corwen, Berwyn R, 1879–83): 7/1
Roberts, J (Ruthin, 1881–2): 2/0
Roberts, J (Bradford, 1906–7): 2/0
Roberts, J G (Arsenal, Birmingham, 1971–6): 22/0
Roberts, J H (Bolton, 1949): 1/0
Roberts, P S (Portsmouth, 1974–5): 4/1
Roberts, R (Druids, Bolton, Preston, 1884–92): 9/1
Roberts, R (Wrexham, 1886–7): 2/0
Roberts, R (Rhos, Crewe, 1891–3): 2/0
Roberts, W (Llangollen, Berwyn R, 1879–83): 6/2
Roberts, W (Wrexham, 1886–7): 4/1
Roberts, W H (Ruthin, Rhyl, 1882–4): 6/1
Robinson, J R C (Charlton, 1996–7): 10/1
Rodrigues, P J (Cardiff, Leicester, Sheff Wed, 1965–74): 40/0
Rogers, J P (Wrexham, 1896): 3/0
Rogers, W (Wrexham, 1931): 2/0
Roose, L R (Aberystwyth, London Welsh, Stoke, Everton, Stoke, Sunderland, 1900–11): 24/0
Rouse, R V (C Palace, 1959): 1/0
Rowlands, A C (Tranmere, 1914): 1/0
Rowley, T (Tranmere, 1959): 1/0
Rush, I (Liverpool, Juventus, Liverpool, 1980–96): 73/28
Russell, M R (Merthyr T, Plymouth, 1912–29): 23/1
Sabine, H W (Oswestry, 1887): 1/1
Saunders, D (Brighton, Oxford, Derby, Liverpool, A Villa, Galatasaray, Nottingham Forest, 1986–97): 61/21
Savage, R W (Crewe, Leicester, 1996–8): 8/1
Savin, G (Oswestry, 1878): 1/0
Sayer, P (Cardiff, 1977–8): 7/0
Scrine, F H (Swansea, 1950): 2/0
Sear, C R (Man City, 1963): 1/0
Shaw, E G (Oswestry, 1882–4): 3/2

Sherwood, A T (Cardiff, Newport, 1947–57): 41/0
Shone, W W (Oswestry, 1879): 1/0
Shortt, W W (Plymouth, 1947–53): 12/0
Showers, D (Cardiff, 1975): 2/0
Sidlow, C (Liverpool, 1947–50): 7/0
Sisson, H (Wrexham Olympic, 1885–6): 3/4
Slatter, N (Bristol R, Oxford, 1983–9): 22/2
Smallman, D P (Wrexham, Everton, 1974–6): 7/1
Southall, N (Everton, 1982–97): 92/0
Speed, G A (Leeds, Everton, Newcastle, 1990–8): 45/3
Sprake, G (Leeds, Birmingham, 1964–75): 37/0
Stansfield, F (Cardiff, 1949): 1/0
Stevenson, B (Leeds, Birmingham, 1978–82): 15/0
Stevenson, N (Swansea, 1982–3): 4/0
Stitfall, R F (Cardiff, 1953–7): 2/0
Sullivan, D (Cardiff, 1953–60): 17/0
Symons, C J (Portsmouth, Man City, 1992–7): 27/1
Tapscott, D R (Arsenal, Cardiff, 1954–9): 14/4
Taylor, G K (C Palace, Sheff Utd, 1996–8): 8/0
Taylor, J (Wrexham, 1898): 1/0
Taylor, O D S (Newtown, 1893–4): 4/0
Thomas, C (Druids, 1899–1900): 2/0
Thomas, D A (Swansea T, 1957–8): 2/0
Thomas, D S (Fulham, 1948–9): 4/0
Thomas, E (Cardiff Corinthians, 1925): 1/0
Thomas, G (Wrexham, 1885): 2/0
Thomas, H (Man Utd, 1927): 1/0
Thomas, M (Wrexham, Man Utd, Everton, Brighton, Stoke, Chelsea, WBA, 1977–86): 51/4
Thomas, M R (Newcastle, 1987): 1/0
Thomas, R J (Swindon, Derby, Cardiff, 1967–78): 50/0
Thomas, T (Bangor, 1898): 2/1
Thomas, W R (Newport, 1931): 2/0
Thomson, D (Druids, 1876): 1/0
Thomson, G F (Druids, 1876–7): 2/0
Toshack, J B (Cardiff, Liverpool, Swansea, 1969–80): 40/13
Townsend, W (Newtown, 1887–93): 2/0
Trainer, H (Wrexham, 1895): 3/2
Trainer, J (Bolton, Preston, 1887–99): 20/0
Trollope, P (Derby, Fulham, 1997–8): 3/0
Turner, H G (Charlton, 1937–9): 8/0
Turner, J (Wrexham, 1892): 1/0
Turner, R E (Wrexham, 1891): 2/0
Turner, W H (Wrexham, 1887–91): 5/0
Van Den Hauwe, P W R (Everton, 1985–9): 13/0
Vaughan, J (Druids, 1893–9): 4/0
Vaughan, J (Oswestry, Bolton, 1879–84): 11/2
Vaughan, J O (Rhyl, 1885–6): 4/0
Vaughan, N (Newport, Cardiff, 1983–5): 10/0
Vaughan, T (Rhyl, 1885): 1/0
Vearncombe, G (Cardiff, 1958–61): 2/0
Vernon, T R (Blackburn, Everton, Stoke, 1957–68): 32/8
Villars, A K (Cardiff, 1974): 3/0
Vizard, E T (Bolton, 1911–27): 22/1
Walley, J T (Watford, 1971): 1/0
Walsh, L (C Palace, Swansea, 1980–2): 18/7
Ward, D (Bristol R, Cardiff, 1959–62): 2/0

Warner, J (Swansea, Man Utd, 1937–9): 2/0

Warren, F W (Cardiff, Middlesbrough, 1929–38): 6/3

Watkins, A E (Leicester Fosse, A Villa, Millwall, 1898–1904): 5/0

Watkins, W M (Stoke, A Villa, Sunderland, Stoke, 1902–8): 10/4

Webster, C (Man Utd, 1957–8): 4/0

Whatley, W J (Tottenham, 1939): 2/0

White, P F (London Welsh, 1896): 1/0

Wilcocks, A R (Oswestry, 1890): 1/0

Wilding, J (Wrexham Olympians, Bootle, Wrexham, 1885–92): 9/4

Williams, A (, 1997): 1/0

Williams, A (Reading, Wolves, 1994–8): 9/0

Williams, A L (Wrexham, 1931): 1/0

Williams, B (Bristol C, 1930): 1/0

Williams, B D (Swansea, Everton, 1928–35): 10/0

Williams, D G (Derby, Ipswich, 1988–96): 13/0

Williams, D M (Norwich, 1986–7): 5/0

Williams, D R (Merthyr T, Sheff Wed, Man Utd, 1921–9): 8/0

Williams, E (Crewe, 1893): 2/0

Williams, E (Druids, 1901–2): 5/0

Williams, G (Chirk, 1893–8): 6/0

Williams, G E (WBA, 1960–9): 26/1

Williams, G G (Swansea, 1961–2): 5/1

Williams, G J J (Cardiff, 1951): 1/0

Williams, G O (Wrexham, 1907): 1/0

Williams, H J (Swansea, 1965–72): 3/0

Williams, H T (Newport, Leeds, 1949–51): 4/0

Williams, J H (Oswestry, 1884): 1/0

Williams, J J (Wrexham, 1939): 1/0

Williams, J T (Middlesbrough, 1925): 1/0

Williams, J W (C Palace, 1912): 2/0

Williams, R (Newcastle, 1935): 2/0

Williams, R P (Caernarvon, 1886): 1/0

Williams, S G (WBA, Southampton, 1954–66): 43/0

Williams, W (Druids, Oswestry, Druids, 1876–83): 11/1

Williams, W (Northampton, 1925): 1/1

Witcomb, D F (WBA, Sheff Wed, 1947): 3/0

Woosnam, A P (Leyton Orient, West Ham, A Villa, 1959–63): 17/4

Woosnam, G (Newton White Star, 1879): 1/0

Worthington, T (Newtown, 1894): 1/0

Wynn, G A (Wrexham, Man City, 1909–14): 11/1

Wynn, W (Chirk, 1903): 1/0

Yorath, T C (Leeds, Coventry, Tottenham, Vancouver W, 1970–81): 59/2

Young, E (Wimbledon, C Palace, Wolves, 1990–6): 21/1

Republic of Ireland

Aherne, T (Belfast C, Luton, 1946–54): 16/0

Aldridge, J W (Oxford, Liverpool, Real Sociedad, Tranmere, 1986–97): 69/19

Ambrose, P (Shamrock R, 1955–64): 5/1

Anderson, J (Preston, Newcastle, 1980–9): 16/1

Andrews, P (Bohemians, 1936): 1/0

Arrigan, T (Waterford, 1938): 1/0

Babb, P A (Coventry, Liverpool, 1994–8): 25/0

Bailham, E (Shamrock R, 1964): 1/0

Barber, E (Shelbourne, Birmingham, 1966): 2/0

Barry, P (Fordsons, 1928–9): 2/0

Beglin, J (Liverpool, 1984–7): 15/0

Bermingham, J (Bohemians, 1929): 1/0

Bermingham, P (St James' Gate, 1935): 1/1

Braddish, S (Dundalk, 1978): 2/0

Bonner, P (Celtic, 1981–96): 80/0

Bradshaw, P (St James' Gate, 1939): 5/4

Brady, F (Fordsons, 1926–7): 2/0

Brady, T R (QPR, 1964): 6/0

Brady, W L (Arsenal, Juventus, Sampdoria, Internazionale, Ascoli, West Ham, 1975–90): 72/9

Branagan, K G (Bolton, 1997): 1/0

Breen, G (Birmingham, Coventry, 1996–8): 15/2

Breen, T (Man Utd, Shamrock R, 1937–47): 5/0

Brennan, F (Drumcondra, 1965): 1/0

Brennan, S A (Man Utd, Waterford, 1965–71): 19/0

Brown, J (Coventry, 1937): 2/0

Browne, W (Bohemians, 1964): 3/0

Buckley, L (Shamrock R, Waregem, 1984–5): 2/0

Burke, F (Cork Ath, 1952): 1/0

Burke, J (Cork, 1934): 1/0

Burke, J (Shamrock R, 1929): 1/0

Byrne, A B (Southampton, 1970–4): 14/0

Byrne, D (Shelbourne, Shamrock R, Coleraine, 1929–34): 3/0

Byrne, J (Bray Unknowns, 1928): 1/1

Byrne, J (QPR, Le Havre, Brighton, Sunderland, Millwall, 1985–93): 23/4

Byrne, P (Shamrock R, 1984–6): 8/0

Byrne, P (Dolphin, Drumcondra, 1931–4): 3/0

Byrne, S (Bohemians, 1931): 1/0

Campbell, A (Racing Santander, 1985): 3/0

Campbell, N (St Patrick's Ath, Fortuna Koln, 1971–7): 11/0

Cannon, H (Bohemians, 1926–8): 2/0

Cantwell, N (West Ham, Man Utd, 1954–67): 36/14

Carey, B P (Man Utd, Leicester, 1992–4): 3/0

Carey, J J (Man Utd, 1938–53): 29/3

Carolan, J (Man Utd, 1960): 2/0

Carroll, B (Shelbourne, 1949–50): 2/0

Carroll, T R (Ipswich, Birmingham, 1968–73): 17/1

Carsley, L (Derby, 1997–8): 6/0

Cascarino, A (Gillingham, Millwall, A Villa, Celtic, Chelsea, Marseille, Nancy, 1986–97): 75/19

Chandler, J (Leeds, 1980): 2/0

Chatton, H A (Shelbourne, Dumbarton, Cork, 1931–4): 3/0

Clarke, J (Drogheda U, 1978): 1/0

Clarke, K (Drumcondra, 1948): 2/0

Clarke, M (Shamrock R, 1950): 1/0

Clinton, T J (Everton, 1951–4): 3/0

Coad, P (Shamrock R, 1947–52): 11/3

Coffey, T (Drumcondra, 1950): 1/0

Colfer, M D (Shelbourne, 1950–1): 2/0

Collins, F (Jacobs, 1927): 1/0

Conmy, O M (Peterborough, 1965–70): 5/0

Connolly, D J (Watford, PSV Eindhoven, Feyenoord, 1996–8): 12/5

Connolly, H (Cork, 1937): 1/0

Connolly, J (Fordsons, 1926): 1/0

Conroy, G A (Stoke, 1970–77): 27/2

Conway, J P (Fulham, Man City, 1967–77): 20/3

Corr, P J (Everton, 1949–50): 4/0

Courtney, E (Cork U, 1946): 1/0

Coyle, O C (Bolton, 1994): 1/0

Coyne, T (Celtic, Tranmere, Motherwell, 1992–7): 22/6

Cummins, G P (Luton, 1954–61): 19/5

Cuneen, T (Limerick, 1951): 1/0

Cunningham, K (Wimbledon, 1996–8): 15/0

Curtis, D P (Shelbourne, Bristol C, Ipswich, Exeter, 1957–64): 17/8

Cusack, S (Limerick, 1953): 1/0

Daish, L S (Cambridge, Coventry, 1992–6): 5/0

Daly, G A (Man Utd, Derby, Coventry, Birmingham, Shrewsbury, 1973–87): 48/13

Daly, J (Shamrock R, 1932–5): 2/0

Daly, M (Wolves, 1978): 2/0

Daly, P (Shamrock R, 1950): 1/0

Davis, T L (Oldham, Tranmere, 1937–8): 4/4

Deacy, E (A Villa, 1982): 4/0

De Mange, K J P P (Liverpool, Hull, 1987–9): 2/0

Delap, R (Derby, 1998): 2/0

Dempsey, J T (Fulham, Chelsea, 1967–72): 19/1

Dennehy, J (Cork Hibernians, Nottingham Forest, Walsall, 1972–7): 11/2

Desmond, P (Middlesbrough, 1950): 4/0

Devine, J (Arsenal, Norwich, 1980–5): 13/0

Donnelly, J (Dundalk, 1935–8): 10/3

Donnelly, T (Drumcondra, Shamrock R, 1938–9): 2/1

Donovan, D C (Everton, 1955–7): 5/0

Donovan, T (A Villa, 1980–1): 2/0

Dowdall, C (Fordsons, Barnsley, Cork, 1928–31): 3/0

Doyle, C (Shelbourne, 1959): 1/0

Doyle, D (Shamrock R, 1926): 1/0

Doyle, L (Dolphin, 1932): 1/0

Duff, D (Blackburn, 1998): 2/0

Duffy, B (Shamrock R, 1950): 1/1

Duggan, H A (Leeds, Newport, 1927–38): 5/1

Dunne, A P (Man Utd, Bolton, 1962–76): 33/0

Dunne, J (Sheff Utd, Arsenal, Southampton, Shamrock R, 1930–9): 15/12

Dunne, J C (Fulham, 1971): 1/0

Dunne, L (Man City, 1935): 2/1

Dunne, P A J (Man Utd, 1965–7): 5/0

Dunne, S (Luton, 1953–60): 15/0

Dunne, T (St Patrick's Ath, 1956–7): 3/0

Dunning, P (Shelbourne, 1971): 2/0

Dunphy, E M (York, Millwall, 1966–71): 23/0

Dwyer, N M (West Ham, Swansea, 1960–5): 14/0

Eccles, P (Shamrock R, 1986): 1/0

Egan, R (Dundalk, 1929): 1/0

Eglington, T J (Shamrock, Everton, 1946–56): 24/2

Ellis, P (Bohemians, 1935–7): 7/1

Fagan, E (Shamrock R, 1973): 1/0

Fagan, F (Man City, Derby, 1955–61): 8/5

Fagan, J (Shamrock R, 1926): 1/0

Fairclough, M (Dundalk, 1982): 2/0

Fallon, S (Celtic, 1951–5): 8/2

Fallon, W J (Notts Co, Sheff Wed, 1935–9): 9/2

Farquharson, T G (Cardiff, 1929–32): 4/0
Farrell, P (Hibernian, 1937): 2/0
Farrell, P D (Shamrock R, Everton, 1946–57): 28/3
Farrelly, G (A Villa, Everton, 1996–8): 5/0
Feenan, J J (Sunderland, 1937): 2/0
Finucane, A (Limerick, 1967–72): 11/0
Fitzgerald, F J (Waterford, 1955–6): 2/1
Fitzgerald, P J (Leeds, Chester, 1961–2): 5/2
Fitzpatrick, K (Limerick, 1970): 1/0
Fitzsimons, A G (Middlesbrough, Lincoln, 1950–9): 26/7
Fleming, C (Middlesbrough, 1996–8): 10/0
Flood, J J (Shamrock R, 1926–32): 5/4
Fogarty, A (Sunderland, Hartlepool, 1960–4): 11/3
Foley, J (Cork, Celtic, 1934–7): 7/0
Foley, M (Shelbourne, 1926): 1/0
Foley, T C (Northampton, 1964–7): 9/0
Foy, T (Shamrock R, 1938–9): 2/0
Fullam, J (Preston, Shamrock R, 1961–70): 11/1
Fullam, R (Shamrock R, 1926–7): 2/1
Gallagher, C (Celtic, 1967): 2/0
Gallagher, M (Hibernian, 1954): 1/0
Gallagher, P (Falkirk, 1932): 1/0
Galvin, A (Tottenham, Sheff Wed, Swindon, 1983–90): 29/1
Gannon, E (Notts Co, Sheff Wed, Shelbourne, 1949–55): 14/0
Gannon, M (Shelbourne, 1972): 1/0
Gaskins, P (Shamrock R, St James' Gate, 1934–8): 7/0
Gavin, J T (Norwich, Tottenham, Norwich, 1950–7): 7/2
Geoghegan, M (St James' Gate, 1937–8): 2/2
Gibbons, A (St Patrick's Ath, 1952–6): 4/0
Gilbert, R (Shamrock R, 1966): 1/0
Giles, C (Doncaster, 1951): 1/0
Giles, M J (Man Utd, Leeds, WBA, Shamrock R, 1960–79): 59/5
Given, S J J (Blackburn, Newcastle, 1996–8): 16/0
Givens, D J (Man Utd, Luton, QPR, Birmingham, Neuchatel Xamax, 1969–82): 56/19
Glen, W (Shamrock R, 1927–36): 8/0
Glynn, D (Drumcondra, 1952–5): 2/1
Godwin, T F (Shamrock R, Leicester, Bournemouth, 1949–58): 13/0
Golding, J (Shamrock R, 1928–30): 2/0
Goodman, J (Wimbledon, 1997): 4/0
Gorman, W C (Bury, Brentford, 1936–47): 13/0
Grace, J (Drumcondra, 1926): 1/0
Grealish, A (Orient, Luton, Brighton, WBA, 1976–86): 45/8
Gregg, E (Bohemians, 1978–80): 8/0
Griffith, R (Walsall, 1935): 1/0
Grimes, A (Man Utd, Coventry, Luton, 1978–88): 18/1
Hale, A (A Villa, Doncaster, Waterford, 1962–72): 13/2
Hamilton, T (Shamrock R, 1959): 2/0
Hand, E K (Portsmouth, 1969–76): 20/2
Harrington, W (Cork, 1936–8): 5/0
Harte, I P (Leeds, 1996–8): 17/2
Hartnett, J B (Middlesbrough, 1949–54): 2/0

Haverty, J (Arsenal, Blackburn, Millwall, Celtic, Bristol R, Shelbourne, 1956–67): 32/3
Hayes, A W P (Southampton, 1979): 1/0
Hayes, W E (Huddersfield, 1947): 2/0
Hayes, W J (Limerick, 1949): 1/0
Healey, R (Cardiff, 1977–80): 2/0
Heighway, S D (Liverpool, Minnesota K, 1971–82): 34/0
Henderson, B (Drumcondra, 1948): 2/0
Hennessy, J (Shelbourne, St Patrick's Ath, 1965–9): 5/0
Herrick, J (Cork Hibernians, Shamrock R, 1972–3): 3/0
Higgins, J (Birmingham, 1951): 1/0
Holmes, J (Coventry, Tottenham, Vancouver W, 1971–81): 30/1
Horlacher, A F (Bohemians, 1930–6): 7/2
Houghton, R J (Oxford, Liverpool, A Villa, C Palace, 1986–97): 73/6
Howlett, G (Brighton, 1984): 1/0
Hoy, M (Dundalk, 1938–9): 6/0
Hughton, C (Tottenham, West Ham, 1980–92): 53/1
Hurley, C J (Millwall, Sunderland, Bolton, 1957–69): 40/2
Hutchinson, F (Drumcondra, 1935): 2/0
Irwin, D J (Man Utd, 1991–8): 48/2
Jordan, D (Wolves, 1937): 2/1
Jordan, W (Bohemians, 1934–8): 2/0
Kavanagh, G (Stoke, 1998): 1/0
Kavanagh, P J (Celtic, 1931–2): 2/0
Keane, R (Wolves, 1998): 3/0
Keane, R M (Nottingham Forest, Man Utd, 1991–7): 37/1
Keane, T R (Swansea T, 1949): 4/0
Kearin, M (Shamrock R, 1972): 1/0
Kearns, F T (West Ham, 1954): 1/0
Kearns, M (Oxford, Walsall, Wolves, 1971–80): 18/0
Kelly, A T (Sheff Utd, 1993–8): 20/0
Kelly, D T (Walsall, West Ham, Leicester, Newcastle, Wolves, Sunderland, 1988–97): 26/9
Kelly, G (Leeds, 1994–8): 27/1
Kelly, J (Derry C, 1932–6): 4/2
Kelly, J A (Drumcondra, Preston, 1957–73): 47/0
Kelly, J P V (Wolves, 1961–2): 5/0
Kelly, M J (Portsmouth, 1988–91): 4/0
Kelly, N (Nottingham Forest, 1954): 1/0
Kendrick, J (Everton, Dolphin, 1927–36): 4/0
Kenna, J J (Blackburn, 1995–8): 23/0
Kennedy, M (Liverpool, Wimbledon, 1996–7): 17/0
Kennedy, W (St James' Gate, 1932–4): 3/0
Keogh, J (Shamrock R, 1966): 1/0
Keogh, S (Shamrock R, 1959): 1/0
Kernaghan, A N (Middlesbrough, Man City, 1993–6): 22/1
Kiernan, F W (Shamrock R, Southampton, 1951–2): 5/0
Kilbane, K (WBA, 1998): 2/0
Kinnear, J P (Tottenham, Brighton, 1967–76): 26/0
Kinsella, J (Shelbourne, 1928): 1/0
Kinsella, M (Charlton, 1998): 2/0
Kinsella, O (Shamrock R, 1932–8): 2/0

Kirkland, A (Shamrock R, 1927): 1/0
Lacey, W (Shelbourne, 1927–30): 3/1
Langan, D (Derby, Birmingham, Oxford, 1978–88): 26/0
Lawler, J F (Fulham, 1953–6): 8/0
Lawlor, J C (Drumcondra, Doncaster, 1949–51): 3/0
Lawlor, M (Shamrock R, 1971–3): 5/0
Lawrenson, M (Preston, Brighton, Liverpool, 1977–88): 38/5
Leech, M (Shamrock R, 1969–73): 8/2
Lennon, C (St James' Gate, 1935): 3/0
Lennox, G (Dolphin, 1931–2): 2/0
Lowry, D (St Patrick's Ath, 1962): 1/0
Lunn, R (Dundalk, 1939): 2/0
Lynch, J (Cork Bohemians, 1934): 1/0
McAlinden, J (Portsmouth, 1946): 2/0
McAteer, J W (Bolton, Liverpool, 1994–7): 24/1
McCann, J (Shamrock R, 1957): 1/1
McCarthy, J (Bohemians, 1926–30): 3/0
McCarthy, M (Man City, Celtic, Lyon, Millwall, 1984–92): 57/2
McCarthy, M (Shamrock R, 1932): 1/0
McConville, T (Dundalk, Waterford, 1972–3): 6/0
McDonagh, J (Shamrock R, 1984–5): 3/0
McDonagh, J (Everton, Bolton, Notts Co, Wichita Wings, 1981–6): 25/0
McEvoy, M A (Blackburn, 1961–7): 67/6
McGee, P (QPR, Preston, 1978–81): 15/4
McGoldrick, E J (C Palace, Arsenal, 1992–5): 15/0
McGowan, D (West Ham, 1949): 3/0
McGowan, J (Cork U, 1947): 1/0
McGrath, M (Blackburn, Bradford, 1958–66): 22/0
McGrath, P (Man Utd, A Villa, Derby, 1985–97): 83/8
McGuire, W (Bohemians, 1936): 1/0
McKenzie, G (Southend, 1938–9): 9/0
Mackey, G (Shamrock R, 1957): 3/0
McLoughlin, A F (Swindon, Southampton, Portsmouth, 1990–8): 33/2
McLoughlin, F (Fordsons, 1930–2): 2/0
McMillan, W (Belfast Celtic, 1946): 2/0
McNally, J B (Luton, 1959–63): 3/0
Macken, A (Derby, 1977): 1/0
Madden, O (Cork, 1936): 1/1
Maguire, J (Shamrock R, 1929): 1/0
Malone, G (Shelbourne, 1949): 1/0
Mancini, T J (QPR, Arsenal, 1974–5): 5/1
Martin, C (Bo'ness, 1927): 1/0
Martin, C J (Glentoran, Leeds, A Villa, 1946–56): 30/60
Martin, M P (Bohemians, Man Utd, Newcastle, 1972–83): 52/0
Maybury, A (Leeds, 1998): 1/0
Meagan, M K (Everton, Huddersfield, 1961–70): 17/0
Meehan, P (Drumcondra, 1934): 1/0
Milligan, M J (Oldham, 1992): 1/0
Monahan, P (Sligo R, 1935): 2/0
Mooney, J (Shamrock R, 1965): 2/1
Moore, A (Middlesbrough, 1996–7): 8/0
Moore, P (Shamrock R, Aberdeen, Shamrock R, 1931–7): 9/7

Moran, K (Man Utd, Sporting Gijon, Blackburn, 1980–94): 71/6

Moroney, T (West Ham, Evergreen U, 1948–54): 12/1

Morris, C B (Celtic, Middlesbrough, 1988–93): 35/0

Moulson, C (Lincoln, Notts Co, 1936–7): 5/0

Moulson, G B (Lincoln, 1948–9): 3/0

Mucklan, C (Drogheda, 1978): 1/0

Muldoon, T (A Villa, 1927): 1/0

Mulligan, P M (Shamrock R, Chelsea, C Palace, WBA, Shamrock R, 1969–80): 50/1

Munroe, L (Shamrock R, 1954): 1/0

Murphy, A (Clyde, 1956): 1/0

Murphy, B (Bohemians, 1986): 1/0

Murphy, J (C Palace, 1980): 3/0

Murray, T (Dundalk, 1950): 1/0

Newman, W (Shelbourne, 1969): 1/0

Nolan, R (Shamrock R, 1957–63): 10/0

O'Brien, F (Philadelphia F, 1980): 3/0

O'Brien, L (Shamrock R, Man Utd, Newcastle, Tranmere, 1986–97): 16/0

O'Brien, M T (Derby, Walsall, Norwich, Watford, 1927–32): 4/0

O'Brien, R (Notts Co, 1976–80): 5/0

O'Byrne, L B (Shamrock R, 1949): 1/0

O'Callaghan, B R (Stoke, 1979–82): 6/0

O'Callaghan, K (Ipswich, Portsmouth, 1981–7): 21/1

O'Connell, A (Dundalk, Bohemians, 1967–71): 2/0

O'Connor, T (Shamrock R, 1950): 4/2

O'Connor, T (Fulham, Dundalk, Bohemians, 1968–73): 7/2

O'Driscoll, J F (Swansea, 1949): 3/0

O'Driscoll, S (Fulham, 1982): 3/0

O'Farrell, F (West Ham, Preston, 1952–9): 9/2

O'Flanagan, K P (Bohemians, Arsenal, 1938–47): 10/3

O'Flanagan, M (Bohemians, 1947): 1/0

O'Hanlon, K G (Rotherham, 1988): 1/0

O'Kane, P (Bohemians, 1935): 3/0

O'Keefe, E (Everton, Port Vale, 1981–5): 5/1

O'Keefe, T (Cork, Waterford, 1934–8): 3/0

O'Leary, D (Arsenal, 1977–93): 68/1

O'Leary, P (Shamrock R, 1980–1): 7/0

O'Mahoney, M T (Bristol R, 1938–9): 6/0

O'Neill, F S (Shamrock, 1962–72): 20/1

O'Neill, J (Everton, 1952–9): 17/0

O'Neill, J (Preston, 1961): 1/0

O'Neill, K P (Norwich, 1996–7): 9/4

O'Neill, W (Dundalk, 1936–9): 11/0

O'Regan, K (Brighton, 1984–5): 4/0

O'Reilly, J (Brideville, Aberdeen, Brideville, St James' Gate, 1932–9): 20/2

O'Reilly, J (Cork U, 1946): 2/1

Peyton, G (Fulham, Bournemouth, Everton, 1977–92): 33/0

Peyton, N (Shamrock R, Leeds, 1957–63): 6/0

Phelan, T (Wimbledon, Man City, Chelsea, Everton, 1992–7): 38/0

Quinn, N J (Arsenal, Man City, Sunderland, 1986–98): 63/16

Reid, C (Brideville, 1931): 1/0

Richardson, D J (Shamrock R, Gillingham, 1972–80): 3/0

Rigby, A (St James' Gate, 1935): 3/0

Ringstead, A (Sheff Utd, 1951–9): 20/7

Robinson, J (Bohemians, Dolphin, 1928–31): 2/0

Robinson, M (Brighton, Liverpool, QPR, 1981–6): 24/4

Roche, P J (Shelbourne, Man Utd, 1972–6): 8/0

Rogers, E (Blackburn, Charlton, 1968–73): 19/5

Ryan, G (Derby, Brighton, 1978–85): 18/1

Ryan, R A (WBA, Derby, 1950–6): 16/3

Savage, D P T (Millwall, 1996): 5/0

Saward, P (Millwall, A Villa, Huddersfield, 1954–63): 18/0

Scannell, T (Southend, 1954): 1/0

Scully, P J (Arsenal, 1989): 1/0

Sheedy, K (Everton, Newcastle, 1984–93): 45/9

Sheridan, J J (Leeds, Sheff Wed, 1988–96): 34/5

Slaven, B (Middlesbrough, 1990–3): 7/1

Sloan, J W (Arsenal, 1946): 2/1

Smyth, M (Shamrock R, 1969): 1/0

Squires, J (Shelbourne, 1934): 1/1

Stapleton, F (Arsenal, Man Utd, Ajax, Le Havre, Blackburn, 1977–90): 71/20

Staunton, S (Liverpool, A Villa, 1989–98): 73/5

Stevenson, A E (Dolphin, Everton, 1932–49): 7/0

Strahan, F (Shelbourne, 1964–6): 5/1

Sullivan, J (Fordsons, 1928): 1/1

Swan, M M G (Drumcondra, 1960): 1/0

Synnott, N (Shamrock R, 1978–9): 3/0

Taylor, T (Waterford, 1959): 1/0

Thomas, P (Waterford, 1974): 2/0

Townsend, A D (Norwich, Chelsea, A Villa, 1989–97): 66/7

Traynor, T J (Southampton, 1954–64): 8/0

Treacy, R C P (WBA, Charlton, Swindon, Preston, WBA, Shamrock R, 1966–1980): 42/5

Tuohy, L (Shamrock R, Newcastle, Shamrock R, 1956–65): 8/4

Turner, C J (Southend, West Ham, 1936–9): 10/0

Turner, P (Celtic, 1963–4): 2/0

Vernon, J (Belfast C, 1946): 2/0

Waddock, G (QPR, Millwall, 1980–90): 21/3

Walsh, D J (Linfield, WBA, A Villa, 1946–54): 20/5

Walsh, J (Linfield, 1982): 1/0

Walsh, M (Blackpool, Everton, QPR, 1976–85): 21/3

Walsh, M (Everton, 1982–3): 4/3

Walsh, W (Man City, 1947–50: 9/0

Waters, J (Grimsby, 1977–80): 2/1

Watters, F (Shelbourne, 1926): 1/0

Weir, E (Clyde, 1939): 3/0

Whelan, R (St Patrick's Ath, 1964): 2/0

Whelan, R (Liverpool, Southend, 1981–95): 53/3

Whelan, W (Man Utd, 1956–7): 4/0

White, J J (Bohemians, 1928): 1/2

Whittaker, R (Chelsea, 1959): 1/0

Williams, J (Shamrock R, 1938): 1/0

INTERNATIONAL
PLAYER RECORDS

GERMAN INTERNATIONAL PLAYERS' RECORDS

This is the full list of total number of appearances and goals by German internationals. French, Dutch, Spanish, Italian, Argentinian and Brazilian lists follow this one. The player's club(s) and season(s) when he won his caps are in brackets and total caps come before total goals. Statistics include the 1998 World Cup finals.

Abramczik, Rudiger (Schalke 04, 1977–79): 19/2
Adam, Karl (1860 Munich, 1951–52): 3
Adamkiewicz, Edmund (Hamburg, 1942): 2/1
Albertz, Jorg (Hamburger, 1996): 2
Albrecht, Erich (Wacker Leipzig, 1909): 1
Albrecht, Ernst (Fortuna Dusseldorf, 1928–34): 15/4
Albu, Gheorghe (Venus Bucharest, 1938): 1/1
Allgower, Karl (VfB Stuttgart, 1980–86): 10
Allofs, Klaus (Fortuna Düsseldorf, Köln, Marseille, 1978–88): 56/17
Allofs, Thomas (Kaiserslautern, Köln, 1985–88): 2
Altvater, Heinrich (Wacker Munich, 1922): 1
Appel, Hans (Blau-Weiss Berlin, 1933–38): 5
Arlt, Willi (Schwaben Augsburg, 1939–42): 11/2
Ascherl, Willy (Schwaben Augsburg, 1924): 1
Au, Alfred (VfR Mannheim, 1921): 1
Auer, Karl (Schwaben Augsburg, 1924–26): 3/2
Augenthaler, Klaus (Bayern Munich, 1983–90): 27
Aumann Raimond (Bayern Munich, 1989–90): 4
Babbel, Marcus (Bayern Munich, 1995–98): 32/1
Bache, Fritz (Wacker 04 Berlin, 1923–24): 2
Balogh, Fritz (VfL Neckarau, 1950): 1
Bantle, Ernst (Fortuna Düsseldorf, 1924): 1
Barufka, Karl (VfB Stuttgart, 1950–51): 3
Base, Joachim (Eintracht Braunschweig, 1968): 1
Basler Mario (Werder Bremen, Bayern Munich, 1994–98): 27/2
Bauer Hans (Borussia Dortmund, 1951–58): 5
Baumann Gunter (Kaiserslautern, 1950–51): 2
Baumgarten Fritz (Germania Berlin, 1908): 1
Baumgartner, Willy (Schwaben, Augsburg, 1908–09): 4
Baumler, Erich (Eintracht Frankfurt, 1956): 1/1
Bauwens, Peco (Schwaben, Augsburg, 1910): 1
Beck, Alfred (St Pauli Hamburg, 1954): 1/1
Beckenbauer, Franz (Bayern Munich, 1965–81): 104/15
Becker, Fritz (Kickers Frankfurt, 1908): 1/2
Beer, Erich (Hertha Berlin, 1975–78): 25/7
Beier, Albert (Hamburg, 1924–31): 9
Beiersdorfer, Dietmar (Hamburg, 1991): 1
Bein, Uwe (Eintracht Frankfurt, 1989–93): 17/3
Bella, Michael (MSV Duisburg, 1968–71): 4
Bender, Jakob (Fortuna Düsseldorf, 1933–35): 9
Benthaus, Helmut (Westfalia Herne, 1958–60): 8
Berg, Walter (Schwaben Augsburg, 1938): 1
Berghausen Alfred (Preussen Duisburg, 1910): 1
Bergmaier, Josef (Blau-Weiss Berlin, 1930–33): 8/1
Bernard, Gunter (Schalke 04, Werder Bremen, 1962–68): 5

Berndt, Hans (1860 Munich, 1937–38): 3/2
Bert, Adalbert (VfB Leipzig, 1910): 1
Berthold, Rudolf Dresdner SC, 1928): 1
Berthold, Thomas (Eintracht Frankfurt, AS Roma [Ita], Verona [Ita], VfB Stuttgart, 1985–94): 62/1
Biallas, Hans (Duisburg, (1938–39): 3/1
Bierhoff, Oliver (Udinese [Ita], 1996–98): 29/20
Biesinger, Ulrich (Borussia Dortmund, 1954–58): 7/2
Billen, Matthias (VfL Osnabruck, 1936): 1
Billmann, Willi (Kaiserslautern, 1937–41): 11
Binder, Franz (Rapid Vienna, 1939–41): 9/10
Binz, Manfred (Eintracht Frankfurt, 1990–92): 14/1
Bittcher, Ulrich (Schalke 04, 1981): 1
Bleidick, Hartwig Borussia Mönchengladbach, 1971): 2
Blum, Ernst (VfB Stuttgart, 1927): 1
Blunk, Wilhelm (Hamburg, 1929): 1
Bobic, Fredi (VfB Stuttgart, 1994–98): 19/2
Bockenfeld, Manfred (Düsseldorf, 1984): 1
Bode, Marco (Werder Bremen, 1995–96): 8
Bogelein, Karl (VfB Stuttgart, 1951): 1
Bokle, Otto (VfB Stuttgart, 1935): 1
Bollmann, Albert (Schwaben Augsburg, 1914): 1
Bommer, Rudolf (Fortuna Düsseldorf, 1984): 6
Bongartz, Hans (Schalke 04, 1976–77): 4
Bonhof, Rainer (Borussia Mönchengladbach, 1972–81): 53/9
Borchers, Ronald (Eintracht Frankfurt, 1978–81): 6
Borck, Walter (MTV Munich, 1911): 1
Borkenhagen, Kurt (Fortuna Düsseldorf, 1952): 1
Borowka, Ulrich (Werder Bremen, 1988): 6
Bosch, Hermann (Karlsruher, 1912–13): 3
Brehme, Andreas (Kaiserslautern, Bayern Munich, Inter Milan [Ita] 1984–88): 86/8
Breitner, Paul (Bayern Munich, Real Madrid [Spa], 1971–82): 48/10
Brenninger, Dieter (Bayern Munich, 1969): 1
Breuer, Theo (Fortuna Düsseldorf, 1933): 2
Breunig, Max (Karlsruhe, Fortuna Düsseldorf, 1910–13): 8/1
Breynk, Andreas (Preussen Duisburg, 1910): 1
Briegel, Hans-Peter (Kaiserslautern, Verona [Ita], 1979–86): 72/4
Brozovic, Miroslav (Gradanski Zagreb, 1942): 1/1
Brülls, Albert (Borussia Dortmund, Borussia Mönchengladbach, 1959–66): 25/9
Brunke, Hans (1860 Munich, 1927–31): 7
Brunnenmeier, Rudolf (1860 Munich,

1964–65): 5/3
Bruns, Hans-Gunter (Borussia Mönchengladbach, 1984): 4
Buchloh, Fritz (VfB Speldorf, 1932–36): 16
Buchwald, Guido (VfB Stuttgart, 1984–94): 76/3
Budzinsky, Lothar (Duisburger SV, 1910): 1
Bulte, Otto (Eintracht Braunschweig, 1910): 1
Burdenski, Dieter (Werder Bremen, 1977–84): 12
Burdenski, Herbert (Schwaben Augsburg, 1941–51): 5/2
Burger, Karl (Schwaben Augsburg, 1909–12): 10
Burgsmüller, Manfred (Borussia Dortmund, 1975–78): 6/4
Burkhardt, Theodor (Germania Brotzingen, 1930) 1
Busch, Willy (Duisburg 99, 1933–36): 13
Cieslarczyk, Hans (Schalke 04, Borussia Dortmund, 1957–58): 7/3
Claus-Oehler, Walter (Arminia Bielefeld, 1923): 2/1
Conen, Edmund (Fortuna Düsseldorf, 1934–42): 28/27
Cullmann, Bernhard (Köln, 1973–80): 40/6
Damminger, Ludwig (Karlsruher, 1935): 3/5
Danner, Dietmar (Borussia Mönchengladbach, 1973–76): 6
Decker, Karl (1942): 8/8
Deike, Fritz (Hannover 96, 1935): 1
Del'Haye, Karl (Borussia Mönchengladbach, Bayern Munich, 1980–81): 4/2
Derwall, Josef (Fortuna Düsseldorf, 1954): 2
Deyhle, Erwin (Kickers Stuttgart, 1939): 1
Diemer, Kurt (Blau-Weiss Berlin, 1912–13): 4
Dietrich, Peter (Borussia Mönchengladbach, 1970): 1
Dietz, Bernhard (MSV Duisburg, 1974–81): 53
Ditgens, Heinz (Blau-Weiss Berlin, 1938): 1
Doll, Thomas (Hamburg, Lazio [Ita], 1991–93): 18/1
Dörfel, Bernd (Hamburg, Eintracht Braunschweig, 1966–69): 15/1
Dörfel, Friedrich (Hamburg, 1942): 2/1
Dörfel, Gerd (Hamburg, 1960–64): 11/6
Dorfner, Hans (Bayern Munich, 1987–89.): 7/1
Dörner, Herbert (Köln, 1956): 2
Dremmler, Wolfgang (Bayern Munich, 1981–84): 27/3
Droz, Rudolf (Preussen Berlin, 1911): 1
Dumke, Otto (Viktoria 89 Berlin, 1911): 2/3
Durek, Ludwig (Fortuna Düsseldorf, FC Vienna, 1940–42): 6/2
Dutton, Edwin (Preussen Berlin, 1909): 1
Dzur, Walter (Dresdner, 1940–41): 3

Eckel, Horst (Kaiserslautern, 1952–58): 32

Eckert, Jakob (Wormatia Worms, 1937): 1

Eckstein, Dieter (Nurnberg, 1986–88): 7

Eder, Norbert (Bayern Munich, 1986): 9

Edy, Eduard (VfB Stuttgart, 1913–22): 3

Effenberg, Stefan (Bayern Munich, Fiorentina [Ita], 1991–94): 32/2

Ehrmann Kurt (Karlsruhe, 1952): 1

Eiberle, Fritz (1860 Munich, 1933): 1

Eichelmann, Paul (Union 92 Berlin, 1908): 2

Eigenstiller, Johann (1968): 1/1

Eikhof, Ernst (Victoria Hamburg, 1923): 3

Eilts, Dieter (Werder Bremen, 1993–97): 31

Elbern Franz (Schwaben Augsburg, 1935–37): 7/1

Emmerich, Heinz (1860 Munich, 1931): 3

Emmerich, Lothar (Borussia Dortmund, 1966): 5/2

Engels, Stefan (Köln, 1982–83): 8

Eppenhoff, Hermann (Schwaben Augsburg, 1940–42): 3/3

Erhardt, Herbert (Schalke 04, Borussia Dortmund, 1953–62): 50/1

Ertl, Georg (Wacker Munich, 1925–27): 7

Eschenlohr, Albert (1860 Munich, 1924): 1

Esser, Franz (Holstein Kiel, 1922): 1

Estram, WJ (1901): 1

Euler, Georg (Köln Sulz 07, 1936): 1

Ewert, Fritz (Köln, 1959–63): 5

Faas, Robert (Kaiserslautern, 1910): 1

Fach, Holger (Bayer Uerdingen, 1988–89): 5

Faeder, Helmut (Hamburg, 1958): 1

Fahrian, Wolfgang (Ulm TSG 1846, 1961–64): 11

Falk, Wilhelm (Wacker Munich, 1927): 1

Falkenmayer, Ralf (Eintracht Frankfurt, 1984–86): 4

Fath, Josef (Wormatia Worms, 1934–38): 13/7

Ferner, Diethelm (Werder Bremen, 1963–77): 3

Fichtel, Klaus (Schalke 04, 1967–71): 23/1

Fick, Willy (Holstein Kiel, 1910): 1/1

Fiederer, Hans (Schwaben Augsburg, 1939–41): 6/3

Fiederer, Leo (Schwaben Augsburg, 1920): 1

Fischer, Erich (Kaiserslautern, 1932–33): 2

Fischer, Klaus (Schalke 04, Köln, 1977–82): 45/32

Fischer, Paul (Viktoria 89 Berlin, 1908): 1

Fischer, Walter (Duisberger, 1911–14): 5

Fitz, Willy (Rapid Vienna, 1942): 1

Fleer, Jurgen (Borussia Mönchengladbach, 1981): 1

Fleischmann, Hans (VfR Mannheim, 1924): 1

Flick, Hermann (Duisburg 99, 1929): 1

Flink, Karl (Kölner BC, 1922): 1

Flohe Heinz (Köln, 1970–78): 39/7

Flotho, Heinz (VfL Osnabruck, 1939): 1

Foda, Franco (Kaiserslautern, 1987): 2

Forderer, Fritz (Karlsruhe, 1908–13): 9/5

Forell, Paul (Kaiserslautern, 1920): 1

Förster, Bernd (VfB Stuttgart, 1979–84): 33

Förster, Karlheinz (VfB Stuttgart, 1978–86): 81/2

Frank, Georg (Schwaben Augsburg, 1927–30): 4/5

Franke, Bernd (Eintracht Braunschweig, 1973–82): 8

Franz, Andreas (Schwaben Augsburg, 1922–26): 10/4

Freund, Steffen (Borussia Dortmund, 1995–98): 20

Fricke, Willi (Arminia Hannover, 1935): 1

Friedel, Georg (Kaiserslautern, 1937): 1

Fritzsche, Walter (Vorwärts Berlin): 1921): 1

Frontzeck, Michael (Borussia Mönchengladbach, VfB Stuttgart, 1984–92): 19

Fuchs, Gottfried (Karlsruhe, 1911–13): 4/4

Funkel, Freidhelm (Kaiserslautern, 1981): 1/1

Funkel, Wolfgang (Bayer Uerdingen, 1986): 2

Fürst, Fritz (Blau-Weiss Berlin, 1913): 1

Gablonsky, Max (Blau-Weiss Berlin, 1910–11): 4

Gaebelein, Arthur (Hohenzollern Halle, 1912): 1

Garrn, Hermann (Victoria Hamburg, 1908–09): 2

Gartner, Ludwig (Olympia Lorsch, 1939–41): 3/1

Gauchel, Josef (1860 Munich, 1936–42): 15/11

Gaudino, Maurizio (Eintracht Frankfurt, 1993–94): 5/1

Gedlich, Richard (Dresdner SC, 1926–27): 2

Gehlhaar, Paul (Hertha Berlin, 1928–31): 2

Gehrts, Adolf (Victoria Hamburg, 1908–10): 2

Geiger, Hans (ASV Nurnberg, Fortuna Düsseldorf, 1926–29): 6

Geiger, Rolf (Schalke 04, VfB Stuttgart, 1956–64): 8/2

Geils, Karl-Heinz (Arminia Bielefeld, 1981): 1

Gellesch, Rudolf (Schwaben Augsburg, 1935–41): 20/1

Gerdau, Willi (Hamburg, 1957): 1

Gerritzen, Felix (Preussen Munster, 1951): 4/1

Gersdorff, Bernd (Eintracht Braunschweig, 1975): 1

Gerwien, Klaus (Eintracht Braunschweig, 1963–68): 6/1

Geye, Rainer (Fortuna Düsseldorf, 1972–75): 5/2

Geyer, Peter (Borussia Dortmund, 1977): 2

Giesemann, Willi (Borussia Dortmund, 1960–65)

Glaser, Dr Josef (Fortuna Düsseldorf, 1909–12): 4

Goede, Erich (Blau-Weiss Berlin, 1939): 1

Goldbrunner, Ludwig (Blau-Weiss Berlin, 1933–40): 37

Görtz, Armin (Köln, 1988): 2

Gottinger, Richard (Schalke 04, 1953): 1

Grabowski, Jürgen (Eintracht Frankfurt, 1966–74): 44/5

Gramlich, Hermann (Villingen 08, 1935): 3

Gramlich, Rudolf (Eintracht Frankfurt, 1931–36): 21

Grau, Gerhard (Hertha Berlin, 1975): 1/1

Groh, Jürgen (Kaiserslautern, Hamburg, 1979–83): 2

Groner, Emil Schwaben Augsburg, 1921): 1

Gros, Wilhelm (Karlsruhe, 1912): 1

Gross, Stefan (Karlsruhe, 1981): 1

Gross, Volkmar (Hertha Berlin, 1970): 1

Grosser, Peter (1860 Munich, 1965–66): 2

Gruber, Hans (Duisburger SV, 1929): 1

Grundel, Heinz (Hamburg, 1985–86): 4

Gunther, Walter (Duisburg 99, 1935–37): 4/2

Haber, Marko (Kaiserslautern, 1995): 2

Haferkamp, Hans (VfL Osnabruck, 1951–52): 4/2

Haftmann, Martin (Dresdner SC, 1927): 1

Hagen, Hans (Schwaben Augsburg, 1920–30): 12

Hahnemann, Wilhelm (Admira Vienna [Aus], 1938–41): 23/16

Haller, Helmut (Augsburg, FC Bologna [Ita], Juventus [Ita] 1958–66): 33/13

Hamann, Dieter (Bayern Munich, 1997–98): 11/1

Hammerl, Franz (Post-SV Munich, 1940): 1

Hanel, Erich (Blau-Weiss Berlin, 1939): 3/1

Hanke, Richard (Fortuna Düsseldorf, 1930): 1/1

Hannes, Wilfried (Borussia Mönchengladbach, 1981–82): 8

Hanreiter, Franz (Vienna, 1940–42): 7

Hanssen, Karl (Altona 33, 1910–11): 3

Hantschick, Otto (Union 92 Berlin, 1908–09): 2

Harder, Otto (Hamburg, 1914–26): 15/14

Haringer, Sigmund (Blau-Weiss Berlin, Wacker Munich, 1931–37): 15

Harpers, Gerhard (Schalke 04, 1953–55): 6

Hartmann, Carl (Union Potsdam, Victoria Hamburg, 1923): 4/2

Hartwig, William (Hamburg, 1979): 2

Hässler, Thomas (Köln, Juventus [Ita], Roma [Ita], Karlsruhe 1988–98): 96/10

Heibach, Hans (Fortuna Düsseldorf, 1938): 1

Heidemann, Hartmut (MSV Duisburg, 1966–68): 3

Heidemann, Matthias (Blau-Weiss Berlin, Werder Bremen, 1933–35): 3

Heidkamp, Conrad (Schwaben Augsburg, Blau-Weiss Berlin, 1927–30): 2

Heinrich, Jürg (SC Freiburg, Borussia Dortmund, 1995–98): 19/2

Heiss, Alfred (1860 Munich, 1962–66): 8/2

Held, Siegfried 'Sigi' (Borussia Dortmund, Kickers Offenbach, 1966–72): 41/6

Helmer, Thomas (Borussia Dortmund, Bayern Munich, 1990–98): 68/6

Hempel, Walter (Schwaben Augsburg, 1908–12): 10

Hense, Robert (Kölner BC, 1910): 1

Hensel, Gustav (Fortuna Düsseldorf, 1908): 1

Herberger, Josef (Schwaben Augsburg, VfR Mannheim, 1921–25): 3/2

Hergert, Heinrich (Fortuna Düsseldorf, 1930–33): 5

Herget, Matthias (Bayer 05 Uerdingen, 1983–88): 39/4

Herkenrath, Fritz (Rot-Weiss Essen, 1954–58): 21

Hermann, Gunter (Werder Bremen, 1988–90): 2

Herrlich, Heiko (Borussia Mönchengladbach, Borussia Dortmund, 1995): 5/1

Herrmann, Günter (Karlsruhe, Schalke 04, 1960–67): 9/1

Herrmann, Richard (FSV Frankfurt, 1950–54): 8/1

Herzog, Dieter (Fortuna Düsseldorf, 1974): 5
Heynckes, Josef (Borussia Mönchengladbach, Hannover 96, 1967–76): 39/13
Hieronymus, Holger (Hamburg, 1981–82): 3
Hiller II, Arthur (Kaiserslautern, 1908–09): 4
Hiller III, Marius (Kaiserslautern, 1910–11): 3/1
Hirsch, Julius (Karlsruhe, Schwaben Augsburg, 1911–13): 5/4
Hirth, Herbert (Hertha Berlin, 1909): 1
Hobsch, Bernd (Werder Bremen, 1993): 1
Hochgesang, Georg (Kaiserslautern, 1924–27): 6/4
Hochstätter, Christian (Borussia Mönchengladbach, 1987): 2
Hoeness, Dieter (VfB Stuttgart, Bayern Munich, 1979–86): 6/4
Hoeness, Ulrich (Bayern Munich, 1972–76): 35/5
Hofer, Franz (Rapid Vienna, 1939): 1
Hoffmann, Rudolf (Viktorai Aschaffenburg, 1955): 1
Hofmann, Ludwig (Blau-Weiss Berlin, 1926–31): 16/4
Hofmann, Richard (Meerane 07, Dresdner SC, 1927–33): 23/20
Hofmeister, Ludwig (Bayern Munich, Stuttgart Kickers, 1912): 2
Hofstätter, Johann (Rapid Vienna, 1940): 1
Hoger, Karl (Schwaben Augsburg, 1914–24): 4
Hohmann, Karl (VfL Benrath, 1930–37): 25/20
Holland, John (1980): 1/1
Hollstein, Ernst (Karlsruhe FV, 1910–12): 4
Holz, Friedel (Duisberg 99, 1938): 1
Hölzenbein, Bernd (Eintracht Frankfurt, 1973–78): 40/6
Horn, Franz (Hamburg, 1928–29): 3
Hornauer, Josef (1860 Munich, 1928–31): 3/2
Hornig, Heinz (Köln, 1965–66): 7
Horster, Thomas (Bayer Leverkusen, 1986–87): 4
Horvat, Ivan 1954): 1/1
Hoschle, Adolf (Kickers Stuttgart, 1920): 1
Höttges, Horst-Dieter (Werder Bremen, 1965–74): 66/1
Hrubesch, Horst (Hamburg, 1980–82): 21/6
Huber, Alfred (Schwaben Augsburg, 1930): 1
Huber, Lorenz (Karlsruhe FV, 1932): 1
Huetti (1901): 1
Hunder, Paul (Viktoria Berlin, 1909–11): 8
Hundt, Eduard (Schwaben Augsburg, 1933–34): 3
Hutter, Willi (Schwaben Augsburg, 1921–22): 2
Illgner, Bodo (Köln, 1987–94): 54
Illmer, Eberhardt (Fortuna Düsseldorf, 1909): 1
Immel, Eike (Borussia Dortmund, VfB Stuttgart, 1980–88): 19
Immig, Franz (Karlsruhe FV, 1939): 2
Islacker, Franz (Rot-Weiss Essen, 1954): 1
Jager, Adolf (Altona 93, 1908–24): 10
Jager, Gunter (Fortuna Düsseldorf, 1958): 1
Jahn, Helmut (Blau-Weiss Berlin, 1939–42): 17
Jakob, Hans (Jahn Regensburg, 1930–39): 37
Jakobs, Ditmar (Tennis Borussia Berlin, Hamburg, 1977–86): 22/1
Jakobs, Johannes (Hannover 96, 1939): 1
Janes, Paul (Fortuna Düsseldorf, 1932–42): 71/7

Janzon, Norbert (Kickers Offenbach, 1975): 1
Jellinek, Franz (Wiener SK, 1940): 1
Jeremies, Jens (1860 Munich, 1997–98): 7
Joppich, Karl (Schwaben Augsburg, 1932): 1
Jordan, Ernst (Cricket-Victoria Magdeburg, 1908): 1
Junghans, Walter (Bayern Munich, 1981): 1
Jungtow, Otto (Hertha Berlin, 1913): 1
Jurissen, Willy (Rot-Weiss Oberhausen, 1935–39): 6
Juskowiak, Erich (Rot-Weiss Oberhausen, Fortuna Düsseldorf, 1951–59): 31/4
Kaburek, Matthias (Rapid, Vienna, 1939): 1
Kahn, Oliver (Bayern Munich, 1995–98): 9
Kalb, Hans (Kaiserslautern, 1920–27): 13/2
Kaltz, Manfred (Hamburg, 1975–83): 70/8
Kapellmann, Hans-Josef (Köln, Bayern Munich, 1973–74): 5
Kapitulski, Helmut (FK Pirmasens, 1958): 1
Kargus, Rudi (Hamburg, 1975–77): 3
Kauer, Erich (1860 Munich, 1930–31): 5
Kaufhold, Gerhard (Kickers Offenbach, 1954): 1
Kelbassa, Alfred (Borussia Dortmund) 1956–58): 6/2
Keller, Ferdinand (1860 Munich, 1975): 1
Kelsch, Walter (VfB Stuttgart, 1979–80): 4/3
Kiessling, Georg (Schwaben Augsburg, 1927–28): 2/1
Kipp, Eugen (Schwaben Augsburg, Sportfreunde Stuttgart, Kickers Stuttgart, 1908–26): 17/10
Kirsei, Willi (Hertha Berlin, 1924): 1
Kirsten, Ulf (Bayer Leverkusen, 1992–98): 35/13
Kitzinger, Albin (Schwaben, Augsburg, 1935–42): 44/2
Klass, Werner (Schwaben Augsburg, 1937): 1
Kleff, Wolfgang (Borussia Mönchengladbach, 1971–73): 6
Kliemann, Uwe (Hertha Berlin, 1975): 2/1
Kling, Eugen (1860 Munich, 1927): 1
Klingler, August (FV Daxlanden, 1942): 5/6
Klinkhammer, Hans (Borussia Mönchengladbach, 1977): 1
Klinsmann, Jürgen (VfB Stuttgart, Inter Milan [Ita], Monaco [Fra], Tottenham Hotspur [Eng], Bayern Munich, Sampdoria [Ita], 1987–1998): 108/47
Klockner, Theo (Schalke 04, 1958–59): 2
Klodt, Bernhard (Schalke 04, 1950–59): 19/3
Klodt, Hans (Schwaben Augsburg, 1938–41): 17
Kmetsch, Sven (Hamburg, 1997–98): 2
Kneib, Wolfgang (Borussia Mönchengladbach, 1977): 1
Knesebeck, Willi (Viktoria Berlin, 1911–12): 2
Knöpfle, Georg (Schwaben Augsburg, Fortuna Düsseldorf): 1928–33): 21
Kobierski, Stanislaus (Fortuna Düsseldorf, 1931–41): 26/9
Koch, Meinolf (Borussia Dortmund, 1981): 1
Kochling, Willi (Rot-Weiss Essen, 1956.): 1
Koenen, Theo (FV Bonn, 1911): 1
Kögl, Ludwig (Bayern Munich, 1985): 2
Kohl, Georg (Nürnberg (1937): 1

Kohler, Georg (Dresdner SC (1925–28): 5
Kohler, Jürgen (SV Waldhof Mannheim, Köln, Bayern Munich, Juventus [Ita], Borussia Dortmund, 1986–98): 77
Kohlmeyer, Werner (Kaiserslautern, 1951–55): 22
Koitka, Heinz-Josef (Eintracht Frankfurt, 1977): 1
Konietzka, Friedhelm "Timo" (Borussia Dortmund, 1962–65) 9/3
Konopka, Harald (Köln, 1975–79)· 3
Kontor, Francois (1967): 1/1
Köpke, Andreas (Nürnberg, Eintracht Frankfurt, Marseille [Fra], 1990–98): 58
Köppel, Horst (VfB Stuttgart, 1968–73): 11/2
Kopplinger, Emil (Kaiserslautern1927): 1
Korbel, Karl-Heinz (Eintracht Frankfurt1974–77): 8
Kordell, Heinz (Schalke 04, 1958): 1
Koslowski, Willi (Schalke 04, 1962): 3/1
Kostedde, Erwin (Kickers Offenbach, Hertha Berlin, 1974–75): 3
Krämer, Werner (Duisburg, 1963–67): 13/3
Kraus, Engelbert (Kickers Offenbach, 1955–64): 9/3
Krause, Emil (Hertha Berlin, 1933): 1
Krause, Walter (Victoria Hamburg, 1920): 1
Holstein, Kiel (1921–24): 5
Krauss, Bernd (1981): 1/1
Krauss, Willy (Carl Zeiss Jena, 1911–12): 2
Kremers, Erwin (Schalke 04, 1972–74): 15/3
Kremers, Helmut (Schalke 04, 1973–75): 8
Kress, Anton (Pforzheim, 1921): 1
Kress, Richard (Eintracht Frankfurt, 1954–61): 9/2
Kress, Willibald (Rot-Weiss Frankfurt, 1929–34): 16
Krogmann, Georg (Holstein Kiel, 1912): 1
Kroth, Thomas (Eintracht Frankfurt, 1985): 1
Kruger, Kurt (Fortuna Düsseldorf, 1940): 1
Krumm, Franz (Blau-Weiss Berlin, 1932–33): 2/1
Kubsch, Heinz (FK Pirmasens, 1954–56): 3
Kubus, Richard (Vorwarts-Rasensport Gleiwitz, 1939): 1
Kugler, Anton (Nürnburg, 1923–27.): 7
Kugler, Paul (Viktoria 89 Berlin, 1911–13): 2
Kuhnle, Paul (Kickers Stuttgart, 1910–11): 2
Kuhnt, Werner (Norden-Nordwest Berlin, 1924): 1
Kund, Willi (Nürnburg, 1930–31): 2/1
Kuntz, Stefan (Kaiserslautern, Besiktas [Tur], Arminia Bielefeld, 1993–97): 25/7
Kupfer, Andreas (Schwaben Augsburg, Schweinfurt 05, 1937–42): 44/1
Kuppers, Hans (1860 Munich, 1962–67): 7/2
Kurbjuhn, Jurgen (Hamburg, 1962–66): 5
Kutterer, Emil (Blau-Weiss Berlin, 1925–28): 8
Kuzorra, Ernst (Schwaben Augsburg, 1927–38): 12/7
Kwiatkowski, Heinz (Borussia Dortmund, 1954–58): 4
Laband, Fritz (Hamburg, 1954): 4
Labbadia, Bruno (Bayern Munich, 1992–95): 2
Lachner, Ludwig (1860 Munich, 1930–34): 8/4

Lameck, Michael (VfL Bochum, 1977–77): 2
Lang, Hans (Schwaben Augsburg, 1922–26): 10
Langenbein, Kurt (VfR Mannheim, 1932–35): 2/1
Langer (1901): 1
Laumen, Herbert (Borussia Mönchengladbach, 1968): 2/1
Lehmann, Jens (Schalke 04, 1998): 2
Lehner, Ernst (Schwaben Augsburg, Blau-Weiss Berlin, 1933–42): 33/6
Leinberger, Ludwig (SpVgg Furth, 1927–33): 22
Leip, Rudolf (Guts Muths Dresden, 1923–24): 3
Lenz, August (Borussia Dortmund, 1935–38): 13/9
Libuda, Reinhard (Schalke 04, Borussia Dortmund, 1963–71): 26/3
Liebrich, Werner (Kaiserslautern, 1951–56): 16
Lindner, Willi (Eintracht Frankfurt, 1933): 1
Littbarski, Pierre (Köln, Racing Club Paris [Fra], 1981–90): 73/18
Loble, Otto (Kickers Stuttgart, 1909–13): 4
Lohneis, Hans (MTV Furth, 1920): 1
Löhr, Johannes (Köln, 1967–70): 20/5
Lohrmann, Theodor (SpVgg Furth, 1920–22): 3
Lorenz, Max (Werder Bremen, Eintracht Braunschweig, 1965–70): 19/1
Lortscher, Ernest (1938): 1/1
Ludewig, Heinz (Duisburger SV, 1914): 1
Ludwig, Johann (Holstein Kiel, 1930–31) 3/2
Ludwig, Karl (SC 99 Köln, Luedecke FC, 1901–08): 2
Luke, Josef (Turn Düsseldorf, 1923): 2
Lütz, Friedel (Eintracht Frankfurt, 1960–66): 12
Lux, Hermann (Tennis Borussia Berlin, 1924–25): 3
Maas, Erich (Eintracht Braunschweig, 1968–70): 3
Magath, Felix (Hamburg, 1977–86): 43/3
Mahlmann, Carl-Heinz (Hamburg, 1932): 1
Mai, Karl (SpVgg Furth, Bayern Munich, 1953–59): 21/1
Maier, Josef 'Sepp' (Bayern Munich, 1966–79): 95
Malecki, Edmund (Hannover 96, 1935–39): 5/2
Malik, Richard (Beuthen 09, 1932–33): 2/1
Maneval, Hellmut (Kickers Stuttgart, 1923): 1
Manglitz, Manfred (MSV Duisburg, Köln, 1965–70): 4
Manner, Ludwig (Hannover 96, 1937–40): 5
Mantel, Hugo (Eintracht Frankfurt, 1927–33): 5
Marischka, Otto (Admira Vienna Austria, 1939): 1
Marohn, Arthur (Viktoria 89 Berlin, 1921): 1
Marschall, Olaf (Kaiserslautern, 1994–98): 7/2
Martin, Bernd (VfB Stuttgart, 1979): 1
Martinek, Alexander (Wacker Vienna, 1940): 1
Martwig, Otto (Tennis Borussia Berlin, 1925–27): 6
Marx, Joseph, (SV Sodingen, 1960): 1/1

Massini, Erich (Preussen Danzig, 1909): 1
Mathies, Paul (Preussen Danzig, 1935): 2
Matthäus, Lothar (Borussia Mönchengladbach, Bayern Munich, Inter Milan [Ita],Bayern Munich, 1980–98): 128/22
Matthes, Paul (Viktoria 96 Magdeburg, 1908): 1
Mauch, Paul (VfB Stuttgart, 1922): 1
Mauritz, Matthias (Fortuna Düsseldorf, 1959): 1
Mebus, Paul (VfL Benrath, Köln, 1951–54): 6
Mechling, Heinrich (FC Freiburg, 1912–13): 2/1
Mehl, Paul (Fortuna Düsseldorf, 1936): 1
Meier, Norbert (Werder Bremen, 1982–85): 16/2
Meissner, Kurt (VfR Mannheim, 1924): 1
Memering, Caspar (Hamburg, 1979–80): 3
Mengel, Hans (Turu Düsseldorf, 1938): 1
Merkel, Max (Wiener SK, 1939): 1
Metzner, Karl-Heinz (Hessen Kassel, 1952–53): 2
Meye, Andre 'Big' (1977): 1/1
Meyer, Peter (Borussia Mönchengladbach, 1967): 1
Milewski, Jürgen (Hamburg, 1981–84): 3
Mill, Frank (Borussia Mönchengladbach, Borussia Dortmund, 1982–90): 17
Miller, Karl (FC St Pauli Hamburg, 1941–42): 12
Miltz, Jakob (TuS Neuendorf, 1954–56): 2
Mock, Hans (Austria Vienna, 1938–42): 5
Mohns, Arthur (Norden-Nordwest Berlin, 1920–22): 5
Möller, Andreas (Borussia Dortmund, Eintracht Frankfurt, Juventus [Ita], 1988–98): 82/31
Möller, Ernst (Holstein Kiel, 1911–13): 9/4
Montag, Otto (Norden-Nordwest Berlin, 1923–25): 4
Moog, Alfons (VfL 99 Köln, 1939–40): 7
Morlock, Max (Nürnburg, 1950–58): 26/20
Mueller, F (1901): 1
Müller, Dieter (Köln, 1976–81): 13/9
Müller, Ernst (Hertha Berlin, 1931): 1
Müller, Friedrich (Dresdner SC, 1931): 2
Müller, Gerhard 'Gerd' (Bayern Munich, 1966–74): 62/67
Müller, Hans (VfB Stuttgart, Inter Milan Italy, 1977–83): 44/5
Müller, Henry (Victoria Hamburg, 1921–28): 9
Müller, Josef (Phonix Ludwigshafen, SpVgg Furth, FV 04 Wurzburg, 1921–28): 12
Müller, Ludwig (Nürnburg, Borussia Mönchengladbach, 1968–69): 6
Munkert, Andreas (Nürnburg, 1935–36): 8
Munzenberg, Reinhold (Alemannia Aachen, 1930–39): 39
Nafziger, Rudolf (Bayern Munich, 1965): 1
Nagelschmitz, Ernst (Bayern Munich, 1926): 1
Neisse, Hermann (Eimsbutteler TV, 1910–11): 3
Netzer, Gunter (Borussia Mönchengladbach, Real Madrid Spain, 1965–75): 37/6
Neubarth, Frank (Werder Bremen, 1988): 1
Neuberger, Willi (Borussia Dortmund, 1968): 2

Neumaier, Robert (Phonix Karlsruhe, 1909–12): 3
Neumann, Arno (Dresdner SC, 1908): 1
Neumann, Herbert (Köln, 1978): 1
Neumer, Leopold (Austria Vienna, 1938): 1
Neuschafer, Hans (Fortuna Düsseldorf, 1956): 1/1
Nickel, Bernhard (Eintracht Frankfurt, 1974–75): 2/1
Nickel, Harald (Borussia Mönchengladbach, 1979–80): 3
Nicodemus, Dr Otto (SV Wiesbaden, 1909): 1
Niederbacher, Max (Kickers Stuttgart, 1925): 1
Niedermayer, Kurt (Bayern Munich, 1980): 1
Nigbur, Norbert (Schalke 04, 1974–81): 7
Noack, Rudolf (Hamburg, 1934–37): 3/1
Nogly, Peter (Hamburg, 1977): 4
Novak, H (1961): 1
Novotny, Jens (Bayer Leverkusen, 1997): 1
Nowak, Hans (Schalke 04, 1961–64): 15
Nowotny, Jens (Bayer Leverkusen, 1997–98): 3
Oberle, Emil (Phonix Karlsruhe, 1909–12): 3
Oehm, Richard (Nürnburg, 1932– 34): 3
Ohlhauser, Ralf (Bayern Munich, 1968): 1
Olk, Werner (Bayern Munich, 1961): 1
Ordenewitz, Frank (Werder Bremen, 1987): 2
Otten, Jonny (Werder Bremen, 1983–84): 6
Overath, Wolfgang (Köln, 1963–81): 82/16
Panse, Herbert (Eimsbutteler TV, 1935): 1/1
Passlack, Stephen (Borussia Mönchengaldbach, 1996): 2
Patzke, Bernd (1860 Munich, Hertha Berlin, 1965–71): 24
Paulsen, Paul (VfB Leipzig, 1924–25): 6/3
Pekarek, Josef (Wacker Vienna, 1939): 1
Pesser, Hans (Rapid Vienna, 1938–40): 12/2
Peters, Wolfgang (Borussia Dortmund, 1957): 1
Pfaff, Alfred (Eintracht Frankfurt, 1953–56): 7/2
Pfeiffer, Michael (Alemmannia Aachen, 1954): 1
Pflipsen, Karlheinz (Borussia Mönchengladbach, 1993): 1
Pflugler, Hans (Bayern Munich, 1987–90): 11
Philipp, Ludwig (Nürnburg, 1910): 2
Picard, Alfred (SSV Ulm, 1939): 1
Pinkall, Kurt (VfL Bochum, 1981):1
Piontek, Josef (Werder Bremen, 1965–66): 6
Pirrung, Josef (Kaiserslautern, 1974–77): 3
Plener, Ernst (Vorwarts Rasensport Gleiwitz, 1940): 2/2
Poetsch, Ernst (Union 92 Berlin, 1908–10): 3
Pohl, Erich (SC 99 Köln, 1923): 2
Pohl, Herbert (Dresdner SC, 1941): 2
Pohler, Ludwig (Hannover 96, 1939): 1
Politz, Kurt (Hamburg, 1934): 1
Popp, Luitpold (Nürnburg, 1920–26): 5/1
Poppe, Walter (Eintracht Braunschweig, 1908): 1
Porges, Ingo (FC St Pauli Hamburg, 1960): 1
Portgen, Ernst (Schalke 04, 1935–37): 3/5
Posipal, Josef (Hamburg, 1951–56): 32/1
Pott, Fritz (Köln, 1962–64): 3

Pottinger, Josef (Bayern Munich, 1926–30): 12/8

Preissler, Alfred (Preussen Munster, 1951): 2

Pyka, Alfred (Westfalia Herne, 1958): 1

Queck, Richard (Eintracht Braunschweig, 1909–14): 3/2

Raftl, Rudolf (Rapid Vienna, 1938–40): 6

Rahn, Helmut (Rot-Weiss Essen, Köln, 1951–60): 40/26

Rahn, Uwe (Borussia Mönchengladbach, 1984–87): 14/5

Rasselnberg, Josef (VfL Banrath, 1933–35): 9/8

Rebele, Hans (1860 Munich, 1965.05.26 1969.03.262

Reck, Oliver (Werder Bremen, 1996): 1

Redder, Theo (Borussia Dortmund, 1964): 1

Reichel, Peter (Eintracht Frankfurt, 1975–77): 4

Reinders, Uwe (Werder Bremen, 1982): 4/1

Reinhardt, Alois (Bayer Leverkusen, 1989–90): 4

Reinhardt, Knut (Bayer Leverkusen, Borussia Dortmund, 1988–92): 7

Reinmann, Baptist (Nürnburg, 1927–29): 4

Reisch, Stefan (Nürnburg, 1962–64): 9

Reiser, Otto (Phonix Karlsruhe, 1911): 1

Reislant, Otto (Wacker Leipzig, 1910): 1

Reissmann, Martin (Gurs Muths Dresden, 1923): 1

Reitermaier, Ernst (Wacker Vienna, 1939): 1

Reitgassl, Willy (Karlsruhe, 1960): 1/1

Retter, Erich (VfB Stuttgart, 1952–56): 14

Retter, Fritz (Sportfreunde Stuttgart, 1922): 1

Reuter, Stefan (Nürnburg, Juventus [Ita], Borussia Dortmund, 1987–98): 69/2

Richter, Leopold (VfB Leipzig, 1909): 1

Richter, Lothar (Chemnitzer FC, 1941): 1

Ricken, Lars (1998): 1

Riedle, Karlheinz (Werder Bremen, Lazio Roma [Ita], Borussia Dortmund, 1988–94): 42/15

Riegel, Carl (Nürnburg, 1920–23): 7

Riegler, Franz (Austria Vienna, 1941–42): 2

Ringel, Karl (Borussia Neunkirchen, 1958): 1

Riso, Hans (Wacker Leipzig, 1910): 1

Riso, Heinrich (VfB Leipzig, 1908–09): 2

Risse, Walter (SC 99 Düsseldorf, Hamburg, 1923–28): 8

Ritschel, Manfred (Kickers Offenbach, 1975): 3/1

Ritter, Oskar (Holstein Kiel, 1925): 1

Rodekamp, Walter (Hannover 96, 1965): 3/1

Rodzinski, Josef (Hamborn 07, 1936): 3

Rohde, Hans (Eimsbutteler TV, 1936–42): 25

Rohr, Oskar (Bayern Munich, 1932): 4/5

Rohrig, Josef (Köln, 1950–56): 12/2

Rohwedder, Otto (Eimsbutteler TV, 1934–37): 5/2

Rokosch, Ernst (SpVgg Furth, 1914): 1

Roleder, Helmut (VfB Stuttgart, 1984): 1

Rolff, Wolfgang (Hamburg, Bayer Leverkusen, 1983–89): 36

Roller, Gustav (Pforzheim, 1924): 1

Ropnack, Helmut (Viktoria 89 Berlin, 1909–13): 8

Rose, Walter (SpVgg Leipzig, 1937): 1

Roth, Franz (Bayern Munich, 1967–70): 4

Ruch, Hans (Union 92 Berlin, Hertha BSC Berlin, 1925–29): 3/2

Ruchay, Fritz (Prussia Samland Konigsberg, 1935): 1

Rummenigge, Karl-Heinz (Bayern Munich, Inter Milan [Ita], 1976–86): 94/45

Rummenigge, Michael (Bayern Munich, 1983–86): 2

Rupp, Bernd (Borussia Mönchengladbach, 1966): 1/1

Russmann, Rolf (Schalke 04, 1977–78): 20/1

Rutz, Willi (VfB Stuttgart, 1932): 1/1

Sabeditsch, Ernst (Vienna Vienna, 1939): 1

Sackenheim, August (Guts Muths Dresden, 1929–31): 4/2

Sammer, Matthias (VfB Stuttgart, Inter Milan Italy, Borussia Dortmund, 1990–97): 51/8

Sawitzki, Gunter (SV Sodingen, VfB Stuttgart, 1956–63): 10

Schade, Horst (SpVgg Furth, Nürnberg, 1951–53): 3/1

Schadler, Erwin (Ulmer FV 94, 1937–1938): 4

Schafer, Hans (Köln, 1952–62): 39/15

Schafer, Herbert (Sportfreunde Siegen, 1957): 1

Schafer, Max (1860 Munich, 1934): 1

Schaletzki, Reinhard (Vorwärts Rasensport Gleiwitz, 1939): 2/1

Schanko, Erich (Borussia Dortmund, 1951–54): 14

Scherm, Karl (ASV Nürnberg, 1926): 2/1

Schilling, Christian (Duisburger SV, 1910): 2

Schlebrowski, Elwin (Borussia Dortmund, 1956): 2

Schlienz, Robert (VfB Stuttgart, 1955–56): 3

Schlosser, Karl (Dresdner SC, 1931): 1/1

Schmaus, Willibald (Vienna, 1938–42): 10

Schmidt, Alfred (Borussia Dortmund, 1957–64): 25/8

Schmidt, Christian (Concordia Berlin, Kickers Stuttgart, 1910–13): 3

Schmidt, Hans (Germania Berlin, 1908):17

Schmidt, Karl (Kaiserslautern, 1955–57): 9

Schmitt, Josef (Nürnburg, 1928): 2/1

Schneider, Georg (Bayern Munich, 1920–21): 3

Schneider, Helmut (SV Waldhof Mannheim, 1940): 1

Schneider, Johannes (VfB Leipzig, 1913): 2

Schneider, Rene (Hansa Rostock, 1995): 1

Schnellinger, Karl-Heinz (Duren 99, Köln, AS Roma [Ita], AC Milan [Ita], 1958–62): 47/1

Schnurle, Fritz (Germania Frankfurt, 1921): 1

Scholl, Mehmet (Bayern Munich, 1995–97): 15/1

Scholz, Heiko (Bayer Leverkusen, 1992): 1

Schon, Helmut (Dresdner SC, 1937–41): 16/17

Schonhoft, Theo (VfL Osnabruck, 1956): 1/1

Schreier, Christian (Bayer Leverkusen, 1984): 1

Schroder, Erich (VfR Köln, 1931): 1

Schroder, Hans (Tennis Borussia Berlin, 1926): 1

Schroder, Helmut (Arminia Bielefeld, 1981): 1/1

Schroder, Willi (Bremen 1860, 1951–57): 12/3

Schubert, Helmut (Dresdner SC, 1941): 3

Schulz, Fritz (Hertha BSC Berlin, 1909): 1

Schulz, Michael (Borussia Dortmund, 1992–93): 7

Schulz, Werner (Arminia Hannover, 1935–38): 4

Schulz, Willi (Union Gunnigfeld, Schalke 04, 1959–70): 66

Schulz I, Karl (Holstein, Kiel, 1925): 2

Schulz II, Karl (Viktoria 89 Berlin, 1929): 1

Schumacher, Harald (Köln, 1979–86): 76

Schumann, Gerrg (Vorwärts Berlin, 1924): 1

Schummelfelder, Josef (Bonner FV, 1913–21): 5

Schuster, Bernd (Köln, Barcelona [Spa], 1979–84): 21/4

Schuster, Dirk (Karlsruhe SC, 1994–95): 3

Schutz, Franz (Eintracht Frankfurt, 1929–32): 11

Schutz, Jürgen (Borussia Dortmund, 1960–63): 6/2

Schwabl, Manfred (Nürnburg, 1987–88):

Schwartz, Hans (Victoria Hamburg, 1934): 2

Schwarzenbeck, Georg (Bayern Munich, 1971–78): 44

Schwedler, Willy (VfB Pankow, 1921): 1

Schweikert, Hermann (Pforzheim, 1909): 1

Seel, Wolfgang (Fortuna Düsseldorf, 1974–77): 6

Seeler, Uwe (Hamburg, 1954–70): 72/43

Seiderer, Leonhard (SpVgg Furth, 1920–24): 8/5

Seliger, Rudolf (MSV Duisburg, 1974–76): 2

Sesta, Karl (Austria Vienna, 1941–42): 3

Shmatovalenko, Sergei (Dynamo Kiev, 1988): 1/1

Siedl, Gerhard (Karlsruhe, Bayern Munich, 1957–59): 6/3

Sieloff, Klaus-Dieter (VfB Stuttgart, Borussia Mönchengladbach, 1964–71): 14/5

Siemensmeyer, Hans (Hannover 96, 1967): 3/2

Sievert, Helmut (Hannover 96, 1936): 1

Siffling, Otto (SV Waldhof Mannheim, 1934–38): 30/17

Simetsreiter, Wilhelm (Bayern Munich, 1935–37): 6/5

Sing, Albert (Kickers Stuttgart, 1940–42): 9/1

Skala, Lothar (Kickers Offenbach, 1975): 1

Skoumal, Stefan (Rapid Vienna, 1938–40): 3

Sobek, Hans (Alemannia Berlin, Hertha BSC Berlin, 1923–31): 10/2

Sold, Wilhelm (FV Saarbrucken, Nürnburg, Tennis Borussia Berlin, 1935–42): 12

Solz, Wolfgang (Eintracht Frankfurt, 1962–64): 2

Sonnrein, Heinrich (Hanau 93, Hannover 96, 1935): 2

Sorkale, Walter (Preussen Berlin, 1911): 1

Stacho, Imrich (Spartak Trnava, 1958): 1/1

Steffen, Bernhard (Fortuna Düsseldorf, 1958–60): 2

Steffenhagen, Arno (Hertha BSC Berlin, 1971): 1

Stegmayer, Roland (1.FC Saarbrucken, 1977): 1

Stein, Erwin (Griesheim 02, 1959): 1/1

Stein, Ulrich (Hamburg, 1983–86): 6

Steiner, Paul (Köln, 1981–90): 2

Steiner, Rudolf (1860 Munich, 1964): 1

Steinmann, Heinz (Schwarz-Weiss Essen, Werder Bremen, 1962–65): 3/1

Stephan, Gunter (Schwarz-Weiss Essen, 1935): 1

Stielike, Ulrich (Borussia Mönchengladbach, Real Madrid Spain, 1975–784): 42/6

Stollenwerk, Georg (Duren 99, Köln, 1951–60): 23/2

Stossel, Kurt (Dresdner SC, 1931): 1

Strack, Gerhard (Köln, 1982–83): 10/1

Strassburger, Wilhelm (Duisburger SV, 1930): 2

Strehl, Heinz (Nürnburg, 1962–65): 4/4

Streitle, Jakob (Bayern Munich, 1938–52): 15

Striebinger, Karl (VfR Mannheim, 1937–38): 3/2

Strobel, Wolfgang (Nürnburg, 1922–24): 4

Stroh, Josef (FK Austria, 1938–39): 4/1

Strunz, Thomas (Bayern Munich, VfB Stuttgart, 1990–96): 34/1

Stubb, Hans (Eintracht Frankfurt, 1930–34): 10/1

Stuhlfauth, Heinrich (Nürnburg, 1920–30): 19

Stuhrk, Erwin (Eimsbutteler TV, 1935): 3

Sturm, Hans (Köln, 1958–62): 3

Sturm, Wilhelm (Borussia Dortmund, 1964): 1

Stürmer, Klaus (Hamburg, 1954–61)2/1

Sukop, Albert (Eintracht Braunschweig, 1935): 1

Sundermann, Hans Jürgen (Rot-Weiss Oberhausen, 1960): 1

Sutor, Hans (Nürnburg, 1920–25): 12/2

Szepan, Fritz (Schalke 04, 1929–39): 34/8

Szymaniak, Horst (Wuppertaler SV, Karlsruhe, Inter Milan, [Ita], Tasmania Berlin, 1956–66): 43/2

Tanzer, Willy (Berliner SC, 1908): 1

Tarnat, Michael (Karlsruhe, Bayern Munich, 1996–98): 15

Tenhagen, Franz-Josef (VfL Bochum, 1977): 3

Termath, Bernhard (Rot-Weiss Essen, 1951–54): 7/4

Tewes, Karl (Viktoria 89 Berlin, 1920–22): 6

Thiel, Otto (Preussen Berlin, 1911): 1

Thielen, Karl-Heinz (Köln, 1964–65): 2

Thom, Andreas (Bayer Leverkusen, 1990–94): 10/2

Thon, Olaf (Schalke 04, Bayern Munich, Schalke 04, 1984–98): 51/3

Tibulski, Hans (Schalke 04, 1931): 1

Tibulski, Otto (Schalke 04, 1936–39): 2

Tiefel, Willi (Eintracht Frankfurt, 1935–36): 7

Tilkowski, Hans (Westfalia Herne, Borussia Dortmund, 1957–67): 39

Todt, Jens (SC Freiburg, 1994–95): 3

Toppmöller, Klaus (Kaiserslautern, 1976–79): 3/1

Trag, Heinrich (Nürnburg, 1921–26): 6/1

Trautmann, Wilhelm (Viktoria Mannheim, 1910): 1

Trimhold, Horst (Schwarz-Weiss Essen, 1962): 1

Turek, Anton (Fortuna Düsseldorf, 1950–54): 20

Ugi, Camillo (VfB Leipzig, Sportfreunde Breslau, 1909–12): 13/1

Ulsass, Lothar (Eintracht Braunschweig, 1965–69): 11/9

Umbach, Josef (SC Mönchengladbach, 1910): 1

Unfried, Gustav (Preussen Berlin, 1910): 1

Urban, Adolf (Schalke 04, 1935–42): 19/8

Urbanek, Hans (Admira Vienna Austria, 1941): 1

Vogts, Hans-Hubert 'Berti' (Borussia Mönchengladbach, 1967–78): 96/2

Volker, Dr Willi (VfB Leipzig, 1914): 1

Volker, Otto (Preussen Berlin, 1913): 1

Volker, Willi (Hertha BSC Berlin, 1929): 1

Volkert, Georg (Nürnburg, Hamburg, 1968–77): 12/1

Völler, Rudi (Werder Bremen, AS Roma [Ita], Marseille [Fra], 1982–94): 90/47

Vollmar, Heinz (SV St Ingbert, Saarbrucken, 1956–59): 12/3

Voss, Kurt (Holstein Kiel, 1925): 2/2

Votava, Miroslav (Borussia Dortmund, 1979–81): 5

Waas, Herbert (Bayer Leverkusen, 1983–88): 11/1

Wagner, Franz (Rapid Vienna, 1938–42): 3

Wagner, Martin (Kaiserslautern, 1992–94): 6

Waldner, Erwin (VfB Stuttgart, 1954–58): 13/2

Walter, Fritz (Kaiserslautern, 1940–58): 61/33

Walter, Ottmar (Kaiserslautern, 1950–56): 21/10

Warnken, Heinz (Komet Bremen, 1935): 1

Weber, Albert (Vorwärts Berlin, 1912): 2

Weber, Heinrich (Kurhessen Kassel, 1928–31): 10

Weber, Josef (Wacker Munich, 1927): 1

Weber, Ralf (Eintracht Frankfurt, 1994–95): 9

Weber, Wolfgang (Köln, 1964–74): 2

Wegele, Karl (Phonix Karlsruhe, 1910–14): 13/2

Weilbacher, Hans (Eintracht Frankfurt, 1955): 1

Weiss, Leonhard (Nürnburg, 1931): 1

Weissenbacher, Viktor (Pforzheim, 1922): 1/1

Welker, Hans (Bayern Munich, 1931): 1

Wellhofer, Georg (SpVgg Furth, 1922): 1

Welsch, Kurt (Borussia Neunkirchen, 1937): 1

Wenauer, Ferdinand (Nürnburg, 1960–62): 4

Wendl, Josef (1860 Munich, 1930–33); 5

Wentorf, Hans (Altona 93, 1928): 2

Wenz, Ludwig (ASV Nürnburg, 1930): 1

Werner, Adolf (Holstein Kiel, Victoria Hamburg, 1909–12): 11

Werner, August (Holstein Kiel, 1925): 2

Werner, Heinz (SV Jena, 1935); 1

Werner Jürgen, (Hamburg, 1961–63): 4/2

Wetzel, Fritz (Pforzheim, 1922): 1

Wewers, Heinz (Rot-Weiss Essen, 1951–58): 12/1

Weymar, Hans (Victoria Hamburg, 1908–10): 4

Widmayer, Werner (Holstein Kiel, 1931): 2

Wieder, Ludwig (Nürnburg, 1923–26): 6/2

Wientjes, Clemens (Rot-Weiss Essen, 1952.): 2

Wiesner, Martin (Karlsruhe SC, 1981): 1

Wiggers, Hermann (Victoria Hamburg, 1911): 1

Wigold, Willi (Fortuna Düsseldorf, 1932–34): 4/3

Wilden, Leo (Köln, 1960–64): 15

Willimowski, Ernst (PSV Chemnitz, 1860 Munich, 1942): 8/13

Willmer, Holger (Köln, 1981): 1

Wimmer, Herbert (Borussia Mönchengladbach, 1968–76): 36/4

Winkler, Paul (Schwarz-Weiss Essen, 1938): 1

Winkler, Willi (Wormatia Worms, 1928): 1

Wohlfahrt, Roland (Bayern Munich, 1986–89): 2

Wolpers, Eduard (Hamburg, 1926): 1

Wolter, Horst (Eintracht Braunschweig, 1967–70): 13

Wolter, Karl (Vorwärts Berlin, 1912–21): 3

Wolter, Thomas (Werder Bremen, 1992): 1

Worm, Ronald (MSV Duisburg, 1975–78): 8/5

Worns, Christian (Bayer Leverkusen, Paris St-Germain [Fra], Bayer Leverkusen, 1992–98): 20

Worpitzky, Willi (Viktoria 89 Berlin, 1909–12): 8/5

Wosz, Dariusz (VfL Bochum, 1997): 6/1

Wunder, Klaus (MSV Duisburg, 1973): 1

Wunderlich, Georg (1860 Furth, Helvetia Bockenheim, Stuttgart Kickers, 1920–21): 5

Wuttke, Wolfram (Kaiserslautern, 1986–88): 4/1

Zaczyk, Klaus (Karlsruhe, 1967): 1/1

Zastrau, Walter (Rot-Weiss Essen, 1958): 1

Zeitler, Hans (VfB Bayreuth, 1952): 1/1

Zembaki, Dieter (Werder Bremen, 1971): 1

Zewe, Gerd (Fortuna Düsseldorf, 1978–79): 4

Ziege, Christian (Bayern Munich, AC Milan [Ita], 1993–98): 41/4

Zielinski, Paul (Union Hamborn, 1934–36): 15

Zilgas, Karl (Victoria Hamburg, 1913): 1

Zimmermann, Gerhard (Fortuna Düsseldorf, 1975): 1

Zimmermann, Herbert (Köln, 1976–79): 15/2

Zinser (1901): 1

Zolper, Dr Karl (CfR Köln, 1925): 1

Zorc, Michael (Borussia Dortmund, 1992–93): 7

Zorner, Dr Karl (SC 99 Köln, 1923): 4

Zwolanowski, Felix (Fortuna Düsseldorf (1940): 2

FRENCH INTERNATIONAL PLAYERS' RECORDS

Abbes, Claude (St Etienne, 1957–58): 9

Abdesselem, Ben Mohamm (Bordeaux, 1953): 1

Accard, Robert (Le Havres, 1922–26): 6/1

Adamczyk, Marcel (Lille, 1963): 1

Adams, Jean-Pierre (Nimes, Nice, 1972–73): 22

Albert, Georges (Paris, 1908): 1

Alcazar, Joseph (Marseille, 1931–35): 11/2

Alle, Charles (Marseille, 1929): 1

Allegre, Andre (UA 1st, 1914): 1

Allemane, Pierre (Racing Club de Paris, 1905–08): 7

Alpsteg, Rene (St Etienne, 1947–52): 12/4

Amisse, Loic (Nantes, 1983): 12/2

Amoros, Manuel (Monaco, Marseille, 1982–92): 83/2

Anatol, Manuel (Racing Club de Paris, 1929–34): 16/1

Andre, Mathieu (Rouen, 1936–37): 3

Anelka, Nicolas (Arsenal [Eng], 1998): 1

Angloma, Jocelyn (Paris St-Germain, Marseille, Torino [Ita], 1990–96): 37/1

Antoinette, Bernard (Rouen, 1937): 2

Anziani, Philippe (Sochaux-Montbeliard, Monaco, Nantes,1984–87): 5/1

Arnaudeau, Henri (Bordeaux, Red Star, 1942–51): 6/1

Artelesa, Marcel (Monaco, Marseille, 1963–66): 21/1

Aston, Alfred (Racing Club de Paris, Red Star, 1934–46): 31/5

Aubour, Marcel (Lyon, Nice, 1964–68): 20

Ayache, William (Nantes, Paris St-Germain, Marseille, 1983–88): 20

Aznar, Emmanuel (Marseille, 1938): 1/1

Ba, Ibrahim (Bordeaux, AC Milan [Ita], 1997–98): 8/2

Baeza, Jean (Monaco, Red Star, 1967–68): 8

Baillot, Henri (Metz, 1948–50): 8/4

Baills, Pascal (Montpellier ,1991): 1

Banide, Maurice (Strasbourg, Mulhouse, Club Francais, Racing Club de Paris, 1929–34): 10/1

Baraffe, Edmond (Toulouse, 1964–66): 3

Barat, M (AS Bon Conseil, 1909): 2

Baratelli, Dominique (Nice, Paris St-Germain, 1972–82): 21

Baratte, Jean (Lille, 1944–52): 32/19

Bard, Henri (Racing Club de France, Paris, 1913–23): 11/3

Bardot, Charles (Philippevillois, Cannes, 1925–32): 6/3

Barron, Paul (Paris, 1923): 1

Baronchelli, Bruno (Nantes, 1981): 6/1

Barreau, Gaston (Levallois, 1911–14): 12

Barthez, Fabien (Marseille, Monaco, 1994–98): 19

Bastien, Jean (Marseille, 1938–45): 4

Bathenay, Dominique (St Etienne, Paris St-Germain, 1975–82): 20/4

Batmale, Jean (Athletique Clichy, Club Francais, Stade Rennais, 1920–24): 5

Baton, Zacharie (Lille, 1906–08): 4

Bats, Joel (Paris St-Germain, Auxerre, 1983–89): 50

Batteux, Albert (Reims, 1948–49): 8/1

Battiston, Patrick (Metz, St Etienne, Bordeaux, Monaco, 1977–89): 56/3

Baumann, Edouard (Racing Club de France, Paris, 1920–24): 8

Bayrou, Georges (Gallia Club Lunel, 1908): 1

Beaucourt, Georges (Lille, 1936): 1

Beaudier, Maurice (Paris, 1921): 3

Beck, Yvan (Sete, St Etienne, 1935–37): 5

Bel, Paul-Emile (Vitry, 1925): 1

Bellocq, Henri (Etoile des Deux Lacs, 1909–11): 6/1

Bellone, Bruno (Monaco, Cannes, 1981–88): 34/2

Belver, Jean (Nice, 1950): 1

Ben Barek, Larbi (Marseille, Red Star, 1938–54): 17/3

Ben, Bouali Abdelkader (Sete, 1937): 1

Ben, Tifour Abdelaziz (Nice, Monaco, Troye, 1952–57): 4

Benouna, Ali (1936): 2

Berdoll, Marc (Angers, Marseille, 1973–75): 16/5

Bereta, Georges (St Etienne, Marseille, 1967–74): 44/4

Berg, Fritz (Goteborg, 1935): 1/1

Berg, Gregoire (Red Star Strasbourg, 1922): 1

Bergeroo, Philippe (Lille, Toulouse, 1980–84): 3

Bernard, Pierre (Sedan-Torcy, Nimes Olympique, St Etienne, 1960–65): 21

Berthelot, Charles (Stade Rennais, 1923): 1

Bertrand, Marcel (Club de France,): 5,

Bertrand-Demanes, Jean-Paul (Nantes, 1973–78): 11

Betta, Andre (Rouen, 1968): 2

Biancheri, Henri (Monaco, 1960): 2

Bibard, Michel (Nantes, Paris St-Germain, 1984–86): 6

Bieganski, Guillaume (Lille, Lens, 1953–61): 9

Bigot, Jules (Lille, 1936–45): 6/1

Bigue, Maurice (Paris, 1911–14): 7

Bihel, Rene (Lille, Le Havre, 1945–47): 6/1

Bijotat, Dominique (Monaco, Bordeaux, 1982–88): 8

Bilot, Charles (Paris, 1904–12): 6

Bilot, Georges (Paris, 1904): 1

Blanc, Laurent (Montpellier Paillade, Napoli [Ita], Nimes Olympique, St Etienne, Auxerre, Marseille, Barcelona [Sp], 1989–98): 73/13

Blanchet, Bernard (Nantes, 1966–72): 17/5

Bliard, Rene (Reims): 7

Bloch, Paul 'Poly' (Mulhouse, 1921): 1

Blondeau, Patrick (Monaco, 1997): 2

Bloquel, Louis (US Boulonnaise, 1924–25): 2

Boghossian, Alain (Sampdoria [Ita], 1997–98): 11

Boissier, Bernard (Nimes Olympique,): 1

Boli, Basile (Auxerre, Marseille,): 45/1

Bollini, Bruno (Racing Club de Paris, 1957–61): 3

Bon, Georges (US Boulonnaise, 1907): 1

Bonello, Georges (Blideen, 1926–27): 3/1

Bongiorni, Emile (Racing Club de Paris, 1945–48): 5/2

Bonifaci, Antoine (Nice, 1953): 12/2

Bonnardel, Philippe (Gallia Club Lunel, Red Star, US Quevillaise, 1920–27): 22

Bonnel, Joseph (Valenciennes-Anzin , Marseille, 1967–69): 2

Bonnet, Rene (AS Francaise, 1914): 1

Bosquier, Bernard (Sochaux-Montbeliard , St Etienne, Marseille, 1966–72):

Bossis, Maxime (Nantes, Racing Club de Paris, 1976–86): 76/1

Boucher, Richard (Toulouse, 1957–61): 3

Bourbotte, Francois (Fives, 1937–42): 17

Bournonville, Louis (Arras, 1913): 1

Boury, Roger (Roubaix-Tourcoing, 1952): 1

Bousdira, Fares (Lens, 1976): 1

Boyer, Jean (CA Sports Generaux , Choisy le Roi , Marseille, 1920–29): 15/7

Bracci, Francois (Marseille, Bordeaux, 1973–82): 18

Brahimi, Said (Toulouse, 1957): 2/1

Bras, Jean-Claude (Valenciennes-Anzin, Liege [Bel], 1969–70): 6/2

Braun, Gabriel (Metz, 1945): 1

Bravo, Daniel (Nice, Marseille, 1982–89): 13/1

Brebion, Gilbert (Etoile des Deux Lacs, 1909): 1

Brisson, Francois (Lens, 1982–84): 2

Broissart, Jose (Racing Club de Paris, St Etienne, 1969–73): 10

Brouzes, Juste (CA Societe Generale , Red Star, 1914–1928): 6/3

Bruat, Marius (Sochaux-Montbeliard, 1953): 1

Bruey, Stephane (Angers, 1957–62): 4/1

Brunel, Fernand (Gallia Club Lunel, 1926): 1/2

Brusseaux, Michel (Sete, 1938): 1

Budzinski, Robert (Nantes, 1965–67): 11

Bulnes, Jose Fernando (1972): 1/1
Bure, Julien (Le Havre,): 1
Buron, Jean-Louis (Rouen, 1963): 4/1
Buscher, Gerard (Brest, 1986–87): 2
Cahuzac, Pierre (Toulouse, 1957): 2
Caillet, Andre (CA Sports Generaux, 1923): 1
Camard, Rene (AS Francaise, 1907): 1
Camerini, Francis (St Etienne, Nice, 1971): 2
Candela, Vincent (Guingamp, AS Roma, 1996–98): 10
Canelle, Fernand (Club Francais, 1904–08): 6
Canthelou, Jacques (Rouen, 1924–28): 11
Cantona, Eric (Auxerre, Montpellier Herault, Marseille, Nimes, Leeds [Eng], Manchester Utd [Eng], 1987–95): 44/19
Capelle, Marcel (Racing Club de Paris, 1930–31): 9
Cardenas, Raul (1954): 1/1
Cardiet, Louis (Stade Rennais, 1965–67): 6
Carnus, Georges (Stade Francais, Paris, St Etienne, Marseille, 1963–73): 36
Carpentier, Daniel (Sedan-Torcy, 1954): 1
Carre, Desire (Nice, 1949): 1
Carre, Roger (Lille, 1947–49): 2
Casolarl, Georges (Monaco, 1963–64): 3
Casoni, Bernard (Toulon, Matra Racing, Marseille, 1988–92): 30
Castaneda, Jean (St Etienne, 1981–82): 9
Cazal, Louis 'Pierrot' (Sete, 1927–30): 6
Cazenave, Hector (Sochaux-Montbeliard, 1937–38): 8
Chaisaz, Raoul (Stade Francais, 1932): 2
Chandelier, Paul (Lille, 1913–14): 3
Chantrel, Augustin (Red Star, CA Sports Generaux, 1928–33): 15
Charbit, Max (Marseille, 1934–35): 4
Charbonnier, L (Auxerre, 1997): 1
Chardar, Andre (Sete, 1930–33): 12/1
Charles, Alfred Daniel (Nimes Olympique, 1964): 4
Charrier, Rene (Marseille, 1975): 2
Chauveau, Yves (Lyon, 1969): 1
Chayrigues, Pierre (Red Star, 1911–1925): 21
Chesneau, Pierre (FC Blideen, 1924): 1
Cheuva, Andre (Lille, SC Fivois, 1929–30): 7/2
Chiarelli, Bernard (Valenciennes-Anzin, 1958): 1
Chiesa, Serge (Marseille, 1969–74)): 12/3
Chillan, Paul (Nimes Olympique, 1963): 2
Chorda, Andre (Nice, Bordeaux, 1960–66): 24
Christophe, Didier (Monaco, 1980–81): 6/1
Cicci, Raymond (Rhiems, 1953): 1/1
Cisowski, Thadee (Metz, Racing Club de Paris, 1951–58): 12/11
Clere, Ernest (Paris, 1924): 1
Coat, Robert (Brest, 1923): 1
Cocard, Christophe (Auxerre): 9/1
Colonna, Dominique (Reims, 1957–61): 13
Combin, Nestor (Lyon, Juventus [Ita], Varese [Its], Torino [Ita], 1964–68): 8/4
Compeyrat, Alfred (Levallois, CA Rosaire, 1909–11): 3
Cornu, Alain (Nice, 1962): 1

Cossou, Lucien (Monaco, 1960–64): 6/4
Coste, Christian (Lille, 1974–75): 5/2
Cottenet, Maurice (Raincy Sports, Paris, Cannes, 1920–25): 17
Cottenier, Jules (Roubaix, 1932–34): 4
Couecou, Didier (Bordeaux, 1967): 1
Coulon, Henri 'Beau' (Paris, 1911): 5
Couriol, Alain (Monaco, Paris St-Germain, 1980–83): 12/2
Courquin, Albert (Lille, 1922): 1
Courtin, Paul (Lens, 1966): 1
Courtois, Roger (Sochaux-Montbeliard, 1933–47): 9
Crozier, Georges (US Parisienne, 1905–06): 2
Crut, Edouard (Marseille, 1924–27): 8/6
Cuissard, Antoine (St Etienne, Lorient, Nice, 1946–54): 27/1
Curbelo, Carlos (Nancy-Lorraine, 1976): 2
Curyl, Stanislas (Sete, 1952): 1
Cypres, Gaston (Paris, 1904–08): 6/2
Cyprien, Jean-Pierre (St Etienne,): 1
Dakoski, Stephane (Nimes Olympique, 1951): 2
Dalger, Christian (Monaco,): 6/2
Dambach, Alfred (Rouen, 1944): 1
Dangles, Marcel (Cette, 1923): 1
Dard, Georges (Marseille, 1947–50): 3/2
Darques, Louis (Paris, 1919–23): 9/1
Darui, Julien (Lille, Red Star, Roubaix-Tourcoing, 1939–45): 25
Dastarac, Sadi (Gallia Club Lunel, 1908): 1
Dauphin, Robert (Stade Français, 1925–29): 15/1
Davy, Jacques (Paris, 1904): 1
De Bourgoing, Hector (Nice, Bordeaux): 3/2
De Michele, Gabriel (Nantes, 1966–67): 2
Dedieu, Rene (Nimes, Montpellier, 1924–27): 6
Defosse, Robert (Lille, 1933–36): 9
Degouve, Jean (Lille, 1913–14): 2
Deladerriere, Leon (Nancy, 1952–58): 11/3
Delamontagne, Patrick (Nancy-Lorraine, Monaco, Stade Levallois, 1981–87): 3
Delannoy, Jacques (Lille, 1932): 1
Delfour, Edmond (Stade Français, Racing Club de France, Roubaix, 1929–38): 41/2
Delmer, Celestin (Amiens, Excelsior, 1930–34): 11
Deloffre, Jean (Ouest Angers, 1967): 1
Delvecchio, Joseph (AS Alfortvillaise, 1910): 1
Denis, Julien (Calais,1908): 2
Denis, Serge (Garenne-Colombes, 1924): 1
Denis, Victor (Tourquennoise, 1908): 1
Depaepe, Maurice (Tourquennoise, 1923): 1
Dereuddre, Rene (Toulouse, 1954–57): 6/1
Desailly, Marcel (Marseille, AC Milan [Ita], Chelsea [Eng], 1993–98): 48/1
Deschamps, Didier (Nantes, Marseille, Bordeaux, Juventus [Ita], 1989–98): 74/4
Desgranges, Jean (Lens,1953): 1/2
Despeyroux, Pascal (Toulouse, 1988): 3
Desrousseaux, Fernand (Tourquennoise, 1908): 1
Desrousseaux, Marcel (Excelsior-Tourcoing,

1935–37): 2
Devaux, Denis (Strasbourg, 1965): 1
Devic, Emilien (Racing Club de France, Red Star, CA Sports Generaux, 1911–21): 8/2
Dewaquez, Jules (Paris, Marseille, 1920–29): 40/12
Dhur, Jacques (Stade Francais, 1927): 1
Di Lorto, Laurent (Marseille, Sochaux-Montbeliard, 1936–38): 11
Di Meco, Eric (Marseille, Monaco, 1989–96): 23
Diagne, Raoul (Racing Club de France, Racing Club de Paris, 1931–40): 18
Dib, Marcel (Monaco, 1988–90): 6
Diomede, Bernard (Auxerre, 1988): 8
Divert, Fabrice (Caen, Montpellier , 1990–92): 1
Djetou, Martin (Monaco, 1996–98): 3
Djorkaeff, Jean (Lyon, Marseille, Paris St-Germain, 1964–72): 48/3
Djorkaeff, Youri (Monaco, Paris St-Germain, Inter Milan [Ita], 1993–98): 44/17
Dogliani, Jean-Pierre (Angers, 1967): 1/1
Dombeck, Stanislas (Stade Rennais, 1958): 1
Domenech, Raymond (Lyon, Strasbourg, 1973–79): 8
Domergue, Jean-François (Toulouse, Marseille, 1984–87): 9/2
Domergue, Marcel (CA Sports Generaux, FC Cette, Nimes, Red Star, 1922–28): 20
Domingo, Marcel (Stade Francais, 1948): 1
Domingo, Rene (St Etienne, 1957): 1
Douis, Yvon (Lille, Le Havre, Monaco, 1957–65): 20/4
Doye, Andre (Bordeaux, 1950–52): 7/5
Droege, Don (Rochester Lancers, 1979): 1/1
Dropsy, Dominique (Strasbourg, 1978–81): 17
Du Rheart, Julien (Montrouge, Club Francais, Red Star, 1906–11): 3
Dubly, Jean (Roubaix, 1908): 1
Dubly, Jules (Tourquennoise, 1914): 1
Dubly, Raymond (Roubaix, 1913–25): 30/4
Dubreucq, Albert (Lille, 1952): 1
Dubus, Gustave (Sete, 0930): 2/1
Ducret, Jean (Etoile des Deux Lacs, Lille, 1910–14): 20/3
Dufour, Robert (Paris, 1924): 1
Dugarry, Christian (Marseille, 1998): 1
Dugarry, Christophe (Bordeaux, AC Milan [Ita], Marseille, 1994–98): 25/3
Duhart, Pierre (Sochaux-Montbeliard, 1935–37): 6/1
Dujardin, Charles (Tourquennoise, 1913): 1
Dupoix, Michel (Racing Club de France, 1924): 1
Dupuis, Maurice (Racing Club de France, 1937–45): 9
Durand, Jean-Philippe (Toulouse, Bordeaux, Marseille, 1988–91): 24
Durand, Raymond (Marseille, 1931): 1
Durbec, Aime (Marseille, 1927): 1
Dusart, Emile (Roubaix, 1914): 1
Dutheil, Raoul (Cannes, 1929): 1
Eloy, Albert (Lille, 1913–14): 2/2
Emon, Albert (Marseille, Monaco, 1975–80): 8/1

Eon, Daniel (Nantes, 1966–67): 3
Esteve, Vincent (Nantes,): 1
Ettori, Jean-Luc (Monaco, 1980–82): 9
Eucher, Rene (AS Francaise): 1
Faivre, Jacques (St Etienne, 1961): 2/2
Fargeon, Philippe (Bordeaux, 1987–88): 7/2
Farison, Gerard (St Etienne, 1976): 1
Faroux (Pantin, 1912): 1
Farvaques, Victor (Tourquennoise, 1928): 1
Faure, Paul (Racing Club de France, 1919): 1
Fenouillere, Rene (Red Star, 1908): 1
Fernandez, Luis (Paris St-Germain, Racing Club de Paris, Matra Racing, Cannes, 1982–92): 35/3
Fernier, (1988): 1/1
Ferratge, Jean-Marc (Toulouse, 1982): 1
Ferreri, Jean-Marc (Auxerre, Bordeaux, 1982–90): 37/3
Ferrero, Bruno (Nancy, 1962): 1
Ferri, Jean-Michel (Nantes, 1994–95): 5
Ferrier, Rene (St Etienne, 1958–64): 24
'Ferry', Ferenc Koczur (St Etienne, 1952): 3
Fidon, Jean (Paris, 1927): 1
Fievet, A (Pantin, 1912): 1
Filez, Adrien (Tourquennoise, 1904–08): 5
Finot, Louis (Paris, 1930–34): 7
Firoud, Abdelkader (Nimes Olympique, 1951–52): 6
Flamion, Pierre (Reims, Marseille, Lyon, AS Troyenne Savinienne, 1948–53): 17/8
Floch, Louis (Monaco, Paris, 1970–72): 16/2
Foix, Jacques (St Etienne, 1953–56): 7/3
Fontaine, Just (Nice, Reims, 1953–56): 21/29
Fosset, Charles (Metz, 1937): 2
Fournier, Laurent (Paris St-Germain, 1992): 3
Francois, Andre (Roubaix, 1906–08): 6/3
Francois, Raymond (Lens, 1936): 1
Fremont, Raymond (Le Havre, 1919): 1
Frey, Andre (Toulouse, 1950): 6
Friess, Emile (Strasbourg, 1922): 2
Frutuoso, Michel (Roubaix, 1937): 1
Fulgenzi, Maxime (UA Sedan-Torcy, 1961): 1
Gabet, Roger (Racing Club de Paris, 1949): 3
Gabrillargues, Louis (Sete, 1934–37): 9
Galey, Marcel (Sete, 1929): 3/1
Gallay, Maurice (Marseille, 1926–29): 13/1
Gallice, Jean (Bordeaux, 1974–76): 7/1
Gallice, Rene (Bordeaux, 1951): 1
Gamblin, Lucien (Red Star, 1911–23): 16
Garande, Patrice (St Etienne, 1988): 1
Garde, Remi (Lyon, 1990–91): 5
Gardien, Rene (Sochaux-Montbeliard, 1953): 2/52
Gardon, Bernard (Nantes, 1973): 1
Garnier, Georges (Club Français, 1904–05): 3
Garriga, Manuel (Bordeaux, 1950): 1
Gastiger, Maurice (FEC Levallois, 1914–20): 3/1
Gautheroux, Jean (Racing Club de France, Excelsior Roubaix-Tourcoing, 1930–36): 2
Gava, Franck (Lyon, Paris St-Germain,

1996–97): 3
Gemmrich, Albert (Strasbourg, 1978): 5/2
Genghini, Bernard (Sochaux-Montbeliard, St Etienne, Monaco, Servette Geneva, 1980–86): 28/4
Gerard, Rene (Olympique Montpellier 1932–33): 7
Germain, Bruno (Matra Racing, 1987): 1
Geronimi, Charles (Garenne Colombes, 1914): 1/1
Geronimi, Georges (Garenne Colombes, 1911): 1
Gianessi, Lazare (Roubaix-Tourcoing, Monaco, 1953–54): 14
Gigot, R (Club Francais, 1905): 1
Gindrat, Alfred (Red Star, 1911–12): 4
Ginola, David (Brest Armorique, Paris St-Germain, Newcastle United [Eng], 1990–95): 17/4
Girard, Rene (Bordeaux, 1981–82): 7/1
Giresse, Alain (Bordeaux, 1974–86): 47/6
Glovacki, Leon (Reims, 1953–55): 11/3
Gnako, Jerome (Monaco, 1992–94): 2
Goma, Alain (Auxerre, 1996): 1
Gondet, Philippe (Nantes, 1965–70): 14/7
Gonzales, Joseph (SC Fivois, 1936): 1
Gosselin, Desire (Stade l'Est, 1926): 1
Gouin, Raymond (JA Levallois, 1909): 2
Goujon, Yvon (Sochaux-Montbeliard, Stade Rennais UC , Rouen, 1960–63):11/6
Grava, Dario (Nice, 1973): 1
Gravelaine, Xavier (Paris St-Germain, 1992–93): 4
Gravelines, Maurice (Lille, 1920–22): 2
Gravier, Ernest (Paris, Cette, 1911–24): 11/1
Gregoire, Jean (Stade Français ,Red Star, 1947–50): 10
Gress, Gilbert (VfB Stuttgart [Ger], Marseille, 1967–71): 3
Gressier, Raoul (Calais, 1908): 1
Grillet, Pierre (Racing Club de Paris, 1954–60): 9/2
Grillon, Andre (Stade Francais, Red Star, Lyon, 1946–51): 15
Gross, Ernest (Red Star Strasbourg, 1924–25): 5/1
Grumellon, Jean (Stade Rennais UC, US Servannaise , 1949–52): 11/5
Gueguen, Ernest (1913): 1
Guerin, Henri (Stade Rennais UC, 1948–49): 3
Guerin, Vincent (Paris St-Germain, 1993–96): 19/2
Guerre, Henri (Patronage Olier, 1909): 1
Guichard, Maurice (US Parisienne, 1904–05): 2
Guillas, Roland (Bordeaux, St Etienne, 1958–62): 9/1
Guillou, Jean-Marc (SC Ouest Angers, Nice, 1974–78): 11/1
Guivarc'h, Stephane (Rennes, Auxerre, 1997–98): 12/1
Guy, Andre (St Etienne, Lille, Lyon, 1964–68): 8/2
Haan, Edmond (Strasbourg, 1953): 4
Hanot, Gabriel (Tourquennoise, AS

Francaise, 1908–19): 12/3
Hausser, Gerard (RC Strasbourg, 1965–66): 14/2
Hediart, Jean (Nancy, 1956): 1
Heine, Charles (RC Strasbourg, 1947): 2
Heisserer, Oscar (RC Strasbourg, Racing Club de Paris, 1936–48): 17/6
Henric, Laurent (Sete, 1928–29): 4
Henry, Thierry (Monaco, 1997–98): 8/3
Herbet, Yves (Sedan-Torcy, Racing Club de Paris, RSC Anderlecht [Bel], Reims, 1965–71): 16/1
Herbin, Robert (St Etienne, 1960–68): 23/3
Heutte, Francois (Racing Club de Paris, 1959–61): 9/4
Hiard, Patrick (Bastia, 1981): 1
Hidalgo, Michel (Monaco, 1962): 1
Hiden, Rodolphe (Racing Club de Paris, 1940): 1
Hiltl, Henri (Racing Club de Paris, Excelsior, 1940–44): 2
Hitzel, Victor (Levallois, 1909): 1
Hoenen, Paul (Saint-Ouen, 1923): 1
Holgard, Henri (Amiens, 1908): 1
Hon, Louis (Stade Francais, Red Star, 1947–49): 12
Horlaville, Daniel (US Quevillaise,. 1969): 1
Hornus, Pierre (Olympique Montpellier, 1931): 3
Houyvet, Georges (Le Havre, 1932): 1
Hugues, Francois (Red Star, Stade Rennais UC, Lyon, 1919–27): 23/1
Huguet, Guy (St Etienne, 1948–52): 12
Huot, Leon (CA Vitry, Olympique d'Alais, 1920–26): 4
Hurtevent, Andre (Abbeville, 1927): 1
Huysmans, Constant (1954): 1/1
Ibrir, Abderrahmar (Toulouse, 1949–50): 6
Ignace, Kowalczyk (Valenciennes-Anzin, Marseille, FC Metz 1935–38): 5/1
Isbecque, Gerard (Roubaix, 1923–24): 4/1
Issa, Pierre (Marseille, 1998): 1/1
Jacolliot, Rene (AS Francaise, 1913): 1
Jacowski, Andre (Stade de Reims, 1952): 2
Jacques, Michel (Sochaux-Montbeliard, 1947): 1
Jacquet, Aime (St Etienne, 1968): 2
Jadrejak, Joseph (Lille, 1947): 3
Janin, Georges (Red Star, 1937): 1
Janvion, Gerard (St Etienne, 1975–82): 40
Jasseron, Lucien (Racing Club de Paris, 1945): 2
Jeannol, Philippe (Paris St-Germain, 1986): 1
Jenicot, Albert (Roubaix, 1908): 3
Jodar, Jean François (Stade de Reims, 1972–75): 6/1
Jonquet, Robert (Stade de Reims, 1948–60): 58
Jordan, Gustave (Racing Club de Paris, 1938–45): 16/1
Jourda, Albert (CA Vitry , Racing Club de Paris, FC Cette, 1914–24): 7
Jourde, Etienne (CA Vitry, Club des Sports Athletiques, 1910–14): 8/1
Jouve, A (Gallia Club Lunel, 1906): 1

Jouve, Roger (Nice, Strasbourg, 1973–79): 7/1
Joyaut, Robert (Red Star, 1923): 4
Julien, Felix (AS Bon Conseil, 1909): 2
Kaelbel, Raymond (Strasbourg, Monaco, 1954–56): 6
Karembeu, Christian (Nantes, Sampdoria [Ita], Real Madrid [Sp], 1992–98): 32/1
Kargu, Edouard (Bordeaux, 1950–53): 11/3
Kastendeuch, Sylvain (Metz, 1987–89): 9
Kaucsar, Joseph (Stade Raphaelois, Olympique Montpellier, 1931–34): 15
Kauffmann, Marcel (Mulhouse, 1930–33): 5
Keller, Curt (Sochaux-Montbeliard, 1937): 1
Keller, Fritz (Strasbourg, 1934–37): 8/3
Keller, Marc (Lyon, Karlsruhe [Ger], 1995–98): 6/1
Kenner, Rene (CA Vitry, 1928): 1
Keruzore, Raymond (Levallois, 1976–78): 2
Khlestov, Dmitri (1993): 1/1
Kopa, Raymond (Stade de Reims, Real Madrid [Sp], Reims, 1952–63): 45/18
Koranyi, Desire (Sete, 1939–42): 5/5
Korb, Pierre (Mulhouse, 1930–34): 12/2
Koza, Casimir (Strasbourg, 1962): 1
Krawczyk, Richard (Lens, 1967): 1
Kress, Jean-Pierre (Strasbourg, 1953):
Lacombe, Bernard (Lyon, St Etienne, Bordeaux, 1973–84): 39/13
Lafont, Maurice (Nice, 1958): 4
Lafouge, Abel Championnet Sports, 1913(): 1
Laigle, Pierre (Lens, Sampdoria [Ita], 1996–97): 8
Lama, Bernard (Paris St-Germain, West Ham [Eng], 1993–98): 37
Lamia, Georges (Nice, 1959–62): 7
Lamouchi, Sabri (Auxerre, 1996–98): 11/1
Lamy, Roger (Racing Club de Paris, 1950): 2
Langenove, Eugene (Paris, 1921): 2
Langiller, Marcel (Paris, Excelsior, Red Star, 1927–35): 30/7
Larios, Jean-François (St Etienne, 1978–82): 17/4
Larque, Jean-Michel (Auxerre, 1969–76): 14/2
Larsen, Soren (1973): 1/1
Laslandes, Lilian (Bordeaux, 1997): 1
Laurent, Jean (Paris, Sochaux-Montbeliard, 1930–32): 9
Laurent, Lucien (Paris, Sochaux, Sochaux-Montbeliard, Mulhouse, 1930–35): 10/2
Laurey, Thierry (Sochaux-Montbeliard, 1989): 1
Lauri, Michel (Sochaux-Montbeliard, 1937): 1
Lavaud, Jean-Claude (Stade Rennais UC, 1967): 1
Le Chenadec, Gilbert (Nantes, 1967):
Le Guen, Paul (Paris St-Germain, 1993–95): 17
Le Roux, Yvon (Stade Brestois, Monaco, Nantes, Marseille, Paris St-Germain, 1983–89): 28/1
Leblond, Michel (Stade de Reims, 1954–57): 4/1
Leboeuf, Frank (Strasbourg, Chelsea [Eng],

1995–98): 16/2
Lech, Georges (Lens, Sochaux-Montbeliard, Stade de Reims, 1963–73): 35/7
Lechantre, Jean (Lille, 1947–49): 3
Lecornu, Patrice (SC Ouest Angers, 1979–81): 3
Leduc, Lucien (Red Star, 1946): 4/1
Lehmann, Maxime (Sochaux-Montbeliard, 1935–36): 2
Lekbello, Artur (1991): 1/1
Lemaitre, Robert (Lille, 1953–54): 2
Lemerre, Roger (Racing Club de Paris-Sedan, Nantes, AS Nancy-Lorraine, 1968–71): 6
Lemoult, Jean-Claude (Paris St-Germain, 1983): 2
Lemriss, Abdel (1988): 1/1
Lenoble, Bernard (Le Havre, 1924): 2
Lerond, Andre (Lyon, Stade Français, 1957–63): 31
Lesmann, E (Saint-Ouen, 1912): 1
Lesur, Henri (Tourquennoise, 1913–14): 6
Letailleur, Lucien (Levallois, 1913): 1
Letizi, Lionel (Metz, 1997–98): 2
Leveugle, Edmond (Roubaix, 1926): 1/1
Lhermine, Marceau (Rouen, 1933): 1
Liberati, Ernest (Amiens, SC Fivois, 1930–34): 19/4
Lieb, Guillaume 'Willy' (FC Bischwiller , Lyon, Mulhouse, 1925–29):
Lienert, Pierre (CA Sports Generaux, 1925): 1
Lietaer, Noel (Excelsior, 1933–34): 7
Liminana, Andre (SC Bel Abbesien, 1925): 2
Lizarazu, Bixente (Bordeaux, Athletic Bilbao [Sp], Bayern Munich [Ger], 1992–98): 38/2
Llense, Rene (Sete, St Etienne, 1935–38): 11
Loko, Patrice (Nantes, Paris St-Germain, 1993–97): 26/6
Loncle, Marcel (Stade Rennais, 1965): 2
Lopez, Christian (St Etienne, Toulouse, 1975–82): 39/1
Loubet, Charly (Nice, Marseille, 1967–74): 37/11
Loubiere, Robert (Gallia Club Lunel, 1914): 1
Louis, Xerces (Lens, 1954–56): 12
Lozes, Antonio (Sochaux, 1930): 3
Luciano, Jean (Nice, 1949–50): 4/1
Ludo, François (Monaco, 1961): 1
Macquart, Edouard (1921): 1
Madar, Michael (Monaco, 1995–96): 3/1
Maes, Eugene (Red Star, 1911–13): 11/15
Mahi, Khennane (Stade Rennais, 1961): 2
Mahjoub, Abderrahma (Nice, Racing Club de Paris, 1954–55): 7
Mahut, Philippe (Metz, St Etienne, 1981–83): 9
Mairesse, Jacques (Cette, Red Star, 1927–34): 6
Makelele, Claude (Nantes, Marseille, 1995–98): 3
Marc, Herve (Stade Rennais UC, 1930): 1
Marcel, Jean-Jacques (Sochaux-

Montbeliard, Marseille, Toulon, Racing Club de Paris, 1953–61): 44/2
Marchal, Marcel (Metz, 1938): 1
Marche, Roger (Stade de Reims, Racing Club de Paris, 1947–59): 63/1
Mariot, Yves (Lyon, 1975): 1
Martini, Bruno (Auxerre, Montpellier, 1987–96): 31
Martins, Corentin (Auxerre,): 14/1
Maryan, Synakowski (UA Sedan-Torcy, Stade Francais, Union St-Gilloise, 1961–65): 13
Maschinot, Andre (Belfort, Sochaux, 1927–30): 5/2
Masnaghetti, Serge (Valenciennes, 1963): 2/1
Massip, Fernand (Red Star, 1): 1
Mathaux, Paul (US Boulonnaise, 1908): 5
Mathe, Jules (Racing Club de Paris, 1939): 2/1
Mathieu, Maurice (Athletique Societe Generale, Red Star, 1914–19): 1
Mattler, Etienne (Sochaux, Sochaux-Montbeliard, 1930–40): 46
Maurice, Florian (Lyon, 1996–97): 3
Meano, Francis (Stade de Reims, 1949–52): 2
Mekhloufi, Rachid (St Etienne, 1956–57): 4
Merchadier, Alain (St Etienne, 1973–75): 5
Mercier, Albert (Racing Club de France, 1919): 1
Mercier, D (Etoile des Deux Lacs, 1910): 3
Mercier, François (Sete, 1942): 1
Mercier, Robert (Club Francais, Racing Club de Paris, 1931–35): 7/3
Meresse, Emilien (SC Fivois, 1936): 1
Mesnier, Louis (Paris, 1904–13): 14/6
Meunier, Maurice (Etoile des Deux Lacs, 1909): 1
Meuris, Georges (Red Star, 1937): 1
Meyer, Maurice (Red Star, 1921): 1
Meynieu, Francis (Bordeaux, 1976): 1
Mezy, Michel (Nimes Olympique, 1970–73): 17/1
Micciche, Carmelo (Metz, 1987): 2/1
Michel, Henri (Nantes, 1967–80): 58/4
Michelin, Pierre (UA Sedan-Torcy, 1963–64): 5
Mihoubi, Ahmed (Toulouse, 1953): 1
Mindonnet, Roger (Nice, 1949): 4
Mistral, Louis (Red Star, Paris, 1920–23): 5
Mitoraj, Roland (St Etienne, 1967–68): 3
Moigneu, Henri (Tourquennoise, 1905–08): 7
Moizan, Alain (Monaco, Lyon, 1979–80): 7
Molitor, Marc (Strasbourg, Nice, 1970–73): 10/4
Monsallier, Jules (Stade Français, Red Star, Sete, 1928–36): 3
Montagne, Charles (Lille,): 3/1
Mony, Alexis (US Boulonnaise, 1920): 1
Mony, Pierre (US Boulonnaise, CA Sports Generaux, 1920–23): 5
Moreel, Georges (Racing Club de Paris, 1949): 1/2
Morel, Pg (Red Star, 1911): 2
Moulene, Georges (Paris,): 1
Mouton, Henri (Etoile des Deux Lacs, 1909): 5/1

Muller, Lucien (Stade de Reims, Real Madrid, [Sp], 1959–64):

Munzenberg, Reinhold (1931): 1/1

Mustapha, Ben M'barek (Bordeaux, 1950): 1

N'Gotty, Bruno (Lyon, Paris St-Germain, 1994–97): 6

Nicol, Steve (1989): 1/1

Nicolai, Eugene (United Sports Club, 1905): 2

Nicolas, Jean (Rouen, 1933–38): 25/20

Nicolas, Paul (Red Star, Amiens, 1920–31): 34/20

Novi, Jacques (Marseille, 1969–72): 19

Novi, Jacques (Marseille, 1971): 1

Novicki, Edmond (Lens, 1936–37): 2/1

Nuic, Aime (Metz, 1935–36): 2

Olagnier, Louis (Gallia Club Lunel, 1920): 1

Oliver, Celestin (UA Sedan-Torcy, 1953–58): 5/3

Olivier, Maurice (Etoile des Deux Lacs, 1910–14): 6

Orlanducci, Charles (Bastia, 1975): 1

Osman, Jean-Claude (Nantes, 1973): 1

Ouedec, Nicolas (Nantes, Barcelona [Sp], 1994–97): 7/1

Ourdouille, Marcel (Lens, 1945): 1

Ouvray, Georges (Paris, 1928): 1/1

Pacot, J (CA Pierrefitte, 1909): 1

Paille, Stephane (Sochaux-Montbeliard, 1986–89): 8/1

Papi, Claude (Bastia, 1973–78): 3

Papin, Jean-Pierre (Club Brugge [Bel], Marseille, AC Milan [Ita], Bayern Munich [Ger], 1986–95): 54/30

Parachini, Antoine (Cette, 1924): 3

Pardo, Bernard (SC Toulon et du Var, Bordeaux, Marseille, 1988–91): 13

Parizon, Patrick (Lille,): 3/1

Parsys, Albert (Tourquennoise, 1914–20): 5

Passi, Gerald (Toulouse, 1987–88): 11/2

Pavillard, Henri (Stade Français, 1928–32): 14/1

Payen, Michel (Rouen, 1937): 3

Pazur, Antoine (Lille, 1953): 1

Pecout, Eric (Nantes, 1979–80): 5/1

Pedros, Reynald (Nantes, Marseille, 1993–96): 22/3

Penverne, Armand (Stade de Reims, Red Star, 1952–59): 39/2

Perez, Christian (Paris St-Germain, 1988–92): 21/2

Peri, Robert (Stade Français, Bordeaux, 1965–67): 3

Petel, E (AS Alfortvillaise, 1910): 1

Petit, Emmanuel (Monaco, Arsenal [Eng], 1990–98): 25/2

Petit, Jean (Monaco, 1977–80): 12/1

Petit, Rene (Stade Bordelais, 1920): 2

Peyroche, Georges (St Etienne, 1960–61): 3

Piantoni, Roger (Nancy, Stade de Reims, 1952–61): 29/6

Piasecki, Francis (Strasbourg, 1978): 3

Picy, Jean (Pantin,1914): 1

Pinel, Marcel (Red Star, 1930): 7/4

Pintenat, Robert (Sochaux-Montbeliard, 1976): 3/1

Pires, Robert (Metz, 1996–98): 16/2

Pironti, Felix (Marseille, 1944): 1

Piumi, Jean-Claude (US Valenciennes-Anzin, 1962–67): 4/1

Platini, Michel (AS Nancy-Lorraine, St Etienne, Juventus [Ita], 1979–87): 62/41

Pleimelding, Pierre (Lille, 1978): 1

Pleimelding, Rene (Toulouse, 1953): 1

Poirier, Paul (Red Star, 1933): 1

Polge, Albert (Nimes, 1933–34): 3

Pouget, Cyrille (Metz, 1996): 3

Poullain, Andre (Club Sports Athletiques, 1913): 3/2

Poullain, Fabrice (Paris St-Germain, 1985–88): 10

Pozo, Felix (Rouen, 1925): 1

Prouff, Jean (Stade Rennais, Stade de Reims, 1946–49): 13/1

Provelli, Louis (US Valenciennes-Anzin, 1967): 1

Prunier, William (Auxerre, 1992): 1

Puget, Andre (Racing Club de Paris, 1907): 1

Quenolle, Roger (Racing Club de Paris, 1949): 2

Quittet, Claude (Sochaux-Montbeliard, Nice, 1967–73): 16

Rahis, Bernard (Nimes Olympique, 1959–61): 3/1

Rambert, Angel (Lyon, 1962–64): 5/1

Rampillon, Gilles (Nantes, 1976–80): 3/1

Ranzoni, Pierre (Stade Français-Red Star, Le Havre, 1949–50): 2

Ravier, Daniel (Lyon, 1973): 2

Remetter, Francois (Metz, Sochaux-Montbeliard, Bordeaux, Limoges, 1953–59): 26

Renaux, Andre (Roubaix, 1908): 1

Renaux, Charles (Roubaix, 1908): 1

Renier, Albert (Le Havre, 1920–24): 4/1

Repellini, Pierre (St Etienne, 1973): 4

Revelli, Herve (St Etienne, Nice, 1966–75): 23/12

Revelli, Patrick (St Etienne, 1973–77): 5/1

Rey, Andre (Metz, 1977–79): 10

Rico, Robert (Stade Rennais UC, 1970): 1

Rigal, Jean (AF Garenne Colombes, 1909–12): 11/1

Rio, Patrice (Nantes, 1976–78): 17

Rio, Roger (Rouen, 1933–37): 18/4

Robin, Claude (Nantes, 1966–67): 4

Robuschi, Laurent (Bordeaux, 1962–66): 5

Roche, Alain (Bordeaux, Paris St-Germain, 1988–96): 25/1

Rochet (CA Boulonnais, 1913): 1

Rocheteau, Dominique (St Etienne, Paris St-Germain, 1975–86): 49/13

Rodighiero, Daniel (Stade Rennais, 1965): 2

Rodriguez, Joseph (Olympique d'Antibes. 1932): 2/1

Rodriguez, Sauveur (Marseille, 1947): 1

Rodzik, Bruno (Stade de Reims, 1960–63): 21

Roessler, Henri (Red Star, 1942): 2

Rohr, Jean-Philippe (Monaco, 1987): 1

Rolhion, Roger (Olympique Montpellier, 1933): 4/2

Rollet, Andre (FEC Levallois, 1927): 4

Romano, Felix (Etoile des Deux Lacs, 1913): 1/1

Romano, Paul (Etoile des Deux Lacs, 1911–12): 3

Rose, Georges (Stade Rennais UC, 1934): 1

Rostagni, Jean-Paul (Monaco, Bordeaux, Paris St-Germain, Paris, 1969–73): 25

Roth, Alfred (Strasbourg, 1920): 1

Rouches, Antoine (Paris, 1921): 1

Rousset, Gilles (Sochaux-Montbeliard, Lyon, 1990–92): 2

Roussey, Laurent (St Etienne, 1982): 2/1

Rouyer, Oliver (AS Nancy-Lorraine, 1981): 18/3

Roy, Serge (Monaco, 1961): 1

Royet, Marius (US Parisienne, 1904–08): 9/2

Ruminski, Cesar (Lille, 1952–54): 7

Rust, Albert (Sochaux-Montbeliard, 1986): 1

Ryssen, Andre (Lille, 1922): 1

Sahnoun, Omar (Nantes, 1977–78): 6

Salva, Marcel (Racing Club de Paris, 1945–52): 13

Salvano, Henri (FC Blideen, 1926): 1/1

Samuel, Jean-Claude (Racing Club de Paris, 1945): 3

Sarramanga, Christian (St Etienne, 1973–76): 4

Sartorius, Emile (Roubaix, 1906–08): 5/2

Sassus, Jean-Luc (St Etienne, 1992): 1

Sauvage, Paul (Stade de Reims, US Valenciennes-Anzin, 1961–65): 6

Sauzee, Frank (Marseille, Monaco, Atalanta Bergamo [Ita], 1988–93): 39/9

Schaff, Albert (CA XIV, 1914): 1

Scharwath, Emile (Strasbourg, Racing Club de Paris, 1932–34): 8

Schmitt, Roland (Sete, Toulouse, 1939–42): 2

Schubart, Louis (Lille, 1906–08): 3

Schultz, Ernest (Toulouse, 1961): 1/1

Scotti, Roger (Marseille, 1950–56): 2

Secember, Jean (Tourquennoise, Excelsior AC, 1932–35): 4/5

Segalen, Yvon (Stade Français, 1929): 3

Sellier, Henri (Etoile des Deux Lacs, 1910): 1

Senac, Didier (Lens, Bordeaux, 1984–87): 3

Senac, Guy (Racing Club de Paris, 1960–61): 2

Sentubery, Raymond (Club Français, 1924–26): 3

Sergent, Victor (Racing Club de France, Stade Raphaelois, 1907–13): 4

Sesia, Georges (Nancy, 1948): 1

Seyler, Pierre (Strasbourg, 1928): 2/1

Siatka, Robert (Stade de Reims, 1960): 1

Siklo, Smid Ladislas (Lens, 1945): 4

Silvestre, Franck (Sochaux-Montbeliard, Sochaux, 1989–92): 11

Simba, Amara (Paris St-Germain, 1991–92): 3/2

Simon, Jacques (Nantes, Bordeaux, 1965–69): 15/1

Simonyi, Andre (Red Star, 1942–45): 4/1

Sinibaldi, Paul (Stade de Reims, 1950): 1

Sinibaldi, Pierre (Stade de Reims, 1946–48): 2

Six, Didier (U.S.Valenciennes-Anzin, Lens, Marseille, Cercle Brugge [Bel], VfB Stuttgart [Ger], Mulhouse, 1976–84): 52/13

Six, Pierre (Lille, 1908): 1

Skiba, Henri (Nice, Stade Français, 1959–61): 3

Soler, Gerard (Sochaux-Montbeliard, Bordeaux, Toulouse, 1974–83): 15/4

Soler, Gerrad (Monaco, 1978): 1

Sollier, Andre (CA Vitry, 1909): 5

Sonor, Luc (Monaco, 1987–89): 9

Sottiault, Julien (US Saint Thomas, 1927): 5/1

Specht, Leonard (Strasbourg, Bordeaux, 1978–85): 18/1

Stako, Edouard (US Valenciennes-Anzin, Stade Français, 1959–64): 3/1

Stievenard, Michel (Lens, 1960): 2

Stopyra, Julien (AS Troyenne Savinienne, 1960): 1

Stopyra, Yannick (Sochaux-Montbeliard, Toulouse, 1980–88): 33/11

Strappe, Andre (Lille, 1949–54): 23/4

Stricanne, Marceau (Le Havre, 1951): 1

Stuttler, Georges (Red Star, 1926): 1

Suaudeau, Jean-Claude (Nantes, 1966–67): 4

Swiatek, Jean (Bordeaux, 1944–50): 5

Synaeghel, Christian (St Etienne, 1974–77): 5

Szczepaniak, Robert (Metz, 1967–68): 5

Taillandier, Jean (Racing Club de Paris, 1960): 3

Taisne, Georges (Amiens,1927): 3/2

Tassin, Andre (Racing Club de France, 1932): 5

Tellechea, Joseph (Sochaux-Montbeliard, 1955–59): 3/1

Tempet, Jean-Pierre (Stade Levallois, 1982–83): 5

Tempowski, Boleslav 'Bolek' (Lille, 1947): 1

Tessier (AS Bon Conseil,l 1909–10): 5

Thedie, Maurice (Amiens, 1925): 1

Theo, Szkudlapsk (Monaco, 1962–63): 2

Thepot, Alex (FEC Levallois, Armoricaine de Brest , Red Star, 1927–35): 31

Thouvenel, Jean-Christophe (Bordeaux, 1983–87): 4

Thuram, Lilian (Monaco, AC Parma [Ita], 1994–98): 37/2

Tibeuf, Philippe (St Etienne, 1990): 2

Tigana, Jean (Lyon, Bordeaux, 1981–88): 52/1

Tillette, Maurice (US Boulonnaise, 1908): 2

Tossier, Ernest (Patronage Olier, 1909): 1

Touffait, Adolphe (Stade Rennais UC, 1932): 1

Toure, Jose (Nantes, Bordeaux, Monaco, 1983–89): 16/4

Tousset, Auguste (Etoile des Deux Lacs, 1910–13): 2/1

Tresor, Marius (Ajacio, Marseille, Bordeaux, 1971–83): 65/4

Trezeguet, David (Monaco, 1988): 11/2

Triantafilos, Yves (St Etienne, 1975): 1

Triboulet, Marcel (FEC Levallois, Racing Club de France, 1911–19): 6/2

Tusseau, Thierry (Nantes, Bordeaux, Racing Club de Paris, 1983–86): 22

Tylinski, Richard (St Etienne, 1957–60): 3

Ujlaki, Joseph (Nimes Olympique, Nice, Racing Club de Paris, 1952–60): 21/10

Vaast, Ernest (Racing Club de Paris, 1945–49): 15/11

Vahirua, Pascal (Auxerre, 1990–94): 22/1

Van Den Driessche, Maurice (Roubaix, 1908): 2

Van Sam, Guy (Racing Club de Paris, 1961): 3

Vanco, Marcel (Paris, Roubaix, 1920–23): 7

Vandooren, Jules (Lille, Stade de Reims, 1933–42): 22

Vandooren, Roger (Lille, CO Roubaix-Tourcoing, 1949–51): 4

Vanucci, Albert (Sochaux-Montbeliard, 1974): 2

Vascout, Henri (CA Vitry, 1910–11): 7

Vasse, Francois (Arras, 1934): 1

Veinante, Emile (Racing Club de France, 1929–40): 24/14

Verbrugge, J (AS Francaise, Red Star, 1906–11): 4

Vercruysse, Philippe (Lens, Bordeaux, Marseille, 1983–89): 12/1

Vergnes, Jacques (Nimes Olympique, 1971): 1/1

Verlet, Joseph (Paris, 1905/11): 7/1

Verriest, Georges (Roubaix, 1933–36): 14/1

Vial, F (CA Vitry, 1911): 1

Vialaret, J (CA XIV, 1908): 1

Vialmonteil, Henri (CA Vitry, 1911–13): 6/2

Vieira, Patrick (Arsenal [Eng], 1997–98): 9

Vignal, Rene (Racing Club de Paris, 1949–54): 17

Vignoli, Marcel (Paris, 1925): 2

Villaplane, Alexandre (Sete, Nimes Olympique, Racing Club de Paris, 1926–30): 25

Vincent, Jean (Lille, Stade de Reims, 1954–61): 46/22

Vogel, Remi (Monaco, 1987): 1

Voyeux, Paul (Lille, 1913): 1

Wagner, Roland (Strasbourg, 1979): 1/1

Wallet, Urbain (Amiens, 1925–29): 21

Walter, Marius 'Maik' (Lille, 1949–50): 2/1

Watteau, Michel (RC Sedan, 1966): 1

Wattine, Raymond (Roubaix, 1923): 1

Wawrzeniak, 'Wagi' Edouard (US Valenciennes Anziri, 1935): 1

Weiler, Walter (1935): 1

Weiskopf Edmond, 'Virage' (Metz, 1939): 1

Wendling, Jean (Stade de Reims, 1963): 26

Wibaut, Ursule (Lille, 1908): 1

Wild, Jacques (Stade Francais, 1927–29): 8

Wilkes, Charles (Le Havre, 1905–08): 4

Wisnieski, Maryan (Lens, 1955–63): 33/12

Xuereb, Daniel (Lyon, Lens, Paris St-Germain, 1981–89): 8/1

Zanon, Jean-Louis (St Etienne, 1983): 1

Zatelli, Mario (Racing Club de Paris, 1939): 1/1

Zehren, Charles (Metz, 1936): 1

Zeiger, J (US Parisienne, 1907): 1

Zenier, Bernard (Metz, AS Nancy-Lorraine, 1977–87): 5/1

Zermani, Emile (Marseille, 1935): 1

Zidane, Zinedine (Bordeaux, Juventus [Ita], 1994–98): 39/9

Zimako, Atre Jacques (St Etienne, Sochaux-Montbeliard, 1977–81): 13/2

Zimny, Simon (Stade de Reims, 1955): 1

Zitouni, Mustapha (Monaco, 1957–58): 4

Zvunka, Victor (Marseille, 1975): 1

DUTCH INTERNATIONAL PLAYERS' RECORDS

Aarts, Kees (ADO Den Haag, 1966): 1
Addicks, Wim (Ajax Amsterdam 1923): 3/2
Akkersdijk, Jack (Velocitas Breda 1908): 2/1
Alberts, Sjaak (Vitesse Arnheim, 1952): 4
Anderiesen, Wim (Ajax Amsterdam 1926–1939): 46
Angenent, Henk (Fortuna '54, 1957): 1
Appel, Bram (Fortuna '54, 1955–57): 11/8
Arntz, Peter (AZ '67 Alkmaar, Go Ahead Eagles, AZ '67 Alkmaar 1975–81): 5
Baay, Henri (Haarlem, 1921): 2
Bak, Aad (Feyenoord, 1956): 1956
Bakers, Piet (PSV Eindhoven, 1951): 124/29
Bakhuys, Beb (ZAC, HBS, 1928–37):
Balkestein, Luuk (Sparta, 1980): 1
Barendregt, Jaap (Feyenord, 1929): 1
Been, M (Feyenoord, 1984): 1
Beeuwkes, Reiner (DFC, 1905–10): 19
Beijers, George (VOC, 1919): 1
Bekker, Kees (HBS, 1906–08): 6
Bennaars, Rinus (DOSKO, Feyenoord, 1951–1963): 14/2
Bergholtz, Gerard (MVV, Feyenoord, RSC Anderlecht [Bel], 1961–67): 12
Berghuis, Frank (VVV Venlo, 1989): 1
Bergkamp, Dennis (Ajax Amsterdam, Inter Milan [Ita], Arsenal [Eng], 1990–1998): 64/35
Bergman, Ko (Blauw-Wit, 1937–47): 8/5
Biesbrouck, Louis (RCH, 1950–54): 18
Bieshaar, Arie (Haarlem, 1920–23): 4
Bijovet, Arie (DFC, 1913): 1
Bleijenberg, Wim (Rigtersbleek, 1953–54): 3
Blind, Danny (Sparta Rotterdam, Ajax Amsterdam, 1986–96): 42/1
Blinker, Regi (Feyenoord, 1993–94): 3
Blomvliet, Henk (Ajax Amsterdam, 1939): 2
Blume, Hans (Quick Nimegen, 1907): 1/1
Boelmans, Ter Spill Pieter (HFC, 1907): 3
Boerdam, Willem (Sparta Rotterdam, 1909–10): 2
Boeve, Peter (Ajax Amsterdam, 1982–86): 16
Bogarde, Winston (Ajax Amsterdam, AC Milan [Ita], FC Barcelona [Spa], 1995–98): 15
Bonsema, Otto (Velocitas G, GVAV, 1932–39): 6/3
Boomsma, Rein (Sparta Rotterdam, 1905): 2
Boskamp, Hans (Ajax Amsterdam, 1952–54):
Boskamp, Johannes (RWD Molenbeek [Belg], 1978):

Bosman, Johnny (Ajax Amsterdam, KV Mechelen [Belg], RSC Anderlecht [Belg], FC Twente, 1986–97): 30/16
Bosschart, Leo (Quick H, 1909–20): 19/1
Bosselaar, Tinus (Feyenoord, Sparta Rotterdam, 1955–62): 17/4
Bosveld, Henk 'Charly' (Spcl Enschede, 1962–64): 2
Bosz, Peter (Feyenoord, 1992–95): 6
Bouman, Piet (DFC, 1912–14): 9
Boutmy, Joop (HBS, 1912–14): 10/1
Bouvy, Nico (DFC, 1912–13): 9/4
Bouwmeester, Frans (NAC Breda, Feyenoord, 1959–68): 5
Bouwmeester, Gerrit (Haarlem, 1912): 1
Brandes, Joop (Feyenoord, 1949): 3/1
Brandts, Ernie (PSV Eindhoven, 1977–85): 28/5
Breeuwer, Klaas (Haarlem, 1924): 1
Breitner, Henk (ADO Den Haag, 1929–33): 6
Brocken, Bud (FC Groningen, 1983): 5
Brokamp, Willy (MVV, 1970–73): 6/6
Brokmann, Theo (Ajax Amsterdam, 1919): 1/1
Bronger, Wim (VOC, 1912): 1
Brooijmans, Jan (Willem II Tilburg, 1955–56): 2
Brouwers, A (NAC Breda, 1969): 1
Brull, Harry (Rapid Joda C, 1959): 2
Brusselers, Toon (PSV Eindhoven, 1955–62): 4/2
Buitenweg, David (UVV, 1921): 1
Buitenweg, Wout (UVV, Hercules, 1913–28): 11/14
Bul, Bertus (Feyenoord, 1923–26): 6
Bulder, Evert (Be Quick Groningen, 1920): 1
Bulder, Jaap (Be Quick Groningen, 1920–23): 6/6
Burgers, Joop (DWS Amsterdam, 1965): 1
Buwalda, Nico (Ajax Amsterdam, 1914): 2
Caldenhove, Bertus (DWS Amsterdam, 1935–40): 25
Camponi, Miel (HVV, 1921): 2
Canjels, Leo (NAC Breda, 1959): 3/2
Canti, Claudio (1993): 1/1
Carlier, Bart (Fortuna '54, 1955–57): 5/2
Choufoer, Herman (ADO Den Haag, 1940): 1
Clavan, Mick (ADO Den Haag, SHS, Holland Sport,): 27/7
Cocu, Philip (PSV Eindhoven, 1996–98): 24/4
Couperus, W (ADO Den Haag, 1970): 1
Cruyff, Johan (Ajax Amsterdam, FC Barcelona [Spa], 1966–77): 48/33
Cruyff, Jordi, (FC Barcelona [Spa],

Manchester United [Eng], 1996): 9/1
Davids, Edgar (Ajax Amsterdam, Juventus [Ita], 1994–98): 16/1
De Bock, Charles (Bloemendaal, 1936): 1/1
De Boer, Frank (Ajax Amsterdam, 1990–98): 61/6
De Boer, Jan (Ajax Amsterdam, 1923–24): 5
De Boer, Piet (KFC, 1937): 1/3
De Boer, Ronald (Ajax Amsterdam, 1993–98): 45/10
De Bruijckere, Sjel (Willem II Tilburg, 1954–56): 7/2
De Bruin, Sjaak (Hermes-DVS, 1929–30): 3
De Bruyn, Kops Frans (HBS, 1906–08): 3
De Goey, Ed (Feyenoord, Chelsea [Eng], 1992–98): 3
De Graaf,12/1 Frits (Limburgia, 1950): 3/2
De Groot, Huug (Sparta, 1912–14): 9/6
De Haas, Theo (Be Quick Groningen, 1923–26): 4/1
De Harder, Bertus (VUC, Holland Sport, 1938–55): 13/1
De Jong, Aad (ADO Den Haag, 1950–52): 5
De Jong, Jerry (PSV Eindhoven, 1990–91): 3
De Jong, Theo (NEC Nijmegen, Feyenoord, 1972–74): 15/3
De Kock, Johan (FC Utrecht, Roda JC Kerkrade, Shalke 04 [Ger], 1993–97): 13/
De Korver, Bok (Sparta Rotterdam, 1905–13): 31/1
De Kreek, Jan (Go Ahead Eagles, 1930): 3
De Kruijff, Andre (Ajax Amsterdam, 1921): 1
De Leeuw, Huib (Willem II Tilburg, 1929): 2
De Munck, Frans (Sittardse Boys, Fortuna '54, DOS Utrecht, 1949–60): 31
De Natris, Jan (Ajax Amsterdam, de Spartaan, Vitesse Arnheim, 1920–25): 23/4
De Neve, Eddy (Velocitas Breda, HBS, 1905–06): 3/6
De Seriere, Guus (HVV, 1911–12): 2
De Vos Willy (DFC, 1905): 2
De Vries, Ab (VSV, 1940): 1
De Vries, Piet (Sparta, 1959): 1
De Vroet, Arie (Feyenoord, 1938–49): 20
De Wit, Rob (Ajax Amsterdam, 1985–86): 8/3
De Wolf, John (FC Groningen, Feyenoord, 1987–94): 6/1
De Wolf, Nico (Haarlem, 1910–13): 5
De Zoete, Piet (ADO Den Haag, 1966–67): 3
De, Kessler 'Tonny' (HVV, 1909–22): 21/9

Dekker, C (FC Amsterdam, 1974): 1

Delsen, Hein (Ajax Amsterdam, 1921–22): 3

Denis, Harry (HBS, 1919–30): 56

Dijkstra, Hennie (ZFC, 1939): 2

Dillen, Coen (PSV Eindhoven, 1954–57): 5/4

Doesburg, Pim (Sparta Rotterdam, PSV Eindhoven, 1967–81): 8

Dozy, Iman (Ajax L, 1907): 4

Drager, Guus (DWS Amsterdam, Ajax Amsterdam, 1939–48): 13/5

Drok, Daaf (RFC, Sparta Rotterdam, 1935–40): 8/4

Drost, Epi (FC Twente 65, 1969–73): 9

Duijnhouwer, Toon (Feyenoord, 1933): 1

Dullens, Willy (Sittardia, 1966): 4

Dumortier, Piet (DOS Utrecht, 1938): 1

Dusbaba, Johnny (RSC Anderlecht [Belg], 1977–78): 4

Eijkenbroek, Hans (Sparta Rotterdam, 1967–70): 18

Elfring, Jan (Alcmaria Victrix, 1926–28): 15/2

Ellerman, Juul (PSV Eindhoven, 1989–1991): 5

Engelsman, Han (Quick Nijmegen, 1948): 1/1

Eshuijs, Jo (Sparta Rotterdam, 1906): 1

Everse, Jan (Neptunus, 1949): 4

Everse, II Jan (Feyenoord, 1975): 2

Eykelkamp, Rene (FC Groningen, KV Mechelen [Belg], PSV Eindhoven, 1988–1995): 6

Faber, (1998): 1

Feith, Constant (HVV, 1906–12): 8/2

Felix, Huub (MVV, 1919): 1

Flinkevleugel, Frits (DWS Amsterdam, 1964–67): 11

Formenoy, Ok (Sparta Rotterdam, 1924–31): 4/4

Fortgens, Ge (Ajax Amsterdam, 1911–12): 8

Francken, Jacques (HFC, 1914): 1/1

Francken, Mannes (HFC, 1906–14): 22/17

Fransen, Piet (GVAV, Feyenoord, 1964–66): 5/1

Fraser, Henk (Roda JC Kerkrade, Feyenoord, 1989–92): 6

Freese, Bertus (Heracles, 1928): 1

Geel, Piet (PVV, 1955): 1

Geels, Ruud (Club Brugge [Belg], Ajax Amsterdam, RSC Anderlecht [Belg], PSV Eindhoven, 1974–81): 20/11

Gerritse, Adje ('t Gooi, 1929): 1

Geurtsen, Frans (DWS Amsterdam, 1964): 1/1

Ghering, Leo (LONGA, 1927–28): 9/6

Gielens, Jan (Hercules, Willem II Tilburg, 1925–26): 9/1

Giesen, Piet (PSV Eindhoven, 1963): 1

Gillhaus, Hans (PSV Eindhoven, Aberdeen [Sco], Vitesse Arnheim, 1987–94): 5/2

Gleenewinkel, Kamperd Karel (HBS, 1905): 2

Gobel, Just (Vitesse Arnheim, 1911–19): 22

Gonsalves, Vic (HBS, 1909–10): 3

Grobbe, Jaap (De Spartaan,1922): 1

Grobbe, Maarten (Excelsior Rotterdam, 1928–29): 2/1

Groen, Appie (Be Quick Groningen, 1922–26): 5/1

Groenendijk, Wim (Feyenoord, 1930): 1

Groeneveld, Piet (Haarlem, 1951): 3

Groosjohan, Ber (VOC, 1920–24): 14/5

Groot, Henk (Ajax Amsterdam, Feyenoord, 1960–69): 39/12

Groskamp, Wim (Quick H, 1908): 1

Gruisen, Gerard (Sittardia, 1953–54): 3

Gullit, Ruud (Haarlem, Feyenoord, PSV Eindhoven, AC Milan [Ita], Sampdoria [Ita], 1981–94): 64/17

Gupffert, Wim (Ajax Amsterdam, 1919–21): 3/2

Haak, Guus (ADO Den Haag, Feyenoord, 1962–63): 14

Haak, Jur (Haarlem, 1912–13): 2/2

Haan, Arie (Ajax Amsterdam, RSC Anderlecht [Belg], 1972–80): 35/6

Haenen, Chiel (MVV Maastricht, 1964): 1

Hakkens, (1980): 1/1

Halle, Jan (Go Ahead Eagles, 1929): 2

Halle, Leo (Go Ahead Eagles, 1928–37): 15

Hansen, Harald (B 93, 1912): 1/1

Hasselbaink, Jimmy Floyd (Leeds United [Eng], 1998): 4/2

Hassink, Jan (PSV Eindhoven, 1926): 2

Heetjans, Lulof (PEC, 1937): 1

Heijnen, Dolf (HVV, 1923): 2/1

Heijnen, Harry (ADO Den Haag, 1966): 1

Heijning, John (HVV, 1907–12): 8

Heijting, Karel (HVV, 1907–10): 17

Helder, Glen (Vitesse Arnhem, Arsenal [Eng], 1995): 4

Hendriks, Wim (Vitesse Arnheim, 1952–53): 3

Henny, Max (HFC, 1907): 1

Hesselink, Willem (Vitesse Arnheim, 1905): 1/1

Hiele, Joop (Feyenoord, SVV Schiedam, 1980–91): 7

Hoekema, Oeki (PSV Eindhoven, 1971): 1/1

Hoekstra, Andre (Feyenoord, 1984): 1/2

Hoekstra, Peter (Ajax Amsterdam, 1995): 5

Hofkens, Wim (RSC Anderlecht [Belg], KV Mechelen [Belg], 1983–89): 5

Hofma, Gerben (Heerenveen, 1950): 3

Hofman, Rene (Roda JC Kerkrade, 1982): 1

Hollander, Dick (DWS Amsterdam, 1964): 1

Holleman, Jan (VUC 1946): 3

Homborg, Frans (Blauw-Wit, 1929): 2

Hoogstede, Ben (NAC Breda, 1921): 4

Horburger, Arnold (VOC, 1910–12): 8

Hordijk, Henk (Ajax Amsterdam, 1919–22): 9

Horsten, Gerrit (Willem II Tilburg, Vitesse Arnheim, 1924–28): 6

Houtkooper, Martin (Haarlem, 1919): 1

Houtman, Peter (Feyenoord, FC Groningen, 1983–85): 8/6

Houwaart, Henk (1969): 1

Hovenkamp, Hugo (AZ '67 Alkmaar, 1977–83): 31/2

Huiberts, Max (Roda JC Kerkrade, 1993): 1

Huijbregts, Cor (BVV, 19550): 3

Huistra, Pieter (FC Twente, Rangers [Sco], 1988–91): 8

Hulshoff, Barry (Ajax Amsterdam, 1971–73): 14/6

Hulsman, Gerrit (Go Ahead Eagles, Feyenoord, 1921–23): 4

Irvine, Brian (1994): 1/1

Israel, Rinus (DWS Amsterdam, Feyenoord, 1964–74): 47/3

Jansen, Nico (FC Amsterdam, 1975): 1

Jansen, Wim (Feyenoord, 1967–80): 65/1

Janssen, Willem (PW, 1907): 3

Janssen Willy, (PSV Eindhoven, 1981): 1

Jeuring, Jan (FC Twente, 1971–73): 2

Jol, Martin (FC Twente, 1980–81): 3

Jole, Jo (Willem II Tilburg, 1923): 2

Jongbloed, Jan (DWS Amsterdam, FC Amsterdam, Roda JC Kerkrade, 1962–78): 24

Jonk, Wim (Ajax Amsterdam, Inter Milan [Ita], PSV Eindhoven, 1992–98): 57/11

Jonker, Jos (AZ '67 Alkmaar, 1980–81): 2

Jurgens, Herman (Sparta Rotterdam, 1908): 2

Keizer, Gerrit (Ajax Amsterdam, 1934): 2

Keizer, Piet (Ajax Amsterdam, 1962–74): 34/11

Kemper, Peter (PSV Eindhoven, 1964–67): 3

Kerkhoffs, Pierre (Spcl Twente 65, PSV Eindhoven, Lausanne Sports, 1960–65): 5

Kerkum, Gerard (Feyenoord, 1960): 1

Kessler, Boelie (HVV, 1919–22): 9/2

Kessler, Dolf (HVV, 19050–06): 3

Kessler, Tonny (HVV, 1907–13): 3/1

Kieft, Wim (Ajax Amsterdam, Pisa SC [Ita], Torino [Ita], PSV Eindhoven, Bordeaux [Fra], PSV Eindhoven, 1981–93): 42/11

Kische, Gerd (FC Hansa Rostock [Ger], 1978): 1/1

Kist, Kees (AZ '67 Alkmaar, 1975–80): 21/4

Klaassens, Jan (VVV, Feyenoord, 1953–63): 56/1

Klijnjan, Jan (DFC, Sparta Rotterdam, 1967–72): 11/

Kluin, Jo (AGOVV, 1928): 1

Kluivert, Patrick (Ajax Amsterdam, AC Milan [Ita], 1994–98): 21/12

Koeman, Erwin (FC Groningen, KV Mechelen [Belg], PSV Eindhoven, FC Barcelona [Spa], 1983–94): 31/

Koeman, Martin (GVAV, 1964): 1

Koeman, Ronald (FC Groningen, Ajax Amsterdam, PSV Eindhoven, FC Barcelona [Spa], 1983–94): 78/13

Koevermans, Wim (Fortuna Sittard, 1988): 1

Kok, Jan (UD, 1908): 1

Koolhof, Jurrie (PSV Eindhoven, 1982–83): 5

Kools, Cor (NAC Breda, 1928–30): 18/3

Koonings, Adriaan (Feyenoord, 1924): 1

Koopal, Coy (VVV Venlo, Willem II Tilburg, 1956): 6/2

Koot, Addick (PSV Eindhoven, 1988–89): 3

Koster, Adri (Roda JC Kerkrade, 1978): 3

Kraak, Piet (Stormvogels, 1946–52): 31

Kraay, Hans (DOS Utrecht, Feyenoord, 1957–64): 8

Kreek, Michel (Go Ahead Eagles, 1993–95): 2

Kreijermaat, Reiner (Feyenoord, 1961): 2

Krijgh, I Kees (BVV, 1950): 1

Krijgh, II Kees (PSV Eindhoven, 1975):

Krol, Ruud (Ajax Amsterdam, Vancouver Whitecaps [Can], Napoli [Ita], 1969–83): 83/3

Krom, Peer (RCH Haarlem, 1926–28): 14/1

Kruiver, Piet (PSV Eindhoven, Feyenoord, 1957–65): 22/22

Kruzen, Hendrie (FC Den Bosch, PSV Eindhoven, KV Kortrijk [Belg], 1987–89): 5

Kuchlin, Therus (HBS, 2925–26): 3/1

Kuipers, Frits (HFC, 1920–23): 5

Kuneman, Harry (HBS, 1908): 1

Kuneman, Jampie (HBS, 1951): 2

Kuppen, Gerard (Feyenoord, Sittard, 1937–46): 3

Kuys, Kees (Haarlem, NAC Breda, 1955–62): 43

La, Chapelle Lo (HVV, 1907): 1

La, Ling Tschenu (Ajax Amsterdam, 1977–82): 14/2

Laamers, Martin (Vitesse Arnheim, 1989–90): 2

Lagarde, Piet (DHC, Spec Enschede, 1962): 2

Lagendaal, Wim (Xerxes, 1930–35): 15/13

Lagerwaard, H (Excelsior Rotterdam, 1953): 1

Lakenberg, Wim (NEC, 1947–50): 2

Landaal, Gep (AGOVV, 1929–30): 10/2

Landman, Wim (Sparta Rotterdam, Holland Sport, SHS, 1952–56): 7

Lankhaar, Joop (Den Haag, 1987): 1

Laseroms, Theo (Sparta Rotterdam,1965–70): 6/1

Latuheru B, (Vitesse, 1989): 1

Le, Fevre Andre (Kampong, 1922–25): 17/1

Legger, Herman (Be Quick Groningen, 1921–22): 2

Lens, Anton (HBS, 1906): 2

Lenstra, Abe (Heerenveen, Spcl Enschede, 1940–59): 46/3

Lietzen, Feike (Blauw–Wit, 1922): 1

Lokhoff, Ton (PSV Eindhoven, 1984–85): 2

Lotsy, Dirk (DFC, 1905–14): 10/1

Louer, Frits (NOAD, 1952–54): 3/1

Lubse, Harry (PSV Eindhoven, 1975): 1/1

Lugthart, Klaas (Be Quick Groningen, 1952): 2

Luiten, Cor (DOS Utrecht, 1953–54): 4

Lungen, Charles (AFC, 1937): 1

Lutjens, Guus (Velocitas Breda, IIVV, 1905–11): 14/5

Maas, Rob (1993): 1

Macneill, Dick (HVV, 1920): 7

Makaay, Roy (Vitesse Arnhem, 1996–97): 2

Mansveld, Aad (FC Den Haag, 1972–73): 6

Massy, Pierre (Roermond, 1926–28): 12/3

Meijer, Erik (MVV Maastricht, 1993): 2

Meijer, H (Ajax Amsterdam, 1987): 1

Meijers, Pauke (NEC, 1953):

Menzo, Stanley (Ajax Amsterdam, 1989–92): 6

Mertens, Sjef (Willem II Tilburg, 1950): 1

Mesman, Ferry (Blauw-Wit, 1950): 1

Metgod, Edward (Haarlem, 1982): 1

Metgod, Johann (AZ '67 Alkmaar, 1981): 1

Metgod, Johnny (AZ '67 Alkmaar, Real Madrid [Spa], 1978–83): 20/4

Meutstege, Willem (Sparta, 1976): 1

Michel, Niek (VSV, 1940): 1

Michels, Rinus (Ajax Amsterdam, 1950–54): 6

Mijnals, Humphrey (Elinkwijk, 1960): 3

Mijnders, Kees (DFC, 1934–38): 7

Mol, Jaap (KFC, 1931–34): 5/1

Molenaar, Keje (Ajax Amsterdam, 1980–81): 2

Mols, Michael (Twente Enschede, 1995–98): 3

Mommers, H (Willem II Tilburg, 1920): 1

Moring, Hennie (Spcl Enschede, 1947–49): 6

Moulijn, Coen (Feyenoord, 1956–69): 37/4

Muhren, Arnold (FC Twente Enschede, Ipswich Town [Eng], Ajax Amsterdam, 1978–88): 23/2

Muhren, Gerrit (Ajax Amsterdam, 1969–73): 10

Mul, Evert (HBS, 1936): 1

Mulder, Youri (Schalke 04 [Ger], 1994–96): 8/3

Mulder, I Jan (RSC Anderlecht [Bel], 1967–70): 5/1

Mulders, Eef PSV Eindhoven, 1971(): 1

Mulders, Henk (Ajax Amsterdam, 1930–33): 2/1

Muller, Bennie (Ajax Amsterdam, 1960–69): 43/2

Muller, Henk (Quick H, 1906): 2/1

Mundt, Miel (HVV, 1908–09): 4

Nagels, Gerrit (1928–33): 3

Nanninga, Dick, (Roda JC Kerkrade, 1978–81): 15/6

Neeskens, Johan (Ajax Amsterdam, FC Bracelona [Spa], Cosmos [USA], 1970–81): 49/18

Noorduijn, Jan (HVV, 1914): 4

Notermans, Jan (Fortuna '54, 1956–60): 24/2

Notten, Rene (FC Twente,Ajax Amsterdam, 1974–75): 5

Numan, Arthur (PSV Eindhoven, 1992–98): 37

Nuninga, Klas (GVAV Ajax Amsterdam, 1963–67): 19/4

Odenthal, Joop (Haarlem, Spcl Enschede, 1951–56): 1

Oldenburg, Kees (Stormvogels, 1926): 1

Ondrus, Anton (1976): 1/1

Oosthoek, Jan (Sparta Rotterdam, 1924): 2

Ophof, Epo (Ajax Amsterdam, 1981–85): 15/2

Oprinsen, Toon (NOAD, 1934): 1

Otten, Louis(Quick H, 1907–11): 12

Otto, H (FC Amsterdam, 1975): 1

Ouderland, Piet (Ajax Amsterdam, 1962–63):

Overbeeke, Louis (DOSKO, 1953–54): 3

Overmars, Marc (Ajax Amsterdam, Arsenal, 1993–98): 46/10

Overweg, Niels (FC Twente, 1975): 4

Paauwe, Bas (Feyenoord, 1932–46): 31/1

Paauwe, Jaap (Feyenoord, 1931–32): 8

Pahlplatz, Theo (FC Twente 65, 1967–72): 13/3

Pantzarios, Nikos (1985): 1/1

Peeper, Marcel (1990): 1

Pellikaan, Henk (LONGA, 1932): 13

Pelser, Fons (Ajax Amsterdam, 1921–22): 6

Peltzer, Herman ('t Zesde, 1909): 1

Peters, Jan (NEC Nijmegan, AZ '67 Alkmaar, 1974–82): 31/4

Peters, II Jan (Feyenoord, 1979): 1

Petersen, Peter (Ajax Amsterdam, 1962–63): 4/1

Petit, Frans (NAC Breda, 1922): 1

Petterson, Ferry (Blauw-Wit, 1922): 2

Pieters, Graafland Eddy (Ajax Amsterdam, Feyenoord, 1957–67): 47

Pijl, Kees (Feyenoord, 1924–26): 9/7

Pijs, Miel (PSV Eindhoven, Sparta Rotterdam, 1965–68): 8/1

Poortvliet, Jan (PSV Eindhoven, 1978–82): 19/1

Potharst, Jan (Ajax Amsterdam, 1945–50): 8

Poulus, Jan (SVV, 1940): 1

Prins, Co (Ajax Amsterdam, 1FC Kaiserslautern, 1960–65): 10/3

Pronk, Tonny (Ajax Amsterdam, 1961–69): 19

Punt, Piet (DFC, 1937): 1

Quadackers, Willy (Fortuna '54, 1964): 1

Quax, Kees (ADO Den Haag, 1926): 3

Ramseyer, Rudolf (1929): 1/1

Reekers, Rob (VfL Bochum, 1988–89): 4

Reeman, Jops (Quick H, 1908): 2/1

Reina, Miguel (1973): 1/1

Reiziger, Michael (Ajax Amsterdam, AC

Milan[Ita], FC Barcelona [Spa], 1994–98): 28

Renders, Jan (PSV Eindhoven, 1962): 4

Rensenbrink, Rob (DWS Amsterdam, Club Brugge[Belg], RSC Anderlecht [Belg], 1968–79): 46/14

Rep, Johnny (Ajax Amsterdam, Valencia CF [Spa], Bastia [Fra], St Etienne [Fra], 1973–1981): 41/12

Ressel, Peter (Feyenoord, 1974): 3

Rijkaard, Frank (Ajax Amsterdam, Real Zaragoza [Spa], AC Milan, 1981–94): 73/8

Rijnders, Nico (Go Ahead Eagles, 1969–70): 8

Rijsbergen, Wim (Feyenoord, 1974–78): 28/1

Rijvers, Kees (NAC Breda, Feyenoord, 1946–60): 32/10

Rodermond, Harry (Be Quick Groningen, 1921–22): 5/3

Roest, Rob (1993): 1/1

Roetert, Wim (Go Ahead Eagles, 1923): 1/2

Roggeveen, Sjaak (Holland Sport, 1969): 3/2

Romeijn, Piet ()Feyenoord, 1967–68: 4/1

Roosen, Wim (Haarlem, 1946–47): 7/1

Roosenburg, Andre (Neptunia/Sneek, 1948–55): 10/1

Roy, Bryan (Ajax Amsterdam, Foggia [Ita], Nottingham Forest [Eng], 1989–95): 32/9

Ruffelse, Cas (Sparta Rotterdam, 1907–20): 8/3

Ruisch, Eef (DFC, 1926–28): 7/2

Ruiter, Jan (RSC Anderlecht [Belg], 1976): 1

Rutjes, Graeme (KV Mechelen [Belg], RSC Anderlecht [Belg], 1989–91): 13/1

Rutten, Fred (FC Twente, 1988): 1

Saeys, Charles (1960): 1/1

Sandberg, Marius (HVV, 1926): 2

Saris, Dre (BVV, 1949): 1

Schaap, Rinus ('t Gooi, 1948–56): 13/1

Schapendonk, Kees (MVV Maastricht, 1981): 1/1

Scheeffer Dolf, (UD, 1927): 1

Schetters, Theo (Ajax Amsterdam, 1927): 1

Schijvenaar, Henk (EDO, 1947–51): 16

Schindeler, Jan (Blauw-Wit, 1925): 1

Schipper, Frits (Heracles, 1928): 1

Schneider, Dick (Feyenoord, 1972–74): 11/2

Schoemaker, Arend (Quich H, 1933): 1

Schoemaker, Jan (,HVV, 1906): 2

Schoenaker, Dick (Ajax Amsterdam, , 1978–85): 13/6

Schot, Joost (NAC Breda, 1922): 1

Schouten, Henk (Holland Sport, Feyenoord, 1955–61): 2

Schreurs, Harry (Roermond, 1928): 2

Schrijvers, Daan (NAC Breda, DWS Amsterdam, PSV Eindhoven, 1962–67): 22/1

Schrijvers, Piet (FC Twente,Ajax Amsterdam, PEC Zwolle, 1971–84): 46

Schrumpf, Jan (SVV, 1950): 2

Schubert, Jan (Ajax Amsterdam, 1939): 2

Schuurman, Carol (ADO Den Haag, 1958–61): 4

Seedorf, Clarence (Ajax Amsterdam, Sampdoria [Ita], Real Madrid [Spa], 1994–98): 32/7

Sigmond, Dick (DFC, HFC, 1923–27): 14/1

Silooy, Sonny (Ajax Amsterdam, Racing Club de Paris [Fra],Ajax Amsterdam, 1983–93): 24

Sissingh, Siebolt (Be Quick Groningen, 1921): 1

Slot, Kees (Blauw-Wit, 1940): 1

Smeets, Felix (HBS, 1927–29): 14/7

Smit, Kick (Haarlem, 1934–46): 29/26

Snelders, Theo (Aberdeen [Sco], 1989): 1

Snethlage, Edu (Quick H, 1907–09): 11/10

Snoek, Dick (Eindhoven, 1950–51): 3

Snouck, Hurgronje Albert (HVV, 1924–25): 6/1

Soetekouw, Frits (de Volewijckers, 1962): 1

Sol, John (HVV, 1908–09): 3

Soons, Sjo (MVV, 1922): 1

Spel, Piet (DWS Amsterdam, 1948): 1

Spelbos, Ronald (AZ '67 Alkmaar, Club Brugge [Belg],Ajax Amsterdam, 1980–87): 21/1

Stam, Bob (VUC, 1939–40): 4

Stam, Jaap (PSV Eindhoven,1996–98): 19/1

Steeman, Henk (Sparta Rotterdam, Quick Nijmegen, 1919–25): 1

Steenbergen, Frans (SVV, 1949): 2

Steenbergen, Piet (Feyenoord, 1950–55): 2

Steiger, Lieuwe (PSV Eindhoven, 1953–54):

Stempels, Noud (Quick H, 1908): 3

Stevens, Huub (PSV Eindhoven, 1979–85): 18/1

Stevens, Piet (Willem II Tilburg, 1921): 5

Stijger, Ko (Blauw-Wit, 1940–46): 2

Stoffelen, Joop (Ajax Amsterdam, 1947–50): 15

Stol, Peet (Haarlem, 1905): 2

Stom, Ben (Velocitas B/HFC, Velocitas Breda, HFC, 1905–08): 9

Strijbosch, P (1930): 1

Strik, Pleun (PSV Eindhoven, 1969–74): 8/1

Stroker, Gerrie (Ajax Amsterdam, 1947): 3

Sturing, Edward (1989–90): 3

Suurbier, Wim (Ajax Amsterdam, Metz, Schalke 04, 1966–78): 60/3

Suvrijn, Wilbert (Fortuna Sittard, Roda JC Kerkrade, 1986–88): 9

Swart, Sjaak (Ajax Amsterdam, 1960–72): 31/10

Tahamata, Simon (Ajax Amsterdam, Standard Liege [Belg],Feyenoord, 1979–86): 22/2

Tap, Gerard (ADO Den Haag, 1928): 1/2

Tap, Wim (ADO Den Haag, 1931): 35/15

Taument, Gaston (Feyenoord, 1992–96): 16/3

Tebak, Frans (Eindhoven, 1952–54): 10

Tekelenburg, Piet (Haarlem, 1919): 2

Ten, Cate Cees (HFC, 1912): 3/1

Ter, Beek Joop (NAC Breda, 1924): 1

Terlouw, Rinus (DCV, Sparta Rotterdam, 1948–54): 33

Tetzner, Hans (Be Quick Groningen, 1923–25): 8

Tetzner, Max (Be Quick Groningen, 1921–22): 3

Thijssen, Frans (FC Twente, Ipswich Town [Eng], 1975–81): 14/3

Thomee, Jan (Concordia, 1907–12): 16/16

Timmermans, Theo (ADO Den Haag, 1949–57): 12/4

Tol, Pier (AZ '67 Alkmaar, 1980–82): 5

Treijtel, Eddy (Feyenoord, 1969–76): 5

Troost, Sjaak (Feyenoord, 1987–88): 4

Trustfull, Orlando (Feyenoord, 1995): 2

Valckx, Stan (Sporting Lisbon,PSV Eindhoven, 1990–96): 20

Valke, Michel (PSV Eindhoven, Feyenoord, 1979–86): 16

Valkenburg, Piet (HBS, 1912): 1

Van Aerle, Berry (PSV Eindhoven, 1987–92): 35

Van Baar, Van Slangen Charles (HBS, 1924–25): 7/3

Van Basten, Marco (Ajax Amsterdam, AC Milan [Ita], 1983–92): 57/23

Van Beek, Jan (Quick K, 1907): 1

Van Berckel, Nol (Quick Nijmegen, 1910–12): 6/2

Van Beurden, Harry (Willem II Tilburg, 1920): 1

Van Beurden, Max (BVV, 1953–54): 5/1

Van Beveren, Jan (Sparta, PSV Eindhoven, 1967–77): 32

Van Boxtel, Piet (NAC Breda, 1927–28):7

Van Breda, Kolff Jan (HVV, 1911–13): 11/1

Van Breukelen, Hans (FC Utrecht, Nottingham Forest [Eng], PSV Eindhoven, 1980–92): 73

Van Bronckhorst, Giovanni (Feyenoord, 1996–97): 7/1

Van Buijtenen, Jan (Hermes-DVS, 1946): 1

Van Bun, Jeu (MVV, 1947–49): 10

Van Daalen, Wiggert (Haarlem, 1925): 1

Van de Griend, Jaap (Hermes-DVS, 1928–29): 5

Van Deinsen, Jan (Feyenoord, 1980): 1

Van Diepenbeek, Jan (Ajax Amsterdam, 1933–35): 4

Van Diermen, Herman (Blauw-Wit, 1920–21): 5

Van Dijk, Dick (FC Twente, Ajax, 1969–71): 7/1

Van Dijk, Ge (Ajax Amsterdam, 1947–48): 2

Van Dijk, Philip (Hercules, 1910): 1

Van Dijke, Kees (Feyenoord, 1925): 3

Van Dolder, Wim ('t Gooi, 1928–29): 3
Van Donkschot, (1982): 1/1
Van Dort, Joop (Ajax Amsterdam, 1920): 5
Van Duivenbode, Theo (Ajax Amsterdam, Feyenoord, 1968–70): 5
Van Ede, Tonny (Sparta Rotterdam,1953): 2
Van Gastel, Jean-Paul (Feyenoord, 1996–97): 2/1
Van Gelder, Koos (VUC, 1926–35): 5/1
Van Gendt, Jan (de Spartaan, 1921–22): 5/5
Van Gobbel, Ulrich (Feyenoord, 1993–94): 9
Van Gogh, Louis (HFC, 1907): 2/2
Van Gorp, Jan (NAC Breda, 1967): 1
Van Haeren, Tonny (Wilhelmina, 1926): 1
Van Hanegem, Wim (Feyenoord, AZ '67 Alkmaar, FC Utrecht, 1968–79): 52/5
Van Heckin,g-Colenbra Guus (Velocitas Breda, 1908): 1
Van Heel, Puck (Feyenoord, 1925–38): 65/2
Van Hemert, Barend (DFC, 1914): 1
Van Heyden, Felix (Quick Nijmegen, 1920): 1
Van Hooijdonk, Pierre (Celtic [Sco], Nottingham Forest [Eng], 1994–98): 15/6
Van Ierssel, Kees (FC Twente, 1973–74): 6
Van Kesteren, Hans (HBS, 1929): 1
Van Kol, Dolf (Ajax Amsterdam, 1925–31): 35/4
Van Kooten, Kees (Go Ahead Eagles, PEC Zwolle, 1981–83): 9/4
Van Kraay, Adri (PSV Eindhoven, 1975–79): 17
Van Leeuwen, Henk (FC Den Haag, 1978): 2/1
Van Leeuwen, Tonny (GVAV, 1967): 2
Van Leijden, Miel (HVV, 1910): 1
Van Leur, Gerard (DOS Utrecht, 1938): 1/1
Van Linge, Evert (Be Quick Groningen, 1919–26): 19/3
Van Loen, John (FC Utrecht, Roda JC Kerkrade, 1985–90): 7/1
Van Loon, Herman (Willem II Tilburg, 1929): 1
Van Male, Adri (Feyenoord, 1932–40): 15
Van Marwijk, Bert (Go Ahead Eagles, 1975): 1
Van Melis, Noud (Eindhoven, Rapid JC, 1950–57): 13/15
Van Mierlo, Toine (Willem II Tilburg, 1980): 3
Van Nee, Hennie (Heracles, 1964–65): 5/2
Van Nellen, Joop (DHC, 1928–37): 27/5
Van Nieuwenhuizen, Kees (Sparta Rotterdam, 1909): 2
Van Nus, Cor (Voorwaarts, 1926): 1
Van Overbeek, Piet (BVV, 1949): 2
Van Raalte, Herman (Blauw-Wit): 1
Van Rappard, Oscar (HBS, 1920): 4
Van Reenen, Piet (Ajax Amsterdam, 1930–33): 4/2

Van Renterghem, Toine (HBS, 1906–07): 3
Van Rijnsoever, Henk (AZ '67 Alkmaar, 1975): 1
Van Roessel, Eduard (NAC Breda, 1920): 2
Van Roessel, Jan (LONGA, Willem II Tilburg, 1949–55): 5/4
Van Run, Sjef (PSV Eindhoven, 1931–35): 25
Van Schijndel, Jan (SVV, 1949–55): 18/1
Van Son, Jos (Willem II Tilburg, 1923): 1
Van Spaandonck, Henk (Neptunas, 1937): 8/4
Van Tiggelen, Adri (FC Groningen, RSC Anderlecht [Belg],PSV Eindhoven, 1983–1992): 56
Van Tilburg, Henk (NOAD, 1921–22): 9
Van Veele, (1982): 1/1
Van Vossen, Peter (Ajax Amsterdam, RSC Anderlecht, [Belg], 1992–95): 18/7
Van Wissen, Fons (MVV, PSV Eindhoven, 1957–64): 30/4
Van Zwieteren, Willy (Sparta Rotterdam, 1929): 1
Van de Kerkhof, Rene (FC Twente,PSV Eindhoven, 1973–82): 47/5
Van de Kerkhof, Willy (PSV Eindhoven, 1974–85): 63/4
Van de Korput, Michel (Feyenoord, Torino [Ita], Köln [Ger], 1979–85): 23
Van de Luer, Eric (Roda JC Kerkrade, 1995): 1
Van de Merwe, Peter (NAC Breda, 1962): 5
Van den Bogert, Louis (DOS Utrecht, 1951–53): 3
Van den Broek, Jan (NAC Breda,PSV Eindhoven, 1927–33): 12/4
Van den Brom, John (Vitesse Arnheim, 1990–93): 2/1
Van den Engel, Herman (DHC, 1940): 1/1
Van den Hoek, Hans (Feyenoord, 1953–54): 2
Van den Hoven, Jo (LONGA, 1937): 1
Van der Gijp, Cor (Emma, Feyenoord, 1954–61): 13/6
Van der Gijp, Rene (Lokeren,PSV Eindhoven, 1982–87): 15/2
Van der Gijp, Wim (Emma, 1954): 1
Van der Hart, Cor (Fortuna '54, 1955–61): 43/2
Van der Heide, Joop (Feyenoord, 1940): 1
Van der Heijden, Evert (Wageningen, 1929–31): 9/1
Van der Hoeven, Cock (Ajax Amsterdam, 1950): 5
Van der Klink, F (Hermes-DVS, 1950): 1
Van der Kluft, Eb (Blauw-Wit, 1921–23): 4
Van der Kuil, Piet (VSV Ajax Amsterdam, PSV Eindhoven, 1952–62): 38/8
Van der Kuylen, Willy (PSV Eindhoven, 1966–77): 22/7
Van der Linden, Henk (Ajax Amsterdam, 1946–47): 7
Van der Linden, Tonny (DOS Utrecht, 1957–63): 23/12

Van der Luer, Eric (Roda JC Kerkrade, 1995): 1
Van der Meulen, Gejus (HFC, 1924): 56
Van der Nagel, Dolf (HFC, 1914): 1
Van der Poel, Frans (Velocitas Breda, 1923): 1
Van der Sar, Edwin (Ajax Amsterdam, 1995–98): 23
Van der Sluijs, Piet (BVV, 1949–50): 5
Van der Sluis, Jan (VOC, 1912): 1/2
Van der Tuyn, Cock (Hermes DVS, 1948–52): 9/2
Van der Veen, Freek (Heracles, 1938–40): 8/1
Van der Vinne, Ferry (HFC, 1906–07): 3/1
Van der Wildt, Koos (VUC, 1929–30): 9
Van der Wolk, Piet (Sparta Rotterdam, 1910–19): 6·
Van der Zalm, Kees (VUC, 1927–29): 3
Van't Schip, Johnny (Ajax Amsterdam, Genoa [Ita]1986–92): 40/2
Vanenburg, Gerald (Ajax Amsterdam, PSV Eindhoven, 1982–92): 42/1
Veenstra, Wietze (Go Ahead Eagles,PSV Eindhoven, 1968–70): 9/1
Veldhoen, Cor (Feyenoord, 1961–67): 27
Veldman, John (Sparta Rotterdam, 1996): 1
Venneker, Hans (Sparta Rotterdam, 1971–72): 4
Vente, Leen (Neptunus,Feyenoord, 1933–40): 21/19
Verdonk, Lambert (PSV Eindhoven, 1964): 4
Verlaat, Frank (AJ Auxerre [Fra], 1995): 1
Verlegh, Rat (NAC Breda, 1923–27): 7/2
Vermetten, Henk (HBS 1924–30): 7
Vermeulen, Pierre (Roda JC Kerkrade, Feyenoord, 1978–83): 9/1
Verweij, Ben (HFC, 1919–1924): 11
Vierklau, Ferdy (Vitesse Arnheim, 1996–97): 2
Villerius, Jan (ADO Den Haag, 1962): 1
Vink, Marciano (Ajax Amsterdam, 1991–93): 3
Vis, Rens (HVV, 1926): 1
Viscaal, Erik (AA Gent [Belg], KAA Gent [Belg], 1992): 5
Visser, Gerrit (Stormvogels, 1924–25): 7/1
Voges, Gerrit (Spcl Enschede, 1956): 2
Volkers, Wim (Ajax Amsterdam, 1924–32): 7/2
Vos, Jan (UVV, 1912–14): 15/10
Vosmaer, Bobby (AZ '67 Alkmaar, 1975): 2
Vrauwdeunt, Manus (Feyenoord, 1937): 1/1
Vreijsen, Martien (NAC Breda, 1980): 1
Vriens, Henk (Willem II Tilburg, 1963): 1
Vroomen, Heinz (Juliana, 1940): 1
Vurens, Edwin (FC Twente, 1995): 1
Walder, Chris (NAC Breda, 1921): 1
Wamsteker, Henk (ASC, HFC, 1925–29): 2
Warnas, Henk (Go Ahead Eagles, 1967–68): 5
Weber, Jaap (Sparta Rotterdam, 1927–28): 14/1

Weber, Mauk (ADO Den Haag, AGOVV,
    ADO Den Haag, 1931–37): 27
Welcker, Caius (Quick H, 1907–11): 17/5
Wels, Frank (Unitas, 1931–38): 36/5
Wery, Henk (DOS Urecht, DOS Utrecht,
    Feyenoord, 1967–73): 12/3
Westra, Van Holthe Willy (Achilles,
    1913–14): 3/1
Wiersma, Roel (Donar, PSV Eindhoven,
    1954–62): 52
Wiertz, Bram (DWS Amsterdam, 1951–52):
    7
Wijnstekers, Bennie (Feyenoord, 1979–85):
    36/1

Wijnveldt, David (UD, 1912–14): 13
Wilders, Cor (Blauw-Wit, 1937–46): 8
Wildschut, Piet (FC Twente,PSV
    Eindhoven, 1978–82): 11/1
Wilkes, Faas (Gornik Zabrze [Pol],
    Valencia CF [Spa], VVV Venlo, Fortuna
    '54, 1946–61): 35/30
Wille, J (EDO, 1940): 1
Winter, Aron (Ajax Amsterdam, Lazio
    [Ita], Inter Milan [Ita], 1987–98): 75/6
Witschge, Richard (Ajax Amsterdam, FC
    Barcelona [Spa], Girondins de Bordeaux
    [Fra], 1989–97): 29/1
Witschge, Rob (Ajax Amsterdam,

Feyenoord, Girondins de Bordeaux
    [Fra], 1989–96): 29/4
Wouters, Jan (FC Utrecht,Ajax
    Amsterdam, Bayern Munchen
    [Ger],PSV Eindhoven, 1982–94): 70/4
Zendan, Boudewijn (PSV Eindhoven,
    1998): 1
Zenden, Boudewijn (PSV Eindhoven,
    1997–98): 7/11
Zoetebier, Edwin (1993): 1
Zondervan, Romeo (FC Twente, 1981): 1
Zuidema, Johan (FC Twente, 1975): 2

Johan Neeskens shoots Holland ahead from the penalty spot after two minutes of the 1974 World Cup Final

SPANISH INTERNATIONAL PLAYERS' RECORDS

Ablanedo, Juan Carlos Iglesias, (Sporting Gijon, 1986–91): 4

Abelardo Fernandez, (Sporting Gijon, Barcelona, 1991–98): 40/2

Adelardo, Rodriguez (Atletico Madrid, 1962–67): 13/2

Acedo, Domingo (Athletic Bilbao, 1920–24): 11/1

Acuna Juan (Deportivo La Coruna,): 1

Aedo, Serafin (Betis Balompie Sevilla, 1935–36): 4

Aguilar, Francisco Javier (Real Madrid, 1971–73): 3

Aguilera, Carlos (Atletico Madrid, 1997–98): 6

Aguirre, Luis Maria (Athletic Bilbao, 1961–65): 7

Alabanda, Sebastian (Betis, 1976): 1

Alcantara, Paulino (Barcelona, 1921–23): 5/6

Alcazar, Antonio (Europa Barcelona, 1925): 2

Alconero, Pedro (Sevilla, 1948–49): 4

Aldana, Adolfo (Deportivo La Coruna, 1993–94): 4/1

Aldecoa, Emilio (Athletic Bilbao, 1948): 1

Alexanco, Jose Ramon (Athletic Bilbao, Barcelona, 1978–82): 34/4

Alfonso, (1998): 1

Alfonso Perez Munoz (Betis Sevilla, 1995): 25/8

Alkorta, Rafael (Athletic Bilbao, Real Madrid, 1990–98): 52

Alonso, Joaquin (Sporting Gijon, 1979–88): 18/1

Alonso, Angel (Real Zaragoza, 1978–80): 3

Alonso, Emilin (Real Madrid, 1936): 1

Alonso, Gabriel (Celta de Vigo, Real Madrid, 1948–52): 12

Alonso, Jesus (Real Madrid, 1942): 3

Alonso, Juan Adelarpe (Real Madrid, 1958–59): 2

Alonso, Miguel A (Real Sociedad San Sebastian, 1980–82): 19/1

Alsua, Rafael (Real Santander, 1954): 2/1

Alvarez, Armando (Deportivo La Coruna, 1996–97): 2

Alvarito, Alvaro Rodriguez (Atletico Madrid, 1960): 2

Amancio, Amaro Varela (Real Madrid, 1962–74): 42/11

Amavisca, Jose Emilio (Real Madrid, 1994–97): 15/1

Amor, Guillermo (Barcelona, 1990–98): 35/4

Andrinua, Genaro (Athletic Bilbao, 1987–90): 29/2

Ansola, Fernando (Real Betis Sevilla, Valencia, 1965–68): 5

Anton, Antonio M Martinez (Valencia, 1969–71): 5

Antunez, Francisco (Sevilla, 1949–51): 4

Aparicio, Alfonso (Atletico Aviacion Madrid, Atletico Madrid, 1945–49): 8

Arabolaza, Patricio (Real Union de Irun, 1920–21): 4/1

Aranaz, Luis (Osasuna Pamplona, 1937–38): 2

Aranzabal, Agustin (Real Sociedad San Sebastian, 1995–97): 5

Aranzabal, Matias (Real Sociedad San Sebastian, 1924–26): 2

Araquistain, Jose (Real Sociedad San Sebastian, Real Madrid, 1960–62): 6

Arbide, Eduardo (Real Sociedad San Sebastian, 1921): 1

Arconada, Luis Miguel (Real Sociedad San Sebastian, 1977–85): 68

Arencibia, Francisco (Atletico Aviacion Madrid, 1942): 1

Areso, Pedro (Betis Balompie Sevilla, 1935): 3

Areta, Esteban (Betis, 1961): 1

Argila, Fernando (Real Oviedo, 1954): 1

Argote, Estanislao (Athletic Bilbao, 1978): 2

Arias, Luis Manuel (Real Oviedo, 1989–92): 4

Arias, Ricardo Panella (Valencia, 1979): 1

Arieta I Ignacio (Athletic Bilbao, 1955): 3/2

Arieta II Anton (Athletic Bilbao, 1971–72): 7/4

Arizcorreta, Trino (Real Sociedad San Sebastian, 1928): 3

Arocha, Angel (Barcelona, 1931): 2/2

Arqueta, Salvador (Athletic Bilbao, 1942): 1

Arrate, Mariano (Real Sociedad San Sebastian, 1920–23): 6/1

Arrillaga, Antonio (Rcal Socicdad San Sebastian, 1927): 1

Arteche, Jose Luis (Athletic Bilbao, 1954–59): 6/1

Arteche, Juan Carlos (Atletico Madrid, 1986–87): 4/1

Artigas, Jose Salvador (Barcelona, 1949): 1

Artola, Juan (Real Sociedad San Sebastian, 1920): 2

Arza, Juan (Sevilla, 1947–52): 2

Asensi, Juan Manuel (Elche, Barcelona, 1972–80): 51/6

Asensi, Vicente (Valencia, 1945–50): 6

Augustin, (Celta de Vigo, 1938): 1

Ayestaran, Miguel (Real Sociedad San Sebastian, 1933): 1

Bakero, Jose Maria (Real Sociedad San Sebastian, Barcelona, 1987–94): 31/7

Ballester, Francisco (Elche, 1969): 1

Bango, Ricardo Gonzalez (Real Oviedo, 1990–91): 2

Banon, Jose (Real Madrid, 1947): 1

Barjaun, Sergi (Barcelona, 1994–98): 34/1

Barjuan, Esclusa Sergi (Barcelona, 1997): 1

Barrachina, Fernando (Valencia, 1969): 1

Barragan, Claudio (Deportivo La Coruna, 1992–93): 6

Basora, Estanislao (Barcelona, 1949–57): 22/13

Bata, Agustin Sauto (Athletic Bilbao, 1931): 1

Becerra, Herado (Atletico Madrid, 1973): 1

Beguiristain, Aitor (Real Sociedad San Sebastian, Barcelona, 1988–94): 22/6

Belauste, Jose Maria (Athletic Bilbao, 1920): 3/1

Belsue, Alberto (Real Zaragoza, 1994–96): 17

Benitez, Antonio (Betis Sevilla, 1974–77): 3

Benito, Gregorio (Real Madrid, 1971–78): 22

Berto, Alberto Martinez (Real Oviedo, 1991): 1

Bertol, Roberto (Athletic Bilbao, 1947–48): 2

Bertolin, Inocencio (Valencia, 1936): 1

Betancort, Antonio (Real Madrid, 1965): 2

Bienzobas, Francisco (Real Sociedad San Sebastian, 1928–29): 2/1

Bilbao, Sabino (Athletic Bilbao, 1920): 2

Biosca, Antonio (Real Betis de Sevilla, 1978): 3

Biosca, Gustavo (Barcelona, 1951–54): 11

Blasco, Gregoria (Athletic Bilbao, 1930–36): 5

Bonet, Francisco (Real Madrid, 1982–83): 4

Bosch, Andres (Barcelona, 1953–55): 6

Bosch, Crisanto (Barcelona, 1929–34): 8/1

Botubot, Manuel (Valencia, 1978): 1

Bravo, Jose (Barcelona, 1942): 1

Bustillo, Miguel Angel (Real Zaragoza, 1968–69): 5/1

Butragueno, Emilio (Real Madrid, 1984–92):69/26

Buyo, Francisco (Sevilla, Real Madrid, 1983–92): 7

Canito, Jose Cano (Barcelona, 1978): 1

Canito, Nicanor Trapero (Athletic Bilbao, 1957): 1

Caldere, Ramon Maria (Barcelona, 1985–88): 18/7

Calleja, Isacio (Atletico Madrid, 1961–72): 13

Callejo, Alberto (Atletico Madrid, 1958): 3

Calvet, Francisco (Barcelona, 1951): 2

Camacho, Jose Antonio (Real Madrid, 1975–88): 81

Camarasa, Francisco Jose (Valencia, 1993–95): 14

Caminero, Jose Luis Perez (Atletico Madrid, 1993–96): 21/8

Campanal, Marcelino (Sevilla, 1952–57): 11

Campanal, Marcelino Gonzalez (Sevilla, 1934–41): 3/2

Campo (1998): 1

Campo, Ivan (Mallorca, 1998): 1

Campos, Francisco (Atletico Aviacion Madrid, 1941–42): 6/5

Canizares, Jose Santiago (Celta de Vigo, 1993–96): 9

Cano, Ruben Andres (Atletico Madrid, 1977–79): 12/3

Canos, Juan Manuel (Elche, 1968): 4

Capon, Jose Luis (Atletico Madrid, 1973–77): 13/1

Cardenosa, Julio (Real Betis de Sevilla,

1977–80): 8

Careaga, Domingo (Arenas de Guecho, 1921–23): 4

Carmelo, Goyemechea (Athletic Bilbao, 1925): 10/3

Carrasco, Francisco Jose (Barcelona, 1979–88): 34/4

Carrete, Jose (Valencia, 1978): 2

Casado, Pedro (Real Madrid, 1961): 1

Castellano, Francisco (Las Palmas, 1968): 2/1

Castellanos, Angel (Granada, 1974): 3

Castillo, Jose (Barcelona, 1931): 1

Carmelo Cedrun (Athletic Bilbao, 1954–63): 13

Celades, Albert (Barcelona, 1998): 2

Celayeta, Genaro (Real Sociedad San Sebastian, 1980): 6

Cervera, Alvaro (Mallorca, Valencia, 1991–92): 4

Chaco, Eduardo Gonzalez (Deportivo La Coruna, 1933–37): 4/7

Chano, Sebastian Cruzado (Tenerife, 1994): 1

Chendo, Miguel Portlan (Real Madrid, 1986–90): 26

Chirri I, Aguirrezabala Marcelino (Athletic Bilbao, 1924–25): 5

Chirri II, Aguirrezabala Ignacio (Athletic Bilbao, 1928–32): 4

Cholin, Ignacio Ma Alcorta, (Real Sociedad, San Sebastian, 1928): 1

Chuzo, Antonio Gonzalez (Atletico Madrid, 1960): 1

Christiansen, Thomas (Barcelona, Sporting Gijon, 1993): 2/1

Churruca, Ignacio (Sporting Gijon, Athletic Bilbao, 1974–77): 16

Ciganda, Jose Angel (Osasuna Pamplona, Athletic Bilbao, 1991–94): 2

Cilaurren, Leonardo (Arenas de Guecho, Athletic Bilbao, 1933–35): 14

Claramunt, Jose (Valencia, 1968–75): 23/4

Clares, Manuel (Castellon, 1973): 1

Clemente, Balbino (Fortuna de Vigo, 1921): 1

Clos, Francisco Javier (Barcelona, 1985): 3/1

Collar, Enrique (Atletico Madrid, 1955–63): 16/4

Conte, Ignacio (Sevilla, 1991): 1

Coque, Gerardo (Real Valladolid, 1952): 1/1

Cortaberria, Ignacio (Real Sociedad San Sebastian, 1976–77): 4

Costas, Enrique Alvarez (Celta de Vigo, Barcelona, 1970–75): 13

Cubells, Eduardo (Valencia, 1925): 5/1

Cuellar, Angel Manuel (Betis Sevilla, 1994–95): 2

Cundi, Secundino Suarez (Sporting Gijon, 1978–81): 9

Curta, Jose Puig (Barcelona, 1947–48): 3

Dani, Daniel Ruiz (Athletic Bilbao, 1977/81): 25/10

De Andres Miguel (Athletic Bilbao, 1984): 1

De Felipe, Pedro Eugenio (Barcelona, 1973): 1

De la Cruz, Jesus Antonio (Granada, Barcelona, 1972–78): 6

Del Bosque Vicente (Real Madrid, 1975–80): 18/1

Del Campo, Victor Jose (Real Madrid, 1923): 1

Del Sol, Luis (Real Madrid, Juventus [Ita],

1960–66): 16/3

Deusto, Juan Antonio (Malaga, 1973): 1

Devora, Ceballos German (Las Palmas, 1968–72): 5

Di Stefano, Alfredo (Real Madrid, 1957–61): 31/23

Diego, Jose (Real Sociedad San Sebastian, 1980): 1

Domenech, Manuel (Sevilla, 1955): 3

Dominguez, Ernesto (Valencia, 1963): 1

Donato, Gama da Silva, (Deportivo La Coruna, 1994): 1/1

Echeberria, Luis Maria (Athletic Bilbao, 1962–63): 4

Echevarria, Jose Maria (Athletic Bilbao, 1941): 1

Echevarria, Roberto (Alaves Vitoria, Athletic Bilbao, 1928–36): 7

Echeveste, Jose (Real Union de Irun, 1922–27): 4

Eguiazabal, Ramon (Real Union de Irun, 1920): 3

Eizaguirre, Guillermo (Sevilla, 1938): 5

Eizaguirre, Ignacio (Valencia, Real Sociedad San Sebastian, 1945–52): 18

Eladio Silvestre (Barcelona, 1966–70): 9

Elicegui, Julio Antonio (Real Union de Irun, 1933): 4/5

Eloy, Olaya (Sporting Gijon, Valencia, 1985–90): 15/4

Emilin, Emilio Alonso (Real Madrid, 1936): 1

Emilin, Emilio Garcia (Real Oviedo, 1942): 2

Epi, Epifanio Fernandez (Donostia San Sebastian, Valencia, 1937–38): 15/4

Errasti, Ciriaco (Alaves de Vitoria, Real Madrid, 1930–38): 16

Errazquin, Juan (Real Union de Irun, 1925–28): 6/6

Escalza, Javier (Athletic Bilbao, 1978): 1

Escola, Jose (Barcelona, 1941–45): 2/1

Escudero, Adrian (Atletico Madrid, 1952–56): 3/1

Estella, Juan Jose (Barcelona, 1982): 1

Etxeberria, Joseba (Athletic Bilbao, 1997–98): 7/2

Fajardo, Desiderio (Atletico Madrid, 1921): 1

Fede, Federico Saiz (Valencia, 1934): 3

Felipe Minambres (Tenerife, 1990–94): 2/2

Felix, Perez Marco (Real Madrid, 1927): 1

Ferreira, Francisco (Athletic Bilbao, Atletico Madrid, 1988–89): 2

Ferrer, Albert (Barcelona, Chelsea [Eng], 1991–98): 34

Foncho, Alfonso Maria Rodriguez, (Barcelona, 1961): 2/1

Fonseca, Gregorio (Real Valladolid, Barcelona, 1992): 4/1

Fortes, Francisco (Barcelona, 1975): 1

Fran, Francisco Javier Gonzalez, (Deportivo La Coruna, 1993–95): 4

Fuertes, Antonio (Valencia, 1952): 1

Fuste, Jose Maria (Barcelona, 1964–69): 8/3

Garcia Remon, Mariano (Real Madrid, 1973): 2

Garcia Soriano, Juan Antonio (Murcia, 1974): 2

Gabilondo, Ramon (Atletico Aviacion Madrid, 1941–42): 5

Gainza, Agustin (Athletic Bilbao, 1945–55): 33/10

Galan, Enrique (Real Oviedo, 1973–74): 2

Galatas, Marcelino (Atletico Madrid, 1927): 1

Gale, Gonzalo (Real Oviedo, 1933): 2

Gallego, Ricardo (Real Madrid, 1982–88): 42/3

Donato Gama da Silva (Deportivo La Coruna, 1994–96): 11/2

Gallego, Francisco Fernandez (Barcelona, 1966–73): 36

Gamborena, Francisco (Real Union de Irun, Arenas de Guecho, 1921–33): 20

Garate, Jose Eulogio (Atletico Madrid, 1961–75): 18/5

Garay, Jesus (Athletic Bilbao, Barcelona, 1953–62): 29/1

Garcia, Fernando (Racing Santander, 1936): 1

Garcia, Jose Maria (Barcelona, 1966–67): 6/1

Garcia Navajas, Antonio (Real Madrid, 1979): 1

Garizurieta, Juan (Athletic Bilbao, 1930): 1

Gaztelu, Jose Agustin Aranzabal (Real Sociedad San Sebastian, 1969–71): 2

Geli, Delfi (Albacete, 1993): 4

Gensana, Enrique (Barcelona, 1957–61): 2

Gento, Francisco (Real Madrid, 1955–69): 43/5

Gil, Ramon (Real Vigo Sporting, 1920): 1

Giner, Fernando (Valencia, 1990–93): 12

Glaria, Jesus (Atletico Madrid, Athletic Bilbao, Barcelona, 1962–69): 20

Goiburu, Severiano (Osasuna, Barcelona, 1926–33): 12/5

Goicoechea, Andoni (Athletic Bilbao, Atletico Madrid, 1983–88): 39/4

Goicoechea, Juan Andoni (Barcelona, Athletic Bilbao, 1990–96): 35/4

Gomez, Fernando (Valencia, 1989–92): 8/2

Gomez, German (Aviacion Nacional Zaragoza, Atletico Aviacion Madrid, 1938–41): 7

Gonsalvo III, Mariano (Barcelona, 1950): 1

Gonzalez, Antero (Alaves de Vitoria, 1928): 1

Miguel Angel Gonzalez (Real Madrid, 1975–78): 18

Fran, Francisco Javier (Deportivo La Coruna, 1995–96): 4

Gonzalvo II, Jose (Barcelona, 1948–50): 8

Gonzalvo III, Manano (Barcelona, 1946–54): 15/1

Gordillo, Rafael (Betis Sevilla, Real Madrid, 1978–88): 75/3

Gorostiza, Guillermo (Athletic Bilbao, Valencia, 1930–41): 19/2

Gorriz, Alberto (Real Sociedad San Sebastian, 1988–90): 12/1

Gracia, Sigfrido (Barcelona, 1959–62): 10

Grosso, Ramon Moreno (Real Madrid, 1967–70): 14/1

Guardiola, Josep (Barcelona, 1992–97): 23/4

Guedes, Juan (Las Palmas, 1968–69): 2

Guerrero, Julen (Athletic Bilbao, 1993–98): 10

Guerri, Francisco (Real Zaragoza, 1983–84): 3

Guillamon, Fernando (Sevilla, 1955–56): 3

Guillot, Vicente (Valencia, 1962–65): 6/4

Guisasola, Agustin (Athletic Bilbao, 1980): 1

Guzman, Antonio (Rayo Vallecano Madrid, 1978): 2

Guzman, Ramon (Barcelona, 1930): 3

Hilario, Juan Marrero (Real Madrid, 1931):

Heredia, Juan Carlos (Barcelona, 1978–79): 3
Hernandez, Rosendo (Barcelona, 1949–50): 4
Herrera, Heriberto (Atletico Madrid, 1957): 1
Herrera, Jesus (Real Madrid, 1960): 1
Herrerita, Eduardo Herrera (Real Oviedo, 1934–38): 7/2
Hierro, Fernando (Real Madrid, 1989–98): 58/17
Higuera, Francisco (Real Zaragoza, 1992–95): 6/2
Hilario, Jose Marrero (Real Madrid, 1935): 1/1
Hita, Juan Lopez (Sevilla, 1970–72): 3
Huete, Felix (Real Madrid, 1946): 1
Idigoras, Santiago (Real Sociedad San Sebastian, 1977): 1
Igoa, Silvestre (Valencia, 1948–50): 10/7
Imaz, Andoni (Real Sociedad San Sebastian, 1993): 1
Ipina, Juan Antonio (Atletico Madrid, Donostia San Sebastian, Real Madrid, Atletico Aviacion Madrid, 1936–46): 7
Iraragorri, Jose (Athletic Bilbao, 1931–36): 7/1
Iribar, Jose Angel (Athletic Bilbao, 1964–76): 49
Iriondo, Rafael (Athletic Bilbao, 1946–47): 2/1
Irureta, Javier Iruretagoyena (Atletico Madrid, 1972–75): 6
Izaguirre, Silverio (Real Sociedad San Sebastian, 1920): 1
Juanin, Juan Bilbao (Osasuna Pamplona, Athletic Bilbao, 1925–27): 2
Jara, Anastasio (Cordoba, 1966): 1
Jauregui, Jose Maria (Arenas de Guecho, 1928): 3
Jimenez, Juan Jose (Real Madrid, 1982–83): 4
Jimenez, Manuel (Sevilla, 1988–90): 16
Jimenez, Manuel Enrique (Sporting Gijon, 1981): 1
Jorge, Gabriel (Barcelona, 1941): 1
Joseito, Jose Iglesias (Real Madrid, 1952): 1
Juanito, Juan Francisco Rodriguez, (Real Zaragoza, Atletico Madrid, 1989–91): 5/1
Juanito, Juan Gomez (Burgos, Real Madrid, 1977–82): 34/8
Juantegui, Antonio (Real Sociedad San Sebastian, 1924): 1
Jugo, Juan (Real Oviedo, 1946): 1
Julio Alberto, Moreno (Barcelona, 1984–88): 34
Juncosa, Jose (Atletico Madrid, 1948–50): 2
Kiko, Narvaez Francisco (Atletico Madrid, 1995–98): 22/5
Kiriki, Luis Iruretagoyena (Real Sociedad San Sebastian, 1928): 3
Kubala, Ladislao (Barcelona, 1953–61): 19/11
Labarta, Amadeo (Real Sociedad San Sebastian, 1928): 3
Laca, Jose Maria (Athletic Bilbao, 1924): 1
Lafuente, Ramin de (Athletic Bilbao, Atletico Madrid, 1924–35): 8
Lanchas, Angel (Barcelona, 1978): 1
Landaburu, Jesus (Barcelona, 1980): 1
Langara, Isidoro (Real Oviedo, 1932–36): 11/17
Lapetra, Carlos (Real Zaragoza, 1963–66): 13/1
Lardin, Jordi (Espanyol, 1997): 1
Larrainzar, Inigo (Athletic Bilbao, 1994): 1
Larranga, Juan Antonio (Real Sociedad San Sebastian, 1988): 1
Larraza, Jesus (Athletic Bilbao, 1924): 1

Larrinaga, Enrique (Racing Santander, 1933): 1/1
Lasa, Miguel (Real Madrid, 1993): 2
Lazcano, Jaime (Real Madrid, 1929–30): 5/1
Leal, Eugenio (Atletico Madrid, 1977–778): 13/1
Lecue, Simon (Betis Sevilla, Real Madrid, 1934–36): 5
Legarreta, Jose (Athletic Bilbao, 1928): 1
Leon, Angel (Real Madrid, 1931): 2
Lesmes, Francisco (Real Valladolid, 1954): 1
Lesmes, Rafael (Real Madrid, 1955–58): 2
Lezama, Raimundo Perez (Athletic Bilbao, 1947): 1
Liceranzu, Inigo (Athletic Bilbao, 1985): 1
Lico, Jose Antonio Morante, (Valencia, 1972): 1
Llorente, Francisco (Real Madrid, 1987): 1/1
Lopetegui, Julian (Logrones, 1994): 1
Lopez, Francisco (Sevilla, 1982–86): 20/1
Lopez, Francisco Jose (Betis, 1977): 1
Lopez, Jose Luis (Real Madrid, 1972–73): 4
Lopez, Juan Manuel (Atletico Madrid, 1992–97): 11
Lopez Rekarte, Luis (Real Sociedad San Sebastian, Barcelona, 1988): 4
Lopez Ufarte, Roberto (Real Sociedad San Sebastian, 1977–82): 15/5
Lora, Enrique (Sevilla, 1970–72): 14/1
Losada, Sebastian (Celta de Vigo, 1995): 1
Luis Aragones (Atletico Madrid, 1965–72): 11/1
Luis Enrique, Martinez (Sporting Gijon, Real Madrid, Barcelona, 1991–98): 35/7
Luis, Garcia (Mallorca, 1988): 1
Martin Dominguez, Jose Antonio (Osasuna Pamplona, 1991): 3
Martin Vazquez, Rafael (Real Madrid, Tenerife, Marseille [Fr] 1987–92): 38/1
Maceda, Jose Antonio (Sporting Gijon, Real Madrid, 1981–86): 35/8
Machin, Francisco (Atletico Aviacion Madrid, 1941): 1
Macias, Jose Diaz (Malaga, 1973): 2
Maguregui, Jose Maria (Athletic Bilbao, 1955–57): 7/1
Manchon, Eduardo (Barcelona, 1954): 1
Manjarin, Javier (Deportivo La Coruna, 1995–97): 13/2
Mano, Daniel (Valencia, 1955): 1
Manolete, Manuel Rios (Deportivo La Coruna, 1972): 2
Manolin, Manuel Martinez (Athletic Bilbao, 1953): 1
Manolo, Manuel Sanchez (Atletico Madrid, 1988–92): 28/9
Manzanedo, Jose F (Valencia, 1977): 1
Maranon, Rafael (Barcelona, 1977–78): 4
Marcet, Francisco (Barcelona, 1951–53): 3/2
Marcos, Alonzo (Atletico Madrid, Barcelona, 1981–85): 22/2
Marculeta, Martin (Real Sociedad San Sebastian, Donostia San Sebastian, Atletico Madrid, 1928–34): 15/1
Maria, Pena Jose (Arenas de Guecho, Real Madrid, 1922–30): 5/1
Marianin, Mariano Arias (Real Oviedo, 1973): 1
Marina, Roberto Simon (Atletico Madrid,

1985): 1
Mariscal, Angel (Real Sociedad San Sebastian, 1928): 2/1
Marrero, Martin (Las Palmas, 1969): 4
Marsal, Ramon (Real Madrid, 1958): 1
Marti, Cristobal (Barcelona, 1930): 3
Martin, Enrique (Osasuna Pamplona, 1982): 2
Martin, Felipe (Las Palmas, 1978–79): 3
Martin, Jose Maria (Barcelona, 1952): 1
Martin, Mariano (Barcelona, 1942–46): 3
Martinez, Eulogio (Barcelona, 1959–62): 8/6
Martinez, Herminio (Sevilla, 1925): 2
Martinez, Jesus (Valencia, 1973–74): 4
Marcelino Martinez (Real Zaragoza, 1961–67): 14/4
Marquitos, Marcos Alonso (Real Madrid, 1955): 2
Martinez, Roberto (Barcelona, Real Madrid, 1973–74): 5/2
Martorell, Alberto (Barcelona, 1941–452): 4
Mateo, Andres (Sevilla, 1942): 3
Mateos, Enrique (Real Madrid, 1957–61): 8/3
Mauri, Mauricio Ugartemendia (Athletic Bilbao, 1955): 4
Matito, Roman (Real Valladolid, 1955): 1
Meana, Manuel (Sporting Gijon, 1921–24): 7/1
Mejido, Alfredo (Sporting Gijon, 1975): 1/1
Melo, Francisco Delgado (Atletico Madrid, 1970): 2
Mencia, Juan Jose (Atletico Madrid, 1951): 1
Mesa, Manuel (Sporting Gijon, 1979–80): 2/1
Mestre, Manuel (Valencia, 1959–61): 2
Michel, Jose Miguel Gonzalez, (Real Madrid, 1985–92): 67/21
Miera, Vicente (Real Madrid, 1961): 1
Mieza, Juan Jose (Athletic Bilbao, 1941): 2
Miguel Gonzalez (Atletico Madrid, 1953–58): 15/2
Migueli, Miguel Bernardo (Barcelona, 1974–77): 32/1
Migueli, Miguel Ramos (Malaga, 1972–73): 2
Milla, Luis (Barcelona, 1989–90): 3
Millan, Jose (Granada, 1945): 1
Mingorance, Jose (Cordoba, 1963): 1
Minguela, Luis Mariano (Real Valladolid, 1989): 1
Miranda, Gerardo (Las Palmas, Barcelona, 1981–85): 9
Moleiro, Jose Morales (Real Madrid, 1945): 1
Molina, Jose Francisco (Atletico Madrid, 1996): 1
Molowny, Luis (Real Madrid, 1950–55): 7/2
Moncho, Gil (Celta de Vigo, 1920): 1
Monjardin, Juan (Real Madrid, 1922–24): 4/3
Montero, Enrique (Sevilla, 1980–81): 3
Montesinos, Eugenio (Barcelona, 1922): 1
Moran, Enrique (Sporting Gijon, Real Betis de Sevilla, 1979–81): 5
Moreno, Tomas Hernandez (Barcelona, 1953): 2
Morientes, Fernando (Real Madrid, 1998): 4/6
Morollon, Emilio (Real Valladolid, 1963): 2
Moya, Gabriel (Real Valladolid, Atletico Madrid, 1989–91):5/1
Muguerza, Jose (Athletic Bilbao, 1930–36): 9
Carlos Munoz (Real Oviedo, 1990–91): 6/6
Mundo, Edmundo Suarez (Valencia, 1941–42): 2/2

Munoz, Miguel (Celta de Vigo, Real Madrid 1948–55): 7

Nadal, Miguel Angel (Barcelona, 1991–98): 45/2

Nando, Fernando Gonzalez (Athletic Bilbao, 1947–51): 8

Nando, Fernando Martinez (Deportivo La Coruna, 1993): 1

Nando, Fernando Munoz (Barcelona, 1990–92): 8

Navarro, Joaquin (Real Madrid, 1952–53): 5

Neme, Nemesio Martin (Pontevere, 1965): 1

Nimo, Jose Ramon (Sevilla, 1983): 1

Nogues, Juan Jose (Barcelona, 1934): 1

Obiols, Jose Garcia (Europa Barcelona, 1930): 1

Oceja, Isaac (Athletic Bilbao, 1941–42): 4

Ochoa, Miguel Angel (Barcelona, 1973): 1

Ochotorena, Jose Manuel (Valencia, 1989–90): 2

Olaso, Alfonso (Atletico Madrid, 1927): 1

Olaso, Luis (Atletico Madrid, 1921–27): 4/1

Oli Johannesen (1996): 1/1

Olivares, Manolo (Alaves de Vitoria, 1930): 1

Olivella, Fernado (Barcelona, 1965): 18

Olmo, Antonio (Barcelona, 1977–80): 13

Ontoria, Sebastian (Real Sociedad San Sebastian, 1950): 1

Orue, Jose Maria (Athletic Bilbao, 1953–57): 3

Osorio, Manuel Fernandez (Barcelona, 1967–68): 2

Otero, Jorge (Celta de Vigo, Valencia, 1993–95): 9

Otero, Luis (Celta de Vigo, Deportivo La Coruna, 1920–24): 4

Pachin, Enrique Perez (Real Madrid, 1960–63): 7

Padron, Jose (Barcelona, 1929–30): 5/2

Pagaza, Francisco (Arenas de Guecho, Racing Santander, 1920–22): 7

Pahino, Manuel Fernandez (Celta de Vigo, Real Madrid, 1948–55): 3/3

Panizo, Jose Luis Lopez (Athletic Bilbao, 1946–53): 14/2

Paquito, Francisco Garcia (Real Oviedo, Valencia, 1962–67): 9

Pardeza, Miguel (Real Zaragoza, 1989–90): 6

Parra, Jose (Barcelona, 1950–51): 7

Parralo, Cristobal (Barcelona, Real Oviedo, 1991–93): 6–1

Pasarin, Luis Casas (Celta de Vigo, 1924–26): 6

Pasieguito, Bernardino Perez (Valencia, 1954): 3

Patricio, Arabolaza (Real Union de Irun, 1920): 1

Paz, Rafael (Sevilla, 1990): 8

Pedraza, Juan Carlos (Atletico Madrid, 1982): 2/1

Pedrito, Pedro Lopez (Deportivo La Coruna, 1945): 1

Pedrol, Esteban (Barcelona, 1935): 1

Peiro, Joaquin (Atletico Madrid, Inter Milan [Ita], 1956–66): 11/5

Pena, Jose Maria (Arenas de Guecho, Real Madrid, 1921–29): 16

Pepin, Jose Casas (Real Betis Sevilla, 1963): 2

Peral, Francisco Suarez (Betis Balompie Sevilla, 1938): 1

Pereda, Jesus Maria (Sevilla, Barcelona, 1960–68): 15/6

Perez, Juan Carlos (Barcelona, 1973–74): 2

Perez, Jose (Hercules Alicante, 1941): 1

Marcelino, Perez (Atletico Madrid, 1977–79): 13

Perez, Venancio (Athletic Bilbao, 1949–54): 11/4

Perez Paya, Jose Luis (Real Madrid, 1955): 2

Pichichi, Rafael Moreno Aranzadi, (Athletic Bilbao, 1920): 5/1

Pier, Pedro Luis Cherubino, (Sporting Gijon, 1994): 1

Piera, Vicente (Barcelona, 1922–31): 15/2

Pina, Marcial (Barcelona, 1966–68): 15

Piquer, Vicente (Valencia, 1961): 1

Pirri, Jose Martinez (Real Madrid, 1966–78): 41/16

Pizzi, Juan Antonio (Tenerife, Barcelona, 1994–98): 21/8

Planas, Javier (Real Zaragoza, 1974): 1

Planelles, Juan Bautista (Castellon, Real Madrid, 1973): 2

Poli, Manuel Polinario Munoz, (Valencia, 1968): 1

Polo, Ramon (Celta de Vigo, 1925–33): 2

Pololo, Miguel Duran (Atletico Madrid, 1921–23): 2

Portas, Conrado (Barcelona, 1927–28): 2

Prat, Jose (Barcelona, 1933): 4

Prats, Francisco (Murcia, Real Madrid, 1927–30): 9

Puchades, Antonio (Valencia, 1949–54): 23

Pujol, Luis (Barcelona, 1969): 1

Puskas, Ferenc (Real Madrid, 1961–62): 4

Querejeta, Jose (Real Madrid, 1947): 2

Quesada, Felix (Real Madrid, 1924–29): 9/1

Quincoces, Jacinto Fernandez (Alaves de Vitoria, Real Madrid, 1928–38): 27

Quincoces, Juan Carlos (Valencia, 1957–59): 7

Quini, Enrique Castro (Sporting Gijon, Barcelona, 1970–82): 35/8

Quino, Jaoquin Sierra (Valencia, Real Betis Sevilla , 1969–72): 7/3

Quique, Enrique Ramos (Atletico Madrid, 1981–85): 4

Quique, Enrique Sanchez (Valencia, 1987–89): 15

Quique, Estebaranz Enrique (Tenerife, Barcelona, 1993): 3

Raich, Jose (Barcelona, 1941): 1

Ramallets, Antonio (Barcelona, 1950–61): 35

Ramoni, Ramon Martinez (Sevilla, 1952): 2

Ramos, Jose Antonio (Barcelona, 1975–77): 4

Raul Gonzalez (Real Madrid, 1996–98): 15/3

Regueiro, Luis (Real Union de Irun, Real Madrid, 1927–36): 25/16

Regueiro, Pedro (Real Union de Irun, Real Madrid, 1928–36): 4

Reija, Severino (Real Zaragoza, 1962–67): 20

Reina, Miguel (Barcelona, 1969–73): 5

Renones, Tomas (Atletico Madrid, 1985–88): 15

Abel, Resino (Atletico Madrid, 1991): 2

Rexach, Carlos (Barcelona, 1969–78): 15/2

Rial, Jose Hector (Real Madrid, 1955–58): 5/1

Riera, Jose Luis (Atletico Madrid, 1949–50): 3

Rife, Joaquin (Barcelona, 1968–70): 4/1

Rincon, Hipolito (Betis, 1983–86): 22/10

Rios, Eusebio (Betis, 1964): 1

Rios, Roberto (Betis, Athletic Bilbao, 1996–98): 11

Rivilla, Feliciano Munoz (Atletico Madrid, 1960–65): 26

Rodilla, Jose Fernando Martinez (Celta de Vigo, 1970): 1

Rodri, Francisco Rodriguez (Barcelona, 1962): 3

Cezar, Rodriguez (Barcelona, 1945–52): 12/6

Robus, Robustiano Bilbao (Arenas de Guecho, 1928): 1

Roberto Fernandez (Valencia, Athletic Bilbao, 1982–1991): 29/1

Rodriguez, Diego (Real Betis de Sevilla, 1988): 1

Rodriguez, Juan Carlos (Atletico Madrid, 1991): 1

Rodriguez, Lozano (Atletico Madrid, 1949): 5

Rodriguez, Oscar (Racing Santander, 1925–27): 2/1

Rogan, Anton (1988): 1/1

Rojo, Jose Chechu (Athletic Bilbao, 1969–78): 18/3

Rojo, Juan Carlos Perez (Barcelona, 1985): 4

Rojo II, Jose Francisco (Athletic Bilbao, 1973): 1

Rousse, Angel (Athletic Bilbao, 1924): 1

Rovira, Isidro (Barcelona, 1941): 2

Rubio, Gaspar (Real Madrid, 1929–30): 4/9

Ru, Juan Jose (Atletico Madrid, 1981): 1

Ruiz, Felix (Real Madrid, 1961–63): 4/1

Ruiz, Sosa Manuel (Sevilla, 1960–61): 5

Sagibarba, Emilio Saqi (Barcelona, 1926): 1

Spencer, Enrique Gomez (Sevilla, 1923): 1

Sacristan, Eusebio (Real Valladolid, Real Madrid, Barcelona, 1987–92): 16/1

Sadurni, Salvador (Barcelona, 1963–69): 10

Saez, Jose Ignacio (Athletic Bilbao, 1968): 3

Sagarzazu, Manuel (Real Union de Irun, 1927): 2

Salinas, Francisco Paxti (Athletic Bilbao, 1988): 2

Salinas, Julio (Athletic Bilbao, Atletico Madrid, Barcelona, Deportivo La Coruna, Sporting Gijon, 1986–96): 56/9

Salva, Salvador Garcia (Real Zaragoza, 1983–84): 6

Salvadore, Sandro (1970): 1/1

Samitier, Jose (Barcelona, 1920–31): 21/2

San, Jose Isidoro (Real Madrid, 1977–79): 13

Sanchez, Fernando (Real Betis de Sevilla, 1998): 2

Sanchez, Jose Vicente (Barcelona, 1978–84): 14

Sanchis, Manuel (Real Madrid, 1965–92): 60/2

Sancho, Agustin (Barcelona, 1920–23): 3

Sans, Juan (Barcelona, 1947): 1

Santamaria, Francisco (Real Zaragoza, 1966): 1

Santamaria, Jose Emilio (Real Madrid, 1958–62): 16

Santi, (1997–98): 2

Santiago, Juan Ramon (Valencia, 1942): 2

Santillana, Carlos Alonso (Real Madrid, 1975–85): 56/15

Santisteban, Juan (Real Madrid, 1957–59): 7

Santos, Eleuterio (Real Zaragoza, 1968): 1

Sarabia, Manuel (Athletic Bilbao, 1983–85): 15/1

Sastre, Jose (Barcelona, 1930): 1/1

Satrustegui, Jesus (Real Sociedad San Sebastian, 1975–82): 32/8

Saura, Enrique (Valencia, 1978–82): 23/4

Segarra, Juan (Barcelona, 1951–62): 25

Seguer, Jose (Barcelona, 1952): 4

Senor, Juan Antonio (Real Zaragoza, Real Madrid, 1982–86): 40/6

Serena, Francisco Rodriguez (Osasuna Pamplona, 1963): 1

Serna, Ricardo (Barcelona, 1988–90): 6

Sesumaga, Felix (Barcelona, Athletic Bilbao, Racing Sama de Langreo, 1920–23): 8/4

Setien, Enrique (Atletico Madrid, 1985–86): 3

Silva, Alfonso (Atletico Madrid, 1949–51): 5/1

Sobrado, Eduardo (Celta de Vigo, 1951): 1

Sol, Juan Cruz (Valencia, Real Madrid, 1970–76): 28–1

Soladrero, Enrique (Real Oviedo, Real Zaragoza, 1935–38): 2

Solana, Jesus Angel (Real Madrid, 1988): 1

Sole, Pedro (Barcelona, 1929–36): 4

Soler, Miguel (Barcelona, Atletico Madrid, 1988–91): 9

Solozabal, Roberto (Atletico Madrid, 1991–93): 12

Solsona, Daniel (Barcelona, Valencia, 1973–81): 7

Suarez, Adolfo (Atletico Madrid, 1928): 1

Suarez, Luis (Barcelona, Inter Milan [Ita], Sampdoria [Ita], 1957–72): 32/14

Tejada, Justo (Barcelona, 1958–61): 8/4

Tendillo, Miguel (Valencia, Real Madrid, 1980–88): 27/1

Teruel, Ricardo (Barcelona, 1941–42): 4

Tomas, Renones Pedro (Atletico Madrid, 1988–89): 4

Toni, Antonio Munoz (Atletico Madrid, 1992–93): 10/2

Tonono, Antonio Alfonso (Las Palmas, 1967–72): 19

Torres, Antonio (Barcelona, 1968–69): 5

Tourino, Juan Carlos (Real Madrid, 1972): 1

Travieso, Manuel Lopez (Athletic Bilbao, 1922): 1/2

Triana, Ramon (Real Madrid, 1929): 1

Trias, Jose (Barcelona, 1941): 1

Ufarte, Jose Armando (Atletico Madrid, 1965–72): 16/2

Uralde, Pedro (Real Sociedad San Sebastian, Atletico Madrid, 1982–86): 3

Uria, Javier Alvarez (Real Oviedo, Real Madrid, Sporting Gijon, 1973–78): 14

Uriarte, Fidel (Athletic Bilbao, 1968–72): 9–1

Urquiaga, Santiago (Athletic Bilbao, 1980–84): 14

Urquizu, Juan (Athletic Bilbao, 1929): 1

Urruticoechea, Francisco Javier (Barcelona, 1978–80): 5

Urtubi, Ismael (Athletic Bilbao, 1984–85): 2

Urzaiz, Ismael (Athletic Bilbao, 1996–97): 2

Victor, Munoz (Real Zaragoza, Barcelona, 1981–88): 60/3

Valderrama, Manuel (Racing Madrid, 1927): 1

Valdez, Ramon Oscar (Valencia, 1972–74): 9/4

Valero, Antonio (Sevilla, 1957): 1

Vallana, Pedro (Arenas de Guecho, 1920–28): 12

Valle, Luis (Real Madrid, 1933): 1

Valverde, Ernesto (Athletic Bilbao, 1990): 1

Vantolra, Martin (Barcelona, Sevilla, 1930–31): 12/3

Vasquez (1988): 1/1

Vasquez, Juan (Aviacion Nacional Zaragoza, 1937–41): 3

Vava, Luciano Sanchez (Elche, 1966–69): 2

Vazquez, Joaquin (Irunes Irun, 1920): 1

Vazquez, Ramon (Sevilla, 1987–88): 3/1

Vega, Jose (Celta de Vigo, 1936–37): 2

Velazquez, Manuel (Real Madrid, 1967–75): 10/2

Veloso, Jose Fidalgo (Deportivo La Coruna, 1962–63): 4/3

Verdugo, Juan (Barcelona, 1978): 1

Vergara, Julian (Recuperacion Levante Zaragoza, Osasuna Pamplona, 1937–38): 2

Verges, Martin (Barcelona, 1957–62): 12/2

Vicente, Jose (Real Madrid, 1961–63): 7

Vidagany, Francisco (Valencia, 1969): 4

Vidal, Antonio (Atletico Madrid, 1948): 1

Vidal, Jose Maria (Real Madrid, 1960–61): 4

Vidal, Manuel (Athletic Bilbao, 1927): 1

Vigo, Esteban (Barcelona, 1981): 3

Villa, Jose Maria (Real Zaragoza, 1964): 2

Villa, Juan Manuel (Real Zaragoza, 1964): 1

Villar, Angel Maria (Athletic Bilbao, 1973–79): 22/3

Villarroya, Francisco Javier Perez (Real Zaragoza, 1989–92): 14

Violeta, Jose Luis (Real Zaragoza, Valencia, 1966–73): 14/1

Vizcaino, Juan (Atletico Madrid, 1991–92): 15

Voro, Salvador Gonzalez (Deportivo La Coruna, 1993–95): 9

Yermo, Jose Maria (Arenas de Guecho, 1927–28): 5/5

Yurrita, Mariano (Real Sociedad San Sebastian, 1929): 2/1

Zabala, Jose Luis (Real Union de Irun, Deportivo Ovetense Oviedo, Barcelona, 1923–24): 4/4

Zaballa, Pedro (Barcelona, 1964): 1/2

Zabalo, Ramon (Barcelona, 1931–36): 11

Zabalza, Pedro Maria (Barcelona, 1968–69): 7

Zaldua, Domingo (Real Sociedad San Sebastian, 1927–28): 5/4

Zaldua, Jose Antonio (Barcelona, 1961–63): 3

Zamora, Jesus Maria (Real Sociedad San Sebastian, 978–82): 30/3

Zamora, Ricardo (Barcelona, Real Madrid, 1920–36): 46

Zarra, Telmo Zarraonandia (Athletic Bilbao, 1945–51): 20/20 **Zarraga**, Jose Maria (Real Madrid, 1955–58): 8

Zoco, Ignacio (Osasuna, Real Madrid, 1961–69): 25/1

Zubieta, Angel (Athletic Bilbao, 1936): 2

Zubizarreta, Andoni (Athletic Bilbao, Barcelona, Valencia, 1985–98): 127

ITALIAN INTERNATIONAL PLAYERS' RECORDS

Aebi, Ermanno (Inter Milan, 1920): 2/3

Agnoletto, Marcello (Sampdoria, 1956): 1

Agroppi, Aldo (Torino, 1972–73): 5

Albertini, Demetrio (AC Milan,1991–98): 14

Albertosi, Enrico (Fiorentina, Cagliari, 1967–75): 37

Aliberti, Giuseppe (Torino, 1923–25): 11

Allemandi, Luigi (Juventus, Ambrosiana Inter, AS Roma, 1925–36): 24

Altafini, Jose (AC Milan, 1961–62): 6/5

Altobelli, Alessandro (Inter Milan, 1980–88): 61/25

Amadei, Amedeo (Inter Milan, Napoli, 1949–53): 13–7

Amoretti, Ugo (Juventus, 1936): 1

Anastasi, Pietro (Varese, Juventus, 1968–75): 25/8

Ancelotti, Carlo (AS Roma, AC Milan, Napoli, 1981–91): 26/1

Andreolo, Michele (Bologna, 1936–42): 27/1

Angelillo, Antonio Valentin (Inter Milan, AS Roma, 1960–61): 2/1

Annovazzi, Carlo (AC Milan, 1947–52): 17

Anquilletti, Angelo (AC Milan, 1969): 2

Antognoni, Giancarlo (Fiorentina, 1974–83): 73/7

Anzolin, Roberto (Juventus, 1966): 1

Apolloni, Luigi (AC Parma, 1994–96): 15

Ara, Guido (Pro Vercelli, 1911–20): 13/1

Arcari, Bruno (Genoa, 1940): 1 1

Ardissone, Mario (Pro Vercelli, 1924): 2

Asti, Giuseppe (Inter Milan, 1920): 1

Auguste, Arsene (Racing, 1974): 1/1

Bacigalupo, Valerio (Torino, 1947–49): 5

Badini, Emilio (Bologna, 1920): 2/1

Baggio, Dino (Inter Milan, Juventus, AC Parma, 1991–98): 50/6

Baggio, Roberto (Fiorentina, Juventus, Juventus Italy, AC Milan, Bologna, AC Parma, 1988–98): 53/28

Bagni, Salvatore (Perugia, Inter Milan, Napoli, 1981–87): 41/4

Baiano, Francesco (Foggia. 1991): 2

Baldi, Gastone (Bologna, 1922–25): 3

Baldini, Giuseppe (Sampdoria, 1949): 1

Ballacci, Dino (Bologna, 1954): 1

Ballarin, Aldo (Torino, 1945–49): 9

Baloncieri, Adolfo (Alessandria, Torino, 1920–30): 47/25

Banchero, Elvio (Alessandria, Genoa, 1928–31): 3/4

Banfi, Janos (KSC Eendracht Aalst [Bel], 1996): 1/1

Barbesino, Luigi (Casale, 1912–14): 5/1

Barbieri, Ottavio (Genoa, 1921–30): 21

Baresi, Franco (Inter Milan, AC Milan, 1982–94): 81/1

Baresi, Giuseppe (Inter Milan, 1979–86): 18

Barison, Paolo (Genoa, Sampdoria, AS Roma, 1959–66): 9/6

Bassetto, Adriano (Atalanta Bergamo, 1954–55): 3

Battistini, Sergio (AC Milan, 1984): 4/1

Battistoni, Giovanni (Liguria, Genoa, 1939): 2

Bean, Gastone (AC Milan, 1957–58): 4

Bearzot, Enzo (Torino, 1955): 1

Becattini, Fosco (Genoa, 1949): 2

Bedin, Gianfranco (Inter Milan, 1966–72): 6

Bellini, Delfo (Genoa, Inter Milan, 1924–27): 8

Bellugi, Mauro (Inter Milan, Bologna, Napoli, 1972–79): 33

Benarrivo, Antonio (AC Parma. 1993–97): 23

Benetti, Romeo (AC Milan, Juventus, AS Roma, 1971–80): 55/2

Berardo, Felice (Piemonte, Pro Vercelli, Genoa, US Torinese, 1911–20): 13/2

Bercellino, Giancarlo (Juventus, 1965–68): 6

Bergamaschi, Mario (AC Milan, Sampdoria, 1954–58): 5

Bergamino, Augusto (Genoa, 1920–23): 5

Bergomi, Giuseppe (Inter Milan, 1982–98): 81/6

Bernardini, Fulvio (Lazio Roma, Inter Milan, AS Roma, 1925–32): 26/3

Bernasconi, Gaudenzio (Sampdoria, 1956): 1

Bernasconi, Gaudenzo (Sampdoria, 1956–59): 5

Berti, Nicola (Inter Milan, 1988–95): 39/3

Bertini, Mario (Fiiorentina, Inter Milan, 1966–72): 25/2

Bertolini, Luigi (Alessandria. Juventus, 1929–35): 26

Bertoni, Sergio (Genoa, 1940): 3/1

Bertuccelli, Alberto (Lucchese, Juventus, 1949–52): 6

Bet, Aldo (AS Roma, 1971): 2

Bettega, Roberto (Juventus, 1975–83): 43/19

Bianchi, Alessandro (Inter Milan, 1992–93): 9

Bianchi, Ottavio (Napoli, 1966): 2

Biavati, Amedeo (Bologna, 1938–47): 18/8

Bigatto, Carlo (Juventus, 1925–27): 5

Binaschi, Angelo (Pro Vercelli, 1911–13): 9

Blason, Ivano (Triestina, 1950): 1

Boffi, Aldo (AC Milan, 1938–39): 2

Boiocchi, Arturo (US Milanese, 1910–14): 6/2

Bolchi, Bruno (Inter Milan, 1961): 3

Bonetti, Dario (AC Milan, 1986): 2

Bonino, Ernesto (Lucchese, 1921–22): 2

Boninsegna, Roberto (Cagliari, Inter Milan, 1967–74): 22/9

Boniperti, Giampiero (Juventus, 1947–60): 38/8

Bonomi, Andrea (AC Milan, 1951): 1

Bontadini, Franco (Inter Milan, 1912): 4/2

Bordon, Ivano (Inter Milan, Sampdoria, 1978–85): 22

Borel, Felice (Juventus, 1933–34): 3/1

Borello, Francesco (Pro Vercelli, 1924): 1

Borgato, Giovanni (Bologna, 1926): 1

Borgonovo, Stefano (Fiorentina, 1989): 3

Bortoletto, Raoul (AS Roma, 1953): 1

Brandts, Ernie (PSV Eindhoven [Hol], 1978): 1/1

Brezzi, Guglielmo (Genoa, Alessandria, 1920–29): 8/5

Brighenti, Sergio (Padova, Sampdoria, 1959–61): 9/2

Bruna, Antonio (Juventus, 1920): 5

Bucci, Luca (AC Parma, 1994–95): 3

Buffon, Gianluigi (AC Parma, 1997–98): 2

Buffon, Lorenzo (AC Milan, Genoa, Inter Milan, 1958–62): 15

Bugatti, Ottavio (Napoli, 1957–58): 5

Bulgarelli, Giacomo (Bologna, 1962–67): 7

Burgnich, Tarcisio (Inter Milan, 1963–74): 66/2

Buriani, Ruben (AC Milan, 1980): 2

Burini, Renzo (AC Milan, Lazio Roma, 1951–55): 4/1

Burlando, Luigi (Doria, Genoa, 1921–25): 19/1

Buscaglia, Pietro (Torino, 1937): 1

Busini, Antonio (Bologna, 1929): 1

Cabrini, Antonio (Juventus, 1978–87): 73/9

Cali, Francesco (Doria, 1910): 2

Caligaris, Umberto (Casale, Juventus, 1922–34): 59

Cameroni, Angelo (Legnano, 1920): 1

Campatelli, Aldo (Ambrosiana Inter, Inter Milan, 1939–50): 7

Campelli, Piero (Inter Milan, 1912–21): 11

Cannavaro, Fabio (AC Parma, 1997–98): 18

Capello, Domenico (Torino, 1910): 2

Capello, Fabio (Juventus, AC Milan, 1972–76): 33/8

Cappellini, Renato (Inter Milan, 1967): 2/1

Cappello, Gino (Bologna, 1949–54): 11/3

Cappioli, Massim (AS Roma, 1994): 1

Capra, Carlo (Torino, 1915): 1

Capra, Egidio (AC Milan, 1937): 2

Carapellese, Riccardo (AC Milan, Torino, Genoa, 1947–56): 16/10

Carboni, Amedeo (AS Roma, 1992–97): 18

Carcano, Carlo (Alessandria, 1915–1921): 5/1

Carnasciali, Daniele (Fiorentina, 1994–96): 2

Carnevale, Andrea (Napoli, 1989–90): 10/2

Carrer, Gustavo (AC Milan, 1911): 2/1

Carrera, Massimo (Juventus, 1992): 1

Carzino, Ercole (Sampierdarenese, 1921): 1

Casanova, Claudio (Genoa, 1914): 1

Casari, Giuseppe (Napoli, 1951): 4

Casiraghi, Pierluigi (Juventus, Lazio Roma, 1991–98): 44/12

Caso, Domenico (Fiorentina, 1974): 1

Castano, Ernesto (Juventus, 1959–69): 7

Castellazi, Armando (Ambrosiana Inter, 1929–34): 3

Castelletti, Sergio (Fiorentina, 1958–62): 7

Castellini, Luciano (Torino, 1977): 1

Castigliano, Eusebio (Torino, 1945–49): 7/1

Cattaneo, Renato (Alessandria, AS Roma, 1931–35): 2/1

Catto, Edoardo (Genoa, 1924): 1

Causio, Franco (Juventus, Udinese, 1972–83): 63/6

Celio, Celestino (Juventus, 1954): 1

Cera, Pierluigi (Caliari, 1969–72): 18

Ceresoli, Carlo (Ambrosiana Inter, Bologna, 1934–38): 8

Cervato, Sergio (Fiorentina, Juventus, 1951–60): 28/4

Cervellati, Cesarino (Bologna, 1951–56): 6

Cesarini, Renato (Juventus, 1931–34): 11/3

Cevenini, Aldo (AC Milan, Inter Milan, 1910–15): 11/4

Cevenini, Luigi (Inter Milan, Novese, Juventus, 1915–29): 29/11

Chiappella, Giuseppe (Fiorentina, 1953–57): 17

Chiarugi, Luciano (Fiorentina, AC Milan, 1969–74): 3

Chiesa, E (AC Parma, 1998): 1

Chiesa, Enrico (Sampdoria, AC Parma, 1996–98): 8/3

Chinaglia, Giorgio (Lazio Roma, 1972–75): 15/6

Cois, Sandro (Fiorentina, 1998): 1

Colaussi, Gino (Triestina, 1935–40): 27/15

Collovati, Fulvio (AC Milan, Inter Milan, 1979–86): 50/3

Colombari, Enrico (Torino, Napoli, 1928–33): 9

Colombo, Umberto (Juventus, 1959–60): 3

Combi, Gianpiero (Juventus, 1924–34): 47

Conte, Antonio (Juventus, 1994–96): 8

Conti, Bruno (AS Roma, 1980–86): 47/5

Conti, Leopoldo (Inter Milan, Ambrosiana Inter, 1920–29): 31/8

Conti, Paolo (AS Roma, 1977–79): 7

Corbelli, Guido (venezia, 1940): 1/1

Cordova, Franco (AS Roma, 1975): 3/1

Corna, Carlo (Pro Vercelli, 1911–15): 8

Corradi, Giuseppe (Juventus, 1952–58): 6

Corsi, Giordano (Bologna, 1935–37): 7

Corso, Mario (Inter Milan, 1961–71): 23/4

Costa, Giovanni (Sestrese, 1924): 1

Costacurta, Alessandro (AC Milan, 1991–98): 58/2

Costagliola, Leonardo (Fiorentina, 1953–54): 3

Costantino, Raffaele (Bari, AS Roma, 1929–33): 23/8

Crippa, Massimo (Napoli, AC Parma, 1988–96): 17

Cuccereddu, Antonello (Juventus, 1975–78): 13

Da Costa, Dino (AS Roma, 1958): 1/1

Damiani, Giuseppe (Juventus, 1974): 2

Danova, Luigi (Torino, 1976): 1

David, Mario (LR Vicenza, AS Roma, AC Milan, 1958–62): 3

De Agostini, Luigi (Verona, Juventus, 1987–91): 36/4

De Marchi, Adevildo (Doria, 1920): 1

De Marchi, Carlo (Torino, 1912): 1

De Napoli, Fernando (Avellino, Napoli, 1986–92): 55/1

De Nardo, Gracco (Spes–Genova, 1920–21): 2

De Pra, Giovanni (Genoa, 1924–28): 19

De Simoni, Mario (US milanese, 1910–14): 7

De Sisti, Giancarlo (Fiorentina, 1967–72): 29/4

De Sordi (Sao Paulo, 1956): 1/1

De Vecchi, Renzo (AC Milan, Genoa, 1910–25): 43

Debernardi, Enrico (Torino, 1910–11): 3/1

Del Piero, Alesandro (Juventus, 1995–95): 23/7

Della Valle, Giuseppe (Bologna, 1923–29): 17/4

Demaria, Atilio (Ambrosiana Inter, 1938): 1

Demaria, Attilio (Ambrosiana Inter, 1932–40): 12/3

Depaoli, Virginio (Brescia, Juventus, 1966): 3/1

Depetrini, Teobaldo (Juventus, 1936–46): 12

Di Biagio, Luigi (AS Roma, 1998): 7/1

Di Chiara, Alberto (AC Parma, 1992–93): 7

Di Gennaro, Antonio (Verona, 1984–86): 15/4

Di Giacomo, Beniamino (Mantova, 1964): 1

Di Livio Angelo (Juventus, 1995–98): 24

Di Matteo, Roberto (Lazio Roma, Chelsea [Eng], 1994–98): 33/2

Di Mauro, Fabrizio(Fiorentina, 1993): 3

Domenghini, Angelo (Atalanta Bergamo, Inter Milan, Caliari, 1963–72): 33/6

Donadoni, Roberto (AC Milan, NY/NJ Metrostars [USA], 1986–96): 64/5

Dossena, Giuseppe (Bologna, Torino, 1981–87): 38/2

Dugoni, Bruno (Modena, AS Roma, 1925–32): 4

Eliani, Alberto (Fiorentina, 1948): 2

Emoli, Flavio (Juventus, 1958–59): 2

Eranio, Stefano (Genoa, AC Milan, 1990–92): 20/3

Esposito, Salvatore (Napoli, 1975): 1

Evani, Alberigo (AC Milan, Sampdoria, 1991–94): 15

Facchetti, Giacinto (Inter Milan, 1963–77): 95/3

Faccio, Ricardo (Ambrosiana Inter, 1935–36): 5

Fanna, Pietro (Verona, Inter Milan, 1983–85): 14

Fantoni, Ottavio (Lazio Roma, 1934): 1

Farina, Giuseppe (Sampdoria, 1956): 1

Faroppa, Vittorio (Piemonte, 1912): 1

Fattori, Osvaldo (Inter Milan, 1949–50): 4

Favalli, Giuseppe (Lazio Roma, 1994): 1

Fayenz, Antonio (Padova, 1925–26): 4

Fedullo, Francesco (Bologna, 1932–33): 2/3

Ferrante, Ugo (Fiorentina, 1970–71): 3

Ferrara, Ciro (Napoli, Juventus, 1987–98): 44

Ferrari, Pietro (Bologna, 1940): 1

Ferrario, Rino (Juventus, 1952–58): 10

Ferraris, Pio (Juventus, 1920–21): 4/1

Ferraris II, Pietro (Napoli, Ambrosiana Inter, Torino, 1935–47): 14/3

Ferraris IV, Attilio (Fortitudo, AS Roma, Lazio Roma, 1926–35): 28

Ferri, Riccardo (Inter Milan, 1986–92): 46/4

Ferrini, Giorgio (Torino, 1962–68): 7

Firmani, Edwing (Sampdoria, 1956–58): 3/2

Fogli, Romano (Bologna, 1958–67): 13

Foni, Alfredo (Juventus, 1937–42): 19

Fontana, Alfio (AC Milan, 1957–60): 3

Fontanesi, Alberto (Spal, 1952): 1

Forlivesi, Giuseppe (Modena, 1920–25): 10/2

Fortunato, Andrea (Juventus, 1993): 1

Fossati, Virgilio (Inter Milan, 1910–15): 12/1

Francini, Giovanni (Torino, Napoli, 1986–88): 8

Franzosi, Angelo (Inter Milan, 1947–49): 2

Fresia, Attilio (Doria, 1913): 1

Fresia, Vincenzo (Pro Vercelli, 1943): 1

Frignani, Amleto (AC Milan, Udinese, 1952–57): 14/6

Frossi, Annibale (Ambrosiana Inter, 1937): 1/1

Furiassi, Zeffiro (Lazio Roma, 1950): 2

Furino, Giuseppe (Juventus, 1970–74): 3

Fuser, Diego (Lazio Roma, 1993–97): 14

Fusi, Luca (Sampdoria, Napoli, Torino, 1988–92): 8

Gabetto, Guglielmo (Torino, 1942–48): 6/5

Galderisi, Giuseppe (Verona, 1985–86): 10

Galia, Roberto (Juventus, 1992): 3

Gallea, Cesare (Torino, 1937): 1

Galletti, Carlo (Doria, 1913): 1

Galli, Carlo (AS Roma, AC Milan, 1953/1959): 13/5

Galli, Giovanni (Fiorentina, 1983–86): 19

Gallina, Giovanni (Casale, 1914): 2

Gandini, Giuseppe (Alessandria, 1925–28): 6

Garre, Oscar Alfredo (1987): 1/1

Garzena, Bruno (Juventus, 1958): 1

Gasperi, Felice (Bologna, 1928–33): 6

Gavinelli, Rodolfo (Piemonte, 1911): 1

Gei, Renato (Sampdoria, 1951): 1

Genovesi, Pietro (Bologna, 1921–29): 10

Genta, Mario (Genoa, 1939): 2

Gentile, Claudio (Juventus, 1975–84): 72/1

Ghezzi, Giorgio (Inter Milan, AC Milan, 1954–61): 6

Ghiggia, Alcide (AS Roma, 1957–59): 5/1

Ghigliano, Carlo (Genoa, 1920): 1

Giacomazzi, Giovanni (Inter Milan, 1954–55): 8

Giacone, Giovanni (Juventus, 1920): 4

Gianni, Mario (Bologna, 1927–33): 6

Giannini, Giuseppe (AS Roma, 1986–91): 47/6

Gimona, Aredio (Palermo, 1951): 1

Giordani, Alberto (Bologna, 1927): 1

Giordano, Bruno (Lazio Roma, Napoli, 1978–85): 13/1

Giovanni, Ferrari (Alessandria, Juventus, Ambrosiana Inter, 1930–38): 44/14

Giovannini, Attilio (Inter Milan, 1949–53): 13

Giuliano, Luigi (AS Roma, 1955): 1

Giunti, Federico (Perugia. 1996): 1

Giustacchini, Giuseppe (Virtis, 1921): 1

Goggio, Gino (Torino, 1914): 1

Gori, Adolfo (Juventus, 1967): 1

Gori, Sergio (Caliari, 1970): 3

Grabbi, Giuseppe (Juventus, 1924): 1

Gratton, Guido (Fiorentina, 1953–59): 11/3

Graziani, Francesco (Torino, Fiorentina, 1975–83): 64/22

Grezar, Giuseppe (Triestina, Torino, 1942–48): 8/1

Griffanti, Luigi (Fiorentina, 1942): 2

Grosso, Pierto (AC Milan, AS Roma, 1952–53): 2

Grosso, Pietro (AC Milan, 1951): 1

Guaita, Enrico (AS Roma, 1934–35): 10/5
Guarisi, Anfilogino (Lazio Roma, 1932–34): 6/1
Guarnacci, Egidio (AS Roma, 1959–60): 3
Guarneri, Aristide (Inter Milan, Bologna, 1963–68): 21/1
Guerini, Vincenzo (Fiorentina, 1974): 1
Guzman, Javier (1970): 1/1
Innocenti, Giovanni (Pro Vercelli, 1913–14): 5
Invernizzi, Giovanni (Inter Milan, 1958): 1
Inzaghi, Filippo (Atalanta Bergamo, Juventus, 1997–98): 6
Janich, Francesco (Bologna, 1962–66): 6
Janni, Antonio (Torino, 1924–29): 23/1
Jong Soo, Chung (Yukong Oil, 1986): 1/1
Juliano, Antonio (Napoli, 1966–74): 18
Lana, Pietro (AC Milan, 1910): 2/3
Landini, Spartaco (Inter Milan, 1966): 4
Lanna, Marco (Sampdoria, AS Roma, 1992–93): 2
Leale, Ettore (Genoa, 1922–24): 2
Lentini, Gainluigi (AC Milan, Torino, Atalanta Bergamo, 1991–96): 13
Leoncini, Gianfranco (Juventus, 1966): 2
Leone, Pietro (Pro Vercelli, 1911–14): 9
Levratto, Virgilio (Vado, Verona, Genoa, 1924–28): 28/11
Libonatti, Julio (Torino, 1926–31): 17/15
Locatelli, Ugo (Ambrosiana Inter, 1937–40): 18
Lodetti, Giovanni (AC Milan, 1964–1968): 17/2
Loik, Ezio (Venezia, Torino, 1942–49): 9/4
Lojacono, Francesco (Fiorentina, AS Roma, 1959–61): 8/5
Lombardo, Attilio (Sampdoria, Juventus, Crystal Palace [Eng], 1990–97): 18/2
Longoni, Angelo (Atalanta Bergamo, 1956): 1/2
Lorenzi, Benito (Inter Milan, 1949–54): 14/4
Losi, Giacomo (AS Roma, 1960–62): 11
Lovati, Cesare (AC Milan, 1920–21): 6
Lovati, Roberto (Lazio Roma, 1957): 2
Lucentini, Arnaldo (Sampdoria, 1951): 1
Magerli, Rolf (): 1/1
Magli, Augusto (Fiorentina, 1950): 1
Magnini, Ardico (Fiorentina, 1953–57): 20
Magnozzi, Mario (Livorno, AC Milan, 1924–32): 29/13
Mai, Karl (1955): 1/1
Maini, Giampiero (Vicenza Italy, 1997): 1
Malatrasi, Saul (Inter Milan, AC Milan, 1965–69): 3
Maldera, Aldo (AC Milan, 1976–79): 10
Maldini, Cesare (AC Milan, 1960–63): 14
Maldini, Paolo (AC Milan, 1988–98): 84/4
Maldini, Paulo (AC Milan, 1994–98): 8/2
Malinverni, Ermanno (Modena, 1947): 1
Mancini, Roberto (Sampdoria, 1984–94): 37/74
Manente, Sergio (Juventus, 1952): 1
Manfredonia, Lionello (Lazio Roma, 1977–78): 4
Manicone, Antonio (Inter Milan, 1993): 1
Mannini, Moreno (Sampdoria, 1992–93): 10
Marangon, Luciano (AS Roma, 1982): 1
Marchegiani, Luca (Torino, Lazio Roma, 1992–96): 9
Marchesi, Rino (Fiorentina, 1961–62): 2
Marchetti, Gian Pietro (Juventus, 1972–73): 5
Marchi, Sergio (Genoa, 1939): 1

Marchini, Liberto (Lucchese, 1936): 1
Marcora, Attilio (Saronno. 1921): 1
Mari, Giacomo (Juventus, Sampdoria, 1950–54): 6
Mariani, Amos (Padova, Lazio Roma, 1959): 2/1
Mariani, Edoardo (Genoa, 1912): 4
Marini, Giampiero (Inter Milan, 1980–83): 20
Marocchi, Giancarlo (Juventus, 1988–91): 11
Marocchino, Domenico (Juventus, 1981): 1
Maroso, Virgilio (Torino, 1945–49): 7/1
Martin, Cesare (Torino, 1923): 1
Martin, Dario (Torino, 1927–30): 2
Martini, Luigi (Lazio Roma, 1974): 1
Martino, Rinaldo (Juventus, 1949): 1
Marucco, Giustiniano (Novara, 1920): 2
Mascheroni, Ernesto (Ambrosiana Inter, 1935): 2
Maschio, Humberto (Atalanta Bergamo, 1962): 2
Masetti, Guido (AS Roma, 1936–39): 2
Massaro, Daniele (Fiorentina, AC Milan, 1982–94): 15
Mattea, Angelo (Casale, Us Torinese, 1914–21): 4/2
Matteoli, Gianfranco (Inter Milan, 1986–87): 6
Mattrel, Carlo (Palermo, 1962): 2
Mattuteia, Francesco (Pro Vercelli, 1924): 1
Mazza, Bruno (Inter Milan, 1953): 1
Mazzola, Alessandro (Inter Milan, 1963–74): 70/22
Mazzola, Valentino (Venezia, Torino, 1942–49): 12/4
Meazza, Giuseppe (Ambrosiana Inter, 1930–39): 54/33
Meeuws, Walter (1977): 1/1
Melli, Alessandro (Parma AC, 1993): 2
Meneghetti, Mario (Novara, 1920): 4
Menegotti, Enzo (Udinese, 1955): 2
Menichelli, Giampaolo (AS Roma, Juventus, 1962–64): 9/1
Menti, Romeo (Torino, 1947–49): 7/5
Merlo, Claudio (Fiorentina, 1969): 1
Meroni, Luigi (Torino, 1966): 6/2
Micelli, Romano (Foggia–Incedit 1965): 1
Migliavacca, Enrico (Novara, 1921–23): 11/3
Mihalic, Marcello (Napoli, 1929): 1/2
Milani, Aurelio (Inter Milan, 1964): 1
Milano, Felice (Pro Vercelli, 1912–13): 5
Milano, Giuseppe (Pro Vercelli, 1911–14): 11
Minelli, Severino (1938): 1/1
Minotti, Lorenzo (AC Parma, 1994–95): 8
Moltrasio, Luigi (Torino, 1954–55): 3
Montesanto, Mario (Bologna, 1934–36): 3
Monti, Feliciano (Padova, 1923–24): 3
Monti, Luisito (Juventus, 1932–36): 18/1
Montico, Antonio (Juventus, 1955): 2
Montouri, Miguel (Fiorentina, 1956–60): 12/2
Monzeglio, Eraldo (Bologna, AS Roma, 1930–38): 36
Mora, Bruno (Sampdoria, Juventus, AC Milan, 1959–65): 22/4
Morando, Clemente (Valenzana, 1921–22): 3
Moreiro, Francesco (Inter Milan, 1998): 1
Morelli Di Popolo, Vittorio (Torino, 1912): 1
Moriero, Francesco (Inter Milan, 1998): 5/2

Morini, Francesco (Juventus, 1973–75): 12
Morini, Giorgio (AS Roma, 1975): 4
Moro, Giuseppe (Bari, Torino, Sampdoria, 1949–53): 9
Moro, Silvano (Padova, 1958): 1
Moscardini, Giovanni (Lucchese, Pisa SC, 191–25): 9/7
Mosso, Eugenio (Torino, 1914): 1
Mozzini, Roberto (Torino, 1976–77): 6
Muccinelli, Ermes (Juventus, AS Roma, 1950–57): 15/4
Munerati, Federico (Juventus, 1926–27): 4
Mussi, Roberto (Torino, AC Parma, 1993–96): 11
Nardin, Stelio (Napoli, 1967): 1
Negri, William (Mantova, Bologna, 1962–65): 12
Negro, Paolo (Lazio Roma, 1994–95): 3
Nela, Sebastiano (AS Roma, 1984–87): 5
Neri, Bruno (Lucchese, Torino, 1936–37): 3
Neri, Giacomo (Genoa, 1939–40): 3/1
Neri, Maino (Inter Milan, 1953–54): 4
Nesta, Alessandro (Lazio Roma, 1996–98): 14
Nesti, Fulvio (Inter Milan, 1953–54): 5/1
Niccolai, Comunardo (Caliari, 1970): 3
Nicole, Bruno (Juventus, AS Roma, 1958–64): 8/3
Nocera, Cosimo (Foggia–Incedit, 1965): 1/1
Novellino, Walter (AC Milan, 1978): 1
Olivieri, Aldo (Lucchese, Torino, 1936–40): 25
Olmi, Renato (Ambrosiana Inter, 1940): 3
Oriali, Gabriele (Inter Milan, 1978–83): 28/1
Orlandini, Andrea (Napoli, 1974–75): 3
Orlando, Alberto (AS Roma, Fiorentina, 1962–65): 5/5
Orsi, Raimondo (Juventus, 1929–35): 35/13
Orzan, Alberto (Fiorentina, 1956–57): 4
Padalino, Pasquale (Fiorentina, 1996): 1
Padovano, Michele (Juventus, 1997): 1
Pagliuca, Gianluca (Sampdoria, Inter Milan, 1991–98): 37
Pagluica, Gianluca (Inter Milan, 1997): 1
Pagotto, Mario (Bologna, 1940): 1
Pandolfini, Egisto (Fiorentina, AS Roma, Inter Milan, 1950–57): 19/7
Panucci, Christian (AC Milan, Real Madrid [Spa], 1994–97): 7/1
Parodi, Giuseppe (Casale, Pro Vercelli, 1913–14): 4
Parola, Carlo (Juventus, 1945–50): 10
Pascutti, Ezio (Bologna, 1958–67): 17/8
Pasinati, Piero (Triestina, 1936–38): 12/5
Patikkis, N (1983): 1/1
Pecci, Eraldo (Torino, 1975–78): 7
Penev, Dimitar (1968): 1/1
Perani, Marino (Bologna, 1966): 4/1
Perazzolo, Mario (Genoa, 1939): 8
Perfumo, Roberto Alfredo (Cruzeiro Belo Horizonte [Bra], 1974): 1/1
Perin, Bernardo (Bologna, 1921–23): 4
Peruchetti, Giuseppe (Brescia, 1936): 2
Peruzzi, Angelo (Juventus, 1995–98): 22
Pesaola, Bruno (Napoli, 1957): 1
Pessotto, Giancula (Juventus, 1998): 1
Pessotto, Gianluca (Juventus, 1996–98): 5
Petris, Gianfranco (Triestina, Fiorentina, 1958–63): 4/1

Petruzzi, Fabio (AS Roma, 1995): 1

Piccaluga, Angelo (Modena, 1929): 2

Picchi, Armando (Inter Milan, Varese, 1964–68): 12

Piccini, Achille (Fiorentina, 1936): 1

Piccinini, Alberto (Juventus, 1949–52): 5

Pietroboni, Silvio (Inter Milan, Ambrosiana Inter, 1927–29): 11

Piola, Silvio (Lazio Roma, Juventus, Novara, 1935–52): 35/30

Pirovano, Giovan Battista (Fiorentina, 1966): 1

Pitto, Alfredo (Bologna, Fiorentina, Ambrosiana Inter, 1928–35): 29/2

Pivatelli, Gino (Bologna, 1955–58): 7/2

Pizzaballa, Pierluigi (Atalanta Bergamo, 1966): 1

Pizziolo, Mario (Fiorentina, 1933–36): 12/1

Poletti, Fabrizio (Torino, 1965–70): 6

Porrini, Sergio (Atalanta Bergamo, 1993): 2

Porta, Roberto (Ambrosiana Inter, 1935): 1

Posio, Celso (Napoli, 1957): 1

Pozzan, Ugo (Bologna, 1956): 2

Pozzi, Alberto (Bologna, 1922–24): 3

Prati, Pierino (AC Milan, AS Roma, 1968–74): 14/7

Prini, Maurilio (Fiorentina, 1956–57): 3

Pruzzo, Roberto (AS Roma, 1978–82): 6

Puia, Giorgio (LR Vicenza, Torino, 1962–78): 7

Pulici, Paolino (Torino, 1973–78): 19/5

Puricelli, Ettore (Bologna, 1939): 1/1

Radice, Luigi (AC Milan, 1962): 5

Rambaudi, Roberto (Lazio Roma, 1994): 2

Rampini, Alessandro (Pro Vercelli, 1920): 1

Rampini, Carlo (Pro Vercelli, 1911–13): 8/3

Rava, Pietro (Juventus, Alessandria, 1937–46): 27

Ravanelli, Fabrizio (Juventus, Middlesbrough [Eng], Marseille [Fra],1995–98): 21/8

Re Cecconi, Luciano (Lazio Roma, 1974): 2

Reguzzoni, Carlo (Bologna, 1940): 1

Remondini, Leandro (Lazio Roma, 1950): 1

Reynaudi, Ettore (Novara, 1920–21): 6

Ricagni, Eduardo (Juventus, Inter Milan, 1953–55): 3/2

Ricci, Secondo (Bologna, 1940): 1

Rigamonti, Mario (Torino, 1947–49): 3

Righetti, Ubaldo (AS Roma, 1983–85): 8

Riva, Luigi (Caliari, 1965–74): 42/35

Rivera, Gianni (AC Milan, 1962–74): 60/14

Rivolta, Enrico (Inter Milan, Ambrosiana Inter, 1928–29): 8/1

Rizzi, Giuseppe (Ausonia, AC Milan, 1910–13): 4/2

Rizzitelli, Ruggerio (AS Roma, 1988): 1

Rizzitelli, Ruggiero (Cesena, AS Roma, 1988–91): 8/2

Rizzo, Francesco (Caliari, 1966): 2/2

Robotti, Enzo (Fiorentina, 1958–65): 15

Rocca, Francesco (AS Roma, 1974–76): 19/3

Rocco, Nereo (Triestina, 1934): 1

Roggero, Rinaldo (Savona, 1920): 1

Roggi, Moreno (Fiorentina, 1974–76): 7

Romano, Felice (Reggiana, 1921–24): 5

Ronzon, Pierluigi (Atalanta Bergamo), 1960: 1

Rosato, Roberto (Torino, AC Milan, 1965–72): 27

Rosetta, Francesco (Fiorentina, 1949–56): 7

Rosetta, Virginio (Pro Vercelli, Juventus, 1920–34): 52

Rossetti, Gino (Torino, 1927–29): 13/9

Rossi, Paolo (LR Vicenza, Perugia, Juventus, AC Milan, 1977–86) : 47/20

Rossi, Paulo (Juventus, 1984): 1

Rossitto, Fabio (Udinese, 1996): 1

Rosso, Severino (Pro Vercelli, 1924): 1

Roversi, Tazio (Bologna, 1971): 1

Ruotolo, Gennaro (Genoa, 1991): 1

Sabadini, Giuseppe (AC Milan, 1973–74): 4

Sabato, Antonio (Inter Milan, 1984): 4

Sala, Claudio (Torino, 1971–78): 18

Sala, Marco (AC Milan, 1912): 1

Sala, Patrizio (Torino, 1976–80): 8

Sallustro, Attila (Napoli, 1929–32): 2/1

Salvadore, Sandro (AC Milan, Juventus, 1960–70): 36

Sansone, Raffaele (Bologna, 1932–39): 3

Santamaria, Aristodemo (Genoa, Novese, 1915–20): 11/3

Santarini, Sergio (AS Roma, 1971–74): 2

Sardelli, Vittorio (Genoa, 1939): 1

Sardi, Enrico (Doria, Genoa, 1912–20): 7/4

Sarti, Benito (Sampdoria, Juventus, 1958–61): 6

Sarti, Giuliano (Fiorentina, Inter Milan, 1959–67): 8

Sartor, (1998): 1

Savoldi, Giuseppe (Atalanta Bergamo, Bologna, Napoli, 1975–): 4/3

Scarabello, Luigi (Genoa, 1939): 1

Schiaffino, Juan (AC Milan, 1954–58): 4

Schiavio, Angelo (Bologna, 1925–34): 21/14

Schillaci, Salvatore (Juventus, 1990–91): 17/7

Scirea, Gaetano (Juventus, 1975–86): 79/2

Sclavi, Ezio (Lazio Roma, 1931–32): 3

Scopelli, Alejandro (AS Roma, 1935): 1

Segato, Armando (Fiorentina, 1953–59): 20

Selvaggi, Franco (Caliari, 1981): 3

Sentimenti, Lucidio (Juventus, Lazio Roma, 1945–53): 9

Serantoni, Pietro (Ambrosiana Inter, Juventus, AS Roma, 1933–39) : 18

Serena, Aldo (Torino, Juventus, Inter Milan, 1984–90): 24/5

Sgarbi, Abdon (AC Milan, 1929):

Signori, Giuseppe (Foggia, Lazio Roma, 1992–95): 27/6

Signori, Guiseppe (Lazio Roma, 1994): 1/1

Silenzi, Andrea (Torino, 1994): 1

Silvestri, Arturo (AC Milan, 1951): 3

Simone, Marco (AC Milan, 1992–96): 4

Sivori, Enrique Omar (Juventus, 1961–62): 9/8

Sormani, Angelo (Mantova, AS Roma, 1962–63): 7/2

Sperone, Mario (Torino, 1927): 2

Spinosi, Luciano (Juventus, 1971–74): 19

Stacchini, Gino (Juventus, 1958–61): 6/3

Statuto, Francesco (AS Roma, 1995): 3

Stroppa, Giovanni (Foggia, 1993–94): 4

Suika, Arunas (Lyn Oslo [Nor], 1995): 1/1

Tacchinardi, Alessio (Juventus, 1995): 1

Tacconi, Stefano (Juventus, 1987–91): 8

Tancredi, Franco (AS Roma, 1984–86): 12

Tansini, Mariano (Cremonese, 1926): 2

Tardelli, Marco (Juventus, Inter Milan, 1976–85): 81/6

Tassotti, Mauro (AC Milan, 1992–94): 7

Ticozzelli, Giuseppe (Alessandria, 1920): 1

Tognon, Omero (AC Milan, 1949–54): 14

Toldo, Francesco (Fiorentina, 1995–96): 6

Torricelli, Moreno (Juventus, 1996–98): 6

Torrisi, Stefano (Bologna, 1997): 1

Tortul, Mario (Sampdoria, 1956): 1

Trapattoni, Giovanni (AC Milan, 1960–64): 17/1

Trebbi, Mario (AC Milan, 1961–63): 2

Trere, Atilio (AC Milan, 1913): 1

Trere, Attilio (Ausonia, AC Milan, 1910–14): 4

Trevisan, Guglielmo (Trestina, 1940): 2/1

Tricella, Roberto (Verona, Juventus, 1984–87): 11

Trivellini, Giuseppe (Brescia 1915–23): 7

Tumburus, Paride (Bologna, 1962–63): 4

Vainoras, Raimondas (Inkaras Grifas Kaunas, 1995): 1/1

Vallana, Pedro (1924): 1/1

Valle, Modesto (Pro Vercelli, 1912–14): 7

Valobra, Attilio (Piemonte, 1913): 1

Varese, Amadeo (Casale, 1914): 5

Varglien, Giovanni (Juventus, 1936–39): 3

Varglien, Mario (Juventus, 1935): 1

Varisco, Francesco (U.S.Milanese, 1910): 2

Vavassori, Giovanni (Juventus, 1961): 1

Vecchina, Giovanni (Padova, Juventus, 1928–31): 2

Venturi, Arcadio (AS Roma, 1951–53): 4

Venturin, Giorgio (Torino, 1992): 1

Vercelli, Luigi (Novese, 1921): 1

Vialli, Gianluca (Sampdoria, Juventus, 1985–92): 60/16

Vierchowod, Pietro (Corno, Sampdoria, 1981–93): 46/2

Vieri, Christian (Juventus, Atletico Madrid [Spa], 1997–98): 13/7

Vieri, Lido (Torino, 1963–68): 4

Vincenzi, Giovanni (Livorno, 1924): 1

Vincenzi, Guido (Inter Milan, 1954–58): 3

Viola, Giovanni (Juventus, 1954–56): 11

Virgili, Giuseppe (Fiorentina, 1955–57): 7/2

Vivolo, Pasquale (Juventus, Lazio Roma, 1952–53): 4/1

Vojak, Antonio (Napoli, 1932): 1

Wilson, Giuseppe (Lazio Roma, 1974): 3

Zaccarelli, Renato (Torino, 1975–80): 25/2

Zaglio, Franco (AS Roma, 1959): 2

Zaldua, D (1927): 1/1

Zanello, Mario (Pro Vercelli, 1927): 2

Zecchini, Luciano (AC Milan, 1974): 3

Zenga, Walter (Inter Milan, 1986–92): 59

Zigoni, Gianfranco (Juventus, 1967): 1

Zoff, Dino (Napoli, Juventus, 1968–83): 113

Zola, Gianfranco (Napoli, AC Parma, Chelsea [Eng], 1991–97): 35/7

Zoratto, Daniele (Parma AC, 1993): 1

Zuffi, Enea (Torino, 1912): 2

ARGENTINIAN INTERNATIONAL PLAYERS' RECORDS

Abatangelo, Donato (Boca Juniors, 1913): 1
Abeledo, J (1960–62): 7
Acevedo, L (1967): 5
Acosta, Alberto Federico (Universidad Catolica Chile, Boca Juniors, 1986–95): 19/2
Acosta, G (1987): 5
Acosta, L (1923): 2/2
Acosta, O (1986–87): 6/1
Adet, Juan Carlos (Sportivo Almagro, 1919): 3/2
Adolfo, H (1989): 1
Aguero, (1976): 2
Aguero, R (1984): 1
Aguire, R (1984): 3
Aguirre, L (1968–69): 8
Aguirre, V (1923): 4/3
Airez, M (1989–90): 4/1
Alarcon, R (1938–41): 2
Alberti, Agustin (Huracan, 1919): 1
Alberti, Jorge (1940–45): 23/1
Albornoz, Josi (1996): 3/1
Albrecht, Jose Rafael (Estudiantes La Plata, San Lorenzo, 1961–69): 38/3
Aldea, Mariano (Hispano Argentina, 1914): 1
Alderete, L (1975): 1/1
Alderete, R (1975): 1
Alfaro, R (1987): 5
Alfaro Moreno Carlos, A (Independiente Avellanada, 1989–91): 12/2
Allegri, A (1951–53): 5
Almeyda, Matias Jesus (River Plate, Lazio Roma [Ita], 1996–98): 21
Almiron, Sergio (Newell's Old Boys, 1985–86): 3/3
Alonso, C (1929): 1
Alonso, Jorge (1928–29): 2/1
Alonso, Norberto (River Plate, 1972–83): 20/4
Altamirano, Ricardo Daniel (Independiente Avellanada, River Plate, 1991–95): 26/1
Alvarez, C (1960): 8
Alvarez (1942): 1/1
Alzua, Inocencio (Atletico San Isidro, 1919): 1
Amadeo, Luis Vernet (Atletico San Isidro, Gimnasia y Esgrima, 1908–10): 5
Ambrossi, R (1951): 3
Ameal, Antonio (River Plate, 1912): 1
Amido, J (1959): 1
Amuchastegui, Luis (1981–83): 3
Anderson, Juan (Lomas, 1901–02): 2/2
Andrada, Edgardo Norberto (1961–69): 20
Angelillo, Antonio Valentin (Boca Juniors, 1956–57): 14/14
Anido, J (1959): 2
Annunziata, M (1922): 4/2
Antonio, Roma (1957): 4
Apraiz, Antonio (Gimnasia y Esgrima, 1912): 1
Aquino, (1988): 2
Araguez, M (1938–40): 10

Araya, Emilio (Gimnasia y Esgrima 1919): 4
Ardiles, Osvaldo Cesar (Huracan, Tottenham Hotspur [Eng],1975–82): 52/8
Arganaraz, S (1923): 1
Arimalo, Germano (Nacional, 1902): 1/1
Arnaldo, J (1943): 2
Arnoldo, J (1942): 1
Arredondo, C (1959): 3
Arregui, C (1983): 4
Arregui, G (1940–41): 8/1
Arrese, I (1933): 1
Arrieta, A (1933–35): 5/1
Arrieta, Luis (Lanus/Ferro, 1939–41): 9/7
Arrilaga, J (1928–31): 4
Arruabarrena, Horacio (1994–95): 5
Arseni, A (0926): 2
Artel, M (1931): 3
Artime, Luis (Atalante, River Plate, Independiente Avellaneda, 1961–67): 16/16
Asad (1995): **2**
Asad, L (1975–76): 7/1
Asteciano, C (1975): 5/5
Astrada, Leonardo Ruben (River Plate, 1991–98): 30/1
Avallay, Roque (1968–74): 18/2
Avio, Ludovico (1958): 2
Ayala, C (1960): 8
Ayala, Roberto Fabian (River Plate, Napoli [Ita], 1994–98): 41/2
Ayala, Ruben H (Atletico Madrid [Sp], 1971–74): 27/13
Babington, Carlos (Huracan, 1973–74): 12/2
Bacchi, S (1926–27): 2
Badalini, Atilio (Gimnasia y Esgrima, Newell's Old Boys, 1916–22): 9/3
Badaracco, Geronimo (Argentino Quilmes, Atletico San Isidro, 1912–18): 13
Baglietto, A (19323): 2
Bagnato (1955): 1
Baiocco (1951): 3/4
Balbo, Abel Eduardo (River Plate, Udinese [Ita], AS Roma [Ita], 1989–96): 34/9
Balbuena, Agustin A (Independiente Avellaneda, 1973–74): 10
Baldonedo, Emilio (Huracan, Newell's Old Boys, 1940): 6/7
Baley, Hector Rodolfo (Huracan, Talleres Cordoba, 1976–82): 11
Ballart, F (Tiro Federal Rosario, 1920): 1
Ballay, J (1955–58): 3
Ballay, R (1976): 1
Ballesteros, G (1940): 4/1
Barbas, Juan Alberto (Racing Club Avellaneda, Real Zaragoza [Sp], Lecce [Ita],1979–85): 33
Bargas, Angel Hugo (Nantes [Fr],1971–74): 32/1
Barros, G (1995): 1
Bartero, J (1987): 5

Bartolucci (1928): 2
Basile, Alfio (1968–69): 9/1
Basilico (1959): 6/8
Bassedas, Christian Gustavo (Velez Sarsfield, 1994–97): 20
Bassio, Carlos Gustavo (Estudiantes La Plata, 1995): 1
Basualdo, Fabian Armando (Mandiyu Corrientes, River Plate, 1986–93): 45
Basualdo, Jose Horacio (VfB Stuttgart [Ger], Velez Sarsfield, 1990–95): 21
Bataglicio (1945): 1
Batista, Sergio Daniel (Racing Club Avellaneda, 1985–90): 40
Batistuta, Gabriel (Boca Juniors, Fiorentina [Ita], 1991–98): 65/44
Battagliero, J (1940–45): 8
Bautista, J (1963): 2
Bauza, Edgardo (Vera Cruz [Mex]. 1981–90): 3
Bearzotti, Felipe (1921–24): 9
Bearzotti, Florindo (Belgrano Rosario , 1920): 4
Becerra, Heraldo (1979): 1
Belen, Raul (Racing Club Avellaneda, 1959–63): 31/9
Belen, S (1940–43): 7/2
Bellis, Ernesto (1934): 1/1
Bello, Fernando (1934): 10
Bello, Juan Jose (Atletico San Isidro, 1912): 2
Beltran (1976): 1
Benavidez, A (1951): 1
Benegas, J (1956–57): 7
Benetiz, V (1959): 1/1
Benitez (1977): 1
Benitez Caceres, Delfin, (Boca Juniors, 1934): 1/1
Berinstain, T (1934): 1
Berizzo, Eduardo (River Plate, 1996–98): 8
Bernao, Raul Emilio (Independiente Avellanada, 1963–69): 14/4
Bernasconi, Diomedes (Estudiantes La Plata, 1914): 2
Beron, J (1960): 2
Berta (1972): 1
Bertetti, E (1931): 1
Berti, Sergio Angel (River Plate, 1991–98): 23/2
Bertolini, J (1921): 2
Bertolotti (1967): 1
Bertolucci, P (1924): 1
Bertoni, Ricardo Daniel (Independiente Avellanada, Fiorentina [Ita], 1974–82): 30/12
Bethular, Angel (Racing Club Avellanada, 1915): 1
Betinotti, C (1959): 1
Biaggo (1995): 1
Biagioli, J (1957): 1
Bianatti, Alberto (Eureka, 1919): 3/1
Bianchi, Carlos (Velez Sarsfield, 1970–72): 15/8
Bianchi, J (1925): 4

Bidoglio, Ludovico (1921–28): 38
Bielli, C (1964): 5
Bincaz, Claudio (Atletico San Isidoro, 1916): 1
Binello (1979): 1
Bisconti (1991): 1
Blanco (1959): 5
Blanco, Antonio (Rosario Central, 1916–25): 9/2
Blanco, Eduardo (Rosario Central, 1918): 2
Blanco, M (1957–61): 2
Blotto, M (1937–42): 6
Bocanelli (1979–80): 4/3
Bochini, Ricardo Enrique (Independiente Avellaneda, 1974–86): 29
Boffi (1921–22): 2
Boggio, Norberto (1958–61): 12
Boigues, J (1926): 1
Boldrini, Ariel (Newell's Old Boys, 1991): 4
Bonano, (1996): 1
Bonelli, R (1954–56): 8/1
Bonnano, Roberto (1959): 6/4
Bonsuck, R (1963): 2
Bordon, M (1979): 4
Borelli, Jorge (Newell's Old Boys, 1993–94): 15
Borelli, Juan Jose (Real Oviedo [Sp], 1997): 1
Borello, I (1953–55): 8/3
Borghi, Claudio (Argentinos Juniors, 1986): 6/1
Borgnia, A (1943): 2
Borrelli, Juan Jose (Panathinaikos [Gre], 1995): 5
Bosich, Juan J (1960): 2
Bossio, Angel (1927–35): 27
Bossio, Carlos Gustavo (Estudiantes La Plata, 1994–96): 10
Botasso, Juan (1929–30): 3
Bottaniz, Victor (Union Santa Fe, 1978): 3
Boveda, J (1972–75): 7/1
Boye, Mario Heriberto (Boca Juniors, 1945–52): 18/8
Bozzo, L (1921): 1
Bravo, Humberto (Talleres Cordoba, 1978): 5
Bravo, Ruben (1950–51): 3/1
Brichetto, Enrique (Boca Juniors, 1919): 1
Brindisi, Miguel Angel (Huracan, 1969–74): 48/17
Broockers, A (1960–62): 6
Brooks, A (1959): 2
Brown, Alfredo (Quilmes, 1912): 3/1
Brown, Alfredo C (Alumni, 1906–11): 10/2
Brown, Carlos C (Alumni, 1903–05): 2
Brown, Eliseo (Alumni, 1906–11): 12/6
Brown, Ernesto A (Alumni, Quilmes, 1902–12): 14/1
Brown, Jorge Gibson (Alumni, Quilmes, 1902–1911): 24/3
Brown, Jose Luis (Racing Club Avellaneda, 1983–89): 41
Brown, Juan Domingo (Alumni, Quilmes, 1906–16): 25/3
Brown, Juan Gibson (Alumni, 1905): 1
Browne, Patricio B (Alumni, 1905–10): 10
Bruno, Alfredo (Gimnasia y Esgrima, 1914): 1
Bruzzone, Roberto (Sportivo Palermo, 1920–21): 3
Buchanan, Carlos J (Alumni, 1902–08): 6
Buchanan, Walter (Alumni, 1902–03): 2
Buck, Sidney R (Quilmes, 1912): 1
Bujedo, F (Racing Club Avellaneda, 1979–83): 3

Bulleri (1982): 1
Burgos, German Adrian (River Plate, 1995–98): 12
Burgos, Lucio (Atletico San Isidoro, 1908): 1/2
Burruchaga, Jorge Luis (Independiente Avellaneda, FC Nantes [Fr], 1983–90): 59/13
Busso, C (1973–74): 5
Busso, J (1919): 3
Busso, M (1984–85): 2
Busso, Mario J (Atlanta, Boca Juniors, 1918–19): 2
Buttice, C (1967–68): 4
Caballero, Pablo Oscar (Velez Sarsfield, 1998): 2
Cabano, Juan (Quilmes, 1914–16): 2/1
Cabrera (1968–89): 10
Caccopardo, E (1925–26): 3
Caceres, Fernando Gabriel (Real Zaragoza [Spa], 1992–97): 24/1
Cagna, Diego (Argentinos Juniors, 1992–98): 12/1
Calandra (1927–28): 2
Calandra, Jorge (Estudiantes La Plata, 1918–20): 3/1
Caldas, G (1921–28): 5/1
Calderon, Gabriel Humberto (Independiente Avellanada, Paris St Germain [Fra], 1980–90): 23/1
Calderon, Jose Luis (Independiente Avellanada, 1997): 5
Caldes, G (1923): 4
Calics, Oscar (San Lorenzo, 1966–67): 6
Calla, Eugenio (1959–60): 12/2
Cambon (1967): 1/1
Camino, Julian (Estudiantes La Plata, 1984): 1
Camino, Julian (Estudiantes La Plata, 1983–85): 7
Campana (1947): 1
Campano, J (1926): 1
Campbell, Colin (Estudiantes La Plata, 1907): 1
Campbell, Guillermo (Alumni, 1908): 1
Camps (1996): 2
Canaveri, Zoilo (Racing Club Avellaneda, 1916): 2
Cancino, E (1923): 1
Caniggia, Claudio Paul (River Plate, Verona [Ita], Atalanta Bergamo [Ita}, AS Roma [Ita]: 32/14
Canteli, J (Newell's Old Boys, 1943): 1/1
Cap, Vladislao Wenceslao (River Plate, 1959–62): 11/1
Carabal, A (1956): 2/3
Carabelli, Norberto (Huracan, 1920): 1
Carbone, B (1959): 1
Carceo, H (1960–61): 5
Cardena (1967): 1
Cardenas, C (1975–76): 6/1
Cardoso (1998): 2
Cardoso, L (1956–63): 14
Cardoso, Rodolfo (Werder Bremen [Ger], Hamburger SV [Ger], 1996–97): 6/1
Cardozo, Raul (Velez Sarsfield, 1997): 4
Caricaberry, Alfredo (1926–34): 16/8
Carnevale, Daniel (Las Palmas [Sp], 1972–74): 27
Carone, R (1967): 5
Carranza, Luis Alberto (Racing Club

Avellaneda, 1994): 1
Carrascosa, Jorge (Juracan, 1970–77): 7
Carre, Pascual (Independiente Avellanada, 1916): 1
Carrizo, Amadeo Raul (River Plate, 1954–64): 20
Casa (1964): 1
Casari (1922): 1
Caspari, J (Santa Fe 1979): 2
Cassan, F (1940): 4/2
Castagno, L (1950): 2
Castagnola, Roberto (Racing Club Avellaneda, 1918–21): 10
Castillo (1995): 1
Castoldi, P (1922): 4
Castro, E (1931): 4/5
Castro, JA (San Lorenzo, 1979): 5/1
Castro, R (1957): 2/1
Cavadini (1936–38): 2/1
Cecconato, Carlos (1953–56): 11/2
Cechi, S (1980): 2
Cejas, Agustin (Racing Club, 1959–70): 9
Celico, Luis (Atlanta, 1919): 4
Celli, Adolfo (Newell's Old Boys, 1919–23): 12
Celli, Ernesto (Newell's Old Boys, 1919–23):5/1
Cerrotti, A (1923–25): 2/1
Cesarini, R (1926): 2/1
Chabiolin, J (1922): 1
Chaires, Jose Arturo (1962): 1/1
Chaldu, Norberto (San Lorenzo, 1964–65): 5
Chambrolin, J (1922): 4
Chamot, Jose Antonio (Foggia [Ita],Lazio Roma [Ita], 1993–98): 38/2
Chaparro, R (Instituto Cordoba, 1982): 1
Chavin, Jaime (Huracan, 1918–21): 4/1
Chazaretta, Enrique Salvador (San Lorenzo, 1973–74): 12
Cherro, F (1937): 1
Cherro, Felipe (1924–26): 6/1
Cherro, Roberto (1926–37): 16/13
Chiappe, Arturo A (River Plate, 1910–16): 14
Chiarrapicco, J (1924): 1
Chiessa, A (1922–23): 10/2
Chividini, Alberto (1929–30): 3
Choperana, P (1924): 1
Ciacci (1962): 1
Ciancio, P (1932): 1
Cielinsky, F (1960–61): 3
Cielinsky, L (1963): 2
Cilley, Luis (Atlantico San Isidro, 1919): 1
Ciocca (1938): 1/1
Clarcke, Edwin (Rosario Central, Porteno, 1918–21): 8/7
Clausen, Nestor Rolando (Independiente Avellanada, FC Sion [Chl], 1983–88): 26/1
Cocco, L (1968–69): 9/2
Cochrane, R (1924): 3
Coletta, S (1936–39): 5
Colman, Juan Carlos (1947–56): 13
Colombo, Bartolome (1937–45): 16
Comas, JA (Velez Sarsfield, 1985): 1
Comaschi (1951): 4
Comino, J (1984): 3
Conde, Norberto (Velez Sarsfield/Atlanta, 1955–58): 12/2
Conigliaro, M (1970): 4/2

Conti, S (1926): 1
Corbatta, Oreste Omar (1956–62): 43/18
Corbella, S (1921): 2
Cordero, L (1974): 1
Corradini (1959): 5
Correa, O (1932): 2
Correa, P (1973): 4
Cortella, Antonio R (Defensor Belgrano, Boca Juniors, 1918–21): 11
Cortez, A (1973): 1
Corti (1989): 1
Coscia, H (San Lorenzo, 1975–79): 10/5
Cosso, Agustin (Velez Sarsfield, San Lorenzo, 1936–38): 2
Coulthurst, Ricardo L (Quilmes, 1906): 1
Cozzi, J (1947): 6
Craviotto, Nestor Oscar (Independiente Avellanada, 1989–93): 11/2
Crespo, Francisco (Tigre, 1914): 3
Crespo, Hernan Jorge (River Plate, AC Parma [Ita], 1995–98): 17/6
Cristante, Rolando (Platense 1995): 6
Crocce, Marcos (Racing Club Avellaneda, 1919): 1
Cruz, Julio (River Plate, 1997): 5
Cruz, Osvaldo (1953–58): 22/3
Cucchiaroni, Ernesto (1955–56): 11
Cucheo, R (1951): 1
Cuciuffo, Jose Luis (Velez Sarsfield, Boca Juniors, 1985–89): 21
Cuello, A (1930–37): 8
Cuper (1984): 3
Cupo (1951): 4/5
D'Ascenso, E (1960): 8/3
Dacquarti, N (1960): 4
Danil, M (1935):
Dannaher, Guillermo (Tiro Federal Rosaria, Quilmes, 1912–1914): 7/4
Daponte, N (1956): 5
De Bourgoing, Hector (1956–57): 5
De Casari, M (1922): 2
De Ciancio (1959): 5
De Jonge, R (1932–35): 8
De la Mata, B (19656–66): 6
De la Mata, Vicente (Independiente Avellanada, Newell's OldBoys, 1937–46): 14/6
De los Santos, A (1922–25): 8
De Mare (1935): 3
De Mare, A (1924): 4
De Maria, Atilio (Instituto Cordoba, 1930–31): 3
De Miguel, Antonio (1922–26): 9/2
De Saa, M (1935): 2
De Vicenzi, A (1931–34): 8/1
De Zorzi, (1945): 7
Decaria M, (1963): 1
Del Felice, A (1931): 3/1
Del Mul (1979): 1
Delgado, B (1923–1926): 8/3
Delgado, Marcelo Alejandro (Racing Club Avellaneda, 1995–98): 12
Dellacha, Pedro Rodolfo (Racing Club Avellaneda, 1953–58): 35
Dellatorre, Jose (1930): 6
Dellavalle, Manuel (Atletico Cen Cordoba, 920–22): 8/1
Delovo (1940): 1

Dertycia, Oscar (Instituto Cordoba, 1984–88): 24/7
Dezotti, Gustavo Abel (Newell's Old Boys, Lazio Roma [Ita], Cremonese [Ita], 1987–90): 11/3
Di Meola, Edgardo (River Plate, 1974): 1
Di Paola, P (1926): 2
Di Stefano, Alfred (River Plate, 1947): 7/7
Diano (1947): 1
Diaz (1998): 1
Diaz, H (1998): 1
Diaz, Hernan Edgardo (River Plate, 1987–97): 26/3
Diaz, I (1936–43): 9
Diaz, Jose (1959): 5
Diaz, O (1979): 1
Diaz, Octavio (River Plate, 1920–28): 12
Diaz, Ramon Angel (River Plate, 1979–82): 5/1
Diaz, Ramon Osvaldo (River Plate, 1981): 1
Diaz, Ruben Osvaldo (Racing, River Plate, 1965–1982): 36/10
Diaz, Zenon (River Plate, 1906–16): 7
Dickinson, Alfredo Lorenzo (Alumni, 1911): 4
Dickinson, Carlos Edgard (Belgrano, 1901–08): 8/2
Dino (1923): 1/1
Ditro, C (1963): 3
Domenech (1986): 1
Dominguez (1984): 2
Dominguez, Rogelio Antonio (River Plate, 1951–62): 24
Dominichi, Jorge (1971–72): 14
Doval (1967): 1
Duggan, Eduardo Patrico (Belgrano, 1902): 1
Echeverria, Raul (Estudiantes la Plata, 1920–22): 8/4
Enrique, Carlos Alberto (River Plate, 1989–91): 12
Enrique, Hector Aldolfo (River Plate, 1986–89): 8
Errea, N (1959–61): 2
Escarra, Roberto Gonzalez (Porteno, 1914): 1
Escudero, Marcelo Alejandro (Newell's Old Boys, 1994–95): 9/2
Esnaider, Juan Eduardo (Real Madrid [Sp], Atletico Madrid [Sp], 1996–97): 3/3
Esperon, G (1940–42): 9/1
Espina, Marcelo (Platense, Colo Colo [Chl], 1994–95): 5/1
Espinoza, J (1943–75): 7
Esponda, A (1930): 1/2
Esposito (1972): 1
Estrada, Juan (1936–41): 17
Etchecopar (1967): 1
Etchegaray, J (1960): 5
Evaristo, Juan (1922–30): 29/1
Evaristo, Mario (1929–30): 9/3
Fabbri, Nestor Ariel (Racing Club Avellaneda, Boca Juniors, 1987–96): 27/2
Fabrini, J (1939): 2/1
Facio, J (1932): 1
Facundo, Hector (San Lorenzo, 1962): 2/1
Facundo, O (1959–62): 4
Faggiani, L (1922): 1
Faina, B (1951): 1
Faina, U (1951): 1

Falcioni, Julio Cesar (America de Cali [Col], 1989–90): 2
Fantaguzzi, J (1986–87): 6
Farro, C (1945): 3
Fattone, J (1939): 1
Fazio, L (1937): 3
Feldman, Dario (Valencia [Sp] (1977): 1
Felice, Roberto (Gimnasia y Esgrima, 1919): 1
Felisari, Alberto (Platense, 1916): 3
Fernandez, E (1963): 7/2
Fernandez, Elias (River Plate, Atletico San Isidoro, 1909–16): 15/1
Fernandez, Emilio (Gimnasia y Esgrima, 1916): 2
Fernandez, J (1963–67): 3
Fernandez, L (1975): 3
Fernandez, M (1947–63): 5/1
Ferrano (1963): 1/1
Ferrario, L (1932–34): 2
Ferraro, J (1945–56): 8/3
Ferreira, Manuel (1923–30): 21/5
Ferreira, Nolo (1930): 1
Ferreiro, Roberto Oscar (Independiente Avellanada, 1963–66): 18
Ferrero, Enzo (Boca Juniors, 1974): 1
Ferrero, R (1974): 2/1
Ferreyra (1943–91): 3/1
Ferreyra, Bernabe (Tigre, River Plate, 1930–36): 3
Ferreyra, JC (1942): 1
Ferreyra, Manuel (1930): 1
Ferro, Antonio (Independiente Avellanada, 1917–19): 8
Ferro, Armando (Independiente Avellanada, 1917): 1
Fidel (1937–38): 3/2
Fidel, M (1940): 1/1
Filgueiras, JM (1950–56): 7
Fillol, Ubaldo Matildo (River Plate, 1974–85): 58
Firpo, Emilio B (Baracas1903): 1
Fischer, Rodolfo Jose (San Lorenzo, 1972): 38/14
Flores, Jose Oscar (1994): 1
Facundo, O (1959): 1
Fonda, J (1945–46): 10
Foresto, A (1926): 1
Fornari, R (1973): 1/1
Forrester (1935): 2
Forrester, Arthur H (Belgrano, 1905–07): 2
Fortunato, Mario (1921–26): 14/1
Fortunato, S (Estudiantes La Plata, 1979): 5
Fossa, J (1927): 1
Fossatti, D (1931): 2
Fournol, 'Calomino' Pedro Bleo (Quilmes, Boca Juniors, 1912–23): 14/5
Francia, Juan (Newell's Old Boys, 1918–22): 7/4
Franco, Dario Javier (Newell's Old Boys, Real Zaragoza [Sp], 1991–94): 22/6
Fredes (1979): 1
Fren, C (1980): 2
Frers, Pablo (Belgrano, 1905): 1
Freschi, Hector (1934): 1
Frumento, Angel (Banfield, 1920): 4
Funes, E (1931): 1
Funes, J (1987): 4

Gabino (1927): 3
Gainzarain, E (1924–28): 3
Gaitan, L (1979):3
Galateo, Alberto (1934): 1/1
Galetto (San Lorenzo, 1995): 1
Gallardo, Marcelo Daniel (River Plate, 1994–98): 30/12
Gallardo, Pedro (Independiente Campana, Independiente Avellanada, 1914): 2/1
Gallego, Americo Ruben (Newell's Old Boys, Old Boys Rosario, River Plate, 1975–81): 72/3
Galleti, C (1974): 1/1
Gallino, Santiago Pio (Gimnasia y Esgrima, 1910–12): 4
Gallo, A (1919): 2
Gallo, C (1967–69): 9
Gallo, Carlos Alberto (Estudiantes La Plata, 1919): 2
Galvan, Ruben (Independiente Avellanada, Talleres Cordoba, 1973–82): 42
Gamboa, Fernando Andres (Rosario Central, 1991): 7
Gandulla, Bernardo (Boca Juniors, 1940): 1
Garabal (1956): 1/1
Garasino, A (1924–25): 3/1
Garceron I, (1950): 2
Garcia (1967): 1/2
Garcia, Candido (River Plate, 1915–18): 5/1
Garcia, Claudio Omar (Racing Club Avellaneda, 1991–94): 12/2
Garcia, Diego (1934–36): 6/5
Garcia, Enrique (1935–43): 30/9
Garcia, H (1950): 1
Garcia, Hector (1938): 1
Garcia, L (1917): 1/1
Garcia, O (1959): 3/1
Garcia, R (1931–58): 4
Garcia, S (1979): 1
Garcia, I Alberto (River Plate, 1909): 1/1
Garcia, II (1967): 1/1
Garcia, Perez C (1951–56): 6
Garcia, Perez JM (1953): 1
Gareca, Ricardo (Boca Juniors, 1983–85): 23/5
Gareca, Ricardo Alberto (1981): 1
Gargiulo, S (1931): 2
Garnero (1995): 2
Garrafa, F (1933–34): 2
Garre, Oscar Alfredo (Ferro Carril Oeste, 1983–88): 39/1
Gaslini, J (1922–25): 5/1
Gaspari, J (1979): 3/1
Gasparini (1979): 1
Gastini, J (1922): 1/1
Gatti, Hugo Orlando (River Plate, Boca Juniors, 1967–77): 18
Gayol (1941): 1
Geloso (1979): 1
Gennoni (1967): 1
Ghisso, C (1972–73): 5/1
Gianserra, F (1956–57): 4
Gierdano, C (1975): 1
Gil, Juan Olegario (Atletico San Isidoro, 1910): 1
Gilli, L (1937): 2
Gimenez, Juan Carlos (1956–57): 11
Ginebra, Miguel (Huracan, 1917): 1

Ginocchio, Armando G (Estudiantes la Plata, Newell's Old Boys, 1907–10): 5
Giudice (1943): 1
Giunta, Blas Armando (Boca Juniors, 1986–91): 11
Giusti, Ricardo Omar (Independiente Avellaneda, 1983–90): 52
Glaria, Ruben (San Lorenzo): 7
Glini, J (1951): 3
Goin, E (1923): 1
Gomez (1960): 1/1
Gomez, E (1940): 2
Gomez, Hector N (1980): 1
Gomez Marcelo (Velez Sarsfield, 1995): 1
Gonzalez, Alberto Mario (Boca Juniors, 1961–67): 17/1
Gonzalez, Carlos (Newell's Old Boys, 1912): 2
Gonzalez, Cristian Alberto (Boca Juniors, 1995): 1
Gonzalez, H (1960): 1
Gonzalez, Ignacio Carlo (Racing Club Avellaneda, 1997): 4
Gonzalez, J (1933): 5
Gonzalez, Manuel Pedro (Newell's Old Boys, 1910–13): 13/10
Gonzalez, Pedro (1969–77): 3
Gonzalez, R (1965): 1/1
Gonzalez, Tomas Medro (Alumni, 1910): 2
Gonzalez, Tristan (Estudiantes La Plata, 1906): 1/1
Gonzalez, V (1921): 2
Gonzalez, Peralta T (1934): 1
Gorosito, Nestor Raul (FC Tirol [Aus], San Lorenzo, 1989–97): 19/9
Gorti (1989): 1
Goycochea, A (1924): 3
Goycochea, Sergio Javier (River Plate, 1986–94): 45
Gracia, Enrique (1935–40): 4
Graciani (Boca Juniors 1986): 1
Gramacho, Roberto (1971): 1
Grant, Haroldo M (Belgrano, 1907–11): 6
Grecco, S (1943): 3
Grieshofer, Conrado (Tiro Federal Rosario, 1913): 1
Griffa, Jorge (1959): 4
Griguol, Carlos Timoteo (1959–63): 13
Griguol, M (1961): 1
Grillo, Ernesto (1952–62): 21/9
Grimoldi, F (1931): 2
Guaita, Enrico (1933–37): 3/1
Gualco, Sebastian (1935–43): 23
Guarrizz (1951): 2/1
Guenzatti, L (1959): 2
Guerini, M (1973): 7/4
Guidi, Carlos (Tiro Federal Rosario, 1913–17): 7/1
Guidi, Juan Hector (1956–61): 36
Guidi, R (1913): 1/3
Guilidori, C (1923–25): 3/1
Gurrutchague, J (Racing Club Avellaneda, 1923–56): 26
Gutierrez, H (1986–87): 6/3
Haedo, J (1931): 1
Hayes, EM (1911–12): 4/7
Hayes, Ennis (Rosario Central, 1915–19): 11/5

Heissinger, Adolfo F (Tigre, 1916–19): 4
Henman, Hector J (Alumni, 1906): 1
Heredia, C (1940): 2
Heredia, JC (1940–42): 6–1
Heredia, Ramon Armando (1971–74): 30/2
Hernandez, Patricio Jose (Estudiantes La Plata, 1979–82): 7
Herrera, A (1933–57): 4
Hiller, Eduardo (Gimnasia y Esgrima, 1916): 2/4
Hospital, Juan (Racing Club Avellaneda, 1912–15): 4
Houseman, Rene Orlando (Huracan, 1973–79): 55/12
Howard, Jorge H (Belgrano ,1903): 1
Hoyos, Guillermo (1980): 4/1
Husain, Claudio (Velez Sarsfield, 1997): 2
Hussein (1995): 1
Iacono, N (1942–51): 4
Iije (1943): 1
Infante, Ricardo (1952–56): 4/1
Infantino (1951): 4
Inigo, D (1957–63): 4
Insua, R (1983–84): 5
Intuni (1951): 4/2
Iraneta, C (1934): 1
Iribarren, Juan (1922–37): 24
Irurieta, J (1924–25): 5/3
Irusta (1964): 1
Ischia, Carlos (Velez Sarsfield, 1980): 2
Islas, Luis Alberto (Independiente Avellanada, Atletico Madrid [Sp], 1984–94): 30
Isola, Carlos (River Plate, 1916–22): 25
Izaguirre, Carlos (Porteno, 1914–23): 9/6
Jacobs, Arturo G (Alumni, Belgrano, 1907–10): 8/1
Jacobs, Arturo O (1906): 1
Jimenez, Jorge (Banfield, 1995): 4
Jimenez, W (1960): 9/2
Johnston, Juan (Quilmes, 1912–13): 2
Juarez, Ernesto (1962–63): 11/2
Juarez, M (1957–58): 4/1
Juarez, N (1957): 1/1
Kempes, Mario Alberto (Rosario Central, Valencia [Sp], 1973–75): 43/21
Kiessel, Ernesto (Huracan, 1920): 1
Killer, Daniel Pedro (Racing Club Avellaneda, 1972–78): 25/3
Kuko, E (1929): 1
La Volpe, Ricardo (San Lorenzo, 1975–76): 8
Labruna, Angel Amadeo (River Plate, 1945–58): 35/18
Lacasia, C (1953): 2
Lafaureta (1923): 1
Laferrara, A (1940–42): 6/5
Laforia, Jose Buruca (Barracas, Alumni, 1902–07): 5
Laginestra (1967): 1 1967.08.22 1
Laguna, Jose (Huracan, 1916–19): 5/4
Laiolo, Jose (Rosario Central, River Plate, 1916–19): 5/3
Lalaurreta, A (1923): 1
Lallana, C (1963–65): 5/3
Lamas, Juan Jose (Estudiantes La Plata, 1913–15): 5
Lamelza, A (1969): 1
Landucci, C (1971–72): 6

Laneri, Alejandro Fabio (Rosario Central, 1991): 1

Lanus, Carlos Galup (1914): 2

Lanzidei (1988): 3

Laraignee, Cesar Antonio (1970–71): 11/3

Larriquy, C (1979): 3

Larrosa, Omar (Independiente Avellanada, 1977–78): 11

Latorre, Diego Fernando (Boca Juniors, 1991): 6/1

Laurenzano, C (1924): 1

Lauri, Miguel Angel (1929–35): 9/2

Lawrie, Henry J (Alumni, 1909–11): 3/1

Lazaraga, C (1921): 1

Lazari (1923): 1

Lazatti, E (1936–37): 4

Lazcano R, (1919): 1

Lazzari, J (1923): 1

Leguizamon, H (1940–43): 3/1

Lejona (1959): 3

Lejone (1959): 1

Lelong, Alberto Latorre (Estudiantes La Plata, 1920): 1

Lennie, A (1912): 2

Leonardi, Jose Bernabe (Ferro Carril Oeste, 1964–67): 9

Leonardi, Roberto (Estudiantes La Plata, 1914–17): 3

Leslie, G (1901): 1/1

Leslie, William (Quilmes, 1902): 1

Lett, Carlos A (Alumni, 1905–11): 3

Lezcano, Delfin (Estudiantes La Plata, 1914): 1/1

Libonatti, Julio (Newell's Old Boys, 1919–25): 15/8

Liztherman (1943): 1

Lloyd, Harold A (Quilmes, 1909): 1

Loizzo, Alberto (1923–25): 14

Lojacono, FR (1956): 8

Lombardi (1998): 2

Lombardo, Francisco (1952–59): 37

Longo (1951): 1

Lopez (1936–98): 7

Lopez, A (1931–34): 7

Lopez, CA (Velez Sarsfield, 1979): 4/1

Lopez, Claudio Javier (Racing Club Avellaneda, Valencia [Sp], 1996–98): 21/5

Lopez, Gustavo Adrian (Independiente Avellanada, Real Zaragoza [Sp], 1994–97): 10/2

Lopez, I (1943): 1

Lopez, J (1924–68): 3

Lopez, Jose Alfredo (Boca Juniors, 1919–21): 9/1

Lopez, Juan Jose (River Plate, 1972–74): 3/2

Lopez, M (1967): 1

Lopez, N (1967–69): 2

Lopez, V (1972): 1

Lorenzo, C (1963): 2

Lorenzo, Nestor Gabriel (Bari [Ita], 1988–90): 12

Loustau, Felix (1945–52): 26/9

Loyarte, E (1924): 5/2

Lucarelli, Jose (Banfield, 1920): 5

Lucarelli, R (1921–22): 2/2

Lucca, M (1988): 4

Lucena, R (1926): 2

Ludana, V (1975): 1

Luduena (1991): 1

Luduena, Luis A (1980): 4/2

Lugo (1956): 1

Luna, C (1964–65): 6

Luna, M (1927): 2/3

Lupo, O (1932): 1

Luque, Leopoldo J (River Plate, 1975–81): 45/19

MacAllister, Carlos (Racing Club Avellaneda, 1987–93): 4

Macchiavello, Enrique (Racing Club Avellaneda, 1919): 1

Maciel (1989): 2

Madero, J (1964–69): 4

Madero I, Juan A (Estudiantes La Plata, 1919): 1

Madurga, Norberto Ruben (1970–71): 13/3

Magistretti, Guillermo S (Tigre, 1919–23): 4

Maglio, J (1925–31): 8/5

Malbernat, Oscar Miguel (1965–70): 14

Malbran, Miguel S (Atletico San Isidoro, 1907–11): 3/2

Maldonado, Rafael (1962): 2

Mallen, Angel H (Belgrano, 1913): 4

Mancuso, Alejandro Victor (Boca Juniors, Velez Sarsfield, 1992–94): 10/1

Manera (1967): 3

Manfredini, P (1959): 2/2

Mantegari (1956): 1

Maradona, Diego Armando (Argentinos Juniors, Boca Juniors, Barcelona [Ita], Napoli [Ita], Sevilla [Ita], 1977–94): 90/34

Marangoni, C (1983–84): 9

Marante, J (1945–47): 9

Marassi (1928): 1

Marchesini, V (1986–87): 6/1

Marcico, A (1992): 1

Marcico, Alberto Jose (Toulouse [Fr], 1984–85): 13

Marcos, Angel (1971): 2

Marcos, S (1969–70): 7/1

Marcovecchio, Alberto (Racing Club Avellaneda, 1912–19): 11/8

Maril, J (1940): 4/1

Marin, Jose (1967–71): 4

Mariotti, J (1962): 1

Marquez, A (Portena, 1912): 1

Marrapodi, R (1954): 2

Martellotto, German (Monterrey [Mex], 1991): 1

Martimo, R (1945): 1/1

Martin (1942): 1

Martin, Alfredo N (Tigre, Boca Juniors, 1917–19): 9/1

Martin, D (1963): 8

Martinez (1951): 4/1

Martinez, A (1932): 2/1

Martinez, Celestino (1936–43): 12

Martinez, Jorge (Independiente Avellanada, 1997): 3

Martinez, Pedro (Huracan, 1917–19): 14

Martinez, Rodolfo (Quilmes, 1914): 1

Martino (1991): 1

Martino, Rinaldo F (San Lorenzo, Boca, 1942–46): 18/7

Marvezzi, JM (1937–41): 8/9

Marzolini, Silvio (Boca Juniors, 1960–69): 28

Mas, Oscar (River Plate, 1965–72): 39/11

Masalis (1967): 1

Masantonio, Herminio (Huracan/Banfield, 1935–42): 19/21

Maschio, Humberto Dionisio (1956–57): 11/12

Mastrangelo, Ernesto Enrique (Atlanta/River/ Union/Boca, 1972): 8/2

Mattozzi, Ernesto (Estudiantil Porteno BA, Racing Club Avellaneda, 1916–19): 20/1

Medici, Secundo (1922–28): 37

Medina, L (1965): 1

Medina, S (1931–32): 3

Medina Bello, Ramon Ismael (River Plate, Yokohama Marinos [Jp], 1991–94): 18/5

Meira, RS (Atletico San Isidoro, 1913): 1

Mendez G, (1923): 1

Mendez, Norberto, (Huracan, Racing/Tigre, 1945–56): 31/19

Mendiburu (1951): 1

Menendez Norberto, (1957–60): 15/5

Menotti, Cesar (1962–68): 11/2

Merlo, Reinaldo (Boca Juniors 1972): 4

Messiano, Juan (1963–65): 5

Meza, Juan Jose (1980): 4/4

Micheli, Rodolfo (1953–56): 13/10

Migone (1959): 1/1

Miguel, Antonio (Newell's Old Boys, 1920): 5

Minella, Jose Maria (1933–41): 24

Minitti (1968–69): 5

Mohamed, Antonio Ricardo (Huracan, 1991): 4/1

Molfino, Aquiles H (Gimnasia y Esgrima, 1914): 1/1

Molina, Pablo (Rosario Central, 1912): 1

Molina, Roberto (1996): 1

Molinari, C (1924–25): 3

Montanez, Oscar (1937–42): 15

Montegari H, (1957): 1

Monti, Luisito (Boca Juniors, 1926–31): 15/7

Montserrat (Boca Juniors, 1993–95): 5

Monzon, Pedro Damian (Independiente Avellanada, 1988–90): 16/1

Moore, Eugenio (Alumni, 1903): 1

Moore, Juan J (Alumni, 1902–05): 3/1

Morales, Hugo Alberto (Lanus, 1996–97): 8/2

Moreno, Jose Manuel (River Plate, 1936–50): 34–19

Morete, Carlos, (Independiente Avellanada, 1973–83): 3/1

Moreyras G, (1929): 1

Morgada (1929): 1

Morgan, Edward O (Quilmes, 1902): 1

Morigi (1996): 1

Morosano (1943): 1

Morroni, Jose (Atletico San Isidoro, 1912–13): 4

Mourino, Eliseo (1952–59): 26

Mouzo, Roberto (Boca Juniors, 1974–83): 4

Moyano, R (1957): 1

Munos, Juan Carlos (1942–45): 11/1

Murphy, Martin (Belgrano, 1908–10): 3

Murray, Juan Antonio (Quilmes, 1907–09): 2

Murua, Juan Carlos (1953–60): 11

Mussimesi, Julio Elias (1952–57): 16

Muttis, Ramon (1923–30): 12

Muttoni, Carlos A (Racing Club Avellaneda, Independiente Avellaneda, 1913–14): 2

Naon, Arturo (San Lorenzo, 1934): 2

Naon, Ricardo (Estudiantes La Plata, 1914): 2

Nardiello Angel, (1959–60): 13/7

Navarro, Ruben Marino (Independiente Avellanada, 1960–63): 32

Nazarino (1927): 1

Nazionale, J (1960): 2

Negri (1943): 1

Negri, Mario Luis (Estudiantil Porteno, 1913): 1

Negri, Osvaldo (1959): 10

Nehin, C (1934): 1

Netto (1995): 1/1

Nicolau, Miguel (1971): 2/1

Nieto, Enrique R (1980): 4

Nobile, C (1923–25): 3

Noseda (1943): 2

Nuin, B (1925): 1

Nuin, R (1959): 1

Oatua, R (1968): 1

Oberti, Alfredo (1971): 1

Ocano, J (Cordoba, 1975–80): 6

Ocano, Victor (1980): 4

Ochandio, Alberto E (Estudiantes La Plata, 1919): 4/3

Ochoa, P (1924–28): 6/1

Ogando, G (1945–52): 5

Ohaco, Alberto Juan (Racing Club Avellaneda, 1912–18): 12/7

Ojeda, Marcelo (Tenerife [Sp], 1997): 1

Olarticoechea, Julio Jorge (Racing Club Avellaneda, 1983–90): 28

Olazar, Francisco (Racing Club Avellaneda, 1916–21): 16/1

Oleniak, Juan Carlos (Argentinos Juniors, 1959–63): 7/5

Olguin, Jorge Mario (San Lorenzo, Independiente Avellanada, 1976–82): 60

Olivari, Alberto J (Atletico San Isidoro, 1912–15): 7

Olivero (1951): 4

Olmedo (1968): 2/1

Omar (1928): 1

Omer, P (1921–23): 6

Onega, Daniel German (River Plate, 1966–72): 13

Onega, Daniel (River Plate, 1966–67): 5/1

Onega, Ermindo Angel (River Plate, 1960–66): 25/10

Ongaro, S (1946): 2

Onzari, Cesareo (1922–24): 15/7

Orio, H (1922): 2

Orlandini, Rodolfo (1927–30): 10

Oropel (1980): 4

Orsi, Raimundo Bibiani (1924–36): 15/4

Ortega, Ariel Arnaldo (River Plate, Valencia [Sp], 1993–98): 56/10

Ortiz, Oscar Alberto (River Plate, Rosario Central, 1975–79): 23/3

Ostua, R (1968): 3

Outes, Norberto (Independiente Avellaneda, 1979): 2

Ovejero, C (1967): 4

Ovide, A (1968): 2

Oviedo, Miguel Angel (Talleres Cordoba, 1975–79): 7

Pachame, R (1967–69): 9

Paez, Raul (San Lorenzo, 1962): 3

Pagani, Marcelo (River Plate, 1961–62): 6/2

Pagnanini, Ruben (Independiente Avellanada, 1978): 4/1

Pairoux (1942): 1

Pallejero (1951): 1

Palma, N (1945–47): 6

Pando, Martin Esteban (1960–62): 13/3

Paolino, Jorge (Racing Club Avellaneda, 1974): 1

Paolino, R (1974): 2

Pardal, M (1921–22): 4

Pardo (1967–68): 5/1

Parducca, F (1925–26): 3

Pasculli, Pedro Pablo (Argentinos Juniors, Lecce [Ita], 1985–87): 16/4

Pascutini, R (1968–69): 3

Passarella, Daniel Alberto (River Plate, Fiorentina [Ita], 1976–86): 70/21

Passet, Oscar (1995–96): 2

Pastoriza, Jose Omar (1970): 20/1

Paternoster, Fernando (1928/30): 16

Pavon, L (1975): 3

Pavoni, JL (1975): 4

Paz, Pablo Ariel (Newell's Old Boys, Banfield, Tenerife [Sp], 1995–98): 13/1

Pazza, Osvaldo (1972): 1

Pearson, Carlos F (Quilmes, 1912): 1

Pedernera, Adolfo (River Plate, 1940–46): 21/8

Pederzoli, A (1960): 1

Pederzoli, H (1960): 1

Pedevilla, C (1934): 1

Peel Yates, Alfredo Luis (Alumni, 1911): 4

Pellegrina, Manuel (Huracan, 1942–45): 4/2

Pellegrino, Mauricio (Velez Sarsfield, 1997): 3

Pellejero (1951): 3/3

Pena, M (1973): 1

Penella (1927): 2

Pentrelli, L (1956): 6

Pepe, Ricardo (Racing Club Avellaneda, 1913–17): 2

Perazzo (1986): 2/2

Percudani, J (1987): 5

Perducca (1928): 1

Perez, A (1957–59): 9/1

Perez, Hugo Leonardo (Independiente Avellaneda, 1993–95): 13/1

Perfumo, Roberto Alfredo (Racing Club Avellaneda, Cruzeiro Belo

Perinetti, Juan Nelusco (Racing Club Avellaneda, 1915–19): 16

Perinetti, Natalio (1924–30): 8/1

Pernia, Vincente Alberto (Boca Juniors, 1973–77): 9

Perotti, C Hugo (Boca Juniors, 1979): 2

Pertino, R (Porteno, 1907): 1

Perucca, Angel (1940–47): 26/2

Pescia, Natalio (1946–54): 12

Petrao, Rodolfo Fraga (River Plate, 1915): 1

Peucelle, Carlos (1928–40): 10

Piaggio, Antonio (Porteno, 1911–14): 6/6

Pianetti, Oscar Antonio (Boca Juniors, 1965–67): 2

Piazza, Oswaldo (St Etienne [Fra], 1972): 8

Pineda (1998): 1

Pineda, Hector Mauricio (Huracan, Boca Juniors, 1997–98): 6/1

Pineda, hector Mauricio (Boca Juniors, 1998): 1

Pizarro, F (1954–57): 6

Pizzuti, Juan Jose (Banfield, River, Racing, Boca, 1959–61): 12/4

Polimeni, Pascual (Quilmes, Porteno, 1912–21): 13/4

Pomar (1927): 1

Ponce (1967–73): 3/1

Ponce, A (1973): 3

Ponce, J (1973): 1

Ponce, Jose Daniel (Estudiantes La Plata, 1983–85): 21/3

Ponce, R (1973): 1

Pontoni, Rene Alejandro (Newell's Old Boys/San Lorenzo, 1942–47): 19/18

Posse (1997): 1

Posse, Martin (Velez Sarsfield, 1997): 2

Potente, Osvaldo R (Boca Juniors, 1971–74): 4/1

Povey, Lui (Newell's Old Boys, 1912–13): 2

Power, A (1923): 2

Poy, M (1973–74): 2

Prado (1940): 1

Prado, E (1954–58): 5/1

Prado, N (1957): 2/1

Pratto (1923): 1

Presta, Juan Salvador (Porteno, 1920–23): 11

Prnia, J (1974): 1

Prospetti, R (1964): 3/2

Pujolas, J (1931): 2

Pumpido, Nery Alberto (River Plate, Betis Sevilla [Sp], 1983–88): 36

Puppo (1956): 1

Quesada, Alfredo (Sporting Cristal, 1976): 1/1

Quintano, A (1969): 1/1

Quintoros, A (1975): 3

Quiroga, Oscar R (1975–80): 6

Rafael, J (1975): 1

Raffo, L (1965): 2

Raffo, N (1967): 2

Raimondo, Miguel Angel (1970–72): 10/1

Ramacciotti, P (1960–61): 6/1

Rambert, Sebastian Pascual (Independiente Avellaneda, 1994–95): 9/5

Ramirez (1995): 1

Ramos, Jose (1942–46): 11

Ramos, Victor Hugo (1983–84): 8/1

Ramos Delgado, Jose Manuel (River Plate, Banfield ,1958–64): 24

Randazzo (1980): 3/1

Ratcliff, Haroldo T (Belgrano, 1908): 1

Rattin, Antonio Ubaldo (Boca Juniors, 1959–69): 35/1

Readigos (1959): 2

Recanattini, Humberto (Sportivo Almagro, 1919–31): 7

Recio (1969): 1

Redondo, Fernando Carlos (Tenerife [Sp], 1992–94): 26/1

Rendo, Alberto (1964–69): 16/6

Reparaz, Arturo (Gimnasia y Esgrima, 1912–14): 5

Reyes, Armando (Racing Club Avellaneda, 1916–19): 20

Reyna, M (1906): 1

Reynoso, J (1960): 1

Rezza, H (1971): 5

Ricardo, H (1945): 7

Righi, J (1964): 3

Rinaldi, Jorge Roberto (Telleres Cordoba, San Lorenzo, Sporting Gijon [Sp], 1979–85): 14

Rinaldi, Osvaldo R (1980): 4

Riquelme, Juan (Boca Juniors, 1997): 1

Rithner, Juan Jose (Porteno, 1910–16): 12

Rithner, Pedro (Baradero, 1914): 1

Rivarola (1935): 2

Rivarola, A (1929): 5

Rivas (1997): 1

Rivet, J (1922): 4

Roa, Carlos Angel (Lanus, Real Mallorca [Sp], 1997–98): 15

Robottaro, L (1975–76): 6

Rocchia, K (1975): 1

Rocha, Juan R (Newell's Old Boys, 1976–77): 3

Rodenak (1951): 1

Rodman, J (Quilmes,): 1

Rodolfi, B (1937–42): 9/1

Rodriguez (Deportivo [Sp], 1945–88): 13/3

Rodriguez, E (1943): 2

Rodriguez, JJ (1959): 7

Rodriguez, JL (1986–87): 2/2

Rodriguez, Leonardo Adrian (San Lorenzo, Atalanta Bergamo [Ita], Borussia Dortmund Germany [Ger], 1991–94): 29/2

Rodriguez, M (1962–63): 8/5

Rodriguez, Raul (1931–32): 3

Rofrano, Nicolas (River Plate, 1917–24): 9

Rogel, Roberto Domingo (Boca Juniors, 1967–74): 11/1

Rogers, Juan Manuel (Provincial Rosario, 1912–13): 3

Rojas, Angel (Boca Juniors, 1958–67): 17/3

Rojo, Enrique (Estudiantes La Plata, 1910): 1

Roldan, Eusebio J (Velez Sarsfield, 1977–80): 3

Rolfo (1979): 1

Roma, Antonio (Boca Juniors, 1956–67): 42

Ronzoni, V (1924): 2

Rosl, Antonio (1967–73): 11

Ross, Guillermo (Alumni, 1907): 1

Rossa, C (1969): 1

Rossi (1980): 1

Rossi, Jose (Atletico San Isidoro, 1913): 1

Rossi, Juan A (Atletico San Isidoro, 1908–09): 2

Rossi, Nestor Raul (1947–58): 27

Rossi, Oscar Raul (San Lorenzo, 1958–63): 17

Rotchen, Pablo Oscar (Independiente Avellanada, 1995–97): 6

Rothschild, Eduardo (Atletico San Isidoro, Gimnasia y Esgrima, 1909–10):3,

Rua, C (1934): 1

Ruggeri, Oscar Alfredo (San Lorenzo, Real Madrid [Sp], 1983–94): 97/7

Ruggilo, N (1950–51): 4

Ruiz, C (1959): 5/1

Rulli, J (1967): 9

Russ, Cirilo P (Quilmes, 1911–12): 4

Russo, Francisco F (Huracan, 1974): 1

Russo, Miguel Angel (Estudiantes La Plata, 1983–87): 16/1

Sa Francisco, Pedro Manuel (Independiente Avellanada, 1973–74): 12

Sabella, Alex (1983–84): 8

Sabio (1940): 2

Sacarella, Antonio (Lanus, 1920): 1

Saccardi, A (1974): 2

Sacchi, Federico (1960–65): 15/1

Sainz, Alberto (River Plate,): 1

Sainz, J (1961–66): 4

Saldana (1992–93): 2

Saldano (1976): 4

Saldias (1959): 4

Salomon, Jose (1940–46): 44

Salomone, E (1968–69): 5

Salvini, J (1945–46): 8/3

Sancet, Roberto (Gimnasia y Esgrima, 1919): 3

Sanchez, M (1925): 3/1

Sanchez, Ruben Omar (Boca Juniors, 1968–74): 15

Sande, Ernesto A (Independiente Avellanada, 1912–16): 10

Sandoval (1928): 1

Sandoval, R (1942): 2/1

Sanfilippo, Jose Francisco (San Lorenzo/Boca/Banfield, 1956–62): 30/20

Sansone, E (1956): 4

Santamaria (1935): 2

Santamaria, Santiago (Newell's Old Boys, 1980–82): 11/2

Santoro, Miguel Angel (Independiente 1964–74): 15

Sanz (1941): 2

Saporiti, E (1979–84): 4

Sarasivar, F (1922): 1

Sarlanga, Jaime (Ferro/Boca/Gimnasia, 1939–43): 5/5

Sarnari (1963): 1/4

Sarnari, C (1966–67): 6/1

Saruppo, B (1921–24): 7/3

Sastre, Antonio (1933–41): 30/6

Sastre, O (1945–47): 3

Saurez, M (1975): 1

Sauri, Ma (1935): 1

Savoy, Raul Armando (Independiente Avellanada, 1963–68): 17/6

Sayanes, Santiago (Gimnasia y Esgrima, Ferro Carril Oeste, 1912–16): 9

Sbarra, Roberto (1940–41): 9

Scarcella (1935): 3

Scarpone, F (1924): 1

Schaidlan, A (1956–57): 12

Schelotto, Guillermo Barros (Gimnasia y Esgrima, 1995–97): 2

Schiarretta, Antonio (Sportivo Barracas, 1918): 1

Schneider, J (1960): 1

Schurrer, Gabriel (Lanus, 1995): 4

Scoffano, Ernesto (Lanus, 1920): 1

Scopelli, Alejandro (1928–37): 8/5

Scotta, Hector (Union, Sa Lorenzo, Ferro, Boca, 1976): 7/5

Scotto (1992): 1

Scursoni, E (1924): 1

Semenewicz, Alejandro Estanislao (1972): 9

Sensini, Roberto Nestor (Velez Sarsfield, Udinese [Ita], AC Parma [Ita], 1987–98): 45

Seoane, Manuel (1921–29): 25/18

Seregni, R (1923–24): 5

Serrizuela, Jose Tiburcio (River Plate, 1990): 8

Sesti, J (1957): 1

Sheridan, JB (Porteno, 1909–10): 2

Silva, J (1967–68): 7/1

Simeone, Carmelo (1959–64): 22

Simeone, Diego (Inter Milan [Ita], Pisa [Ita], Sevilla [Sp], Atletico Madrid [Sp], 1988–98): 72/10

Simmons, Heriberto (River Plate, 1913–16): 2/1

Simon, D (1980): 2

Simon, Juan Ernesto (Boca Juniors, 1989–90): 12

Sinatra, L (1968): 1

Siviski, D (San Lorenzo, 1987–88): 11

Sivo, N (1956): 4

Sivori, Enrique Omar (River Plate, Juventus [Ita], 1956–57): 17/9

Sobrero, Juan Carlos (1943–47): 15

Sola, G (1955–57): 4

Solari, Emilio (1921–26): 28

Solari, Jorge Raul (River Plate, 1966–75): 11

Solorzano (1968): 1

Sorin, Juan Pablo (River Plate, 1995–97): 8/1

Sosa (1979): 1

Sosa, Carlos (1945–46): 10

Sosa, Gabino (1921–27): 15/6

Sosa, Ruben Hector (Racing Club Avellaneda, 1959–62): 18/12

Sotomayor (1996): 1

Spadaro Carlos, (1928–31): 4/1

Spilinga (1959): 2

Squeo Carlos, (Racing Club Avellaneda, 1974): 6

Stabile, Guillermo (1930): 4/8

Stagnaro, A (1926): 1/1

Stanfield, J (1906): 1

Stelman (1959): 1

Stocks, Wilfredo A (1906): 1

Stork (1959): 3/1

Strembel, L (1945–46): 9

Su (1942): 1/3

Suarez, M (1963–75): 3

Suarez, Pedro Arico (1930–40): 13

Suarez, R (1962): 1

Sued, E (1945–47): 6/2

Sune, J (1969–71): 5

Sune, Ruben (1971): 2

Suruppo, B (1924): 3/2

Susan, Jose (Estudiantes La Plata, 1907–08): 2

Susan, Maximiliano A (Estudiantes La Plata, Alumni, 1908–13): 26/9

Taggino, Francisco (Boca Juniors, River Plate, 1913–19): 5

Tapia, Carlos Daniel (Boca Juniors, 1986–88): 9/1

Tapia, J (1980): 1

Tarabini, Anibal (Independiente Avellanada, 1966–69): 5

Tarantini, Alberto Cesar (River Plate, 1974–82): 42/1

Tarasconi, Domingo (1922–28): 29/15

Tardivo (1968): 2

Tarnawsky, A (1959): 1
Tarrio, Oscar (1929–37): 14
Tartalo, Jose R (1980): 4
Tassin, V (1921): 1
Tedesco (1967): 1
Tegliani, J (1973): 1
Telch, Roberto (San Lorenzo, 1964–74): 27/2
Tesorieri, Americo (Boca Juniors, 1919–25): 36
Theiler, J (1986–87): 5
Tittonel (1943): 2
Tobin, Alex (1993): 1/1
Togneri, B (1974): 1
Tojo, Miguel (1971): 2
Tossini, L (1942): 3
Trobbiani, Marcelo Antonio (Boca Juniors, Estudiantes La Plata, Millioarios Bogota [Col], 1973–86): 26/1
Troglio, Pedro Antonio (River Plate, Verona [Ita], Lazio Roma [Ita], 1987–90): 21/2
Troncoso, R (1973–75): 3
Trossero, Enzo Hector (Independiente Avellaneda, Toluca [Mex], 1977–85): 28
Trotta (1995): 3
Unali, (1991): 1
Unate, G (1950): 3/4
Unoste, Carlos Carve (Nacional, 1902): 1/1
Urbieta, S (1934): 1
Urriolabeitia, J (1957): 2
Urruti (1983): 1
Urso, Jacobo E (San Lorenzo, 1919): 1
Uslenghi, Eduardo (Porteno, 1920–21): 13
Vacca, C (1945–46): 7
Vaccaro, Luis (1923–26): 18
Vairo, Federico (1955–58): 41–1
Valdano, Jorge Francisco (Newell's Old Boys, Zaragoza [Spa], Real Madrid [Spa], 1982–90): 23/7
Valencia, Jose Daniel (Talleres Cordoba, 1975–82): 42/5
Vallone, C (1951): 2
Valussi, V (1940–43): 9
Van Tuyne, Jose Danie (Rosario Central, 1979–82): 11
Vanemerak (1985): 1
Vapalpo, J (1923): 1

Varacka, Jose (San Lorenzo, 1956–65): 27
Varallo, Francisco (Boca Juniors, 1930–37): 14/6
Varnazza, S (1950): 1
Vasquez, J (1963–64): 11
Vasta (1979): 1/1
Vazquez (1959): 6
Vazquez, Sergio Fabian (Ferro Carril Oeste, Universidad Catolica [Chi], 1991–94): 30
Veglio, R (1968–69): 9/2
Veira (1967): 1
Veiro, J (1965):
Veloso, Enrique R (1980): 4
Ventureira, Jose (Independiente Avellanada, 1917): 2
Verde (1971): 2
Verdi, L (1971): 12
Vernassa, S (1950): 1/1
Vernazza, Santiago (Platense/River Plate, 1954–55): 3
Vernieres (1936): 1
Veron, Juan (1969–71): 4
Veron, Juan Sebastian (Boca Juniors, Sampdoria [Ita] 1996–98): 20/1
Viale, Jose N (Newell's Old Boys 1908–15): 19/8
Viberti, S (1967): 4
Vidal, Miguel Angel (1960–64): 15
Vidale, J (Gimnasia y Esgrima, 1979): 6
Vidella, R (1941–42): 7
Vieiro, J (1919): 1
Vietes, J (1964–65): 7
Vigliola, J (1923): 2
Vignoles, Horacio H (Belgrano,1913): 1
Villa, L (1950): 1
Villa, Ricardo Julio (Racing Club Avellaneda, 1975–78): 18/1
Villafane (1959): 1
Villagra, J (1926): 2/1
Villarreal, Jose Luis (Boca Juniors, 1991–93): 8
Villaverde, Hugo (Independiente Avellaneda, 1979–80): 6
Visconti, David (Rosario Central, 1991): 4/1
Vivaldo, Nicolas (Racing Club Avellaneda, Porteno, 1917–25): 9/2
Vivas, Nelson David (Boca Juniors, Lugano [Chl], 1994–98): 15/1

Vortura (1923): 1
Watson Hutton, Arnoldo P (Alumni, Belgrano, 1906–13): 17/6
Wehbe, S (1967–69): 3
Weiss, Gottlob E (Barracas, Alumni, 1903–10): 7/1
Wergifker (1935–36): 3
Whaley, Carlos H (Belgrano, 1907): 1
Whebe (1967): 1
Wilde, J (1934): 1
Willington, Daniel Alberto (Velez Sarsfield, 1962–70): 11/1
Wilson, C (1935): 3
Wilson, Carlos T (Atletico San Isidoro, 1907–16): 27
Wolff, Ernesto Enrique (River Plate, 1972–74): 30
Wood, Juan H (Belgrano ,1907): 1
Yacono, Norberto (1942–51): 11
Yazalde, Hector Casimiro (Independiente Avellanada, Sporting Lisbon [Por], 1968–74): 17/3
Yebra (1945): 1
Yudica, J (1956): 4/1
Yustrich, J (1940): 1
Zabaleta, Alberico (Racing Club Avellaneda, 1919): 1
Zamora, Julio Alberto (1992–93): 3
Zanabria, Mario (Boca Juniors 1975): 5/2
Zanetti, Javier Adelmar (Banfield, Inter Milan [Ita], 1994–98): 35/3
Zapata, Gustavo Miguel (River Plate, San Lorenzo, 1991–98): 27
Zarate (1992): 1
Zarate, Roberto (1956–63): 13–6
Zariaga (1942): 1
Zava (1940): 1
Zito (1935): 2
Zorilla, T (1940): 1
Zozaya, Alberto (Estudiantes/Racing, 1933–37): 11/11
Zumelzu, Adolfo (1924–30): 16/4
Zywica (1967): 1

BRAZILIAN INTERNATIONAL PLAYERS' RECORDS

Abatte (1922): 1
Abel (1965–72): 2/1
Abel II (Vasco da Gama, 1978): 1
Acacio (Vasco da Gama,): 6
Acosta (1989): 1/1
Adalberto (1983): 2
Adamstor (1962): 4
Adao, Claudio (1975): 7/11
Adaozinho (1947–48): 2
Adelson (1962): 2
Ademar (1962–65): 6/3
Ademir II (Vasco da Gama, 1987–88): 10
Ademir, Menezes (Vasco da Gama, 1945–53): 39/31
Adevaldo (1963–34): 5
Adhemar (America, 1917): 1
Adilio (Flamengo,1982): 1
Adilson (1939–95): 4/1
Adilson II (1990–91): 5
Ado (1970): 2
Adriano (1995): 1
Afonsinho (San Cristovao, Fluminense, 1936–42): 18/1
Agricola (1932): 1
Airton (1920–63): 5/11
Airton II (1960–64): 7
Aladim (1964): 1
Albertino (1957): 1
Alberto (1968): 4
Alberto, Luis (1975): 8/5
Alberto, 'Pintinho' Carlos (Fluminense, 1976–79): 4
Alberto II, Carlo (1986): 1
Alberto, Torres Carlos (Santos, 1963–77): 58/8
Almir, Albuquerque (Vasco da Gama, 1959–60): 6/1
Alcindo (Gremio Porto Alegre, 1966–67): 6
Aldair, Nasciment: (Benfica [Por], AS Roma [Ita], 1989–97): 62/3
Aldemar (1960–61): 4
Aleixo (Corinthians, 1946): 3
Alemao, Sylvio Serpa (Botafogo, 1923): 6
Alemao II, De Brito Rogerio Ricard (Botafogo, Napoli [Ita], 1983–90): 37/6
Alencar (Sao Paulo, 1946): 4/1
Alexandre, Paes Lopes (Corinthians, 1996): 1
Alexy (1922): 1
Alfeu (1960): 5/1
Alfredinho (Botafogo, 1921–22): 4
Alfredo (1931): 1
Alfredo II (Vasco da Gama,): 6/1
Alfredo, Mostarda (Palmeiras,): 1
Alfredo, Ramos (Sao Paulo, 1955–56): 7
Almeida, Roberto (1981): 2/1
Almir (Santos, 1992–93): 3
Almir II (1990–91): 2
Almir, da Silva (Portuguesa Santista [Sp],

1963): 6/1
Aloisio, Alves (Internacional, Porto Alegre, 1988): 8
Altair (Fluminense, 1959–66): 18
Altamiro, Pereira (San Cristovao, 1963): 1
Altemir (1966): 2
Altivo (1976): 1
Alvariza, Ismael (Brasil Pelotas, 1920): 4/1
Alvaro (San Cristovao, 1955–56): 9/2
Amaral, Alexandre Da Silva (Palmeiras, Parma [Ita], 1995–96): 12
Amaral, Paulo Lima (Guarani Campinas, Corinthians, 1975–79): 41
Amarildo (Botafogo, 1961–66): 23/8
Amaro (1961): 1
Amaro, Silveira (Goitacaz Campos, 1923): 6
Amauri, Albuquerque (Vasco da Gama, 1963): 1
Amauri, Silva (Comercial Ribeirao Preto, 1963): 2
Amilcar (Corinthians, 1916–22): 15/4
Amorim (1942): 2/2
Amoroso (1995): 1
Anderson, Sonny (Barcelona [Sp], 1997): 3/1
Andrada (1976): 1
Andrade, Silva Jorge Luis (Flamengo, 1983–89): 11/1
Andre (1973–76): 2
Andre Cruz (Ponte Preta Campinas, Napoli [Ita], 1988–96): 11
Andre, Luis (Sao Paulo, 1995–96): 2/1
Anselmo (1979–80): 5/3
Antonio II, Marc (Fluminense, Vasco da Gama, 1970–79): 34
Araken (1930): 1
Arati (1952): 1
Araujo, Sergio (Atletico Mineiro, 1987): 3
Arce, Gerardo (1949): 1/1
Argel (1995): 1
Argemiro (Vasco da Gama, 1938–42): 10
Ari (1966): 2
Ari, Nogueira Cesar (Botafogo, 1945–46): 8
Ari de Sousa (America, 1963): 4
Ariel (1934): 1
Arilson (Kaiserslautern [Ger], 1995–96): 6
Arlindo (1966): 2
Arlindo I (1919): 1/2
Arlindo II (1963): 6
Armandinho (1934): 2/1
Arnaldo (Sao Paulo, 1914–19): 15
Aroni (19890): 1
Arturzinho (1984): 1/1
Assis (1984): 2
Augusto (Vasco da Gama, 1947–50): 18/1
Aureo (1966): 2
Avila (1944): 1
Axel (1992): 1
Ay, Clemente (1961): 1

Aymore (1940): 3
Brito, Ruas Hercules (Flamengo, Cruzeiro Belo Horizonte, 1964–73): 46
Baba (1961–68): 4/1
Bahia (Madureira, 1936–37): 4/1
Baia (1979): 3
Baiano, Gil (1990–91): 7
Baiano, Julio (1997): 1
Baidek (1984): 1
Baldochi, Jose Guilherme (Palmeiras, 1970): 1
Baltazar (Corinthians, 1950–56): 19/15
Baltazar II (1980–89): 6/1
Barata (America, 1921): 3
Barbosa (Vasco da Gama, 1945–53): 20
Barto (Sao Bento, 1914–22): 8/2
Batalha (Flamengo, 1925): 1
Batata, Nilton (Santos, 1979): 4/3
Batata, Roberto (1975): 2/1
Batatais (1938–39): 3
Batista (Internacional, Palmeiras, Gremio Porto Alegre, 1981–82): 46
Batista II (Atletico Mineiro, 1987–89): 6/1
Bauer, Jose Carlos (Sao Paulo, 1949–55): 27
Bebeto (Flamengo, Vasco da Gama, Cruzeiro Belo Horizonte, Deportivo La Coruna [Sp], Botafogo, 1985–98): 75/38
Begliomini (Palestra [Ita], Palmeiras, 1942–45): 6
Beiruth (1959): 3/1
Belangero, Roberto (Corinthians, 1955–58): 16
Bellini, Hilderaldo Luiz (Vasco da Gama, Sao Paulo, 1957–66): 49
Benedicto (1930): 2/1
Benedito (1956): 1
Benevenuto (1930): 2
Bernardo (Sao Paulo, 1987–89): 6
Betao (1983): 2
Betinho (1988): 1
Beto, Jaubert Araujo Martins (Botafogo, 1995–96): 4
Bianchi (1975): 1
Bianchini (1965): 3
Bianco (Palestra [Ita], 1919): 5
Bibe (1962): 4
Bigode (Fluminense, 1949–50): 10
Bigua (Flamengo, 1945): 6
Bioro (1939): 1
Bismarck (Vasco da Gama, 1989–90): 12/1
Biu (Santa Cruz, 1959): 3
Boaro, Edson (1979–80): 6/1
Bobo (1989): 3
Bodinho (1956): 5/3
Boiadeiro (Cruzeiro Belo Horizonte, 1993): 5
Bolivar (1972): 1
Boquinha (1957): 1

Bordon (1995): 1
Borgarth (1913): 1/1
Borges, Paulo (1966–68): 14/3
Branco, Claudio, Idraim Vaz Leal (Fluminense, Porto [Por], Genoa [Ita], Corinthians, 1985–95): 73/9
Brandao (Corinthians, 1936–42): 16
Brandaozinho (Portuguesa Santista [Sp], 1952–54): 18
Brant (1940): 1
Brasileiro (1922): 1
Brasinha (1979): 3
Brecha (1976): 1
Brilhante (1930): 1
Britto (Corinthians, 1937–38): 4
Bruno (1960–95): 2
Cabecao (1954): 1
Cacapava (1976): 2
Caetano (Palestra [Italia], 1917): 4/1
Cafu, Marcos Evangelista de Mos (Sao Paulo, Real Zaragoza [Sp], Palmeiras, AS Roma [Ita], 1990–98): 68/2
Caio (Inter Milan [Ita], 1996): 4/3
Cairo (Real Zaragoza [Sp], 1995): 1
Caju (Atletico Paranaense, 1942): 6
Calazans (1956–59): 2
Calu (1979): 3
Calvet (1960–62): 10
Camargo, Joel (1964–70): 21
Campos, Cosme da Silva (Atletico Mineiro, 1975): 5/2
Canali, Heitor (Botafogo, 1934–37): 3
Canario (1956): 7/2
Candiota (Flamengo, 1921): 3/1
Canhoteiro (Sao Paulo, 1947–59): 16/1
Canhotinho, Milton Medeiros (1948–49): 2/2
Cantarelli (1976): 1
Carabina, Valdemar (1961–65): 2
Caravetti (1964): 1
Carbone (1973–74): 6
Cardeal (Brasil Pelotas, 1937): 2
Cardoso (1963): 1
Careca, Oliveira (Guarani Campinas, Sao Paulo, Napoli [Ita], 1982–93): 67/30
Careca II, Hamilton Souza (Cruzeiro Belo Horizonte, 1988–89): 9
Careca III Carlo (Atletico Parana, 1990–91): 10/1
Carlinhos, Carlos A Rodrigues (Guarani Campinas, 1995–96): 6/1
Carlinhos (1964–75): 4
Carlito (1916): 1
Carlos (Portuguesa, 1992–93): 2
Carlos, Antonio (Palmeiras, 1991–93): 11/1
Carlos, Jose (1973): 1
Carlos, Luiz (1968–92): 3
Carlo, Roberto Gallo (Corinthians, Palmeiras, 1975–92): 43
Carlos, Toninho (Santos, 1983): 4
Carlos, Albert (1959): 3
Carlos, Alberto Borges (Palmeiras, 1983): 18/3
Carlos II, Luis (1979–87): 4
Carlos III, Lui (1988): 1/1
Carlos, Winck Luiz (Internacional, 1985–92): 9

Carlos da Silva, Robert (Palmeiras, 1995): 14
Carlyle (1948): 1/1
Carmargo, Joel (1968): 1
Carnera (Palestra [Ita], 1936): 33
Carpeggiani, Paulo Cesar (Internacional, 1974–79): 16
Carregal (1919): 1
Carreiro (San Cristovao, 1937–40): 7
Carvalho, Bruno (1995): 3
Carvalho Leite (Botafogo, 1930–40): 11/7
Casagrande, Valter (Corinthians, 1985–86): 19/8
Casemiro (Sao Paulo, 1916–17): 6
Cassio (1990–91): 2
Castelhano (Santos, 1920): 4
Castilho, Carlos Jose (Fluminense, 1950–62): 27
Celio (1965): 2
Celio Silva (Corinthians, 1992–97): 11
Celso (1972): 1
Cerezo, Toninho (AS Roma [Ita], Atletico Mineiro, 1977–85): 58/5
Cesar (1974–98): 7
Cesar Augusto, Belli Michelon (1998): 1
Cesar, Camassutti Paulo (1981): 1
Cesar I, Paul (1983): 1
Cesar, II (Vasco da Gama, 1981): 2
Cesar, Lima Paulo (Botafogo, 1967–77): 62/10
Cesar Sampaio (Palmeiras, Yokohama Flugels [Jp], 1997–98): 31/5
Chagas, Marinho (1973): 1
Charles (EC Bahia, Flamengo, 1989–95): 14/3
Chaves, Ilton (America, 1967): 3
Chicao (Sao Paulo, 1976–79): 9
Chico (Vasco da Gama, 1945–50): 19/8
Chinezinho (Palmeiras, 1956–61): 16/6
Chiquinho (1973): 2
Christian (1997): 1
Claudio (1968): 6
Claudio, Danni (Internacional, 1963): 5
Claudio, Luis (1979): 4
Claudio, C Pinho (Santos, Corinthians, Sao Paulo, 1942–57): 12/5
Claudio I (1962): 4
Claudiomiro (1971): 5/1
Cleber (Palmeiras, Atletico Mineiro, 1990–98): 11
Cleo (1966): 2
Cleo II (1979–80): 7
Clodo (Paulistano [Sp], 1922–25): 4
Clodoaldo, Tavares Santana (Santos, 1969–76): 42/1
Clovis (Santa Cruz, 1959–62): 8
Coelho (Fluminense, 1923): 3
Conceicao, Flavio (Palmeiras, Deportivo La Coruna [Sp], 1995–98): 27/4
Conceicao, Nei (1970):
Constantino (Santos, 1920): 3
Copeu (1968): 1
Coronel (Vasco da Gama, 1959): 8
Costa, Roberto (1984): 1
Coutinho (Santos, 1960–65): 14/6
Cristian (1997): 1
Cristovao (Gremio Porto Alegre, 1979–89): 13/4
Cruz, Andre (Ponte Preta Campinas [Sp],

Napoli [Ita], 1987–97): 24/2
Cuca (1991): 1
Da Guia, Ademi (Palmeiras, 1965–76): 12
Dada, Dario (1970–73): 5
Dado, Dario (1970): 1
Danilo, Alvim (Vasco da Gama, 1945–53): 25/2
Danival (Atletico Mineiro, 1975): 4/3
Dari (1963): 1
Dario (1959): 3
Dario II (1965): 1
Darnlei (Gremio Porto Alegre, 1995): 3
David (1966): 2
De (1976): 2
De Brito, Waldemar (1934): 2/1
De Maria (Andarai, 1920): 2
De Silva, Mauro (Bragantino, 1992): 1
De Sordi (Sao Paulo, 1955–61): 22
Decio, Esteves (Bangu, 1959–63): 4
Del Debbio (1930): 1
Del Nero (1940): 2
Del Vecchio (Santos, 1956–57): 8/1
Delei (1984): 1
Delem (1960): 7/5
Deley (1979): 3
Dema (1985): 4
Demosthenes (Palmeiras, 1916): 1/1
Dener (Portuguesa Santista [Sp], 1991): 2
Denilson (Sao Paulo, 1996–98): 32/6
Dequinha (Flamengo, 1954–56): 9
Dias, Antonio (Santos, 1917): 4
Dias, Carlos (1992): 1
Dias, Nilson (1977): 1
Dias, Roberto (1962–68): 21/1
Dida (1958–61): 6/4
Dida, Nelson de Jesus (Cruzeiro Belo Horizonte, 1995–97): 15
Dida II (FC Coritiba, 1986): 7/1
Didi (Fluminense, Botafogo, 1952–62): 62/20
Dimas (1964): 1
Dinho (1993): 1
Dino (Flamengo, 1921–23): 6
Dino II (Corinthians, 1942): 4
Dino, Sani (Sao Paulo, 1957–60): 14/1
Diogo, Ivo (1960): 1
Dionisio (1919): 1
Dirceu (Botafogo, Vasco da Gama, 1962–86): 28/3
Dirceu II (1972): 5/2
Dirceu, Lopes Dirceu (Cruzeiro Belo Horizonte, 1967–75): 14/3
Ditao (1965–68): 2
Djalma (Vasco da Gama, 1945): 1
Djalma Dias (1965–69): 14
Djalminha (Palmeiras, 1996–97): 10/4
Doca (1930): 1/1
Dodo, Ricardo Lucas (Sao Paulo, 1997): 5/2
Domingos Da Guia (Bangu, Flamengo, Corinthians, 1931–46): 25
Donizete, Candido Omar (Benfica [Por], 1990–95): 14/2
Doriva, Guidoni Junior (Porto) [Por], 1995–98): 10
Dorval (Santos, 1959–63): 13/1
Douglas (Cruzeiro Belo Horizonte, 1987–89): 14

Duarte (1956): 5
Dudu (1965–66): 9
Dudu I (1965): 1/1
Dudu II (1968–80): 4
Dunga, Carlos (Internacional, Santos, Vasco da Gama, Fiorentina [Ita], Pescara [Ita], VfB Stuttgart [Ger], Jubilo Iwata [Jp], 1983–98): 90/7
Ecio (1960): 2
Eder (Atletico Mineiro, 1979–86): 53/9
Edevaldo (Fluminense, 18/1): 18/1
Edilson (Palmeiras, 1959–95): 10/1
Edinho (Fluminense, Udinese [Ita], 1964–86): 54/4
Edivaldo (Atletico Mineiro, 1986–89): 3
Edmar (1959): 4
Edmar Bernardes dos Santos (Corinthians, Pescara [Ita],): 7/4
Edmudo (Fiorentina [Ita], Palmeiras, Vasco da Gama, 1995–98): 35/10
Edmur (1955): 1
Edson (America, Equador SC Recife, 1956–86): 20
Edson, Boaro (1979): 1
Edson III (Ponte Preta Campinas, Corinthians, 1983–86): 23
Edu, Antunes (1967): 2
Edu, Jonas Eduardo Americo (Santos, 1966–74): 41/8
Edu II Marangon, Carlos Eduardo (Palmeiras, Torino [Ita], Portuguesa de Desportos, 1987–89): 15/1
Eduardo (1963): 8
Eduardo II (1968): 7/1
Eduardo III (Fluminense, 1987–89): 4
Eduardo, Lima (Palmeiras, 1944–47): 10/3
Edval (1976): 1
Egidio, Paulo (1990): 1
Elber (Bayern Munich [Ger], 1998): 3
Elcio (1986): 2
Elcy (Sport Club do Recife, 1959): 1
Elias (Nautico Recife, 1959): 5
Elivelton (Sao Paulo, 1991–93): 12/1
Elton (1960): 6/3
Ely (Vasco da Gama, 1949–54): 17
Elzo (Atletico Mineiro, 1986): 11
Emerson (Bayer Leverkusen) [Ger], 1997–98): 5/1
Eiliano, Marinho (Bangu, 1986): 2/1
Eneas (1974–76): 4/1
Enio, Andrade (1956): 5/1
Enio, Rodrigues (1956–60): 5
Erivelto (1975–76): 5/3
Ernani (1957): 1
Escurinho (1955–56): 8
Esnel (1962): 2
Eudes (1975–76): 7/1
Eurico (1971): 2
Evair, Aparecido Paulino (Guarani Campinas, Atalanta Bergamo [Ita], Palmeiras, 1987–93): 14/3
Evaldo (1963–68): 3/1
Evaraldo I (Gremio Porto Alegre, 1973): 1
Evaristo (Flamengo, 1955–57): 13/8
Everaldo,Marques da Silva (Gremio Porto Alegre, 1967–72): 1967–72

Everaldo II (1983–86): 7
Exorcista, Edu (1976): 4
Fabiano (1995): 1
Fabrico (1995): 1
Fachine (1916): 1
Falcao, Roberto (Internacional, AS Roma [Ita], Sao Paulo, 1972–86): 30/6
Faragassi (1922): 1
Fausto (1930): 4
Fefeu (1966): 1
Feitico (1931): 1
Felix (1965–72): 40
Felix, Mielli Venerando (Fluminense, 1973): 1
Fernando (1930): 3
Fernando, Consul (America, 1963): 3/1
Ferrari (1965): 1
Ferreira (1956)1956: 5/4
Fidelis (Bangu, 1966): 6/1
Figueiro (1956): 4
Filo (Paulistano, 1925): 4
Fischer (1976): 1
Flavio (Internacional, 1963–65): 3
Flavio II (Corinthians, 1963–66): 11/9
Flavio III (1965–68): 3
Flecha (1976): 5
Floriano (Fluminense, 1925): 3
Florindo (1939–40): 6
Florindo II (1956): 5
Florisvaldo (1964): 2
Fonda, J (1945): 1/1
Fontana (1966–70): 8
Formiga (Paulistano [Sp], 1922): 5/2
Formiga II (Santos, Palmeiras, 1955–595): 18
Fortes (Fluminense, 1919–25): 13
Fraga, Chica (1975): 6/1
Frederico (Bangu, 1921): 2
Frederico, Renato (Sao Paulo, Guarani Campinas, Cruzeiro Belo Horizonte, 1979–87): 22/3
Friaca (1947–52): 12/1
Friedenreich, Arthur (Paysandu, Paulistano, 1914–30): 18/9
Fume (1979): 2
Fuscao, Beta (1976): 2
Fuscao, Beto (Gremio Porto Alegre, 1976–77): 7
Galaxe, Rubens (1972): 1
Galo (Flamengo, 1916–19): 7
Galvao, Mario (1989): 1
Galvao, Mauro (1980): 1
Galvao, Mauro (Botafogo, 1980–90): 24
Gamba (1922): 2/3
Garrincha (Botafogo, 1955–73): 50/12
Gaucho, Renato (Flamengo, Botafogo, 1983–93): 41/3
Gelson, Juarez (Flamengo, 1995): 1
Geovani (Vasco da Gama, 1985–91): 23/5
Geraldao (Cruzeiro Belo Horizonte, 1987): 14
Geraldino (Cruzeiro Belo Horizonte, 1963–65): 7
Geraldo, Cleofas Dias Alves (Flamengo, 1975–76): 5
Geraldo, Bastos (Santa Cruz, 1959): 1
Geraldo II, Jose da Silva (Nautico Recife,

1959): 5/2
Geraldo, Scotto (1960): 2
Germano (1959–65): 9/2
Germano, Carlos (1995–97): 8
Gerson (1952–54): 4
Gerson de Oliveira, Nunes (Corinthians, Botafogo, Sao Paulo, 1959–80): 77/20
Gerson II (Atletico Mineiro, 1989–90): 4
Gessy (1960): 4
Getulio II (Atletico Mineiro, Sao Paulo, 1975–81): 19/1
Giba (1991): 1
Gil II Gilberto, Alves (Fluminense, Botafogo, 1976–78): 30/8
Gilberto (1960–62): 5/1
Gilcimar (1979): 4/1
Gilmar (Corinthians, Santos, 1953–95): 99
Gilmar, Da Costa (1989): 1
Gilmar II (Sao Paulo, 1986–87): 3
Gilmar III (1986): 5
Gino (Sao Paulo, 1956–58): 8/3
Giovanni (Santos, Barcelona [Sp], 1995–98): 16/7
Givaldo (Nautico Recife, 1959): 5
Givanildo (Santa Clara University, 1976–77): 7
Goiano (Santa Cruz, 1959): 3
Goliardo (1931): 1
Gomes, Zeze (1979): 2
Goncalves (Botafogo, Cruzeiro Belo Horizonte, Yokohama Flugels [Jp], 1997–98): 24/1
Goncalves, M (Botafogo, 1998): 1
Gonzalez (Deportivo Saprissa, 1989): 2/2
Gottardo, Wilson (Flamengo, 1991): 6
Gradim (1932): 1
Grane (1922–30): 2
Guerreiro, Toninho (1968): 1/1
Guidoni, Junior DORIVA (Atletico Mineiro, 1997): 1
Guimaraes, Dirceu (Vasco da Gama, 1978): 1
Guina (1979): 1
Guto (1983): 3
Hamilton (1957): 2
Haroldo, Domingues (Sao Paulo, 1917–19): 4/4
Haroldo, Rodrigues (Vasco da Gama, 1947–53): 3
Hector (1922): 1
Heitor (1963/83): 5/2
Heitor, Domingues (Palestra [Italia], 1919–30): 7/3
Helcio (Flamengo, 1925): 3
Heleno, De Freitas (Botafogo, 1944–47): 18/15
Helinho (1983): 2
Helio (1956): 3
Helio, Dias (1963): 2
Helvio (1955): 1
Henrique (Flamengo, 1957–86): 9/3
Henrique, Luis (1979–80): 11
Henrique, Luiz (Sao Paulo, Palmeiras, 1991–93): 19/6
Henrique, Paulo (Flamengo, 1967): 10
Henrique II (1986): 1

Hercules (1938–40): 6/3
Hermogenes (1930–31): 5
Hildegardo (1931): 1
Hilton, Chaves (1963): 3/1
Hoffmann, Sylvio (1934): 2
Hugo (1983): 3
Humberto (1954–55): 8/1
Ilton (1956): 2/1
Ilton, Vacari (Guarani Campinas, 1963): 7
Imparatinho (1922): 1/2
Indio (Flamengo, 1954–57): 10/5
Insfran, Jd (1977): 1/1
Ipojucan (Vasco da Gama, 1952–55): 8/1
Iris (1963–64): 6
Irno (1960): 3
Isaias (1944): 2/1
Italia (1930–32): 5
Ivair (1992): 1
Ivan (Botafogo, 1946): 4
Ivan II (1955): 1
Ivan, Mariz (1932): 1
Ivo, Diogo (1960): 3
Ivo, Soares (1964): 2/1
Jackson, Jacques (1979): 1
Jadir (1957–61): 6
Jaime (1976): 1
Jair (Internacional, 1979): 1
Jair da Costa (1962): 1
Jair, Marinho (1961–62): 4
Jair Rosa Pinto (Vasco da Gama, Flamengo, Palmeiras, 1940–56): 39/21
Jairo (1976): 1
Jairzinho, Jair Ventura Filho (Botafogo,): 83/38
Jamelli, Paulo Roberto (Santos, 1996): 6/2
Jandir (1984–85): 5
Japones (Flamengo, 1920): 2
Jarbas (1932): 1
Jarbas II (1976): 1
Jardei (1996): 1
Jardel (1996): 1
Jau (Corinthians, 1936–40): 10
Jayme (Flamengo,): 14/1
Jefferson (1995): 1
Jerson (1979–80): 9/2
Joanino (Atletico Paranaense, 1942): 1
Joao, Carlos (1966): 2/2
Joao, Luiz (1979): 1
Joao, Marcos (1984): 1
Joao, Paulo (1983): 1
Joao Paulo Donizetti, Sergio Luis (Guarani Campinas, Bari [Ita], 1987–91): 23/5
Joao, Reis (1920): 1
Joaoquinzinho (1963): 1
Joaozinho (Cruzeiro Belo Horizonte, 1976–79): 4
Joaozinho I (1986): 2
Joel (Flamengo, 1930–58): 18/4
Joel, Camargo (Santos, 1964–70): 5
Jorge (America, 1963): 5
Jorginho (Palmeiras, Bayern Munchen [Ger], Kashima Antlers [Jp], 1945–92): 60/4
Jorginho I (1945): 1/1
Jorginho II (Flamengo, Montpellier [Fr], Bayer 04 Leverkusen [Ger], 1980–91): 31/3
Jose, Celestino (1959): 3/1

Jose, M Silva (1959): 4/8
Jose, Ricardo (1959): 2/2
Jose, Sales (1959): 2/3
Josimar (Botafogo, 1986–89): 16/2
Juandir (1960): 1
Juarez (1956–60): 6/3
Juary (Santos, 1979): 2
Juliao (Corinthians,): 1
Julinho (Portuguesa, 1952–65): 20/1
Julinho II (1976): 1/1
Julio Cesar (Guarani Campinas, Juventus [Ita], 1986–93): 18
Juninho, Junior Oswaldo (Sao Paulo, Middlesbrough [Eng], Atletico Madrid [Sp], 1980–97): 29/6
Junior (Flamengo, Torino [Ita], 1976–98): 73/5
Junior, Denilson De Souza (Palmeiras, 1998): 1
Junior Baiano (Flamengo, 1997–98): 22/2
Junqueira (Flamengo, 1920–40): 5
Jurandir (1960–68): 15
Jurandyr (Palestina, 1937–44): 8
Juvenal (1950): 10
Kaiser, B (1987): 1/1
Kleber (Palmeiras, 1995): 1
Kuntz (Flamengo, 1920–22): 10
Lagarto (Fluminense, 1925): 4/4
Lagreca (Sao Bento, 1914–17): 11/1
Lais (Fluminense, 1919–22): 9
Lance (1976): 1
Larry (1956): 6/4
Leandro (Flamengo, Vasco da Gama, Internacional, 1981–95): 36/3
Leao, Emerson (Palmeiras, Vasco da Gama, Corinthians, 1970–86): 81
Leite, Joao (Atletico Mineiro, 1981–89): 6
Leite, De Castro (1922): 1
Leivinha (Palmeiras, 1972–74): 21/7
Lele (1940–45): 4/1
Leo (1976): 1
Leon (1972): 1
Leonardo (Sao Paulo, Kashima Antlers [Jp], Paris St Germain [Fr], AC Milan [Ita], 1990–98): 47/6
Leoncio (1966): 2
Leonidas (1956): 6/1
Leonidas, da Silva (Nacional [Uru], Vasco da Gama, Sao Paulo, 1932–46): 19/22
Leonidas II (1967–68): 2
Lima (1963–66): 12/4
Lira (Goias, 1990–93): 8
Lombardo, Attilio (Juventus [Ita], 1997): 1/1
Lopes (1938–40): 7
Lopes, Alexandre (1995–96): 3
Luis, Andre (Sao Paulo, 1995–97): 11/2
Luis, Claudio (1979): 1
Luis, Henrique (1991–92): 2/1
Luisinho (Vasco da Gama, 1991–92): 8/1
Luiz, Joao (1979–80): 5/2
Luiz, 'Borracha' (Flamengo, 1946–63): 5
Luiz, Luz (1934): 2
Luiz, Menezes (Botafogo, 1916–19): 5
Luiz, Mesquita Oliveira (Palestra Italia SP, 1934–44): 11/4
Luiz, Pereira (Palmeiras, 1973–74): 11
Luiz, Trujilo 'Luizinho' (Corinthians, 1956):

16/2
Luizao (Palmeiras,): 1/1
Luizinho (Atletico Mineiro, 1980–87): 34/2
Luizinho I (1976): 1
Lula (Internacional, 1969–76): 10/2
Luna (1966): 1
Luvanor (1979): 3
M Silva, Jose (1959): 1/2
Macale, Tiao (1963): 5
Machado (1938–40): 6
Machado, Ernesto Duarte (Fluminense, 3/2):
Maneca (1950): 6/2
Maneco (1947): 1
Manga (1965–67):
Mano, Wilson (1992): 1
Manoel (1972): 1
Manoel, Sergio (1995–96): 2
Manricio (1959): 1
Maranhao (1959): 5/1
Marcao (1986): 1
Marcelinho (1994–96): 2
Marcelo (Atletico Mineiro, 1975–92): 13/1
Marcelo, Kiremitdjian (1989): 1
Marcial (Atletico Mineiro,): 6
Marcio (Corinthians, 1980–91): 5
Marcio, Rossini (Santos, 1983): 8
Marcio Santos (Internacional, Botafogo, Bordeaux [Fr], Fiorentina [Ita], 1990–95): 37/6
Marco, Antonio (1963): 7/2
Marco Antonio II, Feliciano (1974–76): 2
Marco, Antonio (Vasco da Gama, 1973–77): 3
Marcos (Fluminense, 1914–22): 11
Marcos, Assuncao (1998): 3
Marcos II (Botafogo, 1963): 7/1
Marinho, Caetano (1983): 1
Marinho, Chagas Francisco (Botafogo, 1968–77): 33/4
Marino (1960): 6
Mario (1967): 1
Marinho, Mario Peres Ulibarri (Bantos, Barcelona [Sp], 1972–75): 18
Mario, Seixas (America, 1923): 3
Marlon (1986): 4
Marolla (1980–81): 2
Marques (Corinthians, 1994–96): 3/4
Marquinho (1984): 2
Marquinhos (1990): 1
Martim, Silveira (1932–38): 6
Martinelli (1922): 1
Martinez (1954): 1/1
Martins (San Cristovao, 1919–20): 4
Massinha (Cruzeiro Belo Horizonte,): 4
Mata (1964): 1
Matos (1957): 2
Mauricinho (1983–86): 2
Mauricio (1959): 3
Mauricio II (1991): 1
Maurinho (Sao Paolo, 1954–57): 14/4
Mauro II (1975): 6
Mauro, Ramos Oliveira (Sao Paulo, 1949–63): 21
Mauro Silva (Bragantino, Deportivo La Coruna [Sp], 1991–98): 15
Mazaropi (1976): 1

Mazinho (Lece [Ita], Palmeiras, 1989–94): 34
Mazinho, Iomar (Vasco da Gama, 1989–91): 11/2
Mazzola (Sao Paulo, 1958): 8/4
Medio (1939): 1
Mendonca, Jorge Pinto de (Palmeiras, 1978): 6
Mengalvio (Santos, 1960–63): 14/1
Mesquita (1922): 2
Mica (1979–80): 5/2
Mica, Alfredo Pereira de Mello (Botafogo, 1923): 6
Miguel (Vasco da Gama, Fluminense, 1975–76): 10
Millon (Santos, 1914–19): 7/1
Milton (1960–89): 7/1
Milton II (Coritiba, 1987–88): 7
Mimi (Botafogo, 1916): 2/1
Ministrinho (1930): 1
Miranda, Roberto (1964–72): 13/6
Mirandinha (Sao Paulo, 1974): 7
Mirandinha II (Palmeiras, 1987): 5/1
Moacir (1957–60): 6/2
Moacir II (Atletico Mineiro, 1990–91): 5
Moderato (Flamengo, 1925–30): 5/1
Moises (1973): 1
Moreira (Botafogo, 1967–68): 2
Morovic, Z (1987): 1/1
Mostarda, Alfredo (Palmeiras, 1974): 1
Mozer (Flamengo, Olympique de Marseille [Fr], Benfica [Por], 1983–94): 33
Muller, Correa da Costa, Luis Antonio (Sao Paulo, Torino [Ita],): 55/12
Mura (1964): 2
Narciso, Dos Santos (1995–96): 7
Nado (1966–68): 3
Nair (1965): 1
Nariz (Botafogo,): 4
Nascimento (Fluminense, 1925–40): 7
Natal (1967–68): 13/3
Neca (1976): 3/1
Neco (Corinthians, 1917–22): 14/9
Nei (1976): 2
Neilson (1979): 2
Nelinho (Cruzeiro Belo Horizonte, 1974–76): 21/6
Nelinhope (1957): 2
Nelio (1964): 2
Nelsinho (Sao Paulo, 1987–90): 23/2
Nelson (1959): 4
Nelson, Conceicao (Vasco da Gama, 1923): 6
Nena (1947–50): 5
Nene (1963–65): 5/1
Nery (Flamengo, 1914–16): 6
Nesi (San Cristovao, 1922–23): 8
Nestor (1956): 3
Neto (Corinthians, 1983–93): 19/7
Neto, Chico (Fluminense, 1917): 4
Neto, Jose Rodrigues (Botafogo, 1978): 3
Neto, Rodrigues (1972–77): 10/1
Neves (1962–68): 4
Newton (Flamengo, 1930–47): 8
Ney (1963): 8
Nielsen (1972): 1
Niginho (Palestra [Italia], 1936–37): 4/2

Nilo (Brasil Pelotas, Fluminense, 1923–31): 14/8
Nilson (1989–92): 4
Nininho (Portuguesa de Desportos SP, 1949): 4/3
Nonato (Cruzeiro Belo Horizonte, 1993): 3
Nono (Flamengo, 1921–59): 4
Norival (Fluminense, Flamengo, 1940–46): 20/1
Noronha (Sao Paulo, 1944–50): 16
Nunes, Paulo (Gremio Porto Alegre, 1997): 2
Oberdan (Palmeiras, 1944–45): 9
Octavio (Botafogo, 1949): 4/1
Octavio, Egydio (1914): 1
Odair (1976–91): 3
Odorico (1956): 5
Olavo (Corinthians, 1955–57): 4
Oldair (1966–68): 2
Oliveira, Mauro R (Santos, 1963–65): 8
Oreco (1956–61): 10
Orlando (Flamengo, 1921): 3
Orlando, Azevedo Vianna (Fluminense, 1949): 3/2
Orlando, Pereira (Paulistano SP, 1916): 3
Orlando II (1960): 5
Orlando III (America, 1976): 6
Orlando, Pecanha (Vasco da Gama, Boca Juniors [Arg], 1958–65): 29
Orlando, Carvalho III (1977): 1
Ortunho (1960): 3
Oscar (Ponte Preta Campinas SP, Sao Paulo, 1978–86): 60/2
Oscarino (1930): 1
Oseas (Atletico Paranaense PR, 1996): 2
Osmar (1972): 1
Osni (1976): 1/2
Osny (1976): 1
Osses (1922): 1
Osvaldo, Balisa (1952): 1
Oswaldo (Santos, 1963): 6/3
Oswaldo, Alfredo Silva (Botafogo, 1949): 2
Oswaldo, Gomes (1914): 3
Oswaldo de Carvalho (Vasco da Gama, 1942): 5
Othon (1963–64): 6/5
Otoney (1957): 2
Pagao (Santos, Sao Paulo 1957): 2
Palamone (Botafogo, 1919–22): 7
Palhinha (Cruzeiro Belo Horizonte, Corinthians, 1973–1979): 16/4
Palhinha II (Sao Paulo, 1992–93): 16/5
Pamplona (Botafogo, 1925): 2
Parana (1965–66): 9/1
Parra (1950): 1/1
Pascoal 'Silva' (Vasco da Gama, 1923): 6
Pastor, Mauro (1980): 3
Patesko (1934–42): 15/6
Paula, Ramos (America, 1917): 1
Paulao (1990–92): 8
Paulinho (1942): 8/2
Paulinho II, Paulo Almeida Ribeiro (Flamengo, Vasco da Gama, 1955–57): 14/1
Paulinho III (1983): 3
Paulo, Cesar Lima (Botafogo,): 4
Paulo, Florencio (Siderurgica Sabara MG,

1942): 2
Paulo, Joao (1983): 3
Paulo, Pedro (1968): 1
Paulo, Pisaneschi (Nautico Recife, 1957–59): 5/3
Paulo II, Joao (1988): 1
Paulo Isidoro (Gremio Porto Alegre, Santos, Artemio, 1977–83): 37/3
Paulo Roberto (Gremio Porto Alegre, Vasco da Gama, 1983–89): 3
Paulo Sergio (Bayer 04 Leverkusen [Ger],): 2
Paulo Valentim (Botafogo, 1959): 5/5
Paulo, Vitor (1984–87): 5
Pavao (1955–56): 4
Pedrinho (1972): 1/1
Pedrinho, Pedro Luiz Vicencote (Palmeiras, Vasco da Gama, 1979–83): 13/2
Pedro, Amorim (Fluminense, 1940–42): 5/1
Pedrosa (1934): 2
Pele (Santos, 1957–71): 91/78
Pelliciari, Romeu (1938–40): 13/3
Pennaforte (Flamengo, 1923–25): 8
Pepe (Santos,): 34/15
Pequeno (1957): 2
Peracio (1938–40): 6/3
Pereira (1987): 1
Pereira, Geraldo (1983): 1
Pereira, Luis Edmundo (Palmeiras, 1973–77): 24/1
Peres, Waldir (Sao Paulo, 1975–82): 28
Periperi (1957): 2
Perivaldo (1981–82): 3
Pernambuco (1914): 3
Piazza, Wilson da Silva (Cruzeiro Belo Horizonte, 1967–75): 53
Picagli (Palestra [Ita],): 2
Picasso (Sao Paulo, 1965–68): 4
Picole (1962–76): 5/2
Pindaro (Flamengo, 1914–19): 7
Pinga (1987): 1
Pinga, Jose Lazaro Robles (Portuguesa de Desportos [Sp], 1950–56): 20/9
Pinguela (1957): 2
Pinheiro (1952–56): 18/1
Piolim (1944): 1
Pipi (Palestra [Italia], 1942): 3
Pires (1984): 2
Pirilo (Flamengo, 1942): 5/6
Pita (Sao Paulo, 1975–87): 15/1
Polaco (1986): 3
Poly (1930): 1
Prado (1965): 1
Prates, Cesar (1996): 11
Preguinho (1930): 3/5
Procopio (1963–68): 10
Quarentinha (Flamengo, 1959–63): 14/14
Rafael (1986): 4
Rai (Botafogo, Sao Paulo, Paris St Germain [Fra], 1987–98): 48/15
Raimundinho (1957): 2
Raul (1956): 3/1
Raul II (Cruzeiro Belo Horizonte, 1968–80): 9
Regis (1987): 2
Rei (Vasco da Gama, 1936–37): 2

Reinaldo (Atletico Mineiro, 1975–85): 28/10
Reinaldo, Jose (Atletico Mineiro, 1977): 1/1
Renaldo (1996): 1
Renato (1973–76): 4
Renato Portaluppi (1992–93): 2/1
Rene (1976–86): 4
Ricardinho (1996): 1
Ricardo (1993–95): 2
Ricardo Gomes (Fluminense, Benfica [Por], Paris St Germain [Fr], 1984–94): 49/4
Ricardo Rocha (Guarani Campinas, Sao Paulo, Vasco da Gama, 1987–95): 45/1
Rildo (Botafogo, 1963–69): 39/1
Rinaldo (1964–67): 11/5
Rinaldo II (1990): 1
Riva (1963): 4
Rivaldo, Vito Borba Fereira(Palmeiras, Deportivo La Coruna [Ita], Barcelona [Italia], 1993–98): 22/9
Rivelino, Roberto (Corinthians, Fluminense, 1965–78): 94/26
Robertinho (1980–81): 2
Roberto (1962): 4
Roberto, Carlos (1968): 2
Roberto,Carlo (Palmeiras, Real Madrid [Sp], 1992–97): 24/1
Roberto Dinamite (Vasco da Gama, Barcelona [Sp] 1975–84): 39/7
Roberto, Emilio da Cunha (San Cristovao, 1936–38): 8/3
Roberto, Paulo (Vasco da Gama, 1983–89): 3
Roberto, Batata (Cruzeiro Belo Horizonte): 4/2
Roberto II (1960): 2
Rocha (1981): 1
Rodrigo (Flamengo, Portuguesa Santista, 1920–27): 7/1
Rodrigues Enio(1960): 1
Rodrigues, Raphael (Corinthians, 1922): 4
Rodrigues, Roberto (1959): 5/2
Rodrigues II Francisco (Palmeiras, 1950–55): 20/7
Rodrigues III (1968): 1/1
Rogerio (1997): 1
Rogerio, Hetmanek (Botafogo, 1970): 3
Rogerio II (1979): 2
Rolando (1913): 1/1
Romario (Vasco da Gama, Flamengo, PSV Eindhoven [Hol], Valencia [Sp], Barcelona [Sp],): 65/32
Romeiro (1956): 2
Romeu (Atletico Mineiro, 1975): 6/1
Ronaldao (FC Shimizu S Pulse [Jp], 1995): 6/1
Ronaldo (Cruzeiro Belo Horizonte, PSV Eindhoven [Hol], Barcelona [Sp], Inter Milan [Ita], 1991–98): 52/27
Ronaldo II (Corinthians, 1990–93): 2
Rondinelli (1976): 2
Rosemiro (1975): 7/1
Rossini, Marcio (1983): 5/1
Rubem (1979): 2
Rubens (1952–56): 3
Rubens II (1959): 6
Rueda (Corinthians, 1925): 1
Rui (Sao Paulo, 1944–50): 28/2

Russinho (1930): 2/1
Russo (Fluminense, Vitoria, Sabara, 1979–98): 14/1
Sadi (1966–68): 10/1
Salles, Rubens (1914): 2/1
Sallis (1916): 1/1
Salomon, J (1945): 1/1
Salsara (1956): 1
Salvador (1954): 1
Sandro (1995): 1
Sant'anna (1930): 1
Santo (1963): 2
Santos (1975–75): 6/3
Santos, Djalma (Portuguesa Santista [Sp], Palmeiras, 1952–68): 102/3
Santos, Joao (1990): 1
Santos, Nilton (Botafogo, 1949–62): 75/3
Saul (1966): 2
Savio (Flamengo,): 19/5
Scala (1968): 1
Serafini (1930): 1
Serginho (Sao Paulo, 1979–82): 20/8
Sergio (1981–1992): 4
Sergio, Mario (Sao Paulo, 1982–85): 8
Sergio, Paulo (Corinthians, Bayer 04 Leverkusen [Ger], 1983–92): 10/3
Sergio, Pereira (Paulistano SP, 1919): 4
Sergio I (1956): 1
Sergio II (1956): 2
Sergio III (1966): 2
Sergio IV (1990–91): 6
Sergio, Manoel (1998): 2
Servilio (Corinthians, 1942–45): 6/1
Servilio II (Palmeiras, 1959–60): 9/4
Sidney (Flamengo, 1916): 3
Sidney II (Sao Paulo, 1986): 2
Silas, Ferreira (Madureira RJ, 1963): 2
Silas II (1992): 2
Silas II, Paulo (Sao Paulo, Sporting Lisbon [Por], 1986–90): 33/1
Silva (1966): 4
Silva I (1966): 2/2
Silva II (1979–80): 7/4
Silvinho (1979–95): 6/2
Silvio II (Bragantino, 1991): 2
Simao (Portuguesa de Desportos [Sp], 1949): 7/5
Sisson (Flamengo, 1920): 4
Socrates (Corinthians, Flamengo, 1979–86): 60/21
Soda (America, 1923): 4
Soligo (1960): 3
Solito (1979): 1
Souza (1979): 2/1
Souza, Jose Ivanildo (Corinthians, 1995): 4/1
Suly (1960): 3
Taffarel, Claudio (Atletico Mineiro, Internacional, AC Parma [Ita], Reggiana [Ita], 1987–98): 101
Tales (1968): 1
Tarciso (Gremio Porto Alegre, 1978–79): 2
Tato (1984–85): 3
Tatu (Corinthians, 1922): 5/1
Tecao (1975–76): 8
Telefone (Flamengo, 1920–21): 5
Teophilo (1930–31): 5/1

Teotonio (1957): 2
Tepet (1922): 1
Terezo (1972): 1
Tesourinha (Internacional, 1944–49): 23/10
Thadeu (1939): 1
Tiao (Santa Cruz, 1959): 1
Tim (Portuguesa Santista, Fluminense, 1936–42): 16/1
Tinoco (1934): 1
Tiquinho (1975): 2/1
Tita (Flamengo, Gremio Porto Alegre, Pescara, [Ita], 1979–84): 28/6
Tite (1957): 3/1
Tito (1963): 1
Toninho II, Antonio Dias Santos (1976–79): 19/1
Toninho III (1989): 1
Torres (1992): 1
Torteroli (19223): 1
Tostao (Cruzeiro Belo Horizonte, 1966–72): 51/29
Tracaia (Sport Club do Recife PE, 1959): 5/1
Tuffy (Sirio SP, 1925): 3
Tulio (Botafogo, 1990–91): 12/10
Tunga (Palestra [Ita], 1936–37): 5
Tupazinho (1965): 1/1
Turcao (1955): 1
Ubirajara (1966): 1
Uchoa (1976): 1
Uidemar (FC Goias, 1987–89): 2
Umberto (1964): 1
Urubatao (1957): 1
Vagner II (1979): 6/1
Vaguinho (1971–76): 8
Valber (Sao Paulo, 1992–93): 12
Valber II (Corinthians, 1993): 1
Valdemar (1959): 1
Valdez (1964): 2
Valdir (Atletico Parana, Botafogo RJ, Girondins de Bordeaux [Fr], 1963–93): 10
Valdir II (Palmeiras, 1956–65): 4
Valdir III (Atletico Parana, Girondins de Bordeaux [Fr], 1990–93): 13
Valdo (Paris St Germain, 1960–92): 8/3
Valdo, Candido Filho (Gremio Porto Alegre, 1987–89): 5/3
Valdo II (Gremio Porto Alegre, Benfica [Por], 1987–90): 42/3
Valdeoir (1979–80): 9
Valdomiro (Internacional,): 18/4
Valencia, Jorge (1976): 1
Valtencir (1968): 1/1
Valter (1938): 3
Vanderlei (Atletico Mineiro, 1975): 6
Vantuir (Atletico Mineiro, 1972–75): 7
Vasconcelos (1955): 2
Vasquez (1975): 1/1
Vava (Recife, Vasco da Gama, Palmeiras, Vasco da Gama, Atletico Madrid [Sp], 1955–64): 20/12
Velloso (1990): 1
Veloso (1930–31): 3
Veludo (1954–56): 9
Veve (Flamengo,): 1
Vicente (1962): 4/2
Victor (1932): 1

Victor, Paulo (1985–86): 4

Vidal (Fluminense,): 4

Vinicius, Marcus (1983): 3/1

Viola (Corinthians, 1993–95): 7/2

Vitor (1960–93): 13

Vitor II (Flamengo, 1981–82): 3

Vivinho (1989): 3/1

Volmir (1966–67): 3

Waldemar (Nautico Recife, 1959): 4

Walder (1957): 1

Wallace (1986): 3/3

Walter (1931–56): 3

Walter II (1955–56): 7

Washington (1987–89): 8/3

Washington I (1972): 1

Wassil (1957): 2

Wendell (1973–76): 6

William (Atletico Minciro, 1963): 6

Wilson (Vasco da Gama, 1949): 5

Wladimir (1977–85): 5

Xingo (1922): 1

Yan (1995): 1

Zagallo, Mario (Botafogo, 1958–64): 34/5

Zanata (1987): 1

Zarzur (Vasco da Gama, 1937–40): 8

Ze Alves (1957): 1

Ze Carlos (Cruzeiro Belo Horizonte, Sao Paulo, 1963–68): 12/1

Ze Carlos II (1988–89): 4

Ze Carlos III (1989): 3

Ze De Mello (Santa Cruz, 1959): 5/3

Ze Do Carmo (1988–89): 3/1

Ze Elias (Corinthians, 1995–98): 10

Ze Luiz (1930): 3

Ze Luiz II (1964): 2

Ze Maria (Portuguesa Santista [Sp], Flamengo, AC Parma [Ita], 1996–98): 20/1

Ze Maria II, Jose Maria Rodrigues (Corinthians, Sao Paulo, (1968–78): 52

Ze Roberto (Portuguesa Santista, Real Madris [Sp], 1997): 19/4

Ze Roberto, Jose Roberto Da Silva Juan (Flamengo, 1998): 1

Ze Sergio (Sao Paulo, 1978/81): 25/5

Ze Teodoro (Sao Paulo, 1987): 2

Zemaria (Sport Club do Recife, 1959): 3

Zenon (Gremio Porto Alegre, 1979–84): 5

Zeola (1961): 1

Zequinha (Nautico Recife, Botafogo, 1959–73): 28

Zetti (Sao Paulo, 1993–97): 16

Zeze (Fluminense, 1920–23): 13/3

Ze, Antonio (Fluminense, 1979): 3

Zeze, Procopio (Sao Paulo, 1938–46): 20

Zezinho (Sao Paulo, 1956): 3/1

Zico (Flamengo, 1976–89): 74/52

Zinho, Crizam De Oliveira (Palmeiras, Yokohama Flugels [p], 1989–98): 55/5

Zito (Santos, Botafogo, 1955–66): 44/3

Ziza (1976): 2/1

Zizinho (Flamengo, Bangu, 1942–57): 54/30

Zozimo (Bangu, Rio, 1956–62): 36

Brazil celebrate their Copa America win in 1995

INTERNATIONAL RECORDS

WORLD CUP

Top score (country):
Iran 17–0 vs. Maldives (1997)

Top score (player in finals):
Oleg Salenko (Russia) 5 vs. Cameroon (1994)

Top score (in Final):
Geoff Hurst (England) 3 vs. West Germany (1966)

Top score (agg in finals):
Just Fontaine (France) 13 (1958)

GENERAL INTERNATIONAL

Most career goals:
Artur Friedenreich (Brazil) 1329 (1910–30)

Most career caps:
Majid Mohammed (Saudi Arabia) 147 (1973–93)

EUROPEAN CLUB CUPS

Top score (Champions Cup):
Feyenoord 12–2 vs. KR Reykjavik (1969–70)

Top score (Cup-winners Cup):
Sporting Lisbon 16–1 vs. APOEL Nicosia (1963–64)

Top score (Fairs/UEFA Cup):
Ajax 14–0 vs. Red Boys (1984–85)

Top score (player):
Lothar Emmerich (Borussia Dortmund) 6 vs. Floriana (Cup-winners Cup, 1965)

Top score (one season):
Jürgen Klinsmann (Bayern Munich) 15 (UEFA Cup, 1995–96)

Top score in Champions Cup (one season):
José Altafini (Milan) 13 (Champions Cup, 1962–63)

Top score in Champions Cup (career):
Alfredo Di Stefano (Real Madrid) 49 (1955–64)

Most overall Cup wins (clubs):
Milan 13

Most Champions Cup wins (clubs):
Real Madrid 7 (1956–98)

Most Champions Cup wins (players):
Francisco Gento (Real Madrid) 6 (1956–66)

Most Champions Cup Finals (players):
Francisco Gento (Real Madrid) 8 (1956–66)

HIGHEST WIN

World Cup qualifying round:
Maldives 0, Iran 17 (June 2, 1997).

World Cup Finals:
Hungary 10, El Salvador 1 (Spain, June 15, 1982).
Hungary 9, South Korea 0 (Switzerland, June 17, 1954).
Yugoslavia 9, Zaire 0 (W Germany, June 18, 1974).

MOST GOALS IN A GAME:

International:
Sofus Nielsen (Denmark), 10 goals vs. France, at White City (Olympics, October 22, 1908); Gottfried Fuchs (Germany), 10 goals vs. Russia, in Stockholm (Olympics, July 1, 1912).

World Cup:
Gary Cole (Australia), 7 goals vs. Fiji, in Melbourne (August 14, 1981); Karim Bagheri (Iran), 7 goals vs. Maldives, in Damascus, Syria (June 2, 1997).

World Cup Final:
Geoff Hurst (England), 3 goals vs. West Germany, 1966.
Major European Cup game: Lothar Emmerich (Borussia Dortmund), 6 goals vs. Floriana (Cup-winners Cup, 1965).

RECORD ATTENDANCES

World Cup:
199,854 – Brazil vs. Uruguay (Maracana, Rio), July 16, 1950.

European Cup:
135,826 – Celtic vs. Leeds United (semi-final at Hampden Park), April 15, 1970.

SENDINGS-OFF

Quickest in European competition:
90 seconds, Sergei Dirkach, Dynamo Moscow vs. Ghent, UEFA Cup 3rd Round, 2nd Leg (December 11, 1991).

Quickest in the World Cup:
55 seconds, José Batista, Uruguay vs. Scotland (Neza, Mexico; June 13, 1986).

World record:
10 seconds, Giuseppe Lorenzo, Bologna vs. Parma, Italian Serie A, December 9, 1990.

BRITISH INTERNATIONAL RECORDS

RECORD WINS

British international:
Ireland 0, England 13 (February 18, 1882).
France 0, England 15 (amateur match, 1906).
Ireland 0, England 13 (February 18, 1882).
England 9, Scotland 3 (April 15, 1961).

Biggest England win at Wembley:
England 9, Luxembourg 0 (European Championship qualifier, December 15, 1982).
Scotland 11, Ireland 0 (February 23, 1901).
Northern Ireland 7, Wales 0 (February 1, 1930).
Wales 11, Ireland 0 (March 3, 1888).
Republic of Ireland 8, Malta 0 (European Championship qualifier, November 16, 1983).

ENGLAND

Most caps:
Peter Shilton, 125 (1970–90).

Most goals:
Bobby Charlton, 49 goals in 106 games (1958–70).

Most goals in one match:
Vivian Woodward, 7 goals vs. France, (Paris, amateur international, November 1, 1906 – result, 15–0), and 6 goals vs. Holland (Chelsea, amateur international, December 11, 1909 – result, 9–1)
W. C. Jordan, 6 goals vs. France (Park Royal, amateur international, March 23, 1908 – result, 12–0).
Oliver Vaughton, 5 goals vs. Ireland (Belfast, February 18, 1882 – result, 13–0).
Steve Bloomer, 5 goals vs. Wales (Cardiff, March 16, 1896 – result, 9–1).
Willie Hall, 5 goals vs. Ireland (Old Trafford, November 16, 1938; first three in three minutes, the fastest international hat–trick – result, 7–0).
Malcolm Macdonald, 5 goals vs. Cyprus (Wembley, April 16, 1975 – result, 5–0).

Most hat-tricks:
6, Jimmy Greaves – 3 vs. Luxembourg, October 19, 1960; 3 vs. Scotland, April 15, 1961; 3 vs. Peru, May 20, 1962; 4 vs. Northern Ireland, November 20, 1963; 3 vs. Northern Ireland, 3 October, 1964; 4 vs. Norway, June 29, 1966.
5, Tommy Lawton – 4 vs. Scotland, April 18, 1942; 4 vs. Scotland, October 16, 1943; 3 vs. Scotland, October 14, 1944; 4 vs. Holland, November 27, 1946; 4 vs. Portugal, May 25, 1947.
5, Gary Lineker – 3 vs. Turkey, October 16, 1985; 3 vs. Poland, June 11, 1986; 4 vs. Spain, February 18, 1987; 3 vs. Turkey, October 14, 1987; 4 vs. Malaysia, June 12, 1991.

Youngest international:
James Prinsep, 17 years 252 days, vs. Scotland (April 5, 1879).

Youngest international in 20th century:
Michael Owen, 18 years and 59 days, vs. Chile (February 11, 1998).

Youngest scorer:
Tommy Lawton, 19 years 6 days, vs. Wales (October 22, 1938).

Oldest international:
Stanley Matthews, 42 years 104 days, vs. Denmark (May 15, 1957).

Oldest debutant:
Leslie Compton, 38 years 2 months, vs. Wales (November 15, 1950).

Oldest scorer:
Stanley Matthews, 41 years 248 days, vs. Northern Ireland (May 15, 1957).

Sendings-off:
Alan Mullery, vs. Yugoslavia (Florence, European Championships, June 5, 1968); Alan Ball, vs. Poland (Chorzow, World Cup qualifier, June 6, 1973); Trevor Cherry, vs. Argentina (Buenos Aires, friendly, June 15, 1977); Ray Wilkins, vs. Morocco (Monterrey, World Cup finals, June 6, 1986); David Beckham, vs. Argentina, (St Etienne, World Cup finals June 30 1998)

Record attendances:
(Home): 100,000 (all at Wembley) – vs. Austria, November 28, 1951; vs. Hungary, November 23, 1953; vs. W Germany, December 1, 1954; vs. USSR,

October 22, 1958; vs. Portugal, October 25, 1961; vs. Rest of the World, October 23, 1963; vs. Spain, April 3, 1968; vs. Portugal, December 10, 1969; vs. Northern Ireland, April 21, 1970; vs. West Germany, April 29, 1972; vs. Poland, October 17, 1973; vs. West Germany, March 12, 1975; vs. Scotland, May 26, 1979.
(Away) 160,000 (Maracana, Rio) – vs. Brazil, May 13, 1959.

SCOTLAND

Most caps:
Kenny Dalglish, 102 (1971–86).

Most goals:
Denis Law, 30 goals in 55 matches (1958–74); Kenny Dalglish, 30 goals in 102 matches (1971–86).

Most goals in one match:
Hughie Gallacher, 5 goals vs. Ireland (Belfast, September 23, 1929 – result, 7–3).

Most hat-tricks:
3, Hughie Gallacher – 3 vs. Ireland, February 2, 1926; 3 vs. Wales, October 27, 1928; 5 vs. Ireland, September 23, 1929.
3, Denis Law – 4 vs. Northern Ireland, November 7, 1962; 3 vs. Norway, June 4, 1963; 4 vs. Norway, November 7, 1963.

Youngest international:
Denis Law, 18 years 235 days, vs. Wales (October 18, 1958).

Sendings-off:
Richard Gough, vs. Switzerland (Berne, World Cup qualifier, September 9, 1992); John Spencer, vs. Japan (Hiroshima, Kirin Cup, May 1995); Craig Burley (St Etienne, World Cup finals, June 23, 98)

Record attendances:
(Home) 149,547 (Hampden Park) – vs. England, April 17, 1936.
(Away) 130,000 (Maracana, Rio) – vs. Brazil, May 7, 1972.

NORTHERN IRELAND

Most caps:
Pat Jennings, 119 (1964–86).

Most goals:
Colin Clarke, 13 goals in 38 matches (1986–92).

Most goals in one match:
J Bambrick, 6 goals vs. Wales (February 1, 1930 – result, 7–0).

Most hat-tricks:
1 – W Dalton, 3 vs. Wales (February 7, 1891); O M Stanfield, 3 vs. Canada (September 12, 1891); J Peden, 3 vs. Wales (April 5, 1893); J Bambrick, 6 vs. Wales (February 1, 1930); W McAdams, 3 vs. West Germany (October 26, 1960); J Crossan, 3 vs. Albania (May 7, 1965); George Best, 3 vs. Cyprus (April 21, 1971); Colin Clarke, 3 vs. Faroe Islands (September 11, 1991).

Youngest international:
Norman Whiteside, 17 years 42 days, vs. Yugoslavia (June 17, 1982).

Sendings-off:
W Ferguson, vs. England (October 22, 1966). Iain Dowie, vs. Norway (Belfast, March 1996).

Record attendances:
(Home) 60,000 (Windsor Park, Belfast) – vs. England, October 8, 1960.
(Away) 120,000 (Santiago Bernabeu, Madrid) – vs. Spain, October 15, 1958.

WALES

Most caps:
Neville Southall, 91 (1983–97).

Most goals:
Ian Rush, 28 goals in 73 matches (1980–96).

Most goals in one match:
J Price, 4 goals vs. Ireland (February 25, 1882 – result, 7–1).
J Doughty, 4 goals vs. Ireland (March 3, 1888 – result, 11–0).
Mel Charles, 4 goals vs. Northern Ireland (April 11, 1962 – result, 4–0).
R I Edwards, 4 goals vs. Malta (October 25, 1978 – result, 7–0).
Most hat-tricks: 1 – J Price, 4 vs. Ireland (February 25, 1882); H Sisson, 3 vs. Ireland (April 11, 1885); J Doughty, 4 vs. Ireland (March 3, 1888); A W Green, 3 vs. Ireland (April 2, 1906); G Lowrie, 3 vs. England (February 27, 1943); T Ford, 3 vs. Belgium (November 23, 1949); John Charles, 3 vs. Northern Ireland (April 24, 1955); D Palmer, 3 vs. East Germany (September 25, 1957); Mel Charles, 4 vs. Northern Ireland (April 11, 1962); Cliff Jones, 3 vs. Northern Ireland (April 3, 1963); R I Edwards, 4 vs. Malta (October 25, 1978); John Toshack, 3 vs. Scotland (May 19, 1979).

Youngest international:
Ryan Giggs, 17 years 332 days, vs. Germany (October 16, 1991).

Oldest international:
Billy Meredith, 45 years 229 days, vs. England (March 15, 1920).

Sendings-off:
Cliff Jones, vs. Mexico (Mexico City, May 22, 1962); Iwan Roberts, vs. Japan, Kirin Cup, June 7, 1992); Vinny Jones, vs. Georgia (Cardiff, European Championship qualifier, June 1995).

Record attendances:
(Home) 62,000 (Ninian Park, Cardiff) – vs. England, October 17, 1959.
(Away) 120,000 (Katowice) – vs. Poland, September 26, 1973.

REPUBLIC OF IRELAND

Most caps:
Paul McGrath, 83 (1985–96).

Most goals:
Frank Stapleton, 20 goals in 71 matches (1977–90).

Most goals in one match:
P Moore, 4 goals vs. Belgium (February 25, 1934 – result, 4–4).
Don Givens, 4 goals vs. Turkey (October 29, 1975 – result, 4–0).

Most hat-tricks:
2, Don Givens – 3 vs. USSR, October 30, 1974; 4 vs. Turkey, October 29, 1975.
2, John Aldridge – 3 vs. Turkey, October 17, 1990; 3 vs. Latvia, September 9, 1992.

Youngest international:
Jimmy Holmes, 17 years 200 days, vs. Austria (May 30, 1971).

Record attendances:
(Home) 53,000 (Lansdowne Road, Dublin) – vs. France, October 14, 1981.
(Away) 100,000 (Katowice) – vs. Poland, May 11, 1958.
100,000 (Moscow) – vs. USSR, October 16, 1985.

RECORD INTERNATIONAL DEFEATS:

Hungary 7, England 1 (May 23, 1954).
England 9, Scotland 3 (April 15, 1961).
Ireland 0, England 13 (February 18, 1882).
Scotland 9, Wales 0 (March 23, 1878).
Brazil 7, Republic of Ireland 0 (May 27, 1982).

MISCELLANEOUS INTERNATIONAL RECORDS

EUROPE

ALBANIA

Highest win:
3–0 vs. Turkey (November 13, 1976); 3–0 vs. Algeria (October 10, 1976); 3–0 vs. Moldova (Mar 29, 1995).

Highest defeat:
0–12 vs. Hungary (September 24, 1950).

International appearances:
45 Suleyman Demollari (1983–95).

International goals:
31 Sokol Kushta (1987–96).

Goals in game:
7 Refik Resmja (Partizani vs. Tomori 14–0, 1951; Partizani vs. Apolonja 11–0, 1951; Partizani vs. Kucova 9–0; 1951).

Goalkeeper unbeaten:
1037min Gogunja (Elbasani, 1983–84).

AUSTRIA

Highest win:
9–0 vs. Malta (April 30, 1977).

Highest defeat:
1–11 vs. England (June 8, 1908).

International appearances:
93 Gerhard Hanappi (1948–62); 87 Anton Polster (1982–98); 86 Karl Koller (1952–65); 84 Bruno Pezzey (1975–90); 84 Fredrik Koncilia (1970–85).

Goals in game:
7 Koslicek II (Wacker–Kapfenberg 14–0, 1956–57), 7 Hans Krankl (Rapid-GAK 11–1, 1976–77).

Goalkeeper unbeaten:
940min Otto Konrad (1993–94).

ARMENIA

Highest win:
2–1 vs. Macedonia (August 6, 1995).

Highest defeat:
0–7 vs. Chile (January 4, 1997).

International appearances:
24 Sarkys Hovs.epan (1992–97).

International goals:
3 Ramzik Grigorian.

AZERBAIJAN

Highest win:
3–0 vs. Faroe Islands (February 27, 1996), 3–0 vs. Turkey (Mar 22, 1997).

Highest defeat:
0–10 vs. France (September 6, 1995).

International appearances:
23 Tarian Akhmedov (1992–97).

International goals:
6 Nazim Suleimanov.

BELARUS

Highest win:
2–0 vs. Luxembourg (October 12, 1994) 2–0 vs. Malta (November 12, 1995).

Highest defeat:
0–4 vs. Norway (November 16, 1994), 0–4 Slovakia (March 27, 1996), 1–5 vs. Sweden (June 1, 1996).

International appearances:
21 Serghei Gurenko (1994–97).

International goals:
6 Serghei Gerasimets.

BELGIUM

Highest win:
9–0 vs. Zambia (June 4, 1994).

Highest defeat:
2–11 vs. England (April 17, 1909).

International appearances:
96 Jan Ceulemans (1977–91).

International goals:
30 Paul Van Himst (1960–79).

BULGARIA

Highest win:
7–0 vs. Norway (November 3, 1957), 7–0 vs. Malta (October 14, 1982).

Highest defeat:
0–13 vs. Spain (May 21, 1933).

International appearances:
101 Borislav Mikhailov (1983–97).

International goals:
47 Hristo Bonev (1996).

CYPRUS

Highest win:
3–0 vs. Malta (October 7, 1992).

Highest defeat:
0–12 vs. Germany (May 21, 1969).

International appearances:
69 Yiannakis Yangoudakis (1980–93).

International goals:
8 Andros Sotiriou, Phivos Vrahimis.

Goals in game:
8 Simos Simeonides (Ethnikos vs. Digenis 0–20, 1969).

Goalkeeper unbeaten:
1064min Phanos Stylianou (Anorthosis 1978–79).

CZECH REPUBLIC

Highest win:
6–0 vs. Malta (September 18, 1996).

Highest defeat:
0–3 vs. Switzerland (April 20, 1994).

International appearances:
30 Pavel Kuka (1994–97).

International goals:
14 Pavel Kuka.

Goalkeeper unbeaten:
611min Caloun (Sparta Prague).

CROATIA

Highest win:
7–1 vs. Estonia (September 3, 1995).

Highest defeat:
11–5 vs. Germany (November 1, 1942).

International appearances:
40 Drazin Ladic (1990–98).

International goals:
30 Davor Suker.

DENMARK

Highest win:
17–1 vs. France (October 22, 1908).

Highest defeat:
0–8 vs. Germany (May 15, 1937).

International appearances:
102 Morten Olsen (1970–89).

International goals:
52 Poul Tist Nielsen.

Goalkeeper unbeaten:
438min Peter Schmeichel April 28, 1993–November 17 1993).

ESTONIA

Highest win:
6–0 vs. Lithuania (August 26, 1928).

Highest defeat:
2–10 vs. Finland (August 11, 1922).

International appearances:
.67 Evald Tipner (1924–39).

International goals:
21 Eduard Ellman-Eelma .

Goalkeeper unbeaten:
592min Mart Poom (FC Flora) and Mikhail Burjukov (FC Tevalte).

FAROE ISLANDS

Highest win:
3–0 vs. San Marino (May 26, 1995).

Highest defeat:
0–9 vs. Iceland (July 10, 1985).

International appearances:
52 Kari Reynheim (1983–96).

International goals:
17 Jans Erik Rasmussen.

FRANCE

Highest win:
10–0 vs. Azerbaijan (September 6, 1995).

Highest defeat:
1–17 vs. Denmark (October 22, 1908).

International appearances:
82 Manuel Amoros (1982–92).

International goals:
41 Michel Platini.

Goalkeeper unbeaten:
1176min Gaetan Huard (1992–93).

GEORGIA

Highest win:
7–0 vs. Armenia (March 30, 1997).

Highest defeat:
0–5 Romania (April 24, 1996).

International appearances:
27 Georgi Nemsadze (1992–97).

International goals:
10 Shota Arveladze.

Goalkeeper unbeaten:
1077min Nikolos Chkeidze (Dinamo Tbilisi).

GERMANY

Highest win:
16–0 vs. Russia (July 1, 1912).

Highest defeat:
0–9 vs. England (March 16, 1909).

International appearances:
126 Lothar Matthäus (1980–98).

International goals:
68 Gerd Müller.

Goalkeeper unbeaten:
641min Oliver Reck (Werder Bremen 1987–88).

GREECE

Highest win:
8–0 vs. Syria (September 20, 1948).

Highest defeat:
1–11 Hungary (March 25, 1938).

International appearances:
91 Stratos Apostolakis (1986–97).

Goalkeeper unbeaten:
1088min P Ikonomopoulos (Panathinaikos 1964–65).

HOLLAND

Highest win:
9–0 vs. Norway (July 4, 1912).

Highest defeat:
2–12 vs. England (December 21, 1907).

International appearances:
83 Ruud Krol (1969–83).

International goals:
35 Faas Wilkes.

Goalkeeper unbeaten:
1082min Heinz Stuy (Ajax 1971).

HUNGARY

Highest win:
12–0 vs. Russia (June 12, 1927).

Highest defeat:
0–7 vs. England (June 10, 1908).

International appearances:
100 Jozsef Bozsik (1947–62).

International goals:
83 Ferenc Puskas.

ICELAND

Highest win:
9–0 vs. Faroe Islands (July 10, 1985).

Highest defeat:
2–14 vs. Denmark (August 23, 1967).

International appearances:
74 Gudni Bergsson (1984–97).

International goals:
16 Rickhardur Jonsson.

ISRAEL

Highest win:
9–0 vs. Taiwan (May 24, 1988).

Highest defeat:
0–6 vs. Italy (August 21, 1949).

International appearances:
77 Klinger.

International goals:
22 Nahum Stelmach.

ITALY

Highest win:
5–0 vs. Hungary (May 11, 1930).

Highest defeat:
1–7 vs. Hungary (April 4, 1924).

International appearances:
112 Dino Zoff.

International goals:
35 Gigi Riva.

Goalkeeper unbeaten:
1143min Dino Zoff (1969–72).

LATVIA

Highest win:
8–1 vs. Estonia (August 18, 1942).

Highest defeat:
0–12 vs. Switzerland (May 29, 1927).

International appearances:
64 Eriks Petersons (1929–40).

International goals:
24 Eriks Petersons.

LIECHTENSTEIN

Highest win:
2–0 vs. China (June 6, 1982).

Highest defeat:
1–11 vs. Macedonia (November 9, 1996).

International appearances:
19 Daniel Hasler (1993–97).

International goals:
2 Manfred Moser.

LITHUANIA

Highest win:
7–0 vs. Estonia (May 20, 1995).

Highest defeat:
0–10 vs. Egypt (June 1, 1924).

International appearances:
41 Romualdas Marcinkus (1927–38).

International goals:
13 Antanas Lingys.

LUXEMBOURG

Highest win:
6–0 vs. Afghanistan (July 26, 1948).

Highest defeat:
0–9 vs. Germany (August 4, 1936).

International appearances:
85 Carlos Weiss (1978–97).

International goals:
16 Leon Mart.

MACEDONIA

Highest win:
11–1 vs. Liechtenstein (November 9, 1996).

International appearances:
24 Mitke Stojkovs.ki.

International goals:
5 Zoran Boskovs.ki.

Goalkeeper unbeaten:
948min Lazo Liposki (Sloga Jugomagnat 1996–97)

MALTA

Highest win:
5–0 vs. Azerbaijan (April 19, 1994).

Highest defeat:
1–12 vs. Spain (December 21, 1983).

International appearances:
76 Silvio Vella (1988–97).

International goals:
20 Carmel Busuttil.

Goalkeeper unbeaten:
725min David Cluett (1993–94).

MOLDOVA

Highest win:
5–0 vs. Pakistan (August 18, 1992).

Highest defeat:
1–6 vs. Germany (December 14, 1994).

International appearances:
20 Sergiu Kleschenko (1992–97).

International goals:
5 Sergiu Kleschenko.

Goalkeeper unbeaten:
771min Evgheni Ivanov (Tiligul 1996–97).

NORWAY

Highest win:
12–0 vs. Norway (June 28, 1946).

Highest defeat:
0–12 vs. Denmark(October 7, 1917).

International appearances:
104 Thorjorn Svennsen (1847–61).

International goals:
33 Jorgen Juve.

POLAND

Highest win:
9–0 vs. Norway (September 4, 1963).

Highest defeat:
0–8 vs. Denmark (June 26, 1948).

International appearances:
104 Grzegorz Lato (1971–83).

International goals:
50 Wiodzmierz Lubanski.

Goalkeeper unbeaten:
1003min Piotr Czaja (GKS Katowice 1970).

PORTUGAL

Highest win:
8–0 vs. Liechtenstein (December 18, 1994).

Highest defeat:
0–10 vs. England (May 25, 1947).

International appearances:
70 Joao Pinto I (1983–97).

International goals:
41 Eusebio.

Goalkeeper unbeaten:
1192 Vitor Baia (FC Porto 1991–92).

ROMANIA

Highest win:
9–0 vs. Finland (October 1, 1973).

Highest defeat:
0–9 vs. Hungary (June 6, 1948).

International appearances:
108 Ladislau Boloni (1975–88).

International goals:
30 Gheorghe Hagi.

Goalkeeper unbeaten:
498min D Stingaciu (Steaua 1986–87).

RUSSIA

Highest win:
7–0 vs. San Marino (June 7, 1995).

International appearances:
49 Victor Onopko (1992–97).

International goals:
10 Dimitri Radchenko.

SAN MARINO

Highest defeat:
0–10 vs. Norway (September 9, 1992).

International appearances:
34 William Guerra (1987–97).

SLOVAKIA

Highest win:
6–0 vs. Malta 6 (September 22, 1996).

Highest defeat:
0–6 vs. Argentina (June 22, 1995).

International appearances:
29 Dusan Tittel(1993–97).

International goals:
10 Peter Dubovs.ky.

Goalkeeper unbeaten:
545min Ivo Schumucker (FC Kosice 95–96).

SLOVENIA

Highest win:
7–1 vs. Iceland (February 7, 1996).

Highest defeat:
0–5 vs. France (1920).

International appearances:
27 Robert Englaro (1992–97).

International goals:
11 Saso Udovic.

Goalkeeper unbeaten:
1201min Janko Irglolie (Olimpija 1996).

SPAIN

Highest win:
13–0 Bulgaria (May 21, 1933).

Highest defeat:
1–7 Italy (June 4, 1928).

International appearances:
121 Andoni Zubizarreta (1985–98).

International goals:
26 Emilio Butragueno.

Goalkeeper unbeaten:
1275 Abel (Atletico Madrid 90–91).

SWEDEN

Highest win:
12–0 vs. Latvia (May 29, 1927).

Highest defeat:
1–12 vs. England (August 5, 1948).

International appearances:
138 Thomas Ravelli (1981–97).

International goals:
49 Sven Rydell.

SWITZERLAND

Highest win:
9–0 vs. Lithuania (May 25, 1924).

Highest defeat:
0–9 vs. England (May 20, 1909).

International appearances:
117 Heinz Hermann (1978–91).

International goals:
32 Max Abegglen.

TURKEY

Highest win:
7–0 vs. Syria (November 20, 1949).

Highest defeat:
0–8 vs. Poland (April 24, 1968).

International appearances:
64 Cetin Oguz (1988–97).

International goals:
21 Kucolandonvadis.

YUGOSLAVIA

Highest win:
10–0 vs. Venezuela (June 1, 1972).

Highest defeat:
0–7 vs. Czechoslovakia (October 28, 1925).

International appearances:
85 Dragan Dzajic (1964–79).

International goals:
38 Stjepan Bobek (1946–56).

Goalkeeper unbeaten:
840min Ivica Kralj (Partizan 1996–97).

SOUTH AMERICA

ARGENTINA

Highest win:
12–0 vs. Ecuador (1942).

Highest defeat:
0–6 vs. Uruguay (December 16, 1958).

International appearances:
98 Oscar Ruggeri .

International goals:
41 Gabriel Batistuta.

BOLIVIA

Highest win:
7–0 vs. Venezuela (1993).

Highest defeat:
0–9 vs. Uruguay (1927).

International appearances:
89 Mariano Melgar.

International goals:
16 Victor Ugarte.

BRAZIL

Highest win:
14–0 vs. Nicaragua (October 14, 1975).

Highest defeat:
0–6 vs. Uruguay (September 18, 1920).

International appearances:
101 Claudio Taffarel.

International goals:
77 Pele.

CHILE

Highest win:
7–0 vs. Venezuela (1979).

Highest defeat:
0–7 vs. Brazil (1959).

International appearances:
85 Leonel Sanchez.

International goals:
29 Carlos Caszely.

COLOMBIA

Highest win:
4–0 vs. Venezuela (1979).

Highest defeat:
0–9 vs. Brazil (1957).

International appearances:
103 Carlos Valderrama.

International goals:
25 Arnoldo Iguaran.

ECUADOR

Highest win:
9–1 vs. Peru (1938).

Highest defeat:
0–12 vs. Argentina (1942).

International appearances:
44 Eduardo Hurtado.

International goals:
12 Hurtado.

PARAGUAY

Highest win:
7–0 vs. Bolivia (1949).

Highest defeat:
0–8 vs. Argentina (1926).

International appearances:
78 Roberto Fernandez.

International goals:
13 Saturnino Arrua, Julio Cesar Romero.

PERU
Highest win:
9–1 vs. Ecuador (1938).

Highest defeat:
0–6 vs. Ecuador (1975), vs. Argentina (1978).

International appearances:
110 Hector Chumpitaz.

International goals:
24 Teofilo Cubillas.

URUGUAY
Highest win:
9–0 vs. Bolivia (November 6, 1927).

Highest defeat:
0–6 vs. Argentina (July 20, 1902).

International appearances:
68 Enzo Francescoli.

International goals:
29 Hector Scarone.

VENEZUELA
Highest win:
6–0 vs. Puetro Rico (1946).

Highest defeat:
0–11 vs. Argentina (1975).

International appearances:
42 José Luis Dolguetta.

International goals:
7 José Luis Dolguetta.

BRITISH TOP DIVISION CLUB RECORDS

Highest scores:
Arbroath 36, Bon Accord (Aberdeen) 0 (Scottish Cup 1st Round, September 12, 1885).
Dundee Harp 35, Aberdeen Rovers 0 (Scottish Cup 1st Round, September 12, 1885).

First-class match:
Arbroath 36, Bon Accord 0 (Scottish Cup 1st Round, September 12, 1885).

FA Cup:
Preston North End 26, Hyde United 0 (1st Round, October 15, 1887).

League Cup:
West Ham United 10, Bury 0 (2nd Round, 1st Leg,

October 25, 1983); Liverpool 10, Fulham 0 (2nd Round, 1st Leg, September 23, 1986).

RECORD AGGREGATES:
League Cup:
Liverpool 13, Fulham 2 (10–0h, 3–2a), September 23–October 7, 1986).
West Ham United 12, Bury 1 (2–1a, 10–0h), October 4–25, 1983.
Liverpool 11, Exeter City 0 (5–0h, 6–0a), October 7–28, 1981.

Premier League:
(Home) Manchester United 9, Ipswich Town 0 (March 4, 1995). (Away) Sheffield Wednesday 1, Nottingham Forest 7 (April 1, 1995).

(Former) English First Division:
(Home) WBA 12, Darwen 0 (April 4, 1892); Nottingham Forest 12, Leicester Fosse 0 (April 21, 1909).
(Away) Newcastle United 1, Sunderland 9 (December 5, 1908); Cardiff City 1, Wolverhampton Wanderers 9 (September 3, 1955).

Scottish Premier Division:
(Home) Aberdeen 8, Motherwell 0 (March 26, 1979).
(Away) Hamilton Academicals 0, Celtic 8 (November 5, 1988).

RECORD WINS:
FA Premier League:
Manchester United 9, Ipswich Town 0 (March 4, 1995).

Record away win:
Sheffield Wednesday 1, Nottingham Forest 7 (April 1, 1995).

(Former) First Division:
Aston Villa 12, Accrington 2 (March 12, 1892).
Tottenham Hotspur 10, Everton 4 (October 11, 1958; highest 1st Division aggregate this century).
West Bromwich Albion 12, Darwen 0 (April 4, 1892).
Nottingham Forest 12, Leicester Fosse 0 (April 12, 1909).

Record away wins:
Newcastle United 1, Sunderland 9 (December 5, 1908).
Cardiff City 1, Wolverhampton Wanderers 9 (September 3, 1955).
Scottish Premier Division: Aberdeen 8, Motherwell 0 (March 26, 1979).
Kilmarnock 1, Rangers 8 (September 6, 1980).
Hamilton 0, Celtic 8 (November 5, 1988).
Scottish League Division One: Celtic 11, Dundee 0 (October 26, 1895).
Record British score this century: Stirling Albion 20, Selkirk 0 (Scottish Cup 1st Round, December 8, 1984).

Longest series of consecutive championships:
Three clubs have won the League Championship three years in succession: Huddersfield Town (1923–24, 1924–25, 1925–26), Arsenal (1932–33, 1933–34, 1934–35), and Liverpool (1981–82, 1982–83, 1983–84).
Both Celtic (1965–66, 1966–67, 1967–68, 1968–69, 1969–70, 1970–71, 1971–72, 1972–73, 1973–74) and Rangers (1988–89, 1989–90, 1990–91, 1991–92, 1992–93, 1993–94, 1994–95, 1995–96, 1996–97) have won the Scottish League Championship nine years in succession.

MOST GOALS SCORED IN A SEASON:
Premier League:
Newcastle United (82 goals, 42 games, 1993–94).

(Former) Division One:
Aston Villa (128 goals, 42 games, 1930–31).

Scottish Premier Division:
Rangers (101 goals, 44 games, 1991–92), Dundee United (90 goals, 36 games, 1982–83), Celtic (90 goals, 36 games, 1982–83).

FEWEST GOALS SCORED IN A SEASON:
Premier League:
Leeds United (28 goals, 38 games, 1996–97).

(Former) Division One (min 42 games):
Stoke City (24 goals, 42 games, 1984–85).

Scottish Premier Division:
Hamilton Academicals (19 goals, 36 games, 1988–89); Dunfermline Athletic (22 goals, 44 games, 1991–92).

MOST GOALS AGAINST IN A SEASON:
Premier League:
Swindon Town (100 goals, 42 games, 1993–94).

(Former) First Division:
Blackpool (125 goals, 42 games, 1930–31).

Scottish Premier Division:
Morton (100 goals, 44 games, 1987–88, and from 36 games, 1984–85).

FEWEST GOALS AGAINST IN A SEASON:
Premier League:
Arsenal (28 goals, 42 games, 1993–94); Manchester United (28 goals, 42 games, 1994–95).

(Former) First Division (min 42 games):
Liverpool (16 goals, 42 games, 1978–79).

Scottish Premier Division:
Rangers (19 goals, 36 games, 1989–90); Rangers (23 goals, 44 games, 1986–87); Celtic (23 goals, 44 games, 1987–88).

MOST POINTS IN A SEASON:
Two points for a win:
(Former) First Division:
Liverpool (1978–79), 68 points from 42 matches.

Scottish Premier Division:
Aberdeen (1984–85), 59 points from 36 matches; Rangers (1992–93), 73 points from 44 matches.

Three points for a win:
Premier League:
Manchester United (1993–94), 92 points from 42 matches.

(Former) First Division:
Everton (1984–85), 90 points from 42 matches; Liverpool (1987–88), 90 points from 40 matches.

Scottish Premier Division:
Rangers (1995–96), 87 points from 36 matches.

FEWEST POINTS IN A SEASON:

Premier League:
Ipswich Town (1994–95), 27 points from 42 matches.

(Former) First Division (min 34 games):
Stoke City (1984–85), 17 points from 42 matches.

Scottish Premier Division:
St. Johnstone (1975–76), 11 points from 36 matches; Morton (1987–88), 16 points from 44 matches.

MOST WINS IN A SEASON:

Premier League:
Manchester United (1993–94) and Blackburn Rovers (1994–95), 27 wins from 42 matches.

(Former) First Division:
Tottenham Hotspur (1960–61), 31 wins from 42 matches.

Scottish Premier Division:
Rangers (1995–96) and Aberdeen (1984–85), 27 wins from 36 matches; Rangers (1991–92 and 1992–93), 33 wins from 44 matches.

MOST HOME WINS IN A SEASON:

Five clubs have won every home League match in a season: Liverpool (14 games, in 1893–94), Bury (15, 1894–95), Sheffield Wednesday (17, 1899–1900) and Birmingham City (17, 1902–03), all in the old Second Division, and Brentford in Division Three South (21 games, 1929–30).

Undefeated sequences (at home):
Liverpool went 85 competitive first-team games unbeaten at home between January 23, 1978 (2–3 vs. Birmingham) and January 31, 1981 (1–2 vs. Leicester), comprising 63 in the League, 9 in the League Cup, 7 in European competition and 6 in the FA Cup.
Millwall were unbeaten at home in the League for 59 consecutive matches from 1964–67.
Bradford Park Avenue hold the record for most consecutive home victories, winning 25 successive home games in Division Three North: the last 18 in 1926–27 and the first 7 of the following season.
The longest run of home wins in the top division is 21 by Liverpool: the last 9 of 1971–72 and the first 12 of 1972–73.

Undefeated sequences (at home and away):
Nottingham Forest went 42 League matches unbeaten, spanning the last 26 games of the 1977–78 season, and the first 16 of 1978–79, from November 1977 to the 2–0 defeat to Liverpool on December 9, 1978. The sequence comprised 21 wins and 21 draws.
In all competitions, Forest went 40 games unbeaten between March and December 1978, comprising 21 wins and 19 draws in 29 League matches, 6 League Cup, 4 European Cup and 1 Charity Shield.
Forest also hold the record unbeaten run in the Premiership, going 25 matches undefeated (15 wins, 10 draws), between February and November 1995, before losing 7–0 to Blackburn Rovers.
The longest unbeaten start to a League season is 29 matches, achieved by Leeds United (Division One, 1973–74: 19 wins, 10 draws, goals 51–16) and Liverpool (Division One, 1987–88: 22 wins, 7 draws, goals 67–13).
Burnley hold the record for the most consecutive League matches unbeaten in a season, with 30 First Division games between September 6, 1920 and March 25, 1921 (21 wins, 9 draws, goals 68–17).

Sequences without a win (at home):
In the 1931–32 season, Rochdale went eight home League games without a win in the Third Division North.
Between November 1958 and October 1959, Portsmouth drew 2 and lost 14 out of 16 consecutive home games.

Sequences without a win (at home and away):
Cambridge United went 31 matches (21 lost, 10 drawn) without a League win in the 1983–84 season, between October 8 and April 23, on the way to finishing bottom of the Second Division.
The record for the most consecutive League defeats is held by Darwen in the 1898–99 Division One season. In Division Two in 1988–89, Walsall suffered 15 successive League defeats.
The longest non-winning start to a League season is 25 matches (4 draws, 21 defeats) by Newport County, Division Four (August 15, 1970 to January 9, 1971). Since then, the record is 16 games: Burnley (9 draws, 7 defeats in Division Two, 1979–80); Hull City (10 draws, 6 defeats in Division Two, 1989–90); Sheffield United (4 draws, 12 defeats in Division One, 1990–91).
The worst start to a Premier League season was made by Swindon Town in 1993–94, who went 15 matches without a win (6 draws, 9 defeats).
The worst losing start to a League season was made by Manchester United in 1930–31, who suffered 12 consecutive defeats in Division One.

Most away wins in a season:
Doncaster Rovers won 18 of the 21 League fixtures as Division Three North champions in 1946–47.

FEWEST WINS IN A SEASON:

Premier League:
Swindon Town (1993–94), 5 wins from 42 matches.

(Former) First Division:
Stoke City (1889–90), 3 wins from 22 matches; Woolwich Arsenal (1912–13), 3 wins from 38 matches; Stoke City (1984–85), 3 wins from 42 matches.

Scottish Premier Division:
St. Johnstone (1975–76) and Kilmarnock (1982–83), 3 wins from 36 matches; Morton (1987–88), 3 wins from 44 matches.

MOST DEFEATS IN A SEASON:

Premier League:
Ipswich Town (1994–95), 29 defeats in 42 matches. (Former) First Division: Stoke City (1984–85), 31 defeats in 42 matches.

Scottish Premier Division:
Morton (1984–85), 29 defeats in 36 matches.

FEWEST DEFEATS IN A SEASON:

Premier League:
Manchester United (1993–94), 4 defeats in 42 matches.

(Former) First Division:
Preston North End (1888–89), 0 defeats in 22 matches; Arsenal (1990–91), 1 defeat in 38 matches; Liverpool (1987–88), 2 defeats in 40 matches; Leeds United (1968–69), 2 defeats in 42 matches.

Scottish Premier Division:
Rangers (1995–96), 3 defeats in 36 matches; Celtic (1987–88), 3 defeats in 44 matches.

Scottish Division One:
Rangers (1898–99), 0 defeats in 18 matches; Rangers (1920–21), 1 defeat in 42 matches.

Scottish Division Two:
Clyde (1956–57), Morton (1962–63) and St. Mirren (1967–68) 1 defeat in 36 matches.

New Division One:
Partick Thistle (1975–76), 2 defeats in 26 matches; St. Mirren (1976–77), 2 defeats in 39 matches; Raith Rovers (1992–93) and Falkirk (1993–94), 4 defeats in 44 matches.

New Division Two:
Raith Rovers (1975–76), 1 defeat in 26 matches; Clydebank (1975–76), 3 defeats in 26 matches; Forfar Athletic (1983–84) and Raith Rovers (1986–87), 3 defeats in 39 matches; Livingston (1995–96), 6 defeat in 36 matches.

New Division Three:
Forfar Athletic (1994–95) and Inverness T (1996–97), 6 defeats in 36 matches.

MOST DRAWN GAMES IN A SEASON:

Premier League:
Manchester City (1993–94), Sheffield United (1993–94) and Southampton (1994–95), 18 draws in 42 matches.

(Former) First Division:
Norwich City (1978–79), 23 draws in 42 matches.

Scottish Premier Division:
Aberdeen (1993–94), 21 draws in 44 matches.

Most League Championships:
Liverpool, 18 (1900–01, 1905–06, 1921–22, 1922–23, 1946–47, 1963–64, 1965–66, 1972–73, 1975–76, 1976–77, 1978–79, 1979–80, 1981–82, 1982–83, 1983–84, 1985–86, 1987–88, 1989–90).

Most Premier League Championships:
Manchester United, 4 (1992–93, 1993–94, 1995–96, 1996–97).

Most Scottish League Championships:
Rangers, 47.

Most FA Cup victories:
Manchester United, 9 (1909, 1948, 1963, 1977, 1983, 1985, 1990, 1994, 1996).

Most Scottish FA Cup victories:
Celtic, 30.

Most League Cup victories:
5, by Aston Villa (1961, 1975, 1977, 1994 and 1996) and Liverpool (1981, 1982, 1983, 1984 and 1995).

Most Scottish League Cup victories:
Rangers, 20.

INDIVIDUAL

MOST GOALS IN A GAME:

Premier League:
Andy Cole (Manchester United), 5 goals vs. Ipswich Town (March 4, 1995).

(Former) First Division:
Ted Drake (Arsenal), 7 goals vs. Aston Villa (December 14, 1935); James Ross (Preston North End), 7 goals vs. Stoke City (October 6, 1888).

FA Cup:
Ted MacDougall (Bournemouth), 9 goals vs. Margate (1st Round, November 20, 1971).

FA Cup Final:
Billy Townley (Blackburn Rovers), 3 goals vs. Sheffield Wednesday (Kennington Oval, 1890); Jimmy Logan (Notts County), 3 goals vs. Bolton Wanderers (Everton, 1894); Stan Mortensen (Blackpool), 3 goals vs. Bolton Wanderers (Wembley, 1953).

League Cup:
Frankie Bunn (Oldham Athletic), 6 goals vs. Scarborough (October 25, 1989).

Scottish Premier Division:
Paul Sturrock (Dundee United), 5 goals vs. Morton (November 17, 1984).

Scottish Cup:
John Petrie (Arbroath), 13 goals vs. Bon Accord (1st Round, September 12, 1885); Gerry Baker (St. Mirren), 10 goals vs. Glasgow University (1st Round, January 30, 1960); Joe Baker (Hibernian, Gerry's brother), 9 goals vs. Peebles Rovers (2nd Round, February 11, 1961).

Scottish League Cup:
Jim Fraser (Ayr United), 5 goals vs. Dumbarton (August 13, 1952); Jim Forrest (Rangers), 5 goals vs. Stirling Albion (August 17m 1966).

MOST LEAGUE GOALS IN A SEASON:

Premier League:
Andy Cole (Newcastle United, 1993–94), 34 goals in 40 matches; Alan Shearer (Blackburn Rovers, 1994–95), 34 goals in 42 matches.

(Former) First Division:
Dixie Dean (Everton, 1927–28), 60 goals in 39 matches.

FA Cup:
Sandy Brown (Tottenham Hotspur, 1900–01), 15 goals in 8 matches.

League Cup:
Clive Allen (Tottenham Hotspur, 1986–87), 12 goals in 9 matches.

Scottish Premier Division:
Brian McClair (Celtic, 1986–87), 35 goals.

MOST LEAGUE GOALS IN A CAREER:

Football League:
Arthur Rowley

	Goals	Matches	Seasons
WBA	4	24	1946–48
Fulham	27	56	1948–50
Leicester City	251	303	1950–58
Shrewsbury Town	152	236	1958–65
Totals	434	619	

Scottish League:
Jimmy McGrory

	Goals	Matches	Seasons
Celtic	1	3	1922–23
Clydebank	13	30	1923–24
Celtic	396	375	1924–38
Totals	410	408	1924–38

Most League goals for one club:
349 – Dixie Dean (Everton, 1925–37).

MOST CUP GOALS IN A CAREER:

Pre-war:
Henry Cursham, 48 (Notts County).

Post-war:
Ian Rush, 43 (Liverpool and Newcastle United).

PENALTIES:

Most in a season (individual):
Francis Lee (Manchester City, 1971–72), 13 goals.

Most awarded in one game:
5 – Crystal Palace (4–1 scored, 3 missed) vs. Brighton and Hove Albion (1 scored), Division 2, 1988–89.

Most saved in a season:
8 out of 10, Paul Cooper (Ipswich Town, 1979–80).

Most FA Cup final goals:
5, Ian Rush (Liverpool): 1986 (2), 1989 (2), 1992 (1).

Most League medals:
8, Phil Neal (Liverpool): 1976, 1977, 1979, 1980, 1982, 1983, 1984, 1986.

Most League appearances (750 + matches):
1005, Peter Shilton (286 Leicester City, 110 Stoke City, 202 Nottingham Forest, 188 Southampton, 175 Derby County, 34 Plymouth Argyle, 1 Bolton Wanderers, 9 Leyton Orient), 1966–97.
863, Tommy Hutchison (165 Blackpool, 314 Coventry City, 46 Manchester City, 92 Burnley, 178 Swansea City, 68 Alloa), 1965–91.
824, Terry Paine (713 Southampton, 111 Hereford United), 1957–77.
782, Robbie James (484 Swansea City, 48 Stoke City, 87 QPR, 23 Leicester City, 89 Bradford City, 51 Cardiff City).
777, Alan Oakes (565 Manchester City, 211 Chester City, 1 Port Vale), 1959–84.
771, John Burridge (27 Workington, 134 Blackpool, 65 Aston Villa, 6 Southend United (loan), 88 Crystal Palace, 39 QPR, 74 Wolverhampton Wanderers, 6 Derby County (loan), 109 Sheffield United, 62 Southampton, 67 Newcastle United, 65 Hibernian, 3 Scarborough, 4 Lincoln City, 3 Aberdeen, 3 Dumbarton, 3 Falkirk, 4 Manchester City, 3 Darlington, 6 Queen of the South), 1968–96.
770, John Trollope (all for Swindon Town), 1960–80 – record for one club.
764, Jimmy Dickson (all for Portsmouth), 1946–65.
761, Roy Sproson (all for Port Vale), 1950–72.
758, Ray Clemence (48 Scunthorpe United, 470 Liverpool, 240 Tottenham Hotspur), 1966–87.
758, Billy Bonds (95 Charlton Athletic, 663 West Ham United).
757, Pat Jennings (48 Watford, 472 Tottenham Hotspur, 237 Arsenal), 1963–86.
757, Frank Worthington (171 Huddersfield Town,

210 Leicester City, 84 Bolton Wanderers, 75 Birmingham City, 32 Leeds United, 195 Sunderland, 34 Southampton, 31 Brighton and Hove Albion, 59 Tranmere Rovers, 23 Preston North End, 19 Stockport County), 1966–88.

Consecutive:
401, Harold Bell (401 Tranmere Rovers; 459 in all games), 1946–55.

Most FA Cup appearances:
88, Ian Callaghan (79 Liverpool, 7 Swansea City, 2 Crewe Alexandra).

Most senior matches:
1390, Peter Shilton (1005 League, 86 FA Cup, 102 League Cup, 125 internationals, 13 Under-23s, 4 Football League XI, 20 European Cup, 7 Texaco Cup, 5 Simod Cup, 4 European Super Cup, 4 UEFA Cup, 3 Screen Sport Super Cup, 3 Zenith Data Systems Cup, 2 Autoglass Trophy, 2 Charity Shield, 2 Full Members' Cup, 1 Anglo-Italian Cup, 1 Football League play-offs, 1 World Club Championship).

GOALKEEPING RECORDS:

British record (all competitive games):
Chris Woods (Rangers), in 1196 minutes from November 26, 1986, to January 31, 1987.

Football League:
Steve Death (Reading), 1103 minutes from March 24 to August 18, 1979.

YOUNGEST PLAYERS:

Premier League:
Neil Finn, 17 years 3 days, West Ham United vs. Manchester City, January 1, 1996.

Premier League scorer:
Andy Turner, 17 years 166 days, Tottenham Hotspur vs. Everton, September 5, 1992.

Football League:
Albert Geldard, 15 years 158 days, Bradford Park Avenue vs. Millwall, Division Two, September 16, 1929.
Ken Roberts, 15 years 158 days, Wrexham vs. Bradford Park Avenue, Division Three North, September 1, 1951.

Football League scorer:
Ronnie Dix, 15 years 180 days, Bristol Rovers vs. Norwich City, Division Three South, March 3, 1928.

First Division:
Derek Forster, 15 years 158 days, Sunderland vs. Leicester City, August 22, 1984.

First Division scorer:
Jason Dozzell, 16 years 57 days, as substitute, Ipswich Town vs. Coventry City, February 4, 1984.

First Division hat-tricks:
Alan Shearer, 17 years 240 days, Southampton vs. Arsenal, March 9, 1988.
Jimmy Greaves, 17 years 10 months, Chelsea vs. Portsmouth, December 25, 1957.

FA Cup (any round):
Andy Awford, 15 years 88 days, as substitute, Worcester City vs. Boreham Wood, 3rd Qualifying Round, October 10, 1987.

FA Cup proper:
Scott Endersby, 15 years 288 days, Kettering vs.

Tilbury, 1st Round, November 26, 1977.

FA Cup Final:
James Prinsep, 17 years 245 days, Clapham Rovers vs. Old Etonians, 1879.

FA Cup Final scorer:
Norman Whiteside, 18 years 18 days, Manchester United vs. Brighton and Hove Albion, 1983.

FA Cup Final captain:
David Nish, 21 years 212 days, Leicester City vs. Manchester City, 1969.

League Cup Final scorer:
Norman Whiteside, 17 years 324 days, Manchester United vs. Liverpool, 1983.

League Cup Final captain:
Barry Venison, 20 years 7 months 8 days, Sunderland vs. Norwich City, 1985.

OLDEST PLAYERS:

Football League:
Neil McBain, 52 years 4 months, New Brighton vs. Hartlepool United, Division Three North, March 15, 1947 (McBain was New Brighton's manager and had to play in an emergency).

First Division:
Stanley Matthews, 50 years 5 days, Stoke City vs. Fulham, February 6, 1965.

FA Cup Final:
Walter Hampson, 41 years 8 months, Newcastle United vs. Aston Villa, 1924.

FA Cup:
Billy Meredith, 49 years 8 months, Manchester City vs. Newcastle United, March 29, 1924.

SENDINGS-OFF:

Most in a season:
314 (League alone), 1994–95.

Most in a day:
15 (3 League, 12 FA Cup), November 20, 1982.

Most in the League in a day:
13, December 14, 1985.

Most in the League over a weekend:
15, December 22–23, 1990.

FA Cup Final:
Kevin Moran, Manchester United vs. Everton, 1985.

Others at Wembley:
Boris Stankovic, Yugoslavia vs. Sweden (Olympics), 1948; Antonio Rattin, Argentina vs. England (World Cup), 1966; Billy Bremner (Leeds United) and Kevin Keegan (Liverpool), Charity Shield 1974; Gilbert Dresch, Luxembourg vs. England (World Cup qualifier), 1977; Mike Henry, Sudbury Town vs. Tamworth (FA Vase), 1989; Jason Cook, Colchester United vs. Witton Albion (FA Vase), 1992; Lee Dixon, Arsenal vs. Tottenham Hotspur (FA Cup semi-final), 1993; Peter Swan, Port Vale vs. WBA (play-offs), 1993; Andrei Kanchelskis, Manchester United vs. Aston Villa (Coca-Cola Cup Final), 1994; Michael Wallace and Chris Beaumont (both Stockport County) vs. Burnley (play-offs), 1994; Tetsuji Hashiratani, Japan vs. England (Umbro Cup), 1995; Derek Ward, Northwich Victoria vs. Macclesfield Town (FA Trophy), 1996; Tony Rogers, Dagenham and

Redbridge vs. Woking (FA Trophy), 1997; Brian Statham, Brentford vs. Crewe Alexandra (play-offs), 1997.

Quickest:
19 seconds, Mark Smith, Crewe Alexandra vs. Darlington (away), Division Three (March 12, 1994).

Quickest in Premier League:
72 seconds, Tim Flowers, Blackburn Rovers vs. Leeds United (February 1, 1995).

Quickest in Division One:
85 seconds, Liam O'Brien, Manchester United vs. Southampton (away), January 3, 1987.

Quickest in the FA Cup:
52 seconds, Ian Culverhouse, Swindon Town vs. Everton (away), 3rd Round (January 5, 1997).

Most in one game:
4: Northampton Town (0) vs. Hereford United (4), Division Three (November 11, 1992); Crewe Alexandra (2) vs. Bradford Park Avenue (2), Division Three North (Janaury 8, 1955); Sheffield United (1) vs. Portsmouth (3), Division Two (December 13, 1986); Port Vale (2) vs. Northampton Town (2), Littlewoods Cup (August 18, 1987); Brentford (2) vs. Mansfield Town (2), Division Three (December 12, 1987).

Most sendings-off in a career:
21 – Willie Johnston (7 Rangers, 6 WBA, 4 Vancouver Whitecaps, 3 Hearts, 1 Scotland).

RECORD ATTENDANCES:

Premier League:
55,314 – Manchester United vs. Wimbledon, January 29, 1997.

(Former) First Division:
83,260 – Manchester United vs. Arsenal (Maine Road), January 17, 1948.

Record Football League aggregate (season):
41,271,414 (1948–49) – 88 clubs.

Record Football League aggregate (single day):
1,269,934, December 27, 1949.

Record average home League attendance for season:
57,758, Manchester United, 1967–68.

Last 1 million League crowd aggregate:
1,007,200, December 27, 1971.

Scottish League:
118,567 – Rangers vs. Celtic (Ibrox Stadium), January 2, 1939.

FA Cup Final:
126,047 – Bolton Wanderers vs. West Ham United (Wembley), April 28, 1923.

Scottish Cup:
146,433 – Celtic vs. Aberdeen (Hampden Park), April 24, 1937.

Record cup-tie aggregate:
265,199, at two matches between Rangers and Morton, Scottish Cup Final, 1947–48.

SMALLEST ATTENDANCES:

Lowest post-war League attendance:
450, Rochdale vs. Cambridge United (Division Three, February 2, 1974).

Lowest post-war (Former) First Division crowds:
3,121 – Wimbledon vs. Sheffield Wednesday, October 2, 1991.
3,231 – Wimbledon vs. Luton Town, September 7, 1991 (lowest post-war Saturday top-division crowd).
3,270 – Wimbledon vs. Coventry City, December 28, 1991.
3,496 – Wimbledon vs. Luton Town, February 14, 1990.

Premier League:
3,039 – Wimbledon vs. Everton, January 26, 1993 (smallest top-division attendance since the war).

Smallest League Cup attendance at a top-division ground:
1,987 – Wimbledon vs. Bolton Wanderers (2nd Round, 2nd Leg), October 6, 1992.

PLAYER AWARDS

FIFA WORLD FOOTBALLER OF THE YEAR

1991 Lothar Matthäus (Ger)
1992 Marco Van Basten (Hol)
1993 Roberto Baggio (Ita)
1994 Romario (Bra)
1995 George Weah (Lib)
1996 Ronaldo (Bra)
1997 Ronaldo (Bra)

"WORLD SOCCER" WORLD PLAYER OF THE YEAR

1982 Paolo Rossi (Ita)
1983 Zico (Bra)
1984 Michel Platini (Fra)
1985 Platini (Fra)
1986 Diego Maradona (Arg)
1987 Ruud Gullit (Hol)
1988 Marco Van Basten (Hol)
1989 Gullit (Hol)
1990 Lothar Matthäus (Ger)
1991 Jean-Pierre Papin (Fra)
1992 Van Basten (Hol)
1993 Roberto Baggio (Ita)
1994 Paolo Maldini (Ita)
1995 Gianluca Vialli (Ita)
1996 Ronaldo (Bra)
1997 Ronaldo (Bra)

FRANCE FOOTBALL EUROPEAN FOOTBALLER OF THE YEAR

1956 Stanley Matthews (Eng)
1957 Alfredo Di Stefano (Spa)
1958 Raymond Kopa (Fra)
1959 Di Stefano (Spa)
1960 Luis Suarez (Spa)
1961 Omar Sivori (Ita
1962 Josef Masopust (Cze)
1963 Lev Yashin (SU)
1964 Denis Law (Sco)
1965 Eusebio (Por)
1966 Bobby Charlton (Eng)
1967 Florian Albert (Hun)
1968 George Best (NI)
1969 Gianni Rivera (Ita)
1970 Gerd Müller (Ger)
1971 Johan Cruyff (Hol)
1972 Franz Beckenbauer (WG)
1973 Cruyff (Hol)
1974 Cruyff (Hol)
1975 Oleg Blokhin (SU)
1976 Beckenbauer (Ger)
1977 Allan Simonsen (Den)
1978 Kevin Keegan (Eng)
1979 Keegan (Eng)
1980 Karl-Heinz Rummenigge (WG)
1981 Rummenigge (WG)
1982 Paolo Rossi (Ita)
1983 Michel Platini (Fra)
1984 Platini (Fra)
1985 Platini (Fra)
1986 Igor Belanov (SU)
1987 Ruud Gullit (Hol)
1988 Marco Van Basten (Hol)
1989 Van Basten (Hol)
1990 Lothar Matthäus (Ger)
1991 Jean-Pierre Papin (Fra)
1992 Van Basten (Hol)
1993 Roberto Baggio (Ita)
1994 Hristo Stoichkov (Bul)
1995 George Weah (Lib)

1996 Matthias Sammer (Ger)
1997 Ronaldo (Bra)

EUROPEAN GOLDEN BOOT

(Leading league goalscorer in Europe)
1968 Eusebio (Benfica) 42 goals (Por)
1969 Petar Zhekov (CSKA) 36 goals (Bul)
1970 Gerd Müller (Bayern Munich) 38 goals (Ger)
1971 Josip Skoblar (Marseille) 44 goals (Yug)
1972 Müller (Bayern) 40 goals (Ger)
1973 Eusebio (Benfica) 40 goals (Por)
1974 Hector Yazalde (Sporting) 46 goals (Por)
1975 Dudu Georgescu (Dinamo Bucharest) 33 goals (Rom)
1976 Sotiris Kaiafas (Omonia) 39 goals (Cyp)
1977 Dudu Georgescu (Dinamo Bucharest) 47 goals (Rom)
1978 Hans Krankl (Rapid) 41 goals (Aus)
1979 Kees Kist (Alkmaar) 34 goals (Hol)
1980 Erwin Vandenbergh (Lierse) 39 goals (Bel)
1981 Georgi Slavkov (Trakia) 31 goals (Bul)
1982 Wim Kieft (Ajax) 32 goals (Hol)
1983 Fernando Gomes (Porto) 36 goals (Por)
1984 Ian Rush (Liverpool) 32 goals (Eng)
1985 Fernando Gomes (Porto) 39 goals (Por)
1986 Marco Van Basten (Ajax) 37 goals (Hol)
1987 Rodion Camataru (Dinamo Bucharest) 44 goals (Rom)
1988 Tanju Colak (Galatasaray) 39 goals (Tur)
1989 Dorin Mateut (Dinamo Bucharest) 43 goals (Rom)
1990 Hugo Sanchez (Real Madrid) 38 goals (Spa)
      Hristo Stoichkov (CSKA) 38 goals (Bul)
1991 Darko Pancev (Red Star) 34 goals (Yug)
1992–96 competition suspended
1997 Ronaldo (Barcelona) 34 goals (Spa)
1998 Nikos Machlas (Vitesse Arnhem) 34 goals (Hol)

SOUTH AMERICAN FOOTBALLER OF THE YEAR

1971 Tostao (Bra)
1972 Teofilio Cubillas (Per)
1973 Pele (Bra)
1974 Elias Figueroa (Chl)
1975 Elias Figueroa (Chl)
1976 Elias Figueroa (Chl)
1977 Zico (Bra)
1978 Mario Kempes (Arg)
1979 Diego Maradona (Arg)
1980 Diego Maradona (Arg)
1981 Zico (Bra)
1982 Zico (Bra)
1983 Socrates (Bra)
1984 Enzo Francescoli (Uru)
1985 Romero (Bra)
1986 Alzamendi (Uru)
1987 Carlos Valderrama (Col)
1988 Ruben Paz (Uru)
1989 Bebeto (Bra)
1990 Raul Amarilla (Par)
1991 Oscar Ruggeri (Arg)
1992 Rai (Bra)
1993 Carlos Valderrama (Col)
1994 Cafu (Bra)
1995 Enzo Francescoli (Uru)
1996 José Luis Chilavert (Par)
1997 Marcelo Salas (Chl)

AFRICAN FOOTBALLER OF THE YEAR (FRANCE FOOTBALL MAGAZINE)

1970 Salif Keita (Mali)
1971 Ibrahim Sunday (Gha)
1972 Cherif Souleymane (Gui)
1973 Tshimen Bwanga (Zai)
1974 Paul Moukila (Con)
1975 Ahmed Faras (Mor)
1976 Roger Milla (Cam)
1977 Tarak Dhiab (Tun)
1978 Karim Abdoul Razak (Gha)
1979 Thomas N'Kono (Cam)
1980 Manga Onguene (Cam)
1981 Lakdar Belloumi (Alg)
1982 Thomas N'Kono (Cam)
1983 Mahmoud Al Khatib (Egy)
1984 Theophine Abega (Cam)
1985 Mohamed Timouni (Mor)
1986 Badou Zaki (Mor)
1987 Rabah Madjer (Alg)
1988 Kalusha Bwalya (Zam)
1989 George Weah (Lbr)
1990 Roger Milla (Cam)
1991 Abedi Pele (Gha)
1992 Abedi Pele (Gha)
1993 Abedi Pele (Gha)
1994 George Weah (Lbr)
1995 George Weah (Lbr)
1996 Nwankwo Kanu (Nig)
discontinued

AFRICAN CONFEDERATION AWARD:

1993 Rashidi Yekini (Nig)
1994 Emanuel Amunike (Nig)
1995 George Weah (Lbr)
1996 Nwanko Kanu (Nig)
1997 Victor Ikpeba (Nig)

ASIAN FOOTBALLER OF THE YEAR

1990 Kim Joo-sung (SKo)
1991 Kim Joo-sung (SKo)
1992 no award
1993 Kazau Miura (Jap)
1994 Said Al-Owairan (Sau)
1995 Masami Ihara (Jap)
1996 Khodadad Azizi (Irn)
1997 Hidetoshi Nakata (Jap)

OCEANIA FOOTBALLER OF THE YEAR

1990 Robby Slater (Aus)
1991 Wynton Rufer (NZ)
1992 Wynton Rufer (NZ)
1993 Robby Slater (Aus)
1994 Aurelio Vidmar (Aus)
1995 Christian Karembeu (New Caledonia and Fra)

GLOSSARY

Assistant, Referee's: Formerly a linesman, one of two officials with flags on either touchline who assist the referee in his decisions, especially offside judgements.

Back Heel: A pass to a team-mate made with the hell of a boot.

Back-pass rule: A law approved by FIFA in 1992 which states that a goalkeeper must not handle a ball kicked to him by a team-mate.

Banana kick: A shot favoured mostly by South American players and executed usually from a free kick which bends or swerves around a wall of defenders towards the goal.

Bicycle kick: A shot or pass executed off the ground with the feet above the head.

Booking: An infringement or 'foul' committed by a player which results in a yellow card or caution. Two yellow cards result in an automatic sending-off.

Bosman Ruling: A case won by Belgian footballer Jean-Marc Bosman in December 1995 which gave out-of-contract players within the European Community the right to become free agents. It also removed the limit on the number of foreign players any one club can field.

Cap: Commemorative headgear awarded to a footballer every time he plays for his country in an international match.

Centre circle: The white, painted circle in the middle of the pitch where teams kick off.

Centre forward: A player whose duties are primarily offensive, i.e. to score and/or create goals. Also known as a striker or attacker.

Centre half/ back: A player whose duties are primarily defensive, i.e. to prevent the opposing team from scoring. Also known as a central defender.

Champions League: The premier knock-out competition for European clubs, transformed by UEFA from the old European Cup into a league format followed by knock-out rounds and a final.

Coach: The person who trains and picks the team. Also known as manager.

Copa Libertadores: The South American equivalent of the European Champions League, contested by the continent's top clubs.

Corner: An indirect free-kick awarded to the attacking team in the arc adjacent to the corner flag when the ball is touched by a defending player and travels behind the goal.

Crossbar: The metal or wooden bar supported by the goalposts.

Dead ball: A ball not in play, especially in a free-kick situation.

Defender: A player, either a centre-half or full-back, whose duties are primarily defensive, i.e. to prevent the opposing team from scoring.

Debut: The first appearance made by a player in a specific league, cup or international match at a specific age level, e.g. schoolboy, youth, senior.

Double: The feat of winning two trophies in the same season, usually the domestic league and cup.

European Championship: A tournament contested every four years by UEFA countries and played in a league format followed by knock-out rounds.

Extra time: After 90 minutes of normal time, a further period of 30 minutes divided into halves of 15 minutes used to decide cup ties.

FA Cup: The Football Association Challenge Cup, the oldest football knock-out competition in the world, contested annually by non-league and league clubs in England since 1872.

FIFA: Federation Internationale de Football Association, the governing body of world football, founded in 1904 and based in Switzerland.

Foul: An unfair piece of play resulting in a direct or indirect free kick to the opposing team and often a yellow or red card to the offender.

Free kick: A set kick, awarded after a foul or infringement, allowed to be taken without interference from the opposing team. Direct free-kicks allow shots on goal; indirect free kicks must begin with a pass to a team-mate.

Friendly: A match arranged between two teams outside normal competition, often as a warm-up or a player's testimonial.

Full back: One of two orthodox defensive players who operate on either the left or right side of the pitch.

Full time: The end of the normal period of 90 minutes, signalled by the referee's final whistle.

Goal: The area of posts, crossbar and netting protected by the goalkeeper; a successful attempt to score, i.e. when the whole of the ball crosses the goal line.

Goal difference: The difference in goals scored for and against a team, traditionally used to separate teams tied on points in the same league position.

Goalkeeper: A player stationed to protect the goal, and the only member of a team allowed to handle the ball in the penalty area.

Goal kick: An indirect free-kick awarded to the defending team in the six-yard area of the goal when the ball is touched by an attacking player and travels behind the goal.

Golden Goal: A goal scored during extra time which settles a cup tie instantly, first introduced in a major competition by UEFA at the 1996 European Championship finals in England.

Half time: A 15-minute interval between the two 45-minute periods of normal time.

Hat-trick: The feat of one player scoring three goals in a match.

Header: A pass or effort at goal executed by using the head.

Inside forward: An old fashioned term for an attacking player who operates behind the centre forward or 'target man'.

Inside left/right: An old-fashioned term for a left or right sided midfield player.

Kick off: The start or resumption of a match, conducted by kicking the ball forward to a team-mate from the centre spot in the centre circle.

Loan: A temporary transfer of a player from one club to another, with no fee involved.

Man marking: A defensive system in which each player is assigned a specific opposing player to mark, tackle and defend against throughout a game.

Midfielder: One of usually between three and five players who operates in the middle of the pitch, assisting both defenders and forwards.

Offside law: A rule which states that a player is offside if he is nearer to the opposing team's goal line than the ball and at least two of his opponents. A free kick is awarded to the opposing team. He is not offside if he is level with his opponents.

Own goal: A goal for an attacking team scored inadvertently by a player in the defending team.

Pass: A successful kick or header from one player to a team-mate.

Penalty kick: A direct free-kick on goal taken from the penalty spot and awarded for a foul within the penalty area; only the kicker and opposing goalkeeper are allowed in the penalty area while the kick is being taken.

PFA: Profession Footballers' Association. The official union for players in England, which organises pensions, insurance, post-playing careers and other support services for professional footballers.

Play offs: A series of matches, usually a semi-final and final, used to decide promotion and relegation issues; first introduced in England in May 1987.

Points: The system used to award the winners of a match. Three points for a win was introduced by the English Football League in 1981; one point is awarded for a draw and none for a defeat.

Premier League: The top division in a league; a 22-club English Premier League was launched by the FA in 1992.

Professional foul: An unfair attempt to prevent a player from scoring; in 1990 FIFA deemed it a sending-off offence. In the 1998 World Cup finals, tackling from behind was also outlawed and punishable with a red card.

Promotion: Elevation for a club from a lower division to a higher one, usually after finishing as champions or runners-up, or winning a play-off.

Referee: The official arbiter or umpire in a match who upholds the laws of the games with the help of two assistants.

Relegation: Demotion for a club from a higher division to a lower one, usually after finishing bottom or next-to-bottom.

Save: A goalkeeper's act of preventing an opposing player from scoring, i.e. of stopping the ball from entering the goal.

Scudetto: Italian term for championship or title.

Sending off: Dismissal from the pitch by red card after committing two yellow-card offences or a professional foul.

Set piece: A dead-ball situation, often practised in training and executed with a free-kick near the opposing team's goal.

Substitute: A player who replaces a team-mate on the pitch during a match. From season 1995/96 teams were allowed to use three substitutes in a match, not necessarily including goalkeepers.

Tackle: An attempt to win the ball from an opposing player using the foot or leg. A fair tackle is executed without committing a foul and conceding a free-kick. Tackling from behind or with two feet is outlawed and punishable with a red card.

Throw-in: Throwing the ball from the touchline to restart play, awarded to a team when the ball is touched by an opposing player on its way out of play.

Transfer: The movement of a player from one club to another, usually accompanied by a fee.

Touchline: The line around the pitch inside which play takes place.

UEFA: Union of European Football Associations, the governing body of European football.

Ultras: Continental term for a club's most fanatical supporters.

Wall: A formation of players lined up to protect their goal and defend against a free-kick.

Winger: An attacking midfielder who operates primarily along the touchline.

Wing Back: An old-fashioned term for a player who operates on the left or right side of midfield.

World Cup: A tournament devised by Frenchman Jules Rimet and contested every four years by countries affiliated to FIFA and played in a league format followed by knock-out rounds; the 2002 World Cup finals in Japan and South Korea will be the 17th tournament.

Volley: A shot or pass executed before the ball touches the ground.

Index

Acknowledgements

The publishers would like to thank the following sources for their kind permission to reproduce the pictures in this book:

African Soccer Magazine.
Allsport UK Ltd/Shaun Botterill; Clive Brunskill; Simon Bruty; David Cannon; Graham Chadwick; Chris Cole; Stu Forster; Tom Hauck; Hulton Getty; John Gichigi; Lawrence Griffiths; Mike Hewitt; Trevor Jones; Michael King; Ross Kinnaird; David Leah; Clive Mason; MSI, Doug Pensinger; Gary M.Prior; Steve Powell; Ben Radford; David Rogers; Dan Smith; Mark Thompson; Vandystadt; Claudio Villa.

Colorsport.
Corbis/UPI; Reuters.
Empics.
Mark Leech.
Popperfoto.
Sporting Pictures (UK) Ltd.

Every effort has been made to acknowledge correctly and contact the source and/or copyright holder of each picture, and Carlton Books Limited apologises for any unintentional errors or omissions which will be corrected in future editions of this book.